The I~~n~~
Investor's Guide to

Low-Load
Mutual
Funds

*The Individual
Investor's Guide to*

Low-Load

Mutual

Funds

The American Association
of Individual Investors

13th
Edition

The American Association of Individual Investors is an independent, not-for-profit corporation formed in 1978 for the purpose of assisting individuals in becoming effective managers of their own assets through programs of education, information, and research.

Outside Sales: International Publishing Corporation

Data in this guide was gathered directly from the funds. While the material in this *Guide* cannot be guaranteed to be error free, it has been obtained from sources believed to be reliable.

Preface

Inside the *Guide* are the information and performance statistics you will need to make well-informed decisions on your mutual fund investments. Our goal is to provide pertinent information, organized to minimize your time spent collecting and comparing information on the increasingly large universe of mutual funds.

The data for this *Guide* was gathered from each fund's prospectus and annual report, and from direct contact with each fund. We calculate all performance and risk statistics, and then verify our information. Our objective is full, accurate, and timely disclosure of investment information.

The change in the name of the *Guide*, from *No-Load* to *Low-Load*, recognizes our expanded coverage of funds. Funds with up to a 3% load but no 12b-1 charges are included, and many of these low-load funds waive their loads for pension plan participants. The data pages have been expanded, with 10 years of information reported, when available. All funds, including municipal bond funds and funds with less than a full year of operation, will have full-page coverage and will be found alphabetically in the data pages with all other funds. To get the *Guide* into your hands as quickly as possible and to standardize comparisons, some per share data is now reported on a calendar-year basis instead of on the fiscal year-end of the fund. All performance figures continue to be on a calendar year basis. The reorganized data page includes other additions we hope you will find helpful.

The 1994 edition of the *Low-Load Mutual Fund Guide* covers 826 mutual funds. There are 223 more funds in the *Guide* this year than last year.

John Bajkowski oversaw the development and production of the *Guide*. Mark Fister assisted in the calculation of the performance statistics; Marie Swick supervised the data collection and verification; and Michael Gutierrez, Stephanie Dixon, and Ivana Bevacqua assisted in collecting data. Martha Crawford served as project editor for the *Guide* and Kurt Zauke designed the cover.

Chicago
March 1994

John Markese, Ph.D.
President

Table of Contents

Preface v
Chapter 1: How to Use This Guide 1
Chapter 2: Investing in Mutual Funds 3
   Diversification 3
   Avoiding Excessive Charges 4
   Sorting Out Charges 5
Chapter 3: Mutual Fund Categories 7
   Aggressive Growth Funds 8
   Growth Funds 8
   Growth and Income Funds 9
   Balanced Funds 9
   Bond Funds 10
   International Bond and Stock Funds 10
   Gold Funds 11
   Other Types of Funds 12
Chapter 4 : Understanding Mutual Fund Statements 13
   The Prospectus 13
   Statement of Additional Information 18
   Annual, Semiannual, and Quarterly Reports 19
   Marketing Brochures and Advertisements 19
   Account Statements 20
Chapter 5: Understanding Risk 21
   A Look at Risk 21
   Standard Deviation 22
   Market Risk 22
   Beta 23
   Average Maturity 23
Chapter 6: Which Funds Were Included 25
   Size 25
   Loads 25
Chapter 7: A Key to Terms and Statistics 27
Chapter 8: Fund Performance Rankings 33
   Total Risk and Return Performance for Different Mutual Fund Categories 34
   Total Risk and Return for Domestic Taxable Bond Mutual Funds 34
   The Top 20 Performers: 1993 35
   The Bottom 20 Performers: 1993 35
   The Top 50 Performers: 10 Years, 1984-1993 36

The Top 50 Performers: Five Years, 1989-1993 37
The Top 50 Performers: Three Years, 1991-1993 38
Aggressive Growth Funds 39
Growth Funds 41
Growth and Income Funds 44
Balanced Funds 46
Corporate Bond Funds 47
Corporate High-Yield Bond Funds 48
Government Bond Funds 48
Mortgage-Backed Bond Funds 50
General Bond Funds 51
Tax-Exempt Bond Funds 52
International Stock Funds 55
International Bond Funds 57
Gold Funds 57
Small Capitalization Stock Funds 58
Chapter 9: Individual Fund Listings 61
Appendix A: Special Types of Funds 889
Asset Allocation Funds 889
Funds Investing in Funds 889
Global Funds 890
Index Mutual Funds 891
Sector Funds 891
Small Capitalization Stock Funds 893
Socially Conscious Funds 895
State-Specific Tax-Exempt Bond Funds 895
Appendix B: Changes to the Funds 899
Fund Name Changes 899
Investment Category Changes 900
Funds Dropped from the Guide 900
Index 901

How to Use This Guide 1

Selecting a mutual fund, while less time-consuming than investing in individual securities, does require some homework. No individual should put money into an investment that he or she does not understand. This does not require a detailed investigation of the fund's investments, but it does require some understanding of the investment objectives and strategies of the fund and the possible risks and returns.

This *Guide* is designed to provide you with that understanding. We have kept the chapters brief and to the point, so that individuals new to mutual fund investing will not be overwhelmed with unnecessary details.

Chapters 2 through 5 deal with the basics of investing in mutual funds—diversification; loads; the various categories of mutual funds and what they mean; how to read a mutual fund's prospectus and annual report, as well as any other information they send you; and how to evaluate the risk of a mutual fund.

Those who are familiar with mutual funds may want to skip directly to Chapter 6, which describes how the mutual funds were chosen for inclusion in the *Guide*. Chapter 7 is a key to the terms used in the performance tables and the mutual fund data pages, and includes an explanation of how the returns were calculated and what the different risk measures mean.

Chapter 8 presents the performance tables, which include the historical performance of different categories of mutual funds and their corresponding benchmarks. While past performance is no indication of future performance, it may indicate the quality and consistency of fund management. From this section, you should pick out several mutual funds that meet your investment objectives and risk tolerance. These funds can then be examined more closely in the mutual fund data pages.

Chapter 9 contains the individual fund listings. The funds are listed alphabetically; their ticker symbol and investment category are indicated at the top of the page after the fund's name. These pages provide 10 years of per share data, performance statistics along with risk measures, portfolio information, and shareholder services provided by the fund. Use the address and telephone numbers provided to call or write the funds to request a copy of the prospectus and annual report. Make sure you read the prospectus carefully before investing in any mutual fund.

At the back of the *Guide* is a list of funds that fall into special categories, which include: asset allocation, funds investing in other mutual funds, global, index, sector, small capitalization stocks, socially conscious, and state specific tax-exempt bond funds listed by state. And finally, there is a list of fund changes, including fund name changes, investment category changes, and a list of funds that were dropped from the *Guide*.

Investing in Mutual Funds   2

A mutual fund is an investment company that pools investors' money to invest in securities. An open-end mutual fund continuously issues new shares when investors want to invest in the fund, and it redeems shares when investors want to sell. A mutual fund trades directly with its shareholders, and the share price of the fund represents the market value of the securities that the fund holds.

There are several advantages that mutual funds offer individual investors. They provide:

- Professional investment management at a low cost, even for small accounts;
- A diversified group of securities that only a large portfolio can provide;
- Information through prospectuses and annual reports that facilitates comparisons among funds;
- Special services such as check writing, dividend reinvestment plans, telephone switching, and periodic withdrawal and investment plans;
- Account statements that make it easy to track the value of your investment and that ease the paperwork at tax time.

Successful investing takes time and effort, and it requires special knowledge and relevant, up-to-date information. Investors must spend a considerable amount of energy searching for opportunities and monitoring each investment. Professional investment management is relatively cheap with mutual funds. The typical adviser charges about 0.5% annually for managing a fund's assets. For an individual making a $10,000 investment, that comes to only $50 a year.

Of course, mutual fund investing does not preclude investing in securities on your own. One useful strategy would be to invest in mutual funds and individual securities. The mutual funds would ensure your participation in overall market moves and lend diversification to your portfolio, while the individual securities would provide you with the opportunity to apply your specific investment analysis skills.

DIVERSIFICATION

If there is one ingredient to successful investing that is universally agreed upon, it is the benefit of diversification. This is a concept that is backed by a great deal of research, market experience, and common sense. Diversification reduces risk. Risk to investors is frequently defined as volatility of return—in other words, how much an investment's return might vary over a year. Investors prefer returns that are relatively predictable, and thus less volatile. On the other hand, they want returns that are high, but higher returns are accompanied by higher risks. Diversification eliminates some of the risk without reducing potential returns.

Mutual funds, because of their size and the laws governing their operation, provide investors with diversification that might be difficult for an individual to duplicate. This is true not only for common stock funds, but also for bond funds, municipal bond funds, gold funds, international bond and stock funds—in fact, for almost all mutual funds. Even the sector funds that invest only within one industry offer diversification within that industry. The degree of diversification will vary among funds, but most will provide investors with some amount of diversification.

AVOIDING EXCESSIVE CHARGES

This book is dedicated to no-load and low-load mutual funds. Investors should realize that:

- A load is a sales commission that goes to the seller of the fund shares;
- A load does not go to anyone responsible for managing the fund's assets and does not serve as an incentive for the fund manager to perform better;
- Funds with loads, on average, consistently underperform no-load funds when the load is taken into consideration in performance calculations;
- For every high-performing load fund, there exists a similar no-load or low-load fund that can be purchased more cheaply;
- Loads understate the real commission charged because they reduce the total amount being invested: $10,000 invested in a 6% front-end load fund results in a $600 sales charge and only a $9,400 investment in the fund;
- If a load fund is held over a long time period, the effect of the load, if paid up front, is not diminished as quickly as many people believe; if the money paid for the load had been working for you, as in a no-load fund, it would have been compounding over the whole time period.

The bottom line in any investment is how it performs for you, the investor, and that performance includes consideration of all loads, fees and expenses. There may be some load funds that will do even better factoring in the load, but you have no way of finding that fund in advance. The only guide you have is historical performance, which is not necessarily an indication of future performance. With a heavily loaded fund, you are starting your investment with a significant loss—the load. Avoid unnecessary charges whenever possible.

SORTING OUT CHARGES

It is best to stick with no-load or low-load funds, but they are becoming more difficult to distinguish from heavily loaded funds. The use of high front-end loads has declined, and funds are now turning to other kinds of charges. Some mutual funds sold by brokerage firms, for example, have lowered their front-end loads to 5%, and others have introduced back-end loads (deferred sales charges), which are sales commissions paid when exiting the fund. In both instances, the load is often accompanied by annual charges.

On the other hand, some no-load funds have found that to compete, they must market themselves much more aggressively. To do so, they have introduced charges of their own.

The result has been the introduction of low loads, redemption fees, and annual charges. Low loads—up to 3%—are sometimes added instead of the annual charges. In addition, some funds have instituted a charge for investing or withdrawing money.

Redemption fees work like back-end loads: You pay a percentage of the value of your fund when you get out. Loads are on the amount you have invested, while redemption fees are calculated against the value of your fund assets. Some funds have sliding scale redemption fees, so that the longer you remain invested, the lower the charge when you leave. Some funds use redemption fees to discourage short-term trading, a policy that is designed to protect longer-term investors. These funds usually have redemption fees that disappear after six months.

Probably the most confusing charge is the annual charge, the 12b-1 plan. The adoption of a 12b-1 plan by a fund permits the adviser to use fund assets to pay for distribution costs, including advertising, distribution of fund literature such as prospectuses and annual reports, and sales commissions paid to brokers. Some funds use 12b-1 plans as masked load charges: They levy very high rates on the fund and use the money to pay brokers to sell the fund. Since the charge is annual and based on the value of the investment, this can result in a total cost to a long-term investor that exceeds a high up-front sales load. Other funds use money from 12b-1 plans to pay only distribution costs, and still others have 12b-1 plans but don't use them to levy charges against fund assets. In some instances, the fund adviser may use the 12b-1 plan to pay distribution expenses from his own pocket. A fee table is required in all prospectuses clarifying the impact of a 12b-1 plan and other charges.

The fee table makes the comparison of total expenses among funds easier. Selecting a fund based solely on expenses, including loads and charges, will not give you optimal results, but avoiding funds with high expenses and unnecessary charges is important for long-term performance.

Mutual Fund Categories 3

Mutual funds come in all shapes and sizes; there are over 800 funds covered in this book alone, each with its own characteristics. Many mutual funds, however, have shared investment objectives that generally lead to other characteristics that are similar.

These shared characteristics allow us to divide mutual funds into several broad categories. This chapter defines the mutual fund categories we used for this book. In this guide, the individual fund data pages appear alphabetically; the fund's category is indicated beneath the fund's name.

The following table summarizes some important characteristics of funds by category. Averages for expense ratio, income to assets ratio, portfolio turnover, and portfolio composition illustrate some of the differences in the categories.

Investment Category	Expense Ratio	Yield (%)	Portfolio Turnover (%)	Portfolio Composition (%)				
				Stocks	Bonds	Convertibles	Other	Cash
Aggressive Growth	1.60	0.2	138	90	1	0	0	9
Growth	1.23	0.8	79	83	2	1	2	12
Growth & Income	1.02	2.4	55	80	3	5	3	9
Balanced	1.00	3.3	78	48	32	3	10	7
Corporate Bond	0.71	6.1	162	0	91	1	3	5
Corp. High-Yield Bond	0.99	8.7	85	3	88	1	2	6
Government Bond	0.66	4.7	175	0	95	0	0	5
Mortgage-Backed Bond	0.74	6.4	134	0	96	0	0	4
General Bond	0.76	5.9	197	0	90	0	2	8
Tax-Exempt Bond	0.59	5.1	54	0	98	0	0	2
International Stock	1.62	0.7	70	86	4	1	1	8
International Bond	1.03	6.0	229	0	91	0	2	7
Gold	1.75	0.5	58	85	0	0	5	10
Domestic Equity Fund	1.26	1.2	88	84	2	2	2	10
Small Capitalization Stock	1.36	0.3	88	88	1	0	0	11
Domestic Taxable Bond	0.74	5.8	169	0	92	1	1	6

AGGRESSIVE GROWTH FUNDS

The investment objective of aggressive growth funds is maximum capital gains. They invest aggressively in common stocks and tend to stay fully invested over the market cycle. Sometimes, these funds will borrow money to purchase securities, and some may engage in trading stock options or take positions in stock index futures.

Aggressive growth funds typically provide low income distributions. This is because they tend to be fully invested in common stocks and do not earn a significant amount of interest income. In addition, the common stocks they invest in are generally growth-oriented stocks that pay little or no cash dividends.

Many aggressive growth funds concentrate their assets in particular industries or segments of the market, and their degree of diversification may not be as great as other types of funds. These investment strategies result in increased risk. Thus, they tend to perform better than the overall market during bull markets but fare worse during bear markets.

In general, long-term investors who need not be concerned with monthly or yearly variation in investment return will find investment in this class of funds rewarding. Because of the extreme volatility of return, however, risk-averse investors with a short-term investment horizon may find that these mutual funds lie well outside their comfort zones. During prolonged market declines, aggressive growth funds can sustain severe declines in net asset value.

Market timing is not a strategy we recommend, particularly over the short term. Although the transaction costs of switching in and out of no-load mutual funds are near zero, it can create significant tax liabilities. In addition, the ability to consistently time the market correctly in the short term, after adjusting for risk, costs, and taxes, has not been demonstrated. However, aggressive growth funds, with their high volatility and fully invested position, do make ideal vehicles for those who believe they know the next market move.

GROWTH FUNDS

The investment objective of growth funds is to obtain long-term growth of invested capital. They generally do not engage in speculative tactics such as using financial leverage. On occasion, these funds will use stock or index options or futures to reduce risk by hedging their portfolio positions.

Growth funds typically are more stable than aggressive growth funds. Generally, they invest in growth-oriented firms that are more mature and that pay cash dividends. You are likely to find companies such as Disney, PepsiCo, and McDonald's in the portfolios of growth funds.

The degree of concentration of assets is not as severe as with aggressive growth funds. Additionally, these funds tend to move from fully invested to partially invested positions over the market cycle. They build up cash positions during uncertain market environments.

In general, growth fund performance tends to mirror the market during bull and bear markets. Some growth funds have been able to perform relatively well during recent bear markets because their managers were able to change portfolio composition by a much greater degree or to maintain much higher cash positions than aggressive growth fund managers. However, higher cash positions can also cause the funds to underperform aggressive growth funds during bull markets.

Aggressive investors should consider holding both growth fund shares and aggressive growth fund shares in their overall portfolios. This is an especially appealing strategy for investors who hold aggressive growth mutual funds that invest in small stock growth firms. The portfolios of these funds complement the portfolios of growth funds, leading to greater overall diversification. The combination produces overall returns that will tend to be less volatile than an investment in only aggressive growth funds.

As with aggressive growth funds, these funds can sustain severe declines during prolonged bear markets. Since some portfolio managers of growth funds attempt to time the market over the longer market cycle, using these funds to move in and out of the market for timing purposes may be counterproductive.

GROWTH AND INCOME FUNDS

Growth and income funds generally invest in the common stocks and convertible securities of seasoned, well-established, cash-dividend-paying companies. The funds attempt to provide shareholders with significant income along with long-term growth. They generally attempt to avoid excessive fluctuations in return. One tends to find a high concentration of public utility common stocks and sometimes convertible securities in the portfolios of growth and income funds. The funds also provide higher income distributions, less variability in return, and greater diversification than growth and aggressive growth funds. Names such as equity-income, income, and total return have been attached to funds that have characteristics of growth and income funds. Because of the high current income offered by these kinds of funds, potential investors should keep the tax consequences in mind.

BALANCED FUNDS

The balanced fund category has become less distinct in recent years, and a significant overlap in fund objectives exists between growth and income funds and balanced funds. In general, the portfolios of balanced funds consist of investments in common stocks and substantial investments in bonds and convertible securities. The proportion of stocks and bonds that will be held is usually stated in the investment objective, but usually the portfolio manager has the option of allocating the proportions between some stated range. Some asset allocation funds—funds that have a wide latitude of portfolio composition change—can also be found in the balanced category. Balanced funds are generally less volatile than aggressive growth, growth, and growth and income funds. As with growth and income funds, balanced funds provide a high dividend yield.

BOND FUNDS

Bond mutual funds are attractive to investors because they provide diversification and liquidity, which may not be as readily attainable in direct bond investments.

Because of the potential diversity among bond funds, the funds have been broken down into six categories: corporate, high-yield corporate, government, mortgage-backed, general, and tax-exempt. While many bond funds hold more than one type of bond, the funds have been categorized by the holdings that predominate. Funds in the general category usually hold U.S. government and agency bonds, mortgage-backed bonds, and corporates. Tax-exempt bond funds hold only municipal bonds.

Bond funds have portfolios with a wide range of average maturities. Many funds use their names to characterize their maturity structure. Generally, short term means that the portfolio has a weighted average maturity of less than three years. Intermediate implies an average maturity of three to 10 years, and long term is over 10 years. The longer the maturity, the greater the change in fund value when interest rates change. Longer-term bond funds are riskier than shorter-term funds, and they tend to offer higher yields.

INTERNATIONAL BOND AND STOCK FUNDS

International funds invest in bonds and stocks of foreign firms and governments. Some funds specialize in regions, such as the Pacific or Europe, and others invest worldwide. In addition, some funds—usually termed "global funds"—invest in both foreign and U.S. securities. We have two classifications of international funds—international stock funds and international bond funds—and we provide a portfolio breakdown by country.

International funds provide investors with added diversification. The most important factor when diversifying a portfolio is selecting assets that do not behave similarly to each other under similar economic scenarios. Within the U.S., investors can diversify by selecting securities of firms in different industries. In the international realm, investors take the diversification process one step further by holding securities of firms in different countries. The more independently these foreign markets move in relation to the U.S. stock market, the greater will be the diversification benefit, and the lower the risk.

In addition, international funds overcome some of the difficulties investors face in making foreign investments directly. For instance, individuals have to thoroughly understand the foreign brokerage process, be familiar with the various foreign marketplaces and their economies, be aware of currency fluctuation trends, and have access to reliable financial information. This can be a monumental task for the individual investor.

There are some risks to investing internationally. In addition to the risk inherent in investing in any security, there is an additional exchange rate risk. The return to a U.S. investor from a foreign security depends on both the security's return in its own currency and the rate at which that currency can be exchanged for U.S. dollars. Another uncertainty is political risk, which includes government restriction, taxation, or even total prohibition of the exchange of one currency into another. Of course, the more the mutual fund is diversified among various countries, the less the risk involved.

GOLD FUNDS

Gold mutual funds specialize in investments in both foreign and domestic companies that mine gold and other precious metals. Some funds also hold gold directly through investments in gold coins or bullion. Gold options are another method used to invest in the industry. Mutual fund investments in precious metals range from the conservative to the highly speculative.

Gold and other precious metals mutual funds allow investors interested in this area to invest in a more liquid and diversified vehicle than would be available through a direct purchase.

The appeal of gold and precious metals is that they have performed well during extreme inflationary periods. Over the short term, the price of gold moves in response to a variety of political, economic, and psychological forces. As world tension and anxiety rise, so may the price of gold. In periods of peace and stability, the price of gold may decline. Because gold may perform in an inverse relationship to stocks, bonds, and cash, it may be a stabilizing component in one's portfolio. Silver and platinum react in a similar fashion to gold. Precious metals funds, like the metals themselves, are very volatile, often shooting from the bottom to the top and back to the bottom in fund rankings over the years. Investors should understand, however, that because most gold funds invest in the stock of gold mining companies, they are still subject to some stock market risk.

OTHER TYPES OF FUNDS

There are many specialized mutual funds that do not have their own categories. Instead, they will be found in one of the various categories mentioned above. These funds are classified by their investment objectives rather than by their investment strategies. For instance, several funds specialize in specific sectors or industries, but one industry-specific fund does not necessarily appear in the same category as another industry-specific sector fund. For example, a technology sector fund would likely appear in the aggressive growth category while a utility sector fund would be found in the growth and income category. Other funds that may appear in various categories are small company funds, "socially conscious" funds, index funds, funds investing in funds, and asset allocation funds.

Asset allocation funds, for example, are usually one of two types. Some allocation funds are designed to provide diversification among the various categories of investments and within each investment category. For example, an asset allocation fund may hold minimum percentages in stocks, bonds, cash, and international investments. The second asset allocation strategy used by some funds is to move money around according to what the fund managers believe to be optimal proportions given their expectations for the economy, interest rates, and other market factors. These latter asset allocation funds are market timing funds, distinctly different and with greater risk than the asset allocation funds striving solely for diversification. These market-timing asset allocation funds are noted in the book.

One other fund type deserves a special mention—the index fund. An example of an index fund is Vanguard's Index Trust—500, categorized as a growth and income fund. This fund is designed to match the Standard & Poor's 500 stock index and does so by investing in all 500 stocks in the S&P 500; the amounts invested in each stock are proportional to the firm's market value representation in the S&P 500. Statistics on this fund are quite useful for comparison with other funds, since the index represents a widely followed segment of the market. Index funds are available covering most major segments of the bond and stock markets, domestic and international. Because they are unmanaged, they make no research efforts to select particular stocks or bonds, nor do they make timing decisions. This passive management approach makes the cost of managing an index fund relatively low. A list of specialized funds is at the back of this *Guide*.

Understanding Mutual Fund Statements 4

One of the advantages of mutual fund investing is the wealth of information that mutual funds provide to fund investors and prospective investors. Taken together, the various reports provide investors with vital information concerning financial matters and how the fund is managed, both key elements in the selection process. In fact, mutual fund prospectuses, annual reports, and performance statistics, are key sources of information most investors will need in the selection and monitoring process.

To new mutual fund investors, the information may seem overwhelming. However, regulations governing the industry have standardized the reports: Once you know where to look for information, the location will hold true for almost all funds.

There are basically five types of statements produced by the mutual fund: the prospectus; the statement of additional information; annual, semiannual, and quarterly reports; marketing brochures; and account statements. Actually, the second report—the statement of additional information—is part of the prospectus. However, the Securities and Exchange Commission allows mutual funds to simplify and streamline the prospectus, if they choose, by dividing it into two parts: Part A, which all prospective investors must receive if requested, and Part B—the statement of additional information—which the fund must send investors if they specifically request it. In practice, when most people (including the funds) refer to the prospectus, they are referring to Part A. For simplicity, that is what we will do here as well.

THE PROSPECTUS

The prospectus is the single most important document produced by the mutual fund, and it is must-reading for investors before investing. Current shareholders must be sent new prospectuses when they are updated, at least once every 14 months.

The prospectus is generally organized into sections, and although it must cover specific topics, the overall structure may differ somewhat among funds. The cover usually gives a quick synopsis of the fund: investment category, sales or redemption charges, minimum investment, retirement plans available, address and telephone number. More detailed descriptions are in the body of the prospectus.

Fee Table: All mutual fund prospectuses must include a table near the front that delineates all fees and charges to the investor. The table contains three sections: The first section lists all transaction charges to the investor, including all front-end and back-end loads and redemption fees; the second section lists all annual fund operating expenses, including management fees and any 12b-1 charges, as a percentage of net assets; and the third section is an illustration of the total cost of these fees and charges to an investor over time. The illustration assumes an initial investment of $1,000 and a 5% growth rate for the fund, and states the total dollar cost to an investor if he were to redeem his shares at the end of one year, three years, five years, and 10 years.

The Prospectus Fee Table: An Example

Expenses

The purpose of the following table is to assist you in understanding the various costs and expenses that an investor in the Funds may bear directly or indirectly. For a more complete explanation of the fees and expenses borne by the Funds, see the discussions under the prospectus headings "How to Purchase Shares" and "Management of the Funds", as well as the Statement of Additional Information incorporated by reference into this prospectus.

Shareholder Transaction Expenses

	Oakmark Fund	Oakmark International
Sales Load on Purchases	None	None
Sales Load on Reinvested Dividends	None	None
Deferred Sales Load	None	None
Redemption Fees (a)	None	None
Exchange Fees	$5.00	$5.00

Annual Fund Operating Expenses
(as percentage of net assets)

	Oakmark Fund	Oakmark International
Management Fees	1.00%	1.00%
12b-1 Fees	None	None
Other Expenses	0.70%	1.04%(b)
Total Fund Operating Expenses	1.70%	2.04%(b)

(a) If you request payment of redemption proceeds by wire, you must pay the cost of the wire (currently $5.00).

The following example illustrates the expenses that you would pay on a $1,000 investment in each Fund over various time periods assuming (1) a 5% annual rate of return, (2) the operating expense percentage listed in the table above remains the same through each of the periods, (3) reinvestment of all dividends and capital gain distributions, and (4) redemption at the end of each time period.

	1 Year	3 Years	5 Years	10 Years
The Oakmark Fund	$17	$54	$92	$201
The Oakmark International Fund	$21	$64	n/a	n/a

This example should not be considered a representation of past or future expenses or performance. Actual expenses may be greater or less than those shown.

Source: Oakmark prospectus, March 1, 1993.

Selected Per Share Data and Ratios: An Example

	500 Portfolio									
	Year Ended December 31,									
	1992	1991	1990	1989	1988	1987	1986	1985	1984	1983
Net Asset Value, Beginning of Year	$39.32	$31.24	$33.64	$27.18	$24.65	$24.27	$22.99	$19.52	$19.70	$17.56
Investment Activities										
Income	1.20	1.22	1.24	1.27	1.14	.95	.96	.97	.93	.93
Expenses	(.08)	(.07)	(.07)	(.07)	(.06)	(.07)	(.07)	(.06)	(.05)	(.06)
Net Investment Income	1.12	1.15	1.17	1.20	1.08	.88	.89	.91	.88	.87
Net Realized and Unrealized Gain (Loss) on Investments	1.75	8.20	(2.30)	7.21	2.87	.36	3.30	5.08	.30	2.85
Total from Investment Activities	2.87	9.35	(1.13)	8.41	3.95	1.24	4.19	5.99	1.18	3.72
Distributions										
Net Investment Income	(1.12)	(1.15)	(1.17)	(1.20)	(1.10)	(.69)	(.89)	(.91)	(.88)	(.87)
Realized Net Gain	(.10)	(.12)	(.10)	(.75)	(.32)	(.17)	(2.02)	(1.61)	(.48)	(.71)
Total Distributions	(1.22)	(1.27)	(1.27)	(1.95)	(1.42)	(.86)	(2.91)	(2.52)	(1.36)	(1.58)
Net Asset Value, End of Year	$40.97	$39.32	$31.24	$33.64	$27.18	$24.65	$24.27	$22.99	$19.52	$19.70
Ratio of Expenses to Average Net Assets	.19%	.20%	.22%	.21%	.22%	.26%	.28%	.28%	.27%	.28%
Ratio of Net Investment Income to Average Net Assets	2.81%	3.07%	3.60%	3.62%	4.08%	3.15%	3.40%	4.09%	4.53%	4.22%
Portfolio Turnover Rate	4%	5%	23%	8%	10%	15%	29%	36%	14%	35%
Shares Outstanding, End of Year (thousands)	159,811	110,526	69,555	53,626	38,815	33,527	19,984	17,148	14,841	11,861

Source: *Vanguard Index Trust—500 prospectus, May 1, 1993.*

Selected Per Share Data and Ratios: One of the most important sections of the prospectus contains the selected per share data and ratios, which provides statistics on income and capital changes per share of the fund. The per share figures are given for the life of the fund or 10 years, whichever is less. Also included are important statistical summaries of investment activities throughout each period. Occasionally these financial statements are only referred to in the prospectus and are actually contained in the annual report, which in this instance would accompany the prospectus.

The per share section summarizes the financial activity over the fund's fiscal year, which may or may not correspond to the calendar year, to arrive at the end-of-year net asset value for the fund. The financial activity summarized includes increases in net asset value due to dividend and interest payments received and capital gains from investment activity. Decreases in net asset value are due to capital losses from investment activity, investment expenses, and payouts to fund shareholders in the form of distributions.

Potential investors may want to note the line items in this section. *Investment income* represents the dividends and interest earned by the fund during its fiscal year. *Expenses* reflect such fund costs as the management fee, legal fees, and transfer agent fees. These expenses are given in detail in the statement of operations section of the annual report.

Net investment income is investment income less expenses. This line is important for investors to note because it reflects the level and stability of net income over the time period. A high net investment income would most likely be found in funds that have income rather than growth as their investment category. Since net investment income must be distributed to shareholders to avoid direct taxation of the fund, a high net investment income has the potential of translating into a high tax liability for the investor.

Net realized and unrealized gain (loss) on investments is the change in the value of investments that have been sold (realized) during the year or that continue to be held (unrealized) by the fund.

Distributions to fund shareholders are also detailed. These distributions will include dividends from net investment income for the current fiscal period. Tax law requires that income earned must be distributed in the calendar year earned. Also included in distributions will be any realized net capital gains.

The last line in the per share section will be the *net asset value* at the end of the year, which reflects the value of one share of the fund. It is calculated by determining the total assets of the fund and dividing by the number of mutual fund shares outstanding. The figure will change for a variety of reasons, including changes in investment income, expenses, gains, losses, and distributions. Depending upon the source of change, a decline in net asset value may or may not be due to poor performance. For instance, a decline in net asset value may be due to a distribution of net realized gains on securities.

The financial ratios at the bottom of the per share financial data are important indicators of fund performance and strategy. The *expense ratio* relates expenses incurred by the fund to average net assets. These expenses include the investment advisory fee, legal and accounting fees, and 12b-1 charges to the fund; they do not include fund brokerage costs, loads, or redemption fees. A high expense ratio detracts from your investment return. In general, common stock funds have higher expense ratios than bond funds, and smaller funds have higher expense ratios than larger funds. International funds also tend to have higher expense ratios than domestic funds. Index funds usually have the lowest expense ratios. The average expense ratio for common stock funds is 1.5%, and for bond funds about 1.0%. An expense ratio significantly above 1.5% is cause for concern.

The *ratio of net investment income to average net assets* is very similar to a dividend yield. This, too, should reflect the investment category of the fund. Common stock funds with income as a significant part of their investment objective would be expected to have a ratio in the 2% to 4% range under current market conditions, and aggressive growth funds would have a ratio closer to 0%. Bond funds would normally have ratios more than twice those of common stock funds.

The *portfolio turnover rate* is the lower of purchases or sales divided by average net assets. It reflects how frequently securities are bought and sold by the fund. For purposes of determining the turnover rate for common stock funds, fixed-income securities with a maturity of less than a year are excluded, as are all government securities, short- and long-term. For bond funds, however, long-term U.S. government bonds are included.

Investors should take note of the portfolio turnover rate, because the higher the turnover, the greater the brokerage costs incurred by the fund. Brokerage costs are not reflected in the expense ratio but instead are directly reflected as a decrease in net asset value. In addition, mutual funds with high turnover rates generally have higher capital gains distributions—a potential tax liability. Aggressive growth mutual funds are most likely to have high turnover rates. Some bond funds also have very high portfolio turnover rates. A 100% portfolio turnover rate indicates that the portfolio was completely turned over in a year; a 200% portfolio turnover indicates that the portfolio was completely turned over twice in a year. The portfolio turnover rate for the average mutual fund is around 100% but varies with market conditions and investment category.

Investment Objective/Policy: The investment objective section of the prospectus elaborates on the brief sentence or two from the prospectus cover. In this section, the fund describes the types of investments it will make—whether it is bonds, stocks, convertible securities, options, etc.—along with some general guidelines as to the proportions these securities will represent in the fund's portfolio. The investment objective statement usually indicates whether it will be oriented toward capital gains or income. In this section, the management will also briefly discuss its approach to market timing, risk assumption, and the anticipated level of portfolio turnover. Some prospectuses may indicate any investment restrictions they have placed on the fund, such as purchasing securities on margin, selling short, concentrating in firms or industries, trading foreign securities, and lending securities; this section may also state the allowable proportions in certain investment categories. The restrictions section is usually given in more detail in the statement of additional information.

Fund Management: The fund management section names the investment adviser and gives the advisory fee schedule. Most advisers charge a management fee on a sliding scale that decreases as assets under management increase. Occasionally, some portion of the fund adviser's fees are subject to the fund's performance relative to the market.

Some prospectuses will describe the fund's officers and directors with a short biography of affiliations and relevant experience. For most funds, however, this information is provided in more detail in the statement of additional information. The board of directors is elected by fund shareholders; the fund adviser is selected by the board of directors. The adviser is usually a firm operated by or affiliated with officers of the fund. Information on fund officers and directors is not critical to fund selection. In the prospectus the portfolio manager for the fund is named. The portfolio manager is responsible for the day-to-day investment decisions of the fund and is employed by the fund adviser. Who the portfolio manager is and how long the manager has been in the position can be useful in judging historical performance.

Other Important Sections: There are several other sections in a mutual fund prospectus that investors should be aware of. They will appear under various headings, depending upon the prospectus, but they are not difficult to find.

Mutual funds that have 12b-1 plans must describe them in the prospectus. Under SEC rules, a description of these plans must be prominently and clearly placed in the prospectus, usually in a section titled "Distribution Plan." The distribution plan details the marketing aspects of the fund and how it relates to fund expenses. For instance, advertising, distribution of fund literature, and any arrangements with brokers would be included in the marketing plan; the 12b-1 plan pays for these distribution expenses. Sometimes, these plans do not charge the fund for the expenses but rather allow the adviser to pay for them. The distribution plan section specifies the maximum annual 12b-1 charge that can be made. Funds often charge less than the maximum. The actual charge to the fund of a 12b-1 plan is listed at the front of the prospectus in the fee table.

The capital stock section, or fund share characteristics section, provides shareholders with a summary of their voting rights, participation in dividends and distributions, and the number of authorized and issued shares of the fund. Often, a separate section will discuss the tax treatment that will apply to fund distributions, which may include dividends, interest, and capital gains.

The how-to-buy-shares section gives the minimum initial investment and any subsequent minimums; it will also list load charges or fees. In addition, information on mail, wire, and telephone purchases is provided, along with distribution reinvestment options, automatic exchange, investment and withdrawal plans, and retirement options.

The how-to-redeem-shares section discusses telephone, written, and wire redemption options, including automatic withdrawal plans, with a special section on signature guarantees and other documents that may be needed. Also detailed are any fees for reinvestment or redemption. Shareholder services are usually outlined here, with emphasis on exchanges among funds in a family of funds. This will include any fees for exchanging, any limits on the number of exchanges allowed, and any exchange restrictions.

STATEMENT OF ADDITIONAL INFORMATION

This document elaborates on the prospectus. The investment objectives section is more in-depth, with a list and description of investment restrictions. The management section gives brief biographies of directors and officers, and provides the number of fund shares owned beneficially by the officers and directors named. The investment adviser section, while reiterating the major points made in the prospectus, gives all the expense items and contract provisions of the agreement between the adviser and the fund. If the fund has a 12b-1 plan, further details will likely be in the statement of additional information.

Many times, the statement of additional information will include much more information on the tax consequences of mutual fund distributions and investment. Conditions under which withholding for federal income tax will take place are also provided. The fund's financial statements are incorporated by reference to the annual report to shareholders and generally do not appear in the statement of additional information. Finally, the independent auditors give their opinion on the accuracy of the fund's financial statements.

ANNUAL, SEMIANNUAL, AND QUARTERLY REPORTS

All funds must send their shareholders audited annual and semiannual reports. Mutual funds are allowed to combine their prospectus and annual report; some do this, but many do not.

The annual report describes the fund activities over the past year and provides a listing of all investments of the fund at market value as of the end of the fiscal year. Sometimes the cost basis of each investment is also given. Looking in-depth at the individual securities held by the fund is probably a waste of time. However, it is helpful to be aware of the overall investment categories. For instance, investors should look at the percentage invested in common stocks, bonds, convertible bonds, and any other holdings. In addition, a look at the types of common stocks held and the percentage of fund assets by industry classification gives the investor some indication of how the portfolio will fare in various market environments.

The annual report will also have a balance sheet, which lists all assets and liabilities of the fund by general category. This holds little interest for investors.

The statement of operations, similar to an income statement, is of interest only in that the fund expenses are broken down. For most funds, the management fee is by far the largest expense; the expense ratio in the prospectus conveys much more useful information. The statement of changes in net assets is very close to the financial information provided in the prospectus, but the information is not on a per share basis. Per share information will, however, frequently be detailed in the annual report in a separate section. Footnotes to the financial statements elaborate on the entries, but other than any pending litigation against the fund, they are most often routine.

The quarterly or semiannual reports are current accounts of the investment portfolio and provide more timely views of the fund's investments than does the annual report.

MARKETING BROCHURES AND ADVERTISEMENTS

These will generally provide a brief description of the fund. However, the most important bit of information will be the telephone number to call to receive the fund prospectus and annual report, if you have not received them already.

The SEC has tightened and standardized the rules regarding mutual fund advertising. All mutual funds that use performance figures in their ads must now include one-, three-, five-, and 10-year total return figures. Bond funds that quote yields must use a standardized method for computing yield, and they must include total return figures as well. Finally, any applicable sales commissions must be mentioned in the advertisement.

ACCOUNT STATEMENTS

Mutual funds send out periodic account statements detailing reinvestment of dividend and capital gains distributions, new purchases or redemptions, and any other account activity such as service fees. This statement provides a running account balance by date with share accumulations, an account value to date, and a total of distributions made to date. These statements are invaluable for tax purposes and should be saved. The fund will also send out, in January, a Form 1099-DIV for any distributions made in the previous year and a Form 1099-B if any mutual fund shares were sold.

Understanding Risk $\quad$ 5

Risk tolerance refers to the level of volatility of an investment that an investor finds acceptable. The anticipated holding period of an investment is important because it should affect the investor's risk tolerance. Time is a form of diversification; longer holding periods provide greater diversification across different market environments. Investors who anticipate longer holding periods can take on more risk.

The liquidity needs of an investor similarly help define the types of funds that the investor should consider. Liquidity implies preservation of capital, and if liquidity is important, then mutual funds with smaller variations in value should be considered. A liquid mutual fund is one in which withdrawals from the fund can be made at any time with a reasonable certainty that the per share value will not have dropped sharply. Highly volatile aggressive growth funds are the least liquid, and short-term fixed-income funds are the most liquid.

A LOOK AT RISK

Risk is the most difficult concept for many investors to grasp, and yet much of the mutual fund investment decision depends on an understanding of risk. There are many different ways to categorize investment risk and numerous approaches to the measurement of risk. If we can assume that the volatility of the return on your mutual fund investment is the concern you grapple with when you think of risk, the task of making decisions about risk becomes easier.

Questions about how much value a mutual fund is likely to lose in a down market or how certain it is that a fund will be worth a given amount at the end of the year are the same concerns as volatility of return. Changes in the domestic and international economies, interest rates, exchange rates, corporate profits, consumer confidence, and general expectations all combine to move markets up and down, creating volatility, or risk.

Total risk for a mutual fund measures variation in return from all sources. As an example, variation in return for common stocks is caused by factors unique to the firm, industry variables, and conditions affecting all stocks. Market risk refers to the variables such as interest rates, inflation, and the business cycle that affect all stocks to some degree. In well-diversified portfolios of common stock, the firm and industry risk of the various stocks in the portfolio offset each other; thus, these portfolios tend to have lower total risk, and this total risk is usually composed almost entirely of market risk. For less diversified portfolios, funds that hold very few stocks, or sector funds that concentrate investment in one industry, total risk is usually higher and is composed of firm and industry risk in addition to market risk.

Risk levels based upon total risk are given for all funds with 36 months of performance data. The five categories (high, above average, average, below average, and low) serve as a way to compare the risk inherent in common stock funds, international funds, sector funds, bond funds, or any type of mutual fund. Shorter-term bond funds would be expected to have relatively low total risk while some of the concentrated, less-diversified, aggressive common stock funds would likely be ranked in the high total risk category.

The total risk measure will enable you to construct a portfolio of funds that reflects your risk tolerance and the holding period you anticipate for your portfolio. Portfolios for individuals with low risk tolerance and short holding periods should be composed predominantly of funds that are less volatile, with lower total risk. Individuals with high risk tolerances and longer holding periods can form appropriate portfolios by combining mutual funds with higher total risk.

STANDARD DEVIATION

Total risk is measured by the standard deviation statistic, a numerical measure of how much the return on a mutual fund has varied, no matter what the cause, from the historical average return of the fund. Higher standard deviations indicate higher total risk. The category risk rank measures the total risk of a fund to the average total risk for all funds in the same investment category. The rankings for category risk are high, above average, average, below average, and low. Funds ranked above average and high for category risk should produce returns above the average for the investment category.

The risk index indicates the magnitude of the standard deviation for a fund relative to the average standard deviation for funds in the category. A risk index of 1.20, for example, means that the standard deviation for a fund is 20% higher than the average standard deviation for the category.

MARKET RISK

Market risk is a part of total risk but measures only the sensitivity of the fund to movements in the general market. This is valuable information to the individual investor, particularly when combined with use of the total risk and category risk rank measures, to judge how a mutual fund will perform in different market situations. The market risk measure used for common stock funds is beta; for bond funds, average maturity is used.

BETA

Beta is a measure of the relative volatility inherent in a mutual fund investment. This volatility is compared to some measure of the market such as Standard & Poor's index of 500 common stocks. The market's beta is always 1.0 by definition, and a money market fund's beta is always 0. If you hold a mutual fund with a beta of 1.0, it will move, on average, in tandem with the market. If the market is up 10%, the fund will be up, on average, 10%, and if the market drops 10%, the fund will drop, on average, 10%. A mutual fund with a beta of 1.5 is 50% more volatile than the market: If the market is up 10%, the fund will be up, on average, 50% more, or 15%; conversely, if the market is down 10%, the fund, on average, will be down 15%. A negative beta, a rare occurrence, implies that the mutual fund moves in the opposite direction of the market's movement.

The higher the fund's beta, the greater the volatility of the investment in the fund and the less appropriate the fund would be for shorter holding periods or to meet liquidity needs. Remember that beta is a relative measure: A low beta only implies that the fund's movement is not volatile relative to the market. Its return, however, may be quite variable, resulting in high total risk. For instance, industry-specific sector fund moves may not be related to market volatility, but changes in the industry may cause their returns to fluctuate widely. For a well-diversified stock fund, beta is a very useful measure of risk, but for concentrated funds, beta only captures a portion of the variability that the fund may experience. Betas for gold funds, for example, can be very misleading. Gold funds often have relatively low betas, but these funds are extremely volatile. Their volatility stems from factors that do not affect the common stock market as much. In addition, the betas of gold funds sometimes change significantly from year to year.

AVERAGE MATURITY

For all bond funds, the average maturity of the bonds in the portfolio is reported as a market risk measure, rather than beta. The volatility of a bond fund is determined by how the fund reacts primarily to changes in interest rates, although high-yield (junk) bond funds and international bond funds can be affected significantly by factors other than interest rates. When interest rates rise, bond funds fall in value, and conversely, when interest rates fall, bond mutual funds rise in value. The longer the average maturity of the bond fund, the greater will be the variation in the return on the bond fund when interest rates change. Bond mutual fund investors with less risk tolerance and shorter holding periods should seek shorter maturity funds, and longer-term bond fund investors who are more risk tolerant will find funds with longer maturities a better match.

In the case where a bond fund holds mortgage-backed securities, average maturity may not capture the potential for decline in effective maturity when interest rates fall and mortgages are refinanced. Bond funds that hold corporate bonds and municipal bonds also face changing effective maturities when interest rates decline and bond issuers call bonds before maturity.

Which Funds Were Included

6

The funds that appear in *The Individual Investor's Guide to Low-Load Mutual Funds* were selected from a large universe of funds. Following are the various screens we used to arrive at the final selection.

SIZE

Funds must appear on the National Association of Securities Dealers mutual fund list found in most major newspapers. To qualify for the list, funds must either have at least 1,000 shareholders or more than $25 million under management.

LOADS

The decision as to what constitutes a significant load is difficult, but we took this approach in the *Guide*:

- All funds with front-end loads, back-end loads, or redemption fees of 3% or less were included if the fund did not also have a 12b-1 charge. Funds with redemption fees that disappear after six months that also have 12b-1 charges appear in this *Guide*.
- Funds with 12b-1 plans and no front- or back-end loads were included in the *Guide*; we note, however, if the fund has a 12b-1 plan and what the maximum annual charge is. Investors should carefully assess these plans individually.

A Key to Terms and Statistics

7

Much of the information used in the mutual fund data pages and performance tables is from mutual fund reports (the prospectus and annual and quarterly reports) and our own solicitation of information from the fund. Other statistics, such as fund performance and risk, were calculated by AAII. All numbers are truncated rather than rounded.

When *na* appears in the performance tables or on the mutual fund page, it indicates that the number was not available or does not apply in that particular instance. For example, the 10-year annual return figure would not be available for funds that have been operating less than 10 years. For three-year annual return, category risk, standard deviation, total risk, and beta, funds operating less than three years would not have the number available. We do not compile the bull and bear ratings for funds not operating during the entire bull or bear market period. A dash (—) indicates that the information for that item does not exist. Dashes are used generally during years when the fund was not in operation or did not have a complete calendar year of operations.

The following provides an explanation of the terms we have used in the performance tables and mutual fund data pages. The explanations are listed in the order in which the data and information appear on the mutual fund pages.

Fund Name: The funds are presented alphabetically by fund name.

Ticker: The ticker symbol for each fund is given in parentheses for those investors who may want to access on-line data with their computer or touch-tone phone. The ticker is four letters and is usually followed by an "X," indicating that this is a mutual fund. For example, the Acorn fund ticker symbol is ACRNX.

Investment Category: The fund's investment category is indicated at the top of the page next to the fund's ticker symbol. After evaluating the information and statistics, we placed all mutual funds in exclusive categories by investment category and type of investment. For more complete definitions of the mutual fund investment categories used in the *Guide*, see Chapter 3.

Fund Address and Telephone Number(s): The address and telephone number where investors can write or call to have specific questions answered or to obtain a copy of the prospectus.

Performance

Return (%): Return percentages for the periods below.

3yr Annual: Assuming an investment on January 1, 1991, the annual total return if held through December 31, 1993.

5yr Annual: Assuming an investment on January 1, 1989, the annual total return if held through December 31, 1993.

10yr Annual: Assuming an investment on January 1, 1984, the annual total return if held through December 31, 1993.

Bull: This return reflects the fund's performance in the most recent bull market, starting October 1, 1990, and continuing through December 31, 1993.

Bear: This return reflects the fund's performance in the most recent bear market, from January 1, 1990, through September 30, 1990.

Differ from category (+/−): The difference between the return for the fund and average return for all funds in the same investment category for the *3yr Annual, 5yr Annual, 10yr Annual, Bull,* and *Bear* periods. When the difference from category is negative, the fund underperformed the average fund in its investment category for the period by the percent indicated. The rankings, with possibilities of high, above average, average, below average, low, are relative to all other funds within the same investment category. A rank of high, for example, would indicate that the return is in the highest 20% for that time period of all funds in the investment category.

Total Risk: The total risk of a fund relative to the total risk of all funds in the *Guide.* A high total risk indicates that the fund was in the group that had the greatest volatility of return for all funds, and a low total risk puts it into the group with the lowest volatility of return. Possibilities are high, above average, average, below average, low.

Standard Deviation: A measure of total risk, expressed as an annual return, that indicates the degree of variation in return experienced relative to the average return for a fund. The higher the standard deviation, the greater the total risk of the fund. Standard deviation of any fund can be compared to any other fund.

Category Risk: The total risk of the fund relative to the average total risk for funds within the same investment category. High category risk would, for example, indicate one of the highest total risks in the investment category. The possibilities are high, above average, average, below average, low.

Risk Index: A numerical measure of relative category risk, the risk index is a ratio of the total risk of the fund to the average total risk of funds in the category. Ratios above 1.00 indicate higher than average risk and ratios below 1.00 indicate lower than average risk for the category.

Beta: A risk measure that relates the fund's volatility of returns to the market. The higher the beta of a fund, the higher the market risk of the fund. The figure is based on monthly returns for 36 months. A beta of 1.0 indicates that the fund's returns will on average be as volatile as the market and move in the same direction; a beta higher than 1.0 indicates that if the market rises or falls, the fund will rise or fall respectively but to a greater degree; a beta of less than 1.0 indicates that if the market rises or falls, the fund will rise or fall to a lesser degree. The S&P 500 index always has a beta of 1.0 because it is the measure we selected to represent the overall stock market. Beta is a meaningful figure of risk only for well-diversified common stock portfolios. For sector funds and other concentrated portfolios, beta is less useful than total risk as a measure of risk. Beta was not calculated for bond funds since they do not react in the same way to the factors that affect the stock market. For bond funds, the average maturity of the bond portfolio is more indicative of market risk than beta and is used in place of beta.

Avg Mat: For bond funds, average maturity in years is an indication of market risk. When interest rates rise, bond prices fall and when interest rates fall, bond prices rise. The longer the average maturity of the bonds held in the portfolio, the greater will be the sensitivity of the fund to interest rate changes and thus the greater the risk. The refinancing of mortgages and the calling of outstanding bonds can affect average maturity when interest rates decline. An *na* indicates that the mutual fund did not provide us with an average maturity figure.

Return (%): This is a total return figure, expressed as a percentage and was computed using monthly net asset values per share and shareholder distributions during the year. All distributions were assumed to have been reinvested on the reinvestment date (ex-dividend date or payable date). Rate of return is calculated on the basis of the calendar year. Return figures do not take into account front-end and back-end loads, redemption fees, or one-time or annual account charges, if any. The 12b-1 charge is reflected in the return figure.

Differ from Category (+/–): The difference between the return for the fund and average return for all funds in the same investment category for the time period.

Per Share Data

Dividends, Net Income ($): Per share income distributions for the calendar year.

Distrib'ns, Cap Gains ($): Per share distributions for the year from realized capital gains after netting out realized losses. These distributions vary each year with both the investment success of the fund and the amount of securities sold.

Net Asset Value ($): Net asset value is the sum of all securities held, based on their market value, divided by the number of mutual fund shares outstanding.

Expense Ratio (%): The sum of administrative fees plus adviser management fees and 12b-1 fees divided by the average net asset value of the fund, stated as a percentage. Brokerage costs incurred by the fund are not included in the expense ratio but are instead reflected directly in net asset value. Front-end loads, back-end loads, redemption fees, and account activity charges are not included in this ratio.

Net Income to Assets (%): The income of the fund from dividends and interest after expenses, divided by the average net asset value of the fund. This ratio is similar to a dividend yield and would be higher for income-oriented funds and lower for growth-oriented funds. The figure only reflects income and does not reflect capital gains or losses. It is not total return.

Portfolio Turnover (%): A measure of the trading activity of the fund, which is computed by dividing the lesser of purchases or sales for the year by the monthly average value of the securities owned by the fund during the year. Securities with maturities of less than one year are excluded from the calculation. The result is expressed as a percentage, with 100% implying a complete portfolio turnover within one year.

Total Assets (Millions $): Aggregate fund value in millions of dollars.

Portfolio

Portfolio Manager: The name of the portfolio manager(s) and the year when the manager(s) began managing the fund are noted, providing additional information useful in evaluating past performance. Funds managed by a committee are so noted. For some funds, a recent change in the portfolio manager(s) may indicate that the long-term annual performance figures and other performance classifications are less meaningful.

Investm't Category: Notes the investment category of the fund. Following this is the growth (capital gains) versus income emphasis of the fund, what the geographical distribution is, and any special emphasis of the fund. The possible choices in the section are below.

Growth versus Income Emphasis: Capital Gains, Capital Gains & Income, and Income.

Geographical Distribution: Domestic, Foreign, Country/Region.

Special Emphasis: Asset Allocation, Fund of Funds, Index, Sector, Small Cap, Socially Conscious, and State Specific.

Portfolio: This information was obtained directly from the fund's annual and quarterly reports. The portfolio composition classifies investments by type and gives the percentage of the total portfolio invested in each. Some funds employ leverage (borrowing) to buy securities, and this may result in the portfolio total percent invested exceeding 100%.

Largest Holdings: This may indicate industries, types of securities, government versus corporate bonds, for example, or in the case of international funds, the percentages held by country. For municipal bond funds the percentage held in general obligation bonds is indicated.

Unrealized Net Capital Gains: Indicates percentage of current portfolio that represents net unrealized capital gains (or losses) and potential capital gains distributions.

Shareholder Information

Minimum Investment and Minimum IRA Investment: The minimum initial and subsequent investments, by mail, in the fund are detailed. Minimum investment by telephone or by wire may be different. Often, funds will have a lower minimum IRA investment; this is also indicated.

Maximum Fees:

Load: The maximum load is given, if any, and whether the load is front-end or back-end is indicated.

12b-1: If a fund has a 12b-1 plan, the maximum amount that can be charged is given; remember, though, that while no more than the maximum can be charged, some funds charge less than the maximum, and some do not charge at all.

Other Charges: Charges, such as an annual account fee or an account start-up fee, are noted. Redemption fees are given along with the time period, if appropriate.

Distributions: The months in which income and capital gains distributions are made are indicated, when available.

Exchange: Number Per Year indicates the maximum number of exchanges allowed; Fee indicates any fees charged for exchanges; and Telephone indicates whether telephone exchanges with other funds in the family are permitted. If exchange privileges are allowed, we have indicated whether exchanges are available with a money market fund (money market fund available).

Services: Investor services provided by the fund are detailed. These include the availability for IRA and other pension plans; whether the fund allows for an automatic exchange between funds in the family (auto exchange); whether the fund allows for automatic investments through an investor's checking account (auto invest); and whether the fund allows the automatic and systematic withdrawal of money from the fund (auto withdraw). Since all funds have automatic reinvestment of distributions options, this service was not specifically noted.

Fund Performance Rankings

8

When choosing among mutual funds, most investors start with performance statistics: How well have the various mutual funds performed in the past? If past performance alone could perfectly predict future performance, selection would be easy.

What past performance can tell you is how well the fund's management has handled different market environments, how consistent the fund has been, and how well the fund has done relative to its risk level, relative to other similar funds, and relative to the market.

We present performance statistics in several different forms. First, we provide an overall picture, with the average performance of each mutual fund category for the last five years, along with benchmarks for large and small company domestic stocks, international stocks, bonds, and Treasury bills. The top 20 and bottom 20 mutual fund performers for 1993 are given as a recent reference of performance. The list changes each year and reflects the cyclical nature of financial markets and the changing success of individual mutual fund managers. Lists of the top 50 mutual funds ranked by annual return over the last 10 years, five years and three years are given for a long-term perspective on investment performance.

Since the performance of a fund must be judged relative to similar funds, we have also grouped the funds by investment category and ranked them according to their total return performance for 1993. To make the comparison easier, we have also provided other data. The fund's annual returns for the last three years, five years, and 10 years give a longer-term perspective on the performance of the fund; category and total risk ranks are also given to judge performance.

Key to Fund Categories Used in Performance Tables

AG-Aggressive Growth	**B-CHY**-Corp. High-Yield Bond	**IntlS**-International Stock
Grth-Growth	**B-Gov**-Government Bond	**IntlB**-International Bond
GI-Growth & Income	**B-MB**-Mortgage-Backed Bond	**Gld**-Gold
Bal-Balanced	**B-Gen**-General Bond	
B-Cor-Corporate Bond	**B-TE**-Tax-Exempt Bond	

Total Risk and Return Performance for Different Mutual Fund Categories

Fund Investment Category	Annual Return (%)						Bull	Bear	Total Risk
	1993	1992	1991	1990	1989	5yr			
Aggressive Growth	19.0	10.4	52.4	-6.3	27.0	18.2	125.0	-15.0	high
Growth	13.2	11.0	35.4	-6.1	25.8	14.6	84.7	-12.4	av
Growth & Income	12.6	10.0	27.7	-5.6	21.6	12.5	70.1	-11.6	av
Balanced	13.4	8.1	23.9	-0.5	17.6	12.1	61.6	-5.8	blw av
Corporate Bond	11.4	8.6	16.6	5.3	9.5	10.1	46.1	1.8	low
Corporate High-Yield Bond	19.2	15.8	27.3	-4.2	1.3	10.8	74.9	-3.3	low
Government Bond	10.4	6.2	15.0	6.5	13.9	10.4	46.2	0.5	blw av
Mortgage-Backed Bond	6.8	6.1	14.4	9.5	12.3	9.9	36.7	4.6	low
General Bond	9.2	6.7	14.6	6.9	11.3	9.8	39.4	2.9	low
Tax-Exempt Bond	11.6	8.3	11.3	6.3	9.0	9.2	40.1	2.3	low
International Stock	38.5	-3.5	12.9	-11.1	22.2	8.7	55.1	-15.1	abv av
International Bond	12.7	4.8	14.9	11.5	2.2	11.4	58.1	6.6	low
Gold	86.9	-15.7	-4.8	31.5	24.7	12.3	33.6	45.9	high
Domestic Equity Fund	14.6	10.5	38.0	-6.0	24.9	15.0	91.8	-12.9	av
Small Capitalization Stock	17.2	11.0	51.2	-8.8	24.2	17.4	114.4	-16.2	abv av
Domestic Taxable Bond	10.1	7.2	15.9	6.1	11.3	10.1	45.0	1.7	low
Index Comparisons									
S&P 500	10.0	7.6	30.4	-3.1	31.5	14.5	68.4	-11.1	av
Russell 2000*	18.9	18.4	46.0	-19.5	16.2	13.9	115.9	-23.3	high
MS EAFE**	33.1	-12.1	12.5	-23.3	10.6	2.2	45.5	-30.7	high
Salomon Corporate Bond[†]	12.1	8.8	18.4	7.2	13.9	12.0	50.3	3.1	low
Salomon High-Yield Corp. Bond[†]	17.3	17.8	40.2	-8.1	1.9	12.6	92.3	-7.3	blw av
Salomon Treasury/Agency Bond[†]	10.7	7.2	15.3	8.7	14.2	11.2	44.4	3.1	low
Salomon Mortgage-Backed Bond[†]	7.0	7.3	15.6	10.9	15.1	11.1	39.5	5.6	low
Salomon Investm't-Grade Bond[†]	9.8	7.5	15.9	9.0	14.4	11.3	44.0	3.8	low
Treasury Bills	2.9	3.3	5.6	7.8	8.3	5.6	14.5	5.8	low

Return figures are averages for funds in each category

*Index of small company stocks; Source: Frank Russell Company

**Europe, Australia, Far East Index.; Source: Morgan Stanley

[†]Salomon Brothers Bond Indexes.; Source: Salomon Brothers

Total Risk and Return for Domestic Taxable Bond Mutual Funds

Fund Investment Category	Annual Return (%)						Bull	Bear	Total Risk
	1993	1992	1991	1990	1989	5yr			
Short-Term Bond Funds	5.6	5.6	11.2	7.5	10.3	8.1	28.0	4.6	low
Intermediate-Term Bond Funds	10.0	7.8	16.9	5.8	10.7	10.1	45.2	1.9	low
Long-Term Bond Funds	14.3	7.6	17.0	5.7	13.1	11.3	53.9	-0.4	blw av

The Top 20 Performers: 1993

Type	Fund Name	Annual Return (%)				Category Risk	Total Risk
		1993	3yr	5yr	10yr		
Gld	US Gold Shares	123.9	-2.4	0.1	-4.9	high	high
Gld	Fidelity Sel Precious Metals	111.6	18.8	11.8	4.8	abv av	high
Gld	Blanchard Precious Metals	100.4	16.8	5.8	na	av	high
Gld	Vanguard Spec Port—Gold & PM	93.3	17.6	11.1	na	blw av	high
Gld	US World Gold	89.7	20.4	71.1	na	high	high
Gld	Bull & Bear Gold Investors Ltd	87.6	15.3	7.3	5.2	blw av	high
Gld	Lexington GoldFund	86.9	11.7	6.4	6.8	av	high
IntlS	Fidelity Emerging Markets	81.7	27.1	na	na	abv av	high
Gld	Benham Gold Equities Index	81.2	13.6	8.9	na	high	high
IntlS	T Rowe Price New Asia	78.7	33.3	na	na	high	high
Gld	Fidelity Sel American Gold	78.6	17.5	10.4	na	low	high
IntlS	Fifty-Nine Wall St. Pacific Basin	74.9	28.2	na	na	high	high
IntlS	Scudder Latin America	74.3	na	na	na	na	na
Gld	INVESCO Strat Port—Gold	72.6	13.7	6.5	na	abv av	high
IntlS	Fidelity Pacific-Basin	63.9	19.4	6.6	na	high	high
IntlS	Lexington Worldwide Emerg Mkts	63.3	28.1	18.2	12.2	abv av	high
IntlS	Scudder Pacific Opportunities	60.0	na	na	na	na	na
Gld	Scudder Gold	59.3	10.4	4.4	na	low	high
IntlS	Montgomery Emerging Markets	58.6	na	na	na	na	na
Gld	USAA Gold	58.3	11.6	3.8	na	low	high

The Bottom 20 Performers: 1993

Type	Fund Name	Annual Return (%)				Category Risk	Total Risk
		1993	3yr	5yr	10yr		
AG	INVESCO Strat Port—Health Sci	-8.4	14.8	24.9	na	high	high
Grth	Yacktman	-6.5	na	na	na	na	na
Gl	Reynolds Blue Chip Growth	-5.2	8.8	9.2	na	high	abv av
Grth	Beacon Hill Mutual	-5.1	5.5	8.5	9.2	blw av	av
AG	INVESCO Strat Port—Environm'l	-4.6	-3.2	na	na	av	high
Grth	Rainbow	-4.6	8.5	4.7	6.6	abv av	abv av
Gl	Paine Webber Dividend Growth "D"	-3.2	na	na	na	na	na
Grth	Vanguard US Growth	-1.4	14.1	16.4	13.4	abv av	abv av
Grth	Blanchard American Equity	-1.3	na	na	na	na	na
Bal	Pax World	-1.0	6.3	10.6	10.7	blw av	blw av
AG	Fidelity Sel Environ'l Serv	-0.6	1.8	na	na	blw av	high
Gl	MIM Stock Income	-0.6	7.6	5.3	na	blw av	av
Grth	Century Shares Trust	-0.3	18.5	16.7	15.4	blw av	abv av
Gl	US Real Estate	0.1	17.6	7.0	na	high	high
Grth	FAM Value	0.2	22.7	16.0	na	av	abv av
IntlB	Flex Short Term Global Income	0.3	na	na	na	na	na
Grth	Monetta	0.4	18.2	16.2	na	av	abv av
AG	Fidelity Sel Biotechnology	0.6	21.5	30.1	na	high	high
Grth	Dreyfus Appreciation	0.6	13.4	12.7	na	av	abv av
Grth	Safeco Northwest	1.0	na	na	na	na	na

The Top 50 Performers: 10 Years, 1984-1993

Type	Fund Name	Annual Return (%) 10yr	5yr	3yr	1993	Category Risk	Total Risk
AG	Twentieth Century Giftrust	22.0	29.0	42.0	31.4	high	high
AG	Fidelity Sel Health Care	19.0	22.4	15.8	2.4	high	high
Grth	Fidelity Magellan	18.4	19.3	23.4	24.6	av	abv av
Grth	Acorn	17.9	20.0	34.2	32.3	av	abv av
Grth	Fidelity Contrafund	17.6	26.5	29.6	21.4	abv av	abv av
AG	Berger One Hundred	17.3	28.3	35.4	21.1	abv av	high
AG	Evergreen Limited Market	17.3	14.5	22.1	9.5	blw av	high
IntlS	T Rowe Price Int'l Stock	17.3	12.0	16.1	40.1	av	abv av
IntlS	Vanguard Int'l Growth	16.9	9.4	12.6	44.7	abv av	abv av
AG	Fidelity Growth Company	16.6	22.2	22.9	16.1	blw av	high
AG	Twentieth Century Ultra	16.6	28.0	32.0	21.8	high	high
IntlS	Scudder Int'l	16.4	11.3	14.1	36.5	blw av	abv av
Bal	INVESCO Industrial Income	16.3	18.0	19.8	16.6	high	av
IntlS	Vanguard Trustees' Equity—Int'l	16.1	7.6	9.3	30.5	av	abv av
Grth	Fidelity Retirement Growth	16.0	18.1	25.2	22.1	abv av	abv av
GI	Mutual Qualified	16.0	13.3	22.1	22.7	low	av
Grth	Fidelity Sel Financial Services	15.9	19.6	39.4	17.5	high	high
GI	Fidelity Sel Utilities	15.9	16.0	14.6	12.5	low	av
AG	SteinRoe Special	15.9	19.0	22.5	20.4	low	abv av
GI	Mutual Shares	15.7	12.9	21.1	20.9	low	av
GI	Sequoia	15.6	15.7	19.2	10.7	abv av	abv av
Grth	Century Shares Trust	15.4	16.7	18.5	-0.3	blw av	abv av
GI	Dodge & Cox Stock	15.4	13.9	16.7	18.3	abv av	abv av
Grth	IAI Regional	15.4	14.8	15.1	8.9	low	av
Grth	Scudder Capital Growth	15.4	15.3	22.4	20.0	high	high
GI	Safeco Equity	15.3	17.8	22.3	30.9	high	high
GI	Vanguard Windsor	15.3	11.6	21.3	19.3	abv av	abv av
Grth	Janus	15.2	19.6	19.1	10.8	blw av	abv av
GI	Selected American Shares	15.2	13.5	17.7	5.4	high	abv av
AG	SIT Growth	15.2	18.3	20.6	8.5	av	high
Grth	Neuberger & Berman Manhattan	15.1	14.9	19.1	10.0	abv av	abv av
GI	Neuberger & Berman Guardian	14.9	16.1	22.3	14.4	high	abv av
Bal	Fidelity Puritan	14.6	14.3	20.3	21.4	abv av	av
Grth	Nicholas II	14.6	12.3	17.5	6.4	blw av	av
GI	Vanguard Index Trust—500	14.6	14.3	15.4	9.8	abv av	av
Grth	Founders Growth	14.4	19.5	24.5	25.5	high	high
GI	Neuberger & Berman Partners	14.4	14.3	18.7	16.4	high	high
IntlS	Japan	14.3	-0.1	2.0	23.6	high	high
Bal	Dodge & Cox Balanced	14.2	13.9	15.6	15.9	av	av
AG	Twentieth Century Growth	14.2	18.2	18.8	3.7	abv av	high
Grth	Nicholas	14.1	15.0	19.1	5.8	blw av	abv av
Grth	Babson Enterprise	14.0	16.3	27.4	16.2	av	abv av
Bal	Vanguard Wellesley Income	14.0	13.6	14.8	14.6	blw av	blw av
Grth	Fidelity Trend	13.9	16.8	23.8	19.1	abv av	high
Grth	Gradison McDonald Established Value	13.9	11.6	17.6	20.7	low	av
Grth	Dreyfus Capital Growth	13.8	13.9	17.3	14.7	blw av	av
AG	Founders Special	13.8	20.7	27.1	16.0	av	high
Grth	William Blair Growth Shares	13.8	18.0	21.5	15.5	abv av	abv av
Grth	Columbia Growth	13.6	16.1	19.2	13.0	abv av	abv av
B-CHY	Fidelity Capital & Income	13.6	14.0	27.5	24.8	high	blw av

The Top 50 Performers: Five Years, 1989-1993

Type	Fund Name	Annual Return (%)				Category Risk	Total Risk
		5yr	10yr	3yr	1993		
Gld	US World Gold	71.1	na	20.4	89.7	high	high
AG	Fidelity Sel Biotechnology	30.1	na	21.5	0.6	high	high
AG	CGM Capital Development	29.2	na	44.3	28.6	abv av	high
AG	Twentieth Century Giftrust	29.0	22.0	42.0	31.4	high	high
AG	Berger One Hundred	28.3	17.3	35.4	21.1	abv av	high
AG	Twentieth Century Ultra	28.0	16.6	32.0	21.8	high	high
Grth	INVESCO Strat Port—Financial	27.1	na	37.7	18.4	high	high
AG	PBHG Growth	26.9	na	41.2	44.6	high	high
AG	T Rowe Price Science & Tech	26.8	na	33.2	24.2	high	high
AG	Kaufmann	26.6	na	33.1	18.1	abv av	high
Grth	Fidelity Contrafund	26.5	17.6	29.6	21.4	abv av	abv av
AG	INVESCO Strat Port—Tech	26.0	na	34.2	15.0	high	high
AG	INVESCO Strat Port—Leisure	25.7	na	36.7	35.6	blw av	high
AG	Fidelity Sel Home Finance	25.1	na	48.9	27.2	abv av	high
AG	INVESCO Strat Port—Health Sci	24.9	na	14.8	-8.4	high	high
AG	Oberweis Emerging Growth	24.7	na	34.1	13.3	high	high
AG	Fidelity Sel Medical Delivery	24.5	na	17.6	5.5	high	high
AG	Fidelity Sel Software & Comp	24.2	na	37.9	32.7	high	high
Grth	Fidelity Blue Chip Growth	23.6	na	26.9	24.5	abv av	abv av
AG	Fidelity Sel Technology	23.5	7.3	30.5	28.6	abv av	high
AG	Fidelity Sel Retailing	23.3	na	32.3	13.0	av	high
Grth	Brandywine	23.1	na	28.3	22.5	high	high
AG	Fidelity Sel Electronics	22.7	na	31.5	32.0	abv av	high
AG	Fidelity Sel Health Care	22.4	19.0	15.8	2.4	high	high
Grth	Fidelity Sel Regional Banks	22.4	na	39.8	11.1	high	high
AG	Wasatch Aggressive Equity	22.4	na	24.5	22.5	av	high
AG	Fidelity Growth Company	22.2	16.6	22.9	16.1	blw av	high
AG	Fidelity Sel Broker & Invest Mgmt	22.2	na	41.9	49.3	abv av	high
Grth	Janus Twenty	22.0	na	21.2	3.4	high	high
AG	Legg Mason Special Investment	21.5	na	25.9	24.1	low	abv av
AG	Robertson Stephens Emerg Grth	21.2	na	18.3	7.2	high	high
AG	Fidelity Sel Computers	21.0	na	27.1	28.8	high	high
AG	INVESCO Dynamics	20.9	13.2	31.0	19.0	abv av	high
AG	Founders Special	20.7	-3.0	27.1	16.0	av	high
Grth	Meridian	20.7	na	26.9	13.0	high	high
AG	Fidelity Sel Automotive	20.6	na	38.0	35.3	low	abv av
AG	Founders Frontier	20.4	na	23.7	16.5	av	high
Grth	T Rowe Price New America Growth	20.4	na	27.8	17.4	high	high
AG	MIM Stock Appreciation	20.3	na	27.4	10.4	abv av	high
Grth	Strong Discovery	20.2	na	27.8	22.2	high	high
Grth	Vanguard Spec Port—Health Care	20.0	na	17.2	11.8	high	high
Grth	Acorn	20.0	17.9	34.2	32.3	av	abv av
AG	Fidelity Sel Transportation	19.9	na	35.1	29.3	blw av	high
Grth	Fidelity Sel Telecomm	19.8	na	25.0	29.7	av	abv av
Grth	Fidelity Sel Financial Services	19.6	15.9	39.4	17.5	high	high
Grth	Janus	19.6	15.2	19.1	10.8	blw av	abv av
Gl	Fidelity Convertible Securities	19.5	na	25.8	17.7	blw av	av
Grth	Founders Growth	19.5	14.4	24.5	25.5	high	high
Grth	Fidelity Magellan	19.3	18.4	23.4	24.6	av	abv av
Gl	Schafer Value	19.3	na	27.5	23.9	high	abv av

The Top 50 Performers: Three Years, 1991-1993

Type	Fund Name	Annual Return (%)				Category Risk	Total Risk
		3yr	5yr	10yr	1993		
AG	American Heritage	49.2	17.4	na	41.3	high	high
AG	Fidelity Sel Home Finance	48.9	25.1	na	27.2	abv av	high
AG	CGM Capital Development	44.3	29.2	na	28.6	abv av	high
AG	Twentieth Century Giftrust	42.0	29.0	22.0	31.4	high	high
AG	Fidelity Sel Broker & Invest Mgmt	41.9	22.2	na	49.3	abv av	high
AG	PBHG Growth	41.2	26.9	na	44.6	high	high
Grth	Fidelity Sel Regional Banks	39.8	22.4	na	11.1	high	high
Grth	Fidelity Sel Financial Services	39.4	19.6	15.9	17.5	high	high
AG	Montgomery Small Cap	39.3	na	na	24.3	abv av	high
AG	Fidelity Sel Automotive	38.0	20.6	na	35.3	low	abv av
AG	Fidelity Sel Software & Comp	37.9	24.2	na	32.7	high	high
Grth	INVESCO Strat Port—Financial	37.7	27.1	na	18.4	high	high
AG	INVESCO Strat Port—Leisure	36.7	25.7	na	35.6	blw av	high
AG	Fidelity Sel Dev'ping Communic'ns	35.5	na	na	31.7	av	high
AG	Berger One Hundred	35.4	28.3	17.3	21.1	abv av	high
AG	Fidelity Sel Transportation	35.1	19.9	na	29.3	blw av	high
AG	INVESCO Strat Port—Tech	34.2	26.0	na	15.0	high	high
Grth	Acorn	34.2	20.0	17.9	32.3	av	abv av
AG	Oberweis Emerging Growth	34.1	24.7	na	13.3	high	high
Grth	Regis ICM Small Company Port	33.8	na	na	21.9	abv av	abv av
AG	Strong Common Stock	33.3	na	na	25.1	blw av	high
IntlS	T Rowe Price New Asia	33.3	na	na	78.7	high	high
AG	T Rowe Price Science & Tech	33.2	26.8	na	24.2	high	high
AG	Kaufmann	33.1	26.6	na	18.1	abv av	high
AG	Fidelity Sel Retailing	32.3	23.3	na	13.0	av	high
AG	Fidelity Sel Broadcast & Media	32.2	17.7	na	37.9	blw av	high
AG	Twentieth Century Ultra	32.0	28.0	16.6	21.8	high	high
AG	Fidelity Sel Electronics	31.5	22.7	na	32.0	abv av	high
Grth	Fidelity Low-Priced Stock	31.3	na	na	20.2	av	abv av
AG	INVESCO Dynamics	31.0	20.9	13.2	19.0	abv av	high
AG	Fidelity Sel Constr'n & Hous'g	30.8	18.7	na	33.6	blw av	high
AG	Fidelity Sel Technology	30.5	23.5	7.3	28.6	abv av	high
Grth	Fidelity Contrafund	29.6	26.5	17.6	21.4	abv av	abv av
AG	Fidelity Emerging Growth	29.4	na	na	19.8	abv av	high
AG	Fidelity Sel Leisure	29.1	17.0	na	39.5	low	abv av
Grth	Berwyn	28.6	13.5	na	22.9	abv av	abv av
AG	SteinRoe Capital Opportunities	28.5	15.5	10.0	27.5	blw av	high
Grth	Brandywine	28.3	23.1	na	22.5	high	high
IntlS	Fifty-Nine Wall St. Pacific Basin	28.2	na	na	74.9	high	high
IntlS	Lexington Worldwide Emerg Mkts	28.1	18.2	12.2	63.3	abv av	high
AG	Bull & Bear Special Equities	28.0	13.6	na	16.3	high	high
Grth	Strong Discovery	27.8	20.2	na	22.2	high	high
Grth	T Rowe Price New America Growth	27.8	20.4	na	17.4	high	high
GI	Berger One Hundred & One	27.7	18.2	13.3	23.5	high	abv av
AG	Columbia Special	27.6	19.1	na	21.6	av	high
B-CHY	Fidelity Capital & Income	27.5	14.0	13.6	24.8	high	blw av
GI	Fidelity Equity-Income II	27.5	na	na	18.8	blw av	av
AG	Founders Discovery	27.5	na	na	10.8	abv av	high
GI	Schafer Value	27.5	19.3	na	23.9	high	abv av
Grth	Babson Enterprise	27.4	16.3	14.0	16.2	av	abv av

Aggressive Growth Funds
Ranked by 1993 Total Return

Fund Name	Annual Return (%)				Category Risk	Total Risk
	1993	3yr	5yr	10yr		
Fidelity Sel Broker & Invest Mgmt	49.3	41.9	22.2	na	abv av	high
PBHG Growth	44.6	41.2	26.9	na	high	high
Fidelity Sel Industrial Equipment	43.3	26.4	15.0	na	blw av	abv av
American Heritage	41.3	49.2	17.4	na	high	high
Fidelity Sel Leisure	39.5	29.1	17.0	na	low	abv av
Fidelity Sel Broadcast & Media	37.9	32.2	17.7	na	blw av	high
INVESCO Strat Port—Leisure	35.6	36.7	25.7	na	blw av	high
Fidelity Sel Automotive	35.3	38.0	20.6	na	low	abv av
Fidelity Sel Constr'n & Hous'g	33.6	30.8	18.7	na	blw av	high
Fidelity Sel Software & Comp	32.7	37.9	24.2	na	high	high
Fidelity Sel Electronics	32.0	31.5	22.7	na	abv av	high
Fidelity Sel Dev'ping Communic'ns	31.7	35.5	na	na	av	high
Twentieth Century Giftrust	31.4	42.0	29.0	22.0	high	high
Fidelity Sel Air Transportation	30.8	24.1	14.5	na	av	high
Fidelity Sel Transportation	29.3	35.1	19.9	na	blw av	high
Fidelity Sel Computers	28.8	27.1	21.0	na	high	high
Fidelity Sel Defense & Aerospace	28.8	17.8	11.1	na	low	abv av
Fidelity Sel Technology	28.6	30.5	23.5	7.3	abv av	high
CGM Capital Development	28.6	44.3	29.2	na	abv av	high
SteinRoe Capital Opportunities	27.5	28.5	15.5	10.0	blw av	high
Fidelity Sel Home Finance	27.2	48.9	25.1	na	abv av	high
Forty-Four Wall Street Equity	26.4	23.3	16.2	na	blw av	abv av
Strong Common Stock	25.1	33.3	na	na	blw av	high
Fidelity New Millenium	24.6	na	na	na	na	na
Fidelity Sel Consumer Product	24.6	23.3	na	na	low	abv av
Loomis Sayles Small Cap	24.6	na	na	na	na	na
Montgomery Small Cap	24.3	39.3	na	na	abv av	high
T Rowe Price Science & Tech	24.2	33.2	26.8	na	high	high
Legg Mason Special Investment	24.1	25.9	21.5	na	low	abv av
INVESCO Emerging Growth	23.4	na	na	na	na	na
Baron Asset	23.4	23.5	13.9	na	blw av	abv av
Galaxy Small Company Equity	22.7	na	na	na	na	na
Cappiello-Rushmore Emerging Growth	22.5	na	na	na	na	na
Wasatch Aggressive Equity	22.5	24.5	22.4	na	av	high
Safeco Growth	22.1	24.4	14.3	11.2	high	high
T Rowe Price New Horizons	22.0	27.1	18.5	10.7	av	high
Twentieth Century Ultra	21.8	32.0	28.0	16.6	high	high
Columbia Special	21.6	27.6	19.1	na	av	high
Robertson Stephens Value Plus	21.6	na	na	na	na	na
Fidelity Sel Industrial Materials	21.3	22.8	9.9	na	low	abv av
Berger One Hundred	21.1	35.4	28.3	17.3	abv av	high
Fidelity Sel Energy Services	20.9	-1.4	9.2	na	high	high
SteinRoe Special	20.4	22.5	19.0	15.9	low	abv av
Boston Co Special Growth	20.0	25.0	17.2	12.8	av	high
Fidelity Emerging Growth	19.8	29.4	na	na	abv av	high
INVESCO Dynamics	19.0	31.0	20.9	13.2	abv av	high
Vanguard Small Cap Stock	18.7	26.7	13.0	7.0	blw av	high
Fidelity Sel Paper & Forest Prod	18.5	21.4	9.6	na	blw av	high
T Rowe Price OTC	18.4	23.1	12.1	10.5	low	abv av
Warburg Pincus Emerging Grth	18.1	27.4	17.8	na	av	high

Aggressive Growth Funds (continued)

Ranked by 1993 Total Return

Fund Name	Annual Return (%)				Category Risk	Total Risk
	1993	3yr	5yr	10yr		
Kaufmann	18.1	33.1	26.6	na	abv av	high
Managers Special Equity	17.3	26.5	na	na	low	abv av
Dreyfus New Leaders	17.0	23.0	16.6	na	low	abv av
Salomon Brothers Capital	16.9	17.8	15.7	10.5	blw av	high
INVESCO Strat Port—Energy	16.7	-0.6	3.2	na	av	high
Managers Capital Appreciation	16.6	19.3	na	na	low	abv av
Founders Frontier	16.5	23.7	20.4	na	av	high
Bull & Bear Special Equities	16.3	28.0	13.6	na	high	high
Fidelity Growth Company	16.1	22.9	22.2	16.6	blw av	high
Value Line Leveraged Growth	16.1	18.3	16.6	12.9	av	high
Founders Special	16.0	27.1	20.7	-3.0	av	high
Janus Enterprise	15.6	na	na	na	na	na
Fairmont	15.5	22.8	9.0	9.3	av	high
Vanguard Explorer	15.5	26.7	14.7	7.6	blw av	high
Paine Webber Capital Appreciation "D"	15.2	na	na	na	na	na
INVESCO Strat Port—Tech	15.0	34.2	26.0	na	high	high
GIT Equity—Special Growth	14.8	15.4	10.1	12.7	low	abv av
IAI Emerging Growth	14.7	na	na	na	na	na
Neuberger & Berman Genesis	13.8	23.0	12.8	na	low	abv av
WPG Tudor	13.3	20.2	15.5	12.6	abv av	high
Oberweis Emerging Growth	13.3	34.1	24.7	na	high	high
Fidelity Sel Retailing	13.0	32.3	23.3	na	av	high
Value Line Special Situations	12.9	14.6	11.8	4.5	av	high
Fifty-Nine Wall St. Small Company	12.1	na	na	na	na	na
Vanguard Spec Port—Tech	11.3	23.0	14.7	na	av	high
Founders Discovery	10.8	27.5	na	na	abv av	high
MIM Stock Appreciation	10.4	27.4	20.3	na	abv av	high
Evergreen Limited Market	9.5	22.1	14.5	17.3	blw av	high
Loomis Sayles Growth	9.2	na	na	na	na	na
Janus Venture	9.0	20.1	19.0	na	low	abv av
Fidelity Sel Food & Agriculture	8.8	15.6	18.6	na	low	abv av
Scudder Development	8.8	22.4	18.0	11.2	abv av	high
SIT Growth	8.5	20.6	18.3	15.2	av	high
Fidelity OTC Port	8.3	22.9	18.1	na	low	abv av
USAA Aggressive Growth	8.1	19.3	11.7	7.7	abv av	high
Robertson Stephens Emerg Grth	7.2	18.3	21.2	na	high	high
Evergreen	6.2	17.4	10.4	11.6	low	abv av
Fidelity Sel Medical Delivery	5.5	17.6	24.5	na	high	high
Twentieth Century Vista	5.4	21.4	18.1	12.4	abv av	high
Perritt Capital Growth	5.2	15.8	5.7	na	low	abv av
Twentieth Century Growth	3.7	18.8	18.2	14.2	abv av	high
Prudent Speculator	3.1	19.4	0.6	na	high	high
Fidelity Sel Health Care	2.4	15.8	22.4	19.0	high	high
Fidelity Sel Biotechnology	0.6	21.5	30.1	na	high	high
Fidelity Sel Environ'l Serv	-0.6	1.8	na	na	blw av	high
INVESCO Strat Port—Environm'l	-4.6	-3.2	na	na	av	high
INVESCO Strat Port—Health Sci	-8.4	14.8	24.9	na	high	high
Aggressive Growth Fund Average	**19.0**	**25.4**	**18.2**	**11.9**	**—**	**high**

Growth Funds
Ranked by 1993 Total Return

Fund Name	Annual Return (%)				Category Risk	Total Risk
	1993	3yr	5yr	10yr		
Fidelity Capital Appreciation Port	33.4	19.5	12.8	na	low	av
Acorn	32.3	34.2	20.0	17.9	av	abv av
Oakmark	30.5	na	na	na	na	na
Fidelity Sel Telecomm	29.7	25.0	19.8	na	av	abv av
Vanguard Spec Port—Energy	26.5	10.4	13.7	na	high	high
T Rowe Price Mid-Cap Growth	26.2	na	na	na	na	na
Founders Growth	25.5	24.5	19.5	14.4	high	high
Fidelity Magellan	24.6	23.4	19.3	18.4	av	abv av
Fidelity Blue Chip Growth	24.5	26.9	23.6	na	abv av	abv av
Maxus Equity	24.5	24.4	na	na	av	abv av
First Eagle Fund of America	23.8	23.0	14.2	na	blw av	abv av
T Rowe Price Small Cap Value	23.3	25.9	15.9	na	low	av
Fidelity Value	22.9	23.4	15.0	11.7	low	av
Berwyn	22.9	28.6	13.5	na	abv av	abv av
IAI MidCap Growth	22.8	na	na	na	na	na
Brandywine	22.5	28.3	23.1	na	high	high
Tocqueville	22.5	17.2	13.9	na	low	av
Strong Discovery	22.2	27.8	20.2	na	high	high
Southeastern Asset Mgmt Value Trust	22.2	27.0	16.1	na	blw av	av
Fidelity Retirement Growth	22.1	25.2	18.1	16.0	abv av	abv av
IAI Value	22.0	17.8	12.0	10.5	av	abv av
Regis ICM Small Company Port	21.9	33.8	na	na	abv av	abv av
Gabelli Asset	21.8	18.2	14.6	na	low	av
Fidelity Contrafund	21.4	29.6	26.5	17.6	abv av	abv av
Strong Opportunity	21.1	23.2	14.5	na	av	abv av
Gradison McDonald Established Value	20.7	17.6	11.6	13.9	low	av
M.S.B. Fund	20.5	16.0	13.1	12.0	low	av
Twentieth Century Heritage	20.4	21.7	17.2	na	high	high
SBSF	20.4	15.2	14.7	13.3	low	av
Fidelity Low-Priced Stock	20.2	31.3	na	na	av	abv av
Scudder Capital Growth	20.0	22.4	15.3	15.4	high	high
Weitz Value Port	20.0	20.3	15.0	na	low	av
PRA Real Estate Securities	19.9	20.4	na	na	high	high
Southeastern Asset Mgmt Small Cap	19.8	17.3	8.4	na	blw av	av
Babson Enterprise II	19.7	na	na	na	na	na
Bruce	19.4	10.2	8.9	10.4	abv av	abv av
Fidelity Trend	19.1	23.8	16.8	13.9	abv av	high
Fidelity Sel Energy	19.1	5.1	9.6	8.6	high	high
INVESCO Strat Port—Financial	18.4	37.7	27.1	na	high	high
Harbor Growth	18.3	18.6	13.8	na	high	high
American Pension Investors—Growth	18.2	20.6	12.2	na	high	high
Paine Webber Growth "D"	18.1	na	na	na	na	na
Vanguard Primecap	18.0	19.6	15.1	na	abv av	abv av
INVESCO Growth	17.9	19.9	17.4	12.5	abv av	abv av
Fidelity Sel Financial Services	17.5	39.4	19.6	15.9	high	high
T Rowe Price New America Growth	17.4	27.8	20.4	na	high	high
Eclipse Equity	17.0	22.3	12.9	na	blw av	av
Boston Co Capital Appreciation	16.4	14.1	9.9	13.0	blw av	abv av
Neuberger & Berman Sel Sectors	16.3	20.6	16.4	13.5	av	abv av
Babson Enterprise	16.2	27.4	16.3	14.0	av	abv av

Growth Funds (continued)
Ranked by 1993 Total Return

Fund Name	Annual Return (%)				Category Risk	Total Risk
	1993	3yr	5yr	10yr		
Preferred Growth	16.0	na	na	na	na	na
Warburg Pincus Cap Appreciation	15.8	16.3	13.5	na	av	abv av
AARP Capital Growth	15.8	19.4	13.9	na	high	high
T Rowe Price Capital Appreciation	15.6	15.4	13.0	na	low	blw av
T Rowe Price Growth Stock	15.5	17.8	14.4	13.3	av	abv av
William Blair Growth Shares	15.5	21.5	18.0	13.8	abv av	abv av
Vontobel US Value	15.4	22.4	na	na	abv av	abv av
T Rowe Price New Era	15.3	10.5	8.8	11.3	low	av
Babson Shadow Stock	15.2	23.6	11.1	na	blw av	av
Armstrong Associates	15.0	13.4	9.2	7.9	low	av
Dreyfus Capital Growth	14.7	17.3	13.9	13.8	blw av	av
Fiduciary Capital Growth	14.6	21.3	13.2	9.6	blw av	abv av
Twentieth Century Sel	14.6	12.9	14.8	12.7	abv av	abv av
Evergreen Value Timing	14.4	17.9	14.4	na	low	av
Vanguard Index Trust—Ext Market	14.4	22.2	14.2	na	av	abv av
Fontaine Capital Appreciation	14.0	7.0	na	na	low	blw av
Fidelity Discipline Equity	13.9	20.6	18.8	na	blw av	abv av
Fidelity Stock Selector	13.9	24.2	na	na	av	abv av
Reich & Tang Equity	13.8	17.6	12.5	na	low	av
HighMark Special Growth Equity	13.8	17.0	13.8	na	high	high
New Century Capital Port	13.8	16.1	na	na	av	abv av
Columbia Growth	13.0	19.2	16.1	13.6	abv av	abv av
Meridian	13.0	26.9	20.7	na	high	high
US Growth	12.9	8.3	5.8	2.7	high	high
Salomon Brothers Opportunity	12.8	18.8	11.2	13.1	low	av
SteinRoe Prime Equities	12.8	17.9	16.1	na	low	av
Fidelity Sel Chemical	12.7	19.4	13.8	na	av	abv av
Rushmore OTC Index Plus	12.7	21.0	11.0	na	high	high
Schroder US Equity	12.6	21.5	16.4	12.6	abv av	abv av
Harbor Capital Appreciation	12.1	24.0	18.4	na	high	high
Vanguard Spec Port—Service Econ	12.0	18.5	13.0	na	av	abv av
Sound Shore	11.9	21.5	14.4	na	blw av	abv av
Vanguard Spec Port—Health Care	11.8	17.2	20.0	na	high	high
Scudder Value	11.6	na	na	na	na	na
Benham Equity Growth	11.4	na	na	na	na	na
Legg Mason Value	11.2	18.6	10.7	12.1	av	abv av
Pennsylvania Mutual	11.2	19.4	11.9	na	low	av
Gabelli Growth	11.2	16.0	16.4	na	av	abv av
Fidelity Sel Regional Banks	11.1	39.8	22.4	na	high	high
Clipper	11.1	19.5	14.0	na	blw av	av
Gradison McDonald Opportunity Value	11.0	19.9	13.0	11.7	blw av	av
Janus	10.8	19.1	19.6	15.2	blw av	abv av
Selected Special Shares	10.8	14.6	12.5	10.6	abv av	abv av
Neuberger & Berman Manhattan	10.0	19.1	14.9	15.1	abv av	abv av
IAI Growth & Income	9.9	13.1	11.8	12.1	blw av	av
Portico MidCore Growth	9.9	na	na	na	na	na
Matrix Growth	9.3	15.4	14.8	na	av	abv av
Dreman High Return	9.2	24.5	15.8	na	high	high
Nicholas Limited Edition	9.0	22.1	16.0	na	blw av	abv av
IAI Regional	8.9	15.1	14.8	15.4	low	av

Growth Funds (continued)
Ranked by 1993 Total Return

Fund Name	Annual Return (%)				Category Risk	Total Risk
	1993	3yr	5yr	10yr		
Vista Equity	8.6	14.5	na	na	blw av	abv av
Fidelity Sel Insurance	8.1	21.9	17.6	na	abv av	abv av
Flex Muirfield	8.1	14.4	11.8	na	low	av
Portico Special Growth	8.0	22.3	na	na	high	high
Vanguard Morgan Growth	7.3	14.9	12.9	12.0	av	abv av
Flex Growth	7.2	11.4	9.7	na	low	av
Value Line	6.8	18.5	16.7	12.8	abv av	high
Rightime	6.7	13.1	10.2	na	av	abv av
Nicholas II	6.4	17.5	12.3	14.6	blw av	av
Fremont Growth	6.4	na	na	na	na	na
UMB Heartland Fund	5.9	na	na	na	na	na
Sentry	5.9	13.6	13.8	12.6	low	av
Nicholas	5.8	19.1	15.0	14.1	blw av	abv av
Galaxy Equity Growth	5.3	13.3	na	na	blw av	abv av
Merriman Capital Appreciation	3.6	9.5	na	na	low	av
Wayne Hummer Growth	3.5	13.7	13.9	12.6	low	av
Janus Twenty	3.4	21.2	22.0	na	high	high
SteinRoe Stock	2.8	17.5	17.3	12.0	abv av	abv av
Leeb Personal Finance	2.8	na	na	na	na	na
Northeast Investors Growth	2.3	11.6	13.3	13.5	abv av	abv av
Mathers	2.1	4.8	7.0	11.1	low	low
MIM Stock Growth	2.1	8.3	5.3	na	blw av	abv av
Volumetric	2.0	15.0	10.9	na	abv av	abv av
Gintel	1.9	13.6	11.1	10.2	abv av	abv av
Dreyfus Growth Opportunity	1.7	13.8	9.6	10.1	high	high
Vanguard Index Trust—Growth Port	1.5	na	na	na	na	na
National Industries	1.3	9.9	11.3	8.8	low	av
Safeco Northwest	1.0	na	na	na	na	na
Dreyfus Appreciation	0.6	13.4	12.7	na	av	abv av
Monetta	0.4	18.2	16.2	na	av	abv av
FAM Value	0.2	22.7	16.0	na	av	abv av
Century Shares Trust	-0.3	18.5	16.7	15.4	blw av	abv av
Blanchard American Equity	-1.3	na	na	na	na	na
Vanguard US Growth	-1.4	14.1	16.4	13.4	abv av	abv av
Rainbow	-4.6	8.5	4.7	6.6	abv av	abv av
Beacon Hill Mutual	-5.1	5.5	8.5	9.2	blw av	av
Yacktman	-6.5	na	na	na	na	na
Growth Fund Average	**13.2**	**19.2**	**14.6**	**12.6**	**—**	**av**

Growth and Income Funds
Ranked by 1993 Total Return

Fund Name	1993	3yr	5yr	10yr	Category Risk	Total Risk
Safeco Equity	30.9	22.3	17.8	15.3	high	high
Schafer Value	23.9	27.5	19.3	na	high	abv av
Berger One Hundred & One	23.5	27.7	18.2	13.3	high	abv av
Mutual Beacon	22.9	21.1	13.8	na	low	av
Babson Value	22.8	22.2	13.8	na	abv av	abv av
Mutual Qualified	22.7	22.1	13.3	16.0	low	av
Fidelity Equity-Income	21.3	21.6	12.9	13.5	blw av	av
INVESCO Strat Port—Utilities	21.1	19.7	15.2	na	blw av	av
Mutual Shares	20.9	21.1	12.9	15.7	low	av
T Rowe Price Spectrum Growth	20.9	18.9	na	na	av	av
SBSF Convertible Securities	20.0	19.5	14.0	na	low	blw av
Lindner	19.8	18.5	12.3	13.6	blw av	av
Fidelity Growth & Income	19.5	23.6	17.9	na	high	abv av
T Rowe Price Dividend Growth	19.4	na	na	na	na	na
Vanguard Windsor	19.3	21.3	11.6	15.3	abv av	abv av
Fidelity Equity-Income II	18.8	27.5	na	na	blw av	av
Cohen & Steers Realty Shares	18.7	na	na	na	na	na
Homestead Value	18.7	15.8	na	na	low	av
Dreyfus Growth & Income	18.5	na	na	na	na	na
Dodge & Cox Stock	18.3	16.7	13.9	15.4	abv av	abv av
Fidelity Fund	18.3	16.7	14.2	13.5	av	av
Vanguard Index Trust—Value Port	18.3	na	na	na	na	na
Gabelli Equity Income	17.8	na	na	na	na	na
Fidelity Convertible Securities	17.7	25.8	19.5	na	blw av	av
US Income	17.7	13.2	12.8	9.9	low	av
Philadelphia	17.5	14.1	11.8	10.2	blw av	av
Vanguard Trustees' Equity—US	17.2	16.4	11.1	11.2	abv av	av
Valley Forge	17.1	11.3	8.0	7.4	low	low
Rushmore American GAS Index	16.5	10.2	na	na	abv av	abv av
Columbia Common Stock	16.4	na	na	na	na	na
Neuberger & Berman Partners	16.4	18.7	14.3	14.4	high	high
Seven Seas Series—Matrix Equity	16.2	na	na	na	na	na
Olympic Equity Income	15.7	21.1	12.4	na	abv av	abv av
Fidelity Utilities Income	15.6	15.8	14.7	na	low	av
AARP Growth & Income	15.6	16.9	14.6	na	blw av	av
Scudder Growth & Income	15.5	17.5	14.9	13.5	av	av
Salomon Brothers Investors	15.1	16.9	12.7	11.5	abv av	abv av
Vanguard Spec Port—Utilities Income	15.0	na	na	na	na	na
T Rowe Price Equity Income	14.8	17.9	11.7	na	low	av
Value Line Convertible	14.8	18.9	12.3	na	low	av
Galaxy Equity Value	14.7	15.2	11.6	na	av	av
Vanguard Equity Income	14.6	16.2	11.8	na	av	av
Greenspring	14.6	16.8	10.5	na	low	blw av
Founders Blue Chip	14.4	13.5	14.8	13.4	abv av	av
Neuberger & Berman Guardian	14.4	22.3	16.1	14.9	high	abv av
Legg Mason Total Return	14.0	22.3	12.1	na	blw av	av
WPG Quantitative Equity	13.9	na	na	na	na	na
Vanguard Quantitative Port	13.8	16.6	15.3	na	abv av	av
Vanguard Windsor II	13.6	17.8	13.5	na	av	av
Dreyfus Peoples S&P MidCap Index	13.5	na	na	na	na	na

Growth and Income Funds (continued)
Ranked by 1993 Total Return

Fund Name	Annual Return (%) 1993	3yr	5yr	10yr	Category Risk	Total Risk
Vanguard Convertible Securities	13.5	21.9	14.0	na	blw av	av
America's Utility	13.3	na	na	na	na	na
ASM	13.3	na	na	na	na	na
Lexington Growth & Income	13.2	16.6	12.7	11.2	abv av	abv av
Vanguard Preferred Stock	13.0	14.0	13.3	12.8	low	blw av
Royce Equity Income Series	13.0	20.7	na	na	low	av
Evergreen Total Return	12.9	15.1	10.8	12.2	low	av
T Rowe Price Growth & Income	12.9	19.6	12.6	11.1	av	av
Seven Seas Series—S&P MidCap	12.9	na	na	na	na	na
Fidelity Sel Electric Utilities	12.7	16.1	14.5	na	low	av
HighMark Income Equity	12.7	17.2	12.8	na	high	abv av
Bull & Bear Financial News Composite	12.6	13.1	na	na	av	av
Fidelity Real Estate Investment	12.5	23.2	14.2	na	high	abv av
Fidelity Sel Utilities	12.5	14.6	16.0	15.9	low	av
Managers Income Equity	12.4	16.8	na	na	av	av
BNY Hamilton Equity Income	11.9	na	na	na	na	na
Laurel Stock Port	11.7	17.1	16.6	na	av	av
Bartlett Basic Value	11.6	15.7	9.3	11.3	av	av
Amana Income	11.6	12.0	9.9	na	av	av
USAA Income Stock	11.5	15.2	13.9	na	blw av	av
Primary Trend	11.4	10.1	7.3	na	low	av
Benham Income & Growth	11.3	na	na	na	na	na
BT Investments—Utility	11.0	na	na	na	na	na
Sequoia	10.7	19.2	15.7	15.6	abv av	abv av
UMB Stock	10.6	13.9	11.4	11.7	low	av
Vanguard Index Trust—Tot Stock Mkt	10.6	na	na	na	na	na
INVESCO Value Trust—Value Equity	10.4	16.3	12.4	na	abv av	av
Dreyfus Edison Electric Index	10.4	na	na	na	na	na
Babson Growth	10.2	14.8	10.9	12.0	abv av	av
Copley	10.1	14.9	11.9	13.4	blw av	av
Rushmore Stock Market Index Plus	10.0	12.3	11.0	na	high	abv av
US All American Equity	10.0	13.7	8.8	7.7	av	av
Vanguard Index Trust—500	9.8	15.4	14.3	14.6	abv av	av
Fidelity Market Index	9.6	15.3	na	na	abv av	av
Dreyfus Peoples Index	9.5	15.2	na	na	av	av
Schwab 1000	9.5	na	na	na	na	na
Seven Seas Series—S&P 500	9.5	na	na	na	na	na
WPG Growth & Income	9.5	20.5	14.9	13.0	high	abv av
Portico Equity Index	9.1	14.8	na	na	abv av	av
Dreman Contrarian	9.0	15.3	11.2	na	high	abv av
Woodward Equity Index	9.0	na	na	na	na	na
Corefund Equity Index	8.7	na	na	na	na	na
Preferred Value	8.7	na	na	na	na	na
Harbor Value	8.3	12.1	11.5	na	av	av
Galaxy Equity Income	8.0	12.4	na	na	blw av	av
Gateway Index Plus	7.4	9.9	11.8	10.3	low	low
USAA Growth	7.4	14.7	13.9	10.1	abv av	av
LMH	7.2	11.3	4.6	7.8	blw av	av
Analytic Optioned Equity	6.7	8.6	8.9	9.7	low	blw av
Janus Growth & Income	6.6	na	na	na	na	na

Growth and Income Funds (continued)

Ranked by 1993 Total Return

Fund Name	Annual Return (%) 1993	3yr	5yr	10yr	Category Risk	Total Risk
Portico Growth & Income	6.6	11.1	na	na	blw av	av
Stratton Monthly Dividend Shares	6.5	16.6	12.6	12.8	low	av
Aetna Growth & Income	6.5	na	na	na	na	na
Stratton Growth	6.4	11.5	9.8	9.7	blw av	av
Dreyfus	6.3	12.8	11.4	11.7	av	av
Cappiello-Rushmore Utility Income	6.1	na	na	na	na	na
Selected American Shares	5.4	17.7	13.5	15.2	high	abv av
Gintel ERISA	5.3	11.0	8.4	10.9	abv av	abv av
Dreyfus Third Century	5.2	13.9	12.4	12.0	high	abv av
SIT Growth & Income	3.0	12.8	13.1	na	av	av
Merriman Blue Chip	2.7	6.5	6.6	na	blw av	av
Charter Capital Blue Chip Growth	1.8	11.8	8.5	na	high	high
L. Roy Papp Stock	1.6	15.6	na	na	high	abv av
US Real Estate	0.1	17.6	7.0	na	high	high
MIM Stock Income	-0.6	7.6	5.3	na	blw av	av
Paine Webber Dividend Growth "D"	-3.2	na	na	na	na	na
Reynolds Blue Chip Growth	-5.2	8.8	9.2	na	high	abv av
Growth and Income Fund Average	**12.6**	**16.4**	**12.5**	**12.4**	—	**av**

Balanced Funds

Ranked by 1993 Total Return

Fund Name	Annual Return (%) 1993	3yr	5yr	10yr	Category Risk	Total Risk
Fidelity Asset Manager—Growth	26.3	na	na	na	na	na
USAA Cornerstone	23.7	15.2	11.0	na	abv av	av
Fidelity Asset Manager	23.2	19.7	15.8	na	blw av	blw av
Strong Total Return	22.5	18.0	9.4	12.3	high	abv av
Founders Balanced	21.8	16.6	13.5	11.9	av	av
CGM Mutual	21.8	22.0	17.4	16.6	high	abv av
Fidelity Puritan	21.4	20.3	14.3	14.6	abv av	av
Fremont Global	19.5	14.2	11.1	na	blw av	blw av
Fidelity Balanced	19.2	17.7	14.2	na	blw av	blw av
Merriman Asset Allocation	18.5	11.0	na	na	blw av	blw av
Crabbe Huson Asset Allocation	18.2	17.0	11.3	na	av	blw av
Berwyn Income	16.9	20.5	14.3	na	low	blw av
INVESCO Industrial Income	16.6	19.8	18.0	16.3	high	av
Dodge & Cox Balanced	15.9	15.6	13.9	14.2	av	av
Evergreen Foundation	15.7	23.7	na	na	high	av
Permanent Port	15.5	8.5	5.5	5.2	low	blw av
Fidelity Asset Manager—Income	15.3	na	na	na	na	na
Lindner Dividend	14.9	21.0	13.1	13.6	low	blw av
Vanguard Wellesley Income	14.6	14.8	13.6	14.0	blw av	blw av
Strong Investment	14.4	12.2	10.0	10.4	av	av
Evergreen American Retirement	14.0	14.8	11.3	na	low	blw av
USAA Balanced	13.7	11.0	na	na	low	blw av
Columbia Balanced	13.6	na	na	na	na	na
Lepercq-Istel	13.5	12.0	9.8	7.9	high	av
Vanguard Wellington	13.5	14.8	12.3	13.6	abv av	av

Balanced Funds (continued)
Ranked by 1993 Total Return

Fund Name	Annual Return (%)				Category Risk	Total Risk
	1993	3yr	5yr	10yr		
Vanguard Asset Allocation	13.4	15.2	13.8	na	abv av	av
T Rowe Price Balanced	13.3	14.1	14.0	13.4	av	av
Safeco Income	12.5	15.6	10.4	12.3	abv av	av
Olympic Trust Balanced Income	12.5	14.0	11.7	na	blw av	blw av
T Rowe Price Spectrum Income	12.4	13.1	na	na	low	low
INVESCO Value Trust—Total Return	12.3	15.5	12.8	na	av	av
SteinRoe Total Return	12.3	16.2	13.1	12.0	abv av	av
Dreyfus Balanced	10.8	na	na	na	na	na
Vanguard Star	10.8	15.0	11.7	na	av	av
Janus Balanced	10.5	na	na	na	na	na
Preferred Asset Allocation	10.5	na	na	na	na	na
USAA Income	9.9	12.4	12.2	11.9	low	blw av
Vanguard Balanced Index	9.9	na	na	na	na	na
Aetna	9.7	na	na	na	na	na
Value Line Income	8.2	12.2	12.0	11.1	high	av
Portico Balanced	8.2	na	na	na	na	na
Boston Co Asset Allocation	8.0	13.8	11.9	na	high	av
Galaxy Asset Allocation	8.0	na	na	na	na	na
Twentieth Century Balanced	7.2	13.9	13.6	na	high	abv av
IAI Balanced	4.9	na	na	na	na	na
Bascom Hill Balanced	4.3	12.2	7.9	na	abv av	av
Scudder Balanced	4.1	na	na	na	na	na
MIM Bond Income	2.9	8.3	5.5	na	low	blw av
Pax World	-1.0	6.3	10.6	10.7	blw av	blw av
Balanced Fund Average	**13.4**	**15.0**	**12.1**	**12.0**	—	**blw av**

Corporate Bond Funds
Ranked by 1993 Total Return

Fund Name	Annual Return (%)				Category Risk	Total Risk
	1993	3yr	5yr	10yr		
Loomis Sayles Bond	22.2	na	na	na	na	na
CGM Fixed Income	18.9	na	na	na	na	na
Fidelity Spartan Investment Grade	15.7	na	na	na	na	na
Janus Flexible Income	15.6	17.6	10.1	na	abv av	low
Vanguard Long Term Corp Bond	14.3	14.9	13.1	12.5	high	blw av
SteinRoe Income	13.1	13.0	10.4	na	abv av	low
Paine Webber Investment Gr Inc "D"	12.7	na	na	na	na	na
Merrill Lynch Corp Interm "A"	11.8	11.4	11.0	na	high	blw av
INVESCO Income—Sel Income	11.3	13.3	10.5	10.6	av	low
Strong Short-Term Bond	9.3	10.1	8.7	na	blw av	low
Fidelity Short-Term Bond	9.1	10.1	9.3	na	low	low
Fidelity Spartan Short-Term Bond	9.0	na	na	na	na	na
Strong Advantage	7.8	8.9	8.5	na	low	low
Vanguard Short-Term Corporate	7.0	9.0	9.5	9.9	blw av	low
Homestead Short-Term Bond	6.6	na	na	na	na	na
Janus Short-Term Bond	6.1	na	na	na	na	na
Permanent Port—Versatile Bond	3.7	na	na	na	na	na
Corporate Bond Fund Average	**11.4**	**12.0**	**10.1**	**11.0**	—	**low**

Corporate High-Yield Bond Funds
Ranked by 1993 Total Return

Fund Name	Annual Return (%)				Category Risk	Total Risk
	1993	3yr	5yr	10yr		
Fidelity Capital & Income	24.8	27.5	14.0	13.6	high	blw av
Northeast Investors Trust	23.5	22.4	10.7	12.5	av	blw av
Paine Webber High Income "D"	22.6	na	na	na	na	na
Fidelity Spartan High Income	21.8	25.7	na	na	high	blw av
T Rowe Price High Yield	21.7	22.2	9.9	na	av	blw av
Value Line Aggressive Income	19.0	19.1	10.7	na	av	blw av
Vanguard High Yield Corporate	18.2	20.3	10.8	11.5	blw av	blw av
Safeco High Yield Bond	16.9	18.2	10.2	na	blw av	low
INVESCO Income—High Yield	15.6	17.8	10.1	na	low	low
GIT Income—Maximum	15.0	17.4	9.0	9.3	blw av	blw av
Nicholas Income	12.9	15.3	11.9	11.8	low	low
Corporate High-Yield Bond Fund Avg.	**19.2**	**20.5**	**10.8**	**11.7**	**—**	**low**

Government Bond Funds
Ranked by 1993 Total Return

Fund Name	Annual Return (%)				Category Risk	Total Risk
	1993	3yr	5yr	10yr		
Benham Target Mat Trust—2020	35.6	19.9	na	na	high	high
Benham Target Mat Trust—2015	30.5	19.8	17.3	na	high	abv av
Benham Target Mat Trust—2010	26.2	18.8	16.5	na	high	av
Benham Target Mat Trust—2005	21.5	17.3	15.7	na	high	av
Benham Long-Term Treasury & Agency	17.6	na	na	na	na	na
Vanguard Long-Term US Treasury	16.7	13.7	12.9	na	abv av	av
Fidelity Spartan Long-Term Gov't	16.6	13.9	na	na	abv av	blw av
Vanguard Admiral Long US Treas	16.6	na	na	na	na	na
Dreyfus 100% US Treasury Long Term	16.5	14.0	13.0	na	high	av
Scudder Zero Coupon 2000	16.0	14.6	13.6	na	high	av
CA Investment Trust US Gov't	15.7	13.8	12.6	na	abv av	blw av
Benham Target Mat Trust—2000	15.4	14.7	13.9	na	high	av
Rushmore US Gov't Long-Term	15.3	12.5	12.1	na	high	av
T Rowe Price US Treasury Long Term	12.9	11.5	na	na	abv av	blw av
Fidelity Gov't Securities	12.3	12.0	11.6	10.8	av	blw av
IAI Bond	12.3	12.0	11.7	11.4	abv av	blw av
Rushmore US Gov't Interm-Term	11.8	11.6	11.2	na	abv av	blw av
Vanguard Interm-Term US Treasury	11.4	na	na	na	na	na
Vanguard Admiral Interm US Treas	11.3	na	na	na	na	na
Dreyfus 100% US Treasury Interm Term	11.0	11.0	10.9	na	abv av	av
INVESCO Income—US Gov't Sec	10.2	10.4	10.1	na	av	blw av
GIT Income—Gov't Port	9.6	9.5	9.3	10.4	av	blw av
Founders Gov't Securities	9.2	9.7	9.3	na	av	blw av
Boston Co Interm Term Gov't	9.0	9.3	9.2	na	blw av	low
WPG Gov't Securities	8.8	10.1	10.6	na	blw av	low
INVESCO Value Trust—Interm Gov't	8.7	9.6	9.6	na	blw av	low
IAI Gov't	8.5	na	na	na	na	na
Flex Bond	8.2	8.8	8.7	na	av	blw av
Fundamental US Gov't Strat Income	8.1	na	na	na	na	na
BNY Hamilton Interm Gov't	8.0	na	na	na	na	na

Government Bond Funds (continued)

Ranked by 1993 Total Return

| Fund Name | Annual Return (%) | | | | Category | |
	1993	3yr	5yr	10yr	Risk	Total Risk
Benham Treasury Note	7.9	9.3	9.8	na	blw av	low
T Rowe Price US Treasury Interm	7.9	9.6	na	na	blw av	low
Warburg Pincus Interm Mat Gov't	7.8	9.7	9.9	na	blw av	low
Franklin Short-Interm US Gov't	7.7	8.7	9.1	na	blw av	low
Schwab Short/Interm Gov't Bond	7.7	na	na	na	na	na
Dreyfus Short Interm Gov't	7.3	9.2	9.8	na	low	low
Prudential Gov't Securities Interm Term	7.1	8.7	9.0	na	blw av	low
Dreyfus 100% US Treasury Short Term	7.0	8.9	9.1	na	low	low
Benham Target Mat Trust—1995	6.9	10.0	10.9	na	blw av	low
Vanguard Short-Term Federal	6.9	8.4	9.1	na	low	low
Vanguard Admiral Short US Treas	6.4	na	na	na	na	na
Vanguard Short-Term US Treasury	6.3	na	na	na	na	na
Smith Barney Short-Term US Treasury	6.0	na	na	na	na	na
Columbia US Gov't Securities	5.9	8.1	8.6	na	low	low
Fidelity Spartan Short Intermediate Gov't	5.6	na	na	na	na	na
Benham Short-Term Treasury & Agency	5.2	na	na	na	na	na
Fidelity Short-Interm Gov't	5.2	na	na	na	na	na
Gateway Government Bond Plus	5.0	7.4	8.8	na	av	low
Seven Seas Short Term Gov't Securities	4.7	na	na	na	na	na
Bernstein Gov't Short Duration	4.6	7.0	7.9	na	low	low
Twentieth Century US Gov'ts	4.1	6.6	7.5	8.1	low	low
Smith Barney—Income Return "A"	3.9	6.8	8.0	na	low	low
Capstone Gov't Income	3.3	4.4	3.8	8.1	low	low
Janus Interm Gov't Securities	2.4	na	na	na	na	na
Eaton Vance Short-Term Treasury	2.3	na	na	na	na	na
Permanent Treasury Bill	2.2	3.4	5.1	na	low	low
Government Bond Fund Average	**10.4**	**10.8**	**10.4**	**9.7**	**—**	**blw av**

Mortgage-Backed Bond Funds
Ranked by 1993 Total Return

Fund Name	Annual Return (%)				Category Risk	Total Risk
	1993	3yr	5yr	10yr		
Managers Interm Mortgage	11.4	13.3	na	na	high	low
Bull & Bear US Gov't Securities	10.2	10.1	9.7	na	high	blw av
Value Line US Gov't Securities	9.7	10.7	10.8	11.0	high	low
Dreyfus Investors GNMA	8.7	9.6	9.1	na	abv av	low
Selected US Gov't Income	8.4	8.9	8.9	na	high	low
Montgomery Short Duration Gov't	8.3	na	na	na	na	na
Lexington GNMA Income	7.9	9.5	10.6	10.1	abv av	low
Fidelity Spartan Gov't Income	7.3	9.7	10.6	na	av	low
SIT US Gov't Securities	7.3	8.4	9.4	na	low	low
Dreyfus GNMA	7.1	9.2	9.8	na	av	low
USAA GNMA Trust	7.1	na	na	na	na	na
Safeco US Gov't Securities	7.0	9.4	9.9	na	av	low
Fidelity Mortgage Securities	6.6	8.5	9.8	na	low	low
Benham GNMA Income	6.5	9.8	10.7	na	blw av	low
Fidelity Spartan Ltd Maturity Gov't	6.4	7.9	8.6	na	low	low
Fidelity Spartan Ginnie Mae	6.2	8.8	na	na	blw av	low
Fidelity Ginnie Mae	6.1	8.7	10.0	na	low	low
T Rowe Price GNMA	6.1	9.1	10.2	na	av	low
Scudder GNMA	6.0	9.2	10.1	na	abv av	low
Value Line Adjustable Rate US Gov't	6.0	na	na	na	na	na
AARP GNMA & US Treasury	5.9	8.9	9.6	na	blw av	low
Vanguard GNMA	5.8	9.7	10.8	11.0	abv av	low
Paine Webber U.S. Gov't Income "D"	5.8	na	na	na	na	na
Managers Short Gov't	3.7	6.1	na	na	low	low
Benham Adjustable Rate Gov't	3.5	na	na	na	na	na
T Rowe Price Adjustable Rate US Gov't	2.7	na	na	na	na	na
Mortgage-Backed Bond Fund Average	**6.8**	**9.2**	**9.9**	**10.7**	—	**low**

General Bond Funds
Ranked by 1993 Total Return

Fund Name	Annual Return (%)				Category Risk	Total Risk
	1993	3yr	5yr	10yr		
Strong Income	16.7	13.6	6.6	na	av	low
Fidelity Investment Grade	16.1	14.3	12.3	11.5	abv av	low
SteinRoe Gov't Income	15.0	12.0	11.5	na	high	blw av
Dreyfus A Bonds Plus	14.9	13.8	12.0	11.7	high	blw av
Boston Co Managed Income	14.5	13.3	9.9	10.8	av	low
Merriman Flexible Bond	14.4	10.6	9.3	na	abv av	blw av
Blanchard Flexible Income	13.8	na	na	na	na	na
Morgan Grenfell Fixed Income	13.6	na	na	na	na	na
Galaxy High Quality Bond	12.8	11.5	na	na	high	blw av
Scudder Income	12.7	12.1	11.4	11.4	high	blw av
Strong Gov't Securities	12.6	12.8	11.5	na	abv av	low
Harbor Bond	12.4	13.6	12.4	na	abv av	low
Fidelity Interm Bond	11.9	10.7	10.3	10.7	av	low
Managers Bond	11.5	12.7	na	na	abv av	low
Dodge & Cox Income	11.3	12.2	11.6	na	high	blw av
Legg Mason Investment Grade	11.2	11.2	10.4	na	abv av	low
Babson Bond Trust—Port L	11.1	11.0	10.8	11.0	av	low
Warburg Pincus Fixed Income	11.1	11.4	9.2	na	blw av	low
Portico Bond IMMDEX	10.9	11.6	na	na	abv av	low
AARP High Quality Bond	10.9	10.8	10.4	na	high	blw av
Wayne Hummer Income	10.7	na	na	na	na	na
Aetna Bond	10.7	na	na	na	na	na
Columbia Fixed Income Securities	10.4	11.7	11.5	11.0	abv av	low
Bernstein Interm Duration	10.3	11.3	na	na	av	low
Preferred Fixed Income	10.3	na	na	na	na	na
Vista Bond	10.3	10.7	na	na	abv av	low
Twentieth Century Long-Term Bond	9.9	10.9	10.5	na	high	blw av
Vanguard Bond Index	9.6	10.6	10.8	na	blw av	low
T Rowe Price New Income	9.5	9.9	10.1	10.3	av	low
Dreyfus Short Term Income	9.1	na	na	na	na	na
SteinRoe Interm Bond	8.9	10.5	10.2	11.0	av	low
Maxus Income	8.7	11.8	9.6	na	high	av
Babson Bond Trust—Port S	8.4	9.9	9.7	na	blw av	low
Managers Short & Interm Bond	8.4	10.9	na	na	low	low
UMB Bond	8.3	9.3	9.4	9.9	blw av	low
Brundage Story & Rose Short/Interm	8.3	9.3	na	na	blw av	low
Scudder Short-Term Bond	8.2	9.2	10.1	na	low	low
Connecticut Mutual Inv Acts Income	8.1	9.5	8.7	na	low	low
Laurel Intermediate Income	8.0	na	na	na	na	na
William Blair Income Shares	7.7	9.9	na	na	av	low
HighMark Bond	7.4	9.3	9.7	na	av	low
Bartlett Fixed Income	6.9	9.3	9.3	na	blw av	low
Neuberger & Berman Ltd Mat Bond	6.7	7.8	8.7	na	blw av	low
Legg Mason US Gov't Interm Port	6.6	9.0	9.7	na	blw av	low
T Rowe Price Short-Term Bond	6.6	7.5	8.2	na	blw av	low
Galaxy Short Term Bond	6.4	na	na	na	na	na
Portico Short Term Bond Market	6.3	8.8	na	na	blw av	low
Preferred Short-Term Gov't Securities	5.5	na	na	na	na	na
Bernstein Short Duration Plus	5.4	7.9	8.2	na	low	low
Galaxy Interm Bond	5.4	9.3	8.9	na	high	blw av

General Bond Funds (continued)
Ranked by 1993 Total Return

Fund Name	Annual Return (%)				Category Risk	Total Risk
	1993	3yr	5yr	10yr		
Pacifica Asset Preservation	4.5	6.0	na	na	low	low
Vista Short-Term Bond	4.5	6.1	na	na	low	low
Harbor Short Duration	4.4	na	na	na	na	na
Westcore Trust Short-Term Gov't Bond	4.3	6.9	8.2	na	low	low
Seven Seas Yield Plus	3.4	na	na	na	na	na
IAI Reserve	3.3	4.8	6.3	na	low	low
Neuberger & Berman Ultra Short Bond	3.2	4.7	6.3	na	low	low
General Bond Fund Average	**9.2**	**10.2**	**9.8**	**10.9**	—	low

Tax-Exempt Bond Funds
Ranked by 1993 Total Return

Fund Name	Annual Return (%)				Category Risk	Total Risk
	1993	3yr	5yr	10yr		
Cal Muni	16.7	10.8	8.9	na	abv av	blw av
Evergreen Insured National Tax-Free	15.9	na	na	na	na	na
Fidelity Spartan Florida Muni Income	14.8	na	na	na	na	na
Cal Tax-Free Income	14.7	11.8	10.4	na	high	blw av
Dreyfus CA Interm Muni Bond	14.4	na	na	na	na	na
Fidelity Spartan Muni Income	14.3	11.7	na	na	blw av	low
Scudder Mass Tax-Free	14.3	12.4	10.6	na	abv av	blw av
Benham Nat'l Tax-Free Long-Term	14.2	12.1	10.5	na	high	blw av
Fidelity Spartan CA Muni High Yield	14.0	11.4	na	na	av	blw av
General NY Muni Bond	14.0	12.7	10.2	na	abv av	blw av
T Rowe Price NJ Tax-Free	13.9	na	na	na	na	na
Value Line NY Tax-Exempt Trust	13.9	12.5	9.9	na	high	blw av
Fidelity CA Tax-Free Insured	13.8	11.2	9.9	na	high	blw av
Fidelity Insured Tax-Free	13.8	11.0	9.9	na	abv av	blw av
Fidelity Michigan Tax-Free High Yield	13.8	11.7	10.1	na	av	blw av
Scudder CA Tax Free	13.8	11.9	10.4	10.3	high	blw av
Scudder High Yield Tax-Free	13.8	12.7	10.8	na	abv av	blw av
Benham CA Tax-Free Long-Term	13.7	11.2	9.9	9.6	high	blw av
Fidelity Aggressive Tax-Free	13.7	11.5	10.3	na	low	low
General CA Muni Bond	13.6	11.0	na	na	abv av	blw av
Vanguard Florida Insured Tax Free	13.5	na	na	na	na	na
Schwab Long-Term Tax-Free	13.5	na	na	na	na	na
Benham CA Tax-Free Insured	13.4	11.2	10.1	na	high	blw av
Fidelity CA Tax-Free High Yield	13.4	10.7	9.7	na	av	blw av
USAA Tax Exempt NY Bond	13.4	12.0	na	na	av	blw av
Vanguard Long-Term Muni Bond	13.4	12.0	10.8	11.2	high	blw av
Fidelity Spartan NY Muni High Yield	13.3	12.3	na	na	av	blw av
Scudder Managed Muni Bond	13.3	11.4	10.4	10.8	high	blw av
T Rowe Price NY Tax-Free	13.3	12.0	9.8	na	av	blw av
General Muni Bond	13.3	12.5	11.3	na	abv av	blw av

Tax-Exempt Bond Funds (continued)
Ranked by 1993 Total Return

Fund Name	Annual Return (%)				Category Risk	Total Risk
	1993	3yr	5yr	10yr		
Vanguard NJ Tax Free Insured Long	13.3	11.2	10.3	na	high	blw av
Safeco CA Tax-Free Income	13.2	11.2	10.1	10.7	high	blw av
Benham CA Tax-Free High-Yield	13.1	11.0	9.6	na	blw av	low
Fidelity High Yield Tax Free Port	13.1	10.5	10.2	10.9	blw av	low
Fidelity Muni Bond	13.1	11.3	10.0	10.8	av	blw av
Fidelity Spartan Penn Muni High Yield	13.1	11.5	10.3	na	blw av	low
Scudder Penn Tax Free	13.1	11.5	10.0	na	av	blw av
Fidelity Spartan NJ Muni High Yield	13.0	11.3	10.2	na	av	blw av
Vanguard Insured Long-Term Muni	13.0	11.5	10.4	na	high	blw av
Vanguard NY Insured Tax Free	13.0	11.8	10.4	na	high	blw av
Fidelity Mass Tax-Free High Yield	12.9	11.1	10.0	10.3	blw av	low
Fidelity Spartan Conn Tax-Free High-Yield	12.9	10.5	9.7	na	av	blw av
Scudder NY Tax Free	12.9	12.5	10.3	10.0	high	blw av
T Rowe Price Tax-Free High Yield	12.9	11.4	10.3	na	low	low
Dreyfus NJ Muni Bond	12.9	11.2	10.1	na	av	blw av
Fidelity NY Tax-Free High Yield	12.8	11.7	9.8	na	blw av	low
Fidelity NY Tax-Free Insured	12.8	11.2	9.7	na	av	blw av
Strong Insured Muni Bond	12.8	na	na	na	na	na
Dreyfus Florida Interm Muni	12.8	na	na	na	na	na
Vanguard CA Tax-Free Insured Long	12.8	11.0	10.1	na	high	blw av
Schwab CA Long-Term Tax-Free	12.8	na	na	na	na	na
T Rowe Price Maryland Tax-Free	12.7	10.8	9.6	na	av	blw av
T Rowe Price Tax-Free Income	12.7	11.4	9.8	9.5	abv av	blw av
Dreyfus Conn Interm Muni Bond	12.7	na	na	na	na	na
USAA Tax Exempt CA Bond	12.7	10.6	na	na	abv av	blw av
Vanguard Ohio Tax Free Insur Long	12.7	11.4	na	na	abv av	blw av
Vanguard Penn Tax-Free Insur Long	12.7	11.6	10.5	na	abv av	blw av
Dupree KY Tax-Free Income	12.6	10.7	10.0	9.9	blw av	low
T Rowe Price Tax-Free Insured Interm	12.6	na	na	na	na	na
Dreyfus Muni Bond	12.6	10.9	9.7	10.2	av	blw av
Dreyfus NY Tax-Exempt	12.6	11.2	9.6	9.9	av	blw av
USAA Tax-Exempt Virginia Bond	12.6	11.0	na	na	av	blw av
Vanguard High-Yield Muni Bond	12.6	12.3	10.7	11.5	high	blw av
AARP Insured Tax Free General Bond	12.6	11.1	10.1	na	high	blw av
New York Muni	12.5	13.3	9.5	9.6	high	av
Fidelity Ohio Tax-Free High Yield	12.5	10.8	10.0	na	blw av	low
Safeco Muni Bond	12.5	11.6	10.3	11.5	high	blw av
T Rowe Price Virginia Tax-Free Bond	12.5	na	na	na	na	na
Dreyfus Insured Muni Bond	12.5	10.5	9.4	na	high	blw av
Dreyfus NJ Interm Muni Bond	12.5	na	na	na	na	na
Dreyfus Mass Interm Muni Bond	12.5	na	na	na	na	na
GIT Tax-Free Virginia Port	12.4	9.9	8.5	na	av	blw av
Fidelity Minnesota Tax-Free	12.4	9.4	8.9	na	blw av	low
T Rowe Price CA Tax-Free Bond	12.4	11.1	9.5	na	av	blw av
Dreyfus Mass Tax-Exempt Bond	12.4	10.8	9.2	na	blw av	low
USAA Tax Exempt Long-Term	12.4	11.1	10.1	10.6	av	blw av
Morgan Grenfell Muni Bond	12.4	na	na	na	na	na
Scudder Ohio Tax-Free	12.3	10.9	9.8	na	abv av	blw av
Galaxy NY Muni Bond	12.3	na	na	na	na	na
Fidelity Limited Term Muni	12.2	10.5	9.2	9.7	low	low

Tax-Exempt Bond Funds (continued)
Ranked by 1993 Total Return

Fund Name	Annual Return (%)				Category Risk	Total Risk
	1993	3yr	5yr	10yr		
Babson Tax-Free Income—Port L	12.2	10.9	9.5	10.3	abv av	blw av
Galaxy Tax-Exempt Bond	12.1	na	na	na	na	na
INVESCO Tax-Free Long-Term Bond	12.0	11.1	10.4	11.4	abv av	blw av
Twentieth Century Tax-Exempt Long	12.0	10.5	9.4	na	av	blw av
Rushmore Maryland Tax-Free	11.9	10.0	7.9	8.4	high	blw av
Dreyfus CA Tax Exempt Bond	11.8	9.6	8.8	9.1	abv av	blw av
GIT Tax-Free High Yield	11.7	10.0	8.5	9.6	abv av	blw av
Rushmore Virginia Tax-Free	11.7	10.2	8.5	8.3	abv av	blw av
US Tax Free	11.7	9.6	8.6	na	av	blw av
Dreyfus NY Tax-Exempt Interm	11.5	10.6	9.4	na	blw av	low
Value Line Tax Exempt High Yield	11.5	10.5	9.2	na	abv av	blw av
Vanguard Interm-Term Muni Bond	11.5	10.8	9.9	10.3	blw av	low
Paine Webber Nat'l Tax-Free Income "D"	11.5	na	na	na	na	na
Dreyfus Interm Muni Bond	11.4	10.4	9.3	9.4	blw av	low
USAA Tax Exempt Interm-Term	11.4	10.3	9.3	9.4	low	low
Boston Tax Free Muni Bond	11.2	10.3	9.3	na	av	blw av
Paine Webber Muni High Inc "D"	11.1	na	na	na	na	na
SteinRoe Managed Muni	11.0	10.4	9.7	11.7	abv av	blw av
Dreyfus NY Insured Tax-Exempt	11.0	10.8	9.4	na	av	blw av
Merrill Lynch Muni Interm "A"	11.0	10.0	8.7	na	blw av	low
Paine Webber N.Y. Tax Free Inc"D"	11.0	na	na	na	na	na
Lexington Tax-Exempt Bond Trust	10.9	9.1	8.2	na	av	blw av
Scudder Medium Term Tax Free	10.9	10.6	na	na	low	low
Strong Muni Bond	10.9	12.1	9.6	na	av	blw av
Paine Webber CA Tax-Free Inc. "D"	10.9	na	na	na	na	na
SteinRoe Interm Muni	10.8	9.6	8.9	na	blw av	low
Columbia Muni Bond	10.7	9.6	8.9	na	low	low
Heartland Wisconsin Tax Free	10.7	na	na	na	na	na
Benham CA Tax-Free Interm	10.6	9.3	8.6	8.1	blw av	low
Bull & Bear Muni Income	10.5	10.0	8.5	na	high	blw av
SIT Tax Free Income	10.4	9.0	8.5	na	low	low
SteinRoe High Yield Muni	10.4	8.5	8.9	na	blw av	low
First Hawaii Muni Bond	10.4	9.9	9.0	na	blw av	low
Benham Nat'l Tax-Free Interm Term	10.1	9.6	8.8	na	blw av	low
Warburg Pincus NY Muni Bond	9.9	8.9	7.9	na	low	low
Fremont CA Interm Tax-Free	9.9	9.3	na	na	blw av	low
Neuberger & Berman Muni Securities	9.5	8.4	8.1	na	low	low
Smith Barney Muni Bond Ltd Term "A"	9.3	8.8	8.3	na	low	low
Twentieth Century Tax-Exempt Interm	8.9	8.7	7.8	na	low	low
Oregon Municipal Bond	8.9	8.6	7.9	na	low	low
Bernstein NY Muni Port	8.5	8.6	na	na	low	low
Bernstein Diversified Muni Port	8.4	8.3	na	na	low	low
Bernstein CA Muni Port	8.1	8.1	na	na	low	low
BNY Hamilton Interm NY Tax Exempt	7.9	na	na	na	na	na
Evergreen Short Interm Muni CA	7.7	na	na	na	na	na
Evergreen Short-Interm Muni	7.3	na	na	na	na	na
Fidelity Spartan Short-Interm Muni	7.1	7.3	6.9	na	low	low
Babson Tax-Free Income—Port S	6.7	7.4	7.2	na	low	low
Strong Short-Term Muni Bond	6.7	na	na	na	na	na
Dreyfus Short-Interm Municipal	6.6	7.1	6.9	na	low	low

Tax-Exempt Bond Funds (continued)
Ranked by 1993 Total Return

Fund Name	Annual Return (%)				Category	
	1993	3yr	5yr	10yr	Risk	Total Risk
T Rowe Price Tax-Free Short-Interm	6.3	6.7	6.6	6.5	low	low
Vanguard Limited-Term Muni Bond	6.3	7.3	7.4	na	low	low
Benham CA Tax-Free Short-Term	5.9	na	na	na	na	na
Dupree KY Tax-Free Short to Medium	5.6	6.6	6.8	na	low	low
USAA Tax Exempt Short-Term	5.5	6.3	6.4	6.6	low	low
Merrill Lynch Muni Ltd Mat "A"	4.2	5.7	6.0	na	low	low
Calvert Tax-Free Reserves Ltd Term	4.0	5.1	5.8	6.4	low	low
Vanguard Short-Term Muni Bond	3.8	5.2	5.8	6.0	low	low
Tax-Exempt Bond Fund Average	**11.6**	**10.3**	**9.2**	**9.6**	—	low

International Stock Funds
Ranked by 1993 Total Return

Fund Name	Annual Return (%)				Category	
	1993	3yr	5yr	10yr	Risk	Total Risk
Fidelity Emerging Markets	81.7	27.1	na	na	abv av	high
T Rowe Price New Asia	78.7	33.3	na	na	high	high
Fifty-Nine Wall St. Pacific Basin	74.9	28.2	na	na	high	high
Scudder Latin America	74.3	na	na	na	na	na
Fidelity Pacific-Basin	63.9	19.4	6.6	na	high	high
Lexington Worldwide Emerg Mkts	63.3	28.1	18.2	12.2	abv av	high
Scudder Pacific Opportunities	60.0	na	na	na	na	na
Montgomery Emerging Markets	58.6	na	na	na	na	na
Oakmark Int'l	53.5	na	na	na	na	na
Warburg Pincus Int'l Equity	51.2	20.3	na	na	av	abv av
T Rowe Price Int'l Discovery	49.8	15.0	13.4	na	av	abv av
Acorn Int'l	49.1	na	na	na	na	na
SIT Int'l Growth	48.3	na	na	na	na	na
Strong Int'l Stock	47.7	na	na	na	na	na
International Equity	45.7	13.5	9.6	na	abv av	abv av
Harbor Int'l	45.4	20.7	16.8	na	av	abv av
Vanguard Int'l Growth	44.7	12.6	9.4	16.9	abv av	abv av
INVESCO Int'l—Pacific Basin	42.6	11.7	4.8	na	high	high
Twentieth Century Int'l Equity	42.6	na	na	na	na	na
Preferred Int'l	41.5	na	na	na	na	na
Vontobel EuroPacific	41.4	17.9	na	na	low	abv av
Paine Webber Atlas Global Growth "D"	41.0	na	na	na	na	na
Nomura Pacific Basin	40.4	11.1	7.3	na	high	high
T Rowe Price Int'l Stock	40.1	16.1	12.0	17.3	av	abv av
Fidelity Overseas	40.0	10.4	8.0	na	abv av	abv av
USAA Int'l	39.8	16.5	11.0	na	blw av	abv av
IAI Int'l	39.4	15.0	9.4	na	av	abv av
Loomis Sayles Int'l Equity	38.5	na	na	na	na	na
Managers International Equity	38.2	19.4	na	na	low	av
Scudder Global Small Company	38.1	na	na	na	na	na

International Stock Funds (continued)

Ranked by 1993 Total Return

Fund Name	Annual Return (%)				Category Risk	Total Risk
	1993	3yr	5yr	10yr		
Fidelity Diversified Int'l	36.6	na	na	na	na	na
Fidelity Worldwide	36.5	16.0	na	na	low	abv av
Scudder Int'l	36.5	14.1	11.3	16.4	blw av	abv av
Vanguard Int'l Equity Index—Pacific	35.4	7.0	na	na	high	high
Fidelity Int'l Growth & Income	35.0	12.1	10.2	na	low	abv av
Bernstein Int'l Value	34.5	na	na	na	na	na
Babson-Stewart Ivory Int'l	33.4	14.7	11.6	na	blw av	abv av
Columbia Int'l Stock	33.3	na	na	na	na	na
Lexington Global	31.8	13.6	8.8	na	blw av	abv av
Bartlett Value Int'l	31.3	16.1	na	na	blw av	abv av
Scudder Global	31.1	17.0	15.5	na	low	av
Vanguard Trustees' Equity—Int'l	30.5	9.3	7.6	16.1	av	abv av
Aetna Int'l Growth	30.3	na	na	na	na	na
Founders World Wide Growth	29.8	21.1	na	na	blw av	abv av
Vanguard Int'l Equity Index—Europe	29.2	11.9	na	na	abv av	high
Janus Worldwide	28.4	na	na	na	na	na
Wright Int'l Blue Chip Equity	28.2	13.0	na	na	blw av	abv av
INVESCO Int'l—Int'l Growth	27.8	6.2	3.5	na	abv av	high
T Rowe Price European Stock	27.2	8.8	na	na	av	abv av
Fidelity Europe	27.1	8.8	10.2	na	abv av	abv av
Fifty-Nine Wall St. European	27.1	14.3	na	na	blw av	abv av
Bull & Bear US & Overseas	26.7	14.8	9.8	na	low	abv av
Fidelity Canada	25.4	12.7	11.4	na	low	abv av
Boston Co Int'l	24.5	5.9	2.2	na	high	high
INVESCO Int'l—European	24.5	7.5	9.2	na	abv av	abv av
Blanchard Global Growth	24.4	11.5	8.5	na	low	av
USAA World Growth	24.0	na	na	na	na	na
Japan	23.6	2.0	-0.1	14.3	high	high
T Rowe Price Japan	20.6	na	na	na	na	na
Fidelity Japan	20.4	na	na	na	na	na
US Global Resources	18.5	6.5	4.4	1.0	low	av
US European Income	11.6	1.6	-5.3	na	blw av	abv av
Brinson Global	11.1	na	na	na	na	na
International Stock Fund Average	**38.5**	**14.3**	**8.7**	**13.4**	**—**	**abv av**

International Bond Funds
Ranked by 1993 Total Return

| Fund Name | Annual Return (%) | | | | Category | |
	1993	3yr	5yr	10yr	Risk	Total Risk
Bull & Bear Global Income	24.9	18.5	9.4	7.8	low	blw av
Fidelity Global Bond	21.9	12.7	11.7	na	av	blw av
T Rowe Price Int'l Bond	19.9	13.0	10.1	na	high	av
Warburg Pincus Global Fixed Income	19.6	11.9	na	na	abv av	av
Scudder Int'l Bond	15.8	15.0	14.6	na	high	av
Paine Webber Global Income "D"	13.6	na	na	na	na	na
Fidelity Short Term World Income	12.4	na	na	na	na	na
Benham European Gov't Bond	11.6	na	na	na	na	na
T Rowe Price Global Gov't Bond	11.2	8.6	na	na	blw av	blw av
Blanchard Short-Term Global Inc	8.5	na	na	na	na	na
T Rowe Price Short-Term Global Inc	7.8	na	na	na	na	na
Scudder Short-Term Global Income	6.6	na	na	na	na	na
Alliance World Income Trust	4.0	4.4	na	na	low	low
Flex Short Term Global Income	0.3	na	na	na	na	na
International Bond Fund Average	**12.7**	**12.0**	**11.4**	**7.8**	**—**	**low**

Gold Funds
Ranked by 1993 Total Return

| Fund Name | Annual Return (%) | | | | Category | |
	1993	3yr	5yr	10yr	Risk	Total Risk
US Gold Shares	123.9	-2.4	0.1	-4.9	high	high
Fidelity Sel Precious Metals	111.6	18.8	11.8	4.8	abv av	high
Blanchard Precious Metals	100.4	16.8	5.8	na	av	high
Vanguard Spec Port—Gold & PM	93.3	17.6	11.1	na	blw av	high
US World Gold	89.7	20.4	71.1	na	high	high
Bull & Bear Gold Investors Ltd	87.6	15.3	7.3	5.2	blw av	high
Lexington GoldFund	86.9	11.7	6.4	6.8	av	high
Benham Gold Equities Index	81.2	13.6	8.9	na	high	high
Fidelity Sel American Gold	78.6	17.5	10.4	na	low	high
INVESCO Strat Port—Gold	72.6	13.7	6.5	na	abv av	high
Scudder Gold	59.3	10.4	4.4	na	low	high
USAA Gold	58.3	11.6	3.8	na	low	high
Gold Fund Average	**86.9**	**13.7**	**12.3**	**2.9**	**—**	**high**

Small Capitalization Stock Funds
Ranked by 1993 Total Return

Fund Name	Annual Return (%)				Category Risk	Total Risk
	1993	3yr	5yr	10yr		
T Rowe Price Int'l Discovery	49.8	15.0	13.4	na	av	abv av
Acorn Int'l	49.1	na	na	na	na	na
PBHG Growth	44.6	41.2	26.9	na	high	high
Scudder Global Small Company	38.1	na	na	na	na	na
Acorn	32.3	34.2	20.0	17.9	av	abv av
Twentieth Century Giftrust	31.4	42.0	29.0	22.0	high	high
Fidelity New Millenium	24.6	na	na	na	na	na
Loomis Sayles Small Cap	24.6	na	na	na	na	na
Montgomery Small Cap	24.3	39.3	na	na	abv av	high
Legg Mason Special Investment	24.1	25.9	21.5	na	low	abv av
INVESCO Emerging Growth	23.4	na	na	na	na	na
T Rowe Price Small Cap Value	23.3	25.9	15.9	na	low	av
Galaxy Small Company Equity	22.7	na	na	na	na	na
Cappiello-Rushmore Emerging Growth	22.5	na	na	na	na	na
Strong Discovery	22.2	27.8	20.2	na	high	high
T Rowe Price New Horizons	22.0	27.1	18.5	10.7	av	high
Regis ICM Small Company Port	21.9	33.8	na	na	abv av	abv av
Twentieth Century Ultra	21.8	32.0	28.0	16.6	high	high
Columbia Special	21.6	27.6	19.1	na	av	high
Robertson Stephens Value Plus	21.6	na	na	na	na	na
Fidelity Low-Priced Stock	20.2	31.3	na	na	av	abv av
Fidelity Emerging Growth	19.8	29.4	na	na	abv av	high
Southeastern Asset Mgmt Small Cap	19.8	17.3	8.4	na	blw av	av
Vanguard Small Cap Stock	18.7	26.7	13.0	7.0	blw av	high
T Rowe Price OTC	18.4	23.1	12.1	10.5	low	abv av
Warburg Pincus Emerging Grth	18.1	27.4	17.8	na	av	high
Kaufmann	18.1	33.1	26.6	na	abv av	high
Managers Special Equity	17.3	26.5	na	na	low	abv av
Dreyfus New Leaders	17.0	23.0	16.6	na	low	abv av
Eclipse Equity	17.0	22.3	12.9	na	blw av	av
Founders Frontier	16.5	23.7	20.4	na	av	high
Babson Enterprise	16.2	27.4	16.3	14.0	av	abv av
Vanguard Explorer	15.5	26.7	14.7	7.6	blw av	high
GIT Equity—Special Growth	14.8	15.4	10.1	12.7	low	abv av
IAI Emerging Growth	14.7	na	na	na	na	na
Vanguard Index Trust—Ext Market	14.4	22.2	14.2	na	av	abv av
Neuberger & Berman Genesis	13.8	23.0	12.8	na	low	abv av
HighMark Special Growth Equity	13.8	17.0	13.8	na	high	high
Babson Shadow Stock	13.5	23.1	12.3	na	blw av	av
Oberweis Emerging Growth	13.3	34.1	24.7	na	high	high
Meridian	13.0	26.9	20.7	na	high	high
Fifty-Nine Wall St. Small Company	12.1	na	na	na	na	na
Pennsylvania Mutual	11.2	19.4	11.9	na	low	av
Gradison McDonald Opportunity Value	11.0	19.9	13.0	11.7	blw av	av
Founders Discovery	10.8	27.5	na	na	abv av	high
Evergreen Limited Market	9.5	22.1	14.5	17.3	blw av	high
Janus Venture	9.0	20.1	19.0	na	low	abv av
Nicholas Limited Edition	9.0	22.1	16.0	na	blw av	abv av
Scudder Development	8.8	22.4	18.0	11.2	abv av	high
SIT Growth	8.5	20.6	18.3	15.2	av	high

Small Capitalization Stock Funds (continued)
Ranked by 1993 Total Return

Fund Name	Annual Return (%)				Category Risk	Total Risk
	1993	3yr	5yr	10yr		
USAA Aggressive Growth	8.1	19.3	11.7	7.7	abv av	high
Robertson Stephens Emerg Grth	7.2	18.3	21.2	na	high	high
Nicholas II	6.4	17.5	12.3	14.6	blw av	av
Evergreen	6.2	17.4	10.4	11.6	low	abv av
UMB Heartland Fund	5.9	na	na	na	na	na
Twentieth Century Vista	5.4	21.4	18.1	12.4	abv av	high
Perritt Capital Growth	5.2	15.8	5.7	na	low	abv av
Prudent Speculator	3.1	19.4	0.6	na	high	high
Monetta	0.4	18.2	16.2	na	av	abv av
FAM Value	0.2	22.7	16.0	na	av	abv av
Small Capitalization Stock Fund Avg	17.2	25.3	17.4	13.8	—	abv av

Individual Fund Listings 9

1784 Growth and Income
(SEGWX)

Growth & Income

680 East Swedesford Road
Wayne, PA 19087
(800) 252-1784

fund in existence since 6/14/93

PERFORMANCE

	3yr Annual	5yr Annual	10yr Annual	Bull	Bear
Return (%)	na	na	na	na	na
Differ from Category (+/-)	na	na	na	na	na

Total Risk	Standard Deviation	Category Risk	Risk Index	Beta
na	na	na	na	na

	1993	1992	1991	1990	1989	1988	1987	1986	1985	1984
Return (%)	—	—	—	—	—	—	—	—	—	—
Differ from category (+/-) ...	—	—	—	—	—	—	—	—	—	—

PER SHARE DATA

	1993	1992	1991	1990	1989	1988	1987	1986	1985	1984
Dividends, Net Income ($) .	0.07	—	—	—	—	—	—	—	—	—
Distrib'ns, Cap Gain ($) ...	0.00	—	—	—	—	—	—	—	—	—
Net Asset Value ($)	10.69	—	—	—	—	—	—	—	—	—
Expense Ratio (%)	na	—	—	—	—	—	—	—	—	—
Net Income to Assets (%)	na	—	—	—	—	—	—	—	—	—
Portfolio Turnover (%)	na	—	—	—	—	—	—	—	—	—
Total Assets (Millions $)	97	—	—	—	—	—	—	—	—	—

PORTFOLIO

Portfolio Manager: committee

Investm't Category: Growth & Income

Cap Gain	Asset Allocation
✔ Cap & Income	Fund of Funds
Income	Index
	Sector
✔ Domestic	Small Cap
Foreign	Socially Conscious
Country/Region	State Specific

Portfolio: stocks na bonds na
convertibles na other na cash na

Largest Holdings: na

Unrealized Net Capital Gains: na

SHAREHOLDER INFORMATION

Minimum Investment
Initial: $1,000   Subsequent: $250

Minimum IRA Investment
Initial: $250   Subsequent: $250

Maximum Fees
Load: none   12b-1: 0.25%
Other: none

Distributions
Income: quarterly   Capital Gains: Dec

Exchange Options
Number Per Year: no limit   Fee: none
Telephone: yes (money market fund available)

Services
IRA, other pension, auto invest, auto withdraw

1784 U.S. Gov't Medium Term Income (SEGTX)

680 East Swedesford Road
Wayne, PA 19087
(800) 252-1784

Government Bond

fund in existence since 6/14/93

PERFORMANCE

	3yr Annual	5yr Annual	10yr Annual	Bull	Bear
Return (%)	na	na	na	na	na
Differ from Category (+/-)	na	na	na	na	na

Total Risk	Standard Deviation	Category Risk	Risk Index	Avg Mat
na	na	na	na	4.3 yrs

	1993	1992	1991	1990	1989	1988	1987	1986	1985	1984
Return (%)	—	—	—	—	—	—	—	—	—	—
Differ from category (+/-)	—	—	—	—	—	—	—	—	—	—

PER SHARE DATA

	1993	1992	1991	1990	1989	1988	1987	1986	1985	1984
Dividends, Net Income ($) .	0.36	—	—	—	—	—	—	—	—	—
Distrib'ns, Cap Gain ($) . . .	0.00	—	—	—	—	—	—	—	—	—
Net Asset Value ($)	10.00	—	—	—	—	—	—	—	—	—
Expense Ratio (%)	na	—	—	—	—	—	—	—	—	—
Net Income to Assets (%) . . .	na	—	—	—	—	—	—	—	—	—
Portfolio Turnover (%)	na	—	—	—	—	—	—	—	—	—
Total Assets (Millions $)	96	—	—	—	—	—	—	—	—	—

PORTFOLIO

Portfolio Manager: committee

Investm't Category: Government Bond

Cap Gain	Asset Allocation
Cap & Income	Fund of Funds
✔ Income	Index
	Sector
✔ Domestic	Small Cap
Foreign	Socially Conscious
Country/Region	State Specific

Portfolio: stocks na   bonds na
convertibles na   other na   cash na

Largest Holdings: na

Unrealized Net Capital Gains: na

SHAREHOLDER INFORMATION

Minimum Investment
Initial: $1,000   Subsequent: $250

Minimum IRA Investment
Initial: $250   Subsequent: $250

Maximum Fees
Load: none   12b-1: 0.25%
Other: none

Distributions
Income: monthly   Capital Gains: Dec

Exchange Options
Number Per Year: no limit   Fee: none
Telephone: yes (money market fund available)

Services
IRA, other pension, auto invest, auto withdraw

AARP Capital Growth
(ACGFX)

Growth

P.O. Box 2540
Boston, MA 02208
(800) 253-2277, (617) 439-4640

PERFORMANCE

	3yr Annual	5yr Annual	10yr Annual	Bull	Bear
Return (%)	19.4	13.9	na	89.8	-24.3
Differ from Category (+/-)	0.2 av	-0.6 av	na	5.1 av	-11.9 low

Total Risk	Standard Deviation	Category Risk	Risk Index	Beta
high	14.7%	high	1.4	1.2

	1993	1992	1991	1990	1989	1988	1987	1986	1985	1984
Return (%)	15.8	4.7	40.5	-15.7	33.4	27.3	0.2	15.8	29.4	—
Differ from category (+/-) . . .	2.6	-6.3	5.1	-9.6	7.6	9.6	-1.0	1.3	0.1	—

PER SHARE DATA

	1993	1992	1991	1990	1989	1988	1987	1986	1985	1984
Dividends, Net Income ($) .	0.05	0.14	0.23	0.58	0.18	0.09	0.15	0.18	0.08	—
Distrib'ns, Cap Gain ($) . . .	2.90	1.21	0.93	1.79	1.93	0.42	1.23	0.90	0.18	—
Net Asset Value ($)	34.24	32.09	31.94	23.57	30.83	24.72	19.84	21.19	19.21	—
Expense Ratio (%)	1.05	1.13	1.17	1.11	1.16	1.23	1.24	1.44	1.50	—
Net Income to Assets (%) . .	0.22	0.61	0.90	2.00	0.89	0.37	0.62	1.27	1.95	—
Portfolio Turnover (%)	100	89	100	83	64	45	54	46	41	—
Total Assets (Millions $) . . .	662	424	242	160	180	91	116	55	20	—

PORTFOLIO (as of 9/30/93)

Portfolio Manager: J. Cox - 1984, S. Aronoff - 1989, W. Gadsden - 1989

Investm't Category: Growth

✔ Cap Gain   Asset Allocation
   Cap & Income   Fund of Funds
   Income   Index
     Sector
✔ Domestic   Small Cap
✔ Foreign   Socially Conscious
   Country/Region   State Specific

Portfolio: stocks 91%   bonds 0%
convertibles 2%   other 0%   cash 7%

Largest Holdings: consumer discretionary 21%, media 17%

Unrealized Net Capital Gains: 11% of portfolio value

SHAREHOLDER INFORMATION

Minimum Investment
Initial: $500   Subsequent: $0

Minimum IRA Investment
Initial: $250   Subsequent: $0

Maximum Fees
Load: none   12b-1: none
Other: none

Distributions
Income: Dec   Capital Gains: Dec

Exchange Options
Number Per Year: no limit   Fee: none
Telephone: yes (money market fund available)

Services
IRA, other pension, auto invest, auto withdraw

AARP GNMA & US
Treasury (AGNMX)

P.O. Box 2540
Boston, MA 02208
(800) 253-2277, (617) 439-4640

Mortgage-Backed Bond

	3yr Annual	5yr Annual	10yr Annual	Bull	Bear
Return (%)	8.9	9.6	na	34.8	5.1
Differ from Category (+/-)	-0.3 blw av	-0.3 blw av	na	-1.9 blw av	0.5 abv av

Total Risk	Standard Deviation	Category Risk	Risk Index	Avg Mat
low	2.6%	blw av	1.0	6.4 yrs

	1993	1992	1991	1990	1989	1988	1987	1986	1985	1984
Return (%)	5.9	6.5	14.3	9.7	11.6	7.0	1.9	11.4	17.9	—
Differ from category (+/-). . .	-0.8	0.4	-0.1	0.2	-0.6	0.0	-0.2	0.2	-1.4	—

PER SHARE DATA

	1993	1992	1991	1990	1989	1988	1987	1986	1985	1984
Dividends, Net Income ($).	1.09	1.21	1.25	1.30	1.30	1.36	1.34	1.48	1.58	—
Distrib'ns, Cap Gain ($) . . .	0.00	0.00	0.00	0.00	0.00	0.00	0.00	0.01	0.03	—
Net Asset Value ($)	15.77	15.93	16.13	15.28	15.18	14.82	15.14	16.19	15.94	—
Expense Ratio (%)	0.70	0.72	0.74	0.79	0.79	0.81	0.88	0.90	1.03	—
Net Income to Assets (%) .	7.15	7.69	8.23	8.71	8.76	9.09	8.76	9.49	10.62	—
Portfolio Turnover (%).	105	74	87	61	48	85	51	61	67	—
Total Assets (Millions $). .	6,641	5,231	3,310	2,582	2,518	2,838	2,828	1,905	322	—

PORTFOLIO (as of 9/30/93)

Portfolio Manager: David H. Glen - 1985, Robert E. Pruyne - 1984

Investm't Category: Mortgage-Backed Bond

Cap Gain	Asset Allocation
Cap & Income	Fund of Funds
✔ Income	Index
	Sector
✔ Domestic	Small Cap
Foreign	Socially Conscious
Country/Region	State Specific

Portfolio: stocks 0%   bonds 100%
convertibles 0%   other 0%   cash 0%

Largest Holdings: mortgage-backed 79%, U.S. government 20%

Unrealized Net Capital Gains: 1% of portfolio value

SHAREHOLDER INFORMATION

Minimum Investment
Initial: $500   Subsequent: $0

Minimum IRA Investment
Initial: $250   Subsequent: $0

Maximum Fees
Load: none   12b-1: none
Other: none

Distributions
Income: monthly   Capital Gains: Dec

Exchange Options
Number Per Year: no limit   Fee: none
Telephone: yes (money market fund available)

Services
IRA, other pension, auto invest, auto withdraw

AARP Growth & Income
(AGIFX)
Growth & Income

P.O. Box 2540
Boston, MA 02208
(800) 253-2277, (617) 439-4640

PERFORMANCE

	3yr Annual	5yr Annual	10yr Annual	Bull	Bear
Return (%)	16.9	14.6	na	72.8	-9.5
Differ from Category (+/-)	0.5 abv av	2.1 high	na	2.7 av	2.1 abv av

Total Risk	Standard Deviation	Category Risk	Risk Index	Beta
av	8.3%	blw av	0.9	0.7

	1993	1992	1991	1990	1989	1988	1987	1986	1985	1984
Return (%)	15.6	9.2	26.4	-2.0	26.6	10.9	0.8	19.5	30.2	—
Differ from category (+/-) . . .	3.0	-0.8	-1.3	3.6	5.0	-5.9	0.4	4.3	4.8	—

PER SHARE DATA

	1993	1992	1991	1990	1989	1988	1987	1986	1985	1984
Dividends, Net Income ($) .	0.83	0.92	1.01	1.22	1.06	1.03	0.94	0.69	0.31	—
Distrib'ns, Cap Gain ($) . . .	0.20	0.30	0.47	0.12	0.00	0.00	0.77	0.87	0.08	—
Net Asset Value ($)	32.94	29.41	28.08	23.45	25.36	20.90	19.79	21.28	19.18	—
Expense Ratio (%)	0.84	0.91	0.96	1.03	1.04	1.06	1.08	1.21	1.50	—
Net Income to Assets (%) . .	3.08	3.84	4.61	4.76	4.19	4.52	3.81	4.55	5.62	—
Portfolio Turnover (%)	17	36	54	58	55	61	43	37	12	—
Total Assets (Millions $) . .	1,713	748	392	248	236	228	358	99	26	—

PORTFOLIO (as of 9/30/93)

Portfolio Manager: B. Thorndik - 1984, R. Hoffman - 1990, K. Millard - 1991

Investm't Category: Growth & Income

Cap Gain	Asset Allocation
✔ Cap & Income	Fund of Funds
Income	Index
	Sector
✔ Domestic	Small Cap
✔ Foreign	Socially Conscious
Country/Region	State Specific

Portfolio: stocks 82% bonds 0%
convertibles 12% other 0% cash 6%

Largest Holdings: financial 22%, manufacturing 16%

Unrealized Net Capital Gains: 13% of portfolio value

SHAREHOLDER INFORMATION

Minimum Investment
Initial: $500   Subsequent: $0

Minimum IRA Investment
Initial: $250   Subsequent: $0

Maximum Fees
Load: none   12b-1: none
Other: none

Distributions
Income: quarterly   Capital Gains: Dec

Exchange Options
Number Per Year: no limit   Fee: none
Telephone: yes (money market fund available)

Services
IRA, other pension, auto invest, auto withdraw

AARP High Quality Bond
(AGBFX)

General Bond

P.O. Box 2540
Boston, MA 02208
(800) 253-2277, (617) 439-4640

PERFORMANCE

	3yr Annual	5yr Annual	10yr Annual	Bull	Bear
Return (%)	10.8	10.4	na	43.4	2.0
Differ from Category (+/-)	0.6 av	0.6 abv av	na	4.0 abv av	-0.8 blw av

Total Risk	Standard Deviation	Category Risk	Risk Index	Avg Mat
blw av	4.1%	high	1.4	12.0 yrs

	1993	1992	1991	1990	1989	1988	1987	1986	1985	1984
Return (%)	10.9	6.2	15.4	7.5	12.2	8.0	1.1	11.6	15.7	—
Differ from category (+/-). . .	1.7	-0.5	0.8	0.6	0.8	0.4	-1.4	-2.3	-4.4	—

PER SHARE DATA

	1993	1992	1991	1990	1989	1988	1987	1986	1985	1984
Dividends, Net Income ($) .	0.91	1.00	1.06	1.16	1.21	1.24	1.35	1.33	1.42	—
Distrib'ns, Cap Gain ($) . . .	0.37	0.18	0.00	0.00	0.00	0.00	0.00	0.23	0.05	—
Net Asset Value ($)	16.51	16.07	16.29	15.12	15.20	14.68	14.77	15.96	15.77	—
Expense Ratio (%)	1.01	1.13	1.17	1.14	1.16	1.17	1.18	1.30	1.50	—
Net Income to Assets (%) .	5.64	6.40	7.26	7.86	8.33	8.55	7.81	8.86	9.86	—
Portfolio Turnover (%).	100	63	90	47	58	24	193	62	53	—
Total Assets (Millions $). . . .	623	384	201	151	129	124	108	88	45	—

PORTFOLIO (as of 9/30/93)

Portfolio Manager: Samuel Thorne Jr. - 1984, William Hutchinson - 1987

Investm't Category: General Bond

Cap Gain	Asset Allocation
Cap & Income	Fund of Funds
✔ Income	Index
	Sector
✔ Domestic	Small Cap
Foreign	Socially Conscious
Country/Region	State Specific

Portfolio:	stocks 0%	bonds 93%
convertibles 0%	other 0%	cash 6%

Largest Holdings: mortgage-backed 30%, corporate bonds 28%

Unrealized Net Capital Gains: 5% of portfolio value

SHAREHOLDER INFORMATION

Minimum Investment
Initial: $500   Subsequent: $0

Minimum IRA Investment
Initial: $250   Subsequent: $0

Maximum Fees
Load: none   12b-1: none
Other: none

Distributions
Income: monthly   Capital Gains: Dec

Exchange Options
Number Per Year: no limit   Fee: none
Telephone: yes (money market fund available)

Services
IRA, other pension, auto invest, auto withdraw

AARP Insured Tax Free General Bond (AITGX)

P.O. Box 2540
Boston, MA 02208
(800) 253-2277, (617) 439-4640

Tax-Exempt Bond

PERFORMANCE

	3yr Annual	5yr Annual	10yr Annual	Bull	Bear
Return (%)	11.1	10.1	na	44.4	1.1
Differ from Category (+/-)	0.8 av	0.8 abv av	na	4.3 abv av	-1.2 low

Total Risk	Standard Deviation	Category Risk	Risk Index	Avg Mat
blw av	5.1%	high	1.3	11.8 yrs

	1993	1992	1991	1990	1989	1988	1987	1986	1985	1984
Return (%)	12.6	8.5	12.2	6.3	10.7	12.2	-1.4	16.8	10.2	—
Differ from category (+/-)	1.0	0.2	0.8	0.0	1.7	2.1	-0.2	0.4	-7.1	—

PER SHARE DATA

	1993	1992	1991	1990	1989	1988	1987	1986	1985	1984
Dividends, Net Income ($)	0.87	0.92	0.98	1.03	1.07	1.07	1.07	1.04	0.86	—
Distrib'ns, Cap Gain ($)	0.40	0.42	0.16	0.00	0.25	0.00	0.00	0.19	0.06	—
Net Asset Value ($)	18.54	17.62	17.52	16.68	16.70	16.31	15.55	16.89	15.57	—
Expense Ratio (%)	0.72	0.74	0.77	0.80	0.84	0.92	1.00	1.13	1.29	—
Net Income to Assets (%)	4.90	5.31	5.92	6.29	6.52	6.95	6.58	6.40	6.11	—
Portfolio Turnover (%)	47	62	32	48	149	164	135	135	90	—
Total Assets (Millions $)	2,123	1,488	1,067	771	527	313	238	129	62	—

PORTFOLIO (as of 9/30/93)

Portfolio Manager: Carleton - 1988, Condon - 1989

Investm't Category: Tax-Exempt Bond

Cap Gain	Asset Allocation
Cap & Income	Fund of Funds
✔ Income	Index
	Sector
✔ Domestic	Small Cap
Foreign	Socially Conscious
Country/Region	State Specific

Portfolio: stocks 0% bonds 100%
convertibles 0% other 0% cash 0%

Largest Holdings: general obligation 23%

Unrealized Net Capital Gains: 8% of portfolio value

SHAREHOLDER INFORMATION

Minimum Investment
Initial: $500 Subsequent: $0

Minimum IRA Investment
Initial: na Subsequent: na

Maximum Fees
Load: none 12b-1: none
Other: none

Distributions
Income: monthly Capital Gains: Dec

Exchange Options
Number Per Year: no limit Fee: none
Telephone: yes (money market fund available)

Services
auto invest, auto withdraw

Acorn (ACRNX)

Growth

227 West Monroe
Chicago, IL 60606
(800) 922-6769

this fund is closed to new investors

PERFORMANCE

	3yr Annual	5yr Annual	10yr Annual	Bull	Bear
Return (%)	34.2	20.0	17.9	154.1	-21.3
Differ from Category (+/-)	15.0 high	5.4 high	5.3 high	69.4 high	-8.9 low

Total Risk	Standard Deviation	Category Risk	Risk Index	Beta
abv av	12.3%	av	1.1	0.8

	1993	1992	1991	1990	1989	1988	1987	1986	1985	1984
Return (%)	32.3	24.2	47.3	-17.5	24.9	24.6	4.4	16.8	31.5	4.2
Differ from category (+/-) . .	19.1	13.2	11.9	-11.4	-0.8	6.9	3.2	2.3	2.2	4.2

PER SHARE DATA

	1993	1992	1991	1990	1989	1988	1987	1986	1985	1984
Dividends, Net Income ($) .	0.06	0.13	0.10	0.12	0.11	0.16	0.15	0.10	0.10	0.11
Distrib'ns, Cap Gain ($) . . .	0.59	0.34	0.15	0.44	0.36	0.63	1.08	1.21	0.37	0.33
Net Asset Value ($)	13.95	11.06	9.32	6.51	8.58	7.26	6.48	7.45	7.56	6.17
Expense Ratio (%)	0.68	0.67	0.72	0.82	0.73	0.80	0.82	0.79	0.78	0.85
Net Income to Assets (%) .	0.59	0.72	1.30	1.60	1.59	1.52	1.85	1.71	1.73	2.31
Portfolio Turnover (%).	19	25	25	36	26	36	52	34	32	33
Total Assets (Millions $) . .	2,044	1,450	1,150	767	855	563	418	414	317	210

PORTFOLIO (as of 9/30/93)

Portfolio Manager: Ralph Wanger - 1970

Investm't Category: Growth
✔ Cap Gain   Asset Allocation
  Cap & Income   Fund of Funds
  Income   Index
    Sector
✔ Domestic   ✔ Small Cap
✔ Foreign   Socially Conscious
  Country/Region   State Specific

Portfolio: stocks 97%   bonds 0%
convertibles 0%   other 0%   cash 3%

Largest Holdings: gaming equipment 9%, broadcasting & CATV 9%

Unrealized Net Capital Gains: 42% of portfolio value

SHAREHOLDER INFORMATION

Minimum Investment
Initial: $4,000   Subsequent: $1,000

Minimum IRA Investment
Initial: $200   Subsequent: $200

Maximum Fees
Load: 2.00% redemption   12b-1: none
Other: redemption fee applies for 60 days

Distributions
Income: Jul, Dec   Capital Gains: Dec

Exchange Options
Number Per Year: no limit   Fee: none
Telephone: yes (money market fund available)

Services
IRA, other pension, auto invest, auto withdraw

Acorn Int'l (ACINX)

International Stock

227 West Monroe
Chicago, IL 60606
(800) 922-6769

this fund is closed to new investors

PERFORMANCE

	3yr Annual	5yr Annual	10yr Annual	Bull	Bear
Return (%)	na	na	na	na	na
Differ from Category (+/-)	na	na	na	na	na

Total Risk	Standard Deviation	Category Risk	Risk Index	Beta
na	na	na	na	na

	1993	1992	1991	1990	1989	1988	1987	1986	1985	1984
Return (%)	49.1	—	—	—	—	—	—	—	—	—
Differ from category (+/-)	10.6	—	—	—	—	—	—	—	—	—

PER SHARE DATA

	1993	1992	1991	1990	1989	1988	1987	1986	1985	1984
Dividends, Net Income ($)	0.00	—	—	—	—	—	—	—	—	—
Distrib'ns, Cap Gain ($)	0.00	—	—	—	—	—	—	—	—	—
Net Asset Value ($)	15.94	—	—	—	—	—	—	—	—	—
Expense Ratio (%)	1.40	—	—	—	—	—	—	—	—	—
Net Income to Assets (%)	1.20	—	—	—	—	—	—	—	—	—
Portfolio Turnover (%)	21	—	—	—	—	—	—	—	—	—
Total Assets (Millions $)	954	—	—	—	—	—	—	—	—	—

PORTFOLIO (as of 9/30/93)

Portfolio Manager: Ralph Wanger - 1992

Investm't Category: International Stock

✔ Cap Gain	Asset Allocation
Cap & Income	Fund of Funds
Income	Index
	Sector
✔ Domestic	✔ Small Cap
✔ Foreign	Socially Conscious
Country/Region	State Specific

Portfolio: stocks 92%   bonds 0%
convertibles 0%   other 0%   cash 8%

Largest Holdings: Japan 13%, Hong Kong 8%

Unrealized Net Capital Gains: 6% of portfolio value

SHAREHOLDER INFORMATION

Minimum Investment
Initial: $1,000   Subsequent: $200

Minimum IRA Investment
Initial: $200   Subsequent: $200

Maximum Fees
Load: 2.00% redemption   12b-1: none
Other: redemption fee applies for 60 days

Distributions
Income: Dec   Capital Gains: Dec

Exchange Options
Number Per Year: no limit   Fee: none
Telephone: yes (money market fund available)

Services
IRA, other pension, auto invest, auto withdraw

Aetna (AETFX)

Balanced

151 Farmington Ave.
Hartford, CT 06156
(800) 367-7732

PERFORMANCE

	3yr Annual	5yr Annual	10yr Annual	Bull	Bear
Return (%)	na	na	na	na	na
Differ from Category (+/-)	na	na	na	na	na

Total Risk	Standard Deviation	Category Risk	Risk Index	Beta
na	na	na	na	na

	1993	1992	1991	1990	1989	1988	1987	1986	1985	1984
Return (%)	9.7	6.7	—	—	—	—	—	—	—	—
Differ from category (+/-). . .	-3.7	-1.4	—	—	—	—	—	—	—	—

PER SHARE DATA

	1993	1992	1991	1990	1989	1988	1987	1986	1985	1984
Dividends, Net Income ($).	0.34	0.48	—	—	—	—	—	—	—	—
Distrib'ns, Cap Gain ($) . . .	0.00	0.00	—	—	—	—	—	—	—	—
Net Asset Value ($)	10.82	10.18	—	—	—	—	—	—	—	—
Expense Ratio (%)	na	0.07	—	—	—	—	—	—	—	—
Net Income to Assets (%) . . .	na	4.31	—	—	—	—	—	—	—	—
Portfolio Turnover (%).	na	13	—	—	—	—	—	—	—	—
Total Assets (Millions $).	64	38	—	—	—	—	—	—	—	—

PORTFOLIO (as of 6/30/93)

Portfolio Manager: Charles Dawkins - 1991

Investm't Category: Balanced

Cap Gain	✔ Asset Allocation
✔ Cap & Income	Fund of Funds
Income	Index
	Sector
✔ Domestic	Small Cap
✔ Foreign	Socially Conscious
Country/Region	State Specific

Portfolio: stocks 44% bonds 25%
convertibles 0% other 3% cash 28%

Largest Holdings: finance 5%, bonds—mort-gaged-backed 7%

Unrealized Net Capital Gains: 3% of portfolio value

SHAREHOLDER INFORMATION

Minimum Investment
Initial: $1,000   Subsequent: $100

Minimum IRA Investment
Initial: $500   Subsequent: $100

Maximum Fees
Load: none   12b-1: none
Other: none

Distributions
Income: Jun, Dec   Capital Gains: Dec

Exchange Options
Number Per Year: 5   Fee: none
Telephone: yes (money market fund available)

Services
IRA, other pension, auto invest, auto withdraw

Aetna Bond (AETBX)

General Bond

151 Farmington Ave.
Hartford, CT 06156
(800) 367-7732

PERFORMANCE

	3yr Annual	5yr Annual	10yr Annual	Bull	Bear
Return (%)	na	na	na	na	na
Differ from Category (+/-)	na	na	na	na	na

Total Risk	Standard Deviation	Category Risk	Risk Index	Avg Mat
na	na	na	na	5.8 yrs

	1993	1992	1991	1990	1989	1988	1987	1986	1985	1984
Return (%)	10.7	6.6	—	—	—	—	—	—	—	—
Differ from category (+/-) . . .	1.5	-0.1	—	—	—	—	—	—	—	—

PER SHARE DATA

	1993	1992	1991	1990	1989	1988	1987	1986	1985	1984
Dividends, Net Income ($) .	0.61	0.70	—	—	—	—	—	—	—	—
Distrib'ns, Cap Gain ($) . . .	0.00	0.00	—	—	—	—	—	—	—	—
Net Asset Value ($)	10.37	9.94	—	—	—	—	—	—	—	—
Expense Ratio (%).	na	0.05	—	—	—	—	—	—	—	—
Net Income to Assets (%) . .	2.92	5.44	—	—	—	—	—	—	—	—
Portfolio Turnover (%)	37	57	—	—	—	—	—	—	—	—
Total Assets (Millions $)	47	37	—	—	—	—	—	—	—	—

PORTFOLIO (as of 6/30/93)

Portfolio Manager: Jeanne Wong-Boehm - 1991

Investm't Category: General Bond
Cap Gain	Asset Allocation
Cap & Income	Fund of Funds
✔ Income	Index
	Sector
✔ Domestic	Small Cap
✔ Foreign	Socially Conscious
Country/Region	State Specific

Portfolio: stocks 0%   bonds 85%
convertibles 0%   other 0%   cash 15%

Largest Holdings: mortgage-backed 33%, corporate 24%

Unrealized Net Capital Gains: 3% of portfolio value

SHAREHOLDER INFORMATION

Minimum Investment
Initial: $1,000   Subsequent: $100

Minimum IRA Investment
Initial: $500   Subsequent: $100

Maximum Fees
Load: none   12b-1: none
Other: none

Distributions
Income: monthly   Capital Gains: Dec

Exchange Options
Number Per Year: 5   Fee: none
Telephone: yes (money market fund available)

Services
IRA, other pension, auto invest, auto withdraw

Aetna Growth & Income
(AEGIX)

Growth & Income

151 Farmington Ave.
Hartford, CT 06156
(800) 367-7732

PERFORMANCE

	3yr Annual	5yr Annual	10yr Annual	Bull	Bear
Return (%)	na	na	na	na	na
Differ from Category (+/-)	na	na	na	na	na

Total Risk	Standard Deviation	Category Risk	Risk Index	Beta
na	na	na	na	na

	1993	1992	1991	1990	1989	1988	1987	1986	1985	1984
Return (%)	6.5	7.8	—	—	—	—	—	—	—	—
Differ from category (+/-). . .	-6.1	-2.2	—	—	—	—	—	—	—	—

PER SHARE DATA

	1993	1992	1991	1990	1989	1988	1987	1986	1985	1984
Dividends, Net Income ($).	0.16	0.25	—	—	—	—	—	—	—	—
Distrib'ns, Cap Gain ($) . . .	0.00	0.00	—	—	—	—	—	—	—	—
Net Asset Value ($)	11.03	10.51	—	—	—	—	—	—	—	—
Expense Ratio (%)	na	0.33	—	—	—	—	—	—	—	—
Net Income to Assets (%) . . .	na	2.83	—	—	—	—	—	—	—	—
Portfolio Turnover (%).	0	14	—	—	—	—	—	—	—	—
Total Assets (Millions $). . . .	60	31	—	—	—	—	—	—	—	—

PORTFOLIO (as of 6/30/93)

Portfolio Manager: Richard DiChillo - 1991, Martin Duffy - 1991, Neil Yarhouse - 1991

Investm't Category: Growth & Income
- Cap Gain
- ✔ Cap & Income
- Income
- ✔ Domestic
- ✔ Foreign
- Country/Region
- Asset Allocation
- Fund of Funds
- Index
- Sector
- Small Cap
- Socially Conscious
- State Specific

Portfolio: stocks 81% bonds 0%
convertibles 0% other 0% cash 19%

Largest Holdings: oil 10%, telephone utilities 7%

Unrealized Net Capital Gains: 3% of portfolio value

SHAREHOLDER INFORMATION

Minimum Investment
Initial: $1,000   Subsequent: $100

Minimum IRA Investment
Initial: $500   Subsequent: $100

Maximum Fees
Load: none   12b-1: none
Other: none

Distributions
Income: Jun, Dec   Capital Gains: Dec

Exchange Options
Number Per Year: 5   Fee: none
Telephone: yes (money market fund available)

Services
IRA, other pension, auto invest, auto withdraw

Aetna Int'l Growth
(AEIGX)

International Stock

151 Farmington Ave.
Hartford, CT 06156
(800) 367-7732

PERFORMANCE

	3yr Annual	5yr Annual	10yr Annual	Bull	Bear
Return (%)	na	na	na	na	na
Differ from Category (+/-)	na	na	na	na	na

Total Risk	Standard Deviation	Category Risk	Risk Index	Beta
na	na	na	na	na

	1993	1992	1991	1990	1989	1988	1987	1986	1985	1984
Return (%)	30.3	-10.8	—	—	—	—	—	—	—	—
Differ from category (+/-) . .	-8.2	-7.3	—	—	—	—	—	—	—	—

PER SHARE DATA

	1993	1992	1991	1990	1989	1988	1987	1986	1985	1984
Dividends, Net Income ($) .	0.00	0.03	—	—	—	—	—	—	—	—
Distrib'ns, Cap Gain ($) . . .	0.41	0.00	—	—	—	—	—	—	—	—
Net Asset Value ($)	11.17	8.88	—	—	—	—	—	—	—	—
Expense Ratio (%)	na	0.50	—	—	—	—	—	—	—	—
Net Income to Assets (%) . .	0.43	1.36	—	—	—	—	—	—	—	—
Portfolio Turnover (%)	66	82	—	—	—	—	—	—	—	—
Total Assets (Millions $)	40	27	—	—	—	—	—	—	—	—

PORTFOLIO (as of 6/30/93)

Portfolio Manager: Anna Tong - 1991

Investm't Category: International Stock

✔ Cap Gain	Asset Allocation
Cap & Income	Fund of Funds
Income	Index
	Sector
Domestic	Small Cap
✔ Foreign	Socially Conscious
Country/Region	State Specific

Portfolio: stocks 96% bonds 0%
convertibles 0% other 1% cash 4%

Largest Holdings: Japan 33%, United Kingdom 18%

Unrealized Net Capital Gains: 8% of portfolio value

SHAREHOLDER INFORMATION

Minimum Investment
Initial: $1,000   Subsequent: $100

Minimum IRA Investment
Initial: $500   Subsequent: $100

Maximum Fees
Load: none   12b-1: none
Other: none

Distributions
Income: Dec   Capital Gains: Dec

Exchange Options
Number Per Year: 5   Fee: none
Telephone: yes (money market fund available)

Services
IRA, other pension, auto invest, auto withdraw

Alliance Bond—U.S. Gov't "C" (ABUCX)

Government Bond

P.O. Box 1520
Secaucus, NJ 07096
(800) 221-5672

fund in existence since 5/3/93

PERFORMANCE

	3yr Annual	5yr Annual	10yr Annual	Bull	Bear
Return (%)	na	na	na	na	na
Differ from Category (+/-)	na	na	na	na	na

Total Risk	Standard Deviation	Category Risk	Risk Index	Avg Mat
na	na	na	na	7.8 yrs

	1993	1992	1991	1990	1989	1988	1987	1986	1985	1984
Return (%)	—	—	—	—	—	—	—	—	—	—
Differ from category (+/-)	—	—	—	—	—	—	—	—	—	—

PER SHARE DATA

	1993	1992	1991	1990	1989	1988	1987	1986	1985	1984
Dividends, Net Income ($)	0.39	—	—	—	—	—	—	—	—	—
Distrib'ns, Cap Gain ($)	0.00	—	—	—	—	—	—	—	—	—
Net Asset Value ($)	8.54	—	—	—	—	—	—	—	—	—
Expense Ratio (%)	1.80	—	—	—	—	—	—	—	—	—
Net Income to Assets (%)	6.00	—	—	—	—	—	—	—	—	—
Portfolio Turnover (%)	386	—	—	—	—	—	—	—	—	—
Total Assets (Millions $)	226	—	—	—	—	—	—	—	—	—

PORTFOLIO (as of 10/31/93)

Portfolio Manager: Wayne Lyski - 1985, Paul DeNoon - 1992

Investm't Category: Government Bond
- Cap Gain
- Cap & Income
- ✔ Income
- ✔ Domestic
- Foreign
- Country/Region
- Asset Allocation
- Fund of Funds
- Index
- Sector
- Small Cap
- Socially Conscious
- State Specific

Portfolio: stocks 0% bonds 100%
convertibles 0% other 0% cash 0%

Largest Holdings: U.S. government & agencies 75%, mortgage-backed 23%

Unrealized Net Capital Gains: 1% of portfolio value

SHAREHOLDER INFORMATION

Minimum Investment
Initial: $250   Subsequent: $50

Minimum IRA Investment
Initial: $50   Subsequent: $50

Maximum Fees
Load: none   12b-1: 1.00%
Other: none

Distributions
Income: monthly   Capital Gains: Dec

Exchange Options
Number Per Year: no limit   Fee: none
Telephone: yes (money market fund available)

Services
IRA, other pension, auto exchange, auto invest, auto withdraw

Alliance Mortgage Strategy "C" (ASTCX)

Mortgage-Backed Bond

P.O. Box 1520
Secaucus, NJ 07096
(800) 221-5672

fund in existence since 5/3/93

PERFORMANCE

	3yr Annual	5yr Annual	10yr Annual	Bull	Bear
Return (%)	na	na	na	na	na
Differ from Category (+/-)	na	na	na	na	na

Total Risk	Standard Deviation	Category Risk	Risk Index	Avg Mat
na	na	na	na	9.8 yrs

	1993	1992	1991	1990	1989	1988	1987	1986	1985	1984
Return (%)	—	—	—	—	—	—	—	—	—	—
Differ from category (+/-) ...	—	—	—	—	—	—	—	—	—	—

PER SHARE DATA

	1993	1992	1991	1990	1989	1988	1987	1986	1985	1984
Dividends, Net Income ($) .	0.31	—	—	—	—	—	—	—	—	—
Distrib'ns, Cap Gain ($) ...	0.01	—	—	—	—	—	—	—	—	—
Net Asset Value ($)	9.92	—	—	—	—	—	—	—	—	—
Expense Ratio (%)........	2.33	—	—	—	—	—	—	—	—	—
Net Income to Assets (%)..	5.74	—	—	—	—	—	—	—	—	—
Portfolio Turnover (%)	228	—	—	—	—	—	—	—	—	—
Total Assets (Millions $) ...	135	—	—	—	—	—	—	—	—	—

PORTFOLIO (as of 10/31/93)

Portfolio Manager: Paul Ullman - 1992, Patricia Young - 1992

Investm't Category: Mortgage-Backed Bond

Cap Gain	Asset Allocation
Cap & Income	Fund of Funds
✔ Income	Index
	Sector
✔ Domestic	Small Cap
Foreign	Socially Conscious
Country/Region	State Specific

Portfolio:
stocks 0%　　bonds 97%
convertibles 0%　　other 0%　　cash 3%

Largest Holdings: mortgage-backed 68%, U.S. government 29%

Unrealized Net Capital Gains: 0% of portfolio value

SHAREHOLDER INFORMATION

Minimum Investment
Initial: $250　　Subsequent: $50

Minimum IRA Investment
Initial: $50　　Subsequent: $50

Maximum Fees
Load: none　　12b-1: 1.00%
Other: none

Distributions
Income: monthly　　Capital Gains: Dec

Exchange Options
Number Per Year: no limit　　Fee: none
Telephone: yes (money market fund available)

Services
IRA, other pension, auto exchange, auto invest, auto withdraw

Alliance Municipal Income—CA "C" (ACACX)

P.O. Box 1520
Secaucus, NJ 07096
(800) 221-5672

Tax-Exempt Bond

fund in existence since 5/3/93

	3yr Annual	5yr Annual	10yr Annual	Bull	Bear
Return (%)	na	na	na	na	na
Differ from Category (+/-)	na	na	na	na	na

Total Risk	Standard Deviation	Category Risk	Risk Index	Avg Mat
na	na	na	na	27.0 yrs

	1993	1992	1991	1990	1989	1988	1987	1986	1985	1984
Return (%)	—	—	—	—	—	—	—	—	—	—
Differ from category (+/-)	—	—	—	—	—	—	—	—	—	—

PER SHARE DATA

	1993	1992	1991	1990	1989	1988	1987	1986	1985	1984
Dividends, Net Income ($)	0.35	—	—	—	—	—	—	—	—	—
Distrib'ns, Cap Gain ($)	0.06	—	—	—	—	—	—	—	—	—
Net Asset Value ($)	10.89	—	—	—	—	—	—	—	—	—
Expense Ratio (%)	1.44	—	—	—	—	—	—	—	—	—
Net Income to Assets (%)	4.42	—	—	—	—	—	—	—	—	—
Portfolio Turnover (%)	83	—	—	—	—	—	—	—	—	—
Total Assets (Millions $)	101	—	—	—	—	—	—	—	—	—

PORTFOLIO (as of 10/31/93)

Portfolio Manager: Susan Peabody - 1986

Investm't Category: Tax-Exempt Bond

Cap Gain	Asset Allocation
Cap & Income	Fund of Funds
✔ Income	Index
	Sector
✔ Domestic	Small Cap
Foreign	Socially Conscious
Country/Region	✔ State Specific

Portfolio: stocks 0% bonds 100%
convertibles 0% other 0% cash 0%

Largest Holdings: general obligation 13%

Unrealized Net Capital Gains: 5% of portfolio value

SHAREHOLDER INFORMATION

Minimum Investment
Initial: $250 Subsequent: $50

Minimum IRA Investment
Initial: na Subsequent: na

Maximum Fees
Load: none 12b-1: 1.00%
Other: none

Distributions
Income: monthly Capital Gains: Dec

Exchange Options
Number Per Year: no limit Fee: none
Telephone: yes (money market fund available)

Services
auto exchange, auto invest, auto withdraw

Alliance Municipal Income—National "C"

P.O. Box 1520
Secaucus, NJ 07096
(800) 221-5672

(ALNCX) *Tax-Exempt Bond*

fund in existence since 5/3/93

PERFORMANCE

	3yr Annual	5yr Annual	10yr Annual	Bull	Bear
Return (%)	na	na	na	na	na
Differ from Category (+/-)	na	na	na	na	na

Total Risk	Standard Deviation	Category Risk	Risk Index	Avg Mat
na	na	na	na	22.0 yrs

	1993	1992	1991	1990	1989	1988	1987	1986	1985	1984
Return (%)	—	—	—	—	—	—	—	—	—	—
Differ from category (+/-) . . .	—	—	—	—	—	—	—	—	—	—

PER SHARE DATA

	1993	1992	1991	1990	1989	1988	1987	1986	1985	1984
Dividends, Net Income ($) .	0.35	—	—	—	—	—	—	—	—	—
Distrib'ns, Cap Gain ($) . . .	0.24	—	—	—	—	—	—	—	—	—
Net Asset Value ($)	10.92	—	—	—	—	—	—	—	—	—
Expense Ratio (%)	1.36	—	—	—	—	—	—	—	—	—
Net Income to Assets (%) . .	4.17	—	—	—	—	—	—	—	—	—
Portfolio Turnover (%)	233	—	—	—	—	—	—	—	—	—
Total Assets (Millions $) . . .	125	—	—	—	—	—	—	—	—	—

PORTFOLIO (as of 10/31/93)

Portfolio Manager: Susan Peabody - 1986

Investm't Category: Tax-Exempt Bond

Cap Gain	Asset Allocation
Cap & Income	Fund of Funds
✔ Income	Index
	Sector
✔ Domestic	Small Cap
Foreign	Socially Conscious
Country/Region	State Specific

Portfolio: stocks 0% bonds 94%
convertibles 0% other 0% cash 6%

Largest Holdings: general obligation 6%

Unrealized Net Capital Gains: 4% of portfolio value

SHAREHOLDER INFORMATION

Minimum Investment
Initial: $250   Subsequent: $50

Minimum IRA Investment
Initial: na   Subsequent: na

Maximum Fees
Load: none   12b-1: 1.00%
Other: none

Distributions
Income: monthly   Capital Gains: Dec

Exchange Options
Number Per Year: no limit   Fee: none
Telephone: yes (money market fund available)

Services
auto exchange, auto invest, auto withdraw

Alliance World Income Trust (AWITX)

International Bond

P.O. Box 1520
Secaucus, NJ 07096
(800) 221-5672

	3yr Annual	5yr Annual	10yr Annual	Bull	Bear
Return (%)	4.4	na	na	na	na
Differ from Category (+/-)	-7.6 low	na	na	na	na

Total Risk	Standard Deviation	Category Risk	Risk Index	Avg Mat
low	2.0%	low	0.5	0.4 yrs

	1993	1992	1991	1990	1989	1988	1987	1986	1985	1984
Return (%)	4.0	1.4	7.8	—	—	—	—	—	—	—
Differ from category (+/-). . . .	-8.7	-3.4	-7.1	—	—	—	—	—	—	—

	1993	1992	1991	1990	1989	1988	1987	1986	1985	1984
Dividends, Net Income ($) .	0.07	0.08	0.19	—	—	—	—	—	—	—
Distrib'ns, Cap Gain ($) . . .	0.00	0.00	0.00	—	—	—	—	—	—	—
Net Asset Value ($)	1.89	1.89	1.95	—	—	—	—	—	—	—
Expense Ratio (%)	1.52	1.59	1.85	—	—	—	—	—	—	—
Net Income to Assets (%) .	5.68	7.21	7.29	—	—	—	—	—	—	—
Portfolio Turnover (%).	na	0	0	—	—	—	—	—	—	—
Total Assets (Millions $). . . .	137	319	1,062	—	—	—	—	—	—	—

Portfolio Manager: Charles van Vleet - 1990

Investm't Category: International Bond

Cap Gain	Asset Allocation
Cap & Income	Fund of Funds
✔ Income	Index
	Sector
✔ Domestic	Small Cap
✔ Foreign	Socially Conscious
Country/Region	State Specific

Portfolio: stocks 0% bonds 87%
convertibles 0% other 0% cash 13%

Largest Holdings: U.S government & agency 66%

Unrealized Net Capital Gains: 0% of portfolio value

Minimum Investment
Initial: $10,000 Subsequent: $1,000

Minimum IRA Investment
Initial: $10,000 Subsequent: $1,000

Maximum Fees
Load: none 12b-1: 0.90%
Other: none

Distributions
Income: monthly Capital Gains: Dec

Exchange Options
Number Per Year: no limit Fee: none
Telephone: yes (money market fund available)

Services
IRA, other pension, auto exchange, auto invest, auto withdraw

Amana Income (AMANX)

Growth & Income

1300 N. State Street
Bellingham, WA 98225
(800) 728-8762

PERFORMANCE

	3yr Annual	5yr Annual	10yr Annual	Bull	Bear
Return (%)	12.0	9.9	na	47.3	-7.8
Differ from Category (+/-)	-4.4 low	-2.6 low	na	-22.8 low	3.8 high

Total Risk	Standard Deviation	Category Risk	Risk Index	Beta
av	9.6%	av	1.1	0.7

	1993	1992	1991	1990	1989	1988	1987	1986	1985	1984
Return (%)	11.6	1.8	23.6	-3.3	18.3	13.4	-7.5	—	—	—
Differ from category (+/-)	-1.0	-8.2	-4.1	2.3	-3.3	-3.4	-7.9	—	—	—

PER SHARE DATA

	1993	1992	1991	1990	1989	1988	1987	1986	1985	1984
Dividends, Net Income ($)	0.29	0.31	0.28	0.42	0.42	0.36	0.35	—	—	—
Distrib'ns, Cap Gain ($)	0.13	0.00	0.00	0.00	0.00	0.00	0.50	—	—	—
Net Asset Value ($)	13.19	12.21	12.30	10.19	10.98	9.65	8.84	—	—	—
Expense Ratio (%)	1.58	1.58	1.66	1.76	1.88	2.07	1.81	—	—	—
Net Income to Assets (%)	2.65	2.75	3.73	3.67	3.85	3.17	3.53	—	—	—
Portfolio Turnover (%)	28	18	28	18	70	65	54	—	—	—
Total Assets (Millions $)	10	6	5	4	3	3	3	—	—	—

PORTFOLIO (as of 5/31/93)

Portfolio Manager: Nicholas Kaiser - 1986

Investm't Category: Growth & Income
- Cap Gain
- ✔ Cap & Income
- Income
- ✔ Domestic
- ✔ Foreign
- Country/Region
- Asset Allocation
- Fund of Funds
- Index
- Sector
- Small Cap
- Socially Conscious
- State Specific

Portfolio: stocks 100% bonds 0%
convertibles 0% other 0% cash 0%

Largest Holdings: electric utilities 15%, oil & gas production 10%

Unrealized Net Capital Gains: 14% of portfolio value

SHAREHOLDER INFORMATION

Minimum Investment
Initial: $100   Subsequent: $25

Minimum IRA Investment
Initial: $25   Subsequent: $25

Maximum Fees
Load: none   12b-1: none
Other: none

Distributions
Income: May, Dec   Capital Gains: Dec

Exchange Options
Number Per Year: no limit   Fee: none
Telephone: yes (money market fund available)

Services
IRA, other pension, auto exchange, auto invest, auto withdraw

America's Utility (AMUTX)

Growth & Income

901 East Byrd Street
P.O. Box 26501
Richmond, VA 23261
(800) 487-3863, (804) 649-1315

PERFORMANCE

	3yr Annual	5yr Annual	10yr Annual	Bull	Bear
Return (%)	na	na	na	na	na
Differ from Category (+/-)	na	na	na	na	na

Total Risk	Standard Deviation	Category Risk	Risk Index	Beta
na	na	na	na	na

	1993	1992	1991	1990	1989	1988	1987	1986	1985	1984
Return (%)	13.3	—	—	—	—	—	—	—	—	—
Differ from category (+/-) . . .	0.6	—	—	—	—	—	—	—	—	—

PER SHARE DATA

	1993	1992	1991	1990	1989	1988	1987	1986	1985	1984
Dividends, Net Income ($) .	0.92	—	—	—	—	—	—	—	—	—
Distrib'ns, Cap Gain ($) . . .	0.40	—	—	—	—	—	—	—	—	—
Net Asset Value ($)	23.54	—	—	—	—	—	—	—	—	—
Expense Ratio (%)	1.21	—	—	—	—	—	—	—	—	—
Net Income to Assets (%) .	4.58	—	—	—	—	—	—	—	—	—
Portfolio Turnover (%)	na	—	—	—	—	—	—	—	—	—
Total Assets (Millions $)	131	—	—	—	—	—	—	—	—	—

PORTFOLIO (as of 6/30/93)

Portfolio Manager: Julie Cannell

Investm't Category: Growth & Income

Cap Gain	Asset Allocation
✔ Cap & Income	Fund of Funds
Income	Index
	✔ Sector
✔ Domestic	Small Cap
Foreign	Socially Conscious
Country/Region	State Specific

Portfolio: stocks 92% bonds 0%
convertibles 0% other 0% cash 8%

Largest Holdings: public utility—electric 84%, telecommunicatons 8%

Unrealized Net Capital Gains: 7% of portfolio value

SHAREHOLDER INFORMATION

Minimum Investment
Initial: $1,000   Subsequent: $250

Minimum IRA Investment
Initial: $20   Subsequent: $20

Maximum Fees
Load: none   12b-1: none
Other: none

Distributions
Income: quarterly   Capital Gains: Dec

Exchange Options
Number Per Year: none   Fee: na
Telephone: na

Services
IRA, other pension

American Heritage

(AHERX)

Aggressive Growth

31 W. 52nd St., 8th floor
New York, NY 10019
(800) 828-5050, (212) 474-7308

PERFORMANCE

	3yr Annual	5yr Annual	10yr Annual	Bull	Bear
Return (%)	49.2	17.4	na	223.3	-28.8
Differ from Category (+/-)	23.8 high	-0.8 av	na	98.4 high	-13.8 low

Total Risk	Standard Deviation	Category Risk	Risk Index	Beta
high	24.6%	high	1.6	1.2

	1993	1992	1991	1990	1989	1988	1987	1986	1985	1984
Return (%)	41.3	19.2	97.1	-30.7	-2.8	1.9	-19.8	—	—	—
Differ from category (+/-) . .	22.3	8.8	44.7	-24.4	-29.8	-13.3	-16.4	—	—	—

PER SHARE DATA

	1993	1992	1991	1990	1989	1988	1987	1986	1985	1984
Dividends, Net Income ($) .	0.06	0.08	0.02	0.00	0.00	0.00	0.00	—	—	—
Distrib'ns, Cap Gain ($) . . .	0.00	0.00	0.36	0.00	0.00	0.00	0.09	—	—	—
Net Asset Value ($)	1.53	1.13	1.02	0.72	1.04	1.07	1.05	—	—	—
Expense Ratio (%).	2.10	2.20	6.79	11.04	13.02	11.90	11.80	—	—	—
Net Income to Assets (%) .	-0.46	21.50	-3.72	5.80	-8.00	-8.70	-9.30	—	—	—
Portfolio Turnover (%)	278	776	607	76	81	189	287	—	—	—
Total Assets (Millions $) . . .	150	27	2	1	1	1	1	—	—	—

PORTFOLIO (as of 5/31/93)

Portfolio Manager: Heiko Thieme - 1990

Investm't Category: Aggressive Growth

✔ Cap Gain	Asset Allocation
Cap & Income	Fund of Funds
Income	Index
	Sector
✔ Domestic	Small Cap
Foreign	Socially Conscious
Country/Region	State Specific

Portfolio: stocks 67% bonds 1%
convertibles 0% other 1% cash 31%

Largest Holdings: biotechnology 15%, consumer products 11%

Unrealized Net Capital Gains: 9% of portfolio value

SHAREHOLDER INFORMATION

Minimum Investment
Initial: $5,000   Subsequent: $1,000

Minimum IRA Investment
Initial: $2,000   Subsequent: $0

Maximum Fees
Load: none   12b-1: none
Other: none

Distributions
Income: Dec   Capital Gains: Dec

Exchange Options
Number Per Year: none   Fee: na
Telephone: na

Services
IRA, other pension, auto withdraw

American Pension Investors—Growth (APITX)

Growth

P.O. Box 2529
2303 Yorktown Ave.
Lynchburg, VA 24501
(800) 544-6060, (804) 846-1361

PERFORMANCE

	3yr Annual	5yr Annual	10yr Annual	Bull	Bear
Return (%)	20.6	12.2	na	106.0	-25.5
Differ from Category (+/-)	1.4 abv av	-2.4 blw av	na	21.3 high	-13.1 low

Total Risk	Standard Deviation	Category Risk	Risk Index	Beta
high	15.4%	high	1.5	1.1

	1993	1992	1991	1990	1989	1988	1987	1986	1985	1984
Return (%).............	18.2	1.8	45.9	-12.6	15.6	25.7	-7.6	13.1	—	—
Differ from category (+/-)...	5.0	-9.2	10.5	-6.5	-10.2	8.0	-8.8	-1.4	—	—

PER SHARE DATA

	1993	1992	1991	1990	1989	1988	1987	1986	1985	1984
Dividends, Net Income ($).	0.00	1.15	0.00	0.00	0.05	0.14	0.06	0.56	—	—
Distrib'ns, Cap Gain ($) ...	0.57	0.37	0.95	0.00	2.09	0.00	1.88	0.65	—	—
Net Asset Value ($)	12.83	11.34	11.49	8.53	9.76	10.26	8.26	10.74	—	—
Expense Ratio (%)	2.05	1.97	2.38	2.60	2.66	2.74	2.41	2.59	—	—
Net Income to Assets (%) .	-1.56	-1.24	0.02	0.36	0.78	0.82	1.11	2.00	—	—
Portfolio Turnover (%).....	157	99	206	118	163	165	190	169	—	—
Total Assets (Millions $).....	49	40	30	32	32	27	19	4	—	—

PORTFOLIO (as of 5/31/93)

Portfolio Manager: David Basten - 1985

Investm't Category: Growth

✔ Cap Gain	Asset Allocation
Cap & Income	✔ Fund of Funds
Income	Index
	Sector
✔ Domestic	Small Cap
✔ Foreign	Socially Conscious
Country/Region	State Specific

Portfolio:	stocks 0%	bonds 0%
convertibles 0%	other 100%	cash 0%

Largest Holdings: capital appreciation funds 28%, growth funds 19%

Unrealized Net Capital Gains: 9% of portfolio value

SHAREHOLDER INFORMATION

Minimum Investment
Initial: $500   Subsequent: $100

Minimum IRA Investment
Initial: $500   Subsequent: $100

Maximum Fees
Load: none   12b-1: 1.00%
Other: none

Distributions
Income: Dec   Capital Gains: Dec

Exchange Options
Number Per Year: no limit   Fee: none
Telephone: none

Services
IRA, other pension, auto invest, auto withdraw

Analytic Optioned Equity

(ANALX)

Growth & Income

2222 Martin St.
Suite 230
Irvine, CA 92715
(800) 374-2633, (714) 833-0294

PERFORMANCE

	3yr Annual	5yr Annual	10yr Annual	Bull	Bear
Return (%)	8.6	8.9	9.7	38.3	-5.7
Differ from Category (+/-)	-7.8 low	-3.6 low	-2.7 low	-31.8 low	5.9 high

Total Risk	Standard Deviation	Category Risk	Risk Index	Beta
blw av	5.6%	low	0.6	0.5

	1993	1992	1991	1990	1989	1988	1987	1986	1985	1984
Return (%)	6.7	6.1	13.3	1.5	17.7	15.6	4.2	10.6	16.5	6.7
Differ from category (+/-) . .	-5.9	-3.9	-14.4	7.1	-3.9	-1.2	3.8	-4.6	-8.9	0.5

PER SHARE DATA

	1993	1992	1991	1990	1989	1988	1987	1986	1985	1984
Dividends, Net Income ($) .	0.32	0.28	0.40	0.48	0.50	0.41	0.46	0.44	0.48	0.43
Distrib'ns, Cap Gain ($) . . .	0.48	0.77	0.80	0.78	0.65	0.65	2.47	2.19	1.19	0.02
Net Asset Value ($)	11.96	11.97	12.29	11.92	13.00	12.06	11.38	13.70	14.84	14.31
Expense Ratio (%).	1.06	1.02	1.10	1.11	1.09	1.13	1.17	1.18	1.23	1.30
Net Income to Assets (%) . .	2.52	2.33	3.05	3.68	3.74	3.44	2.68	2.90	3.30	3.65
Portfolio Turnover (%)	40	82	76	72	61	66	84	64	54	45
Total Assets (Millions $)	77	92	100	106	107	102	75	76	85	77

PORTFOLIO (as of 6/30/93)

Portfolio Manager: Charles Dobson - 1978

Investm't Category: Growth & Income

Cap Gain	Asset Allocation
✔ Cap & Income	Fund of Funds
Income	Index
	Sector
✔ Domestic	Small Cap
Foreign	Socially Conscious
Country/Region	State Specific

Portfolio: stocks 76%   bonds 21%
convertibles 0%   other 3%   cash 0%

Largest Holdings: U.S. government bonds 21%, utility—telephone 9%

Unrealized Net Capital Gains: 3% of portfolio value

SHAREHOLDER INFORMATION

Minimum Investment
Initial: $5,000   Subsequent: $500

Minimum IRA Investment
Initial: $0   Subsequent: $0

Maximum Fees
Load: none   12b-1: none
Other: none

Distributions
Income: quarterly   Capital Gains: Dec

Exchange Options
Number Per Year: none   Fee: na
Telephone: na

Services
IRA, other pension, auto withdraw

Armstrong Associates

(ARMSX)

Growth

750 North St. Paul
Lock Box 13, Suite 1300
Dallas, TX 75201
(214) 720-9101

PERFORMANCE

	3yr Annual	5yr Annual	10yr Annual	Bull	Bear
Return (%)	13.4	9.2	7.9	50.2	-9.3
Differ from Category (+/-)	-5.8 low	-5.4 low	-4.7 low	-34.5 low	3.1 abv av

Total Risk	Standard Deviation	Category Risk	Risk Index	Beta
av	8.7%	low	0.8	0.7

	1993	1992	1991	1990	1989	1988	1987	1986	1985	1984
Return (%)	15.0	6.7	18.7	-6.6	14.2	15.5	-0.4	11.5	21.1	-11.4
Differ from category (+/-). . .	1.8	-4.3	-16.7	-0.5	-11.6	-2.2	-1.6	-3.0	-8.2	-11.4

PER SHARE DATA

	1993	1992	1991	1990	1989	1988	1987	1986	1985	1984
Dividends, Net Income ($).	0.00	0.01	0.15	0.23	0.23	0.10	0.14	0.15	0.23	0.14
Distrib'ns, Cap Gain ($) . . .	0.17	0.00	0.02	0.17	0.54	0.23	1.91	0.50	0.00	0.75
Net Asset Value ($)	8.69	7.70	7.24	6.26	7.14	6.94	6.30	7.99	7.76	6.62
Expense Ratio (%)	1.80	1.90	1.90	1.80	1.90	2.00	1.70	1.60	1.70	1.60
Net Income to Assets (%) .	0.20	0.80	2.30	2.90	3.00	1.30	1.00	1.60	3.10	1.90
Portfolio Turnover (%).	17	35	24	44	46	20	51	54	53	96
Total Assets (Millions $).	10	9	9	10	10	10	12	11	10	9

PORTFOLIO (as of 6/30/93)

Portfolio Manager: C.K. Lawson - 1967

Investm't Category: Growth

✔ Cap Gain   Asset Allocation
  Cap & Income   Fund of Funds
  Income   Index
    Sector
✔ Domestic   Small Cap
  Foreign   Socially Conscious
  Country/Region   State Specific

Portfolio: stocks 75% bonds 0%
convertibles 0% other 0% cash 25%

Largest Holdings: broadcasting & media 12%, industrial conglomerate 11%

Unrealized Net Capital Gains: 26% of portfolio value

SHAREHOLDER INFORMATION

Minimum Investment
Initial: $250   Subsequent: $0

Minimum IRA Investment
Initial: $250   Subsequent: $0

Maximum Fees
Load: none   12b-1: none
Other: none

Distributions
Income: Dec   Capital Gains: Dec

Exchange Options
Number Per Year: none Fee: na
Telephone: na

Services
IRA, other pension, auto invest

ASM (ASMUX)

Growth & Income

15438 N. Florida Avenue
Suite 107
Tampa, FL 33613
(800) 445-2763, (813) 963-3150

PERFORMANCE

	3yr Annual	5yr Annual	10yr Annual	Bull	Bear
Return (%)	na	na	na	na	na
Differ from Category (+/-)	na	na	na	na	na

Total Risk	Standard Deviation	Category Risk	Risk Index	Beta
na	na	na	na	na

	1993	1992	1991	1990	1989	1988	1987	1986	1985	1984
Return (%)	13.3	5.6	—	—	—	—	—	—	—	—
Differ from category (+/-) . . .	0.6	-4.4	—	—	—	—	—	—	—	—

PER SHARE DATA

	1993	1992	1991	1990	1989	1988	1987	1986	1985	1984
Dividends, Net Income ($) .	0.44	0.42	—	—	—	—	—	—	—	—
Distrib'ns, Cap Gain ($) . . .	0.00	0.00	—	—	—	—	—	—	—	—
Net Asset Value ($)	9.91	9.15	—	—	—	—	—	—	—	—
Expense Ratio (%).	0.75	0.75	—	—	—	—	—	—	—	—
Net Income to Assets (%) . .	1.20	2.41	—	—	—	—	—	—	—	—
Portfolio Turnover (%)	na	1	—	—	—	—	—	—	—	—
Total Assets (Millions $)	14	7	—	—	—	—	—	—	—	—

PORTFOLIO (as of 4/30/93)

Portfolio Manager: Stephen H. Adler - 1991, William Tapella - 1991

Investm't Category: Growth & Income

Cap Gain	Asset Allocation
✔ Cap & Income	Fund of Funds
Income	Index
	Sector
✔ Domestic	Small Cap
Foreign	Socially Conscious
Country/Region	State Specific

Portfolio: stocks 89% bonds 0%
convertibles 0% other 0% cash 11%

Largest Holdings: oil—international 12%, diversified 10%

Unrealized Net Capital Gains: 3% of portfolio value

SHAREHOLDER INFORMATION

Minimum Investment
Initial: $1,000 Subsequent: $100

Minimum IRA Investment
Initial: $500 Subsequent: $100

Maximum Fees
Load: 0.75% redemption 12b-1: none
Other: redemption fee applies if more than 6/yr

Distributions
Income: quarterly Capital Gains: Dec

Exchange Options
Number Per Year: no limit Fee: none
Telephone: yes (money market fund available)

Services
IRA, auto invest

Babson Bond Trust—Port L (BABIX)

General Bond

Three Crown Center
2440 Pershing Rd., #G-15
Kansas City, MO 64108
(800) 422-2766, (816) 471-5200

PERFORMANCE

	3yr Annual	5yr Annual	10yr Annual	Bull	Bear
Return (%)	11.0	10.8	11.0	43.7	3.3
Differ from Category (+/-)	0.8 abv av	1.0 abv av	0.1 av	4.3 av	0.4 av

Total Risk	Standard Deviation	Category Risk	Risk Index	Avg Mat
low	3.6%	av	1.2	11.7 yrs

	1993	1992	1991	1990	1989	1988	1987	1986	1985	1984
Return (%).............	11.1	7.8	15.0	7.7	13.1	7.1	1.9	13.8	20.6	12.9
Differ from category (+/-)...	1.9	1.1	0.4	0.8	1.8	-0.5	-0.6	-0.1	0.5	0.6

PER SHARE DATA

	1993	1992	1991	1990	1989	1988	1987	1986	1985	1984
Dividends, Net Income ($).	0.12	0.12	0.13	0.13	0.14	0.15	0.15	0.15	0.16	0.17
Distrib'ns, Cap Gain ($) ...	0.05	0.01	0.00	0.00	0.00	0.00	0.00	0.00	0.00	0.00
Net Asset Value ($)	1.63	1.62	1.63	1.54	1.56	1.51	1.56	1.69	1.63	1.50
Expense Ratio (%)	na	0.99	0.98	0.97	0.97	0.97	0.97	1.00	1.00	0.92
Net Income to Assets (%) ...	na	7.67	8.42	8.81	9.19	9.99	9.29	7.75	8.82	8.94
Portfolio Turnover (%).......	na	54	75	51	51	42	54	46	32	27
Total Assets (Millions $)....	160	142	115	91	78	66	65	20	16	11

PORTFOLIO (as of 5/31/93)

Portfolio Manager: Edward Martin - 1984

Investm't Category: General Bond

Cap Gain	Asset Allocation
Cap & Income	Fund of Funds
✔ Income	Index
	Sector
✔ Domestic	Small Cap
Foreign	Socially Conscious
Country/Region	State Specific

Portfolio: stocks 0% bonds 99%
convertibles 0% other 0% cash 1%

Largest Holdings: corporate 56%, U.S. government 26%

Unrealized Net Capital Gains: 3% of portfolio value

SHAREHOLDER INFORMATION

Minimum Investment
Initial: $500   Subsequent: $50

Minimum IRA Investment
Initial: $250   Subsequent: $50

Maximum Fees
Load: none   12b-1: none
Other: none

Distributions
Income: monthly   Capital Gains: Dec

Exchange Options
Number Per Year: no limit   Fee: none
Telephone: yes (money market fund available)

Services
IRA, other pension, auto exchange, auto invest, auto withdraw

Babson Bond Trust—Port S (BBDSX)

General Bond

Three Crown Center
2440 Pershing Rd., #G-15
Kansas City, MO 64108
(800) 422-2766, (816) 471-5200

PERFORMANCE

	3yr Annual	5yr Annual	10yr Annual	Bull	Bear
Return (%)	9.9	9.7	na	37.0	4.7
Differ from Category (+/-)	-0.3 blw av	-0.1 blw av	na	-2.4 blw av	1.8 abv av

Total Risk	Standard Deviation	Category Risk	Risk Index	Avg Mat
low	2.7%	blw av	0.9	7.7 yrs

	1993	1992	1991	1990	1989	1988	1987	1986	1985	1984
Return (%)	8.4	6.9	14.4	8.0	10.8	—	—	—	—	—
Differ from category (+/-)	-0.8	0.2	-0.2	1.1	-0.5	—	—	—	—	—

PER SHARE DATA

	1993	1992	1991	1990	1989	1988	1987	1986	1985	1984
Dividends, Net Income ($)	0.71	0.75	0.79	0.84	0.81	—	—	—	—	—
Distrib'ns, Cap Gain ($)	0.15	0.05	0.02	0.00	0.00	—	—	—	—	—
Net Asset Value ($)	10.33	10.34	10.45	9.90	9.98	—	—	—	—	—
Expense Ratio (%)	na	0.65	0.66	0.78	0.91	—	—	—	—	—
Net Income to Assets (%)	na	7.22	7.98	8.65	8.28	—	—	—	—	—
Portfolio Turnover (%)	na	47	60	35	27	—	—	—	—	—
Total Assets (Millions $)	37	31	14	7	5	—	—	—	—	—

PORTFOLIO (as of 5/31/93)

Portfolio Manager: Edward Martin - 1988

Investm't Category: General Bond
Cap Gain	Asset Allocation
Cap & Income	Fund of Funds
✔ Income	Index
	Sector
✔ Domestic	Small Cap
Foreign	Socially Conscious
Country/Region	State Specific

Portfolio: stocks 0% bonds 98%
convertibles 0% other 0% cash 2%

Largest Holdings: corporate 66%, U. S. government 21%

Unrealized Net Capital Gains: 1% of portfolio value

SHAREHOLDER INFORMATION

Minimum Investment
Initial: $500 Subsequent: $50

Minimum IRA Investment
Initial: $250 Subsequent: $50

Maximum Fees
Load: none 12b-1: none
Other: none

Distributions
Income: monthly Capital Gains: Dec

Exchange Options
Number Per Year: no limit Fee: none
Telephone: yes (money market fund available)

Services
IRA, other pension, auto exchange, auto invest, auto withdraw

Babson Enterprise (BABEX)

Growth

Three Crown Center
2440 Pershing Rd., #G-15
Kansas City, MO 64108
(800) 422-2766, (816) 471-5200

this fund is closed to new investors

PERFORMANCE

	3yr Annual	5yr Annual	10yr Annual	Bull	Bear
Return (%)	27.4	16.3	14.0	116.6	-19.5
Differ from Category (+/-)	8.2 high	1.7 abv av	1.4 abv av	31.9 high	-7.1 blw av

Total Risk	Standard Deviation	Category Risk	Risk Index	Beta
abv av	11.8%	av	1.1	0.7

	1993	1992	1991	1990	1989	1988	1987	1986	1985	1984
Return (%)	16.2	24.5	43.0	-15.8	22.4	32.4	-9.1	9.0	38.6	-4.9
Differ from category (+/-) . . .	3.0	13.5	7.6	-9.7	-3.4	14.7	-10.3	-5.5	9.3	-4.9

PER SHARE DATA

	1993	1992	1991	1990	1989	1988	1987	1986	1985	1984
Dividends, Net Income ($).	0.05	0.08	0.07	0.12	0.18	0.05	0.07	0.04	0.00	0.07
Distrib'ns, Cap Gain ($) . . .	1.10	2.33	0.76	0.30	0.69	0.75	1.68	1.73	0.00	0.12
Net Asset Value ($)	16.51	15.22	14.19	10.55	13.06	11.39	9.22	12.12	12.78	9.22
Expense Ratio (%)	na	1.11	1.17	1.22	1.24	1.37	1.35	1.37	1.58	1.67
Net Income to Assets (%) . . .	na	0.57	0.66	1.08	1.74	0.50	0.23	0.42	0.62	0.73
Portfolio Turnover (%).	na	28	15	10	15	41	24	32	38	14
Total Assets (Millions $). . . .	216	178	121	76	87	52	36	47	34	7

PORTFOLIO (as of 5/31/93)

Portfolio Manager: Peter Schliemann - 1985

Investm't Category: Growth

✔ Cap Gain	Asset Allocation
Cap & Income	Fund of Funds
Income	Index
	Sector
✔ Domestic	✔ Small Cap
Foreign	Socially Conscious
Country/Region	State Specific

Portfolio: stocks 95% bonds 0%
convertibles 0% other 0% cash 5%

Largest Holdings: consumer cyclical 25%, capital goods 20%

Unrealized Net Capital Gains: 15% of portfolio value

SHAREHOLDER INFORMATION

Minimum Investment
Initial: $1,000   Subsequent: $100

Minimum IRA Investment
Initial: $250   Subsequent: $100

Maximum Fees
Load: none   12b-1: none
Other: none

Distributions
Income: Dec   Capital Gains: Dec

Exchange Options
Number Per Year: no limit   Fee: none
Telephone: yes (money market fund available)

Services
IRA, other pension, auto exchange, auto invest, auto withdraw

Babson Enterprise II
(BAETX)
Growth

Three Crown Center
2440 Pershing Rd., #G-15
Kansas City, MO 64108
(800) 422-2766, (816) 471-5200

PERFORMANCE

	3yr Annual	5yr Annual	10yr Annual	Bull	Bear
Return (%)	na	na	na	na	na
Differ from Category (+/-)	na	na	na	na	na

Total Risk	Standard Deviation	Category Risk	Risk Index	Beta
na	na	na	na	na

	1993	1992	1991	1990	1989	1988	1987	1986	1985	1984
Return (%)	19.7	17.2	—	—	—	—	—	—	—	—
Differ from category (+/-)	6.5	6.2	—	—	—	—	—	—	—	—

PER SHARE DATA

	1993	1992	1991	1990	1989	1988	1987	1986	1985	1984
Dividends, Net Income ($)	0.00	0.00	—	—	—	—	—	—	—	—
Distrib'ns, Cap Gain ($)	0.32	0.03	—	—	—	—	—	—	—	—
Net Asset Value ($)	17.60	14.97	—	—	—	—	—	—	—	—
Expense Ratio (%)	na	1.83	—	—	—	—	—	—	—	—
Net Income to Assets (%)	na	-0.11	—	—	—	—	—	—	—	—
Portfolio Turnover (%)	na	14	—	—	—	—	—	—	—	—
Total Assets (Millions $)	30	11	—	—	—	—	—	—	—	—

PORTFOLIO (as of 5/31/93)

Portfolio Manager: Peter Schliemann - 1991, Lance James - 1991

Investm't Category: Growth

✔ Cap Gain	Asset Allocation
Cap & Income	Fund of Funds
Income	Index
	Sector
✔ Domestic	Small Cap
Foreign	Socially Conscious
Country/Region	State Specific

Portfolio: stocks 94% bonds 0%
convertibles 0% other 0% cash 6%

Largest Holdings: consumer cyclical 32%, capital goods 24%

Unrealized Net Capital Gains: 10% of portfolio value

SHAREHOLDER INFORMATION

Minimum Investment
Initial: $1,000 Subsequent: $100

Minimum IRA Investment
Initial: $250 Subsequent: $100

Maximum Fees
Load: none 12b-1: none
Other: none

Distributions
Income: Dec Capital Gains: Dec

Exchange Options
Number Per Year: no limit Fee: none
Telephone: yes (money market fund available)

Services
IRA, other pension, auto exchange, auto invest, auto withdraw

Guide to Low-Load Mutual Funds

Babson Growth (BABSX)

Growth & Income

Three Crown Center
2440 Pershing Rd., #G-15
Kansas City, MO 64108
(800) 422-2766, (816) 471-5200

PERFORMANCE

	3yr Annual	5yr Annual	10yr Annual	Bull	Bear
Return (%)	14.8	10.9	12.0	65.0	-16.7
Differ from Category (+/-)	-1.6 blw av	-1.6 blw av	-0.4 av	-5.1 blw av	-5.1 low

Total Risk	Standard Deviation	Category Risk	Risk Index	Beta
av	10.6%	abv av	1.2	0.9

	1993	1992	1991	1990	1989	1988	1987	1986	1985	1984
Return (%).............	10.2	9.1	26.0	-9.4	22.1	15.9	3.4	18.8	29.6	0.2
Differ from category (+/-)....	-2.4	-0.8	-1.7	-3.8	0.5	-0.8	3.0	3.6	4.2	-6.0

PER SHARE DATA

	1993	1992	1991	1990	1989	1988	1987	1986	1985	1984
Dividends, Net Income ($).	0.18	0.20	0.21	0.26	0.28	0.30	0.45	0.35	0.40	0.20
Distrib'ns, Cap Gain ($) ...	0.55	0.32	0.03	0.54	1.45	2.14	1.50	1.97	1.84	1.48
Net Asset Value ($)	13.08	12.58	12.02	9.75	11.61	10.97	11.59	12.95	12.88	11.89
Expense Ratio (%)	0.86	0.86	0.86	0.86	0.86	0.81	0.74	0.75	0.76	0.75
Net Income to Assets (%) .	1.54	1.69	2.26	2.28	2.53	2.21	2.12	2.65	3.23	2.64
Portfolio Turnover (%)......	13	12	22	23	33	26	14	20	35	52
Total Assets (Millions $)....	246	232	236	259	266	238	289	253	215	208

PORTFOLIO (as of 6/30/93)

Portfolio Manager: David Kirk - 1986

Investm't Category: Growth & Income

Cap Gain	Asset Allocation
✔ Cap & Income	Fund of Funds
Income	Index
	Sector
✔ Domestic	Small Cap
Foreign	Socially Conscious
Country/Region	State Specific

Portfolio: stocks 96% bonds 0%
convertibles 0% other 0% cash 4%

Largest Holdings: consumer cyclical 20%, consumer staples 14%

Unrealized Net Capital Gains: 32% of portfolio value

SHAREHOLDER INFORMATION

Minimum Investment
Initial: $500   Subsequent: $50

Minimum IRA Investment
Initial: $250   Subsequent: $50

Maximum Fees
Load: none   12b-1: none
Other: none

Distributions
Income: Jun, Dec   Capital Gains: Jun, Dec

Exchange Options
Number Per Year: no limit   Fee: none
Telephone: yes (money market fund available)

Services
IRA, other pension, auto exchange, auto invest, auto withdraw

Babson Shadow Stock

(SHSTX)

Growth

Three Crown Center
2440 Pershing Rd., #G-15
Kansas City, MO 64108
(800) 422-2766, (816) 471-5200

PERFORMANCE

	3yr Annual	5yr Annual	10yr Annual	Bull	Bear
Return (%)	23.6	11.1	na	96.5	-22.1
Differ from Category (+/-)	4.4 abv av	-5.5 low	na	11.8 abv av	-9.7 low

Total Risk	Standard Deviation	Category Risk	Risk Index	Beta
av	10.5%	blw av	1.0	0.6

	1993	1992	1991	1990	1989	1988	1987	1986	1985	1984
Return (%)	15.2	17.4	39.9	-19.3	11.2	22.4	—	—	—	—
Differ from category (+/-) . . .	2.0	6.4	4.5	-13.2	-14.6	4.7	—	—	—	—

PER SHARE DATA

	1993	1992	1991	1990	1989	1988	1987	1986	1985	1984
Dividends, Net Income ($) .	0.09	0.08	0.08	0.09	0.17	0.12	—	—	—	—
Distrib'ns, Cap Gain ($) . . .	1.02	0.05	0.00	0.00	0.26	0.10	—	—	—	—
Net Asset Value ($)	12.13	11.72	10.11	7.29	9.14	8.60	—	—	—	—
Expense Ratio (%).	1.25	1.26	1.31	1.29	1.33	1.51	—	—	—	—
Net Income to Assets (%) . .	1.05	0.87	1.20	1.49	1.39	1.57	—	—	—	—
Portfolio Turnover (%)	15	23	0	16	15	7	—	—	—	—
Total Assets (Millions $)	36	26	22	25	26	16	—	—	—	—

PORTFOLIO (as of 6/30/93)

Portfolio Manager: Peter Schliemann - 1987, Nick Whitridge - 1987

Investm't Category: Growth

✔ Cap Gain	Asset Allocation
Cap & Income	Fund of Funds
Income	Index
	Sector
✔ Domestic	✔ Small Cap
Foreign	Socially Conscious
Country/Region	State Specific

Portfolio: stocks 94% bonds 0%
convertibles 0% other 0% cash 6%

Largest Holdings: consumer cyclical 21%, financial 17%

Unrealized Net Capital Gains: 21% of portfolio value

SHAREHOLDER INFORMATION

Minimum Investment
Initial: $2,500   Subsequent: $100

Minimum IRA Investment
Initial: $250   Subsequent: $100

Maximum Fees
Load: none   12b-1: none
Other: none

Distributions
Income: Jun,Dec   Capital Gains: Jun,Dec

Exchange Options
Number Per Year: no limit   Fee: none
Telephone: yes (money market fund available)

Services
IRA, other pension, auto exchange, auto invest, auto withdraw

Babson Tax-Free Income—Port L (BALTX)

Tax-Exempt Bond

Three Crown Center
2440 Pershing Rd., #G-15
Kansas City, MO 64108
(800) 422-2766, (816) 471-5200

PERFORMANCE

	3yr Annual	5yr Annual	10yr Annual	Bull	Bear
Return (%)	10.9	9.5	10.3	43.2	1.3
Differ from Category (+/-)	0.6 av	0.3 av	0.7 av	3.1 abv av	-1.0 blw av

Total Risk	Standard Deviation	Category Risk	Risk Index	Avg Mat
blw av	4.5%	abv av	1.1	19.5 yrs

	1993	1992	1991	1990	1989	1988	1987	1986	1985	1984
Return (%)	12.2	8.3	12.2	6.2	8.7	11.6	-1.8	18.4	20.4	8.9
Differ from category (+/-). . .	0.6	0.0	0.8	-0.1	-0.3	1.5	-0.6	2.0	3.1	0.6

PER SHARE DATA

	1993	1992	1991	1990	1989	1988	1987	1986	1985	1984
Dividends, Net Income ($).	0.45	0.49	0.52	0.55	0.60	0.64	0.61	0.68	0.72	0.72
Distrib'ns, Cap Gain ($) . . .	0.40	0.36	0.03	0.00	0.00	0.00	0.19	0.63	0.00	0.00
Net Asset Value ($)	9.28	9.05	9.17	8.70	8.73	8.60	8.31	9.30	9.02	8.14
Expense Ratio (%)	1.00	0.99	0.98	1.00	0.99	1.00	0.99	1.00	1.00	0.92
Net Income to Assets (%) .	5.03	5.73	6.22	6.47	7.51	7.54	6.80	7.75	8.82	8.94
Portfolio Turnover (%).	126	128	116	121	172	168	123	46	32	27
Total Assets (Millions $).	33	30	29	28	26	21	22	20	16	11

PORTFOLIO (as of 6/30/93)

Portfolio Manager: Joel Vernick - 1987

Investm't Category: Tax-Exempt Bond
Cap Gain	Asset Allocation
Cap & Income	Fund of Funds
✔ Income	Index
	Sector
✔ Domestic	Small Cap
Foreign	Socially Conscious
Country/Region	State Specific

Portfolio: stocks 0% bonds 100%
convertibles 0% other 0% cash 0%

Largest Holdings: general obligation 96%

Unrealized Net Capital Gains: 6% of portfolio value

SHAREHOLDER INFORMATION

Minimum Investment
Initial: $1,000 Subsequent: $100

Minimum IRA Investment
Initial: na Subsequent: na

Maximum Fees
Load: none 12b-1: none
Other: none

Distributions
Income: monthly Capital Gains: Jun, Dec

Exchange Options
Number Per Year: no limit Fee: none
Telephone: yes (money market fund available)

Services
auto exchange, auto invest, auto withdraw

Babson Tax-Free Income—Port S (BASTX)

Tax-Exempt Bond

Three Crown Center
2440 Pershing Rd., #G-15
Kansas City, MO 64108
(800) 422-2766, (816) 471-5200

PERFORMANCE

	3yr Annual	5yr Annual	10yr Annual	Bull	Bear
Return (%)	7.4	7.2	na	28.0	3.4
Differ from Category (+/-)	-2.9 low	-2.0 low	na	-12.1 low	1.1 abv av

Total Risk	Standard Deviation	Category Risk	Risk Index	Avg Mat
low	2.1%	low	0.5	4.7 yrs

	1993	1992	1991	1990	1989	1988	1987	1986	1985	1984
Return (%)	6.7	6.3	9.4	6.5	6.9	5.0	2.6	—	—	—
Differ from category (+/-) ..	-4.9	-2.0	-1.9	0.2	-2.1	-5.1	3.8	—	—	—

PER SHARE DATA

	1993	1992	1991	1990	1989	1988	1987	1986	1985	1984
Dividends, Net Income ($) .	0.48	0.51	0.57	0.59	0.64	0.66	0.61	—	—	—
Distrib'ns, Cap Gain ($) ...	0.05	0.11	0.13	0.00	0.00	0.00	0.00	—	—	—
Net Asset Value ($)	11.05	10.87	10.84	10.58	10.51	10.45	10.59	—	—	—
Expense Ratio (%)........	1.00	1.00	0.99	0.99	0.99	1.00	0.99	—	—	—
Net Income to Assets (%) ..	4.58	5.14	5.57	5.82	6.48	6.01	5.91	—	—	—
Portfolio Turnover (%)	47	81	98	74	115	131	66	—	—	—
Total Assets (Millions $)	31	22	18	18	18	16	16	—	—	—

PORTFOLIO (as of 6/30/93)

Portfolio Manager: Joel Vernick - 1986

Investm't Category: Tax-Exempt Bond

Cap Gain	Asset Allocation
Cap & Income	Fund of Funds
✔ Income	Index
	Sector
✔ Domestic	Small Cap
Foreign	Socially Conscious
Country/Region	State Specific

Portfolio: stocks 0% bonds 100%
convertibles 0% other 0% cash 0%

Largest Holdings: general obligation 95%

Unrealized Net Capital Gains: 4% of portfolio value

SHAREHOLDER INFORMATION

Minimum Investment
Initial: $1,000   Subsequent: $100

Minimum IRA Investment
Initial: na   Subsequent: na

Maximum Fees
Load: none   12b-1: none
Other: none

Distributions
Income: monthly   Capital Gains: June, Dec

Exchange Options
Number Per Year: no limit   Fee: none
Telephone: yes (money market fund available)

Services
auto exchange, auto invest, auto withdraw

Babson Value (BVALX)

Growth & Income

Three Crown Center
2440 Pershing Rd., #G-15
Kansas City, MO 64108
(800) 422-2766, (816) 471-5200

PERFORMANCE

	3yr Annual	5yr Annual	10yr Annual	Bull	Bear
Return (%)	22.2	13.8	na	96.1	-17.3
Differ from Category (+/-)	5.8 high	1.3 abv av	na	26.0 high	-5.7 low

Total Risk	Standard Deviation	Category Risk	Risk Index	Beta
abv av	11.2%	abv av	1.3	0.8

	1993	1992	1991	1990	1989	1988	1987	1986	1985	1984
Return (%)	22.8	15.3	28.9	-11.3	18.2	18.9	3.1	20.8	26.4	—
Differ from category (+/-). .	10.2	5.3	1.2	-5.7	-3.4	2.1	2.7	5.6	1.0	—

PER SHARE DATA

	1993	1992	1991	1990	1989	1988	1987	1986	1985	1984
Dividends, Net Income ($).	0.53	0.62	0.71	0.70	0.50	0.75	0.66	0.87	0.00	—
Distrib'ns, Cap Gain ($) . . .	0.91	0.32	0.00	0.00	0.03	0.07	0.03	0.17	0.00	—
Net Asset Value ($)	25.22	21.75	19.67	15.85	18.68	16.27	14.38	14.64	13.04	—
Expense Ratio (%)	na	1.01	1.01	1.04	1.06	1.11	1.08	1.20	0.93	—
Net Income to Assets (%) . . .	na	3.10	3.82	4.44	4.10	3.87	3.31	3.60	4.79	—
Portfolio Turnover (%).	na	17	31	6	17	24	52	27	13	—
Total Assets (Millions $).	45	34	25	22	20	10	14	6	2	—

PORTFOLIO (as of 5/31/93)

Portfolio Manager: Roland Whitridge - 1984

Investm't Category: Growth & Income

Cap Gain	Asset Allocation
✔ Cap & Income	Fund of Funds
Income	Index
	Sector
✔ Domestic	Small Cap
Foreign	Socially Conscious
Country/Region	State Specific

Portfolio: stocks 94%   bonds 3%
convertibles 0%   other 0%   cash 3%

Largest Holdings: financial services 10%, banks 10%

Unrealized Net Capital Gains: 15% of portfolio value

SHAREHOLDER INFORMATION

Minimum Investment
Initial: $1,000   Subsequent: $100

Minimum IRA Investment
Initial: $250   Subsequent: $100

Maximum Fees
Load: none   12b-1: none
Other: none

Distributions
Income: quarterly   Capital Gains: Dec

Exchange Options
Number Per Year: no limit   Fee: none
Telephone: yes (money market fund available)

Services
IRA, other pension, auto exchange, auto invest, auto withdraw

Babson-Stewart Ivory Int'l (BAINX)

International Stock

Three Crown Center
2440 Pershing Rd., #G-15
Kansas City, MO 64108
(800) 422-2766, (816) 471-5200

PERFORMANCE

	3yr Annual	5yr Annual	10yr Annual	Bull	Bear
Return (%)	14.7	11.6	na	60.8	-14.9
Differ from Category (+/-)	0.4 av	2.9 high	na	5.7 abv av	0.2 av

Total Risk	Standard Deviation	Category Risk	Risk Index	Beta
abv av	12.7%	blw av	1.1	0.4

	1993	1992	1991	1990	1989	1988	1987	1986	1985	1984
Return (%)	33.4	-1.7	15.0	-9.3	26.9	—	—	—	—	—
Differ from category (+/-) . .	-5.1	1.8	2.1	1.8	4.7	—	—	—	—	—

PER SHARE DATA

	1993	1992	1991	1990	1989	1988	1987	1986	1985	1984
Dividends, Net Income ($) .	0.05	0.14	0.11	0.06	0.06	—	—	—	—	—
Distrib'ns, Cap Gain ($) . . .	0.32	0.02	0.00	0.14	0.28	—	—	—	—	—
Net Asset Value ($)	16.20	12.43	12.81	11.24	12.63	—	—	—	—	—
Expense Ratio (%).	1.57	1.58	1.75	1.75	2.68	—	—	—	—	—
Net Income to Assets (%). .	0.88	1.16	1.10	0.36	0.62	—	—	—	—	—
Portfolio Turnover (%)	49	44	52	42	40	—	—	—	—	—
Total Assets (Millions $)	43	18	12	11	4	—	—	—	—	—

PORTFOLIO (as of 6/30/93)

Portfolio Manager: John Wright - 1988

Investm't Category: International Stock

✔ Cap Gain	Asset Allocation
Cap & Income	Fund of Funds
Income	Index
	Sector
Domestic	Small Cap
✔ Foreign	Socially Conscious
Country/Region	State Specific

Portfolio: stocks 97% bonds 0%
convertibles 0% other 0% cash 3%

Largest Holdings: Japan 25%, United Kingdom 19%

Unrealized Net Capital Gains: 10% of portfolio value

SHAREHOLDER INFORMATION

Minimum Investment
Initial: $2,500   Subsequent: $100

Minimum IRA Investment
Initial: $250   Subsequent: $100

Maximum Fees
Load: none   12b-1: none
Other: none

Distributions
Income: Jun, Dec   Capital Gains: Jun, Dec

Exchange Options
Number Per Year: no limit   Fee: none
Telephone: yes (money market fund available)

Services
IRA, other pension, auto exchange, auto invest, auto withdraw

Baron Asset (BARAX)

Aggressive Growth

450 Park Ave.
New York, NY 10022
(800) 992-2766, (212) 759-7700

PERFORMANCE

	3yr Annual	5yr Annual	10yr Annual	Bull	Bear
Return (%)	23.5	13.9	na	106.9	-25.7
Differ from Category (+/-)	-1.9 av	-4.3 blw av	na	-18.1 av	-10.7 low

Total Risk	Standard Deviation	Category Risk	Risk Index	Beta
abv av	13.6%	blw av	0.9	0.9

	1993	1992	1991	1990	1989	1988	1987	1986	1985	1984
Return (%).............	23.4	13.8	34.0	-18.4	24.9	34.4	—	—	—	—
Differ from category (+/-)...	4.4	3.4	-18.4	-12.1	-2.1	19.2	—	—	—	—

PER SHARE DATA

	1993	1992	1991	1990	1989	1988	1987	1986	1985	1984
Dividends, Net Income ($).	0.31	0.00	0.03	0.19	0.15	0.04	—	—	—	—
Distrib'ns, Cap Gain ($) ...	0.45	0.16	0.00	0.00	1.25	0.65	—	—	—	—
Net Asset Value ($)	21.11	17.73	15.71	11.75	14.66	12.87	—	—	—	—
Expense Ratio (%)	1.80	1.70	1.70	1.80	2.10	2.50	—	—	—	—
Net Income to Assets (%) .	-0.70	-0.50	0.50	1.50	1.30	0.50	—	—	—	—
Portfolio Turnover (%).....	108	96	143	98	149	242	—	—	—	—
Total Assets (Millions $).....	62	44	47	40	48	12	—	—	—	—

PORTFOLIO (as of 9/30/93)

Portfolio Manager: Ron Baron - 1987

Investm't Category: Aggressive Growth

✔ Cap Gain	Asset Allocation
Cap & Income	Fund of Funds
Income	Index
	Sector
✔ Domestic	Small Cap
Foreign	Socially Conscious
Country/Region	State Specific

Portfolio: stocks 91% bonds 7%
convertibles 0% other 0% cash 2%

Largest Holdings: amusement & recreation services 12%, health services 10%

Unrealized Net Capital Gains: 29% of portfolio value

SHAREHOLDER INFORMATION

Minimum Investment
Initial: $2,000 Subsequent: $0

Minimum IRA Investment
Initial: $2,000 Subsequent: $0

Maximum Fees
Load: none 12b-1: 0.25%
Other: none

Distributions
Income: Dec Capital Gains: Dec

Exchange Options
Number Per Year: none Fee: na
Telephone: na

Services
IRA

Bartlett Basic Value

(MBBVX)

Growth & Income

36 E. Fourth St.
Suite 400
Cincinnati, OH 45202
(800) 800-4612, (513) 621-4612

PERFORMANCE

	3yr Annual	5yr Annual	10yr Annual	Bull	Bear
Return (%)	15.7	9.3	11.3	67.6	-16.4
Differ from Category (+/-)	-0.6 av	-3.2 low	-1.1 blw av	-2.5 av	-4.8 low

Total Risk	Standard Deviation	Category Risk	Risk Index	Beta
av	9.6%	av	1.1	0.8

	1993	1992	1991	1990	1989	1988	1987	1986	1985	1984
Return (%)	11.6	10.2	25.9	-9.6	11.6	26.2	-3.7	13.6	25.2	8.4
Differ from category (+/-) ..	-1.0	0.2	-1.8	-4.0	-10.0	9.4	-4.1	-1.6	-0.2	2.2

PER SHARE DATA

	1993	1992	1991	1990	1989	1988	1987	1986	1985	1984
Dividends, Net Income ($) .	0.21	0.31	0.38	0.51	0.83	0.51	0.44	0.45	0.55	0.58
Distrib'ns, Cap Gain ($) ...	0.14	0.28	0.00	0.00	0.18	1.15	0.38	1.41	0.18	0.00
Net Asset Value ($)	15.28	14.02	13.28	10.87	12.58	12.18	11.01	12.20	12.37	10.53
Expense Ratio (%)........	1.21	1.22	1.21	1.19	1.23	1.57	1.28	1.56	1.78	1.99
Net Income to Assets (%)..	2.14	2.77	3.87	4.81	4.57	2.75	3.49	4.05	6.01	5.71
Portfolio Turnover (%).....	43	49	92	77	99	97	58	82	36	8
Total Assets (Millions $)	97	89	96	106	100	81	91	52	22	12

PORTFOLIO (as of 9/30/93)

Portfolio Manager: James Miller - 1983, Woodrow Uible - 1983

Investm't Category: Growth & Income

Cap Gain	Asset Allocation
✔ Cap & Income	Fund of Funds
Income	Index
	Sector
✔ Domestic	Small Cap
✔ Foreign	Socially Conscious
Country/Region	State Specific

Portfolio: stocks 86% bonds 12%
convertibles 1% other 1% cash 0%

Largest Holdings: financial services 17%, energy 10%

Unrealized Net Capital Gains: 15% of portfolio value

SHAREHOLDER INFORMATION

Minimum Investment
Initial: $5,000   Subsequent: $100

Minimum IRA Investment
Initial: $250   Subsequent: $100

Maximum Fees
Load: none   12b-1: none
Other: none

Distributions
Income: quarterly   Capital Gains: Dec

Exchange Options
Number Per Year: no limit   Fee: none
Telephone: yes (money market fund available)

Services
IRA, other pension

Bartlett Fixed Income
(BFXFX)
General Bond

36 E. Fourth St.
Suite 400
Cincinnati, OH 45202
(800) 800-4612, (513) 621-4612

PERFORMANCE

	3yr Annual	5yr Annual	10yr Annual	Bull	Bear
Return (%)	9.3	9.3	na	35.8	2.0
Differ from Category (+/-)	-0.8 blw av	-0.5 blw av	na	-3.6 blw av	-0.8 blw av

Total Risk	Standard Deviation	Category Risk	Risk Index	Avg Mat
low	3.0%	blw av	1.0	5.3 yrs

	1993	1992	1991	1990	1989	1988	1987	1986	1985	1984
Return (%)	6.9	6.9	14.3	6.0	12.5	7.6	2.7	—	—	—
Differ from category (+/-) . . .	-2.3	0.2	-0.3	-0.8	1.2	0.0	0.2	—	—	—

PER SHARE DATA

	1993	1992	1991	1990	1989	1988	1987	1986	1985	1984
Dividends, Net Income ($) .	0.49	0.62	0.69	0.74	0.84	0.84	0.84	—	—	—
Distrib'ns, Cap Gain ($) . . .	0.16	0.00	0.00	0.00	0.00	0.00	0.00	—	—	—
Net Asset Value ($)	10.29	10.25	10.19	9.57	9.76	9.46	9.58	—	—	—
Expense Ratio (%)	1.00	1.00	1.00	1.00	1.00	1.00	0.93	—	—	—
Net Income to Assets (%) .	5.81	6.85	7.68	8.56	8.95	8.56	8.57	—	—	—
Portfolio Turnover (%)	175	126	165	95	104	205	192	—	—	—
Total Assets (Millions $)	123	148	159	157	159	157	145	—	—	—

PORTFOLIO (as of 9/30/93)

Portfolio Manager: Dale Rabiner - 1986

Investm't Category: General Bond

Cap Gain	Asset Allocation
Cap & Income	Fund of Funds
✔ Income	Index
	Sector
✔ Domestic	Small Cap
✔ Foreign	Socially Conscious
Country/Region	State Specific

Portfolio: stocks 0%   bonds 95%
convertibles 5%   other 0%   cash 0%

Largest Holdings: corporate 50%, U.S. government & agencies 27%

Unrealized Net Capital Gains: 3% of portfolio value

SHAREHOLDER INFORMATION

Minimum Investment
Initial: $5,000   Subsequent: $100

Minimum IRA Investment
Initial: $250   Subsequent: $100

Maximum Fees
Load: none   12b-1: none
Other: none

Distributions
Income: monthly   Capital Gains: Dec

Exchange Options
Number Per Year: no limit   Fee: none
Telephone: yes (money market fund available)

Services
IRA, other pension

Bartlett Value Int'l (BVLIX)

International Stock

36 E. Fourth St.
Suite 400
Cincinnati, OH 45202
(800) 800-4612, (513) 621-4612

PERFORMANCE

	3yr Annual	5yr Annual	10yr Annual	Bull	Bear
Return (%)	16.1	na	na	61.7	-17.1
Differ from Category (+/-)	1.8 abv av	na	na	6.6 abv av	-2.0 blw av

Total Risk	Standard Deviation	Category Risk	Risk Index	Beta
abv av	12.5%	blw av	1.0	0.6

	1993	1992	1991	1990	1989	1988	1987	1986	1985	1984
Return (%)	31.3	-1.8	21.4	-14.5	—	—	—	—	—	—
Differ from category (+/-)	-7.2	1.7	8.5	-3.4	—	—	—	—	—	—

PER SHARE DATA

	1993	1992	1991	1990	1989	1988	1987	1986	1985	1984
Dividends, Net Income ($)	0.07	0.10	0.21	0.28	—	—	—	—	—	—
Distrib'ns, Cap Gain ($)	0.00	0.00	0.01	0.17	—	—	—	—	—	—
Net Asset Value ($)	12.33	9.45	9.73	8.22	—	—	—	—	—	—
Expense Ratio (%)	2.00	2.00	1.99	1.41	—	—	—	—	—	—
Net Income to Assets (%)	1.13	1.79	3.31	1.80	—	—	—	—	—	—
Portfolio Turnover (%)	19	27	39	155	—	—	—	—	—	—
Total Assets (Millions $)	44	22	24	21	—	—	—	—	—	—

PORTFOLIO (as of 9/30/93)

Portfolio Manager: Madelynn Matlock - 1989

Investm't Category: International Stock

✔ Cap Gain	Asset Allocation
Cap & Income	Fund of Funds
Income	Index
	Sector
✔ Domestic	Small Cap
✔ Foreign	Socially Conscious
Country/Region	State Specific

Portfolio: stocks 90% bonds 0%
convertibles 2% other 0% cash 8%

Largest Holdings: France 11%, United Kingdom 11%

Unrealized Net Capital Gains: 10% of portfolio value

SHAREHOLDER INFORMATION

Minimum Investment
Initial: $5,000   Subsequent: $100

Minimum IRA Investment
Initial: $250   Subsequent: $100

Maximum Fees
Load: none   12b-1: none
Other: none

Distributions
Income: quarterly   Capital Gains: Dec

Exchange Options
Number Per Year: no limit   Fee: none
Telephone: yes (money market fund available)

Services
IRA, other pension

Bascom Hill Balanced

(BHBFX)

Balanced

6411 Mineral Point Road
Madison, WI 53705
(800) 767-0300, (608) 273-2020

PERFORMANCE

	3yr Annual	5yr Annual	10yr Annual	Bull	Bear
Return (%)	12.2	7.9	na	47.6	-11.2
Differ from Category (+/-)	-2.8 low	-4.2 low	na	-14.0 low	-5.4 low

Total Risk	Standard Deviation	Category Risk	Risk Index	Beta
av	7.5%	abv av	1.2	0.6

	1993	1992	1991	1990	1989	1988	1987	1986	1985	1984
Return (%)	4.3	8.4	25.0	-7.3	12.1	7.7	3.6	—	—	—
Differ from category (+/-). . .	-9.1	0.3	1.1	-6.8	-5.5	-4.3	1.3	—	—	—

PER SHARE DATA

	1993	1992	1991	1990	1989	1988	1987	1986	1985	1984
Dividends, Net Income ($).	1.04	0.72	0.77	0.99	1.17	0.91	0.60	—	—	—
Distrib'ns, Cap Gain ($) . . .	1.23	0.52	0.00	0.00	0.45	0.00	0.00	—	—	—
Net Asset Value ($)	22.37	23.65	23.00	19.04	21.62	20.76	20.13	—	—	—
Expense Ratio (%)	na	1.90	1.94	1.96	2.00	2.00	2.00	—	—	—
Net Income to Assets (%) . . .	na	2.53	3.33	5.00	5.60	4.90	4.80	—	—	—
Portfolio Turnover (%).	na	71	64	71	47	0	0	—	—	—
Total Assets (Millions $)	13	15	15	13	14	9	5	—	—	—

PORTFOLIO (as of 6/30/93)

Portfolio Manager: Frank Burgess - 1986

Investm't Category: Balanced

Cap Gain	✔ Asset Allocation
✔ Cap & Income	Fund of Funds
Income	Index
	Sector
✔ Domestic	Small Cap
Foreign	Socially Conscious
Country/Region	State Specific

Portfolio: stocks 52% bonds 32%
convertibles 0% other 0% cash 16%

Largest Holdings: stocks—financial services 18%, U.S. government & agencies 13%

Unrealized Net Capital Gains: 8% of portfolio value

SHAREHOLDER INFORMATION

Minimum Investment
Initial: $1,000   Subsequent: $100

Minimum IRA Investment
Initial: $1,000   Subsequent: $100

Maximum Fees
Load: 3.00% front   12b-1: none
Other: none

Distributions
Income: quarterly   Capital Gains: Dec

Exchange Options
Number Per Year: none   Fee: na
Telephone: na

Services
IRA

BayFunds Bond Port
(BFBPX)

General Bond

P.O. Box 665
Waltham, MA 02254
(800) 229-3863

fund in existence since 3/1/93

PERFORMANCE

	3yr Annual	5yr Annual	10yr Annual	Bull	Bear
Return (%)	na	na	na	na	na
Differ from Category (+/-)	na	na	na	na	na

Total Risk	Standard Deviation	Category Risk	Risk Index	Avg Mat
na	na	na	na	9.7 yrs

	1993	1992	1991	1990	1989	1988	1987	1986	1985	1984
Return (%)	—	—	—	—	—	—	—	—	—	—
Differ from category (+/-) . . .	—	—	—	—	—	—	—	—	—	—

PER SHARE DATA

	1993	1992	1991	1990	1989	1988	1987	1986	1985	1984
Dividends, Net Income ($) .	0.49	—	—	—	—	—	—	—	—	—
Distrib'ns, Cap Gain ($) . . .	0.09	—	—	—	—	—	—	—	—	—
Net Asset Value ($)	10.14	—	—	—	—	—	—	—	—	—
Expense Ratio (%)	0.61	—	—	—	—	—	—	—	—	—
Net Income to Assets (%) . .	6.11	—	—	—	—	—	—	—	—	—
Portfolio Turnover (%)	36	—	—	—	—	—	—	—	—	—
Total Assets (Millions $)	78	—	—	—	—	—	—	—	—	—

PORTFOLIO (as of 6/30/93)

Portfolio Manager: Rick Vincent - 1993

Investm't Category: General Bond

Cap Gain	Asset Allocation
Cap & Income	Fund of Funds
✔ Income	Index
	Sector
✔ Domestic	Small Cap
Foreign	Socially Conscious
Country/Region	State Specific

Portfolio: stocks 0% bonds 99%
convertibles 0% other 0% cash 1%

Largest Holdings: U.S government 57%, corporate 30%

Unrealized Net Capital Gains: 1% of portfolio value

SHAREHOLDER INFORMATION

Minimum Investment
Initial: $2,500   Subsequent: $100

Minimum IRA Investment
Initial: $500   Subsequent: $0

Maximum Fees
Load: none   12b-1: none
Other: none

Distributions
Income: monthly   Capital Gains: Dec

Exchange Options
Number Per Year: no limit   Fee: none
Telephone: yes (money market fund available)

Services
IRA, other pension, auto invest

BayFunds Equity Port
(BFEPX)

Growth

P.O. Box 665
Waltham, MA 02254
(800) 229-3863

fund in existence since 3/1/93

	3yr Annual	5yr Annual	10yr Annual	Bull	Bear
Return (%)	na	na	na	na	na
Differ from Category (+/-)	na	na	na	na	na

Total Risk	Standard Deviation	Category Risk	Risk Index	Beta
na	na	na	na	na

	1993	1992	1991	1990	1989	1988	1987	1986	1985	1984
Return (%)	—	—	—	—	—	—	—	—	—	—
Differ from category (+/-)	—	—	—	—	—	—	—	—	—	—

PER SHARE DATA

	1993	1992	1991	1990	1989	1988	1987	1986	1985	1984
Dividends, Net Income ($)	0.14	—	—	—	—	—	—	—	—	—
Distrib'ns, Cap Gain ($)	0.00	—	—	—	—	—	—	—	—	—
Net Asset Value ($)	10.98	—	—	—	—	—	—	—	—	—
Expense Ratio (%)	0.60	—	—	—	—	—	—	—	—	—
Net Income to Assets (%)	2.20	—	—	—	—	—	—	—	—	—
Portfolio Turnover (%)	19	—	—	—	—	—	—	—	—	—
Total Assets (Millions $)	110	—	—	—	—	—	—	—	—	—

PORTFOLIO (as of 6/30/93)

Portfolio Manager: Geraldine Carroll - 1993

Investm't Category: Growth

✔ Cap Gain	Asset Allocation
Cap & Income	Fund of Funds
Income	Index
	Sector
✔ Domestic	Small Cap
Foreign	Socially Conscious
Country/Region	State Specific

Portfolio: stocks 95% bonds 0%
convertibles 0% other 0% cash 5%

Largest Holdings: banks 7%, retail 6%

Unrealized Net Capital Gains: 4% of portfolio value

SHAREHOLDER INFORMATION

Minimum Investment
Initial: $2,500   Subsequent: $100

Minimum IRA Investment
Initial: $500   Subsequent: $0

Maximum Fees
Load: none   12b-1: none
Other: none

Distributions
Income: monthly   Capital Gains: Dec

Exchange Options
Number Per Year: no limit   Fee: none
Telephone: yes (money market fund available)

Services
IRA, other pension, auto invest

BayFunds Short-Term Yield (BFSTX)

P.O. Box 665
Waltham, MA 02254
(800) 229-3863

General Bond

fund in existence since 3/1/93

PERFORMANCE

	3yr Annual	5yr Annual	10yr Annual	Bull	Bear
Return (%)	na	na	na	na	na
Differ from Category (+/-)	na	na	na	na	na

Total Risk	Standard Deviation	Category Risk	Risk Index	Avg Mat
na	na	na	na	2.5 yrs

	1993	1992	1991	1990	1989	1988	1987	1986	1985	1984
Return (%)	—	—	—	—	—	—	—	—	—	—
Differ from category (+/-) ...	—	—	—	—	—	—	—	—	—	—

PER SHARE DATA

	1993	1992	1991	1990	1989	1988	1987	1986	1985	1984
Dividends, Net Income ($) .	0.43	—	—	—	—	—	—	—	—	—
Distrib'ns, Cap Gain ($) ...	0.00	—	—	—	—	—	—	—	—	—
Net Asset Value ($)	9.91	—	—	—	—	—	—	—	—	—
Expense Ratio (%)........	0.50	—	—	—	—	—	—	—	—	—
Net Income to Assets (%)..	5.63	—	—	—	—	—	—	—	—	—
Portfolio Turnover (%)	47	—	—	—	—	—	—	—	—	—
Total Assets (Millions $) ...	172	—	—	—	—	—	—	—	—	—

PORTFOLIO (as of 6/30/93)

Portfolio Manager: Eric Letendre - 1993

Investm't Category: General Bond

Cap Gain	Asset Allocation
Cap & Income	Fund of Funds
✔ Income	Index
	Sector
✔ Domestic	Small Cap
Foreign	Socially Conscious
Country/Region	State Specific

Portfolio: stocks 0% bonds 94%
convertibles 0% other 0% cash 6%

Largest Holdings: corporate 73%, mortgage-backed 15%

Unrealized Net Capital Gains: 0% of portfolio value

SHAREHOLDER INFORMATION

Minimum Investment
Initial: $2,500 Subsequent: $100

Minimum IRA Investment
Initial: $500 Subsequent: $0

Maximum Fees
Load: none 12b-1: none
Other: none

Distributions
Income: monthly Capital Gains: Dec

Exchange Options
Number Per Year: no limit Fee: none
Telephone: yes (money market fund available)

Services
IRA, other pension, auto invest

Beacon Hill Mutual

(BEHMX)

Growth

75 Federal St.
Boston, MA 02110
(617) 482-0795

PERFORMANCE

	3yr Annual	5yr Annual	10yr Annual	Bull	Bear
Return (%)	5.5	8.5	9.2	32.8	-6.1
Differ from Category (+/-)	-13.7 low	-6.1 low	-3.4 low	-51.9 low	6.3 high

Total Risk	Standard Deviation	Category Risk	Risk Index	Beta
av	10.8%	blw av	1.0	0.8

	1993	1992	1991	1990	1989	1988	1987	1986	1985	1984
Return (%)	-5.1	-1.8	26.3	5.9	20.8	4.2	5.3	5.9	33.5	3.8
Differ from category (+/-). .	-18.3	-12.8	-9.1	12.0	-5.0	-13.5	4.1	-8.6	4.2	3.8

PER SHARE DATA

	1993	1992	1991	1990	1989	1988	1987	1986	1985	1984
Dividends, Net Income ($) .	0.00	0.00	0.00	0.00	0.00	0.00	0.00	0.00	0.00	0.00
Distrib'ns, Cap Gain ($) . . .	0.58	1.36	1.80	1.34	1.88	0.00	0.99	0.00	0.00	0.00
Net Asset Value ($)	31.50	33.86	35.96	30.05	29.66	26.21	25.14	24.65	23.26	17.42
Expense Ratio (%)	2.60	2.80	3.50	3.60	4.00	4.00	3.70	3.50	3.30	3.40
Net Income to Assets (%) .	-0.70	-1.00	-1.20	-1.20	-1.30	-1.60	-1.60	-0.90	-0.20	-0.10
Portfolio Turnover (%).	2	6	3	0	1	0	0	8	1	0
Total Assets (Millions $).	5	5	4	4	3	3	4	3	2	2

PORTFOLIO (as of 6/30/93)

Portfolio Manager: David L. Stone - 1964

Investm't Category: Growth

✔ Cap Gain	Asset Allocation
Cap & Income	Fund of Funds
Income	Index
	Sector
✔ Domestic	Small Cap
Foreign	Socially Conscious
Country/Region	State Specific

Portfolio: stocks 78% bonds 0%
convertibles 0% other 0% cash 22%

Largest Holdings: pharmaceuticals 20%, retail—department & specialty stores 8%

Unrealized Net Capital Gains: 54% of portfolio value

SHAREHOLDER INFORMATION

Minimum Investment
Initial: $0   Subsequent: $0

Minimum IRA Investment
Initial: $0   Subsequent: $0

Maximum Fees
Load: none   12b-1: none
Other: none

Distributions
Income: Jun   Capital Gains: Jun

Exchange Options
Number Per Year: none   Fee: na
Telephone: na

Services
IRA, other pension, auto invest, auto withdraw

Benham Adjustable Rate Gov't (BARGX)

1665 Charleston Rd.
Mountain View, CA 94043
(800) 321-8321, (415) 965-4222

Mortgage-Backed Bond

PERFORMANCE

	3yr Annual	5yr Annual	10yr Annual	Bull	Bear
Return (%)	na	na	na	na	na
Differ from Category (+/-)	na	na	na	na	na

Total Risk	Standard Deviation	Category Risk	Risk Index	Avg Mat
na	na	na	na	na

	1993	1992	1991	1990	1989	1988	1987	1986	1985	1984
Return (%)	3.5	5.2	—	—	—	—	—	—	—	—
Differ from category (+/-)	-3.3	-0.8	—	—	—	—	—	—	—	—

PER SHARE DATA

	1993	1992	1991	1990	1989	1988	1987	1986	1985	1984
Dividends, Net Income ($)	0.56	0.60	—	—	—	—	—	—	—	—
Distrib'ns, Cap Gain ($)	0.00	0.00	—	—	—	—	—	—	—	—
Net Asset Value ($)	9.84	10.05	—	—	—	—	—	—	—	—
Expense Ratio (%)	0.45	0.00	—	—	—	—	—	—	—	—
Net Income to Assets (%)	5.66	7.02	—	—	—	—	—	—	—	—
Portfolio Turnover (%)	82	82	—	—	—	—	—	—	—	—
Total Assets (Millions $)	1,102	886	—	—	—	—	—	—	—	—

PORTFOLIO (as of 3/31/93)

Portfolio Manager: Randy Merk - 1991

Investm't Category: Mortgage-Backed Bond

Cap Gain	Asset Allocation
Cap & Income	Fund of Funds
✔ Income	Index
	Sector
✔ Domestic	Small Cap
Foreign	Socially Conscious
Country/Region	State Specific

Portfolio: stocks 0%   bonds 99%
convertibles 0%   other 0%   cash 1%

Largest Holdings: mortgage-backed 99%

Unrealized Net Capital Gains: 0% of portfolio value

SHAREHOLDER INFORMATION

Minimum Investment
Initial: $1,000   Subsequent: $100

Minimum IRA Investment
Initial: $100   Subsequent: $25

Maximum Fees
Load: none   12b-1: none
Other: none

Distributions
Income: monthly   Capital Gains: Dec

Exchange Options
Number Per Year: 6   Fee: none
Telephone: yes (money market fund available)

Services
IRA, other pension, auto exchange, auto invest, auto withdraw

Benham CA Tax-Free High-Yield (BCHYX)

1665 Charleston Rd.
Mountain View, CA 94043
(800) 321-8321, (415) 965-4222

Tax-Exempt Bond

PERFORMANCE

	3yr Annual	5yr Annual	10yr Annual	Bull	Bear
Return (%)	11.0	9.6	na	41.4	2.3
Differ from Category (+/-)	0.6 av	0.4 av	na	1.3 av	0.0 av

Total Risk	Standard Deviation	Category Risk	Risk Index	Avg Mat
low	3.6%	blw av	0.9	24.4 yrs

	1993	1992	1991	1990	1989	1988	1987	1986	1985	1984
Return (%)	13.1	9.1	10.9	5.6	9.6	12.4	-11.0	—	—	—
Differ from category (+/-)	1.5	0.8	-0.4	-0.6	0.6	2.3	-9.8	—	—	—

PER SHARE DATA

	1993	1992	1991	1990	1989	1988	1987	1986	1985	1984
Dividends, Net Income ($)	0.57	0.57	0.59	0.61	0.65	0.65	0.68	—	—	—
Distrib'ns, Cap Gain ($)	0.12	0.00	0.00	0.00	0.00	0.00	0.00	—	—	—
Net Asset Value ($)	9.60	9.12	8.90	8.58	8.72	8.57	8.23	—	—	—
Expense Ratio (%)	0.60	0.56	0.50	0.24	0.00	0.00	0.00	—	—	—
Net Income to Assets (%)	6.21	6.54	6.79	7.23	7.67	7.85	7.50	—	—	—
Portfolio Turnover (%)	11	33	47	104	50	143	57	—	—	—
Total Assets (Millions $)	116	80	66	45	33	13	8	—	—	—

PORTFOLIO (as of 2/28/93)

Portfolio Manager: G. David MacEwen - 1991

Investm't Category: Tax-Exempt Bond

Cap Gain	Asset Allocation
Cap & Income	Fund of Funds
✔ Income	Index
	Sector
✔ Domestic	Small Cap
Foreign	Socially Conscious
Country/Region	✔ State Specific

Portfolio: stocks 0%   bonds 100%
convertibles 0%   other 0%   cash 0%

Largest Holdings: general obligation 2%

Unrealized Net Capital Gains: 5% of portfolio value

SHAREHOLDER INFORMATION

Minimum Investment
Initial: $1,000   Subsequent: $100

Minimum IRA Investment
Initial: na   Subsequent: na

Maximum Fees
Load: none   12b-1: none
Other: none

Distributions
Income: monthly   Capital Gains: Dec

Exchange Options
Number Per Year: 6   Fee: none
Telephone: yes (money market fund available)

Services
auto exchange, auto invest, auto withdraw

Benham CA Tax-Free Insured (BCINX)

1665 Charleston Rd.
Mountain View, CA 94043
(800) 321-8321, (415) 965-4222

Tax-Exempt Bond

PERFORMANCE

	3yr Annual	5yr Annual	10yr Annual	Bull	Bear
Return (%)	11.2	10.1	na	45.9	0.6
Differ from Category (+/-)	0.8 abv av	0.8 abv av	na	5.8 high	-1.6 low

Total Risk	Standard Deviation	Category Risk	Risk Index	Avg Mat
blw av	5.2%	high	1.3	16.6 yrs

	1993	1992	1991	1990	1989	1988	1987	1986	1985	1984
Return (%)	13.4	9.1	11.2	6.7	10.3	10.1	-6.0	—	—	—
Differ from category (+/-) . . .	1.8	0.8	-0.1	0.4	1.3	0.0	-4.8	—	—	—

PER SHARE DATA

	1993	1992	1991	1990	1989	1988	1987	1986	1985	1984
Dividends, Net Income ($) .	0.53	0.56	0.57	0.58	0.59	0.63	0.64	—	—	—
Distrib'ns, Cap Gain ($) . . .	0.27	0.09	0.00	0.00	0.00	0.00	0.00	—	—	—
Net Asset Value ($)	10.43	9.94	9.74	9.30	9.29	8.98	8.75	—	—	—
Expense Ratio (%)	0.54	0.55	0.59	0.61	0.66	0.00	0.00	—	—	—
Net Income to Assets (%) . .	5.57	5.90	6.18	6.43	6.62	7.39	7.11	—	—	—
Portfolio Turnover (%)	na	54	38	117	74	145	21	—	—	—
Total Assets (Millions $) . . .	223	146	95	60	43	30	13	—	—	—

PORTFOLIO (as of 2/28/93)

Portfolio Manager: G. David MacEwen - 1991

Investm't Category: Tax-Exempt Bond

Cap Gain	Asset Allocation
Cap & Income	Fund of Funds
✔ Income	Index
	Sector
✔ Domestic	Small Cap
Foreign	Socially Conscious
Country/Region	✔ State Specific

Portfolio: stocks 0% bonds 100%
convertibles 0% other 0% cash 0%

Largest Holdings: general obligation 8%

Unrealized Net Capital Gains: 8% of portfolio value

SHAREHOLDER INFORMATION

Minimum Investment
Initial: $1,000 Subsequent: $100

Minimum IRA Investment
Initial: na Subsequent: na

Maximum Fees
Load: none 12b-1: none
Other: none

Distributions
Income: monthly Capital Gains: Dec

Exchange Options
Number Per Year: 6 Fee: none
Telephone: yes (money market fund available)

Services
auto exchange, auto invest, auto withdraw

Benham CA Tax-Free Interm (BCITX)

1665 Charleston Rd.
Mountain View, CA 94043
(800) 321-8321, (415) 965-4222

Tax-Exempt Bond

PERFORMANCE

	3yr Annual	5yr Annual	10yr Annual	Bull	Bear
Return (%)	9.3	8.6	8.1	35.3	3.4
Differ from Category (+/-)	-1.0 low	-0.6 blw av	-1.5 low	-4.8 low	1.1 abv av

Total Risk	Standard Deviation	Category Risk	Risk Index	Avg Mat
low	3.9%	blw av	1.0	8.0 yrs

	1993	1992	1991	1990	1989	1988	1987	1986	1985	1984
Return (%)	10.6	7.0	10.3	6.9	7.9	5.8	0.8	12.5	13.9	5.2
Differ from category (+/-)	-1.0	-1.3	-1.0	0.6	-1.1	-4.3	2.0	-3.9	-3.4	-3.1

PER SHARE DATA

	1993	1992	1991	1990	1989	1988	1987	1986	1985	1984
Dividends, Net Income ($)	0.54	0.57	0.59	0.62	0.62	0.62	0.62	0.66	0.69	0.70
Distrib'ns, Cap Gain ($)	0.08	0.01	0.00	0.00	0.00	0.00	0.00	0.00	0.00	0.00
Net Asset Value ($)	11.38	10.88	10.74	10.30	10.23	10.08	10.12	10.67	10.10	9.50
Expense Ratio (%)	0.51	0.52	0.55	0.58	0.60	0.64	0.67	0.74	0.96	0.97
Net Income to Assets (%)	5.21	5.50	5.84	6.08	6.25	6.19	5.92	6.71	7.11	7.47
Portfolio Turnover (%)	na	49	29	20	40	47	52	23	48	93
Total Assets (Millions $)	469	305	242	191	167	157	167	124	56	30

PORTFOLIO (as of 2/28/93)

Portfolio Manager: G. David MacEwen - 1991

Investm't Category: Tax-Exempt Bond

Cap Gain	Asset Allocation
Cap & Income	Fund of Funds
✔ Income	Index
	Sector
✔ Domestic	Small Cap
Foreign	Socially Conscious
Country/Region	✔ State Specific

Portfolio: stocks 0%   bonds 100%
convertibles 0%   other 0%   cash 0%

Largest Holdings: general obligation 0%

Unrealized Net Capital Gains: 7% of portfolio value

SHAREHOLDER INFORMATION

Minimum Investment
Initial: $1,000   Subsequent: $100

Minimum IRA Investment
Initial: na   Subsequent: na

Maximum Fees
Load: none   12b-1: none
Other: none

Distributions
Income: monthly   Capital Gains: Dec

Exchange Options
Number Per Year: 6   Fee: none
Telephone: yes (money market fund available)

Services
auto exchange, auto invest, auto withdraw

Benham CA Tax-Free Long-Term (BCLTX)

1665 Charleston Rd.
Mountain View, CA 94043
(800) 321-8321, (415) 965-4222

Tax-Exempt Bond

PERFORMANCE

	3yr Annual	5yr Annual	10yr Annual	Bull	Bear
Return (%)	11.2	9.9	9.6	44.9	1.1
Differ from Category (+/-)	0.8 abv av	0.6 abv av	0.0 blw av	4.8 abv av	-1.2 low

Total Risk	Standard Deviation	Category Risk	Risk Index	Avg Mat
blw av	4.9%	high	1.2	20.4 yrs

	1993	1992	1991	1990	1989	1988	1987	1986	1985	1984
Return (%)	13.7	8.1	11.8	6.5	9.7	10.4	-4.5	19.2	17.8	5.6
Differ from category (+/-) ...	2.1	-0.2	0.5	0.2	0.6	0.3	-3.3	2.8	0.5	-2.7

PER SHARE DATA

	1993	1992	1991	1990	1989	1988	1987	1986	1985	1984
Dividends, Net Income ($) .	0.65	0.68	0.69	0.70	0.72	0.73	0.75	0.80	0.84	0.88
Distrib'ns, Cap Gain ($) ...	0.43	0.27	0.00	0.00	0.00	0.00	0.00	0.08	0.00	0.00
Net Asset Value ($)	11.63	11.21	11.28	10.75	10.78	10.51	10.21	11.49	10.43	9.62
Expense Ratio (%)........	0.51	0.52	0.55	0.57	0.58	0.63	0.65	0.74	0.95	0.97
Net Income to Assets (%)..	5.91	6.14	6.48	6.64	6.98	7.19	6.87	7.70	8.58	9.08
Portfolio Turnover (%)	na	72	38	74	78	35	82	47	91	107
Total Assets (Millions $) ...	324	276	247	197	178	143	180	196	83	27

PORTFOLIO (as of 2/28/93)

Portfolio Manager: G. David MacEwen - 1991

Investm't Category: Tax-Exempt Bond

Cap Gain	Asset Allocation
Cap & Income	Fund of Funds
✔ Income	Index
	Sector
✔ Domestic	Small Cap
Foreign	Socially Conscious
Country/Region	✔ State Specific

Portfolio: stocks 0% bonds 100%
convertibles 0% other 0% cash 0%

Largest Holdings: general obligation 0%

Unrealized Net Capital Gains: 8% of portfolio value

SHAREHOLDER INFORMATION

Minimum Investment
Initial: $1,000   Subsequent: $100

Minimum IRA Investment
Initial: na   Subsequent: na

Maximum Fees
Load: none   12b-1: none
Other: none

Distributions
Income: monthly   Capital Gains: Dec

Exchange Options
Number Per Year: 6   Fee: none
Telephone: yes (money market fund available)

Services
auto exchange, auto invest, auto withdraw

Benham CA Tax-Free Short-Term (BCSTX)

1665 Charleston Rd.
Mountain View, CA 94043
(800) 321-8321, (415) 965-4222

Tax-Exempt Bond

PERFORMANCE

	3yr Annual	5yr Annual	10yr Annual	Bull	Bear
Return (%)	na	na	na	na	na
Differ from Category (+/-)	na	na	na	na	na

Total Risk	Standard Deviation	Category Risk	Risk Index	Avg Mat
na	na	na	na	3.5 yrs

	1993	1992	1991	1990	1989	1988	1987	1986	1985	1984
Return (%)	5.9	—	—	—	—	—	—	—	—	—
Differ from category (+/-)	-5.7	—	—	—	—	—	—	—	—	—

PER SHARE DATA

	1993	1992	1991	1990	1989	1988	1987	1986	1985	1984
Dividends, Net Income ($)	0.37	—	—	—	—	—	—	—	—	—
Distrib'ns, Cap Gain ($)	0.03	—	—	—	—	—	—	—	—	—
Net Asset Value ($)	10.35	—	—	—	—	—	—	—	—	—
Expense Ratio (%)	0.12	—	—	—	—	—	—	—	—	—
Net Income to Assets (%)	4.04	—	—	—	—	—	—	—	—	—
Portfolio Turnover (%)	29	—	—	—	—	—	—	—	—	—
Total Assets (Millions $)	125	—	—	—	—	—	—	—	—	—

PORTFOLIO (as of 2/28/93)

Portfolio Manager: G. David MacEwen - 1992

Investm't Category: Tax-Exempt Bond

Cap Gain	Asset Allocation
Cap & Income	Fund of Funds
✔ Income	Index
	Sector
✔ Domestic	Small Cap
Foreign	Socially Conscious
Country/Region	✔ State Specific

Portfolio: stocks 0%   bonds 100%
convertibles 0%   other 0%   cash 0%

Largest Holdings: general obligation 6%

Unrealized Net Capital Gains: 2% of portfolio value

SHAREHOLDER INFORMATION

Minimum Investment
Initial: $1,000   Subsequent: $100

Minimum IRA Investment
Initial: na   Subsequent: na

Maximum Fees
Load: none   12b-1: none
Other: none

Distributions
Income: monthly   Capital Gains: Dec

Exchange Options
Number Per Year: 6   Fee: none
Telephone: yes (money market fund available)

Services
auto exchange, auto invest, auto withdraw

Benham Equity Growth

(BEQGX)

Growth

1665 Charleston Rd.
Mountain View, CA 94043
(800) 321-8321, (415) 965-4222

PERFORMANCE

	3yr Annual	5yr Annual	10yr Annual	Bull	Bear
Return (%)	na	na	na	na	na
Differ from Category (+/-)	na	na	na	na	na

Total Risk	Standard Deviation	Category Risk	Risk Index	Beta
na	na	na	na	na

	1993	1992	1991	1990	1989	1988	1987	1986	1985	1984
Return (%)	11.4	4.1	—	—	—	—	—	—	—	—
Differ from category (+/-) . .	-1.8	-6.9	—	—	—	—	—	—	—	—

PER SHARE DATA

	1993	1992	1991	1990	1989	1988	1987	1986	1985	1984
Dividends, Net Income ($) .	0.23	0.32	—	—	—	—	—	—	—	—
Distrib'ns, Cap Gain ($) . . .	0.65	0.02	—	—	—	—	—	—	—	—
Net Asset Value ($)	12.12	11.68	—	—	—	—	—	—	—	—
Expense Ratio (%).	0.75	0.75	—	—	—	—	—	—	—	—
Net Income to Assets (%) . .	2.25	2.33	—	—	—	—	—	—	—	—
Portfolio Turnover (%)	na	114	—	—	—	—	—	—	—	—
Total Assets (Millions $)	96	74	—	—	—	—	—	—	—	—

PORTFOLIO (as of 6/30/93)

Portfolio Manager: Steve Colton - 1991

Investm't Category: Growth

✔ Cap Gain	Asset Allocation
Cap & Income	Fund of Funds
Income	Index
	Sector
✔ Domestic	Small Cap
Foreign	Socially Conscious
Country/Region	State Specific

Portfolio: stocks 100% bonds 0%
convertibles 0% other 0% cash 0%

Largest Holdings: consumer non-durables 29%, utilities 23%

Unrealized Net Capital Gains: 5% of portfolio value

SHAREHOLDER INFORMATION

Minimum Investment
Initial: $1,000   Subsequent: $100

Minimum IRA Investment
Initial: $100   Subsequent: $100

Maximum Fees
Load: none   12b-1: none
Other: none

Distributions
Income: quarterly   Capital Gains: Dec

Exchange Options
Number Per Year: 6   Fee: none
Telephone: yes (money market fund available)

Services
IRA, other pension, auto exchange, auto invest, auto withdraw

Benham European Gov't Bond (BEGBX)

1665 Charleston Rd.
Mountain View, CA 94043
(800) 321-8321, (415) 965-4222

International Bond

PERFORMANCE

	3yr Annual	5yr Annual	10yr Annual	Bull	Bear
Return (%)	na	na	na	na	na
Differ from Category (+/-)	na	na	na	na	na

Total Risk	Standard Deviation	Category Risk	Risk Index	Avg Mat
na	na	na	na	10.6 yrs

	1993	1992	1991	1990	1989	1988	1987	1986	1985	1984
Return (%)	11.6	—	—	—	—	—	—	—	—	—
Differ from category (+/-) . . .	-1.1	—	—	—	—	—	—	—	—	—

PER SHARE DATA

	1993	1992	1991	1990	1989	1988	1987	1986	1985	1984
Dividends, Net Income ($) .	0.11	—	—	—	—	—	—	—	—	—
Distrib'ns, Cap Gain ($) . . .	0.26	—	—	—	—	—	—	—	—	—
Net Asset Value ($)	10.82	—	—	—	—	—	—	—	—	—
Expense Ratio (%)	0.87	—	—	—	—	—	—	—	—	—
Net Income to Assets (%) .	6.70	—	—	—	—	—	—	—	—	—
Portfolio Turnover (%)	230	—	—	—	—	—	—	—	—	—
Total Assets (Millions $)	354	—	—	—	—	—	—	—	—	—

PORTFOLIO (as of 6/30/93)

Portfolio Manager: Jeff Tyler - 1992

Investm't Category: International Bond

Cap Gain	Asset Allocation
Cap & Income	Fund of Funds
✔ Income	Index
	Sector
Domestic	Small Cap
✔ Foreign	Socially Conscious
✔ Country/Region	State Specific

Portfolio: stocks 0% bonds 100%
convertibles 0% other 0% cash 0%

Largest Holdings: Germany 30%, Italy 15%

Unrealized Net Capital Gains: -1% of portfolio value

SHAREHOLDER INFORMATION

Minimum Investment
Initial: $1,000 Subsequent: $100

Minimum IRA Investment
Initial: $100 Subsequent: $25

Maximum Fees
Load: none 12b-1: none
Other: none

Distributions
Income: quarterly Capital Gains: Dec

Exchange Options
Number Per Year: 6 Fee: none
Telephone: yes (money market fund available)

Services
IRA, other pension, auto exchange, auto invest, auto withdraw

Benham GNMA Income
(BGNMX)

Mortgage-Backed Bond

1665 Charleston Rd.
Mountain View, CA 94043
(800) 321-8321, (415) 965-4222

PERFORMANCE

	3yr Annual	5yr Annual	10yr Annual	Bull	Bear
Return (%)	9.8	10.7	na	39.3	4.8
Differ from Category (+/-)	0.6 high	0.8 high	na	2.6 high	0.2 av

Total Risk	Standard Deviation	Category Risk	Risk Index	Avg Mat
low	2.6%	blw av	1.0	28.3 yrs

	1993	1992	1991	1990	1989	1988	1987	1986	1985	1984
Return (%)	6.5	7.6	15.5	10.1	13.8	8.5	2.7	11.3	—	—
Differ from category (+/-) ..	-0.3	1.5	1.1	0.6	1.5	1.5	0.6	0.1	—	—

PER SHARE DATA

	1993	1992	1991	1990	1989	1988	1987	1986	1985	1984
Dividends, Net Income ($) .	0.69	0.81	0.86	0.89	0.90	0.88	0.87	1.01	—	—
Distrib'ns, Cap Gain ($) ...	0.01	0.00	0.00	0.00	0.00	0.00	0.06	0.00	—	—
Net Asset Value ($)	10.76	10.78	10.80	10.15	10.08	9.69	9.76	10.44	—	—
Expense Ratio (%)........	0.56	0.62	0.72	0.75	0.75	0.73	0.74	0.29	—	—
Net Income to Assets (%)..	7.31	8.18	8.85	9.04	9.11	8.94	8.79	10.52	—	—
Portfolio Turnover (%)	70	97	207	433	497	497	566	264	—	—
Total Assets (Millions $) ..	1,261	724	409	290	253	259	393	169	—	—

PORTFOLIO (as of 3/31/93)

Portfolio Manager: Randall Merk - 1987

Investm't Category: Mortgage-Backed Bond

Cap Gain	Asset Allocation
Cap & Income	Fund of Funds
✔ Income	Index
	Sector
✔ Domestic	Small Cap
Foreign	Socially Conscious
Country/Region	State Specific

Portfolio: stocks 0%   bonds 93%
convertibles 0%   other 0%   cash 7%

Largest Holdings: mortgage-backed 89%, U.S. government 4%

Unrealized Net Capital Gains: 3% of portfolio value

SHAREHOLDER INFORMATION

Minimum Investment
Initial: $1,000   Subsequent: $100

Minimum IRA Investment
Initial: $100   Subsequent: $25

Maximum Fees
Load: none   12b-1: none
Other: none

Distributions
Income: monthly   Capital Gains: Dec

Exchange Options
Number Per Year: 6   Fee: none
Telephone: yes (money market fund available)

Services
IRA, other pension, auto exchange, auto invest, auto withdraw

Benham Gold Equities Index (BGEIX)

1665 Charleston Rd.
Mountain View, CA 94043
(800) 321-8321, (415) 965-4222

Gold

Benham Income & Growth (BIGRX)

Growth & Income

1665 Charleston Rd.
Mountain View, CA 94043
(800) 321-8321, (415) 965-4222

PERFORMANCE

	3yr Annual	5yr Annual	10yr Annual	Bull	Bear
Return (%)	na	na	na	na	na
Differ from Category (+/-)	na	na	na	na	na

Total Risk	Standard Deviation	Category Risk	Risk Index	Beta
na	na	na	na	na

	1993	1992	1991	1990	1989	1988	1987	1986	1985	1984
Return (%)	11.3	7.8	—	—	—	—	—	—	—	—
Differ from category (+/-) . .	-1.3	-2.2	—	—	—	—	—	—	—	—

PER SHARE DATA

	1993	1992	1991	1990	1989	1988	1987	1986	1985	1984
Dividends, Net Income ($) .	0.42	0.41	—	—	—	—	—	—	—	—
Distrib'ns, Cap Gain ($) . . .	0.18	0.03	—	—	—	—	—	—	—	—
Net Asset Value ($)	15.08	14.11	—	—	—	—	—	—	—	—
Expense Ratio (%)	0.75	0.75	—	—	—	—	—	—	—	—
Net Income to Assets (%) . .	3.02	3.16	—	—	—	—	—	—	—	—
Portfolio Turnover (%)	na	63	—	—	—	—	—	—	—	—
Total Assets (Millions $) . . .	232	141	—	—	—	—	—	—	—	—

PORTFOLIO (as of 6/30/93)

Portfolio Manager: Steve Colton - 1991

Investm't Category: Growth & Income

Cap Gain	Asset Allocation
✔ Cap & Income	Fund of Funds
Income	Index
	Sector
✔ Domestic	Small Cap
Foreign	Socially Conscious
Country/Region	State Specific

Portfolio:	stocks 99%	bonds 0%
convertibles 0%	other 0%	cash 1%

Largest Holdings: utilities 27%, consumer nondurables 24%

Unrealized Net Capital Gains: 11% of portfolio value

SHAREHOLDER INFORMATION

Minimum Investment
Initial: $1,000   Subsequent: $100

Minimum IRA Investment
Initial: $100   Subsequent: $25

Maximum Fees
Load: none   12b-1: none
Other: none

Distributions
Income: monthly   Capital Gains: Dec

Exchange Options
Number Per Year: 6   Fee: none
Telephone: yes (money market fund available)

Services
IRA, other pension, auto exchange, auto invest, auto withdraw

Benham Long-Term Treasury & Agency (BLAGX)

1665 Charleston Rd.
Mountain View, CA 94043
(800) 321-8321, (415) 965-4222

Government Bond

PERFORMANCE

	3yr Annual	5yr Annual	10yr Annual	Bull	Bear
Return (%)	na	na	na	na	na
Differ from Category (+/-)	na	na	na	na	na

Total Risk	Standard Deviation	Category Risk	Risk Index	Avg Mat
na	na	na	na	26.9 yrs

	1993	1992	1991	1990	1989	1988	1987	1986	1985	1984
Return (%)	17.6	—	—	—	—	—	—	—	—	—
Differ from category (+/-)	7.2	—	—	—	—	—	—	—	—	—

PER SHARE DATA

	1993	1992	1991	1990	1989	1988	1987	1986	1985	1984
Dividends, Net Income ($)	0.65	—	—	—	—	—	—	—	—	—
Distrib'ns, Cap Gain ($)	0.59	—	—	—	—	—	—	—	—	—
Net Asset Value ($)	10.22	—	—	—	—	—	—	—	—	—
Expense Ratio (%)	0.00	—	—	—	—	—	—	—	—	—
Net Income to Assets (%)	7.18	—	—	—	—	—	—	—	—	—
Portfolio Turnover (%)	56	—	—	—	—	—	—	—	—	—
Total Assets (Millions $)	23	—	—	—	—	—	—	—	—	—

PORTFOLIO (as of 3/31/93)

Portfolio Manager: David Schroeder - 1992

Investm't Category: Government Bond

Cap Gain	Asset Allocation
Cap & Income	Fund of Funds
✔ Income	Index
	Sector
✔ Domestic	Small Cap
Foreign	Socially Conscious
Country/Region	State Specific

Portfolio: stocks 0%   bonds 100%
convertibles 0%   other 0%   cash 0%

Largest Holdings: U.S. government & agencies 100%

Unrealized Net Capital Gains: 4% of portfolio value

SHAREHOLDER INFORMATION

Minimum Investment
Initial: $1,000   Subsequent: $100

Minimum IRA Investment
Initial: $100   Subsequent: $25

Maximum Fees
Load: none   12b-1: none
Other: none

Distributions
Income: monthly   Capital Gains: Dec

Exchange Options
Number Per Year: 6   Fee: none
Telephone: yes (money market fund available)

Services
IRA, other pension, auto exchange, auto invest, auto withdraw

Benham Nat'l Tax-Free Interm Term (BNTIX)

1665 Charleston Rd.
Mountain View, CA 94043
(800) 321-8321, (415) 965-4222

Tax-Exempt Bond

PERFORMANCE

	3yr Annual	5yr Annual	10yr Annual	Bull	Bear
Return (%)	9.6	8.8	na	36.6	3.0
Differ from Category (+/-)	-0.6 blw av	-0.4 blw av	na	-3.5 blw av	0.6 abv av

Total Risk	Standard Deviation	Category Risk	Risk Index	Avg Mat
low	4.0%	blw av	1.0	7.5 yrs

	1993	1992	1991	1990	1989	1988	1987	1986	1985	1984
Return (%)	10.1	7.1	11.6	6.8	8.2	6.6	2.2	14.2	12.5	—
Differ from category (+/-) . .	-1.5	-1.2	0.3	0.5	-0.8	-3.5	3.4	-2.2	-4.8	—

PER SHARE DATA

	1993	1992	1991	1990	1989	1988	1987	1986	1985	1984
Dividends, Net Income ($) .	0.50	0.53	0.58	0.61	0.61	0.63	0.62	0.67	0.74	—
Distrib'ns, Cap Gain ($) . . .	0.11	0.10	0.11	0.00	0.00	0.00	0.00	0.00	0.00	—
Net Asset Value ($)	11.11	10.67	10.58	10.14	10.10	9.92	9.91	10.32	9.66	—
Expense Ratio (%)	0.72	0.65	0.50	0.50	0.50	0.50	0.50	0.27	0.00	—
Net Income to Assets (%) . .	4.81	5.38	5.97	6.12	6.36	6.34	6.27	7.41	8.26	—
Portfolio Turnover (%)	36	85	55	142	49	54	26	44	77	—
Total Assets (Millions $)	76	44	34	25	21	20	20	12	3	—

PORTFOLIO (as of 5/31/93)

Portfolio Manager: G. David MacEwen - 1991

Investm't Category: Tax-Exempt Bond

Cap Gain	Asset Allocation
Cap & Income	Fund of Funds
✔ Income	Index
	Sector
✔ Domestic	Small Cap
Foreign	Socially Conscious
Country/Region	State Specific

Portfolio: stocks 0% bonds 100%
convertibles 0% other 0% cash 0%

Largest Holdings: general obligation 27%

Unrealized Net Capital Gains: 4% of portfolio value

SHAREHOLDER INFORMATION

Minimum Investment
Initial: $1,000   Subsequent: $100

Minimum IRA Investment
Initial: na   Subsequent: na

Maximum Fees
Load: none   12b-1: none
Other: none

Distributions
Income: monthly   Capital Gains: Dec

Exchange Options
Number Per Year: 6   Fee: none
Telephone: yes (money market fund available)

Services
auto exchange, auto invest, auto withdraw

Benham Nat'l Tax-Free Long-Term (BTFLX)

1665 Charleston Rd.
Mountain View, CA 94043
(800) 321-8321, (415) 965-4222

Tax-Exempt Bond

PERFORMANCE

	3yr Annual	5yr Annual	10yr Annual	Bull	Bear
Return (%)	12.1	10.5	na	48.8	1.0
Differ from Category (+/-)	1.8 high	1.3 high	na	8.7 high	-1.3 low

Total Risk	Standard Deviation	Category Risk	Risk Index	Avg Mat
blw av	6.0%	high	1.5	20.8 yrs

	1993	1992	1991	1990	1989	1988	1987	1986	1985	1984
Return (%)	14.2	9.2	12.9	6.7	9.6	11.2	-6.7	18.7	19.1	—
Differ from category (+/-)	2.6	0.8	1.6	0.4	0.6	1.1	-5.5	2.3	1.8	—

PER SHARE DATA

	1993	1992	1991	1990	1989	1988	1987	1986	1985	1984
Dividends, Net Income ($)	0.62	0.64	0.68	0.72	0.73	0.76	0.80	0.88	0.96	—
Distrib'ns, Cap Gain ($)	0.24	0.29	0.23	0.09	0.04	0.00	0.00	0.00	0.00	—
Net Asset Value ($)	12.10	11.38	11.31	10.88	11.00	10.78	10.41	12.00	10.90	—
Expense Ratio (%)	0.72	0.65	0.50	0.50	0.50	0.50	0.50	0.26	0.00	—
Net Income to Assets (%)	5.40	6.00	6.57	6.58	7.14	7.27	7.11	8.61	9.70	—
Portfolio Turnover (%)	105	148	150	215	69	76	102	57	32	—
Total Assets (Millions $)	66	42	35	44	33	25	24	22	7	—

PORTFOLIO (as of 5/31/93)

Portfolio Manager: G. David MacEwen - 1991

Investm't Category: Tax-Exempt Bond

Cap Gain	Asset Allocation
Cap & Income	Fund of Funds
✔ Income	Index
	Sector
✔ Domestic	Small Cap
Foreign	Socially Conscious
Country/Region	State Specific

Portfolio: stocks 0%   bonds 100%
convertibles 0%   other 0%   cash 0%

Largest Holdings: general obligation 3%

Unrealized Net Capital Gains: 7% of portfolio value

SHAREHOLDER INFORMATION

Minimum Investment
Initial: $1,000   Subsequent: $100

Minimum IRA Investment
Initial: na   Subsequent: na

Maximum Fees
Load: none   12b-1: none
Other: none

Distributions
Income: monthly   Capital Gains: Dec

Exchange Options
Number Per Year: 6   Fee: none
Telephone: yes (money market fund available)

Services
auto exchange, auto invest, auto withdraw

Benham Short-Term Treasury & Agency (BSTAX)

1665 Charleston Rd.
Mountain View, CA 94043
(800) 321-8321, (415) 965-4222

Government Bond

PERFORMANCE

	3yr Annual	5yr Annual	10yr Annual	Bull	Bear
Return (%)	na	na	na	na	na
Differ from Category (+/-)	na	na	na	na	na

Total Risk	Standard Deviation	Category Risk	Risk Index	Avg Mat
na	na	na	na	1.8 yrs

	1993	1992	1991	1990	1989	1988	1987	1986	1985	1984
Return (%)	5.2	—	—	—	—	—	—	—	—	—
Differ from category (+/-)	-5.2	—	—	—	—	—	—	—	—	—

PER SHARE DATA

	1993	1992	1991	1990	1989	1988	1987	1986	1985	1984
Dividends, Net Income ($)	0.38	—	—	—	—	—	—	—	—	—
Distrib'ns, Cap Gain ($)	0.03	—	—	—	—	—	—	—	—	—
Net Asset Value ($)	10.00	—	—	—	—	—	—	—	—	—
Expense Ratio (%)	0.00	—	—	—	—	—	—	—	—	—
Net Income to Assets (%)	4.50	—	—	—	—	—	—	—	—	—
Portfolio Turnover (%)	157	—	—	—	—	—	—	—	—	—
Total Assets (Millions $)	24	—	—	—	—	—	—	—	—	—

PORTFOLIO (as of 3/31/93)

Portfolio Manager: David Schroeder - NA

Investm't Category: Government Bond

Cap Gain	Asset Allocation
Cap & Income	Fund of Funds
✔ Income	Index
	Sector
✔ Domestic	Small Cap
Foreign	Socially Conscious
Country/Region	State Specific

Portfolio: stocks 0%   bonds 100%
convertibles 0%   other 0%   cash 0%

Largest Holdings: U.S. government & agencies 100%

Unrealized Net Capital Gains: 1% of portfolio value

SHAREHOLDER INFORMATION

Minimum Investment
Initial: $1,000   Subsequent: $100

Minimum IRA Investment
Initial: $100   Subsequent: $25

Maximum Fees
Load: none   12b-1: none
Other: none

Distributions
Income: monthly   Capital Gains: Dec

Exchange Options
Number Per Year: 6   Fee: none
Telephone: yes (money market fund available)

Services
IRA, other pension, auto exchange, auto invest, auto withdraw

Benham Target Mat Trust—1995 (BTMFX)

1665 Charleston Rd.
Mountain View, CA 94043
(800) 321-8321, (415) 965-4222

Government Bond

PERFORMANCE

	3yr Annual	5yr Annual	10yr Annual	Bull	Bear
Return (%)	10.0	10.9	na	41.4	2.9
Differ from Category (+/-)	-0.8 av	0.5 abv av	na	-4.8 av	2.4 av

Total Risk	Standard Deviation	Category Risk	Risk Index	Avg Mat
low	3.6%	blw av	0.8	2.0 yrs

	1993	1992	1991	1990	1989	1988	1987	1986	1985	1984
Return (%)	6.9	7.3	16.1	9.2	15.3	7.8	-3.8	26.3	—	—
Differ from category (+/-). . .	-3.5	1.1	1.1	2.7	1.4	0.2	-2.0	7.2	—	—

PER SHARE DATA

	1993	1992	1991	1990	1989	1988	1987	1986	1985	1984
Dividends, Net Income ($).	0.00	0.00	0.00	0.00	0.00	0.00	0.00	0.00	—	—
Distrib'ns, Cap Gain ($) . . .	0.00	0.00	0.00	0.00	0.00	0.00	0.00	0.00	—	—
Net Asset Value ($)	94.57	88.43	82.40	70.94	64.96	56.33	52.22	54.33	—	—
Expense Ratio (%)	na	0.62	0.65	0.70	0.70	0.70	0.70	0.70	—	—
Net Income to Assets (%) . . .	na	6.39	7.35	7.74	7.95	8.09	7.70	7.29	—	—
Portfolio Turnover (%).	133	140	110	121	95	108	86	89	—	—
Total Assets (Millions $).	80	95	92	58	39	16	7	5	—	—

PORTFOLIO (as of 9/30/93)

Portfolio Manager: David Schroeder - 1990

Investm't Category: Government Bond

Cap Gain	Asset Allocation
Cap & Income	Fund of Funds
✔ Income	Index
	Sector
✔ Domestic	Small Cap
Foreign	Socially Conscious
Country/Region	State Specific

Portfolio: stocks 0%   bonds 100%
convertibles 0%   other 0%   cash 0%

Largest Holdings: U.S. government 100%

Unrealized Net Capital Gains: 3% of portfolio value

SHAREHOLDER INFORMATION

Minimum Investment
Initial: $1,000   Subsequent: $100

Minimum IRA Investment
Initial: $100   Subsequent: $25

Maximum Fees
Load: none   12b-1: none
Other: none

Distributions
Income: Dec   Capital Gains: Dec

Exchange Options
Number Per Year: 6   Fee: none
Telephone: yes (money market fund available)

Services
IRA, other pension, auto exchange, auto invest, auto withdraw

Benham Target Mat Trust—2000 (BTMTX)

1665 Charleston Rd.
Mountain View, CA 94043
(800) 321-8321, (415) 965-4222

Government Bond

PERFORMANCE

	3yr Annual	5yr Annual	10yr Annual	Bull	Bear
Return (%)	14.7	13.9	na	65.9	-3.1
Differ from Category (+/-)	3.9 high	3.5 high	na	19.7 high	-3.6 low

Total Risk	Standard Deviation	Category Risk	Risk Index	Avg Mat
av	7.0%	high	1.6	7.0 yrs

	1993	1992	1991	1990	1989	1988	1987	1986	1985	1984
Return (%)	15.4	8.4	20.6	6.3	19.8	11.4	-5.9	32.3	—	—
Differ from category (+/-) . . .	5.0	2.2	5.6	-0.2	5.9	3.8	-4.1	13.2	—	—

PER SHARE DATA

	1993	1992	1991	1990	1989	1988	1987	1986	1985	1984
Dividends, Net Income ($) .	0.00	0.00	0.00	0.00	0.00	0.00	0.00	0.00	—	—
Distrib'ns, Cap Gain ($) . . .	0.00	0.00	0.00	0.00	0.00	0.00	0.00	0.00	—	—
Net Asset Value ($)	71.53	61.95	57.11	47.33	44.52	37.16	33.33	35.44	—	—
Expense Ratio (%)	0.64	0.66	0.66	0.70	0.70	0.70	0.70	0.70	—	—
Net Income to Assets (%) . .	6.37	6.90	7.67	7.84	7.81	8.33	8.08	7.34	—	—
Portfolio Turnover (%)	76	93	67	79	49	163	73	39	—	—
Total Assets (Millions $) . . .	288	190	90	53	35	14	6	5	—	—

PORTFOLIO (as of 9/30/93)

Portfolio Manager: David Schroeder - 1990

Investm't Category: Government Bond

Cap Gain	Asset Allocation
Cap & Income	Fund of Funds
✔ Income	Index
	Sector
✔ Domestic	Small Cap
Foreign	Socially Conscious
Country/Region	State Specific

Portfolio: stocks 0% bonds 100%
convertibles 0% other 0% cash 0%

Largest Holdings: U.S. government 100%

Unrealized Net Capital Gains: 8% of portfolio value

SHAREHOLDER INFORMATION

Minimum Investment
Initial: $1,000   Subsequent: $100

Minimum IRA Investment
Initial: $100   Subsequent: $25

Maximum Fees
Load: none   12b-1: none
Other: none

Distributions
Income: Dec   Capital Gains: Dec

Exchange Options
Number Per Year: 6   Fee: none
Telephone: yes (money market fund available)

Services
IRA, other pension, auto exchange, auto invest, auto withdraw

Benham Target Mat Trust—2005 (BTFIX)

1665 Charleston Rd.
Mountain View, CA 94043
(800) 321-8321, (415) 965-4222

Government Bond

PERFORMANCE

	3yr Annual	5yr Annual	10yr Annual	Bull	Bear
Return (%)	17.3	15.7	na	82.2	-8.0
Differ from Category (+/-)	6.5 high	5.3 high	na	36.0 high	-8.5 low

Total Risk	Standard Deviation	Category Risk	Risk Index	Avg Mat
av	9.3%	high	2.2	11.9 yrs

	1993	1992	1991	1990	1989	1988	1987	1986	1985	1984
Return (%)	21.5	9.5	21.4	3.5	23.8	14.4	-10.3	42.2	—	—
Differ from category (+/-). .	11.1	3.3	6.4	-3.0	9.9	6.8	-8.5	23.1	—	—

PER SHARE DATA

	1993	1992	1991	1990	1989	1988	1987	1986	1985	1984
Dividends, Net Income ($).	0.00	0.00	0.00	0.00	0.00	0.00	0.00	0.00	—	—
Distrib'ns, Cap Gain ($) . . .	0.00	0.00	0.00	0.00	0.00	0.00	0.00	0.00	—	—
Net Asset Value ($)	50.57	41.60	37.97	31.26	30.18	24.36	21.28	23.74	—	—
Expense Ratio (%)	0.64	0.63	0.70	0.70	0.70	0.70	0.70	0.70	—	—
Net Income to Assets (%) .	6.76	7.27	7.80	7.93	7.66	8.44	8.31	7.25	—	—
Portfolio Turnover (%).	49	64	85	186	72	27	68	50	—	—
Total Assets (Millions $). . . .	130	169	161	46	25	9	4	3	—	—

PORTFOLIO (as of 9/30/93)

Portfolio Manager: David Schroeder - 1990

Investm't Category: Government Bond

Cap Gain	Asset Allocation
Cap & Income	Fund of Funds
✔ Income	Index
	Sector
✔ Domestic	Small Cap
Foreign	Socially Conscious
Country/Region	State Specific

Portfolio: stocks 0%   bonds 100%
convertibles 0%   other 0%   cash 0%

Largest Holdings: U.S. government 100%

Unrealized Net Capital Gains: 21% of portfolio value

SHAREHOLDER INFORMATION

Minimum Investment
Initial: $1,000   Subsequent: $100

Minimum IRA Investment
Initial: $100   Subsequent: $25

Maximum Fees
Load: none   12b-1: none
Other: none

Distributions
Income: Dec   Capital Gains: Dec

Exchange Options
Number Per Year: 6   Fee: none
Telephone: yes (money market fund available)

Services
IRA, other pension, auto exchange, auto invest, auto withdraw

Benham Target Mat Trust—2010 (BTTNX)

1665 Charleston Rd.
Mountain View, CA 94043
(800) 321-8321, (415) 965-4222

Government Bond

	3yr Annual	5yr Annual	10yr Annual	Bull	Bear
Return (%)	18.8	16.5	na	94.4	-13.4
Differ from Category (+/-)	8.0 high	6.1 high	na	48.2 high	-13.9 low

Total Risk	Standard Deviation	Category Risk	Risk Index	Avg Mat
av	10.7%	high	2.5	16.5 yrs

	1993	1992	1991	1990	1989	1988	1987	1986	1985	1984
Return (%)	26.2	9.7	21.0	0.2	28.0	15.7	-15.2	54.4	—	—
Differ from category (+/-) ..	15.8	3.5	6.0	-6.3	14.1	8.1	-13.4	35.3	—	—

	1993	1992	1991	1990	1989	1988	1987	1986	1985	1984
Dividends, Net Income ($) .	0.00	0.00	0.00	0.00	0.00	0.00	0.00	0.00	—	—
Distrib'ns, Cap Gain ($) ...	0.00	0.00	0.00	0.00	0.00	0.00	0.00	0.00	—	—
Net Asset Value ($)	37.29	29.53	26.90	22.22	22.16	17.31	14.96	17.65	—	—
Expense Ratio (%)........	0.70	0.70	0.70	0.70	0.70	0.70	0.70	0.70	—	—
Net Income to Assets (%)..	6.72	7.20	7.73	7.82	7.34	8.11	8.13	6.71	—	—
Portfolio Turnover (%)....	131	95	131	191	88	259	84	91	—	—
Total Assets (Millions $)	61	56	48	37	42	10	9	5	—	—

PORTFOLIO (as of 9/30/93)

Portfolio Manager: David Schroeder - 1990

Investm't Category: Government Bond

Cap Gain	Asset Allocation
Cap & Income	Fund of Funds
✔ Income	Index
	Sector
✔ Domestic	Small Cap
Foreign	Socially Conscious
Country/Region	State Specific

Portfolio: stocks 0% bonds 100%
convertibles 0% other 0% cash 0%

Largest Holdings: U.S. government 100%

Unrealized Net Capital Gains: 16% of portfolio value

Minimum Investment
Initial: $1,000   Subsequent: $100

Minimum IRA Investment
Initial: $100   Subsequent: $25

Maximum Fees
Load: none   12b-1: none
Other: none

Distributions
Income: Dec   Capital Gains: Dec

Exchange Options
Number Per Year: 6   Fee: none
Telephone: yes (money market fund available)

Services
IRA, other pension, auto exchange, auto invest, auto withdraw

Benham Target Mat Trust—2015 (BTFTX)

1665 Charleston Rd.
Mountain View, CA 94043
(800) 321-8321, (415) 965-4222

Government Bond

PERFORMANCE

	3yr Annual	5yr Annual	10yr Annual	Bull	Bear
Return (%)	19.8	17.3	na	104.0	-18.4
Differ from Category (+/-)	9.0 high	6.9 high	na	57.8 high	-18.9 low

Total Risk	Standard Deviation	Category Risk	Risk Index	Avg Mat
abv av	13.7%	high	3.2	21.7 yrs

	1993	1992	1991	1990	1989	1988	1987	1986	1985	1984
Return (%)	30.5	7.7	22.4	-3.3	33.4	11.0	-19.2	—	—	—
Differ from category (+/-). .	20.1	1.5	7.4	-9.8	19.5	3.4	-17.4	—	—	—

PER SHARE DATA

	1993	1992	1991	1990	1989	1988	1987	1986	1985	1984
Dividends, Net Income ($).	0.00	0.00	0.00	0.00	0.00	0.00	0.11	—	—	—
Distrib'ns, Cap Gain ($) . . .	0.00	0.00	0.00	0.00	0.00	0.00	0.00	—	—	—
Net Asset Value ($)	28.06	21.50	19.95	16.29	16.86	12.63	11.37	—	—	—
Expense Ratio (%)	0.64	0.62	0.61	0.70	0.70	0.70	0.70	—	—	—
Net Income to Assets (%) .	6.65	7.04	7.79	7.74	7.02	7.97	7.99	—	—	—
Portfolio Turnover (%).	138	103	40	81	48	188	509	—	—	—
Total Assets (Millions $).	76	131	222	296	234	12	2	—	—	—

PORTFOLIO (as of 9/30/93)

Portfolio Manager: David Schroeder - 1990

Investm't Category: Government Bond

Cap Gain	Asset Allocation
Cap & Income	Fund of Funds
✔ Income	Index
	Sector
✔ Domestic	Small Cap
Foreign	Socially Conscious
Country/Region	State Specific

Portfolio: stocks 0%   bonds 100%
convertibles 0%   other 0%   cash 0%

Largest Holdings: U.S. government 100%

Unrealized Net Capital Gains: 23% of portfolio value

SHAREHOLDER INFORMATION

Minimum Investment
Initial: $1,000   Subsequent: $100

Minimum IRA Investment
Initial: $100   Subsequent: $25

Maximum Fees
Load: none   12b-1: none
Other: none

Distributions
Income: Dec   Capital Gains: Dec

Exchange Options
Number Per Year: 6   Fee: none
Telephone: yes (money market fund available)

Services
IRA, other pension, auto exchange, auto invest, auto withdraw

Benham Target Mat Trust—2020 (BTTTX)

1665 Charleston Rd.
Mountain View, CA 94043
(800) 321-8321, (415) 965-4222

Government Bond

PERFORMANCE

	3yr Annual	5yr Annual	10yr Annual	Bull	Bear
Return (%)	19.9	na	na	105.1	-19.7
Differ from Category (+/-)	9.1 high	na	na	58.9 high	-20.2 low

Total Risk	Standard Deviation	Category Risk	Risk Index	Avg Mat
high	16.0%	high	3.8	26.5 yrs

	1993	1992	1991	1990	1989	1988	1987	1986	1985	1984
Return (%)	35.6	8.3	17.3	-4.5	—	—	—	—	—	—
Differ from category (+/-) . .	25.2	2.1	2.3	-11.0	—	—	—	—	—	—

PER SHARE DATA

	1993	1992	1991	1990	1989	1988	1987	1986	1985	1984
Dividends, Net Income ($) .	0.00	0.00	0.00	0.00	—	—	—	—	—	—
Distrib'ns, Cap Gain ($) . . .	0.00	0.00	0.00	0.00	—	—	—	—	—	—
Net Asset Value ($)	19.76	14.57	13.45	11.46	—	—	—	—	—	—
Expense Ratio (%).	0.70	0.66	0.67	0.70	—	—	—	—	—	—
Net Income to Assets (%) . .	6.67	7.19	7.50	7.79	—	—	—	—	—	—
Portfolio Turnover (%)	178	144	151	189	—	—	—	—	—	—
Total Assets (Millions $)	48	42	88	53	—	—	—	—	—	—

PORTFOLIO (as of 9/30/93)

Portfolio Manager: David Schroeder - 1990

Investm't Category: Government Bond

Cap Gain	Asset Allocation
Cap & Income	Fund of Funds
✔ Income	Index
	Sector
✔ Domestic	Small Cap
Foreign	Socially Conscious
Country/Region	State Specific

Portfolio: stocks 0% bonds 100%
convertibles 0% other 0% cash 0%

Largest Holdings: U.S. government 100%

Unrealized Net Capital Gains: 20% of portfolio value

SHAREHOLDER INFORMATION

Minimum Investment
Initial: $1,000   Subsequent: $100

Minimum IRA Investment
Initial: $100   Subsequent: $25

Maximum Fees
Load: none   12b-1: none
Other: none

Distributions
Income: Dec   Capital Gains: Dec

Exchange Options
Number Per Year: 6   Fee: none
Telephone: yes (money market fund available)

Services
IRA, other pension, auto exchange, auto invest, auto withdraw

Benham Treasury Note
(CPTNX)

Government Bond

1665 Charleston Rd.
Mountain View, CA 94043
(800) 321-8321, (415) 965-4222

	3yr Annual	5yr Annual	10yr Annual	Bull	Bear
Return (%)	9.3	9.8	na	36.3	4.7
Differ from Category (+/-)	-1.5 blw av	-0.6 av	na	-9.9 blw av	4.2 abv av

Total Risk	Standard Deviation	Category Risk	Risk Index	Avg Mat
low	3.1%	blw av	0.7	3.9 yrs

	1993	1992	1991	1990	1989	1988	1987	1986	1985	1984
Return (%)	7.9	6.5	13.7	9.2	11.9	5.2	-1.0	—	—	—
Differ from category (+/-) . . .	-2.5	0.3	-1.3	2.7	-2.0	-2.4	0.8	—	—	—

PER SHARE DATA

	1993	1992	1991	1990	1989	1988	1987	1986	1985	1984
Dividends, Net Income ($) .	0.48	0.59	0.71	0.75	0.77	0.74	0.73	—	—	—
Distrib'ns, Cap Gain ($) . . .	0.27	0.47	0.00	0.00	0.00	0.00	0.18	—	—	—
Net Asset Value ($)	10.51	10.46	10.85	10.22	10.09	9.74	9.97	—	—	—
Expense Ratio (%)	0.53	0.59	0.73	0.75	0.75	0.75	0.93	—	—	—
Net Income to Assets (%) .	5.18	6.55	7.49	7.66	7.67	7.36	6.26	—	—	—
Portfolio Turnover (%)	299	149	70	217	386	465	396	—	—	—
Total Assets (Millions $)	387	303	159	97	72	54	43	—	—	—

PORTFOLIO (as of 3/31/93)

Portfolio Manager: Jeff Tyler - 1988

Investm't Category: Government Bond

Cap Gain	Asset Allocation
Cap & Income	Fund of Funds
✔ Income	Index
	Sector
✔ Domestic	Small Cap
Foreign	Socially Conscious
Country/Region	State Specific

Portfolio: stocks 0% bonds 100%
convertibles 0% other 0% cash 0%

Largest Holdings: U.S. government 100%

Unrealized Net Capital Gains: 2% of portfolio value

SHAREHOLDER INFORMATION

Minimum Investment
Initial: $1,000   Subsequent: $100

Minimum IRA Investment
Initial: $100   Subsequent: $25

Maximum Fees
Load: none   12b-1: none
Other: none

Distributions
Income: monthly   Capital Gains: Dec

Exchange Options
Number Per Year: 6   Fee: none
Telephone: yes (money market fund available)

Services
IRA, other pension, auto exchange, auto invest, auto withdraw

Benham Utilities Income

(BULIX)

Growth & Income

1665 Charleston Rd.
Mountain View, CA 94043
(800) 321-8321, (415) 965-4222

fund in existence since 3/3/93

PERFORMANCE

	3yr Annual	5yr Annual	10yr Annual	Bull	Bear
Return (%)	na	na	na	na	na
Differ from Category (+/-)	na	na	na	na	na

Total Risk	Standard Deviation	Category Risk	Risk Index	Beta
na	na	na	na	na

	1993	1992	1991	1990	1989	1988	1987	1986	1985	1984
Return (%)	—	—	—	—	—	—	—	—	—	—
Differ from category (+/-) ...	—	—	—	—	—	—	—	—	—	—

PER SHARE DATA

	1993	1992	1991	1990	1989	1988	1987	1986	1985	1984
Dividends, Net Income ($)	0.34	—	—	—	—	—	—	—	—	—
Distrib'ns, Cap Gain ($)	0.07	—	—	—	—	—	—	—	—	—
Net Asset Value ($)	10.24	—	—	—	—	—	—	—	—	—
Expense Ratio (%)	0.06	—	—	—	—	—	—	—	—	—
Net Income to Assets (%)	5.01	—	—	—	—	—	—	—	—	—
Portfolio Turnover (%)	6	—	—	—	—	—	—	—	—	—
Total Assets (Millions $)	188	—	—	—	—	—	—	—	—	—

PORTFOLIO (as of 6/30/93)

Portfolio Manager: Steve Colton - 1993

Investm't Category: Growth & Income

Cap Gain	Asset Allocation
✔ Cap & Income	Fund of Funds
Income	Index
	Sector
✔ Domestic	Small Cap
Foreign	Socially Conscious
Country/Region	State Specific

Portfolio: stocks 82% bonds 12%
convertibles 0% other 0% cash 6%

Largest Holdings: electric utilities 79%, telephone utilities 30%

Unrealized Net Capital Gains: 2% of portfolio value

SHAREHOLDER INFORMATION

Minimum Investment
Initial: $1,000 Subsequent: $100

Minimum IRA Investment
Initial: $100 Subsequent: $25

Maximum Fees
Load: none 12b-1: none
Other: none

Distributions
Income: monthly Capital Gains: Dec

Exchange Options
Number Per Year: 6 Fee: none
Telephone: yes (money market fund available)

Services
IRA, other pension, auto exchange, auto invest, auto withdraw

Guide to Low-Load Mutual Funds

Berger One Hundred
(BEONX)

P.O. Box 5005
Denver, CO 80217
(800) 333-1001, (303) 329-0200

Aggressive Growth

PERFORMANCE

	3yr Annual	5yr Annual	10yr Annual	Bull	Bear
Return (%)	35.4	28.3	17.3	180.8	-16.4
Differ from Category (+/-)	10.0 high	10.1 high	5.4 high	55.8 high	-1.4 av

Total Risk	Standard Deviation	Category Risk	Risk Index	Beta
high	18.8%	abv av	1.2	1.3

	1993	1992	1991	1990	1989	1988	1987	1986	1985	1984
Return (%)............	21.1	8.5	88.8	-5.4	48.2	1.6	15.6	20.0	25.8	-20.1
Differ from category (+/-)...	2.1	-1.9	36.4	0.8	21.2	-13.6	19.0	10.6	-5.2	-10.7

PER SHARE DATA

	1993	1992	1991	1990	1989	1988	1987	1986	1985	1984
Dividends, Net Income ($).	0.00	0.00	0.00	0.00	0.00	0.00	0.00	0.00	0.00	0.11
Distrib'ns, Cap Gain ($) ...	0.00	0.00	0.17	0.58	0.88	0.07	1.58	0.38	0.00	0.00
Net Asset Value ($)	16.81	13.87	12.78	6.87	7.98	5.99	5.97	6.57	5.79	4.60
Expense Ratio (%)	1.69	1.89	2.24	2.13	1.62	1.72	1.61	1.71	2.00	1.90
Net Income to Assets (%) .	-1.00	-0.75	-1.06	-0.71	-0.54	-0.57	-0.27	-0.47	-0.59	1.95
Portfolio Turnover (%)......	74	51	78	145	83	166	106	122	130	272
Total Assets (Millions $)..	1,610	384	77	13	14	11	12	10	8	9

PORTFOLIO (as of 9/30/93)

Portfolio Manager: William Berger - 1974, Rodney Linafelter - 1990

Investm't Category: Aggressive Growth

✔ Cap Gain	Asset Allocation
Cap & Income	Fund of Funds
Income	Index
	Sector
✔ Domestic	Small Cap
✔ Foreign	Socially Conscious
Country/Region	State Specific

Portfolio: stocks 85% bonds 0%
convertibles 0% other 0% cash 15%

Largest Holdings: medical—health maintenance organizations 6%, telecomm. equip. 5%

Unrealized Net Capital Gains: 22% of portfolio value

SHAREHOLDER INFORMATION

Minimum Investment
Initial: $250   Subsequent: $50

Minimum IRA Investment
Initial: $250   Subsequent: $50

Maximum Fees
Load: none   12b-1: 0.75%
Other: none

Distributions
Income: Dec   Capital Gains: Dec

Exchange Options
Number Per Year: 4   Fee: none
Telephone: yes (money market fund available)

Services
IRA, other pension, auto invest, auto withdraw

Berger One Hundred & One (BEOOX)

P.O. Box 5005
Denver, CO 80217
(800) 333-1001, (303) 329-0200

Growth & Income

PERFORMANCE

	3yr Annual	5yr Annual	10yr Annual	Bull	Bear
Return (%)	27.7	18.2	13.3	130.1	-16.6
Differ from Category (+/-)	11.3 high	5.7 high	0.8 av	60.0 high	-5.0 low

Total Risk	Standard Deviation	Category Risk	Risk Index	Beta
abv av	13.4%	high	1.6	1.0

	1993	1992	1991	1990	1989	1988	1987	1986	1985	1984
Return (%)	23.5	4.8	60.9	-7.9	20.2	5.3	-2.8	15.1	29.1	-0.2
Differ from category (+/-) ..	10.9	-5.2	33.2	-2.3	-1.4	-11.5	-3.2	-0.1	3.7	-6.4

PER SHARE DATA

	1993	1992	1991	1990	1989	1988	1987	1986	1985	1984
Dividends, Net Income ($) .	0.08	0.04	0.23	0.11	0.23	0.35	0.40	0.29	0.18	0.28
Distrib'ns, Cap Gain ($) ...	0.00	0.00	0.74	0.00	0.00	0.00	0.68	1.50	0.14	0.00
Net Asset Value ($)	11.92	9.72	9.32	6.47	7.16	6.16	6.19	7.49	8.08	6.54
Expense Ratio (%)........	2.10	2.56	2.66	2.48	2.00	2.00	1.79	1.96	2.00	2.00
Net Income to Assets (%)..	1.05	1.05	1.99	1.74	5.09	3.48	4.04	3.65	2.42	4.24
Portfolio Turnover (%).....	62	42	143	139	132	159	241	187	166	267
Total Assets (Millions $) ...	183	33	4	4	2	2	3	3	2	1

PORTFOLIO (as of 9/30/93)

Portfolio Manager: William Berger - 1974,
Rodney Linafelter - 1990

Investm't Category: Growth & Income
  Cap Gain   Asset Allocation
✔ Cap & Income   Fund of Funds
  Income   Index
               Sector
✔ Domestic   Small Cap
✔ Foreign   Socially Conscious
  Country/Region State Specific

Portfolio: stocks 60%   bonds 1%
convertibles 21%   other 0%   cash 18%

Largest Holdings: diversified operations 6%,
telecommunications services 5%

Unrealized Net Capital Gains: 12% of portfolio value

SHAREHOLDER INFORMATION

Minimum Investment
Initial: $250   Subsequent: $50

Minimum IRA Investment
Initial: $250   Subsequent: $50

Maximum Fees
Load: none   12b-1: 0.75%
Other: none

Distributions
Income: quarterly   Capital Gains: Dec

Exchange Options
Number Per Year: 4   Fee: none
Telephone: yes (money market fund available)

Services
IRA, other pension, auto invest, auto withdraw

Bernstein CA Muni Port
(SNCAX)
Tax-Exempt Bond

767 Fifth Ave.
New York, NY 10153
(212) 756-4097

	3yr Annual	5yr Annual	10yr Annual	Bull	Bear
Return (%)	8.1	na	na	31.3	na
Differ from Category (+/-)	-2.2 low	na	na	-8.8 low	na

Total Risk	Standard Deviation	Category Risk	Risk Index	Avg Mat
low	3.4%	low	0.8	6.8 yrs

	1993	1992	1991	1990	1989	1988	1987	1986	1985	1984
Return (%)	8.1	6.8	9.3	—	—	—	—	—	—	—
Differ from category (+/-). . .	-3.5	-1.5	-1.8	—	—	—	—	—	—	—

	1993	1992	1991	1990	1989	1988	1987	1986	1985	1984
Dividends, Net Income ($).	0.57	0.64	0.67	—	—	—	—	—	—	—
Distrib'ns, Cap Gain ($) . . .	0.02	0.07	0.00	—	—	—	—	—	—	—
Net Asset Value ($)	13.78	13.32	13.17	—	—	—	—	—	—	—
Expense Ratio (%)	0.73	0.77	0.79	—	—	—	—	—	—	—
Net Income to Assets (%) .	4.36	4.96	5.40	—	—	—	—	—	—	—
Portfolio Turnover (%).	23	53	49	—	—	—	—	—	—	—
Total Assets (Millions $). . . .	161	83	50	—	—	—	—	—	—	—

Portfolio Manager: committee

Investm't Category: Tax-Exempt Bond

Cap Gain	Asset Allocation
Cap & Income	Fund of Funds
✔ Income	Index
	Sector
✔ Domestic	Small Cap
Foreign	Socially Conscious
Country/Region	✔ State Specific

Portfolio: stocks 0% bonds 94%
convertibles 0% other 0% cash 6%

Largest Holdings: general obligation 10%

Unrealized Net Capital Gains: 3% of portfolio value

Minimum Investment
Initial: $25,000   Subsequent: $5,000

Minimum IRA Investment
Initial: na   Subsequent: na

Maximum Fees
Load: none   12b-1: none
Other: none

Distributions
Income: monthly   Capital Gains: Dec

Exchange Options
Number Per Year: no limit   Fee: none
Telephone: yes (money market fund not available)

Services
auto withdraw

Bernstein Diversified Muni Port (SNDPX)

767 Fifth Ave.
New York, NY 10153
(212) 756-4097

Tax-Exempt Bond

PERFORMANCE

	3yr Annual	5yr Annual	10yr Annual	Bull	Bear
Return (%)	8.3	na	na	31.7	3.1
Differ from Category (+/-)	-2.0 low	na	na	-8.4 low	0.8 abv av

Total Risk	Standard Deviation	Category Risk	Risk Index	Avg Mat
low	3.2%	low	0.8	6.9 yrs

	1993	1992	1991	1990	1989	1988	1987	1986	1985	1984
Return (%)	8.4	6.5	10.1	6.8	—	—	—	—	—	—
Differ from category (+/-) . .	-3.2	-1.8	-1.2	0.5	—	—	—	—	—	—

PER SHARE DATA

	1993	1992	1991	1990	1989	1988	1987	1986	1985	1984
Dividends, Net Income ($) .	0.61	0.69	0.72	0.73	—	—	—	—	—	—
Distrib'ns, Cap Gain ($) . . .	0.07	0.10	0.03	0.01	—	—	—	—	—	—
Net Asset Value ($)	13.70	13.29	13.25	12.75	—	—	—	—	—	—
Expense Ratio (%)	0.69	0.68	0.71	0.75	—	—	—	—	—	—
Net Income to Assets (%) . .	4.64	5.33	5.69	5.83	—	—	—	—	—	—
Portfolio Turnover (%)	34	48	34	47	—	—	—	—	—	—
Total Assets (Millions $) . . .	480	302	210	158	—	—	—	—	—	—

PORTFOLIO (as of 9/30/93)

Portfolio Manager: committee

Investm't Category: Tax-Exempt Bond

Cap Gain	Asset Allocation
Cap & Income	Fund of Funds
✔ Income	Index
	Sector
✔ Domestic	Small Cap
Foreign	Socially Conscious
Country/Region	State Specific

Portfolio: stocks 0% bonds 96%
convertibles 0% other 0% cash 4%

Largest Holdings: general obligation 22%

Unrealized Net Capital Gains: 3% of portfolio value

SHAREHOLDER INFORMATION

Minimum Investment
Initial: $25,000   Subsequent: $5,000

Minimum IRA Investment
Initial: na   Subsequent: na

Maximum Fees
Load: none   12b-1: none
Other: none

Distributions
Income: monthly   Capital Gains: Dec

Exchange Options
Number Per Year: no limit   Fee: none
Telephone: yes (money market fund not available)

Services
auto withdraw

Bernstein Gov't Short Duration (SNGSX)

767 Fifth Ave.
New York, NY 10153
(212) 756-4097

Government Bond

PERFORMANCE

	3yr Annual	5yr Annual	10yr Annual	Bull	Bear
Return (%)	7.0	7.9	na	26.6	5.6
Differ from Category (+/-)	-3.8 low	-2.5 low	na	-19.6 low	5.1 high

Total Risk	Standard Deviation	Category Risk	Risk Index	Avg Mat
low	1.7%	low	0.4	4.1 yrs

	1993	1992	1991	1990	1989	1988	1987	1986	1985	1984
Return (%)	4.6	5.3	11.2	8.9	9.3	—	—	—	—	—
Differ from category (+/-). . .	-5.8	-0.8	-3.8	2.4	-4.6	—	—	—	—	—

PER SHARE DATA

	1993	1992	1991	1990	1989	1988	1987	1986	1985	1984
Dividends, Net Income ($).	0.41	0.59	0.80	0.95	0.95	—	—	—	—	—
Distrib'ns, Cap Gain ($) . . .	0.14	0.46	0.20	0.05	0.08	—	—	—	—	—
Net Asset Value ($)	12.66	12.65	13.03	12.67	12.60	—	—	—	—	—
Expense Ratio (%)	0.68	0.68	0.70	0.72	0.85	—	—	—	—	—
Net Income to Assets (%) .	3.40	5.02	6.67	7.52	7.82	—	—	—	—	—
Portfolio Turnover (%).	130	221	176	171	141	—	—	—	—	—
Total Assets (Millions $). . . .	189	255	212	160	138	—	—	—	—	—

PORTFOLIO (as of 9/30/93)

Portfolio Manager: committee

Investm't Category: Government Bond

Cap Gain	Asset Allocation
Cap & Income	Fund of Funds
✔ Income	Index
	Sector
✔ Domestic	Small Cap
✔ Foreign	Socially Conscious
Country/Region	State Specific

Portfolio: stocks 0% bonds 100%
convertibles 0% other 0% cash 0%

Largest Holdings: U. S. government 95%

Unrealized Net Capital Gains: 1% of portfolio value

SHAREHOLDER INFORMATION

Minimum Investment
Initial: $25,000   Subsequent: $5,000

Minimum IRA Investment
Initial: $25,000   Subsequent: $5,000

Maximum Fees
Load: none   12b-1: none
Other: none

Distributions
Income: monthly   Capital Gains: Dec

Exchange Options
Number Per Year: no limit   Fee: none
Telephone: yes (money market fund not available)

Services
IRA, other pension, auto withdraw

Bernstein Int'l Value

(SNIVX)

International Stock

767 Fifth Ave.
New York, NY 10153
(212) 756-4097

PERFORMANCE

	3yr Annual	5yr Annual	10yr Annual	Bull	Bear
Return (%)	na	na	na	na	na
Differ from Category (+/-)	na	na	na	na	na

Total Risk	Standard Deviation	Category Risk	Risk Index	Beta
na	na	na	na	na

	1993	1992	1991	1990	1989	1988	1987	1986	1985	1984
Return (%)	34.5	—	—	—	—	—	—	—	—	—
Differ from category (+/-) . .	-4.0	—	—	—	—	—	—	—	—	—

PER SHARE DATA

	1993	1992	1991	1990	1989	1988	1987	1986	1985	1984
Dividends, Net Income ($) .	0.01	—	—	—	—	—	—	—	—	—
Distrib'ns, Cap Gain ($) . . .	0.11	—	—	—	—	—	—	—	—	—
Net Asset Value ($)	15.59	—	—	—	—	—	—	—	—	—
Expense Ratio (%)	1.53	—	—	—	—	—	—	—	—	—
Net Income to Assets (%) . .	1.27	—	—	—	—	—	—	—	—	—
Portfolio Turnover (%)	21	—	—	—	—	—	—	—	—	—
Total Assets (Millions $) . . .	681	—	—	—	—	—	—	—	—	—

PORTFOLIO (as of 9/30/93)

Portfolio Manager: committee

Investm't Category: International Stock

✔ Cap Gain	Asset Allocation
Cap & Income	Fund of Funds
Income	Index
	Sector
Domestic	Small Cap
✔ Foreign	Socially Conscious
Country/Region	State Specific

Portfolio: stocks 98% bonds 0%
convertibles 0% other 0% cash 2%

Largest Holdings: Japan 37%, Germany 17%

Unrealized Net Capital Gains: 9% of portfolio value

SHAREHOLDER INFORMATION

Minimum Investment
Initial: $25,000   Subsequent: $5,000

Minimum IRA Investment
Initial: $25,000   Subsequent: $5,000

Maximum Fees
Load: none   12b-1: none
Other: none

Distributions
Income: Dec   Capital Gains: Dec

Exchange Options
Number Per Year: no limit   Fee: none
Telephone: yes (money market fund not available)

Services
IRA, other pension, auto withdraw

Bernstein Interm Duration (SNIDX)

General Bond

767 Fifth Ave.
New York, NY 10153
(212) 756-4097

PERFORMANCE

	3yr Annual	5yr Annual	10yr Annual	Bull	Bear
Return (%)	11.3	na	na	44.1	2.6
Differ from Category (+/-)	1.1 abv av	na	na	4.7 abv av	-0.3 blw av

Total Risk	Standard Deviation	Category Risk	Risk Index	Avg Mat
low	3.6%	av	1.2	19.2 yrs

	1993	1992	1991	1990	1989	1988	1987	1986	1985	1984
Return (%)	10.3	6.9	16.9	7.1	—	—	—	—	—	—
Differ from category (+/-). . .	1.1	0.2	2.3	0.2	—	—	—	—	—	—

PER SHARE DATA

	1993	1992	1991	1990	1989	1988	1987	1986	1985	1984
Dividends, Net Income ($).	0.75	0.77	0.97	0.95	—	—	—	—	—	—
Distrib'ns, Cap Gain ($) . . .	0.20	0.58	0.15	0.01	—	—	—	—	—	—
Net Asset Value ($)	13.49	13.12	13.57	12.65	—	—	—	—	—	—
Expense Ratio (%)	0.66	0.67	0.68	0.71	—	—	—	—	—	—
Net Income to Assets (%) .	5.59	6.64	7.80	7.77	—	—	—	—	—	—
Portfolio Turnover (%).	60	150	81	119	—	—	—	—	—	—
Total Assets (Millions $). . . .	728	524	375	241	—	—	—	—	—	—

PORTFOLIO (as of 9/30/93)

Portfolio Manager: committee

Investm't Category: General Bond

Cap Gain	Asset Allocation
Cap & Income	Fund of Funds
✔ Income	Index
	Sector
✔ Domestic	Small Cap
✔ Foreign	Socially Conscious
Country/Region	State Specific

Portfolio: stocks 0%   bonds 81%
convertibles 0%   other 0%   cash 19%

Largest Holdings: U. S. government 37%, mortgage-backed 33%

Unrealized Net Capital Gains: 4% of portfolio value

SHAREHOLDER INFORMATION

Minimum Investment
Initial: $25,000   Subsequent: $5,000

Minimum IRA Investment
Initial: $25,000   Subsequent: $5,000

Maximum Fees
Load: none   12b-1: none
Other: none

Distributions
Income: monthly   Capital Gains: Dec

Exchange Options
Number Per Year: no limit   Fee: none
Telephone: yes (money market fund not available)

Services
IRA, other pension, auto withdraw

Bernstein NY Muni Port
(SNNYX)

767 Fifth Ave.
New York, NY 10153
(212) 756-4097

Tax-Exempt Bond

PERFORMANCE

	3yr Annual	5yr Annual	10yr Annual	Bull	Bear
Return (%)	8.6	na	na	32.4	3.1
Differ from Category (+/-)	-1.7 low	na	na	-7.7 low	0.8 abv av

Total Risk	Standard Deviation	Category Risk	Risk Index	Avg Mat
low	3.1%	low	0.7	6.9 yrs

	1993	1992	1991	1990	1989	1988	1987	1986	1985	1984
Return (%)	8.5	6.8	10.4	6.6	—	—	—	—	—	—
Differ from category (+/-) . .	-3.1	-1.5	-0.8	0.3	—	—	—	—	—	—

PER SHARE DATA

	1993	1992	1991	1990	1989	1988	1987	1986	1985	1984
Dividends, Net Income ($) .	0.65	0.72	0.74	0.75	—	—	—	—	—	—
Distrib'ns, Cap Gain ($) . . .	0.07	0.12	0.02	0.01	—	—	—	—	—	—
Net Asset Value ($)	13.71	13.32	13.29	12.77	—	—	—	—	—	—
Expense Ratio (%).	0.69	0.68	0.70	0.74	—	—	—	—	—	—
Net Income to Assets (%) . .	4.91	5.55	5.79	5.94	—	—	—	—	—	—
Portfolio Turnover (%)	34	43	30	36	—	—	—	—	—	—
Total Assets (Millions $) . . .	362	239	191	158	—	—	—	—	—	—

PORTFOLIO (as of 9/30/93)

Portfolio Manager: committee

Investm't Category: Tax-Exempt Bond

Cap Gain	Asset Allocation
Cap & Income	Fund of Funds
✔ Income	Index
	Sector
✔ Domestic	Small Cap
Foreign	Socially Conscious
Country/Region	✔ State Specific

Portfolio: stocks 0% bonds 94%
convertibles 0% other 0% cash 6%

Largest Holdings: general obligation 10%

Unrealized Net Capital Gains: 4% of portfolio value

SHAREHOLDER INFORMATION

Minimum Investment
Initial: $25,000   Subsequent: $5,000

Minimum IRA Investment
Initial: na   Subsequent: na

Maximum Fees
Load: none   12b-1: none
Other: none

Distributions
Income: monthly   Capital Gains: Dec

Exchange Options
Number Per Year: no limit   Fee: none
Telephone: yes (money market fund not available)

Services
auto withdraw

Bernstein Short Duration Plus (SNSDX)

767 Fifth Ave.
New York, NY 10153
(212) 756-4097

General Bond

PERFORMANCE

	3yr Annual	5yr Annual	10yr Annual	Bull	Bear
Return (%)	7.9	8.2	na	29.1	5.1
Differ from Category (+/-)	-2.3 low	-1.6 low	na	-10.3 low	2.2 high

Total Risk	Standard Deviation	Category Risk	Risk Index	Avg Mat
low	1.5%	low	0.5	11.3 yrs

	1993	1992	1991	1990	1989	1988	1987	1986	1985	1984
Return (%)	5.4	6.1	12.3	8.0	9.5	—	—	—	—	—
Differ from category (+/-) . . .	-3.8	-0.6	-2.3	1.1	-1.8	—	—	—	—	—

PER SHARE DATA

	1993	1992	1991	1990	1989	1988	1987	1986	1985	1984
Dividends, Net Income ($) .	0.58	0.67	0.90	0.94	0.97	—	—	—	—	—
Distrib'ns, Cap Gain ($) . . .	0.15	0.35	0.13	0.06	0.10	—	—	—	—	—
Net Asset Value ($)	12.66	12.72	12.97	12.52	12.56	—	—	—	—	—
Expense Ratio (%)	0.66	0.66	0.67	0.68	0.75	—	—	—	—	—
Net Income to Assets (%) .	4.52	5.75	7.42	7.67	7.91	—	—	—	—	—
Portfolio Turnover (%)	112	170	140	155	133	—	—	—	—	—
Total Assets (Millions $)	508	536	435	391	335	—	—	—	—	—

PORTFOLIO (as of 9/30/93)

Portfolio Manager: committee

Investm't Category: General Bond

Cap Gain	Asset Allocation
Cap & Income	Fund of Funds
✔ Income	Index
	Sector
✔ Domestic	Small Cap
✔ Foreign	Socially Conscious
Country/Region	State Specific

Portfolio: stocks 0%   bonds 100%
convertibles 0%   other 0%   cash 0%

Largest Holdings: commercial paper 48%, mortgage-backed 33%, corporate 10%

Unrealized Net Capital Gains: 2% of portfolio value

SHAREHOLDER INFORMATION

Minimum Investment
Initial: $25,000   Subsequent: $5,000

Minimum IRA Investment
Initial: $25,000   Subsequent: $5,000

Maximum Fees
Load: none   12b-1: none
Other: none

Distributions
Income: monthly   Capital Gains: Dec

Exchange Options
Number Per Year: no limit   Fee: none
Telephone: yes (money market fund not available)

Services
IRA, other pension, auto withdraw

Berwyn (BERWX)

Growth

1189 Lancaster Ave.
Berwyn, PA 19312
(800) 824-2249, (215) 640-4330

PERFORMANCE

	3yr Annual	5yr Annual	10yr Annual	Bull	Bear
Return (%)	28.6	13.5	na	109.2	-22.5
Differ from Category (+/-)	9.4 high	-1.1 blw av	na	24.5 high	-10.1 low

Total Risk	Standard Deviation	Category Risk	Risk Index	Beta
abv av	12.9%	abv av	1.2	0.7

	1993	1992	1991	1990	1989	1988	1987	1986	1985	1984
Return (%)	22.9	20.6	43.5	-23.8	16.4	21.5	2.8	14.6	23.5	—
Differ from category (+/-) . . .	9.7	9.6	8.1	-17.7	-9.4	3.8	1.6	0.1	-5.8	—

PER SHARE DATA

	1993	1992	1991	1990	1989	1988	1987	1986	1985	1984
Dividends, Net Income ($) .	0.00	0.04	0.10	0.12	0.09	0.07	0.15	0.09	0.05	—
Distrib'ns, Cap Gain ($) . . .	0.57	1.31	0.27	0.71	0.79	0.46	1.85	0.11	0.00	—
Net Asset Value ($)	17.67	14.85	13.46	9.66	13.82	12.63	10.85	12.41	11.03	—
Expense Ratio (%)	na	1.38	1.38	1.46	1.42	1.45	1.52	1.66	2.00	—
Net Income to Assets (%)	na	0.28	0.91	1.11	0.70	0.60	0.50	1.10	1.42	—
Portfolio Turnover (%)	na	45	33	24	25	20	43	17	24	—
Total Assets (Millions $)	48	31	19	12	14	11	8	6	3	—

PORTFOLIO (as of 6/30/93)

Portfolio Manager: Robert E. Killen - 1984

Investm't Category: Growth

✔ Cap Gain	Asset Allocation
Cap & Income	Fund of Funds
Income	Index
	Sector
✔ Domestic	Small Cap
Foreign	Socially Conscious
Country/Region	State Specific

Portfolio: stocks 97% bonds 0%
convertibles 0% other 1% cash 2%

Largest Holdings: oil, gas exploration & production 9%, manufacture of machinery 8%

Unrealized Net Capital Gains: 16% of portfolio value

SHAREHOLDER INFORMATION

Minimum Investment
Initial: $10,000   Subsequent: $1,000

Minimum IRA Investment
Initial: $1,000   Subsequent: $250

Maximum Fees
Load: 1.00% redemption   12b-1: none
Other: redemption fee applies for 1 year

Distributions
Income: Dec   Capital Gains: Dec

Exchange Options
Number Per Year: 4   Fee: none
Telephone: yes (money market not fund available)

Services
IRA, auto withdraw

Berwyn Income (BERIX)

Balanced

1189 Lancaster Ave.
Berwyn, PA 19312
(800) 824-2249, (215) 640-4330

PERFORMANCE

	3yr Annual	5yr Annual	10yr Annual	Bull	Bear
Return (%)	20.5	14.3	na	81.5	-3.7
Differ from Category (+/-)	5.5 high	2.2 high	na	19.9 high	2.1 abv av

Total Risk	Standard Deviation	Category Risk	Risk Index	Beta
blw av	4.9%	low	0.8	0.1

	1993	1992	1991	1990	1989	1988	1987	1986	1985	1984
Return (%)	16.9	21.7	22.9	-0.1	11.8	11.3	—	—	—	—
Differ from category (+/-). . .	3.5	13.6	-1.0	0.4	-5.8	-0.6	—	—	—	—

PER SHARE DATA

	1993	1992	1991	1990	1989	1988	1987	1986	1985	1984
Dividends, Net Income ($).	0.65	0.69	0.93	0.82	0.79	0.76	—	—	—	—
Distrib'ns, Cap Gain ($) . . .	0.68	0.55	0.05	0.03	0.05	0.05	—	—	—	—
Net Asset Value ($)	11.63	11.12	10.20	9.14	10.03	9.75	—	—	—	—
Expense Ratio (%)	na	1.34	1.34	1.46	1.50	1.75	—	—	—	—
Net Income to Assets (%) . . .	na	6.14	8.40	8.59	8.00	8.29	—	—	—	—
Portfolio Turnover (%).	na	46	14	14	3	17	—	—	—	—
Total Assets (Millions $).	31	12	5	3	3	2	—	—	—	—

PORTFOLIO (as of 8/31/93)

Portfolio Manager: Rob P. Killen - 1992

Investm't Category: Balanced

Cap Gain	Asset Allocation
✔ Cap & Income	Fund of Funds
Income	Index
	Sector
✔ Domestic	Small Cap
Foreign	Socially Conscious
Country/Region	State Specific

Portfolio:	stocks 23%	bonds 61%
convertibles 0%	other 6%	cash 10%

Largest Holdings: aerospace industry 10%, computer & peripheral industries 8%

Unrealized Net Capital Gains: 3% of portfolio value

SHAREHOLDER INFORMATION

Minimum Investment
Initial: $10,000   Subsequent: $1,000

Minimum IRA Investment
Initial: $1,000   Subsequent: $250

Maximum Fees
Load: none   12b-1: none
Other: none

Distributions
Income: quarterly   Capital Gains: Dec

Exchange Options
Number Per Year: 4   Fee: none
Telephone: yes (money market fund not available)

Services
IRA, auto withdraw

Blanchard American Equity (BLAEX)

Growth

41 Madison Avenue
24th Floor
New York, NY 10010
(800) 922-7771

PERFORMANCE

	3yr Annual	5yr Annual	10yr Annual	Bull	Bear
Return (%)	na	na	na	na	na
Differ from Category (+/-)	na	na	na	na	na

Total Risk	Standard Deviation	Category Risk	Risk Index	Beta
na	na	na	na	na

	1993	1992	1991	1990	1989	1988	1987	1986	1985	1984
Return (%)	-1.3	—	—	—	—	—	—	—	—	—
Differ from category (+/-) .	-14.5	—	—	—	—	—	—	—	—	—

PER SHARE DATA

	1993	1992	1991	1990	1989	1988	1987	1986	1985	1984
Dividends, Net Income ($) .	0.00	—	—	—	—	—	—	—	—	—
Distrib'ns, Cap Gain ($) ...	0.00	—	—	—	—	—	—	—	—	—
Net Asset Value ($)	9.87	—	—	—	—	—	—	—	—	—
Expense Ratio (%)........	3.13	—	—	—	—	—	—	—	—	—
Net Income to Assets (%) .	-1.66	—	—	—	—	—	—	—	—	—
Portfolio Turnover (%)	49	—	—	—	—	—	—	—	—	—
Total Assets (Millions $)	19	—	—	—	—	—	—	—	—	—

PORTFOLIO (as of 4/30/93)

Portfolio Manager: Jeffrey Miller - 1992

Investm't Category: Growth

✔ Cap Gain	Asset Allocation
Cap & Income	Fund of Funds
Income	Index
	Sector
✔ Domestic	Small Cap
Foreign	Socially Conscious
Country/Region	State Specific

Portfolio: stocks 75% bonds 0%
convertibles 0% other 0% cash 25%

Largest Holdings: consumer & related 9%, financial services 8%

Unrealized Net Capital Gains: 4% of portfolio value

SHAREHOLDER INFORMATION

Minimum Investment
Initial: $3,000   Subsequent: 200

Minimum IRA Investment
Initial: $2,000   Subsequent: $200

Maximum Fees
Load: none   12b-1: 0.50%
Other: $75 one-time account opening fee

Distributions
Income: Dec   Capital Gains: Dec

Exchange Options
Number Per Year: no limit   Fee: none
Telephone: yes (money market fund available)

Services
IRA, other pension, auto invest, auto withdraw

Blanchard Flexible Income (BLFIX)

General Bond

41 Madison Avenue
24th Floor
New York, NY 10010
(800) 922-7771

	3yr Annual	5yr Annual	10yr Annual	Bull	Bear
Return (%)	na	na	na	na	na
Differ from Category (+/-)	na	na	na	na	na

Total Risk	Standard Deviation	Category Risk	Risk Index	Avg Mat
na	na	na	na	7.9 yrs

	1993	1992	1991	1990	1989	1988	1987	1986	1985	1984
Return (%)	13.8	—	—	—	—	—	—	—	—	—
Differ from category (+/-) . . .	4.6	—	—	—	—	—	—	—	—	—

PER SHARE DATA

	1993	1992	1991	1990	1989	1988	1987	1986	1985	1984
Dividends, Net Income ($) .	0.39	—	—	—	—	—	—	—	—	—
Distrib'ns, Cap Gain ($) . . .	0.09	—	—	—	—	—	—	—	—	—
Net Asset Value ($)	5.15	—	—	—	—	—	—	—	—	—
Expense Ratio (%)	0.20	—	—	—	—	—	—	—	—	—
Net Income to Assets (%) .	9.02	—	—	—	—	—	—	—	—	—
Portfolio Turnover (%)	129	—	—	—	—	—	—	—	—	—
Total Assets (Millions $)	686	—	—	—	—	—	—	—	—	—

PORTFOLIO (as of 4/30/93)

Portfolio Manager: Jack Burks - 1992

Investm't Category: General Bond

Cap Gain	Asset Allocation
Cap & Income	Fund of Funds
✔ Income	Index
	Sector
✔ Domestic	Small Cap
✔ Foreign	Socially Conscious
Country/Region	State Specific

Portfolio: stocks 0% bonds 95%
convertibles 0% other 1% cash 4%

Largest Holdings: foreign government agencies 31%, corporate 29%

Unrealized Net Capital Gains: 1% of portfolio value

SHAREHOLDER INFORMATION

Minimum Investment
Initial: $3,000   Subsequent: $200

Minimum IRA Investment
Initial: $2,000   Subsequent: $200

Maximum Fees
Load: none   12b-1: 0.25%
Other: $75 one-time account opening fee

Distributions
Income: monthly   Capital Gains: Dec

Exchange Options
Number Per Year: no limit   Fee: none
Telephone: yes (money market fund available)

Services
IRA, other pension, auto invest, auto withdraw

Blanchard Global Growth (BGGFX)

International Stock

41 Madison Avenue
24th Floor
New York, NY 10010
(800) 922-7771

PERFORMANCE

	3yr Annual	5yr Annual	10yr Annual	Bull	Bear
Return (%)	11.5	8.5	na	43.5	-9.3
Differ from Category (+/-)	-2.8 blw av	-0.2 blw av	na	-11.6 blw av	5.8 high

Total Risk	Standard Deviation	Category Risk	Risk Index	Beta
av	7.9%	low	0.6	0.4

	1993	1992	1991	1990	1989	1988	1987	1986	1985	1984
Return (%)	24.4	0.6	10.7	-6.3	15.6	7.5	16.3	—	—	—
Differ from category (+/-) .	-14.1	4.2	-2.2	4.8	-6.6	-6.3	4.3	—	—	—

PER SHARE DATA

	1993	1992	1991	1990	1989	1988	1987	1986	1985	1984
Dividends, Net Income ($) .	0.00	0.30	0.31	0.20	0.37	0.10	0.10	—	—	—
Distrib'ns, Cap Gain ($) . . .	1.28	0.18	0.00	0.20	0.50	0.18	0.64	—	—	—
Net Asset Value ($)	10.48	9.47	9.89	9.22	10.28	9.69	9.29	—	—	—
Expense Ratio (%)	2.40	2.31	2.36	2.28	2.29	2.28	3.10	—	—	—
Net Income to Assets (%) . .	1.72	2.31	2.84	2.86	2.27	1.42	0.34	—	—	—
Portfolio Turnover (%)	138	109	78	88	85	119	69	—	—	—
Total Assets (Millions $)	93	127	193	233	244	246	149	—	—	—

PORTFOLIO (as of 4/30/93)

Portfolio Manager: committee

Investm't Category: International Stock

✔ Cap Gain	✔ Asset Allocation
Cap & Income	Fund of Funds
Income	Index
	Sector
✔ Domestic	Small Cap
✔ Foreign	Socially Conscious
Country/Region	State Specific

Portfolio: stocks 70%   bonds 26%
convertibles 0%   other 0%   cash 4%

Largest Holdings: United States 57%, Canada 11%

Unrealized Net Capital Gains: 5% of portfolio value

SHAREHOLDER INFORMATION

Minimum Investment
Initial: $3,000   Subsequent: $200

Minimum IRA Investment
Initial: $2,000   Subsequent: $200

Maximum Fees
Load: none   12b-1: 0.75%
Other: $75 one-time account opening fee

Distributions
Income: Dec   Capital Gains: Dec

Exchange Options
Number Per Year: no limit   Fee: none
Telephone: yes (money market fund available)

Services
IRA, other pension, auto invest, auto withdraw

Blanchard Precious Metals (BLPMX)

Gold

41 Madison Avenue
24th Floor
New York, NY 10010
(800) 922-7771

PERFORMANCE

	3yr Annual	5yr Annual	10yr Annual	Bull	Bear
Return (%)	16.8	5.8	na	41.9	-13.2
Differ from Category (+/-)	3.1 abv av	-6.5 blw av	na	8.3 abv av	-59.1 av

Total Risk	Standard Deviation	Category Risk	Risk Index	Beta
high	26.2%	av	1.0	-0.3

	1993	1992	1991	1990	1989	1988	1987	1986	1985	1984
Return (%)............	100.4	-18.4	-2.3	-22.8	8.0	—	—	—	—	—
Differ from category (+/-)..	13.5	-2.7	2.5	-54.3	-16.7	—	—	—	—	—

PER SHARE DATA

	1993	1992	1991	1990	1989	1988	1987	1986	1985	1984
Dividends, Net Income ($).	0.00	0.00	0.00	0.00	0.02	—	—	—	—	—
Distrib'ns, Cap Gain ($) ...	0.00	0.00	0.00	0.00	0.10	—	—	—	—	—
Net Asset Value ($)	9.64	4.81	5.90	6.04	7.83	—	—	—	—	—
Expense Ratio (%)	2.65	3.09	3.05	2.95	3.99	—	—	—	—	—
Net Income to Assets (%) .	-1.79	-1.57	-1.28	-0.40	0.77	—	—	—	—	—
Portfolio Turnover (%)......	73	62	57	56	20	—	—	—	—	—
Total Assets (Millions $).....	69	20	24	31	25	—	—	—	—	—

PORTFOLIO

Portfolio Manager: Peter Cavelti - 1988

Investm't Category: Gold

✔ Cap Gain	Asset Allocation
Cap & Income	Fund of Funds
Income	Index
	✔ Sector
✔ Domestic	Small Cap
✔ Foreign	Socially Conscious
Country/Region	State Specific

Portfolio: stocks na   bonds na
convertibles na   other na   cash na

Largest Holdings: na

Unrealized Net Capital Gains: na

SHAREHOLDER INFORMATION

Minimum Investment
Initial: $3,000   Subsequent: $200

Minimum IRA Investment
Initial: $2,000   Subsequent: $200

Maximum Fees
Load: none   12b-1: 0.75%
Other: $75 one-time account opening fee

Distributions
Income: Dec   Capital Gains: Dec

Exchange Options
Number Per Year: no limit   Fee: none
Telephone: yes (money market fund available)

Services
IRA, other pension, auto invest, auto withdraw

Blanchard Short-Term Global Inc (BSGIX)

41 Madison Avenue
24th Floor
New York, NY 10010
(800) 922-7771

International Bond

PERFORMANCE

	3yr Annual	5yr Annual	10yr Annual	Bull	Bear
Return (%)	na	na	na	na	na
Differ from Category (+/-)	na	na	na	na	na

Total Risk	Standard Deviation	Category Risk	Risk Index	Avg Mat
na	na	na	na	1.9 yrs

	1993	1992	1991	1990	1989	1988	1987	1986	1985	1984
Return (%)	8.5	3.5	—	—	—	—	—	—	—	—
Differ from category (+/-)	-4.2	-1.3	—	—	—	—	—	—	—	—

PER SHARE DATA

	1993	1992	1991	1990	1989	1988	1987	1986	1985	1984
Dividends, Net Income ($)	0.12	0.13	—	—	—	—	—	—	—	—
Distrib'ns, Cap Gain ($)	0.00	0.00	—	—	—	—	—	—	—	—
Net Asset Value ($)	1.87	1.84	—	—	—	—	—	—	—	—
Expense Ratio (%)	1.44	1.32	—	—	—	—	—	—	—	—
Net Income to Assets (%)	6.97	8.50	—	—	—	—	—	—	—	—
Portfolio Turnover (%)	610	412	—	—	—	—	—	—	—	—
Total Assets (Millions $)	638	1,241	—	—	—	—	—	—	—	—

PORTFOLIO (as of 4/30/93)

Portfolio Manager: Robert McHenry - 1991

Investm't Category: International Bond

Cap Gain	Asset Allocation
Cap & Income	Fund of Funds
✔ Income	Index
	Sector
✔ Domestic	Small Cap
✔ Foreign	Socially Conscious
Country/Region	State Specific

Portfolio: stocks 0% bonds 90%
convertibles 0% other 0% cash 10%

Largest Holdings: United States 41%, Spain 12%

Unrealized Net Capital Gains: 0% of portfolio value

SHAREHOLDER INFORMATION

Minimum Investment
Initial: $3,000   Subsequent: $200

Minimum IRA Investment
Initial: $2,000   Subsequent: $200

Maximum Fees
Load: none   12b-1: 0.25%
Other: $75 one-time account opening fee

Distributions
Income: monthly   Capital Gains: Dec

Exchange Options
Number Per Year: no limit   Fee: none
Telephone: yes (money market fund available)

Services
IRA, other pension, auto invest, auto withdraw

BNY Hamilton Equity Income (BNEIX)

125 West 55th Street
New York, NY 10019
(800) 426-9363

Growth & Income

PERFORMANCE

	3yr Annual	5yr Annual	10yr Annual	Bull	Bear
Return (%)	na	na	na	na	na
Differ from Category (+/-)	na	na	na	na	na

Total Risk	Standard Deviation	Category Risk	Risk Index	Beta
na	na	na	na	na

	1993	1992	1991	1990	1989	1988	1987	1986	1985	1984
Return (%)	11.9	—	—	—	—	—	—	—	—	—
Differ from category (+/-). . .	-0.6	—	—	—	—	—	—	—	—	—

PER SHARE DATA

	1993	1992	1991	1990	1989	1988	1987	1986	1985	1984
Dividends, Net Income ($).	0.28	—	—	—	—	—	—	—	—	—
Distrib'ns, Cap Gain ($) . . .	0.08	—	—	—	—	—	—	—	—	—
Net Asset Value ($)	11.30	—	—	—	—	—	—	—	—	—
Expense Ratio (%)	1.11	—	—	—	—	—	—	—	—	—
Net Income to Assets (%) .	3.00	—	—	—	—	—	—	—	—	—
Portfolio Turnover (%).	na	—	—	—	—	—	—	—	—	—
Total Assets (Millions $). . . .	114	—	—	—	—	—	—	—	—	—

PORTFOLIO (as of 6/30/93)

Portfolio Manager: Robert Knott - 1992

Investm't Category: Growth & Income

Cap Gain	Asset Allocation
✔ Cap & Income	Fund of Funds
Income	Index
	Sector
✔ Domestic	Small Cap
✔ Foreign	Socially Conscious
Country/Region	State Specific

Portfolio: stocks 52% bonds 0%
convertibles 40% other 0% cash 8%

Largest Holdings: natural gas 3%, real estate investment trusts 3%

Unrealized Net Capital Gains: 5% of portfolio value

SHAREHOLDER INFORMATION

Minimum Investment
Initial: $2,000   Subsequent: $100

Minimum IRA Investment
Initial: $250   Subsequent: $40

Maximum Fees
Load: none   12b-1: 0.25%
Other: none

Distributions
Income: none   Capital Gains: Dec

Exchange Options
Number Per Year: no limit   Fee: none
Telephone: yes (money market fund not available)

Services
IRA, auto withdraw

BNY Hamilton Interm Gov't (BNIGX)

125 West 55th Street
New York, NY 10019
(800) 426-9363

Government Bond

PERFORMANCE

	3yr Annual	5yr Annual	10yr Annual	Bull	Bear
Return (%)	na	na	na	na	na
Differ from Category (+/-)	na	na	na	na	na

Total Risk	Standard Deviation	Category Risk	Risk Index	Avg Mat
na	na	na	na	7.5 yrs

	1993	1992	1991	1990	1989	1988	1987	1986	1985	1984
Return (%)	8.0	—	—	—	—	—	—	—	—	—
Differ from category (+/-)	-2.4	—	—	—	—	—	—	—	—	—

PER SHARE DATA

	1993	1992	1991	1990	1989	1988	1987	1986	1985	1984
Dividends, Net Income ($)	0.50	—	—	—	—	—	—	—	—	—
Distrib'ns, Cap Gain ($)	0.02	—	—	—	—	—	—	—	—	—
Net Asset Value ($)	10.12	—	—	—	—	—	—	—	—	—
Expense Ratio (%)	0.80	—	—	—	—	—	—	—	—	—
Net Income to Assets (%)	4.97	—	—	—	—	—	—	—	—	—
Portfolio Turnover (%)	na	—	—	—	—	—	—	—	—	—
Total Assets (Millions $)	73	—	—	—	—	—	—	—	—	—

PORTFOLIO (as of 6/30/93)

Portfolio Manager: Mark Hemenetz - 1992

Investm't Category: Government Bond

Cap Gain	Asset Allocation
Cap & Income	Fund of Funds
✔ Income	Index
	Sector
✔ Domestic	Small Cap
Foreign	Socially Conscious
Country/Region	State Specific

Portfolio:	stocks 0%	bonds 95%
convertibles 0%	other 0%	cash 5%

Largest Holdings: U.S. government & agencies 48%, mortgage-backed 45%

Unrealized Net Capital Gains: 1% of portfolio value

SHAREHOLDER INFORMATION

Minimum Investment
Initial: $2,000   Subsequent: $100

Minimum IRA Investment
Initial: $250   Subsequent: $40

Maximum Fees
Load: none   12b-1: 0.25%
Other: none

Distributions
Income: monthly   Capital Gains: Dec

Exchange Options
Number Per Year: no limit   Fee: none
Telephone: yes (money markt fund not available)

Services
IRA, auto withdraw

BNY Hamilton Interm NY Tax Exempt (BNNYX)

125 West 55th Street
New York, NY 10019
(800) 426-9363

Tax-Exempt Bond

	3yr Annual	5yr Annual	10yr Annual	Bull	Bear
Return (%)	na	na	na	na	na
Differ from Category (+/-)	na	na	na	na	na

Total Risk	Standard Deviation	Category Risk	Risk Index	Avg Mat
na	na	na	na	6.1 yrs

	1993	1992	1991	1990	1989	1988	1987	1986	1985	1984
Return (%)	7.9	—	—	—	—	—	—	—	—	—
Differ from category (+/-). . .	-3.7	—	—	—	—	—	—	—	—	—

PER SHARE DATA

	1993	1992	1991	1990	1989	1988	1987	1986	1985	1984
Dividends, Net Income ($) .	0.38	—	—	—	—	—	—	—	—	—
Distrib'ns, Cap Gain ($) . . .	0.00	—	—	—	—	—	—	—	—	—
Net Asset Value ($)	10.37	—	—	—	—	—	—	—	—	—
Expense Ratio (%)	0.64	—	—	—	—	—	—	—	—	—
Net Income to Assets (%) .	3.73	—	—	—	—	—	—	—	—	—
Portfolio Turnover (%).	na	—	—	—	—	—	—	—	—	—
Total Assets (Millions $). . . .	55	—	—	—	—	—	—	—	—	—

PORTFOLIO (as of 6/30/93)

Portfolio Manager: Colleen Frey - 1992

Investm't Category: Tax-Exempt Bond
Cap Gain	Asset Allocation
Cap & Income	Fund of Funds
✔ Income	Index
	Sector
✔ Domestic	Small Cap
Foreign	Socially Conscious
Country/Region	✔ State Specific

Portfolio: stocks 0% bonds 98%
convertibles 0% other 0% cash 2%

Largest Holdings: general obligation 16%

Unrealized Net Capital Gains: 1% of portfolio value

SHAREHOLDER INFORMATION

Minimum Investment
Initial: $2,000   Subsequent: $100

Minimum IRA Investment
Initial: na   Subsequent: na

Maximum Fees
Load: none   12b-1: 0.25%
Other: none

Distributions
Income: monthly   Capital Gains: Dec

Exchange Options
Number Per Year: no limit   Fee: none
Telephone: yes (money market fund not available)

Services
auto withdraw

Boston Co Asset Allocation (BIAAX)

One Boston Place, 0BO5H
Boston, MA 02108
(800) 225-5267, (800) 343-6324

Balanced

	3yr Annual	5yr Annual	10yr Annual	Bull	Bear
Return (%)	13.8	11.9	na	58.7	-5.9
Differ from Category (+/-)	-1.2 blw av	-0.2 av	na	-2.9 blw av	-0.1 av

Total Risk	Standard Deviation	Category Risk	Risk Index	Beta
av	9.9%	high	1.6	0.9

	1993	1992	1991	1990	1989	1988	1987	1986	1985	1984
Return (%)	8.0	8.3	25.8	1.3	17.9	—	—	—	—	—
Differ from category (+/-) ..	-5.4	0.2	1.9	1.8	0.3	—	—	—	—	—

PER SHARE DATA

	1993	1992	1991	1990	1989	1988	1987	1986	1985	1984
Dividends, Net Income ($) .	0.20	0.24	0.33	0.61	0.44	—	—	—	—	—
Distrib'ns, Cap Gain ($) ...	0.76	0.49	1.12	0.00	0.34	—	—	—	—	—
Net Asset Value ($)	15.17	14.95	14.48	12.69	13.13	—	—	—	—	—
Expense Ratio (%)........	1.27	1.25	1.45	1.25	1.73	—	—	—	—	—
Net Income to Assets (%)..	1.29	2.16	3.63	5.09	6.17	—	—	—	—	—
Portfolio Turnover (%)	32	48	78	39	9	—	—	—	—	—
Total Assets (Millions $)	33	28	24	19	13	—	—	—	—	—

PORTFOLIO (as of 8/31/93)

Portfolio Manager: Edgar Peters - 1988

Investm't Category: Balanced

Cap Gain	✔ Asset Allocation
✔ Cap & Income	Fund of Funds
Income	Index
	Sector
✔ Domestic	Small Cap
Foreign	Socially Conscious
Country/Region	State Specific

Portfolio: stocks 75%   bonds 0%
convertibles 0%   other 0%   cash 25%

Largest Holdings: stocks—financial services 10%, stocks—energy 10%

Unrealized Net Capital Gains: 11% of portfolio value

SHAREHOLDER INFORMATION

Minimum Investment
Initial: $1,000   Subsequent: $0

Minimum IRA Investment
Initial: $500   Subsequent: $0

Maximum Fees
Load: none   12b-1: 0.25%
Other: none

Distributions
Income: Jun, Dec   Capital Gains: Dec

Exchange Options
Number Per Year: no limit   Fee: none
Telephone: yes (money market fund available)

Services
IRA, other pension, auto exchange, auto invest, auto withdraw

Boston Co Capital Appreciation (BCCAX)

Growth

One Boston Place, 0BO5H
Boston, MA 02108
(800) 225-5267, (800) 343-6324

PERFORMANCE

	3yr Annual	5yr Annual	10yr Annual	Bull	Bear
Return (%)	14.1	9.9	13.0	57.8	-18.3
Differ from Category (+/-)	-5.1 blw av	-4.7 low	0.4 av	-26.9 low	-5.9 blw av

Total Risk	Standard Deviation	Category Risk	Risk Index	Beta
abv av	11.0%	blw av	1.0	0.9

	1993	1992	1991	1990	1989	1988	1987	1986	1985	1984
Return (%)	16.4	4.0	22.8	-13.4	24.9	19.5	0.2	22.5	34.9	6.9
Differ from category (+/-). . .	3.2	-7.0	-12.6	-7.3	-0.8	1.8	-1.0	8.0	5.6	6.9

PER SHARE DATA

	1993	1992	1991	1990	1989	1988	1987	1986	1985	1984
Dividends, Net Income ($).	0.29	0.35	0.49	0.54	0.55	0.58	1.32	0.50	0.74	0.68
Distrib'ns, Cap Gain ($) . . .	1.50	2.63	0.56	0.05	7.60	1.87	5.36	5.79	1.56	2.91
Net Asset Value ($)	27.80	25.46	27.40	23.20	27.49	28.65	26.07	32.40	32.11	25.91
Expense Ratio (%)	1.16	1.22	1.20	1.26	1.23	1.31	0.95	0.95	0.96	1.00
Net Income to Assets (%) .	1.10	1.33	1.61	1.96	2.75	2.14	2.16	2.65	3.60	3.69
Portfolio Turnover (%).	na	66	157	180	111	24	46	37	59	47
Total Assets (Millions $). . . .	444	423	509	475	640	543	432	452	369	259

PORTFOLIO (as of 6/30/93)

Portfolio Manager: Guy Scott - 1991

Investm't Category: Growth

✔ Cap Gain	Asset Allocation
Cap & Income	Fund of Funds
Income	Index
	Sector
✔ Domestic	Small Cap
✔ Foreign	Socially Conscious
Country/Region	State Specific

Portfolio: stocks 91% bonds 0%
convertibles 2% other 0% cash 7%

Largest Holdings: energy 13%, financial services 12%

Unrealized Net Capital Gains: 8% of portfolio value

SHAREHOLDER INFORMATION

Minimum Investment
Initial: $1,000 Subsequent: $0

Minimum IRA Investment
Initial: $500 Subsequent: $0

Maximum Fees
Load: none 12b-1: 0.25%
Other: none

Distributions
Income: quarterly Capital Gains: Dec

Exchange Options
Number Per Year: no limit Fee: none
Telephone: yes (money market fund available)

Services
IRA, other pension, auto exchange, auto invest, auto withdraw

Boston Co Int'l (BINTX)

International Stock

One Boston Place, 0BO5H
Boston, MA 02108
(800) 225-5267, (800) 343-6324

PERFORMANCE

	3yr Annual	5yr Annual	10yr Annual	Bull	Bear
Return (%)	5.9	2.2	na	26.1	-23.1
Differ from Category (+/-)	-8.4 low	-6.5 low	na	-29.0 low	-8.0 low

Total Risk	Standard Deviation	Category Risk	Risk Index	Beta
high	15.1%	high	1.3	0.6

	1993	1992	1991	1990	1989	1988	1987	1986	1985	1984
Return (%)	24.5	-10.3	6.6	-18.5	15.4	—	—	—	—	—
Differ from category (+/-) .	-14.0	-6.8	-6.3	-7.4	-6.8	—	—	—	—	—

PER SHARE DATA

	1993	1992	1991	1990	1989	1988	1987	1986	1985	1984
Dividends, Net Income ($) .	0.00	0.00	0.06	0.16	0.18	—	—	—	—	—
Distrib'ns, Cap Gain ($) . . .	0.00	0.00	0.13	0.21	0.09	—	—	—	—	—
Net Asset Value ($)	12.68	10.18	11.36	10.85	13.79	—	—	—	—	—
Expense Ratio (%).	1.79	1.87	1.63	1.63	1.76	—	—	—	—	—
Net Income to Assets (%) . .	0.46	0.24	0.97	1.50	1.52	—	—	—	—	—
Portfolio Turnover (%)	202	110	145	28	47	—	—	—	—	—
Total Assets (Millions $)	5	11	30	31	25	—	—	—	—	—

PORTFOLIO (as of 8/31/93)

Portfolio Manager: Bruce Clark - 1990

Investm't Category: International Stock

✔ Cap Gain	Asset Allocation
Cap & Income	Fund of Funds
Income	Index
	Sector
Domestic	Small Cap
✔ Foreign	Socially Conscious
Country/Region	State Specific

Portfolio: stocks 75% bonds 0%
convertibles 0% other 0% cash 25%

Largest Holdings: Japan 27%, Germany 14%

Unrealized Net Capital Gains: 7% of portfolio value

SHAREHOLDER INFORMATION

Minimum Investment
Initial: $1,000   Subsequent: $0

Minimum IRA Investment
Initial: $500   Subsequent: $0

Maximum Fees
Load: none   12b-1: 0.25%
Other: none

Distributions
Income: Jun, Dec   Capital Gains: Dec

Exchange Options
Number Per Year: 8   Fee: none
Telephone: yes (money market fund available)

Services
IRA, other pension, auto exchange, auto invest, auto withdraw

Boston Co Interm Term Gov't (BGMFX)

Government Bond

One Boston Place, 0BO5H
Boston, MA 02108
(800) 225-5267, (800) 343-6324

PERFORMANCE

	3yr Annual	5yr Annual	10yr Annual	Bull	Bear
Return (%)	9.3	9.2	na	35.6	3.2
Differ from Category (+/-)	-1.5 blw av	-1.2 blw av	na	-10.6 blw av	2.7 av

Total Risk	Standard Deviation	Category Risk	Risk Index	Avg Mat
low	3.6%	blw av	0.8	na

	1993	1992	1991	1990	1989	1988	1987	1986	1985	1984
Return (%)	9.0	5.4	13.5	7.2	10.8	6.2	1.0	—	—	—
Differ from category (+/-)	-1.4	-0.8	-1.5	0.6	-3.1	-1.4	2.8	—	—	—

PER SHARE DATA

	1993	1992	1991	1990	1989	1988	1987	1986	1985	1984
Dividends, Net Income ($)	0.73	0.72	0.74	0.80	0.91	0.80	0.99	—	—	—
Distrib'ns, Cap Gain ($)	0.02	0.00	0.00	0.00	0.00	0.00	0.00	—	—	—
Net Asset Value ($)	13.14	12.76	12.81	11.99	11.97	11.66	11.75	—	—	—
Expense Ratio (%)	1.38	1.67	1.91	1.92	1.85	1.63	1.04	—	—	—
Net Income to Assets (%)	5.74	5.70	6.09	6.87	7.61	6.91	8.20	—	—	—
Portfolio Turnover (%)	na	30	50	300	321	64	122	—	—	—
Total Assets (Millions $)	22	23	16	16	14	14	14	—	—	—

PORTFOLIO (as of 6/30/93)

Portfolio Manager: Almond Goduti - 1990

Investm't Category: Government Bond

Cap Gain	Asset Allocation
Cap & Income	Fund of Funds
✔ Income	Index
	Sector
✔ Domestic	Small Cap
Foreign	Socially Conscious
Country/Region	State Specific

Portfolio: stocks 0% bonds 96%
convertibles 0% other 0% cash 4%

Largest Holdings: U.S. government & agencies 82%, mortgage-backed 14%

Unrealized Net Capital Gains: 6% of portfolio value

SHAREHOLDER INFORMATION

Minimum Investment
Initial: $1,000   Subsequent: $0

Minimum IRA Investment
Initial: $500   Subsequent: $0

Maximum Fees
Load: none   12b-1: 0.25%
Other: none

Distributions
Income: monthly   Capital Gains: Dec

Exchange Options
Number Per Year: no limit   Fee: none
Telephone: yes (money market fund available)

Services
IRA, other pension, auto exchange, auto invest, auto withdraw

Boston Co Managed Income (BOSGX)

General Bond

One Boston Place, 0BO5H
Boston, MA 02108
(800) 225-5267, (800) 343-6324

PERFORMANCE

	3yr Annual	5yr Annual	10yr Annual	Bull	Bear
Return (%)	13.3	9.9	10.8	49.7	1.0
Differ from Category (+/-)	3.1 high	0.1 av	-0.1 blw av	10.3 high	-1.9 low

Total Risk	Standard Deviation	Category Risk	Risk Index	Avg Mat
low	3.4%	av	1.2	9.3 yrs

	1993	1992	1991	1990	1989	1988	1987	1986	1985	1984
Return (%)	14.5	8.7	16.9	3.8	6.1	10.0	5.9	10.0	21.8	12.0
Differ from category (+/-) ...	5.3	2.0	2.3	-3.1	-5.2	2.4	3.4	-3.9	1.7	-0.3

PER SHARE DATA

	1993	1992	1991	1990	1989	1988	1987	1986	1985	1984
Dividends, Net Income ($) .	0.78	0.92	0.86	1.02	0.93	0.95	1.19	0.95	0.99	1.17
Distrib'ns, Cap Gain ($) ...	0.90	0.00	0.00	0.00	0.00	0.00	0.10	0.07	0.00	0.00
Net Asset Value ($)	11.38	11.45	11.41	10.56	11.18	11.43	11.29	11.91	11.80	10.60
Expense Ratio (%)........	1.07	1.02	1.13	1.19	1.15	1.14	0.93	0.88	1.48	1.50
Net Income to Assets (%)..	6.96	7.58	7.91	8.65	8.76	8.81	10.30	10.01	10.77	10.02
Portfolio Turnover (%)	na	216	119	183	142	139	306	71	173	na
Total Assets (Millions $) ...	100	98	84	77	84	65	52	49	16	6

PORTFOLIO (as of 6/30/93)

Portfolio Manager: David Gray - 1990

Investm't Category: General Bond

Cap Gain	Asset Allocation
Cap & Income	Fund of Funds
✔ Income	Index
	Sector
✔ Domestic	Small Cap
✔ Foreign	Socially Conscious
Country/Region	State Specific

Portfolio: stocks 0% bonds 78%
convertibles 8% other 0% cash 14%

Largest Holdings: corporate 36%, mortgage-backed 32%

Unrealized Net Capital Gains: 1% of portfolio value

SHAREHOLDER INFORMATION

Minimum Investment
Initial: $1,000   Subsequent: $0

Minimum IRA Investment
Initial: $500   Subsequent: $0

Maximum Fees
Load: none   12b-1: 0.25%
Other: none

Distributions
Income: monthly   Capital Gains: Dec

Exchange Options
Number Per Year: no limit   Fee: none
Telephone: yes (money market fund available)

Services
IRA, other pension, auto exchange, auto invest, auto withdraw

Boston Co Special Growth (BOSSX)

One Boston Place, 0BO5H
Boston, MA 02108
(800) 225-5267, (800) 343-6324

Aggressive Growth

PERFORMANCE

	3yr Annual	5yr Annual	10yr Annual	Bull	Bear
Return (%)	25.0	17.2	12.8	120.6	-15.6
Differ from Category (+/-)	-0.4 av	-1.0 av	0.8 abv av	-4.4 av	-0.6 av

Total Risk	Standard Deviation	Category Risk	Risk Index	Beta
high	17.6%	av	1.1	1.2

	1993	1992	1991	1990	1989	1988	1987	1986	1985	1984
Return (%)	20.0	26.1	29.2	-4.8	18.8	21.4	-3.8	7.6	34.8	-11.0
Differ from category (+/-). . .	1.0	15.7	-23.2	1.5	-8.2	6.2	-0.4	-1.8	3.8	-1.6

PER SHARE DATA

	1993	1992	1991	1990	1989	1988	1987	1986	1985	1984
Dividends, Net Income ($).	0.00	0.18	0.00	0.02	0.24	0.33	0.81	0.31	0.34	0.09
Distrib'ns, Cap Gain ($) . . .	1.78	1.61	2.82	0.00	2.36	0.00	4.10	4.96	0.00	0.10
Net Asset Value ($)	17.97	16.45	14.59	13.56	14.28	14.27	12.02	17.21	20.95	15.87
Expense Ratio (%)	1.75	1.57	1.70	1.62	1.72	1.58	1.49	1.32	1.35	1.50
Net Income to Assets (%) .	-0.91	-0.71	-0.34	0.19	0.82	2.70	3.25	1.16	1.96	2.83
Portfolio Turnover (%).	na	112	141	222	184	183	322	192	257	261
Total Assets (Millions $). . . .	118	64	42	44	40	35	31	35	53	27

PORTFOLIO (as of 6/30/93)

Portfolio Manager: Guy Scott - 1990

Investm't Category: Aggressive Growth

✔ Cap Gain	Asset Allocation
Cap & Income	Fund of Funds
Income	Index
	Sector
✔ Domestic	Small Cap
✔ Foreign	Socially Conscious
Country/Region	State Specific

Portfolio: stocks 89% bonds 0%
convertibles 0% other 0% cash 11%

Largest Holdings: consumer services—tele-communications 22%, energy 16%

Unrealized Net Capital Gains: 10% of port-folio value

SHAREHOLDER INFORMATION

Minimum Investment
Initial: $1,000   Subsequent: $0

Minimum IRA Investment
Initial: $500   Subsequent: $0

Maximum Fees
Load: none   12b-1: 0.25%
Other: none

Distributions
Income: Dec   Capital Gains: Dec

Exchange Options
Number Per Year: 12   Fee: none
Telephone: yes (money market fund available)

Services
IRA, other pension, auto exchange, auto invest, auto withdraw

Boston Tax Free Muni Bond (BCTBX)

One Boston Place, 0BO5H
Boston, MA 02108
(800) 225-5267, (800) 343-6324

Tax-Exempt Bond

PERFORMANCE

	3yr Annual	5yr Annual	10yr Annual	Bull	Bear
Return (%)	10.3	9.3	na	40.3	1.6
Differ from Category (+/-)	0.0 blw av	0.1 blw av	na	0.2 blw av	-0.6 blw av

Total Risk	Standard Deviation	Category Risk	Risk Index	Avg Mat
blw av	4.2%	av	1.0	6.8 yrs

	1993	1992	1991	1990	1989	1988	1987	1986	1985	1984
Return (%)	11.2	8.2	11.6	6.1	9.8	11.5	2.3	17.8	—	—
Differ from category (+/-) ..	-0.4	-0.1	0.3	-0.2	0.8	1.4	3.5	1.4	—	—

PER SHARE DATA

	1993	1992	1991	1990	1989	1988	1987	1986	1985	1984
Dividends, Net Income ($)	0.57	0.64	0.72	0.76	0.77	0.77	0.74	0.78	—	—
Distrib'ns, Cap Gain ($) ...	0.53	0.29	0.00	0.00	0.31	0.07	0.00	0.00	—	—
Net Asset Value ($)	12.31	12.10	12.08	11.52	11.60	11.59	11.19	11.68	—	—
Expense Ratio (%)........	1.03	0.97	0.81	0.82	0.79	0.79	0.78	0.75	—	—
Net Income to Assets (%)..	4.91	5.82	6.43	6.45	6.82	6.73	6.58	7.25	—	—
Portfolio Turnover (%)	10	30	54	76	101	81	241	5	—	—
Total Assets (Millions $)	38	26	18	15	13	10	9	6	—	—

PORTFOLIO (as of 6/30/93)

Portfolio Manager: Andrew Windmueller - 1988

Investm't Category: Tax-Exempt Bond

Cap Gain	Asset Allocation
Cap & Income	Fund of Funds
✔ Income	Index
	Sector
✔ Domestic	Small Cap
Foreign	Socially Conscious
Country/Region	State Specific

Portfolio: stocks 0%   bonds 99%
convertibles 0%   other 0%   cash 1%

Largest Holdings: na

Unrealized Net Capital Gains: 5% of portfolio value

SHAREHOLDER INFORMATION

Minimum Investment
Initial: $1,000   Subsequent: $0

Minimum IRA Investment
Initial: na   Subsequent: na

Maximum Fees
Load: none   12b-1: 0.25%
Other: none

Distributions
Income: monthly   Capital Gains: Dec

Exchange Options
Number Per Year: no limit   Fee: none
Telephone: yes (money market fund available)

Services
auto exchange, auto invest, auto withdraw

Brandywine (BRWIX)

Growth

3908 Kennett Pike
Greenville, DE 19807
(302) 656-6200

	3yr Annual	5yr Annual	10yr Annual	Bull	Bear
Return (%)	28.3	23.1	na	121.1	-3.7
Differ from Category (+/-)	9.1 high	8.5 high	na	36.4 high	8.7 high

Total Risk	Standard Deviation	Category Risk	Risk Index	Beta
high	16.8%	high	1.6	1.1

	1993	1992	1991	1990	1989	1988	1987	1986	1985	1984
Return (%)	22.5	15.6	49.1	0.6	32.8	17.6	2.6	16.3	—	—
Differ from category (+/-). . .	9.3	4.6	13.7	6.7	7.0	-0.1	1.4	1.8	—	—

PER SHARE DATA

	1993	1992	1991	1990	1989	1988	1987	1986	1985	1984
Dividends, Net Income ($).	0.00	0.01	0.13	0.28	0.03	0.03	0.00	0.02	—	—
Distrib'ns, Cap Gain ($) . . .	2.86	0.54	2.11	0.99	0.68	0.00	0.87	0.00	—	—
Net Asset Value ($)	24.97	22.74	20.17	15.17	16.40	12.87	10.97	11.61	—	—
Expense Ratio (%)	1.10	1.10	1.09	1.12	1.13	1.20	1.20	1.30	—	—
Net Income to Assets (%) .	-0.10	0.20	1.49	0.93	0.23	0.34	-0.18	0.70	—	—
Portfolio Turnover (%).	150	189	188	158	91	107	147	58	—	—
Total Assets (Millions $). .	1,500	695	528	272	170	123	128	57	—	—

PORTFOLIO (as of 9/30/93)

Portfolio Manager: not specified

Investm't Category: Growth

✔ Cap Gain	Asset Allocation
Cap & Income	Fund of Funds
Income	Index
	Sector
✔ Domestic	Small Cap
✔ Foreign	Socially Conscious
Country/Region	State Specific

Portfolio: stocks 90% bonds 0%
convertibles 0% other 0% cash 10%

Largest Holdings: semi-conductors & related 13%, communications 9%

Unrealized Net Capital Gains: 23% of portfolio value

SHAREHOLDER INFORMATION

Minimum Investment
Initial: $25,000   Subsequent: $1,000

Minimum IRA Investment
Initial: $25,000   Subsequent: $1,000

Maximum Fees
Load: none   12b-1: none
Other: none

Distributions
Income: Oct, Dec   Capital Gains: Oct, Dec

Exchange Options
Number Per Year: none   Fee: na
Telephone: na

Services
IRA, auto withdraw

Brinson Global (BPGLX)

International Stock

209 South LaSalle Street
Chicago, IL 60604
(312) 220-7100

	3yr Annual	5yr Annual	10yr Annual	Bull	Bear
Return (%)	na	na	na	na	na
Differ from Category (+/-)	na	na	na	na	na

Total Risk	Standard Deviation	Category Risk	Risk Index	Beta
na	na	na	na	na

	1993	1992	1991	1990	1989	1988	1987	1986	1985	1984
Return (%)	11.1	—	—	—	—	—	—	—	—	—
Differ from category (+/-) .	-27.4	—	—	—	—	—	—	—	—	—

PER SHARE DATA

	1993	1992	1991	1990	1989	1988	1987	1986	1985	1984
Dividends, Net Income ($) .	0.27	—	—	—	—	—	—	—	—	—
Distrib'ns, Cap Gain ($) . . .	0.27	—	—	—	—	—	—	—	—	—
Net Asset Value ($)	10.79	—	—	—	—	—	—	—	—	—
Expense Ratio (%)	1.05	—	—	—	—	—	—	—	—	—
Net Income to Assets (%) . .	3.56	—	—	—	—	—	—	—	—	—
Portfolio Turnover (%)	149	—	—	—	—	—	—	—	—	—
Total Assets (Millions $) . . .	252	—	—	—	—	—	—	—	—	—

PORTFOLIO (as of 6/30/93)

Portfolio Manager: committee

Investm't Category: International Stock

Cap Gain	✔ Asset Allocation
✔ Cap & Income	Fund of Funds
Income	Index
	Sector
✔ Domestic	Small Cap
✔ Foreign	Socially Conscious
Country/Region	State Specific

Portfolio: stocks 28% bonds 50%
convertibles 0% other 0% cash 22%

Largest Holdings: United States 56%

Unrealized Net Capital Gains: 4% of portfolio value

SHAREHOLDER INFORMATION

Minimum Investment
Initial: $100,000   Subsequent: $2,500

Minimum IRA Investment
Initial: na   Subsequent: na

Maximum Fees
Load: none   12b-1: none
Other: none

Distributions
Income: quarterly   Capital Gains: Dec

Exchange Options
Number Per Year: none   Fee: na
Telephone: na

Services

Bruce (BRUFX)

Growth

20 N. Wacker Dr., Suite 2414
Chicago, IL 60606
(312) 236-9160

PERFORMANCE

	3yr Annual	5yr Annual	10yr Annual	Bull	Bear
Return (%)	10.2	8.9	10.4	51.4	-12.4
Differ from Category (+/-)	-9.0 low	-5.7 low	-2.2 low	-33.3 low	0.0 av

Total Risk	Standard Deviation	Category Risk	Risk Index	Beta
abv av	13.9%	abv av	1.3	0.3

	1993	1992	1991	1990	1989	1988	1987	1986	1985	1984
Return (%).............	19.4	10.6	1.4	-1.0	15.6	12.8	-18.0	29.5	38.7	6.1
Differ from category (+/-)...	6.2	-0.4	-34.0	5.1	-10.2	-4.9	-19.2	15.0	9.4	6.1

PER SHARE DATA

	1993	1992	1991	1990	1989	1988	1987	1986	1985	1984
Dividends, Net Income ($).	6.95	2.50	1.97	1.95	2.76	2.52	3.65	1.29	10.20	8.25
Distrib'ns, Cap Gain ($) ...	0.00	0.00	0.00	0.00	0.00	0.00	8.63	0.00	36.94	99.23
Net Asset Value ($)	112.02	99.66	92.37	93.16	96.18	85.66	78.10	109.39	85.34	103.79
Expense Ratio (%)	2.12	2.17	2.47	2.25	1.83	1.92	1.64	2.68	4.89	2.92
Net Income to Assets (%).	6.22	2.49	2.25	1.58	2.92	2.55	2.40	2.30	4.99	3.39
Portfolio Turnover (%)......	13	4	41	20	6	5	11	0	84	98
Total Assets (Millions $)......	2	2	2	3	4	5	7	2	1	1

PORTFOLIO (as of 6/30/93)

Portfolio Manager: Robert Bruce - 1983

Investm't Category: Growth

✔ Cap Gain	Asset Allocation
Cap & Income	Fund of Funds
Income	Index
	Sector
✔ Domestic	Small Cap
Foreign	Socially Conscious
Country/Region	State Specific

Portfolio: stocks 21% bonds 79%
convertibles 0% other 0% cash 0%

Largest Holdings: U.S. government 63%,
property—casualty insurance 6%

Unrealized Net Capital Gains: 11% of portfolio value

SHAREHOLDER INFORMATION

Minimum Investment
Initial: $1,000   Subsequent: $500

Minimum IRA Investment
Initial: $1,000   Subsequent: $500

Maximum Fees
Load: none   12b-1: none
Other: none

Distributions
Income: Dec   Capital Gains: Dec

Exchange Options
Number Per Year: none Fee: na
Telephone: na

Services
IRA, other pension

Brundage Story & Rose Short/Interm (BRSFX)

General Bond

312 Walnut Street
21st Floor
Cincinnati, OH 45202
(800) 543-8721, (513) 629-2000

PERFORMANCE

	3yr Annual	5yr Annual	10yr Annual	Bull	Bear
Return (%)	9.3	na	na	na	na
Differ from Category (+/-)	-0.8 blw av	na	na	na	na

Total Risk	Standard Deviation	Category Risk	Risk Index	Avg Mat
low	2.7%	blw av	0.9	8.8 yrs

	1993	1992	1991	1990	1989	1988	1987	1986	1985	1984
Return (%)	8.3	6.4	13.2	—	—	—	—	—	—	—
Differ from category (+/-)	-0.8	-0.3	-1.4	—	—	—	—	—	—	—

PER SHARE DATA

	1993	1992	1991	1990	1989	1988	1987	1986	1985	1984
Dividends, Net Income ($)	0.63	0.68	0.68	—	—	—	—	—	—	—
Distrib'ns, Cap Gain ($)	0.03	0.00	0.00	—	—	—	—	—	—	—
Net Asset Value ($)	10.76	10.56	10.59	—	—	—	—	—	—	—
Expense Ratio (%)	0.50	0.50	0.50	—	—	—	—	—	—	—
Net Income to Assets (%)	6.28	6.50	7.05	—	—	—	—	—	—	—
Portfolio Turnover (%)	36	24	12	—	—	—	—	—	—	—
Total Assets (Millions $)	73	32	12	—	—	—	—	—	—	—

PORTFOLIO (as of 5/31/93)

Portfolio Manager: Dean Benner - 1991

Investm't Category: General Bond

Cap Gain	Asset Allocation
Cap & Income	Fund of Funds
✔ Income	Index
	Sector
✔ Domestic	Small Cap
Foreign	Socially Conscious
Country/Region	State Specific

Portfolio: stocks 0% bonds 92%
convertibles 0% other 0% cash 8%

Largest Holdings: mortgage-backed 51%, corporate 30%

Unrealized Net Capital Gains: 2% of portfolio value

SHAREHOLDER INFORMATION

Minimum Investment
Initial: $1,000   Subsequent: $0

Minimum IRA Investment
Initial: $250   Subsequent: $0

Maximum Fees
Load: none   12b-1: 0.25%
Other: none

Distributions
Income: monthly   Capital Gains: Dec

Exchange Options
Number Per Year: no limit   Fee: none
Telephone: yes (money market fund available)

Services
IRA, other pension, auto invest, auto withdraw

BT Investments—Utility
(BTIUX)
Growth & Income

280 Park Avenue
Suite 2 West
New York, NY 10017
(800) 365-2223, (212) 454-2709

PERFORMANCE

	3yr Annual	5yr Annual	10yr Annual	Bull	Bear
Return (%)	na	na	na	na	na
Differ from Category (+/-)	na	na	na	na	na

Total Risk	Standard Deviation		Category Risk	Risk Index	Beta
na	na		na	na	na

	1993	1992	1991	1990	1989	1988	1987	1986	1985	1984
Return (%)	11.0	—	—	—	—	—	—	—	—	—
Differ from category (+/-). . .	-1.6	—	—	—	—	—	—	—	—	—

PER SHARE DATA

	1993	1992	1991	1990	1989	1988	1987	1986	1985	1984
Dividends, Net Income ($).	0.38	—	—	—	—	—	—	—	—	—
Distrib'ns, Cap Gain ($) . . .	0.00	—	—	—	—	—	—	—	—	—
Net Asset Value ($)	10.83	—	—	—	—	—	—	—	—	—
Expense Ratio (%)	1.25	—	—	—	—	—	—	—	—	—
Net Income to Assets (%) .	4.02	—	—	—	—	—	—	—	—	—
Portfolio Turnover (%).	0	—	—	—	—	—	—	—	—	—
Total Assets (Millions $). . . .	37	—	—	—	—	—	—	—	—	—

PORTFOLIO (as of 6/30/93)

Portfolio Manager: Murray Stahl - 1992

Investm't Category: Growth & Income
Cap Gain	Asset Allocation
✔ Cap & Income	Fund of Funds
Income	Index
	✔ Sector
✔ Domestic	Small Cap
Foreign	Socially Conscious
Country/Region	State Specific

Portfolio: stocks 88% bonds 0%
convertibles 1% other 1% cash 10%

Largest Holdings: utility—electric 42%, utility—gas pipe line 26%

Unrealized Net Capital Gains: 6% of portfolio value

SHAREHOLDER INFORMATION

Minimum Investment
Initial: $20,000   Subsequent: $5,000

Minimum IRA Investment
Initial: none   Subsequent: none

Maximum Fees
Load: none   12b-1: 0.20%
Other: none

Distributions
Income: quarterly   Capital Gains: Dec

Exchange Options
Number Per Year: no limit   Fee: none
Telephone: yes (money market fund available)

Services
IRA, other pension

Bull & Bear Financial News Composite (BBFNX)

11 Hanover Square
New York, NY 10005
(800) 847-4200, (212) 363-1100

Growth & Income

PERFORMANCE

	3yr Annual	5yr Annual	10yr Annual	Bull	Bear
Return (%)	13.1	na	na	53.5	-14.9
Differ from Category (+/-)	-3.3 blw av	na	na	-16.6 low	-3.3 blw av

Total Risk	Standard Deviation	Category Risk	Risk Index	Beta
av	10.4%	av	1.2	0.8

	1993	1992	1991	1990	1989	1988	1987	1986	1985	1984
Return (%)	12.6	1.4	26.7	-9.8	—	—	—	—	—	—
Differ from category (+/-)	0.0	-8.6	-1.0	-4.2	—	—	—	—	—	—

PER SHARE DATA

	1993	1992	1991	1990	1989	1988	1987	1986	1985	1984
Dividends, Net Income ($)	0.18	0.20	0.55	0.00	—	—	—	—	—	—
Distrib'ns, Cap Gain ($)	0.74	0.00	3.89	0.00	—	—	—	—	—	—
Net Asset Value ($)	18.86	17.55	17.50	18.29	—	—	—	—	—	—
Expense Ratio (%)	1.77	1.79	1.78	1.73	—	—	—	—	—	—
Net Income to Assets (%)	0.95	1.14	1.63	2.06	—	—	—	—	—	—
Portfolio Turnover (%)	na	24	40	217	—	—	—	—	—	—
Total Assets (Millions $)	5	6	7	7	—	—	—	—	—	—

PORTFOLIO (as of 6/30/93)

Portfolio Manager: Thomas Winmill - 1989

Investm't Category: Growth & Income
Cap Gain	Asset Allocation
✔ Cap & Income	Fund of Funds
Income	✔ Index
	Sector
✔ Domestic	Small Cap
Foreign	Socially Conscious
Country/Region	State Specific

Portfolio: stocks 100% bonds 0%
convertibles 0% other 0% cash 0%

Largest Holdings: Financial News Composite Index

Unrealized Net Capital Gains: 9% of portfolio value

SHAREHOLDER INFORMATION

Minimum Investment
Initial: $1,000   Subsequent: $100

Minimum IRA Investment
Initial: $500   Subsequent: $100

Maximum Fees
Load: none   12b-1: 0.25%
Other: none

Distributions
Income: Dec   Capital Gains: Dec

Exchange Options
Number Per Year: no limit   Fee: none
Telephone: yes (money market fund available)

Services
IRA, other pension, auto invest, auto withdraw

Bull & Bear Global Income (BBGLX)

International Bond

11 Hanover Square
New York, NY 10005
(800) 847-4200, (212) 363-1100

PERFORMANCE

	3yr Annual	5yr Annual	10yr Annual	Bull	Bear
Return (%)	18.5	9.4	7.8	64.2	-1.5
Differ from Category (+/-)	6.5 high	-2.0 low	0.0 high	6.1 high	-8.1 low

Total Risk	Standard Deviation	Category Risk	Risk Index	Avg Mat
blw av	4.1%	low	1.0	17.6 yrs

	1993	1992	1991	1990	1989	1988	1987	1986	1985	1984
Return (%).	24.9	13.1	17.9	-3.0	-3.0	4.9	-6.4	5.9	20.9	7.9
Differ from category (+/-). .	12.2	8.3	3.0	-14.5	-5.2	2.5	-19.8	0.0	0.0	0.0

PER SHARE DATA

	1993	1992	1991	1990	1989	1988	1987	1986	1985	1984
Dividends, Net Income ($).	0.72	0.75	0.74	0.96	1.20	1.29	1.62	1.84	1.92	1.95
Distrib'ns, Cap Gain ($) . . .	0.00	0.00	0.00	0.00	0.00	0.00	0.00	0.00	0.00	0.00
Net Asset Value ($)	9.94	8.59	8.29	7.71	8.93	10.43	11.19	13.57	14.55	13.76
Expense Ratio (%)	1.95	1.93	1.95	1.72	1.68	1.71	1.50	1.37	1.16	0.99
Net Income to Assets (%) .	7.44	9.25	10.08	10.99	12.08	11.96	12.40	13.45	13.86	13.77
Portfolio Turnover (%).	172	206	555	134	122	124	85	77	127	95
Total Assets (Millions $). . . .	57	44	43	51	83	124	206	113	33	8

PORTFOLIO (as of 6/30/93)

Portfolio Manager: Clifford McCarthy - 1990

Investm't Category: International Bond
- Cap Gain
- Cap & Income
- ✔ Income

- ✔ Domestic
- ✔ Foreign
- Country/Region

- Asset Allocation
- Fund of Funds
- Index
- Sector
- Small Cap
- Socially Conscious
- State Specific

Portfolio: stocks 0%   bonds 87%
convertibles 1%   other 11%   cash 1%

Largest Holdings: United States 52%, Argentina 6%

Unrealized Net Capital Gains: 6% of portfolio value

SHAREHOLDER INFORMATION

Minimum Investment
Initial: $1,000   Subsequent: $100

Minimum IRA Investment
Initial: $500   Subsequent: $100

Maximum Fees
Load: none   12b-1: 0.50%
Other: none

Distributions
Income: monthly   Capital Gains: Dec

Exchange Options
Number Per Year: no limit   Fee: none
Telephone: yes (money market fund available)

Services
IRA, other pension, auto invest, auto withdraw

Bull & Bear Gold Investors Ltd (BBGIX)

Gold

11 Hanover Square
New York, NY 10005
(800) 847-4200, (212) 363-1100

PERFORMANCE

	3yr Annual	5yr Annual	10yr Annual	Bull	Bear
Return (%)	15.3	7.3	5.2	38.6	-13.7
Differ from Category (+/-)	1.6 av	-5.0 av	2.3 abv av	5.0 av	-59.6 blw av

Total Risk	Standard Deviation	Category Risk	Risk Index	Beta
high	24.6%	blw av	0.9	-0.3

	1993	1992	1991	1990	1989	1988	1987	1986	1985	1984
Return (%)	87.6	-17.1	-1.1	-22.1	19.3	-13.5	30.3	35.0	2.5	-25.1
Differ from category (+/-)	0.6	-1.4	3.7	-53.6	-5.4	5.4	-1.6	-2.6	9.9	1.1

PER SHARE DATA

	1993	1992	1991	1990	1989	1988	1987	1986	1985	1984
Dividends, Net Income ($)	0.00	0.00	0.05	0.03	0.12	0.03	0.00	0.02	0.11	0.14
Distrib'ns, Cap Gain ($)	0.10	0.00	0.00	0.00	0.00	0.00	1.39	0.00	0.00	0.00
Net Asset Value ($)	18.52	9.93	11.99	12.18	15.69	13.26	15.37	12.86	9.55	9.43
Expense Ratio (%)	3.01	2.96	2.59	2.62	2.46	2.33	2.46	2.39	1.74	1.71
Net Income to Assets (%)	-0.29	-0.63	0.34	0.65	0.17	0.10	-0.21	0.18	1.08	1.23
Portfolio Turnover (%)	156	97	95	65	60	52	66	32	30	31
Total Assets (Millions $)	53	25	33	40	38	48	62	20	21	22

PORTFOLIO (as of 6/30/93)

Portfolio Manager: Robert Radsch - 1982

Investm't Category: Gold

✔ Cap Gain	Asset Allocation
Cap & Income	Fund of Funds
Income	Index
	✔ Sector
✔ Domestic	Small Cap
✔ Foreign	Socially Conscious
Country/Region	State Specific

Portfolio: stocks 87%   bonds 0%
convertibles 0%   other 13%   cash 0%

Largest Holdings: N. American gold mining cos. 36%, S. African gold mining cos. 35%

Unrealized Net Capital Gains: 27% of portfolio value

SHAREHOLDER INFORMATION

Minimum Investment
Initial: $1,000   Subsequent: $100

Minimum IRA Investment
Initial: $500   Subsequent: $100

Maximum Fees
Load: none   12b-1: 1.00%
Other: none

Distributions
Income: Dec   Capital Gains: Dec

Exchange Options
Number Per Year: no limit   Fee: none
Telephone: yes (money market fund available)

Services
IRA, other pension, auto invest, auto withdraw

Bull & Bear Muni Income

(BBMIX)

Tax-Exempt Bond

11 Hanover Square
New York, NY 10005
(800) 847-4200, (212) 363-1100

PERFORMANCE

	3yr Annual	5yr Annual	10yr Annual	Bull	Bear
Return (%)	10.0	8.5	na	38.2	0.1
Differ from Category (+/-)	-0.3 blw av	-0.6 low	na	-1.9 blw av	-2.2 low

Total Risk	Standard Deviation	Category Risk	Risk Index	Avg Mat
blw av	5.4%	high	1.3	11.8 yrs

	1993	1992	1991	1990	1989	1988	1987	1986	1985	1984
Return (%).............	10.5	6.0	13.6	3.8	8.9	11.6	-0.8	19.6	22.4	—
Differ from category (+/-)....	-1.1	-2.3	2.3	-2.5	-0.1	1.5	0.3	3.2	5.1	—

PER SHARE DATA

	1993	1992	1991	1990	1989	1988	1987	1986	1985	1984
Dividends, Net Income ($).	0.75	0.89	1.02	1.01	1.13	1.18	1.25	1.30	1.39	—
Distrib'ns, Cap Gain ($)	0.44	0.32	0.86	0.00	0.51	0.00	0.00	0.57	0.00	—
Net Asset Value ($)	17.63	17.06	17.27	16.92	17.29	17.44	16.74	18.17	16.88	—
Expense Ratio (%)	1.61	1.60	1.60	1.50	1.35	1.27	1.18	1.18	1.02	—
Net Income to Assets (%) .	4.42	5.19	5.86	5.94	6.35	7.11	7.18	7.29	8.70	—
Portfolio Turnover (%)......	na	320	511	172	188	70	62	60	46	—
Total Assets (Millions $).....	22	21	20	21	21	19	16	21	11	—

PORTFOLIO (as of 6/30/93)

Portfolio Manager: Cliff McCarthy - 1990

Investm't Category: Tax-Exempt Bond

Cap Gain	Asset Allocation
Cap & Income	Fund of Funds
✔ Income	Index
	Sector
✔ Domestic	Small Cap
Foreign	Socially Conscious
Country/Region	State Specific

Portfolio: stocks 0%   bonds 100%
convertibles 0%   other 0%   cash 0%

Largest Holdings: general obligation 14%

Unrealized Net Capital Gains: 5% of portfolio value

SHAREHOLDER INFORMATION

Minimum Investment
Initial: $1,000   Subsequent: $100

Minimum IRA Investment
Initial: na   Subsequent: na

Maximum Fees
Load: none   12b-1: 0.50%
Other: none

Distributions
Income: monthly   Capital Gains: Dec

Exchange Options
Number Per Year: no limit   Fee: none
Telephone: yes (money market fund available)

Services
auto exchange, auto invest, auto withdraw

Bull & Bear Special Equities (BBSEX)

11 Hanover Square
New York, NY 10005
(800) 847-4200, (212) 363-1100

Aggressive Growth

PERFORMANCE

	3yr Annual	5yr Annual	10yr Annual	Bull	Bear
Return (%)	28.0	13.6	na	87.4	-28.7
Differ from Category (+/-)	2.6 abv av	-4.6 blw av	na	-37.6 low	-13.7 low

Total Risk	Standard Deviation	Category Risk	Risk Index	Beta
high	20.8%	high	1.4	1.2

	1993	1992	1991	1990	1989	1988	1987	1986	1985	1984
Return (%)	16.3	28.3	40.5	-36.3	42.2	22.7	-6.4	—	—	—
Differ from category (+/-)	-2.7	17.9	-11.9	-30.0	15.2	7.5	-3.0	—	—	—

PER SHARE DATA

	1993	1992	1991	1990	1989	1988	1987	1986	1985	1984
Dividends, Net Income ($)	0.00	0.00	0.00	0.00	0.00	0.00	0.00	—	—	—
Distrib'ns, Cap Gain ($)	5.64	0.00	0.00	0.00	4.05	1.15	0.00	—	—	—
Net Asset Value ($)	23.13	24.88	19.38	13.79	21.68	18.17	15.75	—	—	—
Expense Ratio (%)	2.62	3.07	2.83	3.10	3.50	2.94	3.01	—	—	—
Net Income to Assets (%)	-2.51	-2.78	-2.11	-3.19	-3.23	-1.49	-0.82	—	—	—
Portfolio Turnover (%)	na	261	384	475	433	514	751	—	—	—
Total Assets (Millions $)	70	68	17	9	6	3	2	—	—	—

PORTFOLIO (as of 6/30/93)

Portfolio Manager: Brett B. Sneed - 1988

Investm't Category: Aggressive Growth

✔ Cap Gain	Asset Allocation
Cap & Income	Fund of Funds
Income	Index
	Sector
✔ Domestic	Small Cap
✔ Foreign	Socially Conscious
Country/Region	State Specific

Portfolio: stocks 100% bonds 0%
convertibles 0% other 0% cash 0%

Largest Holdings: communications products & equipment 21%, semiconductors 16%

Unrealized Net Capital Gains: 11% of portfolio value

SHAREHOLDER INFORMATION

Minimum Investment
Initial: $1,000   Subsequent: $100

Minimum IRA Investment
Initial: $500   Subsequent: $100

Maximum Fees
Load: none   12b-1: 1.00%
Other: none

Distributions
Income: Dec   Capital Gains: Dec

Exchange Options
Number Per Year: no limit   Fee: none
Telephone: yes (money market fund available)

Services
IRA, other pension, auto invest, auto withdraw

Bull & Bear US & Overseas (BBOSX)

International Stock

11 Hanover Square
New York, NY 10005
(800) 847-4200, (212) 363-1100

PERFORMANCE

	3yr Annual	5yr Annual	10yr Annual	Bull	Bear
Return (%)	14.8	9.8	na	56.2	-11.4
Differ from Category (+/-)	0.5 av	1.1 av	na	1.1 abv av	3.7 abv av

Total Risk	Standard Deviation	Category Risk	Risk Index	Beta
abv av	11.5%	low	1.0	0.6

	1993	1992	1991	1990	1989	1988	1987	1986	1985	1984
Return (%)	26.7	-2.6	22.6	-8.5	15.5	3.7	—	—	—	—
Differ from category (+/-). .	-11.8	0.8	9.7	2.6	-6.7	-10.1	—	—	—	—

PER SHARE DATA

	1993	1992	1991	1990	1989	1988	1987	1986	1985	1984
Dividends, Net Income ($).	0.00	0.00	0.00	0.00	0.02	0.02	—	—	—	—
Distrib'ns, Cap Gain ($) . . .	0.89	0.57	0.96	0.11	0.44	0.00	—	—	—	—
Net Asset Value ($)	8.71	7.59	8.38	7.62	8.48	7.72	—	—	—	—
Expense Ratio (%)	3.57	3.56	3.56	3.50	3.50	3.02	—	—	—	—
Net Income to Assets (%) .	-1.86	0.51	0.90	-0.09	-1.29	0.44	—	—	—	—
Portfolio Turnover (%).	na	175	208	270	178	140	—	—	—	—
Total Assets (Millions $).	11	9	1	1	1	1	—	—	—	—

PORTFOLIO (as of 6/30/93)

Portfolio Manager: Robert Radsch - 1991

Investm't Category: International Stock

Cap Gain	Asset Allocation
✔ Cap & Income	Fund of Funds
Income	Index
	Sector
✔ Domestic	Small Cap
✔ Foreign	Socially Conscious
Country/Region	State Specific

Portfolio: stocks 100% bonds 0%
convertibles 0% other 0% cash 0%

Largest Holdings: United States 29%, Canada 15%

Unrealized Net Capital Gains: 14% of portfolio value

SHAREHOLDER INFORMATION

Minimum Investment
Initial: $1,000   Subsequent: $100

Minimum IRA Investment
Initial: $500   Subsequent: $100

Maximum Fees
Load: none   12b-1: 1.00%
Other: none

Distributions
Income: Dec   Capital Gains: Dec

Exchange Options
Number Per Year: no limit   Fee: none
Telephone: yes (money market fund available)

Services
IRA, other pension, auto invest, auto withdraw

Bull & Bear US Gov't Securities (BBUSX)

11 Hanover Square
New York, NY 10005
(800) 847-4200, (212) 363-1100

Mortgage-Backed Bond

PERFORMANCE

	3yr Annual	5yr Annual	10yr Annual	Bull	Bear
Return (%)	10.1	9.7	na	40.0	2.8
Differ from Category (+/-)	0.8 high	-0.2 blw av	na	3.3 high	-1.8 low

Total Risk	Standard Deviation	Category Risk	Risk Index	Avg Mat
blw av	4.4%	high	1.7	16.2 yrs

	1993	1992	1991	1990	1989	1988	1987	1986	1985	1984
Return (%)	10.2	5.2	15.1	7.8	10.3	4.5	5.4	—	—	—
Differ from category (+/-) . . .	3.4	-0.8	0.6	-1.7	-2.0	-2.5	3.3	—	—	—

PER SHARE DATA

	1993	1992	1991	1990	1989	1988	1987	1986	1985	1984
Dividends, Net Income ($) .	0.69	0.89	0.95	1.01	1.14	1.38	1.46	—	—	—
Distrib'ns, Cap Gain ($) . . .	0.00	0.00	0.00	0.00	0.00	0.00	0.00	—	—	—
Net Asset Value ($)	15.60	14.80	14.95	13.88	13.87	13.65	14.38	—	—	—
Expense Ratio (%)	1.91	1.86	1.86	1.99	1.74	1.96	2.06	—	—	—
Net Income to Assets (%) . .	5.38	6.40	7.14	7.86	8.87	9.95	9.40	—	—	—
Portfolio Turnover (%)	176	140	407	279	217	174	185	—	—	—
Total Assets (Millions $)	21	26	31	33	38	64	47	—	—	—

PORTFOLIO (as of 6/30/93)

Portfolio Manager: Cliff McCarthy - 1990

Investm't Category: Mortgage-Backed Bond
Cap Gain	Asset Allocation
Cap & Income	Fund of Funds
✔ Income	Index
	Sector
✔ Domestic	Small Cap
Foreign	Socially Conscious
Country/Region	State Specific

Portfolio: stocks 0% bonds 100%
convertibles 0% other 0% cash 0%

Largest Holdings: U.S. government 82%, mortgage-backed 18%

Unrealized Net Capital Gains: 4% of portfolio value

SHAREHOLDER INFORMATION

Minimum Investment
Initial: $1,000   Subsequent: $100

Minimum IRA Investment
Initial: $500   Subsequent: $100

Maximum Fees
Load: none   12b-1: 0.25%
Other: none

Distributions
Income: monthly   Capital Gains: Dec

Exchange Options
Number Per Year: no limit   Fee: none
Telephone: yes (money market fund available)

Services
IRA, other pension, auto invest, auto withdraw

CA Investment Trust US Gov't (CAUSX)

44 Montgomery St., Suite 2200
San Francisco, CA 94104
(800) 225-8778, (415) 398-2727

Government Bond

PERFORMANCE

	3yr Annual	5yr Annual	10yr Annual	Bull	Bear
Return (%)	13.8	12.6	na	54.8	3.4
Differ from Category (+/-)	3.0 abv av	2.2 high	na	8.6 abv av	2.9 av

Total Risk	Standard Deviation	Category Risk	Risk Index	Avg Mat
blw av	6.0%	abv av	1.4	24.9 yrs

	1993	1992	1991	1990	1989	1988	1987	1986	1985	1984
Return (%)	15.7	8.4	17.4	8.5	13.4	7.2	1.2	11.9	—	—
Differ from category (+/-) . . .	5.3	2.2	2.4	2.0	-0.5	-0.4	3.0	-7.2	—	—

PER SHARE DATA

	1993	1992	1991	1990	1989	1988	1987	1986	1985	1984
Dividends, Net Income ($) .	0.70	0.72	0.82	0.81	0.85	0.87	0.95	0.82	—	—
Distrib'ns, Cap Gain ($) . . .	0.05	0.05	0.00	0.00	0.00	0.00	0.00	0.00	—	—
Net Asset Value ($)	11.29	10.43	10.38	9.61	9.64	9.29	9.49	10.33	—	—
Expense Ratio (%)	0.52	0.38	0.60	0.60	0.61	0.59	0.34	0.04	—	—
Net Income to Assets (%) .	6.55	7.12	8.73	8.64	9.18	9.24	8.27	9.66	—	—
Portfolio Turnover (%).	52	122	53	78	78	110	115	278	—	—
Total Assets (Millions $)	35	80	21	12	11	10	13	10	—	—

PORTFOLIO (as of 8/31/93)

Portfolio Manager: Phillip McClanahan - 1985

Investm't Category: Government Bond

Cap Gain	Asset Allocation
Cap & Income	Fund of Funds
✔ Income	Index
	Sector
✔ Domestic	Small Cap
Foreign	Socially Conscious
Country/Region	State Specific

Portfolio: stocks 0%   bonds 99%
convertibles 0%   other 0%   cash 1%

Largest Holdings: U.S. government 66%, mortgage-backed 20%

Unrealized Net Capital Gains: 12% of portfolio value

SHAREHOLDER INFORMATION

Minimum Investment
Initial: $10,000   Subsequent: $250

Minimum IRA Investment
Initial: $0   Subsequent: $0

Maximum Fees
Load: none   12b-1: none
Other: none

Distributions
Income: monthly   Capital Gains: Dec

Exchange Options
Number Per Year: no limit   Fee: none
Telephone: yes (money market fund available)

Services
IRA, other pension, auto exchange, auto invest, auto withdraw

Cal Muni (CAMFX)

Tax-Exempt Bond

90 Washington St.
New York, NY 10006
(800) 225-6864, (212) 635-3005

PERFORMANCE

	3yr Annual	5yr Annual	10yr Annual	Bull	Bear
Return (%)	10.8	8.9	na	39.5	1.9
Differ from Category (+/-)	0.5 av	-0.3 blw av	na	-0.6 blw av	-0.4 blw av

Total Risk	Standard Deviation	Category Risk	Risk Index	Avg Mat
blw av	4.6%	abv av	1.1	18.6 yrs

	1993	1992	1991	1990	1989	1988	1987	1986	1985	1984
Return (%)	16.7	7.2	8.8	4.3	8.0	12.2	1.4	9.6	22.1	—
Differ from category (+/-) . . .	5.1	-1.1	-2.5	-2.0	-1.0	2.1	2.6	-6.8	4.8	—

PER SHARE DATA

	1993	1992	1991	1990	1989	1988	1987	1986	1985	1984
Dividends, Net Income ($) .	0.55	0.60	0.57	0.55	0.53	0.60	0.66	0.75	0.81	—
Distrib'ns, Cap Gain ($) . . .	0.19	0.00	0.00	0.00	0.21	0.05	0.16	1.65	0.00	—
Net Asset Value ($)	9.49	8.81	8.80	8.64	8.82	8.87	8.52	9.23	10.67	—
Expense Ratio (%).	1.61	1.63	2.38	2.48	2.49	1.55	1.61	2.33	3.02	—
Net Income to Assets (%) . .	6.24	6.87	6.58	6.36	5.95	6.88	7.66	7.16	7.78	—
Portfolio Turnover (%)	39	19	47	43	86	58	32	34	288	—
Total Assets (Millions $)	16	12	10	10	11	10	8	4	11	—

PORTFOLIO (as of 6/30/93)

Portfolio Manager: Lance Brofman - 1984

Investm't Category: Tax-Exempt Bond
- Cap Gain
- Cap & Income
- ✔ Income
- ✔ Domestic
- Foreign
- Country/Region
- Asset Allocation
- Fund of Funds
- Index
- Sector
- Small Cap
- Socially Conscious
- ✔ State Specific

Portfolio: stocks 0%   bonds 100%
convertibles 0%   other 0%   cash 0%

Largest Holdings: general obligation 34%

Unrealized Net Capital Gains: 5% of portfolio value

SHAREHOLDER INFORMATION

Minimum Investment
Initial: $1,000   Subsequent: $100

Minimum IRA Investment
Initial: na   Subsequent: na

Maximum Fees
Load: none   12b-1: 0.50%
Other: none

Distributions
Income: monthly   Capital Gains: Dec

Exchange Options
Number Per Year: no limit   Fee: none
Telephone: yes (money market fund available)

Services
auto exchange, auto invest, auto withdraw

Cal Tax-Free Income
(CFNTX)

Tax-Exempt Bond

44 Montgomery St., Suite 2200
San Francisco, CA 94104
(800) 225-8778, (415) 398-2727

PERFORMANCE

	3yr Annual	5yr Annual	10yr Annual	Bull	Bear
Return (%)	11.8	10.4	na	46.0	2.3
Differ from Category (+/-)	1.5 high	1.2 high	na	5.9 high	0.0 av

Total Risk	Standard Deviation	Category Risk	Risk Index	Avg Mat
blw av	5.6%	high	1.4	22.1 yrs

	1993	1992	1991	1990	1989	1988	1987	1986	1985	1984
Return (%)	14.7	8.8	12.1	6.7	9.9	11.3	-1.2	22.7	—	—
Differ from category (+/-). . .	3.1	0.5	0.8	0.4	0.8	1.2	0.0	6.3	—	—

PER SHARE DATA

	1993	1992	1991	1990	1989	1988	1987	1986	1985	1984
Dividends, Net Income ($).	0.67	0.71	0.73	0.76	0.79	0.80	0.89	0.79	—	—
Distrib'ns, Cap Gain ($) . . .	0.28	0.08	0.00	0.00	0.00	0.00	0.00	0.00	—	—
Net Asset Value ($)	13.18	12.36	12.13	11.52	11.54	11.25	10.86	11.90	—	—
Expense Ratio (%)	0.60	0.60	0.60	0.59	0.60	0.61	0.39	0.03	—	—
Net Income to Assets (%) .	5.41	5.98	6.43	6.67	7.06	7.43	7.22	8.01	—	—
Portfolio Turnover (%).	25	45	44	42	48	102	87	50	—	—
Total Assets (Millions $). . . .	279	217	137	86	70	39	37	21	—	—

PORTFOLIO (as of 8/31/93)

Portfolio Manager: Phillip McClanahan - 1985

Investm't Category: Tax-Exempt Bond
    Cap Gain   Asset Allocation
    Cap & Income   Fund of Funds
 ✔ Income   Index
                  Sector
 ✔ Domestic   Small Cap
    Foreign   Socially Conscious
    Country/Region ✔ State Specific

Portfolio: stocks 0%   bonds 100%
convertibles 0%   other 0%   cash 0%

Largest Holdings: general obligation 5%

Unrealized Net Capital Gains: 12% of portfolio value

SHAREHOLDER INFORMATION

Minimum Investment
Initial: $10,000   Subsequent: $250

Minimum IRA Investment
Initial: na   Subsequent: na

Maximum Fees
Load: none   12b-1: none
Other: none

Distributions
Income: monthly   Capital Gains: Dec

Exchange Options
Number Per Year: no limit   Fee: none
Telephone: yes (money market fund available)

Services
auto exchange, auto invest, auto withdraw

Calvert Tax-Free Reserves Ltd Term (CTFLX)

Tax-Exempt Bond

4550 Montgomery Avenue
Suite 1000 North
Bethesda, MD 20814
(800) 368-2748, (301) 951-4820

PERFORMANCE

	3yr Annual	5yr Annual	10yr Annual	Bull	Bear
Return (%)	5.1	5.8	6.4	18.6	4.4
Differ from Category (+/-)	-5.2 low	-3.4 low	-3.2 low	-21.5 low	2.1 high

Total Risk	Standard Deviation	Category Risk	Risk Index	Avg Mat
low	1.6%	low	0.4	1.0 yrs

	1993	1992	1991	1990	1989	1988	1987	1986	1985	1984
Return (%)	4.0	5.0	6.4	6.4	7.2	6.9	3.6	8.5	8.6	7.3
Differ from category (+/-) ..	-7.6	-3.3	-4.9	0.1	-1.8	-3.2	4.8	-7.9	-8.7	-1.0

PER SHARE DATA

	1993	1992	1991	1990	1989	1988	1987	1986	1985	1984
Dividends, Net Income ($) .	0.38	0.49	0.62	0.66	0.67	0.60	0.59	0.64	0.71	0.68
Distrib'ns, Cap Gain ($) ...	0.00	0.00	0.00	0.00	0.00	0.00	0.00	0.03	0.01	0.00
Net Asset Value ($)	10.72	10.68	10.65	10.61	10.61	10.55	10.45	10.67	10.48	10.33
Expense Ratio (%)........	0.68	0.71	0.73	0.77	0.78	0.81	0.76	0.81	0.88	0.95
Net Income to Assets (%)..	3.67	4.58	5.99	6.35	6.35	5.71	5.59	6.00	6.65	6.84
Portfolio Turnover (%)	na	5	1	12	21	68	52	67	90	155
Total Assets (Millions $) ...	678	568	294	152	133	145	148	189	77	52

PORTFOLIO (as of 6/30/93)

Portfolio Manager: Reno Martini - 1982

Investm't Category: Tax-Exempt Bond

Cap Gain	Asset Allocation
Cap & Income	Fund of Funds
✔ Income	Index
	Sector
✔ Domestic	Small Cap
Foreign	Socially Conscious
Country/Region	State Specific

Portfolio:	stocks 0%	bonds 100%
convertibles 0%	other 0%	cash 0%

Largest Holdings: general obligation 5%

Unrealized Net Capital Gains: 0% of portfolio value

SHAREHOLDER INFORMATION

Minimum Investment
Initial: $2,000   Subsequent: $250

Minimum IRA Investment
Initial: na   Subsequent: na

Maximum Fees
Load: 2.00% front   12b-1: none
Other: none

Distributions
Income: monthly   Capital Gains: Dec

Exchange Options
Number Per Year: 8   Fee: none
Telephone: yes (money market fund available)

Services
auto exchange, auto invest, auto withdraw

Cappiello-Rushmore Emerging Growth (CREGX)

4922 Fairmont Ave.
Bethesda, MD 20814
(800) 621-7874, (301) 657-1517

Aggressive Growth

PERFORMANCE

	3yr Annual	5yr Annual	10yr Annual	Bull	Bear
Return (%)	na	na	na	na	na
Differ from Category (+/-)	na	na	na	na	na

Total Risk	Standard Deviation	Category Risk	Risk Index	Beta
na	na	na	na	na

	1993	1992	1991	1990	1989	1988	1987	1986	1985	1984
Return (%).............	22.5	—	—	—	—	—	—	—	—	—
Differ from category (+/-)...	3.5	—	—	—	—	—	—	—	—	—

PER SHARE DATA

	1993	1992	1991	1990	1989	1988	1987	1986	1985	1984
Dividends, Net Income ($).	0.00	—	—	—	—	—	—	—	—	—
Distrib'ns, Cap Gain ($)...	0.13	—	—	—	—	—	—	—	—	—
Net Asset Value ($).....	12.52	—	—	—	—	—	—	—	—	—
Expense Ratio (%).......	1.50	—	—	—	—	—	—	—	—	—
Net Income to Assets (%)	-0.63	—	—	—	—	—	—	—	—	—
Portfolio Turnover (%).....	67	—	—	—	—	—	—	—	—	—
Total Assets (Millions $).....	12	—	—	—	—	—	—	—	—	—

PORTFOLIO (as of 6/30/93)

Portfolio Manager: Frank Cappiell - 1992

Investm't Category: Aggressive Growth

- ✔ Cap Gain
- Cap & Income
- Income

- Asset Allocation
- Fund of Funds
- Index
- Sector

- ✔ Domestic
- Foreign
- Country/Region

- ✔ Small Cap
- Socially Conscious
- State Specific

Portfolio:	stocks 81%	bonds 0%
convertibles 0%	other 0%	cash 19%

Largest Holdings: electric products 15%, computer & business equipment 11%

Unrealized Net Capital Gains: 4% of portfolio value

SHAREHOLDER INFORMATION

Minimum Investment
Initial: $2,500   Subsequent: $0

Minimum IRA Investment
Initial: $500   Subsequent: $0

Maximum Fees
Load: none   12b-1: none
Other: none

Distributions
Income: Dec   Capital Gains: Dec

Exchange Options
Number Per Year: no limit   Fee: none
Telephone: yes (money market fund available)

Services
IRA, other pension, auto exchange, auto invest, auto withdraw

Cappiello-Rushmore Utility Income (CRUTX)

4922 Fairmont Ave.
Bethesda, MD 20814
(800) 621-7874, (301) 657-1517

Growth & Income

PERFORMANCE

	3yr Annual	5yr Annual	10yr Annual	Bull	Bear
Return (%)	na	na	na	na	na
Differ from Category (+/-)	na	na	na	na	na

Total Risk	Standard Deviation	Category Risk	Risk Index	Beta
na	na	na	na	na

	1993	1992	1991	1990	1989	1988	1987	1986	1985	1984
Return (%)	6.1	—	—	—	—	—	—	—	—	—
Differ from category (+/-)	-6.5	—	—	—	—	—	—	—	—	—

PER SHARE DATA

	1993	1992	1991	1990	1989	1988	1987	1986	1985	1984
Dividends, Net Income ($)	0.36	—	—	—	—	—	—	—	—	—
Distrib'ns, Cap Gain ($)	0.01	—	—	—	—	—	—	—	—	—
Net Asset Value ($)	10.47	—	—	—	—	—	—	—	—	—
Expense Ratio (%)	1.05	—	—	—	—	—	—	—	—	—
Net Income to Assets (%)	3.31	—	—	—	—	—	—	—	—	—
Portfolio Turnover (%)	15	—	—	—	—	—	—	—	—	—
Total Assets (Millions $)	11	—	—	—	—	—	—	—	—	—

PORTFOLIO (as of 6/30/93)

Portfolio Manager: Frank Cappiello - 1992

Investm't Category: Growth & Income

Cap Gain	Asset Allocation
✔ Cap & Income	Fund of Funds
Income	Index
	✔ Sector
✔ Domestic	Small Cap
Foreign	Socially Conscious
Country/Region	State Specific

Portfolio: stocks 85% bonds 0%
convertibles 0% other 0% cash 15%

Largest Holdings: electric power 36%, gas & electric 26%

Unrealized Net Capital Gains: 3% of portfolio value

SHAREHOLDER INFORMATION

Minimum Investment
Initial: $2,500   Subsequent: $0

Minimum IRA Investment
Initial: $500   Subsequent: $0

Maximum Fees
Load: none   12b-1: none
Other: none

Distributions
Income: quarterly   Capital Gains: Dec

Exchange Options
Number Per Year: no limit   Fee: none
Telephone: yes (money market fund available)

Services
IRA, other pension, auto exchange, auto invest, auto withdraw

Capstone Gov't Income
(CGVIX)

Government Bond

P.O. Box 3167
1100 Milam, Suite 3500
Houston, TX 77253
(800) 262-6631

	3yr Annual	5yr Annual	10yr Annual	Bull	Bear
Return (%)	4.4	3.8	8.1	13.6	-0.6
Differ from Category (+/-)	-6.4 low	-6.6 low	-1.6 low	-32.6 low	-1.2 blw av

Total Risk	Standard Deviation	Category Risk	Risk Index	Avg Mat
low	1.2%	low	0.2	1.6 yrs

	1993	1992	1991	1990	1989	1988	1987	1986	1985	1984
Return (%)	3.3	3.5	6.5	-1.0	7.2	11.7	3.7	16.1	20.4	11.2
Differ from category (+/-). . .	-7.1	-2.7	-8.5	-7.5	-6.7	4.1	5.5	-3.0	1.3	-1.8

PER SHARE DATA

	1993	1992	1991	1990	1989	1988	1987	1986	1985	1984
Dividends, Net Income ($).	0.09	0.09	0.17	0.44	0.47	0.43	0.52	0.47	0.47	0.47
Distrib'ns, Cap Gain ($) . . .	0.00	0.00	0.00	0.00	0.00	0.00	0.00	0.00	0.00	0.00
Net Asset Value ($)	4.80	4.74	4.67	4.55	5.05	5.17	5.03	5.36	5.06	4.64
Expense Ratio (%)	1.07	0.96	1.67	1.40	1.24	1.29	1.29	1.52	1.72	1.30
Net Income to Assets (%) .	3.40	4.69	5.29	9.06	8.75	8.51	8.90	9.18	10.32	11.67
Portfolio Turnover (%).	162	633	754	82	70	100	102	186	236	171
Total Assets (Millions $).	90	30	38	18	20	25	23	19	12	8

PORTFOLIO (as of 6/30/93)

Portfolio Manager: Edward Jaroski - 1987, Howard Potter - 1991

Investm't Category: Government Bond

Cap Gain	Asset Allocation
Cap & Income	Fund of Funds
✔ Income	Index
	Sector
✔ Domestic	Small Cap
Foreign	Socially Conscious
Country/Region	State Specific

Portfolio: stocks 0%   bonds 69%
convertibles 0%   other 0%   cash 31%

Largest Holdings: U.S. government 69%

Unrealized Net Capital Gains: 35% of port-folio value

SHAREHOLDER INFORMATION

Minimum Investment
Initial: $10,000   Subsequent: $0

Minimum IRA Investment
Initial: $10,000   Subsequent: $0

Maximum Fees
Load: none   12b-1: 0.20%
Other: none

Distributions
Income: Dec   Capital Gains: Dec

Exchange Options
Number Per Year: 12   Fee: none
Telephone: yes (money market fund available)

Services
IRA, other pension, auto invest, auto withdraw

Century Shares Trust
(CENSX)

Growth

One Liberty Square
Boston, MA 02109
(800) 321-1928, (617) 482-3060

PERFORMANCE

	3yr Annual	5yr Annual	10yr Annual	Bull	Bear
Return (%)	18.5	16.7	15.4	92.6	-20.3
Differ from Category (+/-)	-0.6 av	2.1 abv av	2.8 high	7.9 abv av	-7.9 low

Total Risk	Standard Deviation	Category Risk	Risk Index	Beta
abv av	11.3%	blw av	1.1	0.7

	1993	1992	1991	1990	1989	1988	1987	1986	1985	1984
Return (%)	-0.3	26.9	31.5	-7.8	41.6	15.6	-8.0	9.6	43.4	15.5
Differ from category (+/-)	-13.5	15.9	-3.9	-1.7	15.8	-2.1	-9.2	-4.9	14.1	15.5

PER SHARE DATA

	1993	1992	1991	1990	1989	1988	1987	1986	1985	1984
Dividends, Net Income ($)	0.44	0.41	0.46	0.50	0.50	0.54	0.50	0.50	0.54	0.60
Distrib'ns, Cap Gain ($)	1.10	0.56	0.56	0.57	0.70	1.90	1.61	1.11	0.91	0.91
Net Asset Value ($)	24.04	25.68	21.03	16.82	19.42	14.62	14.76	18.30	18.22	14.02
Expense Ratio (%)	0.40	0.84	0.95	1.03	0.93	0.87	0.81	0.77	0.84	0.95
Net Income to Assets (%)	0.88	1.84	2.28	2.82	2.78	3.45	2.60	2.57	3.14	4.30
Portfolio Turnover (%)	na	5	0	3	3	3	2	6	6	4
Total Assets (Millions $)	241	260	158	130	151	110	109	140	123	76

PORTFOLIO (as of 6/30/93)

Portfolio Manager: Allan W. Fulkerson - 1976

Investm't Category: Growth

Cap Gain	Asset Allocation
✔ Cap & Income	Fund of Funds
Income	Index
	✔ Sector
✔ Domestic	Small Cap
Foreign	Socially Conscious
Country/Region	State Specific

Portfolio: stocks 89% bonds 4%
convertibles 3% other 0% cash 4%

Largest Holdings: insurance 82%, banking institutions 7%

Unrealized Net Capital Gains: 51% of portfolio value

SHAREHOLDER INFORMATION

Minimum Investment
Initial: $500   Subsequent: $25

Minimum IRA Investment
Initial: $500   Subsequent: $25

Maximum Fees
Load: none   12b-1: none
Other: none

Distributions
Income: Jun, Dec   Capital Gains: Dec

Exchange Options
Number Per Year: none Fee: na
Telephone: na

Services
IRA, other pension, auto withdraw

CGM Capital Development (LOMCX)

222 Berkley St., 19th Fl.
Boston, MA 02116
(800) 345-4048, (617) 859-7714

Aggressive Growth

this fund is closed to new investors

PERFORMANCE

	3yr Annual	5yr Annual	10yr Annual	Bull	Bear
Return (%)	44.3	29.2	na	240.8	-10.3
Differ from Category (+/-)	18.9 high	11.0 high	na	115.8 high	4.7 abv av

Total Risk	Standard Deviation	Category Risk	Risk Index	Beta
high	20.3%	abv av	1.3	1.6

	1993	1992	1991	1990	1989	1988	1987	1986	1985	1984
Return (%)	28.6	17.4	99.0	1.4	17.8	-0.2	—	—	—	—
Differ from category (+/-). . .	9.6	7.0	46.6	7.7	-9.2	-15.4	—	—	—	—

PER SHARE DATA

	1993	1992	1991	1990	1989	1988	1987	1986	1985	1984
Dividends, Net Income ($).	0.07	0.20	0.05	0.10	0.34	0.62	—	—	—	—
Distrib'ns, Cap Gain ($) . . .	7.51	2.67	11.07	0.00	0.00	0.01	—	—	—	—
Net Asset Value ($)	27.71	27.43	25.80	18.55	18.37	15.87	—	—	—	—
Expense Ratio (%)	0.85	0.86	0.88	0.93	0.92	0.92	—	—	—	—
Net Income to Assets (%) .	0.42	0.79	0.21	0.40	1.26	3.89	—	—	—	—
Portfolio Turnover (%).	139	163	272	226	254	301	—	—	—	—
Total Assets (Millions $). . . .	523	395	326	176	190	194	—	—	—	—

PORTFOLIO (as of 9/30/93)

Portfolio Manager: G. Kenneth Heebner - 1976

Investm't Category: Aggressive Growth

✔ Cap Gain	Asset Allocation
Cap & Income	Fund of Funds
Income	Index
	Sector
✔ Domestic	Small Cap
Foreign	Socially Conscious
Country/Region	State Specific

Portfolio: stocks 100% bonds 0%
convertibles 0% other 0% cash 0%

Largest Holdings: housing & building materials 20%, basic materials 12%

Unrealized Net Capital Gains: 17% of portfolio value

SHAREHOLDER INFORMATION

Minimum Investment
Initial: $2,500 Subsequent: $50

Minimum IRA Investment
Initial: $1,000 Subsequent: $50

Maximum Fees
Load: none 12b-1: none
Other: none

Distributions
Income: Dec Capital Gains: Dec

Exchange Options
Number Per Year: 4 Fee: none
Telephone: yes (money market fund available)

Services
IRA, other pension, auto exchange, auto invest, auto withdraw

CGM Fixed Income
(CFXIX)
Corporate Bond

222 Berkley St.
19th Fl.
Boston, MA 02116
(800) 345-4048, (617) 859-7714

PERFORMANCE

	3yr Annual	5yr Annual	10yr Annual	Bull	Bear
Return (%)	na	na	na	na	na
Differ from Category (+/-)	na	na	na	na	na

Total Risk	Standard Deviation	Category Risk	Risk Index	Avg Mat
na	na	na	na	13.0 yrs

	1993	1992	1991	1990	1989	1988	1987	1986	1985	1984
Return (%)	18.9	—	—	—	—	—	—	—	—	—
Differ from category (+/-) ...	7.5	—	—	—	—	—	—	—	—	—

PER SHARE DATA

	1993	1992	1991	1990	1989	1988	1987	1986	1985	1984
Dividends, Net Income ($) .	0.67	—	—	—	—	—	—	—	—	—
Distrib'ns, Cap Gain ($) ...	0.31	—	—	—	—	—	—	—	—	—
Net Asset Value ($)	11.17	—	—	—	—	—	—	—	—	—
Expense Ratio (%)........	0.85	—	—	—	—	—	—	—	—	—
Net Income to Assets (%)..	6.41	—	—	—	—	—	—	—	—	—
Portfolio Turnover (%)....	206	—	—	—	—	—	—	—	—	—
Total Assets (Millions $)	32	—	—	—	—	—	—	—	—	—

PORTFOLIO (as of 9/30/93)

Portfolio Manager: Janis H. Saul - 1992, G. Kenneth Heebner - 1992

Investm't Category: Corporate Bond
Cap Gain	Asset Allocation
Cap & Income	Fund of Funds
✔ Income	Index
	Sector
✔ Domestic	Small Cap
✔ Foreign	Socially Conscious
Country/Region	State Specific

Portfolio: stocks 0% bonds 67%
convertibles 0% other 30% cash 3%

Largest Holdings: housing & building materials 9%, basic materials 8%

Unrealized Net Capital Gains: 2% of portfolio value

SHAREHOLDER INFORMATION

Minimum Investment
Initial: $2,500   Subsequent: $50

Minimum IRA Investment
Initial: $1,000   Subsequent: $50

Maximum Fees
Load: none   12b-1: none
Other: none

Distributions
Income: monthly   Capital Gains: none

Exchange Options
Number Per Year: 4   Fee: none
Telephone: yes (money market fund available)

Services
IRA, other pension, auto exchange, auto invest, auto withdraw

CGM Mutual (LOMMX)

Balanced

222 Berkley St.
19th Fl.
Boston, MA 02116
(800) 345-4048, (617) 859-7714

PERFORMANCE

	3yr Annual	5yr Annual	10yr Annual	Bull	Bear
Return (%)	22.0	17.4	na	97.9	-7.0
Differ from Category (+/-)	7.0 high	5.3 high	na	36.3 high	-1.2 blw av

Total Risk	Standard Deviation	Category Risk	Risk Index	Beta
abv av	12.2%	high	2.0	1.0

	1993	1992	1991	1990	1989	1988	1987	1986	1985	1984
Return (%)	21.8	6.0	40.8	1.1	21.5	3.1	13.6	—	—	—
Differ from category (+/-). . .	8.4	-2.1	16.9	1.6	3.9	-8.9	11.3	—	—	—

PER SHARE DATA

	1993	1992	1991	1990	1989	1988	1987	1986	1985	1984
Dividends, Net Income ($).	0.86	0.93	0.97	0.93	0.93	1.10	1.06	—	—	—
Distrib'ns, Cap Gain ($) . . .	1.93	1.42	2.64	0.00	0.94	0.00	4.52	—	—	—
Net Asset Value ($)	28.88	26.02	26.80	21.64	22.34	19.94	20.40	—	—	—
Expense Ratio (%)	0.93	0.93	0.93	0.97	0.97	1.01	0.93	—	—	—
Net Income to Assets (%) .	3.51	3.74	3.80	4.00	4.26	5.25	3.69	—	—	—
Portfolio Turnover (%).	86	121	201	159	218	218	197	—	—	—
Total Assets (Millions $). . . .	947	549	402	296	312	293	303	—	—	—

PORTFOLIO (as of 9/30/93)

Portfolio Manager: G. Kenneth Heebner - 1976

Investm't Category: Balanced
Cap Gain	Asset Allocation
✔ Cap & Income	Fund of Funds
Income	Index
	Sector
✔ Domestic	Small Cap
Foreign	Socially Conscious
Country/Region	State Specific

Portfolio: stocks 64% bonds 28%
convertibles 7% other 0% cash 1%

Largest Holdings: U.S. government 28%, stocks—special situations 14%

Unrealized Net Capital Gains: 15% of portfolio value

SHAREHOLDER INFORMATION

Minimum Investment
Initial: $2,500   Subsequent: $50

Minimum IRA Investment
Initial: $1,000   Subsequent: $50

Maximum Fees
Load: none   12b-1: none
Other: none

Distributions
Income: quarterly   Capital Gains: Dec

Exchange Options
Number Per Year: 4   Fee: none
Telephone: yes (money market fund available)

Services
IRA, other pension, auto exchange, auto invest, auto withdraw

Charter Capital Blue Chip Growth (CCBGX)

4920 W. Vliet St.
Milwaukee, WI 53208
(414) 257-1842

Growth & Income

PERFORMANCE

	3yr Annual	5yr Annual	10yr Annual	Bull	Bear
Return (%)	11.8	8.5	na	56.2	-11.7
Differ from Category (+/-)	-4.6 low	-4.0 low	na	-13.9 blw av	-0.1 av

Total Risk	Standard Deviation	Category Risk	Risk Index	Beta
high	14.1%	high	1.6	1.1

	1993	1992	1991	1990	1989	1988	1987	1986	1985	1984
Return (%)	1.8	-5.6	45.7	-1.6	9.1	1.8	-4.9	16.0	13.5	—
Differ from category (+/-) .	-10.8	-15.6	18.0	4.0	-12.5	-15.0	-5.3	0.8	-11.9	—

PER SHARE DATA

	1993	1992	1991	1990	1989	1988	1987	1986	1985	1984
Dividends, Net Income ($) .	0.00	0.00	0.00	0.15	0.36	0.36	0.37	0.40	0.29	—
Distrib'ns, Cap Gain ($) . . .	0.00	0.00	0.00	0.00	0.00	0.00	1.56	0.72	0.17	—
Net Asset Value ($)	13.10	12.86	13.63	9.35	9.67	9.19	9.38	11.50	10.87	—
Expense Ratio (%)	na	2.15	2.28	2.29	2.07	1.73	1.73	1.87	1.95	—
Net Income to Assets (%) . . .	na	-0.60	-0.39	1.61	2.95	2.65	1.74	3.41	3.99	—
Portfolio Turnover (%)	na	166	112	314	194	226	107	232	179	—
Total Assets (Millions $)	9	12	13	8	12	25	40	30	24	—

PORTFOLIO (as of 6/30/93)

Portfolio Manager: Lauren Toll - 1988, F. John Mirek - 1993

Investm't Category: Growth & Income
Cap Gain	Asset Allocation
✔ Cap & Income	Fund of Funds
Income	Index
	Sector
✔ Domestic	Small Cap
Foreign	Socially Conscious
Country/Region	State Specific

Portfolio: stocks 92% bonds 0%
convertibles 0% other 0% cash 8%

Largest Holdings: capital goods 32%, consumer 20%

Unrealized Net Capital Gains: 3% of portfolio value

SHAREHOLDER INFORMATION

Minimum Investment
Initial: $50   Subsequent: $50

Minimum IRA Investment
Initial: $50   Subsequent: $50

Maximum Fees
Load: none   12b-1: none
Other: none

Distributions
Income: Dec   Capital Gains: Dec

Exchange Options
Number Per Year: none Fee: na
Telephone: na

Services
IRA, other pension, auto withdraw

Clipper (CFIMX)

Growth

9601 Wilshire Blvd., Suite 800
Beverly Hills, CA 90210
(800) 776-5033, (310) 247-3940

PERFORMANCE

	3yr Annual	5yr Annual	10yr Annual	Bull	Bear
Return (%)	19.5	14.0	na	91.2	-17.4
Differ from Category (+/-)	0.3 av	-0.6 av	na	6.5 abv av	-5.0 blw av

Total Risk	Standard Deviation	Category Risk	Risk Index	Beta
av	10.6%	blw av	1.0	0.8

	1993	1992	1991	1990	1989	1988	1987	1986	1985	1984
Return (%)	11.1	15.9	32.5	-7.5	22.1	19.6	2.8	18.7	26.4	—
Differ from category (+/-)	-2.1	4.9	-2.9	-1.4	-3.7	1.9	1.6	4.2	-2.9	—

PER SHARE DATA

	1993	1992	1991	1990	1989	1988	1987	1986	1985	1984
Dividends, Net Income ($)	0.75	0.95	1.18	1.14	1.00	0.94	3.28	0.00	0.83	—
Distrib'ns, Cap Gain ($)	6.72	3.01	1.97	0.21	1.55	1.68	5.88	1.41	0.37	—
Net Asset Value ($)	50.02	51.74	48.10	38.80	43.45	37.74	33.76	41.55	36.17	—
Expense Ratio (%)	1.13	1.12	1.15	1.15	1.17	1.24	1.25	1.28	1.50	—
Net Income to Assets (%)	1.56	2.02	2.67	2.71	2.54	2.44	4.00	4.26	5.19	—
Portfolio Turnover (%)	85	46	42	23	26	33	140	40	15	—
Total Assets (Millions $)	280	210	161	125	128	86	76	73	35	—

PORTFOLIO (as of 9/30/93)

Portfolio Manager: James H. Gipson - 1984

Investm't Category: Growth

✔ Cap Gain	Asset Allocation
Cap & Income	Fund of Funds
Income	Index
	Sector
✔ Domestic	Small Cap
✔ Foreign	Socially Conscious
Country/Region	State Specific

Portfolio: stocks 94%   bonds 5%
convertibles 0%   other 0%   cash 1%

Largest Holdings: insurance & financial services 21%, health care 16%

Unrealized Net Capital Gains: 11% of portfolio value

SHAREHOLDER INFORMATION

Minimum Investment
Initial: $5,000   Subsequent: $1,000

Minimum IRA Investment
Initial: $1,000   Subsequent: $200

Maximum Fees
Load: none   12b-1: none
Other: none

Distributions
Income: Dec   Capital Gains: Dec

Exchange Options
Number Per Year: none   Fee: na
Telephone: na

Services
IRA

Cohen & Steers Realty Shares (CSRSX)

Growth & Income

757 Third Ave.
New York, NY 10017
(212) 832-3232

	3yr Annual	5yr Annual	10yr Annual	Bull	Bear
Return (%)	na	na	na	na	na
Differ from Category (+/-)	na	na	na	na	na

Total Risk	Standard Deviation	Category Risk	Risk Index	Beta
na	na	na	na	na

	1993	1992	1991	1990	1989	1988	1987	1986	1985	1984
Return (%)	18.7	20.0	—	—	—	—	—	—	—	—
Differ from category (+/-)	6.1	10.0	—	—	—	—	—	—	—	—

PER SHARE DATA

	1993	1992	1991	1990	1989	1988	1987	1986	1985	1984
Dividends, Net Income ($)	1.51	1.80	—	—	—	—	—	—	—	—
Distrib'ns, Cap Gain ($)	1.68	0.23	—	—	—	—	—	—	—	—
Net Asset Value ($)	31.92	29.58	—	—	—	—	—	—	—	—
Expense Ratio (%)	1.13	1.25	—	—	—	—	—	—	—	—
Net Income to Assets (%)	4.76	5.92	—	—	—	—	—	—	—	—
Portfolio Turnover (%)	36	15	—	—	—	—	—	—	—	—
Total Assets (Millions $)	167	50	—	—	—	—	—	—	—	—

PORTFOLIO (as of 6/30/93)

Portfolio Manager: Martin Cohen - 1991, Robert Steers - 1991

Investm't Category: Growth & Income

Cap Gain	Asset Allocation
✔ Cap & Income	Fund of Funds
Income	Index
	✔ Sector
✔ Domestic	Small Cap
✔ Foreign	Socially Conscious
Country/Region	State Specific

Portfolio: stocks 95% bonds 0%
convertibles 0% other 0% cash 5%

Largest Holdings: shopping center 50%, health care 19%

Unrealized Net Capital Gains: 9% of portfolio value

SHAREHOLDER INFORMATION

Minimum Investment
Initial: $100,000   Subsequent: $5,000

Minimum IRA Investment
Initial: $100,000   Subsequent: $5,000

Maximum Fees
Load: none   12b-1: none
Other: none

Distributions
Income: quarterly   Capital Gains: Dec

Exchange Options
Number Per Year: none   Fee: na
Telephone: na

Services
IRA

Columbia Balanced
(CBALX)
Balanced

1301 S.W. Fifth Ave.
P.O. Box 1350
Portland, OR 97207
(800) 547-1707, (503) 222-3600

	3yr Annual	5yr Annual	10yr Annual	Bull	Bear
Return (%)	na	na	na	na	na
Differ from Category (+/-)	na	na	na	na	na

Total Risk	Standard Deviation	Category Risk	Risk Index	Beta
na	na	na	na	na

	1993	1992	1991	1990	1989	1988	1987	1986	1985	1984
Return (%)	13.6	8.8	—	—	—	—	—	—	—	—
Differ from category (+/-) . . .	0.2	0.6	—	—	—	—	—	—	—	—

PER SHARE DATA

	1993	1992	1991	1990	1989	1988	1987	1986	1985	1984
Dividends, Net Income ($) .	0.56	0.56	—	—	—	—	—	—	—	—
Distrib'ns, Cap Gain ($) . . .	0.58	0.07	—	—	—	—	—	—	—	—
Net Asset Value ($)	17.91	16.80	—	—	—	—	—	—	—	—
Expense Ratio (%)	0.70	0.81	—	—	—	—	—	—	—	—
Net Income to Assets (%) .	3.53	4.08	—	—	—	—	—	—	—	—
Portfolio Turnover (%).	133	138	—	—	—	—	—	—	—	—
Total Assets (Millions $). . . .	193	90	—	—	—	—	—	—	—	—

PORTFOLIO (as of 6/30/93)

Portfolio Manager: Mike Powers - 1991

Investm't Category: Balanced

Cap Gain	Asset Allocation
✔ Cap & Income	Fund of Funds
Income	Index
	Sector
✔ Domestic	Small Cap
✔ Foreign	Socially Conscious
Country/Region	State Specific

Portfolio: stocks 52% bonds 40%
convertibles 2% other 0% cash 6%

Largest Holdings: bonds—mortgage-backed
14%, bonds—U.S. government 12%

Unrealized Net Capital Gains: 6% of portfolio value

SHAREHOLDER INFORMATION

Minimum Investment
Initial: $1,000   Subsequent: $100

Minimum IRA Investment
Initial: $1,000   Subsequent: $100

Maximum Fees
Load: none   12b-1: none
Other: none

Distributions
Income: quarterly   Capital Gains: Dec

Exchange Options
Number Per Year: no limit   Fee: none
Telephone: yes (money market fund available)

Services
IRA, other pension, auto exchange, auto invest, auto withdraw

Columbia Common Stock (CMSTX)

Growth & Income

1301 S.W. Fifth Ave.
P.O. Box 1350
Portland, OR 97207
(800) 547-1707, (503) 222-3600

PERFORMANCE

	3yr Annual	5yr Annual	10yr Annual	Bull	Bear
Return (%)	na	na	na	na	na
Differ from Category (+/-)	na	na	na	na	na

Total Risk	Standard Deviation	Category Risk	Risk Index	Beta
na	na	na	na	na

	1993	1992	1991	1990	1989	1988	1987	1986	1985	1984
Return (%)	16.4	9.9	—	—	—	—	—	—	—	—
Differ from category (+/-) ...	3.8	-0.1	—	—	—	—	—	—	—	—

PER SHARE DATA

	1993	1992	1991	1990	1989	1988	1987	1986	1985	1984
Dividends, Net Income ($) .	0.20	0.23	—	—	—	—	—	—	—	—
Distrib'ns, Cap Gain ($) ...	0.83	0.17	—	—	—	—	—	—	—	—
Net Asset Value ($)	15.29	14.04	—	—	—	—	—	—	—	—
Expense Ratio (%)........	0.80	0.86	—	—	—	—	—	—	—	—
Net Income to Assets (%)..	1.58	1.97	—	—	—	—	—	—	—	—
Portfolio Turnover (%).....	76	68	—	—	—	—	—	—	—	—
Total Assets (Millions $) ...	102	51	—	—	—	—	—	—	—	—

PORTFOLIO (as of 6/30/93)

Portfolio Manager: Terry L. Chambers - 1991

Investm't Category: Growth & Income
Cap Gain	Asset Allocation
✔ Cap & Income	Fund of Funds
Income	Index
	Sector
✔ Domestic	Small Cap
✔ Foreign	Socially Conscious
Country/Region	State Specific

Portfolio: stocks 90% bonds 0%
convertibles 3% other 0% cash 7%

Largest Holdings: technology 10%, banking & finance 10%

Unrealized Net Capital Gains: 10% of portfolio value

SHAREHOLDER INFORMATION

Minimum Investment
Initial: $1,000   Subsequent: $100

Minimum IRA Investment
Initial: $1,000   Subsequent: $100

Maximum Fees
Load: none   12b-1: none
Other: none

Distributions
Income: quarterly   Capital Gains: Dec

Exchange Options
Number Per Year: no limit   Fee: none
Telephone: yes (money market fund available)

Services
IRA, other pension, auto exchange, auto invest, auto withdraw

Columbia Fixed Income Securities (CFISX)

General Bond

1301 S.W. Fifth Ave.
P.O. Box 1350
Portland, OR 97207
(800) 547-1707, (503) 222-3600

PERFORMANCE

	3yr Annual	5yr Annual	10yr Annual	Bull	Bear
Return (%)	11.7	11.5	11.0	46.1	3.2
Differ from Category (+/-)	1.5 abv av	1.7 high	0.1 av	6.7 abv av	0.3 av

Total Risk	Standard Deviation	Category Risk	Risk Index	Avg Mat
low	4.0%	abv av	1.4	7.2 yrs

	1993	1992	1991	1990	1989	1988	1987	1986	1985	1984
Return (%)............	10.4	7.9	16.8	8.2	14.3	7.7	1.3	12.3	20.1	12.2
Differ from category (+/-)...	1.2	1.2	2.2	1.3	3.0	0.1	-1.2	-1.6	0.0	-0.1

PER SHARE DATA

	1993	1992	1991	1990	1989	1988	1987	1986	1985	1984
Dividends, Net Income ($).	0.84	0.95	0.99	1.02	1.04	1.04	1.03	1.21	1.39	1.44
Distrib'ns, Cap Gain ($) ...	0.36	0.40	0.18	0.00	0.00	0.00	0.27	0.00	0.00	0.00
Net Asset Value ($)	13.44	13.28	13.59	12.72	12.75	12.11	12.23	13.37	13.05	12.14
Expense Ratio (%)	0.65	0.66	0.68	0.73	0.74	0.77	0.82	0.79	0.88	1.05
Net Income to Assets (%) .	6.40	7.03	7.63	8.20	8.27	8.44	8.21	9.15	11.03	12.17
Portfolio Turnover (%).....	151	196	159	132	114	133	114	97	94	97
Total Assets (Millions $)....	300	263	207	134	111	103	100	124	83	38

PORTFOLIO (as of 6/30/93)

Portfolio Manager: committee

Investm't Category: General Bond

Cap Gain	Asset Allocation
Cap & Income	Fund of Funds
✔ Income	Index
	Sector
✔ Domestic	Small Cap
Foreign	Socially Conscious
Country/Region	State Specific

Portfolio: stocks 0% bonds 94%
convertibles 0% other 0% cash 6%

Largest Holdings: mortgage-backed 32%, corporate 31%

Unrealized Net Capital Gains: 4% of portfolio value

SHAREHOLDER INFORMATION

Minimum Investment
Initial: $1,000   Subsequent: $100

Minimum IRA Investment
Initial: $1,000   Subsequent: $100

Maximum Fees
Load: none   12b-1: none
Other: none

Distributions
Income: monthly   Capital Gains: Dec

Exchange Options
Number Per Year: no limit   Fee: none
Telephone: yes (money market fund available)

Services
IRA, other pension, auto exchange, auto invest, auto withdraw

Columbia Growth (CLMBX)

Growth

1301 S.W. Fifth Ave.
P.O. Box 1350
Portland, OR 97207
(800) 547-1707, (503) 222-3600

PERFORMANCE

	3yr Annual	5yr Annual	10yr Annual	Bull	Bear
Return (%)	19.2	16.1	13.6	78.6	-8.1
Differ from Category (+/-)	0.0 av	1.5 abv av	1.0 abv av	-6.1 av	4.3 abv av

Total Risk	Standard Deviation	Category Risk	Risk Index	Beta
abv av	12.7%	abv av	1.2	1.0

	1993	1992	1991	1990	1989	1988	1987	1986	1985	1984
Return (%)	13.0	11.8	34.2	-3.3	29.0	10.8	14.7	6.9	32.0	-5.5
Differ from category (+/-) ..	-0.2	0.8	-1.2	2.8	3.2	-6.9	13.5	-7.6	2.7	-5.5

PER SHARE DATA

	1993	1992	1991	1990	1989	1988	1987	1986	1985	1984
Dividends, Net Income ($) .	0.18	0.20	0.38	0.47	0.54	0.51	0.60	0.40	0.33	0.18
Distrib'ns, Cap Gain ($) ...	3.02	2.98	2.44	0.46	3.40	0.63	5.33	6.47	0.00	2.41
Net Asset Value ($)	26.38	26.18	26.26	21.68	23.40	21.21	20.19	22.88	28.02	21.52
Expense Ratio (%)........	0.82	0.86	0.90	0.96	0.96	1.04	1.04	1.00	1.06	1.18
Net Income to Assets (%)..	0.71	0.77	1.50	2.08	2.14	2.33	1.46	0.78	1.81	1.78
Portfolio Turnover (%)	110	116	164	172	166	179	197	130	92	90
Total Assets (Millions $) ...	611	518	432	271	267	204	194	200	250	155

PORTFOLIO (as of 6/30/93)

Portfolio Manager: Alec MacMillan - 1992

Investm't Category: Growth
- ✔ Cap Gain
- Cap & Income
- Income
- Asset Allocation
- Fund of Funds
- Index
- Sector
- ✔ Domestic
- Foreign
- Country/Region
- Small Cap
- Socially Conscious
- State Specific

Portfolio: stocks 96% bonds 0%
convertibles 0% other 0% cash 4%

Largest Holdings: consumer non-durables 20%, technology 16%

Unrealized Net Capital Gains: 12% of portfolio value

SHAREHOLDER INFORMATION

Minimum Investment
Initial: $1,000   Subsequent: $100

Minimum IRA Investment
Initial: $1,000   Subsequent: $100

Maximum Fees
Load: none   12b-1: none
Other: none

Distributions
Income: Dec   Capital Gains: Dec

Exchange Options
Number Per Year: no limit   Fee: none
Telephone: yes (money market fund available)

Services
IRA, other pension, auto exchange, auto invest, auto withdraw

Columbia Int'l Stock
(CMISX)
International Stock

1301 S.W. Fifth Ave.
P.O. Box 1350
Portland, OR 97207
(800) 547-1707, (503) 222-3600

PERFORMANCE

	3yr Annual	5yr Annual	10yr Annual	Bull	Bear
Return (%)	na	na	na	na	na
Differ from Category (+/-)	na	na	na	na	na

Total Risk	Standard Deviation	Category Risk	Risk Index	Beta
na	na	na	na	na

	1993	1992	1991	1990	1989	1988	1987	1986	1985	1984
Return (%)	33.3	—	—	—	—	—	—	—	—	—
Differ from category (+/-). . .	-5.2	—	—	—	—	—	—	—	—	—

PER SHARE DATA

	1993	1992	1991	1990	1989	1988	1987	1986	1985	1984
Dividends, Net Income ($).	0.00	—	—	—	—	—	—	—	—	—
Distrib'ns, Cap Gain ($) . . .	0.31	—	—	—	—	—	—	—	—	—
Net Asset Value ($)	12.96	—	—	—	—	—	—	—	—	—
Expense Ratio (%)	1.88	—	—	—	—	—	—	—	—	—
Net Income to Assets (%) .	0.11	—	—	—	—	—	—	—	—	—
Portfolio Turnover (%).	81	—	—	—	—	—	—	—	—	—
Total Assets (Millions $)	77	—	—	—	—	—	—	—	—	—

PORTFOLIO (as of 6/30/93)

Portfolio Manager: James McAlear — 1992

Investm't Category: International Stock

✔ Cap Gain	Asset Allocation
Cap & Income	Fund of Funds
Income	Index
	Sector
✔ Domestic	Small Cap
✔ Foreign	Socially Conscious
Country/Region	State Specific

Portfolio: stocks 96% bonds 0%
convertibles 2% other 2% cash 0%

Largest Holdings: Japan 31%, France 18%

Unrealized Net Capital Gains: 3% of portfolio value

SHAREHOLDER INFORMATION

Minimum Investment
Initial: $1,000   Subsequent: $100

Minimum IRA Investment
Initial: $1,000   Subsequent: $100

Maximum Fees
Load: none   12b-1: none
Other: none

Distributions
Income: Dec   Capital Gains: Dec

Exchange Options
Number Per Year: no limit   Fee: none
Telephone: yes (money market fund available)

Services
IRA, other pension, auto exchange, auto invest, auto withdraw

Columbia Muni Bond

(CMBFX)

Tax-Exempt Bond

1301 S.W. Fifth Ave.
P.O. Box 1350
Portland, OR 97207
(800) 547-1707, (503) 222-3600

PERFORMANCE

	3yr Annual	5yr Annual	10yr Annual	Bull	Bear
Return (%)	9.6	8.9	na	36.9	2.8
Differ from Category (+/-)	-0.6 blw av	-0.3 blw av	na	-3.2 blw av	0.5 av

Total Risk	Standard Deviation	Category Risk	Risk Index	Avg Mat
low	3.3%	low	0.8	15.6 yrs

	1993	1992	1991	1990	1989	1988	1987	1986	1985	1984
Return (%)	10.7	6.4	11.7	6.8	8.9	10.2	1.2	16.7	19.7	—
Differ from category (+/-) ..	-0.8	-1.9	0.4	0.5	-0.1	0.1	2.4	0.3	2.4	—

PER SHARE DATA

	1993	1992	1991	1990	1989	1988	1987	1986	1985	1984
Dividends, Net Income ($) .	0.66	0.69	0.72	0.74	0.76	0.76	0.76	0.83	0.88	—
Distrib'ns, Cap Gain ($) ...	0.07	0.11	0.02	0.01	0.01	0.03	0.00	0.00	0.00	—
Net Asset Value ($)	12.71	12.17	12.22	11.65	11.64	11.42	11.11	11.75	10.82	—
Expense Ratio (%)........	0.58	0.59	0.59	0.60	0.61	0.63	0.66	0.65	0.76	—
Net Income to Assets (%) ..	5.34	5.69	6.07	6.50	6.59	6.71	6.84	7.17	8.51	—
Portfolio Turnover (%)	12	18	15	7	11	10	21	3	17	—
Total Assets (Millions $) ...	429	342	285	208	167	141	119	118	58	—

PORTFOLIO (as of 6/30/93)

Portfolio Manager: Thomas Thomsen - 1984

Investm't Category: Tax-Exempt Bond
Cap Gain	Asset Allocation
Cap & Income	Fund of Funds
✔ Income	Index
	Sector
✔ Domestic	Small Cap
Foreign	Socially Conscious
Country/Region	State Specific

Portfolio: stocks 0% bonds 99%
convertibles 0% other 0% cash 1%

Largest Holdings: general obligation 32%

Unrealized Net Capital Gains: 7% of portfolio value

SHAREHOLDER INFORMATION

Minimum Investment
Initial: $1,000   Subsequent: $100

Minimum IRA Investment
Initial: na   Subsequent: na

Maximum Fees
Load: none   12b-1: none
Other: none

Distributions
Income: monthly   Capital Gains: Dec

Exchange Options
Number Per Year: no limit   Fee: none
Telephone: yes (money market fund available)

Services
auto exchange, auto invest, auto withdraw

Columbia Special (CLSPX)

Aggressive Growth

1301 S.W. Fifth Ave.
P.O. Box 1350
Portland, OR 97207
(800) 547-1707, (503) 222-3600

PERFORMANCE

	3yr Annual	5yr Annual	10yr Annual	Bull	Bear
Return (%)	27.6	19.1	na	139.3	-23.7
Differ from Category (+/-)	2.2 abv av	0.8 av	na	14.3 abv av	-8.7 low

Total Risk	Standard Deviation	Category Risk	Risk Index	Beta
high	16.4%	av	1.1	1.2

	1993	1992	1991	1990	1989	1988	1987	1986	1985	1984
Return (%)	21.6	13.6	50.4	-12.3	31.9	42.5	3.0	15.8	—	—
Differ from category (+/-)	2.6	3.2	-2.0	-6.0	4.9	27.3	6.4	6.4	—	—

PER SHARE DATA

	1993	1992	1991	1990	1989	1988	1987	1986	1985	1984
Dividends, Net Income ($)	0.00	0.00	0.00	0.02	0.01	0.00	0.00	0.00	—	—
Distrib'ns, Cap Gain ($)	3.32	1.04	0.76	0.00	1.05	1.86	0.00	0.24	—	—
Net Asset Value ($)	19.51	18.79	17.45	12.12	13.85	11.32	9.26	8.99	—	—
Expense Ratio (%)	1.13	1.19	1.22	1.32	1.35	1.38	1.44	1.54	—	—
Net Income to Assets (%)	0.00	-0.25	-0.16	0.05	0.18	0.06	-0.63	-0.47	—	—
Portfolio Turnover (%)	183	117	115	147	124	244	333	203	—	—
Total Assets (Millions $)	797	471	264	122	96	31	21	20	—	—

PORTFOLIO (as of 6/30/93)

Portfolio Manager: Alan Folkman - 1985

Investm't Category: Aggressive Growth

✔ Cap Gain
Cap & Income
Income

Asset Allocation
Fund of Funds
Index
Sector

✔ Domestic
✔ Foreign
Country/Region

✔ Small Cap
Socially Conscious
State Specific

Portfolio: stocks 85% bonds 0%
convertibles 0% other 0% cash 15%

Largest Holdings: technology 17%, machinery & capital spending 14%

Unrealized Net Capital Gains: 11% of portfolio value

SHAREHOLDER INFORMATION

Minimum Investment
Initial: $2,000 Subsequent: $100

Minimum IRA Investment
Initial: $2,000 Subsequent: $100

Maximum Fees
Load: none 12b-1: none
Other: none

Distributions
Income: Dec Capital Gains: Dec

Exchange Options
Number Per Year: no limit Fee: none
Telephone: yes (money market fund available)

Services
IRA, other pension, auto exchange, auto invest, auto withdraw

Columbia US Gov't Securities (CUGGX)

Government Bond

1301 S.W. Fifth Ave.
P.O. Box 1350
Portland, OR 97207
(800) 547-1707, (503) 222-3600

PERFORMANCE

	3yr Annual	5yr Annual	10yr Annual	Bull	Bear
Return (%)	8.1	8.6	na	30.7	5.5
Differ from Category (+/-)	-2.7 low	-1.8 low	na	-15.5 low	5.0 high

Total Risk	Standard Deviation	Category Risk	Risk Index	Avg Mat
low	2.5%	low	0.6	2.4 yrs

	1993	1992	1991	1990	1989	1988	1987	1986	1985	1984
Return (%)	5.9	5.8	12.7	9.2	9.6	5.3	4.1	—	—	—
Differ from category (+/-)	-4.5	-0.4	-2.3	2.7	-4.3	-2.3	5.9	—	—	—

PER SHARE DATA

	1993	1992	1991	1990	1989	1988	1987	1986	1985	1984
Dividends, Net Income ($)	0.31	0.39	0.53	0.61	0.62	0.56	0.51	—	—	—
Distrib'ns, Cap Gain ($)	0.15	0.20	0.46	0.00	0.00	0.00	0.00	—	—	—
Net Asset Value ($)	8.36	8.35	8.47	8.43	8.30	8.17	8.30	—	—	—
Expense Ratio (%)	0.73	0.76	0.76	0.85	0.85	0.85	0.85	—	—	—
Net Income to Assets (%)	3.83	4.60	6.18	7.33	7.66	6.88	6.34	—	—	—
Portfolio Turnover (%)	454	289	309	222	159	394	147	—	—	—
Total Assets (Millions $)	36	35	35	23	13	9	7	—	—	—

PORTFOLIO (as of 6/30/93)

Portfolio Manager: committee

Investm't Category: Government Bond

Cap Gain	Asset Allocation
Cap & Income	Fund of Funds
✔ Income	Index
	Sector
✔ Domestic	Small Cap
Foreign	Socially Conscious
Country/Region	State Specific

Portfolio: stocks 0%   bonds 98%
convertibles 0%   other 0%   cash 2%

Largest Holdings: U.S. government 98%

Unrealized Net Capital Gains: 0% of portfolio value

SHAREHOLDER INFORMATION

Minimum Investment
Initial: $1,000   Subsequent: $100

Minimum IRA Investment
Initial: $1,000   Subsequent: $100

Maximum Fees
Load: none   12b-1: none
Other: none

Distributions
Income: monthly   Capital Gains: Dec

Exchange Options
Number Per Year: no limit   Fee: none
Telephone: yes (money market fund available)

Services
IRA, other pension, auto exchange, auto invest, auto withdraw

Connecticut Mutual Inv Acts Income (CINAX)

140 Garden Street
Hartford, CT 06154
(800) 322-2642

General Bond

PERFORMANCE

	3yr Annual	5yr Annual	10yr Annual	Bull	Bear
Return (%)	9.5	8.7	na	32.4	5.6
Differ from Category (+/-)	-0.7 blw av	-1.1 low	na	-7.0 low	2.7 high

Total Risk	Standard Deviation	Category Risk	Risk Index	Avg Mat
low	1.9%	low	0.6	3.8 yrs

	1993	1992	1991	1990	1989	1988	1987	1986	1985	1984
Return (%)	8.1	6.5	14.1	6.3	9.5	6.7	2.0	—	—	—
Differ from category (+/-)	-1.1	-0.2	-0.5	-0.6	-1.8	-0.9	-0.5	—	—	—

PER SHARE DATA

	1993	1992	1991	1990	1989	1988	1987	1986	1985	1984
Dividends, Net Income ($)	0.67	0.78	0.81	0.94	0.88	0.85	0.76	—	—	—
Distrib'ns, Cap Gain ($)	0.00	0.00	0.00	0.00	0.00	0.00	0.50	—	—	—
Net Asset Value ($)	9.86	9.75	9.91	9.44	9.79	9.77	9.97	—	—	—
Expense Ratio (%)	0.63	0.63	1.12	1.24	1.27	1.24	1.27	—	—	—
Net Income to Assets (%)	6.70	8.09	8.44	9.78	8.93	8.43	7.32	—	—	—
Portfolio Turnover (%)	155	109	50	90	52	150	231	—	—	—
Total Assets (Millions $)	49	38	22	19	18	16	15	—	—	—

PORTFOLIO (as of 6/30/93)

Portfolio Manager: Stephen Libera - na

Investm't Category: General Bond
Cap Gain	Asset Allocation
Cap & Income	Fund of Funds
✔ Income	Index
	Sector
✔ Domestic	Small Cap
Foreign	Socially Conscious
Country/Region	State Specific

Portfolio: stocks 0%   bonds 80%
convertibles 0%   other 0%   cash 20%

Largest Holdings: corporate 60%, mortgage-backed 20%

Unrealized Net Capital Gains: 1% of portfolio value

SHAREHOLDER INFORMATION

Minimum Investment
Initial: $1,000   Subsequent: $0

Minimum IRA Investment
Initial: $0   Subsequent: $0

Maximum Fees
Load: 2.00% front   12b-1: none
Other: none

Distributions
Income: monthly   Capital Gains: Aug, Dec

Exchange Options
Number Per Year: 12   Fee: $5
Telephone: yes (money market fund available)

Services
IRA, other pension, auto invest, auto withdraw

Copley (COPLX)

Growth & Income

315 Pleasant St., 5th Fl.
P.O. Box 3287
Fall River, MA 02722
(508) 674-8459

PERFORMANCE

	3yr Annual	5yr Annual	10yr Annual	Bull	Bear
Return (%)	14.9	11.9	13.4	59.4	-6.2
Differ from Category (+/-)	-1.5 blw av	-0.6 blw av	1.0 av	-10.7 blw av	5.4 high

Total Risk	Standard Deviation	Category Risk	Risk Index	Beta
av	9.0%	blw av	1.0	0.3

	1993	1992	1991	1990	1989	1988	1987	1986	1985	1984
Return (%)	10.1	17.6	17.1	-1.5	17.8	19.8	-8.2	17.7	24.6	23.9
Differ from category (+/-) . .	-2.5	7.6	-10.6	4.1	-3.8	3.0	-8.6	2.5	-0.8	17.7

PER SHARE DATA

	1993	1992	1991	1990	1989	1988	1987	1986	1985	1984
Dividends, Net Income ($) .	0.00	0.00	0.00	0.00	0.00	0.00	0.00	0.00	0.00	0.00
Distrib'ns, Cap Gain ($) . . .	0.00	0.00	0.00	0.00	0.00	0.00	0.00	0.00	0.00	0.00
Net Asset Value ($)	21.35	19.38	16.47	14.06	14.28	12.12	10.11	11.02	9.36	7.51
Expense Ratio (%).	1.14	1.38	1.50	1.86	1.38	1.72	1.43	1.47	1.50	1.40
Net Income to Assets (%). .	5.93	4.86	5.34	5.81	6.45	5.58	5.20	7.26	7.90	8.49
Portfolio Turnover (%)	5	7	16	3	24	10	16	19	29	39
Total Assets (Millions $)	70	32	28	29	21	26	34	21	8	6

PORTFOLIO (as of 8/31/93)

Portfolio Manager: Irving Levine - 1978

Investm't Category: Growth & Income

Cap Gain	Asset Allocation
✔ Cap & Income	Fund of Funds
Income	Index
	Sector
✔ Domestic	Small Cap
Foreign	Socially Conscious
Country/Region	State Specific

Portfolio:	stocks 97%	bonds 0%
convertibles 0%	other 3%	cash 0%

Largest Holdings: electric power companies 23%, electric & gas 22%

Unrealized Net Capital Gains: 37% of portfolio value

SHAREHOLDER INFORMATION

Minimum Investment
Initial: $1,000   Subsequent: $100

Minimum IRA Investment
Initial: $100   Subsequent: $100

Maximum Fees
Load: none   12b-1: none
Other: none

Distributions
Income: none   Capital Gains: none

Exchange Options
Number Per Year: none   Fee: na
Telephone: na

Services
IRA, other pension, auto withdraw

Corefund Equity Index
(VEIFX)

Growth & Income

680 E. Swedesford Rd.
Wayne, PA 19087
(800) 355-2673

PERFORMANCE

	3yr Annual	5yr Annual	10yr Annual	Bull	Bear
Return (%)	na	na	na	na	na
Differ from Category (+/-)	na	na	na	na	na

Total Risk	Standard Deviation	Category Risk	Risk Index	Beta
na	na	na	na	na

	1993	1992	1991	1990	1989	1988	1987	1986	1985	1984
Return (%)	8.7	6.7	—	—	—	—	—	—	—	—
Differ from category (+/-). . . .	-3.9	-3.3	—	—	—	—	—	—	—	—

PER SHARE DATA

	1993	1992	1991	1990	1989	1988	1987	1986	1985	1984
Dividends, Net Income ($).	0.44	0.48	—	—	—	—	—	—	—	—
Distrib'ns, Cap Gain ($) . . .	0.00	0.40	—	—	—	—	—	—	—	—
Net Asset Value ($)	21.61	20.30	—	—	—	—	—	—	—	—
Expense Ratio (%)	0.49	0.57	—	—	—	—	—	—	—	—
Net Income to Assets (%) .	2.82	2.66	—	—	—	—	—	—	—	—
Portfolio Turnover (%).	4	27	—	—	—	—	—	—	—	—
Total Assets (Millions $).....	77	20	—	—	—	—	—	—	—	—

PORTFOLIO (as of 6/30/93)

Portfolio Manager: not specified

Investm't Category: Growth & Income

Cap Gain	Asset Allocation
✔ Cap & Income	Fund of Funds
Income	✔ Index
	Sector
✔ Domestic	Small Cap
Foreign	Socially Conscious
Country/Region	State Specific

Portfolio: stocks 99% bonds 0%
convertibles 0% other 0% cash 1%

Largest Holdings: S&P 500 Composite Price
Index

Unrealized Net Capital Gains: 15% of portfolio value

SHAREHOLDER INFORMATION

Minimum Investment
Initial: $2,500   Subsequent: $0

Minimum IRA Investment
Initial: $2,500   Subsequent: $0

Maximum Fees
Load: none   12b-1: none
Other: none

Distributions
Income: quarterly   Capital Gains: Jun, Dec

Exchange Options
Number Per Year: no limit   Fee: none
Telephone: yes (money market fund available)

Services
IRA, other pension, auto invest, auto withdraw

Crabbe Huson Asset Allocation (CHAAX)

Balanced

121 S.W. Morrison St.
Suite 1425
Portland, OR 97204
(800) 541-9732, (503) 295-0919

PERFORMANCE

	3yr Annual	5yr Annual	10yr Annual	Bull	Bear
Return (%)	17.0	11.3	na	69.4	-5.9
Differ from Category (+/-)	2.0 abv av	-0.8 blw av	na	7.8 abv av	-0.1 av

Total Risk	Standard Deviation	Category Risk	Risk Index	Beta
blw av	6.2%	av	1.0	0.5

	1993	1992	1991	1990	1989	1988	1987	1986	1985	1984
Return (%)	18.2	12.1	21.2	-0.6	7.5	—	—	—	—	—
Differ from category (+/-) . . .	4.8	4.0	-2.7	-0.2	-10.1	—	—	—	—	—

PER SHARE DATA

	1993	1992	1991	1990	1989	1988	1987	1986	1985	1984
Dividends, Net Income ($) .	0.21	0.32	0.46	0.45	0.05	—	—	—	—	—
Distrib'ns, Cap Gain ($) . . .	0.71	0.30	0.18	0.00	0.36	—	—	—	—	—
Net Asset Value ($)	13.07	11.87	11.15	9.78	10.34	—	—	—	—	—
Expense Ratio (%).	1.42	1.52	1.76	1.90	1.91	—	—	—	—	—
Net Income to Assets (%). .	2.18	3.02	3.97	4.51	5.02	—	—	—	—	—
Portfolio Turnover (%)	140	155	158	162	88	—	—	—	—	—
Total Assets (Millions $)	7	55	24	13	13	—	—	—	—	—

PORTFOLIO (as of 4/30/93)

Portfolio Manager: Richard Huson - 1989

Investm't Category: Balanced

Cap Gain	✔ Asset Allocation
✔ Cap & Income	Fund of Funds
Income	Index
	Sector
✔ Domestic	Small Cap
Foreign	Socially Conscious
Country/Region	State Specific

Portfolio: stocks 49% bonds 33%
convertibles 4% other 0% cash 14%

Largest Holdings: bonds—U.S. government
& agency 26%, stocks—retail 7%

Unrealized Net Capital Gains: 5% of portfolio value

SHAREHOLDER INFORMATION

Minimum Investment
Initial: $1,000 Subsequent: $500

Minimum IRA Investment
Initial: $1,000 Subsequent: $500

Maximum Fees
Load: none 12b-1: 1.00%
Other: none

Distributions
Income: quarterly Capital Gains: Dec

Exchange Options
Number Per Year: no limit Fee: none
Telephone: yes (money market fund available)

Services
IRA, other pension, auto invest, auto withdraw

Dodge & Cox Balanced
(DODBX)

Balanced

One Sansome St., 35th Fl.
San Francisco, CA 94104
(415) 434-0311

PERFORMANCE

	3yr Annual	5yr Annual	10yr Annual	Bull	Bear
Return (%)	15.6	13.9	14.2	66.9	-6.4
Differ from Category (+/-)	0.6 abv av	1.8 abv av	2.2 high	5.3 abv av	-0.6 av

Total Risk	Standard Deviation	Category Risk	Risk Index	Beta
av	7.1%	av	1.1	0.6

	1993	1992	1991	1990	1989	1988	1987	1986	1985	1984
Return (%)............	15.9	10.5	20.7	0.8	23.0	11.5	7.1	18.8	32.4	4.7
Differ from category (+/-)...	2.5	2.4	-3.2	1.4	5.4	-0.5	4.8	1.3	8.7	-2.7

PER SHARE DATA

	1993	1992	1991	1990	1989	1988	1987	1986	1985	1984
Dividends, Net Income ($).	1.67	1.73	1.76	1.81	1.76	1.68	1.70	1.62	1.70	1.73
Distrib'ns, Cap Gain ($) ...	1.06	0.07	0.28	0.33	0.70	0.46	2.67	3.55	0.37	0.82
Net Asset Value ($)	46.40	42.44	40.09	35.03	36.85	32.09	30.72	32.62	31.93	25.92
Expense Ratio (%)	0.61	0.63	0.65	0.70	0.72	0.77	0.72	0.73	0.75	0.76
Net Income to Assets (%) .	3.87	4.27	4.78	5.24	4.98	5.19	4.69	4.86	6.03	6.76
Portfolio Turnover (%)......	na	6	10	10	12	9	15	14	26	7
Total Assets (Millions $)....	504	269	179	83	51	39	34	28	25	19

PORTFOLIO (as of 9/30/93)

Portfolio Manager: committee

Investm't Category: Balanced

Cap Gain	Asset Allocation
✔ Cap & Income	Fund of Funds
Income	Index
	Sector
✔ Domestic	Small Cap
Foreign	Socially Conscious
Country/Region	State Specific

Portfolio: stocks 57% bonds 36%
convertibles 0% other 0% cash 7%

Largest Holdings: bonds—mortgage backed 15%, stocks—finance 11%

Unrealized Net Capital Gains: 17% of portfolio value

SHAREHOLDER INFORMATION

Minimum Investment
Initial: $2,500 Subsequent: $100

Minimum IRA Investment
Initial: $1,000 Subsequent: $100

Maximum Fees
Load: none 12b-1: none
Other: none

Distributions
Income: quarterly Capital Gains: Dec

Exchange Options
Number Per Year: none Fee: na
Telephone: na

Services
IRA, auto invest, auto withdraw

Dodge & Cox Income
(DODIX)

General Bond

One Sansome St., 35th Fl.
San Francisco, CA 94104
(415) 434-0311

PERFORMANCE

	3yr Annual	5yr Annual	10yr Annual	Bull	Bear
Return (%)	12.2	11.6	na	48.8	2.1
Differ from Category (+/-)	2.0 high	1.8 high	na	9.4 high	-0.8 blw av

Total Risk	Standard Deviation	Category Risk	Risk Index	Avg Mat
blw av	4.3%	high	1.5	10.0 yrs

	1993	1992	1991	1990	1989	1988	1987	1986	1985	1984
Return (%)	11.3	7.7	17.9	7.4	14.0	—	—	—	—	—
Differ from category (+/-)	2.1	1.0	3.3	0.5	2.7	—	—	—	—	—

PER SHARE DATA

	1993	1992	1991	1990	1989	1988	1987	1986	1985	1984
Dividends, Net Income ($)	0.77	0.81	0.81	0.81	0.68	—	—	—	—	—
Distrib'ns, Cap Gain ($)	0.17	0.09	0.02	0.00	0.00	—	—	—	—	—
Net Asset Value ($)	11.89	11.55	11.59	10.61	10.68	—	—	—	—	—
Expense Ratio (%)	0.60	0.62	0.64	0.68	0.66	—	—	—	—	—
Net Income to Assets (%)	6.72	7.14	7.63	7.99	7.85	—	—	—	—	—
Portfolio Turnover (%)	na	12	15	13	3	—	—	—	—	—
Total Assets (Millions $)	183	136	96	52	33	—	—	—	—	—

PORTFOLIO (as of 9/30/93)

Portfolio Manager: committee

Investm't Category: General Bond

Cap Gain	Asset Allocation
Cap & Income	Fund of Funds
✔ Income	Index
	Sector
✔ Domestic	Small Cap
Foreign	Socially Conscious
Country/Region	State Specific

Portfolio: stocks 0% bonds 96%
convertibles 0% other 0% cash 4%

Largest Holdings: corporate 41%, mortgage-backed 35%

Unrealized Net Capital Gains: 8% of portfolio value

SHAREHOLDER INFORMATION

Minimum Investment
Initial: $2,500   Subsequent: $100

Minimum IRA Investment
Initial: $1,000   Subsequent: $100

Maximum Fees
Load: none   12b-1: none
Other: none

Distributions
Income: quarterly   Capital Gains: Dec

Exchange Options
Number Per Year: none   Fee: na
Telephone: na

Services
IRA, auto invest, auto withdraw

Dodge & Cox Stock
(DODGX)

Growth & Income

One Sansome St., 35th Fl.
San Francisco, CA 94104
(415) 434-0311

PERFORMANCE

	3yr Annual	5yr Annual	10yr Annual	Bull	Bear
Return (%)	16.7	13.9	15.4	75.3	-13.7
Differ from Category (+/-)	0.3 av	1.4 abv av	3.0 high	5.2 abv av	-2.1 blw av

Total Risk	Standard Deviation	Category Risk	Risk Index	Beta
abv av	11.0%	abv av	1.3	0.9

	1993	1992	1991	1990	1989	1988	1987	1986	1985	1984
Return (%).	18.3	10.8	21.4	-5.0	26.9	13.7	11.9	18.3	37.8	5.1
Differ from category (+/-). . .	5.7	0.8	-6.3	0.6	5.3	-3.1	11.5	3.1	12.4	-1.1

PER SHARE DATA

	1993	1992	1991	1990	1989	1988	1987	1986	1985	1984
Dividends, Net Income ($).	1.04	1.11	1.24	1.35	1.23	1.07	1.04	0.93	1.01	1.02
Distrib'ns, Cap Gain ($) . . .	2.84	0.15	0.87	0.28	0.81	1.11	1.57	3.90	1.23	1.88
Net Asset Value ($)	53.23	48.37	44.85	38.79	42.57	35.26	32.94	31.66	30.95	24.45
Expense Ratio (%)	0.63	0.64	0.64	0.65	0.65	0.68	0.65	0.66	0.68	0.68
Net Income to Assets (%) .	2.06	2.43	2.87	3.47	3.12	3.09	2.68	2.95	3.80	4.26
Portfolio Turnover (%).	na	7	5	7	4	10	12	10	22	14
Total Assets (Millions $). . . .	449	336	281	173	152	82	68	45	39	28

PORTFOLIO (as of 9/30/93)

Portfolio Manager: committee

Investm't Category: Growth & Income

Cap Gain	Asset Allocation
✔ Cap & Income	Fund of Funds
Income	Index
	Sector
✔ Domestic	Small Cap
Foreign	Socially Conscious
Country/Region	State Specific

Portfolio: stocks 94% bonds 0%
convertibles 0% other 0% cash 6%

Largest Holdings: finance 18%, consumer 15%

Unrealized Net Capital Gains: 28% of portfolio value

SHAREHOLDER INFORMATION

Minimum Investment
Initial: $2,500   Subsequent: $100

Minimum IRA Investment
Initial: $1,000   Subsequent: $100

Maximum Fees
Load: none   12b-1: none
Other: none

Distributions
Income: quarterly   Capital Gains: Dec

Exchange Options
Number Per Year: none Fee: na
Telephone: na

Services
IRA, auto invest, auto withdraw

Dreman Contrarian

(DRCPX)

Growth & Income

10 Exchange Place
Suite 2050
Jersey City, NJ 07302
(800) 533-1608

	3yr Annual	5yr Annual	10yr Annual	Bull	Bear
Return (%)	15.3	11.2	na	72.5	-16.5
Differ from Category (+/-)	-1.1 av	-1.3 blw av	na	2.4 av	-4.9 low

Total Risk	Standard Deviation	Category Risk	Risk Index	Beta
abv av	13.3%	high	1.5	1.1

	1993	1992	1991	1990	1989	1988	1987	1986	1985	1984
Return (%)	9.0	11.3	26.5	-6.0	18.2	—	—	—	—	—
Differ from category (+/-)	-3.6	1.3	-1.2	-0.4	-3.4	—	—	—	—	—

PER SHARE DATA

	1993	1992	1991	1990	1989	1988	1987	1986	1985	1984
Dividends, Net Income ($)	0.22	0.26	0.27	0.26	0.29	—	—	—	—	—
Distrib'ns, Cap Gain ($)	0.84	0.00	0.11	0.28	0.80	—	—	—	—	—
Net Asset Value ($)	13.62	13.50	12.38	10.11	11.34	—	—	—	—	—
Expense Ratio (%)	1.25	1.25	1.25	1.25	1.25	—	—	—	—	—
Net Income to Assets (%)	1.69	2.04	2.35	2.46	2.59	—	—	—	—	—
Portfolio Turnover (%)	7	28	36	37	45	—	—	—	—	—
Total Assets (Millions $)	17	14	14	11	9	—	—	—	—	—

PORTFOLIO (as of 6/30/93)

Portfolio Manager: David Dreman - 1988

Investm't Category: Growth & Income

Cap Gain	Asset Allocation
✔ Cap & Income	Fund of Funds
Income	Index
	Sector
✔ Domestic	Small Cap
Foreign	Socially Conscious
Country/Region	State Specific

Portfolio: stocks 100% bonds 0%
convertibles 0% other 0% cash 0%

Largest Holdings: financial services 13%,
banks/regional 9%

Unrealized Net Capital Gains: 22% of portfolio value

SHAREHOLDER INFORMATION

Minimum Investment
Initial: $1,000   Subsequent: $100

Minimum IRA Investment
Initial: $100   Subsequent: $100

Maximum Fees
Load: 1.00% redemption   12b-1: none
Other: redemption fee applies for 1 year

Distributions
Income: quarterly   Capital Gains: Dec

Exchange Options
Number Per Year: no limit   Fee: none
Telephone: yes (money market fund available)

Services
IRA, other pension, auto invest auto withdraw

Dreman High Return

(DRHRX)

Growth

10 Exchange Place
Suite 2050
Jersey City, NJ 07302
(800) 533-1608

PERFORMANCE

	3yr Annual	5yr Annual	10yr Annual	Bull	Bear
Return (%)	24.5	15.8	na	124.1	-21.2
Differ from Category (+/-)	5.3 high	1.2 abv av	na	39.4 high	-8.8 low

Total Risk	Standard Deviation	Category Risk	Risk Index	Beta
high	16.3%	high	1.5	1.3

	1993	1992	1991	1990	1989	1988	1987	1986	1985	1984
Return (%)	9.2	19.7	47.5	-8.6	18.4	—	—	—	—	—
Differ from category (+/-)	-4.0	8.7	12.1	-2.5	-7.4	—	—	—	—	—

PER SHARE DATA

	1993	1992	1991	1990	1989	1988	1987	1986	1985	1984
Dividends, Net Income ($)	0.21	0.24	0.29	0.35	0.43	—	—	—	—	—
Distrib'ns, Cap Gain ($)	0.24	0.12	0.20	0.07	2.25	—	—	—	—	—
Net Asset Value ($)	15.50	14.62	12.53	8.85	10.14	—	—	—	—	—
Expense Ratio (%)	1.25	1.25	1.25	1.25	1.25	—	—	—	—	—
Net Income to Assets (%)	1.40	1.88	2.52	3.61	3.83	—	—	—	—	—
Portfolio Turnover (%)	3	13	37	204	156	—	—	—	—	—
Total Assets (Millions $)	29	14	7	3	3	—	—	—	—	—

PORTFOLIO (as of 6/30/93)

Portfolio Manager: David Dreman - 1988

Investm't Category: Growth

Cap Gain	Asset Allocation
✔ Cap & Income	Fund of Funds
Income	Index
	Sector
✔ Domestic	Small Cap
Foreign	Socially Conscious
Country/Region	State Specific

Portfolio: stocks 100% bonds 0%
convertibles 0% other 0% cash 0%

Largest Holdings: banks/regional 14%, financial services 12%

Unrealized Net Capital Gains: 13% of portfolio value

SHAREHOLDER INFORMATION

Minimum Investment
Initial: $1,000   Subsequent: $100

Minimum IRA Investment
Initial: $100   Subsequent: $100

Maximum Fees
Load: 1.00% redemption   12b-1: none
Other: redemption fee applies for 1 year

Distributions
Income: quarterly   Capital Gains: Dec

Exchange Options
Number Per Year: no limit   Fee: none
Telephone: yes (money market fund available)

Services
IRA, other pension, auto invest, auto withdraw

Dreyfus (DREVX)

Growth & Income

200 Park Ave.
New York, NY 10166
(800) 645-6561, (718) 895-1206

PERFORMANCE

	3yr Annual	5yr Annual	10yr Annual	Bull	Bear
Return (%)	12.8	11.4	11.7	52.7	-9.0
Differ from Category (+/-)	-3.6 low	-1.1 blw av	-0.6 blw av	-17.4 low	2.6 abv av

Total Risk	Standard Deviation	Category Risk	Risk Index	Beta
av	9.9%	av	1.1	0.8

	1993	1992	1991	1990	1989	1988	1987	1986	1985	1984
Return (%)	6.3	5.5	28.0	-3.3	23.6	8.7	8.6	16.3	25.0	3.3
Differ from category (+/-) ..	-6.3	-4.5	0.3	2.3	2.0	-8.1	8.2	1.1	-0.4	-2.9

PER SHARE DATA

	1993	1992	1991	1990	1989	1988	1987	1986	1985	1984
Dividends, Net Income ($) .	0.32	0.23	0.34	0.50	0.58	0.45	0.76	0.58	0.49	0.74
Distrib'ns, Cap Gain ($) ...	0.66	0.34	0.28	0.36	0.35	0.16	2.56	2.70	0.98	2.66
Net Asset Value ($)	13.10	13.27	13.14	10.80	12.07	10.55	10.28	12.55	13.86	12.45
Expense Ratio (%)..........	na	0.74	0.78	0.77	0.75	0.77	0.71	0.74	0.75	0.76
Net Income to Assets (%)	na	2.08	2.65	4.20	4.73	4.62	3.51	3.77	4.24	3.99
Portfolio Turnover (%).....	55	55	80	99	104	179	110	149	83	50
Total Assets (Millions $) ..	3,082	3,148	2,998	2,526	2,537	2,262	2,369	2,308	2,165	1,921

PORTFOLIO (as of 6/30/93)

Portfolio Manager: Wolodymyr Wronskyj - 1986

Investm't Category: Growth & Income

Cap Gain	Asset Allocation
✔ Cap & Income	Fund of Funds
Income	Index
	Sector
✔ Domestic	Small Cap
✔ Foreign	Socially Conscious
Country/Region	State Specific

Portfolio: stocks 77% bonds 0%
convertibles 0% other 0% cash 23%

Largest Holdings: consumer staples 16%, finance 14%

Unrealized Net Capital Gains: 19% of portfolio value

SHAREHOLDER INFORMATION

Minimum Investment
Initial: $2,500   Subsequent: $100

Minimum IRA Investment
Initial: $750   Subsequent: $0

Maximum Fees
Load: none   12b-1: none
Other: none

Distributions
Income: quarterly   Capital Gains: Dec

Exchange Options
Number Per Year: no limit   Fee: none
Telephone: yes (money market fund available)

Services
IRA, other pension, auto exchange, auto invest, auto withdraw

Dreyfus 100% US Treasury Interm Term

(DRGIX) *Government Bond*

200 Park Ave.
New York, NY 10166
(800) 645-6561, (718) 895-1206

	3yr Annual	5yr Annual	10yr Annual	Bull	Bear
Return (%)	11.0	10.9	na	43.1	4.0
Differ from Category (+/-)	0.2 abv av	0.5 abv av	na	-3.1 av	3.5 abv av

Total Risk	Standard Deviation	Category Risk	Risk Index	Avg Mat
av	6.8%	abv av	1.6	6.9 yrs

	1993	1992	1991	1990	1989	1988	1987	1986	1985	1984
Return (%)	11.0	7.1	15.2	8.5	12.8	5.7	—	—	—	—
Differ from category (+/-)	0.6	0.8	0.2	2.0	-1.1	-1.9	—	—	—	—

PER SHARE DATA

	1993	1992	1991	1990	1989	1988	1987	1986	1985	1984
Dividends, Net Income ($)	0.94	1.00	1.06	1.12	1.13	1.15	—	—	—	—
Distrib'ns, Cap Gain ($)	0.00	0.00	0.00	0.00	0.00	0.00	—	—	—	—
Net Asset Value ($)	13.60	13.12	13.22	12.48	12.59	12.22	—	—	—	—
Expense Ratio (%)	0.60	0.52	0.62	0.80	0.80	0.47	—	—	—	—
Net Income to Assets (%)	7.03	7.68	8.44	9.15	9.16	9.18	—	—	—	—
Portfolio Turnover (%)	na	116	22	4	6	21	—	—	—	—
Total Assets (Millions $)	253	231	183	71	61	62	—	—	—	—

PORTFOLIO (as of 6/30/93)

Portfolio Manager: Barbara Kenworthy - 1987

Investm't Category: Government Bond

Cap Gain	Asset Allocation
Cap & Income	Fund of Funds
✔ Income	Index
	Sector
✔ Domestic	Small Cap
Foreign	Socially Conscious
Country/Region	State Specific

Portfolio: stocks 0% bonds 100%
convertibles 0% other 0% cash 0%

Largest Holdings: U.S. government 100%

Unrealized Net Capital Gains: 2% of portfolio value

SHAREHOLDER INFORMATION

Minimum Investment
Initial: $2,500   Subsequent: $100

Minimum IRA Investment
Initial: na   Subsequent: na

Maximum Fees
Load: none   12b-1: none
Other: none

Distributions
Income: monthly   Capital Gains: Dec

Exchange Options
Number Per Year: no limit   Fee: none
Telephone: yes (money market fund available)

Services
auto exchange, auto invest, auto withdraw

Dreyfus 100% US Treasury Long Term

200 Park Ave.
New York, NY 10166
(800) 645-6561, (718) 895-1206

(DRGBX)   *Government Bond*

PERFORMANCE

	3yr Annual	5yr Annual	10yr Annual	Bull	Bear
Return (%)	14.0	13.0	na	58.9	-0.1
Differ from Category (+/-)	3.2 high	2.6 high	na	12.7 abv av	-0.6 blw av

Total Risk	Standard Deviation	Category Risk	Risk Index	Avg Mat
av	7.7%	high	1.8	19.4 yrs

	1993	1992	1991	1990	1989	1988	1987	1986	1985	1984
Return (%)	16.5	7.5	18.2	7.0	16.2	8.1	—	—	—	—
Differ from category (+/-)	6.1	1.3	3.2	0.5	2.3	0.5	—	—	—	—

PER SHARE DATA

	1993	1992	1991	1990	1989	1988	1987	1986	1985	1984
Dividends, Net Income ($)	1.02	1.07	1.13	1.16	1.16	1.16	—	—	—	—
Distrib'ns, Cap Gain ($)	0.00	0.00	0.00	0.00	0.00	0.00	—	—	—	—
Net Asset Value ($)	15.68	14.37	14.42	13.26	13.56	12.74	—	—	—	—
Expense Ratio (%)	0.69	0.56	0.25	0.00	0.00	0.00	—	—	—	—
Net Income to Assets (%)	6.91	7.63	8.34	9.05	8.79	9.04	—	—	—	—
Portfolio Turnover (%)	420	97	21	31	40	19	—	—	—	—
Total Assets (Millions $)	211	239	217	43	24	10	—	—	—	—

PORTFOLIO (as of 6/30/93)

Portfolio Manager: Barbara Kenworthy - 1987

Investm't Category: Government Bond

Cap Gain	Asset Allocation
Cap & Income	Fund of Funds
✔ Income	Index
	Sector
✔ Domestic	Small Cap
Foreign	Socially Conscious
Country/Region	State Specific

Portfolio: stocks 0%   bonds 99%
convertibles 0%   other 0%   cash 1%

Largest Holdings: U.S. government 99%

Unrealized Net Capital Gains: 1% of portfolio value

SHAREHOLDER INFORMATION

Minimum Investment
Initial: $2,500   Subsequent: $100

Minimum IRA Investment
Initial: na   Subsequent: na

Maximum Fees
Load: none   12b-1: none
Other: none

Distributions
Income: monthly   Capital Gains: Dec

Exchange Options
Number Per Year: no limit   Fee: none
Telephone: yes (money market fund available)

Services
auto exchange, auto invest, auto withdraw

Dreyfus 100% US Treasury Short Term

200 Park Ave.
New York, NY 10166
(800) 645-6561, (718) 895-1206

(DRTSX) *Government Bond*

PERFORMANCE

	3yr Annual	5yr Annual	10yr Annual	Bull	Bear
Return (%)	8.9	9.1	na	35.9	1.0
Differ from Category (+/-)	-1.9 blw av	-1.3 blw av	na	-10.3 blw av	0.5 blw av

Total Risk	Standard Deviation	Category Risk	Risk Index	Avg Mat
low	2.8%	low	0.6	2.6 yrs

	1993	1992	1991	1990	1989	1988	1987	1986	1985	1984
Return (%)	7.0	7.0	12.9	6.2	12.8	7.8	—	—	—	—
Differ from category (+/-). . .	-3.4	0.8	-2.1	-0.3	-1.1	0.2	—	—	—	—

PER SHARE DATA

	1993	1992	1991	1990	1989	1988	1987	1986	1985	1984
Dividends, Net Income ($) .	1.25	1.35	1.12	1.13	1.19	1.19	—	—	—	—
Distrib'ns, Cap Gain ($) . . .	0.00	0.00	0.00	0.00	0.00	0.00	—	—	—	—
Net Asset Value ($)	15.75	15.91	16.18	15.40	15.62	14.96	—	—	—	—
Expense Ratio (%)	0.05	0.03	0.00	0.00	0.00	0.00	—	—	—	—
Net Income to Assets (%) .	7.86	8.34	8.60	7.50	7.84	7.75	—	—	—	—
Portfolio Turnover (%).	na	138	60	0	0	0	—	—	—	—
Total Assets (Millions $). . . .	190	144	29	2	2	4	—	—	—	—

PORTFOLIO (as of 6/30/93)

Portfolio Manager: Barbara Kenworthy - 1987

Investm't Category: Government Bond

Cap Gain	Asset Allocation
Cap & Income	Fund of Funds
✔ Income	Index
	Sector
✔ Domestic	Small Cap
Foreign	Socially Conscious
Country/Region	State Specific

Portfolio: stocks 0% bonds 99%
convertibles 0% other 0% cash 1%

Largest Holdings: U.S. government 99%

Unrealized Net Capital Gains: 0% of portfolio value

SHAREHOLDER INFORMATION

Minimum Investment
Initial: $2,500 Subsequent: $100

Minimum IRA Investment
Initial: na Subsequent: na

Maximum Fees
Load: none 12b-1: none
Other: none

Distributions
Income: monthly Capital Gains: Dec

Exchange Options
Number Per Year: no limit Fee: none
Telephone: yes (money market fund available)

Services
auto exchange, auto invest, auto withdraw

Dreyfus A Bonds Plus
(DRBDX)

General Bond

200 Park Ave.
New York, NY 10166
(800) 645-6561, (718) 895-1206

PERFORMANCE

	3yr Annual	5yr Annual	10yr Annual	Bull	Bear
Return (%)	13.8	12.0	11.7	55.8	-0.6
Differ from Category (+/-)	3.6 high	2.2 high	0.8 high	16.4 high	-3.5 low

Total Risk	Standard Deviation	Category Risk	Risk Index	Avg Mat
blw av	4.9%	high	1.7	17.4 yrs

	1993	1992	1991	1990	1989	1988	1987	1986	1985	1984
Return (%)	14.9	8.2	18.7	4.7	14.2	9.0	-0.3	13.9	23.2	12.5
Differ from category (+/-) . . .	5.7	1.5	4.1	-2.2	2.9	1.4	-2.8	0.0	3.1	0.2

PER SHARE DATA

	1993	1992	1991	1990	1989	1988	1987	1986	1985	1984
Dividends, Net Income ($) .	1.00	1.07	1.10	1.15	1.18	1.18	1.34	1.32	1.42	1.49
Distrib'ns, Cap Gain ($) . . .	0.58	0.20	0.00	0.00	0.00	0.00	0.21	0.25	0.00	0.00
Net Asset Value ($)	15.18	14.62	14.74	13.44	13.98	13.34	13.36	14.99	14.61	13.16
Expense Ratio (%)	0.93	0.88	0.85	0.86	0.93	0.88	0.84	0.87	0.93	0.93
Net Income to Assets (%) . .	7.07	7.88	8.59	8.52	8.90	8.87	8.72	10.34	11.85	11.29
Portfolio Turnover (%)	81	67	26	40	66	49	79	61	20	5
Total Assets (Millions $) . . .	638	447	340	300	262	254	320	222	123	105

PORTFOLIO (as of 9/30/93)

Portfolio Manager: Barbara Kenworthy - 1985

Investm't Category: General Bond

Cap Gain	Asset Allocation
Cap & Income	Fund of Funds
✔ Income	Index
	Sector
✔ Domestic	Small Cap
✔ Foreign	Socially Conscious
Country/Region	State Specific

Portfolio: stocks 0%   bonds 96%
convertibles 0%   other 0%   cash 4%

Largest Holdings: corporate 57%, mortgage-backed 16%

Unrealized Net Capital Gains: 8% of portfolio value

SHAREHOLDER INFORMATION

Minimum Investment
Initial: $2,500   Subsequent: $100

Minimum IRA Investment
Initial: $750   Subsequent: $0

Maximum Fees
Load: none   12b-1: none
Other: none

Distributions
Income: monthly   Capital Gains: Dec

Exchange Options
Number Per Year: no limit   Fee: none
Telephone: yes (money market fund available)

Services
IRA, other pension, auto exchange, auto invest, auto withdraw

Dreyfus Appreciation
(DGAGX)
Growth

200 Park Ave.
New York, NY 10166
(800) 645-6561, (718) 895-1206

PERFORMANCE

	3yr Annual	5yr Annual	10yr Annual	Bull	Bear
Return (%)	13.4	12.7	na	58.5	-9.6
Differ from Category (+/-)	-5.8 low	-1.9 blw av	na	-26.2 low	2.8 abv av

Total Risk	Standard Deviation	Category Risk	Risk Index	Beta
abv av	12.0%	av	1.1	1.0

	1993	1992	1991	1990	1989	1988	1987	1986	1985	1984
Return (%).............	0.6	4.6	38.4	-1.8	27.2	16.6	4.5	15.1	35.3	—
Differ from category (+/-)..	-12.5	-6.4	3.0	4.3	1.4	-1.1	3.3	0.6	6.0	—

PER SHARE DATA

	1993	1992	1991	1990	1989	1988	1987	1986	1985	1984
Dividends, Net Income ($).	0.26	0.12	0.20	0.23	0.16	0.16	0.14	0.01	0.12	—
Distrib'ns, Cap Gain ($) ...	0.06	0.07	0.24	0.77	0.68	0.07	0.95	0.10	0.00	—
Net Asset Value ($)	14.92	15.15	14.67	10.94	12.20	10.28	9.03	9.67	8.51	—
Expense Ratio (%)	na	1.14	1.30	1.24	1.18	1.74	1.63	1.50	1.51	—
Net Income to Assets (%) ...	na	1.46	1.69	2.21	1.38	1.41	0.65	0.65	1.15	—
Portfolio Turnover (%)......	na	3	13	179	130	137	179	183	198	—
Total Assets (Millions $)....	241	208	81	40	46	41	40	27	5	—

PORTFOLIO (as of 6/30/93)

Portfolio Manager: not specified

Investm't Category: Growth

✔ Cap Gain	Asset Allocation
Cap & Income	Fund of Funds
Income	Index
	Sector
✔ Domestic	Small Cap
✔ Foreign	Socially Conscious
Country/Region	State Specific

Portfolio: stocks 89%   bonds 2%
convertibles 0%   other 5%   cash 4%

Largest Holdings: health care 15%, consumer staples 15%

Unrealized Net Capital Gains: 5% of portfolio value

SHAREHOLDER INFORMATION

Minimum Investment
Initial: $2,500   Subsequent: $100

Minimum IRA Investment
Initial: $750   Subsequent: $0

Maximum Fees
Load: none   12b-1: 0.20%
Other: none

Distributions
Income: Dec   Capital Gains: Dec

Exchange Options
Number Per Year: no limit   Fee: none
Telephone: yes (money market fund available)

Services
IRA, other pension, auto exchange, auto invest, auto withdraw

Dreyfus Balanced
(DRBAX)
Balanced

200 Park Ave.
New York, NY 10166
(800) 645-6561, (718) 895-1206

PERFORMANCE

	3yr Annual	5yr Annual	10yr Annual	Bull	Bear
Return (%)	na	na	na	na	na
Differ from Category (+/-)	na	na	na	na	na

Total Risk	Standard Deviation	Category Risk	Risk Index	Beta
na	na	na	na	na

	1993	1992	1991	1990	1989	1988	1987	1986	1985	1984
Return (%)	10.8	—	—	—	—	—	—	—	—	—
Differ from category (+/-) . .	-2.6	—	—	—	—	—	—	—	—	—

PER SHARE DATA

	1993	1992	1991	1990	1989	1988	1987	1986	1985	1984
Dividends, Net Income ($) .	0.40	—	—	—	—	—	—	—	—	—
Distrib'ns, Cap Gain ($) . . .	0.13	—	—	—	—	—	—	—	—	—
Net Asset Value ($)	13.46	—	—	—	—	—	—	—	—	—
Expense Ratio (%).	na	—	—	—	—	—	—	—	—	—
Net Income to Assets (%)	na	—	—	—	—	—	—	—	—	—
Portfolio Turnover (%)	na	—	—	—	—	—	—	—	—	—
Total Assets (Millions $)	63	—	—	—	—	—	—	—	—	—

PORTFOLIO (as of 8/31/93)

Portfolio Manager: not specified

Investm't Category: Balanced
Cap Gain	✔ Asset Allocation
✔ Cap & Income	Fund of Funds
Income	Index
	Sector
✔ Domestic	Small Cap
Foreign	Socially Conscious
Country/Region	State Specific

Portfolio: stocks 40%   bonds 48%
convertibles 0%   other 0%   cash 12%

Largest Holdings: bonds—U.S. government
agencies 24%, stocks—consumer 7%

Unrealized Net Capital Gains: 2% of portfolio value

SHAREHOLDER INFORMATION

Minimum Investment
Initial: $2,500   Subsequent: $100

Minimum IRA Investment
Initial: $750   Subsequent: $0

Maximum Fees
Load: none   12b-1: none
Other: none

Distributions
Income: quarterly   Capital Gains: Dec

Exchange Options
Number Per Year: no limit   Fee: none
Telephone: yes (money market fund available)

Services
IRA, other pension, auto exchange, auto invest,
auto withdraw

Dreyfus CA Interm Muni Bond (DCIMX)

200 Park Ave.
New York, NY 10166
(800) 645-6561, (718) 895-1206

Tax-Exempt Bond

PERFORMANCE

	3yr Annual	5yr Annual	10yr Annual	Bull	Bear
Return (%)	na	na	na	na	na
Differ from Category (+/-)	na	na	na	na	na

Total Risk	Standard Deviation	Category Risk	Risk Index	Avg Mat
na	na	na	na	8.9 yrs

	1993	1992	1991	1990	1989	1988	1987	1986	1985	1984
Return (%).............	14.4	—	—	—	—	—	—	—	—	—
Differ from category (+/-)...	2.8	—	—	—	—	—	—	—	—	—

PER SHARE DATA

	1993	1992	1991	1990	1989	1988	1987	1986	1985	1984
Dividends, Net Income ($).	0.72	—	—	—	—	—	—	—	—	—
Distrib'ns, Cap Gain ($) ...	0.00	—	—	—	—	—	—	—	—	—
Net Asset Value ($)	13.97	—	—	—	—	—	—	—	—	—
Expense Ratio (%)	0.00	—	—	—	—	—	—	—	—	—
Net Income to Assets (%) .	5.61	—	—	—	—	—	—	—	—	—
Portfolio Turnover (%).......	6	—	—	—	—	—	—	—	—	—
Total Assets (Millions $)....	305	—	—	—	—	—	—	—	—	—

PORTFOLIO (as of 9/30/93)

Portfolio Manager: Laurence Troutman - 1992

Investm't Category: Tax-Exempt Bond

Cap Gain	Asset Allocation
Cap & Income	Fund of Funds
✔ Income	Index
	Sector
✔ Domestic	Small Cap
Foreign	Socially Conscious
Country/Region	✔ State Specific

Portfolio: stocks 0% bonds 93%
convertibles 0% other 0% cash 7%

Largest Holdings: na

Unrealized Net Capital Gains: 3% of portfolio value

SHAREHOLDER INFORMATION

Minimum Investment
Initial: $2,500   Subsequent: $100

Minimum IRA Investment
Initial: na   Subsequent: na

Maximum Fees
Load: none   12b-1: none
Other: none

Distributions
Income: monthly   Capital Gains: Nov

Exchange Options
Number Per Year: no limit   Fee: none
Telephone: yes (money market fund available)

Services
auto exchange, auto invest, auto withdraw

Dreyfus CA Tax Exempt Bond (DRCAX)

200 Park Ave.
New York, NY 10166
(800) 645-6561, (718) 895-1206

Tax-Exempt Bond

PERFORMANCE

	3yr Annual	5yr Annual	10yr Annual	Bull	Bear
Return (%)	9.6	8.8	9.1	36.4	3.0
Differ from Category (+/-)	-0.6 blw av	-0.4 blw av	-0.5 blw av	-3.7 blw av	0.6 abv av

Total Risk	Standard Deviation	Category Risk	Risk Index	Avg Mat
blw av	4.6%	abv av	1.1	23.7 yrs

	1993	1992	1991	1990	1989	1988	1987	1986	1985	1984
Return (%)	11.8	6.6	10.3	6.7	8.5	9.6	-1.6	17.7	18.0	4.9
Differ from category (+/-) . . .	0.2	-1.7	-1.0	0.4	-0.5	-0.5	-0.4	1.3	0.6	-3.4

PER SHARE DATA

	1993	1992	1991	1990	1989	1988	1987	1986	1985	1984
Dividends, Net Income ($) .	0.86	0.90	0.95	1.01	1.03	1.05	1.06	1.09	1.13	1.18
Distrib'ns, Cap Gain ($) . . .	0.16	0.15	0.03	0.00	0.00	0.00	0.00	0.00	0.00	0.00
Net Asset Value ($)	15.56	14.86	14.96	14.50	14.58	14.42	14.15	15.47	14.13	13.00
Expense Ratio (%).	0.68	0.68	0.68	0.68	0.70	0.71	0.70	0.72	0.75	0.55
Net Income to Assets (%) . .	5.88	6.32	6.82	7.10	7.32	7.37	7.08	7.85	8.75	8.92
Portfolio Turnover (%)	41	46	56	35	40	60	32	19	27	35
Total Assets (Millions $) . .	1,843	1,751	1,630	1,497	1,385	1,175	1,175	973	529	216

PORTFOLIO (as of 5/31/93)

Portfolio Manager: Larry Troutman - 1986

Investm't Category: Tax-Exempt Bond

Cap Gain	Asset Allocation
Cap & Income	Fund of Funds
✔ Income	Index
	Sector
✔ Domestic	Small Cap
Foreign	Socially Conscious
Country/Region	✔ State Specific

Portfolio: stocks 0% bonds 97%
convertibles 0% other 0% cash 3%

Largest Holdings: na

Unrealized Net Capital Gains: 6% of portfolio value

SHAREHOLDER INFORMATION

Minimum Investment
Initial: $2,500   Subsequent: $100

Minimum IRA Investment
Initial: na   Subsequent: na

Maximum Fees
Load: none   12b-1: none
Other: none

Distributions
Income: monthly   Capital Gains: Nov

Exchange Options
Number Per Year: no limit   Fee: none
Telephone: yes (money market fund available)

Services
auto exchange, auto invest, auto withdraw

Dreyfus Capital Growth
(DRLEX)

200 Park Ave.
New York, NY 10166
(800) 645-6561, (718) 895-1206

Growth

	3yr Annual	5yr Annual	10yr Annual	Bull	Bear
Return (%)	17.3	13.9	13.8	73.7	-8.3
Differ from Category (+/-)	-1.9 blw av	-0.6 av	1.2 abv av	-11.0 blw av	4.1 abv av

Total Risk	Standard Deviation	Category Risk	Risk Index	Beta
av	10.5%	blw av	1.0	0.8

	1993	1992	1991	1990	1989	1988	1987	1986	1985	1984
Return (%)	14.7	6.2	32.6	-1.4	20.4	1.8	11.1	19.3	30.5	8.5
Differ from category (+/-). . .	1.5	-4.8	-2.8	4.7	-5.4	-15.9	9.9	4.8	1.2	8.5

PER SHARE DATA

	1993	1992	1991	1990	1989	1988	1987	1986	1985	1984
Dividends, Net Income ($).	0.80	0.23	0.38	0.75	0.69	0.63	0.40	0.51	0.77	0.55
Distrib'ns, Cap Gain ($) . . .	2.22	1.37	1.37	0.00	0.00	0.00	3.66	4.73	1.94	1.03
Net Asset Value ($)	16.38	16.98	17.50	14.62	15.61	13.55	13.94	16.23	18.07	16.04
Expense Ratio (%)	1.02	1.07	1.14	1.34	1.58	1.31	na	1.01	1.20	2.34
Net Income to Assets (%) .	1.24	1.74	2.13	3.97	5.32	3.91	1.98	2.69	4.12	3.73
Portfolio Turnover (%).	102	141	81	89	124	111	123	141	82	82
Total Assets (Millions $). . . .	618	521	494	401	484	472	631	486	407	397

PORTFOLIO (as of 9/30/93)

Portfolio Manager: Howard Stein - 1968

Investm't Category: Growth

✔ Cap Gain	Asset Allocation
Cap & Income	Fund of Funds
Income	Index
	Sector
✔ Domestic	Small Cap
✔ Foreign	Socially Conscious
Country/Region	State Specific

Portfolio: stocks 56% bonds 0%
convertibles 2% other 0% cash 42%

Largest Holdings: consumer growth staples 16%, energy 11%

Unrealized Net Capital Gains: 11% of portfolio value

SHAREHOLDER INFORMATION

Minimum Investment
Initial: $2,500   Subsequent: $100

Minimum IRA Investment
Initial: $750   Subsequent: $0

Maximum Fees
Load: 3.00% front   12b-1: none
Other: none

Distributions
Income: Dec   Capital Gains: Dec

Exchange Options
Number Per Year: 2   Fee: none
Telephone: yes (money market fund available)

Services
IRA, other pension, auto exchange, auto invest, auto withdraw

Dreyfus Conn Interm Muni Bond (DCTIX)

200 Park Ave.
New York, NY 10166
(800) 645-6561, (718) 895-1206

Tax-Exempt Bond

PERFORMANCE

	3yr Annual	5yr Annual	10yr Annual	Bull	Bear
Return (%)	na	na	na	na	na
Differ from Category (+/-)	na	na	na	na	na

Total Risk	Standard Deviation	Category Risk	Risk Index	Avg Mat
na	na	na	na	9.1 yrs

	1993	1992	1991	1990	1989	1988	1987	1986	1985	1984
Return (%)	12.7	—	—	—	—	—	—	—	—	—
Differ from category (+/-) . . .	1.1	—	—	—	—	—	—	—	—	—

PER SHARE DATA

	1993	1992	1991	1990	1989	1988	1987	1986	1985	1984
Dividends, Net Income ($) .	0.68	—	—	—	—	—	—	—	—	—
Distrib'ns, Cap Gain ($) . . .	0.00	—	—	—	—	—	—	—	—	—
Net Asset Value ($)	13.77	—	—	—	—	—	—	—	—	—
Expense Ratio (%)	0.00	—	—	—	—	—	—	—	—	—
Net Income to Assets (%) . .	5.21	—	—	—	—	—	—	—	—	—
Portfolio Turnover (%)	37	—	—	—	—	—	—	—	—	—
Total Assets (Millions $) . . .	137	—	—	—	—	—	—	—	—	—

PORTFOLIO (as of 9/30/93)

Portfolio Manager: Stephen Kris - 1992

Investm't Category: Tax-Exempt Bond

Cap Gain	Asset Allocation
Cap & Income	Fund of Funds
✔ Income	Index
	Sector
✔ Domestic	Small Cap
Foreign	Socially Conscious
Country/Region	✔ State Specific

Portfolio: stocks 0%   bonds 95%
convertibles 0%   other 0%   cash 5%

Largest Holdings: na

Unrealized Net Capital Gains: 4% of portfolio value

SHAREHOLDER INFORMATION

Minimum Investment
Initial: $2,500   Subsequent: $100

Minimum IRA Investment
Initial: na   Subsequent: na

Maximum Fees
Load: none   12b-1: none
Other: none

Distributions
Income: monthly   Capital Gains: Dec

Exchange Options
Number Per Year: no limit   Fee: none
Telephone: yes (money market fund available)

Services
auto exchange, auto invest, auto withdraw

Dreyfus Edison Electric Index (DEEIX)

200 Park Ave.
New York, NY 10166
(800) 645-6561, (718) 895-1206

Growth & Income

PERFORMANCE

	3yr Annual	5yr Annual	10yr Annual	Bull	Bear
Return (%)	na	na	na	na	na
Differ from Category (+/-)	na	na	na	na	na

Total Risk	Standard Deviation	Category Risk	Risk Index	Beta
na	na	na	na	na

	1993	1992	1991	1990	1989	1988	1987	1986	1985	1984
Return (%)	10.4	7.4	—	—	—	—	—	—	—	—
Differ from category (+/-). . .	-2.2	-2.6	—	—	—	—	—	—	—	—

PER SHARE DATA

	1993	1992	1991	1990	1989	1988	1987	1986	1985	1984
Dividends, Net Income ($).	0.66	0.65	—	—	—	—	—	—	—	—
Distrib'ns, Cap Gain ($) . . .	0.21	0.00	—	—	—	—	—	—	—	—
Net Asset Value ($)	13.78	13.26	—	—	—	—	—	—	—	—
Expense Ratio (%)	0.29	0.24	—	—	—	—	—	—	—	—
Net Income to Assets (%) .	2.57	5.31	—	—	—	—	—	—	—	—
Portfolio Turnover (%).	1	3	—	—	—	—	—	—	—	—
Total Assets (Millions $). . . .	107	37	—	—	—	—	—	—	—	—

PORTFOLIO (as of 4/30/93)

Portfolio Manager: not specified

Investm't Category: Growth & Income
Cap Gain	Asset Allocation
✔ Cap & Income	Fund of Funds
Income	✔ Index
	✔ Sector
✔ Domestic	Small Cap
Foreign	Socially Conscious
Country/Region	State Specific

Portfolio: stocks 97% bonds 0%
convertibles 0% other 0% cash 3%

Largest Holdings: Edison Electric Institute Index

Unrealized Net Capital Gains: 7% of portfolio value

SHAREHOLDER INFORMATION

Minimum Investment
Initial: $2,500   Subsequent: $100

Minimum IRA Investment
Initial: $750   Subsequent: $0

Maximum Fees
Load: none   12b-1: none
Other: none

Distributions
Income: quarterly   Capital Gains: Dec

Exchange Options
Number Per Year: no limit   Fee: none
Telephone: none

Services
IRA, other pension, auto invest,

Dreyfus Florida Interm Muni (DFLIX)

200 Park Ave.
New York, NY 10166
(800) 645-6561, (718) 895-1206

Tax-Exempt Bond

PERFORMANCE

	3yr Annual	5yr Annual	10yr Annual	Bull	Bear
Return (%)	na	na	na	na	na
Differ from Category (+/-)	na	na	na	na	na

Total Risk	Standard Deviation	Category Risk	Risk Index	Avg Mat
na	na	na	na	9.3 yrs

	1993	1992	1991	1990	1989	1988	1987	1986	1985	1984
Return (%)	12.8	—	—	—	—	—	—	—	—	—
Differ from category (+/-) . . .	1.2	—	—	—	—	—	—	—	—	—

PER SHARE DATA

	1993	1992	1991	1990	1989	1988	1987	1986	1985	1984
Dividends, Net Income ($) .	0.70	—	—	—	—	—	—	—	—	—
Distrib'ns, Cap Gain ($) . . .	0.01	—	—	—	—	—	—	—	—	—
Net Asset Value ($)	13.85	—	—	—	—	—	—	—	—	—
Expense Ratio (%).	0.09	—	—	—	—	—	—	—	—	—
Net Income to Assets (%) . .	5.42	—	—	—	—	—	—	—	—	—
Portfolio Turnover (%)	13	—	—	—	—	—	—	—	—	—
Total Assets (Millions $) . . .	529	—	—	—	—	—	—	—	—	—

PORTFOLIO (as of 6/30/93)

Portfolio Manager: Stephen Kris - 1992

Investm't Category: Tax-Exempt Bond

Cap Gain	Asset Allocation
Cap & Income	Fund of Funds
✔ Income	Index
	Sector
✔ Domestic	Small Cap
Foreign	Socially Conscious
Country/Region	✔ State Specific

Portfolio: stocks 0%   bonds 100%
convertibles 0%   other 0%   cash 0%

Largest Holdings: na

Unrealized Net Capital Gains: 5% of portfolio value

SHAREHOLDER INFORMATION

Minimum Investment
Initial: $2,500   Subsequent: $100

Minimum IRA Investment
Initial: na   Subsequent: na

Maximum Fees
Load: none   12b-1: none
Other: none

Distributions
Income: monthly   Capital Gains: August

Exchange Options
Number Per Year: no limit   Fee: none
Telephone: yes (money market fund available)

Services
auto exchange, auto invest, auto withdraw

Dreyfus GNMA (DRGMX)

Mortgage-Backed Bond

200 Park Ave.
New York, NY 10166
(800) 645-6561, (718) 895-1206

PERFORMANCE

	3yr Annual	5yr Annual	10yr Annual	Bull	Bear
Return (%)	9.2	9.8	na	36.1	5.1
Differ from Category (+/-)	0.0 av	-0.1 blw av	na	-0.6 av	0.5 abv av

Total Risk	Standard Deviation	Category Risk	Risk Index	Avg Mat
low	2.7%	av	1.0	24.3 yrs

	1993	1992	1991	1990	1989	1988	1987	1986	1985	1984
Return (%).	7.1	6.3	14.4	9.7	11.5	6.3	2.4	9.7	—	—
Differ from category (+/-). . .	0.3	0.2	0.0	0.2	-0.8	-0.6	0.3	-1.5	—	—

PER SHARE DATA

	1993	1992	1991	1990	1989	1988	1987	1986	1985	1984
Dividends, Net Income ($).	1.03	1.12	1.23	1.28	1.29	1.29	1.45	1.48	—	—
Distrib'ns, Cap Gain ($) . . .	0.00	0.00	0.00	0.00	0.00	0.00	0.02	0.00	—	—
Net Asset Value ($)	15.15	15.12	15.32	14.54	14.49	14.21	14.59	15.70	—	—
Expense Ratio (%)	0.93	0.95	0.97	0.97	0.99	1.01	1.01	0.96	—	—
Net Income to Assets (%) .	7.20	8.05	8.81	8.98	8.89	8.98	8.87	10.27	—	—
Portfolio Turnover (%).	155	61	26	272	473	288	257	245	—	—
Total Assets (Millions $). .	1,801	1,575	1,583	1,496	1,616	1,981	2,397	1,738	—	—

PORTFOLIO (as of 4/30/93)

Portfolio Manager: Garitt Kono - 1993

Investm't Category: Mortgage-Backed Bond

Cap Gain	Asset Allocation
Cap & Income	Fund of Funds
✔ Income	Index
	Sector
✔ Domestic	Small Cap
Foreign	Socially Conscious
Country/Region	State Specific

Portfolio: stocks 0% bonds 99%
convertibles 0% other 0% cash 1%

Largest Holdings: mortgage-backed 94%

Unrealized Net Capital Gains: 2% of portfolio value

SHAREHOLDER INFORMATION

Minimum Investment
Initial: $2,500   Subsequent: $100

Minimum IRA Investment
Initial: $750   Subsequent: $0

Maximum Fees
Load: none   12b-1: 0.20%
Other: none

Distributions
Income: monthly   Capital Gains: Dec

Exchange Options
Number Per Year: no limit   Fee: none
Telephone: yes (money market fund available)

Services
IRA, other pension, auto exchange, auto invest, auto withdraw

Dreyfus Growth & Income (DGRIX)

Growth & Income

200 Park Ave.
New York, NY 10166
(800) 645-6561, (718) 895-1206

PERFORMANCE

	3yr Annual	5yr Annual	10yr Annual	Bull	Bear
Return (%)	na	na	na	na	na
Differ from Category (+/-)	na	na	na	na	na

Total Risk	Standard Deviation	Category Risk	Risk Index	Beta
na	na	na	na	na

	1993	1992	1991	1990	1989	1988	1987	1986	1985	1984
Return (%)	18.5	20.1	—	—	—	—	—	—	—	—
Differ from category (+/-) . . .	5.9	10.1	—	—	—	—	—	—	—	—

PER SHARE DATA

	1993	1992	1991	1990	1989	1988	1987	1986	1985	1984
Dividends, Net Income ($) .	0.35	0.27	—	—	—	—	—	—	—	—
Distrib'ns, Cap Gain ($) . . .	0.03	0.00	—	—	—	—	—	—	—	—
Net Asset Value ($)	17.04	14.73	—	—	—	—	—	—	—	—
Expense Ratio (%)	1.24	1.02	—	—	—	—	—	—	—	—
Net Income to Assets (%) . .	2.92	2.30	—	—	—	—	—	—	—	—
Portfolio Turnover (%)	85	127	—	—	—	—	—	—	—	—
Total Assets (Millions $) . .	1,263	99	—	—	—	—	—	—	—	—

PORTFOLIO (as of 10/31/93)

Portfolio Manager: Richard Hoey - 1992

Investm't Category: Growth & Income

Cap Gain	Asset Allocation
✔ Cap & Income	Fund of Funds
Income	Index
	Sector
✔ Domestic	Small Cap
✔ Foreign	Socially Conscious
Country/Region	State Specific

Portfolio: stocks 57% bonds 0%
convertibles 31% other 0% cash 12%

Largest Holdings: telecommunications 12%, financial 9%

Unrealized Net Capital Gains: 9% of portfolio value

SHAREHOLDER INFORMATION

Minimum Investment
Initial: $2,500   Subsequent: $100

Minimum IRA Investment
Initial: $750   Subsequent: $0

Maximum Fees
Load: none   12b-1: none
Other: none

Distributions
Income: quarterly   Capital Gains: Dec

Exchange Options
Number Per Year: no limit   Fee: none
Telephone: yes (money market fund available)

Services
IRA, other pension, auto exchange, auto invest, auto withdraw

Dreyfus Growth Opportunity (DREQX)

Growth

200 Park Ave.
New York, NY 10166
(800) 645-6561, (718) 895-1206

PERFORMANCE

	3yr Annual	5yr Annual	10yr Annual	Bull	Bear
Return (%)	13.8	9.6	10.1	57.8	-12.5
Differ from Category (+/-)	-5.4 low	-5.0 low	-2.5 low	-26.9 low	-0.1 av

Total Risk	Standard Deviation	Category Risk	Risk Index	Beta
high	16.2%	high	1.5	1.2

	1993	1992	1991	1990	1989	1988	1987	1986	1985	1984
Return (%)	1.7	-4.2	51.4	-6.5	14.7	17.8	6.7	15.2	30.6	-12.1
Differ from category (+/-) . .	-11.5	-15.2	16.0	-0.4	-11.1	0.1	5.5	0.6	1.3	-12.1

PER SHARE DATA

	1993	1992	1991	1990	1989	1988	1987	1986	1985	1984
Dividends, Net Income ($) .	0.00	0.02	0.13	0.27	0.46	0.40	0.43	0.20	0.21	0.17
Distrib'ns, Cap Gain ($) . . .	2.60	0.00	0.00	0.01	0.80	0.02	2.07	2.59	0.33	0.88
Net Asset Value ($)	10.74	13.14	13.73	9.16	10.12	9.94	8.81	10.50	11.59	9.38
Expense Ratio (%)	1.00	0.95	0.98	1.00	1.04	0.91	0.95	0.98	1.02	0.99
Net Income to Assets (%) .	0.11	0.85	2.32	3.13	3.50	3.69	1.62	1.87	2.04	1.85
Portfolio Turnover (%).	90	57	147	126	83	129	73	56	44	59
Total Assets (Millions $)	490	632	512	526	571	492	516	477	441	369

PORTFOLIO (as of 2/28/93)

Portfolio Manager: Richard Shields - 1990

Investm't Category: Growth

✔ Cap Gain	Asset Allocation
Cap & Income	Fund of Funds
Income	Index
	Sector
✔ Domestic	Small Cap
✔ Foreign	Socially Conscious
Country/Region	State Specific

Portfolio: stocks 77% bonds 0%
convertibles 0% other 1% cash 22%

Largest Holdings: consumer growth staples 35%, consumer cyclical 15%

Unrealized Net Capital Gains: 14% of portfolio value

SHAREHOLDER INFORMATION

Minimum Investment
Initial: $2,500   Subsequent: $100

Minimum IRA Investment
Initial: $750   Subsequent: $0

Maximum Fees
Load: none   12b-1: none
Other: none

Distributions
Income: Dec   Capital Gains: Dec

Exchange Options
Number Per Year: no limit   Fee: none
Telephone: yes (money market fund available)

Services
IRA, other pension, auto exchange, auto invest, auto withdraw

Dreyfus Insured Muni Bond (DTBDX)

200 Park Ave.
New York, NY 10166
(800) 645-6561, (718) 895-1206

Tax-Exempt Bond

PERFORMANCE

	3yr Annual	5yr Annual	10yr Annual	Bull	Bear
Return (%)	10.5	9.4	na	40.9	2.5
Differ from Category (+/-)	0.2 blw av	0.2 av	na	0.8 av	0.2 av

Total Risk	Standard Deviation	Category Risk	Risk Index	Avg Mat
blw av	5.0%	high	1.2	23.0 yrs

	1993	1992	1991	1990	1989	1988	1987	1986	1985	1984
Return (%)	12.5	7.7	11.3	7.0	8.7	10.1	-1.9	17.0	—	—
Differ from category (+/-) . . .	0.8	-0.6	0.0	0.6	-0.3	0.0	-0.6	0.6	—	—

PER SHARE DATA

	1993	1992	1991	1990	1989	1988	1987	1986	1985	1984
Dividends, Net Income ($) .	1.02	1.08	1.10	1.15	1.16	1.19	1.21	1.27	—	—
Distrib'ns, Cap Gain ($) . . .	0.70	0.21	0.00	0.00	0.00	0.00	0.00	0.00	—	—
Net Asset Value ($)	19.08	18.54	18.46	17.63	17.60	17.30	16.83	18.40	—	—
Expense Ratio (%).	0.93	0.96	0.96	0.99	1.00	0.90	0.84	0.73	—	—
Net Income to Assets (%) . .	5.69	6.07	6.50	6.63	6.96	7.11	6.78	7.60	—	—
Portfolio Turnover (%)	80	51	62	67	68	96	75	51	—	—
Total Assets (Millions $) . . .	290	241	219	191	186	177	198	144	—	—

PORTFOLIO (as of 4/30/93)

Portfolio Manager: Lawrence Troutman - 1985

Investm't Category: Tax-Exempt Bond

Cap Gain	Asset Allocation
Cap & Income	Fund of Funds
✔ Income	Index
	Sector
✔ Domestic	Small Cap
Foreign	Socially Conscious
Country/Region	State Specific

Portfolio: stocks 0% bonds 100%
convertibles 0% other 0% cash 0%

Largest Holdings: na

Unrealized Net Capital Gains: 7% of portfolio value

SHAREHOLDER INFORMATION

Minimum Investment
Initial: $2,500   Subsequent: $100

Minimum IRA Investment
Initial: na   Subsequent: na

Maximum Fees
Load: none   12b-1: 0.21%
Other: none

Distributions
Income: monthly   Capital Gains: Nov

Exchange Options
Number Per Year: no limit   Fee: none
Telephone: yes (money market fund available)

Services
auto exchange, auto invest, auto withdraw

Dreyfus Interm Muni Bond (DITEX)

Tax-Exempt Bond

200 Park Ave.
New York, NY 10166
(800) 645-6561, (718) 895-1206

PERFORMANCE

	3yr Annual	5yr Annual	10yr Annual	Bull	Bear
Return (%)	10.4	9.3	9.4	38.8	3.4
Differ from Category (+/-)	0.1 blw av	0.1 blw av	-0.2 blw av	-1.3 blw av	1.1 abv av

Total Risk	Standard Deviation	Category Risk	Risk Index	Avg Mat
low	3.6%	blw av	0.9	9.9 yrs

	1993	1992	1991	1990	1989	1988	1987	1986	1985	1984
Return (%)	11.4	8.7	11.1	6.7	8.7	8.0	1.1	15.4	16.0	7.4
Differ from category (+/-). . .	-0.2	0.4	-0.2	0.4	-0.3	-2.1	2.3	-1.0	-1.3	-0.8

PER SHARE DATA

	1993	1992	1991	1990	1989	1988	1987	1986	1985	1984
Dividends, Net Income ($).	0.77	0.84	0.90	0.94	0.96	0.97	0.97	1.01	1.02	1.02
Distrib'ns, Cap Gain ($) . . .	0.16	0.31	0.07	0.00	0.00	0.00	0.00	0.00	0.00	0.00
Net Asset Value ($)	14.60	13.97	13.95	13.48	13.54	13.37	13.30	14.12	13.16	12.28
Expense Ratio (%)	0.71	0.70	0.68	0.71	0.71	0.73	0.71	0.75	0.81	0.68
Net Income to Assets (%) .	5.68	6.47	6.84	7.01	7.27	7.21	7.07	7.76	8.23	8.31
Portfolio Turnover (%).	60	48	31	40	34	49	50	34	21	29
Total Assets (Millions $). .	1,836	1,406	1,237	1,113	1,056	1,015	1,090	920	548	228

PORTFOLIO (as of 5/31/93)

Portfolio Manager: Monica Wieboldt - 1985

Investm't Category: Tax-Exempt Bond

Cap Gain	Asset Allocation
Cap & Income	Fund of Funds
✔ Income	Index
	Sector
✔ Domestic	Small Cap
Foreign	Socially Conscious
Country/Region	State Specific

Portfolio:	stocks 0%	bonds 97%
convertibles 0%	other 0%	cash 3%

Largest Holdings: na

Unrealized Net Capital Gains: 6% of portfolio value

SHAREHOLDER INFORMATION

Minimum Investment
Initial: $2,500   Subsequent: $100

Minimum IRA Investment
Initial: na   Subsequent: na

Maximum Fees
Load: none   12b-1: none
Other: none

Distributions
Income: monthly   Capital Gains: Nov

Exchange Options
Number Per Year: no limit   Fee: none
Telephone: yes (money market fund available)

Services
auto exchange, auto invest, auto withdraw

Dreyfus Investors GNMA
(DIGFX)

200 Park Ave.
New York, NY 10166
(800) 645-6561, (718) 895-1206

Mortgage-Backed Bond

PERFORMANCE

	3yr Annual	5yr Annual	10yr Annual	Bull	Bear
Return (%)	9.6	9.1	na	34.7	6.1
Differ from Category (+/-)	0.4 abv av	-0.8 low	na	-2.0 low	1.5 high

Total Risk	Standard Deviation	Category Risk	Risk Index	Avg Mat
low	3.5%	abv av	1.4	18.0 yrs

	1993	1992	1991	1990	1989	1988	1987	1986	1985	1984
Return (%)	8.7	6.9	13.2	8.5	8.4	10.5	—	—	—	—
Differ from category (+/-) . . .	1.9	0.8	-1.2	-1.0	-3.9	3.5	—	—	—	—

PER SHARE DATA

	1993	1992	1991	1990	1989	1988	1987	1986	1985	1984
Dividends, Net Income ($) .	1.11	1.16	1.06	1.20	1.22	1.34	—	—	—	—
Distrib'ns, Cap Gain ($) . . .	0.00	0.00	0.00	0.00	0.00	0.00	—	—	—	—
Net Asset Value ($)	15.39	15.20	15.34	14.55	14.55	14.59	—	—	—	—
Expense Ratio (%).	0.00	0.00	0.00	0.00	0.00	0.00	—	—	—	—
Net Income to Assets (%). .	7.41	7.70	7.78	8.29	8.64	8.97	—	—	—	—
Portfolio Turnover (%)	na	31	40	0	288	1,026	—	—	—	—
Total Assets (Millions $)	54	45	25	3	3	2	—	—	—	—

PORTFOLIO (as of 6/30/93)

Portfolio Manager: Garitt Kono - 1993

Investm't Category: Mortgage-Backed Bond

Cap Gain	Asset Allocation
Cap & Income	Fund of Funds
✔ Income	Index
	Sector
✔ Domestic	Small Cap
Foreign	Socially Conscious
Country/Region	State Specific

Portfolio: stocks 0%   bonds 94%
convertibles 0%   other 0%   cash 6%

Largest Holdings: mortgage-backed 87%, U.S. government 7%

Unrealized Net Capital Gains: 3% of portfolio value

SHAREHOLDER INFORMATION

Minimum Investment
Initial: $2,500   Subsequent: $100

Minimum IRA Investment
Initial: na   Subsequent: na

Maximum Fees
Load: none   12b-1: none
Other: none

Distributions
Income: monthly   Capital Gains: Dec

Exchange Options
Number Per Year: no limit   Fee: none
Telephone: yes (money market fund available)

Services
auto exchange, auto invest, auto withdraw

Dreyfus Mass Interm Muni Bond (DMAIX)

200 Park Ave.
New York, NY 10166
(800) 645-6561, (718) 895-1206

Tax-Exempt Bond

PERFORMANCE

	3yr Annual	5yr Annual	10yr Annual	Bull	Bear
Return (%)	na	na	na	na	na
Differ from Category (+/-)	na	na	na	na	na

Total Risk	Standard Deviation	Category Risk	Risk Index	Avg Mat
na	na	na	na	8.9 yrs

	1993	1992	1991	1990	1989	1988	1987	1986	1985	1984
Return (%)	12.5	—	—	—	—	—	—	—	—	—
Differ from category (+/-)	0.8	—	—	—	—	—	—	—	—	—

PER SHARE DATA

	1993	1992	1991	1990	1989	1988	1987	1986	1985	1984
Dividends, Net Income ($)	0.68	—	—	—	—	—	—	—	—	—
Distrib'ns, Cap Gain ($)	0.00	—	—	—	—	—	—	—	—	—
Net Asset Value ($)	13.72	—	—	—	—	—	—	—	—	—
Expense Ratio (%)	0.00	—	—	—	—	—	—	—	—	—
Net Income to Assets (%)	5.17	—	—	—	—	—	—	—	—	—
Portfolio Turnover (%)	9	—	—	—	—	—	—	—	—	—
Total Assets (Millions $)	89	—	—	—	—	—	—	—	—	—

PORTFOLIO (as of 9/30/93)

Portfolio Manager: Laurence Troutman - 1992

Investm't Category: Tax-Exempt Bond

Cap Gain	Asset Allocation
Cap & Income	Fund of Funds
✔ Income	Index
	Sector
✔ Domestic	Small Cap
Foreign	Socially Conscious
Country/Region	✔ State Specific

Portfolio: stocks 0% bonds 88%
convertibles 0% other 0% cash 12%

Largest Holdings: na

Unrealized Net Capital Gains: 8% of portfolio value

SHAREHOLDER INFORMATION

Minimum Investment
Initial: $2,500   Subsequent: $100

Minimum IRA Investment
Initial: na   Subsequent: na

Maximum Fees
Load: none   12b-1: none
Other: none

Distributions
Income: monthly   Capital Gains: Nov

Exchange Options
Number Per Year: no limit   Fee: none
Telephone: yes (money market fund available)

Services
auto exchange, auto invest, auto withdraw

Dreyfus Mass Tax-Exempt Bond (DMEBX)

200 Park Ave.
New York, NY 10166
(800) 645-6561, (718) 895-1206

Tax-Exempt Bond

PERFORMANCE

	3yr Annual	5yr Annual	10yr Annual	Bull	Bear
Return (%)	10.8	9.2	na	41.6	1.9
Differ from Category (+/-)	0.5 av	0.0 blw av	na	1.5 av	-0.4 blw av

Total Risk	Standard Deviation	Category Risk	Risk Index	Avg Mat
low	3.8%	blw av	0.9	23.0 yrs

	1993	1992	1991	1990	1989	1988	1987	1986	1985	1984
Return (%)	12.4	7.4	12.6	6.0	7.7	10.5	-3.4	17.9	—	—
Differ from category (+/-)	0.8	-0.8	1.3	-0.3	-1.3	0.4	-2.2	1.5	—	—

PER SHARE DATA

	1993	1992	1991	1990	1989	1988	1987	1986	1985	1984
Dividends, Net Income ($)	0.93	0.97	1.03	1.08	1.08	1.09	1.09	1.16	—	—
Distrib'ns, Cap Gain ($)	0.44	0.00	0.00	0.00	0.00	0.00	0.00	0.00	—	—
Net Asset Value ($)	17.13	16.51	16.30	15.44	15.62	15.54	15.09	16.75	—	—
Expense Ratio (%)	0.81	0.84	0.81	0.83	0.83	0.79	0.64	0.26	—	—
Net Income to Assets (%)	5.83	6.30	6.87	6.92	7.06	7.18	6.75	7.66	—	—
Portfolio Turnover (%)	85	68	50	55	18	71	39	103	—	—
Total Assets (Millions $)	192	157	121	108	99	84	82	54	—	—

PORTFOLIO (as of 5/31/93)

Portfolio Manager: Lawrence Troutman - 1986

Investm't Category: Tax-Exempt Bond

Cap Gain	Asset Allocation
Cap & Income	Fund of Funds
✔ Income	Index
	Sector
✔ Domestic	Small Cap
Foreign	Socially Conscious
Country/Region	✔ State Specific

Portfolio: stocks 0%   bonds 94%
convertibles 0%   other 0%   cash 6%

Largest Holdings: na

Unrealized Net Capital Gains: 4% of portfolio value

SHAREHOLDER INFORMATION

Minimum Investment
Initial: $2,500   Subsequent: $100

Minimum IRA Investment
Initial: na   Subsequent: na

Maximum Fees
Load: none   12b-1: none
Other: none

Distributions
Income: monthly   Capital Gains: Dec

Exchange Options
Number Per Year: no limit   Fee: none
Telephone: yes (money market fund available)

Services
auto exchange, auto invest, auto withdraw

Dreyfus Muni Bond
(DRTAX)

Tax-Exempt Bond

200 Park Ave.
New York, NY 10166
(800) 645-6561, (718) 895-1206

PERFORMANCE

	3yr Annual	5yr Annual	10yr Annual	Bull	Bear
Return (%)	10.9	9.7	10.2	41.0	3.1
Differ from Category (+/-)	0.6 av	0.5 av	0.6 av	0.8 av	0.8 abv av

Total Risk	Standard Deviation		Category Risk	Risk Index	Avg Mat
blw av	4.1%		av	1.0	23.3 yrs

	1993	1992	1991	1990	1989	1988	1987	1986	1985	1984
Return (%)	12.6	8.4	11.9	6.4	9.3	11.5	-1.7	17.3	19.4	8.6
Differ from category (+/-). . .	1.0	0.1	0.6	0.1	0.3	1.4	-0.5	0.8	2.1	0.3

PER SHARE DATA

	1993	1992	1991	1990	1989	1988	1987	1986	1985	1984
Dividends, Net Income ($).	0.77	0.82	0.85	0.90	0.90	0.91	0.92	0.97	1.02	1.02
Distrib'ns, Cap Gain ($) . . .	0.32	0.27	0.00	0.00	0.00	0.00	0.00	0.00	0.00	0.00
Net Asset Value ($)	13.36	12.87	12.92	12.35	12.48	12.27	11.86	13.01	11.97	10.95
Expense Ratio (%)	0.69	0.68	0.67	0.67	0.68	0.71	0.68	0.69	0.69	0.71
Net Income to Assets (%) .	5.96	6.49	7.05	7.23	7.41	7.68	7.34	8.16	9.11	9.22
Portfolio Turnover (%).	45	68	36	28	36	51	67	53	27	22
Total Assets (Millions $). .	4,675	4,273	4,082	3,594	3,486	3,245	3,528	3,648	2,724	2,020

PORTFOLIO

Portfolio Manager: Richard Moynihan - 1976

Investm't Category: Tax-Exempt Bond

Cap Gain	Asset Allocation
Cap & Income	Fund of Funds
✔ Income	Index
	Sector
✔ Domestic	Small Cap
Foreign	Socially Conscious
Country/Region	State Specific

Portfolio: stocks 0%   bonds 95%
convertibles 0%   other 0%   cash 5%

Largest Holdings: na

Unrealized Net Capital Gains: 8% of portfolio value

SHAREHOLDER INFORMATION

Minimum Investment
Initial: $2,500   Subsequent: $100

Minimum IRA Investment
Initial: na   Subsequent: na

Maximum Fees
Load: none   12b-1: none
Other: none

Distributions
Income: monthly   Capital Gains: Dec

Exchange Options
Number Per Year: no limit   Fee: none
Telephone: yes (money market fund available)

Services
auto exchange, auto invest, auto withdraw

Dreyfus New Leaders
(DNLDX)

200 Park Ave.
New York, NY 10166
(800) 645-6561, (718) 895-1206

Aggressive Growth

PERFORMANCE

	3yr Annual	5yr Annual	10yr Annual	Bull	Bear
Return (%)	23.0	16.6	na	91.8	-14.4
Differ from Category (+/-)	-2.4 blw av	-1.6 blw av	na	-33.2 blw av	0.6 av

Total Risk	Standard Deviation	Category Risk	Risk Index	Beta
abv av	12.1%	low	0.8	0.8

	1993	1992	1991	1990	1989	1988	1987	1986	1985	1984
Return (%)	17.0	9.4	45.3	-11.8	31.2	23.3	-5.0	12.3	—	—
Differ from category (+/-) . .	-2.0	-1.0	-7.1	-5.5	4.2	8.1	-1.6	2.9	—	—

PER SHARE DATA

	1993	1992	1991	1990	1989	1988	1987	1986	1985	1984
Dividends, Net Income ($) .	0.07	0.14	0.22	0.47	0.37	0.21	0.17	0.00	—	—
Distrib'ns, Cap Gain ($) . . .	3.34	2.93	2.74	1.07	1.08	0.00	0.00	0.00	—	—
Net Asset Value ($)	34.13	32.17	32.29	24.25	29.27	23.41	19.16	20.34	—	—
Expense Ratio (%).	na	1.21	1.29	1.42	1.37	1.50	1.41	1.30	—	—
Net Income to Assets (%)	na	0.43	0.76	1.31	1.60	0.90	0.35	0.66	—	—
Portfolio Turnover (%)	na	119	108	129	114	120	177	195	—	—
Total Assets (Millions $) . . .	349	234	194	102	196	112	80	65	—	—

PORTFOLIO (as of 6/30/93)

Portfolio Manager: Thomas Frank - 1985

Investm't Category: Aggressive Growth

✔ Cap Gain	Asset Allocation
Cap & Income	Fund of Funds
Income	Index
	Sector
✔ Domestic	✔ Small Cap
✔ Foreign	Socially Conscious
Country/Region	State Specific

Portfolio: stocks 77% bonds 0%
convertibles 1% other 0% cash 22%

Largest Holdings: capital goods 8%, technology 8%

Unrealized Net Capital Gains: 16% of portfolio value

SHAREHOLDER INFORMATION

Minimum Investment
Initial: $2,500   Subsequent: $100

Minimum IRA Investment
Initial: $750   Subsequent: $0

Maximum Fees
Load: 1.00% redemption   12b-1: 0.25%
Other: redemption fee applies for 6 mos

Distributions
Income: Dec   Capital Gains: Dec

Exchange Options
Number Per Year: no limit   Fee: none
Telephone: yes (money market fund available)

Services
IRA, other pension, auto exchange, auto invest, auto withdraw

Dreyfus NJ Interm Muni Bond (DNJIX)

200 Park Ave.
New York, NY 10166
(800) 645-6561, (718) 895-1206

Tax-Exempt Bond

PERFORMANCE

	3yr Annual	5yr Annual	10yr Annual	Bull	Bear
Return (%)	na	na	na	na	na
Differ from Category (+/-)	na	na	na	na	na

Total Risk	Standard Deviation	Category Risk	Risk Index	Avg Mat
na	na	na	na	9.3 yrs

	1993	1992	1991	1990	1989	1988	1987	1986	1985	1984
Return (%)	12.5	—	—	—	—	—	—	—	—	—
Differ from category (+/-) . . .	0.8	—	—	—	—	—	—	—	—	—

PER SHARE DATA

	1993	1992	1991	1990	1989	1988	1987	1986	1985	1984
Dividends, Net Income ($) .	0.68	—	—	—	—	—	—	—	—	—
Distrib'ns, Cap Gain ($) . . .	0.00	—	—	—	—	—	—	—	—	—
Net Asset Value ($)	13.93	—	—	—	—	—	—	—	—	—
Expense Ratio (%)	0.00	—	—	—	—	—	—	—	—	—
Net Income to Assets (%) .	5.27	—	—	—	—	—	—	—	—	—
Portfolio Turnover (%)	32	—	—	—	—	—	—	—	—	—
Total Assets (Millions $)	240	—	—	—	—	—	—	—	—	—

PORTFOLIO (as of 9/30/93)

Portfolio Manager: Stephen Kris - 1992

Investm't Category: Tax-Exempt Bond

Cap Gain	Asset Allocation
Cap & Income	Fund of Funds
✔ Income	Index
	Sector
✔ Domestic	Small Cap
Foreign	Socially Conscious
Country/Region	✔ State Specific

Portfolio: stocks 0% bonds 98%
convertibles 0% other 0% cash 2%

Largest Holdings: na

Unrealized Net Capital Gains: 4% of portfolio value

SHAREHOLDER INFORMATION

Minimum Investment
Initial: $2,500   Subsequent: $100

Minimum IRA Investment
Initial: na   Subsequent: na

Maximum Fees
Load: none   12b-1: none
Other: none

Distributions
Income: monthly   Capital Gains: Nov

Exchange Options
Number Per Year: no limit   Fee: none
Telephone: yes (money market fund available)

Services
auto exchange, auto invest, auto withdraw

Dreyfus NJ Muni Bond
(DRNJX)

Tax-Exempt Bond

200 Park Ave.
New York, NY 10166
(800) 645-6561, (718) 895-1206

PERFORMANCE

	3yr Annual	5yr Annual	10yr Annual	Bull	Bear
Return (%)	11.2	10.1	na	43.2	3.6
Differ from Category (+/-)	0.8 abv av	0.8 abv av	na	3.1 abv av	1.3 abv av

Total Risk	Standard Deviation	Category Risk	Risk Index	Avg Mat
blw av	4.4%	av	1.1	23.4 yrs

	1993	1992	1991	1990	1989	1988	1987	1986	1985	1984
Return (%)	12.9	8.7	11.9	7.9	9.1	12.6	—	—	—	—
Differ from category (+/-) . . .	1.3	0.4	0.6	1.6	0.1	2.5	—	—	—	—

PER SHARE DATA

	1993	1992	1991	1990	1989	1988	1987	1986	1985	1984
Dividends, Net Income ($) .	0.78	0.79	0.81	0.83	0.83	0.88	—	—	—	—
Distrib'ns, Cap Gain ($) . . .	0.02	0.20	0.03	0.00	0.04	0.00	—	—	—	—
Net Asset Value ($)	14.03	13.17	13.06	12.47	12.36	12.16	—	—	—	—
Expense Ratio (%)	0.73	0.73	0.75	0.77	0.82	0.39	—	—	—	—
Net Income to Assets (%) . .	5.87	6.06	6.36	6.74	6.77	7.36	—	—	—	—
Portfolio Turnover (%)	6	34	23	25	35	61	—	—	—	—
Total Assets (Millions $) . . .	724	614	516	350	257	175	—	—	—	—

PORTFOLIO (as of 6/30/93)

Portfolio Manager: Samuel Weinstock - 1988

Investm't Category: Tax-Exempt Bond

Cap Gain	Asset Allocation
Cap & Income	Fund of Funds
✔ Income	Index
	Sector
✔ Domestic	Small Cap
Foreign	Socially Conscious
Country/Region	✔ State Specific

Portfolio: stocks 0%   bonds 100%
convertibles 0%   other 0%   cash 0%

Largest Holdings: na

Unrealized Net Capital Gains: 9% of portfolio value

SHAREHOLDER INFORMATION

Minimum Investment
Initial: $2,500   Subsequent: $100

Minimum IRA Investment
Initial: na   Subsequent: na

Maximum Fees
Load: none   12b-1: 0.25%
Other: none

Distributions
Income: monthly   Capital Gains: Dec

Exchange Options
Number Per Year: no limit   Fee: none
Telephone: yes (money market fund available)

Services
auto exchange, auto invest, auto withdraw

Dreyfus NY Insured Tax-Exempt (DNYBX)

200 Park Ave.
New York, NY 10166
(800) 645-6561, (718) 895-1206

Tax-Exempt Bond

PERFORMANCE

	3yr Annual	5yr Annual	10yr Annual	Bull	Bear
Return (%)	10.8	9.4	na	42.2	1.4
Differ from Category (+/-)	0.5 av	0.2 av	na	2.1 av	-0.8 blw av

Total Risk	Standard Deviation	Category Risk	Risk Index	Avg Mat
blw av	4.2%	av	1.0	24.4 yrs

	1993	1992	1991	1990	1989	1988	1987	1986	1985	1984
Return (%)	11.0	8.5	13.0	5.9	8.7	11.3	—	—	—	—
Differ from category (+/-)	-0.6	0.2	1.7	-0.4	-0.3	1.2	—	—	—	—

PER SHARE DATA

	1993	1992	1991	1990	1989	1988	1987	1986	1985	1984
Dividends, Net Income ($)	0.60	0.62	0.65	0.71	0.70	0.72	—	—	—	—
Distrib'ns, Cap Gain ($)	0.21	0.04	0.00	0.00	0.00	0.00	—	—	—	—
Net Asset Value ($)	12.04	11.60	11.33	10.64	10.75	10.56	—	—	—	—
Expense Ratio (%)	0.95	0.90	0.88	0.50	0.50	0.23	—	—	—	—
Net Income to Assets (%)	5.18	5.49	6.01	6.74	6.64	7.00	—	—	—	—
Portfolio Turnover (%)	19	16	16	63	54	32	—	—	—	—
Total Assets (Millions $)	197	180	148	92	66	45	—	—	—	—

PORTFOLIO (as of 6/30/93)

Portfolio Manager: Lawrence Troutman - 1987

Investm't Category: Tax-Exempt Bond

Cap Gain	Asset Allocation
Cap & Income	Fund of Funds
✔ Income	Index
	Sector
✔ Domestic	Small Cap
Foreign	Socially Conscious
Country/Region	✔ State Specific

Portfolio: stocks 0% bonds 99%
convertibles 0% other 0% cash 1%

Largest Holdings: na

Unrealized Net Capital Gains: 8% of portfolio value

SHAREHOLDER INFORMATION

Minimum Investment
Initial: $2,500   Subsequent: $100

Minimum IRA Investment
Initial: na   Subsequent: na

Maximum Fees
Load: none   12b-1: 0.26%
Other: none

Distributions
Income: monthly   Capital Gains: Dec

Exchange Options
Number Per Year: no limit   Fee: none
Telephone: yes (money market fund available)

Services
auto exchange, auto invest, auto withdraw

Dreyfus NY Tax-Exempt
(DRNYX)

Tax-Exempt Bond

200 Park Ave.
New York, NY 10166
(800) 645-6561, (718) 895-1206

PERFORMANCE

	3yr Annual	5yr Annual	10yr Annual	Bull	Bear
Return (%)	11.2	9.6	9.9	42.5	1.9
Differ from Category (+/-)	0.8 abv av	0.4 av	0.3 av	2.4 av	-0.4 blw av

Total Risk	Standard Deviation	Category Risk	Risk Index	Avg Mat
blw av	4.1%	av	1.0	21.7 yrs

	1993	1992	1991	1990	1989	1988	1987	1986	1985	1984
Return (%)	12.6	8.8	12.4	5.5	8.9	10.1	-2.6	17.0	20.6	8.0
Differ from category (+/-) . . .	1.0	0.5	1.1	-0.8	-0.1	0.0	-1.4	0.6	3.3	-0.3

PER SHARE DATA

	1993	1992	1991	1990	1989	1988	1987	1986	1985	1984
Dividends, Net Income ($) .	0.90	0.98	1.02	1.05	1.06	1.07	1.08	1.12	1.15	1.15
Distrib'ns, Cap Gain ($) . . .	0.37	0.22	0.00	0.00	0.00	0.00	0.00	0.00	0.00	0.00
Net Asset Value ($)	16.15	15.51	15.40	14.67	14.94	14.73	14.39	15.89	14.59	13.14
Expense Ratio (%).	0.70	0.68	0.70	0.70	0.68	0.72	0.71	0.71	0.76	0.76
Net Income to Assets (%). .	6.03	6.69	7.08	7.12	7.34	7.41	7.04	7.83	8.74	8.61
Portfolio Turnover (%)	51	40	26	31	38	57	38	14	28	43
Total Assets (Millions $) . .	2,145	1,898	1,752	1,681	1,643	1,463	1,538	1,245	652	252

PORTFOLIO (as of 5/31/93)

Portfolio Manager: Monica Wieboldt - 1985

Investm't Category: Tax-Exempt Bond

Cap Gain	Asset Allocation
Cap & Income	Fund of Funds
✔ Income	Index
	Sector
✔ Domestic	Small Cap
Foreign	Socially Conscious
Country/Region	✔ State Specific

Portfolio: stocks 0% bonds 94%
convertibles 0% other 0% cash 6%

Largest Holdings: na

Unrealized Net Capital Gains: 8% of portfolio value

SHAREHOLDER INFORMATION

Minimum Investment
Initial: $2,500   Subsequent: $100

Minimum IRA Investment
Initial: na   Subsequent: na

Maximum Fees
Load: none   12b-1: none
Other: none

Distributions
Income: monthly   Capital Gains: Dec

Exchange Options
Number Per Year: no limit   Fee: none
Telephone: yes (money market fund available)

Services
auto exchange, auto invest, auto withdraw

Dreyfus NY Tax-Exempt Interm (DRNIX)

200 Park Ave.
New York, NY 10166
(800) 645-6561, (718) 895-1206

Tax-Exempt Bond

PERFORMANCE

	3yr Annual	5yr Annual	10yr Annual	Bull	Bear
Return (%)	10.6	9.4	na	40.2	2.5
Differ from Category (+/-)	0.3 av	0.2 av	na	0.1 blw av	0.2 av

Total Risk	Standard Deviation	Category Risk	Risk Index	Avg Mat
low	3.6%	blw av	0.9	9.5 yrs

	1993	1992	1991	1990	1989	1988	1987	1986	1985	1984
Return (%)	11.5	9.3	11.1	6.0	9.2	9.5	—	—	—	—
Differ from category (+/-). . .	-0.1	1.0	-0.2	-0.3	0.2	-0.6	—	—	—	—

PER SHARE DATA

	1993	1992	1991	1990	1989	1988	1987	1986	1985	1984
Dividends, Net Income ($).	0.89	0.97	1.02	1.11	1.10	1.08	—	—	—	—
Distrib'ns, Cap Gain ($) . . .	0.03	0.11	0.08	0.05	0.00	0.00	—	—	—	—
Net Asset Value ($)	18.69	17.63	17.15	16.48	16.68	16.32	—	—	—	—
Expense Ratio (%)	0.85	0.85	0.60	0.30	0.24	0.00	—	—	—	—
Net Income to Assets (%) .	5.25	5.95	6.48	6.75	6.80	6.58	—	—	—	—
Portfolio Turnover (%).	17	29	56	38	7	1	—	—	—	—
Total Assets (Millions $). . . .	416	174	113	94	58	25	—	—	—	—

PORTFOLIO (as of 5/31/93)

Portfolio Manager: Monica Wieboldt - 1987

Investm't Category: Tax-Exempt Bond

Cap Gain	Asset Allocation
Cap & Income	Fund of Funds
✔ Income	Index
	Sector
✔ Domestic	Small Cap
Foreign	Socially Conscious
Country/Region	✔ State Specific

Portfolio: stocks 0% bonds 96%
convertibles 0% other 0% cash 4%

Largest Holdings: na

Unrealized Net Capital Gains: 4% of portfolio value

SHAREHOLDER INFORMATION

Minimum Investment
Initial: $2,500   Subsequent: $100

Minimum IRA Investment
Initial: na   Subsequent: na

Maximum Fees
Load: none   12b-1: 0.25%
Other: none

Distributions
Income: monthly   Capital Gains: Nov

Exchange Options
Number Per Year: no limit   Fee: none
Telephone: yes (money market fund available)

Services
auto exchange, auto invest, auto withdraw

Dreyfus Peoples Index
(PEOPX)

Growth & Income

200 Park Ave.
New York, NY 10166
(800) 645-6561, (718) 895-1206

PERFORMANCE

	3yr Annual	5yr Annual	10yr Annual	Bull	Bear
Return (%)	15.2	na	na	66.7	-12.8
Differ from Category (+/-)	-1.2 blw av	na	na	-3.4 av	-1.2 blw av

Total Risk	Standard Deviation	Category Risk	Risk Index	Beta
av	10.4%	av	1.2	0.9

	1993	1992	1991	1990	1989	1988	1987	1986	1985	1984
Return (%)	9.5	7.7	29.8	-5.1	—	—	—	—	—	—
Differ from category (+/-) . .	-3.1	-2.3	2.1	0.5	—	—	—	—	—	—

PER SHARE DATA

	1993	1992	1991	1990	1989	1988	1987	1986	1985	1984
Dividends, Net Income ($) .	0.31	0.40	0.37	0.21	—	—	—	—	—	—
Distrib'ns, Cap Gain ($) . . .	0.66	0.03	0.00	0.00	—	—	—	—	—	—
Net Asset Value ($)	15.93	15.43	14.73	11.64	—	—	—	—	—	—
Expense Ratio (%).	na	0.00	0.00	0.00	—	—	—	—	—	—
Net Income to Assets (%)	na	3.04	3.45	3.46	—	—	—	—	—	—
Portfolio Turnover (%)	na	3	1	1	—	—	—	—	—	—
Total Assets (Millions $) . . .	295	93	69	29	—	—	—	—	—	—

PORTFOLIO (as of 4/30/93)

Portfolio Manager: Geraldine Hom - 1990

Investm't Category: Growth & Income
Cap Gain	Asset Allocation
✔ Cap & Income	Fund of Funds
Income	✔ Index
	Sector
✔ Domestic	Small Cap
Foreign	Socially Conscious
Country/Region	State Specific

Portfolio: stocks 95% bonds 0%
convertibles 0% other 0% cash 5%

Largest Holdings: S&P 500 Composite Stock Price Index

Unrealized Net Capital Gains: 10% of portfolio value

SHAREHOLDER INFORMATION

Minimum Investment
Initial: $2,500   Subsequent: $100

Minimum IRA Investment
Initial: $750   Subsequent: $0

Maximum Fees
Load: 1.00% redemption   12b-1: none
Other: redemption fee applies for 6 mos

Distributions
Income: Dec   Capital Gains: Dec

Exchange Options
Number Per Year: no limit   Fee: none
Telephone: none

Services
IRA, other pension, auto invest

Dreyfus Peoples S&P MidCap Index (PESPX)

200 Park Ave.
New York, NY 10166
(800) 645-6561, (718) 895-1206

Growth & Income

PERFORMANCE

	3yr Annual	5yr Annual	10yr Annual	Bull	Bear
Return (%)	na	na	na	na	na
Differ from Category (+/-)	na	na	na	na	na

Total Risk	Standard Deviation	Category Risk	Risk Index	Beta
na	na	na	na	na

	1993	1992	1991	1990	1989	1988	1987	1986	1985	1984
Return (%)	13.5	11.9	—	—	—	—	—	—	—	—
Differ from category (+/-). . .	0.8	1.9	—	—	—	—	—	—	—	—

PER SHARE DATA

	1993	1992	1991	1990	1989	1988	1987	1986	1985	1984
Dividends, Net Income ($).	0.27	0.26	—	—	—	—	—	—	—	—
Distrib'ns, Cap Gain ($) . . .	0.55	0.25	—	—	—	—	—	—	—	—
Net Asset Value ($)	17.19	15.87	—	—	—	—	—	—	—	—
Expense Ratio (%)	na	0.00	—	—	—	—	—	—	—	—
Net Income to Assets (%) . . .	na	2.22	—	—	—	—	—	—	—	—
Portfolio Turnover (%).	na	16	—	—	—	—	—	—	—	—
Total Assets (Millions $).	74	46	—	—	—	—	—	—	—	—

PORTFOLIO (as of 4/30/93)

Portfolio Manager: not specified

Investm't Category: Growth & Income
Cap Gain	Asset Allocation
✔ Cap & Income	Fund of Funds
Income	✔ Index
	Sector
✔ Domestic	Small Cap
Foreign	Socially Conscious
Country/Region	State Specific

Portfolio: stocks 96% bonds 0%
convertibles 0% other 0% cash 4%

Largest Holdings: S&P MidCap 400 Index

Unrealized Net Capital Gains: 6% of portfolio value

SHAREHOLDER INFORMATION

Minimum Investment
Initial: $2,500 Subsequent: $100

Minimum IRA Investment
Initial: $750 Subsequent: $0

Maximum Fees
Load: 1.00% redemption 12b-1: none
Other: redemption fee applies for 6 mos

Distributions
Income: Dec Capital Gains: Dec

Exchange Options
Number Per Year: no limit Fee: none
Telephone: none

Services
IRA, other pension, auto invest

Dreyfus Short Interm Gov't (DSIGX)

200 Park Ave.
New York, NY 10166
(800) 645-6561, (718) 895-1206

Government Bond

PERFORMANCE

	3yr Annual	5yr Annual	10yr Annual	Bull	Bear
Return (%)	9.2	9.8	na	34.8	6.3
Differ from Category (+/-)	-1.6 blw av	-0.6 av	na	-11.4 blw av	5.8 high

Total Risk	Standard Deviation	Category Risk	Risk Index	Avg Mat
low	2.8%	low	0.6	2.9 yrs

	1993	1992	1991	1990	1989	1988	1987	1986	1985	1984
Return (%)	7.3	7.0	13.4	10.0	11.2	5.6	—	—	—	—
Differ from category (+/-)	-3.1	0.8	-1.6	3.5	-2.7	-2.0	—	—	—	—

PER SHARE DATA

	1993	1992	1991	1990	1989	1988	1987	1986	1985	1984
Dividends, Net Income ($)	0.77	0.81	0.83	0.98	1.02	0.95	—	—	—	—
Distrib'ns, Cap Gain ($)	0.05	0.27	0.20	0.00	0.00	0.00	—	—	—	—
Net Asset Value ($)	11.37	11.39	11.69	11.28	11.20	11.03	—	—	—	—
Expense Ratio (%)	0.39	0.35	0.49	0.00	0.00	0.00	—	—	—	—
Net Income to Assets (%)	6.66	7.00	7.41	8.90	9.24	8.56	—	—	—	—
Portfolio Turnover (%)	317	226	132	25	17	89	—	—	—	—
Total Assets (Millions $)	556	334	144	63	32	18	—	—	—	—

PORTFOLIO (as of 05/31/93)

Portfolio Manager: Barbara Kenworthy - 1987

Investm't Category: Government Bond

Cap Gain	Asset Allocation
Cap & Income	Fund of Funds
✔ Income	Index
	Sector
✔ Domestic	Small Cap
Foreign	Socially Conscious
Country/Region	State Specific

Portfolio: stocks 0% bonds 99%
convertibles 0% other 0% cash 1%

Largest Holdings: U. S. government 83%, mortgage-backed 16%

Unrealized Net Capital Gains: 1% of portfolio value

SHAREHOLDER INFORMATION

Minimum Investment
Initial: $2,500   Subsequent: $100

Minimum IRA Investment
Initial: $750   Subsequent: $0

Maximum Fees
Load: none   12b-1: none
Other: none

Distributions
Income: monthly   Capital Gains: Dec

Exchange Options
Number Per Year: no limit   Fee: none
Telephone: yes (money market fund available)

Services
IRA, other pension, auto exchange, auto invest, auto withdraw

Dreyfus Short Term Income (DSTIX)

200 Park Ave.
New York, NY 10166
(800) 645-6561, (718) 895-1206

General Bond

PERFORMANCE

	3yr Annual	5yr Annual	10yr Annual	Bull	Bear
Return (%)	na	na	na	na	na
Differ from Category (+/-)	na	na	na	na	na

Total Risk	Standard Deviation	Category Risk	Risk Index	Avg Mat
na	na	na	na	3.0 yrs

	1993	1992	1991	1990	1989	1988	1987	1986	1985	1984
Return (%)	9.1	—	—	—	—	—	—	—	—	—
Differ from category (+/-). . .	-0.1	—	—	—	—	—	—	—	—	—

PER SHARE DATA

	1993	1992	1991	1990	1989	1988	1987	1986	1985	1984
Dividends, Net Income ($) .	0.91	—	—	—	—	—	—	—	—	—
Distrib'ns, Cap Gain ($) . . .	0.00	—	—	—	—	—	—	—	—	—
Net Asset Value ($)	12.42	—	—	—	—	—	—	—	—	—
Expense Ratio (%)	0.00	—	—	—	—	—	—	—	—	—
Net Income to Assets (%) .	7.58	—	—	—	—	—	—	—	—	—
Portfolio Turnover (%).	na	—	—	—	—	—	—	—	—	—
Total Assets (Millions $). . . .	325	—	—	—	—	—	—	—	—	—

PORTFOLIO (as of 7/31/93)

Portfolio Manager: Barbara Kenworthy - 1992

Investm't Category: General Bond
- Cap Gain
- Cap & Income
- ✔ Income

- ✔ Domestic
- ✔ Foreign
- Country/Region

- Asset Allocation
- Fund of Funds
- Index
- Sector
- Small Cap
- Socially Conscious
- State Specific

Portfolio: stocks 0%   bonds 94%
convertibles 0%   other 0%   cash 6%

Largest Holdings: corporate 90%, U.S. government 4%

Unrealized Net Capital Gains: 0% of portfolio value

SHAREHOLDER INFORMATION

Minimum Investment
Initial: $2,500   Subsequent: $100

Minimum IRA Investment
Initial: $750   Subsequent: $0

Maximum Fees
Load: none   12b-1: 0.20%
Other: none

Distributions
Income: monthly   Capital Gains: Dec

Exchange Options
Number Per Year: no limit   Fee: none
Telephone: yes (money market fund available)

Services
IRA, other pension, auto exchange, auto invest, auto withdraw

Dreyfus Short-Interm Municipal (DSIBX)

200 Park Ave.
New York, NY 10166
(800) 645-6561, (718) 895-1206

Tax-Exempt Bond

PERFORMANCE

	3yr Annual	5yr Annual	10yr Annual	Bull	Bear
Return (%)	7.1	6.9	na	25.8	4.4
Differ from Category (+/-)	-3.2 low	-2.3 low	na	-14.3 low	2.1 high

Total Risk	Standard Deviation	Category Risk	Risk Index	Avg Mat
low	1.3%	low	0.3	2.6 yrs

	1993	1992	1991	1990	1989	1988	1987	1986	1985	1984
Return (%)	6.6	6.7	8.2	6.6	6.5	5.7	—	—	—	—
Differ from category (+/-) ..	-5.0	-1.6	-3.1	0.3	-2.5	-4.4	—	—	—	—

PER SHARE DATA

	1993	1992	1991	1990	1989	1988	1987	1986	1985	1984
Dividends, Net Income ($) .	0.57	0.65	0.71	0.77	0.78	0.74	—	—	—	—
Distrib'ns, Cap Gain ($) ...	0.01	0.02	0.00	0.00	0.00	0.00	—	—	—	—
Net Asset Value ($)	13.31	13.05	12.88	12.58	12.55	12.54	—	—	—	—
Expense Ratio (%)........	0.75	0.72	0.59	0.50	0.43	0.00	—	—	—	—
Net Income to Assets (%)..	4.76	5.42	6.07	6.29	6.01	5.81	—	—	—	—
Portfolio Turnover (%)	31	64	67	100	126	63	—	—	—	—
Total Assets (Millions $) ...	575	188	77	64	60	47	—	—	—	—

PORTFOLIO (as of 9/30/93)

Portfolio Manager: Samuel Weinstock - 1987

Investm't Category: Tax-Exempt Bond
- Cap Gain
- Cap & Income
- ✔ Income
- Asset Allocation
- Fund of Funds
- Index
- Sector
- ✔ Domestic
- Foreign
- Country/Region
- Small Cap
- Socially Conscious
- State Specific

Portfolio: stocks 0% bonds 97%
convertibles 0% other 0% cash 3%

Largest Holdings: na

Unrealized Net Capital Gains: 2% of portfolio value

SHAREHOLDER INFORMATION

Minimum Investment
Initial: $2,500 Subsequent: $100

Minimum IRA Investment
Initial: na Subsequent: na

Maximum Fees
Load: none 12b-1: 0.10%
Other: none

Distributions
Income: monthly Capital Gains: Dec

Exchange Options
Number Per Year: no limit Fee: none
Telephone: yes (money market fund available)

Services
auto exchange, auto invest, auto withdraw

Dreyfus Third Century
(DRTHX)
Growth & Income

200 Park Ave.
New York, NY 10166
(800) 645-6561, (718) 895-1206

PERFORMANCE

	3yr Annual	5yr Annual	10yr Annual	Bull	Bear
Return (%)	13.9	12.4	12.0	66.6	-8.0
Differ from Category (+/-)	-2.5 blw av	-0.1 av	-0.4 av	-3.5 av	3.6 abv av

Total Risk	Standard Deviation	Category Risk	Risk Index	Beta
abv av	11.9%	high	1.4	0.9

	1993	1992	1991	1990	1989	1988	1987	1986	1985	1984
Return (%)	5.2	1.9	38.0	3.4	17.3	23.2	2.6	4.5	29.7	1.3
Differ from category (+/-)	-7.4	-8.1	10.3	9.0	-4.3	6.4	2.2	-10.7	4.3	-4.9

PER SHARE DATA

	1993	1992	1991	1990	1989	1988	1987	1986	1985	1984
Dividends, Net Income ($)	0.03	0.04	0.07	0.11	0.18	0.30	0.36	0.31	0.20	0.20
Distrib'ns, Cap Gain ($)	0.61	0.05	0.21	0.22	0.18	0.25	1.27	0.95	0.50	0.52
Net Asset Value ($)	8.26	8.48	8.42	6.33	6.45	5.82	5.18	6.51	7.50	6.39
Expense Ratio (%)	1.11	1.08	1.04	1.05	1.04	1.02	0.99	0.97	1.01	1.03
Net Income to Assets (%)	0.48	0.83	1.10	3.19	4.71	2.94	2.95	3.72	3.39	2.73
Portfolio Turnover (%)	67	48	73	163	53	37	33	63	44	25
Total Assets (Millions $)	517	443	266	196	169	153	170	176	174	114

PORTFOLIO (as of 5/31/93)

Portfolio Manager: Diane Coffey - 1990

Investm't Category: Growth & Income
Cap Gain	Asset Allocation
✔ Cap & Income	Fund of Funds
Income	Index
	Sector
✔ Domestic	Small Cap
Foreign	✔ Socially Conscious
Country/Region	State Specific

Portfolio: stocks 75% bonds 0%
convertibles 0% other 0% cash 25%

Largest Holdings: banking 10%, drugs 8%

Unrealized Net Capital Gains: 13% of portfolio value

SHAREHOLDER INFORMATION

Minimum Investment
Initial: $2,500   Subsequent: $100

Minimum IRA Investment
Initial: $750   Subsequent: $0

Maximum Fees
Load: none   12b-1: none
Other: none

Distributions
Income: Dec   Capital Gains: Dec

Exchange Options
Number Per Year: no limit   Fee: none
Telephone: yes (money market fund available)

Services
IRA, other pension, auto exchange, auto invest, auto withdraw

Dupree KY Tax-Free Income (KYTFX)

Tax-Exempt Bond

P.O. Box 1149
Lexington, KY 40589
(800) 866-0614, (606) 254-7741

PERFORMANCE

	3yr Annual	5yr Annual	10yr Annual	Bull	Bear
Return (%)	10.7	10.0	9.9	40.0	4.2
Differ from Category (+/-)	0.4 av	0.8 abv av	0.3 av	-0.1 blw av	1.9 high

Total Risk	Standard Deviation	Category Risk	Risk Index	Avg Mat
low	3.5%	blw av	0.8	10.9 yrs

	1993	1992	1991	1990	1989	1988	1987	1986	1985	1984
Return (%)	12.6	9.0	10.6	7.3	10.7	10.3	-0.8	16.8	15.8	8.1
Differ from category (+/-) . . .	1.0	0.6	-0.6	1.0	1.7	0.2	0.3	0.4	-1.5	-0.2

PER SHARE DATA

	1993	1992	1991	1990	1989	1988	1987	1986	1985	1984
Dividends, Net Income ($) .	0.41	0.43	0.44	0.45	0.46	0.47	0.47	0.52	0.56	0.58
Distrib'ns, Cap Gain ($) . . .	0.04	0.00	0.00	0.00	0.00	0.00	0.00	0.00	0.00	0.00
Net Asset Value ($)	7.72	7.28	7.09	6.83	6.80	6.58	6.41	6.96	6.43	6.06
Expense Ratio (%).	0.67	0.71	0.75	0.76	0.78	0.81	0.79	0.78	0.76	0.81
Net Income to Assets (%). .	5.79	6.28	6.63	6.82	7.44	7.40	7.32	8.39	9.31	9.40
Portfolio Turnover (%)	31	12	18	36	44	87	54	28	30	57
Total Assets (Millions $) . . .	271	169	114	88	73	61	62	36	19	9

PORTFOLIO (as of 6/30/93)

Portfolio Manager: William Griggs - 1989

Investm't Category: Tax-Exempt Bond

Cap Gain	Asset Allocation
Cap & Income	Fund of Funds
✔ Income	Index
	Sector
✔ Domestic	Small Cap
Foreign	Socially Conscious
Country/Region	✔ State Specific

Portfolio: stocks 0% bonds 100%
convertibles 0% other 0% cash 0%

Largest Holdings: general obligation 0%

Unrealized Net Capital Gains: 7% of portfolio value

SHAREHOLDER INFORMATION

Minimum Investment
Initial: $100   Subsequent: $100

Minimum IRA Investment
Initial: na   Subsequent: na

Maximum Fees
Load: none   12b-1: none
Other: none

Distributions
Income: quarterly   Capital Gains: Jun, Dec

Exchange Options
Number Per Year: no limit   Fee: none
Telephone: yes (money market fund not available)

Services
auto exchange, auto invest, auto withdraw

Dupree KY Tax-Free Short to Medium (KYSMX)

Tax-Exempt Bond

P.O. Box 1149
Lexington, KY 40589
(800) 866-0614, (606) 254-7741

PERFORMANCE

	3yr Annual	5yr Annual	10yr Annual	Bull	Bear
Return (%)	6.6	6.8	na	24.0	4.4
Differ from Category (+/-)	-3.7 low	-2.4 low	na	-16.1 low	2.1 high

Total Risk	Standard Deviation	Category Risk	Risk Index	Avg Mat
low	1.3%	low	0.3	3.8 yrs

	1993	1992	1991	1990	1989	1988	1987	1986	1985	1984
Return (%)	5.6	6.8	7.2	6.8	7.4	5.1	—	—	—	—
Differ from category (+/-). . .	-6.0	-1.5	-4.1	0.5	-1.6	-5.0	—	—	—	—

PER SHARE DATA

	1993	1992	1991	1990	1989	1988	1987	1986	1985	1984
Dividends, Net Income ($) .	0.21	0.24	0.26	0.29	0.29	0.28	—	—	—	—
Distrib'ns, Cap Gain ($) . . .	0.00	0.00	0.00	0.00	0.00	0.00	—	—	—	—
Net Asset Value ($)	5.30	5.23	5.13	5.04	5.00	4.94	—	—	—	—
Expense Ratio (%)	0.76	0.76	0.76	0.76	0.75	0.75	—	—	—	—
Net Income to Assets (%) .	4.37	4.96	5.58	5.79	5.88	5.48	—	—	—	—
Portfolio Turnover (%).	22	29	26	58	41	103	—	—	—	—
Total Assets (Millions $). . . .	70	34	13	6	7	3	—	—	—	—

PORTFOLIO (as of 6/30/93)

Portfolio Manager: William Griggs - 1989

Investm't Category: Tax-Exempt Bond
- Cap Gain
- Cap & Income
- ✔ Income

- Asset Allocation
- Fund of Funds
- Index
- Sector
- Small Cap
- Socially Conscious
- ✔ State Specific

- ✔ Domestic
- Foreign
- Country/Region

Portfolio: stocks 0% bonds 100%
convertibles 0% other 0% cash 0%

Largest Holdings: general obligation 0%

Unrealized Net Capital Gains: 2% of portfolio value

SHAREHOLDER INFORMATION

Minimum Investment
Initial: $100   Subsequent: $100

Minimum IRA Investment
Initial: na   Subsequent: na

Maximum Fees
Load: none   12b-1: none
Other: none

Distributions
Income: monthly   Capital Gains: Dec

Exchange Options
Number Per Year: no limit   Fee: none
Telephone: yes (money market fund not available)

Services
auto exchange, auto invest, auto withdraw

Eaton Vance Short-Term Treasury (EVTYX)

Government Bond

24 Federal Street
Boston, MA 02110
(800) 225-6265, (617) 482-8260

PERFORMANCE

	3yr Annual	5yr Annual	10yr Annual	Bull	Bear
Return (%)	na	na	na	na	na
Differ from Category (+/-)	na	na	na	na	na

Total Risk	Standard Deviation	Category Risk	Risk Index	Avg Mat
na	na	na	na	5.3 yrs

	1993	1992	1991	1990	1989	1988	1987	1986	1985	1984
Return (%)	2.3	3.1	—	—	—	—	—	—	—	—
Differ from category (+/-)	-8.1	-3.1	—	—	—	—	—	—	—	—

PER SHARE DATA

	1993	1992	1991	1990	1989	1988	1987	1986	1985	1984
Dividends, Net Income ($)	0.00	0.00	—	—	—	—	—	—	—	—
Distrib'ns, Cap Gain ($)	0.00	0.00	—	—	—	—	—	—	—	—
Net Asset Value ($)	55.58	54.30	—	—	—	—	—	—	—	—
Expense Ratio (%)	0.60	0.60	—	—	—	—	—	—	—	—
Net Income to Assets (%)	2.39	3.01	—	—	—	—	—	—	—	—
Portfolio Turnover (%)	0	0	—	—	—	—	—	—	—	—
Total Assets (Millions $)	41	5	—	—	—	—	—	—	—	—

PORTFOLIO (as of 6/30/93)

Portfolio Manager: Michael Terry - 1991

Investm't Category: Government Bond

Cap Gain	Asset Allocation
Cap & Income	Fund of Funds
✔ Income	Index
	Sector
✔ Domestic	Small Cap
Foreign	Socially Conscious
Country/Region	State Specific

Portfolio: stocks 0%   bonds 100%
convertibles 0%   other 0%   cash 0%

Largest Holdings: U.S. government 100%

Unrealized Net Capital Gains: 0% of portfolio value

SHAREHOLDER INFORMATION

Minimum Investment
Initial: $5,000   Subsequent: $50

Minimum IRA Investment
Initial: $50   Subsequent: $50

Maximum Fees
Load: none   12b-1: 0.25%
Other: none

Distributions
Income: monthly   Capital Gains: Dec

Exchange Options
Number Per Year: no limit   Fee: none
Telephone: yes (money market fund not available)

Services
IRA, other pension

Eclipse Equity (EEQFX)

Growth

P.O. Box 2196
Peachtree City, GA 30269
(800) 872-2710, (404) 631-0414

PERFORMANCE

	3yr Annual	5yr Annual	10yr Annual	Bull	Bear
Return (%)	22.3	12.9	na	92.2	-17.6
Differ from Category (+/-)	3.1 abv av	-1.7 blw av	na	7.5 abv av	-5.2 blw av

Total Risk	Standard Deviation	Category Risk	Risk Index	Beta
av	10.8%	blw av	1.0	0.8

	1993	1992	1991	1990	1989	1988	1987	1986	1985	1984
Return (%)	17.0	19.3	31.1	-13.6	16.3	12.7	—	—	—	—
Differ from category (+/-). . .	3.8	8.3	-4.3	-7.5	-9.5	-5.0	—	—	—	—

PER SHARE DATA

	1993	1992	1991	1990	1989	1988	1987	1986	1985	1984
Dividends, Net Income ($).	0.07	0.15	0.15	0.31	0.27	0.40	—	—	—	—
Distrib'ns, Cap Gain ($) . . .	2.02	0.64	0.00	0.00	0.63	0.00	—	—	—	—
Net Asset Value ($)	13.35	13.20	11.73	9.07	10.86	10.12	—	—	—	—
Expense Ratio (%)	1.12	1.15	1.18	1.18	1.09	1.12	—	—	—	—
Net Income to Assets (%) .	0.72	1.17	1.48	2.57	2.40	4.05	—	—	—	—
Portfolio Turnover (%).	na	111	119	154	46	31	—	—	—	—
Total Assets (Millions $). . . .	198	163	149	110	184	161	—	—	—	—

PORTFOLIO (as of 6/30/93)

Portfolio Manager: Wesley McCain - 1987

Investm't Category: Growth

✔ Cap Gain	Asset Allocation
Cap & Income	Fund of Funds
Income	Index
	Sector
✔ Domestic	✔ Small Cap
✔ Foreign	Socially Conscious
Country/Region	State Specific

Portfolio: stocks 94% bonds 0%
convertibles 0% other 0% cash 6%

Largest Holdings: retail 17%, utilities—electric 10%

Unrealized Net Capital Gains: 8% of portfolio value

SHAREHOLDER INFORMATION

Minimum Investment
Initial: $1,000   Subsequent: $0

Minimum IRA Investment
Initial: $1,000   Subsequent: $0

Maximum Fees
Load: none   12b-1: none
Other: none

Distributions
Income: Dec   Capital Gains: Dec

Exchange Options
Number Per Year: no limit   Fee: none
Telephone: yes (money market fund available)

Services
IRA, other pension, auto invest, auto withdraw

Evergreen (EVGRX)

Aggressive Growth

2500 Westchester Ave.
Purchase, NY 10577
(800) 235-0064, (914) 694-2020

PERFORMANCE

	3yr Annual	5yr Annual	10yr Annual	Bull	Bear
Return (%)	17.4	10.4	11.6	80.5	-20.8
Differ from Category (+/-)	-8.0 low	-7.8 low	-0.3 av	-44.5 low	-5.8 blw av

Total Risk	Standard Deviation	Category Risk	Risk Index	Beta
abv av	12.3%	low	0.8	1.0

	1993	1992	1991	1990	1989	1988	1987	1986	1985	1984
Return (%)	6.2	8.7	40.0	-11.7	15.0	22.9	-2.9	12.9	35.4	0.0
Differ from category (+/-) .	-12.8	-1.7	-12.4	-5.4	-12.0	7.7	0.5	3.5	4.4	9.4

PER SHARE DATA

	1993	1992	1991	1990	1989	1988	1987	1986	1985	1984
Dividends, Net Income ($) .	0.09	0.06	0.17	0.18	0.36	0.20	0.37	0.14	0.16	0.17
Distrib'ns, Cap Gain ($) ...	0.60	0.61	0.68	0.25	0.61	0.56	1.67	1.65	0.41	1.19
Net Asset Value ($)	14.20	14.03	13.54	10.34	12.21	11.49	9.98	12.47	12.67	9.94
Expense Ratio (%)........	1.12	1.13	1.15	1.15	1.11	1.03	1.03	1.04	1.08	1.10
Net Income to Assets (%)..	0.60	0.56	1.45	1.83	2.46	1.70	1.32	1.41	1.73	1.83
Portfolio Turnover (%)	21	32	35	39	40	42	46	48	59	53
Total Assets (Millions $) ...	629	722	754	525	867	751	808	638	334	239

PORTFOLIO (as of 9/30/93)

Portfolio Manager: Stephen Lieber - 1971

Investm't Category: Aggressive Growth
- ✔ Cap Gain
- Cap & Income
- Income
- Asset Allocation
- Fund of Funds
- Index
- Sector
- ✔ Domestic
- Foreign
- Country/Region
- ✔ Small Cap
- Socially Conscious
- State Specific

Portfolio:　stocks 98%　bonds 0%
convertibles 0%　other 0%　cash 2%

Largest Holdings: banks 20%, finance & insurance 15%

Unrealized Net Capital Gains: 32% of portfolio value

SHAREHOLDER INFORMATION

Minimum Investment
Initial: $2,000　Subsequent: $0

Minimum IRA Investment
Initial: $0　Subsequent: $0

Maximum Fees
Load: none　12b-1: none
Other: none

Distributions
Income: Dec　Capital Gains: Dec

Exchange Options
Number Per Year: no limit　Fee: $5 (first 4 free)
Telephone: yes (money market fund available)

Services
IRA, other pension, auto exchange, auto invest, auto withdraw

Evergreen American Retirement (EAMRX)

2500 Westchester Ave.
Purchase, NY 10577
(800) 235-0064, (914) 694-2020

Balanced

PERFORMANCE

	3yr Annual	5yr Annual	10yr Annual	Bull	Bear
Return (%)	14.8	11.3	na	59.2	-5.2
Differ from Category (+/-)	-0.2 av	-0.8 blw av	na	-2.4 av	0.6 abv av

Total Risk	Standard Deviation	Category Risk	Risk Index	Beta
blw av	5.1%	low	0.8	0.4

	1993	1992	1991	1990	1989	1988	1987	1986	1985	1984
Return (%)	14.0	11.8	18.7	-0.4	13.4	—	—	—	—	—
Differ from category (+/-). . .	0.6	3.7	-5.2	0.1	-4.2	—	—	—	—	—

PER SHARE DATA

	1993	1992	1991	1990	1989	1988	1987	1986	1985	1984
Dividends, Net Income ($).	0.60	0.61	0.60	0.60	0.58	—	—	—	—	—
Distrib'ns, Cap Gain ($) . . .	0.26	0.17	0.21	0.15	0.41	—	—	—	—	—
Net Asset Value ($)	11.60	10.95	10.52	9.59	10.41	—	—	—	—	—
Expense Ratio (%)	1.41	1.51	1.50	1.50	1.88	—	—	—	—	—
Net Income to Assets (%) .	6.58	6.23	5.91	6.04	5.49	—	—	—	—	—
Portfolio Turnover (%).	na	151	97	33	152	—	—	—	—	—
Total Assets (Millions $).	37	24	16	12	12	—	—	—	—	—

PORTFOLIO (as of 6/30/93)

Portfolio Manager: Irene D. O'Neill - 1988

Investm't Category: Balanced

Cap Gain	Asset Allocation
✔ Cap & Income	Fund of Funds
Income	Index
	Sector
✔ Domestic	Small Cap
Foreign	Socially Conscious
Country/Region	State Specific

Portfolio: stocks 52% bonds 31%
convertibles 7% other 7% cash 3%

Largest Holdings: U.S. government 10%, utilities—electric 10%

Unrealized Net Capital Gains: 7% of portfolio value

SHAREHOLDER INFORMATION

Minimum Investment
Initial: $2,000   Subsequent: $0

Minimum IRA Investment
Initial: $0   Subsequent: $0

Maximum Fees
Load: none   12b-1: none
Other: none

Distributions
Income: quarterly   Capital Gains: Dec

Exchange Options
Number Per Year: no limit   Fee: $5 (first 4 free)
Telephone: yes (money market fund available)

Services
IRA, other pension, auto exchange, auto invest, auto withdraw

Evergreen Foundation
(EFONX)
Balanced

2500 Westchester Ave.
Purchase, NY 10577
(800) 235-0064, (914) 694-2020

	3yr Annual	5yr Annual	10yr Annual	Bull	Bear
Return (%)	23.7	na	na	110.4	-4.1
Differ from Category (+/-)	8.7 high	na	na	48.8 high	1.7 abv av

Total Risk	Standard Deviation	Category Risk	Risk Index	Beta
av	9.2%	high	1.5	0.7

	1993	1992	1991	1990	1989	1988	1987	1986	1985	1984
Return (%)	15.7	19.9	36.3	6.5	—	—	—	—	—	—
Differ from category (+/-)	2.3	11.8	12.4	7.0	—	—	—	—	—	—

	1993	1992	1991	1990	1989	1988	1987	1986	1985	1984
Dividends, Net Income ($)	0.31	0.23	0.33	1.17	—	—	—	—	—	—
Distrib'ns, Cap Gain ($)	0.40	0.63	0.96	0.51	—	—	—	—	—	—
Net Asset Value ($)	13.12	11.98	10.75	8.95	—	—	—	—	—	—
Expense Ratio (%)	1.23	1.40	1.20	0.00	—	—	—	—	—	—
Net Income to Assets (%)	2.93	2.93	2.86	15.07	—	—	—	—	—	—
Portfolio Turnover (%)	60	127	178	131	—	—	—	—	—	—
Total Assets (Millions $)	246	64	11	2	—	—	—	—	—	—

Portfolio Manager: Stephen A. Lieber - 1990

Investm't Category: Balanced
Cap Gain	✔ Asset Allocation
✔ Cap & Income	Fund of Funds
Income	Index
	Sector
✔ Domestic	Small Cap
Foreign	Socially Conscious
Country/Region	State Specific

Portfolio: stocks 57% bonds 30%
convertibles 4% other 0% cash 9%

Largest Holdings: U.S. government & agencies 30%, finance & insurance 11%

Unrealized Net Capital Gains: 6% of portfolio value

Minimum Investment
Initial: $500   Subsequent: $0

Minimum IRA Investment
Initial: $0   Subsequent: $0

Maximum Fees
Load: none   12b-1: none
Other: none

Distributions
Income: quarterly   Capital Gains: Dec

Exchange Options
Number Per Year: no limit   Fee: $5 (first 4 free)
Telephone: yes (money market fund available)

Services
IRA, other pension, auto exchange, auto invest, auto withdraw

Evergreen Insured National Tax-Free (EINSX)

2500 Westchester Ave.
Purchase, NY 10577
(800) 235-0064, (914) 694-2020

Tax-Exempt Bond

PERFORMANCE

	3yr Annual	5yr Annual	10yr Annual	Bull	Bear
Return (%)	na	na	na	na	na
Differ from Category (+/-)	na	na	na	na	na

Total Risk	Standard Deviation	Category Risk	Risk Index	Avg Mat
na	na	na	na	18.3 yrs

	1993	1992	1991	1990	1989	1988	1987	1986	1985	1984
Return (%)	15.9	—	—	—	—	—	—	—	—	—
Differ from category (+/-)	4.3	—	—	—	—	—	—	—	—	—

PER SHARE DATA

	1993	1992	1991	1990	1989	1988	1987	1986	1985	1984
Dividends, Net Income ($)	0.58	—	—	—	—	—	—	—	—	—
Distrib'ns, Cap Gain ($)	0.16	—	—	—	—	—	—	—	—	—
Net Asset Value ($)	10.82	—	—	—	—	—	—	—	—	—
Expense Ratio (%)	0.00	—	—	—	—	—	—	—	—	—
Net Income to Assets (%)	5.51	—	—	—	—	—	—	—	—	—
Portfolio Turnover (%)	166	—	—	—	—	—	—	—	—	—
Total Assets (Millions $)	38	—	—	—	—	—	—	—	—	—

PORTFOLIO (as of 8/31/93)

Portfolio Manager: James Colby - 1992

Investm't Category: Tax-Exempt Bond

Cap Gain	Asset Allocation
Cap & Income	Fund of Funds
✔ Income	Index
	Sector
✔ Domestic	Small Cap
Foreign	Socially Conscious
Country/Region	State Specific

Portfolio: stocks 0% bonds 100%
convertibles 0% other 0% cash 0%

Largest Holdings: general obligation 8%

Unrealized Net Capital Gains: 3% of portfolio value

SHAREHOLDER INFORMATION

Minimum Investment
Initial: $2,000   Subsequent: $100

Minimum IRA Investment
Initial: na   Subsequent: na

Maximum Fees
Load: none   12b-1: none
Other: none

Distributions
Income: monthly   Capital Gains: Dec

Exchange Options
Number Per Year: no limit   Fee: $5 (first 4 free)
Telephone: yes (money market fund available)

Services
auto exchange, auto invest, auto withdraw

Evergreen Limited Market (EVLMX)

Aggressive Growth

2500 Westchester Ave.
Purchase, NY 10577
(800) 235-0064, (914) 694-2020

PERFORMANCE

	3yr Annual	5yr Annual	10yr Annual	Bull	Bear
Return (%)	22.1	14.5	17.3	86.4	-12.4
Differ from Category (+/-)	-3.3 blw av	-3.7 blw av	5.4 high	-38.6 low	2.6 abv av

Total Risk	Standard Deviation	Category Risk	Risk Index	Beta
high	14.5%	blw av	0.9	0.8

	1993	1992	1991	1990	1989	1988	1987	1986	1985	1984
Return (%)	9.5	10.1	51.0	-10.4	20.8	26.0	-3.2	14.9	53.9	15.9
Differ from category (+/-) . .	-9.5	-0.3	-1.4	-4.1	-6.2	10.8	0.2	5.5	22.9	25.3

PER SHARE DATA

	1993	1992	1991	1990	1989	1988	1987	1986	1985	1984
Dividends, Net Income ($) .	0.00	0.00	0.14	0.52	0.36	0.05	0.00	0.00	0.00	0.20
Distrib'ns, Cap Gain ($) . . .	1.27	1.69	1.00	0.57	3.67	0.28	0.94	2.61	1.16	0.00
Net Asset Value ($)	21.70	20.99	20.63	14.46	17.37	17.79	14.38	15.74	15.82	11.12
Expense Ratio (%)	1.24	1.25	1.32	1.33	1.30	1.47	1.44	1.44	1.67	1.40
Net Income to Assets (%) .	-0.07	0.22	3.32	2.25	0.86	0.01	-0.20	-0.10	-0.05	2.15
Portfolio Turnover (%)	29	55	59	46	45	47	43	56	69	27
Total Assets (Millions $) . . .	104	62	46	38	37	23	21	19	9	5

PORTFOLIO (as of 5/31/93)

Portfolio Manager: Derrick E. Wenger - 1993

Investm't Category: Aggressive Growth

✔ Cap Gain	Asset Allocation
Cap & Income	Fund of Funds
Income	Index
	Sector
✔ Domestic	✔ Small Cap
Foreign	Socially Conscious
Country/Region	State Specific

Portfolio: stocks 86%   bonds 0%
convertibles 0%   other 0%   cash 14%

Largest Holdings: consumer products 21%, banks 12%

Unrealized Net Capital Gains: 13% of portfolio value

SHAREHOLDER INFORMATION

Minimum Investment
Initial: $5,000   Subsequent: $0

Minimum IRA Investment
Initial: $2,000   Subsequent: $0

Maximum Fees
Load: none   12b-1: none
Other: none

Distributions
Income: Dec   Capital Gains: Dec

Exchange Options
Number Per Year: no limit   Fee: $5 (first 4 free)
Telephone: yes (money market fund available)

Services
IRA, other pension, auto exchange, auto invest, auto withdraw

Evergreen Short Interm Muni CA (EMUCX)

2500 Westchester Ave.
Purchase, NY 10577
(800) 235-0064, (914) 694-2020

Tax-Exempt Bond

PERFORMANCE

	3yr Annual	5yr Annual	10yr Annual	Bull	Bear
Return (%)	na	na	na	na	na
Differ from Category (+/-)	na	na	na	na	na

Total Risk	Standard Deviation	Category Risk	Risk Index	Avg Mat
na	na	na	na	4.5 yrs

	1993	1992	1991	1990	1989	1988	1987	1986	1985	1984
Return (%)	7.7	—	—	—	—	—	—	—	—	—
Differ from category (+/-) . . .	-3.9	—	—	—	—	—	—	—	—	—

PER SHARE DATA

	1993	1992	1991	1990	1989	1988	1987	1986	1985	1984
Dividends, Net Income ($) .	0.44	—	—	—	—	—	—	—	—	—
Distrib'ns, Cap Gain ($) . . .	0.01	—	—	—	—	—	—	—	—	—
Net Asset Value ($)	10.41	—	—	—	—	—	—	—	—	—
Expense Ratio (%)	0.30	—	—	—	—	—	—	—	—	—
Net Income to Assets (%) .	3.96	—	—	—	—	—	—	—	—	—
Portfolio Turnover (%).	37	—	—	—	—	—	—	—	—	—
Total Assets (Millions $).	30	—	—	—	—	—	—	—	—	—

PORTFOLIO (as of 8/31/93)

Portfolio Manager: Steven Shachat - 1992

Investm't Category: Tax-Exempt Bond
Cap Gain	Asset Allocation
Cap & Income	Fund of Funds
✔ Income	Index
	Sector
✔ Domestic	Small Cap
Foreign	Socially Conscious
Country/Region	✔ State Specific

Portfolio: stocks 0%   bonds 97%
convertibles 0%   other 0%   cash 3%

Largest Holdings: general obligation 5%

Unrealized Net Capital Gains: 2% of portfolio value

SHAREHOLDER INFORMATION

Minimum Investment
Initial: $2,000   Subsequent: $100

Minimum IRA Investment
Initial: na   Subsequent: na

Maximum Fees
Load: none   12b-1: none
Other: none

Distributions
Income: monthly   Capital Gains: Dec

Exchange Options
Number Per Year: no limit   Fee: $5 (first 4 free)
Telephone: yes (money market fund available)

Services
auto exchange, auto invest, auto withdraw

Evergreen Short-Interm Muni (EMUNX)

Tax-Exempt Bond

2500 Westchester Ave.
Purchase, NY 10577
(800) 235-0064, (914) 694-2020

PERFORMANCE

	3yr Annual	5yr Annual	10yr Annual	Bull	Bear
Return (%)	na	na	na	na	na
Differ from Category (+/-)	na	na	na	na	na

Total Risk	Standard Deviation	Category Risk	Risk Index	Avg Mat
na	na	na	na	4.7 yrs

	1993	1992	1991	1990	1989	1988	1987	1986	1985	1984
Return (%)	7.3	7.3	—	—	—	—	—	—	—	—
Differ from category (+/-)	-4.3	-1.0	—	—	—	—	—	—	—	—

PER SHARE DATA

	1993	1992	1991	1990	1989	1988	1987	1986	1985	1984
Dividends, Net Income ($)	0.49	0.49	—	—	—	—	—	—	—	—
Distrib'ns, Cap Gain ($)	0.04	0.00	—	—	—	—	—	—	—	—
Net Asset Value ($)	10.58	10.38	—	—	—	—	—	—	—	—
Expense Ratio (%)	0.40	0.17	—	—	—	—	—	—	—	—
Net Income to Assets (%)	4.73	4.85	—	—	—	—	—	—	—	—
Portfolio Turnover (%)	37	57	—	—	—	—	—	—	—	—
Total Assets (Millions $)	63	54	—	—	—	—	—	—	—	—

PORTFOLIO (as of 8/31/93)

Portfolio Manager: Steven Shachat - 1991

Investm't Category: Tax-Exempt Bond

Cap Gain	Asset Allocation
Cap & Income	Fund of Funds
✔ Income	Index
	Sector
✔ Domestic	Small Cap
Foreign	Socially Conscious
Country/Region	State Specific

Portfolio:	stocks 0%	bonds 99%
convertibles 0%	other 0%	cash 1%

Largest Holdings: general obligation 22%

Unrealized Net Capital Gains: 3% of portfolio value

SHAREHOLDER INFORMATION

Minimum Investment
Initial: $2,000   Subsequent: $100

Minimum IRA Investment
Initial: na   Subsequent: na

Maximum Fees
Load: none   12b-1: none
Other: none

Distributions
Income: monthly   Capital Gains: Dec

Exchange Options
Number Per Year: no limit   Fee: $5 (first 4 free)
Telephone: yes (money market fund available)

Services
auto exchange, auto invest, auto withdraw

Evergreen Total Return
(EVTRX)

Growth & Income

2500 Westchester Ave.
Purchase, NY 10577
(800) 235-0064, (914) 694-2020

	3yr Annual	5yr Annual	10yr Annual	Bull	Bear
Return (%)	15.1	10.8	12.2	64.7	-13.0
Differ from Category (+/-)	-1.3 blw av	-1.7 low	-0.2 av	-5.4 blw av	-1.4 blw av

Total Risk	Standard Deviation	Category Risk	Risk Index	Beta
av	7.8%	low	0.9	0.6

	1993	1992	1991	1990	1989	1988	1987	1986	1985	1984
Return (%)	12.9	10.0	22.9	-6.2	16.8	15.7	-7.9	20.1	29.8	13.9
Differ from category (+/-). . .	0.3	0.0	-4.8	-0.6	-4.8	-1.1	-8.3	4.9	4.4	7.7

PER SHARE DATA

	1993	1992	1991	1990	1989	1988	1987	1986	1985	1984
Dividends, Net Income ($) .	1.08	1.08	1.08	1.08	1.08	1.08	1.33	1.09	0.97	0.94
Distrib'ns, Cap Gain ($) . . .	1.20	0.45	0.00	0.00	0.00	0.01	0.87	1.10	0.97	1.32
Net Asset Value ($)	19.62	19.43	19.12	16.49	18.76	17.01	15.66	19.18	17.87	15.52
Expense Ratio (%)	1.18	1.21	1.23	1.18	1.02	1.01	1.02	1.11	1.31	1.09
Net Income to Assets (%) .	5.65	5.73	5.90	5.64	6.36	5.80	5.68	6.06	6.18	6.21
Portfolio Turnover (%).	164	137	137	89	86	81	44	65	82	67
Total Assets (Millions $). .	1,180	1,032	1,151	1,292	1,312	1,355	1,636	408	83	47

PORTFOLIO (as of 9/30/93)

Portfolio Manager: Nola M. Falcone - 1978

Investm't Category: Growth & Income

Cap Gain	Asset Allocation
✔ Cap & Income	Fund of Funds
Income	Index
	Sector
✔ Domestic	Small Cap
Foreign	Socially Conscious
Country/Region	State Specific

Portfolio:	stocks 73%	bonds 0%
convertibles 24%	other 0%	cash 3%

Largest Holdings: utilities—electric 18%, banks 9%

Unrealized Net Capital Gains: 0% of portfolio value

SHAREHOLDER INFORMATION

Minimum Investment
Initial: $2,000   Subsequent: $0

Minimum IRA Investment
Initial: $0   Subsequent: $0

Maximum Fees
Load: none   12b-1: none
Other: none

Distributions
Income: quarterly   Capital Gains: Dec

Exchange Options
Number Per Year: no limit   Fee: $5 (first 4 free)
Telephone: yes (money market fund available)

Services
IRA, other pension, auto exchange, auto invest, auto withdraw

Evergreen Value Timing
(EVVTX)

2500 Westchester Ave.
Purchase, NY 10577
(800) 235-0064, (914) 694-2020

Growth

PERFORMANCE

	3yr Annual	5yr Annual	10yr Annual	Bull	Bear
Return (%)	17.9	14.4	na	78.7	-12.3
Differ from Category (+/-)	-1.3 av	-0.2 av	na	-6.0 av	0.1 av

Total Risk	Standard Deviation	Category Risk	Risk Index	Beta
av	10.4%	low	1.0	0.9

	1993	1992	1991	1990	1989	1988	1987	1986	1985	1984
Return (%)	14.4	13.8	25.8	-4.4	25.4	24.5	-4.3	—	—	—
Differ from category (+/-) . . .	1.2	2.8	-9.6	1.7	-0.4	6.8	-5.5	—	—	—

PER SHARE DATA

	1993	1992	1991	1990	1989	1988	1987	1986	1985	1984
Dividends, Net Income ($) .	0.14	0.14	0.19	0.30	0.52	0.19	0.24	—	—	—
Distrib'ns, Cap Gain ($) . . .	0.67	0.46	0.30	0.47	0.75	0.86	0.00	—	—	—
Net Asset Value ($)	15.41	14.18	12.99	10.72	12.03	10.62	9.38	—	—	—
Expense Ratio (%).	1.27	1.33	1.41	1.50	1.54	1.56	1.76	—	—	—
Net Income to Assets (%) . .	1.02	1.18	1.55	2.62	4.13	1.70	1.90	—	—	—
Portfolio Turnover (%)	na	30	23	41	53	41	48	—	—	—
Total Assets (Millions $)	77	64	48	36	32	24	22	—	—	—

PORTFOLIO (as of 6/30/93)

Portfolio Manager: Edmund H. Nicklin - 1986

Investm't Category: Growth

✔ Cap Gain	Asset Allocation
Cap & Income	Fund of Funds
Income	Index
	Sector
✔ Domestic	Small Cap
Foreign	Socially Conscious
Country/Region	State Specific

Portfolio: stocks 89%   bonds 2%
convertibles 0%   other 0%   cash 9%

Largest Holdings: banks & thrifts 14%, business equipment & services 11%

Unrealized Net Capital Gains: 23% of portfolio value

SHAREHOLDER INFORMATION

Minimum Investment
Initial: $2,000   Subsequent: $0

Minimum IRA Investment
Initial: $0   Subsequent: $0

Maximum Fees
Load: none   12b-1: none
Other: none

Distributions
Income: Dec   Capital Gains: Dec

Exchange Options
Number Per Year: no limit   Fee: $5 (first 4 free)
Telephone: yes (money market fund available)

Services
IRA, other pension, auto exchange, auto invest, auto withdraw

Fairmont (FAIMX)

Aggressive Growth

1346 S. Third St.
Louisville, KY 40208
(800) 262-9936, (502) 636-5633

PERFORMANCE

	3yr Annual	5yr Annual	10yr Annual	Bull	Bear
Return (%)	22.8	9.0	9.3	96.4	-26.5
Differ from Category (+/-)	-2.6 blw av	-9.2 low	-2.6 blw av	-28.6 blw av	-11.5 low

Total Risk	Standard Deviation	Category Risk	Risk Index	Beta
high	17.1%	av	1.1	1.0

	1993	1992	1991	1990	1989	1988	1987	1986	1985	1984
Return (%)	15.5	14.0	40.5	-22.1	6.8	3.1	-7.7	14.0	32.1	10.7
Differ from category (+/-) . . .	-3.5	3.6	-11.9	-15.8	-20.2	-12.1	-4.3	4.6	1.1	20.1

PER SHARE DATA

	1993	1992	1991	1990	1989	1988	1987	1986	1985	1984
Dividends, Net Income ($) .	0.00	0.00	0.08	0.30	0.20	0.23	0.18	0.19	0.25	0.26
Distrib'ns, Cap Gain ($) . . .	0.00	0.00	0.00	0.00	0.00	0.00	0.08	3.85	0.92	0.47
Net Asset Value ($)	22.43	19.41	17.02	12.17	16.01	15.18	14.95	16.50	18.07	14.76
Expense Ratio (%)	1.78	1.79	1.79	1.68	1.37	1.25	1.18	1.48	2.05	2.15
Net Income to Assets (%) .	-0.24	-0.85	0.51	1.53	1.01	1.30	0.91	1.22	1.41	2.28
Portfolio Turnover (%).	159	132	115	128	90	158	145	129	123	103
Total Assets (Millions $)	19	17	17	16	43	64	79	60	24	14

PORTFOLIO (as of 6/30/93)

Portfolio Manager: Morton H. Sachs - 1981

Investm't Category: Aggressive Growth

✔ Cap Gain	Asset Allocation
Cap & Income	Fund of Funds
Income	Index
	Sector
✔ Domestic	Small Cap
Foreign	Socially Conscious
Country/Region	State Specific

Portfolio: stocks 97% bonds 0%
convertibles 0% other 0% cash 3%

Largest Holdings: health care management 22%, banking 14%

Unrealized Net Capital Gains: 7% of portfolio value

SHAREHOLDER INFORMATION

Minimum Investment
Initial: $1,000   Subsequent: $0

Minimum IRA Investment
Initial: $1,000   Subsequent: $0

Maximum Fees
Load: none   12b-1: none
Other: none

Distributions
Income: Dec   Capital Gains: Dec

Exchange Options
Number Per Year: no limit   Fee: none
Telephone: none

Services
IRA, other pension

FAM Value (FAMVX)

Growth

118 North Grand Street
P.O. Box 399
Cobleskill, NY 12043
(800) 932-3271

this fund is closed to new investors

PERFORMANCE

	3yr Annual	5yr Annual	10yr Annual	Bull	Bear
Return (%)	22.7	16.0	na	96.6	-10.9
Differ from Category (+/-)	3.5 abv av	1.4 abv av	na	11.9 abv av	1.5 av

Total Risk	Standard Deviation	Category Risk	Risk Index	Beta
abv av	11.4%	av	1.1	0.5

	1993	1992	1991	1990	1989	1988	1987	1986	1985	1984
Return (%)	0.2	25.0	47.6	-5.3	20.3	35.5	-17.1	—	—	—
Differ from category (+/-) .	-13.0	14.0	12.2	0.8	-5.5	17.8	-18.3	—	—	—

PER SHARE DATA

	1993	1992	1991	1990	1989	1988	1987	1986	1985	1984
Dividends, Net Income ($) .	0.09	0.10	0.08	0.08	0.05	0.25	0.10	—	—	—
Distrib'ns, Cap Gain ($) . . .	0.05	0.48	0.82	0.02	0.06	0.00	0.01	—	—	—
Net Asset Value ($)	20.40	20.50	16.87	12.06	12.85	10.78	8.14	—	—	—
Expense Ratio (%)	1.50	1.50	1.49	1.53	1.51	1.48	1.54	—	—	—
Net Income to Assets (%) . .	0.60	0.81	0.66	0.72	0.56	2.89	1.47	—	—	—
Portfolio Turnover (%)	10	10	14	9	15	12	16	—	—	—
Total Assets (Millions $) . . .	217	45	14	6	5	2	1	—	—	—

PORTFOLIO (as of 6/30/93)

Portfolio Manager: Thomas Putnam - 1987, Diane VanBuren - 1987

Investm't Category: Growth

✔ Cap Gain	Asset Allocation
Cap & Income	Fund of Funds
Income	Index
	Sector
✔ Domestic	✔ Small Cap
Foreign	Socially Conscious
Country/Region	State Specific

Portfolio:
stocks 89%   bonds 0%
convertibles 0%   other 0%   cash 11%

Largest Holdings: insurance 21%, banking 15%

Unrealized Net Capital Gains: 2% of portfolio value

SHAREHOLDER INFORMATION

Minimum Investment
Initial: $2,000   Subsequent: $100

Minimum IRA Investment
Initial: $100   Subsequent: $50

Maximum Fees
Load: none   12b-1: none
Other: none

Distributions
Income: Dec   Capital Gains: Dec

Exchange Options
Number Per Year: none   Fee: na
Telephone: na

Services
IRA, other pension, auto invest

Fidelity Fund (FFIDX)

Growth & Income

82 Devonshire St.
Boston, MA 02109
(800) 544-8888, (801) 534-1910

PERFORMANCE

	3yr Annual	5yr Annual	10yr Annual	Bull	Bear
Return (%)	16.7	14.2	13.5	68.0	-9.9
Differ from Category (+/-)	0.3 av	1.7 abv av	1.1 abv av	-2.1 av	1.7 abv av

Total Risk	Standard Deviation	Category Risk	Risk Index	Beta
av	10.2%	av	1.2	0.8

	1993	1992	1991	1990	1989	1988	1987	1986	1985	1984
Return (%).	18.3	8.4	24.1	-5.0	28.8	17.8	3.2	15.5	28.0	1.5
Differ from category (+/-). . .	5.7	-1.6	-3.6	0.6	7.2	1.0	2.8	0.3	2.6	-4.7

PER SHARE DATA

	1993	1992	1991	1990	1989	1988	1987	1986	1985	1984
Dividends, Net Income ($).	0.43	0.47	0.50	0.74	0.68	0.56	0.47	0.66	0.72	0.71
Distrib'ns, Cap Gain ($) . . .	2.55	0.57	1.15	0.00	1.17	0.00	2.72	4.08	0.10	4.40
Net Asset Value ($)	19.27	18.94	18.47	16.30	17.93	15.42	13.58	16.05	18.08	14.82
Expense Ratio (%)	0.66	0.67	0.68	0.66	0.64	0.67	0.67	0.60	0.66	0.66
Net Income to Assets (%) .	2.94	2.37	2.84	4.04	3.76	3.69	2.75	3.48	4.25	5.06
Portfolio Turnover (%).	261	151	267	259	191	175	211	214	215	200
Total Assets (Millions $). .	1,669	1,354	1,320	1,064	1,087	892	870	780	761	618

PORTFOLIO (as of 6/30/93)

Portfolio Manager: Beth Terrana - 1993

Investm't Category: Growth & Income
- Cap Gain
- ✔ Cap & Income
- Income
- ✔ Domestic
- ✔ Foreign
- Country/Region
- Asset Allocation
- Fund of Funds
- Index
- Sector
- Small Cap
- Socially Conscious
- State Specific

Portfolio: stocks 67%   bonds 9%
convertibles 5%   other 0%   cash 19%

Largest Holdings: stocks—energy 12%, stocks—technology 9%

Unrealized Net Capital Gains: 8% of portfolio value

SHAREHOLDER INFORMATION

Minimum Investment
Initial: $2,500   Subsequent: $250

Minimum IRA Investment
Initial: $500   Subsequent: $250

Maximum Fees
Load: none   12b-1: none
Other: none

Distributions
Income: quarterly   Capital Gains: Feb, Dec

Exchange Options
Number Per Year: 4   Fee: none
Telephone: yes (money market fund available)

Services
IRA, other pension, auto exchange, auto invest, auto withdraw

Fidelity Aggressive Tax-Free (FATFX)

82 Devonshire St.
Boston, MA 02109
(800) 544-8888, (801) 534-1910

Tax-Exempt Bond

PERFORMANCE

	3yr Annual	5yr Annual	10yr Annual	Bull	Bear
Return (%)	11.5	10.3	na	42.6	4.5
Differ from Category (+/-)	1.2 abv av	1.1 high	na	2.5 av	2.2 high

Total Risk	Standard Deviation	Category Risk	Risk Index	Avg Mat
low	3.4%	low	0.8	20.7 yrs

	1993	1992	1991	1990	1989	1988	1987	1986	1985	1984
Return (%)	13.7	9.1	11.7	7.4	9.5	13.4	1.3	17.6	—	—
Differ from category (+/-) ...	2.1	0.8	0.4	1.1	0.5	3.3	2.5	1.2	—	—

PER SHARE DATA

	1993	1992	1991	1990	1989	1988	1987	1986	1985	1984
Dividends, Net Income ($) .	0.78	0.83	0.86	0.88	0.88	0.89	0.89	0.92	—	—
Distrib'ns, Cap Gain ($) ...	0.34	0.12	0.05	0.00	0.00	0.00	0.00	0.00	—	—
Net Asset Value ($)	12.34	11.88	11.80	11.43	11.49	11.33	10.82	11.56	—	—
Expense Ratio (%)........	0.65	0.64	0.68	0.66	0.68	0.73	0.74	0.65	—	—
Net Income to Assets (%)..	6.47	7.01	7.46	7.79	7.68	7.98	8.06	8.17	—	—
Portfolio Turnover (%)	50	43	30	46	46	46	68	17	—	—
Total Assets (Millions $) ...	948	761	654	551	546	456	353	394	—	—

PORTFOLIO (as of 6/30/93)

Portfolio Manager: Ann Punzak - 1985

Investm't Category: Tax-Exempt Bond

Cap Gain	Asset Allocation
Cap & Income	Fund of Funds
✔ Income	Index
	Sector
✔ Domestic	Small Cap
Foreign	Socially Conscious
Country/Region	State Specific

Portfolio: stocks 0% bonds 100%
convertibles 0% other 0% cash 0%

Largest Holdings: general obligation 5%

Unrealized Net Capital Gains: 6% of portfolio value

SHAREHOLDER INFORMATION

Minimum Investment
Initial: $2,500   Subsequent: $250

Minimum IRA Investment
Initial: na   Subsequent: na

Maximum Fees
Load: 1.00% redemption   12b-1: none
Other: redemption fee applies for 6 mos

Distributions
Income: monthly   Capital Gains: Feb, Dec

Exchange Options
Number Per Year: 4   Fee: none
Telephone: yes (money market fund available)

Services
auto exchange, auto invest, auto withdraw

Fidelity Asset Manager
(FASMX)
Balanced

82 Devonshire St.
Boston, MA 02109
(800) 544-8888, (801) 534-1910

PERFORMANCE

	3yr Annual	5yr Annual	10yr Annual	Bull	Bear
Return (%)	19.7	15.8	na	86.2	-2.7
Differ from Category (+/-)	4.7 high	3.7 high	na	24.6 high	3.1 high

Total Risk	Standard Deviation	Category Risk	Risk Index	Beta
blw av	5.6%	blw av	0.9	0.4

	1993	1992	1991	1990	1989	1988	1987	1986	1985	1984
Return (%)	23.2	12.7	23.6	5.3	15.2	—	—	—	—	—
Differ from category (+/-). . .	9.8	4.6	-0.3	5.8	-2.4	—	—	—	—	—

PER SHARE DATA

	1993	1992	1991	1990	1989	1988	1987	1986	1985	1984
Dividends, Net Income ($).	0.58	0.47	0.44	0.64	0.37	—	—	—	—	—
Distrib'ns, Cap Gain ($) . . .	0.43	0.18	0.50	0.00	0.23	—	—	—	—	—
Net Asset Value ($)	15.40	13.37	12.46	10.87	10.94	—	—	—	—	—
Expense Ratio (%)	1.09	1.17	1.17	1.17	1.58	—	—	—	—	—
Net Income to Assets (%) .	4.28	5.58	5.74	5.89	5.88	—	—	—	—	—
Portfolio Turnover (%).	98	134	134	105	167	—	—	—	—	—
Total Assets (Millions $). .	8,958	2,762	743	316	245	—	—	—	—	—

PORTFOLIO (as of 9/30/93)

Portfolio Manager: Bob Beckwitt - 1988

Investm't Category: Balanced

Cap Gain	✔ Asset Allocation
✔ Cap & Income	Fund of Funds
Income	Index
	Sector
✔ Domestic	Small Cap
✔ Foreign	Socially Conscious
Country/Region	State Specific

Portfolio: stocks 50% bonds 30%
convertibles 0% other 7% cash 13%

Largest Holdings: bonds—foreign government 16%, stocks—finance 11%

Unrealized Net Capital Gains: 7% of portfolio value

SHAREHOLDER INFORMATION

Minimum Investment
Initial: $2,500   Subsequent: $250

Minimum IRA Investment
Initial: $500   Subsequent: $250

Maximum Fees
Load: none   12b-1: none
Other: none

Distributions
Income: quarterly   Capital Gains: Dec

Exchange Options
Number Per Year: 4   Fee: none
Telephone: yes (money market fund available)

Services
IRA, other pension, auto exchange, auto invest, auto withdraw

Fidelity Asset Manager—Growth (FASGX)

82 Devonshire St.
Boston, MA 02109
(800) 544-8888, (801) 534-1910

Balanced

PERFORMANCE

	3yr Annual	5yr Annual	10yr Annual	Bull	Bear
Return (%)	na	na	na	na	na
Differ from Category (+/-)	na	na	na	na	na

Total Risk	Standard Deviation	Category Risk	Risk Index	Beta
na	na	na	na	na

	1993	1992	1991	1990	1989	1988	1987	1986	1985	1984
Return (%)	26.3	19.0	—	—	—	—	—	—	—	—
Differ from category (+/-)	12.9	10.9	—	—	—	—	—	—	—	—

PER SHARE DATA

	1993	1992	1991	1990	1989	1988	1987	1986	1985	1984
Dividends, Net Income ($)	0.09	0.15	—	—	—	—	—	—	—	—
Distrib'ns, Cap Gain ($)	0.50	0.07	—	—	—	—	—	—	—	—
Net Asset Value ($)	14.25	11.77	—	—	—	—	—	—	—	—
Expense Ratio (%)	1.19	1.64	—	—	—	—	—	—	—	—
Net Income to Assets (%)	3.02	3.50	—	—	—	—	—	—	—	—
Portfolio Turnover (%)	97	693	—	—	—	—	—	—	—	—
Total Assets (Millions $)	1,717	94	—	—	—	—	—	—	—	—

PORTFOLIO (as of 09/30/93)

Portfolio Manager: Bob Beckwitt - 1991

Investm't Category: Balanced

Cap Gain	✔ Asset Allocation
✔ Cap & Income	Fund of Funds
Income	Index
	Sector
✔ Domestic	Small Cap
✔ Foreign	Socially Conscious
Country/Region	State Specific

Portfolio: stocks 65%   bonds 22%
convertibles 0%   other 5%   cash 8%

Largest Holdings: stocks—finance 16%, bonds—foreign government 15%

Unrealized Net Capital Gains: 7% of portfolio value

SHAREHOLDER INFORMATION

Minimum Investment
Initial: $2,500   Subsequent: $250

Minimum IRA Investment
Initial: $500   Subsequent: $250

Maximum Fees
Load: none   12b-1: none
Other: none

Distributions
Income: Dec   Capital Gains: Dec

Exchange Options
Number Per Year: 4   Fee: none
Telephone: yes (money market fund available)

Services
IRA, other pension, auto exchange, auto invest, auto withdraw

Fidelity Asset Manager—Income (FASIX)

82 Devonshire St.
Boston, MA 02109
(800) 544-8888, (801) 534-1910

Balanced

PERFORMANCE

	3yr Annual	5yr Annual	10yr Annual	Bull	Bear
Return (%)	na	na	na	na	na
Differ from Category (+/-)	na	na	na	na	na

Total Risk	Standard Deviation	Category Risk	Risk Index	Beta
na	na	na	na	na

	1993	1992	1991	1990	1989	1988	1987	1986	1985	1984
Return (%).	15.3	—	—	—	—	—	—	—	—	—
Differ from category (+/-). . .	1.9	—	—	—	—	—	—	—	—	—

PER SHARE DATA

	1993	1992	1991	1990	1989	1988	1987	1986	1985	1984
Dividends, Net Income ($) .	0.49	—	—	—	—	—	—	—	—	—
Distrib'ns, Cap Gain ($) . . .	0.07	—	—	—	—	—	—	—	—	—
Net Asset Value ($)	11.06	—	—	—	—	—	—	—	—	—
Expense Ratio (%)	0.65	—	—	—	—	—	—	—	—	—
Net Income to Assets (%) .	5.19	—	—	—	—	—	—	—	—	—
Portfolio Turnover (%).	47	—	—	—	—	—	—	—	—	—
Total Assets (Millions $). . . .	284	—	—	—	—	—	—	—	—	—

PORTFOLIO (as of 9/30/93)

Portfolio Manager: Bob Beckwitt - 1992

Investm't Category: Balanced
- Cap Gain
- ✔ Cap & Income
- Income

- ✔ Domestic
- ✔ Foreign
- Country/Region

- ✔ Asset Allocation
- Fund of Funds
- Index
- Sector
- Small Cap
- Socially Conscious
- State Specific

Portfolio: stocks 23%   bonds 57%
convertibles 5%   other 7%   cash 8%

Largest Holdings: bonds—finance 19%,
bonds—foreign government 14%

Unrealized Net Capital Gains: 2% of portfolio value

SHAREHOLDER INFORMATION

Minimum Investment
Initial: $2,500   Subsequent: $250

Minimum IRA Investment
Initial: $500   Subsequent: $250

Maximum Fees
Load: none   12b-1: none
Other: none

Distributions
Income: monthly   Capital Gains: Sep, Dec

Exchange Options
Number Per Year: 4   Fee: none
Telephone: yes (money market fund available)

Services
IRA, other pension, auto exchange, auto invest, auto withdraw

Fidelity Balanced (FBALX)

Balanced

82 Devonshire St.
Boston, MA 02109
(800) 544-8888, (801) 534-1910

PERFORMANCE

	3yr Annual	5yr Annual	10yr Annual	Bull	Bear
Return (%)	17.7	14.2	na	71.8	-5.4
Differ from Category (+/-)	2.7 abv av	2.1 high	na	10.2 high	0.4 av

Total Risk	Standard Deviation	Category Risk	Risk Index	Beta
blw av	5.8%	blw av	0.9	0.4

	1993	1992	1991	1990	1989	1988	1987	1986	1985	1984
Return (%)	19.2	7.9	26.7	-0.4	19.7	15.7	1.9	—	—	—
Differ from category (+/-) . . .	5.8	-0.2	2.8	0.1	2.1	3.7	-0.4	—	—	—

PER SHARE DATA

	1993	1992	1991	1990	1989	1988	1987	1986	1985	1984
Dividends, Net Income ($) .	0.60	0.66	0.60	0.68	1.00	0.68	0.60	—	—	—
Distrib'ns, Cap Gain ($) . . .	0.63	0.36	0.44	0.00	0.21	0.00	0.07	—	—	—
Net Asset Value ($)	13.39	12.29	12.35	10.63	11.37	10.55	9.72	—	—	—
Expense Ratio (%)	0.93	0.96	0.98	0.97	1.13	1.30	1.19	—	—	—
Net Income to Assets (%) . .	5.07	5.68	5.93	6.74	8.90	6.29	6.03	—	—	—
Portfolio Turnover (%)	162	242	238	223	168	213	161	—	—	—
Total Assets (Millions $) . .	4,638	1,366	458	268	146	125	167	—	—	—

PORTFOLIO (as of 7/31/93)

Portfolio Manager: Bob Haber - 1988

Investm't Category: Balanced

Cap Gain	Asset Allocation
✔ Cap & Income	Fund of Funds
Income	Index
	Sector
✔ Domestic	Small Cap
Foreign	Socially Conscious
Country/Region	State Specific

Portfolio: stocks 31% bonds 47%
convertibles 13% other 0% cash 9%

Largest Holdings: U.S. government & agencies 11%, stocks—finance 7%

Unrealized Net Capital Gains: 3% of portfolio value

SHAREHOLDER INFORMATION

Minimum Investment
Initial: $2,500   Subsequent: $250

Minimum IRA Investment
Initial: $500   Subsequent: $250

Maximum Fees
Load: none   12b-1: none
Other: none

Distributions
Income: quarterly   Capital Gains: Sep, Dec

Exchange Options
Number Per Year: 4   Fee: none
Telephone: yes (money market fund available)

Services
IRA, other pension, auto exchange, auto invest, auto withdraw

Fidelity Blue Chip Growth (FBGRX)

82 Devonshire St.
Boston, MA 02109
(800) 544-8888, (801) 534-1910

Growth

PERFORMANCE

	3yr Annual	5yr Annual	10yr Annual	Bull	Bear
Return (%)	26.9	23.6	na	123.5	-5.2
Differ from Category (+/-)	7.7 high	9.0 high	na	38.8 high	7.2 high

Total Risk	Standard Deviation	Category Risk	Risk Index	Beta
abv av	13.9%	abv av	1.3	1.2

	1993	1992	1991	1990	1989	1988	1987	1986	1985	1984
Return (%)	24.5	6.1	54.8	3.5	36.2	5.9	—	—	—	—
Differ from category (+/-). .	11.3	-4.9	19.4	9.6	10.4	-11.8	—	—	—	—

PER SHARE DATA

	1993	1992	1991	1990	1989	1988	1987	1986	1985	1984
Dividends, Net Income ($).	0.00	0.14	0.07	0.15	0.11	0.02	—	—	—	—
Distrib'ns, Cap Gain ($) . . .	4.12	0.62	0.00	0.00	0.17	0.00	—	—	—	—
Net Asset Value ($)	24.17	22.83	22.25	14.43	14.09	10.56	—	—	—	—
Expense Ratio (%)	1.25	1.27	1.26	1.26	1.56	2.74	—	—	—	—
Net Income to Assets (%) .	0.46	0.55	0.80	1.14	0.97	0.14	—	—	—	—
Portfolio Turnover (%). . . .	319	71	99	68	83	40	—	—	—	—
Total Assets (Millions $). .	1,069	476	219	131	54	41	—	—	—	—

PORTFOLIO (as of 7/31/93)

Portfolio Manager: Michael Gordon - 1993

Investm't Category: Growth

✔ Cap Gain	Asset Allocation
Cap & Income	Fund of Funds
Income	Index
	Sector
✔ Domestic	Small Cap
✔ Foreign	Socially Conscious
Country/Region	State Specific

Portfolio: stocks 86% bonds 0%
convertibles 0% other 0% cash 14%

Largest Holdings: energy 18%, technology 16%

Unrealized Net Capital Gains: 9% of portfolio value

SHAREHOLDER INFORMATION

Minimum Investment
Initial: $2,500   Subsequent: $250

Minimum IRA Investment
Initial: $500   Subsequent: $250

Maximum Fees
Load: 3.00% front   12b-1: none
Other: none

Distributions
Income: Sep   Capital Gains: Sep

Exchange Options
Number Per Year: 4   Fee: none
Telephone: yes (money market fund available)

Services
IRA, other pension, auto exchange, auto invest, auto withdraw

Fidelity Canada (FICDX)

International Stock

82 Devonshire St.
Boston, MA 02109
(800) 544-8888, (801) 534-1910

PERFORMANCE

	3yr Annual	5yr Annual	10yr Annual	Bull	Bear
Return (%)	12.7	11.4	na	48.6	-8.8
Differ from Category (+/-)	-1.6 av	2.7 abv av	na	-6.5 blw av	6.3 high

Total Risk	Standard Deviation	Category Risk	Risk Index	Beta
abv av	11.6%	low	1.0	0.4

	1993	1992	1991	1990	1989	1988	1987	1986	1985	1984
Return (%)	25.4	-2.8	17.6	-5.4	26.9	19.4	—	—	—	—
Differ from category (+/-) .	-13.1	0.6	4.7	5.7	4.7	5.6	—	—	—	—

PER SHARE DATA

	1993	1992	1991	1990	1989	1988	1987	1986	1985	1984
Dividends, Net Income ($) .	0.00	0.01	0.00	0.05	0.00	0.11	—	—	—	—
Distrib'ns, Cap Gain ($) ...	0.03	0.00	0.92	0.85	0.68	0.15	—	—	—	—
Net Asset Value ($)	18.19	14.53	14.98	13.53	15.29	12.59	—	—	—	—
Expense Ratio (%)........	2.00	2.00	2.01	2.05	2.06	2.02	—	—	—	—
Net Income to Assets (%) .	-0.66	-0.11	0.17	0.34	0.16	4.24	—	—	—	—
Portfolio Turnover (%)	131	55	68	164	152	401	—	—	—	—
Total Assets (Millions $) ...	104	21	23	17	24	10	—	—	—	—

PORTFOLIO (as of 10/31/93)

Portfolio Manager: George Domolky - 1987

Investm't Category: International Stock
✔ Cap Gain	Asset Allocation
Cap & Income	Fund of Funds
Income	Index
	Sector
Domestic	Small Cap
✔ Foreign	Socially Conscious
✔ Country/Region	State Specific

Portfolio: stocks 94% bonds 0%
convertibles 1% other 0% cash 5%

Largest Holdings: Canada 90%, United States 3%

Unrealized Net Capital Gains: 10% of portfolio value

SHAREHOLDER INFORMATION

Minimum Investment
Initial: $2,500   Subsequent: $250

Minimum IRA Investment
Initial: $500   Subsequent: $250

Maximum Fees
Load: 3.00% front   12b-1: none
Other: none

Distributions
Income: Dec   Capital Gains: Dec

Exchange Options
Number Per Year: 2   Fee: none
Telephone: yes (money market fund available)

Services
IRA, other pension, auto exchange, auto invest, auto withdraw

Fidelity Capital & Income
(FAGIX)

82 Devonshire St.
Boston, MA 02109
(800) 544-8888, (801) 534-1910

Corporate High-Yield Bond

PERFORMANCE

	3yr Annual	5yr Annual	10yr Annual	Bull	Bear
Return (%)	27.5	14.0	13.6	104.8	-2.5
Differ from Category (+/-)	7.0 high	3.2 high	1.9 high	29.9 high	0.8 abv av

Total Risk	Standard Deviation	Category Risk	Risk Index	Avg Mat
blw av	5.3%	high	1.4	6.9 yrs

	1993	1992	1991	1990	1989	1988	1987	1986	1985	1984
Return (%).............	24.8	28.0	29.8	-3.8	-3.1	12.5	1.2	18.0	25.5	10.4
Differ from category (+/-)...	5.6	12.2	2.5	0.4	-4.4	0.2	0.2	2.8	2.0	-0.4

PER SHARE DATA

	1993	1992	1991	1990	1989	1988	1987	1986	1985	1984
Dividends, Net Income ($).	0.83	0.66	0.73	0.75	1.07	1.00	1.05	1.10	1.14	1.16
Distrib'ns, Cap Gain ($) ...	0.00	0.00	0.00	0.00	0.00	0.00	0.28	0.31	0.00	0.00
Net Asset Value ($)	9.86	8.61	7.28	6.23	7.26	8.56	8.53	9.72	9.51	8.59
Expense Ratio (%)	0.91	0.80	0.81	0.81	0.77	0.88	0.78	0.80	0.83	0.85
Net Income to Assets (%) .	7.45	9.77	11.26	12.70	11.96	11.38	10.99	11.30	12.54	13.51
Portfolio Turnover (%).....	102	132	108	95	72	68	116	104	157	71
Total Assets (Millions $)..	2,744	1,580	952	1,062	1,741	1,530	1,720	1,645	782	395

PORTFOLIO (as of 4/30/93)

Portfolio Manager: David Breazzano - 1991, Dan Harmetz - 1991

Investm't Category: Corp. High-Yield Bond

Cap Gain	Asset Allocation
✔ Cap & Income	Fund of Funds
Income	Index
	Sector
✔ Domestic	Small Cap
✔ Foreign	Socially Conscious
Country/Region	State Specific

Portfolio: stocks 4% bonds 72%
convertibles 4% other 11% cash 9%

Largest Holdings: media & leisure 14%, construction & real estate 9%

Unrealized Net Capital Gains: 7% of portfolio value

SHAREHOLDER INFORMATION

Minimum Investment
Initial: $2,500   Subsequent: $250

Minimum IRA Investment
Initial: $500   Subsequent: $100

Maximum Fees
Load: 1.50% redemption 12b-1: none
Other: redemption fee applies for 1 year

Distributions
Income: monthly   Capital Gains: Jun

Exchange Options
Number Per Year: 4   Fee: none
Telephone: yes (money market fund available)

Services
IRA, other pension, auto exchange, auto invest, auto withdraw

Fidelity Capital Appreciation Port (FDCAX)

Growth

82 Devonshire St.
Boston, MA 02109
(800) 544-8888, (801) 534-1910

PERFORMANCE

	3yr Annual	5yr Annual	10yr Annual	Bull	Bear
Return (%)	19.5	12.8	na	80.3	-20.1
Differ from Category (+/-)	0.3 av	-1.8 blw av	na	-4.4 av	-7.7 low

Total Risk	Standard Deviation	Category Risk	Risk Index	Beta
av	10.4%	low	1.0	0.5

	1993	1992	1991	1990	1989	1988	1987	1986	1985	1984
Return (%)	33.4	16.3	9.9	-15.6	26.9	37.6	19.2	—	—	—
Differ from category (+/-) ..	20.2	5.3	-25.5	-9.5	1.1	19.9	18.0	—	—	—

PER SHARE DATA

	1993	1992	1991	1990	1989	1988	1987	1986	1985	1984
Dividends, Net Income ($) .	0.10	0.18	0.62	0.17	0.23	0.12	0.01	—	—	—
Distrib'ns, Cap Gain ($) ...	1.06	0.60	2.13	0.00	1.22	0.00	0.81	—	—	—
Net Asset Value ($)	16.92	13.57	12.34	13.84	16.63	14.29	10.48	—	—	—
Expense Ratio (%)........	0.86	0.71	0.83	1.14	1.14	1.36	1.25	—	—	—
Net Income to Assets (%)..	0.93	1.63	3.87	1.61	1.84	1.35	0.56	—	—	—
Portfolio Turnover (%)....	120	99	72	56	73	120	203	—	—	—
Total Assets (Millions $) ..	1,411	1,009	1,110	1,354	2,155	1,436	867	—	—	—

PORTFOLIO (as of 10/31/93)

Portfolio Manager: Tom Sweeney - 1986

Investm't Category: Growth

✔ Cap Gain   Asset Allocation
   Cap & Income   Fund of Funds
   Income   Index
     Sector
✔ Domestic   Small Cap
✔ Foreign   Socially Conscious
   Country/Region   State Specific

Portfolio: stocks 88%   bonds 0%
convertibles 0%   other 0%   cash 12%

Largest Holdings: transportation 17%, basic industries 17%

Unrealized Net Capital Gains: 12% of portfolio value

SHAREHOLDER INFORMATION

Minimum Investment
Initial: $2,500   Subsequent: $250

Minimum IRA Investment
Initial: $500   Subsequent: $250

Maximum Fees
Load: 3.00% front   12b-1: none
Other: none

Distributions
Income: Dec   Capital Gains: Dec

Exchange Options
Number Per Year: 4   Fee: none
Telephone: yes (money market fund available)

Services
IRA, other pension, auto exchange, auto invest, auto withdraw

Fidelity CA Tax-Free High Yield (FCTFX)

82 Devonshire St.
Boston, MA 02109
(800) 544-8888, (801) 534-1910

Tax-Exempt Bond

PERFORMANCE

	3yr Annual	5yr Annual	10yr Annual	Bull	Bear
Return (%)	10.7	9.7	na	40.7	3.2
Differ from Category (+/-)	0.4 av	0.5 av	na	0.6 av	0.8 abv av

Total Risk	Standard Deviation	Category Risk	Risk Index	Avg Mat
blw av	4.2%	av	1.0	20.9 yrs

	1993	1992	1991	1990	1989	1988	1987	1986	1985	1984
Return (%)	13.4	8.7	10.1	6.9	9.6	11.7	-3.6	17.5	16.5	—
Differ from category (+/-)	1.8	0.4	-1.2	0.6	0.6	1.6	-2.4	1.1	-0.8	—

PER SHARE DATA

	1993	1992	1991	1990	1989	1988	1987	1986	1985	1984
Dividends, Net Income ($)	0.72	0.73	0.74	0.75	0.76	0.75	0.76	0.80	0.92	—
Distrib'ns, Cap Gain ($)	0.27	0.00	0.00	0.00	0.00	0.00	0.05	0.05	0.00	—
Net Asset Value ($)	12.42	11.86	11.62	11.26	11.26	10.99	10.54	11.80	10.81	—
Expense Ratio (%)	0.60	0.59	0.58	0.60	0.61	0.73	0.68	0.72	1.00	—
Net Income to Assets (%)	6.17	6.52	6.71	6.73	7.05	7.15	6.68	7.75	9.53	—
Portfolio Turnover (%)	32	23	15	34	21	52	46	16	14	—
Total Assets (Millions $)	592	529	523	514	494	399	461	323	30	—

PORTFOLIO (as of 2/28/93)

Portfolio Manager: John F. Haley Jr. - 1985

Investm't Category: Tax-Exempt Bond

Cap Gain	Asset Allocation
Cap & Income	Fund of Funds
✔ Income	Index
	Sector
✔ Domestic	Small Cap
Foreign	Socially Conscious
Country/Region	✔ State Specific

Portfolio: stocks 0% bonds 100%
convertibles 0% other 0% cash 0%

Largest Holdings: general obligation 0%

Unrealized Net Capital Gains: 10% of portfolio value

SHAREHOLDER INFORMATION

Minimum Investment
Initial: $2,500   Subsequent: $250

Minimum IRA Investment
Initial: na   Subsequent: na

Maximum Fees
Load: none   12b-1: none
Other: none

Distributions
Income: monthly   Capital Gains: April, Dec

Exchange Options
Number Per Year: 4   Fee: none
Telephone: yes (money market fund available)

Services
auto exchange, auto invest, auto withdraw

Fidelity CA Tax-Free Insured (FCXIX)

82 Devonshire St.
Boston, MA 02109
(800) 544-8888, (801) 534-1910

Tax-Exempt Bond

PERFORMANCE

	3yr Annual	5yr Annual	10yr Annual	Bull	Bear
Return (%)	11.2	9.9	na	43.7	2.6
Differ from Category (+/-)	0.8 abv av	0.6 abv av	na	3.6 abv av	0.3 av

Total Risk	Standard Deviation	Category Risk	Risk Index	Avg Mat
blw av	4.9%	high	1.2	20.2 yrs

	1993	1992	1991	1990	1989	1988	1987	1986	1985	1984
Return (%)	13.8	9.1	10.9	7.0	8.7	11.6	-4.5	—	—	—
Differ from category (+/-) . . .	2.2	0.8	-0.4	0.6	-0.3	1.5	-3.3	—	—	—

PER SHARE DATA

	1993	1992	1991	1990	1989	1988	1987	1986	1985	1984
Dividends, Net Income ($) .	0.58	0.60	0.59	0.61	0.61	0.60	0.61	—	—	—
Distrib'ns, Cap Gain ($) . . .	0.20	0.00	0.00	0.00	0.00	0.00	0.00	—	—	—
Net Asset Value ($)	11.07	10.45	10.15	9.72	9.68	9.49	9.07	—	—	—
Expense Ratio (%)	0.63	0.66	0.72	0.75	0.83	0.65	0.45	—	—	—
Net Income to Assets (%) . .	5.72	6.06	6.30	6.38	6.54	6.70	6.27	—	—	—
Portfolio Turnover (%)	27	19	14	10	32	76	28	—	—	—
Total Assets (Millions $) . . .	312	178	114	87	69	43	35	—	—	—

PORTFOLIO (as of 2/28/93)

Portfolio Manager: John F. Haley Jr. - 1986

Investm't Category: Tax-Exempt Bond

Cap Gain	Asset Allocation
Cap & Income	Fund of Funds
✔ Income	Index
	Sector
✔ Domestic	Small Cap
Foreign	Socially Conscious
Country/Region	✔ State Specific

Portfolio: stocks 0%   bonds 100%
convertibles 0%   other 0%   cash 0%

Largest Holdings: general obligation 0%

Unrealized Net Capital Gains: 9% of portfolio value

SHAREHOLDER INFORMATION

Minimum Investment
Initial: $2,500   Subsequent: $250

Minimum IRA Investment
Initial: na   Subsequent: na

Maximum Fees
Load: none   12b-1: none
Other: none

Distributions
Income: monthly   Capital Gains: April, Dec

Exchange Options
Number Per Year: 4   Fee: none
Telephone: yes (money market fund available)

Services
auto exchange, auto invest, auto withdraw

Fidelity Contrafund
(FCNTX)

Growth

82 Devonshire St.
Boston, MA 02109
(800) 544-8888, (801) 534-1910

PERFORMANCE

	3yr Annual	5yr Annual	10yr Annual	Bull	Bear
Return (%)	29.6	26.5	17.6	141.2	-6.0
Differ from Category (+/-)	10.4 high	11.9 high	5.0 high	56.5 high	6.4 high

Total Risk	Standard Deviation	Category Risk	Risk Index	Beta
abv av	12.9%	abv av	1.2	1.0

	1993	1992	1991	1990	1989	1988	1987	1986	1985	1984
Return (%)	21.4	15.8	54.9	3.9	43.1	21.0	-1.9	13.1	27.0	-8.2
Differ from category (+/-). . .	8.2	4.8	19.5	10.0	17.3	3.3	-3.1	-1.4	-2.3	-8.2

PER SHARE DATA

	1993	1992	1991	1990	1989	1988	1987	1986	1985	1984
Dividends, Net Income ($).	0.18	0.20	0.10	0.09	0.25	0.31	0.00	0.25	0.25	0.29
Distrib'ns, Cap Gain ($) . . .	2.25	1.92	1.06	0.00	1.07	0.00	0.43	2.15	0.00	1.69
Net Asset Value ($)	30.84	27.47	25.60	17.35	16.78	12.65	10.72	11.29	12.16	9.77
Expense Ratio (%)	1.13	0.87	0.89	1.06	0.95	0.98	0.92	0.88	0.95	0.99
Net Income to Assets (%) .	0.58	1.19	1.01	3.02	4.01	3.01	1.26	1.68	3.84	2.82
Portfolio Turnover (%).	230	297	217	320	266	250	196	190	135	234
Total Assets (Millions $). .	6,345	1,986	1,000	332	298	106	86	84	86	80

PORTFOLIO (as of 6/30/93)

Portfolio Manager: Will Danoff - 1990

Investm't Category: Growth

✔ Cap Gain
  Cap & Income
  Income

  Asset Allocation
  Fund of Funds
  Index
  Sector

✔ Domestic
✔ Foreign
  Country/Region

  Small Cap
  Socially Conscious
  State Specific

Portfolio: stocks 83% bonds 1%
convertibles 0% other 0% cash 16%

Largest Holdings: energy 16%, technology 16%

Unrealized Net Capital Gains: 10% of portfolio value

SHAREHOLDER INFORMATION

Minimum Investment
Initial: $2,500   Subsequent: $250

Minimum IRA Investment
Initial: $500   Subsequent: $250

Maximum Fees
Load: 3.00% front   12b-1: none
Other: none

Distributions
Income: Dec   Capital Gains: Dec

Exchange Options
Number Per Year: 4   Fee: none
Telephone: yes (money market fund available)

Services
IRA, other pension, auto exchange, auto invest, auto withdraw

Fidelity Convertible Securities (FCVSX)

Growth & Income

82 Devonshire St.
Boston, MA 02109
(800) 544-8888, (801) 534-1910

PERFORMANCE

	3yr Annual	5yr Annual	10yr Annual	Bull	Bear
Return (%)	25.8	19.5	na	111.8	-8.6
Differ from Category (+/-)	9.4 high	7.0 high	na	41.7 high	3.0 abv av

Total Risk	Standard Deviation	Category Risk	Risk Index	Beta
av	8.5%	blw av	1.0	0.6

	1993	1992	1991	1990	1989	1988	1987	1986	1985	1984
Return (%)	17.7	22.0	38.7	-2.8	26.2	15.8	—	—	—	—
Differ from category (+/-) . . .	5.1	12.0	11.0	2.8	4.6	-1.0	—	—	—	—

PER SHARE DATA

	1993	1992	1991	1990	1989	1988	1987	1986	1985	1984
Dividends, Net Income ($) .	0.73	0.67	0.63	0.62	0.76	0.72	—	—	—	—
Distrib'ns, Cap Gain ($) . . .	1.09	0.40	0.37	0.00	0.00	0.00	—	—	—	—
Net Asset Value ($)	16.45	15.55	13.67	10.65	11.60	9.83	—	—	—	—
Expense Ratio (%).	0.95	0.96	1.17	1.31	1.38	1.60	—	—	—	—
Net Income to Assets (%) . .	4.93	4.82	4.99	5.63	7.48	6.20	—	—	—	—
Portfolio Turnover (%)	298	258	152	223	207	191	—	—	—	—
Total Assets (Millions $) . .	1,057	412	126	57	60	45	—	—	—	—

PORTFOLIO (as of 5/31/93)

Portfolio Manager: Andrew Offit - 1992

Investm't Category: Growth & Income

Cap Gain	Asset Allocation
✔ Cap & Income	Fund of Funds
Income	Index
	Sector
✔ Domestic	Small Cap
✔ Foreign	Socially Conscious
Country/Region	State Specific

Portfolio: stocks 5%   bonds 1%
convertibles 84%   other 0%   cash 10%

Largest Holdings: transportation 12%, finance 7%

Unrealized Net Capital Gains: 6% of portfolio value

SHAREHOLDER INFORMATION

Minimum Investment
Initial: $2,500   Subsequent: $250

Minimum IRA Investment
Initial: $500   Subsequent: $250

Maximum Fees
Load: none   12b-1: none
Other: none

Distributions
Income: quarterly   Capital Gains: Dec

Exchange Options
Number Per Year: 4   Fee: none
Telephone: yes (money market fund available)

Services
IRA, other pension, auto exchange, auto invest, auto withdraw

Fidelity Discipline Equity
(FDEQX)
Growth

82 Devonshire St.
Boston, MA 02109
(800) 544-8888, (801) 534-1910

PERFORMANCE

	3yr Annual	5yr Annual	10yr Annual	Bull	Bear
Return (%)	20.6	18.8	na	93.1	-9.8
Differ from Category (+/-)	1.4 abv av	4.2 high	na	8.4 abv av	2.6 abv av

Total Risk	Standard Deviation	Category Risk	Risk Index	Beta
abv av	11.0%	blw av	1.0	0.9

	1993	1992	1991	1990	1989	1988	1987	1986	1985	1984
Return (%).............	13.9	13.2	36.0	-0.6	36.3	—	—	—	—	—
Differ from category (+/-)...	0.6	2.2	0.6	5.4	10.5	—	—	—	—	—

PER SHARE DATA

	1993	1992	1991	1990	1989	1988	1987	1986	1985	1984
Dividends, Net Income ($).	0.20	0.18	0.23	0.30	0.12	—	—	—	—	—
Distrib'ns, Cap Gain ($) ...	1.04	0.99	1.32	0.00	0.12	—	—	—	—	—
Net Asset Value ($)	18.18	17.07	16.14	13.11	13.52	—	—	—	—	—
Expense Ratio (%)	1.09	1.16	1.19	1.24	1.94	—	—	—	—	—
Net Income to Assets (%) .	1.39	1.79	2.05	2.29	2.04	—	—	—	—	—
Portfolio Turnover (%).....	279	255	210	171	118	—	—	—	—	—
Total Assets (Millions $)....	790	341	154	96	71	—	—	—	—	—

PORTFOLIO (as of 10/31/93)

Portfolio Manager: Brad Lewis - 1988

Investm't Category: Growth

✔ Cap Gain	Asset Allocation
Cap & Income	Fund of Funds
Income	Index
	Sector
✔ Domestic	Small Cap
✔ Foreign	Socially Conscious
Country/Region	State Specific

Portfolio:
stocks 80% bonds 0%
convertibles 0% other 0% cash 20%

Largest Holdings: utilities 15%, finance 13%

Unrealized Net Capital Gains: 8% of portfolio value

SHAREHOLDER INFORMATION

Minimum Investment
Initial: $2,500   Subsequent: $250

Minimum IRA Investment
Initial: $500   Subsequent: $250

Maximum Fees
Load: none   12b-1: none
Other: none

Distributions
Income: Dec   Capital Gains: Dec

Exchange Options
Number Per Year: 4   Fee: none
Telephone: yes (money market fund available)

Services
IRA, other pension, auto exchange, auto invest, auto withdraw

Fidelity Diversified Int'l

(FDIVX)

International Stock

82 Devonshire St.
Boston, MA 02109
(800) 544-8888, (801) 534-1910

PERFORMANCE

	3yr Annual	5yr Annual	10yr Annual	Bull	Bear
Return (%)	na	na	na	na	na
Differ from Category (+/-)	na	na	na	na	na

Total Risk	Standard Deviation	Category Risk	Risk Index	Beta
na	na	na	na	na

	1993	1992	1991	1990	1989	1988	1987	1986	1985	1984
Return (%)	36.6	-13.8	—	—	—	—	—	—	—	—
Differ from category (+/-) ..	-1.9	-10.3	—	—	—	—	—	—	—	—

PER SHARE DATA

	1993	1992	1991	1990	1989	1988	1987	1986	1985	1984
Dividends, Net Income ($) .	0.00	0.10	—	—	—	—	—	—	—	—
Distrib'ns, Cap Gain ($) ...	0.10	0.00	—	—	—	—	—	—	—	—
Net Asset Value ($)	11.60	8.57	—	—	—	—	—	—	—	—
Expense Ratio (%)........	1.47	2.00	—	—	—	—	—	—	—	—
Net Income to Assets (%)..	0.84	1.38	—	—	—	—	—	—	—	—
Portfolio Turnover (%).....	56	56	—	—	—	—	—	—	—	—
Total Assets (Millions $) ...	247	36	—	—	—	—	—	—	—	—

PORTFOLIO (as of 10/31/93)

Portfolio Manager: Greg Fraser - 1991

Investm't Category: International Stock

✔ Cap Gain	Asset Allocation
Cap & Income	Fund of Funds
Income	Index
	Sector
Domestic	Small Cap
✔ Foreign	Socially Conscious
Country/Region	State Specific

Portfolio: stocks 85%   bonds 1%
convertibles 0%   other 2%   cash 12%

Largest Holdings: Japan 19%, United Kingdom 13%

Unrealized Net Capital Gains: 7% of portfolio value

SHAREHOLDER INFORMATION

Minimum Investment
Initial: $2,500   Subsequent: $250

Minimum IRA Investment
Initial: $500   Subsequent: $250

Maximum Fees
Load: 3.00% front   12b-1: none
Other: none

Distributions
Income: Dec   Capital Gains: Dec

Exchange Options
Number Per Year: 4   Fee: none
Telephone: yes (money market fund available)

Services
IRA, other pension, auto exchange, auto invest, auto withdraw

Fidelity Emerging Growth (FDEGX)

82 Devonshire St.
Boston, MA 02109
(800) 544-8888, (801) 534-1910

Aggressive Growth

PERFORMANCE

	3yr Annual	5yr Annual	10yr Annual	Bull	Bear
Return (%)	29.4	na	na	na	na
Differ from Category (+/-)	4.0 abv av	na	na	na	na

Total Risk	Standard Deviation	Category Risk	Risk Index	Beta
high	17.9%	abv av	1.2	1.3

	1993	1992	1991	1990	1989	1988	1987	1986	1985	1984
Return (%)	19.8	8.3	67.0	—	—	—	—	—	—	—
Differ from category (+/-)	0.8	-2.1	14.6	—	—	—	—	—	—	—

PER SHARE DATA

	1993	1992	1991	1990	1989	1988	1987	1986	1985	1984
Dividends, Net Income ($)	0.00	0.01	0.00	—	—	—	—	—	—	—
Distrib'ns, Cap Gain ($)	3.57	0.14	0.38	—	—	—	—	—	—	—
Net Asset Value ($)	17.33	17.58	16.38	—	—	—	—	—	—	—
Expense Ratio (%)	1.19	1.09	1.37	—	—	—	—	—	—	—
Net Income to Assets (%)	-0.08	0.56	-0.10	—	—	—	—	—	—	—
Portfolio Turnover (%)	379	531	326	—	—	—	—	—	—	—
Total Assets (Millions $)	641	614	530	—	—	—	—	—	—	—

PORTFOLIO (as of 5/31/93)

Portfolio Manager: Larry Greenberg - 1993

Investm't Category: Aggressive Growth

✔ Cap Gain	Asset Allocation
Cap & Income	Fund of Funds
Income	Index
	Sector
✔ Domestic	✔ Small Cap
✔ Foreign	Socially Conscious
Country/Region	State Specific

Portfolio: stocks 96%   bonds 0%
convertibles 0%   other 0%   cash 4%

Largest Holdings: retail & wholesale 13%, computer services & software 12%

Unrealized Net Capital Gains: 11% of portfolio value

SHAREHOLDER INFORMATION

Minimum Investment
Initial: $2,500   Subsequent: $250

Minimum IRA Investment
Initial: $500   Subsequent: $250

Maximum Fees
Load: 3.00% front   12b-1: none
Other: 0.75% redemption fee (90 days)

Distributions
Income: Feb, Dec   Capital Gains: Feb, Dec

Exchange Options
Number Per Year: 4   Fee: none
Telephone: yes (money market fund available)

Services
IRA, other pension, auto exchange, auto invest, auto withdraw

Fidelity Emerging Markets (FEMKX)

82 Devonshire St.
Boston, MA 02109
(800) 544-8888, (801) 534-1910

International Stock

PERFORMANCE

	3yr Annual	5yr Annual	10yr Annual	Bull	Bear
Return (%)	27.1	na	na	na	na
Differ from Category (+/-)	12.8 high	na	na	na	na

Total Risk	Standard Deviation	Category Risk	Risk Index	Beta
high	14.1%	abv av	1.2	0.2

	1993	1992	1991	1990	1989	1988	1987	1986	1985	1984
Return (%)	81.7	5.8	6.7	—	—	—	—	—	—	—
Differ from category (+/-) . .	43.2	9.3	-6.2	—	—	—	—	—	—	—

PER SHARE DATA

	1993	1992	1991	1990	1989	1988	1987	1986	1985	1984
Dividends, Net Income ($) .	0.05	0.07	0.07	—	—	—	—	—	—	—
Distrib'ns, Cap Gain ($) . . .	0.00	0.15	0.14	—	—	—	—	—	—	—
Net Asset Value ($)	19.70	10.87	10.49	—	—	—	—	—	—	—
Expense Ratio (%)	1.91	2.60	2.60	—	—	—	—	—	—	—
Net Income to Assets (%) . .	0.44	0.90	1.34	—	—	—	—	—	—	—
Portfolio Turnover (%)	57	159	45	—	—	—	—	—	—	—
Total Assets (Millions $) . .	1,675	13	6	—	—	—	—	—	—	—

PORTFOLIO (as of 10/31/93)

Portfolio Manager: Richard Hazelwood - 1993

Investm't Category: International Stock
- ✔ Cap Gain
- Cap & Income
- Income
- Domestic
- ✔ Foreign
- Country/Region
- Asset Allocation
- Fund of Funds
- Index
- Sector
- Small Cap
- Socially Conscious
- State Specific

Portfolio: stocks 89% bonds 2%
convertibles 0% other 0% cash 9%

Largest Holdings: Malaysia 20%, Mexico 16%

Unrealized Net Capital Gains: 14% of portfolio value

SHAREHOLDER INFORMATION

Minimum Investment
Initial: $2,500   Subsequent: $250

Minimum IRA Investment
Initial: $500   Subsequent: $250

Maximum Fees
Load: 3.00% front   12b-1: none
Other: 1.50% redemption fee (90 days)

Distributions
Income: Dec   Capital Gains: Dec

Exchange Options
Number Per Year: 4   Fee: none
Telephone: yes (money market fund available)

Services
IRA, other pension, auto exchange, auto invest, auto withdraw

Fidelity Equity-Income
(FEQIX)

Growth & Income

82 Devonshire St.
Boston, MA 02109
(800) 544-8888, (801) 534-1910

PERFORMANCE

	3yr Annual	5yr Annual	10yr Annual	Bull	Bear
Return (%)	21.6	12.9	13.5	91.1	-18.9
Differ from Category (+/-)	5.2 high	0.4 av	1.1 abv av	21.0 high	-7.3 low

Total Risk	Standard Deviation	Category Risk	Risk Index	Beta
av	8.9%	blw av	1.0	0.7

	1993	1992	1991	1990	1989	1988	1987	1986	1985	1984
Return (%)	21.3	14.6	29.4	-13.9	18.6	22.4	-1.6	16.8	25.0	10.5
Differ from category (+/-). . .	8.7	4.6	1.7	-8.3	-3.0	5.6	-2.0	1.6	-0.4	4.3

PER SHARE DATA

	1993	1992	1991	1990	1989	1988	1987	1986	1985	1984
Dividends, Net Income ($).	1.15	1.08	1.20	1.55	1.75	1.51	1.51	1.70	1.70	1.63
Distrib'ns, Cap Gain ($) . . .	0.11	0.00	0.00	0.30	1.16	0.00	3.92	3.08	0.51	3.12
Net Asset Value ($)	33.84	29.01	26.31	21.34	26.90	25.20	21.85	27.29	27.51	23.95
Expense Ratio (%)	0.67	0.68	0.70	0.71	0.63	0.66	0.65	0.66	0.72	0.80
Net Income to Assets (%) .	4.02	4.80	6.20	6.10	6.50	5.50	5.80	7.10	7.90	7.00
Portfolio Turnover (%).	84	111	107	92	68	120	110	118	123	118
Total Assets (Millions $). .	6,582	4,422	3,941	4,751	4,401	3,683	3,818	2,362	1,351	780

PORTFOLIO (as of 7/31/93)

Portfolio Manager: Stephen Peterson - 1993

Investm't Category: Growth & Income

Cap Gain	Asset Allocation
✔ Cap & Income	Fund of Funds
Income	Index
	Sector
✔ Domestic	Small Cap
Foreign	Socially Conscious
Country/Region	State Specific

Portfolio: stocks 73%   bonds 7%
convertibles 14%   other 2%   cash 4%

Largest Holdings: finance 16%, utilities 12%

Unrealized Net Capital Gains: 17% of portfolio value

SHAREHOLDER INFORMATION

Minimum Investment
Initial: $2,500   Subsequent: $250

Minimum IRA Investment
Initial: $500   Subsequent: $250

Maximum Fees
Load: 2.00% front   12b-1: none
Other: none

Distributions
Income: quarterly   Capital Gains: Mar, Dec

Exchange Options
Number Per Year: 4   Fee: none
Telephone: yes (money market fund available)

Services
IRA, other pension, auto exchange, auto invest, auto withdraw

Fidelity Equity-Income II
(FEQTX)
Growth & Income

82 Devonshire St.
Boston, MA 02109
(800) 544-8888, (801) 534-1910

PERFORMANCE

	3yr Annual	5yr Annual	10yr Annual	Bull	Bear
Return (%)	27.5	na	na	121.5	na
Differ from Category (+/-)	11.1 high	na	na	51.4 high	na

Total Risk	Standard Deviation	Category Risk	Risk Index	Beta
av	8.5%	blw av	1.0	0.6

	1993	1992	1991	1990	1989	1988	1987	1986	1985	1984
Return (%)	18.8	19.0	46.5	—	—	—	—	—	—	—
Differ from category (+/-) . . .	6.2	9.0	18.8	—	—	—	—	—	—	—

PER SHARE DATA

	1993	1992	1991	1990	1989	1988	1987	1986	1985	1984
Dividends, Net Income ($) .	0.44	0.37	0.46	—	—	—	—	—	—	—
Distrib'ns, Cap Gain ($) . . .	0.73	0.36	0.17	—	—	—	—	—	—	—
Net Asset Value ($)	18.41	16.51	14.52	—	—	—	—	—	—	—
Expense Ratio (%).	0.91	1.01	1.52	—	—	—	—	—	—	—
Net Income to Assets (%). .	2.62	3.09	3.83	—	—	—	—	—	—	—
Portfolio Turnover (%)	54	89	206	—	—	—	—	—	—	—
Total Assets (Millions $) . .	4,992	1,942	292	—	—	—	—	—	—	—

PORTFOLIO (as of 5/31/93)

Portfolio Manager: Brian Posner - 1992

Investm't Category: Growth & Income

Cap Gain	Asset Allocation
✔ Cap & Income	Fund of Funds
Income	Index
	Sector
✔ Domestic	Small Cap
✔ Foreign	Socially Conscious
Country/Region	State Specific

Portfolio: stocks 72% bonds 2%
convertibles 8% other 0% cash 18%

Largest Holdings: basic industries 11%, energy 11%

Unrealized Net Capital Gains: 8% of portfolio value

SHAREHOLDER INFORMATION

Minimum Investment
Initial: $2,500   Subsequent: $250

Minimum IRA Investment
Initial: $500   Subsequent: $250

Maximum Fees
Load: none   12b-1: none
Other: none

Distributions
Income: quarterly   Capital Gains: Jan, Dec

Exchange Options
Number Per Year: 4   Fee: none
Telephone: yes (money market fund available)

Services
IRA, other pension, auto exchange, auto invest, auto withdraw

Fidelity Europe (FIEUX)

International Stock

82 Devonshire St.
Boston, MA 02109
(800) 544-8888, (801) 534-1910

PERFORMANCE

	3yr Annual	5yr Annual	10yr Annual	Bull	Bear
Return (%)	8.8	10.2	na	32.9	-7.3
Differ from Category (+/-)	-5.5 low	1.5 abv av	na	-22.2 low	7.8 high

Total Risk	Standard Deviation	Category Risk	Risk Index	Beta
abv av	13.6%	abv av	1.1	0.6

	1993	1992	1991	1990	1989	1988	1987	1986	1985	1984
Return (%)	27.1	-2.5	4.1	-4.5	32.3	5.8	14.9	—	—	—
Differ from category (+/-). .	-11.4	1.0	-8.8	6.6	10.1	-8.0	2.9	—	—	—

PER SHARE DATA

	1993	1992	1991	1990	1989	1988	1987	1986	1985	1984
Dividends, Net Income ($).	0.07	0.28	0.50	0.37	0.18	0.28	0.00	—	—	—
Distrib'ns, Cap Gain ($) . . .	0.00	0.00	0.00	0.00	0.00	0.00	0.00	—	—	—
Net Asset Value ($)	19.12	15.10	15.79	15.67	16.81	12.85	12.41	—	—	—
Expense Ratio (%)	1.25	1.22	1.31	1.45	1.89	2.66	1.91	—	—	—
Net Income to Assets (%) .	1.44	2.38	2.83	2.87	1.67	0.97	0.48	—	—	—
Portfolio Turnover (%).	76	95	80	148	160	180	241	—	—	—
Total Assets (Millions $). . . .	499	431	297	389	97	102	131	—	—	—

PORTFOLIO (as of 10/31/93)

Portfolio Manager: Sally Walden - 1992

Investm't Category: International Stock

✔ Cap Gain	Asset Allocation
Cap & Income	Fund of Funds
Income	Index
	Sector
Domestic	Small Cap
✔ Foreign	Socially Conscious
✔ Country/Region	State Specific

Portfolio: stocks 94% bonds 0%
convertibles 0% other 4% cash 2%

Largest Holdings: United Kingdom 27%, France 14%

Unrealized Net Capital Gains: 14% of portfolio value

SHAREHOLDER INFORMATION

Minimum Investment
Initial: $2,500   Subsequent: $250

Minimum IRA Investment
Initial: $500   Subsequent: $250

Maximum Fees
Load: 3.00% front   12b-1: none
Other: none

Distributions
Income: Dec   Capital Gains: Dec

Exchange Options
Number Per Year: 2   Fee: none
Telephone: yes (money market fund available)

Services
IRA, other pension, auto exchange, auto invest, auto withdraw

Fidelity Ginnie Mae
(FGMNX)

Mortgage-Backed Bond

82 Devonshire St.
Boston, MA 02109
(800) 544-8888, (801) 534-1910

PERFORMANCE

	3yr Annual	5yr Annual	10yr Annual	Bull	Bear
Return (%)	8.7	10.0	na	35.1	5.1
Differ from Category (+/-)	-0.5 blw av	0.1 av	na	-1.6 blw av	0.5 abv av

Total Risk	Standard Deviation	Category Risk	Risk Index	Avg Mat
low	2.3%	low	0.9	7.0 yrs

	1993	1992	1991	1990	1989	1988	1987	1986	1985	1984
Return (%)	6.1	6.6	13.5	10.4	13.8	7.1	1.1	13.0	—	—
Differ from category (+/-) ..	-0.6	0.5	-0.8	0.8	1.5	0.1	-1.0	1.8	—	—

PER SHARE DATA

	1993	1992	1991	1990	1989	1988	1987	1986	1985	1984
Dividends, Net Income ($) .	0.62	0.74	0.83	0.85	0.85	0.84	0.87	0.94	—	—
Distrib'ns, Cap Gain ($) ...	0.25	0.00	0.00	0.00	0.00	0.00	0.00	0.00	—	—
Net Asset Value ($)	10.86	11.07	11.10	10.56	10.38	9.91	10.05	10.81	—	—
Expense Ratio (%)........	0.80	0.80	0.83	0.83	0.85	0.87	0.79	0.75	—	—
Net Income to Assets (%)..	7.26	7.73	8.24	8.71	9.03	8.57	8.28	9.13	—	—
Portfolio Turnover (%)	259	114	125	96	291	361	177	106	—	—
Total Assets (Millions $) ...	893	914	797	658	651	722	869	652	—	—

PORTFOLIO (as of 7/31/93)

Portfolio Manager: Bob Ives - 1993

Investm't Category: Mortgage-Backed Bond

Cap Gain	Asset Allocation
Cap & Income	Fund of Funds
✔ Income	Index
	Sector
✔ Domestic	Small Cap
✔ Foreign	Socially Conscious
Country/Region	State Specific

Portfolio: stocks 0% bonds 96%
convertibles 0% other 0% cash 4%

Largest Holdings: mortgage-backed 95%

Unrealized Net Capital Gains: 1% of portfolio value

SHAREHOLDER INFORMATION

Minimum Investment
Initial: $2,500   Subsequent: $250

Minimum IRA Investment
Initial: $500   Subsequent: $250

Maximum Fees
Load: none   12b-1: none
Other: none

Distributions
Income: monthly   Capital Gains: Sep, Dec

Exchange Options
Number Per Year: 4   Fee: none
Telephone: yes (money market fund available)

Services
IRA, other pension, auto exchange, auto invest, auto withdraw

Fidelity Global Balanced
(FGBLX)

International Stock

82 Devonshire St.
Boston, MA 02109
(800) 544-8888, (801) 534-1910

fund in existence since 2/1/93

PERFORMANCE

	3yr Annual	5yr Annual	10yr Annual	Bull	Bear
Return (%)	na	na	na	na	na
Differ from Category (+/-)	na	na	na	na	na

Total Risk	Standard Deviation	Category Risk	Risk Index	Beta
na	na	na	na	na

	1993	1992	1991	1990	1989	1988	1987	1986	1985	1984
Return (%)	—	—	—	—	—	—	—	—	—	—
Differ from category (+/-)	—	—	—	—	—	—	—	—	—	—

PER SHARE DATA

	1993	1992	1991	1990	1989	1988	1987	1986	1985	1984
Dividends, Net Income ($) .	0.25	—	—	—	—	—	—	—	—	—
Distrib'ns, Cap Gain ($) . . .	0.28	—	—	—	—	—	—	—	—	—
Net Asset Value ($)	13.16	—	—	—	—	—	—	—	—	—
Expense Ratio (%)	2.12	—	—	—	—	—	—	—	—	—
Net Income to Assets (%) .	4.02	—	—	—	—	—	—	—	—	—
Portfolio Turnover (%).	172	—	—	—	—	—	—	—	—	—
Total Assets (Millions $). . . .	360	—	—	—	—	—	—	—	—	—

PORTFOLIO (as of 7/31/93)

Portfolio Manager: Bob Haber - 1993

Investm't Category: International Stock

Cap Gain	✔ Asset Allocation
✔ Cap & Income	Fund of Funds
Income	Index
	Sector
✔ Domestic	Small Cap
✔ Foreign	Socially Conscious
Country/Region	State Specific

Portfolio: stocks 45% bonds 33%
convertibles 9% other 0% cash 13%

Largest Holdings: Mexico 12%, United States 10%

Unrealized Net Capital Gains: 0% of portfolio value

SHAREHOLDER INFORMATION

Minimum Investment
Initial: $2,500   Subsequent: $250

Minimum IRA Investment
Initial: $500   Subsequent: $250

Maximum Fees
Load: none   12b-1: none
Other: none

Distributions
Income: quarterly   Capital Gains: Sep, Dec

Exchange Options
Number Per Year: 4   Fee: none
Telephone: yes (money market fund available)

Services
IRA, other pension, auto exchange, auto invest, auto withdraw

Fidelity Global Bond
(FGBDX)

International Bond

82 Devonshire St.
Boston, MA 02109
(800) 544-8888, (801) 534-1910

PERFORMANCE

	3yr Annual	5yr Annual	10yr Annual	Bull	Bear
Return (%)	12.7	11.7	na	49.9	7.4
Differ from Category (+/-)	0.6 av	0.3 abv av	na	-8.2 low	0.8 blw av

Total Risk	Standard Deviation	Category Risk	Risk Index	Avg Mat
blw av	4.5%	av	1.1	11.4 yrs

	1993	1992	1991	1990	1989	1988	1987	1986	1985	1984
Return (%)	21.9	4.3	12.7	12.2	7.9	3.6	19.1	—	—	—
Differ from category (+/-) . . .	9.2	-0.5	-2.2	0.6	5.7	1.2	5.7	—	—	—

PER SHARE DATA

	1993	1992	1991	1990	1989	1988	1987	1986	1985	1984
Dividends, Net Income ($) .	0.85	1.08	0.89	1.05	0.49	0.89	0.68	—	—	—
Distrib'ns, Cap Gain ($) . . .	0.25	0.00	0.00	0.00	0.00	0.00	0.00	—	—	—
Net Asset Value ($)	12.61	11.34	11.90	11.38	11.08	10.72	11.21	—	—	—
Expense Ratio (%).	1.15	1.23	1.35	1.40	1.50	1.14	0.95	—	—	—
Net Income to Assets (%) . .	7.84	8.02	7.92	7.82	7.56	7.61	7.14	—	—	—
Portfolio Turnover (%)	172	81	228	154	150	227	297	—	—	—
Total Assets (Millions $) . . .	687	332	160	126	57	59	44	—	—	—

PORTFOLIO (as of 6/30/93)

Portfolio Manager: John Kelly - 1993

Investm't Category: International Bond

Cap Gain	Asset Allocation
✔ Cap & Income	Fund of Funds
Income	Index
	Sector
✔ Domestic	Small Cap
✔ Foreign	Socially Conscious
Country/Region	State Specific

Portfolio:	stocks 0%	bonds 91%
convertibles 1%	other 0%	cash 8%

Largest Holdings: Argentina 12%, Mexico 12%

Unrealized Net Capital Gains: 0% of portfolio value

SHAREHOLDER INFORMATION

Minimum Investment
Initial: $2,500   Subsequent: $250

Minimum IRA Investment
Initial: $500   Subsequent: $250

Maximum Fees
Load: none   12b-1: none
Other: none

Distributions
Income: monthly   Capital Gains: Dec

Exchange Options
Number Per Year: 4   Fee: none
Telephone: yes (money market fund available)

Services
IRA, other pension, auto exchange, auto invest, auto withdraw

Fidelity Gov't Securities
(FGOVX)

82 Devonshire St.
Boston, MA 02109
(800) 544-8888, (801) 534-1910

Government Bond

PERFORMANCE

	3yr Annual	5yr Annual	10yr Annual	Bull	Bear
Return (%)	12.0	11.6	10.8	48.3	3.8
Differ from Category (+/-)	1.2 abv av	1.2 abv av	1.1 abv av	2.1 abv av	3.3 abv av

Total Risk	Standard Deviation	Category Risk	Risk Index	Avg Mat
blw av	4.4%	av	1.0	17.8 yrs

	1993	1992	1991	1990	1989	1988	1987	1986	1985	1984
Return (%).	12.3	7.9	15.9	9.5	12.6	6.3	1.0	14.6	17.7	11.2
Differ from category (+/-). . .	1.9	1.7	0.8	3.0	-1.3	-1.3	2.8	-4.5	-1.4	-1.8

PER SHARE DATA

	1993	1992	1991	1990	1989	1988	1987	1986	1985	1984
Dividends, Net Income ($).	0.67	0.73	0.80	0.83	0.78	0.83	0.85	0.90	0.98	1.00
Distrib'ns, Cap Gain ($) . . .	0.31	0.25	0.00	0.00	0.00	0.00	0.00	0.00	0.00	0.00
Net Asset Value ($)	10.34	10.10	10.30	9.64	9.61	9.27	9.52	10.28	9.80	9.24
Expense Ratio (%)	0.69	0.70	0.70	0.66	0.73	0.79	0.87	0.84	0.81	0.85
Net Income to Assets (%) .	6.64	7.31	8.23	8.84	8.29	8.87	8.68	8.72	10.46	11.14
Portfolio Turnover (%).	311	219	257	302	312	283	253	138	137	na
Total Assets (Millions $). . . .	744	581	522	469	560	568	683	752	270	89

PORTFOLIO (as of 3/31/93)

Portfolio Manager: Curtis Hollingsworth - 1990

Investm't Category: Government Bond

Cap Gain	Asset Allocation
Cap & Income	Fund of Funds
✔ Income	Index
	Sector
✔ Domestic	Small Cap
Foreign	Socially Conscious
Country/Region	State Specific

Portfolio: stocks 0%   bonds 100%
convertibles 0%   other 0%   cash 0%

Largest Holdings: U. S. government & agencies 100%

Unrealized Net Capital Gains: 5% of portfolio value

SHAREHOLDER INFORMATION

Minimum Investment
Initial: $2,500   Subsequent: $250

Minimum IRA Investment
Initial: $500   Subsequent: $250

Maximum Fees
Load: none   12b-1: none
Other: none

Distributions
Income: monthly   Capital Gains: Feb

Exchange Options
Number Per Year: 4   Fee: none
Telephone: yes (money market fund available)

Services
IRA, other pension, auto exchange, auto invest, auto withdraw

Fidelity Growth & Income (FGRIX)

82 Devonshire St.
Boston, MA 02109
(800) 544-8888, (801) 534-1910

Growth & Income

PERFORMANCE

	3yr Annual	5yr Annual	10yr Annual	Bull	Bear
Return (%)	23.6	17.9	na	101.9	-12.7
Differ from Category (+/-)	7.2 high	5.4 high	na	31.8 high	-1.1 av

Total Risk	Standard Deviation	Category Risk	Risk Index	Beta
abv av	11.6%	high	1.3	0.9

	1993	1992	1991	1990	1989	1988	1987	1986	1985	1984
Return (%)	19.5	11.5	41.8	-6.7	29.6	22.9	5.7	34.9	—	—
Differ from category (+/-)	6.9	1.5	14.1	-1.1	8.0	6.1	5.3	19.7	—	—

PER SHARE DATA

	1993	1992	1991	1990	1989	1988	1987	1986	1985	1984
Dividends, Net Income ($)	0.51	0.56	0.37	0.57	0.75	0.62	0.44	0.15	—	—
Distrib'ns, Cap Gain ($)	0.76	2.40	0.63	0.21	1.27	0.00	1.35	0.00	—	—
Net Asset Value ($)	22.22	19.71	20.49	15.22	17.17	14.85	12.60	13.33	—	—
Expense Ratio (%)	0.83	0.86	0.87	0.87	0.89	1.02	1.09	1.21	—	—
Net Income to Assets (%)	2.67	2.49	2.62	3.43	4.76	3.69	2.96	3.12	—	—
Portfolio Turnover (%)	87	221	215	108	97	135	165	69	—	—
Total Assets (Millions $)	7,642	4,199	2,686	1,910	1,428	1,188	1,629	365	—	—

PORTFOLIO (as of 7/31/93)

Portfolio Manager: Steven Kaye - 1993

Investm't Category: Growth & Income

Cap Gain	Asset Allocation
✔ Cap & Income	Fund of Funds
Income	Index
	Sector
✔ Domestic	Small Cap
✔ Foreign	Socially Conscious
Country/Region	State Specific

Portfolio: stocks 72%   bonds 13%
convertibles 11%   other 0%   cash 4%

Largest Holdings: finance 14%, utilities 12%

Unrealized Net Capital Gains: 12% of portfolio value

SHAREHOLDER INFORMATION

Minimum Investment
Initial: $2,500   Subsequent: $250

Minimum IRA Investment
Initial: $500   Subsequent: $250

Maximum Fees
Load: 3.00% front   12b-1: none
Other: none

Distributions
Income: quarterly   Capital Gains: Sep, Dec

Exchange Options
Number Per Year: 4   Fee: none
Telephone: yes (money market fund available)

Services
IRA, other pension, auto exchange, auto invest, auto withdraw

Fidelity Growth Company (FDGRX)

82 Devonshire St.
Boston, MA 02109
(800) 544-8888, (801) 534-1910

Aggressive Growth

PERFORMANCE

	3yr Annual	5yr Annual	10yr Annual	Bull	Bear
Return (%)	22.9	22.2	16.6	117.5	-11.4
Differ from Category (+/-)	-2.5 blw av	4.0 abv av	4.7 abv av	-7.5 av	3.6 abv av

Total Risk	Standard Deviation	Category Risk	Risk Index	Beta
high	15.1%	blw av	1.0	1.2

	1993	1992	1991	1990	1989	1988	1987	1986	1985	1984
Return (%)	16.1	7.9	48.3	3.5	41.6	16.0	-1.6	13.0	39.9	-5.4
Differ from category (+/-)	-2.9	-2.5	-4.1	9.8	14.6	0.8	1.8	3.6	8.9	4.0

PER SHARE DATA

	1993	1992	1991	1990	1989	1988	1987	1986	1985	1984
Dividends, Net Income ($)	0.07	0.09	0.07	0.00	0.14	0.10	0.01	0.07	0.07	0.02
Distrib'ns, Cap Gain ($)	2.92	1.48	1.73	0.00	2.00	0.00	0.83	4.65	0.00	0.28
Net Asset Value ($)	29.06	27.64	27.09	19.60	18.92	15.00	13.02	14.11	16.83	12.10
Expense Ratio (%)	1.11	1.09	1.07	1.14	0.95	1.03	1.02	1.11	1.18	1.17
Net Income to Assets (%)	0.48	0.52	0.75	1.51	1.42	0.70	0.00	0.23	0.55	0.62
Portfolio Turnover (%)	246	250	174	189	269	257	212	120	129	143
Total Assets (Millions $)	2,512	1,752	1,133	535	283	129	112	180	147	109

PORTFOLIO (as of 5/31/93)

Portfolio Manager: Bob Stansky - 1987

Investm't Category: Aggressive Growth

✔ Cap Gain
　Cap & Income
　Income

　Asset Allocation
　Fund of Funds
　Index
　Sector

✔ Domestic
✔ Foreign
　Country/Region

　Small Cap
　Socially Conscious
　State Specific

Portfolio: stocks 83%　bonds 0%
convertibles 0%　other 0%　cash 17%

Largest Holdings: technology 26%, finance 15%

Unrealized Net Capital Gains: 11% of portfolio value

SHAREHOLDER INFORMATION

Minimum Investment
Initial: $2,500　Subsequent: $250

Minimum IRA Investment
Initial: $500　Subsequent: $250

Maximum Fees
Load: 3.00% front　12b-1: none
Other: none

Distributions
Income: Jan, Dec　Capital Gains: Jan, Dec

Exchange Options
Number Per Year: 4　Fee: none
Telephone: yes (money market fund available)

Services
IRA, other pension, auto exchange, auto invest, auto withdraw

Fidelity High Yield Tax Free Port (FHIGX)

82 Devonshire St.
Boston, MA 02109
(800) 544-8888, (801) 534-1910

Tax-Exempt Bond

PERFORMANCE

	3yr Annual	5yr Annual	10yr Annual	Bull	Bear
Return (%)	10.5	10.2	10.9	41.2	3.6
Differ from Category (+/-)	0.2 blw av	1.0 abv av	1.3 high	1.1 av	1.3 abv av

Total Risk	Standard Deviation	Category Risk	Risk Index	Avg Mat
low	3.6%	blw av	0.9	19.4 yrs

	1993	1992	1991	1990	1989	1988	1987	1986	1985	1984
Return (%)	13.1	8.3	10.1	8.4	11.3	12.2	-2.8	18.8	21.4	9.9
Differ from category (+/-) ...	1.5	0.0	-1.2	2.1	2.3	2.1	-1.6	2.4	4.1	1.6

PER SHARE DATA

	1993	1992	1991	1990	1989	1988	1987	1986	1985	1984
Dividends, Net Income ($) .	0.76	0.80	0.83	0.85	0.88	0.89	0.93	0.98	1.03	1.07
Distrib'ns, Cap Gain ($) ...	0.50	0.18	0.15	0.23	0.38	0.00	0.11	0.43	0.00	0.00
Net Asset Value ($)	12.95	12.60	12.58	12.36	12.44	12.36	11.87	13.29	12.44	11.18
Expense Ratio (%)........	0.56	0.57	0.56	0.57	0.58	0.60	0.71	0.57	0.56	0.59
Net Income to Assets (%) ..	5.98	6.40	6.72	6.96	7.10	7.48	7.38	7.63	8.83	9.75
Portfolio Turnover (%)	56	47	44	58	71	47	80	49	57	73
Total Assets (Millions $) ..	2,164	2,075	1,996	1,785	1,738	1,574	1,610	2,449	1,600	1,040

PORTFOLIO (as of 6/30/93)

Portfolio Manager: Anne Punzak - 1993

Investm't Category: Tax-Exempt Bond

Cap Gain	Asset Allocation
Cap & Income	Fund of Funds
✔ Income	Index
	Sector
✔ Domestic	Small Cap
Foreign	Socially Conscious
Country/Region	State Specific

Portfolio: stocks 0%   bonds 100%
convertibles 0%   other 0%   cash 0%

Largest Holdings: general obligation 11%

Unrealized Net Capital Gains: 7% of portfolio value

SHAREHOLDER INFORMATION

Minimum Investment
Initial: $2,500   Subsequent: $250

Minimum IRA Investment
Initial: na   Subsequent: na

Maximum Fees
Load: none   12b-1: none
Other: none

Distributions
Income: monthly   Capital Gains: Dec

Exchange Options
Number Per Year: 4   Fee: none
Telephone: yes (money market fund available)

Services
auto exchange, auto invest, auto withdraw

Fidelity Insured Tax-Free
(FMUIX)

82 Devonshire St.
Boston, MA 02109
(800) 544-8888, (801) 534-1910

Tax-Exempt Bond

PERFORMANCE

	3yr Annual	5yr Annual	10yr Annual	Bull	Bear
Return (%)	11.0	9.9	na	42.7	2.8
Differ from Category (+/-)	0.6 av	0.6 abv av	na	2.6 av	0.5 av

Total Risk	Standard Deviation	Category Risk	Risk Index	Avg Mat
blw av	4.7%	abv av	1.2	19.8 yrs

	1993	1992	1991	1990	1989	1988	1987	1986	1985	1984
Return (%).............	13.8	7.9	11.5	7.0	9.4	11.1	-2.1	18.4	—	—
Differ from category (+/-)...	2.2	-0.4	0.2	0.6	0.4	1.0	-0.8	2.0	—	—

PER SHARE DATA

	1993	1992	1991	1990	1989	1988	1987	1986	1985	1984
Dividends, Net Income ($).	0.65	0.68	0.70	0.71	0.71	0.70	0.72	0.74	—	—
Distrib'ns, Cap Gain ($) ...	0.28	0.10	0.00	0.00	0.00	0.00	0.01	0.00	—	—
Net Asset Value ($)	12.37	11.72	11.63	11.09	11.05	10.78	10.36	11.33	—	—
Expense Ratio (%)	0.62	0.63	0.65	0.67	0.70	0.70	0.62	0.60	—	—
Net Income to Assets (%) .	5.57	5.91	6.23	6.52	6.57	6.64	6.73	6.52	—	—
Portfolio Turnover (%)......	63	69	62	66	51	35	57	23	—	—
Total Assets (Millions $)....	448	371	303	199	175	154	145	146	—	—

PORTFOLIO (as of 6/30/93)

Portfolio Manager: Gary Wickwire - 1993

Investm't Category: Tax-Exempt Bond

Cap Gain	Asset Allocation
Cap & Income	Fund of Funds
✔ Income	Index
	Sector
✔ Domestic	Small Cap
Foreign	Socially Conscious
Country/Region	State Specific

Portfolio: stocks 0% bonds 100%
convertibles 0% other 0% cash 0%

Largest Holdings: general obligation 11%

Unrealized Net Capital Gains: na

SHAREHOLDER INFORMATION

Minimum Investment
Initial: $2,500   Subsequent: $250

Minimum IRA Investment
Initial: na   Subsequent: na

Maximum Fees
Load: none   12b-1: none
Other: none

Distributions
Income: monthly   Capital Gains: Feb, Dec

Exchange Options
Number Per Year: 4   Fee: none
Telephone: yes (money market fund available)

Services
auto exchange, auto invest, auto withdraw

Fidelity Int'l Growth & Income (FIGRX)

International Stock

82 Devonshire St.
Boston, MA 02109
(800) 544-8888, (801) 534-1910

PERFORMANCE

	3yr Annual	5yr Annual	10yr Annual	Bull	Bear
Return (%)	12.1	10.2	na	52.0	-10.2
Differ from Category (+/-)	-2.2 blw av	1.5 abv av	na	-3.1 blw av	4.9 abv av

Total Risk	Standard Deviation	Category Risk	Risk Index	Beta
abv av	11.2%	low	0.9	0.3

	1993	1992	1991	1990	1989	1988	1987	1986	1985	1984
Return (%)	35.0	-3.3	8.0	-3.2	19.1	11.5	8.3	—	—	—
Differ from category (+/-) . .	-3.5	0.2	-4.9	7.9	-3.1	-2.3	-3.7	—	—	—

PER SHARE DATA

	1993	1992	1991	1990	1989	1988	1987	1986	1985	1984
Dividends, Net Income ($) .	0.05	0.31	0.17	0.43	0.15	0.20	0.09	—	—	—
Distrib'ns, Cap Gain ($) . . .	0.05	0.00	0.00	0.00	0.00	0.00	0.00	—	—	—
Net Asset Value ($)	17.57	13.09	13.87	13.00	13.88	11.79	10.75	—	—	—
Expense Ratio (%)	1.52	1.62	1.89	1.98	1.92	2.58	2.72	—	—	—
Net Income to Assets (%) . .	0.87	2.78	2.86	2.31	1.98	1.08	1.23	—	—	—
Portfolio Turnover (%)	24	76	117	102	147	112	158	—	—	—
Total Assets (Millions $) . .	1,061	60	50	35	26	32	41	—	—	—

PORTFOLIO (as of 10/31/93)

Portfolio Manager: Rick Mace - 1993

Investm't Category: International Stock

Cap Gain	Asset Allocation
✔ Cap & Income	Fund of Funds
Income	Index
	Sector
✔ Domestic	Small Cap
✔ Foreign	Socially Conscious
Country/Region	State Specific

Portfolio: stocks 67%   bonds 8%
convertibles 0%   other 6%   cash 19%

Largest Holdings: Japan 15%, United Kingdom 8%

Unrealized Net Capital Gains: 7% of portfolio value

SHAREHOLDER INFORMATION

Minimum Investment
Initial: $2,500   Subsequent: $250

Minimum IRA Investment
Initial: $500   Subsequent: $250

Maximum Fees
Load: 2.00% front   12b-1: none
Other: none

Distributions
Income: Dec   Capital Gains: Dec

Exchange Options
Number Per Year: 2   Fee: none
Telephone: yes (money market fund available)

Services
IRA, other pension, auto exchange, auto invest, auto withdraw

Fidelity Interm Bond
(FTHRX)

General Bond

82 Devonshire St.
Boston, MA 02109
(800) 544-8888, (801) 534-1910

PERFORMANCE

	3yr Annual	5yr Annual	10yr Annual	Bull	Bear
Return (%)	10.7	10.3	10.7	41.2	3.4
Differ from Category (+/-)	0.5 av	0.5 abv av	-0.2 blw av	1.8 av	0.5 abv av

Total Risk	Standard Deviation	Category Risk	Risk Index	Avg Mat
low	3.5%	av	1.2	8.9 yrs

	1993	1992	1991	1990	1989	1988	1987	1986	1985	1984
Return (%)	11.9	6.0	14.4	7.5	11.7	7.2	1.9	13.0	20.7	13.5
Differ from category (+/-). . .	2.7	-0.6	-0.2	0.6	0.4	-0.4	-0.6	-0.8	0.6	1.2

PER SHARE DATA

	1993	1992	1991	1990	1989	1988	1987	1986	1985	1984
Dividends, Net Income ($).	0.75	0.77	0.76	0.81	0.88	0.87	1.60	0.66	0.74	1.10
Distrib'ns, Cap Gain ($) . . .	0.09	0.05	0.00	0.00	0.00	0.00	0.10	0.21	0.00	0.00
Net Asset Value ($)	10.78	10.41	10.62	10.00	10.10	9.87	10.04	11.55	11.03	9.83
Expense Ratio (%)	0.61	0.63	0.66	0.72	0.62	0.87	0.86	0.75	0.79	0.73
Net Income to Assets (%) .	7.44	7.45	8.05	8.57	9.35	8.76	9.17	9.27	10.73	11.62
Portfolio Turnover (%).	51	80	73	82	101	59	67	101	68	80
Total Assets (Millions $). .	1,838	1,235	878	661	528	504	370	367	244	151

PORTFOLIO (as of 4/30/93)

Portfolio Manager: Michael Gray - 1987

Investm't Category: General Bond

Cap Gain	Asset Allocation
Cap & Income	Fund of Funds
✔ Income	Index
	Sector
✔ Domestic	Small Cap
✔ Foreign	Socially Conscious
Country/Region	State Specific

Portfolio: stocks 0% bonds 96%
convertibles 0% other 0% cash 4%

Largest Holdings: U.S. government & agencies 35%, corporate 33%

Unrealized Net Capital Gains: 4% of portfolio value

SHAREHOLDER INFORMATION

Minimum Investment
Initial: $2,500   Subsequent: $250

Minimum IRA Investment
Initial: $500   Subsequent: $100

Maximum Fees
Load: none   12b-1: none
Other: none

Distributions
Income: monthly   Capital Gains: Jun, Dec

Exchange Options
Number Per Year: 4   Fee: none
Telephone: yes (money market fund available)

Services
IRA, other pension, auto exchange, auto invest, auto withdraw

Fidelity Investment Grade (FBNDX)

General Bond

82 Devonshire St.
Boston, MA 02109
(800) 544-8888, (801) 534-1910

PERFORMANCE

	3yr Annual	5yr Annual	10yr Annual	Bull	Bear
Return (%)	14.3	12.3	11.5	54.0	3.0
Differ from Category (+/-)	4.1 high	2.5 high	0.6 high	14.6 high	0.1 av

Total Risk	Standard Deviation	Category Risk	Risk Index	Avg Mat
low	3.8%	abv av	1.3	13.0 yrs

	1993	1992	1991	1990	1989	1988	1987	1986	1985	1984
Return (%)	16.1	8.3	18.9	6.0	13.0	7.8	0.1	13.5	21.1	11.7
Differ from category (+/-) . . .	6.9	1.6	4.3	-0.8	1.7	0.2	-2.4	-0.4	1.0	-0.6

PER SHARE DATA

	1993	1992	1991	1990	1989	1988	1987	1986	1985	1984
Dividends, Net Income ($) .	0.55	0.55	0.59	0.60	0.60	0.59	0.62	0.69	0.76	0.78
Distrib'ns, Cap Gain ($) . . .	0.00	0.00	0.00	0.00	0.00	0.00	0.00	0.00	0.00	0.00
Net Asset Value ($)	7.89	7.30	7.28	6.67	6.88	6.65	6.73	7.36	7.12	6.58
Expense Ratio (%)	0.68	0.70	0.67	0.70	0.66	0.76	0.68	0.67	0.79	0.76
Net Income to Assets (%) . .	7.74	8.29	8.84	8.76	8.91	8.95	9.17	10.53	12.22	11.40
Portfolio Turnover (%)	74	77	101	103	128	118	127	243	164	164
Total Assets (Millions $) . .	1,044	943	455	359	334	316	384	250	166	134

PORTFOLIO (as of 4/30/93)

Portfolio Manager: Michael Gray - 1987

Investm't Category: General Bond

Cap Gain	Asset Allocation
Cap & Income	Fund of Funds
✔ Income	Index
	Sector
✔ Domestic	Small Cap
✔ Foreign	Socially Conscious
Country/Region	State Specific

Portfolio: stocks 0% bonds 91%
convertibles 3% other 0% cash 6%

Largest Holdings: corporate 37%, U.S. government & agencies 27%

Unrealized Net Capital Gains: 5% of portfolio value

SHAREHOLDER INFORMATION

Minimum Investment
Initial: $2,500   Subsequent: $250

Minimum IRA Investment
Initial: $500   Subsequent: $100

Maximum Fees
Load: none   12b-1: none
Other: none

Distributions
Income: monthly   Capital Gains: Jun, Dec

Exchange Options
Number Per Year: 4   Fee: none
Telephone: yes (money market fund available)

Services
IRA, other pension, auto exchange, auto invest, auto withdraw

Fidelity Japan (FJAPX)

International Stock

82 Devonshire St.
Boston, MA 02109
(800) 544-8888, (801) 534-1910

PERFORMANCE

	3yr Annual	5yr Annual	10yr Annual	Bull	Bear
Return (%)	na	na	na	na	na
Differ from Category (+/-)	na	na	na	na	na

Total Risk	Standard Deviation	Category Risk	Risk Index	Beta
na	na	na	na	na

	1993	1992	1991	1990	1989	1988	1987	1986	1985	1984
Return (%)	20.4	—	—	—	—	—	—	—	—	—
Differ from category (+/-). .	-18.1	—	—	—	—	—	—	—	—	—

PER SHARE DATA

	1993	1992	1991	1990	1989	1988	1987	1986	1985	1984
Dividends, Net Income ($).	0.00	—	—	—	—	—	—	—	—	—
Distrib'ns, Cap Gain ($) . . .	0.39	—	—	—	—	—	—	—	—	—
Net Asset Value ($)	11.61	—	—	—	—	—	—	—	—	—
Expense Ratio (%)	1.71	—	—	—	—	—	—	—	—	—
Net Income to Assets (%) .	-0.77	—	—	—	—	—	—	—	—	—
Portfolio Turnover (%).	257	—	—	—	—	—	—	—	—	—
Total Assets (Millions $). . . .	97	—	—	—	—	—	—	—	—	—

PORTFOLIO (as of 10/31/93)

Portfolio Manager: John R. Hickling - 1993

Investm't Category: International Stock

✔ Cap Gain	Asset Allocation
Cap & Income	Fund of Funds
Income	Index
	Sector
Domestic	Small Cap
✔ Foreign	Socially Conscious
✔ Country/Region	State Specific

Portfolio: stocks 96% bonds 0%
convertibles 1% other 1% cash 2%

Largest Holdings: Japan 90%, Korea 6%

Unrealized Net Capital Gains: 1% of portfolio value

SHAREHOLDER INFORMATION

Minimum Investment
Initial: $2,500   Subsequent: $250

Minimum IRA Investment
Initial: $500   Subsequent: $250

Maximum Fees
Load: 3.00% front   12b-1: none
Other: none

Distributions
Income: Dec   Capital Gains: Dec

Exchange Options
Number Per Year: 4   Fee: none
Telephone: yes (money market fund available)

Services
IRA, other pension, auto exchange, auto invest, auto withdraw

Fidelity Latin America
(FLATX)

82 Devonshire St.
Boston, MA 02109
(800) 544-8888, (801) 534-1910

International Stock

fund in existence since 4/19/93

PERFORMANCE

	3yr Annual	5yr Annual	10yr Annual	Bull	Bear
Return (%)	na	na	na	na	na
Differ from Category (+/-)	na	na	na	na	na

Total Risk	Standard Deviation	Category Risk	Risk Index	Beta
na	na	na	na	na

	1993	1992	1991	1990	1989	1988	1987	1986	1985	1984
Return (%)	—	—	—	—	—	—	—	—	—	—
Differ from category (+/-) ...	—	—	—	—	—	—	—	—	—	—

PER SHARE DATA

	1993	1992	1991	1990	1989	1988	1987	1986	1985	1984
Dividends, Net Income ($) .	0.05	—	—	—	—	—	—	—	—	—
Distrib'ns, Cap Gain ($) ...	0.05	—	—	—	—	—	—	—	—	—
Net Asset Value ($)	16.10	—	—	—	—	—	—	—	—	—
Expense Ratio (%)........	1.94	—	—	—	—	—	—	—	—	—
Net Income to Assets (%)..	1.21	—	—	—	—	—	—	—	—	—
Portfolio Turnover (%).....	72	—	—	—	—	—	—	—	—	—
Total Assets (Millions $) ...	718	—	—	—	—	—	—	—	—	—

PORTFOLIO (as of 10/31/93)

Portfolio Manager: Patti Satterthwaite - 1993

Investm't Category: International Stock

Cap Gain	Asset Allocation
✔ Cap & Income	Fund of Funds
Income	Index
	Sector
✔ Domestic	Small Cap
✔ Foreign	Socially Conscious
Country/Region	State Specific

Portfolio: stocks 74%   bonds 19%
convertibles 0%   other 2%   cash 5%

Largest Holdings: Mexico 41%, Brazil 15%

Unrealized Net Capital Gains: 9% of portfolio value

SHAREHOLDER INFORMATION

Minimum Investment
Initial: $2,500   Subsequent: $250

Minimum IRA Investment
Initial: $500   Subsequent: $250

Maximum Fees
Load: 3.00% front   12b-1: none
Other: 1.50% redemption fee (90 days)

Distributions
Income: Dec   Capital Gains: Dec

Exchange Options
Number Per Year: 4   Fee: none
Telephone: yes (money market fund available)

Services
IRA, other pension, auto exchange, auto invest, auto withdraw

Fidelity Limited Term Muni (FLTMX)

82 Devonshire St.
Boston, MA 02109
(800) 544-8888, (801) 534-1910

Tax-Exempt Bond

PERFORMANCE

	3yr Annual	5yr Annual	10yr Annual	Bull	Bear
Return (%)	10.5	9.2	9.7	38.8	3.9
Differ from Category (+/-)	0.2 blw av	0.0 blw av	0.1 av	-1.3 blw av	1.6 high

Total Risk	Standard Deviation	Category Risk	Risk Index	Avg Mat
low	3.4%	low	0.8	10.1 yrs

	1993	1992	1991	1990	1989	1988	1987	1986	1985	1984
Return (%)	12.2	8.1	11.1	6.9	7.8	8.2	1.1	15.1	17.3	9.8
Differ from category (+/-)	0.6	-0.2	-0.2	0.6	-1.2	-1.9	2.3	-1.3	0.0	1.5

PER SHARE DATA

	1993	1992	1991	1990	1989	1988	1987	1986	1985	1984
Dividends, Net Income ($)	0.51	0.57	0.60	0.61	0.61	0.60	0.57	0.61	0.63	0.63
Distrib'ns, Cap Gain ($)	0.23	0.10	0.15	0.05	0.00	0.00	0.00	0.00	0.00	0.00
Net Asset Value ($)	9.99	9.60	9.52	9.27	9.31	9.23	9.10	9.58	8.88	8.15
Expense Ratio (%)	0.60	0.64	0.68	0.67	0.66	0.67	0.74	0.68	0.71	0.79
Net Income to Assets (%)	5.26	5.94	6.41	6.63	6.70	6.51	6.29	6.55	7.41	7.93
Portfolio Turnover (%)	109	50	42	72	55	30	59	30	73	152
Total Assets (Millions $)	1,192	976	696	468	443	441	459	580	315	214

PORTFOLIO (as of 6/30/93)

Portfolio Manager: David Murphy - 1989

Investm't Category: Tax-Exempt Bond

Cap Gain	Asset Allocation
Cap & Income	Fund of Funds
✔ Income	Index
	Sector
✔ Domestic	Small Cap
Foreign	Socially Conscious
Country/Region	State Specific

Portfolio: stocks 0% bonds 100%
convertibles 0% other 0% cash 0%

Largest Holdings: general obligation 23%

Unrealized Net Capital Gains: 5% of portfolio value

SHAREHOLDER INFORMATION

Minimum Investment
Initial: $2,500   Subsequent: $250

Minimum IRA Investment
Initial: na   Subsequent: na

Maximum Fees
Load: none   12b-1: none
Other: none

Distributions
Income: monthly   Capital Gains: Feb, Dec

Exchange Options
Number Per Year: 4   Fee: none
Telephone: yes (money market fund available)

Services
auto exchange, auto invest, auto withdraw

Fidelity Low-Priced Stock (FLPSX)

82 Devonshire St.
Boston, MA 02109
(800) 544-8888, (801) 534-1910

Growth

PERFORMANCE

	3yr Annual	5yr Annual	10yr Annual	Bull	Bear
Return (%)	31.3	na	na	142.3	-6.5
Differ from Category (+/-)	12.1 high	na	na	57.6 high	5.9 high

Total Risk	Standard Deviation	Category Risk	Risk Index	Beta
abv av	12.4%	av	1.2	0.8

	1993	1992	1991	1990	1989	1988	1987	1986	1985	1984
Return (%)	20.2	28.9	46.2	0.0	—	—	—	—	—	—
Differ from category (+/-) ...	7.0	17.9	10.8	6.1	—	—	—	—	—	—

PER SHARE DATA

	1993	1992	1991	1990	1989	1988	1987	1986	1985	1984
Dividends, Net Income ($) .	0.15	0.10	0.15	0.14	—	—	—	—	—	—
Distrib'ns, Cap Gain ($) ...	1.62	0.68	0.60	0.25	—	—	—	—	—	—
Net Asset Value ($)	17.30	15.96	13.05	9.47	—	—	—	—	—	—
Expense Ratio (%)........	1.12	1.20	1.36	1.92	—	—	—	—	—	—
Net Income to Assets (%)..	1.00	1.27	2.14	3.77	—	—	—	—	—	—
Portfolio Turnover (%).....	47	82	84	126	—	—	—	—	—	—
Total Assets (Millions $) ..	2,030	928	256	116	—	—	—	—	—	—

PORTFOLIO (as of 1/31/93)

Portfolio Manager: Joel Tillinghast - 1989

Investm't Category: Growth
- ✔ Cap Gain
- Cap & Income
- Income
- ✔ Domestic
- ✔ Foreign
- Country/Region
- Asset Allocation
- Fund of Funds
- Index
- Sector
- ✔ Small Cap
- Socially Conscious
- State Specific

Portfolio: stocks 53% bonds 0%
convertibles 0% other 0% cash 46%

Largest Holdings: finance 9%, technology 9%

Unrealized Net Capital Gains: 11% of portfolio value

SHAREHOLDER INFORMATION

Minimum Investment
Initial: $2,500   Subsequent: $250

Minimum IRA Investment
Initial: $500   Subsequent: $250

Maximum Fees
Load: 3.00% front   12b-1: none
Other: 1.50% redemption fee (90 days)

Distributions
Income: Sep, Dec   Capital Gains: Sep, Dec

Exchange Options
Number Per Year: 4   Fee: none
Telephone: yes (money market fund available)

Services
IRA, other pension, auto exchange, auto invest, auto withdraw

Fidelity Magellan (FMAGX)

Growth

82 Devonshire St.
Boston, MA 02109
(800) 544-8888, (801) 534-1910

PERFORMANCE

	3yr Annual	5yr Annual	10yr Annual	Bull	Bear
Return (%)	23.4	19.3	18.4	106.0	-12.8
Differ from Category (+/-)	4.2 abv av	4.7 high	5.8 high	21.3 high	-0.4 av

Total Risk	Standard Deviation	Category Risk	Risk Index	Beta
abv av	12.0%	av	1.1	1.0

	1993	1992	1991	1990	1989	1988	1987	1986	1985	1984
Return (%).............	24.6	7.0	41.0	-4.5	34.5	22.7	1.0	23.7	43.1	2.0
Differ from category (+/-)..	11.4	-4.0	5.6	1.6	8.7	5.0	-0.2	9.2	13.8	2.0

PER SHARE DATA

	1993	1992	1991	1990	1989	1988	1987	1986	1985	1984
Dividends, Net Income ($).	0.75	1.25	1.30	0.82	1.24	0.89	0.72	0.46	0.64	0.37
Distrib'ns, Cap Gain ($) ...	6.50	8.82	5.43	2.42	3.82	0.00	9.02	6.84	1.78	3.69
Net Asset Value ($)	70.85	63.01	68.61	53.93	59.85	48.32	40.10	48.69	45.21	33.69
Expense Ratio (%)	1.00	1.05	1.06	1.03	1.08	1.14	1.08	1.08	1.12	1.04
Net Income to Assets (%) .	2.11	1.57	2.47	2.54	2.13	1.33	1.18	1.95	2.79	1.47
Portfolio Turnover (%).....	155	172	135	82	87	101	96	96	126	85
Total Assets (Millions $).	31,088	19,825	14,807	13,162	9,626	8,438	9,889	6,086	2,363	1,611

PORTFOLIO (as of 9/30/93)

Portfolio Manager: Jeff Vinik - 1992

Investm't Category: Growth

✔ Cap Gain	Asset Allocation
Cap & Income	Fund of Funds
Income	Index
	Sector
✔ Domestic	Small Cap
✔ Foreign	Socially Conscious
Country/Region	State Specific

Portfolio: stocks 93% bonds 2%
convertibles 2% other 0% cash 3%

Largest Holdings: technology 22%, energy 16%

Unrealized Net Capital Gains: 20% of portfolio value

SHAREHOLDER INFORMATION

Minimum Investment
Initial: $2,500   Subsequent: $250

Minimum IRA Investment
Initial: $500   Subsequent: $250

Maximum Fees
Load: 3.00% front   12b-1: none
Other: none

Distributions
Income: Dec   Capital Gains: Dec

Exchange Options
Number Per Year: 4   Fee: none
Telephone: yes (money market fund available)

Services
IRA, other pension, auto exchange, auto invest, auto withdraw

Fidelity Market Index
(FSMKX)

Growth & Income

82 Devonshire St.
Boston, MA 02109
(800) 544-8888, (801) 534-1910

PERFORMANCE

	3yr Annual	5yr Annual	10yr Annual	Bull	Bear
Return (%)	15.3	na	na	66.9	na
Differ from Category (+/-)	-1.1 av	na	na	-3.2 av	na

Total Risk	Standard Deviation	Category Risk	Risk Index	Beta
av	10.5%	abv av	1.2	1.0

	1993	1992	1991	1990	1989	1988	1987	1986	1985	1984
Return (%)	9.6	7.3	30.3	—	—	—	—	—	—	—
Differ from category (+/-) ..	-3.0	-2.7	2.6	—	—	—	—	—	—	—

PER SHARE DATA

	1993	1992	1991	1990	1989	1988	1987	1986	1985	1984
Dividends, Net Income ($) .	0.80	0.81	0.82	—	—	—	—	—	—	—
Distrib'ns, Cap Gain ($) ...	0.18	0.00	0.07	—	—	—	—	—	—	—
Net Asset Value ($)	34.60	32.49	31.07	—	—	—	—	—	—	—
Expense Ratio (%)........	0.44	0.35	0.28	—	—	—	—	—	—	—
Net Income to Assets (%)..	2.54	2.84	3.52	—	—	—	—	—	—	—
Portfolio Turnover (%)	0	1	1	—	—	—	—	—	—	—
Total Assets (Millions $) ...	300	230	112	—	—	—	—	—	—	—

PORTFOLIO (as of 10/1/93)

Portfolio Manager: Jennifer Farrelly - 1994

Investm't Category: Growth & Income

Cap Gain	Asset Allocation
✔ Cap & Income	Fund of Funds
Income	✔ Index
	Sector
✔ Domestic	Small Cap
Foreign	Socially Conscious
Country/Region	State Specific

Portfolio: stocks 96% bonds 0%
convertibles 0% other 0% cash 4%

Largest Holdings: S&P 500 Composite Stock Price Index 96%

Unrealized Net Capital Gains: 19% of portfolio value

SHAREHOLDER INFORMATION

Minimum Investment
Initial: $2,500   Subsequent: $250

Minimum IRA Investment
Initial: $500   Subsequent: $100

Maximum Fees
Load: 0.50% redemption   12b-1: none
Other: redemption fee applies for 6 mos

Distributions
Income: quarterly   Capital Gains: Jun, Dec

Exchange Options
Number Per Year: 4   Fee: none
Telephone: yes (money market fund available)

Services
IRA, other pension, auto exchange, auto invest, auto withdraw

Fidelity Mass Tax-Free High Yield (FDMMX)

82 Devonshire St.
Boston, MA 02109
(800) 544-8888, (801) 534-1910

Tax-Exempt Bond

PERFORMANCE

	3yr Annual	5yr Annual	10yr Annual	Bull	Bear
Return (%)	11.1	10.0	10.3	42.6	3.3
Differ from Category (+/-)	0.8 av	0.8 abv av	0.6 av	2.5 av	1.0 abv av

Total Risk	Standard Deviation	Category Risk	Risk Index	Avg Mat
low	3.5%	blw av	0.8	20.3 yrs

	1993	1992	1991	1990	1989	1988	1987	1986	1985	1984
Return (%)	12.9	9.2	11.3	7.3	9.2	10.6	-1.2	16.8	19.6	8.4
Differ from category (+/-)	1.3	0.8	0.0	1.0	0.2	0.5	0.0	0.4	2.3	0.1

PER SHARE DATA

	1993	1992	1991	1990	1989	1988	1987	1986	1985	1984
Dividends, Net Income ($)	0.71	0.72	0.75	0.79	0.80	0.80	0.80	0.82	0.90	0.94
Distrib'ns, Cap Gain ($)	0.25	0.07	0.07	0.10	0.00	0.00	0.02	0.00	0.00	0.00
Net Asset Value ($)	12.13	11.64	11.41	11.04	11.16	10.98	10.68	11.66	10.72	9.78
Expense Ratio (%)	0.55	0.57	0.56	0.57	0.56	0.61	0.64	0.64	0.76	0.89
Net Income to Assets (%)	6.08	6.43	7.05	7.20	7.33	7.56	6.85	7.82	9.01	10.02
Portfolio Turnover (%)	50	18	29	31	26	25	36	13	12	102
Total Assets (Millions $)	1,378	1,235	842	737	663	580	642	500	203	56

PORTFOLIO (as of 7/31/93)

Portfolio Manager: Guy Wickwire - 1983

Investm't Category: Tax-Exempt Bond
Cap Gain	Asset Allocation
Cap & Income	Fund of Funds
✔ Income	Index
	Sector
✔ Domestic	Small Cap
Foreign	Socially Conscious
Country/Region	✔ State Specific

Portfolio:	stocks 0%	bonds 100%
convertibles 0%	other 0%	cash 0%

Largest Holdings: general obligation 15%

Unrealized Net Capital Gains: 7% of portfolio value

SHAREHOLDER INFORMATION

Minimum Investment
Initial: $2,500   Subsequent: $250

Minimum IRA Investment
Initial: na   Subsequent: na

Maximum Fees
Load: none   12b-1: none
Other: none

Distributions
Income: monthly   Capital Gains: Sep, Dec

Exchange Options
Number Per Year: 4   Fee: none
Telephone: yes (money market fund available)

Services
auto exchange, auto invest, auto withdraw

Fidelity Michigan Tax-Free High Yield

82 Devonshire St.
Boston, MA 02109
(800) 544-8888, (801) 534-1910

(FMHTX) *Tax-Exempt Bond*

PERFORMANCE

	3yr Annual	5yr Annual	10yr Annual	Bull	Bear
Return (%)	11.7	10.1	na	44.0	2.0
Differ from Category (+/-)	1.4 high	0.8 abv av	na	3.9 abv av	-0.3 blw av

Total Risk	Standard Deviation	Category Risk	Risk Index	Avg Mat
blw av	4.1%	av	1.0	20.4 yrs

	1993	1992	1991	1990	1989	1988	1987	1986	1985	1984
Return (%)	13.8	9.5	12.0	5.1	10.2	13.0	-2.8	19.0	—	—
Differ from category (+/-) . . .	2.2	1.2	0.6	-1.2	1.2	2.9	-1.6	2.6	—	—

PER SHARE DATA

	1993	1992	1991	1990	1989	1988	1987	1986	1985	1984
Dividends, Net Income ($) .	0.71	0.73	0.74	0.75	0.76	0.75	0.76	0.79	—	—
Distrib'ns, Cap Gain ($) . . .	0.23	0.01	0.00	0.00	0.00	0.00	0.03	0.00	—	—
Net Asset Value ($)	12.34	11.71	11.41	10.89	11.10	10.79	10.25	11.38	—	—
Expense Ratio (%).	0.60	0.61	0.62	0.64	0.68	0.75	0.72	0.60	—	—
Net Income to Assets (%). .	5.94	6.36	6.73	6.98	6.92	7.12	7.25	7.03	—	—
Portfolio Turnover (%)	12	15	12	18	19	24	44	24	—	—
Total Assets (Millions $) . . .	560	464	379	279	234	171	128	127	—	—

PORTFOLIO (as of 6/30/93)

Portfolio Manager: Peter Allegrini - 1985

Investm't Category: Tax-Exempt Bond

Cap Gain	Asset Allocation
Cap & Income	Fund of Funds
✔ Income	Index
	Sector
✔ Domestic	Small Cap
Foreign	Socially Conscious
Country/Region	✔ State Specific

Portfolio: stocks 0% bonds 100%
convertibles 0% other 0% cash 0%

Largest Holdings: general obligation 16%

Unrealized Net Capital Gains: 9% of portfolio value

SHAREHOLDER INFORMATION

Minimum Investment
Initial: $2,500   Subsequent: $250

Minimum IRA Investment
Initial: na   Subsequent: na

Maximum Fees
Load: none   12b-1: none
Other: none

Distributions
Income: monthly   Capital Gains: Feb, Dec

Exchange Options
Number Per Year: 4   Fee: none
Telephone: yes (money market fund available)

Services
auto exchange, auto invest, auto withdraw

Fidelity Minnesota Tax-Free (FIMIX)

82 Devonshire St.
Boston, MA 02109
(800) 544-8888, (801) 534-1910

Tax-Exempt Bond

PERFORMANCE

	3yr Annual	5yr Annual	10yr Annual	Bull	Bear
Return (%)	9.4	8.9	na	36.4	3.1
Differ from Category (+/-)	-0.8 blw av	-0.3 blw av	na	-3.7 blw av	0.8 abv av

Total Risk	Standard Deviation	Category Risk	Risk Index	Avg Mat
low	3.5%	blw av	0.8	21.8 yrs

	1993	1992	1991	1990	1989	1988	1987	1986	1985	1984
Return (%)	12.4	7.6	8.4	7.2	9.2	12.6	-3.8	17.0	—	—
Differ from category (+/-)	0.8	-0.6	-2.9	0.8	0.2	2.5	-2.6	0.6	—	—

PER SHARE DATA

	1993	1992	1991	1990	1989	1988	1987	1986	1985	1984
Dividends, Net Income ($)	0.64	0.67	0.68	0.69	0.71	0.71	0.72	0.77	—	—
Distrib'ns, Cap Gain ($)	0.00	0.00	0.00	0.00	0.00	0.00	0.03	0.00	—	—
Net Asset Value ($)	11.52	10.85	10.73	10.55	10.52	10.31	9.82	10.99	—	—
Expense Ratio (%)	0.63	0.67	0.72	0.76	0.80	0.82	0.79	0.60	—	—
Net Income to Assets (%)	5.85	6.25	6.47	6.72	6.84	7.06	7.04	7.05	—	—
Portfolio Turnover (%)	31	12	14	29	25	31	63	23	—	—
Total Assets (Millions $)	339	281	222	167	131	100	79	93	—	—

PORTFOLIO (as of 6/30/93)

Portfolio Manager: Steve Harvey - 1993

Investm't Category: Tax-Exempt Bond
Cap Gain	Asset Allocation
Cap & Income	Fund of Funds
✔ Income	Index
	Sector
✔ Domestic	Small Cap
Foreign	Socially Conscious
Country/Region	✔ State Specific

Portfolio: stocks 0%   bonds 100%
convertibles 0%   other 0%   cash 0%

Largest Holdings: general obligation 0%

Unrealized Net Capital Gains: 6% of portfolio value

SHAREHOLDER INFORMATION

Minimum Investment
Initial: $2,500   Subsequent: $250

Minimum IRA Investment
Initial: na   Subsequent: na

Maximum Fees
Load: none   12b-1: none
Other: none

Distributions
Income: monthly   Capital Gains: Feb, Dec

Exchange Options
Number Per Year: 4   Fee: none
Telephone: yes (money market fund available)

Services
auto exchange, auto invest, auto withdraw

Fidelity Mortgage Securities (FMSFX)

82 Devonshire St.
Boston, MA 02109
(800) 544-8888, (801) 534-1910

Mortgage-Backed Bond

PERFORMANCE

	3yr Annual	5yr Annual	10yr Annual	Bull	Bear
Return (%)	8.5	9.8	na	34.2	5.0
Differ from Category (+/-)	-0.6 low	-0.1 blw av	na	-2.5 low	0.4 av

Total Risk	Standard Deviation	Category Risk	Risk Index	Avg Mat
low	2.2%	low	0.8	5.3 yrs

	1993	1992	1991	1990	1989	1988	1987	1986	1985	1984
Return (%)	6.6	5.4	13.6	10.3	13.6	6.6	2.6	11.2	19.6	—
Differ from category (+/-) ..	-0.2	-0.6	-0.8	0.8	1.3	-0.4	0.5	0.0	0.3	—

PER SHARE DATA

	1993	1992	1991	1990	1989	1988	1987	1986	1985	1984
Dividends, Net Income ($) .	0.63	0.75	0.82	0.83	0.84	0.82	0.90	0.99	1.15	—
Distrib'ns, Cap Gain ($) ...	0.07	0.00	0.00	0.00	0.00	0.00	0.00	0.02	0.00	—
Net Asset Value ($)	10.73	10.73	10.91	10.38	10.21	9.77	9.94	10.58	10.48	—
Expense Ratio (%)........	0.78	0.80	0.82	0.82	0.88	0.90	0.80	0.75	0.75	—
Net Income to Assets (%)..	7.25	7.57	8.39	8.78	8.72	8.96	8.79	9.13	11.53	—
Portfolio Turnover (%)	280	146	209	110	271	245	160	106	72	—
Total Assets (Millions $) ...	377	441	410	388	421	485	603	652	140	—

PORTFOLIO (as of 1/31/93)

Portfolio Manager: Kevin Grant - 1993

Investm't Category: Mortgage-Backed Bond

Cap Gain	Asset Allocation
Cap & Income	Fund of Funds
✔ Income	Index
	Sector
✔ Domestic	Small Cap
✔ Foreign	Socially Conscious
Country/Region	State Specific

Portfolio: stocks 0%   bonds 78%
convertibles 0%   other 1%   cash 21%

Largest Holdings: mortgage-backed 78%

Unrealized Net Capital Gains: 1% of portfolio value

SHAREHOLDER INFORMATION

Minimum Investment
Initial: $2,500   Subsequent: $250

Minimum IRA Investment
Initial: $500   Subsequent: $250

Maximum Fees
Load: none   12b-1: none
Other: none

Distributions
Income: monthly   Capital Gains: Sep, Dec

Exchange Options
Number Per Year: 4   Fee: none
Telephone: yes (money market fund available)

Services
IRA, other pension, auto exchange, auto invest, auto withdraw

Fidelity Muni Bond
(FMBDX)

Tax-Exempt Bond

82 Devonshire St.
Boston, MA 02109
(800) 544-8888, (801) 534-1910

PERFORMANCE

	3yr Annual	5yr Annual	10yr Annual	Bull	Bear
Return (%)	11.3	10.0	10.8	43.0	3.0
Differ from Category (+/-)	1.0 abv av	0.8 abv av	1.2 abv av	2.9 abv av	0.6 abv av

Total Risk	Standard Deviation	Category Risk	Risk Index	Avg Mat
blw av	4.4%	av	1.1	21.4 yrs

	1993	1992	1991	1990	1989	1988	1987	1986	1985	1984
Return (%)	13.1	8.9	11.9	6.8	9.5	12.2	-1.5	19.5	20.0	9.0
Differ from category (+/-). . .	1.5	0.6	0.6	0.5	0.5	2.1	-0.3	3.1	2.7	0.6

PER SHARE DATA

	1993	1992	1991	1990	1989	1988	1987	1986	1985	1984
Dividends, Net Income ($).	0.48	0.51	0.52	0.53	0.55	0.55	0.55	0.55	0.57	0.59
Distrib'ns, Cap Gain ($) . . .	0.40	0.18	0.07	0.00	0.00	0.00	0.00	0.00	0.00	0.00
Net Asset Value ($)	8.69	8.50	8.47	8.13	8.13	7.95	7.60	8.28	7.42	6.70
Expense Ratio (%)	0.49	0.49	0.50	0.50	0.50	0.51	0.57	0.51	0.46	0.53
Net Income to Assets (%) .	5.67	6.11	6.35	6.71	6.90	7.11	7.03	6.90	8.06	8.98
Portfolio Turnover (%).	79	53	33	49	64	46	72	72	145	93
Total Assets (Millions $). .	1,273	1,192	1,163	1,071	1,053	984	903	1,141	906	741

PORTFOLIO (as of 6/30/93)

Portfolio Manager: Gary Swayze - 1985

Investm't Category: Tax-Exempt Bond

Cap Gain	Asset Allocation
Cap & Income	Fund of Funds
✔ Income	Index
	Sector
✔ Domestic	Small Cap
Foreign	Socially Conscious
Country/Region	State Specific

Portfolio: stocks 0%   bonds 100%
convertibles 0%   other 0%   cash 0%

Largest Holdings: general obligation 6%

Unrealized Net Capital Gains: 7% of portfolio value

SHAREHOLDER INFORMATION

Minimum Investment
Initial: $2,500   Subsequent: $250

Minimum IRA Investment
Initial: na   Subsequent: na

Maximum Fees
Load: none   12b-1: none
Other: none

Distributions
Income: monthly   Capital Gains: Feb, Dec

Exchange Options
Number Per Year: 4   Fee: none
Telephone: yes (money market fund available)

Services
auto exchange, auto invest, auto withdraw

Fidelity New Millenium
(FMILX)

Aggressive Growth

82 Devonshire St.
Boston, MA 02109
(800) 544-8888, (801) 534-1910

PERFORMANCE

	3yr Annual	5yr Annual	10yr Annual	Bull	Bear
Return (%)	na	na	na	na	na
Differ from Category (+/-)	na	na	na	na	na

Total Risk	Standard Deviation	Category Risk	Risk Index	Beta
na	na	na	na	na

	1993	1992	1991	1990	1989	1988	1987	1986	1985	1984
Return (%)	24.6	—	—	—	—	—	—	—	—	—
Differ from category (+/-) . . .	5.6	—	—	—	—	—	—	—	—	—

PER SHARE DATA

	1993	1992	1991	1990	1989	1988	1987	1986	1985	1984
Dividends, Net Income ($) .	0.00	—	—	—	—	—	—	—	—	—
Distrib'ns, Cap Gain ($) . . .	0.25	—	—	—	—	—	—	—	—	—
Net Asset Value ($)	12.30	—	—	—	—	—	—	—	—	—
Expense Ratio (%).	1.77	—	—	—	—	—	—	—	—	—
Net Income to Assets (%) .	-0.29	—	—	—	—	—	—	—	—	—
Portfolio Turnover (%)	297	—	—	—	—	—	—	—	—	—
Total Assets (Millions $) . . .	271	—	—	—	—	—	—	—	—	—

PORTFOLIO (as of 5/31/93)

Portfolio Manager: Neal Miller - 1992

Investm't Category: Aggressive Growth
- ✔ Cap Gain
- Cap & Income
- Income
- ✔ Domestic
- ✔ Foreign
- Country/Region
- Asset Allocation
- Fund of Funds
- Index
- Sector
- ✔ Small Cap
- Socially Conscious
- State Specific

Portfolio: stocks 93%   bonds 0%
convertibles 0%   other 0%   cash 7%

Largest Holdings: technology 23%, durable 9%

Unrealized Net Capital Gains: 6% of portfolio value

SHAREHOLDER INFORMATION

Minimum Investment
Initial: $2,500   Subsequent: $250

Minimum IRA Investment
Initial: $500   Subsequent: $250

Maximum Fees
Load: 3.00% front   12b-1: none
Other: none

Distributions
Income: Dec   Capital Gains: Dec

Exchange Options
Number Per Year: 4   Fee: none
Telephone: yes (money market fund available)

Services
IRA, other pension, auto exchange, auto invest, auto withdraw

Fidelity NY Tax-Free High Yield (FTFMX)

Tax-Exempt Bond

82 Devonshire St.
Boston, MA 02109
(800) 544-8888, (801) 534-1910

PERFORMANCE

	3yr Annual	5yr Annual	10yr Annual	Bull	Bear
Return (%)	11.7	9.8	na	43.2	2.3
Differ from Category (+/-)	1.4 high	0.6 av	na	3.1 abv av	0.0 av

Total Risk	Standard Deviation	Category Risk	Risk Index	Avg Mat
low	4.0%	blw av	1.0	20.9 yrs

	1993	1992	1991	1990	1989	1988	1987	1986	1985	1984
Return (%)	12.8	8.9	13.3	5.0	9.2	11.9	-2.4	16.7	20.8	—
Differ from category (+/-)	1.2	0.6	2.0	-1.3	0.2	1.8	-1.2	0.3	3.5	—

PER SHARE DATA

	1993	1992	1991	1990	1989	1988	1987	1986	1985	1984
Dividends, Net Income ($)	0.72	0.77	0.77	0.79	0.81	0.78	0.80	0.82	0.92	—
Distrib'ns, Cap Gain ($)	0.46	0.00	0.00	0.00	0.00	0.00	0.10	0.17	0.00	—
Net Asset Value ($)	12.97	12.57	12.28	11.56	11.78	11.55	11.06	12.26	11.41	—
Expense Ratio (%)	0.61	0.61	0.59	0.61	0.63	0.67	0.60	0.67	1.00	—
Net Income to Assets (%)	6.08	6.52	6.81	6.87	6.99	7.10	6.76	7.61	9.05	—
Portfolio Turnover (%)	45	30	45	34	49	64	51	62	8	—
Total Assets (Millions $)	482	412	386	381	368	312	352	202	28	—

PORTFOLIO (as of 7/31/93)

Portfolio Manager: Norm Lind - 1993

Investm't Category: Tax-Exempt Bond

Cap Gain	Asset Allocation
Cap & Income	Fund of Funds
✔ Income	Index
	Sector
✔ Domestic	Small Cap
Foreign	Socially Conscious
Country/Region	✔ State Specific

Portfolio: stocks 0%   bonds 100%
convertibles 0%   other 0%   cash 0%

Largest Holdings: general obligation 0%

Unrealized Net Capital Gains: 6% of portfolio value

SHAREHOLDER INFORMATION

Minimum Investment
Initial: $2,500   Subsequent: $250

Minimum IRA Investment
Initial: na   Subsequent: na

Maximum Fees
Load: none   12b-1: none
Other: none

Distributions
Income: monthly   Capital Gains: Jun, Dec

Exchange Options
Number Per Year: 4   Fee: none
Telephone: yes (money market fund available)

Services
auto exchange, auto invest, auto withdraw

Fidelity NY Tax-Free Insured (FNTIX)

82 Devonshire St.
Boston, MA 02109
(800) 544-8888, (801) 534-1910

Tax-Exempt Bond

PERFORMANCE

	3yr Annual	5yr Annual	10yr Annual	Bull	Bear
Return (%)	11.2	9.7	na	42.6	2.5
Differ from Category (+/-)	0.8 abv av	0.5 av	na	2.5 av	0.2 av

Total Risk	Standard Deviation	Category Risk	Risk Index	Avg Mat
blw av	4.1%	av	1.0	20.4 yrs

	1993	1992	1991	1990	1989	1988	1987	1986	1985	1984
Return (%)	12.8	8.5	12.4	6.1	9.0	11.2	-3.1	17.3	—	—
Differ from category (+/-)	1.2	0.2	1.1	-0.2	0.0	1.1	-1.9	0.8	—	—

PER SHARE DATA

	1993	1992	1991	1990	1989	1988	1987	1986	1985	1984
Dividends, Net Income ($)	0.65	0.67	0.68	0.69	0.69	0.68	0.69	0.70	—	—
Distrib'ns, Cap Gain ($)	0.31	0.00	0.00	0.00	0.00	0.00	0.00	0.00	—	—
Net Asset Value ($)	12.24	11.73	11.46	10.84	10.89	10.65	10.22	11.28	—	—
Expense Ratio (%)	0.61	0.62	0.64	0.65	0.65	0.67	0.60	0.60	—	—
Net Income to Assets (%)	5.73	6.17	6.45	6.47	6.55	6.72	6.31	6.81	—	—
Portfolio Turnover (%)	39	17	33	18	31	29	30	8	—	—
Total Assets (Millions $)	409	309	247	206	180	155	172	63	—	—

PORTFOLIO (as of 7/31/93)

Portfolio Manager: David Murphy - 1992

Investm't Category: Tax-Exempt Bond

Cap Gain	Asset Allocation
Cap & Income	Fund of Funds
✔ Income	Index
	Sector
✔ Domestic	Small Cap
Foreign	Socially Conscious
Country/Region	✔ State Specific

Portfolio: stocks 0% bonds 100%
convertibles 0% other 0% cash 0%

Largest Holdings: general obligation 12%

Unrealized Net Capital Gains: 6% of portfolio value

SHAREHOLDER INFORMATION

Minimum Investment
Initial: $2,500 Subsequent: $250

Minimum IRA Investment
Initial: na Subsequent: na

Maximum Fees
Load: none 12b-1: none
Other: none

Distributions
Income: monthly Capital Gains: Jun, Dec

Exchange Options
Number Per Year: 4 Fee: none
Telephone: yes (money market fund available)

Services
auto exchange, auto invest, auto withdraw

Fidelity Ohio Tax-Free High Yield (FOHFX)

82 Devonshire St.
Boston, MA 02109
(800) 544-8888, (801) 534-1910

Tax-Exempt Bond

PERFORMANCE

	3yr Annual	5yr Annual	10yr Annual	Bull	Bear
Return (%)	10.8	10.0	na	42.1	3.0
Differ from Category (+/-)	0.5 av	0.8 abv av	na	2.0 av	0.6 abv av

Total Risk	Standard Deviation	Category Risk	Risk Index	Avg Mat
low	4.0%	blw av	1.0	19.0 yrs

	1993	1992	1991	1990	1989	1988	1987	1986	1985	1984
Return (%).	12.5	8.6	11.4	7.4	9.9	12.9	-2.3	16.4	—	—
Differ from category (+/-). . .	0.8	0.3	0.1	1.1	0.8	2.8	-1.1	0.0	—	—

PER SHARE DATA

	1993	1992	1991	1990	1989	1988	1987	1986	1985	1984
Dividends, Net Income ($).	0.69	0.71	0.71	0.72	0.72	0.72	0.74	0.77	—	—
Distrib'ns, Cap Gain ($) . . .	0.25	0.00	0.00	0.00	0.00	0.00	0.00	0.00	—	—
Net Asset Value ($)	12.02	11.55	11.32	10.84	10.79	10.50	9.97	10.97	—	—
Expense Ratio (%)	0.59	0.61	0.64	0.66	0.71	0.73	0.79	0.60	—	—
Net Income to Assets (%) .	5.99	6.31	6.53	6.82	6.79	7.08	7.09	7.01	—	—
Portfolio Turnover (%).	45	20	11	12	22	23	36	32	—	—
Total Assets (Millions $). . . .	456	385	328	242	201	153	117	107	—	—

PORTFOLIO (as of 6/30/93)

Portfolio Manager: Peter Allegrini - 1985

Investm't Category: Tax-Exempt Bond
- Cap Gain
- Cap & Income
- ✔ Income

- Asset Allocation
- Fund of Funds
- Index
- Sector

- ✔ Domestic
- Foreign
- Country/Region

- Small Cap
- Socially Conscious
- ✔ State Specific

Portfolio: stocks 0% bonds 100%
convertibles 0% other 0% cash 0%

Largest Holdings: general obligation 26%

Unrealized Net Capital Gains: 7% of portfolio value

SHAREHOLDER INFORMATION

Minimum Investment
Initial: $2,500   Subsequent: $250

Minimum IRA Investment
Initial: na   Subsequent: na

Maximum Fees
Load: none   12b-1: none
Other: none

Distributions
Income: monthly   Capital Gains: Feb, Dec

Exchange Options
Number Per Year: 4   Fee: none
Telephone: yes (money market fund available)

Services
auto exchange, auto invest, auto withdraw

Fidelity OTC Port
(FOCPX)
Aggressive Growth

82 Devonshire St.
Boston, MA 02109
(800) 544-8888, (801) 534-1910

PERFORMANCE

	3yr Annual	5yr Annual	10yr Annual	Bull	Bear
Return (%)	22.9	18.1	na	102.0	-12.4
Differ from Category (+/-)	-2.5 blw av	-0.1 av	na	-23.0 blw av	2.6 abv av

Total Risk	Standard Deviation	Category Risk	Risk Index	Beta
abv av	13.1%	low	0.8	0.9

	1993	1992	1991	1990	1989	1988	1987	1986	1985	1984
Return (%)	8.3	14.9	49.1	-4.7	30.3	22.8	1.5	11.3	68.6	—
Differ from category (+/-) .	-10.7	4.5	-3.3	1.6	3.3	7.6	4.9	1.9	37.6	—

PER SHARE DATA

	1993	1992	1991	1990	1989	1988	1987	1986	1985	1984
Dividends, Net Income ($) .	0.10	0.25	0.11	0.05	0.50	0.30	0.01	0.01	0.00	—
Distrib'ns, Cap Gain ($) . . .	3.42	2.24	2.51	0.57	2.41	0.00	1.93	1.27	0.44	—
Net Asset Value ($)	24.14	25.65	24.78	18.54	20.14	17.68	14.64	16.47	15.93	—
Expense Ratio (%).	1.08	1.17	1.29	1.35	1.32	1.42	1.36	1.31	1.50	—
Net Income to Assets (%). .	0.53	0.59	1.00	2.30	2.02	0.90	0.12	0.57	0.51	—
Portfolio Turnover (%)	213	245	198	212	118	193	191	132	122	—
Total Assets (Millions $) . .	1,306	1,037	864	697	772	933	1,274	784	74	—

PORTFOLIO (as of 7/31/93)

Portfolio Manager: Alan Radlo - 1990

Investm't Category: Aggressive Growth

✔ Cap Gain	Asset Allocation
Cap & Income	Fund of Funds
Income	Index
	Sector
✔ Domestic	Small Cap
Foreign	Socially Conscious
Country/Region	State Specific

Portfolio: stocks 77% bonds 0%
convertibles 0% other 0% cash 23%

Largest Holdings: finance 29%, health 14%

Unrealized Net Capital Gains: 8% of portfolio value

SHAREHOLDER INFORMATION

Minimum Investment
Initial: $2,500   Subsequent: $250

Minimum IRA Investment
Initial: $500   Subsequent: $250

Maximum Fees
Load: 3.00% front   12b-1: none
Other: none

Distributions
Income: Sep   Capital Gains: Sep

Exchange Options
Number Per Year: 4   Fee: none
Telephone: yes (money market fund available)

Services
IRA, other pension, auto exchange, auto invest, auto withdraw

Fidelity Overseas (FOSFX)

International Stock

82 Devonshire St.
Boston, MA 02109
(800) 544-8888, (801) 534-1910

PERFORMANCE

	3yr Annual	5yr Annual	10yr Annual	Bull	Bear
Return (%)	10.4	8.0	na	41.4	-11.0
Differ from Category (+/-)	-3.9 blw av	-0.6 blw av	na	-13.7 blw av	4.1 abv av

Total Risk	Standard Deviation	Category Risk	Risk Index	Beta
abv av	13.7%	abv av	1.1	0.4

	1993	1992	1991	1990	1989	1988	1987	1986	1985	1984
Return (%)	40.0	-11.4	8.6	-6.6	16.9	8.2	18.3	69.2	78.6	—
Differ from category (+/-). . .	1.5	-7.9	-4.3	4.5	-5.3	-5.6	6.3	18.9	38.0	—

PER SHARE DATA

	1993	1992	1991	1990	1989	1988	1987	1986	1985	1984
Dividends, Net Income ($) .	0.43	0.37	0.43	0.68	0.28	0.57	0.00	0.00	0.00	—
Distrib'ns, Cap Gain ($) . . .	0.00	2.10	1.16	0.86	1.06	0.00	9.41	2.14	0.12	—
Net Asset Value ($)	27.43	19.90	25.26	24.79	28.20	25.30	23.92	28.68	18.25	—
Expense Ratio (%)	1.27	1.52	1.53	1.26	1.06	1.38	1.71	1.57	1.72	—
Net Income to Assets (%) .	1.00	1.78	2.19	1.34	1.06	1.21	-0.53	-0.32	0.73	—
Portfolio Turnover (%).	64	122	132	96	100	115	122	107	63	—
Total Assets (Millions $). .	1,515	801	969	1,011	876	1,149	1,393	1,766	119	—

PORTFOLIO (as of 10/31/93)

Portfolio Manager: John R. Hickling - 1993

Investm't Category: International Stock

✔ Cap Gain	Asset Allocation
Cap & Income	Fund of Funds
Income	Index
	Sector
Domestic	Small Cap
✔ Foreign	Socially Conscious
Country/Region	State Specific

Portfolio: stocks 83%   bonds 3%
convertibles 0%   other 7%   cash 7%

Largest Holdings: Japan 18%, United Kingdom 13%

Unrealized Net Capital Gains: 16% of portfolio value

SHAREHOLDER INFORMATION

Minimum Investment
Initial: $2,500   Subsequent: $250

Minimum IRA Investment
Initial: $500   Subsequent: $250

Maximum Fees
Load: 3.00% front   12b-1: none
Other: none

Distributions
Income: Dec   Capital Gains: Dec

Exchange Options
Number Per Year: 2   Fee: none
Telephone: yes (money market fund available)

Services
IRA, other pension, auto exchange, auto invest, auto withdraw

Fidelity Pacific-Basin

(FPBFX)

International Stock

82 Devonshire St.
Boston, MA 02109
(800) 544-8888, (801) 534-1910

PERFORMANCE

	3yr Annual	5yr Annual	10yr Annual	Bull	Bear
Return (%)	19.4	6.6	na	76.9	-29.8
Differ from Category (+/-)	5.1 high	-2.1 blw av	na	21.8 high	-14.7 low

Total Risk	Standard Deviation	Category Risk	Risk Index	Beta
high	17.4%	high	1.5	0.1

	1993	1992	1991	1990	1989	1988	1987	1986	1985	1984
Return (%)	63.9	-7.6	12.5	-27.1	11.4	10.4	24.9	—	—	—
Differ from category (+/-) ..	25.4	-4.1	-0.4	-16.0	-10.8	-3.4	12.9	—	—	—

PER SHARE DATA

	1993	1992	1991	1990	1989	1988	1987	1986	1985	1984
Dividends, Net Income ($) .	0.12	0.10	0.00	0.15	0.00	0.09	0.15	—	—	—
Distrib'ns, Cap Gain ($) ...	0.27	0.00	0.00	0.00	0.62	0.01	0.00	—	—	—
Net Asset Value ($)	18.80	11.74	12.83	11.40	15.87	14.82	13.52	—	—	—
Expense Ratio (%)........	1.59	1.84	1.88	1.59	1.40	1.80	2.10	—	—	—
Net Income to Assets (%)..	0.15	0.65	0.12	0.88	-0.18	0.04	-0.83	—	—	—
Portfolio Turnover (%)	77	105	143	118	133	228	324	—	—	—
Total Assets (Millions $) ...	500	116	95	86	111	136	159	—	—	—

PORTFOLIO (as of 10/31/93)

Portfolio Manager: Simon Fraser - 1993

Investm't Category: International Stock

✔ Cap Gain	Asset Allocation
Cap & Income	Fund of Funds
Income	Index
	Sector
Domestic	Small Cap
✔ Foreign	Socially Conscious
✔ Country/Region	State Specific

Portfolio: stocks 96% bonds 0%
convertibles 3% other 0% cash 1%

Largest Holdings: Indonesia 5%, Hong Kong 15%

Unrealized Net Capital Gains: 16% of portfolio value

SHAREHOLDER INFORMATION

Minimum Investment
Initial: $2,500   Subsequent: $250

Minimum IRA Investment
Initial: $500   Subsequent: $250

Maximum Fees
Load: 3.00% front   12b-1: none
Other: none

Distributions
Income: Dec   Capital Gains: Dec

Exchange Options
Number Per Year: 2   Fee: none
Telephone: yes (money market fund available)

Services
IRA, other pension, auto exchange, auto invest, auto withdraw

Fidelity Puritan (FPURX)

Balanced

82 Devonshire St.
Boston, MA 02109
(800) 544-8888, (801) 534-1910

PERFORMANCE

	3yr Annual	5yr Annual	10yr Annual	Bull	Bear
Return (%)	20.3	14.3	14.6	85.3	-11.8
Differ from Category (+/-)	5.3 high	2.2 high	2.6 high	23.7 high	-6.0 low

Total Risk	Standard Deviation	Category Risk	Risk Index	Beta
av	7.5%	abv av	1.2	0.6

	1993	1992	1991	1990	1989	1988	1987	1986	1985	1984
Return (%).............	21.4	15.4	24.4	-6.3	19.5	18.8	-1.7	20.7	28.7	10.6
Differ from category (+/-)...	8.0	7.3	0.5	-5.8	1.9	6.8	-4.0	3.2	5.0	3.2

PER SHARE DATA

	1993	1992	1991	1990	1989	1988	1987	1986	1985	1984
Dividends, Net Income ($).	0.72	0.81	0.80	0.80	0.99	0.91	0.93	0.92	0.97	0.97
Distrib'ns, Cap Gain ($) ...	1.36	0.68	0.00	0.00	0.54	0.00	0.76	0.75	1.16	0.81
Net Asset Value ($)	15.75	14.74	14.14	12.05	13.70	12.76	11.53	13.34	12.52	11.57
Expense Ratio (%)	0.74	0.64	0.66	0.65	0.64	0.72	0.70	0.63	0.61	0.60
Net Income to Assets (%) .	4.89	6.23	5.94	6.30	7.41	6.58	6.40	7.50	8.40	8.05
Portfolio Turnover (%)......	76	102	108	58	77	88	63	85	133	74
Total Assets (Millions $)..	8,934	5,577	4,943	4,768	4,948	4,283	4,955	2,206	1,083	772

PORTFOLIO (as of 7/31/93)

Portfolio Manager: Richard Fentin - 1987

Investm't Category: Balanced

Cap Gain	Asset Allocation
✔ Cap & Income	Fund of Funds
Income	Index
	Sector
✔ Domestic	Small Cap
✔ Foreign	Socially Conscious
Country/Region	State Specific

Portfolio: stocks 50% bonds 44%
convertibles 6% other 3% cash 3%

Largest Holdings: stocks—basic industries 8%, stocks—energy 8%

Unrealized Net Capital Gains: 10% of portfolio value

SHAREHOLDER INFORMATION

Minimum Investment
Initial: $2,500   Subsequent: $250

Minimum IRA Investment
Initial: $500   Subsequent: $250

Maximum Fees
Load: 2.00% front   12b-1: none
Other: none

Distributions
Income: quarterly   Capital Gains: Sep, Dec

Exchange Options
Number Per Year: 4   Fee: none
Telephone: yes (money market fund available)

Services
IRA, other pension, auto exchange, auto invest, auto withdraw

Fidelity Real Estate Investment (FRESX)

82 Devonshire St.
Boston, MA 02109
(800) 544-8888, (801) 534-1910

Growth & Income

PERFORMANCE

	3yr Annual	5yr Annual	10yr Annual	Bull	Bear
Return (%)	23.2	14.2	na	97.2	-13.3
Differ from Category (+/-)	6.8 high	1.7 abv av	na	27.1 high	-1.7 blw av

Total Risk	Standard Deviation	Category Risk	Risk Index	Beta
abv av	12.2%	high	1.4	0.6

	1993	1992	1991	1990	1989	1988	1987	1986	1985	1984
Return (%)	12.5	19.5	39.1	-8.6	13.7	10.3	-7.6	—	—	—
Differ from category (+/-) . .	-0.1	9.5	11.4	-3.0	-7.9	-6.5	-8.0	—	—	—

PER SHARE DATA

	1993	1992	1991	1990	1989	1988	1987	1986	1985	1984
Dividends, Net Income ($) .	0.60	0.43	0.49	0.50	0.54	0.58	0.60	—	—	—
Distrib'ns, Cap Gain ($) . . .	0.00	0.00	0.00	0.00	0.00	0.00	0.00	—	—	—
Net Asset Value ($)	13.57	12.60	10.94	8.26	9.59	8.92	8.62	—	—	—
Expense Ratio (%).	1.16	1.24	1.47	1.39	1.28	1.50	1.50	—	—	—
Net Income to Assets (%) . .	5.81	5.84	8.45	7.11	6.87	6.26	7.17	—	—	—
Portfolio Turnover (%)	82	84	49	70	42	89	6	—	—	—
Total Assets (Millions $) . . .	409	76	45	50	63	71	86	—	—	—

PORTFOLIO (as of 7/31/93)

Portfolio Manager: Barry Greenfield - 1986

Investm't Category: Growth & Income

Cap Gain	Asset Allocation
✔ Cap & Income	Fund of Funds
Income	Index
	✔ Sector
✔ Domestic	Small Cap
Foreign	Socially Conscious
Country/Region	State Specific

Portfolio:	stocks 79%	bonds 0%
convertibles 13%	other 1%	cash 7%

Largest Holdings: real estate investment trusts 74%, stocks—media & leisure 3%

Unrealized Net Capital Gains: 8% of portfolio value

SHAREHOLDER INFORMATION

Minimum Investment
Initial: $2,500   Subsequent: $250

Minimum IRA Investment
Initial: $500   Subsequent: $250

Maximum Fees
Load: none   12b-1: none
Other: none

Distributions
Income: quarterly   Capital Gains: Mar, Dec

Exchange Options
Number Per Year: 4   Fee: none
Telephone: yes (money market fund available)

Services
IRA, other pension, auto exchange, auto invest, auto withdraw

Fidelity Retirement Growth (FDFFX)

Growth

82 Devonshire St.
Boston, MA 02109
(800) 544-8888, (801) 534-1910

PERFORMANCE

	3yr Annual	5yr Annual	10yr Annual	Bull	Bear
Return (%)	25.2	18.1	16.0	110.1	-15.9
Differ from Category (+/-)	6.0 high	3.5 high	3.4 high	25.4 high	-3.5 blw av

Total Risk	Standard Deviation	Category Risk	Risk Index	Beta
abv av	12.8%	abv av	1.2	1.1

	1993	1992	1991	1990	1989	1988	1987	1986	1985	1984
Return (%).............	22.1	10.5	45.5	-10.1	30.4	15.5	9.3	14.1	28.9	3.2
Differ from category (+/-)...	8.9	-0.5	10.1	-4.0	4.6	-2.2	8.1	-0.4	-0.4	3.2

PER SHARE DATA

	1993	1992	1991	1990	1989	1988	1987	1986	1985	1984
Dividends, Net Income ($).	0.14	0.15	0.20	0.10	0.37	0.20	0.37	0.34	0.23	0.03
Distrib'ns, Cap Gain ($) ...	1.75	3.53	1.04	0.56	0.00	0.00	6.68	0.98	0.15	0.41
Net Asset Value ($)	18.14	16.44	18.23	13.45	15.66	12.31	10.84	16.31	15.63	12.52
Expense Ratio (%)	1.05	1.02	0.83	0.98	0.92	1.09	0.97	1.07	1.14	1.13
Net Income to Assets (%) .	0.72	1.01	1.56	2.34	2.51	1.79	1.25	1.11	2.86	3.08
Portfolio Turnover (%)......	93	138	119	127	139	156	171	161	100	97
Total Assets (Millions $)..	2,970	2,166	1,577	1,292	1,448	1,244	993	915	600	388

PORTFOLIO (as of 5/31/93)

Portfolio Manager: Harris Leviton - 1992

Investm't Category: Growth

✔ Cap Gain   Asset Allocation
   Cap & Income   Fund of Funds
   Income   Index
     Sector
✔ Domestic   Small Cap
✔ Foreign   Socially Conscious
   Country/Region   State Specific

Portfolio:	stocks 86%	bonds 0%
convertibles 5%	other 0%	cash 9%

Largest Holdings: finance 12%, health 9%

Unrealized Net Capital Gains: 13% of portfolio value

SHAREHOLDER INFORMATION

Minimum Investment
Initial: $500   Subsequent: $250

Minimum IRA Investment
Initial: $500   Subsequent: $250

Maximum Fees
Load: none   12b-1: none
Other: none

Distributions
Income: Jan, Dec   Capital Gains: Jan, Dec

Exchange Options
Number Per Year: 4   Fee: none
Telephone: yes (money market fund available)

Services
IRA, other pension, auto exchange, auto invest, auto withdraw

Fidelity Select Air Transportation (FSAIX)

Aggressive Growth

82 Devonshire St.
Boston, MA 02109
(800) 544-8888, (801) 534-1910

PERFORMANCE

	3yr Annual	5yr Annual	10yr Annual	Bull	Bear
Return (%)	24.1	14.5	na	109.6	-25.3
Differ from Category (+/-)	-1.3 av	-3.7 blw av	na	-15.4 av	-10.3 low

Total Risk	Standard Deviation	Category Risk	Risk Index	Beta
high	17.0%	av	1.1	1.0

	1993	1992	1991	1990	1989	1988	1987	1986	1985	1984
Return (%)	30.8	6.5	37.0	-18.1	26.3	29.0	-20.6	13.7	—	—
Differ from category (+/-) . .	11.8	-3.9	-15.4	-11.8	-0.6	13.8	-17.2	4.3	—	—

PER SHARE DATA

	1993	1992	1991	1990	1989	1988	1987	1986	1985	1984
Dividends, Net Income ($) .	0.00	0.00	0.00	0.00	0.00	0.00	0.01	0.00	—	—
Distrib'ns, Cap Gain ($) . . .	0.27	0.36	0.25	0.00	0.56	0.00	1.04	0.00	—	—
Net Asset Value ($)	17.09	13.27	12.81	9.54	11.66	9.68	7.50	10.81	—	—
Expense Ratio (%)	2.48	2.51	2.48	2.55	2.52	2.62	1.58	1.92	—	—
Net Income to Assets (%) .	-0.90	-1.04	-0.34	-0.03	-0.18	-0.75	0.36	-0.60	—	—
Portfolio Turnover (%)	96	261	106	143	115	340	611	1,125	—	—
Total Assets (Millions $)	16	6	4	4	11	2	4	1	—	—

PORTFOLIO (as of 8/31/93)

Portfolio Manager: Brenda Reed - 1992

Investm't Category: Aggressive Growth

✔ Cap Gain	Asset Allocation
Cap & Income	Fund of Funds
Income	Index
	✔ Sector
✔ Domestic	Small Cap
✔ Foreign	Socially Conscious
Country/Region	State Specific

Portfolio: stocks 94% bonds 0%
convertibles 0% other 0% cash 6%

Largest Holdings: air transportation 66%, trucking & freight 10%

Unrealized Net Capital Gains: 5% of portfolio value

SHAREHOLDER INFORMATION

Minimum Investment
Initial: $2,500   Subsequent: $250

Minimum IRA Investment
Initial: $500   Subsequent: $100

Maximum Fees
Load: 3.00% front   12b-1: none
Other: $7.50 redemption fee (30 days or more)

Distributions
Income: April, Dec   Capital Gains: April, Dec

Exchange Options
Number Per Year: 4   Fee: $7.50
Telephone: yes (money market fund available)

Services
IRA, other pension, auto exchange, auto invest, auto withdraw

Fidelity Select American Gold (FSAGX)

82 Devonshire St.
Boston, MA 02109
(800) 544-8888, (801) 534-1910

Gold

PERFORMANCE

	3yr Annual	5yr Annual	10yr Annual	Bull	Bear
Return (%)	17.5	10.4	na	44.7	-7.0
Differ from Category (+/-)	3.8 abv av	-1.9 abv av	na	11.1 abv av	-52.9high

Total Risk	Standard Deviation	Category Risk	Risk Index	Beta
high	24.0%	low	0.9	-0.1

	1993	1992	1991	1990	1989	1988	1987	1986	1985	1984
Return (%)	78.6	-3.0	-6.1	-17.2	22.0	-12.4	40.5	18.0	—	—
Differ from category (+/-). . .	-8.3	12.7	-1.3	-48.7	-2.7	6.5	8.6	-19.6	—	—

PER SHARE DATA

	1993	1992	1991	1990	1989	1988	1987	1986	1985	1984
Dividends, Net Income ($).	0.00	0.00	0.00	0.00	0.00	0.00	0.05	0.00	—	—
Distrib'ns, Cap Gain ($) . . .	0.00	0.00	0.00	0.00	0.00	0.00	0.18	0.00	—	—
Net Asset Value ($)	23.55	13.18	13.60	14.49	17.50	14.34	16.38	11.83	—	—
Expense Ratio (%)	1.59	1.75	1.75	1.85	2.03	2.33	1.21	1.50	—	—
Net Income to Assets (%) .	-0.44	-0.47	-0.29	-0.38	-0.61	0.06	1.13	0.81	—	—
Portfolio Turnover (%).	30	40	38	68	56	89	78	52	—	—
Total Assets (Millions $). . . .	364	130	164	195	175	206	435	5	—	—

PORTFOLIO (as of 8/31/93)

Portfolio Manager: Malcolm MacNaught - 1985

Investm't Category: Gold

✔ Cap Gain	Asset Allocation
Cap & Income	Fund of Funds
Income	Index
	✔ Sector
✔ Domestic	Small Cap
✔ Foreign	Socially Conscious
Country/Region	State Specific

Portfolio: stocks 78% bonds 0%
convertibles 1% other 7% cash 14%

Largest Holdings: Canadian gold mining cos. 58%, United States mining cos. 15%

Unrealized Net Capital Gains: 19% of portfolio value

SHAREHOLDER INFORMATION

Minimum Investment
Initial: $2,500   Subsequent: $250

Minimum IRA Investment
Initial: $500   Subsequent: $100

Maximum Fees
Load: 3.00% front   12b-1: none
Other: $7.50 redemption fee (30 days or more)

Distributions
Income: April, Dec   Capital Gains: April, Dec

Exchange Options
Number Per Year: 4   Fee: $7.50
Telephone: yes (money market fund available)

Services
IRA, other pension, auto exchange, auto invest, auto withdraw

Fidelity Select Automotive (FSAVX)

82 Devonshire St.
Boston, MA 02109
(800) 544-8888, (801) 534-1910

Aggressive Growth

PERFORMANCE

	3yr Annual	5yr Annual	10yr Annual	Bull	Bear
Return (%)	38.0	20.6	na	183.3	-13.3
Differ from Category (+/-)	12.6 high	2.4 abv av	na	58.4 high	1.7 av

Total Risk	Standard Deviation	Category Risk	Risk Index	Beta
abv av	13.1%	low	0.8	0.7

	1993	1992	1991	1990	1989	1988	1987	1986	1985	1984
Return (%)	35.3	41.6	37.3	-6.7	4.1	20.0	6.5	—	—	—
Differ from category (+/-) ..	16.3	31.2	-15.1	-0.4	-22.9	4.8	9.9	—	—	—

PER SHARE DATA

	1993	1992	1991	1990	1989	1988	1987	1986	1985	1984
Dividends, Net Income ($) .	0.05	0.05	0.00	0.18	0.40	0.00	0.03	—	—	—
Distrib'ns, Cap Gain ($) ...	1.26	0.36	0.69	0.00	0.00	0.00	0.46	—	—	—
Net Asset Value ($)	24.91	19.49	14.07	10.80	11.74	11.67	9.72	—	—	—
Expense Ratio (%)........	1.57	2.48	2.25	2.42	2.63	2.49	1.63	—	—	—
Net Income to Assets (%)..	0.72	0.36	2.06	1.84	1.22	0.91	1.90	—	—	—
Portfolio Turnover (%)....	140	29	219	121	149	311	284	—	—	—
Total Assets (Millions $) ...	194	178	1	1	1	8	5	—	—	—

PORTFOLIO (as of 8/31/93)

Portfolio Manager: Richard Patton - 1993

Investm't Category: Aggressive Growth
- ✔ Cap Gain
- Cap & Income
- Income
- Asset Allocation
- Fund of Funds
- Index
- ✔ Sector
- ✔ Domestic
- ✔ Foreign
- Country/Region
- Small Cap
- Socially Conscious
- State Specific

Portfolio: stocks 100% bonds 0%
convertibles 0% other 0% cash 0%

Largest Holdings: autos, tires, & accessories 79%, conglomerates 7%

Unrealized Net Capital Gains: 20% of portfolio value

SHAREHOLDER INFORMATION

Minimum Investment
Initial: $2,500   Subsequent: $250

Minimum IRA Investment
Initial: $500   Subsequent: $100

Maximum Fees
Load: 3.00% front   12b-1: none
Other: $7.50 redemption fee (30 days or more)

Distributions
Income: April, Dec   Capital Gains: April, Dec

Exchange Options
Number Per Year: 4   Fee: $7.50
Telephone: yes (money market fund available)

Services
IRA, other pension, auto exchange, auto invest, auto withdraw

Fidelity Select Biotechnology (FBIOX)

Aggressive Growth

82 Devonshire St.
Boston, MA 02109
(800) 544-8888, (801) 534-1910

PERFORMANCE

	3yr Annual	5yr Annual	10yr Annual	Bull	Bear
Return (%)	21.5	30.1	na	109.3	23.8
Differ from Category (+/-)	-3.9 blw av	11.9 high	na	-15.7 av	38.8 high

Total Risk	Standard Deviation	Category Risk	Risk Index	Beta
high	24.9%	high	1.6	1.5

	1993	1992	1991	1990	1989	1988	1987	1986	1985	1984
Return (%)	0.6	-10.3	99.0	44.3	43.9	4.1	-3.3	3.4	—	—
Differ from category (+/-)	-18.3	-20.7	46.6	50.6	16.9	-11.1	0.1	-6.0	—	—

PER SHARE DATA

	1993	1992	1991	1990	1989	1988	1987	1986	1985	1984
Dividends, Net Income ($)	0.00	0.00	0.01	0.00	0.00	0.00	0.00	0.00	—	—
Distrib'ns, Cap Gain ($)	0.00	3.89	2.52	0.67	0.23	0.00	0.28	0.00	—	—
Net Asset Value ($)	28.61	28.41	36.42	19.94	14.30	10.10	9.70	10.35	—	—
Expense Ratio (%)	1.50	1.50	1.63	2.07	2.21	2.51	1.38	1.41	—	—
Net Income to Assets (%)	-0.37	-0.34	0.24	-0.31	-0.43	-1.31	-0.41	0.74	—	—
Portfolio Turnover (%)	79	160	166	290	80	205	431	937	—	—
Total Assets (Millions $)	589	679	482	70	46	47	75	39	—	—

PORTFOLIO (as of 8/31/93)

Portfolio Manager: Karen Firestone - 1992

Investm't Category: Aggressive Growth

✔ Cap Gain   Asset Allocation
   Cap & Income   Fund of Funds
   Income   Index
             ✔ Sector
✔ Domestic   Small Cap
✔ Foreign   Socially Conscious
   Country/Region   State Specific

Portfolio: stocks 86%   bonds 0%
convertibles 0%   other 0%   cash 14%

Largest Holdings: drugs & pharmaceuticals 78%, drugs 24%

Unrealized Net Capital Gains: 0% of portfolio value

SHAREHOLDER INFORMATION

Minimum Investment
Initial: $2,500   Subsequent: $250

Minimum IRA Investment
Initial: $500   Subsequent: $100

Maximum Fees
Load: 3.00% front   12b-1: none
Other: $7.50 redemption fee (30 days or more)

Distributions
Income: April, Dec   Capital Gains: April, Dec

Exchange Options
Number Per Year: 4   Fee: $7.50
Telephone: yes (money market fund available)

Services
IRA, other pension, auto exchange, auto invest, auto withdraw

Fidelity Select Broadcast & Media (FBMPX)

82 Devonshire St.
Boston, MA 02109
(800) 544-8888, (801) 534-1910

Aggressive Growth

PERFORMANCE

	3yr Annual	5yr Annual	10yr Annual	Bull	Bear
Return (%)	32.2	17.7	na	161.8	-34.9
Differ from Category (+/-)	6.8 abv av	-0.5 av	na	36.9 abv av	-19.9 low

Total Risk	Standard Deviation	Category Risk	Risk Index	Beta
high	14.4%	blw av	0.9	0.9

	1993	1992	1991	1990	1989	1988	1987	1986	1985	1984
Return (%)	37.9	21.4	37.8	-26.2	32.5	26.8	19.9	—	—	—
Differ from category (+/-) . .	18.9	11.0	-14.6	-19.9	5.5	11.6	23.3	—	—	—

PER SHARE DATA

	1993	1992	1991	1990	1989	1988	1987	1986	1985	1984
Dividends, Net Income ($) .	0.00	0.00	0.00	0.00	0.00	0.00	0.00	—	—	—
Distrib'ns, Cap Gain ($) . . .	0.63	0.23	0.00	0.00	2.57	0.75	0.77	—	—	—
Net Asset Value ($)	23.84	17.82	14.86	10.78	14.61	12.98	10.87	—	—	—
Expense Ratio (%).	2.49	2.49	2.53	2.51	2.66	2.48	1.50	—	—	—
Net Income to Assets (%) .	-0.52	-1.22	-0.43	-0.14	-1.01	-0.52	0.25	—	—	—
Portfolio Turnover (%)	70	111	150	75	437	325	224	—	—	—
Total Assets (Millions $)	66	8	5	7	45	17	7	—	—	—

PORTFOLIO (as of 8/31/93)

Portfolio Manager: Stephen DuFour - 1993

Investm't Category: Aggressive Growth

✔ Cap Gain   Asset Allocation
  Cap & Income   Fund of Funds
  Income   Index
     ✔ Sector
✔ Domestic   Small Cap
✔ Foreign   Socially Conscious
  Country/Region   State Specific

Portfolio: stocks 91%   bonds 0%
convertibles 0%   other 0%   cash 9%

Largest Holdings: broadcasting 20%, cellular 17%

Unrealized Net Capital Gains: 10% of portfolio value

SHAREHOLDER INFORMATION

Minimum Investment
Initial: $2,500   Subsequent: $250

Minimum IRA Investment
Initial: $500   Subsequent: $100

Maximum Fees
Load: 3.00% front   12b-1: none
Other: $7.50 redemption fee (30 days or more)

Distributions
Income: April, Dec   Capital Gains: April, Dec

Exchange Options
Number Per Year: 4   Fee: $7.50
Telephone: yes (money market fund available)

Services
IRA, other pension, auto exchange, auto invest, auto withdraw

Fidelity Select Broker & Invest Mgmt (FSLBX)

82 Devonshire St.
Boston, MA 02109
(800) 544-8888, (801) 534-1910

Aggressive Growth

PERFORMANCE

	3yr Annual	5yr Annual	10yr Annual	Bull	Bear
Return (%)	41.9	22.2	na	203.7	-21.0
Differ from Category (+/-)	16.5 high	4.0 abv av	na	78.7 high	-6.0 blw av

Total Risk	Standard Deviation	Category Risk	Risk Index	Beta
high	19.5%	abv av	1.3	1.3

	1993	1992	1991	1990	1989	1988	1987	1986	1985	1984
Return (%)	49.3	5.1	82.2	-16.1	14.0	18.5	-36.8	9.5	—	—
Differ from category (+/-). .	30.3	-5.3	29.8	-9.8	-13.0	3.3	-33.4	0.1	—	—

PER SHARE DATA

	1993	1992	1991	1990	1989	1988	1987	1986	1985	1984
Dividends, Net Income ($).	0.00	0.00	0.00	0.09	0.15	0.09	0.02	0.01	—	—
Distrib'ns, Cap Gain ($) . . .	1.47	0.00	0.00	0.00	0.00	0.00	1.15	0.01	—	—
Net Asset Value ($)	18.30	13.34	12.69	6.97	8.42	7.52	6.42	12.12	—	—
Expense Ratio (%)	2.21	2.17	2.50	2.50	2.54	2.58	1.67	1.52	—	—
Net Income to Assets (%) .	0.02	0.16	0.93	0.91	1.18	0.09	0.68	1.39	—	—
Portfolio Turnover (%). . . .	111	254	62	142	185	447	603	347	—	—
Total Assets (Millions $). . . .	84	17	11	2	4	4	13	42	—	—

PORTFOLIO (as of 8/31/93)

Portfolio Manager: Arieh Coll - 1993

Investm't Category: Aggressive Growth
✔ Cap Gain	Asset Allocation
Cap & Income	Fund of Funds
Income	Index
	✔ Sector
✔ Domestic	Small Cap
✔ Foreign	Socially Conscious
Country/Region	State Specific

Portfolio: stocks 89% bonds 0%
convertibles 0% other 0% cash 11%

Largest Holdings: securities industry 76%, credit & other finance 13%

Unrealized Net Capital Gains: 10% of portfolio value

SHAREHOLDER INFORMATION

Minimum Investment
Initial: $2,500 Subsequent: $250

Minimum IRA Investment
Initial: $500 Subsequent: $100

Maximum Fees
Load: 3.00% front 12b-1: none
Other: $7.50 redemption fee (30 days or more)

Distributions
Income: April, Dec Capital Gains: April, Dec

Exchange Options
Number Per Year: 4 Fee: $7.50
Telephone: yes (money market fund available)

Services
IRA, other pension, auto exchange, auto invest, auto withdraw

Fidelity Select Chemical

(FSCHX)

Growth

82 Devonshire St.
Boston, MA 02109
(800) 544-8888, (801) 534-1910

PERFORMANCE

	3yr Annual	5yr Annual	10yr Annual	Bull	Bear
Return (%)	19.4	13.8	na	91.6	-14.8
Differ from Category (+/-)	0.2 av	-0.8 blw av	na	6.9 abv av	-2.4 blw av

Total Risk	Standard Deviation	Category Risk	Risk Index	Beta
abv av	11.9%	av	1.1	0.9

	1993	1992	1991	1990	1989	1988	1987	1986	1985	1984
Return (%)	12.7	8.9	38.6	-4.1	17.3	20.9	14.8	26.8	—	—
Differ from category (+/-) . .	-0.5	-2.1	3.2	2.0	-8.5	3.2	13.6	12.3	—	—

PER SHARE DATA

	1993	1992	1991	1990	1989	1988	1987	1986	1985	1984
Dividends, Net Income ($) .	0.23	0.31	0.18	0.10	0.15	0.00	0.00	0.00	—	—
Distrib'ns, Cap Gain ($) . . .	3.05	3.36	0.70	0.60	1.13	0.00	0.03	0.05	—	—
Net Asset Value ($)	29.42	29.16	30.20	22.49	24.14	21.70	17.94	15.66	—	—
Expense Ratio (%).	1.89	2.16	2.50	2.37	2.24	1.93	1.52	1.50	—	—
Net Income to Assets (%) . .	1.21	0.40	1.21	1.65	1.27	1.61	1.03	1.24	—	—
Portfolio Turnover (%)	214	87	87	99	117	179	170	125	—	—
Total Assets (Millions $)	26	39	20	21	44	118	86	45	—	—

PORTFOLIO (as of 8/31/93)

Portfolio Manager: Steve Wymer - 1993

Investm't Category: Growth

✔ Cap Gain	Asset Allocation
Cap & Income	Fund of Funds
Income	Index
	✔ Sector
✔ Domestic	Small Cap
✔ Foreign	Socially Conscious
Country/Region	State Specific

Portfolio: stocks 96% bonds 0%
convertibles 0% other 0% cash 4%

Largest Holdings: chemicals & plastics 77%, oil & gas 7%

Unrealized Net Capital Gains: 9% of portfolio value

SHAREHOLDER INFORMATION

Minimum Investment
Initial: $2,500   Subsequent: $250

Minimum IRA Investment
Initial: $500   Subsequent: $100

Maximum Fees
Load: 3.00% front   12b-1: none
Other: $7.50 redemption fee (30 days or more)

Distributions
Income: April, Dec   Capital Gains: April, Dec

Exchange Options
Number Per Year: 4   Fee: $7.50
Telephone: yes (money market fund available)

Services
IRA, other pension, auto exchange, auto invest, auto withdraw

Fidelity Select Computers (FDCPX)

Aggressive Growth

82 Devonshire St.
Boston, MA 02109
(800) 544-8888, (801) 534-1910

PERFORMANCE

	3yr Annual	5yr Annual	10yr Annual	Bull	Bear
Return (%)	27.1	21.0	na	157.0	-5.3
Differ from Category (+/-)	1.7 av	2.8 abv av	na	33.3 abv av	9.7 high

Total Risk	Standard Deviation	Category Risk	Risk Index	Beta
high	24.1%	high	1.6	1.5

	1993	1992	1991	1990	1989	1988	1987	1986	1985	1984
Return (%)............	28.8	21.9	30.7	18.4	6.8	-5.0	-6.3	7.8	—	—
Differ from category (+/-)...	9.8	11.5	-21.7	24.7	-20.2	-20.2	-2.9	-1.6	—	—

PER SHARE DATA

	1993	1992	1991	1990	1989	1988	1987	1986	1985	1984
Dividends, Net Income ($).	0.00	0.00	0.27	0.12	0.00	0.00	0.00	0.00	—	—
Distrib'ns, Cap Gain ($) ...	1.80	0.00	0.21	0.00	0.00	0.00	0.33	0.03	—	—
Net Asset Value ($)	24.35	20.44	16.76	13.20	11.25	10.53	11.09	12.21	—	—
Expense Ratio (%)	1.81	2.17	2.26	2.64	2.56	2.62	1.58	1.68	—	—
Net Income to Assets (%) .	-0.98	-0.18	2.94	-0.94	-1.18	-0.75	0.32	-0.05	—	—
Portfolio Turnover (%).....	254	568	695	596	466	284	259	269	—	—
Total Assets (Millions $).....	60	32	29	27	15	23	118	24	—	—

PORTFOLIO (as of 8/31/93)

Portfolio Manager: Harry Lange - 1992

Investm't Category: Aggressive Growth

✔ Cap Gain   Asset Allocation
  Cap & Income   Fund of Funds
  Income   Index
              ✔ Sector
✔ Domestic   Small Cap
✔ Foreign   Socially Conscious
  Country/Region State Specific

Portfolio: stocks 99%   bonds 1%
convertibles 0%   other 0%   cash 0%

Largest Holdings: computers & office equipment 45%, computer software & services 27%

Unrealized Net Capital Gains: 18% of portfolio value

SHAREHOLDER INFORMATION

Minimum Investment
Initial: $2,500   Subsequent: $250

Minimum IRA Investment
Initial: $500   Subsequent: $100

Maximum Fees
Load: 3.00% front   12b-1: none
Other: $7.50 redemption fee (30 days or more)

Distributions
Income: April, Dec   Capital Gains: April, Dec

Exchange Options
Number Per Year: 4   Fee: $7.50
Telephone: yes (money market fund available)

Services
IRA, other pension, auto exchange, auto invest, auto withdraw

Fidelity Select Construction & Housing

82 Devonshire St.
Boston, MA 02109
(800) 544-8888, (801) 534-1910

(FSHOX) *Aggressive Growth*

PERFORMANCE

	3yr Annual	5yr Annual	10yr Annual	Bull	Bear
Return (%)	30.8	18.7	na	159.3	-21.9
Differ from Category (+/-)	5.4 abv av	0.5 av	na	34.4 abv av	-6.9 blw av

Total Risk	Standard Deviation	Category Risk	Risk Index	Beta
high	14.8%	blw av	1.0	1.0

	1993	1992	1991	1990	1989	1988	1987	1986	1985	1984
Return (%)	33.6	18.7	41.3	-9.6	16.5	29.1	-12.4	—	—	—
Differ from category (+/-) . .	14.6	8.3	-11.1	-3.3	-10.5	13.9	-9.0	—	—	—

PER SHARE DATA

	1993	1992	1991	1990	1989	1988	1987	1986	1985	1984
Dividends, Net Income ($) .	0.00	0.00	0.00	0.15	0.07	0.05	0.00	—	—	—
Distrib'ns, Cap Gain ($) . . .	0.21	0.00	0.87	1.27	1.62	0.27	0.12	—	—	—
Net Asset Value ($)	19.59	14.84	12.51	9.55	11.89	11.65	9.28	—	—	—
Expense Ratio (%).	2.02	2.50	2.48	2.41	2.56	2.70	1.46	—	—	—
Net Income to Assets (%) . .	0.20	-0.49	0.08	-0.03	1.16	-0.41	0.57	—	—	—
Portfolio Turnover (%)	60	183	137	185	225	330	590	—	—	—
Total Assets (Millions $)	58	26	4	1	1	3	6	—	—	—

PORTFOLIO (as of 8/31/93)

Portfolio Manager: Katherine Collins - 1992

Investm't Category: Aggressive Growth
- ✔ Cap Gain
-   Cap & Income
-   Income
- ✔ Domestic
- ✔ Foreign
-   Country/Region
-   Asset Allocation
-   Fund of Funds
-   Index
- ✔ Sector
-   Small Cap
-   Socially Conscious
-   State Specific

Portfolio: stocks 87% bonds 0%
convertibles 0% other 1% cash 12%

Largest Holdings: building materials 33%, construction 13%

Unrealized Net Capital Gains: 16% of portfolio value

SHAREHOLDER INFORMATION

Minimum Investment
Initial: $2,500   Subsequent: $250

Minimum IRA Investment
Initial: $500   Subsequent: $100

Maximum Fees
Load: 3.00% front   12b-1: none
Other: $7.50 redemption fee (30 days or more)

Distributions
Income: April, Dec   Capital Gains: April, Dec

Exchange Options
Number Per Year: 4   Fee: $7.50
Telephone: yes (money market fund available)

Services
IRA, other pension, auto exchange, auto invest, auto withdraw

Fidelity Select Consumer Product (FSCPX)

82 Devonshire St.
Boston, MA 02109
(800) 544-8888, (801) 534-1910

Aggressive Growth

PERFORMANCE

	3yr Annual	5yr Annual	10yr Annual	Bull	Bear
Return (%)	23.3	na	na	113.1	na
Differ from Category (+/-)	-2.1 av	na	na	-11.9 av	na

Total Risk	Standard Deviation	Category Risk	Risk Index	Beta
abv av	12.9%	low	0.8	1.0

	1993	1992	1991	1990	1989	1988	1987	1986	1985	1984
Return (%)	24.6	8.5	38.5	—	—	—	—	—	—	—
Differ from category (+/-). . .	5.6	-1.9	-13.9	—	—	—	—	—	—	—

PER SHARE DATA

	1993	1992	1991	1990	1989	1988	1987	1986	1985	1984
Dividends, Net Income ($).	0.00	0.00	0.00	—	—	—	—	—	—	—
Distrib'ns, Cap Gain ($) . . .	1.40	0.97	0.21	—	—	—	—	—	—	—
Net Asset Value ($)	15.41	13.51	13.38	—	—	—	—	—	—	—
Expense Ratio (%)	2.47	2.48	2.43	—	—	—	—	—	—	—
Net Income to Assets (%)	-0.80	-0.56	0.62	—	—	—	—	—	—	—
Portfolio Turnover (%).	215	140	108	—	—	—	—	—	—	—
Total Assets (Millions $).	9	7	1	—	—	—	—	—	—	—

PORTFOLIO (as of 8/31/93)

Portfolio Manager: Steve Pesek - 1993

Investm't Category: Aggressive Growth

✔ Cap Gain	Asset Allocation
Cap & Income	Fund of Funds
Income	Index
	✔ Sector
✔ Domestic	Small Cap
✔ Foreign	Socially Conscious
Country/Region	State Specific

Portfolio: stocks 89%   bonds 0%
convertibles 0%   other 0%   cash 11%

Largest Holdings: broadcasting 12%, household products 9%

Unrealized Net Capital Gains: 14% of portfolio value

SHAREHOLDER INFORMATION

Minimum Investment
Initial: $2,500   Subsequent: $250

Minimum IRA Investment
Initial: $500   Subsequent: $100

Maximum Fees
Load: 3.00% front   12b-1: none
Other: $7.50 redemption fee (30 days or more)

Distributions
Income: April, Dec   Capital Gains: April, Dec

Exchange Options
Number Per Year: 4   Fee: $7.50
Telephone: yes (money market fund available)

Services
IRA, other pension, auto exchange, auto invest, auto withdraw

Fidelity Select Defense & Aerospace (FSDAX)

82 Devonshire St.
Boston, MA 02109
(800) 544-8888, (801) 534-1910

Aggressive Growth

PERFORMANCE

	3yr Annual	5yr Annual	10yr Annual	Bull	Bear
Return (%)	17.8	11.1	na	77.8	-12.2
Differ from Category (+/-)	-7.6 low	-7.1 low	na	-47.2 low	2.8 abv av

Total Risk	Standard Deviation	Category Risk	Risk Index	Beta
abv av	12.7%	low	0.8	0.7

	1993	1992	1991	1990	1989	1988	1987	1986	1985	1984
Return (%)	28.8	0.0	26.9	-4.5	8.8	4.3	-23.1	4.8	26.3	—
Differ from category (+/-) . . .	9.8	-10.4	-25.5	1.8	-18.2	-10.9	-19.7	-4.6	-4.7	—

PER SHARE DATA

	1993	1992	1991	1990	1989	1988	1987	1986	1985	1984
Dividends, Net Income ($) .	0.10	0.00	0.05	0.11	0.00	0.00	0.00	0.02	0.10	—
Distrib'ns, Cap Gain ($) . . .	0.62	0.00	0.00	0.00	0.00	0.00	0.46	0.20	0.00	—
Net Asset Value ($)	18.27	14.75	14.75	11.67	12.35	11.35	10.88	14.79	14.31	—
Expense Ratio (%)	2.48	2.46	2.49	2.43	2.53	2.33	1.54	1.60	1.50	—
Net Income to Assets (%) .	-0.14	-0.10	0.78	0.34	-0.39	-0.91	0.16	0.33	1.13	—
Portfolio Turnover (%)	87	32	162	96	62	162	264	280	271	—
Total Assets (Millions $)	2	1	3	1	1	2	4	11	10	—

PORTFOLIO (as of 8/31/93)

Portfolio Manager: Steve Binder - 1992

Investm't Category: Aggressive Growth
✔ Cap Gain	Asset Allocation
Cap & Income	Fund of Funds
Income	Index
	✔ Sector
✔ Domestic	Small Cap
✔ Foreign	Socially Conscious
Country/Region	State Specific

Portfolio: stocks 100% bonds 0%
convertibles 0% other 0% cash 0%

Largest Holdings: aerospace & defense 49%, defense electronics 25%

Unrealized Net Capital Gains: 6% of portfolio value

SHAREHOLDER INFORMATION

Minimum Investment
Initial: $2,500   Subsequent: $250

Minimum IRA Investment
Initial: $500   Subsequent: $100

Maximum Fees
Load: 3.00% front   12b-1: none
Other: $7.50 redemption fee (30 days or more)

Distributions
Income: April, Dec   Capital Gains: April, Dec

Exchange Options
Number Per Year: 4   Fee: $7.50
Telephone: yes (money market fund available)

Services
IRA, other pension, auto exchange, auto invest, auto withdraw

Fidelity Select Developing Communications (FSDCX)

82 Devonshire St.
Boston, MA 02109
(800) 544-8888, (801) 534-1910

Aggressive Growth

PERFORMANCE

	3yr Annual	5yr Annual	10yr Annual	Bull	Bear
Return (%)	35.5	na	na	223.3	na
Differ from Category (+/-)	10.1 high	na	na	98.4 high	na

Total Risk	Standard Deviation	Category Risk	Risk Index	Beta
high	17.6%	av	1.1	1.2

	1993	1992	1991	1990	1989	1988	1987	1986	1985	1984
Return (%)	31.7	17.2	61.3	—	—	—	—	—	—	—
Differ from category (+/-)	12.7	6.8	8.9	—	—	—	—	—	—	—

PER SHARE DATA

	1993	1992	1991	1990	1989	1988	1987	1986	1985	1984
Dividends, Net Income ($)	0.00	0.00	0.00	—	—	—	—	—	—	—
Distrib'ns, Cap Gain ($)	1.47	0.02	0.79	—	—	—	—	—	—	—
Net Asset Value ($)	19.24	15.91	13.60	—	—	—	—	—	—	—
Expense Ratio (%)	1.88	2.50	2.50	—	—	—	—	—	—	—
Net Income to Assets (%)	-0.59	-0.61	-1.23	—	—	—	—	—	—	—
Portfolio Turnover (%)	77	25	469	—	—	—	—	—	—	—
Total Assets (Millions $)	239	39	7	—	—	—	—	—	—	—

PORTFOLIO (as of 8/31/93)

Portfolio Manager: Paul Antico - 1993

Investm't Category: Aggressive Growth
- ✔ Cap Gain
- Cap & Income
- Income
- Asset Allocation
- Fund of Funds
- Index
- ✔ Sector
- ✔ Domestic
- ✔ Foreign
- Country/Region
- Small Cap
- Socially Conscious
- State Specific

Portfolio: stocks 85% bonds 0%
convertibles 0% other 0% cash 15%

Largest Holdings: computer software & services 27%, cellular 11%

Unrealized Net Capital Gains: 11% of portfolio value

SHAREHOLDER INFORMATION

Minimum Investment
Initial: $2,500   Subsequent: $250

Minimum IRA Investment
Initial: $500   Subsequent: $100

Maximum Fees
Load: 3.00% front   12b-1: none
Other: $7.50 redemption fee (30 days or more)

Distributions
Income: April, Dec   Capital Gains: April, Dec

Exchange Options
Number Per Year: 4   Fee: $7.50
Telephone: yes (money market fund available)

Services
IRA, other pension, auto exchange, auto invest, auto withdraw

Fidelity Select Electric Utilities (FSEUX)

82 Devonshire St.
Boston, MA 02109
(800) 544-8888, (801) 534-1910

Growth & Income

PERFORMANCE

	3yr Annual	5yr Annual	10yr Annual	Bull	Bear
Return (%)	16.1	14.5	na	75.6	-12.5
Differ from Category (+/-)	-0.3 av	2.0 abv av	na	5.5 abv av	-0.8 av

Total Risk	Standard Deviation	Category Risk	Risk Index	Beta
av	7.6%	low	0.8	0.3

	1993	1992	1991	1990	1989	1988	1987	1986	1985	1984
Return (%)	12.7	9.8	26.3	-1.8	28.2	20.0	—	—	—	—
Differ from category (+/-) . . .	0.1	-0.2	-1.4	3.8	6.6	3.2	—	—	—	—

PER SHARE DATA

	1993	1992	1991	1990	1989	1988	1987	1986	1985	1984
Dividends, Net Income ($) .	0.37	0.43	0.50	0.15	0.21	0.40	—	—	—	—
Distrib'ns, Cap Gain ($) . . .	0.82	1.01	0.31	0.15	0.00	0.00	—	—	—	—
Net Asset Value ($)	13.15	12.75	13.01	11.03	11.56	9.20	—	—	—	—
Expense Ratio (%)	1.70	1.83	2.27	2.30	2.52	2.49	—	—	—	—
Net Income to Assets (%) . .	3.20	3.63	4.17	3.80	3.95	4.22	—	—	—	—
Portfolio Turnover (%)	55	76	50	62	125	159	—	—	—	—
Total Assets (Millions $)	23	25	24	23	10	13	—	—	—	—

PORTFOLIO (as of 8/31/93)

Portfolio Manager: John Muresianu - 1992

Investm't Category: Growth & Income

Cap Gain	Asset Allocation
✔ Cap & Income	Fund of Funds
Income	Index
	✔ Sector
✔ Domestic	Small Cap
✔ Foreign	Socially Conscious
Country/Region	State Specific

Portfolio: stocks 97% bonds 0%
convertibles 0% other 0% cash 3%

Largest Holdings: electric utility 92%, gas 5%

Unrealized Net Capital Gains: 24% of portfolio value

SHAREHOLDER INFORMATION

Minimum Investment
Initial: $2,500   Subsequent: $250

Minimum IRA Investment
Initial: $500   Subsequent: $100

Maximum Fees
Load: 3.00% front   12b-1: none
Other: $7.50 redemption fee (30 days or more)

Distributions
Income: April, Dec   Capital Gains: April, Dec

Exchange Options
Number Per Year: 4   Fee: $7.50
Telephone: yes (money market fund available)

Services
IRA, other pension, auto exchange, auto invest, auto withdraw

Fidelity Select Electronics (FSELX)

82 Devonshire St.
Boston, MA 02109
(800) 544-8888, (801) 534-1910

Aggressive Growth

PERFORMANCE

	3yr Annual	5yr Annual	10yr Annual	Bull	Bear
Return (%)	31.5	22.7	na	157.8	-6.5
Differ from Category (+/-)	6.1 abv av	4.5 abv av	na	32.9 abv av	8.5 high

Total Risk	Standard Deviation	Category Risk	Risk Index	Beta
high	20.3%	abv av	1.3	1.3

	1993	1992	1991	1990	1989	1988	1987	1986	1985	1984
Return (%)	32.0	27.4	35.2	5.8	15.6	-8.4	-13.4	-23.8	—	—
Differ from category (+/-)	13.0	17.0	-17.2	12.1	-11.4	-23.6	-10.0	-33.2	—	—

PER SHARE DATA

	1993	1992	1991	1990	1989	1988	1987	1986	1985	1984
Dividends, Net Income ($)	0.00	0.00	0.00	0.00	0.00	0.00	0.00	0.00	—	—
Distrib'ns, Cap Gain ($)	2.75	0.00	0.00	0.00	0.00	0.00	0.00	0.00	—	—
Net Asset Value ($)	15.78	14.12	11.08	8.19	7.75	6.70	7.32	8.46	—	—
Expense Ratio (%)	1.69	2.16	2.26	2.57	2.79	2.54	1.61	1.77	—	—
Net Income to Assets (%)	-0.50	-1.07	-0.45	-0.02	-1.51	-1.02	0.05	0.85	—	—
Portfolio Turnover (%)	293	299	268	378	697	686	511	326	—	—
Total Assets (Millions $)	43	34	18	26	8	12	16	10	—	—

PORTFOLIO (as of 8/31/93)

Portfolio Manager: Steve Shaprio - 1992

Investm't Category: Aggressive Growth

✔ Cap Gain	Asset Allocation
Cap & Income	Fund of Funds
Income	Index
	✔ Sector
✔ Domestic	Small Cap
✔ Foreign	Socially Conscious
Country/Region	State Specific

Portfolio: stocks 69% bonds 0%
convertibles 4% other 0% cash 27%

Largest Holdings: electronics 34%, computers & office equipment 10%

Unrealized Net Capital Gains: 11% of portfolio value

SHAREHOLDER INFORMATION

Minimum Investment
Initial: $2,500   Subsequent: $250

Minimum IRA Investment
Initial: $500   Subsequent: $100

Maximum Fees
Load: 3.00% front   12b-1: none
Other: $7.50 redemption fee (30 days or more)

Distributions
Income: April, Dec   Capital Gains: April, Dec

Exchange Options
Number Per Year: 4   Fee: $7.50
Telephone: yes (money market fund available)

Services
IRA, other pension, auto exchange, auto invest, auto withdraw

Fidelity Select Energy
(FSENX)

Growth

82 Devonshire St.
Boston, MA 02109
(800) 544-8888, (801) 534-1910

PERFORMANCE

	3yr Annual	5yr Annual	10yr Annual	Bull	Bear
Return (%)	5.1	9.6	8.6	3.8	6.9
Differ from Category (+/-)	-14.1 low	-5.0 low	-4.0 low	-80.9 low	19.3 high

Total Risk	Standard Deviation	Category Risk	Risk Index	Beta
high	15.6%	high	1.5	0.6

	1993	1992	1991	1990	1989	1988	1987	1986	1985	1984
Return (%)	19.1	-2.3	0.0	-4.4	42.8	15.9	-1.7	5.4	17.9	2.3
Differ from category (+/-) . . .	5.9	-13.3	-35.4	1.7	17.0	-1.8	-2.9	-9.1	-11.4	2.3

PER SHARE DATA

	1993	1992	1991	1990	1989	1988	1987	1986	1985	1984
Dividends, Net Income ($) .	0.02	0.27	0.15	0.15	0.07	0.31	0.02	0.00	0.62	0.12
Distrib'ns, Cap Gain ($) . . .	0.56	0.00	0.01	1.43	0.21	0.00	0.27	0.00	0.00	0.00
Net Asset Value ($)	16.43	14.32	14.95	15.13	17.47	12.44	11.01	11.53	10.93	9.83
Expense Ratio (%).	1.71	1.78	1.79	1.94	1.77	2.09	1.50	1.54	1.35	1.25
Net Income to Assets (%). .	1.88	1.16	0.99	1.69	2.48	1.72	3.31	5.11	4.33	3.30
Portfolio Turnover (%)	72	81	61	74	168	183	226	167	163	174
Total Assets (Millions $)	72	77	92	83	80	109	104	33	52	83

PORTFOLIO (as of 8/31/93)

Portfolio Manager: Bob Bertleson - 1992

Investm't Category: Growth

✔ Cap Gain
  Cap & Income
  Income
✔ Domestic
✔ Foreign
  Country/Region

  Asset Allocation
  Fund of Funds
  Index
✔ Sector
  Small Cap
  Socially Conscious
  State Specific

Portfolio: stocks 91%   bonds 0%
convertibles 0%   other 0%   cash 9%

Largest Holdings: oil & gas 86%, trucking & freight 1%

Unrealized Net Capital Gains: 15% of portfolio value

SHAREHOLDER INFORMATION

Minimum Investment
Initial: $2,500   Subsequent: $250

Minimum IRA Investment
Initial: $500   Subsequent: $100

Maximum Fees
Load: 3.00% front   12b-1: none
Other: $7.50 redemption fee (30 days or more)

Distributions
Income: April, Dec   Capital Gains: April, Dec

Exchange Options
Number Per Year: 4   Fee: $7.50
Telephone: yes (money market fund available)

Services
IRA, other pension, auto exchange, auto invest, auto withdraw

Fidelity Select Energy Services (FSESX)

Aggressive Growth

82 Devonshire St.
Boston, MA 02109
(800) 544-8888, (801) 534-1910

PERFORMANCE

	3yr Annual	5yr Annual	10yr Annual	Bull	Bear
Return (%)	-1.4	9.2	na	-17.9	18.7
Differ from Category (+/-)	-26.8 low	-9.0 low	na	-142.8 low	33.7 high

Total Risk	Standard Deviation	Category Risk	Risk Index	Beta
high	22.3%	high	1.5	0.9

	1993	1992	1991	1990	1989	1988	1987	1986	1985	1984
Return (%)	20.9	3.4	-23.4	1.7	59.4	-0.3	-11.7	-15.7	—	—
Differ from category (+/-)	1.9	-7.0	-75.8	8.0	32.4	-15.5	-8.3	-25.1	—	—

PER SHARE DATA

	1993	1992	1991	1990	1989	1988	1987	1986	1985	1984
Dividends, Net Income ($)	0.05	0.00	0.00	0.01	0.00	0.00	0.00	0.00	—	—
Distrib'ns, Cap Gain ($)	0.00	0.00	0.00	0.00	0.00	0.00	0.00	0.00	—	—
Net Asset Value ($)	11.61	9.64	9.32	12.18	11.99	7.52	7.55	8.56	—	—
Expense Ratio (%)	1.76	2.07	1.82	2.29	2.53	2.71	1.49	1.51	—	—
Net Income to Assets (%)	0.13	-1.13	-0.02	-0.42	-0.45	-1.06	1.03	2.57	—	—
Portfolio Turnover (%)	236	89	62	128	78	461	575	54	—	—
Total Assets (Millions $)	38	41	73	61	44	33	19	1	—	—

PORTFOLIO (as of 8/31/93)

Portfolio Manager: Bill Mankivsky - 1991

Investm't Category: Aggressive Growth
- ✔ Cap Gain   Asset Allocation
-    Cap & Income   Fund of Funds
-    Income   Index
-    ✔ Sector
- ✔ Domestic   Small Cap
- ✔ Foreign   Socially Conscious
-    Country/Region   State Specific

Portfolio: stocks 81%   bonds 3%
convertibles 7%   other 0%   cash 9%

Largest Holdings: energy services 74%, iron & steel 3%

Unrealized Net Capital Gains: 16% of portfolio value

SHAREHOLDER INFORMATION

Minimum Investment
Initial: $2,500   Subsequent: $250

Minimum IRA Investment
Initial: $500   Subsequent: $100

Maximum Fees
Load: 3.00% front   12b-1: none
Other: $7.50 redemption fee (30 days or more)

Distributions
Income: April, Dec   Capital Gains: April, Dec

Exchange Options
Number Per Year: 4   Fee: $7.50
Telephone: yes (money market fund available)

Services
IRA, other pension, auto exchange, auto invest, auto withdraw

Fidelity Select Environmental Services

82 Devonshire St.
Boston, MA 02109
(800) 544-8888, (801) 534-1910

(FSLEX)   *Aggressive Growth*

PERFORMANCE

	3yr Annual	5yr Annual	10yr Annual	Bull	Bear
Return (%)	1.8	na	na	13.7	-9.5
Differ from Category (+/-)	-23.6 low	na	na	-111.3 low	5.5 abv av

Total Risk	Standard Deviation	Category Risk	Risk Index	Beta
high	15.3%	blw av	1.0	0.9

	1993	1992	1991	1990	1989	1988	1987	1986	1985	1984
Return (%)	-0.6	-1.3	7.6	-2.4	—	—	—	—	—	—
Differ from category (+/-) .	-19.6	-11.7	-44.8	3.9	—	—	—	—	—	—

PER SHARE DATA

	1993	1992	1991	1990	1989	1988	1987	1986	1985	1984
Dividends, Net Income ($) .	0.00	0.00	0.00	0.00	—	—	—	—	—	—
Distrib'ns, Cap Gain ($) . . .	0.00	0.38	0.41	0.00	—	—	—	—	—	—
Net Asset Value ($)	11.20	11.27	11.84	11.42	—	—	—	—	—	—
Expense Ratio (%).	1.99	2.03	2.03	2.25	—	—	—	—	—	—
Net Income to Assets (%) .	-0.70	-0.74	-0.30	0.16	—	—	—	—	—	—
Portfolio Turnover (%)	176	130	122	72	—	—	—	—	—	—
Total Assets (Millions $)	49	65	100	101	—	—	—	—	—	—

PORTFOLIO (as of 8/31/93)

Portfolio Manager: Philip Barton - 1993

Investm't Category: Aggressive Growth

✔ Cap Gain	Asset Allocation
Cap & Income	Fund of Funds
Income	Index
	✔ Sector
✔ Domestic	Small Cap
✔ Foreign	Socially Conscious
Country/Region	State Specific

Portfolio: stocks 95%   bonds 0%
convertibles 0%   other 0%   cash 5%

Largest Holdings: pollution control 58%, engineering 8%

Unrealized Net Capital Gains: -1% of portfolio value

SHAREHOLDER INFORMATION

Minimum Investment
Initial: $2,500   Subsequent: $250

Minimum IRA Investment
Initial: $500   Subsequent: $100

Maximum Fees
Load: 3.00% front   12b-1: none
Other: $7.50 redemption fee (30 days or more)

Distributions
Income: April, Dec   Capital Gains: April, Dec

Exchange Options
Number Per Year: 4   Fee: $7.50
Telephone: yes (money market fund available)

Services
IRA, other pension, auto exchange, auto invest, auto withdraw

Fidelity Select Financial Services (FIDSX)

82 Devonshire St.
Boston, MA 02109
(800) 544-8888, (801) 534-1910

Growth

PERFORMANCE

	3yr Annual	5yr Annual	10yr Annual	Bull	Bear
Return (%)	39.4	19.6	15.9	207.3	-33.1
Differ from Category (+/-)	20.2 high	5.0 high	3.3 high	122.6 high	-20.7 low

Total Risk	Standard Deviation	Category Risk	Risk Index	Beta
high	17.1%	high	1.6	1.3

	1993	1992	1991	1990	1989	1988	1987	1986	1985	1984
Return (%)	17.5	42.8	61.6	-24.3	19.3	12.0	-16.5	15.0	41.2	17.9
Differ from category (+/-)	4.3	31.8	26.2	-18.2	-6.5	-5.7	-17.7	0.5	11.9	17.9

PER SHARE DATA

	1993	1992	1991	1990	1989	1988	1987	1986	1985	1984
Dividends, Net Income ($)	0.20	0.50	0.34	0.51	0.33	0.81	0.11	0.20	0.28	0.09
Distrib'ns, Cap Gain ($)	7.32	3.38	0.00	0.00	0.18	0.00	1.54	0.33	0.00	0.03
Net Asset Value ($)	49.79	48.83	37.14	23.22	31.39	26.73	24.57	31.56	27.86	19.96
Expense Ratio (%)	1.54	1.85	2.49	2.22	1.07	2.47	1.57	1.26	1.50	1.51
Net Income to Assets (%)	0.86	1.49	2.22	2.03	3.53	1.58	1.65	3.05	4.17	3.21
Portfolio Turnover (%)	100	164	237	308	186	81	40	136	170	191
Total Assets (Millions $)	128	91	35	21	32	28	56	234	68	13

PORTFOLIO (as of 8/31/93)

Portfolio Manager: Steve Binder - 1993

Investm't Category: Growth

✔ Cap Gain	Asset Allocation
Cap & Income	Fund of Funds
Income	Index
	✔ Sector
✔ Domestic	Small Cap
✔ Foreign	Socially Conscious
Country/Region	State Specific

Portfolio: stocks 99%   bonds 0%
convertibles 0%   other 0%   cash 1%

Largest Holdings: banks 60%, credit & other finance 11%

Unrealized Net Capital Gains: 14% of portfolio value

SHAREHOLDER INFORMATION

Minimum Investment
Initial: $2,500   Subsequent: $250

Minimum IRA Investment
Initial: $500   Subsequent: $100

Maximum Fees
Load: 3.00% front   12b-1: none
Other: $7.50 redemption fee (30 days or more)

Distributions
Income: April, Dec   Capital Gains: April, Dec

Exchange Options
Number Per Year: 4   Fee: $7.50
Telephone: yes (money market fund available)

Services
IRA, other pension, auto exchange, auto invest, auto withdraw

Fidelity Select Food & Agriculture (FDFAX)

Aggressive Growth

82 Devonshire St.
Boston, MA 02109
(800) 544-8888, (801) 534-1910

PERFORMANCE

	3yr Annual	5yr Annual	10yr Annual	Bull	Bear
Return (%)	15.6	18.6	na	71.2	-1.2
Differ from Category (+/-)	-9.8 low	0.4 av	na	-53.8 low	13.8 high

Total Risk	Standard Deviation	Category Risk	Risk Index	Beta
abv av	10.9%	low	0.7	0.9

	1993	1992	1991	1990	1989	1988	1987	1986	1985	1984
Return (%)	8.8	6.0	34.0	9.3	38.8	26.7	7.5	22.5	—	—
Differ from category (+/-) .	-10.2	-4.4	-18.4	15.6	11.8	11.5	10.9	13.1	—	—

PER SHARE DATA

	1993	1992	1991	1990	1989	1988	1987	1986	1985	1984
Dividends, Net Income ($) .	0.07	0.10	0.10	0.27	0.03	0.05	0.02	0.00	—	—
Distrib'ns, Cap Gain ($) . . .	2.68	1.57	1.59	0.79	2.17	0.00	0.55	0.00	—	—
Net Asset Value ($)	30.75	30.93	30.86	24.39	23.29	18.42	14.57	14.10	—	—
Expense Ratio (%).	1.67	1.83	2.22	2.53	2.50	2.45	1.67	1.75	—	—
Net Income to Assets (%) . .	0.21	0.46	0.85	0.82	0.48	-0.41	0.71	1.70	—	—
Portfolio Turnover (%)	515	63	124	267	248	215	608	576	—	—
Total Assets (Millions $) . . .	175	108	64	25	15	9	11	9	—	—

PORTFOLIO (as of 8/31/93)

Portfolio Manager: Bill Mankivsky - 1993

Investm't Category: Aggressive Growth
- ✔ Cap Gain
- Cap & Income
- Income
- Asset Allocation
- Fund of Funds
- Index
- ✔ Sector
- Small Cap
- ✔ Domestic
- ✔ Foreign
- Country/Region
- Socially Conscious
- State Specific

Portfolio: stocks 92% bonds 0%
convertibles 0% other 0% cash 8%

Largest Holdings: foods 48%, beverages 19%

Unrealized Net Capital Gains: 9% of portfolio value

SHAREHOLDER INFORMATION

Minimum Investment
Initial: $2,500   Subsequent: $250

Minimum IRA Investment
Initial: $500   Subsequent: $100

Maximum Fees
Load: 3.00% front   12b-1: none
Other: $7.50 redemption fee (30 days or more)

Distributions
Income: April, Dec   Capital Gains: April, Dec

Exchange Options
Number Per Year: 4   Fee: $7.50
Telephone: yes (money market fund available)

Services
IRA, other pension, auto exchange, auto invest, auto withdraw

Fidelity Select Health Care (FSPHX)

82 Devonshire St.
Boston, MA 02109
(800) 544-8888, (801) 534-1910

Aggressive Growth

PERFORMANCE

	3yr Annual	5yr Annual	10yr Annual	Bull	Bear
Return (%)	15.8	22.4	19.0	80.1	7.1
Differ from Category (+/-)	-9.6 low	4.2 abv av	7.1 high	-44.9 low	22.1 high

Total Risk	Standard Deviation	Category Risk	Risk Index	Beta
high	20.9%	high	1.4	1.4

	1993	1992	1991	1990	1989	1988	1987	1986	1985	1984
Return (%)	2.4	-17.4	83.6	24.3	42.4	8.8	-0.6	21.9	59.4	-1.0
Differ from category (+/-)	-16.6	-27.8	31.2	30.6	15.4	-6.4	2.8	12.5	28.4	8.4

PER SHARE DATA

	1993	1992	1991	1990	1989	1988	1987	1986	1985	1984
Dividends, Net Income ($)	0.07	0.15	0.34	0.20	0.12	0.28	0.00	0.00	0.04	0.05
Distrib'ns, Cap Gain ($)	0.00	8.51	8.81	5.67	0.83	0.00	0.92	0.36	0.00	0.09
Net Asset Value ($)	63.62	62.19	85.95	52.98	47.58	34.13	31.62	32.78	27.15	17.06
Expense Ratio (%)	1.46	1.44	1.53	1.74	1.41	1.64	1.39	1.29	1.26	1.21
Net Income to Assets (%)	0.24	-0.02	1.28	1.61	0.95	0.06	-0.01	0.53	0.56	0.54
Portfolio Turnover (%)	112	154	159	126	114	122	213	217	159	139
Total Assets (Millions $)	560	838	624	217	210	208	341	251	145	65

PORTFOLIO (as of 8/31/93)

Portfolio Manager: Charles Mangum - 1992

Investm't Category: Aggressive Growth
✔ Cap Gain   Asset Allocation
  Cap & Income   Fund of Funds
  Income   Index
                  ✔ Sector
✔ Domestic   Small Cap
✔ Foreign   Socially Conscious
  Country/Region   State Specific

Portfolio: stocks 89%   bonds 0%
convertibles 1%   other 0%   cash 10%

Largest Holdings: drugs & pharmaceuticals 58%, medical equipment & supplies 17%

Unrealized Net Capital Gains: -1% of portfolio value

SHAREHOLDER INFORMATION

Minimum Investment
Initial: $2,500   Subsequent: $250

Minimum IRA Investment
Initial: $500   Subsequent: $100

Maximum Fees
Load: 3.00% front   12b-1: none
Other: $7.50 redemption fee (30 days or more)

Distributions
Income: April, Dec   Capital Gains: April, Dec

Exchange Options
Number Per Year: 4   Fee: $7.50
Telephone: yes (money market fund available)

Services
IRA, other pension, auto exchange, auto invest, auto withdraw

Fidelity Select Home Finance (FSVLX)

82 Devonshire St.
Boston, MA 02109
(800) 544-8888, (801) 534-1910

Aggressive Growth

PERFORMANCE

	3yr Annual	5yr Annual	10yr Annual	Bull	Bear
Return (%)	48.9	25.1	na	271.2	-24.3
Differ from Category (+/-)	23.5 high	6.9 high	na	146.2 high	-9.3 low

Total Risk	Standard Deviation	Category Risk	Risk Index	Beta
high	18.7%	abv av	1.2	1.2

	1993	1992	1991	1990	1989	1988	1987	1986	1985	1984
Return (%)	27.2	57.8	64.6	-15.0	9.3	18.4	-7.9	27.5	—	—
Differ from category (+/-)	8.2	47.4	12.2	-8.7	-17.7	3.2	-4.5	18.1	—	—

PER SHARE DATA

	1993	1992	1991	1990	1989	1988	1987	1986	1985	1984
Dividends, Net Income ($)	0.00	0.00	0.14	0.14	0.03	0.12	0.00	0.00	—	—
Distrib'ns, Cap Gain ($)	1.40	0.28	0.00	0.00	0.49	0.00	3.50	0.00	—	—
Net Asset Value ($)	24.44	20.35	13.09	8.05	9.65	9.30	7.96	12.88	—	—
Expense Ratio (%)	1.55	2.08	2.50	2.53	2.56	2.57	1.53	1.54	—	—
Net Income to Assets (%)	0.61	0.40	1.78	0.83	1.13	0.17	-0.05	5.76	—	—
Portfolio Turnover (%)	61	134	159	282	216	456	335	312	—	—
Total Assets (Millions $)	156	49	8	5	5	6	24	36	—	—

PORTFOLIO (as of 8/31/93)

Portfolio Manager: David Ellison - 1985

Investm't Category: Aggressive Growth
- ✔ Cap Gain
- Cap & Income
- Income
- Asset Allocation
- Fund of Funds
- Index
- ✔ Sector
- ✔ Domestic
- ✔ Foreign
- Country/Region
- Small Cap
- Socially Conscious
- State Specific

Portfolio: stocks 97% bonds 1%
convertibles 0% other 0% cash 2%

Largest Holdings: savings & loans 77%, banks 14%

Unrealized Net Capital Gains: 15% of portfolio value

SHAREHOLDER INFORMATION

Minimum Investment
Initial: $2,500   Subsequent: $250

Minimum IRA Investment
Initial: $500   Subsequent: $100

Maximum Fees
Load: 3.00% front   12b-1: none
Other: $7.50 redemption fee (30 days or more)

Distributions
Income: April, Dec   Capital Gains: April, Dec

Exchange Options
Number Per Year: 4   Fee: $7.50
Telephone: yes (money market fund available)

Services
IRA, other pension, auto exchange, auto invest, auto withdraw

Fidelity Select Industrial Equipment (FSCGX)

82 Devonshire St.
Boston, MA 02109
(800) 544-8888, (801) 534-1910

Aggressive Growth

PERFORMANCE

	3yr Annual	5yr Annual	10yr Annual	Bull	Bear
Return (%)	26.4	15.0	na	110.8	-18.8
Differ from Category (+/-)	1.0 av	-3.2 blw av	na	-14.2 av	-3.8 av

Total Risk	Standard Deviation	Category Risk	Risk Index	Beta
abv av	13.7%	blw av	0.9	0.7

	1993	1992	1991	1990	1989	1988	1987	1986	1985	1984
Return (%)	43.3	11.3	26.8	-15.5	17.9	4.8	-9.2	—	—	—
Differ from category (+/-). .	24.3	0.8	-25.6	-9.2	-9.1	-10.4	-5.8	—	—	—

PER SHARE DATA

	1993	1992	1991	1990	1989	1988	1987	1986	1985	1984
Dividends, Net Income ($) .	0.00	0.00	0.10	0.09	0.00	0.00	0.00	—	—	—
Distrib'ns, Cap Gain ($) . . .	0.40	0.00	0.00	0.00	0.00	0.00	0.23	—	—	—
Net Asset Value ($)	19.14	13.65	12.26	9.76	11.63	9.86	9.40	—	—	—
Expense Ratio (%)	2.49	2.49	2.52	2.59	2.58	2.65	1.70	—	—	—
Net Income to Assets (%) .	0.15	-0.57	0.09	1.06	-0.66	-0.37	0.38	—	—	—
Portfolio Turnover (%).	407	167	43	132	164	407	514	—	—	—
Total Assets (Millions $).	85	7	1	3	2	5	2	—	—	—

PORTFOLIO (as of 8/31/93)

Portfolio Manager: Albert Ruback - 1991

Investm't Category: Aggressive Growth

✔ Cap Gain   Asset Allocation
   Cap & Income   Fund of Funds
   Income   Index
      ✔ Sector
✔ Domestic   Small Cap
✔ Foreign   Socially Conscious
   Country/Region   State Specific

Portfolio: stocks 96%   bonds 0%
convertibles 0%   other 0%   cash 4%

Largest Holdings: industrial machinery & equipment 66%, autos, tires, & accessories 13%

Unrealized Net Capital Gains: 8% of portfolio value

SHAREHOLDER INFORMATION

Minimum Investment
Initial: $2,500   Subsequent: $250

Minimum IRA Investment
Initial: $500   Subsequent: $100

Maximum Fees
Load: 3.00% front   12b-1: none
Other: $7.50 redemption fee (30 days or more)

Distributions
Income: April, Dec   Capital Gains: April, Dec

Exchange Options
Number Per Year: 4   Fee: $7.50
Telephone: yes (money market fund available)

Services
IRA, other pension, auto exchange, auto invest, auto withdraw

Fidelity Select Industrial Materials (FSDPX)

82 Devonshire St.
Boston, MA 02109
(800) 544-8888, (801) 534-1910

Aggressive Growth

PERFORMANCE

	3yr Annual	5yr Annual	10yr Annual	Bull	Bear
Return (%)	22.8	9.9	na	100.9	-23.6
Differ from Category (+/-)	-2.6 blw av	-8.3 low	na	-24.1 blw av	-8.6 low

Total Risk	Standard Deviation	Category Risk	Risk Index	Beta
abv av	12.9%	low	0.8	0.9

	1993	1992	1991	1990	1989	1988	1987	1986	1985	1984
Return (%)	21.3	12.4	35.8	-17.1	4.4	10.8	15.6	—	—	—
Differ from category (+/-)	2.3	2.0	-16.6	-10.8	-22.6	-4.4	19.0	—	—	—

PER SHARE DATA

	1993	1992	1991	1990	1989	1988	1987	1986	1985	1984
Dividends, Net Income ($)	0.05	0.08	0.06	0.34	0.00	0.21	0.02	—	—	—
Distrib'ns, Cap Gain ($)	0.00	0.00	0.00	0.00	0.00	0.00	0.00	—	—	—
Net Asset Value ($)	20.47	16.92	15.13	11.19	13.86	13.27	12.17	—	—	—
Expense Ratio (%)	2.02	2.47	2.49	2.59	2.68	2.43	1.56	—	—	—
Net Income to Assets (%)	0.86	0.25	1.30	1.22	-0.54	0.53	0.15	—	—	—
Portfolio Turnover (%)	273	222	148	250	289	455	414	—	—	—
Total Assets (Millions $)	36	22	2	3	8	42	27	—	—	—

PORTFOLIO (as of 8/31/93)

Portfolio Manager: Louis Salemy - 1992

Investm't Category: Aggressive Growth
- ✔ Cap Gain
- Cap & Income
- Income
- ✔ Domestic
- ✔ Foreign
- Country/Region
- Asset Allocation
- Fund of Funds
- Index
- ✔ Sector
- Small Cap
- Socially Conscious
- State Specific

Portfolio:

stocks 86%	bonds 0%	
convertibles 0%	other 0%	cash 14%

Largest Holdings: metals & mining 20%, railroads 18%

Unrealized Net Capital Gains: 5% of portfolio value

SHAREHOLDER INFORMATION

Minimum Investment
Initial: $2,500   Subsequent: $250

Minimum IRA Investment
Initial: $500   Subsequent: $100

Maximum Fees
Load: 3.00% front   12b-1: none
Other: $7.50 redemption fee (30 days or more)

Distributions
Income: April, Dec   Capital Gains: April, Dec

Exchange Options
Number Per Year: 4   Fee: $7.50
Telephone: yes (money market fund available)

Services
IRA, other pension, auto exchange, auto invest, auto withdraw

Fidelity Select Insurance
(FSPCX)
Growth

82 Devonshire St.
Boston, MA 02109
(800) 544-8888, (801) 534-1910

PERFORMANCE

	3yr Annual	5yr Annual	10yr Annual	Bull	Bear
Return (%)	21.9	17.6	na	104.8	-20.2
Differ from Category (+/-)	2.7 abv av	3.0 high	na	20.1 abv av	-7.8 low

Total Risk	Standard Deviation	Category Risk	Risk Index	Beta
abv av	12.8%	abv av	1.2	0.8

	1993	1992	1991	1990	1989	1988	1987	1986	1985	1984
Return (%)	8.1	22.5	36.6	-9.8	37.8	17.4	-12.1	7.6	—	—
Differ from category (+/-)	-5.1	11.5	1.2	-3.7	12.0	-0.3	-13.3	-6.9	—	—

PER SHARE DATA

	1993	1992	1991	1990	1989	1988	1987	1986	1985	1984
Dividends, Net Income ($)	0.00	0.02	0.25	0.00	0.15	0.09	0.14	0.00	—	—
Distrib'ns, Cap Gain ($)	1.96	1.71	0.00	0.00	0.00	0.00	0.00	0.00	—	—
Net Asset Value ($)	20.03	20.33	18.30	13.60	15.08	11.05	9.49	10.97	—	—
Expense Ratio (%)	2.49	2.47	2.49	2.50	2.53	2.48	1.63	1.51	—	—
Net Income to Assets (%)	-0.26	0.22	1.58	1.15	0.98	0.28	0.53	1.34	—	—
Portfolio Turnover (%)	81	112	98	158	95	174	718	299	—	—
Total Assets (Millions $)	18	2	2	2	3	3	7	5	—	—

PORTFOLIO (as of 8/31/93)

Portfolio Manager: Bob Chow - 1993

Investm't Category: Growth

✔ Cap Gain	Asset Allocation
Cap & Income	Fund of Funds
Income	Index
	✔ Sector
✔ Domestic	Small Cap
✔ Foreign	Socially Conscious
Country/Region	State Specific

Portfolio: stocks 95% bonds 0%
convertibles 0% other 0% cash 5%

Largest Holdings: property—casualty & rein-
surance 66%, life insurance 14%

Unrealized Net Capital Gains: 12% of portfolio value

SHAREHOLDER INFORMATION

Minimum Investment
Initial: $2,500   Subsequent: $250

Minimum IRA Investment
Initial: $500   Subsequent: $100

Maximum Fees
Load: 3.00% front   12b-1: none
Other: $7.50 redemption fee (30 days or more)

Distributions
Income: April, Dec   Capital Gains: April, Dec

Exchange Options
Number Per Year: 4   Fee: $7.50
Telephone: yes (money market fund available)

Services
IRA, other pension, auto exchange, auto invest,
auto withdraw

Fidelity Select Leisure

(FDLSX)

Aggressive Growth

82 Devonshire St.
Boston, MA 02109
(800) 544-8888, (801) 534-1910

PERFORMANCE

	3yr Annual	5yr Annual	10yr Annual	Bull	Bear
Return (%)	29.1	17.0	na	140.1	-30.2
Differ from Category (+/-)	3.7 abv av	-1.2 blw av	na	15.1 abv av	-15.2 low

Total Risk	Standard Deviation	Category Risk	Risk Index	Beta
abv av	12.2%	low	0.8	0.9

	1993	1992	1991	1990	1989	1988	1987	1986	1985	1984
Return (%)	39.5	16.2	32.9	-22.2	31.2	26.0	5.6	15.7	56.4	—
Differ from category (+/-) ..	20.5	5.8	-19.5	-15.9	4.2	10.8	9.0	6.3	25.4	—

PER SHARE DATA

	1993	1992	1991	1990	1989	1988	1987	1986	1985	1984
Dividends, Net Income ($) .	0.00	0.00	0.00	0.23	0.07	0.00	0.00	0.00	0.02	—
Distrib'ns, Cap Gain ($) ...	3.26	0.00	0.00	0.00	2.03	0.40	2.03	0.03	0.00	—
Net Asset Value ($)	45.22	35.09	30.19	22.71	29.52	24.13	19.49	20.51	17.76	—
Expense Ratio (%)........	1.90	2.21	2.27	1.96	1.73	1.96	1.55	1.41	1.50	—
Net Income to Assets (%) .	-0.39	-0.28	0.34	0.86	0.50	-0.13	-0.16	0.48	1.16	—
Portfolio Turnover (%)	109	45	75	124	249	229	148	148	243	—
Total Assets (Millions $) ...	115	40	40	49	91	56	72	207	27	—

PORTFOLIO (as of 8/31/93)

Portfolio Manager: Deborah Wheeler - 1992

Investm't Category: Aggressive Growth

✔ Cap Gain
Cap & Income
Income
✔ Domestic
✔ Foreign
Country/Region

Asset Allocation
Fund of Funds
Index
✔ Sector
Small Cap
Socially Conscious
State Specific

Portfolio: stocks 86% bonds 0%
convertibles 1% other 0% cash 13%

Largest Holdings: broadcasting 21%, entertainment 12%

Unrealized Net Capital Gains: 15% of portfolio value

SHAREHOLDER INFORMATION

Minimum Investment
Initial: $2,500 Subsequent: $250

Minimum IRA Investment
Initial: $500 Subsequent: $100

Maximum Fees
Load: 3.00% front 12b-1: none
Other: $7.50 redemption fee (30 days or more)

Distributions
Income: April, Dec Capital Gains: April, Dec

Exchange Options
Number Per Year: 4 Fee: $7.50
Telephone: yes (money market fund available)

Services
IRA, other pension, auto exchange, auto invest, auto withdraw

Fidelity Select Medical Delivery (FSHCX)

82 Devonshire St.
Boston, MA 02109
(800) 544-8888, (801) 534-1910

Aggressive Growth

PERFORMANCE

	3yr Annual	5yr Annual	10yr Annual	Bull	Bear
Return (%)	17.6	24.5	na	98.7	-4.7
Differ from Category (+/-)	-7.8 low	6.3 high	na	-26.3 blw av	10.3 high

Total Risk	Standard Deviation	Category Risk	Risk Index	Beta
high	24.5%	high	1.6	1.3

	1993	1992	1991	1990	1989	1988	1987	1986	1985	1984
Return (%)	5.5	-13.1	77.8	16.2	58.0	15.7	-12.0	—	—	—
Differ from category (+/-). .	-13.5	-23.5	25.4	22.5	31.0	0.5	-8.6	—	—	—

PER SHARE DATA

	1993	1992	1991	1990	1989	1988	1987	1986	1985	1984
Dividends, Net Income ($).	0.00	0.00	0.00	0.00	0.05	0.00	0.02	—	—	—
Distrib'ns, Cap Gain ($) . . .	0.00	1.55	1.24	0.39	0.26	0.00	0.36	—	—	—
Net Asset Value ($)	19.10	18.10	22.76	13.65	12.09	7.85	6.78	—	—	—
Expense Ratio (%)	1.77	1.69	1.94	2.16	2.48	2.48	1.49	—	—	—
Net Income to Assets (%) .	-0.89	-0.71	-0.07	1.43	0.59	-0.65	0.62	—	—	—
Portfolio Turnover (%).	155	181	165	253	92	264	221	—	—	—
Total Assets (Millions $). . . .	148	129	131	23	20	3	3	—	—	—

PORTFOLIO (as of 8/31/93)

Portfolio Manager: Louis Salemy - 1993

Investm't Category: Aggressive Growth

✔ Cap Gain	Asset Allocation
Cap & Income	Fund of Funds
Income	Index
	✔ Sector
✔ Domestic	Small Cap
✔ Foreign	Socially Conscious
Country/Region	State Specific

Portfolio: stocks 76% bonds 0%
convertibles 0% other 0% cash 24%

Largest Holdings: medical facilities management 56%, drugs & pharmaceuticals 12%

Unrealized Net Capital Gains: 3% of portfolio value

SHAREHOLDER INFORMATION

Minimum Investment
Initial: $2,500 Subsequent: $250

Minimum IRA Investment
Initial: $500 Subsequent: $100

Maximum Fees
Load: 3.00% front 12b-1: none
Other: $7.50 redemption fee (30 days or more)

Distributions
Income: April, Dec Capital Gains: April, Dec

Exchange Options
Number Per Year: 4 Fee: $7.50
Telephone: yes (money market fund available)

Services
IRA, other pension, auto exchange, auto invest, auto withdraw

Fidelity Select Natural Gas Port (FSNGX)

82 Devonshire St.
Boston, MA 02109
(800) 544-8888, (801) 534-1910

Growth

fund in existence since 4/21/93

PERFORMANCE

	3yr Annual	5yr Annual	10yr Annual	Bull	Bear
Return (%)	na	na	na	na	na
Differ from Category (+/-)	na	na	na	na	na

Total Risk	Standard Deviation	Category Risk	Risk Index	Beta
na	na	na	na	na

	1993	1992	1991	1990	1989	1988	1987	1986	1985	1984
Return (%)	—	—	—	—	—	—	—	—	—	—
Differ from category (+/-) ...	—	—	—	—	—	—	—	—	—	—

PER SHARE DATA

	1993	1992	1991	1990	1989	1988	1987	1986	1985	1984
Dividends, Net Income ($) .	0.00	—	—	—	—	—	—	—	—	—
Distrib'ns, Cap Gain ($) ...	0.12	—	—	—	—	—	—	—	—	—
Net Asset Value ($)	9.36	—	—	—	—	—	—	—	—	—
Expense Ratio (%)........	2.09	—	—	—	—	—	—	—	—	—
Net Income to Assets (%) ..	0.61	—	—	—	—	—	—	—	—	—
Portfolio Turnover (%)	0	—	—	—	—	—	—	—	—	—
Total Assets (Millions $)	48	—	—	—	—	—	—	—	—	—

PORTFOLIO (as of 8/31/93)

Portfolio Manager: John Muresianu - 1993

Investm't Category: Growth

Cap Gain	Asset Allocation
✔ Cap & Income	Fund of Funds
Income	Index
	✔ Sector
✔ Domestic	Small Cap
✔ Foreign	Socially Conscious
Country/Region	State Specific

Portfolio: stocks 86%   bonds 0%
convertibles 0%   other 0%   cash 14%

Largest Holdings: oil & gas 40%, gas 40%

Unrealized Net Capital Gains: 6% of portfolio value

SHAREHOLDER INFORMATION

Minimum Investment
Initial: $2,500   Subsequent: $250

Minimum IRA Investment
Initial: $500   Subsequent: $100

Maximum Fees
Load: 3.00% front   12b-1: none
Other: $7.50 redemption fee (30 days or more)

Distributions
Income: April, Dec   Capital Gains: April, Dec

Exchange Options
Number Per Year: 4   Fee: $7.50
Telephone: yes (money market fund available)

Services
IRA, other pension, auto exchange, auto invest, auto withdraw

Fidelity Select Paper & Forest Prod (FSPFX)

82 Devonshire St.
Boston, MA 02109
(800) 544-8888, (801) 534-1910

Aggressive Growth

PERFORMANCE

	3yr Annual	5yr Annual	10yr Annual	Bull	Bear
Return (%)	21.4	9.6	na	105.1	-25.9
Differ from Category (+/-)	-4.0 blw av	-8.6 low	na	-19.9 av	-10.9 low

Total Risk	Standard Deviation	Category Risk	Risk Index	Beta
high	14.4%	blw av	0.9	0.7

	1993	1992	1991	1990	1989	1988	1987	1986	1985	1984
Return (%)	18.5	12.0	34.7	-15.1	4.0	6.7	3.9	—	—	—
Differ from category (+/-)	-0.5	1.6	-17.7	-8.8	-23.0	-8.5	7.3	—	—	—

PER SHARE DATA

	1993	1992	1991	1990	1989	1988	1987	1986	1985	1984
Dividends, Net Income ($)	0.01	0.09	0.30	0.17	0.15	0.03	0.04	—	—	—
Distrib'ns, Cap Gain ($)	0.00	0.00	0.00	0.00	0.00	0.00	1.04	—	—	—
Net Asset Value ($)	18.08	15.26	13.70	10.41	12.47	12.13	11.39	—	—	—
Expense Ratio (%)	2.21	2.05	2.49	2.57	2.54	2.52	1.29	—	—	—
Net Income to Assets (%)	0.49	0.92	1.73	0.92	0.07	-0.20	1.61	—	—	—
Portfolio Turnover (%)	222	421	171	221	154	209	466	—	—	—
Total Assets (Millions $)	49	28	12	5	9	15	110	—	—	—

PORTFOLIO (as of 8/31/93)

Portfolio Manager: Scott Offen - 1993

Investm't Category: Aggressive Growth
- ✔ Cap Gain
-   Cap & Income
-   Income
- ✔ Domestic
- ✔ Foreign
-   Country/Region
-   Asset Allocation
-   Fund of Funds
-   Index
- ✔ Sector
-   Small Cap
-   Socially Conscious
-   State Specific

Portfolio: stocks 89% bonds 0%
convertibles 0% other 0% cash 11%

Largest Holdings: paper & forest products 76%, printing 11%

Unrealized Net Capital Gains: 4% of portfolio value

SHAREHOLDER INFORMATION

Minimum Investment
Initial: $2,500   Subsequent: $250

Minimum IRA Investment
Initial: $500   Subsequent: $100

Maximum Fees
Load: 3.00% front   12b-1: none
Other: $7.50 redemption fee (30 days or more)

Distributions
Income: April, Dec   Capital Gains: April, Dec

Exchange Options
Number Per Year: 4   Fee: $7.50
Telephone: yes (money market fund available)

Services
IRA, other pension, auto exchange, auto invest, auto withdraw

Fidelity Select Precious Metals (FDPMX)

82 Devonshire St.
Boston, MA 02109
(800) 544-8888, (801) 534-1910

Gold

PERFORMANCE

	3yr Annual	5yr Annual	10yr Annual	Bull	Bear
Return (%)	18.8	11.8	4.8	52.3	-13.0
Differ from Category (+/-)	5.1 high	-0.5 high	1.9 blw av	18.7 high	-58.9 av

Total Risk	Standard Deviation	Category Risk	Risk Index	Beta
high	26.5%	abv av	1.0	-0.4

	1993	1992	1991	1990	1989	1988	1987	1986	1985	1984
Return (%)	111.6	-21.8	1.5	-21.0	32.1	-23.8	37.5	32.9	-10.5	-26.1
Differ from category (+/-) . .	24.7	-6.1	6.3	-52.5	7.4	-4.9	5.6	-4.7	-3.1	0.1

PER SHARE DATA

	1993	1992	1991	1990	1989	1988	1987	1986	1985	1984
Dividends, Net Income ($) .	0.21	0.17	0.10	0.15	0.18	0.46	0.07	0.09	0.39	0.19
Distrib'ns, Cap Gain ($) . . .	0.00	0.00	0.00	0.00	0.00	0.00	0.12	0.00	0.00	0.02
Net Asset Value ($)	18.13	8.67	11.31	11.24	14.44	11.06	15.14	11.15	8.49	9.85
Expense Ratio (%)	1.73	1.81	1.79	1.93	1.88	2.02	1.50	1.48	1.11	1.16
Net Income to Assets (%) . .	1.12	0.92	1.52	1.01	2.18	2.42	3.44	4.16	3.65	3.81
Portfolio Turnover (%)	36	44	41	98	72	86	84	65	46	26
Total Assets (Millions $) . . .	466	130	155	192	180	242	647	116	189	219

PORTFOLIO (as of 8/31/93)

Portfolio Manager: Malcolm MacNaught - 1981

Investm't Category: Gold

✔ Cap Gain	Asset Allocation
Cap & Income	Fund of Funds
Income	Index
	✔ Sector
✔ Domestic	Small Cap
✔ Foreign	Socially Conscious
Country/Region	State Specific

Portfolio: stocks 83% bonds 0%
convertibles 1% other 6% cash 10%

Largest Holdings: South African gold mining co. 38%, Canadian gold mining co. 25%

Unrealized Net Capital Gains: 12% of portfolio value

SHAREHOLDER INFORMATION

Minimum Investment
Initial: $2,500   Subsequent: $250

Minimum IRA Investment
Initial: $500   Subsequent: $250

Maximum Fees
Load: 3.00% front   12b-1: none
Other: $7.50 redemption fee (30 days or more)

Distributions
Income: Dec   Capital Gains: Dec

Exchange Options
Number Per Year: 4   Fee: $7.50
Telephone: yes (money market fund available)

Services
IRA, other pension, auto exchange, auto invest, auto withdraw

Fidelity Select Regional Banks (FSRBX)

82 Devonshire St.
Boston, MA 02109
(800) 544-8888, (801) 534-1910

Growth

PERFORMANCE

	3yr Annual	5yr Annual	10yr Annual	Bull	Bear
Return (%)	39.8	22.4	na	224.1	-33.0
Differ from Category (+/-)	20.6 high	7.8 high	na	139.3 high	-20.6 low

Total Risk	Standard Deviation	Category Risk	Risk Index	Beta
high	103.2%	high	10.0	-0.5

	1993	1992	1991	1990	1989	1988	1987	1986	1985	1984
Return (%)	11.1	48.5	65.7	-20.6	26.6	25.7	-3.0	—	—	—
Differ from category (+/-). . .	-2.1	37.5	30.3	-14.5	0.8	8.0	-4.2	—	—	—

PER SHARE DATA

	1993	1992	1991	1990	1989	1988	1987	1986	1985	1984
Dividends, Net Income ($).	0.15	0.11	0.15	0.15	0.11	0.20	0.06	—	—	—
Distrib'ns, Cap Gain ($) . . .	3.92	0.81	0.52	0.00	0.64	0.46	0.15	—	—	—
Net Asset Value ($)	17.49	19.44	13.75	8.74	11.21	9.45	8.05	—	—	—
Expense Ratio (%)	1.49	1.77	2.51	2.55	2.53	2.48	1.63	—	—	—
Net Income to Assets (%) .	1.06	1.80	2.34	1.74	2.24	1.61	2.10	—	—	—
Portfolio Turnover (%).	63	89	110	411	352	291	227	—	—	—
Total Assets (Millions $). . . .	116	156	24	5	17	9	2	—	—	—

PORTFOLIO (as of 8/31/93)

Portfolio Manager: Steve Binder - 1990

Investm't Category: Growth

✔ Cap Gain	Asset Allocation
Cap & Income	Fund of Funds
Income	Index
	✔ Sector
✔ Domestic	Small Cap
✔ Foreign	Socially Conscious
Country/Region	State Specific

Portfolio: stocks 100% bonds 0%
convertibles 0% other 0% cash 0%

Largest Holdings: banks 98%, credit & other finance 2%

Unrealized Net Capital Gains: 13% of portfolio value

SHAREHOLDER INFORMATION

Minimum Investment
Initial: $2,500   Subsequent: $250

Minimum IRA Investment
Initial: $500   Subsequent: $100

Maximum Fees
Load: 3.00% front   12b-1: none
Other: $7.50 redemption fee (30 days or more)

Distributions
Income: April, Dec   Capital Gains: April, Dec

Exchange Options
Number Per Year: 4   Fee: $7.50
Telephone: yes (money market fund available)

Services
IRA, other pension, auto exchange, auto invest, auto withdraw

Fidelity Select Retailing
(FSRPX)

Aggressive Growth

82 Devonshire St.
Boston, MA 02109
(800) 544-8888, (801) 534-1910

PERFORMANCE

	3yr Annual	5yr Annual	10yr Annual	Bull	Bear
Return (%)	32.3	23.3	na	165.2	-16.9
Differ from Category (+/-)	6.9 abv av	5.1 abv av	na	40.2 abv av	-1.9 av

Total Risk	Standard Deviation	Category Risk	Risk Index	Beta
high	16.1%	av	1.0	1.0

	1993	1992	1991	1990	1989	1988	1987	1986	1985	1984
Return (%)	13.0	22.0	68.1	-5.0	29.5	38.7	-7.3	14.1	—	—
Differ from category (+/-) . .	-6.0	11.6	15.7	1.3	2.5	23.5	-3.9	4.7	—	—

PER SHARE DATA

	1993	1992	1991	1990	1989	1988	1987	1986	1985	1984
Dividends, Net Income ($) .	0.00	0.00	0.00	0.00	0.16	0.02	0.23	0.00	—	—
Distrib'ns, Cap Gain ($) . . .	2.63	1.17	0.50	0.03	2.57	0.18	0.76	0.00	—	—
Net Asset Value ($)	25.14	24.64	21.28	12.98	13.70	12.74	9.34	11.19	—	—
Expense Ratio (%).	1.77	1.87	2.54	2.50	2.51	2.47	1.54	1.67	—	—
Net Income to Assets (%) .	-0.44	-0.13	-0.34	2.13	0.48	0.13	0.39	0.63	—	—
Portfolio Turnover (%)	171	205	115	212	290	294	596	812	—	—
Total Assets (Millions $)	68	48	18	8	9	15	9	3	—	—

PORTFOLIO (as of 8/31/93)

Portfolio Manager: Mary English - 1993

Investm't Category: Aggressive Growth

✔ Cap Gain	Asset Allocation
Cap & Income	Fund of Funds
Income	Index
	✔ Sector
✔ Domestic	Small Cap
✔ Foreign	Socially Conscious
Country/Region	State Specific

Portfolio: stocks 94% bonds 0%
convertibles 0% other 0% cash 6%

Largest Holdings: general merchandise stores 28%, misc. retail & wholesale 26%

Unrealized Net Capital Gains: 9% of portfolio value

SHAREHOLDER INFORMATION

Minimum Investment
Initial: $2,500   Subsequent: $250

Minimum IRA Investment
Initial: $500   Subsequent: $100

Maximum Fees
Load: 3.00% front   12b-1: none
Other: $7.50 redemption fee (30 days or more)

Distributions
Income: April, Dec   Capital Gains: April, Dec

Exchange Options
Number Per Year: 4   Fee: $7.50
Telephone: yes (money market fund available)

Services
IRA, other pension, auto exchange, auto invest, auto withdraw

Fidelity Select Software & Computer (FSCSX)

82 Devonshire St.
Boston, MA 02109
(800) 544-8888, (801) 534-1910

Aggressive Growth

PERFORMANCE

	3yr Annual	5yr Annual	10yr Annual	Bull	Bear
Return (%)	37.9	24.2	na	223.6	-18.2
Differ from Category (+/-)	12.5 high	6.0 high	na	98.6 high	-3.2 av

Total Risk	Standard Deviation	Category Risk	Risk Index	Beta
high	22.0%	high	1.4	1.4

	1993	1992	1991	1990	1989	1988	1987	1986	1985	1984
Return (%).............	32.7	35.5	45.8	0.8	12.0	9.0	9.4	13.8	—	—
Differ from category (+/-)..	13.7	25.1	-6.6	7.1	-15.0	-6.2	12.8	4.4	—	—

PER SHARE DATA

	1993	1992	1991	1990	1989	1988	1987	1986	1985	1984
Dividends, Net Income ($).	0.00	0.00	0.00	0.00	0.00	0.00	0.00	0.00	—	—
Distrib'ns, Cap Gain ($) ...	6.48	0.00	2.50	0.00	0.86	0.00	0.68	0.00	—	—
Net Asset Value ($)	27.55	26.43	19.50	15.32	15.19	14.34	13.15	12.65	—	—
Expense Ratio (%)	1.64	1.98	2.50	2.56	2.63	2.51	1.51	1.65	—	—
Net Income to Assets (%)	-0.37	-1.30	-0.84	-1.30	-1.51	-0.61	0.08	-0.35	—	—
Portfolio Turnover (%).....	402	348	326	284	434	134	220	193	—	—
Total Assets (Millions $)....	162	89	17	10	14	23	103	17	—	—

PORTFOLIO (as of 8/31/93)

Portfolio Manager: Arieh Coll - 1991

Investm't Category: Aggressive Growth
- ✔ Cap Gain
- Cap & Income
- Income
- Asset Allocation
- Fund of Funds
- Index
- ✔ Sector
- ✔ Domestic
- ✔ Foreign
- Country/Region
- Small Cap
- Socially Conscious
- State Specific

Portfolio:	stocks 92%	bonds 0%
convertibles 0%	other 6%	cash 2%

Largest Holdings: computer software & services 35%, communications equipment 27%

Unrealized Net Capital Gains: 9% of portfolio value

SHAREHOLDER INFORMATION

Minimum Investment
Initial: $2,500   Subsequent: $250

Minimum IRA Investment
Initial: $500   Subsequent: $100

Maximum Fees
Load: 3.00% front   12b-1: none
Other: $7.50 redemption fee (30 days or more)

Distributions
Income: April, Dec   Capital Gains: April, Dec

Exchange Options
Number Per Year: 4   Fee: $7.50
Telephone: yes (money market fund available)

Services
IRA, other pension, auto exchange, auto invest, auto withdraw

Fidelity Select Technology (FSPTX)

82 Devonshire St.
Boston, MA 02109
(800) 544-8888, (801) 534-1910

Aggressive Growth

PERFORMANCE

	3yr Annual	5yr Annual	10yr Annual	Bull	Bear
Return (%)	30.5	23.5	7.3	178.8	-11.8
Differ from Category (+/-)	5.1 abv av	5.3 high	-4.6 low	53.8 high	3.2 abv av

Total Risk	Standard Deviation	Category Risk	Risk Index	Beta
high	20.0%	abv av	1.3	1.4

	1993	1992	1991	1990	1989	1988	1987	1986	1985	1984
Return (%)	28.6	8.7	58.9	10.5	16.9	-2.6	-11.7	-7.4	7.5	-16.8
Differ from category (+/-)	9.6	-1.7	6.5	16.8	-10.1	-17.8	-8.3	-16.8	-23.5	-7.4

PER SHARE DATA

	1993	1992	1991	1990	1989	1988	1987	1986	1985	1984
Dividends, Net Income ($)	0.13	0.00	0.16	0.00	0.00	0.00	0.00	0.00	0.39	0.00
Distrib'ns, Cap Gain ($)	3.70	2.75	0.00	0.00	0.00	0.00	0.80	0.08	0.00	0.08
Net Asset Value ($)	38.73	33.79	33.92	21.46	19.42	16.60	17.06	20.27	21.99	20.87
Expense Ratio (%)	1.64	1.72	1.83	2.09	1.86	1.76	1.44	1.26	1.04	1.04
Net Income to Assets (%)	0.52	-0.84	0.61	-0.76	-0.67	-0.71	-0.21	-0.21	1.24	0.12
Portfolio Turnover (%)	259	353	442	327	397	140	73	85	126	147
Total Assets (Millions $)	174	105	117	78	105	137	296	318	565	462

PORTFOLIO (as of 8/31/93)

Portfolio Manager: Harry Lange - 1993

Investm't Category: Aggressive Growth
✔ Cap Gain	Asset Allocation
Cap & Income	Fund of Funds
Income	Index
	✔ Sector
✔ Domestic	Small Cap
✔ Foreign	Socially Conscious
Country/Region	State Specific

Portfolio: stocks 91% bonds 0%
convertibles 0% other 6% cash 3%

Largest Holdings: computer services & software 35%, communications equipment 31%

Unrealized Net Capital Gains: 15% of portfolio value

SHAREHOLDER INFORMATION

Minimum Investment
Initial: $2,500 Subsequent: $250

Minimum IRA Investment
Initial: $500 Subsequent: $100

Maximum Fees
Load: 3.00% front 12b-1: none
Other: $7.50 redemption fee (30 days or more)

Distributions
Income: April, Dec Capital Gains: April, Dec

Exchange Options
Number Per Year: 4 Fee: $7.50
Telephone: yes (money market fund available)

Services
IRA, other pension, auto exchange, auto invest, auto withdraw

Fidelity Select Telecomm (FSTCX)

Growth

82 Devonshire St.
Boston, MA 02109
(800) 544-8888, (801) 534-1910

PERFORMANCE

	3yr Annual	5yr Annual	10yr Annual	Bull	Bear
Return (%)	25.0	19.8	na	123.9	-26.9
Differ from Category (+/-)	5.8 high	5.2 high	na	39.2 high	-14.5 low

Total Risk	Standard Deviation	Category Risk	Risk Index	Beta
abv av	11.8%	av	1.1	0.8

	1993	1992	1991	1990	1989	1988	1987	1986	1985	1984
Return (%)	29.7	15.3	30.8	-16.3	50.8	27.7	15.2	19.8	—	—
Differ from category (+/-)	16.5	4.3	-4.6	-10.2	25.0	10.0	14.0	5.3	—	—

PER SHARE DATA

	1993	1992	1991	1990	1989	1988	1987	1986	1985	1984
Dividends, Net Income ($)	0.20	0.18	0.28	0.43	0.12	0.12	0.02	0.00	—	—
Distrib'ns, Cap Gain ($)	4.18	0.48	0.00	0.00	0.98	0.03	0.36	0.00	—	—
Net Asset Value ($)	37.54	32.51	28.79	22.23	27.11	18.73	14.78	13.18	—	—
Expense Ratio (%)	1.74	1.90	1.97	1.85	2.12	2.48	1.52	1.51	—	—
Net Income to Assets (%)	1.16	1.32	1.35	1.83	1.63	1.64	1.12	2.00	—	—
Portfolio Turnover (%)	115	20	262	341	224	162	284	237	—	—
Total Assets (Millions $)	409	78	55	77	116	36	11	4	—	—

PORTFOLIO (as of 8/31/93)

Portfolio Manager: Fergus Shiel - 1992

Investm't Category: Growth

✔ Cap Gain	Asset Allocation
Cap & Income	Fund of Funds
Income	Index
	✔ Sector
✔ Domestic	Small Cap
✔ Foreign	Socially Conscious
Country/Region	State Specific

Portfolio: stocks 92% bonds 0%
convertibles 3% other 0% cash 5%

Largest Holdings: telephone services 48%, cellular 10%

Unrealized Net Capital Gains: 12% of portfolio value

SHAREHOLDER INFORMATION

Minimum Investment
Initial: $2,500   Subsequent: $250

Minimum IRA Investment
Initial: $500   Subsequent: $100

Maximum Fees
Load: 3.00% front   12b-1: none
Other: $7.50 redemption fee (30 days or more)

Distributions
Income: April, Dec   Capital Gains: April, Dec

Exchange Options
Number Per Year: 4   Fee: $7.50
Telephone: yes (money market fund available)

Services
IRA, other pension, auto exchange, auto invest, auto withdraw

Fidelity Select Transportation (FSRFX)

Aggressive Growth

82 Devonshire St.
Boston, MA 02109
(800) 544-8888, (801) 534-1910

PERFORMANCE

	3yr Annual	5yr Annual	10yr Annual	Bull	Bear
Return (%)	35.1	19.9	na	161.8	-26.1
Differ from Category (+/-)	9.7 high	1.7 abv av	na	36.9 abv av	-11.1 low

Total Risk	Standard Deviation	Category Risk	Risk Index	Beta
high	14.1%	blw av	0.9	1.1

	1993	1992	1991	1990	1989	1988	1987	1986	1985	1984
Return (%)	29.3	23.7	54.1	-21.5	28.4	38.4	-17.4	—	—	—
Differ from category (+/-) ..	10.3	13.3	1.7	-15.2	1.4	23.2	-14.0	—	—	—

PER SHARE DATA

	1993	1992	1991	1990	1989	1988	1987	1986	1985	1984
Dividends, Net Income ($) .	0.00	0.00	0.03	0.00	0.00	0.00	0.00	—	—	—
Distrib'ns, Cap Gain ($) ...	1.96	0.36	0.00	0.50	2.32	0.00	0.13	—	—	—
Net Asset Value ($)	20.76	17.64	14.55	9.47	12.58	11.63	8.40	—	—	—
Expense Ratio (%)........	2.48	2.43	2.39	2.50	2.50	2.41	1.60	—	—	—
Net Income to Assets (%).	-0.53	-0.34	0.52	-0.20	-0.33	-0.59	0.01	—	—	—
Portfolio Turnover (%)	116	423	187	156	172	255	218	—	—	—
Total Assets (Millions $)	10	3	1	1	3	1	1	—	—	—

PORTFOLIO (as of 8/31/93)

Portfolio Manager: Beso Sikharulidze - 1993

Investm't Category: Aggressive Growth

✔ Cap Gain	Asset Allocation
Cap & Income	Fund of Funds
Income	Index
	✔ Sector
✔ Domestic	Small Cap
✔ Foreign	Socially Conscious
Country/Region	State Specific

Portfolio: stocks 100% bonds 0%
convertibles 0% other 0% cash 0%

Largest Holdings: railroads 30%, air transportation 16%

Unrealized Net Capital Gains: 23% of portfolio value

SHAREHOLDER INFORMATION

Minimum Investment
Initial: $2,500   Subsequent: $250

Minimum IRA Investment
Initial: $500   Subsequent: $100

Maximum Fees
Load: 3.00% front   12b-1: none
Other: $7.50 redemption fee (30 days or more)

Distributions
Income: April, Dec   Capital Gains: April, Dec

Exchange Options
Number Per Year: 4   Fee: $7.50
Telephone: yes (money market fund available)

Services
IRA, other pension, auto exchange, auto invest, auto withdraw

Fidelity Select Utilities
(FSUTX)
Growth & Income

82 Devonshire St.
Boston, MA 02109
(800) 544-8888, (801) 534-1910

PERFORMANCE

	3yr Annual	5yr Annual	10yr Annual	Bull	Bear
Return (%)	14.6	16.0	15.9	64.6	-8.0
Differ from Category (+/-)	-1.8 blw av	3.5 high	3.5 high	-5.5 blw av	3.6 abv av

Total Risk	Standard Deviation	Category Risk	Risk Index	Beta
av	7.8%	low	0.9	0.3

	1993	1992	1991	1990	1989	1988	1987	1986	1985	1984
Return (%)............	12.5	10.5	21.0	0.5	39.0	16.4	-9.2	24.0	31.7	20.8
Differ from category (+/-)...	-0.1	0.5	-6.7	6.1	17.4	-0.4	-9.6	8.8	6.3	14.6

PER SHARE DATA

	1993	1992	1991	1990	1989	1988	1987	1986	1985	1984
Dividends, Net Income ($).	1.13	1.33	1.69	0.60	0.81	1.42	0.44	0.21	0.48	0.23
Distrib'ns, Cap Gain ($) ...	4.94	1.70	1.19	0.58	0.00	0.00	0.83	0.14	0.00	0.00
Net Asset Value ($)	37.58	38.80	38.01	34.02	35.05	25.90	23.49	27.31	22.30	17.33
Expense Ratio (%)	1.42	1.51	1.65	1.67	1.21	1.94	1.45	1.42	1.50	1.51
Net Income to Assets (%) .	3.71	4.58	4.75	3.93	5.33	4.71	4.88	6.31	7.14	7.42
Portfolio Turnover (%)......	34	45	45	75	75	143	161	96	52	105
Total Assets (Millions $)....	279	206	197	124	84	85	99	86	56	17

PORTFOLIO (as of 8/31/93)

Portfolio Manager: John Muresianu - 1992

Investm't Category: Growth & Income

Cap Gain	Asset Allocation
✔ Cap & Income	Fund of Funds
Income	Index
	✔ Sector
✔ Domestic	Small Cap
✔ Foreign	Socially Conscious
Country/Region	State Specific

Portfolio: stocks 94% bonds 2%
convertibles 1% other 0% cash 3%

Largest Holdings: electric utility 42%, telephone services 26%

Unrealized Net Capital Gains: 17% of portfolio value

SHAREHOLDER INFORMATION

Minimum Investment
Initial: $2,500   Subsequent: $250

Minimum IRA Investment
Initial: $500   Subsequent: $100

Maximum Fees
Load: 3.00% front   12b-1: none
Other: $7.50 redemption fee (30 days or more)

Distributions
Income: April, Dec   Capital Gains: April, Dec

Exchange Options
Number Per Year: 4   Fee: $7.50
Telephone: yes (money market fund available)

Services
IRA, other pension, auto exchange, auto invest, auto withdraw

Fidelity Short-Interm Gov't (FFXSX)

82 Devonshire St.
Boston, MA 02109
(800) 544-8888, (801) 534-1910

Government Bond

PERFORMANCE

	3yr Annual	5yr Annual	10yr Annual	Bull	Bear
Return (%)	na	na	na	na	na
Differ from Category (+/-)	na	na	na	na	na

Total Risk	Standard Deviation	Category Risk	Risk Index	Avg Mat
na	na	na	na	4.8 yrs

	1993	1992	1991	1990	1989	1988	1987	1986	1985	1984
Return (%)	5.2	4.6	—	—	—	—	—	—	—	—
Differ from category (+/-) ..	-5.2	-1.6	—	—	—	—	—	—	—	—

PER SHARE DATA

	1993	1992	1991	1990	1989	1988	1987	1986	1985	1984
Dividends, Net Income ($) .	0.58	0.64	—	—	—	—	—	—	—	—
Distrib'ns, Cap Gain ($) ...	0.00	0.07	—	—	—	—	—	—	—	—
Net Asset Value ($)	9.86	9.93	—	—	—	—	—	—	—	—
Expense Ratio (%)........	0.61	0.28	—	—	—	—	—	—	—	—
Net Income to Assets (%)..	7.19	7.91	—	—	—	—	—	—	—	—
Portfolio Turnover (%)....	348	419	—	—	—	—	—	—	—	—
Total Assets (Millions $) ...	152	173	—	—	—	—	—	—	—	—

PORTFOLIO (as of 9/30/93)

Portfolio Manager: Curtis Hollingsworth - 1991

Investm't Category: Government Bond

Cap Gain	Asset Allocation
Cap & Income	Fund of Funds
✔ Income	Index
	Sector
✔ Domestic	Small Cap
Foreign	Socially Conscious
Country/Region	State Specific

Portfolio: stocks 0% bonds 100%
convertibles 0% other 0% cash 0%

Largest Holdings: U. S. government 59%, mortgage-backed 41%

Unrealized Net Capital Gains: 0% of portfolio value

SHAREHOLDER INFORMATION

Minimum Investment
Initial: $2,500   Subsequent: $250

Minimum IRA Investment
Initial: $500   Subsequent: $250

Maximum Fees
Load: none   12b-1: none
Other: none

Distributions
Income: monthly   Capital Gains: Nov, Dec

Exchange Options
Number Per Year: 4   Fee: none
Telephone: yes (money market fund available)

Services
IRA, other pension, auto exchange, auto invest, auto withdraw

Fidelity Short-Term Bond (FSHBX)

82 Devonshire St.
Boston, MA 02109
(800) 544-8888, (801) 534-1910

Corporate Bond

PERFORMANCE

	3yr Annual	5yr Annual	10yr Annual	Bull	Bear
Return (%)	10.1	9.3	na	35.2	4.4
Differ from Category (+/-)	-1.9 blw av	-0.8 blw av	na	-10.9 blw av	2.6 abv av

Total Risk	Standard Deviation	Category Risk	Risk Index	Avg Mat
low	1.8%	low	0.6	2.5 yrs

	1993	1992	1991	1990	1989	1988	1987	1986	1985	1984
Return (%)	9.1	7.3	14.0	5.7	10.5	5.7	3.9	—	—	—
Differ from category (+/-) . . .	-2.3	-1.3	-2.6	0.4	1.0	-3.3	2.1	—	—	—

PER SHARE DATA

	1993	1992	1991	1990	1989	1988	1987	1986	1985	1984
Dividends, Net Income ($) .	0.66	0.74	0.81	0.80	0.80	0.81	0.83	—	—	—
Distrib'ns, Cap Gain ($) . . .	0.00	0.00	0.00	0.00	0.00	0.00	0.00	—	—	—
Net Asset Value ($)	9.55	9.38	9.45	9.05	9.34	9.21	9.50	—	—	—
Expense Ratio (%)	0.77	0.86	0.83	0.83	0.89	0.88	0.90	—	—	—
Net Income to Assets (%) .	7.68	8.23	8.65	8.28	8.77	8.77	8.40	—	—	—
Portfolio Turnover (%)	63	87	164	148	171	251	149	—	—	—
Total Assets (Millions $) . .	2,476	983	235	197	236	382	137	—	—	—

PORTFOLIO (as of 4/30/93)

Portfolio Manager: Donald G. Taylor - 1989

Investm't Category: Corporate Bond

Cap Gain	Asset Allocation
Cap & Income	Fund of Funds
✔ Income	Index
	Sector
✔ Domestic	Small Cap
✔ Foreign	Socially Conscious
Country/Region	State Specific

Portfolio: stocks 0% bonds 88%
convertibles 0% other 9% cash 3%

Largest Holdings: finance 35%, utilities 9%

Unrealized Net Capital Gains: 1% of portfolio value

SHAREHOLDER INFORMATION

Minimum Investment
Initial: $2,500 Subsequent: $250

Minimum IRA Investment
Initial: $500 Subsequent: $100

Maximum Fees
Load: none 12b-1: none
Other: none

Distributions
Income: monthly Capital Gains: Jun, Dec

Exchange Options
Number Per Year: 4 Fee: none
Telephone: yes (money market fund available)

Services
IRA, other pension, auto exchange, auto invest, auto withdraw

Fidelity Short Term World Income (FSHWX)

82 Devonshire St.
Boston, MA 02109
(800) 544-8888, (801) 534-1910

International Bond

PERFORMANCE

	3yr Annual	5yr Annual	10yr Annual	Bull	Bear
Return (%)	na	na	na	na	na
Differ from Category (+/-)	na	na	na	na	na

Total Risk	Standard Deviation	Category Risk	Risk Index	Avg Mat
na	na	na	na	2.8 yrs

	1993	1992	1991	1990	1989	1988	1987	1986	1985	1984
Return (%)	12.4	4.9	—	—	—	—	—	—	—	—
Differ from category (+/-) . .	-0.3	0.1	—	—	—	—	—	—	—	—

PER SHARE DATA

	1993	1992	1991	1990	1989	1988	1987	1986	1985	1984
Dividends, Net Income ($) .	0.67	0.72	—	—	—	—	—	—	—	—
Distrib'ns, Cap Gain ($) . . .	0.00	0.00	—	—	—	—	—	—	—	—
Net Asset Value ($)	10.19	9.69	—	—	—	—	—	—	—	—
Expense Ratio (%).	1.05	1.09	—	—	—	—	—	—	—	—
Net Income to Assets (%). .	8.72	9.04	—	—	—	—	—	—	—	—
Portfolio Turnover (%)	189	154	—	—	—	—	—	—	—	—
Total Assets (Millions $) . . .	419	649	—	—	—	—	—	—	—	—

PORTFOLIO (as of 6/30/93)

Portfolio Manager: Judy Pagliuca - 1991

Investm't Category: International Bond

Cap Gain	Asset Allocation
Cap & Income	Fund of Funds
✔ Income	Index
	Sector
✔ Domestic	Small Cap
✔ Foreign	Socially Conscious
Country/Region	State Specific

Portfolio: stocks 0% bonds 92%
convertibles 0% other 5% cash 3%

Largest Holdings: Mexico 24%, United States 19%

Unrealized Net Capital Gains: -2% of portfolio value

SHAREHOLDER INFORMATION

Minimum Investment
Initial: $2,500 Subsequent: $250

Minimum IRA Investment
Initial: $500 Subsequent: $250

Maximum Fees
Load: none 12b-1: none
Other: none

Distributions
Income: monthly Capital Gains: Dec

Exchange Options
Number Per Year: 4 Fee: none
Telephone: yes (money market fund available)

Services
IRA, other pension, auto exchange, auto invest, auto withdraw

Fidelity Southeast Asia
(FSEAX)

International Stock

82 Devonshire St.
Boston, MA 02109
(800) 544-8888, (801) 534-1910

fund in existence since 4/19/93

PERFORMANCE

	3yr Annual	5yr Annual	10yr Annual	Bull	Bear
Return (%)	na	na	na	na	na
Differ from Category (+/-)	na	na	na	na	na

Total Risk	Standard Deviation	Category Risk	Risk Index	Beta
na	na	na	na	na

	1993	1992	1991	1990	1989	1988	1987	1986	1985	1984
Return (%)	—	—	—	—	—	—	—	—	—	—
Differ from category (+/-).	—	—	—	—	—	—	—	—	—	—

PER SHARE DATA

	1993	1992	1991	1990	1989	1988	1987	1986	1985	1984
Dividends, Net Income ($).	0.07	—	—	—	—	—	—	—	—	—
Distrib'ns, Cap Gain ($) . . .	0.00	—	—	—	—	—	—	—	—	—
Net Asset Value ($)	16.41	—	—	—	—	—	—	—	—	—
Expense Ratio (%)	2.00	—	—	—	—	—	—	—	—	—
Net Income to Assets (%) .	0.45	—	—	—	—	—	—	—	—	—
Portfolio Turnover (%).	14	—	—	—	—	—	—	—	—	—
Total Assets (Millions $). .	1,044	—	—	—	—	—	—	—	—	—

PORTFOLIO (as of 10/31/93)

Portfolio Manager: Allan Liu - 1993

Investm't Category: International Stock
- ✔ Cap Gain
- Cap & Income
- Income
- ✔ Domestic
- ✔ Foreign
- Country/Region
- Asset Allocation
- Fund of Funds
- Index
- Sector
- Small Cap
- Socially Conscious
- State Specific

Portfolio: stocks 92% bonds 0%
convertibles 1% other 1% cash 6%

Largest Holdings: Hong Kong 37%, Thailand 18%

Unrealized Net Capital Gains: 14% of portfolio value

SHAREHOLDER INFORMATION

Minimum Investment
Initial: $2,500   Subsequent: $250

Minimum IRA Investment
Initial: $500   Subsequent: $250

Maximum Fees
Load: 3.00% front   12b-1: none
Other: 1.50% redemption fee (90 days)

Distributions
Income: Dec   Capital Gains: Dec

Exchange Options
Number Per Year: 4   Fee: none
Telephone: yes (money market fund available)

Services
IRA, other pension, auto exchange, auto invest, auto withdraw

Fidelity Spartan CA Muni High Yield (FSCAX)

82 Devonshire St.
Boston, MA 02109
(800) 544-8888, (801) 534-1910

Tax-Exempt Bond

PERFORMANCE

	3yr Annual	5yr Annual	10yr Annual	Bull	Bear
Return (%)	11.4	na	na	45.3	3.0
Differ from Category (+/-)	1.1 abv av	na	na	5.2 abv av	0.6 abv av

Total Risk	Standard Deviation	Category Risk	Risk Index	Avg Mat
blw av	4.4%	av	1.1	22.1 yrs

	1993	1992	1991	1990	1989	1988	1987	1986	1985	1984
Return (%)	14.0	8.8	11.6	8.1	—	—	—	—	—	—
Differ from category (+/-) . . .	2.4	0.5	0.3	1.8	—	—	—	—	—	—

PER SHARE DATA

	1993	1992	1991	1990	1989	1988	1987	1986	1985	1984
Dividends, Net Income ($) .	0.63	0.66	0.67	0.71	—	—	—	—	—	—
Distrib'ns, Cap Gain ($) . . .	0.38	0.05	0.00	0.00	—	—	—	—	—	—
Net Asset Value ($)	11.23	10.79	10.61	10.15	—	—	—	—	—	—
Expense Ratio (%).	0.40	0.36	0.19	0.00	—	—	—	—	—	—
Net Income to Assets (%). .	6.07	6.36	7.02	7.42	—	—	—	—	—	—
Portfolio Turnover (%)	26	13	15	5	—	—	—	—	—	—
Total Assets (Millions $) . . .	599	479	282	107	—	—	—	—	—	—

PORTFOLIO (as of 8/31/93)

Portfolio Manager: John F. Haley Jr. - 1989

Investm't Category: Tax-Exempt Bond

Cap Gain	Asset Allocation
Cap & Income	Fund of Funds
✔ Income	Index
	Sector
✔ Domestic	Small Cap
Foreign	Socially Conscious
Country/Region	✔ State Specific

Portfolio:	stocks 0%	bonds 100%
convertibles 0%	other 0%	cash 0%

Largest Holdings: general obligation 0%

Unrealized Net Capital Gains: 8% of portfolio value

SHAREHOLDER INFORMATION

Minimum Investment
Initial: $10,000   Subsequent: $1,000

Minimum IRA Investment
Initial: na   Subsequent: na

Maximum Fees
Load: 0.50% redemption   12b-1: none
Other: redemption fee applies for 6 mos

Distributions
Income: monthly   Capital Gains: Jun, Dec

Exchange Options
Number Per Year: 4   Fee: $5
Telephone: yes (money market fund available)

Services
auto exchange, auto invest, auto withdraw

Fidelity Spartan Conn Tax-Free High-Yield

82 Devonshire St.
Boston, MA 02109
(800) 544-8888, (801) 534-1910

(FICNX)   *Tax-Exempt Bond*

PERFORMANCE

	3yr Annual	5yr Annual	10yr Annual	Bull	Bear
Return (%)	10.5	9.7	na	40.8	2.4
Differ from Category (+/-)	0.2 blw av	0.5 av	na	0.6 av	0.1 av

Total Risk	Standard Deviation	Category Risk	Risk Index	Avg Mat
blw av	4.3%	av	1.1	20.7 yrs

	1993	1992	1991	1990	1989	1988	1987	1986	1985	1984
Return (%)	12.9	8.2	10.5	6.6	10.4	10.1	—	—	—	—
Differ from category (+/-). . .	1.3	-0.1	-0.8	0.3	1.4	0.0	—	—	—	—

PER SHARE DATA

	1993	1992	1991	1990	1989	1988	1987	1986	1985	1984
Dividends, Net Income ($) .	0.67	0.69	0.68	0.68	0.70	0.71	—	—	—	—
Distrib'ns, Cap Gain ($) . . .	0.33	0.00	0.00	0.04	0.02	0.00	—	—	—	—
Net Asset Value ($)	11.70	11.28	11.09	10.68	10.72	10.39	—	—	—	—
Expense Ratio (%)	0.55	0.55	0.55	0.62	0.54	0.11	—	—	—	—
Net Income to Assets (%) .	5.99	6.21	6.34	6.51	6.62	7.10	—	—	—	—
Portfolio Turnover (%).	26	11	6	18	8	11	—	—	—	—
Total Assets (Millions $)	449	414	347	252	180	74	—	—	—	—

PORTFOLIO (as of 06/30/93)

Portfolio Manager: Peter Allegrini - 1987

Investm't Category: Tax-Exempt Bond
Cap Gain	Asset Allocation
Cap & Income	Fund of Funds
✔ Income	Index
	Sector
✔ Domestic	Small Cap
Foreign	Socially Conscious
Country/Region	✔ State Specific

Portfolio: stocks 0%   bonds 100%
convertibles 0%   other 0%   cash 0%

Largest Holdings: general obligation 18%

Unrealized Net Capital Gains: 8% of portfolio value

SHAREHOLDER INFORMATION

Minimum Investment
Initial: $10,000   Subsequent: $1,000

Minimum IRA Investment
Initial: na   Subsequent: na

Maximum Fees
Load: 0.50% redemption   12b-1: none
Other: redemption fee applies for 6 mos

Distributions
Income: monthly   Capital Gains: Jan, Dec

Exchange Options
Number Per Year: 4   Fee: $5
Telephone: yes (money market fund available)

Services
auto exchange, auto invest, auto withdraw

Fidelity Spartan Florida Muni Income (FFLIX)

82 Devonshire St.
Boston, MA 02109
(800) 544-8888, (801) 534-1910

Tax-Exempt Bond

PERFORMANCE

	3yr Annual	5yr Annual	10yr Annual	Bull	Bear
Return (%)	na	na	na	na	na
Differ from Category (+/-)	na	na	na	na	na

Total Risk	Standard Deviation	Category Risk	Risk Index	Avg Mat
na	na	na	na	19.6 yrs

	1993	1992	1991	1990	1989	1988	1987	1986	1985	1984
Return (%)	14.8	—	—	—	—	—	—	—	—	—
Differ from category (+/-) . . .	3.2	—	—	—	—	—	—	—	—	—

PER SHARE DATA

	1993	1992	1991	1990	1989	1988	1987	1986	1985	1984
Dividends, Net Income ($) .	0.61	—	—	—	—	—	—	—	—	—
Distrib'ns, Cap Gain ($) . . .	0.20	—	—	—	—	—	—	—	—	—
Net Asset Value ($)	11.33	—	—	—	—	—	—	—	—	—
Expense Ratio (%).	0.10	—	—	—	—	—	—	—	—	—
Net Income to Assets (%). .	5.78	—	—	—	—	—	—	—	—	—
Portfolio Turnover (%)	38	—	—	—	—	—	—	—	—	—
Total Assets (Millions $) . . .	445	—	—	—	—	—	—	—	—	—

PORTFOLIO (as of 5/31/93)

Portfolio Manager: Anne Punzak - 1992

Investm't Category: Tax-Exempt Bond
Cap Gain	Asset Allocation
Cap & Income	Fund of Funds
✔ Income	Index
	Sector
✔ Domestic	Small Cap
Foreign	Socially Conscious
Country/Region	✔ State Specific

Portfolio: stocks 0% bonds 100%
convertibles 0% other 0% cash 0%

Largest Holdings: general obligation 0%

Unrealized Net Capital Gains: 3% of portfolio value

SHAREHOLDER INFORMATION

Minimum Investment
Initial: $10,000   Subsequent: $1,000

Minimum IRA Investment
Initial: na   Subsequent: na

Maximum Fees
Load: 0.50% redemption   12b-1: none
Other: redemption fee applies for 6 mos

Distributions
Income: monthly   Capital Gains: Dec

Exchange Options
Number Per Year: 4   Fee: $5
Telephone: yes (money market fund available)

Services
auto exchange, auto invest, auto withdraw

Fidelity Spartan Ginnie Mae (SGNMX)

82 Devonshire St.
Boston, MA 02109
(800) 544-8888, (801) 534-1910

Mortgage-Backed Bond

PERFORMANCE

	3yr Annual	5yr Annual	10yr Annual	Bull	Bear
Return (%)	8.8	na	na	na	na
Differ from Category (+/-)	-0.4 blw av	na	na	na	na

Total Risk	Standard Deviation	Category Risk	Risk Index	Avg Mat
low	2.5%	blw av	1.0	7.0 yrs

	1993	1992	1991	1990	1989	1988	1987	1986	1985	1984
Return (%)	6.2	6.4	13.7	—	—	—	—	—	—	—
Differ from category (+/-)	-0.6	0.3	-0.6	—	—	—	—	—	—	—

PER SHARE DATA

	1993	1992	1991	1990	1989	1988	1987	1986	1985	1984
Dividends, Net Income ($)	0.56	0.75	0.84	—	—	—	—	—	—	—
Distrib'ns, Cap Gain ($)	0.07	0.24	0.02	—	—	—	—	—	—	—
Net Asset Value ($)	10.10	10.11	10.46	—	—	—	—	—	—	—
Expense Ratio (%)	0.41	0.17	0.25	—	—	—	—	—	—	—
Net Income to Assets (%)	7.63	8.09	8.69	—	—	—	—	—	—	—
Portfolio Turnover (%)	241	168	41	—	—	—	—	—	—	—
Total Assets (Millions $)	566	838	423	—	—	—	—	—	—	—

PORTFOLIO (as of 8/31/93)

Portfolio Manager: Bob Ives - 1993

Investm't Category: Mortgage-Backed Bond

Cap Gain	Asset Allocation
Cap & Income	Fund of Funds
✔ Income	Index
	Sector
✔ Domestic	Small Cap
✔ Foreign	Socially Conscious
Country/Region	State Specific

Portfolio: stocks 0% bonds 98%
convertibles 0% other 2% cash 0%

Largest Holdings: mortgage-backed 97%, U.S. government agencies 1%

Unrealized Net Capital Gains: 1% of portfolio value

SHAREHOLDER INFORMATION

Minimum Investment
Initial: $10,000   Subsequent: $1,000

Minimum IRA Investment
Initial: $10,000   Subsequent: $1,000

Maximum Fees
Load: none   12b-1: none
Other: $5 account close-out fee

Distributions
Income: monthly   Capital Gains: Oct, Dec

Exchange Options
Number Per Year: 4   Fee: $5
Telephone: yes (money market fund available)

Services
IRA, other pension, auto exchange, auto invest, auto withdraw

Fidelity Spartan Gov't Income (SPGVX)

82 Devonshire St.
Boston, MA 02109
(800) 544-8888, (801) 534-1910

Mortgage-Backed Bond

PERFORMANCE

	3yr Annual	5yr Annual	10yr Annual	Bull	Bear
Return (%)	9.7	10.6	na	39.3	3.2
Differ from Category (+/-)	0.5 abv av	0.6 abv av	na	2.6 high	-1.4 low

Total Risk	Standard Deviation	Category Risk	Risk Index	Avg Mat
low	3.0%	av	1.2	13.3 yrs

	1993	1992	1991	1990	1989	1988	1987	1986	1985	1984
Return (%)	7.3	7.1	15.1	9.1	15.2	—	—	—	—	—
Differ from category (+/-) . . .	0.5	1.0	0.6	-0.4	2.9	—	—	—	—	—

PER SHARE DATA

	1993	1992	1991	1990	1989	1988	1987	1986	1985	1984
Dividends, Net Income ($) .	0.61	0.76	0.83	0.85	0.93	—	—	—	—	—
Distrib'ns, Cap Gain ($) . . .	0.26	0.41	0.04	0.04	0.03	—	—	—	—	—
Net Asset Value ($)	10.68	10.78	11.21	10.56	10.54	—	—	—	—	—
Expense Ratio (%).	0.65	0.65	0.53	0.16	0.65	—	—	—	—	—
Net Income to Assets (%) . .	7.11	7.77	8.35	9.02	9.26	—	—	—	—	—
Portfolio Turnover (%)	170	59	96	68	277	—	—	—	—	—
Total Assets (Millions $) . . .	380	483	431	283	21	—	—	—	—	—

PORTFOLIO (as of 4/30/93)

Portfolio Manager: Bob Ives - 1993

Investm't Category: Mortgage-Backed Bond

Cap Gain	Asset Allocation
Cap & Income	Fund of Funds
✔ Income	Index
	Sector
✔ Domestic	Small Cap
Foreign	Socially Conscious
Country/Region	State Specific

Portfolio: stocks 0% bonds 84%
convertibles 0% other 0% cash 16%

Largest Holdings: mortgage-backed 65%, U.S. government & agencies 19%

Unrealized Net Capital Gains: 2% of portfolio value

SHAREHOLDER INFORMATION

Minimum Investment
Initial: $10,000   Subsequent: $1,000

Minimum IRA Investment
Initial: $10,000   Subsequent: $1,000

Maximum Fees
Load: none   12b-1: none
Other: $5 account close-out fee

Distributions
Income: monthly   Capital Gains: Jun, Dec

Exchange Options
Number Per Year: 4   Fee: $5
Telephone: yes (money market fund available)

Services
IRA, other pension, auto exchange, auto invest, auto withdraw

Fidelity Spartan High Income (SPHIX)

Corporate High-Yield Bond

82 Devonshire St.
Boston, MA 02109
(800) 544-8888, (801) 534-1910

PERFORMANCE

	3yr Annual	5yr Annual	10yr Annual	Bull	Bear
Return (%)	25.7	na	na	103.1	na
Differ from Category (+/-)	5.2 high	na	na	28.2 high	na

Total Risk	Standard Deviation	Category Risk	Risk Index	Avg Mat
blw av	4.9%	high	1.3	7.2 yrs

	1993	1992	1991	1990	1989	1988	1987	1986	1985	1984
Return (%).............	21.8	21.4	34.3	—	—	—	—	—	—	—
Differ from category (+/-)...	2.6	5.6	7.0	—	—	—	—	—	—	—

PER SHARE DATA

	1993	1992	1991	1990	1989	1988	1987	1986	1985	1984
Dividends, Net Income ($).	1.12	1.25	1.29	—	—	—	—	—	—	—
Distrib'ns, Cap Gain ($) ...	0.79	0.37	0.32	—	—	—	—	—	—	—
Net Asset Value ($)	12.17	11.65	11.00	—	—	—	—	—	—	—
Expense Ratio (%)	0.70	0.70	0.70	—	—	—	—	—	—	—
Net Income to Assets (%) .	9.57	11.43	11.98	—	—	—	—	—	—	—
Portfolio Turnover (%).....	136	99	72	—	—	—	—	—	—	—
Total Assets (Millions $)....	671	371	101	—	—	—	—	—	—	—

PORTFOLIO (as of 4/30/93)

Portfolio Manager: David Glancy - 1993

Investm't Category: Corp. High-Yield Bond
Cap Gain	Asset Allocation
✔ Cap & Income	Fund of Funds
Income	Index
	Sector
✔ Domestic	Small Cap
✔ Foreign	Socially Conscious
Country/Region	State Specific

Portfolio: stocks 2% bonds 76%
convertibles 3% other 7% cash 12%

Largest Holdings: basic industries 12%, media & leisure 11%

Unrealized Net Capital Gains: 4% of portfolio value

SHAREHOLDER INFORMATION

Minimum Investment
Initial: $10,000   Subsequent: $1,000

Minimum IRA Investment
Initial: $10,000   Subsequent: $1,000

Maximum Fees
Load: 1.00% redemption 12b-1: none
Other: redemption fee applies for 9 mos

Distributions
Income: monthly   Capital Gains: Jun, Dec

Exchange Options
Number Per Year: 4   Fee: $5
Telephone: yes (money market fund available)

Services
IRA, other pension, auto exchange, auto invest, auto withdraw

Fidelity Spartan
Investment Grade (FSIBX)

Corporate Bond

82 Devonshire St.
Boston, MA 02109
(800) 544-8888, (801) 534-1910

PERFORMANCE

	3yr Annual	5yr Annual	10yr Annual	Bull	Bear
Return (%)	na	na	na	na	na
Differ from Category (+/-)	na	na	na	na	na

Total Risk	Standard Deviation	Category Risk	Risk Index	Avg Mat
na	na	na	na	19.8 yrs

	1993	1992	1991	1990	1989	1988	1987	1986	1985	1984
Return (%)	15.7	—	—	—	—	—	—	—	—	—
Differ from category (+/-)	4.3	—	—	—	—	—	—	—	—	—

PER SHARE DATA

	1993	1992	1991	1990	1989	1988	1987	1986	1985	1984
Dividends, Net Income ($)	0.78	—	—	—	—	—	—	—	—	—
Distrib'ns, Cap Gain ($)	0.00	—	—	—	—	—	—	—	—	—
Net Asset Value ($)	10.68	—	—	—	—	—	—	—	—	—
Expense Ratio (%)	0.65	—	—	—	—	—	—	—	—	—
Net Income to Assets (%)	7.58	—	—	—	—	—	—	—	—	—
Portfolio Turnover (%)	55	—	—	—	—	—	—	—	—	—
Total Assets (Millions $)	122	—	—	—	—	—	—	—	—	—

PORTFOLIO (as of 9/30/93)

Portfolio Manager: Michael Gray - 1992

Investm't Category: Corporate Bond

Cap Gain	Asset Allocation
Cap & Income	Fund of Funds
✔ Income	Index
	Sector
✔ Domestic	Small Cap
✔ Foreign	Socially Conscious
Country/Region	State Specific

Portfolio: stocks 0% bonds 91%
convertibles 0% other 0% cash 9%

Largest Holdings: finance 16%, foreign government 12%

Unrealized Net Capital Gains: 5% of portfolio value

SHAREHOLDER INFORMATION

Minimum Investment
Initial: $10,000   Subsequent: $1,000

Minimum IRA Investment
Initial: $10,000   Subsequent: $1,000

Maximum Fees
Load: none   12b-1: none
Other: $5 account close-out fee

Distributions
Income: monthly   Capital Gains: June, Dec

Exchange Options
Number Per Year: 4   Fee: $5
Telephone: yes (money market fund available)

Services
IRA, other pension, auto exchange, auto invest, auto withdraw

Fidelity Spartan
Long-Term Gov't (SLTGX)

82 Devonshire St.
Boston, MA 02109
(800) 544-8888, (801) 534-1910

Government Bond

PERFORMANCE

	3yr Annual	5yr Annual	10yr Annual	Bull	Bear
Return (%)	13.9	na	na	63.0	na
Differ from Category (+/-)	3.1 high	na	na	16.8 high	na

Total Risk	Standard Deviation	Category Risk	Risk Index	Avg Mat
blw av	5.9%	abv av	1.4	22.7 yrs

	1993	1992	1991	1990	1989	1988	1987	1986	1985	1984
Return (%)	16.6	8.0	17.3	—	—	—	—	—	—	—
Differ from category (+/-) . . .	6.2	1.8	2.3	—	—	—	—	—	—	—

PER SHARE DATA

	1993	1992	1991	1990	1989	1988	1987	1986	1985	1984
Dividends, Net Income ($) .	0.84	0.84	0.74	—	—	—	—	—	—	—
Distrib'ns, Cap Gain ($) . . .	0.52	0.18	0.08	—	—	—	—	—	—	—
Net Asset Value ($)	12.40	11.82	11.92	—	—	—	—	—	—	—
Expense Ratio (%)	0.65	0.65	0.65	—	—	—	—	—	—	—
Net Income to Assets (%) .	7.35	7.30	7.26	—	—	—	—	—	—	—
Portfolio Turnover (%).	135	335	256	—	—	—	—	—	—	—
Total Assets (Millions $)	71	63	34	—	—	—	—	—	—	—

PORTFOLIO (as of 7/31/93)

Portfolio Manager: Curt Hollingsworth - 1993

Investm't Category: Government Bond

Cap Gain	Asset Allocation
Cap & Income	Fund of Funds
✔ Income	Index
	Sector
✔ Domestic	Small Cap
✔ Foreign	Socially Conscious
Country/Region	State Specific

Portfolio:
stocks 0%   bonds 70%
convertibles 0%   other 0%   cash 30%

Largest Holdings: U.S. government & agencies 52%, mortgage-backed 18%

Unrealized Net Capital Gains: 10% of portfolio value

SHAREHOLDER INFORMATION

Minimum Investment
Initial: $10,000   Subsequent: $1,000

Minimum IRA Investment
Initial: $10,000   Subsequent: $1,000

Maximum Fees
Load: none   12b-1: none
Other: $5 account close-out fee

Distributions
Income: quarterly   Capital Gains: Dec

Exchange Options
Number Per Year: 4   Fee: $5
Telephone: yes (money market fund available)

Services
IRA, other pension, auto exchange, auto invest, auto withdraw

Fidelity Spartan Ltd Maturity Gov't (FSTGX)

82 Devonshire St.
Boston, MA 02109
(800) 544-8888, (801) 534-1910

Mortgage-Backed Bond

PERFORMANCE

	3yr Annual	5yr Annual	10yr Annual	Bull	Bear
Return (%)	7.9	8.6	na	29.9	5.8
Differ from Category (+/-)	-1.3 low	-1.3 low	na	-6.8 low	1.2 high

Total Risk	Standard Deviation	Category Risk	Risk Index	Avg Mat
low	1.7%	low	0.6	5.1 yrs

	1993	1992	1991	1990	1989	1988	1987	1986	1985	1984
Return (%)	6.4	5.7	11.9	9.1	10.3	—	—	—	—	—
Differ from category (+/-)	-0.4	-0.4	-2.5	-0.4	-2.0	—	—	—	—	—

PER SHARE DATA

	1993	1992	1991	1990	1989	1988	1987	1986	1985	1984
Dividends, Net Income ($)	0.57	0.60	0.82	0.81	0.82	—	—	—	—	—
Distrib'ns, Cap Gain ($)	0.23	0.05	0.06	0.01	0.00	—	—	—	—	—
Net Asset Value ($)	10.00	10.17	10.25	9.99	9.96	—	—	—	—	—
Expense Ratio (%)	0.65	0.61	0.50	0.83	0.68	—	—	—	—	—
Net Income to Assets (%)	8.05	8.24	8.63	8.28	8.20	—	—	—	—	—
Portfolio Turnover (%)	324	330	288	270	806	—	—	—	—	—
Total Assets (Millions $)	1,389	1,770	881	132	126	—	—	—	—	—

PORTFOLIO (as of 7/31/93)

Portfolio Manager: Curtis Hollingsworth - 1988

Investm't Category: Mortgage-Backed Bond

Cap Gain	Asset Allocation
Cap & Income	Fund of Funds
✔ Income	Index
	Sector
✔ Domestic	Small Cap
✔ Foreign	Socially Conscious
Country/Region	State Specific

Portfolio: stocks 0% bonds 94%
convertibles 0% other 0% cash 6%

Largest Holdings: mortgage-backed 72%, U.S. government & agencies 22%

Unrealized Net Capital Gains: 0% of portfolio value

SHAREHOLDER INFORMATION

Minimum Investment
Initial: $10,000   Subsequent: $1,000

Minimum IRA Investment
Initial: $10,000   Subsequent: $1,000

Maximum Fees
Load: none   12b-1: none
Other: $5 account close-out fee

Distributions
Income: monthly   Capital Gains: Sep, Dec

Exchange Options
Number Per Year: 4   Fee: $5
Telephone: yes (money market fund available)

Services
IRA, other pension, auto invest, auto withdraw

Fidelity Spartan Muni Income (FSMIX)

Tax-Exempt Bond

82 Devonshire St.
Boston, MA 02109
(800) 544-8888, (801) 534-1910

PERFORMANCE

	3yr Annual	5yr Annual	10yr Annual	Bull	Bear
Return (%)	11.7	na	na	45.1	na
Differ from Category (+/-)	1.4 high	na	na	5.0 abv av	na

Total Risk	Standard Deviation	Category Risk	Risk Index	Avg Mat
low	4.0%	blw av	1.0	20.2 yrs

	1993	1992	1991	1990	1989	1988	1987	1986	1985	1984
Return (%).	14.3	8.3	12.6	—	—	—	—	—	—	—
Differ from category (+/-). . .	2.7	0.0	1.3	—	—	—	—	—	—	—

PER SHARE DATA

	1993	1992	1991	1990	1989	1988	1987	1986	1985	1984
Dividends, Net Income ($).	0.64	0.69	0.72	—	—	—	—	—	—	—
Distrib'ns, Cap Gain ($) . . .	0.55	0.07	0.04	—	—	—	—	—	—	—
Net Asset Value ($)	10.93	10.64	10.55	—	—	—	—	—	—	—
Expense Ratio (%)	0.47	0.36	0.23	—	—	—	—	—	—	—
Net Income to Assets (%) .	6.09	6.68	7.24	—	—	—	—	—	—	—
Portfolio Turnover (%).	50	62	78	—	—	—	—	—	—	—
Total Assets (Millions $). . . .	863	870	551	—	—	—	—	—	—	—

PORTFOLIO (as of 8/31/93)

Portfolio Manager: Norman Lind - 1990

Investm't Category: Tax-Exempt Bond

Cap Gain	Asset Allocation
Cap & Income	Fund of Funds
✔ Income	Index
	Sector
✔ Domestic	Small Cap
Foreign	Socially Conscious
Country/Region	State Specific

Portfolio: stocks 0%   bonds 100%
convertibles 0%   other 0%   cash 0%

Largest Holdings: Washington 10%, Colorado 9%, general obligation 6%

Unrealized Net Capital Gains: 5% of portfolio value

SHAREHOLDER INFORMATION

Minimum Investment
Initial: $10,000   Subsequent: $1,000

Minimum IRA Investment
Initial: na   Subsequent: na

Maximum Fees
Load: 0.50% redemption   12b-1: none
Other: redemption fee applies for 6 mos

Distributions
Income: monthly   Capital Gains: Oct, Dec

Exchange Options
Number Per Year: 4   Fee: $5
Telephone: yes (money market fund available)

Services
auto exchange, auto invest, auto withdraw

Fidelity Spartan NJ Muni High Yield (FNJHX)

82 Devonshire St.
Boston, MA 02109
(800) 544-8888, (801) 534-1910

Tax-Exempt Bond

PERFORMANCE

	3yr Annual	5yr Annual	10yr Annual	Bull	Bear
Return (%)	11.3	10.2	na	43.9	2.7
Differ from Category (+/-)	1.0 abv av	1.0 abv av	na	3.8 abv av	0.4 av

Total Risk	Standard Deviation	Category Risk	Risk Index	Avg Mat
blw av	4.3%	av	1.1	19.3 yrs

	1993	1992	1991	1990	1989	1988	1987	1986	1985	1984
Return (%)	13.0	8.7	12.3	7.1	10.3	10.8	—	—	—	—
Differ from category (+/-)	1.4	0.4	1.0	0.8	1.3	0.6	—	—	—	—

PER SHARE DATA

	1993	1992	1991	1990	1989	1988	1987	1986	1985	1984
Dividends, Net Income ($)	0.63	0.69	0.69	0.67	0.70	0.74	—	—	—	—
Distrib'ns, Cap Gain ($)	0.15	0.16	0.08	0.00	0.08	0.00	—	—	—	—
Net Asset Value ($)	11.82	11.18	11.10	10.61	10.56	10.31	—	—	—	—
Expense Ratio (%)	0.55	0.51	0.52	0.65	0.56	0.00	—	—	—	—
Net Income to Assets (%)	5.69	6.22	6.44	6.47	6.76	7.52	—	—	—	—
Portfolio Turnover (%)	23	33	42	82	90	140	—	—	—	—
Total Assets (Millions $)	428	343	290	210	159	90	—	—	—	—

PORTFOLIO (as of 5/31/93)

Portfolio Manager: David L. Murphy - 1991

Investm't Category: Tax-Exempt Bond

Cap Gain	Asset Allocation
Cap & Income	Fund of Funds
✔ Income	Index
	Sector
✔ Domestic	Small Cap
Foreign	Socially Conscious
Country/Region	✔ State Specific

Portfolio:	stocks 0%	bonds 100%
convertibles 0%	other 0%	cash 0%

Largest Holdings: general obligation 13%

Unrealized Net Capital Gains: 7% of portfolio value

SHAREHOLDER INFORMATION

Minimum Investment
Initial: $10,000   Subsequent: $1,000

Minimum IRA Investment
Initial: na   Subsequent: na

Maximum Fees
Load: 0.50% redemption   12b-1: none
Other: redemption fee applies for 6 mos; $5 account close-out fee

Distributions
Income: monthly   Capital Gains: Jan, Dec

Exchange Options
Number Per Year: 4   Fee: $5
Telephone: yes (money market fund available)

Services
auto exchange, auto invest, auto withdraw

Fidelity Spartan NY Muni High Yield (FSNYX)

82 Devonshire St.
Boston, MA 02109
(800) 544-8888, (801) 534-1910

Tax-Exempt Bond

PERFORMANCE

	3yr Annual	5yr Annual	10yr Annual	Bull	Bear
Return (%)	12.3	na	na	46.5	na
Differ from Category (+/-)	2.0 high	na	na	6.4 high	na

Total Risk	Standard Deviation	Category Risk	Risk Index	Avg Mat
blw av	4.4%	av	1.1	23.6 yrs

	1993	1992	1991	1990	1989	1988	1987	1986	1985	1984
Return (%)	13.3	9.4	14.4	—	—	—	—	—	—	—
Differ from category (+/-)	1.7	1.1	3.1	—	—	—	—	—	—	—

PER SHARE DATA

	1993	1992	1991	1990	1989	1988	1987	1986	1985	1984
Dividends, Net Income ($)	0.62	0.65	0.68	—	—	—	—	—	—	—
Distrib'ns, Cap Gain ($)	0.28	0.11	0.02	—	—	—	—	—	—	—
Net Asset Value ($)	11.31	10.80	10.60	—	—	—	—	—	—	—
Expense Ratio (%)	0.48	0.38	0.19	—	—	—	—	—	—	—
Net Income to Assets (%)	6.03	6.51	7.21	—	—	—	—	—	—	—
Portfolio Turnover (%)	35	21	40	—	—	—	—	—	—	—
Total Assets (Millions $)	442	292	163	—	—	—	—	—	—	—

PORTFOLIO (as of 7/31/93)

Portfolio Manager: Norm Lind - 1993

Investm't Category: Tax-Exempt Bond

Cap Gain	Asset Allocation
Cap & Income	Fund of Funds
✔ Income	Index
	Sector
✔ Domestic	Small Cap
Foreign	Socially Conscious
Country/Region	✔ State Specific

Portfolio: stocks 0% bonds 100%
convertibles 0% other 0% cash 0%

Largest Holdings: general obligation 0%

Unrealized Net Capital Gains: 7% of portfolio value

SHAREHOLDER INFORMATION

Minimum Investment
Initial: $10,000   Subsequent: $1,000

Minimum IRA Investment
Initial: na   Subsequent: na

Maximum Fees
Load: 0.50% redemption   12b-1: none
Other: redemption fee applies for 6 mos; $5 account close-out fee

Distributions
Income: monthly   Capital Gains: Jun, Dec

Exchange Options
Number Per Year: 4   Fee: $5
Telephone: yes (money market fund available)

Services
auto exchange, auto invest, auto withdraw

Fidelity Spartan Penn Muni High Yield (FPXTX)

Tax-Exempt Bond

82 Devonshire St.
Boston, MA 02109
(800) 544-8888, (801) 534-1910

PERFORMANCE

	3yr Annual	5yr Annual	10yr Annual	Bull	Bear
Return (%)	11.5	10.3	na	45.1	2.6
Differ from Category (+/-)	1.2 abv av	1.1 high	na	5.0 abv av	0.3 av

Total Risk	Standard Deviation	Category Risk	Risk Index	Avg Mat
low	4.0%	blw av	1.0	20.0 yrs

	1993	1992	1991	1990	1989	1988	1987	1986	1985	1984
Return (%)	13.1	9.1	12.4	7.2	9.8	14.3	-5.8	—	—	—
Differ from category (+/-) . . .	1.5	0.8	1.1	0.8	0.8	4.2	-4.6	—	—	—

PER SHARE DATA

	1993	1992	1991	1990	1989	1988	1987	1986	1985	1984
Dividends, Net Income ($) .	0.67	0.69	0.70	0.70	0.67	0.66	0.69	—	—	—
Distrib'ns, Cap Gain ($) . . .	0.14	0.00	0.00	0.00	0.00	0.00	0.00	—	—	—
Net Asset Value ($)	11.13	10.59	10.37	9.88	9.90	9.66	9.06	—	—	—
Expense Ratio (%).	0.55	0.55	0.55	0.60	0.78	0.84	0.63	—	—	—
Net Income to Assets (%) . .	6.31	6.65	6.96	7.22	6.90	7.05	7.28	—	—	—
Portfolio Turnover (%)	18	8	6	8	23	31	54	—	—	—
Total Assets (Millions $) . . .	303	242	199	143	104	63	42	—	—	—

PORTFOLIO (as of 6/30/93)

Portfolio Manager: Steve Harvey - 1993

Investm't Category: Tax-Exempt Bond

Cap Gain	Asset Allocation
Cap & Income	Fund of Funds
✔ Income	Index
	Sector
✔ Domestic	Small Cap
Foreign	Socially Conscious
Country/Region	✔ State Specific

Portfolio: stocks 0% bonds 100%
convertibles 0% other 0% cash 0%

Largest Holdings: general obligation 13%

Unrealized Net Capital Gains: 9% of portfolio value

SHAREHOLDER INFORMATION

Minimum Investment
Initial: $10,000   Subsequent: $1,000

Minimum IRA Investment
Initial: na   Subsequent: na

Maximum Fees
Load: 0.50% redemption 12b-1: none
Other: redemption fee applies for 6 mos

Distributions
Income: monthly   Capital Gains: Feb, Dec

Exchange Options
Number Per Year: 4   Fee: $5
Telephone: yes (money market fund available)

Services
auto exchange, auto invest, auto withdraw

Fidelity Spartan Short Intermediate Gov't (SPSIX)

82 Devonshire St.
Boston, MA 02109
(800) 544-8888, (801) 534-1910

Government Bond

PERFORMANCE

	3yr Annual	5yr Annual	10yr Annual	Bull	Bear
Return (%)	na	na	na	na	na
Differ from Category (+/-)	na	na	na	na	na

Total Risk	Standard Deviation	Category Risk	Risk Index	Avg Mat
na	na	na	na	4.9 yrs

	1993	1992	1991	1990	1989	1988	1987	1986	1985	1984
Return (%)	5.6	—	—	—	—	—	—	—	—	—
Differ from category (+/-). . .	-4.8	—	—	—	—	—	—	—	—	—

PER SHARE DATA

	1993	1992	1991	1990	1989	1988	1987	1986	1985	1984
Dividends, Net Income ($).	0.65	—	—	—	—	—	—	—	—	—
Distrib'ns, Cap Gain ($) . . .	0.00	—	—	—	—	—	—	—	—	—
Net Asset Value ($)	9.91	—	—	—	—	—	—	—	—	—
Expense Ratio (%)	0.02	—	—	—	—	—	—	—	—	—
Net Income to Assets (%) .	7.28	—	—	—	—	—	—	—	—	—
Portfolio Turnover (%). . . .	587	—	—	—	—	—	—	—	—	—
Total Assets (Millions $).	65	—	—	—	—	—	—	—	—	—

PORTFOLIO (as of 10/31/93)

Portfolio Manager: Curt Hollingsworth - 1992

Investm't Category: Government Bond

Cap Gain	Asset Allocation
Cap & Income	Fund of Funds
✔ Income	Index
	Sector
✔ Domestic	Small Cap
Foreign	Socially Conscious
Country/Region	State Specific

Portfolio: stocks 0%   bonds 100%
convertibles 0%   other 0%   cash 0%

Largest Holdings: U.S. government 57%, mortgage-backed 43%

Unrealized Net Capital Gains: 0% of portfolio value

SHAREHOLDER INFORMATION

Minimum Investment
Initial: $10,000   Subsequent: $1,000

Minimum IRA Investment
Initial: $10,000   Subsequent: $1,000

Maximum Fees
Load: none   12b-1: none
Other: $5 account close-out fee

Distributions
Income: monthly   Capital Gains: Jun, Dec

Exchange Options
Number Per Year: 4   Fee: $5
Telephone: yes (money market fund available)

Services
IRA, other pension, auto exchange, auto invest, auto withdraw

Fidelity Spartan Short-Interm Muni (FSTFX)

82 Devonshire St.
Boston, MA 02109
(800) 544-8888, (801) 534-1910

Tax-Exempt Bond

PERFORMANCE

	3yr Annual	5yr Annual	10yr Annual	Bull	Bear
Return (%)	7.3	6.9	na	26.5	4.1
Differ from Category (+/-)	-3.0 low	-2.3 low	na	-13.6 low	1.8 high

Total Risk	Standard Deviation	Category Risk	Risk Index	Avg Mat
low	1.6%	low	0.4	3.8 yrs

	1993	1992	1991	1990	1989	1988	1987	1986	1985	1984
Return (%)	7.1	6.1	8.8	6.4	6.2	4.8	0.2	—	—	—
Differ from category (+/-) . .	-4.5	-2.2	-2.5	0.1	-2.8	-5.3	1.4	—	—	—

PER SHARE DATA

	1993	1992	1991	1990	1989	1988	1987	1986	1985	1984
Dividends, Net Income ($)	0.45	0.48	0.55	0.56	0.53	0.51	0.43	—	—	—
Distrib'ns, Cap Gain ($) . . .	0.00	0.00	0.00	0.00	0.00	0.00	0.00	—	—	—
Net Asset Value ($)	10.11	9.88	9.78	9.52	9.49	9.45	9.51	—	—	—
Expense Ratio (%).	0.55	0.55	0.55	0.60	0.58	0.35	0.60	—	—	—
Net Income to Assets (%) . .	4.55	4.95	5.68	5.90	5.69	5.48	4.58	—	—	—
Portfolio Turnover (%)	56	28	59	75	82	96	180	—	—	—
Total Assets (Millions $) . .	1,204	659	244	59	58	77	59	—	—	—

PORTFOLIO (as of 6/30/93)

Portfolio Manager: David Murphy - 1989

Investm't Category: Tax-Exempt Bond

Cap Gain	Asset Allocation
Cap & Income	Fund of Funds
✔ Income	Index
	Sector
✔ Domestic	Small Cap
Foreign	Socially Conscious
Country/Region	State Specific

Portfolio: stocks 0% bonds 100%
convertibles 0% other 0% cash 0%

Largest Holdings: general obligation 22%

Unrealized Net Capital Gains: 2% of portfolio value

SHAREHOLDER INFORMATION

Minimum Investment
Initial: $10,000   Subsequent: $1,000

Minimum IRA Investment
Initial: na   Subsequent: na

Maximum Fees
Load: none   12b-1: none
Other: none

Distributions
Income: monthly   Capital Gains: Feb, Dec

Exchange Options
Number Per Year: 4   Fee: $5
Telephone: yes (money market fund available)

Services
auto exchange, auto invest, auto withdraw

Fidelity Spartan
Short-Term Bond (FTBDX)

82 Devonshire St.
Boston, MA 02109
(800) 544-8888, (801) 534-1910

Corporate Bond

PERFORMANCE

	3yr Annual	5yr Annual	10yr Annual	Bull	Bear
Return (%)	na	na	na	na	na
Differ from Category (+/-)	na	na	na	na	na

Total Risk	Standard Deviation	Category Risk	Risk Index	Avg Mat
na	na	na	na	2.6 yrs

	1993	1992	1991	1990	1989	1988	1987	1986	1985	1984
Return (%).	9.0	—	—	—	—	—	—	—	—	—
Differ from category (+/-). . .	-2.4	—	—	—	—	—	—	—	—	—

PER SHARE DATA

	1993	1992	1991	1990	1989	1988	1987	1986	1985	1984
Dividends, Net Income ($).	0.72	—	—	—	—	—	—	—	—	—
Distrib'ns, Cap Gain ($) . . .	0.01	—	—	—	—	—	—	—	—	—
Net Asset Value ($)	9.97	—	—	—	—	—	—	—	—	—
Expense Ratio (%)	0.20	—	—	—	—	—	—	—	—	—
Net Income to Assets (%) .	7.32	—	—	—	—	—	—	—	—	—
Portfolio Turnover (%).	112	—	—	—	—	—	—	—	—	—
Total Assets (Millions $). .	1,529	—	—	—	—	—	—	—	—	—

PORTFOLIO (as of 9/30/93)

Portfolio Manager: Donald G. Taylor - 1992

Investm't Category: Corporate Bond

Cap Gain	Asset Allocation
Cap & Income	Fund of Funds
✔ Income	Index
	Sector
✔ Domestic	Small Cap
✔ Foreign	Socially Conscious
Country/Region	State Specific

Portfolio: stocks 0% bonds 84%
convertibles 0% other 3% cash 13%

Largest Holdings: finance 33%, foreign government 16%

Unrealized Net Capital Gains: 0% of portfolio value

SHAREHOLDER INFORMATION

Minimum Investment
Initial: $10,000   Subsequent: $1,000

Minimum IRA Investment
Initial: $10,000   Subsequent: $1,000

Maximum Fees
Load: none   12b-1: none
Other: $5 account close-out fee

Distributions
Income: monthly   Capital Gains: Dec

Exchange Options
Number Per Year: 4   Fee: $5
Telephone: yes (money market fund available)

Services
IRA, other pension, auto exchange, auto invest, auto withdraw

Fidelity Stock Selector

(FDSSX)

Growth

82 Devonshire St.
Boston, MA 02109
(800) 544-8888, (801) 534-1910

PERFORMANCE

	3yr Annual	5yr Annual	10yr Annual	Bull	Bear
Return (%)	24.2	na	na	114.0	na
Differ from Category (+/-)	5.0 high	na	na	29.3 high	na

Total Risk	Standard Deviation	Category Risk	Risk Index	Beta
abv av	12.4%	av	1.2	1.0

	1993	1992	1991	1990	1989	1988	1987	1986	1985	1984
Return (%)	13.9	15.4	45.9	—	—	—	—	—	—	—
Differ from category (+/-)	0.6	4.4	10.5	—	—	—	—	—	—	—

PER SHARE DATA

	1993	1992	1991	1990	1989	1988	1987	1986	1985	1984
Dividends, Net Income ($)	0.24	0.10	0.08	—	—	—	—	—	—	—
Distrib'ns, Cap Gain ($)	1.06	0.31	0.47	—	—	—	—	—	—	—
Net Asset Value ($)	18.75	17.61	15.63	—	—	—	—	—	—	—
Expense Ratio (%)	1.10	1.22	1.43	—	—	—	—	—	—	—
Net Income to Assets (%)	1.52	1.43	1.20	—	—	—	—	—	—	—
Portfolio Turnover (%)	192	268	317	—	—	—	—	—	—	—
Total Assets (Millions $)	650	260	99	—	—	—	—	—	—	—

PORTFOLIO

Portfolio Manager: Brad Lewis - 1990

Investm't Category: Growth

✔ Cap Gain	Asset Allocation
Cap & Income	Fund of Funds
Income	Index
	Sector
✔ Domestic	Small Cap
✔ Foreign	Socially Conscious
Country/Region	State Specific

Portfolio: stocks 81%   bonds 0%
convertibles 0%   other 0%   cash 19%

Largest Holdings: stocks—finance 26%, stocks—utilities 18%

Unrealized Net Capital Gains: 10% of portfolio value

SHAREHOLDER INFORMATION

Minimum Investment
Initial: $2,500   Subsequent: $250

Minimum IRA Investment
Initial: $500   Subsequent: $250

Maximum Fees
Load: 3.00% front   12b-1: none
Other: none

Distributions
Income: Dec   Capital Gains: Dec

Exchange Options
Number Per Year: 4   Fee: none
Telephone: yes (money market fund available)

Services
IRA, other pension, auto exchange, auto invest, auto withdraw

Fidelity Trend (FTRNX)

Growth

82 Devonshire St.
Boston, MA 02109
(800) 544-8888, (801) 534-1910

PERFORMANCE

	3yr Annual	5yr Annual	10yr Annual	Bull	Bear
Return (%)	23.8	16.8	13.9	104.5	-18.9
Differ from Category (+/-)	4.6 high	2.2 abv av	1.3 abv av	19.8 abv av	-6.5 blw av

Total Risk	Standard Deviation	Category Risk	Risk Index	Beta
high	14.0%	abv av	1.3	1.2

	1993	1992	1991	1990	1989	1988	1987	1986	1985	1984
Return (%)	19.1	16.7	36.0	-12.6	31.6	24.3	-4.1	13.2	28.2	-2.1
Differ from category (+/-) . . .	5.9	5.7	1.0	-6.5	5.8	6.6	-5.3	-1.3	-1.1	-2.1

PER SHARE DATA

	1993	1992	1991	1990	1989	1988	1987	1986	1985	1984
Dividends, Net Income ($) .	0.27	0.43	0.48	0.23	0.62	0.51	0.43	0.61	0.79	0.82
Distrib'ns, Cap Gain ($) . . .	5.06	3.23	1.79	0.14	4.22	1.06	6.20	10.64	1.25	0.00
Net Asset Value ($)	59.08	54.19	49.63	38.25	44.22	37.43	31.40	39.83	45.02	36.86
Expense Ratio (%)	0.83	0.56	0.53	0.61	0.58	0.47	0.49	0.52	0.52	0.56
Net Income to Assets (%) .	0.55	1.14	1.43	1.51	1.76	2.01	1.49	2.00	2.40	2.90
Portfolio Turnover (%)	63	47	57	48	67	49	128	71	62	57
Total Assets (Millions $) . .	1,396	1,115	892	702	889	702	599	669	712	602

PORTFOLIO (as of 6/30/93)

Portfolio Manager: Alan Leifer - 1987

Investm't Category: Growth

✔ Cap Gain	Asset Allocation
Cap & Income	Fund of Funds
Income	Index
	Sector
✔ Domestic	Small Cap
✔ Foreign	Socially Conscious
Country/Region	State Specific

Portfolio: stocks 90% bonds 0%
convertibles 1% other 0% cash 9%

Largest Holdings: finance 17%, health 11%

Unrealized Net Capital Gains: 20% of portfolio value

SHAREHOLDER INFORMATION

Minimum Investment
Initial: $2,500   Subsequent: $250

Minimum IRA Investment
Initial: $500   Subsequent: $250

Maximum Fees
Load: none   12b-1: none
Other: none

Distributions
Income: Feb, Dec   Capital Gains: Feb, Dec

Exchange Options
Number Per Year: 4   Fee: none
Telephone: yes (money market fund available)

Services
IRA, other pension, auto exchange, auto invest, auto withdraw

Fidelity Utilities Income
(FIUIX)
Growth & Income

82 Devonshire St.
Boston, MA 02109
(800) 544-8888, (801) 534-1910

	3yr Annual	5yr Annual	10yr Annual	Bull	Bear
Return (%)	15.8	14.7	na	70.7	-7.3
Differ from Category (+/-)	-0.6 av	2.2 high	na	0.6 av	4.3 high

Total Risk	Standard Deviation	Category Risk	Risk Index	Beta
av	7.7%	low	0.9	0.3

	1993	1992	1991	1990	1989	1988	1987	1986	1985	1984
Return (%)	15.6	10.9	21.1	1.8	25.9	14.7	—	—	—	—
Differ from category (+/-)	3.0	0.8	-6.6	7.4	4.3	-2.1	—	—	—	—

PER SHARE DATA

	1993	1992	1991	1990	1989	1988	1987	1986	1985	1984
Dividends, Net Income ($)	0.52	0.60	0.63	0.69	0.76	0.52	—	—	—	—
Distrib'ns, Cap Gain ($)	0.22	0.38	0.18	0.30	0.31	0.03	—	—	—	—
Net Asset Value ($)	15.18	13.79	13.38	11.79	12.60	10.93	—	—	—	—
Expense Ratio (%)	0.87	0.95	0.93	1.02	1.47	2.00	—	—	—	—
Net Income to Assets (%)	4.57	5.11	5.93	6.19	6.14	5.36	—	—	—	—
Portfolio Turnover (%)	73	39	43	61	10	0	—	—	—	—
Total Assets (Millions $)	1,462	647	220	157	129	31	—	—	—	—

PORTFOLIO (as of 7/31/93)

Portfolio Manager: John Muresianu - 1992

Investm't Category: Growth & Income

Cap Gain	Asset Allocation
✔ Cap & Income	Fund of Funds
Income	Index
	✔ Sector
✔ Domestic	Small Cap
✔ Foreign	Socially Conscious
Country/Region	State Specific

Portfolio: stocks 86% bonds 4%
convertibles 1% other 2% cash 7%

Largest Holdings: utilities 78%, energy 3%

Unrealized Net Capital Gains: 9% of portfolio value

SHAREHOLDER INFORMATION

Minimum Investment
Initial: $2,500   Subsequent: $250

Minimum IRA Investment
Initial: $500   Subsequent: $250

Maximum Fees
Load: none   12b-1: none
Other: none

Distributions
Income: quarterly   Capital Gains: Mar, Dec

Exchange Options
Number Per Year: 4   Fee: none
Telephone: yes (money market fund available)

Services
IRA, other pension, auto exchange, auto invest, auto withdraw

Fidelity Value (FDVLX)

Growth

82 Devonshire St.
Boston, MA 02109
(800) 544-8888, (801) 534-1910

PERFORMANCE

	3yr Annual	5yr Annual	10yr Annual	Bull	Bear
Return (%)	23.4	15.0	11.7	96.6	-16.6
Differ from Category (+/-)	4.2 abv av	0.4 av	-0.8 blw av	11.9 abv av	-4.2 blw av

Total Risk	Standard Deviation	Category Risk	Risk Index	Beta
av	9.7%	low	0.9	0.7

	1993	1992	1991	1990	1989	1988	1987	1986	1985	1984
Return (%)	22.9	21.1	26.1	-12.8	22.9	29.0	-8.6	14.7	22.0	-8.6
Differ from category (+/-). . .	9.7	10.1	-9.3	-6.7	-2.9	11.3	-9.8	0.2	-7.3	-8.6

PER SHARE DATA

	1993	1992	1991	1990	1989	1988	1987	1986	1985	1984
Dividends, Net Income ($).	0.34	0.23	0.85	1.17	0.30	0.47	0.15	0.00	0.41	0.49
Distrib'ns, Cap Gain ($) . . .	2.80	0.15	0.00	0.00	2.85	0.00	0.37	1.99	0.00	0.00
Net Asset Value ($)	40.23	35.35	29.50	24.10	28.99	26.14	20.63	23.06	21.76	18.17
Expense Ratio (%)	1.11	1.00	0.98	1.06	1.13	1.11	1.07	1.07	1.13	1.26
Net Income to Assets (%) .	1.43	2.01	2.93	4.55	1.45	4.74	1.02	2.20	3.43	4.84
Portfolio Turnover (%).	117	81	137	165	386	480	442	281	246	398
Total Assets (Millions $). .	1,695	331	124	92	139	135	92	143	101	114

PORTFOLIO (as of 10/31/93)

Portfolio Manager: Jeff Ubben - 1992

Investm't Category: Growth

✔ Cap Gain
   Cap & Income
   Income

✔ Domestic
✔ Foreign
   Country/Region

   Asset Allocation
   Fund of Funds
   Index
   Sector
   Small Cap
   Socially Conscious
   State Specific

Portfolio: stocks 84%   bonds 4%
convertibles 2%   other 0%   cash 10%

Largest Holdings: basic industries 15%, energy 13%

Unrealized Net Capital Gains: 8% of portfolio value

SHAREHOLDER INFORMATION

Minimum Investment
Initial: $2,500   Subsequent: $250

Minimum IRA Investment
Initial: $500   Subsequent: $250

Maximum Fees
Load: none   12b-1: none
Other: none

Distributions
Income: Dec   Capital Gains: Dec

Exchange Options
Number Per Year: 4   Fee: none
Telephone: yes (money market fund available)

Services
IRA, other pension, auto exchange, auto invest, auto withdraw

Fidelity Worldwide
(FWWFX)

82 Devonshire St.
Boston, MA 02109
(800) 544-8888, (801) 534-1910

International Stock

PERFORMANCE

	3yr Annual	5yr Annual	10yr Annual	Bull	Bear
Return (%)	16.0	na	na	na	na
Differ from Category (+/-)	1.7 abv av	na	na	na	na

Total Risk	Standard Deviation	Category Risk	Risk Index	Beta
abv av	11.2%	low	0.9	0.6

	1993	1992	1991	1990	1989	1988	1987	1986	1985	1984
Return (%)	36.5	6.2	7.8	—	—	—	—	—	—	—
Differ from category (+/-) . .	-2.0	9.7	-5.1	—	—	—	—	—	—	—

PER SHARE DATA

	1993	1992	1991	1990	1989	1988	1987	1986	1985	1984
Dividends, Net Income ($) .	0.10	0.25	0.10	—	—	—	—	—	—	—
Distrib'ns, Cap Gain ($) . . .	0.15	0.00	0.00	—	—	—	—	—	—	—
Net Asset Value ($)	13.03	9.73	9.41	—	—	—	—	—	—	—
Expense Ratio (%).	1.40	1.51	1.69	—	—	—	—	—	—	—
Net Income to Assets (%). .	1.99	2.02	2.19	—	—	—	—	—	—	—
Portfolio Turnover (%)	57	130	129	—	—	—	—	—	—	—
Total Assets (Millions $) . . .	336	103	105	—	—	—	—	—	—	—

PORTFOLIO (as of 10/31/93)

Portfolio Manager: Penelope Dobkin - 1990

Investm't Category: International Stock

✔ Cap Gain
  Cap & Income
  Income

  Asset Allocation
  Fund of Funds
  Index
  Sector

✔ Domestic
✔ Foreign
  Country/Region

  Small Cap
  Socially Conscious
  State Specific

Portfolio: stocks 78% bonds 4%
convertibles 2% other 2% cash 14%

Largest Holdings: United States 18%, Japan 11%

Unrealized Net Capital Gains: 9% of portfolio value

SHAREHOLDER INFORMATION

Minimum Investment
Initial: $2,500   Subsequent: $250

Minimum IRA Investment
Initial: $500   Subsequent: $250

Maximum Fees
Load: 3.00% front   12b-1: none
Other: none

Distributions
Income: Dec   Capital Gains: Dec

Exchange Options
Number Per Year: 4   Fee: none
Telephone: yes (money market fund available)

Services
IRA, other pension, auto exchange, auto invest, auto withdraw

Fiduciary Capital Growth
(FCGFX)
Growth

225 E. Mason St.
Milwaukee, WI 53202
(414) 226-4555

PERFORMANCE

	3yr Annual	5yr Annual	10yr Annual	Bull	Bear
Return (%)	21.3	13.2	9.6	95.6	-19.2
Differ from Category (+/-)	2.1 abv av	-1.4 blw av	-3.0 low	10.9 abv av	-6.8 blw av

Total Risk	Standard Deviation	Category Risk	Risk Index	Beta
abv av	11.1%	blw av	1.0	0.8

	1993	1992	1991	1990	1989	1988	1987	1986	1985	1984
Return (%).............	14.6	14.4	36.2	-11.6	17.9	18.7	-8.9	0.0	29.9	-4.1
Differ from category (+/-)...	1.4	3.4	0.8	-5.5	-7.9	1.0	-10.1	-14.5	0.6	-4.1

PER SHARE DATA

	1993	1992	1991	1990	1989	1988	1987	1986	1985	1984
Dividends, Net Income ($).	0.05	0.10	0.16	0.23	0.19	0.03	0.14	0.10	0.19	0.30
Distrib'ns, Cap Gain ($) ...	1.29	1.85	1.22	0.92	0.00	0.00	3.45	3.68	0.03	0.20
Net Asset Value ($)	19.63	18.33	17.87	14.23	17.54	15.04	12.69	17.90	21.42	16.68
Expense Ratio (%)	1.20	1.30	1.50	1.40	1.30	1.30	1.10	1.20	1.30	1.50
Net Income to Assets (%) .	0.04	0.60	1.20	1.10	0.80	0.30	0.60	0.40	1.20	2.00
Portfolio Turnover (%)......	33	59	63	55	42	43	83	56	37	26
Total Assets (Millions $).....	48	38	31	20	40	42	55	51	41	28

PORTFOLIO (as of 9/30/93)

Portfolio Manager: Ted Kellner - 1981, Don Wilson - 1981

Investm't Category: Growth

✔ Cap Gain	Asset Allocation
Cap & Income	Fund of Funds
Income	Index
	Sector
✔ Domestic	Small Cap
✔ Foreign	Socially Conscious
Country/Region	State Specific

Portfolio: stocks 82%   bonds 5%
convertibles 0%   other 0%   cash 13%

Largest Holdings: software/service 19%, retail trade 14%

Unrealized Net Capital Gains: 16% of portfolio value

SHAREHOLDER INFORMATION

Minimum Investment
Initial: $1,000   Subsequent: $100

Minimum IRA Investment
Initial: $1,000   Subsequent: $100

Maximum Fees
Load: none   12b-1: none
Other: none

Distributions
Income: Oct, Dec   Capital Gains: Oct, Dec

Exchange Options
Number Per Year: no limit   Fee: none
Telephone: none

Services
IRA, other pension, auto invest, auto withdraw

Fifty-Nine Wall St.
European (FNEEX)

6 St. James Avenue
Boston, MA 02116
(212) 493-8100

International Stock

PERFORMANCE

	3yr Annual	5yr Annual	10yr Annual	Bull	Bear
Return (%)	14.3	na	na	na	na
Differ from Category (+/-)	0.0 av	na	na	na	na

Total Risk	Standard Deviation	Category Risk	Risk Index	Beta
abv av	12.2%	blw av	1.0	0.6

	1993	1992	1991	1990	1989	1988	1987	1986	1985	1984
Return (%)	27.1	7.5	9.2	—	—	—	—	—	—	—
Differ from category (+/-)	-11.4	11.0	-3.7	—	—	—	—	—	—	—

PER SHARE DATA

	1993	1992	1991	1990	1989	1988	1987	1986	1985	1984
Dividends, Net Income ($)	1.47	0.36	0.20	—	—	—	—	—	—	—
Distrib'ns, Cap Gain ($)	0.06	1.92	0.02	—	—	—	—	—	—	—
Net Asset Value ($)	31.66	26.19	26.48	—	—	—	—	—	—	—
Expense Ratio (%)	1.50	1.50	1.50	—	—	—	—	—	—	—
Net Income to Assets (%)	1.28	1.71	1.54	—	—	—	—	—	—	—
Portfolio Turnover (%)	37	50	58	—	—	—	—	—	—	—
Total Assets (Millions $)	3	27	14	—	—	—	—	—	—	—

PORTFOLIO (as of 10/31/93)

Portfolio Manager: John Nielsen - 1990,
Henry Frantzen - 1992

Investm't Category: International Stock
- ✔ Cap Gain
- Cap & Income
- Income
- Domestic
- ✔ Foreign
- ✔ Country/Region
- Asset Allocation
- Fund of Funds
- Index
- Sector
- Small Cap
- Socially Conscious
- State Specific

Portfolio: stocks 100% bonds 0%
convertibles 0%   other 0%   cash 0%

Largest Holdings: United Kingdom 35%, Germany 15%

Unrealized Net Capital Gains: 9% of portfolio value

SHAREHOLDER INFORMATION

Minimum Investment
Initial: $25,000   Subsequent: $25,000

Minimum IRA Investment
Initial: na   Subsequent: na

Maximum Fees
Load: 1.25% redemption   12b-1: none
Other: none

Distributions
Income: Dec   Capital Gains: Dec

Exchange Options
Number Per Year: none   Fee: na
Telephone: na

Services

Fifty-Nine Wall St. Pacific Basin (FNPEX)

6 St. James Avenue
Boston, MA 02116
(212) 493-8100

International Stock

PERFORMANCE

	3yr Annual	5yr Annual	10yr Annual	Bull	Bear
Return (%)	28.2	na	na	na	na
Differ from Category (+/-)	13.9 high	na	na	na	na

Total Risk	Standard Deviation	Category Risk	Risk Index	Beta
high	18.4%	high	1.6	0.3

	1993	1992	1991	1990	1989	1988	1987	1986	1985	1984
Return (%).............	74.9	6.1	13.6	—	—	—	—	—	—	—
Differ from category (+/-)..	36.4	9.6	0.6	—	—	—	—	—	—	—

PER SHARE DATA

	1993	1992	1991	1990	1989	1988	1987	1986	1985	1984
Dividends, Net Income ($).	0.71	0.01	0.34	—	—	—	—	—	—	—
Distrib'ns, Cap Gain ($) . . .	0.70	0.95	0.21	—	—	—	—	—	—	—
Net Asset Value ($)	46.10	27.29	26.63	—	—	—	—	—	—	—
Expense Ratio (%)	1.50	1.50	1.50	—	—	—	—	—	—	—
Net Income to Assets (%) .	0.62	0.43	0.64	—	—	—	—	—	—	—
Portfolio Turnover (%).....	79	84	56	—	—	—	—	—	—	—
Total Assets (Millions $)......	2	31	20	—	—	—	—	—	—	—

PORTFOLIO (as of 10/31/93)

Portfolio Manager: John Nielsen - 1990, Henry Frantzen - 1992

Investm't Category: International Stock

✔ Cap Gain	Asset Allocation
Cap & Income	Fund of Funds
Income	Index
	Sector
Domestic	Small Cap
✔ Foreign	Socially Conscious
✔ Country/Region	State Specific

Portfolio: stocks 100% bonds 0%
convertibles 0% other 0% cash 0%

Largest Holdings: Japan 13%, Malaysia 12%

Unrealized Net Capital Gains: 25% of portfolio value

SHAREHOLDER INFORMATION

Minimum Investment
Initial: $25,000 Subsequent: $25,000

Minimum IRA Investment
Initial: na Subsequent: na

Maximum Fees
Load: 1.25% redemption 12b-1: none
Other: none

Distributions
Income: Dec Capital Gains: Dec

Exchange Options
Number Per Year: none Fee: na
Telephone: na

Services

Fifty-Nine Wall St. Small Company (FNSMX)

6 St. James Avenue
Boston, MA 02116
(212) 493-8100

Aggressive Growth

PERFORMANCE

	3yr Annual	5yr Annual	10yr Annual	Bull	Bear
Return (%)	na	na	na	na	na
Differ from Category (+/-)	na	na	na	na	na

Total Risk	Standard Deviation	Category Risk	Risk Index	Beta
na	na	na	na	na

	1993	1992	1991	1990	1989	1988	1987	1986	1985	1984
Return (%)	12.1	10.6	—	—	—	—	—	—	—	—
Differ from category (+/-) . .	-6.9	0.2	—	—	—	—	—	—	—	—

PER SHARE DATA

	1993	1992	1991	1990	1989	1988	1987	1986	1985	1984
Dividends, Net Income ($) .	0.00	0.00	—	—	—	—	—	—	—	—
Distrib'ns, Cap Gain ($) . . .	0.88	0.11	—	—	—	—	—	—	—	—
Net Asset Value ($)	12.50	11.96	—	—	—	—	—	—	—	—
Expense Ratio (%)	1.10	1.10	—	—	—	—	—	—	—	—
Net Income to Assets (%) . .	0.04	0.16	—	—	—	—	—	—	—	—
Portfolio Turnover (%)	116	67	—	—	—	—	—	—	—	—
Total Assets (Millions $)	3	20	—	—	—	—	—	—	—	—

PORTFOLIO (as of 10/31/93)

Portfolio Manager: D. Murphy - 1991, J. Nielsen - 1991, C. Mellon -1993

Investm't Category: Aggressive Growth
- ✔ Cap Gain
- Cap & Income
- Income
- Asset Allocation
- Fund of Funds
- Index
- Sector
- ✔ Domestic
- Foreign
- Country/Region
- ✔ Small Cap
- Socially Conscious
- State Specific

Portfolio: stocks 100%   bonds 0%
convertibles 0%   other 0%   cash 0%

Largest Holdings: finance 15%, electronic technology 12%

Unrealized Net Capital Gains: 10% of portfolio value

SHAREHOLDER INFORMATION

Minimum Investment
Initial: $25,000   Subsequent: $25,000

Minimum IRA Investment
Initial: na   Subsequent: na

Maximum Fees
Load: 0.50% redemption   12b-1: none
Other: none

Distributions
Income: Dec   Capital Gains: Dec

Exchange Options
Number Per Year: none   Fee: na
Telephone: na

Services

First Eagle Fund of America (FEAFX)

Growth

45 Broadway, 27th Fl.
New York, NY 10006
(800) 451-3623, (212) 943-9200

PERFORMANCE

	3yr Annual	5yr Annual	10yr Annual	Bull	Bear
Return (%)	23.0	14.2	na	78.9	-14.2
Differ from Category (+/-)	3.8 abv av	-0.4 av	na	-5.8 av	-1.8 blw av

Total Risk	Standard Deviation	Category Risk	Risk Index	Beta
abv av	11.0%	blw av	1.0	0.7

	1993	1992	1991	1990	1989	1988	1987	1986	1985	1984
Return (%)	23.8	24.3	20.9	-17.5	26.6	22.7	—	—	—	—
Differ from category (+/-). .	10.6	13.3	-14.5	-11.4	0.8	5.0	—	—	—	—

PER SHARE DATA

	1993	1992	1991	1990	1989	1988	1987	1986	1985	1984
Dividends, Net Income ($).	0.00	0.00	0.08	0.28	0.10	0.00	—	—	—	—
Distrib'ns, Cap Gain ($) . . .	1.62	1.17	0.74	0.00	1.40	0.34	—	—	—	—
Net Asset Value ($)	15.04	13.48	11.85	10.51	13.11	11.56	—	—	—	—
Expense Ratio (%)	2.90	3.00	2.00	1.10	2.00	3.30	—	—	—	—
Net Income to Assets (%) .	1.50	-1.00	0.80	1.30	1.30	0.20	—	—	—	—
Portfolio Turnover (%).	141	145	92	72	52	55	—	—	—	—
Total Assets (Millions $). . . .	109	77	74	67	84	54	—	—	—	—

PORTFOLIO (as of 10/31/93)

Portfolio Manager: Harold J. Levy - 1987, David L. Cohen - 1989

Investm't Category: Growth

✔ Cap Gain	Asset Allocation
Cap & Income	Fund of Funds
Income	Index
	Sector
✔ Domestic	Small Cap
✔ Foreign	Socially Conscious
Country/Region	State Specific

Portfolio: stocks 93% bonds 0%
convertibles 0% other 1% cash 6%

Largest Holdings: banking/financial 32%, consumer products 16%

Unrealized Net Capital Gains: 22% of portfolio value

SHAREHOLDER INFORMATION

Minimum Investment
Initial: $5,000   Subsequent: $1,000

Minimum IRA Investment
Initial: $2,000   Subsequent: $1,000

Maximum Fees
Load: 1.00% redemption   12b-1: none
Other: redemption fee applies for 2 years

Distributions
Income: Nov   Capital Gains: Nov

Exchange Options
Number Per Year: none Fee: na
Telephone: na

Services
IRA, other pension

First Hawaii Muni Bond

(SURFX)

Tax-Exempt Bond

1270 Queen Emma St., Suite 607
Honolulu, HI 96813
(808) 599-2400

PERFORMANCE

	3yr Annual	5yr Annual	10yr Annual	Bull	Bear
Return (%)	9.9	9.0	na	38.4	1.9
Differ from Category (+/-)	-0.4 blw av	-0.2 blw av	na	-1.7 blw av	-0.4 blw av

Total Risk	Standard Deviation	Category Risk	Risk Index	Avg Mat
low	3.5%	blw av	0.8	14.9 yrs

	1993	1992	1991	1990	1989	1988	1987	1986	1985	1984
Return (%)	10.4	8.6	10.5	6.2	9.2	—	—	—	—	—
Differ from category (+/-) . .	-1.2	0.3	-0.8	-0.1	0.2	—	—	—	—	—

PER SHARE DATA

	1993	1992	1991	1990	1989	1988	1987	1986	1985	1984
Dividends, Net Income ($) .	0.57	0.60	0.61	0.62	0.65	—	—	—	—	—
Distrib'ns, Cap Gain ($) . . .	0.06	0.01	0.00	0.09	0.00	—	—	—	—	—
Net Asset Value ($)	11.37	10.89	10.61	10.18	10.28	—	—	—	—	—
Expense Ratio (%).	0.95	0.95	0.91	0.83	0.54	—	—	—	—	—
Net Income to Assets (%) . .	5.21	5.67	6.05	6.16	6.40	—	—	—	—	—
Portfolio Turnover (%)	28	18	7	47	22	—	—	—	—	—
Total Assets (Millions $)	58	39	26	15	7	—	—	—	—	—

PORTFOLIO (as of 9/30/93)

Portfolio Manager: Louis Davanzo - 1991

Investm't Category: Tax-Exempt Bond

Cap Gain	Asset Allocation
Cap & Income	Fund of Funds
✔ Income	Index
	Sector
✔ Domestic	Small Cap
Foreign	Socially Conscious
Country/Region	✔ State Specific

Portfolio: stocks 0%   bonds 100%
convertibles 0%   other 0%   cash 0%

Largest Holdings: general obligation 24%

Unrealized Net Capital Gains: 7% of portfolio value

SHAREHOLDER INFORMATION

Minimum Investment
Initial: $1,000   Subsequent: $100

Minimum IRA Investment
Initial: na   Subsequent: na

Maximum Fees
Load: none   12b-1: 0.60%
Other: none

Distributions
Income: monthly   Capital Gains: Nov

Exchange Options
Number Per Year: none   Fee: na
Telephone: na

Services
auto exchange, auto invest, auto withdraw

Flex Bond (FLXBX)

Government Bond

6000 Memorial Dr.
P.O. Box 7177
Dublin, OH 43017
(800) 325-3539, (614) 766-7000

PERFORMANCE

	3yr Annual	5yr Annual	10yr Annual	Bull	Bear
Return (%)	8.8	8.7	na	34.4	3.8
Differ from Category (+/-)	-2.0 blw av	-1.7 low	na	-11.8 blw av	3.3 abv av

Total Risk	Standard Deviation	Category Risk	Risk Index	Avg Mat
blw av	4.7%	av	1.1	na

	1993	1992	1991	1990	1989	1988	1987	1986	1985	1984
Return (%)	8.2	3.2	15.3	8.3	8.7	2.7	-0.6	12.5	—	—
Differ from category (+/-) . . .	-2.2	-3.0	0.3	1.8	-5.2	-4.9	1.2	-6.6	—	—

PER SHARE DATA

	1993	1992	1991	1990	1989	1988	1987	1986	1985	1984
Dividends, Net Income ($) .	0.85	0.99	1.22	1.33	1.54	1.49	1.65	1.88	—	—
Distrib'ns, Cap Gain ($) . . .	0.00	0.00	0.00	0.00	0.00	0.00	0.30	0.17	—	—
Net Asset Value ($)	20.18	19.46	19.84	18.37	18.24	18.25	19.22	21.31	—	—
Expense Ratio (%)	1.00	1.00	0.93	0.99	0.81	0.83	0.75	0.78	—	—
Net Income to Assets (%) .	4.68	5.13	6.59	7.33	8.54	7.85	8.31	8.74	—	—
Portfolio Turnover (%)	na	101	214	500	0	188	258	150	—	—
Total Assets (Millions $)	13	11	9	6	5	6	13	13	—	—

PORTFOLIO (as of 6/30/93)

Portfolio Manager: Philip Voelker - 1988

Investm't Category: Government Bond
Cap Gain	Asset Allocation
Cap & Income	Fund of Funds
✔ Income	Index
	Sector
✔ Domestic	Small Cap
Foreign	Socially Conscious
Country/Region	State Specific

Portfolio: stocks 0% bonds 93%
convertibles 0% other 0% cash 7%

Largest Holdings: U.S. government 93%

Unrealized Net Capital Gains: 3% of portfolio value

SHAREHOLDER INFORMATION

Minimum Investment
Initial: $2,500   Subsequent: $100

Minimum IRA Investment
Initial: $500   Subsequent: $100

Maximum Fees
Load: none   12b-1: 0.20%
Other: none

Distributions
Income: monthly   Capital Gains: Dec

Exchange Options
Number Per Year: no limit   Fee: none
Telephone: yes (money market fund available)

Services
IRA, other pension, auto invest, auto withdraw

Flex Growth (FLCGX)

Growth

6000 Memorial Dr.
P.O. Box 7177
Dublin, OH 43017
(800) 325-3539, (614) 766-7000

PERFORMANCE

	3yr Annual	5yr Annual	10yr Annual	Bull	Bear
Return (%)	11.4	9.7	na	45.0	-0.3
Differ from Category (+/-)	-7.8 low	-4.9 low	na	-39.7 low	12.1 high

Total Risk	Standard Deviation	Category Risk	Risk Index	Beta
av	10.1%	low	0.9	0.7

	1993	1992	1991	1990	1989	1988	1987	1986	1985	1984
Return (%)	7.2	6.3	21.4	4.3	10.1	-5.7	7.5	11.8	—	—
Differ from category (+/-) . .	-6.0	-4.7	-14.0	10.4	-15.7	-23.4	6.3	-2.7	—	—

PER SHARE DATA

	1993	1992	1991	1990	1989	1988	1987	1986	1985	1984
Dividends, Net Income ($) .	0.15	0.11	0.33	0.56	0.31	0.77	0.05	0.27	—	—
Distrib'ns, Cap Gain ($) . . .	0.00	0.00	0.00	0.00	0.00	0.19	0.00	1.14	—	—
Net Asset Value ($)	13.45	12.70	12.05	10.21	10.33	9.67	11.27	10.52	—	—
Expense Ratio (%)	1.53	1.51	1.42	1.46	1.55	1.50	1.48	1.49	—	—
Net Income to Assets (%) . .	0.73	1.31	2.98	4.90	2.63	2.06	1.79	2.32	—	—
Portfolio Turnover (%)	na	39	265	436	50	313	326	152	—	—
Total Assets (Millions $)	26	26	33	25	30	5	13	10	—	—

PORTFOLIO (as of 6/30/93)

Portfolio Manager: Philip Voelker - 1989

Investm't Category: Growth

✔ Cap Gain	Asset Allocation
Cap & Income	Fund of Funds
Income	Index
	Sector
✔ Domestic	Small Cap
Foreign	Socially Conscious
Country/Region	State Specific

Portfolio: stocks 78% bonds 0%
convertibles 0% other 0% cash 22%

Largest Holdings: petroleum 6%, machinery (construction & mining) 4%

Unrealized Net Capital Gains: 0% of portfolio value

SHAREHOLDER INFORMATION

Minimum Investment
Initial: $2,500   Subsequent: $100

Minimum IRA Investment
Initial: $500   Subsequent: $100

Maximum Fees
Load: none   12b-1: 0.20%
Other: none

Distributions
Income: quarterly   Capital Gains: Dec

Exchange Options
Number Per Year: no limit   Fee: none
Telephone: yes (money market fund available)

Services
IRA, other pension, auto invest, auto withdraw

Flex Muirfield (FLMFX)

Growth

6000 Memorial Dr.
P.O. Box 7177
Dublin, OH 43017
(800) 325-3539, (614) 766-7000

PERFORMANCE

	3yr Annual	5yr Annual	10yr Annual	Bull	Bear
Return (%)	14.4	11.8	na	56.6	-1.8
Differ from Category (+/-)	-4.8 blw av	-2.8 low	na	-28.1 low	10.6 high

Total Risk	Standard Deviation	Category Risk	Risk Index	Beta
av	10.1%	low	0.9	0.8

	1993	1992	1991	1990	1989	1988	1987	1986	1985	1984
Return (%)	8.1	6.9	29.8	2.4	13.9	—	—	—	—	—
Differ from category (+/-)	-5.1	-4.1	-5.6	8.5	-11.9	—	—	—	—	—

PER SHARE DATA

	1993	1992	1991	1990	1989	1988	1987	1986	1985	1984
Dividends, Net Income ($)	0.02	0.06	0.27	0.10	0.07	—	—	—	—	—
Distrib'ns, Cap Gain ($)	1.31	0.52	0.00	0.63	0.10	—	—	—	—	—
Net Asset Value ($)	5.36	6.25	6.43	5.22	5.84	—	—	—	—	—
Expense Ratio (%)	1.31	1.40	1.50	1.52	1.53	—	—	—	—	—
Net Income to Assets (%)	-0.27	1.05	1.25	4.46	1.65	—	—	—	—	—
Portfolio Turnover (%)	na	324	107	649	202	—	—	—	—	—
Total Assets (Millions $)	81	55	43	30	26	—	—	—	—	—

PORTFOLIO (as of 6/30/93)

Portfolio Manager: Robert Meeder, Jr. - 1988

Investm't Category: Growth

✔ Cap Gain	Asset Allocation
Cap & Income	✔ Fund of Funds
Income	Index
	Sector
✔ Domestic	Small Cap
Foreign	Socially Conscious
Country/Region	State Specific

Portfolio: stocks 0%   bonds 0%
convertibles 0%   other 84%   cash 16%

Largest Holdings: Neuberger & Berman Selected Sector Fund 9%, Mutual Shares Fund 9%

Unrealized Net Capital Gains: 5% of portfolio value

SHAREHOLDER INFORMATION

Minimum Investment
Initial: $2,500   Subsequent: $100

Minimum IRA Investment
Initial: $500   Subsequent: $100

Maximum Fees
Load: none   12b-1: 0.20%
Other: none

Distributions
Income: quarterly   Capital Gains: Dec

Exchange Options
Number Per Year: no limit   Fee: none
Telephone: yes (money market fund available)

Services
IRA, other pension, auto invest, auto withdraw

Flex Short Term Global Income (FLGIX)

International Bond

6000 Memorial Dr.
P.O. Box 7177
Dublin, OH 43017
(800) 325-3539, (614) 766-7000

PERFORMANCE

	3yr Annual	5yr Annual	10yr Annual	Bull	Bear
Return (%)	na	na	na	na	na
Differ from Category (+/-)	na	na	na	na	na

Total Risk	Standard Deviation	Category Risk	Risk Index	Avg Mat
na	na	na	na	na

	1993	1992	1991	1990	1989	1988	1987	1986	1985	1984
Return (%)	0.3	—	—	—	—	—	—	—	—	—
Differ from category (+/-)	-12.4	—	—	—	—	—	—	—	—	—

PER SHARE DATA

	1993	1992	1991	1990	1989	1988	1987	1986	1985	1984
Dividends, Net Income ($)	0.38	—	—	—	—	—	—	—	—	—
Distrib'ns, Cap Gain ($)	0.00	—	—	—	—	—	—	—	—	—
Net Asset Value ($)	9.41	—	—	—	—	—	—	—	—	—
Expense Ratio (%)	0.81	—	—	—	—	—	—	—	—	—
Net Income to Assets (%)	4.83	—	—	—	—	—	—	—	—	—
Portfolio Turnover (%)	na	—	—	—	—	—	—	—	—	—
Total Assets (Millions $)	14	—	—	—	—	—	—	—	—	—

PORTFOLIO (as of 6/30/93)

Portfolio Manager: Joseph Zarr - 1992

Investm't Category: International Bond

Cap Gain	Asset Allocation
Cap & Income	Fund of Funds
✔ Income	Index
	Sector
✔ Domestic	Small Cap
✔ Foreign	Socially Conscious
Country/Region	State Specific

Portfolio:	stocks 0%	bonds 55%
convertibles 0%	other 0%	cash 45%

Largest Holdings: United States 55%

Unrealized Net Capital Gains: 0% of portfolio value

SHAREHOLDER INFORMATION

Minimum Investment
Initial: $2,500   Subsequent: $100

Minimum IRA Investment
Initial: $500   Subsequent: $100

Maximum Fees
Load: none   12b-1: 0.20%
Other: none

Distributions
Income: monthly   Capital Gains: Dec

Exchange Options
Number Per Year: no limit   Fee: none
Telephone: yes (money market fund available)

Services
IRA, other pension, auto invest, auto withdraw

Fontaine Capital Appreciation (FAPPX)

Growth

210 W. Pennsylvania Ave.
Suite 240
Towson, MD 21204
(800) 247-1550, (410) 825-7894

PERFORMANCE

	3yr Annual	5yr Annual	10yr Annual	Bull	Bear
Return (%)	7.0	na	na	26.2	3.0
Differ from Category (+/-)	-12.2 low	na	na	-58.5 low	15.4 high

Total Risk	Standard Deviation	Category Risk	Risk Index	Beta
blw av	6.1%	low	0.5	0.2

	1993	1992	1991	1990	1989	1988	1987	1986	1985	1984
Return (%)	14.0	-3.9	11.8	6.1	—	—	—	—	—	—
Differ from category (+/-) . . .	0.8	-14.9	-23.6	12.2	—	—	—	—	—	—

PER SHARE DATA

	1993	1992	1991	1990	1989	1988	1987	1986	1985	1984
Dividends, Net Income ($).	0.13	0.11	0.63	0.39	—	—	—	—	—	—
Distrib'ns, Cap Gain ($) . . .	0.06	0.62	0.20	0.04	—	—	—	—	—	—
Net Asset Value ($)	10.75	9.60	10.78	10.40	—	—	—	—	—	—
Expense Ratio (%)	1.50	1.50	1.50	1.50	—	—	—	—	—	—
Net Income to Assets (%) . . .	na	3.12	4.14	5.26	—	—	—	—	—	—
Portfolio Turnover (%).	na	129	79	288	—	—	—	—	—	—
Total Assets (Millions $).	7	15	16	4	—	—	—	—	—	—

PORTFOLIO (as of 6/30/93)

Portfolio Manager: Richard H. Fontaine - 1989

Investm't Category: Growth

Cap Gain	Asset Allocation
✔ Cap & Income	Fund of Funds
Income	Index
	Sector
✔ Domestic	Small Cap
✔ Foreign	Socially Conscious
Country/Region	State Specific

Portfolio: stocks 36% bonds 0%
convertibles 0% other 0% cash 64%

Largest Holdings: gold mining 14%, office automation 12%

Unrealized Net Capital Gains: 0% of portfolio value

SHAREHOLDER INFORMATION

Minimum Investment
Initial: $1,000   Subsequent: $100

Minimum IRA Investment
Initial: $250   Subsequent: $100

Maximum Fees
Load: none   12b-1: none
Other: none

Distributions
Income: Dec   Capital Gains: Dec

Exchange Options
Number Per Year: 8   Fee: none
Telephone: none

Services
IRA, other pension

Forty-Four Wall Street Equity (FWLEX)

26 Broadway, Suite 205
New York, NY 10004
(800) 543-2620, (212) 248-8080

Aggressive Growth

PERFORMANCE

	3yr Annual	5yr Annual	10yr Annual	Bull	Bear
Return (%)	23.3	16.2	na	100.1	-14.2
Differ from Category (+/-)	-2.1 av	-2.0 blw av	na	-24.9 blw av	0.8 av

Total Risk	Standard Deviation	Category Risk	Risk Index	Beta
abv av	13.6%	blw av	0.9	0.6

	1993	1992	1991	1990	1989	1988	1987	1986	1985	1984
Return (%)	26.4	18.1	25.6	-8.6	23.5	32.3	-41.9	16.8	22.3	—
Differ from category (+/-) ...	7.4	7.7	-26.8	-2.3	-3.5	17.1	-38.5	7.4	-8.7	—

PER SHARE DATA

	1993	1992	1991	1990	1989	1988	1987	1986	1985	1984
Dividends, Net Income ($) .	0.00	0.70	0.00	0.00	0.00	0.00	0.00	0.00	0.00	—
Distrib'ns, Cap Gain ($) ...	1.76	0.23	0.00	0.00	0.00	0.00	0.00	0.00	0.00	—
Net Asset Value ($)	6.41	6.47	6.27	4.99	5.46	4.42	3.34	5.75	4.92	—
Expense Ratio (%)........	4.39	5.33	4.42	4.28	4.68	5.88	5.35	6.11	6.62	—
Net Income to Assets (%).	-0.62	-1.11	-1.19	-0.44	-2.13	-5.23	-4.88	-5.16	-5.98	—
Portfolio Turnover (%)....	167	136	87	235	238	81	98	82	112	—
Total Assets (Millions $)	8	4	4	4	4	4	12	13	10	—

PORTFOLIO (as of 6/30/93)

Portfolio Manager: Mark D. Beckerman - 1988

Investm't Category: Aggressive Growth

✔ Cap Gain   Asset Allocation
   Cap & Income   Fund of Funds
   Income   Index
     Sector
✔ Domestic   Small Cap
✔ Foreign   Socially Conscious
   Country/Region   State Specific

Portfolio: stocks 83%   bonds 3%
convertibles 0%   other 7%   cash 7%

Largest Holdings: real estate 16%, apparel 9%

Unrealized Net Capital Gains: 3% of portfolio value

SHAREHOLDER INFORMATION

Minimum Investment
Initial: $1,000   Subsequent: $100

Minimum IRA Investment
Initial: $1,000   Subsequent: $100

Maximum Fees
Load: none   12b-1: none
Other: none

Distributions
Income: Dec   Capital Gains: Dec

Exchange Options
Number Per Year: none   Fee: na
Telephone: na

Services
IRA, other pension, auto invest, auto withdraw

Founders Balanced

(FRINX)

Balanced

Founders Financial Center
2930 E. Third Ave.
Denver, CO 80206
(800) 525-2440, (303) 394-4404

PERFORMANCE

	3yr Annual	5yr Annual	10yr Annual	Bull	Bear
Return (%)	16.6	13.5	11.9	64.9	-8.5
Differ from Category (+/-)	1.6 abv av	1.4 abv av	-0.1 blw av	3.3 abv av	-2.7 low

Total Risk	Standard Deviation	Category Risk	Risk Index	Beta
av	6.8%	av	1.1	0.5

	1993	1992	1991	1990	1989	1988	1987	1986	1985	1984
Return (%)............	21.8	6.0	22.8	-4.9	25.2	11.0	1.8	14.5	12.7	11.6
Differ from category (+/-)...	8.4	-2.1	-1.1	-4.4	7.6	-1.0	-0.5	-3.0	-11.0	4.2

PER SHARE DATA

	1993	1992	1991	1990	1989	1988	1987	1986	1985	1984
Dividends, Net Income ($).	0.20	0.27	0.31	0.35	0.32	0.37	0.40	0.33	0.40	0.46
Distrib'ns, Cap Gain ($) ...	0.95	0.09	0.33	0.00	0.32	0.00	0.87	0.43	0.15	0.32
Net Asset Value ($)	8.93	8.30	8.19	7.22	7.97	6.89	6.55	7.65	7.37	7.07
Expense Ratio (%)	1.42	1.88	1.73	1.65	1.52	1.64	1.66	1.59	1.50	1.50
Net Income to Assets (%) .	2.67	3.57	4.01	4.63	4.19	5.39	4.03	4.44	5.88	6.67
Portfolio Turnover (%).....	149	96	133	103	85	182	133	178	126	145
Total Assets (Millions $).....	74	32	19	14	15	13	17	12	9	7

PORTFOLIO (as of 6/30/93)

Portfolio Manager: Pat Adams - 1993

Investm't Category: Balanced

Cap Gain	Asset Allocation
✔ Cap & Income	Fund of Funds
Income	Index
	Sector
✔ Domestic	Small Cap
✔ Foreign	Socially Conscious
Country/Region	State Specific

Portfolio: stocks 51% bonds 24%
convertibles 8% other 6% cash 11%

Largest Holdings: U.S. government 17%, stocks—retail 8%

Unrealized Net Capital Gains: 6% of portfolio value

SHAREHOLDER INFORMATION

Minimum Investment
Initial: $1,000   Subsequent: $100

Minimum IRA Investment
Initial: $500   Subsequent: $100

Maximum Fees
Load: none   12b-1: 0.25%
Other: none

Distributions
Income: quarterly   Capital Gains: Dec

Exchange Options
Number Per Year: 4   Fee: none
Telephone: yes (money market fund available)

Services
IRA, other pension, auto exchange, auto invest, auto withdraw

Founders Blue Chip

(FRMUX)

Growth & Income

Founders Financial Center
2930 E. Third Ave.
Denver, CO 80206
(800) 525-2440, (303) 394-4404

PERFORMANCE

	3yr Annual	5yr Annual	10yr Annual	Bull	Bear
Return (%)	13.5	14.8	13.4	56.4	-5.9
Differ from Category (+/-)	-2.9 blw av	2.3 high	1.0 av	-13.7 blw av	5.7 high

Total Risk	Standard Deviation	Category Risk	Risk Index	Beta
av	10.7%	abv av	1.2	0.9

	1993	1992	1991	1990	1989	1988	1987	1986	1985	1984
Return (%)	14.4	-0.2	28.3	0.4	35.5	10.0	1.9	17.3	31.9	1.8
Differ from category (+/-) ...	1.8	-10.2	0.6	6.0	13.9	-6.8	1.5	2.1	6.5	-4.4

PER SHARE DATA

	1993	1992	1991	1990	1989	1988	1987	1986	1985	1984
Dividends, Net Income ($) .	0.03	0.08	0.11	0.16	0.16	0.18	0.23	0.28	0.37	0.31
Distrib'ns, Cap Gain ($) ...	1.38	0.65	0.74	0.51	1.04	0.25	1.71	3.21	1.84	1.16
Net Asset Value ($)	6.49	6.91	7.67	6.67	7.32	6.31	6.14	7.87	9.75	9.38
Expense Ratio (%)........	1.29	1.23	1.10	1.07	0.98	1.00	0.87	0.74	0.70	0.66
Net Income to Assets (%)..	0.80	1.13	1.52	2.35	2.03	2.81	2.11	2.64	3.69	3.07
Portfolio Turnover (%)....	183	103	95	82	64	58	56	42	18	17
Total Assets (Millions $) ...	306	290	290	234	232	173	240	175	138	134

PORTFOLIO (as of 6/30/93)

Portfolio Manager: Pat Adams - 1993

Investm't Category: Growth & Income

Cap Gain	Asset Allocation
✔ Cap & Income	Fund of Funds
Income	Index
	Sector
✔ Domestic	Small Cap
✔ Foreign	Socially Conscious
Country/Region	State Specific

Portfolio: stocks 80% bonds 0%
convertibles 1% other 3% cash 16%

Largest Holdings: retail 9%, banking 8%

Unrealized Net Capital Gains: 10% of portfolio value

SHAREHOLDER INFORMATION

Minimum Investment
Initial: $1,000   Subsequent: $100

Minimum IRA Investment
Initial: $500   Subsequent: $100

Maximum Fees
Load: none   12b-1: 0.25%
Other: none

Distributions
Income: quarterly   Capital Gains: Dec

Exchange Options
Number Per Year: 4   Fee: none
Telephone: yes (money market fund available)

Services
IRA, other pension, auto exchange, auto invest, auto withdraw

Founders Discovery
(FDISX)
Aggressive Growth

Founders Financial Center
2930 E. Third Ave.
Denver, CO 80206
(800) 525-2440, (303) 394-4404

PERFORMANCE

	3yr Annual	5yr Annual	10yr Annual	Bull	Bear
Return (%)	27.5	na	na	133.0	0.6
Differ from Category (+/-)	2.1 abv av	na	na	8.0 abv av	15.7 high

Total Risk	Standard Deviation	Category Risk	Risk Index	Beta
high	17.7%	abv av	1.2	1.1

	1993	1992	1991	1990	1989	1988	1987	1986	1985	1984
Return (%)	10.8	15.1	62.4	13.1	—	—	—	—	—	—
Differ from category (+/-) . . .	-8.2	4.7	10.0	19.4	—	—	—	—	—	—

PER SHARE DATA

	1993	1992	1991	1990	1989	1988	1987	1986	1985	1984
Dividends, Net Income ($) .	0.00	0.06	0.00	0.09	—	—	—	—	—	—
Distrib'ns, Cap Gain ($) . . .	0.51	0.17	0.67	0.00	—	—	—	—	—	—
Net Asset Value ($)	21.55	19.93	17.52	11.22	—	—	—	—	—	—
Expense Ratio (%)	1.69	1.85	1.77	2.03	—	—	—	—	—	—
Net Income to Assets (%) .	-0.95	-0.67	-0.55	1.68	—	—	—	—	—	—
Portfolio Turnover (%).	94	111	165	271	—	—	—	—	—	—
Total Assets (Millions $). . . .	230	152	47	7	—	—	—	—	—	—

PORTFOLIO (as of 6/30/93)

Portfolio Manager: Michael Haines - 1989

Investm't Category: Aggressive Growth

✔ Cap Gain	Asset Allocation
Cap & Income	Fund of Funds
Income	Index
	Sector
✔ Domestic	✔ Small Cap
✔ Foreign	Socially Conscious
Country/Region	State Specific

Portfolio: stocks 86% bonds 0%
convertibles 0% other 0% cash 14%

Largest Holdings: retail 11%, computer software 9%

Unrealized Net Capital Gains: 10% of portfolio value

SHAREHOLDER INFORMATION

Minimum Investment
Initial: $1,000   Subsequent: $100

Minimum IRA Investment
Initial: $500   Subsequent: $100

Maximum Fees
Load: none   12b-1: 0.25%
Other: none

Distributions
Income: Dec   Capital Gains: Dec

Exchange Options
Number Per Year: 4   Fee: none
Telephone: yes (money market fund available)

Services
IRA, other pension, auto exchange, auto invest, auto withdraw

Founders Frontier

(FOUNX)

Aggressive Growth

Founders Financial Center
2930 E. Third Ave.
Denver, CO 80206
(800) 525-2440, (303) 394-4404

PERFORMANCE

	3yr Annual	5yr Annual	10yr Annual	Bull	Bear
Return (%)	23.7	20.4	na	104.7	-14.3
Differ from Category (+/-)	-1.7 av	2.2 abv av	na	-20.3 blw av	0.6 av

Total Risk	Standard Deviation	Category Risk	Risk Index	Beta
high	15.6%	av	1.0	1.1

	1993	1992	1991	1990	1989	1988	1987	1986	1985	1984
Return (%)	16.5	8.9	49.3	-7.4	44.3	29.2	—	—	—	—
Differ from category (+/-) . .	-2.5	-1.5	-3.1	-1.1	17.3	14.0	—	—	—	—

PER SHARE DATA

	1993	1992	1991	1990	1989	1988	1987	1986	1985	1984
Dividends, Net Income ($) .	0.00	0.00	0.01	0.16	0.05	0.00	—	—	—	—
Distrib'ns, Cap Gain ($) . . .	1.20	1.30	0.92	0.08	0.84	0.77	—	—	—	—
Net Asset Value ($)	27.94	25.03	24.21	16.87	18.49	13.45	—	—	—	—
Expense Ratio (%).	1.73	1.83	1.68	1.71	1.46	1.89	—	—	—	—
Net Income to Assets (%) .	-0.60	-0.58	0.05	0.78	0.38	-0.43	—	—	—	—
Portfolio Turnover (%)	116	155	158	207	198	312	—	—	—	—
Total Assets (Millions $) . . .	200	146	103	39	50	9	—	—	—	—

PORTFOLIO (as of 6/30/93)

Portfolio Manager: Michael Haines - 1987

Investm't Category: Aggressive Growth

✔ Cap Gain	Asset Allocation
Cap & Income	Fund of Funds
Income	Index
	Sector
✔ Domestic	✔ Small Cap
✔ Foreign	Socially Conscious
Country/Region	State Specific

Portfolio: stocks 78% bonds 0%
convertibles 0% other 0% cash 22%

Largest Holdings: telecommunications 8%, retail 7%

Unrealized Net Capital Gains: 12% of portfolio value

SHAREHOLDER INFORMATION

Minimum Investment
Initial: $1,000 Subsequent: $100

Minimum IRA Investment
Initial: $500 Subsequent: $100

Maximum Fees
Load: none 12b-1: 0.25%
Other: none

Distributions
Income: Dec Capital Gains: Dec

Exchange Options
Number Per Year: 4 Fee: none
Telephone: yes (money market fund available)

Services
IRA, other pension, auto exchange, auto invest, auto withdraw

Founders Gov't Securities (FGVSX)

Government Bond

Founders Financial Center
2930 E. Third Ave.
Denver, CO 80206
(800) 525-2440, (303) 394-4404

PERFORMANCE

	3yr Annual	5yr Annual	10yr Annual	Bull	Bear
Return (%)	9.7	9.3	na	39.0	-0.6
Differ from Category (+/-)	-1.1 av	-1.1 blw av	na	-7.2 av	-1.2 blw av

Total Risk	Standard Deviation	Category Risk	Risk Index	Avg Mat
blw av	4.3%	av	1.0	13.0 yrs

	1993	1992	1991	1990	1989	1988	1987	1986	1985	1984
Return (%)	9.2	5.3	14.8	4.4	13.3	—	—	—	—	—
Differ from category (+/-)	-1.2	-0.8	-0.2	-2.1	-0.6	—	—	—	—	—

PER SHARE DATA

	1993	1992	1991	1990	1989	1988	1987	1986	1985	1984
Dividends, Net Income ($)	0.46	0.51	0.59	0.69	0.79	—	—	—	—	—
Distrib'ns, Cap Gain ($)	0.64	0.31	0.18	0.00	0.00	—	—	—	—	—
Net Asset Value ($)	10.02	10.19	10.48	9.85	10.13	—	—	—	—	—
Expense Ratio (%)	1.15	1.18	1.12	1.03	0.65	—	—	—	—	—
Net Income to Assets (%)	4.23	4.83	5.89	7.15	7.90	—	—	—	—	—
Portfolio Turnover (%)	455	204	261	103	195	—	—	—	—	—
Total Assets (Millions $)	31	25	18	7	7	—	—	—	—	—

PORTFOLIO (as of 6/30/93)

Portfolio Manager: Montgomery Cleworth - 1993

Investm't Category: Government Bond

Cap Gain	Asset Allocation
Cap & Income	Fund of Funds
✔ Income	Index
	Sector
✔ Domestic	Small Cap
Foreign	Socially Conscious
Country/Region	State Specific

Portfolio:	stocks 0%	bonds 93%
convertibles 0%	other 0%	cash 7%

Largest Holdings: U.S. government securities 93%

Unrealized Net Capital Gains: 2% of portfolio value

SHAREHOLDER INFORMATION

Minimum Investment
Initial: $1,000   Subsequent: $100

Minimum IRA Investment
Initial: $500   Subsequent: $100

Maximum Fees
Load: none   12b-1: 0.25%
Other: none

Distributions
Income: monthly   Capital Gains: Dec

Exchange Options
Number Per Year: 4   Fee: none
Telephone: yes (money market fund available)

Services
IRA, other pension, auto exchange, auto invest, auto withdraw

Founders Growth (FRGRX)

Growth

Founders Financial Center
2930 E. Third Ave.
Denver, CO 80206
(800) 525-2440, (303) 394-4404

PERFORMANCE

	3yr Annual	5yr Annual	10yr Annual	Bull	Bear
Return (%)	24.5	19.5	14.4	101.9	-14.5
Differ from Category (+/-)	5.3 high	4.9 high	1.8 abv av	17.2 abv av	-2.1 blw av

Total Risk	Standard Deviation	Category Risk	Risk Index	Beta
high	15.2%	high	1.4	1.1

	1993	1992	1991	1990	1989	1988	1987	1986	1985	1984
Return (%)	25.5	4.3	47.3	-10.6	41.7	4.8	10.0	19.6	28.7	-11.0
Differ from category (+/-) . .	12.3	-6.7	11.9	-4.5	15.9	-12.9	8.8	5.1	-0.6	-11.0

PER SHARE DATA

	1993	1992	1991	1990	1989	1988	1987	1986	1985	1984
Dividends, Net Income ($) .	0.00	0.00	0.06	0.13	0.07	0.15	0.13	0.10	0.16	0.18
Distrib'ns, Cap Gain ($) . . .	0.84	1.15	0.87	0.01	1.27	0.00	1.61	1.35	0.00	0.00
Net Asset Value ($)	12.38	10.54	11.22	8.27	9.41	7.61	7.41	8.30	8.14	6.45
Expense Ratio (%)	1.42	1.54	1.45	1.45	1.28	1.38	1.25	1.27	1.17	1.22
Net Income to Assets (%) .	-0.11	0.06	0.65	1.53	0.77	1.74	0.99	1.19	2.49	2.52
Portfolio Turnover (%)	202	216	161	178	167	179	147	142	186	203
Total Assets (Millions $) . . .	352	145	141	88	112	53	58	61	42	41

PORTFOLIO (as of 6/30/93)

Portfolio Manager: Edward F. Keely - 1993, Scott Schoelzel - 1991

Investm't Category: Growth
- ✔ Cap Gain
- Cap & Income
- Income
- ✔ Domestic
- ✔ Foreign
- Country/Region
- Asset Allocation
- Fund of Funds
- Index
- Sector
- Small Cap
- Socially Conscious
- State Specific

Portfolio: stocks 74% bonds 0%
convertibles 0% other 0% cash 26%

Largest Holdings: computer networking 11%, computer software 9%

Unrealized Net Capital Gains: 15% of portfolio value

SHAREHOLDER INFORMATION

Minimum Investment
Initial: $1,000 Subsequent: $100

Minimum IRA Investment
Initial: $500 Subsequent: $100

Maximum Fees
Load: none 12b-1: 0.25%
Other: none

Distributions
Income: Dec Capital Gains: Dec

Exchange Options
Number Per Year: 4 Fee: none
Telephone: yes (money market fund available)

Services
IRA, other pension, auto exchange, auto invest, auto withdraw

Founders Special (FRSPX)

Aggressive Growth

Founders Financial Center
2930 E. Third Ave.
Denver, CO 80206
(800) 525-2440, (303) 394-4404

PERFORMANCE

	3yr Annual	5yr Annual	10yr Annual	Bull	Bear
Return (%)	27.1	20.7	13.8	129.5	-19.7
Differ from Category (+/-)	1.7 av	2.5 abv av	1.9 abv av	4.5 abv av	-4.7 blw av

Total Risk	Standard Deviation	Category Risk	Risk Index	Beta
high	16.0%	av	1.0	1.2

	1993	1992	1991	1990	1989	1988	1987	1986	1985	1984
Return (%)	16.0	8.2	63.6	-10.4	39.2	13.1	5.2	18.7	15.1	-12.4
Differ from category (+/-). . .	-3.0	-2.2	11.2	-4.1	12.2	-2.1	8.6	9.3	-15.9	-3.0

PER SHARE DATA

	1993	1992	1991	1990	1989	1988	1987	1986	1985	1984
Dividends, Net Income ($) .	0.00	0.00	0.04	0.10	0.15	0.03	0.02	0.06	0.50	0.11
Distrib'ns, Cap Gain ($) . . .	1.33	0.45	0.57	0.80	0.81	0.30	0.72	0.69	0.61	0.00
Net Asset Value ($)	7.67	7.76	7.59	5.03	6.64	5.47	5.14	5.59	5.34	4.68
Expense Ratio (%)	1.37	1.23	1.15	1.20	1.06	1.12	1.14	1.06	1.02	1.11
Net Income to Assets (%) .	0.04	-0.05	0.76	1.54	1.95	0.59	0.45	0.73	0.85	2.20
Portfolio Turnover (%).	271	223	102	146	151	160	210	138	192	191
Total Assets (Millions $)	436	457	226	58	95	63	66	70	95	81

PORTFOLIO (as of 6/30/93)

Portfolio Manager: Charles Hooper - 1991

Investm't Category: Aggressive Growth

✔ Cap Gain	Asset Allocation
Cap & Income	Fund of Funds
Income	Index
	Sector
✔ Domestic	Small Cap
✔ Foreign	Socially Conscious
Country/Region	State Specific

Portfolio: stocks 91% bonds 0%
convertibles 0% other 0% cash 8%

Largest Holdings: banking 13%, semiconductors 9%

Unrealized Net Capital Gains: 8% of portfolio value

SHAREHOLDER INFORMATION

Minimum Investment
Initial: $1,000 Subsequent: $100

Minimum IRA Investment
Initial: $500 Subsequent: $100

Maximum Fees
Load: none 12b-1: 0.25%
Other: none

Distributions
Income: Dec Capital Gains: Dec

Exchange Options
Number Per Year: 4 Fee: none
Telephone: yes (money market fund available)

Services
IRA, other pension, auto exchange, auto invest, auto withdraw

Founders World Wide Growth (FWWGX)

International Stock

Founders Financial Center
2930 E. Third Ave.
Denver, CO 80206
(800) 525-2440, (303) 394-4404

PERFORMANCE

	3yr Annual	5yr Annual	10yr Annual	Bull	Bear
Return (%)	21.1	na	na	86.7	1.5
Differ from Category (+/-)	6.8 high	na	na	31.6 high	16.6 high

Total Risk	Standard Deviation	Category Risk	Risk Index	Beta
abv av	12.7%	blw av	1.1	0.8

	1993	1992	1991	1990	1989	1988	1987	1986	1985	1984
Return (%)	29.8	1.5	34.8	6.6	—	—	—	—	—	—
Differ from category (+/-) . .	-8.7	5.0	21.9	17.7	—	—	—	—	—	—

PER SHARE DATA

	1993	1992	1991	1990	1989	1988	1987	1986	1985	1984
Dividends, Net Income ($) .	0.00	0.00	0.03	0.28	—	—	—	—	—	—
Distrib'ns, Cap Gain ($) . . .	0.40	0.00	0.03	0.00	—	—	—	—	—	—
Net Asset Value ($)	17.94	14.13	13.92	10.38	—	—	—	—	—	—
Expense Ratio (%)	2.01	2.06	1.90	2.10	—	—	—	—	—	—
Net Income to Assets (%) . .	0.34	0.01	0.38	3.21	—	—	—	—	—	—
Portfolio Turnover (%)	119	152	84	170	—	—	—	—	—	—
Total Assets (Millions $)	90	37	20	6	—	—	—	—	—	—

PORTFOLIO (as of 6/30/93)

Portfolio Manager: Michael Gerding - 1990

Investm't Category: International Stock

✔ Cap Gain	Asset Allocation
Cap & Income	Fund of Funds
Income	Index
	Sector
✔ Domestic	Small Cap
✔ Foreign	Socially Conscious
Country/Region	State Specific

Portfolio: stocks 87% bonds 0%
convertibles 0% other 0% cash 13%

Largest Holdings: United States 16%, United Kingdom 9%

Unrealized Net Capital Gains: 1% of portfolio value

SHAREHOLDER INFORMATION

Minimum Investment
Initial: $1,000   Subsequent: $100

Minimum IRA Investment
Initial: $500   Subsequent: $100

Maximum Fees
Load: none   12b-1: 0.25%
Other: none

Distributions
Income: Dec   Capital Gains: Dec

Exchange Options
Number Per Year: 4   Fee: none
Telephone: yes (money market fund available)

Services
IRA, other pension, auto exchange, auto invest, auto withdraw

Franklin Short-Interm US Gov't (FRGVX)

777 Mariners Island Blvd.
San Mateo, CA 94404
(800) 342-5236

Government Bond

PERFORMANCE

	3yr Annual	5yr Annual	10yr Annual	Bull	Bear
Return (%)	8.7	9.1	na	33.0	6.0
Differ from Category (+/-)	-2.1 blw av	-1.3 blw av	na	-13.2 blw av	5.5 high

Total Risk	Standard Deviation	Category Risk	Risk Index	Avg Mat
low	3.1%	blw av	0.7	3.9 yrs

	1993	1992	1991	1990	1989	1988	1987	1986	1985	1984
Return (%)	7.7	6.6	12.0	9.6	9.6	5.7	—	—	—	—
Differ from category (+/-)	-2.7	0.4	-3.0	3.1	-4.3	-1.9	—	—	—	—

PER SHARE DATA

	1993	1992	1991	1990	1989	1988	1987	1986	1985	1984
Dividends, Net Income ($)	0.51	0.58	0.80	0.86	0.82	0.73	—	—	—	—
Distrib'ns, Cap Gain ($)	0.09	0.25	0.07	0.00	0.00	0.00	—	—	—	—
Net Asset Value ($)	10.61	10.42	10.59	10.29	10.22	10.11	—	—	—	—
Expense Ratio (%)	0.56	0.71	0.48	0.27	0.25	0.14	—	—	—	—
Net Income to Assets (%)	5.40	5.90	7.56	7.60	7.72	6.50	—	—	—	—
Portfolio Turnover (%)	78	102	71	151	112	13	—	—	—	—
Total Assets (Millions $)	270	164	49	31	29	13	—	—	—	—

PORTFOLIO (as of 7/31/93)

Portfolio Manager: Jack Lemein - 1987

Investm't Category: Government Bond

Cap Gain	Asset Allocation
Cap & Income	Fund of Funds
✔ Income	Index
	Sector
✔ Domestic	Small Cap
Foreign	Socially Conscious
Country/Region	State Specific

Portfolio: stocks 0% bonds 99%
convertibles 0% other 1% cash 0%

Largest Holdings: U.S. government 99%

Unrealized Net Capital Gains: 2% of portfolio value

SHAREHOLDER INFORMATION

Minimum Investment
Initial: $100 Subsequent: $25

Minimum IRA Investment
Initial: $0 Subsequent: $0

Maximum Fees
Load: 2.25% front 12b-1: none
Other: 2.25% load on reinvested dividends

Distributions
Income: monthly Capital Gains: June, Dec

Exchange Options
Number Per Year: no limit Fee: none
Telephone: yes (money market fund available)

Services
IRA, other pension, auto invest, auto withdraw

Fremont CA Interm Tax-Free (FCATX)

Tax-Exempt Bond

50 Fremont St., Suite 3600
San Francisco, CA 94105
(800) 548-4539, (415) 768-9000

PERFORMANCE

	3yr Annual	5yr Annual	10yr Annual	Bull	Bear
Return (%)	9.3	na	na	na	na
Differ from Category (+/-)	-1.0 low	na	na	na	na

Total Risk	Standard Deviation	Category Risk	Risk Index	Avg Mat
low	3.5%	blw av	0.8	8.4 yrs

	1993	1992	1991	1990	1989	1988	1987	1986	1985	1984
Return (%)	9.9	7.2	10.7	—	—	—	—	—	—	—
Differ from category (+/-) ..	-1.7	-1.1	-0.6	—	—	—	—	—	—	—

PER SHARE DATA

	1993	1992	1991	1990	1989	1988	1987	1986	1985	1984
Dividends, Net Income ($) .	0.55	0.56	0.59	—	—	—	—	—	—	—
Distrib'ns, Cap Gain ($) ...	0.08	0.02	0.06	—	—	—	—	—	—	—
Net Asset Value ($)	11.09	10.69	10.53	—	—	—	—	—	—	—
Expense Ratio (%)........	0.52	0.54	0.35	—	—	—	—	—	—	—
Net Income to Assets (%)..	5.11	5.38	5.88	—	—	—	—	—	—	—
Portfolio Turnover (%).....	23	18	39	—	—	—	—	—	—	—
Total Assets (Millions $)	62	44	34	—	—	—	—	—	—	—

PORTFOLIO (as of 4/30/93)

Portfolio Manager: William M. Feeney - 1990

Investm't Category: Tax-Exempt Bond

Cap Gain	Asset Allocation
Cap & Income	Fund of Funds
✔ Income	Index
	Sector
✔ Domestic	Small Cap
Foreign	Socially Conscious
Country/Region	✔ State Specific

Portfolio: stocks 0% bonds 100%
convertibles 0% other 0% cash 0%

Largest Holdings: general obligation 14%

Unrealized Net Capital Gains: 5% of portfolio value

SHAREHOLDER INFORMATION

Minimum Investment
Initial: $2,000   Subsequent: $200

Minimum IRA Investment
Initial: na   Subsequent: na

Maximum Fees
Load: none   12b-1: none
Other: none

Distributions
Income: monthly   Capital Gains: Oct

Exchange Options
Number Per Year: no limit   Fee: none
Telephone: yes (money market fund available)

Services
auto exchange, auto invest, auto withdraw

Fremont Global (FMAFX)

Balanced

50 Fremont St., Suite 3600
San Francisco, CA 94105
(800) 548-4539, (415) 768-9000

PERFORMANCE

	3yr Annual	5yr Annual	10yr Annual	Bull	Bear
Return (%)	14.2	11.1	na	58.2	-7.3
Differ from Category (+/-)	-0.8 av	-1.0 blw av	na	-3.4 blw av	-1.5 blw av

Total Risk	Standard Deviation	Category Risk	Risk Index	Beta
blw av	6.1%	blw av	1.0	0.4

	1993	1992	1991	1990	1989	1988	1987	1986	1985	1984
Return (%)	19.5	5.2	18.6	-1.7	15.9	—	—	—	—	—
Differ from category (+/-)	6.1	-2.9	-5.3	-1.2	-1.7	—	—	—	—	—

PER SHARE DATA

	1993	1992	1991	1990	1989	1988	1987	1986	1985	1984
Dividends, Net Income ($)	0.33	0.43	0.36	0.52	0.48	—	—	—	—	—
Distrib'ns, Cap Gain ($)	0.06	0.15	0.03	0.02	0.14	—	—	—	—	—
Net Asset Value ($)	13.62	11.74	11.74	10.25	11.02	—	—	—	—	—
Expense Ratio (%)	1.01	1.09	1.12	1.10	1.02	—	—	—	—	—
Net Income to Assets (%)	3.30	3.41	4.34	5.01	5.30	—	—	—	—	—
Portfolio Turnover (%)	49	50	81	36	51	—	—	—	—	—
Total Assets (Millions $)	214	102	74	55	44	—	—	—	—	—

PORTFOLIO (as of 4/30/93)

Portfolio Manager: P. Landini - 1988, D. Redo - 1988, J. Rhodes - 1988

Investm't Category: Balanced
Cap Gain	✔ Asset Allocation
✔ Cap & Income	Fund of Funds
Income	Index
	Sector
✔ Domestic	Small Cap
✔ Foreign	Socially Conscious
Country/Region	State Specific

Portfolio: stocks 51% bonds 36%
convertibles 0% other 2% cash 11%

Largest Holdings: international stocks 25%, international bonds 22%

Unrealized Net Capital Gains: 9% of portfolio value

SHAREHOLDER INFORMATION

Minimum Investment
Initial: $2,000   Subsequent: $200

Minimum IRA Investment
Initial: $1,000   Subsequent: $0

Maximum Fees
Load: none   12b-1: none
Other: none

Distributions
Income: quarterly   Capital Gains: Oct, Dec

Exchange Options
Number Per Year: no limit   Fee: none
Telephone: yes (money market fund available)

Services
IRA, other pension, auto exchange, auto invest, auto withdraw

Fremont Growth (FEQFX)

Growth

50 Fremont St., Suite 3600
San Francisco, CA 94105
(800) 548-4539, (415) 768-9000

PERFORMANCE

	3yr Annual	5yr Annual	10yr Annual	Bull	Bear
Return (%)	na	na	na	na	na
Differ from Category (+/-)	na	na	na	na	na

Total Risk	Standard Deviation	Category Risk	Risk Index	Beta
na	na	na	na	na

	1993	1992	1991	1990	1989	1988	1987	1986	1985	1984
Return (%)	6.4	—	—	—	—	—	—	—	—	—
Differ from category (+/-) . .	-6.8	—	—	—	—	—	—	—	—	—

PER SHARE DATA

	1993	1992	1991	1990	1989	1988	1987	1986	1985	1984
Dividends, Net Income ($) .	0.15	—	—	—	—	—	—	—	—	—
Distrib'ns, Cap Gain ($) . . .	0.00	—	—	—	—	—	—	—	—	—
Net Asset Value ($)	11.18	—	—	—	—	—	—	—	—	—
Expense Ratio (%)	0.90	—	—	—	—	—	—	—	—	—
Net Income to Assets (%) . .	1.16	—	—	—	—	—	—	—	—	—
Portfolio Turnover (%)	38	—	—	—	—	—	—	—	—	—
Total Assets (Millions $)	42	—	—	—	—	—	—	—	—	—

PORTFOLIO (as of 4/30/93)

Portfolio Manager: Andrew Pang - 1992,
Eugene Sit - 1992

Investm't Category: Growth

✔ Cap Gain   Asset Allocation
  Cap & Income   Fund of Funds
  Income   Index
                  Sector
✔ Domestic   Small Cap
  Foreign   Socially Conscious
  Country/Region State Specific

Portfolio: stocks 95%   bonds 0%
convertibles 0%   other 0%   cash 5%

Largest Holdings: financial services 17%, technology 14%

Unrealized Net Capital Gains: 5% of portfolio value

SHAREHOLDER INFORMATION

Minimum Investment
Initial: $2,000   Subsequent: $200

Minimum IRA Investment
Initial: $1,000   Subsequent: $0

Maximum Fees
Load: none   12b-1: none
Other: none

Distributions
Income: quarterly   Capital Gains: Oct, Dec

Exchange Options
Number Per Year: no limit   Fee: none
Telephone: yes (money market fund available)

Services
IRA, other pension, auto exchange, auto invest, auto withdraw

Fundamental US Gov't Strat Income (FUSIX)

90 Washington St.
New York, NY 10006
(800) 225-6864, (212) 635-3005

Government Bond

PERFORMANCE

	3yr Annual	5yr Annual	10yr Annual	Bull	Bear
Return (%)	na	na	na	na	na
Differ from Category (+/-)	na	na	na	na	na

Total Risk	Standard Deviation	Category Risk	Risk Index	Avg Mat
na	na	na	na	20.9 yrs

	1993	1992	1991	1990	1989	1988	1987	1986	1985	1984
Return (%)	8.1	—	—	—	—	—	—	—	—	—
Differ from category (+/-)	-2.3	—	—	—	—	—	—	—	—	—

PER SHARE DATA

	1993	1992	1991	1990	1989	1988	1987	1986	1985	1984
Dividends, Net Income ($)	0.16	—	—	—	—	—	—	—	—	—
Distrib'ns, Cap Gain ($)	0.00	—	—	—	—	—	—	—	—	—
Net Asset Value ($)	2.01	—	—	—	—	—	—	—	—	—
Expense Ratio (%)	1.27	—	—	—	—	—	—	—	—	—
Net Income to Assets (%)	8.11	—	—	—	—	—	—	—	—	—
Portfolio Turnover (%)	na	—	—	—	—	—	—	—	—	—
Total Assets (Millions $)	62	—	—	—	—	—	—	—	—	—

PORTFOLIO (as of 6/30/93)

Portfolio Manager: Vince Malanga - 1992

Investm't Category: Government Bond

Cap Gain	Asset Allocation
Cap & Income	Fund of Funds
✔ Income	Index
	Sector
✔ Domestic	Small Cap
Foreign	Socially Conscious
Country/Region	State Specific

Portfolio: stocks 0%   bonds 100%
convertibles 0%   other 0%   cash 0%

Largest Holdings: U.S. government & agencies 79%, mortgage-backed 21%

Unrealized Net Capital Gains: 15% of portfolio value

SHAREHOLDER INFORMATION

Minimum Investment
Initial: $2,500   Subsequent: $100

Minimum IRA Investment
Initial: $2,000   Subsequent: $100

Maximum Fees
Load: none   12b-1: 0.25%
Other: $50 account opening fee

Distributions
Income: monthly   Capital Gains: Dec

Exchange Options
Number Per Year: no limit   Fee: none
Telephone: yes (money market fund available)

Services
IRA, other pension, auto invest, auto withdraw

Gabelli Asset (GABAX)

Growth

One Corporate Center
Rye, NY 10580
(800) 422-3554, (914) 921-5100

PERFORMANCE

	3yr Annual	5yr Annual	10yr Annual	Bull	Bear
Return (%)	18.2	14.6	na	78.3	-11.8
Differ from Category (+/-)	-1.0 av	0.0 av	na	-6.4 av	0.6 av

Total Risk	Standard Deviation	Category Risk	Risk Index	Beta
av	8.2%	low	0.8	0.6

	1993	1992	1991	1990	1989	1988	1987	1986	1985	1984
Return (%)	21.8	14.8	18.1	-4.9	26.1	31.1	16.1	—	—	—
Differ from category (+/-) . . .	8.6	3.8	-17.3	1.2	0.3	13.4	14.9	—	—	—

PER SHARE DATA

	1993	1992	1991	1990	1989	1988	1987	1986	1985	1984
Dividends, Net Income ($) .	0.16	0.25	0.38	0.76	0.55	0.37	0.09	—	—	—
Distrib'ns, Cap Gain ($) . . .	0.75	0.50	0.11	0.00	0.72	1.23	0.40	—	—	—
Net Asset Value ($)	23.30	19.88	17.96	15.63	17.26	14.69	12.61	—	—	—
Expense Ratio (%).	1.31	1.31	1.30	1.20	1.26	1.31	1.26	—	—	—
Net Income to Assets (%) . .	0.94	1.42	2.34	4.51	4.17	2.04	1.19	—	—	—
Portfolio Turnover (%)	na	14	20	56	49	47	90	—	—	—
Total Assets (Millions $) . . .	948	633	484	343	360	143	77	—	—	—

PORTFOLIO (as of 9/30/93)

Portfolio Manager: Mario J. Gabelli - 1986

Investm't Category: Growth

✔ Cap Gain	Asset Allocation
Cap & Income	Fund of Funds
Income	Index
	Sector
✔ Domestic	Small Cap
✔ Foreign	Socially Conscious
Country/Region	State Specific

Portfolio: stocks 83% bonds 1%
convertibles 3% other 1% cash 12%

Largest Holdings: industrial equipment & supplies 10%, automotive parts & accessories 8%

Unrealized Net Capital Gains: 22% of portfolio value

SHAREHOLDER INFORMATION

Minimum Investment
Initial: $1,000   Subsequent: $0

Minimum IRA Investment
Initial: $1,000   Subsequent: $0

Maximum Fees
Load: none   12b-1: 0.25%
Other: none

Distributions
Income: Dec   Capital Gains: Dec

Exchange Options
Number Per Year: no limit   Fee: none
Telephone: yes (money market fund available)

Services
IRA, other pension, auto invest, auto withdraw

Gabelli Equity Income
(GABEX)

Growth & Income

One Corporate Center
Rye, NY 10580
(800) 422-3554, (914) 921-5100

PERFORMANCE

	3yr Annual	5yr Annual	10yr Annual	Bull	Bear
Return (%)	na	na	na	na	na
Differ from Category (+/-)	na	na	na	na	na

Total Risk	Standard Deviation	Category Risk	Risk Index	Beta
na	na	na	na	na

	1993	1992	1991	1990	1989	1988	1987	1986	1985	1984
Return (%)	17.8	9.7	—	—	—	—	—	—	—	—
Differ from category (+/-) . . .	5.2	-0.3	—	—	—	—	—	—	—	—

PER SHARE DATA

	1993	1992	1991	1990	1989	1988	1987	1986	1985	1984
Dividends, Net Income ($) .	0.28	0.27	—	—	—	—	—	—	—	—
Distrib'ns, Cap Gain ($) . . .	0.68	0.05	—	—	—	—	—	—	—	—
Net Asset Value ($)	11.57	10.64	—	—	—	—	—	—	—	—
Expense Ratio (%)	1.78	1.93	—	—	—	—	—	—	—	—
Net Income to Assets (%) .	2.62	2.65	—	—	—	—	—	—	—	—
Portfolio Turnover (%)	76	22	—	—	—	—	—	—	—	—
Total Assets (Millions $)	54	45	—	—	—	—	—	—	—	—

PORTFOLIO (as of 9/30/93)

Portfolio Manager: Mario Gabelli - 1992

Investm't Category: Growth & Income
Cap Gain	Asset Allocation
✔ Cap & Income	Fund of Funds
Income	Index
	Sector
✔ Domestic	Small Cap
✔ Foreign	Socially Conscious
Country/Region	State Specific

Portfolio: stocks 76% bonds 0%
convertibles 17% other 0% cash 7%

Largest Holdings: financial services 12%, industrial equipment & supplies 12%

Unrealized Net Capital Gains: 12% of portfolio value

SHAREHOLDER INFORMATION

Minimum Investment
Initial: $1,000   Subsequent: $0

Minimum IRA Investment
Initial: $1,000   Subsequent: $0

Maximum Fees
Load: 4.50% front   12b-1: 0.25%
Other: none

Distributions
Income: quarterly   Capital Gains: Dec

Exchange Options
Number Per Year: no limit   Fee: none
Telephone: yes (money market fund available)

Services
IRA, other pension, auto invest, auto withdraw

Gabelli Growth (GABGX)

Growth

One Corporate Center
Rye, NY 10580
(800) 422-3554, (914) 921-5100

PERFORMANCE

	3yr Annual	5yr Annual	10yr Annual	Bull	Bear
Return (%)	16.0	16.4	na	65.8	-7.7
Differ from Category (+/-)	-3.2 blw av	1.8 abv av	na	-18.9 blw av	4.7 abv av

Total Risk	Standard Deviation	Category Risk	Risk Index	Beta
abv av	11.9%	av	1.1	1.0

	1993	1992	1991	1990	1989	1988	1987	1986	1985	1984
Return (%)	11.2	4.4	34.3	-1.9	40.1	39.1	—	—	—	—
Differ from category (+/-) . .	-2.0	-6.6	-1.1	4.2	14.3	21.4	—	—	—	—

PER SHARE DATA

	1993	1992	1991	1990	1989	1988	1987	1986	1985	1984
Dividends, Net Income ($) .	0.09	0.08	0.15	0.38	0.17	0.19	—	—	—	—
Distrib'ns, Cap Gain ($) . . .	0.67	0.56	0.41	0.07	0.48	0.33	—	—	—	—
Net Asset Value ($)	23.26	21.59	21.28	16.27	17.07	12.65	—	—	—	—
Expense Ratio (%).	1.39	1.41	1.45	1.50	1.85	2.30	—	—	—	—
Net Income to Assets (%). .	0.44	0.46	0.97	2.67	2.24	0.72	—	—	—	—
Portfolio Turnover (%)	na	46	50	75	48	82	—	—	—	—
Total Assets (Millions $) . . .	696	625	423	203	113	12	—	—	—	—

PORTFOLIO (as of 6/30/93)

Portfolio Manager: Elizabeth Bramwell - 1987

Investm't Category: Growth

✔ Cap Gain	Asset Allocation
Cap & Income	Fund of Funds
Income	Index
	Sector
✔ Domestic	Small Cap
✔ Foreign	Socially Conscious
Country/Region	State Specific

Portfolio: stocks 84% bonds 0%
convertibles 0% other 2% cash 14%

Largest Holdings: industrial products 10%, telecommunications 10%

Unrealized Net Capital Gains: 14% of portfolio value

SHAREHOLDER INFORMATION

Minimum Investment
Initial: $1,000   Subsequent: $0

Minimum IRA Investment
Initial: $1,000   Subsequent: $0

Maximum Fees
Load: none   12b-1: 0.25%
Other: none

Distributions
Income: Dec   Capital Gains: Dec

Exchange Options
Number Per Year: no limit   Fee: none
Telephone: yes (money market fund available)

Services
IRA, other pension, auto invest, auto withdraw

Galaxy Asset Allocation
(GAAAX)

440 Lincoln St.
Worcester, MA 01653
(800) 628-0414

Balanced

PERFORMANCE

	3yr Annual	5yr Annual	10yr Annual	Bull	Bear
Return (%)	na	na	na	na	na
Differ from Category (+/-)	na	na	na	na	na

Total Risk	Standard Deviation	Category Risk	Risk Index	Beta
na	na	na	na	na

	1993	1992	1991	1990	1989	1988	1987	1986	1985	1984
Return (%).	8.0	6.5	—	—	—	—	—	—	—	—
Differ from category (+/-). . .	-5.4	-1.6	—	—	—	—	—	—	—	—

PER SHARE DATA

	1993	1992	1991	1990	1989	1988	1987	1986	1985	1984
Dividends, Net Income ($) .	0.24	0.19	—	—	—	—	—	—	—	—
Distrib'ns, Cap Gain ($) . . .	0.00	0.00	—	—	—	—	—	—	—	—
Net Asset Value ($)	11.04	10.45	—	—	—	—	—	—	—	—
Expense Ratio (%)	1.01	1.11	—	—	—	—	—	—	—	—
Net Income to Assets (%) .	2.90	2.80	—	—	—	—	—	—	—	—
Portfolio Turnover (%).	7	2	—	—	—	—	—	—	—	—
Total Assets (Millions $). . . .	112	11	—	—	—	—	—	—	—	—

PORTFOLIO (as of 4/30/93)

Portfolio Manager: Fred E. Thompson - 1991

Investm't Category: Balanced

Cap Gain	✔ Asset Allocation
✔ Cap & Income	Fund of Funds
Income	Index
	Sector
✔ Domestic	Small Cap
✔ Foreign	Socially Conscious
Country/Region	State Specific

Portfolio: stocks 50% bonds 29%
convertibles 0% other 5% cash 16%

Largest Holdings: bonds—U.S. government 27%, stocks—consumer staples 13%

Unrealized Net Capital Gains: 2% of portfolio value

SHAREHOLDER INFORMATION

Minimum Investment
Initial: $2,500   Subsequent: $100

Minimum IRA Investment
Initial: $500   Subsequent: $100

Maximum Fees
Load: none   12b-1: 0.25%
Other: none

Distributions
Income: quarterly   Capital Gains: Dec

Exchange Options
Number Per Year: no limit   Fee: none
Telephone: yes (money market fund available)

Services
IRA, other pension, auto invest, auto withdraw

Galaxy Equity Growth
(GAEGX)

Growth

440 Lincoln St.
Worcester, MA 01653
(800) 628-0414

PERFORMANCE

	3yr Annual	5yr Annual	10yr Annual	Bull	Bear
Return (%)	13.3	na	na	na	na
Differ from Category (+/-)	-5.9 low	na	na	na	na

Total Risk	Standard Deviation	Category Risk	Risk Index	Beta
abv av	10.9%	blw av	1.0	1.0

	1993	1992	1991	1990	1989	1988	1987	1986	1985	1984
Return (%)	5.3	6.1	30.3	—	—	—	—	—	—	—
Differ from category (+/-)	-7.9	-4.9	-5.1	—	—	—	—	—	—	—

PER SHARE DATA

	1993	1992	1991	1990	1989	1988	1987	1986	1985	1984
Dividends, Net Income ($)	0.16	0.15	0.19	—	—	—	—	—	—	—
Distrib'ns, Cap Gain ($)	0.14	0.00	0.00	—	—	—	—	—	—	—
Net Asset Value ($)	13.87	13.47	12.85	—	—	—	—	—	—	—
Expense Ratio (%)	0.98	0.95	0.83	—	—	—	—	—	—	—
Net Income to Assets (%)	1.15	1.37	1.46	—	—	—	—	—	—	—
Portfolio Turnover (%)	16	22	16	—	—	—	—	—	—	—
Total Assets (Millions $)	435	225	92	—	—	—	—	—	—	—

PORTFOLIO (as of 4/30/93)

Portfolio Manager: Robert G. Armknecht - 1990

Investm't Category: Growth

✔ Cap Gain   Asset Allocation
   Cap & Income   Fund of Funds
   Income   Index
       Sector
✔ Domestic   Small Cap
   Foreign   Socially Conscious
   Country/Region   State Specific

Portfolio: stocks 85%   bonds 0%
convertibles 0%   other 7%   cash 8%

Largest Holdings: consumer staples 22%, technology 12%

Unrealized Net Capital Gains: 9% of portfolio value

SHAREHOLDER INFORMATION

Minimum Investment
Initial: $2,500   Subsequent: $100

Minimum IRA Investment
Initial: $500   Subsequent: $100

Maximum Fees
Load: none   12b-1: 0.25%
Other: none

Distributions
Income: quarterly   Capital Gains: Dec

Exchange Options
Number Per Year: no limit   Fee: none
Telephone: yes (money market fund available)

Services
IRA, other pension, auto invest, auto withdraw

Galaxy Equity Income
(GAEIX)

Growth & Income

440 Lincoln St.
Worcester, MA 01653
(800) 628-0414

PERFORMANCE

	3yr Annual	5yr Annual	10yr Annual	Bull	Bear
Return (%)	12.4	na	na	na	na
Differ from Category (+/-)	-4.0 low	na	na	na	na

Total Risk	Standard Deviation	Category Risk	Risk Index	Beta
av	8.7%	blw av	1.0	0.8

	1993	1992	1991	1990	1989	1988	1987	1986	1985	1984
Return (%)	8.0	7.4	22.3	—	—	—	—	—	—	—
Differ from category (+/-). . .	-4.6	-2.6	-5.4	—	—	—	—	—	—	—

PER SHARE DATA

	1993	1992	1991	1990	1989	1988	1987	1986	1985	1984
Dividends, Net Income ($) .	0.29	0.27	0.35	—	—	—	—	—	—	—
Distrib'ns, Cap Gain ($) . . .	0.25	0.04	0.19	—	—	—	—	—	—	—
Net Asset Value ($)	12.58	12.16	11.63	—	—	—	—	—	—	—
Expense Ratio (%)	1.06	1.03	0.85	—	—	—	—	—	—	—
Net Income to Assets (%) .	2.57	2.84	2.72	—	—	—	—	—	—	—
Portfolio Turnover (%).	27	18	77	—	—	—	—	—	—	—
Total Assets (Millions $). . . .	129	21	7	—	—	—	—	—	—	—

PORTFOLIO (as of 4/30/93)

Portfolio Manager: J. Edward Klisiewicz - 1990

Investm't Category: Growth & Income

Cap Gain	Asset Allocation
✔ Cap & Income	Fund of Funds
Income	Index
	Sector
✔ Domestic	Small Cap
✔ Foreign	Socially Conscious
Country/Region	State Specific

Portfolio: stocks 82% bonds 4%
convertibles 0% other 1% cash 13%

Largest Holdings: consumer staples 18%, energy 11%

Unrealized Net Capital Gains: 4% of portfolio value

SHAREHOLDER INFORMATION

Minimum Investment
Initial: $2,500   Subsequent: $100

Minimum IRA Investment
Initial: $500   Subsequent: $100

Maximum Fees
Load: none   12b-1: 0.25%
Other: none

Distributions
Income: quarterly   Capital Gains: Dec

Exchange Options
Number Per Year: no limit   Fee: none
Telephone: yes (money market fund available)

Services
IRA, other pension, auto invest, auto withdraw

Galaxy Equity Value
(GALEX)

Growth & Income

440 Lincoln St.
Worcester, MA 01653
(800) 628-0414

PERFORMANCE

	3yr Annual	5yr Annual	10yr Annual	Bull	Bear
Return (%)	15.2	11.6	na	65.1	-10.2
Differ from Category (+/-)	-1.2 blw av	-0.8 blw av	na	-5.0 blw av	1.4 av

Total Risk	Standard Deviation	Category Risk	Risk Index	Beta
av	9.9%	av	1.1	0.8

	1993	1992	1991	1990	1989	1988	1987	1986	1985	1984
Return (%)	14.7	8.2	23.3	-3.1	16.9	—	—	—	—	—
Differ from category (+/-) . . .	2.1	-1.8	-4.4	2.5	-4.7	—	—	—	—	—

PER SHARE DATA

	1993	1992	1991	1990	1989	1988	1987	1986	1985	1984
Dividends, Net Income ($) .	0.18	0.24	0.36	0.38	0.37	—	—	—	—	—
Distrib'ns, Cap Gain ($) . . .	0.28	0.41	0.43	0.34	0.70	—	—	—	—	—
Net Asset Value ($)	12.84	11.60	11.35	9.90	10.98	—	—	—	—	—
Expense Ratio (%).	0.96	0.93	0.93	0.95	0.97	—	—	—	—	—
Net Income to Assets (%) . .	1.78	2.24	3.25	3.66	3.25	—	—	—	—	—
Portfolio Turnover (%)	50	136	40	94	44	—	—	—	—	—
Total Assets (Millions $) . . .	190	134	100	93	92	—	—	—	—	—

PORTFOLIO (as of 4/30/93)

Portfolio Manager: G. Jay Evans - 1992

Investm't Category: Growth & Income

Cap Gain	Asset Allocation
✔ Cap & Income	Fund of Funds
Income	Index
	Sector
✔ Domestic	Small Cap
Foreign	Socially Conscious
Country/Region	State Specific

Portfolio: stocks 88% bonds 0%
convertibles 0% other 9% cash 3%

Largest Holdings: financial 18%, consumer cyclical 14%

Unrealized Net Capital Gains: 8% of portfolio value

SHAREHOLDER INFORMATION

Minimum Investment
Initial: $2,500   Subsequent: $100

Minimum IRA Investment
Initial: $500   Subsequent: $100

Maximum Fees
Load: none   12b-1: 0.25%
Other: none

Distributions
Income: quarterly   Capital Gains: Dec

Exchange Options
Number Per Year: no limit   Fee: none
Telephone: yes (money market fund available)

Services
IRA, other pension, auto invest, auto withdraw

Galaxy High Quality Bond (GAHQX)

General Bond

440 Lincoln St.
Worcester, MA 01653
(800) 628-0414

PERFORMANCE

	3yr Annual	5yr Annual	10yr Annual	Bull	Bear
Return (%)	11.5	na	na	na	na
Differ from Category (+/-)	1.3 abv av	na	na	na	na

Total Risk	Standard Deviation	Category Risk	Risk Index	Avg Mat
blw av	4.9%	high	1.7	8.5 yrs

	1993	1992	1991	1990	1989	1988	1987	1986	1985	1984
Return (%)	12.8	6.7	15.1	—	—	—	—	—	—	—
Differ from category (+/-)	3.6	0.0	0.5	—	—	—	—	—	—	—

PER SHARE DATA

	1993	1992	1991	1990	1989	1988	1987	1986	1985	1984
Dividends, Net Income ($)	0.64	0.69	0.70	—	—	—	—	—	—	—
Distrib'ns, Cap Gain ($)	0.27	0.16	0.07	—	—	—	—	—	—	—
Net Asset Value ($)	10.89	10.49	10.65	—	—	—	—	—	—	—
Expense Ratio (%)	0.74	0.87	0.95	—	—	—	—	—	—	—
Net Income to Assets (%)	6.18	6.55	7.25	—	—	—	—	—	—	—
Portfolio Turnover (%)	128	121	145	—	—	—	—	—	—	—
Total Assets (Millions $)	161	109	58	—	—	—	—	—	—	—

PORTFOLIO (as of 4/30/93)

Portfolio Manager: Kenneth W. Thomae - 1990

Investm't Category: General Bond

Cap Gain	Asset Allocation
Cap & Income	Fund of Funds
✔ Income	Index
	Sector
✔ Domestic	Small Cap
Foreign	Socially Conscious
Country/Region	State Specific

Portfolio: stocks 0%   bonds 93%
convertibles 0%   other 0%   cash 7%

Largest Holdings: U. S. government & agencies 65%, corporate 24%

Unrealized Net Capital Gains: 4% of portfolio value

SHAREHOLDER INFORMATION

Minimum Investment
Initial: $2,500   Subsequent: $100

Minimum IRA Investment
Initial: $500   Subsequent: $100

Maximum Fees
Load: none   12b-1: 0.25%
Other: none

Distributions
Income: monthly   Capital Gains: Dec

Exchange Options
Number Per Year: no limit   Fee: none
Telephone: yes (money market fund available)

Services
IRA, other pension, auto invest, auto withdraw

Galaxy Interm Bond
(GALBX)

General Bond

440 Lincoln St.
Worcester, MA 01653
(800) 628-0414

PERFORMANCE

	3yr Annual	5yr Annual	10yr Annual	Bull	Bear
Return (%)	9.3	8.9	na	36.8	1.2
Differ from Category (+/-)	-0.9 blw av	-0.8 blw av	na	-2.6 blw av	-1.7 low

Total Risk	Standard Deviation	Category Risk	Risk Index	Avg Mat
blw av	4.1%	high	1.4	9.2 yrs

	1993	1992	1991	1990	1989	1988	1987	1986	1985	1984
Return (%)	5.4	7.1	15.7	5.8	11.5	—	—	—	—	—
Differ from category (+/-) ..	-3.8	0.4	1.1	-1.1	0.2	—	—	—	—	—

PER SHARE DATA

	1993	1992	1991	1990	1989	1988	1987	1986	1985	1984
Dividends, Net Income ($) .	0.63	0.69	0.74	0.75	0.83	—	—	—	—	—
Distrib'ns, Cap Gain ($) ...	0.11	0.10	0.00	0.00	0.00	—	—	—	—	—
Net Asset Value ($)	10.54	10.70	10.75	9.98	10.17	—	—	—	—	—
Expense Ratio (%)........	0.81	0.80	0.96	0.98	0.99	—	—	—	—	—
Net Income to Assets (%)..	5.68	6.52	7.25	7.69	8.19	—	—	—	—	—
Portfolio Turnover (%)	153	103	150	162	112	—	—	—	—	—
Total Assets (Millions $) ...	434	199	100	81	71	—	—	—	—	—

PORTFOLIO (as of 4/30/93)

Portfolio Manager: Bruce R. Barton - 1988

Investm't Category: General Bond

Cap Gain	Asset Allocation
Cap & Income	Fund of Funds
✔ Income	Index
	Sector
✔ Domestic	Small Cap
Foreign	Socially Conscious
Country/Region	State Specific

Portfolio:	stocks 0%	bonds 97%
convertibles 0%	other 3%	cash 0%

Largest Holdings: corporate 34%, U. S. government & agencies 29%

Unrealized Net Capital Gains: 3% of portfolio value

SHAREHOLDER INFORMATION

Minimum Investment
Initial: $2,500   Subsequent: $100

Minimum IRA Investment
Initial: $500   Subsequent: $100

Maximum Fees
Load: none   12b-1: 0.25%
Other: none

Distributions
Income: monthly   Capital Gains: Dec

Exchange Options
Number Per Year: no limit   Fee: none
Telephone: yes (money market fund available)

Services
IRA, other pension, auto invest, auto withdraw

Galaxy NY Muni Bond
(GANYX)

440 Lincoln St.
Worcester, MA 01653
(800) 628-0414

Tax-Exempt Bond

PERFORMANCE

	3yr Annual	5yr Annual	10yr Annual	Bull	Bear
Return (%)	na	na	na	na	na
Differ from Category (+/-)	na	na	na	na	na

Total Risk	Standard Deviation	Category Risk	Risk Index	Avg Mat
na	na	na	na	14.2 yrs

	1993	1992	1991	1990	1989	1988	1987	1986	1985	1984
Return (%)	12.3	8.2	—	—	—	—	—	—	—	—
Differ from category (+/-). . .	0.6	-0.1	—	—	—	—	—	—	—	—

PER SHARE DATA

	1993	1992	1991	1990	1989	1988	1987	1986	1985	1984
Dividends, Net Income ($).	0.48	0.46	—	—	—	—	—	—	—	—
Distrib'ns, Cap Gain ($) . . .	0.00	0.00	—	—	—	—	—	—	—	—
Net Asset Value ($)	11.10	10.34	—	—	—	—	—	—	—	—
Expense Ratio (%)	0.87	0.65	—	—	—	—	—	—	—	—
Net Income to Assets (%) .	4.54	5.22	—	—	—	—	—	—	—	—
Portfolio Turnover (%).	3	19	—	—	—	—	—	—	—	—
Total Assets (Millions $)	72	20	—	—	—	—	—	—	—	—

PORTFOLIO (as of 10/31/93)

Portfolio Manager: Maria C. Schwenzer - 1991

Investm't Category: Tax-Exempt Bond

Cap Gain	Asset Allocation
Cap & Income	Fund of Funds
✔ Income	Index
	Sector
✔ Domestic	Small Cap
Foreign	Socially Conscious
Country/Region	✔ State Specific

Portfolio: stocks 0% bonds 90%
convertibles 0% other 10% cash 0%

Largest Holdings: general obligation 3%

Unrealized Net Capital Gains: 3% of portfolio value

SHAREHOLDER INFORMATION

Minimum Investment
Initial: $2,500   Subsequent: $100

Minimum IRA Investment
Initial: na   Subsequent: na

Maximum Fees
Load: none   12b-1: 0.25%
Other: none

Distributions
Income: monthly   Capital Gains: Dec

Exchange Options
Number Per Year: no limit   Fee: none
Telephone: yes (money market fund available)

Services
auto invest, auto withdraw

Galaxy Short Term Bond
(GASTX)

General Bond

440 Lincoln St.
Worcester, MA 01653
(800) 628-0414

PERFORMANCE

	3yr Annual	5yr Annual	10yr Annual	Bull	Bear
Return (%)	na	na	na	na	na
Differ from Category (+/-)	na	na	na	na	na

Total Risk	Standard Deviation	Category Risk	Risk Index	Avg Mat
na	na	na	na	1.9 yrs

	1993	1992	1991	1990	1989	1988	1987	1986	1985	1984
Return (%)	6.4	5.8	—	—	—	—	—	—	—	—
Differ from category (+/-)	-2.8	-0.8	—	—	—	—	—	—	—	—

PER SHARE DATA

	1993	1992	1991	1990	1989	1988	1987	1986	1985	1984
Dividends, Net Income ($)	0.45	0.50	—	—	—	—	—	—	—	—
Distrib'ns, Cap Gain ($)	0.05	0.01	—	—	—	—	—	—	—	—
Net Asset Value ($)	10.17	10.05	—	—	—	—	—	—	—	—
Expense Ratio (%)	0.83	0.90	—	—	—	—	—	—	—	—
Net Income to Assets (%)	4.86	5.77	—	—	—	—	—	—	—	—
Portfolio Turnover (%)	100	114	—	—	—	—	—	—	—	—
Total Assets (Millions $)	88	57	—	—	—	—	—	—	—	—

PORTFOLIO (as of 4/30/93)

Portfolio Manager: Ken Thomae - 1991

Investm't Category: General Bond
Cap Gain	Asset Allocation
Cap & Income	Fund of Funds
✔ Income	Index
	Sector
✔ Domestic	Small Cap
✔ Foreign	Socially Conscious
Country/Region	State Specific

Portfolio: stocks 0%   bonds 92%
convertibles 0%   other 8%   cash 0%

Largest Holdings: U. S. government & agencies 59%, corporate 30%

Unrealized Net Capital Gains: 1% of portfolio value

SHAREHOLDER INFORMATION

Minimum Investment
Initial: $2,500   Subsequent: $100

Minimum IRA Investment
Initial: $500   Subsequent: $0

Maximum Fees
Load: none   12b-1: 0.25%
Other: none

Distributions
Income: monthly   Capital Gains: Dec

Exchange Options
Number Per Year: no limit   Fee: none
Telephone: yes (money market fund available)

Services
IRA, other pension, auto invest, auto withdraw

Galaxy Small Company Equity (GASEX)

440 Lincoln St.
Worcester, MA 01653
(800) 628-0414

Aggressive Growth

PERFORMANCE

	3yr Annual	5yr Annual	10yr Annual	Bull	Bear
Return (%)	na	na	na	na	na
Differ from Category (+/-)	na	na	na	na	na

Total Risk	Standard Deviation	Category Risk	Risk Index	Beta
na	na	na	na	na

	1993	1992	1991	1990	1989	1988	1987	1986	1985	1984
Return (%)	22.7	1.1	—	—	—	—	—	—	—	—
Differ from category (+/-). . .	3.7	-9.3	—	—	—	—	—	—	—	—

PER SHARE DATA

	1993	1992	1991	1990	1989	1988	1987	1986	1985	1984
Dividends, Net Income ($).	0.00	0.00	—	—	—	—	—	—	—	—
Distrib'ns, Cap Gain ($) . . .	0.05	0.00	—	—	—	—	—	—	—	—
Net Asset Value ($)	12.37	10.12	—	—	—	—	—	—	—	—
Expense Ratio (%)	1.22	1.06	—	—	—	—	—	—	—	—
Net Income to Assets (%) .	-0.69	-0.63	—	—	—	—	—	—	—	—
Portfolio Turnover (%).	57	87	—	—	—	—	—	—	—	—
Total Assets (Millions $). . . .	65	29	—	—	—	—	—	—	—	—

PORTFOLIO (as of 4/30/93)

Portfolio Manager: Steve Barbaro - 1991

Investm't Category: Aggressive Growth

✔ Cap Gain
  Cap & Income
  Income

  Asset Allocation
  Fund of Funds
  Index
  Sector

✔ Domestic
  Foreign
  Country/Region

✔ Small Cap
  Socially Conscious
  State Specific

Portfolio: stocks 95%   bonds 0%
convertibles 0%   other 5%   cash 0%

Largest Holdings: technology 24%, consumer cyclical 14%

Unrealized Net Capital Gains: 12% of portfolio value

SHAREHOLDER INFORMATION

Minimum Investment
Initial: $2,500   Subsequent: $100

Minimum IRA Investment
Initial: $500   Subsequent: $0

Maximum Fees
Load: none   12b-1: 0.25%
Other: none

Distributions
Income: quarterly   Capital Gains: Dec

Exchange Options
Number Per Year: no limit   Fee: none
Telephone: yes (money market fund available)

Services
IRA, other pension, auto invest, auto withdraw

Galaxy Tax-Exempt Bond (GABDX)

440 Lincoln St.
Worcester, MA 01653
(800) 628-0414

Tax-Exempt Bond

PERFORMANCE

	3yr Annual	5yr Annual	10yr Annual	Bull	Bear
Return (%)	na	na	na	na	na
Differ from Category (+/-)	na	na	na	na	na

Total Risk	Standard Deviation	Category Risk	Risk Index	Avg Mat
na	na	na	na	12.4 yrs

	1993	1992	1991	1990	1989	1988	1987	1986	1985	1984
Return (%)	12.1	9.2	—	—	—	—	—	—	—	—
Differ from category (+/-)	0.5	0.8	—	—	—	—	—	—	—	—

PER SHARE DATA

	1993	1992	1991	1990	1989	1988	1987	1986	1985	1984
Dividends, Net Income ($)	0.53	0.43	—	—	—	—	—	—	—	—
Distrib'ns, Cap Gain ($)	0.10	0.00	—	—	—	—	—	—	—	—
Net Asset Value ($)	11.07	10.47	—	—	—	—	—	—	—	—
Expense Ratio (%)	0.64	0.42	—	—	—	—	—	—	—	—
Net Income to Assets (%)	5.00	5.03	—	—	—	—	—	—	—	—
Portfolio Turnover (%)	38	11	—	—	—	—	—	—	—	—
Total Assets (Millions $)	145	15	—	—	—	—	—	—	—	—

PORTFOLIO (as of 10/31/93)

Portfolio Manager: Mary M. McGoldrick - 1991

Investm't Category: Tax-Exempt Bond

Cap Gain	Asset Allocation
Cap & Income	Fund of Funds
✔ Income	Index
	Sector
✔ Domestic	Small Cap
Foreign	Socially Conscious
Country/Region	State Specific

Portfolio:	stocks 0%	bonds 100%
convertibles 0%	other 0%	cash 0%

Largest Holdings: general obligation 8%

Unrealized Net Capital Gains: 5% of portfolio value

SHAREHOLDER INFORMATION

Minimum Investment
Initial: $2,500   Subsequent: $100

Minimum IRA Investment
Initial: na   Subsequent: na

Maximum Fees
Load: none   12b-1: 0.25%
Other: none

Distributions
Income: monthly   Capital Gains: Dec

Exchange Options
Number Per Year: no limit   Fee: none
Telephone: yes (money market fund available)

Services
auto invest, auto withdraw

Gateway Government Bond Plus (GATBX)

Government Bond

400 TechneCenter Dr., Suite 220
Milford, OH 45150
(800) 354-6339, (513) 248-2700

PERFORMANCE

	3yr Annual	5yr Annual	10yr Annual	Bull	Bear
Return (%)	7.4	8.8	na	31.7	1.4
Differ from Category (+/-)	-3.4 low	-1.6 blw av	na	-14.5 low	0.8 av

Total Risk	Standard Deviation	Category Risk	Risk Index	Avg Mat
low	4.0%	av	0.9	8.4 yrs

	1993	1992	1991	1990	1989	1988	1987	1986	1985	1984
Return (%)	5.0	1.8	16.0	7.6	14.5	—	—	—	—	—
Differ from category (+/-) . . .	-5.4	-4.4	1.0	1.1	0.6	—	—	—	—	—

PER SHARE DATA

	1993	1992	1991	1990	1989	1988	1987	1986	1985	1984
Dividends, Net Income ($) .	0.55	0.65	0.72	0.72	0.84	—	—	—	—	—
Distrib'ns, Cap Gain ($) . . .	0.00	0.00	0.25	0.17	0.01	—	—	—	—	—
Net Asset Value ($)	10.36	10.40	10.87	10.27	10.41	—	—	—	—	—
Expense Ratio (%)	0.85	1.02	1.20	1.18	1.18	—	—	—	—	—
Net Income to Assets (%) .	5.33	6.18	6.71	7.24	7.19	—	—	—	—	—
Portfolio Turnover (%).	0	4	71	30	0	—	—	—	—	—
Total Assets (Millions $)	17	25	7	9	8	—	—	—	—	—

PORTFOLIO (as of 6/30/93)

Portfolio Manager: Walter G. Sall - 1988

Investm't Category: Government Bond

Cap Gain	Asset Allocation
Cap & Income	Fund of Funds
✔ Income	Index
	Sector
✔ Domestic	Small Cap
Foreign	Socially Conscious
Country/Region	State Specific

Portfolio:	stocks 0%	bonds 100%
convertibles 0%	other 0%	cash 0%

Largest Holdings: U.S. government 100%

Unrealized Net Capital Gains: 8% of portfolio value

SHAREHOLDER INFORMATION

Minimum Investment
Initial: $1,000   Subsequent: $100

Minimum IRA Investment
Initial: $1,000   Subsequent: $100

Maximum Fees
Load: none   12b-1: none
Other: none

Distributions
Income: monthly   Capital Gains: Dec

Exchange Options
Number Per Year: no limit   Fee: none
Telephone: yes (money market fund available)

Services
IRA, other pension, auto invest, auto withdraw

Gateway Index Plus
(GATEX)
Growth & Income

400 TechneCenter Dr., Suite 220
Milford, OH 45150
(800) 354-6339, (513) 248-2700

PERFORMANCE

	3yr Annual	5yr Annual	10yr Annual	Bull	Bear
Return (%)	9.9	11.8	10.3	44.8	1.1
Differ from Category (+/-)	-6.5 low	-0.6 blw av	-2.1 blw av	-25.3 low	12.7 high

Total Risk	Standard Deviation	Category Risk	Risk Index	Beta
low	3.7%	low	0.4	0.2

	1993	1992	1991	1990	1989	1988	1987	1986	1985	1984
Return (%)	7.4	5.1	17.7	10.1	19.4	19.7	-5.6	12.6	15.9	3.9
Differ from category (+/-) . .	-5.2	-4.9	-10.0	15.7	-2.2	2.9	-6.0	-2.6	-9.5	-2.3

PER SHARE DATA

	1993	1992	1991	1990	1989	1988	1987	1986	1985	1984
Dividends, Net Income ($) .	0.28	0.28	0.30	0.40	0.37	0.20	0.33	0.34	0.46	0.56
Distrib'ns, Cap Gain ($) . . .	0.50	0.23	0.50	3.00	0.43	0.00	1.92	1.46	1.22	0.64
Net Asset Value ($)	15.85	15.51	15.24	13.64	15.49	13.67	11.60	14.63	14.69	14.22
Expense Ratio (%).	1.03	1.11	1.22	1.34	1.40	2.08	1.48	1.49	1.50	1.45
Net Income to Assets (%) . .	1.77	1.96	2.17	2.59	2.21	1.75	1.83	2.23	2.81	3.84
Portfolio Turnover (%)	15	15	31	79	30	10	175	85	96	103
Total Assets (Millions $) . . .	205	213	81	38	32	27	27	45	28	21

PORTFOLIO (as of 6/30/93)

Portfolio Manager: Peter Thayer - 1977

Investm't Category: Growth & Income

Cap Gain	Asset Allocation
✔ Cap & Income	Fund of Funds
Income	Index
	Sector
✔ Domestic	Small Cap
Foreign	Socially Conscious
Country/Region	State Specific

Portfolio: stocks 100%   bonds 0%
convertibles 0%   other 0%   cash 0%

Largest Holdings: consumer cyclical 18%, consumer non-cyclical 17%

Unrealized Net Capital Gains: 7% of portfolio value

SHAREHOLDER INFORMATION

Minimum Investment
Initial: $1,000   Subsequent: $100

Minimum IRA Investment
Initial: $1,000   Subsequent: $100

Maximum Fees
Load: none   12b-1: none
Other: none

Distributions
Income: quarterly   Capital Gains: Dec

Exchange Options
Number Per Year: no limit   Fee: none
Telephone: yes (money market fund available)

Services
IRA, other pension, auto invest, auto withdraw

General CA Muni Bond
(GCABX)

Tax-Exempt Bond

200 Park Ave.
New York, NY 10166
(800) 645-6561, (718) 895-1206

PERFORMANCE

	3yr Annual	5yr Annual	10yr Annual	Bull	Bear
Return (%)	11.0	na	na	42.2	3.7
Differ from Category (+/-)	0.6 av	na	na	2.1 av	1.4 high

Total Risk	Standard Deviation	Category Risk	Risk Index	Avg Mat
blw av	4.6%	abv av	1.1	23.0 yrs

	1993	1992	1991	1990	1989	1988	1987	1986	1985	1984
Return (%)	13.6	8.6	10.9	7.7	—	—	—	—	—	—
Differ from category (+/-) . . .	2.0	0.3	-0.4	1.4	—	—	—	—	—	—

PER SHARE DATA

	1993	1992	1991	1990	1989	1988	1987	1986	1985	1984
Dividends, Net Income ($) .	0.80	0.83	0.88	0.92	—	—	—	—	—	—
Distrib'ns, Cap Gain ($) . . .	0.06	0.08	0.00	0.00	—	—	—	—	—	—
Net Asset Value ($)	14.19	13.28	13.11	12.66	—	—	—	—	—	—
Expense Ratio (%)	0.64	0.37	0.21	0.00	—	—	—	—	—	—
Net Income to Assets (%) .	5.96	6.47	7.06	7.35	—	—	—	—	—	—
Portfolio Turnover (%)	30	24	3	10	—	—	—	—	—	—
Total Assets (Millions $)	697	374	272	98	—	—	—	—	—	—

PORTFOLIO (as of 9/30/93)

Portfolio Manager: Paul Disdier - 1989

Investm't Category: Tax-Exempt Bond

Cap Gain	Asset Allocation
Cap & Income	Fund of Funds
✔ Income	Index
	Sector
✔ Domestic	Small Cap
Foreign	Socially Conscious
Country/Region	✔ State Specific

Portfolio: stocks 0% bonds 100%
convertibles 0% other 0% cash 0%

Largest Holdings: na

Unrealized Net Capital Gains: 10% of portfolio value

SHAREHOLDER INFORMATION

Minimum Investment
Initial: $2,500   Subsequent: $100

Minimum IRA Investment
Initial: na   Subsequent: na

Maximum Fees
Load: none   12b-1: 0.25%
Other: none

Distributions
Income: monthly   Capital Gains: Nov

Exchange Options
Number Per Year: no limit   Fee: none
Telephone: yes (money market fund available)

Services
auto exchange, auto invest, auto withdraw

General Muni Bond

(GMBDX)

Tax-Exempt Bond

200 Park Ave.
New York, NY 10166
(800) 645-6561, (718) 895-1206

	3yr Annual	5yr Annual	10yr Annual	Bull	Bear
Return (%)	12.5	11.3	na	48.2	3.6
Differ from Category (+/-)	2.2 high	2.1 high	na	8.1 high	1.3 abv av

Total Risk	Standard Deviation	Category Risk	Risk Index	Avg Mat
blw av	4.8%	abv av	1.2	22.4 yrs

	1993	1992	1991	1990	1989	1988	1987	1986	1985	1984
Return (%)	13.3	9.8	14.6	7.6	11.4	12.5	-5.5	17.1	21.0	—
Differ from category (+/-) . . .	1.7	1.5	3.3	1.3	2.4	2.4	-4.3	0.6	3.7	—

PER SHARE DATA

	1993	1992	1991	1990	1989	1988	1987	1986	1985	1984
Dividends, Net Income ($) .	0.90	0.99	1.06	1.09	1.01	0.96	0.98	1.07	1.17	—
Distrib'ns, Cap Gain ($) . . .	0.22	0.14	0.04	0.00	0.00	0.00	0.24	0.00	0.00	—
Net Asset Value ($)	15.84	15.02	14.76	13.90	13.97	13.48	12.87	14.89	13.69	—
Expense Ratio (%)	0.41	0.01	0.00	0.28	0.80	0.80	0.77	0.41	0.00	—
Net Income to Assets (%) . .	6.46	7.30	7.83	7.58	7.27	7.30	7.22	8.66	9.57	—
Portfolio Turnover (%)	64	38	50	110	218	67	105	87	71	—
Total Assets (Millions $) . .	1,251	720	309	109	35	37	63	39	5	—

PORTFOLIO (as of 2/28/93)

Portfolio Manager: Paul Disdier - 1988

Investm't Category: Tax-Exempt Bond

Cap Gain	Asset Allocation
Cap & Income	Fund of Funds
✔ Income	Index
	Sector
✔ Domestic	Small Cap
Foreign	Socially Conscious
Country/Region	State Specific

Portfolio: stocks 0% bonds 100%
convertibles 0% other 0% cash 0%

Largest Holdings: na

Unrealized Net Capital Gains: 7% of portfolio value

SHAREHOLDER INFORMATION

Minimum Investment
Initial: $2,500   Subsequent: $100

Minimum IRA Investment
Initial: na   Subsequent: na

Maximum Fees
Load: none   12b-1: 0.20%
Other: none

Distributions
Income: monthly   Capital Gains: June, Nov

Exchange Options
Number Per Year: no limit   Fee: none
Telephone: yes (money market fund available)

Services
auto exchange, auto invest, auto withdraw

General NY Muni Bond
(GNYMX)

Tax-Exempt Bond

200 Park Ave.
New York, NY 10166
(800) 645-6561, (718) 895-1206

PERFORMANCE

	3yr Annual	5yr Annual	10yr Annual	Bull	Bear
Return (%)	12.7	10.2	na	48.5	2.8
Differ from Category (+/-)	2.4 high	1.0 abv av	na	8.4 high	0.5 av

Total Risk	Standard Deviation	Category Risk	Risk Index	Avg Mat
blw av	4.6%	abv av	1.1	20.7 yrs

	1993	1992	1991	1990	1989	1988	1987	1986	1985	1984
Return (%)	14.0	10.0	14.0	6.6	6.5	5.9	1.3	14.1	14.8	—
Differ from category (+/-). . .	2.4	1.7	2.7	0.3	-2.5	-4.2	2.5	-2.3	-2.5	—

PER SHARE DATA

	1993	1992	1991	1990	1989	1988	1987	1986	1985	1984
Dividends, Net Income ($).	1.15	1.21	1.29	1.35	1.05	1.00	1.04	1.17	1.29	—
Distrib'ns, Cap Gain ($) . . .	0.29	0.26	0.00	0.00	0.00	0.00	0.00	0.00	0.00	—
Net Asset Value ($)	21.14	19.85	19.44	18.25	18.43	18.31	18.25	19.05	17.77	—
Expense Ratio (%)	0.69	0.62	0.36	0.07	1.32	1.10	0.89	0.46	0.21	—
Net Income to Assets (%) .	5.64	6.32	6.95	7.36	5.60	5.49	5.66	6.44	7.47	—
Portfolio Turnover (%).	23	43	19	60	27	32	67	37	31	—
Total Assets (Millions $). . . .	400	284	209	103	38	47	53	56	13	—

PORTFOLIO (as of 10/31/93)

Portfolio Manager: Monica Wieboldt - 1988

Investm't Category: Tax-Exempt Bond

Cap Gain	Asset Allocation
Cap & Income	Fund of Funds
✔ Income	Index
	Sector
✔ Domestic	Small Cap
Foreign	Socially Conscious
Country/Region	✔ State Specific

Portfolio: stocks 0% bonds 98%
convertibles 0% other 0% cash 2%

Largest Holdings: na

Unrealized Net Capital Gains: 9% of portfolio value

SHAREHOLDER INFORMATION

Minimum Investment
Initial: $2,500   Subsequent: $100

Minimum IRA Investment
Initial: na   Subsequent: na

Maximum Fees
Load: none   12b-1: 0.20%
Other: none

Distributions
Income: monthly   Capital Gains: Dec

Exchange Options
Number Per Year: no limit   Fee: none
Telephone: yes (money market fund available)

Services
auto exchange, auto invest, auto withdraw

GE U.S. Equity (GEEQX)

Growth

3003 Summer Street
Stamford, CT 06905
(800) 242-0134

fund in existence since 1/5/93

PERFORMANCE

	3yr Annual	5yr Annual	10yr Annual	Bull	Bear
Return (%)	na	na	na	na	na
Differ from Category (+/-)	na	na	na	na	na

Total Risk	Standard Deviation	Category Risk	Risk Index	Beta
na	na	na	na	na

	1993	1992	1991	1990	1989	1988	1987	1986	1985	1984
Return (%)	—	—	—	—	—	—	—	—	—	—
Differ from category (+/-) . . .	—	—	—	—	—	—	—	—	—	—

PER SHARE DATA

	1993	1992	1991	1990	1989	1988	1987	1986	1985	1984
Dividends, Net Income ($) .	0.20	—	—	—	—	—	—	—	—	—
Distrib'ns, Cap Gain ($) . . .	0.17	—	—	—	—	—	—	—	—	—
Net Asset Value ($)	16.26	—	—	—	—	—	—	—	—	—
Expense Ratio (%)	0.50	—	—	—	—	—	—	—	—	—
Net Income to Assets (%) . .	1.86	—	—	—	—	—	—	—	—	—
Portfolio Turnover (%)	15	—	—	—	—	—	—	—	—	—
Total Assets (Millions $)	75	—	—	—	—	—	—	—	—	—

PORTFOLIO (as of 9/30/93)

Portfolio Manager: Eugene Bolton - 1993

Investm't Category: Growth

✔ Cap Gain	Asset Allocation
Cap & Income	Fund of Funds
Income	Index
	Sector
✔ Domestic	Small Cap
Foreign	Socially Conscious
Country/Region	State Specific

Portfolio: stocks 82% bonds 0%
convertibles 6% other 0% cash 12%

Largest Holdings: banks & financial services 11%, energy & energy related 9%

Unrealized Net Capital Gains: 3% of portfolio value

SHAREHOLDER INFORMATION

Minimum Investment
Initial: $500 Subsequent: $100

Minimum IRA Investment
Initial: $250 Subsequent: $100

Maximum Fees
Load: none 12b-1: 0.25%
Other: none

Distributions
Income: Dec Capital Gains: Dec

Exchange Options
Number Per Year: no limit Fee: none
Telephone: yes (money market fund available)

Services
IRA, other pension, auto invest, auto withdraw

Gintel (GINLX)

Growth

6 Greenwich Office Park
Greenwich, CT 06831
(800) 243-5808, (203) 622-6400

PERFORMANCE

	3yr Annual	5yr Annual	10yr Annual	Bull	Bear
Return (%)	13.6	11.1	10.2	47.9	-7.3
Differ from Category (+/-)	-5.6 low	-3.5 low	-2.4 low	-36.8 low	5.1 abv av

Total Risk	Standard Deviation	Category Risk	Risk Index	Beta
abv av	13.1%	abv av	1.2	0.8

	1993	1992	1991	1990	1989	1988	1987	1986	1985	1984
Return (%)	1.9	24.6	15.5	-6.6	23.8	29.3	-14.1	20.8	20.0	-2.5
Differ from category (+/-). .	-11.3	13.6	-19.9	-0.5	-2.0	11.6	-15.3	6.3	-9.3	-2.5

PER SHARE DATA

	1993	1992	1991	1990	1989	1988	1987	1986	1985	1984
Dividends, Net Income ($).	0.50	0.10	0.30	0.48	1.44	0.00	0.32	0.28	0.32	0.22
Distrib'ns, Cap Gain ($) . . .	1.13	0.25	0.93	0.00	0.00	0.00	1.01	6.15	0.74	1.63
Net Asset Value ($)	15.11	16.45	13.48	12.75	14.18	12.70	9.81	12.70	15.96	14.29
Expense Ratio (%)	2.20	1.70	1.40	1.50	1.40	1.60	1.30	1.20	1.20	1.70
Net Income to Assets (%) .	-0.40	0.90	1.90	3.10	7.40	2.50	1.30	1.60	2.30	1.70
Portfolio Turnover (%).	na	56	66	75	65	85	111	77	25	30
Total Assets (Millions $). . . .	138	165	77	79	95	83	121	130	116	104

PORTFOLIO (as of 6/30/93)

Portfolio Manager: Robert Gintel - 1981, Cecil Godman - 1992

Investm't Category: Growth

✔ Cap Gain	Asset Allocation
Cap & Income	Fund of Funds
Income	Index
	Sector
✔ Domestic	Small Cap
✔ Foreign	Socially Conscious
Country/Region	State Specific

Portfolio: stocks 87% bonds 0%
convertibles 0% other 0% cash 13%

Largest Holdings: copper producer 17%, transportation communication 16%

Unrealized Net Capital Gains: 21% of portfolio value

SHAREHOLDER INFORMATION

Minimum Investment
Initial: $5,000   Subsequent: $0

Minimum IRA Investment
Initial: $5,000   Subsequent: $0

Maximum Fees
Load: none   12b-1: none
Other: none

Distributions
Income: Dec   Capital Gains: Dec

Exchange Options
Number Per Year: no limit   Fee: none
Telephone: yes (money market fund available)

Services
IRA, other pension, auto invest, auto withdraw

Gintel ERISA (GINTX)

Growth & Income

6 Greenwich Office Park
Greenwich, CT 06831
(800) 243-5808, (203) 622-6400

PERFORMANCE

	3yr Annual	5yr Annual	10yr Annual	Bull	Bear
Return (%)	11.0	8.4	10.9	39.9	-7.2
Differ from Category (+/-)	-5.4 low	-4.1 low	-1.5 blw av	-30.2 low	4.4 high

Total Risk	Standard Deviation	Category Risk	Risk Index	Beta
abv av	11.4%	abv av	1.3	0.8

	1993	1992	1991	1990	1989	1988	1987	1986	1985	1984
Return (%)	5.3	14.4	13.5	-5.1	15.4	21.9	-0.8	22.5	24.0	2.2
Differ from category (+/-) ..	-7.3	4.4	-14.2	0.5	-6.2	5.1	-1.2	7.3	-1.4	-4.0

PER SHARE DATA

	1993	1992	1991	1990	1989	1988	1987	1986	1985	1984
Dividends, Net Income ($) .	2.27	0.63	0.83	1.35	3.43	0.00	1.99	1.20	1.10	0.82
Distrib'ns, Cap Gain ($) ...	5.53	0.00	0.91	0.00	5.99	0.00	13.41	1.46	1.88	2.77
Net Asset Value ($)	29.41	35.38	31.49	29.29	32.31	36.34	29.79	45.23	39.48	34.70
Expense Ratio (%)........	2.00	1.70	1.50	1.60	1.30	1.30	1.20	1.30	1.30	1.40
Net Income to Assets (%)..	0.80	1.50	2.40	3.50	5.90	2.50	2.90	1.80	3.00	3.70
Portfolio Turnover (%)	na	80	97	97	85	100	109	69	100	109
Total Assets (Millions $)	51	56	73	79	86	81	75	89	85	72

PORTFOLIO (as of 6/30/93)

Portfolio Manager: Robert Gintel - 1982,
Cecil Godman - 1992

Investm't Category: Growth & Income

Cap Gain	Asset Allocation
✔ Cap & Income	Fund of Funds
Income	Index
	Sector
✔ Domestic	Small Cap
Foreign	Socially Conscious
Country/Region	State Specific

Portfolio: stocks 49%   bonds 0%
convertibles 0%   other 0%   cash 51%

Largest Holdings: mortgage investments
12%, transportation communication 8%

Unrealized Net Capital Gains: 7% of portfolio value

SHAREHOLDER INFORMATION

Minimum Investment
Initial: $10,000   Subsequent: $0

Minimum IRA Investment
Initial: $2,000   Subsequent: $0

Maximum Fees
Load: none   12b-1: none
Other: none

Distributions
Income: Dec   Capital Gains: Dec

Exchange Options
Number Per Year: no limit   Fee: none
Telephone: yes (money market fund available)

Services
IRA, other pension, auto invest, auto withdraw

GIT Equity—Special Growth (GTSGX)

Aggressive Growth

1655 N. Fort Myer Dr.
Suite 1000
Arlington, VA 22209
(800) 336-3063, (703) 528-6500

PERFORMANCE

	3yr Annual	5yr Annual	10yr Annual	Bull	Bear
Return (%)	15.4	10.1	12.7	63.0	-20.5
Differ from Category (+/-)	-10.0 low	-8.1 low	0.8 av	-62.0 low	-5.5 blw av

Total Risk	Standard Deviation	Category Risk	Risk Index	Beta
abv av	11.5%	low	0.7	0.7

	1993	1992	1991	1990	1989	1988	1987	1986	1985	1984
Return (%)	14.8	6.7	25.7	-15.8	26.3	23.4	-2.0	15.1	47.1	-1.2
Differ from category (+/-)	-4.2	-3.7	-26.7	-9.5	-0.7	8.2	1.4	5.7	16.1	8.2

PER SHARE DATA

	1993	1992	1991	1990	1989	1988	1987	1986	1985	1984
Dividends, Net Income ($)	0.17	0.12	0.20	0.32	0.39	0.11	0.23	0.11	0.08	0.19
Distrib'ns, Cap Gain ($)	0.98	0.13	0.20	0.00	0.57	1.06	1.99	0.25	0.00	0.00
Net Asset Value ($)	21.37	19.63	18.64	15.16	18.40	15.38	13.43	16.03	14.23	9.74
Expense Ratio (%)	1.35	1.39	1.40	1.47	1.50	1.50	1.50	1.35	1.09	0.36
Net Income to Assets (%)	0.44	0.95	1.82	2.59	2.24	0.73	0.92	1.38	1.29	3.85
Portfolio Turnover (%)	13	24	6	15	27	29	8	35	30	18
Total Assets (Millions $)	39	59	51	37	18	16	20	10	2	1

PORTFOLIO (as of 3/31/93)

Portfolio Manager: Richard Carney - 1983

Investm't Category: Aggressive Growth
✔ Cap Gain   Asset Allocation
  Cap & Income   Fund of Funds
  Income   Index
                    Sector
✔ Domestic   ✔ Small Cap
✔ Foreign   Socially Conscious
  Country/Region   State Specific

Portfolio: stocks 92%   bonds 0%
convertibles 0%   other 0%   cash 8%

Largest Holdings: household furnishings 11%, drugs & health care 11%

Unrealized Net Capital Gains: 1% of portfolio value

SHAREHOLDER INFORMATION

Minimum Investment
Initial: $2,500   Subsequent: $0

Minimum IRA Investment
Initial: $500   Subsequent: $0

Maximum Fees
Load: none   12b-1: none
Other: none

Distributions
Income: Mar, Dec   Capital Gains: Mar, Dec

Exchange Options
Number Per Year: no limit   Fee: none
Telephone: yes (money market fund available)

Services
IRA, other pension, auto invest, auto withdraw

GIT Income—Gov't Port
(GTTAX)
Government Bond

1655 N. Fort Myer Dr.
Suite 1000
Arlington, VA 22209
(800) 336-3063, (703) 528-6500

PERFORMANCE

	3yr Annual	5yr Annual	10yr Annual	Bull	Bear
Return (%)	9.5	9.3	10.4	38.6	1.7
Differ from Category (+/-)	-1.3 blw av	-1.1 blw av	0.6 av	-7.6 av	1.2 av

Total Risk	Standard Deviation	Category Risk	Risk Index	Avg Mat
blw av	4.5%	av	1.0	8.0 yrs

	1993	1992	1991	1990	1989	1988	1987	1986	1985	1984
Return (%)	9.6	5.3	13.8	7.1	11.1	7.1	-1.0	13.6	24.8	14.7
Differ from category (+/-) ..	-0.8	-0.8	-1.2	0.6	-2.8	-0.5	0.8	-5.5	5.7	1.7

PER SHARE DATA

	1993	1992	1991	1990	1989	1988	1987	1986	1985	1984
Dividends, Net Income ($) .	0.38	0.55	0.65	0.72	0.80	0.78	0.87	0.94	1.04	1.14
Distrib'ns, Cap Gain ($) ...	0.77	0.53	0.04	0.04	0.00	0.24	0.21	0.00	0.00	0.00
Net Asset Value ($)	10.01	10.21	10.77	10.12	10.21	9.95	10.28	11.51	11.01	9.77
Expense Ratio (%)........	1.52	1.53	1.65	1.51	1.50	1.47	1.41	1.12	0.89	0.00
Net Income to Assets (%)..	4.78	6.28	7.13	7.76	7.94	8.18	7.99	9.82	11.78	12.90
Portfolio Turnover (%)	357	123	116	86	45	36	31	26	63	0
Total Assets (Millions $)	3	7	6	6	7	6	9	8	4	2

PORTFOLIO (as of 3/31/93)

Portfolio Manager: John Edwards - 1988

Investm't Category: Government Bond

Cap Gain	Asset Allocation
Cap & Income	Fund of Funds
✔ Income	Index
	Sector
✔ Domestic	Small Cap
Foreign	Socially Conscious
Country/Region	State Specific

Portfolio: stocks 0%   bonds 85%
convertibles 0%   other 0%   cash 15%

Largest Holdings: U.S. government 85%

Unrealized Net Capital Gains: 0% of portfolio value

SHAREHOLDER INFORMATION

Minimum Investment
Initial: $2,500   Subsequent: $0

Minimum IRA Investment
Initial: $500   Subsequent: $0

Maximum Fees
Load: none   12b-1: none
Other: none

Distributions
Income: monthly   Capital Gains: Dec

Exchange Options
Number Per Year: no limit   Fee: none
Telephone: yes (money market fund available)

Services
IRA, other pension, auto invest, auto withdraw

GIT Income—Maximum

(GITMX)

Corporate High-Yield Bond

1655 N. Fort Myer Dr.
Suite 1000
Arlington, VA 22209
(800) 336-3063, (703) 528-6500

PERFORMANCE

	3yr Annual	5yr Annual	10yr Annual	Bull	Bear
Return (%)	17.4	9.0	9.3	61.2	-7.1
Differ from Category (+/-)	-3.1 low	-1.8 low	-2.4 low	-13.7 low	-3.8 blw av

Total Risk	Standard Deviation	Category Risk	Risk Index	Avg Mat
blw av	4.1%	blw av	1.1	7.0 yrs

	1993	1992	1991	1990	1989	1988	1987	1986	1985	1984
Return (%)	15.0	12.0	25.6	-7.5	2.8	10.0	-2.7	10.5	22.0	9.6
Differ from category (+/-)	-4.2	-3.8	-1.7	-3.3	1.5	-2.3	-3.7	-4.7	-1.5	-1.2

PER SHARE DATA

	1993	1992	1991	1990	1989	1988	1987	1986	1985	1984
Dividends, Net Income ($)	0.61	0.68	0.68	0.81	0.88	0.86	0.95	1.10	1.16	1.25
Distrib'ns, Cap Gain ($)	0.00	0.00	0.00	0.00	0.00	0.00	0.00	0.00	0.00	0.00
Net Asset Value ($)	7.66	7.22	7.09	6.23	7.59	8.24	8.30	9.48	9.59	8.91
Expense Ratio (%)	1.52	1.54	1.66	1.51	1.50	1.45	1.39	1.10	0.93	0.00
Net Income to Assets (%)	9.26	9.95	11.57	11.16	10.45	10.48	10.87	12.23	13.75	13.47
Portfolio Turnover (%)	73	124	54	93	80	78	127	47	66	16
Total Assets (Millions $)	7	6	5	7	10	11	17	12	7	3

PORTFOLIO (as of 3/31/93)

Portfolio Manager: John Edwards - 1988

Investm't Category: Corp. High-Yield Bond

Cap Gain	Asset Allocation
✔ Cap & Income	Fund of Funds
Income	Index
	Sector
✔ Domestic	Small Cap
Foreign	Socially Conscious
Country/Region	State Specific

Portfolio: stocks 0% bonds 85%
convertibles 0% other 0% cash 15%

Largest Holdings: food retail 17%, automotive 8%

Unrealized Net Capital Gains: 0% of portfolio value

SHAREHOLDER INFORMATION

Minimum Investment
Initial: $2,500   Subsequent: $0

Minimum IRA Investment
Initial: $500   Subsequent: $0

Maximum Fees
Load: none   12b-1: none
Other: none

Distributions
Income: monthly   Capital Gains: Dec

Exchange Options
Number Per Year: no limit   Fee: none
Telephone: yes (money market fund available)

Services
IRA, other pension, auto invest, auto withdraw

GIT Tax-Free High Yield

(GTFHX)

Tax-Exempt Bond

1655 N. Fort Myer Dr.
Suite 1000
Arlington, VA 22209
(800) 336-3063, (703) 528-6500

PERFORMANCE

	3yr Annual	5yr Annual	10yr Annual	Bull	Bear
Return (%)	10.0	8.5	9.6	38.8	1.2
Differ from Category (+/-)	-0.3 blw av	-0.6 low	0.0 blw av	-1.3 blw av	-1.1 blw av

Total Risk	Standard Deviation	Category Risk	Risk Index	Avg Mat
blw av	4.6%	abv av	1.1	22.0 yrs

	1993	1992	1991	1990	1989	1988	1987	1986	1985	1984
Return (%)	11.7	8.1	10.2	5.3	7.2	8.5	0.2	19.3	19.0	8.0
Differ from category (+/-) . . .	0.1	-0.2	-1.1	-1.0	-1.8	-1.6	1.4	2.9	1.7	-0.3

PER SHARE DATA

	1993	1992	1991	1990	1989	1988	1987	1986	1985	1984
Dividends, Net Income ($) .	0.51	0.60	0.61	0.68	0.72	0.74	0.80	0.84	0.87	0.89
Distrib'ns, Cap Gain ($) . . .	0.93	0.21	0.00	0.00	0.00	0.00	0.07	0.64	0.16	0.00
Net Asset Value ($)	10.92	11.12	11.06	10.62	10.75	10.72	10.58	11.45	10.90	10.09
Expense Ratio (%).	1.10	1.17	1.24	1.24	1.19	1.16	0.99	1.16	1.29	1.14
Net Income to Assets (%) . .	4.80	5.47	5.95	6.54	6.78	7.15	7.18	7.60	8.54	8.84
Portfolio Turnover (%)	80	114	91	41	58	77	66	117	173	252
Total Assets (Millions $)	41	41	40	40	41	40	45	43	34	27

PORTFOLIO (as of 9/30/93)

Portfolio Manager: Rick Fontanilla - 1991

Investm't Category: Tax-Exempt Bond
Cap Gain	Asset Allocation
Cap & Income	Fund of Funds
✔ Income	Index
	Sector
✔ Domestic	Small Cap
Foreign	Socially Conscious
Country/Region	State Specific

Portfolio: stocks 0% bonds 98%
convertibles 0% other 0% cash 2%

Largest Holdings: general obligation 22%

Unrealized Net Capital Gains: 3% of portfolio value

SHAREHOLDER INFORMATION

Minimum Investment
Initial: $2,500   Subsequent: $0

Minimum IRA Investment
Initial: na   Subsequent: na

Maximum Fees
Load: none   12b-1: none
Other: none

Distributions
Income: monthly   Capital Gains: Nov

Exchange Options
Number Per Year: no limit   Fee: none
Telephone: yes (money market fund available)

Services
auto invest, auto withdraw

GIT Tax-Free Virginia Port (GTVAX)

Tax-Exempt Bond

1655 N. Fort Myer Dr.
Suite 1000
Arlington, VA 22209
(800) 336-3063, (703) 528-6500

PERFORMANCE

	3yr Annual	5yr Annual	10yr Annual	Bull	Bear
Return (%)	9.9	8.5	na	37.6	2.1
Differ from Category (+/-)	-0.4 blw av	-0.6 low	na	-2.5 blw av	-0.2 blw av

Total Risk	Standard Deviation	Category Risk	Risk Index	Avg Mat
blw av	4.1%	av	1.0	21.0 yrs

	1993	1992	1991	1990	1989	1988	1987	1986	1985	1984
Return (%)	12.4	7.5	9.8	5.9	7.3	8.2	—	—	—	—
Differ from category (+/-)	0.8	-0.8	-1.5	-0.4	-1.7	-1.9	—	—	—	—

PER SHARE DATA

	1993	1992	1991	1990	1989	1988	1987	1986	1985	1984
Dividends, Net Income ($)	0.55	0.58	0.60	0.61	0.62	0.68	—	—	—	—
Distrib'ns, Cap Gain ($)	0.59	0.11	0.11	0.00	0.00	0.13	—	—	—	—
Net Asset Value ($)	11.78	11.53	11.41	11.08	11.07	10.92	—	—	—	—
Expense Ratio (%)	1.10	1.13	1.18	1.25	1.22	0.72	—	—	—	—
Net Income to Assets (%)	4.80	5.20	5.47	5.69	5.71	6.41	—	—	—	—
Portfolio Turnover (%)	80	74	73	11	34	58	—	—	—	—
Total Assets (Millions $)	44	37	31	25	20	19	—	—	—	—

PORTFOLIO (as of 9/30/93)

Portfolio Manager: Rick Fontanilla - 1991

Investm't Category: Tax-Exempt Bond

Cap Gain	Asset Allocation
Cap & Income	Fund of Funds
✔ Income	Index
	Sector
✔ Domestic	Small Cap
Foreign	Socially Conscious
Country/Region	✔ State Specific

Portfolio: stocks 0% bonds 100%
convertibles 0% other 0% cash 0%

Largest Holdings: general obligation 24%

Unrealized Net Capital Gains: 6% of portfolio value

SHAREHOLDER INFORMATION

Minimum Investment
Initial: $2,500   Subsequent: None

Minimum IRA Investment
Initial: na   Subsequent: na

Maximum Fees
Load: none   12b-1: none
Other: none

Distributions
Income: monthly   Capital Gains: Nov

Exchange Options
Number Per Year: no limit   Fee: none
Telephone: yes (money market fund available)

Services
auto invest, auto withdraw

Gradison McDonald Established Value (GETGX)

580 Walnut St.
Cincinnati, OH 45202
(800) 869-5999, (513) 579-5700

Growth

PERFORMANCE

	3yr Annual	5yr Annual	10yr Annual	Bull	Bear
Return (%)	17.6	11.6	13.9	72.8	-13.4
Differ from Category (+/-)	-1.6 blw av	-3.0 low	1.3 abv av	-11.9 blw av	-1.0 av

Total Risk	Standard Deviation	Category Risk	Risk Index	Beta
av	10.0%	low	0.9	0.8

	1993	1992	1991	1990	1989	1988	1987	1986	1985	1984
Return (%)	20.7	10.2	22.2	-8.0	16.0	15.1	12.4	22.0	28.7	4.5
Differ from category (+/-) . . .	7.5	-0.8	-13.2	-1.9	-9.8	-2.6	11.2	7.5	-0.6	4.5

PER SHARE DATA

	1993	1992	1991	1990	1989	1988	1987	1986	1985	1984
Dividends, Net Income ($) .	0.21	0.30	0.44	0.37	0.72	0.50	0.68	0.33	0.28	0.25
Distrib'ns, Cap Gain ($) . . .	1.00	0.27	0.27	0.40	0.50	0.31	1.26	1.18	0.00	0.00
Net Asset Value ($)	22.71	19.87	18.60	15.85	18.07	16.64	15.18	15.21	13.73	10.91
Expense Ratio (%).	1.28	1.31	1.39	1.40	1.45	1.57	1.61	1.72	2.00	2.00
Net Income to Assets (%). .	1.48	2.12	3.10	4.14	3.34	2.67	2.50	2.63	2.68	3.71
Portfolio Turnover (%)	28	68	74	64	50	26	76	79	70	19
Total Assets (Millions $) . . .	244	176	150	135	102	69	54	30	12	6

PORTFOLIO (as of 7/31/93)

Portfolio Manager: William Leugers - 1983

Investm't Category: Growth

✔ Cap Gain	Asset Allocation
Cap & Income	Fund of Funds
Income	Index
	Sector
✔ Domestic	Small Cap
Foreign	Socially Conscious
Country/Region	State Specific

Portfolio: stocks 70% bonds 0%
convertibles 0% other 0% cash 30%

Largest Holdings: industrial products 11%, aerospace/defense companies 10%

Unrealized Net Capital Gains: 24% of portfolio value

SHAREHOLDER INFORMATION

Minimum Investment
Initial: $1,000   Subsequent: $50

Minimum IRA Investment
Initial: $1,000   Subsequent: $50

Maximum Fees
Load: none   12b-1: 0.25%
Other: none

Distributions
Income: quarterly   Capital Gains: May, Nov

Exchange Options
Number Per Year: no limit   Fee: none
Telephone: yes (money market fund available)

Services
IRA, auto invest, auto withdraw

Gradison McDonald
Opportunity Value (GOGFX)

Growth

580 Walnut St.
Cincinnati, OH 45202
(800) 869-5999, (513) 579-5700

PERFORMANCE

	3yr Annual	5yr Annual	10yr Annual	Bull	Bear
Return (%)	19.9	13.0	11.7	90.4	-21.2
Differ from Category (+/-)	0.6 av	-1.6 blw av	-0.8 blw av	5.7 av	-8.8 low

Total Risk	Standard Deviation	Category Risk	Risk Index	Beta
av	10.7%	blw av	1.0	0.7

	1993	1992	1991	1990	1989	1988	1987	1986	1985	1984
Return (%)	11.0	14.3	35.9	-13.0	23.1	23.5	-5.3	12.9	28.0	-3.2
Differ from category (+/-). . .	-2.2	3.3	0.5	-6.9	-2.7	5.8	-6.5	-1.6	-1.3	-3.2

PER SHARE DATA

	1993	1992	1991	1990	1989	1988	1987	1986	1985	1984
Dividends, Net Income ($).	0.07	0.10	0.27	0.25	0.33	0.27	0.11	0.10	0.02	0.00
Distrib'ns, Cap Gain ($) . . .	0.80	0.63	0.67	0.06	0.25	0.62	0.12	0.73	0.00	0.00
Net Asset Value ($)	18.38	17.37	15.90	12.45	14.67	12.40	10.77	11.64	10.99	8.60
Expense Ratio (%)	1.44	1.49	1.61	1.52	1.84	1.83	1.73	2.00	2.00	2.00
Net Income to Assets (%) .	0.61	1.32	2.03	2.47	1.84	1.22	0.90	0.26	0.29	0.25
Portfolio Turnover (%).	39	64	64	37	36	74	65	83	99	108
Total Assets (Millions $).	88	47	29	23	20	18	20	14	4	3

PORTFOLIO (as of 4/30/93)

Portfolio Manager: William Leugers - 1983

Investm't Category: Growth
- ✔ Cap Gain
- Cap & Income
- Income
- Asset Allocation
- Fund of Funds
- Index
- Sector
- ✔ Domestic
- Foreign
- Country/Region
- ✔ Small Cap
- Socially Conscious
- State Specific

Portfolio: stocks 66% bonds 0%
convertibles 0% other 0% cash 34%

Largest Holdings: banks 9%, retail trade 9%

Unrealized Net Capital Gains: 18% of portfolio value

SHAREHOLDER INFORMATION

Minimum Investment
Initial: $1,000   Subsequent: $50

Minimum IRA Investment
Initial: $1,000   Subsequent: $50

Maximum Fees
Load: none   12b-1: 0.25%
Other: none

Distributions
Income: May, Dec   Capital Gains: May, Dec

Exchange Options
Number Per Year: no limit   Fee: none
Telephone: yes (money market fund available)

Services
IRA, auto invest, auto withdraw

Greenspring (GRSPX)

Growth & Income

2330 West Joppa Road
Suite 110
Lutherville, MD 21093
(800) 366-3863, (410) 823-5353

PERFORMANCE

	3yr Annual	5yr Annual	10yr Annual	Bull	Bear
Return (%)	16.8	10.5	na	55.7	-4.2
Differ from Category (+/-)	0.4 av	-2.0 low	na	-14.4 blw av	7.4 high

Total Risk	Standard Deviation	Category Risk	Risk Index	Beta
blw av	5.4%	low	0.6	0.3

	1993	1992	1991	1990	1989	1988	1987	1986	1985	1984
Return (%)	14.6	16.5	19.3	-6.5	10.6	15.9	9.1	15.9	20.1	—
Differ from category (+/-) ...	2.0	6.5	-8.4	-0.8	-11.0	-0.8	8.7	0.6	-5.3	—

PER SHARE DATA

	1993	1992	1991	1990	1989	1988	1987	1986	1985	1984
Dividends, Net Income ($) .	0.39	0.50	0.51	0.68	0.78	1.24	1.64	0.73	1.13	—
Distrib'ns, Cap Gain ($) ...	1.41	0.72	0.06	0.00	0.18	0.04	1.25	1.46	0.03	—
Net Asset Value ($)	13.96	13.78	12.91	11.31	12.83	12.49	11.89	13.61	13.85	—
Expense Ratio (%)........	1.31	1.48	1.33	1.31	1.27	1.29	1.36	1.46	1.49	—
Net Income to Assets (%)..	2.78	3.68	3.79	4.82	6.23	11.13	8.57	5.55	5.96	—
Portfolio Turnover (%)....	121	100	70	90	106	199	929	502	350	—
Total Assets (Millions $)	30	20	19	19	22	21	18	14	13	—

PORTFOLIO (as of 9/30/93)

Portfolio Manager: Charles vK. Carlson - 1987

Investm't Category: Growth & Income

Cap Gain	Asset Allocation
✔ Cap & Income	Fund of Funds
Income	Index
	Sector
✔ Domestic	Small Cap
Foreign	Socially Conscious
Country/Region	State Specific

Portfolio: stocks 40% bonds 30%
convertibles 4% other 5% cash 21%

Largest Holdings: financial services 15%, real estate 13%

Unrealized Net Capital Gains: 9% of portfolio value

SHAREHOLDER INFORMATION

Minimum Investment
Initial: $1,000   Subsequent: $100

Minimum IRA Investment
Initial: $1,000   Subsequent: $100

Maximum Fees
Load: none   12b-1: none
Other: none

Distributions
Income: Jul, Dec   Capital Gains: Dec

Exchange Options
Number Per Year: none   Fee: na
Telephone: na

Services
IRA, other pension, auto withdraw

Harbor Bond (HABDX)

General Bond

One SeaGate
Toledo, OH 43666
(800) 422-1050, (419) 247-2477

PERFORMANCE

	3yr Annual	5yr Annual	10yr Annual	Bull	Bear
Return (%)	13.6	12.4	na	55.0	2.1
Differ from Category (+/-)	3.4 high	2.6 high	na	15.6 high	-0.8 blw av

Total Risk	Standard Deviation	Category Risk	Risk Index	Avg Mat
low	4.0%	abv av	1.4	8.5 yrs

	1993	1992	1991	1990	1989	1988	1987	1986	1985	1984
Return (%)	12.4	9.1	19.6	7.9	13.6	7.1	—	—	—	—
Differ from category (+/-). . .	3.2	2.4	5.0	1.0	2.3	-0.5	—	—	—	—

PER SHARE DATA

	1993	1992	1991	1990	1989	1988	1987	1986	1985	1984
Dividends, Net Income ($).	0.64	0.74	0.86	0.84	0.82	0.66	—	—	—	—
Distrib'ns, Cap Gain ($) . . .	0.50	0.24	0.25	0.00	0.09	0.07	—	—	—	—
Net Asset Value ($)	11.31	11.10	11.11	10.29	10.36	9.96	—	—	—	—
Expense Ratio (%)	0.70	0.77	0.86	1.22	1.21	1.55	—	—	—	—
Net Income to Assets (%) .	7.03	7.30	8.12	8.30	8.20	7.42	—	—	—	—
Portfolio Turnover (%). . . .	107	53	58	91	91	124	—	—	—	—
Total Assets (Millions $). . . .	174	65	40	24	21	11	—	—	—	—

PORTFOLIO (as of 4/30/93)

Portfolio Manager: William Gross - 1987

Investm't Category: General Bond

Cap Gain	Asset Allocation
Cap & Income	Fund of Funds
✔ Income	Index
	Sector
✔ Domestic	Small Cap
✔ Foreign	Socially Conscious
Country/Region	State Specific

Portfolio:	stocks 0%	bonds 89%
convertibles 0%	other 0%	cash 11%

Largest Holdings: mortgage-backed 45%, corporate 41%

Unrealized Net Capital Gains: 2% of portfolio value

SHAREHOLDER INFORMATION

Minimum Investment
Initial: $2,000   Subsequent: $500

Minimum IRA Investment
Initial: $500   Subsequent: $100

Maximum Fees
Load: none   12b-1: none
Other: none

Distributions
Income: quarterly   Capital Gains: Dec

Exchange Options
Number Per Year: no limit   Fee: none
Telephone: yes (money market fund available)

Services
IRA, other pension, auto exchange, auto invest, auto withdraw

Harbor Capital Appreciation (HACAX)

Growth

One SeaGate
Toledo, OH 43666
(800) 422-1050, (419) 247-2477

PERFORMANCE

	3yr Annual	5yr Annual	10yr Annual	Bull	Bear
Return (%)	24.0	18.4	na	114.4	-12.5
Differ from Category (+/-)	4.8 high	3.8 high	na	29.7 high	-0.1 av

Total Risk	Standard Deviation	Category Risk	Risk Index	Beta
high	15.8%	high	1.5	1.2

	1993	1992	1991	1990	1989	1988	1987	1986	1985	1984
Return (%)	12.1	9.9	54.7	-1.7	24.1	15.2	—	—	—	—
Differ from category (+/-) . .	-1.1	-1.1	19.3	4.4	-1.7	-2.5	—	—	—	—

PER SHARE DATA

	1993	1992	1991	1990	1989	1988	1987	1986	1985	1984
Dividends, Net Income ($) .	0.03	0.01	0.04	0.14	0.20	0.17	—	—	—	—
Distrib'ns, Cap Gain ($) . . .	1.12	2.03	0.97	0.85	1.17	0.38	—	—	—	—
Net Asset Value ($)	16.37	15.65	16.11	11.09	12.31	11.05	—	—	—	—
Expense Ratio (%)	0.85	0.91	0.89	0.88	0.92	0.99	—	—	—	—
Net Income to Assets (%) . .	0.22	0.12	0.47	1.18	1.77	1.48	—	—	—	—
Portfolio Turnover (%)	97	69	90	162	75	48	—	—	—	—
Total Assets (Millions $) . . .	150	77	80	55	60	46	—	—	—	—

PORTFOLIO (as of 4/30/93)

Portfolio Manager: Spiros Segalas - 1990

Investm't Category: Growth

✔ Cap Gain	Asset Allocation
Cap & Income	Fund of Funds
Income	Index
	Sector
✔ Domestic	Small Cap
Foreign	Socially Conscious
Country/Region	State Specific

Portfolio: stocks 96% bonds 0%
convertibles 0% other 0% cash 4%

Largest Holdings: insurance 11%, retailing 8%

Unrealized Net Capital Gains: 12% of portfolio value

SHAREHOLDER INFORMATION

Minimum Investment
Initial: $2,000   Subsequent: $500

Minimum IRA Investment
Initial: $500   Subsequent: $100

Maximum Fees
Load: none   12b-1: none
Other: none

Distributions
Income: Dec   Capital Gains: Dec

Exchange Options
Number Per Year: no limit   Fee: none
Telephone: yes (money market fund available)

Services
IRA, other pension, auto exchange, auto invest, auto withdraw

Harbor Growth (HAGWX)

Growth

One SeaGate
Toledo, OH 43666
(800) 422-1050, (419) 247-2477

	3yr Annual	5yr Annual	10yr Annual	Bull	Bear
Return (%)	18.6	13.8	na	92.0	-18.8
Differ from Category (+/-)	-0.6 av	-0.8 blw av	na	7.3 abv av	-6.4 blw av

Total Risk	Standard Deviation	Category Risk	Risk Index	Beta
high	18.3%	high	1.7	1.3

	1993	1992	1991	1990	1989	1988	1987	1986	1985	1984
Return (%)	18.3	-6.3	50.4	-6.6	22.9	14.2	2.9	—	—	—
Differ from category (+/-). . .	5.1	-17.3	15.0	-0.5	-2.9	-3.5	1.7	—	—	—

	1993	1992	1991	1990	1989	1988	1987	1986	1985	1984
Dividends, Net Income ($).	0.01	0.00	0.04	0.08	0.10	0.11	0.10	—	—	—
Distrib'ns, Cap Gain ($) . . .	0.00	1.36	2.30	0.93	0.48	0.00	0.79	—	—	—
Net Asset Value ($)	13.88	11.74	14.02	10.94	12.81	10.91	9.65	—	—	—
Expense Ratio (%)	0.89	0.90	0.91	0.93	1.03	1.06	1.33	—	—	—
Net Income to Assets (%) .	0.04	0.14	0.32	0.74	0.75	1.14	0.72	—	—	—
Portfolio Turnover (%).	257	83	98	96	104	53	56	—	—	—
Total Assets (Millions $). . . .	189	191	211	123	139	116	99	—	—	—

Portfolio Manager: Arthur E. Nicholas - 1993

Investm't Category: Growth

✔ Cap Gain
  Cap & Income
  Income

  Asset Allocation
  Fund of Funds
  Index
  Sector

✔ Domestic
  Foreign
  Country/Region

  Small Cap
  Socially Conscious
  State Specific

Portfolio:	stocks 96%	bonds 0%
convertibles 0%	other 0%	cash 4%

Largest Holdings: telecommunications 13%, computer & office equipment 9%

Unrealized Net Capital Gains: 5% of portfolio value

Minimum Investment
Initial: $2,000   Subsequent: $500

Minimum IRA Investment
Initial: $500   Subsequent: $100

Maximum Fees
Load: none   12b-1: none
Other: none

Distributions
Income: Dec   Capital Gains: Dec

Exchange Options
Number Per Year: no limit   Fee: none
Telephone: yes (money market fund available)

Services
IRA, other pension, auto exchange, auto invest, auto withdraw

Harbor Int'l (HAINX)

International Stock

One SeaGate
Toledo, OH 43666
(800) 422-1050, (419) 247-2477

this fund is closed to new investors

PERFORMANCE

	3yr Annual	5yr Annual	10yr Annual	Bull	Bear
Return (%)	20.7	16.8	na	79.2	-11.2
Differ from Category (+/-)	6.4 high	8.1 high	na	24.1 high	3.9 abv av

Total Risk	Standard Deviation	Category Risk	Risk Index	Beta
abv av	13.4%	av	1.1	0.6

	1993	1992	1991	1990	1989	1988	1987	1986	1985	1984
Return (%)	45.4	-0.2	21.4	-9.7	36.8	37.7	—	—	—	—
Differ from category (+/-) ...	6.9	3.3	8.5	1.4	14.6	23.9	—	—	—	—

PER SHARE DATA

	1993	1992	1991	1990	1989	1988	1987	1986	1985	1984
Dividends, Net Income ($)	0.21	0.21	0.21	0.33	0.17	0.10	—	—	—	—
Distrib'ns, Cap Gain ($) ...	0.00	0.17	0.00	0.34	0.72	0.75	—	—	—	—
Net Asset Value ($)	24.32	16.87	17.30	14.42	16.74	12.90	—	—	—	—
Expense Ratio (%)........	1.26	1.28	1.35	1.40	1.15	1.78	—	—	—	—
Net Income to Assets (%)..	0.59	1.98	1.76	2.82	1.56	0.87	—	—	—	—
Portfolio Turnover (%).....	24	25	19	28	21	27	—	—	—	—
Total Assets (Millions $) ..	2,609	701	206	64	29	10	—	—	—	—

PORTFOLIO (as of 4/30/93)

Portfolio Manager: Hakan Castegren - 1987

Investm't Category: International Stock
- ✔ Cap Gain
- Cap & Income
- Income
- Domestic
- ✔ Foreign
- Country/Region
- Asset Allocation
- Fund of Funds
- Index
- Sector
- Small Cap
- Socially Conscious
- State Specific

Portfolio: stocks 92% bonds 0%
convertibles 0% other 0% cash 8%

Largest Holdings: Switzerland 16%, United Kingdom 16%

Unrealized Net Capital Gains: 7% of portfolio value

SHAREHOLDER INFORMATION

Minimum Investment
Initial: $2,000   Subsequent: $500

Minimum IRA Investment
Initial: $500   Subsequent: $100

Maximum Fees
Load: none   12b-1: none
Other: none

Distributions
Income: Dec   Capital Gains: Dec

Exchange Options
Number Per Year: no limit   Fee: none
Telephone: yes (money market fund available)

Services
IRA, other pension, auto exchange, auto invest, auto withdraw

Harbor Short Duration
(HASDX)
General Bond

One SeaGate
Toledo, OH 43666
(800) 422-1050, (419) 247-2477

	3yr Annual	5yr Annual	10yr Annual	Bull	Bear
Return (%)	na	na	na	na	na
Differ from Category (+/-)	na	na	na	na	na

Total Risk	Standard Deviation	Category Risk	Risk Index	Avg Mat
na	na	na	na	2.2 yrs

	1993	1992	1991	1990	1989	1988	1987	1986	1985	1984
Return (%)	4.4	—	—	—	—	—	—	—	—	—
Differ from category (+/-). . .	-4.8	—	—	—	—	—	—	—	—	—

PER SHARE DATA

	1993	1992	1991	1990	1989	1988	1987	1986	1985	1984
Dividends, Net Income ($) .	1.15	—	—	—	—	—	—	—	—	—
Distrib'ns, Cap Gain ($) . . .	0.00	—	—	—	—	—	—	—	—	—
Net Asset Value ($)	9.25	—	—	—	—	—	—	—	—	—
Expense Ratio (%)	0.69	—	—	—	—	—	—	—	—	—
Net Income to Assets (%) .	4.19	—	—	—	—	—	—	—	—	—
Portfolio Turnover (%). . .	1,212	—	—	—	—	—	—	—	—	—
Total Assets (Millions $). . . .	144	—	—	—	—	—	—	—	—	—

PORTFOLIO (as of 4/30/93)

Portfolio Manager: Adnen Akant - 1992

Investm't Category: General Bond

Cap Gain	Asset Allocation
Cap & Income	Fund of Funds
✔ Income	Index
	Sector
✔ Domestic	Small Cap
✔ Foreign	Socially Conscious
Country/Region	State Specific

Portfolio: stocks 0%   bonds 73%
convertibles 0%   other 0%   cash 27%

Largest Holdings: U. S. government 48%,
asset-backed 27%

Unrealized Net Capital Gains: 0% of portfolio value

SHAREHOLDER INFORMATION

Minimum Investment
Initial: $2,000   Subsequent: $500

Minimum IRA Investment
Initial: $500   Subsequent: $100

Maximum Fees
Load: none   12b-1: none
Other: none

Distributions
Income: monthly   Capital Gains: Dec

Exchange Options
Number Per Year: no limit   Fee: none
Telephone: yes (money market fund available)

Services
IRA, other pension, auto exchange, auto invest, auto withdraw

Harbor Value (HAVLX)

Growth & Income

One SeaGate
Toledo, OH 43666
(800) 422-1050, (419) 247-2477

Heartland Wisconsin Tax Free (HRWIX)

790 North Milwaukee Street
Milwaukee, WI 53202
(800) 432-7856, (414) 347-7777

Tax-Exempt Bond

PERFORMANCE

	3yr Annual	5yr Annual	10yr Annual	Bull	Bear
Return (%)	na	na	na	na	na
Differ from Category (+/-)	na	na	na	na	na

Total Risk	Standard Deviation	Category Risk	Risk Index	Avg Mat
na	na	na	na	19.3 yrs

	1993	1992	1991	1990	1989	1988	1987	1986	1985	1984
Return (%)	10.7	—	—	—	—	—	—	—	—	—
Differ from category (+/-). . .	-0.8	—	—	—	—	—	—	—	—	—

PER SHARE DATA

	1993	1992	1991	1990	1989	1988	1987	1986	1985	1984
Dividends, Net Income ($) .	0.49	—	—	—	—	—	—	—	—	—
Distrib'ns, Cap Gain ($) . . .	0.01	—	—	—	—	—	—	—	—	—
Net Asset Value ($)	10.38	—	—	—	—	—	—	—	—	—
Expense Ratio (%)	0.80	—	—	—	—	—	—	—	—	—
Net Income to Assets (%) .	4.80	—	—	—	—	—	—	—	—	—
Portfolio Turnover (%).	8	—	—	—	—	—	—	—	—	—
Total Assets (Millions $).	10	—	—	—	—	—	—	—	—	—

PORTFOLIO (as of 6/30/93)

Portfolio Manager: Patrick Retzer - 1992

Investm't Category: Tax-Exempt Bond

Cap Gain	Asset Allocation
Cap & Income	Fund of Funds
✔ Income	Index
	Sector
✔ Domestic	Small Cap
Foreign	Socially Conscious
Country/Region	✔ State Specific

Portfolio: stocks 0% bonds 100%
convertibles 0% other 0% cash 0%

Largest Holdings: general obligation 17%

Unrealized Net Capital Gains: 2% of portfolio value

SHAREHOLDER INFORMATION

Minimum Investment
Initial: $10,000   Subsequent: $1,000

Minimum IRA Investment
Initial: na   Subsequent: na

Maximum Fees
Load: 3.00% front   12b-1: none
Other: none

Distributions
Income: monthly   Capital Gains: Dec

Exchange Options
Number Per Year: no limit   Fee: none
Telephone: yes (money market fund available)

Services
auto invest, auto withdraw

HighMark Bond (HMBDX)

General Bond

1900 East Dublin-Granville Rd.
Columbus, OH 43229
(800) 433-6884

PERFORMANCE

	3yr Annual	5yr Annual	10yr Annual	Bull	Bear
Return (%)	9.3	9.7	na	37.6	2.7
Differ from Category (+/-)	-0.8 blw av	-0.1 blw av	na	-1.8 blw av	-0.2 blw av

Total Risk	Standard Deviation	Category Risk	Risk Index	Avg Mat
low	3.6%	av	1.2	9.5 yrs

	1993	1992	1991	1990	1989	1988	1987	1986	1985	1984
Return (%)	7.4	8.3	12.2	8.1	12.7	6.2	—	—	—	—
Differ from category (+/-) . .	-1.8	1.6	-2.4	1.2	1.4	-1.4	—	—	—	—

PER SHARE DATA

	1993	1992	1991	1990	1989	1988	1987	1986	1985	1984
Dividends, Net Income ($) .	0.66	0.64	0.77	0.77	0.81	0.77	—	—	—	—
Distrib'ns, Cap Gain ($) . . .	0.05	0.24	0.03	0.00	0.00	0.00	—	—	—	—
Net Asset Value ($)	10.76	10.68	10.70	10.30	10.28	9.88	—	—	—	—
Expense Ratio (%).	0.93	0.91	0.79	1.01	1.18	1.04	—	—	—	—
Net Income to Assets (%) . .	6.41	6.23	7.61	7.77	8.24	8.63	—	—	—	—
Portfolio Turnover (%)	59	80	66	54	25	0	—	—	—	—
Total Assets (Millions $)	75	22	11	7	5	3	—	—	—	—

PORTFOLIO (as of 7/31/93)

Portfolio Manager: not specified

Investm't Category: General Bond

Cap Gain	Asset Allocation
Cap & Income	Fund of Funds
✔ Income	Index
	Sector
✔ Domestic	Small Cap
✔ Foreign	Socially Conscious
Country/Region	State Specific

Portfolio: stocks 0%   bonds 97%
convertibles 0%   other 0%   cash 3%

Largest Holdings: U.S. government 51%, corporate 32%

Unrealized Net Capital Gains: 3% of portfolio value

SHAREHOLDER INFORMATION

Minimum Investment
Initial: $1,000   Subsequent: $100

Minimum IRA Investment
Initial: na   Subsequent: na

Maximum Fees
Load: none   12b-1: none
Other: none

Distributions
Income: monthly   Capital Gains: Dec

Exchange Options
Number Per Year: no limit   Fee: none
Telephone: yes (money market fund available)

Services
auto invest, auto withdraw

HighMark Income Equity
(HMIEX)

Growth & Income

1900 East Dublin-Granville Rd.
Columbus, OH 43229
(800) 433-6884

PERFORMANCE

	3yr Annual	5yr Annual	10yr Annual	Bull	Bear
Return (%)	17.2	12.8	na	72.3	-15.5
Differ from Category (+/-)	0.8 abv av	0.3 av	na	2.2 av	-3.9 blw av

Total Risk	Standard Deviation	Category Risk	Risk Index	Beta
abv av	12.2%	high	1.4	0.7

	1993	1992	1991	1990	1989	1988	1987	1986	1985	1984
Return (%)	12.7	9.4	30.4	-9.5	25.4	20.7	0.8	12.2	29.6	—
Differ from category (+/-) . . .	0.1	-0.6	2.7	-3.9	3.8	3.9	0.4	-3.0	4.2	—

PER SHARE DATA

	1993	1992	1991	1990	1989	1988	1987	1986	1985	1984
Dividends, Net Income ($) .	0.37	0.38	0.41	0.52	0.51	0.54	0.46	0.44	0.50	—
Distrib'ns, Cap Gain ($) . . .	0.32	0.00	0.00	0.84	1.05	0.00	0.00	0.00	0.00	—
Net Asset Value ($)	12.16	11.42	10.80	8.63	11.03	10.07	8.81	9.17	7.96	—
Expense Ratio (%)	1.15	1.16	1.17	1.15	1.19	1.41	1.12	0.97	0.80	—
Net Income to Assets (%) .	3.27	3.76	4.81	4.82	4.61	5.45	4.50	4.96	6.71	—
Portfolio Turnover (%).	30	23	33	37	29	6	21	12	5	—
Total Assets (Millions $). . . .	206	74	49	41	40	31	28	20	7	—

PORTFOLIO (as of 7/31/93)

Portfolio Manager: not specified

Investm't Category: Growth & Income

Cap Gain	Asset Allocation
✔ Cap & Income	Fund of Funds
Income	Index
	Sector
✔ Domestic	Small Cap
✔ Foreign	Socially Conscious
Country/Region	State Specific

Portfolio: stocks 92%   bonds 0%
convertibles 0%   other 0%   cash 8%

Largest Holdings: oil & gas 14%, telecommni-cations 13%

Unrealized Net Capital Gains: 12% of portfolio value

SHAREHOLDER INFORMATION

Minimum Investment
Initial: $1,000   Subsequent: $100

Minimum IRA Investment
Initial: na   Subsequent: na

Maximum Fees
Load: none   12b-1: none
Other: none

Distributions
Income: monthly   Capital Gains: Dec

Exchange Options
Number Per Year: no limit   Fee: none
Telephone: yes (money market fund available)

Services
auto invest, auto withdraw

HighMark Special Growth Equity (HMSGX)

Growth

1900 East Dublin-Granville Rd.
Columbus, OH 43229
(800) 433-6884

PERFORMANCE

	3yr Annual	5yr Annual	10yr Annual	Bull	Bear
Return (%)	17.0	13.8	na	83.4	-10.7
Differ from Category (+/-)	-2.2 blw av	-0.8 blw av	na	-1.3 av	1.7 av

Total Risk	Standard Deviation	Category Risk	Risk Index	Beta
high	16.0%	high	1.5	1.1

	1993	1992	1991	1990	1989	1988	1987	1986	1985	1984
Return (%)	13.8	-3.6	46.1	2.0	16.8	10.6	-0.6	1.9	16.2	—
Differ from category (+/-) . . .	0.6	-14.6	10.7	8.1	-9.0	-7.1	-1.8	-12.6	-13.1	—

PER SHARE DATA

	1993	1992	1991	1990	1989	1988	1987	1986	1985	1984
Dividends, Net Income ($) .	0.00	0.00	0.05	0.02	0.06	0.00	0.06	0.17	0.14	—
Distrib'ns, Cap Gain ($) . . .	0.00	0.76	0.30	0.00	0.69	0.69	0.00	0.00	0.00	—
Net Asset Value ($)	14.19	12.46	13.74	9.68	9.52	8.79	8.57	8.68	8.68	—
Expense Ratio (%)	1.57	0.93	0.81	1.64	1.21	0.85	1.08	0.98	0.67	—
Net Income to Assets (%) .	-0.88	-0.02	0.82	-0.01	0.74	-0.05	0.33	0.53	1.21	—
Portfolio Turnover (%)	46	49	40	50	45	2	34	38	27	—
Total Assets (Millions $)	4	5	3	2	1	1	1	1	1	—

PORTFOLIO (as of 7/31/93)

Portfolio Manager: not specified

Investm't Category: Growth

✔ Cap Gain
  Cap & Income
  Income
✔ Domestic
✔ Foreign
  Country/Region

  Asset Allocation
  Fund of Funds
  Index
  Sector
✔ Small Cap
  Socially Conscious
  State Specific

Portfolio: stocks 97% bonds 0%
convertibles 0% other 0% cash 3%

Largest Holdings: retail 13%, business services 10%

Unrealized Net Capital Gains: 11% of portfolio value

SHAREHOLDER INFORMATION

Minimum Investment
Initial: $1,000   Subsequent: $100

Minimum IRA Investment
Initial: na   Subsequent: na

Maximum Fees
Load: none   12b-1: none
Other: none

Distributions
Income: quarterly   Capital Gains: Dec

Exchange Options
Number Per Year: no limit   Fee: none
Telephone: yes (money market fund available)

Services
auto invest, auto withdraw

Homestead Short-Term Bond (HOSBX)

Corporate Bond

1800 Massachusetts Ave., N.W.
Washington, DC 20036
(800) 258-3030

PERFORMANCE

	3yr Annual	5yr Annual	10yr Annual	Bull	Bear
Return (%)	na	na	na	na	na
Differ from Category (+/-)	na	na	na	na	na

Total Risk	Standard Deviation	Category Risk	Risk Index	Avg Mat
na	na	na	na	2.8 yrs

	1993	1992	1991	1990	1989	1988	1987	1986	1985	1984
Return (%)	6.6	6.2	—	—	—	—	—	—	—	—
Differ from category (+/-). . . .	-4.8	-2.4	—	—	—	—	—	—	—	—

PER SHARE DATA

	1993	1992	1991	1990	1989	1988	1987	1986	1985	1984
Dividends, Net Income ($).	0.23	0.26	—	—	—	—	—	—	—	—
Distrib'ns, Cap Gain ($) . . .	0.00	0.00	—	—	—	—	—	—	—	—
Net Asset Value ($)	5.19	5.10	—	—	—	—	—	—	—	—
Expense Ratio (%)	0.75	0.75	—	—	—	—	—	—	—	—
Net Income to Assets (%) .	4.78	5.20	—	—	—	—	—	—	—	—
Portfolio Turnover (%).	5	19	—	—	—	—	—	—	—	—
Total Assets (Millions $).	36	10	—	—	—	—	—	—	—	—

PORTFOLIO (as of 6/30/93)

Portfolio Manager: Douglas Kern - 1991

Investm't Category: Corporate Bond

Cap Gain	Asset Allocation
Cap & Income	Fund of Funds
✔ Income	Index
	Sector
✔ Domestic	Small Cap
Foreign	Socially Conscious
Country/Region	State Specific

Portfolio: stocks 0% bonds 89%
convertibles 0% other 0% cash 11%

Largest Holdings: finance 35%, basic industries 10%

Unrealized Net Capital Gains: 1% of portfolio value

SHAREHOLDER INFORMATION

Minimum Investment
Initial: $1,000   Subsequent: $100

Minimum IRA Investment
Initial: $250   Subsequent: $100

Maximum Fees
Load: none   12b-1: none
Other: none

Distributions
Income: monthly   Capital Gains: Dec

Exchange Options
Number Per Year: 4   Fee: none
Telephone: yes (money market fund available)

Services
IRA, other pension, auto invest, auto withdraw

Homestead Value (HOVLX)

Growth & Income

1800 Massachusetts Ave., N.W.
Washington, DC 20036
(800) 258-3030

PERFORMANCE

	3yr Annual	5yr Annual	10yr Annual	Bull	Bear
Return (%)	15.8	na	na	na	na
Differ from Category (+/-)	-0.6 av	na	na	na	na

Total Risk	Standard Deviation	Category Risk	Risk Index	Beta
av	7.9%	low	0.9	0.6

	1993	1992	1991	1990	1989	1988	1987	1986	1985	1984
Return (%)	18.7	11.6	17.1	—	—	—	—	—	—	—
Differ from category (+/-) ...	6.1	1.6	-10.6	—	—	—	—	—	—	—

PER SHARE DATA

	1993	1992	1991	1990	1989	1988	1987	1986	1985	1984
Dividends, Net Income ($) .	0.21	0.24	0.38	—	—	—	—	—	—	—
Distrib'ns, Cap Gain ($) ...	0.07	0.07	0.01	—	—	—	—	—	—	—
Net Asset Value ($)	14.54	12.49	11.48	—	—	—	—	—	—	—
Expense Ratio (%)........	1.25	1.25	1.25	—	—	—	—	—	—	—
Net Income to Assets (%)..	2.09	2.33	3.80	—	—	—	—	—	—	—
Portfolio Turnover (%)	0	5	26	—	—	—	—	—	—	—
Total Assets (Millions $)	54	19	10	—	—	—	—	—	—	—

PORTFOLIO (as of 6/30/93)

Portfolio Manager: Stuart E. Teach - 1990

Investm't Category: Growth & Income

Cap Gain	Asset Allocation
✔ Cap & Income	Fund of Funds
Income	Index
	Sector
✔ Domestic	Small Cap
Foreign	Socially Conscious
Country/Region	State Specific

Portfolio:	stocks 82%	bonds 0%
convertibles 0%	other 0%	cash 18%

Largest Holdings: consumer non-durables 14%, basic industries 14%

Unrealized Net Capital Gains: 11% of portfolio value

SHAREHOLDER INFORMATION

Minimum Investment
Initial: $1,000   Subsequent: $100

Minimum IRA Investment
Initial: $250   Subsequent: $100

Maximum Fees
Load: none   12b-1: none
Other: none

Distributions
Income: June, Dec   Capital Gains: Dec

Exchange Options
Number Per Year: 4   Fee: none
Telephone: yes (money market fund available)

Services
IRA, other pension, auto invest, auto withdraw

IAI Balanced (IABLX)

Balanced

3700 First Bank Place
P.O. Box 357
Minneapolis, MN 55440
(800) 945-3863, (612) 376-2700

PERFORMANCE

	3yr Annual	5yr Annual	10yr Annual	Bull	Bear
Return (%)	na	na	na	na	na
Differ from Category (+/-)	na	na	na	na	na

Total Risk	Standard Deviation	Category Risk	Risk Index	Beta
na	na	na	na	na

	1993	1992	1991	1990	1989	1988	1987	1986	1985	1984
Return (%).............	4.9	—	—	—	—	—	—	—	—	—
Differ from category (+/-)...	-8.5	—	—	—	—	—	—	—	—	—

PER SHARE DATA

	1993	1992	1991	1990	1989	1988	1987	1986	1985	1984
Dividends, Net Income ($).	0.25	—	—	—	—	—	—	—	—	—
Distrib'ns, Cap Gain ($) ...	0.20	—	—	—	—	—	—	—	—	—
Net Asset Value ($)	10.83	—	—	—	—	—	—	—	—	—
Expense Ratio (%)	1.25	—	—	—	—	—	—	—	—	—
Net Income to Assets (%) .	2.18	—	—	—	—	—	—	—	—	—
Portfolio Turnover (%).....	83	—	—	—	—	—	—	—	—	—
Total Assets (Millions $).....	65	—	—	—	—	—	—	—	—	—

PORTFOLIO (as of 9/30/93)

Portfolio Manager: Mark Simenstead & James Diedrich - 1993

Investm't Category: Balanced

Cap Gain	✔ Asset Allocation
✔ Cap & Income	Fund of Funds
Income	Index
	Sector
✔ Domestic	Small Cap
Foreign	Socially Conscious
Country/Region	State Specific

Portfolio: stocks 57% bonds 43%
convertibles 0% other 0% cash 0%

Largest Holdings: bonds—U.S. government 15%, stocks—energy 8%

Unrealized Net Capital Gains: 7% of portfolio value

SHAREHOLDER INFORMATION

Minimum Investment
Initial: $5,000   Subsequent: $100

Minimum IRA Investment
Initial: $2000   Subsequent: $100

Maximum Fees
Load: none   12b-1: 0.25%
Other: none

Distributions
Income: Jun, Dec   Capital Gains: Jun, Dec

Exchange Options
Number Per Year: 4   Fee: none
Telephone: yes (money market fund available)

Services
IRA, other pension, auto exchange, auto invest, auto withdraw

IAI Bond (IAIBX)

Government Bond

3700 First Bank Place
P.O. Box 357
Minneapolis, MN 55440
(800) 945-3863, (612) 376-2700

PERFORMANCE

	3yr Annual	5yr Annual	10yr Annual	Bull	Bear
Return (%)	12.0	11.7	11.4	51.5	-0.6
Differ from Category (+/-)	1.2 abv av	1.3 abv av	1.7 high	5.3 abv av	-1.1 blw av

Total Risk	Standard Deviation	Category Risk	Risk Index	Avg Mat
blw av	5.3%	abv av	1.2	15.1 yrs

	1993	1992	1991	1990	1989	1988	1987	1986	1985	1984
Return (%)	12.3	6.7	17.3	7.0	15.8	6.3	2.0	12.1	20.0	15.9
Differ from category (+/-) ...	1.9	0.5	2.3	0.5	1.9	-1.3	3.8	-7.0	0.8	2.9

PER SHARE DATA

	1993	1992	1991	1990	1989	1988	1987	1986	1985	1984
Dividends, Net Income ($) .	0.63	0.74	0.74	0.76	0.71	0.71	0.97	0.89	0.97	1.00
Distrib'ns, Cap Gain ($) ...	0.81	0.76	0.09	0.00	0.02	0.00	0.09	0.27	0.00	0.00
Net Asset Value ($)	9.76	9.99	10.82	10.00	10.10	9.39	9.51	10.39	10.37	9.54
Expense Ratio (%)........	1.10	1.10	0.88	0.90	0.90	0.80	0.70	0.70	0.70	0.80
Net Income to Assets (%)..	6.03	7.43	7.56	7.50	7.70	7.70	8.50	9.60	11.20	10.40
Portfolio Turnover (%)....	160	126	43	78	115	20	35	76	22	40
Total Assets (Millions $)	98	107	109	80	50	41	46	31	22	16

PORTFOLIO (as of 9/30/93)

Portfolio Manager: Larry Hill - 1984

Investm't Category: Government Bond
Cap Gain	Asset Allocation
Cap & Income	Fund of Funds
✔ Income	Index
	Sector
✔ Domestic	Small Cap
✔ Foreign	Socially Conscious
Country/Region	State Specific

Portfolio: stocks 0%   bonds 90%
convertibles 0%   other 0%   cash 10%

Largest Holdings: U.S. government & agencies 49%, mortgage-backed 27%

Unrealized Net Capital Gains: 4% of portfolio value

SHAREHOLDER INFORMATION

Minimum Investment
Initial: $5,000   Subsequent: $100

Minimum IRA Investment
Initial: $2,000   Subsequent: $100

Maximum Fees
Load: none   12b-1: 0.25%
Other: none

Distributions
Income: quarterly   Capital Gains: Jun, Dec

Exchange Options
Number Per Year: 4   Fee: none
Telephone: yes (money market fund available)

Services
IRA, other pension, auto exchange, auto invest, auto withdraw

IAI Emerging Growth
(IAEGX)
Aggressive Growth

3700 First Bank Place
P.O. Box 357
Minneapolis, MN 55440
(800) 945-3863, (612) 376-2700

PERFORMANCE

	3yr Annual	5yr Annual	10yr Annual	Bull	Bear
Return (%)	na	na	na	na	na
Differ from Category (+/-)	na	na	na	na	na

Total Risk	Standard Deviation	Category Risk	Risk Index	Beta
na	na	na	na	na

	1993	1992	1991	1990	1989	1988	1987	1986	1985	1984
Return (%)	14.7	22.4	—	—	—	—	—	—	—	—
Differ from category (+/-). . .	-4.3	12.0	—	—	—	—	—	—	—	—

PER SHARE DATA

	1993	1992	1991	1990	1989	1988	1987	1986	1985	1984
Dividends, Net Income ($) .	0.00	0.00	—	—	—	—	—	—	—	—
Distrib'ns, Cap Gain ($) . . .	0.34	0.75	—	—	—	—	—	—	—	—
Net Asset Value ($)	15.74	14.03	—	—	—	—	—	—	—	—
Expense Ratio (%)	1.25	1.25	—	—	—	—	—	—	—	—
Net Income to Assets (%) .	-0.72	0.14	—	—	—	—	—	—	—	—
Portfolio Turnover (%).	96	127	—	—	—	—	—	—	—	—
Total Assets (Millions $). . . .	212	38	—	—	—	—	—	—	—	—

PORTFOLIO (as of 9/30/93)

Portfolio Manager: Rick Leggott - 1991

Investm't Category: Aggressive Growth
- ✔ Cap Gain
- Cap & Income
- Income
- Asset Allocation
- Fund of Funds
- Index
- Sector
- ✔ Domestic
- ✔ Foreign
- Country/Region
- ✔ Small Cap
- Socially Conscious
- State Specific

Portfolio:
stocks 84%   bonds 0%
convertibles 0%   other 0%   cash 16%

Largest Holdings: electronics & information 16%, merchandising 16%

Unrealized Net Capital Gains: 19% of portfolio value

SHAREHOLDER INFORMATION

Minimum Investment
Initial: $5,000   Subsequent: $100

Minimum IRA Investment
Initial: $2,000   Subsequent: $100

Maximum Fees
Load: none   12b-1: 0.25%
Other: none

Distributions
Income: Jun, Dec   Capital Gains: Jun, Dec

Exchange Options
Number Per Year: 4   Fee: none
Telephone: yes (money market fund available)

Services
IRA, other pension, auto exchange, auto invest, auto withdraw

IAI Gov't (IAGVX)

Government Bond

3700 First Bank Place
P.O. Box 357
Minneapolis, MN 55440
(800) 945-3863, (612) 376-2700

PERFORMANCE

	3yr Annual	5yr Annual	10yr Annual	Bull	Bear
Return (%)	na	na	na	na	na
Differ from Category (+/-)	na	na	na	na	na

Total Risk	Standard Deviation	Category Risk	Risk Index	Avg Mat
na	na	na	na	5.3 yrs

	1993	1992	1991	1990	1989	1988	1987	1986	1985	1984
Return (%)	8.5	5.6	—	—	—	—	—	—	—	—
Differ from category (+/-)	-1.9	-0.6	—	—	—	—	—	—	—	—

PER SHARE DATA

	1993	1992	1991	1990	1989	1988	1987	1986	1985	1984
Dividends, Net Income ($)	0.55	0.58	—	—	—	—	—	—	—	—
Distrib'ns, Cap Gain ($)	0.21	0.34	—	—	—	—	—	—	—	—
Net Asset Value ($)	10.33	10.23	—	—	—	—	—	—	—	—
Expense Ratio (%)	1.10	1.10	—	—	—	—	—	—	—	—
Net Income to Assets (%)	5.40	5.16	—	—	—	—	—	—	—	—
Portfolio Turnover (%)	236	170	—	—	—	—	—	—	—	—
Total Assets (Millions $)	41	31	—	—	—	—	—	—	—	—

PORTFOLIO (as of 9/30/93)

Portfolio Manager: Scott Bettin - 1991

Investm't Category: Government Bond
Cap Gain	Asset Allocation
Cap & Income	Fund of Funds
✔ Income	Index
	Sector
✔ Domestic	Small Cap
Foreign	Socially Conscious
Country/Region	State Specific

Portfolio: stocks 0%   bonds 100%
convertibles 0%   other 0%   cash 0%

Largest Holdings: mortgage-backed 48%, U.S. government 46%

Unrealized Net Capital Gains: 0% of portfolio value

SHAREHOLDER INFORMATION

Minimum Investment
Initial: $5,000   Subsequent: $100

Minimum IRA Investment
Initial: $2,000   Subsequent: $100

Maximum Fees
Load: none   12b-1: 0.25%
Other: none

Distributions
Income: quarterly   Capital Gains: Jun, Dec

Exchange Options
Number Per Year: 4   Fee: none
Telephone: yes (money market fund available)

Services
IRA, other pension, auto exchange, auto invest, auto withdraw

IAI Growth & Income

(IASKX)

Growth

3700 First Bank Place
P.O. Box 357
Minneapolis, MN 55440
(800) 945-3863, (612) 376-2700

PERFORMANCE

	3yr Annual	5yr Annual	10yr Annual	Bull	Bear
Return (%)	13.1	11.8	12.1	50.8	-10.4
Differ from Category (+/-)	-6.1 low	-2.8 low	-0.5 blw av	-33.9 low	2.0 av

Total Risk	Standard Deviation	Category Risk	Risk Index	Beta
av	10.5%	blw av	1.0	0.8

	1993	1992	1991	1990	1989	1988	1987	1986	1985	1984
Return (%)	9.9	3.9	26.7	-6.8	29.6	8.3	15.5	13.1	23.7	2.8
Differ from category (+/-) . . .	-3.3	-7.1	-8.7	-0.6	3.8	-9.4	14.3	-1.4	-5.6	2.8

PER SHARE DATA

	1993	1992	1991	1990	1989	1988	1987	1986	1985	1984
Dividends, Net Income ($) .	0.06	0.08	0.15	0.28	0.42	0.22	0.37	0.37	0.47	0.41
Distrib'ns, Cap Gain ($) . . .	1.68	0.68	0.94	1.69	2.76	1.10	1.34	1.80	0.46	1.39
Net Asset Value ($)	14.51	14.85	15.10	12.84	15.79	14.70	14.79	14.25	14.54	12.64
Expense Ratio (%)	1.25	1.25	1.05	1.00	0.90	0.80	0.80	0.70	0.70	0.69
Net Income to Assets (%) .	0.61	1.03	2.19	2.10	1.80	1.70	2.10	2.90	3.90	3.00
Portfolio Turnover (%)	175	210	69	66	48	36	68	50	62	69
Total Assets (Millions $)	123	113	91	77	77	83	84	69	60	48

PORTFOLIO (as of 9/30/93)

Portfolio Manager: Julian Carlin - 1991

Investm't Category: Growth

✔ Cap Gain   Asset Allocation
  Cap & Income   Fund of Funds
  Income   Index
    Sector
✔ Domestic   Small Cap
✔ Foreign   Socially Conscious
  Country/Region   State Specific

Portfolio:	stocks 76%	bonds 6%
convertibles 0%	other 6%	cash 12%

Largest Holdings: electronics & information 12%, utilities 11%

Unrealized Net Capital Gains: 10% of portfolio value

SHAREHOLDER INFORMATION

Minimum Investment
Initial: $5,000   Subsequent: $100

Minimum IRA Investment
Initial: $2,000   Subsequent: $100

Maximum Fees
Load: none   12b-1: 0.25%
Other: none

Distributions
Income: Jun, Dec   Capital Gains: Jun, Dec

Exchange Options
Number Per Year: 4   Fee: none
Telephone: yes (money market fund available)

Services
IRA, other pension, auto exchange, auto invest, auto withdraw

IAI International (IAINX)

International Stock

3700 First Bank Place
P.O. Box 357
Minneapolis, MN 55440
(800) 945-3863, (612) 376-2700

PERFORMANCE

	3yr Annual	5yr Annual	10yr Annual	Bull	Bear
Return (%)	15.0	9.4	na	60.0	-17.2
Differ from Category (+/-)	0.6 abv av	0.6 av	na	4.9 abv av	-2.1 blw av

Total Risk	Standard Deviation	Category Risk	Risk Index	Beta
abv av	12.8%	av	1.1	0.5

	1993	1992	1991	1990	1989	1988	1987	1986	1985	1984
Return (%)	39.4	-6.3	16.5	-13.0	18.3	18.0	—	—	—	—
Differ from category (+/-) . . .	0.8	-2.8	3.6	-1.9	-3.9	4.2	—	—	—	—

PER SHARE DATA

	1993	1992	1991	1990	1989	1988	1987	1986	1985	1984
Dividends, Net Income ($) .	0.34	0.03	0.21	0.00	0.29	0.10	—	—	—	—
Distrib'ns, Cap Gain ($) . . .	0.04	0.41	0.33	0.14	0.63	0.00	—	—	—	—
Net Asset Value ($)	13.61	10.08	11.22	10.15	11.84	10.85	—	—	—	—
Expense Ratio (%).	1.91	2.00	1.73	1.90	2.10	2.13	—	—	—	—
Net Income to Assets (%). .	1.42	1.39	2.79	1.00	1.20	-0.16	—	—	—	—
Portfolio Turnover (%)	28	35	41	33	71	53	—	—	—	—
Total Assets (Millions $) . . .	122	36	34	30	16	12	—	—	—	—

PORTFOLIO (as of 9/30/93)

Portfolio Manager: Roy Gillson - 1990

Investm't Category: International Stock

✔ Cap Gain	Asset Allocation
Cap & Income	Fund of Funds
Income	Index
	Sector
Domestic	Small Cap
✔ Foreign	Socially Conscious
Country/Region	State Specific

Portfolio: stocks 97% bonds 0%
convertibles 0% other 0% cash 3%

Largest Holdings: Japan 20%, United Kingdom 15%

Unrealized Net Capital Gains: 9% of portfolio value

SHAREHOLDER INFORMATION

Minimum Investment
Initial: $5,000   Subsequent: $100

Minimum IRA Investment
Initial: $2,000   Subsequent: $100

Maximum Fees
Load: none   12b-1: 0.25%
Other: none

Distributions
Income: Jun, Dec   Capital Gains: Jun, Dec

Exchange Options
Number Per Year: 4   Fee: none
Telephone: yes (money market fund available)

Services
IRA, other pension, auto exchange, auto invest, auto withdraw

IAI MidCap Growth

(IAMCX)

Growth

3700 First Bank Place
P.O. Box 357
Minneapolis, MN 55440
(800) 945-3863, (612) 376-2700

PERFORMANCE

	3yr Annual	5yr Annual	10yr Annual	Bull	Bear
Return (%)	na	na	na	na	na
Differ from Category (+/-)	na	na	na	na	na

Total Risk	Standard Deviation	Category Risk	Risk Index	Beta
na	na	na	na	na

	1993	1992	1991	1990	1989	1988	1987	1986	1985	1984
Return (%)	22.8	—	—	—	—	—	—	—	—	—
Differ from category (+/-) . . .	9.6	—	—	—	—	—	—	—	—	—

PER SHARE DATA

	1993	1992	1991	1990	1989	1988	1987	1986	1985	1984
Dividends, Net Income ($) .	0.00	—	—	—	—	—	—	—	—	—
Distrib'ns, Cap Gain ($) . . .	0.15	—	—	—	—	—	—	—	—	—
Net Asset Value ($)	13.93	—	—	—	—	—	—	—	—	—
Expense Ratio (%)	1.25	—	—	—	—	—	—	—	—	—
Net Income to Assets (%) .	0.24	—	—	—	—	—	—	—	—	—
Portfolio Turnover (%)	57	—	—	—	—	—	—	—	—	—
Total Assets (Millions $)	41	—	—	—	—	—	—	—	—	—

PORTFOLIO (as of 9/30/93)

Portfolio Manager: Susan Zak - 1993

Investm't Category: Growth

✔ Cap Gain	Asset Allocation
Cap & Income	Fund of Funds
Income	Index
	Sector
✔ Domestic	Small Cap
✔ Foreign	Socially Conscious
Country/Region	State Specific

Portfolio: stocks 91% bonds 0%
convertibles 0% other 2% cash 7%

Largest Holdings: electronics & information 9%, leisure & entertainment 9%

Unrealized Net Capital Gains: 14% of portfolio value

SHAREHOLDER INFORMATION

Minimum Investment
Initial: $5,000   Subsequent: $100

Minimum IRA Investment
Initial: $2,000   Subsequent: $100

Maximum Fees
Load: none   12b-1: 0.25%
Other: none

Distributions
Income: Jun, Dec   Capital Gains: Jun, Dec

Exchange Options
Number Per Year: 4   Fee: none
Telephone: yes (money market fund available)

Services
IRA, other pension, auto exchange, auto invest, auto withdraw

IAI Regional (IARGX)

Growth

3700 First Bank Place
P.O. Box 357
Minneapolis, MN 55440
(800) 945-3863, (612) 376-2700

PERFORMANCE

	3yr Annual	5yr Annual	10yr Annual	Bull	Bear
Return (%)	15.1	14.8	15.4	64.0	-7.3
Differ from Category (+/-)	-4.1 blw av	0.2 av	2.8 high	-20.7 blw av	5.1 abv av

Total Risk	Standard Deviation	Category Risk	Risk Index	Beta
av	10.2%	low	0.9	0.8

	1993	1992	1991	1990	1989	1988	1987	1986	1985	1984
Return (%)	8.9	3.5	35.3	-0.3	31.1	18.7	5.1	24.6	38.8	-2.4
Differ from category (+/-) ..	-4.3	-7.5	-0.1	5.8	5.3	1.0	3.9	10.1	9.5	-2.4

PER SHARE DATA

	1993	1992	1991	1990	1989	1988	1987	1986	1985	1984
Dividends, Net Income ($) .	0.17	0.22	0.24	0.33	0.50	0.27	0.39	0.41	0.42	0.47
Distrib'ns, Cap Gain ($) ...	1.82	0.51	2.07	0.82	3.97	0.56	3.21	6.44	0.40	1.11
Net Asset Value ($)	21.45	21.58	21.62	17.79	18.98	17.99	15.86	18.42	20.53	15.51
Expense Ratio (%)........	1.25	1.25	1.01	1.00	1.00	0.80	0.80	0.80	0.90	1.00
Net Income to Assets (%)..	1.09	1.20	2.27	2.30	2.00	1.60	1.80	3.00	2.60	3.10
Portfolio Turnover (%)	139	141	169	116	94	85	133	80	77	116
Total Assets (Millions $) ...	616	529	284	138	102	86	102	56	44	38

PORTFOLIO (as of 9/30/93)

Portfolio Manager: Julian Carlin - 1980

Investm't Category: Growth

✔ Cap Gain	Asset Allocation
Cap & Income	Fund of Funds
Income	Index
	Sector
✔ Domestic	Small Cap
Foreign	Socially Conscious
Country/Region	State Specific

Portfolio: stocks 78%   bonds 0%
convertibles 0%   other 3%   cash 19%

Largest Holdings: consumer goods 12%, utilities 10%

Unrealized Net Capital Gains: 10% of portfolio value

SHAREHOLDER INFORMATION

Minimum Investment
Initial: $5,000   Subsequent: $100

Minimum IRA Investment
Initial: $2,000   Subsequent: $100

Maximum Fees
Load: none   12b-1: 0.25%
Other: none

Distributions
Income: Jun, Dec   Capital Gains: Jun, Dec

Exchange Options
Number Per Year: 4   Fee: none
Telephone: yes (money market fund available)

Services
IRA, other pension, auto exchange, auto invest, auto withdraw

IAI Reserve (IARVX)

General Bond

3700 First Bank Place
P.O. Box 357
Minneapolis, MN 55440
(800) 945-3863, (612) 376-2700

PERFORMANCE

	3yr Annual	5yr Annual	10yr Annual	Bull	Bear
Return (%)	4.8	6.3	na	17.9	5.8
Differ from Category (+/-)	-5.4 low	-3.5 low	na	-21.5 low	2.9 high

Total Risk	Standard Deviation	Category Risk	Risk Index	Avg Mat
low	69%	low	0.2	1.0 yrs

	1993	1992	1991	1990	1989	1988	1987	1986	1985	1984
Return (%).	3.3	3.2	7.9	8.3	8.7	6.7	5.8	—	—	—
Differ from category (+/-). . .	-5.9	-3.5	-6.7	1.4	-2.6	-0.8	3.3	—	—	—

PER SHARE DATA

	1993	1992	1991	1990	1989	1988	1987	1986	1985	1984
Dividends, Net Income ($).	0.37	0.39	0.59	0.79	0.78	0.69	0.69	—	—	—
Distrib'ns, Cap Gain ($) . . .	0.01	0.08	0.07	0.00	0.00	0.00	0.00	—	—	—
Net Asset Value ($)	10.04	10.09	10.24	10.13	10.11	10.04	10.07	—	—	—
Expense Ratio (%)	0.85	0.85	0.85	0.85	0.80	0.80	0.80	—	—	—
Net Income to Assets (%) .	3.49	5.63	7.09	7.90	7.20	5.90	5.60	—	—	—
Portfolio Turnover (%).	538	218	87	63	64	0	30	—	—	—
Total Assets (Millions $). . . .	100	108	104	79	66	68	35	—	—	—

PORTFOLIO (as of 9/30/93)

Portfolio Manager: Timothy Palmer - 1991

Investm't Category: General Bond

Cap Gain	Asset Allocation
Cap & Income	Fund of Funds
✔ Income	Index
	Sector
✔ Domestic	Small Cap
✔ Foreign	Socially Conscious
Country/Region	State Specific

Portfolio: stocks 0%   bonds 100%
convertibles 0%   other 0%   cash 0%

Largest Holdings: corporate 35%, commercial paper 32%

Unrealized Net Capital Gains: 0% of portfolio value

SHAREHOLDER INFORMATION

Minimum Investment
Initial: $5,000   Subsequent: $100

Minimum IRA Investment
Initial: $2,000   Subsequent: $100

Maximum Fees
Load: none   12b-1: 0.10%
Other: none

Distributions
Income: monthly   Capital Gains: Dec

Exchange Options
Number Per Year: 4   Fee: none
Telephone: yes (money market fund available)

Services
IRA, other pension, auto exchange, auto invest, auto withdraw

IAI Value (IAAPX)

Growth

3700 First Bank Place
P.O. Box 357
Minneapolis, MN 55440
(800) 945-3863, (612) 376-2700

PERFORMANCE

	3yr Annual	5yr Annual	10yr Annual	Bull	Bear
Return (%)	17.8	12.0	10.5	74.2	-17.0
Differ from Category (+/-)	-1.4 av	-2.6 blw av	-2.1 low	-10.5 blw av	-4.6 blw av

Total Risk	Standard Deviation	Category Risk	Risk Index	Beta
abv av	11.9%	av	1.1	0.8

	1993	1992	1991	1990	1989	1988	1987	1986	1985	1984
Return (%)	22.0	11.9	19.7	-11.6	22.5	24.3	14.1	1.9	12.9	-5.5
Differ from category (+/-) ...	8.8	0.8	-15.7	-5.5	-3.3	6.6	12.9	-12.6	-16.4	-5.5

PER SHARE DATA

	1993	1992	1991	1990	1989	1988	1987	1986	1985	1984
Dividends, Net Income ($) .	0.13	0.00	0.15	0.17	0.17	0.09	0.16	0.18	0.20	0.21
Distrib'ns, Cap Gain ($) ...	1.36	0.10	0.44	2.24	1.97	0.08	1.67	0.30	0.19	0.14
Net Asset Value ($)	12.11	11.18	10.09	8.94	12.60	12.08	9.87	10.18	10.45	9.65
Expense Ratio (%)........	1.25	1.25	1.10	1.00	1.00	1.00	1.00	1.00	1.00	1.00
Net Income to Assets (%)..	0.68	1.24	2.00	1.30	1.00	1.00	1.30	2.10	2.60	2.90
Portfolio Turnover (%)....	118	125	57	70	53	63	86	85	35	20
Total Assets (Millions $)	30	32	22	26	28	21	22	24	18	12

PORTFOLIO (as of 9/30/93)

Portfolio Manager: Doug Platt - 1991

Investm't Category: Growth

✔ Cap Gain	Asset Allocation
Cap & Income	Fund of Funds
Income	Index
	Sector
✔ Domestic	Small Cap
✔ Foreign	Socially Conscious
Country/Region	State Specific

Portfolio:	stocks 80%	bonds 0%
convertibles 0%	other 7%	cash 13%

Largest Holdings: merchandising 17%, consumer goods 15%

Unrealized Net Capital Gains: 9% of portfolio value

SHAREHOLDER INFORMATION

Minimum Investment
Initial: $5,000   Subsequent: $100

Minimum IRA Investment
Initial: $2,000   Subsequent: $100

Maximum Fees
Load: none   12b-1: 0.25%
Other: none

Distributions
Income: Jun, Dec   Capital Gains: Jun

Exchange Options
Number Per Year: 4   Fee: none
Telephone: yes (money market fund available)

Services
IRA, other pension, auto exchange, auto invest, auto withdraw

International Equity
(SCIEX)

International Stock

787 Seventh Ave.
New York, NY 10019
(800) 344-8332, (212) 841-3841

	3yr Annual	5yr Annual	10yr Annual	Bull	Bear
Return (%)	13.5	9.6	na	56.6	-17.2
Differ from Category (+/-)	-0.8 av	0.8 av	na	1.5 abv av	-2.1 blw av

Total Risk	Standard Deviation	Category Risk	Risk Index	Beta
abv av	13.7%	abv av	1.1	0.4

	1993	1992	1991	1990	1989	1988	1987	1986	1985	1984
Return (%)	45.7	-4.0	4.5	-11.3	22.1	19.4	3.7	49.6	—	—
Differ from category (+/-). . .	7.2	-0.5	-8.4	-0.2	-0.1	5.6	-8.3	-0.6	—	—

PER SHARE DATA

	1993	1992	1991	1990	1989	1988	1987	1986	1985	1984
Dividends, Net Income ($).	0.07	0.11	0.23	0.25	0.44	0.03	0.00	0.01	—	—
Distrib'ns, Cap Gain ($) . . .	0.00	0.00	0.05	1.23	0.08	0.04	1.33	0.67	—	—
Net Asset Value ($)	21.94	15.11	15.86	15.44	19.10	16.07	13.52	14.37	—	—
Expense Ratio (%)	0.96	0.93	1.07	1.12	1.12	1.30	1.64	2.47	—	—
Net Income to Assets (%) .	0.84	1.62	1.59	0.83	1.27	0.38	0.42	-0.12	—	—
Portfolio Turnover (%).	65	49	51	56	72	86	85	77	—	—
Total Assets (Millions $). . . .	363	160	108	62	49	30	33	9	—	—

PORTFOLIO (as of 4/30/93)

Portfolio Manager: Mark J. Smith - 1989

Investm't Category: International Stock
- ✔ Cap Gain
- Cap & Income
- Income
- Domestic
- ✔ Foreign
- Country/Region
- Asset Allocation
- Fund of Funds
- Index
- Sector
- Small Cap
- Socially Conscious
- State Specific

Portfolio: stocks 100% bonds 0%
convertibles 0% other 0% cash 0%

Largest Holdings: Japan 28%, United Kingdom 17%

Unrealized Net Capital Gains: 12% of portfolio value

SHAREHOLDER INFORMATION

Minimum Investment
Initial: $2,500   Subsequent: $100

Minimum IRA Investment
Initial: $250   Subsequent: $100

Maximum Fees
Load: none   12b-1: 0.50%
Other: none

Distributions
Income: Dec   Capital Gains: Dec

Exchange Options
Number Per Year: none   Fee: na
Telephone: na

Services
IRA

INVESCO Dynamics
(FIDYX)
Aggressive Growth

P.O. Box 173706
Denver, CO 80217
(800) 525-8085, (303) 930-6300

PERFORMANCE

	3yr Annual	5yr Annual	10yr Annual	Bull	Bear
Return (%)	31.0	20.9	13.2	141.8	-12.8
Differ from Category (+/-)	5.6 abv av	2.7 abv av	1.3 abv av	16.8 abv av	2.2 av

Total Risk	Standard Deviation	Category Risk	Risk Index	Beta
high	17.8%	abv av	1.2	1.2

	1993	1992	1991	1990	1989	1988	1987	1986	1985	1984
Return (%)	19.0	13.1	66.9	-6.3	22.6	9.1	3.7	6.4	29.1	-13.8
Differ from category (+/-) . . .	0.0	2.7	14.5	0.0	-4.4	-6.1	7.1	-3.0	-1.9	-4.4

PER SHARE DATA

	1993	1992	1991	1990	1989	1988	1987	1986	1985	1984
Dividends, Net Income ($) .	0.00	0.00	0.00	0.11	0.11	0.08	0.02	0.05	0.09	0.15
Distrib'ns, Cap Gain ($) . . .	0.80	0.28	1.20	0.00	0.28	0.00	1.36	2.09	0.00	1.38
Net Asset Value ($)	12.83	11.50	10.47	7.09	7.70	6.61	6.14	7.06	8.56	6.71
Expense Ratio (%)	1.20	1.18	1.15	0.98	0.98	1.02	0.92	0.90	0.78	0.66
Net Income to Assets (%) .	-0.38	-0.17	0.59	1.47	1.77	0.28	0.27	0.63	1.30	1.44
Portfolio Turnover (%)	144	174	243	225	237	199	234	246	152	56
Total Assets (Millions $) . . .	311	154	101	61	90	84	91	87	73	66

PORTFOLIO (as of 4/30/93)

Portfolio Manager: Tim Miller - 1993

Investm't Category: Aggressive Growth
- ✔ Cap Gain
-   Cap & Income
-   Income
-   Asset Allocation
-   Fund of Funds
-   Index
-   Sector
- ✔ Domestic
-   Foreign
-   Country/Region
-   Small Cap
-   Socially Conscious
-   State Specific

Portfolio: stocks 70% bonds 0%
convertibles 0% other 0% cash 30%

Largest Holdings: retail 12%, computer networks 6%

Unrealized Net Capital Gains: 14% of portfolio value

SHAREHOLDER INFORMATION

Minimum Investment
Initial: $1,000   Subsequent: $50

Minimum IRA Investment
Initial: $250   Subsequent: $50

Maximum Fees
Load: none   12b-1: 0.25%
Other: none

Distributions
Income: Apr, Dec   Capital Gains: Apr, Dec

Exchange Options
Number Per Year: 4   Fee: none
Telephone: yes (money market fund available)

Services
IRA, other pension, auto exchange, auto invest, auto withdraw

INVESCO Emerging Growth (FIEGX)

Aggressive Growth

P.O. Box 173706
Denver, CO 80217
(800) 525-8085, (303) 930-6300

PERFORMANCE

	3yr Annual	5yr Annual	10yr Annual	Bull	Bear
Return (%)	na	na	na	na	na
Differ from Category (+/-)	na	na	na	na	na

Total Risk	Standard Deviation	Category Risk	Risk Index	Beta
na	na	na	na	na

	1993	1992	1991	1990	1989	1988	1987	1986	1985	1984
Return (%).	23.4	25.7	—	—	—	—	—	—	—	—
Differ from category (+/-). . .	4.4	15.3	—	—	—	—	—	—	—	—

PER SHARE DATA

	1993	1992	1991	1990	1989	1988	1987	1986	1985	1984
Dividends, Net Income ($).	0.00	0.00	—	—	—	—	—	—	—	—
Distrib'ns, Cap Gain ($) . . .	0.00	0.00	—	—	—	—	—	—	—	—
Net Asset Value ($)	12.11	9.82	—	—	—	—	—	—	—	—
Expense Ratio (%)	1.54	1.93	—	—	—	—	—	—	—	—
Net Income to Assets (%) .	-0.70	-0.95	—	—	—	—	—	—	—	—
Portfolio Turnover (%).	153	50	—	—	—	—	—	—	—	—
Total Assets (Millions $). . . .	218	26	—	—	—	—	—	—	—	—

PORTFOLIO (as of 12/30/93)

Portfolio Manager: Doug Pratt - 1993

Investm't Category: Aggressive Growth

✔ Cap Gain	Asset Allocation
Cap & Income	Fund of Funds
Income	Index
	Sector
✔ Domestic	✔ Small Cap
✔ Foreign	Socially Conscious
Country/Region	State Specific

Portfolio: stocks 88% bonds 0%
convertibles 0% other 0% cash 12%

Largest Holdings: retail 14%, electronics 9%

Unrealized Net Capital Gains: 13% of portfolio value

SHAREHOLDER INFORMATION

Minimum Investment
Initial: $1,000   Subsequent: $50

Minimum IRA Investment
Initial: $250   Subsequent: $50

Maximum Fees
Load: none   12b-1: 0.25%
Other: none

Distributions
Income: May   Capital Gains: May, Dec

Exchange Options
Number Per Year: 4   Fee: none
Telephone: yes (money market fund available)

Services
IRA, other pension, auto exchange, auto invest, auto withdraw

INVESCO Growth

(FLRFX)

Growth

P.O. Box 173706
Denver, CO 80217
(800) 525-8085, (303) 930-6300

PERFORMANCE

	3yr Annual	5yr Annual	10yr Annual	Bull	Bear
Return (%)	19.9	17.4	12.5	84.3	-7.5
Differ from Category (+/-)	0.6 av	2.8 high	-0.1 av	-0.4 av	4.9 abv av

Total Risk	Standard Deviation	Category Risk	Risk Index	Beta
abv av	13.6%	abv av	1.3	1.1

	1993	1992	1991	1990	1989	1988	1987	1986	1985	1984
Return (%)	17.9	2.9	42.0	-1.1	31.2	5.8	0.0	8.1	28.4	-1.1
Differ from category (+/-) ...	4.7	-8.1	6.6	5.0	5.4	-11.9	-1.2	-6.4	-0.8	-1.1

PER SHARE DATA

	1993	1992	1991	1990	1989	1988	1987	1986	1985	1984
Dividends, Net Income ($) .	0.03	0.04	0.07	0.10	0.10	0.07	0.07	0.10	0.14	0.15
Distrib'ns, Cap Gain ($) ...	0.44	0.54	0.47	0.02	0.00	0.00	0.63	1.02	0.45	0.03
Net Asset Value ($)	5.54	5.12	5.59	4.36	4.55	3.55	3.42	3.96	4.66	4.16
Expense Ratio (%)........	1.04	1.04	1.00	0.78	0.82	0.81	0.77	0.71	0.68	0.64
Net Income to Assets (%) ..	0.72	0.93	1.52	2.17	2.60	1.84	1.56	4.85	5.72	5.92
Portfolio Turnover (%).....	77	77	69	86	90	116	250	160	54	54
Total Assets (Millions $) ...	510	408	428	340	383	328	481	341	249	182

PORTFOLIO (as of 8/31/93)

Portfolio Manager: R. Dalton Sim - 1987

Investm't Category: Growth

✔ Cap Gain	Asset Allocation
Cap & Income	Fund of Funds
Income	Index
	Sector
✔ Domestic	Small Cap
Foreign	Socially Conscious
Country/Region	State Specific

Portfolio:	stocks 91%	bonds 0%
convertibles 0%	other 0%	cash 9%

Largest Holdings: utilities 10%, finance related 8%

Unrealized Net Capital Gains: 20% of portfolio value

SHAREHOLDER INFORMATION

Minimum Investment
Initial: $1,000   Subsequent: $50

Minimum IRA Investment
Initial: $250   Subsequent: $50

Maximum Fees
Load: none   12b-1: 0.25%
Other: none

Distributions
Income: quarterly   Capital Gains: Aug, Nov

Exchange Options
Number Per Year: 4   Fee: none
Telephone: yes (money market fund available)

Services
IRA, other pension, auto exchange, auto invest, auto withdraw

INVESCO Income— High Yield (FHYPX)

Corporate High-Yield Bond

P.O. Box 173706
Denver, CO 80217
(800) 525-8085, (303) 930-6300

PERFORMANCE

	3yr Annual	5yr Annual	10yr Annual	Bull	Bear
Return (%)	17.8	10.1	na	63.7	-4.6
Differ from Category (+/-)	-2.7 blw av	-0.6 blw av	na	-11.2 blw av	-1.3 abv av

Total Risk	Standard Deviation	Category Risk	Risk Index	Avg Mat
low	3.3%	low	0.9	9.2 yrs

	1993	1992	1991	1990	1989	1988	1987	1986	1985	1984
Return (%)	15.6	14.5	23.4	-4.5	3.6	13.4	3.6	14.5	26.5	—
Differ from category (+/-). . .	-3.6	-1.3	-3.9	-0.3	2.3	1.1	2.6	-0.6	3.0	—

PER SHARE DATA

	1993	1992	1991	1990	1989	1988	1987	1986	1985	1984
Dividends, Net Income ($) .	0.59	0.62	0.68	0.84	0.95	0.93	0.94	1.01	1.03	—
Distrib'ns, Cap Gain ($) . . .	0.00	0.00	0.00	0.00	0.00	0.00	0.00	0.17	0.00	—
Net Asset Value ($)	7.43	6.97	6.66	6.00	7.16	7.82	7.75	8.38	8.37	—
Expense Ratio (%)	0.97	1.00	1.05	0.93	0.83	0.82	0.86	0.76	0.93	—
Net Income to Assets (%) .	8.28	9.29	10.57	12.57	12.27	11.72	11.22	11.35	12.97	—
Portfolio Turnover (%).	68	120	64	28	53	42	89	134	96	—
Total Assets (Millions $). . . .	294	212	99	40	49	61	38	46	18	—

PORTFOLIO (as of 8/31/93)

Portfolio Manager: William Veronda - 1984

Investm't Category: Corp. High-Yield Bond

Cap Gain	Asset Allocation
✔ Cap & Income	Fund of Funds
Income	Index
	Sector
✔ Domestic	Small Cap
Foreign	Socially Conscious
Country/Region	State Specific

Portfolio: stocks 0% bonds 97%
convertibles 0% other 0% cash 3%

Largest Holdings: retail 11%, manufacturing 11%

Unrealized Net Capital Gains: 3% of portfolio value

SHAREHOLDER INFORMATION

Minimum Investment
Initial: $1,000   Subsequent: $50

Minimum IRA Investment
Initial: $250   Subsequent: $50

Maximum Fees
Load: none   12b-1: 0.25%
Other: none

Distributions
Income: monthly   Capital Gains: Dec

Exchange Options
Number Per Year: 4   Fee: none
Telephone: yes (money market fund available)

Services
IRA, other pension, auto exchange, auto invest, auto withdraw

INVESCO Income—
Select Income (FBDSX)

P.O. Box 173706
Denver, CO 80217
(800) 525-8085, (303) 930-6300

Corporate Bond

PERFORMANCE

	3yr Annual	5yr Annual	10yr Annual	Bull	Bear
Return (%)	13.3	10.5	10.6	50.9	1.3
Differ from Category (+/-)	1.3 abv av	0.4 abv av	-0.4 av	4.8 abv av	-0.5 blw av

Total Risk	Standard Deviation	Category Risk	Risk Index	Avg Mat
low	2.6%	av	0.9	12.2 yrs

	1993	1992	1991	1990	1989	1988	1987	1986	1985	1984
Return (%)	11.3	10.4	18.6	4.9	8.1	10.3	-1.5	18.8	22.6	5.2
Differ from category (+/-) . .	-0.1	1.8	2.0	-0.4	-1.4	1.3	-3.3	4.1	2.9	-5.9

PER SHARE DATA

	1993	1992	1991	1990	1989	1988	1987	1986	1985	1984
Dividends, Net Income ($) .	0.49	0.52	0.52	0.58	0.62	0.60	0.63	0.68	0.72	0.73
Distrib'ns, Cap Gain ($) . . .	0.18	0.09	0.00	0.00	0.00	0.00	0.00	0.31	0.00	0.00
Net Asset Value ($)	6.57	6.53	6.50	5.96	6.26	6.39	6.36	7.10	6.84	6.22
Expense Ratio (%).	1.15	1.14	1.15	1.01	0.99	1.00	0.99	0.85	0.97	0.23
Net Income to Assets (%) . .	7.40	7.97	8.57	9.67	9.92	9.47	9.36	9.19	11.10	11.74
Portfolio Turnover (%)	157	178	117	38	121	143	131	153	146	188
Total Assets (Millions $) . . .	155	123	94	46	33	30	20	24	15	8

PORTFOLIO (as of 8/31/93)

Portfolio Manager: Ron Lout - 1990

Investm't Category: Corporate Bond

Cap Gain	Asset Allocation
Cap & Income	Fund of Funds
✔ Income	Index
	Sector
✔ Domestic	Small Cap
Foreign	Socially Conscious
Country/Region	State Specific

Portfolio: stocks 0%   bonds 100%
convertibles 0%   other 0%   cash 0%

Largest Holdings: utilities 16%, mortgage-backed 16%

Unrealized Net Capital Gains: 2% of portfolio value

SHAREHOLDER INFORMATION

Minimum Investment
Initial: $1,000   Subsequent: $50

Minimum IRA Investment
Initial: $250   Subsequent: $50

Maximum Fees
Load: none   12b-1: 0.25%
Other: none

Distributions
Income: monthly   Capital Gains: Dec

Exchange Options
Number Per Year: 4   Fee: none
Telephone: yes (money market fund available)

Services
IRA, other pension, auto exchange, auto invest, auto withdraw

INVESCO Income—US Gov't Sec (FBDGX)

Government Bond

P.O. Box 173706
Denver, CO 80217
(800) 525-8085, (303) 930-6300

PERFORMANCE

	3yr Annual	5yr Annual	10yr Annual	Bull	Bear
Return (%)	10.4	10.1	na	43.9	0.3
Differ from Category (+/-)	-0.4 av	-0.3 av	na	-2.3 abv av	-0.2 blw av

Total Risk	Standard Deviation	Category Risk	Risk Index	Avg Mat
blw av	5.2%	av	1.2	23.1 yrs

	1993	1992	1991	1990	1989	1988	1987	1986	1985	1984
Return (%)	10.2	5.7	15.5	7.2	12.4	6.1	-5.0	14.2	—	—
Differ from category (+/-). . .	-0.2	-0.5	0.5	0.6	-1.5	-1.5	-3.2	-4.9	—	—

PER SHARE DATA

	1993	1992	1991	1990	1989	1988	1987	1986	1985	1984
Dividends, Net Income ($).	0.42	0.45	0.49	0.53	0.55	0.52	0.52	0.61	—	—
Distrib'ns, Cap Gain ($) . . .	0.15	0.00	0.00	0.00	0.00	0.00	0.00	0.02	—	—
Net Asset Value ($)	7.79	7.61	7.65	7.08	7.14	6.87	6.98	7.90	—	—
Expense Ratio (%)	1.40	1.27	1.27	1.07	1.04	1.19	1.29	0.74	—	—
Net Income to Assets (%) .	5.36	6.08	6.78	7.58	7.98	7.75	7.06	7.53	—	—
Portfolio Turnover (%).	149	115	67	38	159	221	284	61	—	—
Total Assets (Millions $). . . .	35	36	29	21	19	9	8	7	—	—

PORTFOLIO (as of 8/31/93)

Portfolio Manager: Ron Lout - 1988

Investm't Category: Government Bond

Cap Gain	Asset Allocation
Cap & Income	Fund of Funds
✔ Income	Index
	Sector
✔ Domestic	Small Cap
Foreign	Socially Conscious
Country/Region	State Specific

Portfolio:	stocks 0%	bonds 94%
convertibles 0%	other 0%	cash 6%

Largest Holdings: mortgage-backed 54%, U.S. government & agencies 39%

Unrealized Net Capital Gains: 8% of portfolio value

SHAREHOLDER INFORMATION

Minimum Investment
Initial: $1,000   Subsequent: $50

Minimum IRA Investment
Initial: $250   Subsequent: $50

Maximum Fees
Load: none   12b-1: 0.25%
Other: none

Distributions
Income: monthly   Capital Gains: Dec

Exchange Options
Number Per Year: 4   Fee: none
Telephone: yes (money market fund available)

Services
IRA, other pension, auto exchange, auto invest, auto withdraw

INVESCO Industrial Income (FIIIX)

P.O. Box 173706
Denver, CO 80217
(800) 525-8085, (303) 930-6300

Balanced

PERFORMANCE

	3yr Annual	5yr Annual	10yr Annual	Bull	Bear
Return (%)	19.8	18.0	16.3	86.5	-6.7
Differ from Category (+/-)	4.8 high	5.9 high	4.3 high	24.9 high	-0.8 av

Total Risk	Standard Deviation	Category Risk	Risk Index	Beta
av	10.4%	high	1.7	0.8

	1993	1992	1991	1990	1989	1988	1987	1986	1985	1984
Return (%)	16.6	0.8	46.2	0.8	31.8	15.3	4.8	14.6	30.7	9.7
Differ from category (+/-) ...	3.2	-7.2	22.3	1.4	14.2	3.3	2.5	-2.9	7.0	2.3

PER SHARE DATA

	1993	1992	1991	1990	1989	1988	1987	1986	1985	1984
Dividends, Net Income ($) .	0.43	0.29	0.31	0.37	0.41	0.36	0.36	0.41	0.47	0.54
Distrib'ns, Cap Gain ($) ...	0.54	0.38	0.46	0.41	0.73	0.00	0.88	2.41	0.66	0.95
Net Asset Value ($)	11.93	11.10	11.70	8.61	9.32	7.98	7.24	8.00	9.37	8.16
Expense Ratio (%)........	0.96	0.98	0.93	0.76	0.78	0.78	0.74	0.71	0.68	0.63
Net Income to Assets (%) ..	2.94	2.75	3.92	4.14	5.08	4.29	3.96	4.85	5.72	5.92
Portfolio Turnover (%)	121	119	104	132	124	148	195	160	54	54
Total Assets (Millions $) ..	3,897	2,093	882	572	400	381	451	341	249	182

PORTFOLIO (as of 6/30/93)

Portfolio Manager: Ron Lout - 1992, Charles P. Mayer - 1993

Investm't Category: Balanced

Cap Gain	Asset Allocation
✔ Cap & Income	Fund of Funds
Income	Index
	Sector
✔ Domestic	Small Cap
Foreign	Socially Conscious
Country/Region	State Specific

Portfolio: stocks 68% bonds 21%
convertibles 0% other 1% cash 9%

Largest Holdings: bonds—corporate 15%, stocks—oil & gas related 9%

Unrealized Net Capital Gains: 9% of portfolio value

SHAREHOLDER INFORMATION

Minimum Investment
Initial: $1,000   Subsequent: $50

Minimum IRA Investment
Initial: $250   Subsequent: $50

Maximum Fees
Load: none   12b-1: 0.25%
Other: none

Distributions
Income: quarterly   Capital Gains: Jun, Dec

Exchange Options
Number Per Year: 4   Fee: none
Telephone: yes (money market fund available)

Services
IRA, other pension, auto exchange, auto invest, auto withdraw

INVESCO
International—European

P.O. Box 173706
Denver, CO 80217
(800) 525-8085, (303) 930-6300

(FEURX) *International Stock*

PERFORMANCE

	3yr Annual	5yr Annual	10yr Annual	Bull	Bear
Return (%)	7.5	9.2	na	34.5	-6.9
Differ from Category (+/-)	-6.8 low	0.5 av	na	-20.6 low	8.2 high

Total Risk	Standard Deviation	Category Risk	Risk Index	Beta
abv av	13.9%	abv av	1.2	0.7

	1993	1992	1991	1990	1989	1988	1987	1986	1985	1984
Return (%)	24.5	-7.5	7.9	0.6	24.2	10.5	-4.5	—	—	—
Differ from category (+/-). .	-14.0	-4.0	-5.0	11.8	2.0	-3.3	-16.5	—	—	—

PER SHARE DATA

	1993	1992	1991	1990	1989	1988	1987	1986	1985	1984
Dividends, Net Income ($) .	0.13	0.19	0.36	0.25	0.13	0.07	0.05	—	—	—
Distrib'ns, Cap Gain ($) . . .	0.00	0.00	0.00	0.00	0.00	0.00	0.00	—	—	—
Net Asset Value ($)	12.83	10.41	11.48	10.99	11.17	9.11	8.31	—	—	—
Expense Ratio (%)	na	1.29	1.43	1.29	1.78	1.88	1.50	—	—	—
Net Income to Assets (%) . . .	na	2.23	1.83	3.38	1.57	1.08	1.44	—	—	—
Portfolio Turnover (%).	44	87	61	20	118	75	131	—	—	—
Total Assets (Millions $). . . .	306	117	75	84	11	7	10	—	—	—

PORTFOLIO (as of 4/30/93)

Portfolio Manager: Jerry Mill - 1986; Steven Chamberlain - 1990

Investm't Category: International Stock

✔ Cap Gain	Asset Allocation
Cap & Income	Fund of Funds
Income	Index
	Sector
Domestic	Small Cap
✔ Foreign	Socially Conscious
✔ Country/Region	State Specific

Portfolio:	stocks 86%	bonds 0%
convertibles 0%	other 0%	cash 14%

Largest Holdings: United Kingdom 32%, France 16%

Unrealized Net Capital Gains: 3% of portfolio value

SHAREHOLDER INFORMATION

Minimum Investment
Initial: $1,000   Subsequent: $50

Minimum IRA Investment
Initial: $250   Subsequent: $50

Maximum Fees
Load: none   12b-1: none
Other: none

Distributions
Income: Oct   Capital Gains: Oct

Exchange Options
Number Per Year: 4   Fee: none
Telephone: yes (money market fund available)

Services
IRA, other pension, auto exchange, auto invest, auto withdraw

INVESCO International— Int'l Growth (FSIGX)

P.O. Box 173706
Denver, CO 80217
(800) 525-8085, (303) 930-6300

International Stock

PERFORMANCE

	3yr Annual	5yr Annual	10yr Annual	Bull	Bear
Return (%)	6.2	3.5	na	31.0	-21.6
Differ from Category (+/-)	-8.1 low	-5.2 low	na	-24.1 low	-6.5 low

Total Risk	Standard Deviation	Category Risk	Risk Index	Beta
high	14.4%	abv av	1.2	0.6

	1993	1992	1991	1990	1989	1988	1987	1986	1985	1984
Return (%)	27.8	-12.6	7.3	-14.3	15.7	16.6	—	—	—	—
Differ from category (+/-) .	-10.7	-9.1	-5.6	-3.2	-6.5	2.8	—	—	—	—

PER SHARE DATA

	1993	1992	1991	1990	1989	1988	1987	1986	1985	1984
Dividends, Net Income ($) .	0.06	0.11	0.17	0.02	0.16	0.09	—	—	—	—
Distrib'ns, Cap Gain ($) . . .	0.00	0.00	0.00	0.05	0.50	0.00	—	—	—	—
Net Asset Value ($)	16.01	12.57	14.52	13.69	16.08	14.48	—	—	—	—
Expense Ratio (%)	na	1.36	1.48	1.48	1.24	1.26	—	—	—	—
Net Income to Assets (%)	na	0.83	1.17	1.85	1.18	1.14	—	—	—	—
Portfolio Turnover (%)	na	50	71	78	35	73	—	—	—	—
Total Assets (Millions $)	91	35	42	39	41	12	—	—	—	—

PORTFOLIO (as of 6/30/93)

Portfolio Manager: W. Lindsay Davidson - 1989, Phillip Ehrman - 1993

Investm't Category: International Stock
- ✔ Cap Gain
- Cap & Income
- Income
- Domestic
- ✔ Foreign
- Country/Region
- Asset Allocation
- Fund of Funds
- Index
- Sector
- Small Cap
- Socially Conscious
- State Specific

Portfolio: stocks 91% bonds 1%
convertibles 0% other 0% cash 8%

Largest Holdings: Japan 27%, United Kingdom 17%

Unrealized Net Capital Gains: 6% of portfolio value

SHAREHOLDER INFORMATION

Minimum Investment
Initial: $1,000   Subsequent: $50

Minimum IRA Investment
Initial: $250   Subsequent: $50

Maximum Fees
Load: none   12b-1: none
Other: none

Distributions
Income: quarterly   Capital Gains: Dec

Exchange Options
Number Per Year: 4   Fee: none
Telephone: yes (money market fund available)

Services
IRA, other pension, auto exchange, auto invest, auto withdraw

INVESCO International— Pacific Basin (FPBSX)

P.O. Box 173706
Denver, CO 80217
(800) 525-8085, (303) 930-6300

International Stock

PERFORMANCE

	3yr Annual	5yr Annual	10yr Annual	Bull	Bear
Return (%)	11.7	4.8	na	45.8	-27.6
Differ from Category (+/-)	-2.6 blw av	-3.9 low	na	-9.3 blw av	-12.5 low

Total Risk	Standard Deviation	Category Risk	Risk Index	Beta
high	16.6%	high	1.4	0.5

	1993	1992	1991	1990	1989	1988	1987	1986	1985	1984
Return (%).............	42.6	-13.5	13.1	-24.4	20.1	23.1	9.7	71.8	27.3	—
Differ from category (+/-)...	4.1	-10.0	0.2	-13.3	-2.1	9.3	-2.3	21.5	-13.3	—

PER SHARE DATA

	1993	1992	1991	1990	1989	1988	1987	1986	1985	1984
Dividends, Net Income ($).	0.04	0.05	0.10	0.09	0.01	0.00	0.07	0.03	0.03	—
Distrib'ns, Cap Gain ($) ...	0.31	0.00	0.00	0.28	0.00	0.00	3.11	1.72	0.00	—
Net Asset Value ($)	15.27	10.96	12.75	11.35	15.49	12.91	10.48	12.69	8.52	—
Expense Ratio (%)	na	1.78	1.87	1.79	1.62	1.62	1.26	1.47	1.50	—
Net Income to Assets (%) ...	na	0.66	0.99	0.36	0.13	-0.12	0.39	0.39	0.99	—
Portfolio Turnover (%)......	na	123	89	93	86	69	155	199	161	—
Total Assets (Millions $)....	270	26	28	17	24	28	36	8	2	—

PORTFOLIO (as of 4/30/93)

Portfolio Manager: Julian Pickstone - 1993, Doug Pratt - 1993

Investm't Category: International Stock

✔ Cap Gain	Asset Allocation
Cap & Income	Fund of Funds
Income	Index
	Sector
Domestic	Small Cap
✔ Foreign	Socially Conscious
✔ Country/Region	State Specific

Portfolio: stocks 71% bonds 0%
convertibles 0% other 0% cash 29%

Largest Holdings: Japan 43%, Hong Kong 12%

Unrealized Net Capital Gains: 6% of portfolio value

SHAREHOLDER INFORMATION

Minimum Investment
Initial: $1,000   Subsequent: $50

Minimum IRA Investment
Initial: $250   Subsequent: $50

Maximum Fees
Load: none   12b-1: none
Other: none

Distributions
Income: Oct   Capital Gains: Oct

Exchange Options
Number Per Year: 4   Fee: none
Telephone: yes (money market fund available)

Services
IRA, other pension, auto exchange, auto invest, auto withdraw

INVESCO Strategic Portfolio—Energy (FSTEX)

P.O. Box 173706
Denver, CO 80217
(800) 525-8085, (303) 930-6300

Aggressive Growth

PERFORMANCE

	3yr Annual	5yr Annual	10yr Annual	Bull	Bear
Return (%)	-0.6	3.2	na	-19.2	1.0
Differ from Category (+/-)	-26.1 low	-15.0 low	na	-144.2 low	16.0 high

Total Risk	Standard Deviation	Category Risk	Risk Index	Beta
high	17.3%	av	1.1	0.7

	1993	1992	1991	1990	1989	1988	1987	1986	1985	1984
Return (%)	16.7	-13.2	-3.4	-16.5	43.5	14.9	4.9	7.1	13.6	—
Differ from category (+/-)	-2.3	-23.6	-55.8	-10.2	16.5	-0.3	8.3	-2.3	-17.4	—

PER SHARE DATA

	1993	1992	1991	1990	1989	1988	1987	1986	1985	1984
Dividends, Net Income ($)	0.10	0.01	0.10	0.10	0.24	0.14	0.14	0.13	0.15	—
Distrib'ns, Cap Gain ($)	0.00	0.00	0.00	0.00	0.00	0.00	0.64	0.17	0.00	—
Net Asset Value ($)	10.37	8.97	10.36	10.83	13.10	9.32	8.23	8.60	8.32	—
Expense Ratio (%)	na	1.73	1.69	1.42	1.75	1.90	1.30	1.50	1.50	—
Net Income to Assets (%)	na	0.32	0.83	1.04	1.73	0.99	1.32	2.85	2.34	—
Portfolio Turnover (%)	na	370	337	321	109	177	452	629	235	—
Total Assets (Millions $)	42	17	12	20	9	6	12	1	0	—

PORTFOLIO (as of 4/30/93)

Portfolio Manager: Tim Miller - 1992

Investm't Category: Aggressive Growth
- ✔ Cap Gain
- Cap & Income
- Income
- Asset Allocation
- Fund of Funds
- Index
- ✔ Sector
- ✔ Domestic
- Foreign
- Country/Region
- Small Cap
- Socially Conscious
- State Specific

Portfolio: stocks 94% bonds 0%
convertibles 0% other 2% cash 4%

Largest Holdings: exploration & production 29%, international 20%

Unrealized Net Capital Gains: 10% of portfolio value

SHAREHOLDER INFORMATION

Minimum Investment
Initial: $1,000   Subsequent: $50

Minimum IRA Investment
Initial: $250   Subsequent: $50

Maximum Fees
Load: none   12b-1: none
Other: none

Distributions
Income: Oct   Capital Gains: Oct

Exchange Options
Number Per Year: 4   Fee: none
Telephone: yes (money market fund available)

Services
IRA, other pension, auto exchange, auto invest, auto withdraw

INVESCO Strategic Portfolio—Environm'l

(FSEVX)   *Aggressive Growth*

P.O. Box 173706
Denver, CO 80217
(800) 525-8085, (303) 930-6300

PERFORMANCE

	3yr Annual	5yr Annual	10yr Annual	Bull	Bear
Return (%)	-3.2	na	na	na	na
Differ from Category (+/-)	-28.6 low	na	na	na	na

Total Risk	Standard Deviation	Category Risk	Risk Index	Beta
high	16.1%	av	1.0	0.8

	1993	1992	1991	1990	1989	1988	1987	1986	1985	1984
Return (%).	-4.6	-18.6	16.7	—	—	—	—	—	—	—
Differ from category (+/-). .	-23.6	-29.0	-35.7	—	—	—	—	—	—	—

PER SHARE DATA

	1993	1992	1991	1990	1989	1988	1987	1986	1985	1984
Dividends, Net Income ($).	0.00	0.00	0.00	—	—	—	—	—	—	—
Distrib'ns, Cap Gain ($) . . .	0.00	0.00	0.00	—	—	—	—	—	—	—
Net Asset Value ($)	7.24	7.60	9.34	—	—	—	—	—	—	—
Expense Ratio (%)	na	1.85	2.50	—	—	—	—	—	—	—
Net Income to Assets (%) . . .	na	-1.23	-1.81	—	—	—	—	—	—	—
Portfolio Turnover (%).	155	113	69	—	—	—	—	—	—	—
Total Assets (Millions $).	50	18	8	—	—	—	—	—	—	—

PORTFOLIO (as of 4/30/93)

Portfolio Manager: John Schroer - 1993

Investm't Category: Aggressive Growth
✔ Cap Gain	Asset Allocation
Cap & Income	Fund of Funds
Income	Index
	✔ Sector
✔ Domestic	Small Cap
✔ Foreign	Socially Conscious
Country/Region	State Specific

Portfolio: stocks 95% bonds 5%
convertibles 0% other 0% cash 0%

Largest Holdings: pollution control—services 21%, pollution control—equipment 7%

Unrealized Net Capital Gains: -12% of portfolio value

SHAREHOLDER INFORMATION

Minimum Investment
Initial: $1,000   Subsequent: $50

Minimum IRA Investment
Initial: $250   Subsequent: $50

Maximum Fees
Load: none   12b-1: none
Other: none

Distributions
Income: Oct   Capital Gains: Oct

Exchange Options
Number Per Year: 4   Fee: none
Telephone: yes (money market fund available)

Services
IRA, other pension, auto exchange, auto invest, auto withdraw

INVESCO Strategic Portfolio—Financial (FSFSX)

P.O. Box 173706
Denver, CO 80217
(800) 525-8085, (303) 930-6300

Growth

PERFORMANCE

	3yr Annual	5yr Annual	10yr Annual	Bull	Bear
Return (%)	37.7	27.1	na	203.2	-20.0
Differ from Category (+/-)	18.5 high	12.5 high	na	118.5 high	-7.6 low

Total Risk	Standard Deviation	Category Risk	Risk Index	Beta
high	16.4%	high	1.5	1.1

	1993	1992	1991	1990	1989	1988	1987	1986	1985	1984
Return (%)	18.4	26.7	74.0	-7.1	36.9	17.1	-11.0	—	—	—
Differ from category (+/-)	5.2	15.7	38.6	-1.0	11.1	-0.6	-12.2	—	—	—

PER SHARE DATA

	1993	1992	1991	1990	1989	1988	1987	1986	1985	1984
Dividends, Net Income ($)	0.20	0.18	0.11	0.00	0.09	0.11	0.07	—	—	—
Distrib'ns, Cap Gain ($)	4.30	0.90	0.10	0.02	0.80	0.00	0.12	—	—	—
Net Asset Value ($)	15.91	17.24	14.57	8.49	9.19	7.38	6.40	—	—	—
Expense Ratio (%)	na	1.07	1.13	2.50	2.50	1.95	1.50	—	—	—
Net Income to Assets (%)	na	1.28	1.76	-0.16	1.05	1.71	1.18	—	—	—
Portfolio Turnover (%)	na	208	249	528	217	175	284	—	—	—
Total Assets (Millions $)	346	190	95	1	2	2	1	—	—	—

PORTFOLIO (as of 4/30/93)

Portfolio Manager: Douglas N. Pratt - 1992

Investm't Category: Growth

✔ Cap Gain	Asset Allocation
Cap & Income	Fund of Funds
Income	Index
	✔ Sector
✔ Domestic	Small Cap
Foreign	Socially Conscious
Country/Region	State Specific

Portfolio: stocks 100% bonds 0%
convertibles 0% other 0% cash 0%

Largest Holdings: banking 46%, insurance 20%

Unrealized Net Capital Gains: 3% of portfolio value

SHAREHOLDER INFORMATION

Minimum Investment
Initial: $1,000   Subsequent: $50

Minimum IRA Investment
Initial: $250   Subsequent: $50

Maximum Fees
Load: none   12b-1: none
Other: none

Distributions
Income: Oct   Capital Gains: Oct

Exchange Options
Number Per Year: 4   Fee: none
Telephone: yes (money market fund available)

Services
IRA, other pension, auto exchange, auto invest, auto withdraw

INVESCO Strategic Portfolio—Gold (FGLDX)

P.O. Box 173706
Denver, CO 80217
(800) 525-8085, (303) 930-6300

Gold

PERFORMANCE

	3yr Annual	5yr Annual	10yr Annual	Bull	Bear
Return (%)	13.7	6.5	na	34.6	-15.9
Differ from Category (+/-)	0.0 av	-5.8 av	na	1.0 av	-61.8 low

Total Risk	Standard Deviation	Category Risk	Risk Index	Beta
high	26.6%	abv av	1.0	-0.3

	1993	1992	1991	1990	1989	1988	1987	1986	1985	1984
Return (%)	72.6	-8.2	-7.1	-23.0	21.3	-20.0	15.9	38.6	-4.4	—
Differ from category (+/-)	-14.3	7.5	-2.3	-54.5	-3.4	-1.1	-16.0	1.0	3.0	—

PER SHARE DATA

	1993	1992	1991	1990	1989	1988	1987	1986	1985	1984
Dividends, Net Income ($)	0.00	0.00	0.00	0.00	0.02	0.06	0.06	0.08	0.10	—
Distrib'ns, Cap Gain ($)	0.00	0.00	0.00	0.00	0.00	0.00	0.04	0.05	0.00	—
Net Asset Value ($)	6.75	3.91	4.26	4.58	5.97	4.94	6.25	5.49	4.06	—
Expense Ratio (%)	na	1.41	1.47	1.32	1.63	1.58	1.15	1.50	1.50	—
Net Income to Assets (%)	na	-0.23	-0.25	0.26	0.68	0.62	0.98	2.35	2.72	—
Portfolio Turnover (%)	142	101	43	107	77	47	124	232	46	—
Total Assets (Millions $)	251	46	46	36	34	33	38	5	2	—

PORTFOLIO (as of 4/30/93)

Portfolio Manager: Dan Leonard - 1989

Investm't Category: Gold

✔ Cap Gain
    Asset Allocation
    Cap & Income   Fund of Funds
    Income   Index
    ✔ Sector
✔ Domestic   Small Cap
✔ Foreign   Socially Conscious
    Country/Region   State Specific

Portfolio:	stocks 80%	bonds 0%
convertibles 0%	other 0%	cash 20%

Largest Holdings: exploration & mining companies 65%, oil & gas related 5%

Unrealized Net Capital Gains: 15% of portfolio value

SHAREHOLDER INFORMATION

Minimum Investment
Initial: $1,000   Subsequent: $50

Minimum IRA Investment
Initial: $250   Subsequent: $50

Maximum Fees
Load: none   12b-1: none
Other: none

Distributions
Income: Oct   Capital Gains: Oct

Exchange Options
Number Per Year: 4   Fee: none
Telephone: yes (money market fund available)

Services
IRA, other pension, auto exchange, auto invest, auto withdraw

INVESCO Strategic Portfolio—Health Sci

(FHLSX)   *Aggressive Growth*

P.O. Box 173706
Denver, CO 80217
(800) 525-8085, (303) 930-6300

PERFORMANCE

	3yr Annual	5yr Annual	10yr Annual	Bull	Bear
Return (%)	14.8	24.9	na	83.7	3.7
Differ from Category (+/-)	-10.6 low	6.7 high	na	-41.3 low	18.7 high

Total Risk	Standard Deviation	Category Risk	Risk Index	Beta
high	23.1%	high	1.5	1.4

	1993	1992	1991	1990	1989	1988	1987	1986	1985	1984
Return (%)	-8.4	-13.7	91.8	25.7	59.4	16.0	7.0	29.5	31.4	—
Differ from category (+/-) .	-27.4	-24.1	39.4	32.0	32.4	0.8	10.4	20.1	0.4	—

PER SHARE DATA

	1993	1992	1991	1990	1989	1988	1987	1986	1985	1984
Dividends, Net Income ($)	0.00	0.10	0.10	0.17	0.10	0.00	0.00	0.00	0.00	—
Distrib'ns, Cap Gain ($) ...	0.00	0.44	3.47	0.21	1.95	0.00	0.93	1.37	0.00	—
Net Asset Value ($)	35.14	38.38	45.17	25.62	20.76	14.39	12.40	12.50	10.69	—
Expense Ratio (%)..........	na	1.00	1.03	1.12	1.42	1.65	1.42	1.50	1.50	—
Net Income to Assets (%)	na	0.26	0.55	1.18	0.79	-0.48	-0.17	-0.28	0.19	—
Portfolio Turnover (%)	87	91	100	242	272	280	364	470	203	—
Total Assets (Millions $) ...	558	757	745	88	27	10	10	4	1	—

PORTFOLIO (as of 4/30/93)

Portfolio Manager: Barry Kurokawa - 1992

Investm't Category: Aggressive Growth
- ✔ Cap Gain
- Cap & Income
- Income
- Asset Allocation
- Fund of Funds
- Index
- ✔ Sector
- ✔ Domestic
- Foreign
- Country/Region
- Small Cap
- Socially Conscious
- State Specific

Portfolio: stocks 79%   bonds 1%
convertibles 0%   other 6%   cash 14%

Largest Holdings: health maintenance organizations 12%, biotechnology 12%

Unrealized Net Capital Gains: -3% of portfolio value

SHAREHOLDER INFORMATION

Minimum Investment
Initial: $1,000   Subsequent: $50

Minimum IRA Investment
Initial: $250   Subsequent: $50

Maximum Fees
Load: none   12b-1: none
Other: none

Distributions
Income: Oct   Capital Gains: Oct

Exchange Options
Number Per Year: 4   Fee: none
Telephone: yes (money market fund available)

Services
IRA, other pension, auto exchange, auto invest, auto withdraw

INVESCO Strategic Portfolio—Leisure (FLISX)

Aggressive Growth

P.O. Box 173706
Denver, CO 80217
(800) 525-8085, (303) 930-6300

PERFORMANCE

	3yr Annual	5yr Annual	10yr Annual	Bull	Bear
Return (%)	36.7	25.7	na	192.3	-22.1
Differ from Category (+/-)	11.3 high	7.5 high	na	67.4 high	-7.1 blw av

Total Risk	Standard Deviation	Category Risk	Risk Index	Beta
high	14.2%	blw av	0.9	0.9

	1993	1992	1991	1990	1989	1988	1987	1986	1985	1984
Return (%)	35.6	23.4	52.7	-10.9	38.2	28.5	0.6	18.8	32.2	—
Differ from category (+/-)	16.6	13.0	0.3	-4.6	11.2	13.3	4.1	9.4	1.2	—

PER SHARE DATA

	1993	1992	1991	1990	1989	1988	1987	1986	1985	1984
Dividends, Net Income ($)	0.00	0.00	0.00	0.03	0.20	0.00	0.00	0.00	0.03	—
Distrib'ns, Cap Gain ($)	1.89	0.98	2.12	0.67	1.99	0.00	1.43	2.76	0.00	—
Net Asset Value ($)	23.28	18.55	15.94	11.93	14.34	11.94	9.29	10.69	11.18	—
Expense Ratio (%)	na	1.51	1.86	1.84	1.38	1.89	1.50	1.50	1.50	—
Net Income to Assets (%)	na	-0.33	-0.24	0.10	1.44	0.16	-0.37	-0.11	0.57	—
Portfolio Turnover (%)	116	148	122	89	119	136	376	458	160	—
Total Assets (Millions $)	223	40	14	5	13	6	3	2	1	—

PORTFOLIO (as of 4/30/93)

Portfolio Manager: Timothy L. Miller - 1992

Investm't Category: Aggressive Growth

✔ Cap Gain	Asset Allocation
Cap & Income	Fund of Funds
Income	Index
	✔ Sector
✔ Domestic	Small Cap
Foreign	Socially Conscious
Country/Region	State Specific

Portfolio: stocks 90% bonds 0%
convertibles 0% other 0% cash 10%

Largest Holdings: retail 18%, broadcasting 7%

Unrealized Net Capital Gains: 6% of portfolio value

SHAREHOLDER INFORMATION

Minimum Investment
Initial: $1,000   Subsequent: $50

Minimum IRA Investment
Initial: $250   Subsequent: $50

Maximum Fees
Load: none   12b-1: none
Other: none

Distributions
Income: Oct   Capital Gains: Oct

Exchange Options
Number Per Year: 4   Fee: none
Telephone: yes (money market fund available)

Services
IRA, other pension, auto exchange, auto invest, auto withdraw

INVESCO Strategic Portfolio—Tech (FTCHX)

P.O. Box 173706
Denver, CO 80217
(800) 525-8085, (303) 930-6300

Aggressive Growth

PERFORMANCE

	3yr Annual	5yr Annual	10yr Annual	Bull	Bear
Return (%)	34.2	26.0	na	184.8	-7.8
Differ from Category (+/-)	8.8 high	7.8 high	na	59.8 high	7.2 high

Total Risk	Standard Deviation	Category Risk	Risk Index	Beta
high	21.8%	high	1.4	1.3

	1993	1992	1991	1990	1989	1988	1987	1986	1985	1984
Return (%)	15.0	18.8	76.9	8.5	21.4	14.2	-5.2	21.7	27.3	—
Differ from category (+/-) . .	-4.0	8.4	24.5	14.8	-5.6	-1.0	-1.8	12.3	-3.7	—

PER SHARE DATA

	1993	1992	1991	1990	1989	1988	1987	1986	1985	1984
Dividends, Net Income ($) .	0.00	0.00	0.00	0.00	0.00	0.00	0.00	0.00	0.00	—
Distrib'ns, Cap Gain ($) . . .	3.22	0.00	4.38	0.00	0.00	0.00	0.00	1.06	0.00	—
Net Asset Value ($)	23.59	23.31	19.62	13.77	12.69	10.45	9.15	9.67	8.85	—
Expense Ratio (%).	na	1.12	1.19	1.25	1.59	1.72	1.47	1.50	1.50	—
Net Income to Assets (%)	na	-0.45	-0.53	-0.06	-0.62	-0.90	-0.68	-0.71	0.03	—
Portfolio Turnover (%)	184	169	307	345	259	356	556	368	175	—
Total Assets (Millions $) . . .	248	165	63	20	9	10	9	4	2	—

PORTFOLIO (as of 4/30/93)

Portfolio Manager: Dan Leonard - 1985

Investm't Category: Aggressive Growth
- ✔ Cap Gain
- Cap & Income
- Income
- Asset Allocation
- Fund of Funds
- Index
- ✔ Sector
- Small Cap
- ✔ Domestic
- Foreign
- Country/Region
- Socially Conscious
- State Specific

Portfolio:	stocks 94%	bonds 0%
convertibles 0%	other 1%	cash 5%

Largest Holdings: telecommunications 31%, computer software 13%

Unrealized Net Capital Gains: 5% of portfolio value

SHAREHOLDER INFORMATION

Minimum Investment
Initial: $1,000   Subsequent: $50

Minimum IRA Investment
Initial: $250   Subsequent: $50

Maximum Fees
Load: none   12b-1: none
Other: none

Distributions
Income: Oct   Capital Gains: Oct

Exchange Options
Number Per Year: 4   Fee: none
Telephone: yes (money market fund available)

Services
IRA, other pension, auto exchange, auto invest, auto withdraw

INVESCO Strategic Portfolio—Utilities (FSTUX)

P.O. Box 173706
Denver, CO 80217
(800) 525-8085, (303) 930-6300

Growth & Income

PERFORMANCE

	3yr Annual	5yr Annual	10yr Annual	Bull	Bear
Return (%)	19.7	15.2	na	84.9	-16.4
Differ from Category (+/-)	3.3 abv av	2.7 high	na	14.8 high	-4.8 low

Total Risk	Standard Deviation	Category Risk	Risk Index	Beta
av	8.5%	blw av	1.0	0.5

	1993	1992	1991	1990	1989	1988	1987	1986	1985	1984
Return (%)	21.1	10.7	28.0	-10.0	31.4	14.2	-4.9	—	—	—
Differ from category (+/-)	8.5	0.6	0.3	-4.4	9.8	-2.6	-5.3	—	—	—

PER SHARE DATA

	1993	1992	1991	1990	1989	1988	1987	1986	1985	1984
Dividends, Net Income ($)	0.26	0.25	0.34	0.34	0.37	0.37	0.47	—	—	—
Distrib'ns, Cap Gain ($)	2.00	0.77	0.00	0.00	0.71	0.00	0.00	—	—	—
Net Asset Value ($)	10.68	10.69	10.64	8.61	9.96	8.47	7.76	—	—	—
Expense Ratio (%)	na	1.13	1.21	1.26	1.35	1.39	1.39	—	—	—
Net Income to Assets (%)	na	2.73	4.19	3.48	4.07	4.93	5.07	—	—	—
Portfolio Turnover (%)	202	226	151	264	220	164	84	—	—	—
Total Assets (Millions $)	178	108	69	31	24	18	16	—	—	—

PORTFOLIO (as of 4/30/93)

Portfolio Manager: Brian Kelly - 1993

Investm't Category: Growth & Income

Cap Gain	Asset Allocation
✔ Cap & Income	Fund of Funds
Income	Index
	✔ Sector
✔ Domestic	Small Cap
Foreign	Socially Conscious
Country/Region	State Specific

Portfolio: stocks 92% bonds 0%
convertibles 0% other 0% cash 8%

Largest Holdings: gas & electric utilities 49%, telecommunications 20%

Unrealized Net Capital Gains: 9% of portfolio value

SHAREHOLDER INFORMATION

Minimum Investment
Initial: $1,000   Subsequent: $50

Minimum IRA Investment
Initial: $250   Subsequent: $50

Maximum Fees
Load: none   12b-1: none
Other: none

Distributions
Income: quarterly   Capital Gains: Oct

Exchange Options
Number Per Year: 4   Fee: none
Telephone: yes (money market fund available)

Services
IRA, other pension, auto exchange, auto invest, auto withdraw

INVESCO Tax-Free Long-Term Bond (FTIFX)

P.O. Box 173706
Denver, CO 80217
(800) 525-8085, (303) 930-6300

Tax-Exempt Bond

PERFORMANCE

	3yr Annual	5yr Annual	10yr Annual	Bull	Bear
Return (%)	11.1	10.4	11.4	44.5	1.6
Differ from Category (+/-)	0.8 av	1.2 high	1.8 high	4.4 abv av	-0.6 blw av

Total Risk	Standard Deviation	Category Risk	Risk Index	Avg Mat
blw av	4.7%	abv av	1.2	25.1 yrs

	1993	1992	1991	1990	1989	1988	1987	1986	1985	1984
Return (%)	12.0	8.7	12.5	7.1	11.6	15.0	-4.0	22.1	22.8	9.1
Differ from category (+/-) . . .	0.4	0.4	1.2	0.8	2.6	4.9	-2.8	5.7	5.5	0.8

PER SHARE DATA

	1993	1992	1991	1990	1989	1988	1987	1986	1985	1984
Dividends, Net Income ($) .	0.84	0.90	0.93	0.98	1.00	1.00	1.02	1.17	1.24	1.25
Distrib'ns, Cap Gain ($) . . .	0.37	0.33	0.16	0.00	0.00	0.00	0.47	1.38	0.70	0.08
Net Asset Value ($)	16.54	15.90	15.81	15.08	15.05	14.42	13.46	15.59	15.00	13.95
Expense Ratio (%).	1.03	1.02	0.93	0.75	0.74	0.77	0.70	0.68	0.65	0.58
Net Income to Assets (%). .	5.43	5.90	6.39	6.67	7.06	7.33	7.04	7.86	9.05	8.87
Portfolio Turnover (%)	30	28	25	27	27	41	98	92	156	88
Total Assets (Millions $) . . .	342	272	208	179	144	109	118	108	85	60

PORTFOLIO (as of 6/30/93)

Portfolio Manager: William Veronda - 1984

Investm't Category: Tax-Exempt Bond

Cap Gain	Asset Allocation
Cap & Income	Fund of Funds
✔ Income	Index
	Sector
✔ Domestic	Small Cap
Foreign	Socially Conscious
Country/Region	State Specific

Portfolio: stocks 0% bonds 98%
convertibles 0% other 0% cash 2%

Largest Holdings: general obligation 98%

Unrealized Net Capital Gains: 0% of portfolio value

SHAREHOLDER INFORMATION

Minimum Investment
Initial: $1,000 Subsequent: $50

Minimum IRA Investment
Initial: na Subsequent: na

Maximum Fees
Load: none 12b-1: 0.25%
Other: none

Distributions
Income: monthly Capital Gains: Jun, Dec

Exchange Options
Number Per Year: no limit Fee: none
Telephone: yes (money market fund available)

Services
auto exchange, auto invest, auto withdraw

INVESCO Value Trust— Interm Gov't (FIGBX)

P.O. Box 173706
Denver, CO 80217
(800) 525-8085, (303) 930-6300

Government Bond

PERFORMANCE

	3yr Annual	5yr Annual	10yr Annual	Bull	Bear
Return (%)	9.6	9.6	na	37.6	4.3
Differ from Category (+/-)	-1.2 av	-0.8 av	na	-8.6 av	3.8 abv av

Total Risk	Standard Deviation	Category Risk	Risk Index	Avg Mat
low	3.5%	blw av	0.8	4.4 yrs

	1993	1992	1991	1990	1989	1988	1987	1986	1985	1984
Return (%)	8.7	6.0	14.1	9.1	10.5	5.4	-0.5	—	—	—
Differ from category (+/-). . .	-1.7	-0.2	-0.8	2.6	-3.4	-2.2	1.3	—	—	—

PER SHARE DATA

	1993	1992	1991	1990	1989	1988	1987	1986	1985	1984
Dividends, Net Income ($).	0.71	0.90	0.89	0.99	1.02	0.95	0.61	—	—	—
Distrib'ns, Cap Gain ($) . . .	0.34	0.04	0.00	0.00	0.00	0.00	0.00	—	—	—
Net Asset Value ($)	12.72	12.68	12.89	12.13	12.07	11.89	12.19	—	—	—
Expense Ratio (%)	na	0.97	0.93	0.85	0.85	0.85	0.93	—	—	—
Net Income to Assets (%) . . .	na	6.38	7.28	8.16	8.45	7.92	7.31	—	—	—
Portfolio Turnover (%).	na	93	51	31	52	6	28	—	—	—
Total Assets (Millions $).	40	30	24	18	20	18	15	—	—	—

PORTFOLIO (as of 6/30/93)

Portfolio Manager: James Baker - 1993

Investm't Category: Government Bond

Cap Gain	Asset Allocation
Cap & Income	Fund of Funds
✔ Income	Index
	Sector
✔ Domestic	Small Cap
✔ Foreign	Socially Conscious
Country/Region	State Specific

Portfolio: stocks 0% bonds 97%
convertibles 0% other 0% cash 3%

Largest Holdings: U.S. government 97%

Unrealized Net Capital Gains: 3% of portfolio value

SHAREHOLDER INFORMATION

Minimum Investment
Initial: $1,000,000   Subsequent: $50

Minimum IRA Investment
Initial: $1,000,000   Subsequent: $50

Maximum Fees
Load: none   12b-1: none
Other: none

Distributions
Income: quarterly   Capital Gains: Dec

Exchange Options
Number Per Year: 4   Fee: none
Telephone: yes (money market fund available)

Services
IRA, other pension, auto exchange, auto invest, auto withdraw

INVESCO Value Trust— Total Return (FSFLX)

P.O. Box 173706
Denver, CO 80217
(800) 525-8085, (303) 930-6300

Balanced

PERFORMANCE

	3yr Annual	5yr Annual	10yr Annual	Bull	Bear
Return (%)	15.5	12.8	na	65.2	-7.0
Differ from Category (+/-)	0.5 abv av	0.6 av	na	3.6 abv av	-1.2 blw av

Total Risk	Standard Deviation	Category Risk	Risk Index	Beta
av	6.7%	av	1.1	0.6

	1993	1992	1991	1990	1989	1988	1987	1986	1985	1984
Return (%)	12.3	9.8	24.9	-0.3	19.1	11.5	—	—	—	—
Differ from category (+/-) ..	-1.1	1.7	1.0	0.2	1.5	-0.5	—	—	—	—

PER SHARE DATA

	1993	1992	1991	1990	1989	1988	1987	1986	1985	1984
Dividends, Net Income ($) .	0.68	0.64	0.71	0.74	0.78	0.51	—	—	—	—
Distrib'ns, Cap Gain ($) ...	0.33	0.18	0.55	0.05	0.13	0.02	—	—	—	—
Net Asset Value ($)	18.26	17.18	16.43	14.21	15.08	13.46	—	—	—	—
Expense Ratio (%)........	0.93	0.88	0.92	1.00	1.00	1.00	—	—	—	—
Net Income to Assets (%)..	3.51	4.06	4.62	5.22	5.46	5.56	—	—	—	—
Portfolio Turnover (%)	28	13	49	24	28	13	—	—	—	—
Total Assets (Millions $) ...	231	137	82	55	45	28	—	—	—	—

PORTFOLIO (as of 8/31/93)

Portfolio Manager: Edward Mitchell - 1987

Investm't Category: Balanced

Cap Gain	✔ Asset Allocation
✔ Cap & Income	Fund of Funds
Income	Index
	Sector
✔ Domestic	Small Cap
✔ Foreign	Socially Conscious
Country/Region	State Specific

Portfolio: stocks 70% bonds 27%
convertibles 0% other 0% cash 3%

Largest Holdings: bonds—U.S. government 27%, stocks—diversified companies 11%

Unrealized Net Capital Gains: 10% of portfolio value

SHAREHOLDER INFORMATION

Minimum Investment
Initial: $1,000,000   Subsequent: $50

Minimum IRA Investment
Initial: $1,000,000   Subsequent: $50

Maximum Fees
Load: none   12b-1: none
Other: none

Distributions
Income: quarterly   Capital Gains: Dec

Exchange Options
Number Per Year: 4   Fee: none
Telephone: yes (money market fund available)

Services
IRA, other pension, auto exchange, auto invest, auto withdraw

INVESCO Value Trust— Value Equity (FSEQX)

Growth & Income

P.O. Box 173706
Denver, CO 80217
(800) 525-8085, (303) 930-6300

PERFORMANCE

	3yr Annual	5yr Annual	10yr Annual	Bull	Bear
Return (%)	16.3	12.4	na	74.0	-14.7
Differ from Category (+/-)	-0.1 av	-0.1 av	na	3.9 av	-3.1 blw av

Total Risk	Standard Deviation	Category Risk	Risk Index	Beta
av	10.5%	abv av	1.2	0.9

	1993	1992	1991	1990	1989	1988	1987	1986	1985	1984
Return (%)	10.4	4.9	35.8	-5.7	21.3	13.3	-0.2	—	—	—
Differ from category (+/-)	-2.2	-5.1	8.1	-0.1	-0.3	-3.5	-0.6	—	—	—

PER SHARE DATA

	1993	1992	1991	1990	1989	1988	1987	1986	1985	1984
Dividends, Net Income ($)	0.36	0.34	0.39	0.47	0.48	0.31	0.37	—	—	—
Distrib'ns, Cap Gain ($)	0.87	0.12	1.84	0.06	0.83	0.00	0.00	—	—	—
Net Asset Value ($)	17.41	16.91	16.57	13.88	15.30	13.72	12.39	—	—	—
Expense Ratio (%)	1.00	0.91	0.98	1.00	1.00	1.00	1.00	—	—	—
Net Income to Assets (%)	2.07	2.19	2.39	3.00	3.29	3.48	2.95	—	—	—
Portfolio Turnover (%)	52	37	64	23	30	16	20	—	—	—
Total Assets (Millions $)	86	79	40	30	37	27	15	—	—	—

PORTFOLIO (as of 8/31/93)

Portfolio Manager: Michael Harhai - 1993

Investm't Category: Growth & Income

Cap Gain	Asset Allocation
✔ Cap & Income	Fund of Funds
Income	Index
	Sector
✔ Domestic	Small Cap
✔ Foreign	Socially Conscious
Country/Region	State Specific

Portfolio: stocks 98% bonds 0%
convertibles 0% other 0% cash 2%

Largest Holdings: diversified companies 14%, insurance 10%

Unrealized Net Capital Gains: 9% of portfolio value

SHAREHOLDER INFORMATION

Minimum Investment
Initial: $1,000,000   Subsequent: $50

Minimum IRA Investment
Initial: $1,000,000   Subsequent: $50

Maximum Fees
Load: none   12b-1: none
Other: none

Distributions
Income: quarterly   Capital Gains: Dec

Exchange Options
Number Per Year: 4   Fee: none
Telephone: yes (money market fund available)

Services
IRA, other pension, auto exchange, auto invest, auto withdraw

Janus (JANSX)

Growth

100 Fillmore St., Suite 300
Denver, CO 80206
(800) 525-3713, (303) 333-3863

PERFORMANCE

	3yr Annual	5yr Annual	10yr Annual	Bull	Bear
Return (%)	19.1	19.6	15.2	80.2	-6.8
Differ from Category (+/-)	-0.1 av	5.0 high	2.6 high	-4.5 av	5.6 abv av

Total Risk	Standard Deviation	Category Risk	Risk Index	Beta
abv av	11.1%	blw av	1.0	0.9

	1993	1992	1991	1990	1989	1988	1987	1986	1985	1984
Return (%)	10.8	6.8	42.7	-0.6	46.3	16.5	4.1	11.2	24.5	-0.1
Differ from category (+/-) . .	-2.4	-4.2	7.3	5.4	20.5	-1.2	2.9	-3.3	-4.8	-0.1

PER SHARE DATA

	1993	1992	1991	1990	1989	1988	1987	1986	1985	1984
Dividends, Net Income ($) .	0.38	0.29	0.18	0.30	0.18	0.56	0.98	0.00	0.54	1.30
Distrib'ns, Cap Gain ($) . . .	0.93	0.90	0.90	0.00	2.50	0.00	1.60	2.20	0.73	0.34
Net Asset Value ($)	19.39	18.68	18.60	13.79	14.21	11.55	10.39	12.47	13.19	11.61
Expense Ratio (%).	0.92	0.97	0.98	1.02	0.92	0.98	1.01	1.00	1.03	1.06
Net Income to Assets (%). .	1.55	1.54	1.77	2.11	1.68	4.99	1.55	2.82	4.01	4.26
Portfolio Turnover (%)	127	153	132	307	205	175	214	254	163	162
Total Assets (Millions $) . .	9,234	4,989	2,598	1,050	673	392	388	474	410	319

PORTFOLIO (as of 10/31/93)

Portfolio Manager: James P. Craig — 1986

Investm't Category: Growth

✔ Cap Gain	Asset Allocation
Cap & Income	Fund of Funds
Income	Index
	Sector
✔ Domestic	Small Cap
✔ Foreign	Socially Conscious
Country/Region	State Specific

Portfolio: stocks 79% bonds 8%
convertibles 0% other 0% cash 13%

Largest Holdings: banking 15%, bonds—U.S. government 8%

Unrealized Net Capital Gains: 9% of portfolio value

SHAREHOLDER INFORMATION

Minimum Investment
Initial: $1,000   Subsequent: $50

Minimum IRA Investment
Initial: $250   Subsequent: $50

Maximum Fees
Load: none   12b-1: none
Other: none

Distributions
Income: Dec   Capital Gains: Dec

Exchange Options
Number Per Year: 4   Fee: none
Telephone: yes (money market fund available)

Services
IRA, other pension, auto exchange, auto invest, auto withdraw

Janus Balanced (JABAX)

Balanced

100 Fillmore St., Suite 300
Denver, CO 80206
(800) 525-3713, (303) 333-3863

PERFORMANCE

	3yr Annual	5yr Annual	10yr Annual	Bull	Bear
Return (%)	na	na	na	na	na
Differ from Category (+/-)	na	na	na	na	na

Total Risk	Standard Deviation	Category Risk	Risk Index	Beta
na	na	na	na	na

	1993	1992	1991	1990	1989	1988	1987	1986	1985	1984
Return (%)	10.5	—	—	—	—	—	—	—	—	—
Differ from category (+/-). . .	-2.9	—	—	—	—	—	—	—	—	—

PER SHARE DATA

	1993	1992	1991	1990	1989	1988	1987	1986	1985	1984
Dividends, Net Income ($).	0.22	—	—	—	—	—	—	—	—	—
Distrib'ns, Cap Gain ($) . . .	0.00	—	—	—	—	—	—	—	—	—
Net Asset Value ($)	12.19	—	—	—	—	—	—	—	—	—
Expense Ratio (%)	1.70	—	—	—	—	—	—	—	—	—
Net Income to Assets (%) .	2.15	—	—	—	—	—	—	—	—	—
Portfolio Turnover (%).	131	—	—	—	—	—	—	—	—	—
Total Assets (Millions $). . . .	78	—	—	—	—	—	—	—	—	—

PORTFOLIO (as of 10/31/93)

Portfolio Manager: James P. Craig — 1993

Investm't Category: Balanced

Cap Gain	✔ Asset Allocation
✔ Cap & Income	Fund of Funds
Income	Index
	Sector
✔ Domestic	Small Cap
Foreign	Socially Conscious
Country/Region	State Specific

Portfolio: stocks 46% bonds 11%
convertibles 0% other 41% cash 2%

Largest Holdings: stocks—banking 18%, stocks—real estate investment trusts 9%

Unrealized Net Capital Gains: 6% of portfolio value

SHAREHOLDER INFORMATION

Minimum Investment
Initial: $1,000   Subsequent: $50

Minimum IRA Investment
Initial: $250   Subsequent: $50

Maximum Fees
Load: none   12b-1: none
Other: none

Distributions
Income: quarterly   Capital Gains: Dec

Exchange Options
Number Per Year: 4   Fee: none
Telephone: yes (money market fund available)

Services
IRA, other pension, auto exchange, auto invest, auto withdraw

Janus Enterprise (JAENX)

Aggressive Growth

100 Fillmore St., Suite 300
Denver, CO 80206
(800) 525-3713, (303) 333-3863

PERFORMANCE

	3yr Annual	5yr Annual	10yr Annual	Bull	Bear
Return (%)	na	na	na	na	na
Differ from Category (+/-)	na	na	na	na	na

Total Risk	Standard Deviation	Category Risk	Risk Index	Beta
na	na	na	na	na

	1993	1992	1991	1990	1989	1988	1987	1986	1985	1984
Return (%)	15.6	—	—	—	—	—	—	—	—	—
Differ from category (+/-) . .	-3.4	—	—	—	—	—	—	—	—	—

PER SHARE DATA

	1993	1992	1991	1990	1989	1988	1987	1986	1985	1984
Dividends, Net Income ($) .	0.01	—	—	—	—	—	—	—	—	—
Distrib'ns, Cap Gain ($) . . .	0.54	—	—	—	—	—	—	—	—	—
Net Asset Value ($)	21.92	—	—	—	—	—	—	—	—	—
Expense Ratio (%).	1.36	—	—	—	—	—	—	—	—	—
Net Income to Assets (%) . .	0.14	—	—	—	—	—	—	—	—	—
Portfolio Turnover (%)	201	—	—	—	—	—	—	—	—	—
Total Assets (Millions $) . . .	254	—	—	—	—	—	—	—	—	—

PORTFOLIO (as of 10/31/93)

Portfolio Manager: James Goff - 1992

Investm't Category: Aggressive Growth

✔ Cap Gain	Asset Allocation
Cap & Income	Fund of Funds
Income	Index
	Sector
✔ Domestic	Small Cap
✔ Foreign	Socially Conscious
Country/Region	State Specific

Portfolio: stocks 85% bonds 2%
convertibles 1% other 0% cash 12%

Largest Holdings: retail 12%, drugs 12%

Unrealized Net Capital Gains: 9% of portfolio value

SHAREHOLDER INFORMATION

Minimum Investment
Initial: $1,000   Subsequent: $50

Minimum IRA Investment
Initial: $250   Subsequent: $50

Maximum Fees
Load: none   12b-1: none
Other: none

Distributions
Income: Dec   Capital Gains: Dec

Exchange Options
Number Per Year: 4   Fee: none
Telephone: yes (money market fund available)

Services
IRA, other pension, auto exchange, auto invest, auto withdraw

Janus Federal Tax-Exempt (JATEX)

Tax-Exempt Bond

100 Fillmore St., Suite 300
Denver, CO 80206
(800) 525-3713, (303) 333-3863

fund in existence since 5/3/93

PERFORMANCE

	3yr Annual	5yr Annual	10yr Annual	Bull	Bear
Return (%)	na	na	na	na	na
Differ from Category (+/-)	na	na	na	na	na

Total Risk	Standard Deviation	Category Risk	Risk Index	Avg Mat
na	na	na	na	23.0 yrs

	1993	1992	1991	1990	1989	1988	1987	1986	1985	1984
Return (%)	—	—	—	—	—	—	—	—	—	—
Differ from category (+/-). . . .	—	—	—	—	—	—	—	—	—	—

PER SHARE DATA

	1993	1992	1991	1990	1989	1988	1987	1986	1985	1984
Dividends, Net Income ($).	0.20	—	—	—	—	—	—	—	—	—
Distrib'ns, Cap Gain ($) . . .	0.01	—	—	—	—	—	—	—	—	—
Net Asset Value ($)	7.31	—	—	—	—	—	—	—	—	—
Expense Ratio (%)	0.75	—	—	—	—	—	—	—	—	—
Net Income to Assets (%) .	4.58	—	—	—	—	—	—	—	—	—
Portfolio Turnover (%).	124	—	—	—	—	—	—	—	—	—
Total Assets (Millions $).	29	—	—	—	—	—	—	—	—	—

PORTFOLIO (as of 10/31/93)

Portfolio Manager: Ronald V. Speaker - 1993

Investm't Category: Tax-Exempt Bond

Cap Gain	Asset Allocation
Cap & Income	Fund of Funds
✔ Income	Index
	Sector
✔ Domestic	Small Cap
Foreign	Socially Conscious
Country/Region	State Specific

Portfolio: stocks 0%   bonds 100%
convertibles 0%   other 0%   cash 0%

Largest Holdings: general obligation 15%

Unrealized Net Capital Gains: 1% of portfolio value

SHAREHOLDER INFORMATION

Minimum Investment
Initial: $1,000   Subsequent: $50

Minimum IRA Investment
Initial: na   Subsequent: na

Maximum Fees
Load: none   12b-1: none
Other: none

Distributions
Income: monthly   Capital Gains: Dec

Exchange Options
Number Per Year: 4   Fee: none
Telephone: yes (money market fund available)

Services
auto exchange, auto invest, auto withdraw

Janus Flexible Income

(JAFIX)

Corporate Bond

100 Fillmore St., Suite 300
Denver, CO 80206
(800) 525-3713, (303) 333-3863

PERFORMANCE

	3yr Annual	5yr Annual	10yr Annual	Bull	Bear
Return (%)	17.6	10.1	na	71.4	-9.3
Differ from Category (+/-)	5.6 high	0.0 av	na	25.3 high	-11.1 low

Total Risk	Standard Deviation	Category Risk	Risk Index	Avg Mat
low	3.2%	abv av	1.1	12.9 yrs

	1993	1992	1991	1990	1989	1988	1987	1986	1985	1984
Return (%)	15.6	11.7	25.9	-4.5	4.1	10.6	—	—	—	—
Differ from category (+/-) ...	4.2	3.1	9.3	-9.8	-5.4	1.6	—	—	—	—

PER SHARE DATA

	1993	1992	1991	1990	1989	1988	1987	1986	1985	1984
Dividends, Net Income ($) .	0.75	0.78	0.89	0.90	0.97	0.93	—	—	—	—
Distrib'ns, Cap Gain ($) ...	0.22	0.02	0.00	0.00	0.07	0.00	—	—	—	—
Net Asset Value ($)	9.74	9.31	9.09	8.00	9.35	9.99	—	—	—	—
Expense Ratio (%)........	1.00	1.00	1.00	1.00	1.00	1.00	—	—	—	—
Net Income to Assets (%)..	7.96	8.98	9.38	11.24	10.00	9.32	—	—	—	—
Portfolio Turnover (%)	201	210	88	96	75	76	—	—	—	—
Total Assets (Millions $) ...	466	205	72	14	18	10	—	—	—	—

PORTFOLIO (as of 10/31/93)

Portfolio Manager: Ronald Speaker - 1991

Investm't Category: Corporate Bond
Cap Gain	Asset Allocation
Cap & Income	Fund of Funds
✔ Income	Index
	Sector
✔ Domestic	Small Cap
✔ Foreign	Socially Conscious
Country/Region	State Specific

Portfolio: stocks 0% bonds 86%
convertibles 4% other 6% cash 4%

Largest Holdings: insurance 15%, energy 11%

Unrealized Net Capital Gains: 3% of portfolio value

SHAREHOLDER INFORMATION

Minimum Investment
Initial: $1,000   Subsequent: $50

Minimum IRA Investment
Initial: $250   Subsequent: $50

Maximum Fees
Load: none   12b-1: none
Other: none

Distributions
Income: monthly   Capital Gains: Dec

Exchange Options
Number Per Year: 4   Fee: none
Telephone: yes (money market fund available)

Services
IRA, other pension, auto exchange, auto invest, auto withdraw

Janus Growth & Income
(JAGIX)
Growth & Income

100 Fillmore St., Suite 300
Denver, CO 80206
(800) 525-3713, (303) 333-3863

PERFORMANCE

	3yr Annual	5yr Annual	10yr Annual	Bull	Bear
Return (%)	na	na	na	na	na
Differ from Category (+/-)	na	na	na	na	na

Total Risk	Standard Deviation	Category Risk	Risk Index	Beta
na	na	na	na	na

	1993	1992	1991	1990	1989	1988	1987	1986	1985	1984
Return (%)	6.6	5.3	—	—	—	—	—	—	—	—
Differ from category (+/-). . .	-6.0	-4.7	—	—	—	—	—	—	—	—

PER SHARE DATA

	1993	1992	1991	1990	1989	1988	1987	1986	1985	1984
Dividends, Net Income ($).	0.16	0.15	—	—	—	—	—	—	—	—
Distrib'ns, Cap Gain ($) . . .	0.33	0.00	—	—	—	—	—	—	—	—
Net Asset Value ($)	14.69	14.24	—	—	—	—	—	—	—	—
Expense Ratio (%)	1.28	1.52	—	—	—	—	—	—	—	—
Net Income to Assets (%) .	1.13	1.61	—	—	—	—	—	—	—	—
Portfolio Turnover (%).	138	120	—	—	—	—	—	—	—	—
Total Assets (Millions $). . . .	512	243	—	—	—	—	—	—	—	—

PORTFOLIO (as of 10/31/93)

Portfolio Manager: Thomas Marsico - 1991

Investm't Category: Growth & Income

Cap Gain	Asset Allocation
✔ Cap & Income	Fund of Funds
Income	Index
	Sector
✔ Domestic	Small Cap
✔ Foreign	Socially Conscious
Country/Region	State Specific

Portfolio: stocks 76% bonds 13%
convertibles 0% other 5% cash 6%

Largest Holdings: banking 18%, telecommunications 9%

Unrealized Net Capital Gains: 10% of portfolio value

SHAREHOLDER INFORMATION

Minimum Investment
Initial: $1,000   Subsequent: $50

Minimum IRA Investment
Initial: $250   Subsequent: $50

Maximum Fees
Load: none   12b-1: none
Other: none

Distributions
Income: quarterly   Capital Gains: Dec

Exchange Options
Number Per Year: 4   Fee: none
Telephone: yes (money market fund available)

Services
IRA, other pension, auto exchange, auto invest, auto withdraw

Janus Interm Gov't Securities (JAIGX)

100 Fillmore St., Suite 300
Denver, CO 80206
(800) 525-3713, (303) 333-3863

Government Bond

PERFORMANCE

	3yr Annual	5yr Annual	10yr Annual	Bull	Bear
Return (%)	na	na	na	na	na
Differ from Category (+/-)	na	na	na	na	na

Total Risk	Standard Deviation	Category Risk	Risk Index	Avg Mat
na	na	na	na	4.6 yrs

	1993	1992	1991	1990	1989	1988	1987	1986	1985	1984
Return (%)	2.4	4.8	—	—	—	—	—	—	—	—
Differ from category (+/-) ..	-8.0	-1.4	—	—	—	—	—	—	—	—

PER SHARE DATA

	1993	1992	1991	1990	1989	1988	1987	1986	1985	1984
Dividends, Net Income ($) .	0.21	0.26	—	—	—	—	—	—	—	—
Distrib'ns, Cap Gain ($) ...	0.00	0.11	—	—	—	—	—	—	—	—
Net Asset Value ($)	5.13	5.22	—	—	—	—	—	—	—	—
Expense Ratio (%)........	0.91	1.00	—	—	—	—	—	—	—	—
Net Income to Assets (%)..	4.27	4.95	—	—	—	—	—	—	—	—
Portfolio Turnover (%)....	371	270	—	—	—	—	—	—	—	—
Total Assets (Millions $)	56	70	—	—	—	—	—	—	—	—

PORTFOLIO (as of 10/31/93)

Portfolio Manager: Ronald Speaker - 1991

Investm't Category: Government Bond

Cap Gain	Asset Allocation
Cap & Income	Fund of Funds
✔ Income	Index
	Sector
✔ Domestic	Small Cap
Foreign	Socially Conscious
Country/Region	State Specific

Portfolio: stocks 0%   bonds 100%
convertibles 0%   other 0%   cash 0%

Largest Holdings: U. S. government 100%

Unrealized Net Capital Gains: 2% of portfolio value

SHAREHOLDER INFORMATION

Minimum Investment
Initial: $1,000   Subsequent: $50

Minimum IRA Investment
Initial: $250   Subsequent: $50

Maximum Fees
Load: none   12b-1: none
Other: none

Distributions
Income: monthly   Capital Gains: Dec

Exchange Options
Number Per Year: 4   Fee: none
Telephone: yes (money market fund available)

Services
IRA, other pension, auto exchange, auto invest, auto withdraw

Janus Mercury (JAMRX)

Growth

100 Fillmore St., Suite 300
Denver, CO 80206
(800) 525-3713, (303) 333-3863

fund in existence since 5/3/93

PERFORMANCE

	3yr Annual	5yr Annual	10yr Annual	Bull	Bear
Return (%)	na	na	na	na	na
Differ from Category (+/-)	na	na	na	na	na

Total Risk	Standard Deviation	Category Risk	Risk Index	Beta
na	na	na	na	na

	1993	1992	1991	1990	1989	1988	1987	1986	1985	1984
Return (%)	—	—	—	—	—	—	—	—	—	—
Differ from category (+/-)	—	—	—	—	—	—	—	—	—	—

PER SHARE DATA

	1993	1992	1991	1990	1989	1988	1987	1986	1985	1984
Dividends, Net Income ($)	0.00	—	—	—	—	—	—	—	—	—
Distrib'ns, Cap Gain ($)	0.00	—	—	—	—	—	—	—	—	—
Net Asset Value ($)	11.94	—	—	—	—	—	—	—	—	—
Expense Ratio (%)	1.75	—	—	—	—	—	—	—	—	—
Net Income to Assets (%)	-0.40	—	—	—	—	—	—	—	—	—
Portfolio Turnover (%)	151	—	—	—	—	—	—	—	—	—
Total Assets (Millions $)	123	—	—	—	—	—	—	—	—	—

PORTFOLIO (as of 10/31/93)

Portfolio Manager: Warren Lammert — 1993

Investm't Category: Growth

✔ Cap Gain	Asset Allocation
Cap & Income	Fund of Funds
Income	Index
	Sector
✔ Domestic	Small Cap
✔ Foreign	Socially Conscious
Country/Region	State Specific

Portfolio: stocks 87% bonds 0%
convertibles 2% other 6% cash 5%

Largest Holdings: auto related 8%, retail 7%

Unrealized Net Capital Gains: 10% of portfolio value

SHAREHOLDER INFORMATION

Minimum Investment
Initial: $1,000   Subsequent: $50

Minimum IRA Investment
Initial: $250   Subsequent: $50

Maximum Fees
Load: none   12b-1: none
Other: none

Distributions
Income: Dec   Capital Gains: Dec

Exchange Options
Number Per Year: 4   Fee: none
Telephone: yes (money market fund available)

Services
IRA, other pension, auto exchange, auto invest, auto withdraw

Janus Short-Term Bond
(JASBX)
Corporate Bond

100 Fillmore St., Suite 300
Denver, CO 80206
(800) 525-3713, (303) 333-3863

PERFORMANCE

	3yr Annual	5yr Annual	10yr Annual	Bull	Bear
Return (%)	na	na	na	na	na
Differ from Category (+/-)	na	na	na	na	na

Total Risk	Standard Deviation	Category Risk	Risk Index	Avg Mat
na	na	na	na	2.8 yrs

	1993	1992	1991	1990	1989	1988	1987	1986	1985	1984
Return (%)	6.1	—	—	—	—	—	—	—	—	—
Differ from category (+/-)	-5.3	—	—	—	—	—	—	—	—	—

PER SHARE DATA

	1993	1992	1991	1990	1989	1988	1987	1986	1985	1984
Dividends, Net Income ($)	0.14	—	—	—	—	—	—	—	—	—
Distrib'ns, Cap Gain ($)	0.01	—	—	—	—	—	—	—	—	—
Net Asset Value ($)	3.00	—	—	—	—	—	—	—	—	—
Expense Ratio (%)	0.83	—	—	—	—	—	—	—	—	—
Net Income to Assets (%)	4.86	—	—	—	—	—	—	—	—	—
Portfolio Turnover (%)	372	—	—	—	—	—	—	—	—	—
Total Assets (Millions $)	53	—	—	—	—	—	—	—	—	—

PORTFOLIO (as of 10/31/93)

Portfolio Manager: Ronald V. Speaker - 1992

Investm't Category: Corporate Bond

Cap Gain	Asset Allocation
Cap & Income	Fund of Funds
✔ Income	Index
	Sector
✔ Domestic	Small Cap
Foreign	Socially Conscious
Country/Region	State Specific

Portfolio: stocks 0%   bonds 100%
convertibles 0%   other 0%   cash 0%

Largest Holdings: U. S government 47%, electric utilities 9%

Unrealized Net Capital Gains: 0% of portfolio value

SHAREHOLDER INFORMATION

Minimum Investment
Initial: $1,000   Subsequent: $50

Minimum IRA Investment
Initial: $250   Subsequent: $50

Maximum Fees
Load: none   12b-1: none
Other: none

Distributions
Income: monthly   Capital Gains: Dec

Exchange Options
Number Per Year: 4   Fee: none
Telephone: yes (money market fund available)

Services
IRA, other pension, auto exchange, auto invest, auto withdraw

Janus Twenty (JAVLX)

Growth

100 Fillmore St., Suite 300
Denver, CO 80206
(800) 525-3713, (303) 333-3863

this fund is closed to new investors

PERFORMANCE

	3yr Annual	5yr Annual	10yr Annual	Bull	Bear
Return (%)	21.2	22.0	na	93.3	-7.1
Differ from Category (+/-)	2.0 abv av	7.4 high	na	8.6 abv av	5.3 abv av

Total Risk	Standard Deviation	Category Risk	Risk Index	Beta
high	15.6%	high	1.5	1.3

	1993	1992	1991	1990	1989	1988	1987	1986	1985	1984
Return (%)	3.4	1.9	69.2	0.5	50.8	19.0	-11.6	12.4	—	—
Differ from category (+/-) . . .	-9.8	-9.1	33.8	6.6	25.0	1.3	-12.8	-2.1	—	—

PER SHARE DATA

	1993	1992	1991	1990	1989	1988	1987	1986	1985	1984
Dividends, Net Income ($).	0.25	0.18	0.02	0.18	0.01	0.80	0.40	0.80	—	—
Distrib'ns, Cap Gain ($) . . .	0.45	0.19	0.42	0.00	0.42	0.00	1.17	0.81	—	—
Net Asset Value ($)	24.42	24.29	24.19	14.56	14.66	10.01	9.08	12.07	—	—
Expense Ratio (%)	1.05	1.12	1.07	1.32	1.88	1.70	1.79	2.00	—	—
Net Income to Assets (%) .	0.87	1.27	1.30	1.28	0.68	3.35	2.98	3.55	—	—
Portfolio Turnover (%).	99	79	163	228	220	317	202	152	—	—
Total Assets (Millions $). .	3,473	2,435	556	175	20	13	19	10	—	—

PORTFOLIO (as of 10/31/93)

Portfolio Manager: Thomas Marsico - 1988

Investm't Category: Growth

✔ Cap Gain	Asset Allocation
Cap & Income	Fund of Funds
Income	Index
	Sector
✔ Domestic	Small Cap
✔ Foreign	Socially Conscious
Country/Region	State Specific

Portfolio: stocks 89% bonds 5%
convertibles 0% other 0% cash 6%

Largest Holdings: banking 16%, financial services 12%

Unrealized Net Capital Gains: 14% of portfolio value

SHAREHOLDER INFORMATION

Minimum Investment
Initial: $1,000   Subsequent: $50

Minimum IRA Investment
Initial: $250   Subsequent: $50

Maximum Fees
Load: none   12b-1: none
Other: none

Distributions
Income: Dec   Capital Gains: Dec

Exchange Options
Number Per Year: 4   Fee: none
Telephone: yes (money market fund available)

Services
IRA, other pension, auto exchange, auto invest, auto withdraw

Janus Venture (JAVTX)

Aggressive Growth

100 Fillmore St., Suite 300
Denver, CO 80206
(800) 525-3713, (303) 333-3863

this fund is closed to new investors

PERFORMANCE

	3yr Annual	5yr Annual	10yr Annual	Bull	Bear
Return (%)	20.1	19.0	na	88.7	-8.5
Differ from Category (+/-)	-5.3 blw av	0.8 av	na	-36.3 blw av	6.5 abv av

Total Risk	Standard Deviation	Category Risk	Risk Index	Beta
abv av	11.0%	low	0.7	0.8

	1993	1992	1991	1990	1989	1988	1987	1986	1985	1984
Return (%)	9.0	7.4	47.8	-0.3	38.7	19.6	5.1	20.4	—	—
Differ from category (+/-) .	-10.0	-3.0	-4.6	6.0	11.7	4.4	8.5	11.0	—	—

PER SHARE DATA

	1993	1992	1991	1990	1989	1988	1987	1986	1985	1984
Dividends, Net Income ($) .	0.52	1.16	0.24	0.10	0.43	1.52	0.14	1.48	—	—
Distrib'ns, Cap Gain ($) ...	4.36	0.71	3.43	0.89	2.35	0.00	4.17	1.04	—	—
Net Asset Value ($)	48.88	49.30	47.63	34.71	35.85	27.85	24.55	27.45	—	—
Expense Ratio (%)........	0.97	1.07	1.04	1.16	1.28	1.41	1.44	1.95	—	—
Net Income to Assets (%)..	1.29	1.32	2.10	1.24	1.10	5.11	0.40	1.47	—	—
Portfolio Turnover (%)	139	124	167	184	219	299	250	248	—	—
Total Assets (Millions $) ..	1,724	1,545	893	257	58	34	46	30	—	—

PORTFOLIO (as of 10/31/93)

Portfolio Manager: Jim Goff - 1993, Warren Lammert - 1993

Investm't Category: Aggressive Growth
✔ Cap Gain	Asset Allocation
Cap & Income	Fund of Funds
Income	Index
	Sector
✔ Domestic	✔ Small Cap
✔ Foreign	Socially Conscious
Country/Region	State Specific

Portfolio: stocks 76%   bonds 0%
convertibles 0%   other 1%   cash 23%

Largest Holdings: insurance 15%, banking 11%

Unrealized Net Capital Gains: 11% of portfolio value

SHAREHOLDER INFORMATION

Minimum Investment
Initial: $1,000   Subsequent: $50

Minimum IRA Investment
Initial: $250   Subsequent: $50

Maximum Fees
Load: none   12b-1: none
Other: none

Distributions
Income: Dec   Capital Gains: Dec

Exchange Options
Number Per Year: 4   Fee: none
Telephone: yes (money market fund available)

Services
IRA, other pension, auto exchange, auto invest, auto withdraw

Janus Worldwide (JAWWX)

International Stock

100 Fillmore St., Suite 300
Denver, CO 80206
(800) 525-3713, (303) 333-3863

PERFORMANCE

	3yr Annual	5yr Annual	10yr Annual	Bull	Bear
Return (%)	na	na	na	na	na
Differ from Category (+/-)	na	na	na	na	na

Total Risk	Standard Deviation	Category Risk	Risk Index	Beta
na	na	na	na	na

	1993	1992	1991	1990	1989	1988	1987	1986	1985	1984
Return (%)	28.4	9.0	—	—	—	—	—	—	—	—
Differ from category (+/-). .	-10.1	12.5	—	—	—	—	—	—	—	—

PER SHARE DATA

	1993	1992	1991	1990	1989	1988	1987	1986	1985	1984
Dividends, Net Income ($).	0.27	0.22	—	—	—	—	—	—	—	—
Distrib'ns, Cap Gain ($) . . .	0.37	0.00	—	—	—	—	—	—	—	—
Net Asset Value ($)	25.03	20.00	—	—	—	—	—	—	—	—
Expense Ratio (%)	1.32	1.73	—	—	—	—	—	—	—	—
Net Income to Assets (%) .	0.92	1.74	—	—	—	—	—	—	—	—
Portfolio Turnover (%).	124	147	—	—	—	—	—	—	—	—
Total Assets (Millions $). .	1,022	161	—	—	—	—	—	—	—	—

PORTFOLIO (as of 10/31/93)

Portfolio Manager: Helen Hayes - 1992

Investm't Category: International Stock

✔ Cap Gain	Asset Allocation
Cap & Income	Fund of Funds
Income	Index
	Sector
✔ Domestic	Small Cap
✔ Foreign	Socially Conscious
Country/Region	State Specific

Portfolio:	stocks 83%	bonds 0%
convertibles 0%	other 3%	cash 14%

Largest Holdings: United States 22%, Switzerland 15%

Unrealized Net Capital Gains: 11% of portfolio value

SHAREHOLDER INFORMATION

Minimum Investment
Initial: $1,000   Subsequent: $50

Minimum IRA Investment
Initial: $250   Subsequent: $50

Maximum Fees
Load: none   12b-1: none
Other: none

Distributions
Income: Dec   Capital Gains: Dec

Exchange Options
Number Per Year: 4   Fee: none
Telephone: yes (money market fund available)

Services
IRA, other pension, auto exchange, auto invest, auto withdraw

Japan (SJPNX)

International Stock

160 Federal St.
Boston, MA 02110
(800) 225-2470, (617) 439-4640

PERFORMANCE

	3yr Annual	5yr Annual	10yr Annual	Bull	Bear
Return (%)	2.0	-0.1	14.3	17.5	-24.3
Differ from Category (+/-)	-12.3 low	-8.8 low	0.8 blw av	-37.6 low	-9.2 low

Total Risk	Standard Deviation	Category Risk	Risk Index	Beta
high	22.0%	high	1.9	0.1

	1993	1992	1991	1990	1989	1988	1987	1986	1985	1984
Return (%)	23.6	-16.7	3.1	-16.2	11.6	19.4	33.0	77.5	38.8	-1.7
Differ from category (+/-) .	-14.9	-13.2	-9.8	-5.1	-10.6	5.6	21.0	27.2	-1.8	7.8

PER SHARE DATA

	1993	1992	1991	1990	1989	1988	1987	1986	1985	1984
Dividends, Net Income ($) .	0.28	0.00	0.00	0.20	0.10	0.01	0.19	0.01	0.07	0.10
Distrib'ns, Cap Gain ($) ...	0.38	0.00	0.40	0.99	3.58	3.88	9.08	4.67	1.36	1.05
Net Asset Value ($)	10.33	8.90	10.69	10.76	14.27	16.24	16.97	20.28	15.53	12.60
Expense Ratio (%)........	1.29	1.42	1.26	1.05	1.02	1.01	0.90	0.70	0.64	0.66
Net Income to Assets (%) .	-0.39	-0.31	-0.15	0.72	0.34	0.28	0.41	0.51	0.63	0.73
Portfolio Turnover (%)	85	47	46	53	60	39	34	38	23	27
Total Assets (Millions $) ...	431	409	335	313	401	404	394	584	360	269

PORTFOLIO (as of 6/30/93)

Portfolio Manager: Seung Kwak - 1989, Elizabeth J. Allen - 1990

Investm't Category: International Stock

✔ Cap Gain	Asset Allocation
Cap & Income	Fund of Funds
Income	Index
	Sector
Domestic	Small Cap
✔ Foreign	Socially Conscious
✔ Country/Region	State Specific

Portfolio: stocks 92% bonds 0%
convertibles 6% other 0% cash 2%

Largest Holdings: Japan 92%

Unrealized Net Capital Gains: 14% of portfolio value

SHAREHOLDER INFORMATION

Minimum Investment
Initial: $1,000 Subsequent: $100

Minimum IRA Investment
Initial: $500 Subsequent: $50

Maximum Fees
Load: none 12b-1: none
Other: none

Distributions
Income: Dec Capital Gains: Dec

Exchange Options
Number Per Year: no limit Fee: none
Telephone: yes (money market fund available)

Services
IRA, other pension, auto exchange, auto invest, auto withdraw

Kaufmann (KAUFX)

Aggressive Growth

17 Battery Place, Suite 2624
New York, NY 10004
(800) 237-0132, (212) 344-2661

PERFORMANCE

	3yr Annual	5yr Annual	10yr Annual	Bull	Bear
Return (%)	33.1	26.6	na	173.6	-19.0
Differ from Category (+/-)	7.7 high	8.4 high	na	48.6 high	-4.0 blw av

Total Risk	Standard Deviation	Category Risk	Risk Index	Beta
high	18.1%	abv av	1.2	1.1

	1993	1992	1991	1990	1989	1988	1987	1986	1985	1984
Return (%)............	18.1	11.3	79.4	-6.1	46.8	58.5	-37.1	—	—	—
Differ from category (+/-)...	-0.8	0.8	27.0	0.2	19.8	43.3	-33.7	—	—	—

PER SHARE DATA

	1993	1992	1991	1990	1989	1988	1987	1986	1985	1984
Dividends, Net Income ($).	0.00	0.00	0.00	0.00	0.00	0.00	0.00	—	—	—
Distrib'ns, Cap Gain ($) ...	0.03	0.00	0.08	0.00	0.00	0.00	0.00	—	—	—
Net Asset Value ($)	3.45	2.95	2.65	1.53	1.63	1.11	0.69	—	—	—
Expense Ratio (%)	2.67	2.94	3.64	3.45	2.36	2.00	2.00	—	—	—
Net Income to Assets (%) .	-1.39	-1.74	-1.96	-2.56	-1.41	-0.23	0.92	—	—	—
Portfolio Turnover (%)......	80	51	128	195	202	343	228	—	—	—
Total Assets (Millions $)....	980	314	141	40	36	6	2	—	—	—

PORTFOLIO (as of 6/30/93)

Portfolio Manager: Lawrence Auriana - 1986,
Hans Utsch - 1986

Investm't Category: Aggressive Growth
- ✔ Cap Gain
- Cap & Income
- Income
- Asset Allocation
- Fund of Funds
- Index
- Sector
- ✔ Domestic
- ✔ Foreign
- Country/Region
- ✔ Small Cap
- Socially Conscious
- State Specific

Portfolio: stocks 99%   bonds 1%
convertibles 0%   other 0%   cash 0%

Largest Holdings: medical services 14%, computer hardware & software 11%

Unrealized Net Capital Gains: 11% of portfolio value

SHAREHOLDER INFORMATION

Minimum Investment
Initial: $1,500   Subsequent: $100

Minimum IRA Investment
Initial: $500   Subsequent: $50

Maximum Fees
Load: 0.20% redemption   12b-1: 0.75%
Other: none

Distributions
Income: Dec   Capital Gains: Dec

Exchange Options
Number Per Year: no limit   Fee: none
Telephone: yes (money market fund available)

Services
IRA, other pension, auto invest, auto withdraw

Laurel Intermediate Income (LRIIX)

909 A St.
Tacoma, WA 98402
(800) 235-4331

General Bond

PERFORMANCE

	3yr Annual	5yr Annual	10yr Annual	Bull	Bear
Return (%)	na	na	na	na	na
Differ from Category (+/-)	na	na	na	na	na

Total Risk	Standard Deviation	Category Risk	Risk Index	Avg Mat
na	na	na	na	4.2 yrs

	1993	1992	1991	1990	1989	1988	1987	1986	1985	1984
Return (%)	8.0	6.1	—	—	—	—	—	—	—	—
Differ from category (+/-)	-1.2	-0.6	—	—	—	—	—	—	—	—

PER SHARE DATA

	1993	1992	1991	1990	1989	1988	1987	1986	1985	1984
Dividends, Net Income ($)	0.48	0.60	—	—	—	—	—	—	—	—
Distrib'ns, Cap Gain ($)	0.05	0.08	—	—	—	—	—	—	—	—
Net Asset Value ($)	10.86	10.57	—	—	—	—	—	—	—	—
Expense Ratio (%)	0.60	0.51	—	—	—	—	—	—	—	—
Net Income to Assets (%)	4.81	5.91	—	—	—	—	—	—	—	—
Portfolio Turnover (%)	111	67	—	—	—	—	—	—	—	—
Total Assets (Millions $)	94	20	—	—	—	—	—	—	—	—

PORTFOLIO (as of 4/30/93)

Portfolio Manager: Laurie Carroll - 1991, Chris Pellegrino - 1991

Investm't Category: General Bond

Cap Gain	Asset Allocation
Cap & Income	Fund of Funds
✔ Income	Index
	Sector
✔ Domestic	Small Cap
Foreign	Socially Conscious
Country/Region	State Specific

Portfolio: stocks 0%   bonds 96%
convertibles 0%   other 0%   cash 4%

Largest Holdings: U.S. government 66%, corporate 30%

Unrealized Net Capital Gains: 1% of portfolio value

SHAREHOLDER INFORMATION

Minimum Investment
Initial: $1,000   Subsequent: $100

Minimum IRA Investment
Initial: $250   Subsequent: $100

Maximum Fees
Load: none   12b-1: 0.35%
Other: none

Distributions
Income: monthly   Capital Gains: Dec

Exchange Options
Number Per Year: no limit   Fee: none
Telephone: yes (money market fund available)

Services
IRA, auto invest, auto withdraw

Laurel Stock Port (LRSPX)

Growth & Income

909 A St.
Tacoma, WA 98402
(800) 235-4331

PERFORMANCE

	3yr Annual	5yr Annual	10yr Annual	Bull	Bear
Return (%)	17.1	16.6	na	75.7	-8.3
Differ from Category (+/-)	0.6 abv av	4.1 high	na	5.6 abv av	3.3 abv av

Total Risk	Standard Deviation	Category Risk	Risk Index	Beta
av	10.1%	av	1.2	0.9

	1993	1992	1991	1990	1989	1988	1987	1986	1985	1984
Return (%)	11.7	7.5	33.6	0.2	34.3	10.7	—	—	—	—
Differ from category (+/-) . . .	-0.8	-2.5	5.9	5.8	12.7	-6.1	—	—	—	—

PER SHARE DATA

	1993	1992	1991	1990	1989	1988	1987	1986	1985	1984
Dividends, Net Income ($) .	0.27	0.26	0.25	0.28	0.30	0.15	—	—	—	—
Distrib'ns, Cap Gain ($) . . .	0.39	1.07	0.52	0.05	0.66	0.00	—	—	—	—
Net Asset Value ($)	18.26	16.94	17.00	13.34	13.65	10.92	—	—	—	—
Expense Ratio (%)	0.90	0.90	0.90	0.82	0.35	0.35	—	—	—	—
Net Income to Assets (%) .	1.79	1.73	1.92	2.22	2.85	2.58	—	—	—	—
Portfolio Turnover (%).	64	84	69	76	93	42	—	—	—	—
Total Assets (Millions $). . . .	203	44	26	10	3	2	—	—	—	—

PORTFOLIO (as of 4/30/93)

Portfolio Manager: Bert J. Mullins - 1988

Investm't Category: Growth & Income
Cap Gain	Asset Allocation
✔ Cap & Income	Fund of Funds
Income	Index
	Sector
✔ Domestic	Small Cap
Foreign	Socially Conscious
Country/Region	State Specific

Portfolio: stocks 93% bonds 0%
convertibles 0% other 0% cash 7%

Largest Holdings: consumer basics 18%, technology 12%

Unrealized Net Capital Gains: 7% of portfolio value

SHAREHOLDER INFORMATION

Minimum Investment
Initial: $1,000   Subsequent: $100

Minimum IRA Investment
Initial: $250   Subsequent: $100

Maximum Fees
Load: none   12b-1: 0.35%
Other: none

Distributions
Income: quarterly   Capital Gains: Dec

Exchange Options
Number Per Year: no limit   Fee: none
Telephone: yes (money market fund available)

Services
IRA, auto invest, auto withdraw

Leeb Personal Finance
(LBPFX)
Growth

312 Walnut St., 21st Fl.
Cincinnati, OH 45202
(800) 545-0103, (513) 629-2070

PERFORMANCE

	3yr Annual	5yr Annual	10yr Annual	Bull	Bear
Return (%)	na	na	na	na	na
Differ from Category (+/-)	na	na	na	na	na

Total Risk	Standard Deviation	Category Risk	Risk Index	Beta
na	na	na	na	na

	1993	1992	1991	1990	1989	1988	1987	1986	1985	1984
Return (%)	2.8	6.2	—	—	—	—	—	—	—	—
Differ from category (+/-)	-10.4	-4.8	—	—	—	—	—	—	—	—

PER SHARE DATA

	1993	1992	1991	1990	1989	1988	1987	1986	1985	1984
Dividends, Net Income ($)	0.16	0.14	—	—	—	—	—	—	—	—
Distrib'ns, Cap Gain ($)	0.18	0.10	—	—	—	—	—	—	—	—
Net Asset Value ($)	10.73	10.78	—	—	—	—	—	—	—	—
Expense Ratio (%)	1.50	1.47	—	—	—	—	—	—	—	—
Net Income to Assets (%)	1.60	2.21	—	—	—	—	—	—	—	—
Portfolio Turnover (%)	na	75	—	—	—	—	—	—	—	—
Total Assets (Millions $)	54	28	—	—	—	—	—	—	—	—

PORTFOLIO (as of 6/30/93)

Portfolio Manager: Stephen Leeb - 1991

Investm't Category: Growth

✔ Cap Gain   Asset Allocation
   Cap & Income   Fund of Funds
   Income   Index
     Sector
✔ Domestic   Small Cap
   Foreign   Socially Conscious
   Country/Region   State Specific

Portfolio: stocks 25%   bonds 5%
convertibles 0%   other 0%   cash 70%

Largest Holdings: finance & insurance 8%, multi-industry 4%

Unrealized Net Capital Gains: 2% of portfolio value

SHAREHOLDER INFORMATION

Minimum Investment
Initial: $2,500   Subsequent: $0

Minimum IRA Investment
Initial: $250   Subsequent: $0

Maximum Fees
Load: none   12b-1: none
Other: none

Distributions
Income: Jun, Dec   Capital Gains: Dec

Exchange Options
Number Per Year: none   Fee: na
Telephone: na

Services
IRA, other pension, auto invest, auto withdraw

Legg Mason Global Gov't Trust (LMGGX)

International Bond

111 S. Calvert St.
Baltimore, MD 21203
(800) 822-5544, (410) 539-0000

fund in existence since 4/15/93

PERFORMANCE

	3yr Annual	5yr Annual	10yr Annual	Bull	Bear
Return (%)	na	na	na	na	na
Differ from Category (+/-)	na	na	na	na	na

Total Risk	Standard Deviation	Category Risk	Risk Index	Avg Mat
na	na	na	na	8.7 yrs

	1993	1992	1991	1990	1989	1988	1987	1986	1985	1984
Return (%)	—	—	—	—	—	—	—	—	—	—
Differ from category (+/-). . . .	—	—	—	—	—	—	—	—	—	—

PER SHARE DATA

	1993	1992	1991	1990	1989	1988	1987	1986	1985	1984
Dividends, Net Income ($).	0.35	—	—	—	—	—	—	—	—	—
Distrib'ns, Cap Gain ($) . . .	0.03	—	—	—	—	—	—	—	—	—
Net Asset Value ($)	10.27	—	—	—	—	—	—	—	—	—
Expense Ratio (%)	0.20	—	—	—	—	—	—	—	—	—
Net Income to Assets (%) .	5.22	—	—	—	—	—	—	—	—	—
Portfolio Turnover (%).	134	—	—	—	—	—	—	—	—	—
Total Assets (Millions $). . . .	163	—	—	—	—	—	—	—	—	—

PORTFOLIO (as of 6/30/93)

Portfolio Manager: Keith Gardner - 1993

Investm't Category: International Bond

Cap Gain	Asset Allocation
✔ Cap & Income	Fund of Funds
Income	Index
	Sector
✔ Domestic	Small Cap
✔ Foreign	Socially Conscious
Country/Region	State Specific

Portfolio: stocks 0%   bonds 96%
convertibles 0%   other 0%   cash 4%

Largest Holdings: United States 50%, Japan 11%

Unrealized Net Capital Gains: 0% of portfolio value

SHAREHOLDER INFORMATION

Minimum Investment
Initial: $1,000   Subsequent: $100

Minimum IRA Investment
Initial: $1,000   Subsequent: $100

Maximum Fees
Load: none   12b-1: 0.75%
Other: none

Distributions
Income: monthly   Capital Gains: Dec

Exchange Options
Number Per Year: 4   Fee: none
Telephone: yes (money market fund available)

Services
IRA, other pension, auto exchange, auto invest, auto withdraw

Legg Mason Investment Grade (LMIGX)

111 S. Calvert St.
Baltimore, MD 21203
(800) 822-5544, (410) 539-0000

General Bond

PERFORMANCE

	3yr Annual	5yr Annual	10yr Annual	Bull	Bear
Return (%)	11.2	10.4	na	43.8	1.3
Differ from Category (+/-)	1.0 abv av	0.6 abv av	na	4.4 abv av	-1.6 low

Total Risk	Standard Deviation	Category Risk	Risk Index	Avg Mat
low	3.9%	abv av	1.3	10.3 yrs

	1993	1992	1991	1990	1989	1988	1987	1986	1985	1984
Return (%)	11.2	6.7	15.9	5.7	12.9	7.6	—	—	—	—
Differ from category (+/-)	2.0	0.0	1.3	-1.2	1.6	0.0	—	—	—	—

PER SHARE DATA

	1993	1992	1991	1990	1989	1988	1987	1986	1985	1984
Dividends, Net Income ($)	0.62	0.66	0.75	0.84	0.82	0.77	—	—	—	—
Distrib'ns, Cap Gain ($)	0.85	0.03	0.02	0.04	0.00	0.02	—	—	—	—
Net Asset Value ($)	10.40	10.71	10.71	9.97	10.29	9.88	—	—	—	—
Expense Ratio (%)	0.85	0.85	0.71	0.50	0.80	1.00	—	—	—	—
Net Income to Assets (%)	5.80	6.10	7.30	8.30	8.10	7.70	—	—	—	—
Portfolio Turnover (%)	347	317	213	55	92	146	—	—	—	—
Total Assets (Millions $)	68	48	36	23	14	10	—	—	—	—

PORTFOLIO (as of 6/30/93)

Portfolio Manager: Kent S. Engel - 1987

Investm't Category: General Bond

Cap Gain	Asset Allocation
Cap & Income	Fund of Funds
✔ Income	Index
	Sector
✔ Domestic	Small Cap
✔ Foreign	Socially Conscious
Country/Region	State Specific

Portfolio: stocks 0% bonds 85%
convertibles 0% other 0% cash 15%

Largest Holdings: corporate 42%, asset-backed 15%

Unrealized Net Capital Gains: 3% of portfolio value

SHAREHOLDER INFORMATION

Minimum Investment
Initial: $1,000   Subsequent: $100

Minimum IRA Investment
Initial: $1,000   Subsequent: $100

Maximum Fees
Load: none   12b-1: 0.50%
Other: none

Distributions
Income: monthly   Capital Gains: Feb, Dec

Exchange Options
Number Per Year: 4   Fee: none
Telephone: yes (money market fund available)

Services
IRA, other pension, auto exchange, auto invest, auto withdraw

Legg Mason Special Investment (LMASX)

Aggressive Growth

111 S. Calvert St.
Baltimore, MD 21203
(800) 822-5544, (410) 539-0000

PERFORMANCE

	3yr Annual	5yr Annual	10yr Annual	Bull	Bear
Return (%)	25.9	21.5	na	114.9	-6.6
Differ from Category (+/-)	0.5 av	3.3 abv av	na	-10.1 av	8.4 high

Total Risk	Standard Deviation	Category Risk	Risk Index	Beta
abv av	12.3%	low	0.8	0.7

	1993	1992	1991	1990	1989	1988	1987	1986	1985	1984
Return (%)	24.1	15.3	39.4	0.5	32.0	19.6	-10.5	7.4	—	—
Differ from category (+/-) . . .	5.1	4.9	-13.0	6.8	5.0	4.4	-7.1	-2.0	—	—

PER SHARE DATA

	1993	1992	1991	1990	1989	1988	1987	1986	1985	1984
Dividends, Net Income ($) .	0.02	0.10	0.02	0.27	0.07	0.00	0.07	0.01	—	—
Distrib'ns, Cap Gain ($) . . .	0.14	1.10	0.07	1.32	0.00	0.00	0.88	0.21	—	—
Net Asset Value ($)	22.14	17.98	16.78	12.12	13.63	10.38	8.68	10.51	—	—
Expense Ratio (%)	2.00	2.10	2.30	2.30	2.50	2.50	2.50	2.50	—	—
Net Income to Assets (%) .	0.20	0.08	1.40	1.00	0.70	1.00	0.00	1.20	—	—
Portfolio Turnover (%)	32	57	76	116	122	159	77	41	—	—
Total Assets (Millions $)	491	202	107	68	44	44	56	34	—	—

PORTFOLIO (as of 9/30/93)

Portfolio Manager: William H. Miller III - 1985

Investm't Category: Aggressive Growth
✔ Cap Gain	Asset Allocation
Cap & Income	Fund of Funds
Income	Index
	Sector
✔ Domestic	✔ Small Cap
✔ Foreign	Socially Conscious
Country/Region	State Specific

Portfolio: stocks 94% bonds 2%
convertibles 0% other 1% cash 3%

Largest Holdings: finance 12%, entertainment 11%

Unrealized Net Capital Gains: 0% of portfolio value

SHAREHOLDER INFORMATION

Minimum Investment
Initial: $1,000   Subsequent: $100

Minimum IRA Investment
Initial: $1,000   Subsequent: $100

Maximum Fees
Load: none   12b-1: 1.00%
Other: none

Distributions
Income: Dec   Capital Gains: May, Dec

Exchange Options
Number Per Year: 4   Fee: none
Telephone: yes (money market fund available)

Services
IRA, other pension, auto exchange, auto invest, auto withdraw

Legg Mason Total Return (LMTRX)

Growth & Income

111 S. Calvert St.
Baltimore, MD 21203
(800) 822-5544, (410) 539-0000

PERFORMANCE

	3yr Annual	5yr Annual	10yr Annual	Bull	Bear
Return (%)	22.3	12.1	na	96.0	-22.2
Differ from Category (+/-)	5.9 high	-0.4 blw av	na	25.9 high	-10.6 low

Total Risk	Standard Deviation	Category Risk	Risk Index	Beta
av	9.0%	blw av	1.0	0.7

	1993	1992	1991	1990	1989	1988	1987	1986	1985	1984
Return (%)	14.0	14.3	40.4	-16.8	16.2	21.7	-7.7	1.4	—	—
Differ from category (+/-) ...	1.4	4.3	12.7	-11.2	-5.4	4.9	-8.1	-13.8	—	—

PER SHARE DATA

	1993	1992	1991	1990	1989	1988	1987	1986	1985	1984
Dividends, Net Income ($) .	0.40	0.30	0.18	0.28	0.20	0.12	0.23	0.15	—	—
Distrib'ns, Cap Gain ($) ...	0.34	0.00	0.00	0.07	0.18	0.00	1.39	0.03	—	—
Net Asset Value ($)	14.00	12.98	11.64	8.43	10.54	9.40	7.83	10.04	—	—
Expense Ratio (%)........	1.95	2.30	2.50	2.40	2.40	2.30	2.40	2.20	—	—
Net Income to Assets (%)..	3.10	3.10	3.10	2.00	1.60	1.90	1.70	3.80	—	—
Portfolio Turnover (%)	40	38	62	39	26	50	83	40	—	—
Total Assets (Millions $) ...	171	52	23	27	30	35	47	44	—	—

PORTFOLIO (as of 9/30/93)

Portfolio Manager: William H. Miller III - 1985, Nancy T. Dennin - 1992

Investm't Category: Growth & Income

Cap Gain	Asset Allocation
✔ Cap & Income	Fund of Funds
Income	Index
	Sector
✔ Domestic	Small Cap
✔ Foreign	Socially Conscious
Country/Region	State Specific

Portfolio: stocks 78% bonds 4%
convertibles 0% other 13% cash 5%

Largest Holdings: banking 17%, real estate 11%

Unrealized Net Capital Gains: 10% of portfolio value

SHAREHOLDER INFORMATION

Minimum Investment
Initial: $1,000   Subsequent: $100

Minimum IRA Investment
Initial: $1,000   Subsequent: $100

Maximum Fees
Load: none   12b-1: 1.00%
Other: none

Distributions
Income: quarterly   Capital Gains: May, Dec

Exchange Options
Number Per Year: 4   Fee: none
Telephone: yes (money market fund available)

Services
IRA, other pension, auto exchange, auto invest, auto withdraw

Legg Mason US Gov't Interm Port (LGINX)

111 S. Calvert St.
Baltimore, MD 21203
(800) 822-5544, (410) 539-0000

General Bond

PERFORMANCE

	3yr Annual	5yr Annual	10yr Annual	Bull	Bear
Return (%)	9.0	9.7	na	36.2	3.6
Differ from Category (+/-)	-1.2 blw av	-0.1 blw av	na	-3.2 blw av	0.6 abv av

Total Risk	Standard Deviation	Category Risk	Risk Index	Avg Mat
low	2.9%	blw av	1.0	4.0 yrs

	1993	1992	1991	1990	1989	1988	1987	1986	1985	1984
Return (%)	6.6	6.2	14.3	9.0	12.7	6.4	—	—	—	—
Differ from category (+/-)	-2.6	-0.5	-0.3	2.1	1.4	-1.2	—	—	—	—

PER SHARE DATA

	1993	1992	1991	1990	1989	1988	1987	1986	1985	1984
Dividends, Net Income ($)	0.52	0.60	0.71	0.78	0.79	0.74	—	—	—	—
Distrib'ns, Cap Gain ($)	0.46	0.10	0.21	0.00	0.00	0.00	—	—	—	—
Net Asset Value ($)	10.43	10.72	10.77	10.29	10.20	9.79	—	—	—	—
Expense Ratio (%)	0.90	0.90	0.80	0.60	0.80	1.00	—	—	—	—
Net Income to Assets (%)	4.90	5.50	6.70	7.70	7.90	7.40	—	—	—	—
Portfolio Turnover (%)	507	513	643	67	57	133	—	—	—	—
Total Assets (Millions $)	299	307	212	74	43	27	—	—	—	—

PORTFOLIO (as of 6/30/93)

Portfolio Manager: Stephen A. Walsh - 1991

Investm't Category: General Bond

Cap Gain	Asset Allocation
Cap & Income	Fund of Funds
✔ Income	Index
	Sector
✔ Domestic	Small Cap
Foreign	Socially Conscious
Country/Region	State Specific

Portfolio: stocks 0%   bonds 96%
convertibles 0%   other 0%   cash 4%

Largest Holdings: mortgage-backed 46%, U.S. government & agencies 26%

Unrealized Net Capital Gains: 1% of portfolio value

SHAREHOLDER INFORMATION

Minimum Investment
Initial: $1,000   Subsequent: $100

Minimum IRA Investment
Initial: $1,000   Subsequent: $100

Maximum Fees
Load: none   12b-1: 0.50%
Other: none

Distributions
Income: monthly   Capital Gains: Feb, Dec

Exchange Options
Number Per Year: 4   Fee: none
Telephone: yes (money market fund available)

Services
IRA, other pension, auto exchange, auto invest, auto withdraw

Legg Mason Value
(LMVTX)

Growth

111 S. Calvert St.
Baltimore, MD 21203
(800) 822-5544, (410) 539-0000

	3yr Annual	5yr Annual	10yr Annual	Bull	Bear
Return (%)	18.6	10.7	12.1	76.6	-21.4
Differ from Category (+/-)	-0.6 av	-3.9 low	-0.5 blw av	-8.1 blw av	-9.0 low

Total Risk	Standard Deviation	Category Risk	Risk Index	Beta
abv av	11.5%	av	1.1	1.0

	1993	1992	1991	1990	1989	1988	1987	1986	1985	1984
Return (%)	11.2	11.4	34.7	-16.9	20.0	25.7	-7.4	9.4	31.7	12.7
Differ from category (+/-) . .	-2.0	0.4	-0.6	-10.8	-5.8	8.0	-8.6	-5.1	2.4	12.7

PER SHARE DATA

	1993	1992	1991	1990	1989	1988	1987	1986	1985	1984
Dividends, Net Income ($) .	0.23	0.15	0.22	0.36	0.33	0.18	0.25	0.20	0.17	0.17
Distrib'ns, Cap Gain ($) . . .	0.15	0.00	0.00	0.03	0.73	0.00	1.39	1.39	0.43	0.17
Net Asset Value ($)	18.87	17.32	15.70	11.84	14.69	13.14	10.60	13.05	13.35	10.65
Expense Ratio (%).	1.86	1.90	1.90	1.86	1.96	1.97	2.00	2.07	2.41	2.50
Net Income to Assets (%). .	1.10	1.70	2.50	2.20	1.60	1.50	1.50	2.00	2.30	2.50
Portfolio Turnover (%)	21	39	39	31	30	48	43	32	37	17
Total Assets (Millions $) . . .	902	746	690	809	721	666	819	599	163	61

PORTFOLIO (as of 9/30/93)

Portfolio Manager: William H. Miller III - 1982

Investm't Category: Growth

✔ Cap Gain	Asset Allocation
Cap & Income	Fund of Funds
Income	Index
	Sector
✔ Domestic	Small Cap
✔ Foreign	Socially Conscious
Country/Region	State Specific

Portfolio: stocks 92%   bonds 3%
convertibles 0%   other 2%   cash 3%

Largest Holdings: finance 20%, banking 19%

Unrealized Net Capital Gains: 27% of portfolio value

SHAREHOLDER INFORMATION

Minimum Investment
Initial: $1,000   Subsequent: $100

Minimum IRA Investment
Initial: $1,000   Subsequent: $100

Maximum Fees
Load: none   12b-1: 1.00%
Other: none

Distributions
Income: quarterly   Capital Gains: Dec

Exchange Options
Number Per Year: 4   Fee: none
Telephone: yes (money market fund available)

Services
IRA, other pension, auto exchange, auto invest, auto withdraw

Lepercq-Istel (ISTLX)

Balanced

1675 Broadway, 16th Fl.
New York, NY 10019
(800) 338-1579, (212) 698-0749

PERFORMANCE

	3yr Annual	5yr Annual	10yr Annual	Bull	Bear
Return (%)	12.0	9.8	7.9	45.8	-10.1
Differ from Category (+/-)	-3.0 low	-2.3 low	-4.1 low	-15.8 low	-4.3 low

Total Risk	Standard Deviation	Category Risk	Risk Index	Beta
av	8.7%	high	1.4	0.6

	1993	1992	1991	1990	1989	1988	1987	1986	1985	1984
Return (%)	13.5	5.4	17.3	-6.6	21.7	7.0	2.2	8.1	20.0	-4.9
Differ from category (+/-). . .	0.1	-2.7	-6.6	-6.1	4.1	-5.0	-0.1	-9.4	-3.7	-12.3

PER SHARE DATA

	1993	1992	1991	1990	1989	1988	1987	1986	1985	1984
Dividends, Net Income ($).	0.31	0.40	0.52	0.62	0.62	0.54	0.56	0.63	0.74	0.60
Distrib'ns, Cap Gain ($) . . .	0.92	0.22	0.00	0.00	0.37	0.23	0.85	1.08	1.47	0.73
Net Asset Value ($)	14.84	14.17	14.05	12.46	14.00	12.33	12.23	13.29	13.89	13.58
Expense Ratio (%)	1.49	1.53	1.54	1.50	1.48	1.50	1.44	1.67	1.12	1.04
Net Income to Assets (%) .	2.00	2.90	3.80	4.57	4.41	4.13	2.69	3.01	3.81	3.77
Portfolio Turnover (%).	na	20	22	24	48	72	67	44	27	25
Total Assets (Millions $).	16	17	17	19	22	20	22	23	28	91

PORTFOLIO (as of 12/31/93)

Portfolio Manager: Bruno Desforges - 1986

Investm't Category: Balanced
Cap Gain	Asset Allocation
✔ Cap & Income	Fund of Funds
Income	Index
	Sector
✔ Domestic	Small Cap
✔ Foreign	Socially Conscious
Country/Region	State Specific

Portfolio: stocks 72% bonds 20%
convertibles 0% other 0% cash 8%

Largest Holdings: stocks—energy 21%,
bonds—U.S. government 20%

Unrealized Net Capital Gains: 16% of portfolio value

SHAREHOLDER INFORMATION

Minimum Investment
Initial: $500   Subsequent: 1 share

Minimum IRA Investment
Initial: $500   Subsequent: 1 share

Maximum Fees
Load: none   12b-1: 1.00%
Other: none

Distributions
Income: Jul, Dec   Capital Gains: Dec

Exchange Options
Number Per Year: none   Fee: na
Telephone: na

Services
IRA, other pension, auto withdraw

Lexington Global

(LXGLX)

International Stock

Park 80 W. Plaza 2
P.O. Box 1515
Saddle Brook, NJ 07662
(800) 526-0056, (201) 845-7300

PERFORMANCE

	3yr Annual	5yr Annual	10yr Annual	Bull	Bear
Return (%)	13.6	8.8	na	55.5	-21.3
Differ from Category (+/-)	-0.6 av	0.1 av	na	0.4 av	-6.2 low

Total Risk	Standard Deviation	Category Risk	Risk Index	Beta
abv av	12.2%	blw av	1.0	0.7

	1993	1992	1991	1990	1989	1988	1987	1986	1985	1984
Return (%)	31.8	-3.5	15.5	-16.7	25.1	16.3	—	—	—	—
Differ from category (+/-) . .	-6.7	0.0	2.6	-5.6	2.9	2.5	—	—	—	—

PER SHARE DATA

	1993	1992	1991	1990	1989	1988	1987	1986	1985	1984
Dividends, Net Income ($) .	0.05	0.07	0.15	0.12	0.01	0.50	—	—	—	—
Distrib'ns, Cap Gain ($) . . .	1.05	0.00	0.12	0.30	0.76	0.07	—	—	—	—
Net Asset Value ($)	13.51	11.09	11.57	10.26	12.83	10.89	—	—	—	—
Expense Ratio (%).	1.50	1.52	1.57	1.59	1.64	1.80	—	—	—	—
Net Income to Assets (%). .	1.41	0.55	0.79	0.99	0.13	0.12	—	—	—	—
Portfolio Turnover (%)	74	81	76	82	114	97	—	—	—	—
Total Assets (Millions $)	78	50	54	51	57	38	—	—	—	—

PORTFOLIO (as of 6/30/93)

Portfolio Manager: Caesar Bryan - 1987

Investm't Category: International Stock

✔ Cap Gain	Asset Allocation
Cap & Income	Fund of Funds
Income	Index
	Sector
✔ Domestic	Small Cap
✔ Foreign	Socially Conscious
Country/Region	State Specific

Portfolio: stocks 100% bonds 0%
convertibles 0% other 0% cash 0%

Largest Holdings: Japan 27%, United States 27%

Unrealized Net Capital Gains: 9% of portfolio value

SHAREHOLDER INFORMATION

Minimum Investment
Initial: $1,000   Subsequent: $50

Minimum IRA Investment
Initial: $250   Subsequent: $50

Maximum Fees
Load: none   12b-1: none
Other: none

Distributions
Income: Aug, Dec   Capital Gains: Dec

Exchange Options
Number Per Year: no limit   Fee: none
Telephone: yes (money market fund available)

Services
IRA, other pension, auto exchange, auto invest, auto withdraw

Lexington GNMA Income (LEXNX)

Mortgage-Backed Bond

Park 80 W. Plaza 2
P.O. Box 1515
Saddle Brook, NJ 07662
(800) 526-0056, (201) 845-7300

PERFORMANCE

	3yr Annual	5yr Annual	10yr Annual	Bull	Bear
Return (%)	9.5	10.6	10.1	39.0	3.2
Differ from Category (+/-)	0.3 abv av	0.6 abv av	-0.6 low	2.3 abv av	-1.4 low

Total Risk	Standard Deviation	Category Risk	Risk Index	Avg Mat
low	3.5%	abv av	1.4	na

	1993	1992	1991	1990	1989	1988	1987	1986	1985	1984
Return (%)	7.9	5.1	15.7	9.1	15.5	6.8	1.5	11.7	17.2	11.9
Differ from category (+/-)	1.1	-1.0	1.3	-0.4	3.2	-0.2	-0.6	0.5	-2.1	-1.4

PER SHARE DATA

	1993	1992	1991	1990	1989	1988	1987	1986	1985	1984
Dividends, Net Income ($)	0.58	0.60	0.63	0.66	0.68	0.64	0.72	0.74	0.92	0.81
Distrib'ns, Cap Gain ($)	0.00	0.00	0.00	0.00	0.00	0.00	0.03	0.00	0.00	0.00
Net Asset Value ($)	8.32	8.26	8.45	7.90	7.88	7.45	7.58	8.22	8.06	7.74
Expense Ratio (%)	1.04	1.01	1.02	1.04	1.03	1.07	0.98	0.86	1.01	1.22
Net Income to Assets (%)	7.21	7.31	7.97	8.43	8.88	8.31	8.49	9.30	11.06	11.89
Portfolio Turnover (%)	29	180	139	113	103	233	89	300	167	133
Total Assets (Millions $)	160	132	122	98	96	97	108	141	87	25

PORTFOLIO (as of 6/30/93)

Portfolio Manager: Denis Jamison - 1981

Investm't Category: Mortgage-Backed Bond

Cap Gain	Asset Allocation
Cap & Income	Fund of Funds
✔ Income	Index
	Sector
✔ Domestic	Small Cap
Foreign	Socially Conscious
Country/Region	State Specific

Portfolio: stocks 0% bonds 94%
convertibles 0% other 0% cash 6%

Largest Holdings: mortgage-backed 94%

Unrealized Net Capital Gains: 5% of portfolio value

SHAREHOLDER INFORMATION

Minimum Investment
Initial: $1,000   Subsequent: $50

Minimum IRA Investment
Initial: $250   Subsequent: $50

Maximum Fees
Load: none   12b-1: none
Other: none

Distributions
Income: monthly   Capital Gains: Dec

Exchange Options
Number Per Year: no limit   Fee: none
Telephone: yes (money market fund available)

Services
IRA, other pension, auto exchange, auto invest, auto withdraw

Lexington GoldFund

(LEXMX)

Gold

Park 80 W. Plaza 2
P.O. Box 1515
Saddle Brook, NJ 07662
(800) 526-0056, (201) 845-7300

PERFORMANCE

	3yr Annual	5yr Annual	10yr Annual	Bull	Bear
Return (%)	11.7	6.4	6.8	25.4	-11.7
Differ from Category (+/-)	-2.0 blw av	-5.9 blw av	3.9 high	-8.2 blw av	-57.6 abv av

Total Risk	Standard Deviation	Category Risk	Risk Index	Beta
high	26.1%	av	1.0	-0.4

	1993	1992	1991	1990	1989	1988	1987	1986	1985	1984
Return (%)	86.9	-20.5	-6.1	-20.6	23.6	-15.0	46.3	32.6	12.9	-24.0
Differ from category (+/-) ...	0.0	-4.8	-1.3	-52.1	-1.1	3.9	14.4	-5.0	20.3	2.2

PER SHARE DATA

	1993	1992	1991	1990	1989	1988	1987	1986	1985	1984
Dividends, Net Income ($)	0.01	0.01	0.03	0.03	0.05	0.05	0.05	0.01	0.03	0.03
Distrib'ns, Cap Gain ($) ...	0.00	0.00	0.00	0.00	0.00	0.00	0.31	0.00	0.00	0.10
Net Asset Value ($)	6.90	3.70	4.68	5.03	6.39	5.21	6.19	4.49	3.40	3.05
Expense Ratio (%)........	1.76	1.69	1.43	1.36	1.42	1.61	1.29	1.52	1.52	1.52
Net Income to Assets (%)..	0.24	0.58	0.81	0.68	1.14	0.78	0.57	1.11	0.71	1.14
Portfolio Turnover (%).....	18	13	22	12	16	20	14	14	30	17
Total Assets (Millions $) ...	161	72	96	106	155	93	105	24	12	7

PORTFOLIO (as of 6/30/93)

Portfolio Manager: Caesar Bryan - 1987

Investm't Category: Gold

✔ Cap Gain	Asset Allocation
Cap & Income	Fund of Funds
Income	Index
	✔ Sector
✔ Domestic	Small Cap
✔ Foreign	Socially Conscious
Country/Region	State Specific

Portfolio:	stocks 96%	bonds 0%
convertibles 0%	other 4%	cash 0%

Largest Holdings: N. American gold mining cos. 52%, S. African gold mining cos. 32%

Unrealized Net Capital Gains: 17% of portfolio value

SHAREHOLDER INFORMATION

Minimum Investment
Initial: $1,000   Subsequent: $50

Minimum IRA Investment
Initial: $250   Subsequent: $50

Maximum Fees
Load: none   12b-1: 0.25%
Other: none

Distributions
Income: Aug, Dec   Capital Gains: Dec

Exchange Options
Number Per Year: no limit   Fee: none
Telephone: yes (money market fund available)

Services
IRA, other pension, auto exchange, auto invest, auto withdraw

Lexington Growth & Income (LEXRX)

Growth & Income

Park 80 W. Plaza 2
P.O. Box 1515
Saddle Brook, NJ 07662
(800) 526-0056, (201) 845-7300

PERFORMANCE

	3yr Annual	5yr Annual	10yr Annual	Bull	Bear
Return (%)	16.6	12.7	11.2	68.0	-15.1
Differ from Category (+/-)	0.2 av	0.2 av	-1.2 blw av	-2.1 av	-3.5 blw av

Total Risk	Standard Deviation	Category Risk	Risk Index	Beta
abv av	11.1%	abv av	1.3	0.9

	1993	1992	1991	1990	1989	1988	1987	1986	1985	1984
Return (%)	13.2	12.3	24.8	-10.2	27.5	9.4	0.0	20.5	26.3	-4.1
Differ from category (+/-) . . .	0.6	2.3	-2.9	-4.6	5.9	-7.4	-0.4	5.3	0.8	-10.3

PER SHARE DATA

	1993	1992	1991	1990	1989	1988	1987	1986	1985	1984
Dividends, Net Income ($) .	0.20	0.31	0.34	0.30	0.60	0.44	0.51	0.66	0.60	0.80
Distrib'ns, Cap Gain ($) . . .	2.02	1.84	1.02	0.00	1.54	0.00	5.52	2.33	0.10	2.73
Net Asset Value ($)	16.16	16.25	16.39	14.24	16.19	14.39	13.57	19.16	18.62	15.37
Expense Ratio (%)	1.28	1.20	1.13	1.04	1.02	1.10	0.96	0.96	1.00	1.00
Net Income to Assets (%) .	1.33	2.57	2.19	3.91	2.82	3.20	2.37	2.52	3.52	4.20
Portfolio Turnover (%)	94	88	80	67	64	81	95	81	86	59
Total Assets (Millions $)	136	126	121	105	128	111	113	124	114	99

PORTFOLIO (as of 6/30/93)

Portfolio Manager: William Stack - 1991

Investm't Category: Growth & Income

Cap Gain	Asset Allocation
✔ Cap & Income	Fund of Funds
Income	Index
	Sector
✔ Domestic	Small Cap
✔ Foreign	Socially Conscious
Country/Region	State Specific

Portfolio: stocks 94%   bonds 0%
convertibles 2%   other 0%   cash 4%

Largest Holdings: banking 12%, petroleum (integrated) 7%

Unrealized Net Capital Gains: 9% of portfolio value

SHAREHOLDER INFORMATION

Minimum Investment
Initial: $1,000   Subsequent: $50

Minimum IRA Investment
Initial: $250   Subsequent: $50

Maximum Fees
Load: none   12b-1: 0.25%
Other: none

Distributions
Income: quarterly   Capital Gains: Dec

Exchange Options
Number Per Year: no limit   Fee: none
Telephone: yes (money market fund available)

Services
IRA, other pension, auto exchange, auto invest, auto withdraw

Lexington Tax-Exempt Bond Trust (LEBDX)

Tax-Exempt Bond

Park 80 W. Plaza 2
P.O. Box 1515
Saddle Brook, NJ 07662
(800) 526-0056, (201) 845-7300

PERFORMANCE

	3yr Annual	5yr Annual	10yr Annual	Bull	Bear
Return (%)	9.1	8.2	na	35.0	2.5
Differ from Category (+/-)	-1.2 low	-1.0 low	na	-5.1 low	0.2 av

Total Risk	Standard Deviation	Category Risk	Risk Index	Avg Mat
blw av	4.2%	av	1.0	10.2 yrs

	1993	1992	1991	1990	1989	1988	1987	1986	1985	1984
Return (%)	10.9	6.5	10.0	6.5	7.3	10.2	0.0	—	—	—
Differ from category (+/-) . .	-0.6	-1.8	-1.3	0.2	-1.7	0.1	1.2	—	—	—

PER SHARE DATA

	1993	1992	1991	1990	1989	1988	1987	1986	1985	1984
Dividends, Net Income ($) .	0.55	0.61	0.67	0.70	0.63	0.63	0.85	—	—	—
Distrib'ns, Cap Gain ($) . . .	0.00	0.00	0.00	0.00	0.00	0.00	0.00	—	—	—
Net Asset Value ($)	10.95	10.39	10.35	10.05	10.12	10.03	9.69	—	—	—
Expense Ratio (%).	1.42	1.50	1.12	1.08	1.20	1.33	0.00	—	—	—
Net Income to Assets (%) . .	5.31	5.92	6.64	7.20	6.22	6.33	7.95	—	—	—
Portfolio Turnover (%)	19	31	29	45	47	67	67	—	—	—
Total Assets (Millions $)	14	13	12	11	13	13	3	—	—	—

PORTFOLIO (as of 6/30/93)

Portfolio Manager: Denis Jamison - 1987

Investm't Category: Tax-Exempt Bond
Cap Gain	Asset Allocation
Cap & Income	Fund of Funds
✔ Income	Index
	Sector
✔ Domestic	Small Cap
Foreign	Socially Conscious
Country/Region	State Specific

Portfolio: stocks 0%   bonds 100%
convertibles 0%   other 0%   cash 0%

Largest Holdings: general obligation 19%

Unrealized Net Capital Gains: 6% of portfolio value

SHAREHOLDER INFORMATION

Minimum Investment
Initial: $1,000   Subsequent: $50

Minimum IRA Investment
Initial: na   Subsequent: na

Maximum Fees
Load: none   12b-1: none
Other: none

Distributions
Income: monthly   Capital Gains: Dec

Exchange Options
Number Per Year: no limit   Fee: none
Telephone: yes (money market fund available)

Services
auto exchange, auto invest, auto withdraw

Lexington Worldwide Emerging Mkts (LEXGX)

International Stock

Park 80 W. Plaza 2
P.O. Box 1515
Saddle Brook, NJ 07662
(800) 526-0056, (201) 845-7300

PERFORMANCE

	3yr Annual	5yr Annual	10yr Annual	Bull	Bear
Return (%)	28.1	18.2	12.2	122.0	-18.8
Differ from Category (+/-)	13.8 high	9.5 high	-1.2 low	66.9 high	-3.7 blw av

Total Risk	Standard Deviation	Category Risk	Risk Index	Beta
high	14.4%	abv av	1.2	0.6

	1993	1992	1991	1990	1989	1988	1987	1986	1985	1984
Return (%)	63.3	3.7	24.1	-14.4	28.1	10.4	0.2	20.6	26.6	-18.3
Differ from category (+/-). .	24.8	7.2	11.2	-3.3	5.9	-3.4	-11.8	-29.7	-14.0	-8.8

PER SHARE DATA

	1993	1992	1991	1990	1989	1988	1987	1986	1985	1984
Dividends, Net Income ($).	0.00	0.10	0.10	0.23	0.20	0.11	0.38	0.20	0.11	0.30
Distrib'ns, Cap Gain ($) . . .	0.17	0.60	1.48	0.43	0.17	0.00	3.67	0.00	0.00	0.07
Net Asset Value ($)	13.96	8.66	9.03	8.56	10.79	8.72	8.00	11.80	9.97	7.98
Expense Ratio (%)	1.95	1.89	1.97	1.42	1.36	1.33	1.34	1.32	1.43	1.50
Net Income to Assets (%) .	0.89	0.75	0.79	2.52	1.18	1.27	1.26	1.24	2.00	1.78
Portfolio Turnover (%).	130	91	112	52	59	48	83	54	151	141
Total Assets (Millions $). . . .	248	30	25	22	29	26	26	29	28	22

PORTFOLIO (as of 6/30/93)

Portfolio Manager: William Stack - 1991, Caesar Bryan - 1991

Investm't Category: International Stock

✔ Cap Gain	Asset Allocation
Cap & Income	Fund of Funds
Income	Index
	Sector
✔ Domestic	Small Cap
✔ Foreign	Socially Conscious
Country/Region	State Specific

Portfolio: stocks 87% bonds 0%
convertibles 0% other 0% cash 13%

Largest Holdings: Mexico 16%, Malaysia 9%

Unrealized Net Capital Gains: 7% of portfolio value

SHAREHOLDER INFORMATION

Minimum Investment
Initial: $1,000 Subsequent: $50

Minimum IRA Investment
Initial: $250 Subsequent: $50

Maximum Fees
Load: none 12b-1: none
Other: none

Distributions
Income: Dec Capital Gains: Dec

Exchange Options
Number Per Year: no limit Fee: none
Telephone: yes (money market fund available)

Services
IRA, other pension, auto exchange, auto invest, auto withdraw

Lindner (LDNRX)

Growth & Income

7711 Carondelet Ave.
P.O. Box 11208
St. Louis, MO 63105
(314) 727-5305

PERFORMANCE

	3yr Annual	5yr Annual	10yr Annual	Bull	Bear
Return (%)	18.5	12.3	13.6	64.9	-10.3
Differ from Category (+/-)	2.1 abv av	-0.2 av	1.2 abv av	-5.2 blw av	1.3 av

Total Risk	Standard Deviation	Category Risk	Risk Index	Beta
av	8.5%	blw av	1.0	0.5

	1993	1992	1991	1990	1989	1988	1987	1986	1985	1984
Return (%)	19.8	12.7	23.4	-11.3	21.2	20.3	8.8	14.0	19.5	12.8
Differ from category (+/-) ...	7.2	2.7	-4.3	-5.7	-0.4	3.5	8.4	-1.2	-5.9	6.6

PER SHARE DATA

	1993	1992	1991	1990	1989	1988	1987	1986	1985	1984
Dividends, Net Income ($) .	0.45	0.52	0.66	0.85	1.10	0.70	1.01	1.49	1.71	0.89
Distrib'ns, Cap Gain ($) ...	0.53	0.15	0.00	0.70	0.64	0.15	1.57	4.08	0.86	1.58
Net Asset Value ($)	23.22	20.22	18.55	15.58	19.21	17.31	15.12	16.12	19.16	18.34
Expense Ratio (%)........	0.80	0.80	0.83	0.74	0.92	1.07	0.89	0.58	0.65	0.88
Net Income to Assets (%)..	2.52	3.05	4.64	4.84	4.93	3.76	4.56	5.83	7.44	6.22
Portfolio Turnover (%)	18	11	13	19	18	21	39	32	46	40
Total Assets (Millions $) ..	1,504	979	783	716	535	404	406	390	397	339

PORTFOLIO (as of 6/30/93)

Portfolio Manager: R. Lange - 1977, E. Ryback - 1982, L. Callahan - 1993

Investm't Category: Growth & Income

Cap Gain	Asset Allocation
✔ Cap & Income	Fund of Funds
Income	Index
	Sector
✔ Domestic	Small Cap
✔ Foreign	Socially Conscious
Country/Region	State Specific

Portfolio: stocks 85% bonds 5%
convertibles 2% other 2% cash 6%

Largest Holdings: utilities 13%, financial services 11%

Unrealized Net Capital Gains: 19% of portfolio value

SHAREHOLDER INFORMATION

Minimum Investment
Initial: $2,000   Subsequent: $100

Minimum IRA Investment
Initial: $250   Subsequent: $100

Maximum Fees
Load: 2.00% redemption   12b-1: none
Other: redemption fee applies for 60 days

Distributions
Income: Aug, Dec   Capital Gains: Aug, Dec

Exchange Options
Number Per Year: none   Fee: na
Telephone: na

Services
IRA, auto withdraw

Lindner Dividend

(LDDVX)

Balanced

7711 Carondelet Ave.
P.O. Box 11208
St. Louis, MO 63105
(314) 727-5305

PERFORMANCE

	3yr Annual	5yr Annual	10yr Annual	Bull	Bear
Return (%)	21.0	13.1	13.6	72.8	-4.1
Differ from Category (+/-)	6.0 high	1.0 av	1.6 abv av	11.2 high	1.7 abv av

Total Risk	Standard Deviation	Category Risk	Risk Index	Beta
blw av	4.4%	low	0.7	0.2

	1993	1992	1991	1990	1989	1988	1987	1986	1985	1984
Return (%)............	14.9	21.1	27.3	-6.5	11.8	24.2	-4.0	20.7	17.1	15.2
Differ from category (+/-)...	1.5	13.0	3.4	-6.0	-5.8	12.2	-6.3	3.2	-6.6	7.8

PER SHARE DATA

	1993	1992	1991	1990	1989	1988	1987	1986	1985	1984
Dividends, Net Income ($).	1.74	1.86	1.99	1.86	2.19	1.76	1.87	2.17	1.76	1.27
Distrib'ns, Cap Gain ($) ...	0.57	0.10	0.00	0.02	0.00	0.05	1.16	3.25	0.00	0.86
Net Asset Value ($)	27.32	25.84	23.06	19.77	23.11	22.67	19.87	23.74	24.42	22.52
Expense Ratio (%)	0.74	0.80	0.87	0.87	0.97	1.04	1.00	0.95	1.14	0.41
Net Income to Assets (%) .	7.10	9.75	8.98	8.90	7.57	7.43	7.43	8.08	8.40	2.83
Portfolio Turnover (%)......	13	24	3	5	2	17	56	26	10	1
Total Assets (Millions $)..	1,371	267	164	143	97	52	67	67	51	1

PORTFOLIO (as of 8/31/93)

Portfolio Manager: Eric Ryback - 1982

Investm't Category: Balanced

Cap Gain	Asset Allocation
✔ Cap & Income	Fund of Funds
Income	Index
	Sector
✔ Domestic	Small Cap
Foreign	Socially Conscious
Country/Region	State Specific

Portfolio: stocks 17% bonds 22%
convertibles 12% other 48% cash 1%

Largest Holdings: stocks—utilities 16%, stocks—financial services 13%

Unrealized Net Capital Gains: 7% of portfolio value

SHAREHOLDER INFORMATION

Minimum Investment
Initial: $2,000   Subsequent: $100

Minimum IRA Investment
Initial: $250   Subsequent: 100

Maximum Fees
Load: 2.00% redemption   12b-1: none
Other: redemption fee applies for 60 days

Distributions
Income: quarterly   Capital Gains: Apr, Dec

Exchange Options
Number Per Year: none   Fee: na
Telephone: na

Services
IRA, auto withdraw

LMH (LMHFX)

Growth & Income

560 Hudson St.
Hackensack, NJ 07601
(201) 641-4960

PERFORMANCE

	3yr Annual	5yr Annual	10yr Annual	Bull	Bear
Return (%)	11.3	4.6	7.8	46.5	-23.3
Differ from Category (+/-)	-5.1 low	-7.9 low	-4.6 low	-23.6 low	-11.7 low

Total Risk	Standard Deviation	Category Risk	Risk Index	Beta
av	8.5%	blw av	1.0	0.7

	1993	1992	1991	1990	1989	1988	1987	1986	1985	1984
Return (%)	7.2	8.5	18.4	-18.5	12.0	17.9	-6.2	14.0	22.7	9.3
Differ from category (+/-) . .	-5.4	-1.5	-9.3	-12.9	-9.6	1.1	-6.6	-1.2	-2.7	3.1

PER SHARE DATA

	1993	1992	1991	1990	1989	1988	1987	1986	1985	1984
Dividends, Net Income ($) .	0.23	0.37	0.43	0.63	0.71	0.81	2.37	1.09	0.51	0.10
Distrib'ns, Cap Gain ($) . . .	0.00	0.00	0.00	0.09	2.36	0.00	3.13	4.41	0.80	0.10
Net Asset Value ($)	18.56	17.52	16.48	14.28	18.44	19.20	16.97	24.01	25.85	22.23
Expense Ratio (%).	2.50	2.63	2.39	1.81	1.55	1.44	1.29	1.25	1.42	2.60
Net Income to Assets (%). .	1.58	1.86	2.61	2.40	3.65	4.09	4.11	3.83	3.24	2.82
Portfolio Turnover (%)	53	76	133	59	26	72	19	50	25	13
Total Assets (Millions $)	6	8	10	27	38	40	77	84	77	30

PORTFOLIO (as of 6/30/93)

Portfolio Manager: Leonard M. Heine Jr. - 1983, N. Russell Wayne - 1991

Investm't Category: Growth & Income
Cap Gain	Asset Allocation
✔ Cap & Income	Fund of Funds
Income	Index
	Sector
✔ Domestic	Small Cap
Foreign	Socially Conscious
Country/Region	State Specific

Portfolio: stocks 100% bonds 0%
convertibles 0%   other 0%   cash 0%

Largest Holdings: utilities—electric & gas 14%, drugs 12%

Unrealized Net Capital Gains: 10% of portfolio value

SHAREHOLDER INFORMATION

Minimum Investment
Initial: $1,000   Subsequent: $100

Minimum IRA Investment
Initial: $500   Subsequent: $100

Maximum Fees
Load: none   12b-1: none
Other: none

Distributions
Income: Dec   Capital Gains: Dec

Exchange Options
Number Per Year: no limit   Fee: $5 (telephone)
Telephone: yes (money market fund available)

Services
IRA, auto invest

Loomis Sayles Bond
(LSBDX)

Corporate Bond

One Financial Center
Boston, MA 02111
(800) 633-3330, (617) 482-2450

PERFORMANCE

	3yr Annual	5yr Annual	10yr Annual	Bull	Bear
Return (%)	na	na	na	na	na
Differ from Category (+/-)	na	na	na	na	na

Total Risk	Standard Deviation	Category Risk	Risk Index	Avg Mat
na	na	na	na	16.6 yrs

	1993	1992	1991	1990	1989	1988	1987	1986	1985	1984
Return (%).............	22.2	14.2	—	—	—	—	—	—	—	—
Differ from category (+/-)..	10.8	5.6	—	—	—	—	—	—	—	—

PER SHARE DATA

	1993	1992	1991	1990	1989	1988	1987	1986	1985	1984
Dividends, Net Income ($).	0.80	0.75	—	—	—	—	—	—	—	—
Distrib'ns, Cap Gain ($) ...	0.45	0.54	—	—	—	—	—	—	—	—
Net Asset Value ($)	11.37	10.36	—	—	—	—	—	—	—	—
Expense Ratio (%)	1.00	1.00	—	—	—	—	—	—	—	—
Net Income to Assets (%) .	8.75	7.50	—	—	—	—	—	—	—	—
Portfolio Turnover (%).....	127	101	—	—	—	—	—	—	—	—
Total Assets (Millions $).....	63	18	—	—	—	—	—	—	—	—

PORTFOLIO (as of 6/30/93)

Portfolio Manager: Daniel Fuss - 1991

Investm't Category: Corporate Bond
Cap Gain	Asset Allocation
Cap & Income	Fund of Funds
✔ Income	Index
	Sector
✔ Domestic	Small Cap
✔ Foreign	Socially Conscious
Country/Region	State Specific

Portfolio: stocks 0%   bonds 65%
convertibles 18%   other 10%   cash 7%

Largest Holdings: aircraft 17%, food & beverage 5%

Unrealized Net Capital Gains: 3% of portfolio value

SHAREHOLDER INFORMATION

Minimum Investment
Initial: $2,500   Subsequent: $50

Minimum IRA Investment
Initial: $250   Subsequent: $50

Maximum Fees
Load: none   12b-1: none
Other: none

Distributions
Income: quarterly   Capital Gains: Dec

Exchange Options
Number Per Year: 4   Fee: none
Telephone: yes (money market fund available)

Services
IRA, other pension, auto invest, auto withdraw

Loomis Sayles Growth
(LSGRX)

One Financial Center
Boston, MA 02111
(800) 633-3330, (617) 482-2450

Aggressive Growth

PERFORMANCE

	3yr Annual	5yr Annual	10yr Annual	Bull	Bear
Return (%)	na	na	na	na	na
Differ from Category (+/-)	na	na	na	na	na

Total Risk	Standard Deviation	Category Risk	Risk Index	Beta
na	na	na	na	na

	1993	1992	1991	1990	1989	1988	1987	1986	1985	1984
Return (%)	9.2	3.8	—	—	—	—	—	—	—	—
Differ from category (+/-) . .	-9.8	-6.6	—	—	—	—	—	—	—	—

PER SHARE DATA

	1993	1992	1991	1990	1989	1988	1987	1986	1985	1984
Dividends, Net Income ($) .	0.00	0.00	—	—	—	—	—	—	—	—
Distrib'ns, Cap Gain ($) . . .	0.60	0.00	—	—	—	—	—	—	—	—
Net Asset Value ($)	13.02	12.47	—	—	—	—	—	—	—	—
Expense Ratio (%)	1.28	1.50	—	—	—	—	—	—	—	—
Net Income to Assets (%) .	-0.05	-0.45	—	—	—	—	—	—	—	—
Portfolio Turnover (%)	63	98	—	—	—	—	—	—	—	—
Total Assets (Millions $)	32	24	—	—	—	—	—	—	—	—

PORTFOLIO (as of 6/30/93)

Portfolio Manager: Jerome Castellini - 1991

Investm't Category: Aggressive Growth

✔ Cap Gain	Asset Allocation
Cap & Income	Fund of Funds
Income	Index
	Sector
✔ Domestic	Small Cap
✔ Foreign	Socially Conscious
Country/Region	State Specific

Portfolio: stocks 98% bonds 0%
convertibles 0% other 0% cash 2%

Largest Holdings: oil—independent producers 8%, oil—service 8%

Unrealized Net Capital Gains: 12% of portfolio value

SHAREHOLDER INFORMATION

Minimum Investment
Initial: $2,500   Subsequent: $50

Minimum IRA Investment
Initial: $250   Subsequent: $50

Maximum Fees
Load: none   12b-1: none
Other: none

Distributions
Income: Dec   Capital Gains: Dec

Exchange Options
Number Per Year: 4   Fee: none
Telephone: yes (money market fund available)

Services
IRA, other pension, auto invest, auto withdraw

Loomis Sayles
International Equity (LSIEX)

One Financial Center
Boston, MA 02111
(800) 633-3330, (617) 482-2450

International Stock

PERFORMANCE

	3yr Annual	5yr Annual	10yr Annual	Bull	Bear
Return (%)	na	na	na	na	na
Differ from Category (+/-)	na	na	na	na	na

Total Risk	Standard Deviation	Category Risk	Risk Index	Beta
na	na	na	na	na

	1993	1992	1991	1990	1989	1988	1987	1986	1985	1984
Return (%)	38.5	-5.0	—	—	—	—	—	—	—	—
Differ from category (+/-)	0.0	-1.5	—	—	—	—	—	—	—	—

PER SHARE DATA

	1993	1992	1991	1990	1989	1988	1987	1986	1985	1984
Dividends, Net Income ($)	0.10	0.10	—	—	—	—	—	—	—	—
Distrib'ns, Cap Gain ($)	0.35	0.00	—	—	—	—	—	—	—	—
Net Asset Value ($)	12.90	9.64	—	—	—	—	—	—	—	—
Expense Ratio (%)	1.50	1.50	—	—	—	—	—	—	—	—
Net Income to Assets (%)	2.68	1.64	—	—	—	—	—	—	—	—
Portfolio Turnover (%)	137	101	—	—	—	—	—	—	—	—
Total Assets (Millions $)	59	14	—	—	—	—	—	—	—	—

PORTFOLIO (as of 6/30/93)

Portfolio Manager: Frank Jedlicka - 1991

Investm't Category: International Stock

✔ Cap Gain	Asset Allocation
Cap & Income	Fund of Funds
Income	Index
	Sector
Domestic	Small Cap
✔ Foreign	Socially Conscious
Country/Region	State Specific

Portfolio: stocks 95%   bonds 0%
convertibles 0%   other 0%   cash 5%

Largest Holdings: Australia 10%, Portugal 10%

Unrealized Net Capital Gains: 5% of portfolio value

SHAREHOLDER INFORMATION

Minimum Investment
Initial: $2,500   Subsequent: $50

Minimum IRA Investment
Initial: $250   Subsequent: $50

Maximum Fees
Load: none   12b-1: none
Other: none

Distributions
Income: Dec   Capital Gains: Dec

Exchange Options
Number Per Year: 4   Fee: none
Telephone: yes (money market fund available)

Services
IRA, other pension, auto invest, auto withdraw

Loomis Sayles Small Cap

(LSSCX)

Aggressive Growth

One Financial Center
Boston, MA 02111
(800) 633-3330, (617) 482-2450

PERFORMANCE

	3yr Annual	5yr Annual	10yr Annual	Bull	Bear
Return (%)	na	na	na	na	na
Differ from Category (+/-)	na	na	na	na	na

Total Risk	Standard Deviation	Category Risk	Risk Index	Beta
na	na	na	na	na

	1993	1992	1991	1990	1989	1988	1987	1986	1985	1984
Return (%)	24.6	13.1	—	—	—	—	—	—	—	—
Differ from category (+/-) ...	5.6	2.7	—	—	—	—	—	—	—	—

PER SHARE DATA

	1993	1992	1991	1990	1989	1988	1987	1986	1985	1984
Dividends, Net Income ($) .	0.00	0.00	—	—	—	—	—	—	—	—
Distrib'ns, Cap Gain ($) ...	1.90	1.22	—	—	—	—	—	—	—	—
Net Asset Value ($)	14.13	12.88	—	—	—	—	—	—	—	—
Expense Ratio (%)........	1.45	1.50	—	—	—	—	—	—	—	—
Net Income to Assets (%) .	-0.41	-0.79	—	—	—	—	—	—	—	—
Portfolio Turnover (%)....	126	109	—	—	—	—	—	—	—	—
Total Assets (Millions $)	69	39	—	—	—	—	—	—	—	—

PORTFOLIO (as of 6/30/93)

Portfolio Manager: Barbara Friedman - 1991, Jeffrey Petherick - 1993

Investm't Category: Aggressive Growth
- ✔ Cap Gain
- Cap & Income
- Income
- ✔ Domestic
- Foreign
- Country/Region
- Asset Allocation
- Fund of Funds
- Index
- Sector
- ✔ Small Cap
- Socially Conscious
- State Specific

Portfolio: stocks 89% bonds 0%
convertibles 0% other 0% cash 11%

Largest Holdings: health care services 9%, oil services 7%

Unrealized Net Capital Gains: 1% of portfolio value

SHAREHOLDER INFORMATION

Minimum Investment
Initial: $2,500   Subsequent: $50

Minimum IRA Investment
Initial: $250   Subsequent: $50

Maximum Fees
Load: none   12b-1: none
Other: none

Distributions
Income: Dec   Capital Gains: Dec

Exchange Options
Number Per Year: 4   Fee: none
Telephone: yes (money market fund available)

Services
IRA, other pension, auto invest, auto withdraw

L. Roy Papp Stock (LRPSX)

Growth & Income

4400 North 32nd Street
Suite 280
Phoenix, AZ 85018
(800) 421-4004, (602) 956-1115

	3yr Annual	5yr Annual	10yr Annual	Bull	Bear
Return (%)	15.6	na	na	75.1	-9.5
Differ from Category (+/-)	-0.8 av	na	na	5.0 abv av	2.1 abv av

Total Risk	Standard Deviation	Category Risk	Risk Index	Beta
abv av	11.5%	high	1.3	0.9

	1993	1992	1991	1990	1989	1988	1987	1986	1985	1984
Return (%)	1.6	13.5	33.8	2.5	—	—	—	—	—	—
Differ from category (+/-)	-11.0	3.5	6.1	8.1	—	—	—	—	—	—

PER SHARE DATA

	1993	1992	1991	1990	1989	1988	1987	1986	1985	1984
Dividends, Net Income ($)	0.13	0.13	0.13	0.12	—	—	—	—	—	—
Distrib'ns, Cap Gain ($)	0.09	0.16	0.34	0.10	—	—	—	—	—	—
Net Asset Value ($)	14.98	14.96	13.45	10.42	—	—	—	—	—	—
Expense Ratio (%)	1.25	1.25	1.25	1.25	—	—	—	—	—	—
Net Income to Assets (%)	2.25	2.28	2.46	2.82	—	—	—	—	—	—
Portfolio Turnover (%)	2	11	11	28	—	—	—	—	—	—
Total Assets (Millions $)	38	22	13	6	—	—	—	—	—	—

PORTFOLIO (as of 6/30/93)

Portfolio Manager: L. Roy Papp - 1989,
Rosellen Papp - 1989

Investm't Category: Growth & Income
Cap Gain	Asset Allocation
✔ Cap & Income	Fund of Funds
Income	Index
	Sector
✔ Domestic	Small Cap
Foreign	Socially Conscious
Country/Region	State Specific

Portfolio: stocks 99% bonds 0%
convertibles 0% other 0% cash 1%

Largest Holdings: electrical equipment 14%, food & beverage 13%

Unrealized Net Capital Gains: 8% of portfolio value

SHAREHOLDER INFORMATION

Minimum Investment
Initial: $10,000   Subsequent: $2,000

Minimum IRA Investment
Initial: $2,000   Subsequent: $2,000

Maximum Fees
Load: none   12b-1: none
Other: none

Distributions
Income: June, Dec   Capital Gains: Dec

Exchange Options
Number Per Year: none   Fee: na
Telephone: na

Services
IRA

Managers Bond (MGFIX)

General Bond

200 Connecticut Avenue
Norwalk, CT 06854
(800) 835-3879

PERFORMANCE

	3yr Annual	5yr Annual	10yr Annual	Bull	Bear
Return (%)	12.7	na	na	na	na
Differ from Category (+/-)	2.5 high	na	na	na	na

Total Risk	Standard Deviation	Category Risk	Risk Index	Avg Mat
low	3.7%	abv av	1.3	20.1 yrs

	1993	1992	1991	1990	1989	1988	1987	1986	1985	1984
Return (%)	11.5	7.8	19.0	—	—	—	—	—	—	—
Differ from category (+/-) ...	2.3	1.1	4.4	—	—	—	—	—	—	—

PER SHARE DATA

	1993	1992	1991	1990	1989	1988	1987	1986	1985	1984
Dividends, Net Income ($) .	1.50	1.48	1.72	—	—	—	—	—	—	—
Distrib'ns, Cap Gain ($) ...	0.67	0.94	0.44	—	—	—	—	—	—	—
Net Asset Value ($)	22.18	21.88	22.60	—	—	—	—	—	—	—
Expense Ratio (%)........	1.15	0.93	1.02	—	—	—	—	—	—	—
Net Income to Assets (%)..	6.36	6.61	7.82	—	—	—	—	—	—	—
Portfolio Turnover (%)	660	292	181	—	—	—	—	—	—	—
Total Assets (Millions $)	44	39	36	—	—	—	—	—	—	—

PORTFOLIO (as of 6/30/93)

Portfolio Manager: not specified

Investm't Category: General Bond

Cap Gain	Asset Allocation
Cap & Income	Fund of Funds
✔ Income	Index
	Sector
✔ Domestic	Small Cap
✔ Foreign	Socially Conscious
Country/Region	State Specific

Portfolio: stocks 0% bonds 82%
convertibles 12% other 4% cash 2%

Largest Holdings: corporate 64%, foreign government 10%

Unrealized Net Capital Gains: 2% of portfolio value

SHAREHOLDER INFORMATION

Minimum Investment
Initial: $10,000   Subsequent: $0

Minimum IRA Investment
Initial: $10,000   Subsequent: $0

Maximum Fees
Load: none   12b-1: none
Other: none

Distributions
Income: monthly   Capital Gains: Dec

Exchange Options
Number Per Year: no limit   Fee: none
Telephone: yes (money market fund available)

Services
IRA, auto exchange, auto withdraw

Managers Capital Appreciation (MGCAX)

Aggressive Growth

200 Connecticut Avenue
Norwalk, CT 06854
(800) 835-3879

PERFORMANCE

	3yr Annual	5yr Annual	10yr Annual	Bull	Bear
Return (%)	19.3	na	na	na	na
Differ from Category (+/-)	-6.1 blw av	na	na	na	na

Total Risk	Standard Deviation	Category Risk	Risk Index	Beta
abv av	12.0%	low	0.8	0.9

	1993	1992	1991	1990	1989	1988	1987	1986	1985	1984
Return (%)	16.6	10.4	31.9	—	—	—	—	—	—	—
Differ from category (+/-). . .	-2.4	0.0	-20.5	—	—	—	—	—	—	—

PER SHARE DATA

	1993	1992	1991	1990	1989	1988	1987	1986	1985	1984
Dividends, Net Income ($).	0.18	0.07	0.27	—	—	—	—	—	—	—
Distrib'ns, Cap Gain ($) . . .	3.30	1.19	2.61	—	—	—	—	—	—	—
Net Asset Value ($)	25.17	24.67	23.47	—	—	—	—	—	—	—
Expense Ratio (%)	1.19	1.05	1.31	—	—	—	—	—	—	—
Net Income to Assets (%) .	1.43	0.33	1.07	—	—	—	—	—	—	—
Portfolio Turnover (%).	120	175	259	—	—	—	—	—	—	—
Total Assets (Millions $).	71	56	53	—	—	—	—	—	—	—

PORTFOLIO (as of 6/30/93)

Portfolio Manager: not specified

Investm't Category: Aggressive Growth

✔ Cap Gain	Asset Allocation
Cap & Income	Fund of Funds
Income	Index
	Sector
✔ Domestic	Small Cap
Foreign	Socially Conscious
Country/Region	State Specific

Portfolio: stocks 85% bonds 0%
convertibles 0% other 0% cash 15%

Largest Holdings: technology 15%, finance & insurance 12%

Unrealized Net Capital Gains: 10% of portfolio value

SHAREHOLDER INFORMATION

Minimum Investment
Initial: $10,000   Subsequent: $0

Minimum IRA Investment
Initial: $10,000   Subsequent: $0

Maximum Fees
Load: none   12b-1: none
Other: none

Distributions
Income: monthly   Capital Gains: Dec

Exchange Options
Number Per Year: no limit   Fee: none
Telephone: yes (money market fund available)

Services
IRA, auto exchange, auto withdraw

Managers Income Equity

200 Connecticut Avenue
Norwalk, CT 06854
(800) 835-3879

(MGIEX)

Growth & Income

PERFORMANCE

	3yr Annual	5yr Annual	10yr Annual	Bull	Bear
Return (%)	16.8	na	na	na	na
Differ from Category (+/-)	0.4 av	na	na	na	na

Total Risk	Standard Deviation	Category Risk	Risk Index	Beta
av	9.4%	av	1.1	0.8

	1993	1992	1991	1990	1989	1988	1987	1986	1985	1984
Return (%)	12.4	9.7	29.3	—	—	—	—	—	—	—
Differ from category (+/-) . .	-0.2	-0.3	1.6	—	—	—	—	—	—	—

PER SHARE DATA

	1993	1992	1991	1990	1989	1988	1987	1986	1985	1984
Dividends, Net Income ($) .	0.75	1.03	1.20	—	—	—	—	—	—	—
Distrib'ns, Cap Gain ($) . . .	2.08	2.97	1.17	—	—	—	—	—	—	—
Net Asset Value ($)	27.89	27.38	28.63	—	—	—	—	—	—	—
Expense Ratio (%).	1.30	1.20	1.16	—	—	—	—	—	—	—
Net Income to Assets (%) . .	2.79	3.52	4.00	—	—	—	—	—	—	—
Portfolio Turnover (%)	40	41	63	—	—	—	—	—	—	—
Total Assets (Millions $)	41	49	70	—	—	—	—	—	—	—

PORTFOLIO (as of 6/30/93)

Portfolio Manager: not specified

Investm't Category: Growth & Income

Cap Gain	Asset Allocation
✔ Cap & Income	Fund of Funds
Income	Index
	Sector
✔ Domestic	Small Cap
Foreign	Socially Conscious
Country/Region	State Specific

Portfolio: stocks 93% bonds 0%
convertibles 1% other 2% cash 4%

Largest Holdings: utilities 19%, finance & insurance 15%

Unrealized Net Capital Gains: 12% of portfolio value

SHAREHOLDER INFORMATION

Minimum Investment
Initial: $10,000   Subsequent: $0

Minimum IRA Investment
Initial: $10,000   Subsequent: $0

Maximum Fees
Load: none   12b-1: none
Other: none

Distributions
Income: monthly   Capital Gains: Dec

Exchange Options
Number Per Year: no limit   Fee: none
Telephone: yes (money market fund available)

Services
IRA, auto exchange, auto withdraw

Managers Interm Mortgage (MGIGX)

Mortgage-Backed Bond

200 Connecticut Avenue
Norwalk, CT 06854
(800) 835-3879

PERFORMANCE

	3yr Annual	5yr Annual	10yr Annual	Bull	Bear
Return (%)	13.3	na	na	na	na
Differ from Category (+/-)	4.1 high	na	na	na	na

Total Risk	Standard Deviation	Category Risk	Risk Index	Avg Mat
low	3.9%	high	1.5	3.4 yrs

	1993	1992	1991	1990	1989	1988	1987	1986	1985	1984
Return (%)	11.4	10.5	18.1	—	—	—	—	—	—	—
Differ from category (+/-). . .	4.6	4.4	3.7	—	—	—	—	—	—	—

PER SHARE DATA

	1993	1992	1991	1990	1989	1988	1987	1986	1985	1984
Dividends, Net Income ($).	2.28	2.40	2.05	—	—	—	—	—	—	—
Distrib'ns, Cap Gain ($) . . .	0.57	0.41	0.00	—	—	—	—	—	—	—
Net Asset Value ($)	20.64	21.13	21.77	—	—	—	—	—	—	—
Expense Ratio (%)	0.75	0.79	0.68	—	—	—	—	—	—	—
Net Income to Assets (%)	12.16	11.30	9.91	—	—	—	—	—	—	—
Portfolio Turnover (%).	212	278	171	—	—	—	—	—	—	—
Total Assets (Millions $). . . .	275	115	165	—	—	—	—	—	—	—

PORTFOLIO (as of 6/30/93)

Portfolio Manager: not specified

Investm't Category: Mortgage-Backed Bond

Cap Gain	Asset Allocation
Cap & Income	Fund of Funds
✔ Income	Index
	Sector
✔ Domestic	Small Cap
Foreign	Socially Conscious
Country/Region	State Specific

Portfolio: stocks 0% bonds 97%
convertibles 0% other 0% cash 3%

Largest Holdings: mortgage-backed 97%

Unrealized Net Capital Gains: 1% of portfolio value

SHAREHOLDER INFORMATION

Minimum Investment
Initial: $10,000 Subsequent: $0

Minimum IRA Investment
Initial: $10,000 Subsequent: $0

Maximum Fees
Load: none 12b-1: none
Other: none

Distributions
Income: monthly Capital Gains: Dec

Exchange Options
Number Per Year: no limit Fee: none
Telephone: yes (money market fund available)

Services
IRA, auto exchange, auto withdraw

Managers International Equity (MGITX)

International Stock

200 Connecticut Avenue
Norwalk, CT 06854
(800) 835-3879

PERFORMANCE

	3yr Annual	5yr Annual	10yr Annual	Bull	Bear
Return (%)	19.4	na	na	na	na
Differ from Category (+/-)	5.1 high	na	na	na	na

Total Risk	Standard Deviation	Category Risk	Risk Index	Beta
av	10.8%	low	0.9	0.5

	1993	1992	1991	1990	1989	1988	1987	1986	1985	1984
Return (%)	38.2	4.2	18.1	—	—	—	—	—	—	—
Differ from category (+/-)	-0.3	7.7	5.2	—	—	—	—	—	—	—

PER SHARE DATA

	1993	1992	1991	1990	1989	1988	1987	1986	1985	1984
Dividends, Net Income ($)	0.40	0.21	0.36	—	—	—	—	—	—	—
Distrib'ns, Cap Gain ($)	0.30	0.00	0.07	—	—	—	—	—	—	—
Net Asset Value ($)	35.92	26.52	25.65	—	—	—	—	—	—	—
Expense Ratio (%)	1.52	1.45	1.69	—	—	—	—	—	—	—
Net Income to Assets (%)	1.17	0.97	1.50	—	—	—	—	—	—	—
Portfolio Turnover (%)	42	51	157	—	—	—	—	—	—	—
Total Assets (Millions $)	67	23	14	—	—	—	—	—	—	—

PORTFOLIO (as of 6/30/93)

Portfolio Manager: Willie Holzer - 1986

Investm't Category: International Stock

✔ Cap Gain	Asset Allocation
Cap & Income	Fund of Funds
Income	Index
	Sector
✔ Domestic	Small Cap
✔ Foreign	Socially Conscious
Country/Region	State Specific

Portfolio:	stocks 87%	bonds 13%
convertibles 0%	other 0%	cash 0%

Largest Holdings: Japan 15%, Switzerland 10%

Unrealized Net Capital Gains: 10% of portfolio value

SHAREHOLDER INFORMATION

Minimum Investment
Initial: $10,000   Subsequent: $0

Minimum IRA Investment
Initial: $10,000   Subsequent: $0

Maximum Fees
Load: none   12b-1: none
Other: none

Distributions
Income: monthly   Capital Gains: Dec

Exchange Options
Number Per Year: no limit   Fee: none
Telephone: yes (money market fund available)

Services
IRA, auto exchange, auto withdraw

Managers Short & Interm Bond (MGSIX)

General Bond

200 Connecticut Avenue
Norwalk, CT 06854
(800) 835-3879

PERFORMANCE

	3yr Annual	5yr Annual	10yr Annual	Bull	Bear
Return (%)	10.9	na	na	na	na
Differ from Category (+/-)	0.6 av	na	na	na	na

Total Risk	Standard Deviation	Category Risk	Risk Index	Avg Mat
low	2.0%	low	0.7	2.7 yrs

	1993	1992	1991	1990	1989	1988	1987	1986	1985	1984
Return (%)	8.4	11.5	12.7	—	—	—	—	—	—	—
Differ from category (+/-). . .	-0.8	4.8	-1.9	—	—	—	—	—	—	—

PER SHARE DATA

	1993	1992	1991	1990	1989	1988	1987	1986	1985	1984
Dividends, Net Income ($) .	1.38	1.70	1.48	—	—	—	—	—	—	—
Distrib'ns, Cap Gain ($) . . .	0.00	0.00	0.00	—	—	—	—	—	—	—
Net Asset Value ($)	21.23	20.89	20.33	—	—	—	—	—	—	—
Expense Ratio (%)	0.86	0.86	0.96	—	—	—	—	—	—	—
Net Income to Assets (%) .	6.91	8.33	7.41	—	—	—	—	—	—	—
Portfolio Turnover (%).	132	117	536	—	—	—	—	—	—	—
Total Assets (Millions $). . . .	112	72	52	—	—	—	—	—	—	—

PORTFOLIO (as of 6/30/93)

Portfolio Manager: not specified

Investm't Category: General Bond

Cap Gain	Asset Allocation
Cap & Income	Fund of Funds
✔ Income	Index
	Sector
✔ Domestic	Small Cap
✔ Foreign	Socially Conscious
Country/Region	State Specific

Portfolio: stocks 0% bonds 95%
convertibles 0% other 0% cash 5%

Largest Holdings: mortgage-backed 57%, corporate 30%

Unrealized Net Capital Gains: 1% of portfolio value

SHAREHOLDER INFORMATION

Minimum Investment
Initial: $10,000   Subsequent: $0

Minimum IRA Investment
Initial: $10,000   Subsequent: $0

Maximum Fees
Load: none   12b-1: none
Other: none

Distributions
Income: monthly   Capital Gains: Dec

Exchange Options
Number Per Year: no limit   Fee: none
Telephone: yes (money market fund available)

Services
IRA, auto exchange, auto withdraw

Managers Short Gov't
(MGSGX)

Mortgage-Backed Bond

200 Connecticut Avenue
Norwalk, CT 06854
(800) 835-3879

PERFORMANCE

	3yr Annual	5yr Annual	10yr Annual	Bull	Bear
Return (%)	6.1	na	na	na	na
Differ from Category (+/-)	-3.1 low	na	na	na	na

Total Risk	Standard Deviation		Category Risk	Risk Index	Avg Mat
low	1.4%		low	0.5	3.2 yrs

	1993	1992	1991	1990	1989	1988	1987	1986	1985	1984
Return (%)	3.7	3.9	10.8	—	—	—	—	—	—	—
Differ from category (+/-)	-3.1	-2.2	-3.6	—	—	—	—	—	—	—

PER SHARE DATA

	1993	1992	1991	1990	1989	1988	1987	1986	1985	1984
Dividends, Net Income ($)	1.24	1.26	1.58	—	—	—	—	—	—	—
Distrib'ns, Cap Gain ($)	0.00	0.00	0.00	—	—	—	—	—	—	—
Net Asset Value ($)	19.35	19.86	20.35	—	—	—	—	—	—	—
Expense Ratio (%)	0.88	0.76	0.58	—	—	—	—	—	—	—
Net Income to Assets (%)	8.94	6.24	6.08	—	—	—	—	—	—	—
Portfolio Turnover (%)	137	168	84	—	—	—	—	—	—	—
Total Assets (Millions $)	87	142	144	—	—	—	—	—	—	—

PORTFOLIO (as of 6/30/93)

Portfolio Manager: not specified

Investm't Category: Mortgage-Backed Bond

Cap Gain	Asset Allocation
Cap & Income	Fund of Funds
✔ Income	Index
	Sector
✔ Domestic	Small Cap
Foreign	Socially Conscious
Country/Region	State Specific

Portfolio: stocks 0% bonds 99%
convertibles 0% other 0% cash 1%

Largest Holdings: mortgage-backed 99%

Unrealized Net Capital Gains: -1% of portfolio value

SHAREHOLDER INFORMATION

Minimum Investment
Initial: $10,000   Subsequent: $0

Minimum IRA Investment
Initial: $10,000   Subsequent: $0

Maximum Fees
Load: none   12b-1: none
Other: none

Distributions
Income: monthly   Capital Gains: Dec

Exchange Options
Number Per Year: no limit   Fee: none
Telephone: yes (money market fund available)

Services
IRA, auto exchange, auto withdraw

Managers Special Equity
(MGSEX)

Aggressive Growth

200 Connecticut Avenue
Norwalk, CT 06854
(800) 835-3879

PERFORMANCE

	3yr Annual	5yr Annual	10yr Annual	Bull	Bear
Return (%)	26.5	na	na	na	na
Differ from Category (+/-)	1.1 av	na	na	na	na

Total Risk	Standard Deviation	Category Risk	Risk Index	Beta
abv av	12.7%	low	0.8	0.9

	1993	1992	1991	1990	1989	1988	1987	1986	1985	1984
Return (%)	17.3	15.6	49.2	—	—	—	—	—	—	—
Differ from category (+/-). . .	-1.7	5.2	-3.2	—	—	—	—	—	—	—

PER SHARE DATA

	1993	1992	1991	1990	1989	1988	1987	1986	1985	1984
Dividends, Net Income ($).	0.00	0.05	0.23	—	—	—	—	—	—	—
Distrib'ns, Cap Gain ($) . . .	3.37	3.70	1.74	—	—	—	—	—	—	—
Net Asset Value ($)	38.90	36.14	34.50	—	—	—	—	—	—	—
Expense Ratio (%)	1.28	1.29	1.30	—	—	—	—	—	—	—
Net Income to Assets (%) .	0.00	0.14	0.73	—	—	—	—	—	—	—
Portfolio Turnover (%).	66	54	69	—	—	—	—	—	—	—
Total Assets (Millions $). . . .	100	53	40	—	—	—	—	—	—	—

PORTFOLIO (as of 6/30/93)

Portfolio Manager: not specified

Investm't Category: Aggressive Growth

✔ Cap Gain	Asset Allocation
Cap & Income	Fund of Funds
Income	Index
	Sector
✔ Domestic	✔ Small Cap
Foreign	Socially Conscious
Country/Region	State Specific

Portfolio: stocks 93% bonds 0%
convertibles 0% other 0% cash 7%

Largest Holdings: finance & insurance 20%, general business 14%

Unrealized Net Capital Gains: 17% of portfolio value

SHAREHOLDER INFORMATION

Minimum Investment
Initial: $10,000   Subsequent: $0

Minimum IRA Investment
Initial: $10,000   Subsequent: $0

Maximum Fees
Load: none   12b-1: none
Other: none

Distributions
Income: monthly   Capital Gains: Dec

Exchange Options
Number Per Year: no limit   Fee: none
Telephone: yes (money market fund available)

Services
IRA, auto exchange, auto withdraw

Mathers (MATRX)

Growth

100 Corporate N., Suite 201
Bannockburn, IL 60015
(800) 962-3863, (708) 295-7400

PERFORMANCE

	3yr Annual	5yr Annual	10yr Annual	Bull	Bear
Return (%)	4.8	7.0	11.1	18.5	7.3
Differ from Category (+/-)	-14.4 low	-7.6 low	-1.5 blw av	-66.2 low	19.7 high

Total Risk	Standard Deviation	Category Risk	Risk Index	Beta
low	3.5%	low	0.3	na

	1993	1992	1991	1990	1989	1988	1987	1986	1985	1984
Return (%)	2.1	3.1	9.4	10.3	10.3	13.6	27.0	13.9	27.4	-2.5
Differ from category (+/-) .	-11.1	-7.9	-26.0	16.4	-15.5	-4.1	25.8	-0.6	-1.9	-2.5

PER SHARE DATA

	1993	1992	1991	1990	1989	1988	1987	1986	1985	1984
Dividends, Net Income ($) .	0.23	0.50	0.74	0.83	0.97	0.33	0.87	0.81	0.55	0.86
Distrib'ns, Cap Gain ($) ...	0.00	0.00	0.55	0.23	1.73	0.50	5.97	7.38	1.82	2.68
Net Asset Value ($)	15.11	15.02	15.06	14.95	14.52	15.60	14.46	16.96	22.65	19.97
Expense Ratio (%)........	0.89	0.88	0.93	0.98	1.01	0.98	0.82	0.77	0.74	0.69
Net Income to Assets (%)..	1.39	3.33	5.39	6.29	5.45	2.18	2.37	1.76	3.69	2.90
Portfolio Turnover (%)	136	212	80	190	303	148	202	174	278	71
Total Assets (Millions $) ...	434	554	517	300	215	201	152	134	187	182

PORTFOLIO (as of 6/30/93)

Portfolio Manager: Henry G. Van der Eb Jr. - 1975

Investm't Category: Growth

✔ Cap Gain	Asset Allocation
Cap & Income	Fund of Funds
Income	Index
	Sector
✔ Domestic	Small Cap
✔ Foreign	Socially Conscious
Country/Region	State Specific

Portfolio: stocks 33% bonds 0%
convertibles 0% other 0% cash 67%

Largest Holdings: gold mining companies 9%, pollution control 8%

Unrealized Net Capital Gains: 2% of portfolio value

SHAREHOLDER INFORMATION

Minimum Investment
Initial: $1,000   Subsequent: $200

Minimum IRA Investment
Initial: $0   Subsequent: $0

Maximum Fees
Load: none   12b-1: none
Other: none

Distributions
Income: Dec   Capital Gains: Dec

Exchange Options
Number Per Year: none   Fee: na
Telephone: na

Services
IRA, other pension, auto invest, auto withdraw

Matrix Growth (GATGX)

Growth

300 Main St
Cincinnati, OH 45202
(800) 354-6339, (513) 621-2875

PERFORMANCE

	3yr Annual	5yr Annual	10yr Annual	Bull	Bear
Return (%)	15.4	14.8	na	69.9	-13.5
Differ from Category (+/-)	-3.8 blw av	0.2 av	na	-14.8 blw av	-1.1 av

Total Risk	Standard Deviation	Category Risk	Risk Index	Beta
abv av	11.7%	av	1.1	1.0

	1993	1992	1991	1990	1989	1988	1987	1986	1985	1984
Return (%)	9.3	4.9	34.2	-4.5	36.0	-2.0	0.6	—	—	—
Differ from category (+/-). . .	-3.9	-6.1	-1.2	1.6	10.2	-19.7	-0.5	—	—	—

PER SHARE DATA

	1993	1992	1991	1990	1989	1988	1987	1986	1985	1984
Dividends, Net Income ($).	0.05	0.09	0.14	0.20	0.28	0.09	0.11	—	—	—
Distrib'ns, Cap Gain ($) . . .	0.79	0.56	0.64	0.00	1.11	0.00	0.00	—	—	—
Net Asset Value ($)	14.51	14.05	14.01	11.03	11.76	9.67	9.96	—	—	—
Expense Ratio (%)	1.69	1.50	1.50	1.50	1.50	1.49	1.49	—	—	—
Net Income to Assets (%) .	0.40	0.68	1.17	1.59	2.99	0.78	0.27	—	—	—
Portfolio Turnover (%).	na	51	70	79	130	132	157	—	—	—
Total Assets (Millions $). . . .	19	19	17	11	9	4	4	—	—	—

PORTFOLIO (as of 6/30/93)

Portfolio Manager: Peter Williams - 1988

Investm't Category: Growth

✔ Cap Gain	Asset Allocation
Cap & Income	Fund of Funds
Income	Index
	Sector
✔ Domestic	Small Cap
Foreign	Socially Conscious
Country/Region	State Specific

Portfolio: stocks 94% bonds 0%
convertibles 0% other 0% cash 6%

Largest Holdings: consumer cyclical 18%, financial 16%

Unrealized Net Capital Gains: 23% of portfolio value

SHAREHOLDER INFORMATION

Minimum Investment
Initial: $1,000   Subsequent: $100

Minimum IRA Investment
Initial: $1,000   Subsequent: $100

Maximum Fees
Load: none   12b-1: none
Other: none

Distributions
Income: Dec   Capital Gains: Dec

Exchange Options
Number Per Year: no limit   Fee: none
Telephone: yes (money market fund not available)

Services
IRA, other pension, auto invest, auto withdraw

Maxus Equity (MXSEX)

Growth

28601 Chagrin Blvd.
Suite 500
Cleveland, OH 44122
(216) 292-3434

PERFORMANCE

	3yr Annual	5yr Annual	10yr Annual	Bull	Bear
Return (%)	24.4	na	na	101.4	-14.6
Differ from Category (+/-)	5.2 high	na	na	16.7 abv av	-2.2 blw av

Total Risk	Standard Deviation	Category Risk	Risk Index	Beta
abv av	11.9%	av	1.1	0.7

	1993	1992	1991	1990	1989	1988	1987	1986	1985	1984
Return (%)	24.5	13.5	36.4	-10.8	—	—	—	—	—	—
Differ from category (+/-) . .	11.3	2.5	1.0	-4.7	—	—	—	—	—	—

PER SHARE DATA

	1993	1992	1991	1990	1989	1988	1987	1986	1985	1984
Dividends, Net Income ($) .	0.14	0.08	0.49	0.00	—	—	—	—	—	—
Distrib'ns, Cap Gain ($) . . .	1.52	0.58	0.00	0.00	—	—	—	—	—	—
Net Asset Value ($)	13.60	12.28	11.41	8.73	—	—	—	—	—	—
Expense Ratio (%)	na	2.89	3.94	5.25	—	—	—	—	—	—
Net Income to Assets (%)	na	0.80	0.52	-0.19	—	—	—	—	—	—
Portfolio Turnover (%)	na	187	189	221	—	—	—	—	—	—
Total Assets (Millions $)	12	6	3	2	—	—	—	—	—	—

PORTFOLIO (as of 6/30/93)

Portfolio Manager: Richard Barone - 1989

Investm't Category: Growth
- ✔ Cap Gain
- Cap & Income
- Income
- ✔ Asset Allocation
- Fund of Funds
- Index
- Sector
- ✔ Domestic
- Foreign
- Country/Region
- Small Cap
- Socially Conscious
- State Specific

Portfolio: stocks 88% bonds 12%
convertibles 0% other 0% cash 0%

Largest Holdings: information technology 12%, financial services 12%

Unrealized Net Capital Gains: 12% of portfolio value

SHAREHOLDER INFORMATION

Minimum Investment
Initial: $1,000   Subsequent: $100

Minimum IRA Investment
Initial: $1,000   Subsequent: $100

Maximum Fees
Load: none   12b-1: 0.50%
Other: none

Distributions
Income: Dec   Capital Gains: Dec

Exchange Options
Number Per Year: no limit   Fee: none
Telephone: yes (money market fund not available)

Services
IRA, other pension, auto exchange, auto withdraw

Maxus Income (MXSFX)

General Bond

28601 Chagrin Blvd.
Suite 500
Cleveland, OH 44122
(216) 292-3434

PERFORMANCE

	3yr Annual	5yr Annual	10yr Annual	Bull	Bear
Return (%)	11.8	9.6	na	45.0	-1.8
Differ from Category (+/-)	1.6 abv av	-0.2 blw av	na	5.6 abv av	-4.7 low

Total Risk	Standard Deviation	Category Risk	Risk Index	Avg Mat
av	7.4%	high	2.6	6.1 yrs

	1993	1992	1991	1990	1989	1988	1987	1986	1985	1984
Return (%)	8.7	7.8	19.2	1.7	11.4	7.8	3.5	6.5	—	—
Differ from category (+/-)	-0.5	1.1	4.6	-5.2	0.1	0.2	1.0	-7.4	—	—

PER SHARE DATA

	1993	1992	1991	1990	1989	1988	1987	1986	1985	1984
Dividends, Net Income ($)	0.67	0.78	0.81	0.74	0.89	0.61	1.05	0.27	—	—
Distrib'ns, Cap Gain ($)	0.20	0.16	0.00	0.00	0.33	0.00	0.36	0.01	—	—
Net Asset Value ($)	10.94	10.88	10.98	9.94	10.52	10.57	10.37	11.39	—	—
Expense Ratio (%)	na	1.94	2.00	2.00	2.00	2.00	2.01	2.01	—	—
Net Income to Assets (%)	na	7.18	7.59	7.43	6.25	5.64	5.33	4.15	—	—
Portfolio Turnover (%)	na	91	108	155	145	139	168	215	—	—
Total Assets (Millions $)	36	29	18	13	13	11	11	11	—	—

PORTFOLIO (as of 6/30/93)

Portfolio Manager: Richard Barone - 1985

Investm't Category: General Bond

Cap Gain	✔ Asset Allocation
✔ Cap & Income	Fund of Funds
Income	Index
	Sector
✔ Domestic	Small Cap
Foreign	Socially Conscious
Country/Region	State Specific

Portfolio: stocks 0%   bonds 51%
convertibles 14%   other 32%   cash 3%

Largest Holdings: U.S. government 49%, closed-end investment companies 25%

Unrealized Net Capital Gains: 2% of portfolio value

SHAREHOLDER INFORMATION

Minimum Investment
Initial: $1,000   Subsequent: $100

Minimum IRA Investment
Initial: $1,000   Subsequent: $100

Maximum Fees
Load: none   12b-1: 0.50%
Other: none

Distributions
Income: monthly   Capital Gains: Dec

Exchange Options
Number Per Year: no limit   Fee: none
Telephone: yes (money market fund not available)

Services
IRA, other pension, auto exchange, auto withdraw

Maxus Prism (MXSPX)

Growth & Income

28601 Chagrin Blvd., Suite 500
Cleveland, OH 44122
(216) 292-3434

fund in existence since 5/1/93

PERFORMANCE

	3yr Annual	5yr Annual	10yr Annual	Bull	Bear
Return (%)	na	na	na	na	na
Differ from Category (+/-)	na	na	na	na	na

Total Risk	Standard Deviation	Category Risk	Risk Index	Beta
na	na	na	na	na

	1993	1992	1991	1990	1989	1988	1987	1986	1985	1984
Return (%)	—	—	—	—	—	—	—	—	—	—
Differ from category (+/-) ...	—	—	—	—	—	—	—	—	—	—

PER SHARE DATA

	1993	1992	1991	1990	1989	1988	1987	1986	1985	1984
Dividends, Net Income ($) .	0.00	—	—	—	—	—	—	—	—	—
Distrib'ns, Cap Gain ($) ...	0.90	—	—	—	—	—	—	—	—	—
Net Asset Value ($)	9.96	—	—	—	—	—	—	—	—	—
Expense Ratio (%)..........	na	—	—	—	—	—	—	—	—	—
Net Income to Assets (%)....	na	—	—	—	—	—	—	—	—	—
Portfolio Turnover (%)......	na	—	—	—	—	—	—	—	—	—
Total Assets (Millions $)	2	—	—	—	—	—	—	—	—	—

PORTFOLIO (as of 6/30/93)

Portfolio Manager: Robert Beausoleil - 1993

Investm't Category: Growth & Income

Cap Gain	Asset Allocation
✔ Cap & Income	✔ Fund of Funds
Income	Index
	Sector
✔ Domestic	Small Cap
✔ Foreign	Socially Conscious
Country/Region	State Specific

Portfolio: stocks 0%   bonds 0%
convertibles 0%   other 100%   cash 0%

Largest Holdings: general equity funds—mid-cap 29%, general equity funds—smallcap 21%

Unrealized Net Capital Gains: 2% of portfolio value

SHAREHOLDER INFORMATION

Minimum Investment
Initial: $1,000   Subsequent: $100

Minimum IRA Investment
Initial: $1,000   Subsequent: $100

Maximum Fees
Load: none   12b-1: 0.50%
Other: none

Distributions
Income: Dec   Capital Gains: Dec

Exchange Options
Number Per Year: no limit   Fee: none
Telephone: yes (money market fund not available)

Services
IRA, other pension, auto exchange, auto withdraw

Meridian (MERDX)

Growth

60 E. Sir Francis Drake Blvd.
Wood Island, Suite 306
Larkspur, CA 94939
(800) 446-6662, (415) 461-6237

PERFORMANCE

	3yr Annual	5yr Annual	10yr Annual	Bull	Bear
Return (%)	26.9	20.7	na	122.3	-3.6
Differ from Category (+/-)	7.7 high	6.1 high	na	37.6 high	8.8 high

Total Risk	Standard Deviation	Category Risk	Risk Index	Beta
high	15.3%	high	1.4	1.1

	1993	1992	1991	1990	1989	1988	1987	1986	1985	1984
Return (%)	13.0	15.5	56.8	4.6	19.5	18.0	-7.8	13.1	27.1	—
Differ from category (+/-) . . .	-0.2	4.5	21.4	10.7	-6.3	0.3	-9.0	-1.4	-2.2	—

PER SHARE DATA

	1993	1992	1991	1990	1989	1988	1987	1986	1985	1984
Dividends, Net Income ($) .	0.02	0.03	0.09	0.11	0.47	0.00	0.02	0.07	0.10	—
Distrib'ns, Cap Gain ($) . . .	0.43	0.56	1.69	1.04	0.64	0.00	1.21	1.15	0.00	—
Net Asset Value ($)	25.87	23.29	20.75	14.55	15.09	13.59	11.51	13.57	13.01	—
Expense Ratio (%)	1.47	1.75	1.68	2.08	2.01	1.85	1.72	1.91	2.00	—
Net Income to Assets (%) .	-0.01	0.24	0.98	0.14	2.83	-0.59	0.15	0.80	2.58	—
Portfolio Turnover (%).	61	61	85	66	62	58	88	75	156	—
Total Assets (Millions $). . . .	153	18	12	11	10	11	19	18	4	—

PORTFOLIO (as of 6/30/93)

Portfolio Manager: Richard F. Aster Jr. - 1984

Investm't Category: Growth
- ✔ Cap Gain
-   Cap & Income
-   Income
- ✔ Domestic
-   Foreign
-   Country/Region
-   Asset Allocation
-   Fund of Funds
-   Index
-   Sector
- ✔ Small Cap
-   Socially Conscious
-   State Specific

Portfolio: stocks 70% bonds 2%
convertibles 0% other 1% cash 27%

Largest Holdings: health services 10%, cellular communications 9%

Unrealized Net Capital Gains: 12% of portfolio value

SHAREHOLDER INFORMATION

Minimum Investment
Initial: $1,000   Subsequent: $50

Minimum IRA Investment
Initial: $1,000   Subsequent: $50

Maximum Fees
Load: none   12b-1: none
Other: none

Distributions
Income: Sep   Capital Gains: Sep, Dec

Exchange Options
Number Per Year: none   Fee: na
Telephone: na

Services
IRA, auto invest, auto withdraw

Merrill Lynch Corp Interm "A" (MLITX)

Box 9011
Princeton, NJ 08543
(609) 282-2800

Corporate Bond

PERFORMANCE

	3yr Annual	5yr Annual	10yr Annual	Bull	Bear
Return (%)	11.4	11.0	na	43.7	4.4
Differ from Category (+/-)	-0.6 av	0.8 high	na	-2.4 av	2.6 abv av

Total Risk	Standard Deviation	Category Risk	Risk Index	Avg Mat
blw av	4.6%	high	1.7	7.0 yrs

	1993	1992	1991	1990	1989	1988	1987	1986	1985	1984
Return (%)	11.8	7.2	15.4	8.4	12.3	7.5	0.6	14.4	19.7	—
Differ from category (+/-) ...	0.4	-1.4	-1.2	3.1	2.8	-1.5	-1.2	-0.3	0.0	—

PER SHARE DATA

	1993	1992	1991	1990	1989	1988	1987	1986	1985	1984
Dividends, Net Income ($) .	0.74	0.85	0.91	0.96	0.98	0.96	0.94	1.02	1.16	—
Distrib'ns, Cap Gain ($) ...	0.28	0.13	0.00	0.00	0.00	0.00	0.00	0.00	0.00	—
Net Asset Value ($)	11.92	11.60	11.77	11.05	11.13	10.83	10.99	11.87	11.32	—
Expense Ratio (%)........	0.58	0.62	0.67	0.71	0.72	0.62	0.61	0.62	0.50	—
Net Income to Assets (%) ..	6.42	7.54	8.35	8.86	8.97	8.83	8.09	9.12	11.00	—
Portfolio Turnover (%)....	180	95	133	103	149	152	153	67	48	—
Total Assets (Millions $) ...	190	154	103	88	87	98	111	105	48	—

PORTFOLIO (as of 9/30/93)

Portfolio Manager: Jay Harbeck - 1992

Investm't Category: Corporate Bond

Cap Gain	Asset Allocation
Cap & Income	Fund of Funds
✔ Income	Index
	Sector
✔ Domestic	Small Cap
Foreign	Socially Conscious
Country/Region	State Specific

Portfolio: stocks 0%   bonds 95%
convertibles 0%   other 0%   cash 5%

Largest Holdings: industrials 28%, financial services 16%

Unrealized Net Capital Gains: 4% of portfolio value

SHAREHOLDER INFORMATION

Minimum Investment
Initial: $1,000   Subsequent: $100

Minimum IRA Investment
Initial: $250   Subsequent: $0

Maximum Fees
Load: 2.00% front   12b-1: none
Other: none

Distributions
Income: monthly   Capital Gains: Dec

Exchange Options
Number Per Year: no limit   Fee: none
Telephone: yes (money market fund available)

Services
IRA, other pension, auto exchange, auto invest, auto withdraw

Merrill Lynch Muni Interm "A" (MLMIX)

Box 9011
Princeton, NJ 08543
(609) 282-2800

Tax-Exempt Bond

PERFORMANCE

	3yr Annual	5yr Annual	10yr Annual	Bull	Bear
Return (%)	10.0	8.7	na	37.5	2.1
Differ from Category (+/-)	-0.3 blw av	-0.5 blw av	na	-2.6 blw av	-0.2 blw av

Total Risk	Standard Deviation	Category Risk	Risk Index	Avg Mat
low	3.9%	blw av	1.0	10.6 yrs

	1993	1992	1991	1990	1989	1988	1987	1986	1985	1984
Return (%).	11.0	7.8	11.2	5.4	8.0	—	—	—	—	—
Differ from category (+/-). . .	-0.6	-0.5	-0.1	-0.8	-1.0	—	—	—	—	—

PER SHARE DATA

	1993	1992	1991	1990	1989	1988	1987	1986	1985	1984
Dividends, Net Income ($).	0.53	0.58	0.59	0.59	0.60	—	—	—	—	—
Distrib'ns, Cap Gain ($) . . .	0.00	0.00	0.00	0.00	0.00	—	—	—	—	—
Net Asset Value ($)	10.42	9.89	9.73	9.31	9.41	—	—	—	—	—
Expense Ratio (%)	0.75	0.86	0.85	0.92	0.90	—	—	—	—	—
Net Income to Assets (%) .	5.35	5.97	6.34	6.39	6.50	—	—	—	—	—
Portfolio Turnover (%).	83	74	130	236	68	—	—	—	—	—
Total Assets (Millions $). . . .	179	14	7	2	1	—	—	—	—	—

PORTFOLIO (as of 10/31/93)

Portfolio Manager: Fred Steube - 1987

Investm't Category: Tax-Exempt Bond

Cap Gain	Asset Allocation
Cap & Income	Fund of Funds
✔ Income	Index
	Sector
✔ Domestic	Small Cap
Foreign	Socially Conscious
Country/Region	State Specific

Portfolio: stocks 0% bonds 100%
convertibles 0% other 0% cash 0%

Largest Holdings: general obligation 41%

Unrealized Net Capital Gains: 5% of portfolio value

SHAREHOLDER INFORMATION

Minimum Investment
Initial: $1,000   Subsequent: $50

Minimum IRA Investment
Initial: na   Subsequent: na

Maximum Fees
Load: 2.00% front   12b-1: none
Other: none

Distributions
Income: monthly   Capital Gains: Oct

Exchange Options
Number Per Year: no limit   Fee: none
Telephone: yes (money market fund available)

Services
auto exchange, auto invest, auto withdraw

Merrill Lynch Muni Ltd Mat "A" (MLLMX)

Box 9011
Princeton, NJ 08543
(609) 282-2800

Tax-Exempt Bond

PERFORMANCE

	3yr Annual	5yr Annual	10yr Annual	Bull	Bear
Return (%)	5.7	6.0	na	20.5	4.1
Differ from Category (+/-)	-4.6 low	-3.2 low	na	-19.6 low	1.8 high

Total Risk	Standard Deviation	Category Risk	Risk Index	Avg Mat
low	1.1%	low	0.2	1.3 yrs

	1993	1992	1991	1990	1989	1988	1987	1986	1985	1984
Return (%)	4.2	5.6	7.3	6.0	6.9	5.8	3.0	7.4	6.6	—
Differ from category (+/-)	-7.4	-2.7	-4.0	-0.3	-2.1	-4.3	4.2	-9.0	-10.7	—

PER SHARE DATA

	1993	1992	1991	1990	1989	1988	1987	1986	1985	1984
Dividends, Net Income ($)	0.38	0.45	0.53	0.59	0.58	0.55	0.51	0.56	0.62	—
Distrib'ns, Cap Gain ($)	0.00	0.00	0.00	0.00	0.00	0.00	0.00	0.00	0.00	—
Net Asset Value ($)	10.01	9.97	9.88	9.72	9.74	9.68	9.68	9.90	9.75	—
Expense Ratio (%)	0.41	0.40	0.40	0.40	0.41	0.40	0.40	0.42	0.43	—
Net Income to Assets (%)	4.13	5.02	5.88	6.21	6.00	5.42	5.27	6.04	6.83	—
Portfolio Turnover (%)	65	96	93	106	229	146	20	7	81	—
Total Assets (Millions $)	887	613	351	352	386	567	796	623	428	—

PORTFOLIO (as of 6/30/93)

Portfolio Manager: Peter Hayes - 1987

Investm't Category: Tax-Exempt Bond

Cap Gain	Asset Allocation
Cap & Income	Fund of Funds
✔ Income	Index
	Sector
✔ Domestic	Small Cap
Foreign	Socially Conscious
Country/Region	State Specific

Portfolio: stocks 0% bonds 100%
convertibles 0% other 0% cash 0%

Largest Holdings: general obligation 24%

Unrealized Net Capital Gains: 1% of portfolio value

SHAREHOLDER INFORMATION

Minimum Investment
Initial: $1,000   Subsequent: $100

Minimum IRA Investment
Initial: na   Subsequent: na

Maximum Fees
Load: 0.75% front   12b-1: none
Other: none

Distributions
Income: monthly   Capital Gains: Dec

Exchange Options
Number Per Year: no limit   Fee: none
Telephone: yes (money market fund available)

Services
auto exchange, auto invest, auto withdraw

Merriman Asset Allocation (MTASX)

1200 Westlake Ave. N.
Seattle, WA 98109
(800) 423-4893, (206) 285-8877

Balanced

PERFORMANCE

	3yr Annual	5yr Annual	10yr Annual	Bull	Bear
Return (%)	11.0	na	na	38.6	-0.4
Differ from Category (+/-)	-4.0 low	na	na	-23.0 low	5.4 high

Total Risk	Standard Deviation	Category Risk	Risk Index	Beta
blw av	5.9%	blw av	0.9	0.3

	1993	1992	1991	1990	1989	1988	1987	1986	1985	1984
Return (%)	18.5	2.7	12.2	0.8	—	—	—	—	—	—
Differ from category (+/-). . .	5.1	-5.4	-11.7	1.3	—	—	—	—	—	—

PER SHARE DATA

	1993	1992	1991	1990	1989	1988	1987	1986	1985	1984
Dividends, Net Income ($) .	0.14	0.22	0.28	0.46	—	—	—	—	—	—
Distrib'ns, Cap Gain ($) . . .	0.56	0.53	0.00	0.00	—	—	—	—	—	—
Net Asset Value ($)	11.71	10.48	10.94	10.00	—	—	—	—	—	—
Expense Ratio (%)	1.52	1.52	1.52	1.53	—	—	—	—	—	—
Net Income to Assets (%) .	1.52	2.87	3.03	5.01	—	—	—	—	—	—
Portfolio Turnover (%).	2	133	312	416	—	—	—	—	—	—
Total Assets (Millions $).	30	27	28	23	—	—	—	—	—	—

PORTFOLIO (as of 3/31/93)

Portfolio Manager: Paul A. Merriman - 1989

Investm't Category: Balanced

Cap Gain	✔ Asset Allocation
✔ Cap & Income	✔ Fund of Funds
Income	Index
	Sector
✔ Domestic	Small Cap
✔ Foreign	Socially Conscious
Country/Region	State Specific

Portfolio: stocks 0% bonds 0%
convertibles 0% other 83% cash 17%

Largest Holdings: equity funds 27%, fixed-income funds 22%

Unrealized Net Capital Gains: 5% of portfolio value

SHAREHOLDER INFORMATION

Minimum Investment
Initial: $1,000   Subsequent: $100

Minimum IRA Investment
Initial: $250   Subsequent: $100

Maximum Fees
Load: none   12b-1: none
Other: none

Distributions
Income: quarterly   Capital Gains: Dec

Exchange Options
Number Per Year: no limit   Fee: $5
Telephone: yes (money market fund available)

Services
IRA, other pension, auto invest, auto withdraw

Merriman Blue Chip
(MTBCX)
Growth & Income

1200 Westlake Ave. N.
Seattle, WA 98109
(800) 423-4893, (206) 285-8877

PERFORMANCE

	3yr Annual	5yr Annual	10yr Annual	Bull	Bear
Return (%)	6.5	6.6	na	23.8	1.3
Differ from Category (+/-)	-9.9 low	-5.9 low	na	-46.3 low	12.9 high

Total Risk	Standard Deviation	Category Risk	Risk Index	Beta
av	8.3%	blw av	0.9	0.6

	1993	1992	1991	1990	1989	1988	1987	1986	1985	1984
Return (%)	2.7	-1.2	19.1	3.8	9.7	—	—	—	—	—
Differ from category (+/-) ..	-9.9	-11.2	-8.6	9.4	-11.9	—	—	—	—	—

PER SHARE DATA

	1993	1992	1991	1990	1989	1988	1987	1986	1985	1984
Dividends, Net Income ($) .	0.08	0.18	0.18	0.43	0.31	—	—	—	—	—
Distrib'ns, Cap Gain ($) ...	0.00	1.11	0.00	0.13	0.00	—	—	—	—	—
Net Asset Value ($)	11.05	10.84	12.30	10.49	10.66	—	—	—	—	—
Expense Ratio (%)........	1.64	1.60	1.71	1.83	2.00	—	—	—	—	—
Net Income to Assets (%)..	1.14	1.64	2.47	4.16	4.12	—	—	—	—	—
Portfolio Turnover (%)....	200	91	149	329	48	—	—	—	—	—
Total Assets (Millions $)	14	22	20	15	9	—	—	—	—	—

PORTFOLIO (as of 3/31/93)

Portfolio Manager: Paul A. Merriman - 1989

Investm't Category: Growth & Income

Cap Gain	Asset Allocation
✔ Cap & Income	Fund of Funds
Income	Index
	Sector
✔ Domestic	Small Cap
Foreign	Socially Conscious
Country/Region	State Specific

Portfolio: stocks 52% bonds 0%
convertibles 0% other 0% cash 48%

Largest Holdings: consumer non-durables 18%, technology 7%

Unrealized Net Capital Gains: 4% of portfolio value

SHAREHOLDER INFORMATION

Minimum Investment
Initial: $1,000   Subsequent: $100

Minimum IRA Investment
Initial: $250   Subsequent: $100

Maximum Fees
Load: none   12b-1: none
Other: none

Distributions
Income: quarterly   Capital Gains: Dec

Exchange Options
Number Per Year: no limit   Fee: $5
Telephone: yes (money market fund available)

Services
IRA, other pension, auto invest, auto withdraw

Merriman Capital Appreciation (MNCAX)

1200 Westlake Ave. N.
Seattle, WA 98109
(800) 423-4893, (206) 285-8877

Growth

PERFORMANCE

	3yr Annual	5yr Annual	10yr Annual	Bull	Bear
Return (%)	9.5	na	na	35.7	0.0
Differ from Category (+/-)	-9.7 low	na	na	-49.0 low	12.4 high

Total Risk	Standard Deviation	Category Risk	Risk Index	Beta
av	8.1%	low	0.7	0.5

	1993	1992	1991	1990	1989	1988	1987	1986	1985	1984
Return (%)	3.6	4.1	21.8	3.1	—	—	—	—	—	—
Differ from category (+/-). . .	-9.6	-6.9	-13.6	9.2	—	—	—	—	—	—

PER SHARE DATA

	1993	1992	1991	1990	1989	1988	1987	1986	1985	1984
Dividends, Net Income ($).	0.07	0.12	0.22	0.44	—	—	—	—	—	—
Distrib'ns, Cap Gain ($) . . .	0.46	1.14	0.00	0.00	—	—	—	—	—	—
Net Asset Value ($)	10.94	11.07	11.85	9.91	—	—	—	—	—	—
Expense Ratio (%)	1.54	1.46	1.48	1.53	—	—	—	—	—	—
Net Income to Assets (%) .	0.48	2.48	1.73	4.79	—	—	—	—	—	—
Portfolio Turnover (%).	241	122	119	429	—	—	—	—	—	—
Total Assets (Millions $).	33	44	46	18	—	—	—	—	—	—

PORTFOLIO (as of 3/31/93)

Portfolio Manager: Paul A. Merriman - 1989

Investm't Category: Growth

✔ Cap Gain	Asset Allocation
Cap & Income	✔ Fund of Funds
Income	Index
	Sector
✔ Domestic	Small Cap
✔ Foreign	Socially Conscious
Country/Region	State Specific

Portfolio: stocks 0%   bonds 0%
convertibles 0%   other 53%   cash 47%

Largest Holdings: equity funds 53%

Unrealized Net Capital Gains: 2% of portfolio value

SHAREHOLDER INFORMATION

Minimum Investment
Initial: $1,000   Subsequent: $100

Minimum IRA Investment
Initial: $250   Subsequent: $100

Maximum Fees
Load: none   12b-1: none
Other: none

Distributions
Income: quarterly   Capital Gains: Dec

Exchange Options
Number Per Year: no limit   Fee: $5
Telephone: yes (money market fund available)

Services
IRA, other pension, auto invest, auto withdraw

Merriman Flexible Bond

(MTGVX)

General Bond

1200 Westlake Ave. N.
Seattle, WA 98109
(800) 423-4893, (206) 285-8877

PERFORMANCE

	3yr Annual	5yr Annual	10yr Annual	Bull	Bear
Return (%)	10.6	9.3	na	40.4	2.4
Differ from Category (+/-)	-0.2 av	-1.1 blw av	na	-5.8 av	1.9 av

Total Risk	Standard Deviation	Category Risk	Risk Index	Avg Mat
blw av	5.7%	abv av	1.3	7.9 yrs

	1993	1992	1991	1990	1989	1988	1987	1986	1985	1984
Return (%)	14.4	4.5	13.3	6.1	8.4	—	—	—	—	—
Differ from category (+/-) . . .	4.0	-1.7	-1.7	-0.4	-5.5	—	—	—	—	—

PER SHARE DATA

	1993	1992	1991	1990.	1989	1988	1987	1986	1985	1984
Dividends, Net Income ($) .	0.62	0.58	0.61	0.62	0.60	—	—	—	—	—
Distrib'ns, Cap Gain ($) . . .	0.65	0.45	0.00	0.00	0.18	—	—	—	—	—
Net Asset Value ($)	10.27	10.11	10.69	10.02	10.05	—	—	—	—	—
Expense Ratio (%).	1.52	1.51	1.55	1.56	1.50	—	—	—	—	—
Net Income to Assets (%). .	4.56	6.26	6.03	6.41	7.14	—	—	—	—	—
Portfolio Turnover (%). . . .	272	2	202	234	270	—	—	—	—	—
Total Assets (Millions $)	12	11	11	10	7	—	—	—	—	—

PORTFOLIO (as of 3/31/93)

Portfolio Manager: Paul A. Merriman - 1988

Investm't Category: General Bond

Cap Gain	Asset Allocation
Cap & Income	Fund of Funds
✔ Income	Index
	Sector
✔ Domestic	Small Cap
Foreign	Socially Conscious
Country/Region	State Specific

Portfolio: stocks 0%   bonds 27%
convertibles 0%   other 67%   cash 6%

Largest Holdings: U.S. government 27%, corporate 49%

Unrealized Net Capital Gains: 2% of portfolio value

SHAREHOLDER INFORMATION

Minimum Investment
Initial: $1,000   Subsequent: $100

Minimum IRA Investment
Initial: $250   Subsequent: $100

Maximum Fees
Load: none   12b-1: none
Other: none

Distributions
Income: quarterly   Capital Gains: Dec

Exchange Options
Number Per Year: no limit   Fee: $5
Telephone: yes (money market fund available)

Services
IRA, other pension, auto invest, auto withdraw

MiM Bond Income (MIBIX)

Balanced

4500 Rockside Rd., Suite 440
Cleveland, OH 44131
(800) 233-1240, (216) 642-3000

PERFORMANCE

	3yr Annual	5yr Annual	10yr Annual	Bull	Bear
Return (%)	8.3	5.5	na	29.5	-1.7
Differ from Category (+/-)	-6.7 low	-6.6 low	na	-32.1 low	4.1 high

Total Risk	Standard Deviation	Category Risk	Risk Index	Beta
blw av	4.2%	low	0.6	0.2

	1993	1992	1991	1990	1989	1988	1987	1986	1985	1984
Return (%)	2.9	6.7	15.6	0.1	3.0	10.3	-1.1	—	—	—
Differ from category (+/-)	-10.5	-1.4	-8.3	0.6	-14.6	-1.7	-3.4	—	—	—

PER SHARE DATA

	1993	1992	1991	1990	1989	1988	1987	1986	1985	1984
Dividends, Net Income ($)	0.23	0.38	0.57	0.84	0.69	0.58	0.66	—	—	—
Distrib'ns, Cap Gain ($)	0.00	0.00	0.00	0.00	0.00	0.00	0.00	—	—	—
Net Asset Value ($)	9.41	9.37	9.15	8.44	9.28	9.68	9.31	—	—	—
Expense Ratio (%)	2.75	2.80	2.70	2.30	2.30	2.30	2.50	—	—	—
Net Income to Assets (%)	2.76	5.00	7.10	8.00	7.30	6.80	4.60	—	—	—
Portfolio Turnover (%)	95	64	25	18	42	40	50	—	—	—
Total Assets (Millions $)	3	4	4	5	10	6	1	—	—	—

PORTFOLIO (as of 9/30/93)

Portfolio Manager: Harvey Salkin - 1986

Investm't Category: Balanced

Cap Gain	Asset Allocation
✔ Cap & Income	Fund of Funds
Income	Index
	Sector
✔ Domestic	Small Cap
✔ Foreign	Socially Conscious
Country/Region	State Specific

Portfolio: stocks 37% bonds 1%
convertibles 55% other 0% cash 7%

Largest Holdings: stocks—drug 15%, convertible bonds—aerospace/defense 11%

Unrealized Net Capital Gains: 1% of portfolio value

SHAREHOLDER INFORMATION

Minimum Investment
Initial: $250   Subsequent: $50

Minimum IRA Investment
Initial: $0   Subsequent: $0

Maximum Fees
Load: none   12b-1: 0.70%
Other: none

Distributions
Income: quarterly   Capital Gains: Dec

Exchange Options
Number Per Year: no limit   Fee: none
Telephone: yes (money market fund available)

Services
IRA, other pension, auto exchange, auto invest, auto withdraw

MIM Stock Appreciation
(MISAX)
Aggressive Growth

4500 Rockside Rd., Suite 440
Cleveland, OH 44131
(800) 233-1240, (216) 642-3000

	3yr Annual	5yr Annual	10yr Annual	Bull	Bear
Return (%)	27.4	20.3	na	135.0	-7.4
Differ from Category (+/-)	2.0 abv av	2.1 abv av	na	10.0 abv av	7.6 high

Total Risk	Standard Deviation	Category Risk	Risk Index	Beta
high	18.8%	abv av	1.2	1.3

	1993	1992	1991	1990	1989	1988	1987	1986	1985	1984
Return (%)	10.4	5.8	76.9	5.1	16.3	-2.1	—	—	—	—
Differ from category (+/-) . .	-8.6	-4.6	24.5	11.4	-10.7	-17.3	—	—	—	—

PER SHARE DATA

	1993	1992	1991	1990	1989	1988	1987	1986	1985	1984
Dividends, Net Income ($) .	0.00	0.00	0.00	0.00	0.17	0.06	—	—	—	—
Distrib'ns, Cap Gain ($) . . .	0.95	0.34	1.82	0.00	0.00	0.00	—	—	—	—
Net Asset Value ($)	15.43	14.84	14.35	9.14	8.69	7.63	—	—	—	—
Expense Ratio (%)	2.47	2.70	2.90	2.70	3.10	2.70	—	—	—	—
Net Income to Assets (%) .	-1.85	-1.10	-1.70	-0.60	2.20	0.40	—	—	—	—
Portfolio Turnover (%)	216	288	240	185	71	207	—	—	—	—
Total Assets (Millions $)	58	29	10	4	1	2	—	—	—	—

PORTFOLIO (as of 9/30/93)

Portfolio Manager: Arthur Bonnel - 1987

Investm't Category: Aggressive Growth
✔ Cap Gain	Asset Allocation
Cap & Income	Fund of Funds
Income	Index
	Sector
✔ Domestic	Small Cap
Foreign	Socially Conscious
Country/Region	State Specific

Portfolio: stocks 98% bonds 0%
convertibles 0% other 0% cash 2%

Largest Holdings: semiconductor 14%, computer software & services 14%

Unrealized Net Capital Gains: 19% of portfolio value

SHAREHOLDER INFORMATION

Minimum Investment
Initial: $250 Subsequent: $50

Minimum IRA Investment
Initial: $0 Subsequent: $0

Maximum Fees
Load: none 12b-1: 0.70%
Other: none

Distributions
Income: quarterly Capital Gains: Dec

Exchange Options
Number Per Year: no limit Fee: none
Telephone: yes (money market fund available)

Services
IRA, other pension, auto exchange, auto invest, auto withdraw

MIM Stock Growth
(MISGX)
Growth

4500 Rockside Rd., Suite 440
Cleveland, OH 44131
(800) 233-1240, (216) 642-3000

PERFORMANCE

	3yr Annual	5yr Annual	10yr Annual	Bull	Bear
Return (%)	8.3	5.3	na	36.3	-12.2
Differ from Category (+/-)	-10.9 low	-9.3 low	na	-48.4 low	0.2 av

Total Risk	Standard Deviation	Category Risk	Risk Index	Beta
abv av	10.9%	blw av	1.0	0.8

	1993	1992	1991	1990	1989	1988	1987	1986	1985	1984
Return (%).............	2.1	-1.9	26.9	-5.9	8.3	15.2	-10.9	—	—	—
Differ from category (+/-)..	-11.1	-12.9	-8.5	0.2	-17.5	-2.5	-12.1	—	—	—

PER SHARE DATA

	1993	1992	1991	1990	1989	1988	1987	1986	1985	1984
Dividends, Net Income ($).	0.00	0.00	0.09	0.24	0.34	0.27	0.43	—	—	—
Distrib'ns, Cap Gain ($) ...	0.00	0.01	0.00	0.00	0.00	0.00	0.03	—	—	—
Net Asset Value ($)	11.40	11.16	11.39	9.06	9.89	9.44	8.44	—	—	—
Expense Ratio (%)	2.79	2.90	2.90	2.70	2.80	2.80	2.50	—	—	—
Net Income to Assets (%) .	-0.77	0.00	1.40	2.70	3.90	3.80	3.70	—	—	—
Portfolio Turnover (%).....	137	105	67	42	38	58	50	—	—	—
Total Assets (Millions $)......	9	9	7	6	7	2	1	—	—	—

PORTFOLIO (as of 9/30/93)

Portfolio Manager: Martin Weisberg - 1993

Investm't Category: Growth

✔ Cap Gain	Asset Allocation
Cap & Income	Fund of Funds
Income	Index
	Sector
✔ Domestic	Small Cap
Foreign	Socially Conscious
Country/Region	State Specific

Portfolio: stocks 99% bonds 0%
convertibles 0% other 0% cash 1%

Largest Holdings: bank 9%, retail—special lines 7%

Unrealized Net Capital Gains: 14% of portfolio value

SHAREHOLDER INFORMATION

Minimum Investment
Initial: $250   Subsequent: $50

Minimum IRA Investment
Initial: $0   Subsequent: $0

Maximum Fees
Load: none   12b-1: 0.70%
Other: none

Distributions
Income: quarterly   Capital Gains: Dec

Exchange Options
Number Per Year: no limit   Fee: none
Telephone: yes (money market fund available)

Services
IRA, other pension, auto exchange, auto invest, auto withdraw

MIM Stock Income

(MICIX)

Growth & Income

4500 Rockside Rd., Suite 440
Cleveland, OH 44131
(800) 233-1240, (216) 642-3000

PERFORMANCE

	3yr Annual	5yr Annual	10yr Annual	Bull	Bear
Return (%)	7.6	5.3	na	33.0	-9.4
Differ from Category (+/-)	-8.8 low	-7.2 low	na	-37.1 low	2.2 abv av

Total Risk	Standard Deviation	Category Risk	Risk Index	Beta
av	8.9%	blw av	1.0	0.7

	1993	1992	1991	1990	1989	1988	1987	1986	1985	1984
Return (%)	-0.6	5.1	19.3	-3.3	7.8	15.8	-2.0	—	—	—
Differ from category (+/-) .	-13.2	-4.9	-8.4	2.3	-13.8	-1.0	-2.4	—	—	—

PER SHARE DATA

	1993	1992	1991	1990	1989	1988	1987	1986	1985	1984
Dividends, Net Income ($) .	0.02	0.19	0.22	0.30	0.45	0.34	0.70	—	—	—
Distrib'ns, Cap Gain ($) . . .	0.00	0.96	0.22	0.08	0.00	0.00	0.09	—	—	—
Net Asset Value ($)	10.40	10.50	11.12	9.72	10.46	10.12	9.04	—	—	—
Expense Ratio (%)	2.61	2.60	2.70	2.50	2.60	2.50	1.70	—	—	—
Net Income to Assets (%) . .	0.53	2.10	2.50	3.70	4.80	4.80	7.10	—	—	—
Portfolio Turnover (%)	272	222	139	86	65	78	70	—	—	—
Total Assets (Millions $)	7	12	11	10	13	5	1	—	—	—

PORTFOLIO (as of 9/30/93)

Portfolio Manager: Harvey Salkin - 1986

Investm't Category: Growth & Income

Cap Gain	Asset Allocation
✔ Cap & Income	Fund of Funds
Income	Index
	Sector
✔ Domestic	Small Cap
Foreign	Socially Conscious
Country/Region	State Specific

Portfolio: stocks 100% bonds 0%
convertibles 0% other 0% cash 0%

Largest Holdings: banks 13%, medical supplies 7%

Unrealized Net Capital Gains: 2% of portfolio value

SHAREHOLDER INFORMATION

Minimum Investment
Initial: $250   Subsequent: $50

Minimum IRA Investment
Initial: $0   Subsequent: $0

Maximum Fees
Load: none   12b-1: 0.70%
Other: none

Distributions
Income: quarterly   Capital Gains: Dec

Exchange Options
Number Per Year: no limit   Fee: none
Telephone: yes (money market fund available)

Services
IRA, other pension, auto exchange, auto invest, auto withdraw

Monetta (MONTX)

Growth

1776-A S. Naperville Rd., #207
Wheaton, IL 60187
(800) 666-3882, (708) 462-9800

this fund is closed to new investors

PERFORMANCE

	3yr Annual	5yr Annual	10yr Annual	Bull	Bear
Return (%)	18.2	16.2	na	93.5	-4.8
Differ from Category (+/-)	-1.0 av	1.6 abv av	na	8.8 abv av	7.6 high

Total Risk	Standard Deviation	Category Risk	Risk Index	Beta
abv av	12.2%	av	1.1	0.7

	1993	1992	1991	1990	1989	1988	1987	1986	1985	1984
Return (%)	0.4	5.4	55.8	11.3	15.2	23.0	1.5	—	—	—
Differ from category (+/-)	-12.8	-5.6	20.4	17.4	-10.6	5.3	0.3	—	—	—

PER SHARE DATA

	1993	1992	1991	1990	1989	1988	1987	1986	1985	1984
Dividends, Net Income ($)	0.12	0.04	0.05	0.10	0.21	0.07	0.14	—	—	—
Distrib'ns, Cap Gain ($)	0.40	0.55	1.30	0.58	0.76	1.91	0.00	—	—	—
Net Asset Value ($)	15.54	15.99	15.73	10.96	10.44	9.93	9.68	—	—	—
Expense Ratio (%)	na	1.45	1.42	1.50	1.57	1.50	2.31	—	—	—
Net Income to Assets (%)	na	0.16	0.93	1.09	2.18	0.96	1.33	—	—	—
Portfolio Turnover (%)	na	127	154	207	258	170	333	—	—	—
Total Assets (Millions $)	52	408	57	6	4	3	2	—	—	—

PORTFOLIO (as of 6/30/93)

Portfolio Manager: Robert S. Bacarella - 1986

Investm't Category: Growth

✔ Cap Gain	Asset Allocation
Cap & Income	Fund of Funds
Income	Index
	Sector
✔ Domestic	✔ Small Cap
Foreign	Socially Conscious
Country/Region	State Specific

Portfolio: stocks 92% bonds 0%
convertibles 0% other 0% cash 8%

Largest Holdings: electrical & electronic 14%,
banks and savings & loans 12%

Unrealized Net Capital Gains: 6% of portfolio value

SHAREHOLDER INFORMATION

Minimum Investment
Initial: $100   Subsequent: $50

Minimum IRA Investment
Initial: $100   Subsequent: $50

Maximum Fees
Load: none   12b-1: none
Other: none

Distributions
Income: Jun, Dec   Capital Gains: Dec

Exchange Options
Number Per Year: none Fee: na
Telephone: na

Services
IRA, other pension, auto invest

Montgomery Emerging Markets (MNEMX)

600 Montgomery St.
San Francisco, CA 94111
(800) 572-3863, (415) 627-2400

International Stock

PERFORMANCE

	3yr Annual	5yr Annual	10yr Annual	Bull	Bear
Return (%)	na	na	na	na	na
Differ from Category (+/-)	na	na	na	na	na

Total Risk	Standard Deviation	Category Risk	Risk Index	Beta
na	na	na	na	na

	1993	1992	1991	1990	1989	1988	1987	1986	1985	1984
Return (%)	58.6	—	—	—	—	—	—	—	—	—
Differ from category (+/-)	20.1	—	—	—	—	—	—	—	—	—

PER SHARE DATA

	1993	1992	1991	1990	1989	1988	1987	1986	1985	1984
Dividends, Net Income ($)	0.01	—	—	—	—	—	—	—	—	—
Distrib'ns, Cap Gain ($)	0.25	—	—	—	—	—	—	—	—	—
Net Asset Value ($)	15.58	—	—	—	—	—	—	—	—	—
Expense Ratio (%)	1.90	—	—	—	—	—	—	—	—	—
Net Income to Assets (%)	0.66	—	—	—	—	—	—	—	—	—
Portfolio Turnover (%)	21	—	—	—	—	—	—	—	—	—
Total Assets (Millions $)	576	—	—	—	—	—	—	—	—	—

PORTFOLIO (as of 6/30/93)

Portfolio Manager: Josephine Jimenez - 1992, Bryan Sudweeks - 1992

Investm't Category: International Stock
✔ Cap Gain   Asset Allocation
   Cap & Income   Fund of Funds
   Income   Index
                    Sector
   Domestic   Small Cap
✔ Foreign   Socially Conscious
   Country/Region   State Specific

Portfolio: stocks 82%   bonds 0%
convertibles 0%   other 0%   cash 18%

Largest Holdings: Brazil 14%, Mexico 9%

Unrealized Net Capital Gains: 7% of portfolio value

SHAREHOLDER INFORMATION

Minimum Investment
Initial: $2,000   Subsequent: $100

Minimum IRA Investment
Initial: $2,000   Subsequent: $100

Maximum Fees
Load: none   12b-1: none
Other: none

Distributions
Income: July, Dec   Capital Gains: July, Dec

Exchange Options
Number Per Year: no limit   Fee: none
Telephone: yes (money market fund available)

Services
IRA, other pension, auto exchange, auto invest, auto withdraw

Montgomery Short Duration Gov't (MNSGX)

600 Montgomery St.
San Francisco, CA 94111
(800) 572-3863, (415) 627-2400

Mortgage-Backed Bond

PERFORMANCE

	3yr Annual	5yr Annual	10yr Annual	Bull	Bear
Return (%)	na	na	na	na	na
Differ from Category (+/-)	na	na	na	na	na

Total Risk	Standard Deviation	Category Risk	Risk Index	Avg Mat
na	na	na	na	27.8 yrs

	1993	1992	1991	1990	1989	1988	1987	1986	1985	1984
Return (%)	8.3	—	—	—	—	—	—	—	—	—
Differ from category (+/-)	1.5	—	—	—	—	—	—	—	—	—

PER SHARE DATA

	1993	1992	1991	1990	1989	1988	1987	1986	1985	1984
Dividends, Net Income ($)	0.66	—	—	—	—	—	—	—	—	—
Distrib'ns, Cap Gain ($)	0.07	—	—	—	—	—	—	—	—	—
Net Asset Value ($)	10.10	—	—	—	—	—	—	—	—	—
Expense Ratio (%)	0.22	—	—	—	—	—	—	—	—	—
Net Income to Assets (%)	6.02	—	—	—	—	—	—	—	—	—
Portfolio Turnover (%)	213	—	—	—	—	—	—	—	—	—
Total Assets (Millions $)	27	—	—	—	—	—	—	—	—	—

PORTFOLIO (as of 6/30/93)

Portfolio Manager: Jim Midanek - 1991

Investm't Category: Mortgage-Backed Bond

Cap Gain	Asset Allocation
Cap & Income	Fund of Funds
✔ Income	Index
	Sector
✔ Domestic	Small Cap
Foreign	Socially Conscious
Country/Region	State Specific

Portfolio: stocks 0%   bonds 100%
convertibles 0%   other 0%   cash 0%

Largest Holdings: mortgage-backed 79%, U.S. government 21%

Unrealized Net Capital Gains: 0% of portfolio value

SHAREHOLDER INFORMATION

Minimum Investment
Initial: $2,000   Subsequent: $100

Minimum IRA Investment
Initial: $2,000   Subsequent: $100

Maximum Fees
Load: none   12b-1: none
Other: none

Distributions
Income: monthly   Capital Gains: Dec

Exchange Options
Number Per Year: no limit   Fee: none
Telephone: yes (money market fund available)

Services
IRA, other pension, auto exchange, auto invest, auto withdraw

Montgomery Small Cap

(MNSCX)

Aggressive Growth

600 Montgomery St.
San Francisco, CA 94111
(800) 572-3863, (415) 627-2400

this fund is closed to new investors

PERFORMANCE

	3yr Annual	5yr Annual	10yr Annual	Bull	Bear
Return (%)	39.3	na	na	204.1	na
Differ from Category (+/-)	13.9 high	na	na	79.1 high	na

Total Risk	Standard Deviation	Category Risk	Risk Index	Beta
high	20.2%	abv av	1.3	1.4

	1993	1992	1991	1990	1989	1988	1987	1986	1985	1984
Return (%)	24.3	9.5	98.7	—	—	—	—	—	—	—
Differ from category (+/-) . . .	5.3	-0.8	46.3	—	—	—	—	—	—	—

PER SHARE DATA

	1993	1992	1991	1990	1989	1988	1987	1986	1985	1984
Dividends, Net Income ($) .	0.00	0.00	0.00	—	—	—	—	—	—	—
Distrib'ns, Cap Gain ($) . . .	1.51	0.00	3.52	—	—	—	—	—	—	—
Net Asset Value ($)	17.67	15.54	14.18	—	—	—	—	—	—	—
Expense Ratio (%).	1.40	1.50	1.45	—	—	—	—	—	—	—
Net Income to Assets (%) .	-0.68	-0.44	-0.45	—	—	—	—	—	—	—
Portfolio Turnover (%)	130	81	188	—	—	—	—	—	—	—
Total Assets (Millions $) . . .	250	177	27	—	—	—	—	—	—	—

PORTFOLIO (as of 6/30/93)

Portfolio Manager: Stuart O. Roberts - 1990

Investm't Category: Aggressive Growth

✔ Cap Gain	Asset Allocation
Cap & Income	Fund of Funds
Income	Index
	Sector
✔ Domestic	✔ Small Cap
Foreign	Socially Conscious
Country/Region	State Specific

Portfolio: stocks 92% bonds 0%
convertibles 0% other 0% cash 8%

Largest Holdings: telecommunications 19%,
consumer/leisure time products 16%

Unrealized Net Capital Gains: 19% of portfolio value

SHAREHOLDER INFORMATION

Minimum Investment
Initial: $2,000   Subsequent: $100

Minimum IRA Investment
Initial: $2,000   Subsequent: $100

Maximum Fees
Load: none   12b-1: none
Other: none

Distributions
Income: Jun, Dec   Capital Gains: Jun, Dec

Exchange Options
Number Per Year: no limit   Fee: none
Telephone: yes (money market fund available)

Services
IRA, other pension, auto exchange, auto invest,
auto withdraw

Morgan Grenfell Fixed Income (MFINX)

680 E. Swedesford Rd.
Wayne, PA 19087
(800) 338-4345, (215) 254-1000

General Bond

PERFORMANCE

	3yr Annual	5yr Annual	10yr Annual	Bull	Bear
Return (%)	na	na	na	na	na
Differ from Category (+/-)	na	na	na	na	na

Total Risk	Standard Deviation	Category Risk	Risk Index	Avg Mat
na	na	na	na	6.1 yrs

	1993	1992	1991	1990	1989	1988	1987	1986	1985	1984
Return (%)	13.6	—	—	—	—	—	—	—	—	—
Differ from category (+/-). . .	4.4	—	—	—	—	—	—	—	—	—

PER SHARE DATA

	1993	1992	1991	1990	1989	1988	1987	1986	1985	1984
Dividends, Net Income ($).	0.63	—	—	—	—	—	—	—	—	—
Distrib'ns, Cap Gain ($) . . .	0.10	—	—	—	—	—	—	—	—	—
Net Asset Value ($)	10.64	—	—	—	—	—	—	—	—	—
Expense Ratio (%)	0.55	—	—	—	—	—	—	—	—	—
Net Income to Assets (%) .	6.01	—	—	—	—	—	—	—	—	—
Portfolio Turnover (%).	196	—	—	—	—	—	—	—	—	—
Total Assets (Millions $). . . .	151	—	—	—	—	—	—	—	—	—

PORTFOLIO

Portfolio Manager: David Baldt - 1992

Investm't Category: General Bond

Cap Gain	Asset Allocation
Cap & Income	Fund of Funds
✔ Income	Index
	Sector
✔ Domestic	Small Cap
Foreign	Socially Conscious
Country/Region	State Specific

Portfolio: stocks na bonds na
convertibles na other na cash na

Largest Holdings: na

Unrealized Net Capital Gains: na

SHAREHOLDER INFORMATION

Minimum Investment
Initial: $50,000   Subsequent: $1,000

Minimum IRA Investment
Initial: na   Subsequent: na

Maximum Fees
Load: none   12b-1: none
Other: none

Distributions
Income: monthly   Capital Gains: Dec

Exchange Options
Number Per Year: none Fee: na
Telephone: na

Services

Morgan Grenfell Muni Bond (MGMBX)

680 E. Swedesford Rd.
Wayne, PA 19087
(800) 338-4345, (215) 254-1000

Tax-Exempt Bond

PERFORMANCE

	3yr Annual	5yr Annual	10yr Annual	Bull	Bear
Return (%)	na	na	na	na	na
Differ from Category (+/-)	na	na	na	na	na

Total Risk	Standard Deviation	Category Risk	Risk Index	Avg Mat
na	na	na	na	8.7 yrs

	1993	1992	1991	1990	1989	1988	1987	1986	1985	1984
Return (%)	12.4	11.9	—	—	—	—	—	—	—	—
Differ from category (+/-)	0.8	3.6	—	—	—	—	—	—	—	—

PER SHARE DATA

	1993	1992	1991	1990	1989	1988	1987	1986	1985	1984
Dividends, Net Income ($)	0.65	0.73	—	—	—	—	—	—	—	—
Distrib'ns, Cap Gain ($)	0.37	0.00	—	—	—	—	—	—	—	—
Net Asset Value ($)	10.98	10.71	—	—	—	—	—	—	—	—
Expense Ratio (%)	0.55	0.55	—	—	—	—	—	—	—	—
Net Income to Assets (%)	5.94	6.31	—	—	—	—	—	—	—	—
Portfolio Turnover (%)	160	143	—	—	—	—	—	—	—	—
Total Assets (Millions $)	146	94	—	—	—	—	—	—	—	—

PORTFOLIO

Portfolio Manager: David Baldt - 1991

Investm't Category: Tax-Exempt Bond

Cap Gain	Asset Allocation
Cap & Income	Fund of Funds
✔ Income	Index
	Sector
✔ Domestic	Small Cap
Foreign	Socially Conscious
Country/Region	State Specific

Portfolio: stocks na bonds na
convertibles na other na cash na

Largest Holdings: na

Unrealized Net Capital Gains: na

SHAREHOLDER INFORMATION

Minimum Investment
Initial: $50,000   Subsequent: $1,000

Minimum IRA Investment
Initial: na   Subsequent: na

Maximum Fees
Load: none   12b-1: none
Other: none

Distributions
Income: monthly   Capital Gains: Dec

Exchange Options
Number Per Year: none   Fee: na
Telephone: na

Services

M.S.B. Fund (MSBFX)

Growth

330 Madison Ave.
New York, NY 10017
(212) 551-1920

PERFORMANCE

	3yr Annual	5yr Annual	10yr Annual	Bull	Bear
Return (%)	16.0	13.1	12.0	69.1	-14.4
Differ from Category (+/-)	-3.2 blw av	-1.5 blw av	-0.6 blw av	-15.6 blw av	-2.0 blw av

Total Risk	Standard Deviation	Category Risk	Risk Index	Beta
av	10.4%	low	1.0	0.7

	1993	1992	1991	1990	1989	1988	1987	1986	1985	1984
Return (%)	20.5	10.6	16.9	-7.2	27.9	9.5	4.6	12.7	27.7	2.2
Differ from category (+/-). . .	7.3	-0.4	-18.5	-1.1	2.1	-8.2	3.4	-1.8	-1.6	2.2

PER SHARE DATA

	1993	1992	1991	1990	1989	1988	1987	1986	1985	1984
Dividends, Net Income ($).	0.17	0.28	0.20	0.40	0.25	0.37	0.33	0.61	0.49	0.70
Distrib'ns, Cap Gain ($) . . .	1.92	0.21	2.11	1.58	2.86	2.11	3.88	3.70	1.43	1.70
Net Asset Value ($)	16.79	15.67	14.62	14.54	17.82	16.40	17.23	20.60	21.97	19.00
Expense Ratio (%)	1.12	1.13	1.86	1.39	1.20	1.19	0.98	0.94	0.79	0.50
Net Income to Assets (%) .	1.00	1.43	1.36	2.38	1.30	2.06	1.32	2.08	2.94	3.70
Portfolio Turnover (%).	na	13	17	31	29	19	37	8	21	19
Total Assets (Millions $). . . .	46	41	41	42	52	49	49	50	51	43

PORTFOLIO (as of 6/30/93)

Portfolio Manager: Mark F. Trautman - 1993

Investm't Category: Growth

✔ Cap Gain	Asset Allocation
Cap & Income	Fund of Funds
Income	Index
	Sector
✔ Domestic	Small Cap
Foreign	Socially Conscious
Country/Region	State Specific

Portfolio: stocks 89% bonds 0%
convertibles 0% other 0% cash 11%

Largest Holdings: retail—speciality 8%, publishing—newspaper 6%

Unrealized Net Capital Gains: 23% of portfolio value

SHAREHOLDER INFORMATION

Minimum Investment
Initial: $50 Subsequent: $25

Minimum IRA Investment
Initial: na Subsequent: na

Maximum Fees
Load: none 12b-1: none
Other: none

Distributions
Income: quarterly Capital Gains: Dec

Exchange Options
Number Per Year: none Fee: na
Telephone: na

Services
auto invest, auto withdraw

Mutual Beacon (BEGRX)

Growth & Income

51 John F. Kennedy Pkwy.
Short Hills, NJ 07078
(800) 448-3863, (201) 912-2100

PERFORMANCE

	3yr Annual	5yr Annual	10yr Annual	Bull	Bear
Return (%)	21.1	13.8	na	79.3	-9.0
Differ from Category (+/-)	4.7 high	1.3 abv av	na	9.2 abv av	2.6 abv av

Total Risk	Standard Deviation	Category Risk	Risk Index	Beta
av	7.0%	low	0.8	0.4

	1993	1992	1991	1990	1989	1988	1987	1986	1985	1984
Return (%)	22.9	22.9	17.5	-8.1	17.4	28.9	12.7	15.4	24.5	—
Differ from category (+/-) . .	10.3	12.9	-10.2	-2.5	-4.2	12.1	12.3	0.2	-0.8	—

PER SHARE DATA

	1993	1992	1991	1990	1989	1988	1987	1986	1985	1984
Dividends, Net Income ($) .	0.37	0.46	0.74	1.08	1.17	0.80	0.50	0.31	0.25	—
Distrib'ns, Cap Gain ($) . . .	1.82	1.10	0.33	0.25	1.55	1.41	1.04	0.93	0.00	—
Net Asset Value ($)	31.09	27.10	23.36	20.80	24.09	22.85	19.47	18.64	17.24	—
Expense Ratio (%).	0.73	0.81	0.85	0.85	0.70	0.60	0.85	1.16	1.39	—
Net Income to Assets (%) . .	1.51	1.90	3.07	4.59	5.00	3.60	2.50	2.86	1.99	—
Portfolio Turnover (%)	na	58	57	58	67	87	73	113	72	—
Total Assets (Millions $) . .	1,060	534	399	388	409	214	159	65	9	—

PORTFOLIO (as of 6/30/93)

Portfolio Manager: Michael F. Price - 1985

Investm't Category: Growth & Income
Cap Gain	Asset Allocation
✔ Cap & Income	Fund of Funds
Income	Index
	Sector
✔ Domestic	Small Cap
✔ Foreign	Socially Conscious
Country/Region	State Specific

Portfolio: stocks 71% bonds 12%
convertibles 0% other 2% cash 15%

Largest Holdings: banking & financial institutions 11%, consumer products & services 8%

Unrealized Net Capital Gains: 13% of portfolio value

SHAREHOLDER INFORMATION

Minimum Investment
Initial: $5,000   Subsequent: $100

Minimum IRA Investment
Initial: $2,000   Subsequent: $100

Maximum Fees
Load: none   12b-1: none
Other: none

Distributions
Income: Jun, Dec   Capital Gains: Jun, Dec

Exchange Options
Number Per Year: no limit   Fee: none
Telephone: none

Services
IRA, other pension, auto invest, auto withdraw

Mutual Discovery (MDISX)

Growth

51 John F. Kennedy Pkwy.
Short Hills, NJ 07078
(800) 448-3863, (201) 912-2100
fund in existence since 1/4/93
this fund is closed to new investors

PERFORMANCE

	3yr Annual	5yr Annual	10yr Annual	Bull	Bear
Return (%)	na	na	na	na	na
Differ from Category (+/-)	na	na	na	na	na

Total Risk	Standard Deviation	Category Risk	Risk Index	Beta
na	na	na	na	na

	1993	1992	1991	1990	1989	1988	1987	1986	1985	1984
Return (%)	—	—	—	—	—	—	—	—	—	—
Differ from category (+/-). . . .	—	—	—	—	—	—	—	—	—	—

PER SHARE DATA

	1993	1992	1991	1990	1989	1988	1987	1986	1985	1984
Dividends, Net Income ($).	0.09	—	—	—	—	—	—	—	—	—
Distrib'ns, Cap Gain ($) . . .	0.43	—	—	—	—	—	—	—	—	—
Net Asset Value ($)	13.05	—	—	—	—	—	—	—	—	—
Expense Ratio (%)	1.29	—	—	—	—	—	—	—	—	—
Net Income to Assets (%) .	1.42	—	—	—	—	—	—	—	—	—
Portfolio Turnover (%).	na	—	—	—	—	—	—	—	—	—
Total Assets (Millions $). . . .	546	—	—	—	—	—	—	—	—	—

PORTFOLIO (as of 6/30/93)

Portfolio Manager: Michael Price - 1985

Investm't Category: Growth

✔ Cap Gain	Asset Allocation
Cap & Income	Fund of Funds
Income	Index
	Sector
✔ Domestic	✔ Small Cap
✔ Foreign	Socially Conscious
Country/Region	State Specific

Portfolio: stocks 80% bonds 9%
convertibles 0% other 2% cash 9%

Largest Holdings: banking & financial institutions 17%, health care 11%

Unrealized Net Capital Gains: 3% of portfolio value

SHAREHOLDER INFORMATION

Minimum Investment
Initial: $1,000   Subsequent: $50

Minimum IRA Investment
Initial: $1,000   Subsequent: $50

Maximum Fees
Load: none   12b-1: none
Other: none

Distributions
Income: July, Dec   Capital Gains: Dec

Exchange Options
Number Per Year: no limit   Fee: none
Telephone: none

Services
IRA, other pension, auto invest, auto withdraw

Mutual Qualified (MQIFX)

Growth & Income

51 John F. Kennedy Pkwy.
Short Hills, NJ 07078
(800) 448-3863, (201) 912-2100

this fund is closed to new investors

PERFORMANCE

	3yr Annual	5yr Annual	10yr Annual	Bull	Bear
Return (%)	22.1	13.3	16.0	87.9	-12.7
Differ from Category (+/-)	5.7 high	0.8 av	3.6 high	17.8 high	-1.1 av

Total Risk	Standard Deviation	Category Risk	Risk Index	Beta
av	6.8%	low	0.8	0.4

	1993	1992	1991	1990	1989	1988	1987	1986	1985	1984
Return (%)	22.7	22.6	21.1	-10.1	14.3	30.1	7.8	16.8	25.5	14.6
Differ from category (+/-) . .	10.1	12.6	-6.6	-4.5	-7.3	13.3	7.4	1.6	0.1	8.4

PER SHARE DATA

	1993	1992	1991	1990	1989	1988	1987	1986	1985	1984
Dividends, Net Income ($) .	0.37	0.49	0.67	1.23	1.36	0.82	0.87	0.85	0.61	0.34
Distrib'ns, Cap Gain ($) . . .	2.56	1.02	0.37	0.37	2.39	1.62	1.44	1.55	1.17	1.13
Net Asset Value ($)	27.00	24.43	21.18	18.37	22.21	22.71	19.37	20.04	19.22	16.75
Expense Ratio (%).	0.79	0.82	0.87	0.89	0.70	0.62	0.71	0.68	0.70	0.81
Net Income to Assets (%). .	1.51	2.10	3.09	5.40	5.61	3.96	3.43	4.55	4.27	3.58
Portfolio Turnover (%)	na	47	52	46	73	85	74	123	95	106
Total Assets (Millions $) . .	1,540	1,251	1,110	1,075	1,470	1,094	686	561	432	178

PORTFOLIO (as of 6/30/93)

Portfolio Manager: Michael F. Price - 1980

Investm't Category: Growth & Income

Cap Gain	Asset Allocation
✔ Cap & Income	Fund of Funds
Income	Index
	Sector
✔ Domestic	Small Cap
✔ Foreign	Socially Conscious
Country/Region	State Specific

Portfolio: stocks 72% bonds 11%
convertibles 0% other 3% cash 14%

Largest Holdings: consumer products & services 12%, banking & financial institutions 9%

Unrealized Net Capital Gains: 16% of portfolio value

SHAREHOLDER INFORMATION

Minimum Investment
Initial: $1,000   Subsequent: $50

Minimum IRA Investment
Initial: $1,000   Subsequent: $50

Maximum Fees
Load: none   12b-1: none
Other: none

Distributions
Income: Jun, Dec   Capital Gains: Jun, Dec

Exchange Options
Number Per Year: no limit   Fee: none
Telephone: none

Services
IRA, other pension, auto invest, auto withdraw

Mutual Shares (MUTHX)

Growth & Income

51 John F. Kennedy Pkwy.
Short Hills, NJ 07078
(800) 448-3863, (201) 912-2100

this fund is closed to new investors

	3yr Annual	5yr Annual	10yr Annual	Bull	Bear
Return (%)	21.1	12.9	15.7	83.5	-12.7
Differ from Category (+/-)	4.7 high	0.4 av	3.3 high	13.4 abv av	-1.1 av

Total Risk	Standard Deviation	Category Risk	Risk Index	Beta
av	6.7%	low	0.8	0.4

	1993	1992	1991	1990	1989	1988	1987	1986	1985	1984
Return (%)	20.9	21.3	20.9	-9.8	14.8	30.6	6.3	16.9	26.5	14.4
Differ from category (+/-)	8.3	11.3	-6.8	-4.2	-6.8	13.8	5.9	1.7	1.1	8.2

PER SHARE DATA

	1993	1992	1991	1990	1989	1988	1987	1986	1985	1984
Dividends, Net Income ($)	1.38	1.59	2.00	3.34	4.09	2.63	2.52	2.33	1.88	1.42
Distrib'ns, Cap Gain ($)	6.31	3.16	1.63	0.88	6.55	5.05	4.09	4.52	4.12	4.83
Net Asset Value ($)	80.96	73.36	64.49	56.39	67.16	67.77	57.83	60.39	57.54	50.30
Expense Ratio (%)	0.75	0.78	0.82	0.85	0.65	0.67	0.68	0.70	0.67	0.73
Net Income to Assets (%)	1.65	2.18	3.08	4.88	5.57	4.16	3.32	4.07	4.08	3.42
Portfolio Turnover (%)	na	41	48	43	72	90	78	122	91	102
Total Assets (Millions $)	3,527	2,913	2,640	2,521	3,403	2,552	1,685	1,403	1,076	496

PORTFOLIO (as of 6/30/93)

Portfolio Manager: Michael F. Price - 1975

Investm't Category: Growth & Income

Cap Gain	Asset Allocation
✔ Cap & Income	Fund of Funds
Income	Index
	Sector
✔ Domestic	Small Cap
✔ Foreign	Socially Conscious
Country/Region	State Specific

Portfolio: stocks 69% bonds 11%
convertibles 0% other 2% cash 18%

Largest Holdings: consumer products & services 11%, banking & financial institutions 9%

Unrealized Net Capital Gains: 17% of portfolio value

SHAREHOLDER INFORMATION

Minimum Investment
Initial: $5,000   Subsequent: $100

Minimum IRA Investment
Initial: $2,000   Subsequent: $100

Maximum Fees
Load: none   12b-1: none
Other: none

Distributions
Income: Jun, Dec   Capital Gains: Jun, Dec

Exchange Options
Number Per Year: no limit   Fee: none
Telephone: none

Services
IRA, other pension, auto invest, auto withdraw

National Industries
(NAIDX)
Growth

5990 Greenwood Plaza Blvd.
Englewood, CO 80111
(303) 220-8500

PERFORMANCE

	3yr Annual	5yr Annual	10yr Annual	Bull	Bear
Return (%)	9.9	11.3	8.8	45.7	-5.7
Differ from Category (+/-)	-9.3 low	-3.3 low	-3.8 low	-39.0 low	6.7 high

Total Risk	Standard Deviation	Category Risk	Risk Index	Beta
av	10.2%	low	0.9	0.8

	1993	1992	1991	1990	1989	1988	1987	1986	1985	1984
Return (%)	1.3	-0.5	31.9	3.2	24.4	12.6	2.5	9.8	10.5	-2.2
Differ from category (+/-) .	-11.9	-11.5	-3.5	9.3	-1.4	-5.1	1.3	-4.7	-18.8	-2.2

PER SHARE DATA

	1993	1992	1991	1990	1989	1988	1987	1986	1985	1984
Dividends, Net Income ($) .	0.06	0.14	0.21	0.23	0.20	0.12	0.10	0.37	0.34	0.38
Distrib'ns, Cap Gain ($) ...	0.30	1.88	1.10	0.34	1.47	0.50	1.15	1.82	0.18	1.17
Net Asset Value ($)	12.71	12.90	15.01	12.37	12.53	11.41	10.69	11.64	12.66	11.94
Expense Ratio (%)..........	na	1.50	1.48	1.70	1.69	1.70	1.65	1.70	1.70	1.70
Net Income to Assets (%)....	na	0.99	1.46	1.69	1.52	1.04	0.64	0.90	2.00	2.80
Portfolio Turnover (%)......	na	45	22	64	83	32	68	73	70	56
Total Assets (Millions $)	33	35	34	30	32	27	24	27	27	27

PORTFOLIO (as of 5/31/93)

Portfolio Manager: Richard Barrett - 1984

Investm't Category: Growth

✔ Cap Gain	Asset Allocation
Cap & Income	Fund of Funds
Income	Index
	Sector
✔ Domestic	Small Cap
✔ Foreign	Socially Conscious
Country/Region	State Specific

Portfolio: stocks 87%   bonds 0%
convertibles 0%   other 0%   cash 13%

Largest Holdings: health care 19%, electronics, instrumentation & computer peripherals 9%

Unrealized Net Capital Gains: 19% of portfolio value

SHAREHOLDER INFORMATION

Minimum Investment
Initial: $250   Subsequent: $25

Minimum IRA Investment
Initial: na   Subsequent: na

Maximum Fees
Load: none   12b-1: none
Other: none

Distributions
Income: Dec   Capital Gains: Dec

Exchange Options
Number Per Year: none   Fee: na
Telephone: na

Services
auto withdraw

Neuberger & Berman Genesis (NBGNX)

605 Third Ave., 2nd Fl.
New York, NY 10158
(800) 877-9700, (212) 476-8800

Aggressive Growth

PERFORMANCE

	3yr Annual	5yr Annual	10yr Annual	Bull	Bear
Return (%)	23.0	12.8	na	97.9	-21.1
Differ from Category (+/-)	-2.4 blw av	-5.4 low	na	-27.1 blw av	-6.1 blw av

Total Risk	Standard Deviation	Category Risk	Risk Index	Beta
abv av	12.3%	low	0.8	0.8

	1993	1992	1991	1990	1989	1988	1987	1986	1985	1984
Return (%).	13.8	15.6	41.5	-16.2	17.2	—	—	—	—	—
Differ from category (+/-). . .	-5.2	5.2	-10.9	-9.9	-9.8	—	—	—	—	—

PER SHARE DATA

	1993	1992	1991	1990	1989	1988	1987	1986	1985	1984
Dividends, Net Income ($).	0.00	0.00	0.00	0.03	0.01	—	—	—	—	—
Distrib'ns, Cap Gain ($) . . .	0.75	0.00	0.09	0.00	0.11	—	—	—	—	—
Net Asset Value ($)	8.26	7.92	6.85	4.91	5.91	—	—	—	—	—
Expense Ratio (%)	1.65	2.00	2.00	2.00	2.00	—	—	—	—	—
Net Income to Assets (%) .	0.15	-0.14	0.60	0.41	0.51	—	—	—	—	—
Portfolio Turnover (%).	54	23	46	37	10	—	—	—	—	—
Total Assets (Millions $). . . .	122	72	28	21	18	—	—	—	—	—

PORTFOLIO (as of 8/31/93)

Portfolio Manager: Stephen Milman - 1988

Investm't Category: Aggressive Growth

✔ Cap Gain	Asset Allocation
Cap & Income	Fund of Funds
Income	Index
	Sector
✔ Domestic	✔ Small Cap
✔ Foreign	Socially Conscious
Country/Region	State Specific

Portfolio: stocks 97% bonds 0%
convertibles 0% other 0% cash 3%

Largest Holdings: industrial & commercial products & services 15%, retailing 9%

Unrealized Net Capital Gains: 12% of portfolio value

SHAREHOLDER INFORMATION

Minimum Investment
Initial: $1,000   Subsequent: $100

Minimum IRA Investment
Initial: $250   Subsequent: $100

Maximum Fees
Load: none   12b-1: none
Other: none

Distributions
Income: Dec   Capital Gains: Dec

Exchange Options
Number Per Year: no limit   Fee: none
Telephone: yes (money market fund available)

Services
IRA, other pension, auto exchange, auto invest, auto withdraw

Neuberger & Berman Guardian (NGUAX)

Growth & Income

605 Third Ave., 2nd Fl.
New York, NY 10158
(800) 877-9700, (212) 476-8800

PERFORMANCE

	3yr Annual	5yr Annual	10yr Annual	Bull	Bear
Return (%)	22.3	16.1	14.9	104.1	-14.5
Differ from Category (+/-)	5.9 high	3.6 high	2.5 high	34.0 high	-2.9 blw av

Total Risk	Standard Deviation	Category Risk	Risk Index	Beta
abv av	11.8%	high	1.4	1.0

	1993	1992	1991	1990	1989	1988	1987	1986	1985	1984
Return (%)	14.4	19.0	34.3	-4.7	21.5	28.0	-1.0	11.8	25.0	7.2
Differ from category (+/-) ...	1.8	9.0	6.6	0.8	-0.1	11.2	-1.4	-3.4	-0.4	1.0

PER SHARE DATA

	1993	1992	1991	1990	1989	1988	1987	1986	1985	1984
Dividends, Net Income ($) .	0.30	0.25	0.31	0.35	0.35	0.35	0.49	0.49	0.58	0.47
Distrib'ns, Cap Gain ($) ...	0.40	0.66	0.90	0.16	1.18	1.22	1.40	1.50	2.14	0.37
Net Asset Value ($)	18.60	16.87	14.96	12.07	13.22	12.16	10.74	12.71	13.10	12.81
Expense Ratio (%)........	0.81	0.82	0.84	0.86	0.84	0.84	0.74	0.73	0.76	0.77
Net Income to Assets (%)..	2.01	1.90	2.46	2.89	2.59	2.80	2.72	3.59	4.58	3.81
Portfolio Turnover (%).....	27	41	59	58	52	73	91	70	57	32
Total Assets (Millions $) ..	2,000	803	629	496	569	539	461	531	388	344

PORTFOLIO (as of 8/31/93)

Portfolio Manager: Kent Simons - 1982

Investm't Category: Growth & Income

Cap Gain	Asset Allocation
✔ Cap & Income	Fund of Funds
Income	Index
	Sector
✔ Domestic	Small Cap
✔ Foreign	Socially Conscious
Country/Region	State Specific

Portfolio: stocks 86% bonds 1%
convertibles 0% other 1% cash 12%

Largest Holdings: communications 10%, technology 9%

Unrealized Net Capital Gains: 20% of portfolio value

SHAREHOLDER INFORMATION

Minimum Investment
Initial: $1,000   Subsequent: $100

Minimum IRA Investment
Initial: $250   Subsequent: $100

Maximum Fees
Load: none   12b-1: none
Other: none

Distributions
Income: quarterly   Capital Gains: Dec

Exchange Options
Number Per Year: no limit   Fee: none
Telephone: yes (money market fund available)

Services
IRA, other pension, auto exchange, auto invest, auto withdraw

Neuberger & Berman Ltd Maturity Bond (NLMBX)

605 Third Ave., 2nd Fl.
New York, NY 10158
(800) 877-9700, (212) 476-8800

General Bond

PERFORMANCE

	3yr Annual	5yr Annual	10yr Annual	Bull	Bear
Return (%)	7.8	8.7	na	29.5	5.4
Differ from Category (+/-)	-2.4 low	-1.1 low	na	-9.9 low	2.5 high

Total Risk	Standard Deviation	Category Risk	Risk Index	Avg Mat
low	2.1%	blw av	0.7	3.1 yrs

	1993	1992	1991	1990	1989	1988	1987	1986	1985	1984
Return (%)	6.7	5.1	11.8	8.7	11.1	6.7	3.6	—	—	—
Differ from category (+/-). . .	-2.5	-1.6	-2.8	1.8	-0.2	-0.8	1.1	—	—	—

PER SHARE DATA

	1993	1992	1991	1990	1989	1988	1987	1986	1985	1984
Dividends, Net Income ($).	0.56	0.61	0.69	0.79	0.82	0.73	0.68	—	—	—
Distrib'ns, Cap Gain ($) . . .	0.05	0.05	0.00	0.00	0.00	0.00	0.00	—	—	—
Net Asset Value ($)	10.36	10.30	10.44	10.00	9.96	9.74	9.83	—	—	—
Expense Ratio (%)	0.65	0.65	0.65	0.65	0.65	0.50	0.50	—	—	—
Net Income to Assets (%) .	5.79	6.02	7.07	8.09	8.33	6.97	6.71	—	—	—
Portfolio Turnover (%).	76	113	88	88	121	158	41	—	—	—
Total Assets (Millions $). . . .	348	273	163	101	108	107	70	—	—	—

PORTFOLIO (as of 4/30/93)

Portfolio Manager: Theresa Havell - 1986

Investm't Category: General Bond

Cap Gain	Asset Allocation
Cap & Income	Fund of Funds
✔ Income	Index
	Sector
✔ Domestic	Small Cap
Foreign	Socially Conscious
Country/Region	State Specific

Portfolio: stocks 0%   bonds 92%
convertibles 0%   other 0%   cash 8%

Largest Holdings: U.S government 42%,
mortgage-backed 18%

Unrealized Net Capital Gains: 0% of portfolio value

SHAREHOLDER INFORMATION

Minimum Investment
Initial: $2,000   Subsequent: $100

Minimum IRA Investment
Initial: $250   Subsequent: $100

Maximum Fees
Load: none   12b-1: none
Other: none

Distributions
Income: monthly   Capital Gains: Dec

Exchange Options
Number Per Year: no limit   Fee: none
Telephone: yes (money market fund available)

Services
IRA, other pension, auto exchange, auto invest,
auto withdraw

Neuberger & Berman Manhattan (NMANX)

605 Third Ave., 2nd Fl.
New York, NY 10158
(800) 877-9700, (212) 476-8800

Growth

PERFORMANCE

	3yr Annual	5yr Annual	10yr Annual	Bull	Bear
Return (%)	19.1	14.9	15.1	82.9	-14.7
Differ from Category (+/-)	-0.1 av	0.3 av	2.5 high	-1.8 av	-2.3 blw av

Total Risk	Standard Deviation	Category Risk	Risk Index	Beta
abv av	13.9%	abv av	1.3	1.1

	1993	1992	1991	1990	1989	1988	1987	1986	1985	1984
Return (%)	10.0	17.7	30.8	-8.0	29.0	18.3	0.4	16.8	37.1	7.0
Differ from category (+/-) . .	-3.2	6.7	-4.6	-1.9	3.2	0.6	-0.8	2.3	7.8	7.0

PER SHARE DATA

	1993	1992	1991	1990	1989	1988	1987	1986	1985	1984
Dividends, Net Income ($) .	0.01	0.05	0.10	0.15	0.18	0.16	0.26	0.08	0.10	0.18
Distrib'ns, Cap Gain ($) . . .	2.06	1.68	0.40	0.15	1.05	0.04	0.95	1.24	0.00	0.00
Net Asset Value ($)	11.11	11.99	11.65	9.29	10.44	9.04	7.81	8.95	8.86	6.56
Expense Ratio (%).	1.04	1.07	1.09	1.14	1.12	1.18	1.00	1.10	1.43	1.52
Net Income to Assets (%). .	0.20	0.57	1.28	1.44	1.60	1.55	1.60	1.34	1.76	1.85
Portfolio Turnover (%).	76	83	78	91	77	70	111	96	155	186
Total Assets (Millions $) . . .	525	401	429	356	405	342	329	293	167	79

PORTFOLIO (as of 8/31/93)

Portfolio Manager: Mark Goldstein - 1992

Investm't Category: Growth

✔ Cap Gain	Asset Allocation
Cap & Income	Fund of Funds
Income	Index
	Sector
✔ Domestic	Small Cap
✔ Foreign	Socially Conscious
Country/Region	State Specific

Portfolio: stocks 100% bonds 0%
convertibles 0% other 0% cash 0%

Largest Holdings: financial services 19%, consumer goods & services 17%

Unrealized Net Capital Gains: 14% of portfolio value

SHAREHOLDER INFORMATION

Minimum Investment
Initial: $1,000   Subsequent: $100

Minimum IRA Investment
Initial: $250   Subsequent: $100

Maximum Fees
Load: none   12b-1: none
Other: none

Distributions
Income: Dec   Capital Gains: Dec

Exchange Options
Number Per Year: no limit   Fee: none
Telephone: yes (money market fund available)

Services
IRA, other pension, auto exchange, auto invest, auto withdraw

Neuberger & Berman Muni Securities (NBMUX)

605 Third Ave., 2nd Fl.
New York, NY 10158
(800) 877-9700, (212) 476-8800

Tax-Exempt Bond

PERFORMANCE

	3yr Annual	5yr Annual	10yr Annual	Bull	Bear
Return (%)	8.4	8.1	na	31.7	3.5
Differ from Category (+/-)	-1.9 low	-1.1 low	na	-8.4 low	1.2 abv av

Total Risk	Standard Deviation	Category Risk	Risk Index	Avg Mat
low	3.3%	low	0.8	8.2 yrs

	1993	1992	1991	1990	1989	1988	1987	1986	1985	1984
Return (%)	9.5	6.9	9.0	6.8	8.2	6.7	—	—	—	—
Differ from category (+/-). . .	-2.1	-1.4	-2.3	0.5	-0.8	-3.4	—	—	—	—

PER SHARE DATA

	1993	1992	1991	1990	1989	1988	1987	1986	1985	1984
Dividends, Net Income ($) .	0.46	0.53	0.57	0.63	0.63	0.59	—	—	—	—
Distrib'ns, Cap Gain ($) . . .	0.12	0.09	0.00	0.00	0.00	0.00	—	—	—	—
Net Asset Value ($)	11.01	10.61	10.53	10.21	10.17	10.00	—	—	—	—
Expense Ratio (%)	0.62	0.50	0.50	0.50	0.50	0.50	—	—	—	—
Net Income to Assets (%) .	4.33	5.16	5.61	6.28	6.26	5.90	—	—	—	—
Portfolio Turnover (%).	35	46	10	42	17	23	—	—	—	—
Total Assets (Millions $). . . .	106	37	26	14	11	10	—	—	—	—

PORTFOLIO (as of 10/31/93)

Portfolio Manager: Havell - 1987, Giuliano - 1987

Investm't Category: Tax-Exempt Bond

Cap Gain	Asset Allocation
Cap & Income	Fund of Funds
✔ Income	Index
	Sector
✔ Domestic	Small Cap
Foreign	Socially Conscious
Country/Region	State Specific

Portfolio: stocks 0%   bonds 100%
convertibles 0%   other 0%   cash 0%

Largest Holdings: general obligation 10%

Unrealized Net Capital Gains: 2% of portfolio value

SHAREHOLDER INFORMATION

Minimum Investment
Initial: $2,000   Subsequent: $100

Minimum IRA Investment
Initial: na   Subsequent: na

Maximum Fees
Load: none   12b-1: none
Other: none

Distributions
Income: monthly   Capital Gains: Dec

Exchange Options
Number Per Year: no limit   Fee: none
Telephone: yes (money market fund available)

Services
auto exchange, auto invest, auto withdraw

Neuberger & Berman Partners (NPRTX)

Growth & Income

605 Third Ave., 2nd Fl.
New York, NY 10158
(800) 877-9700, (212) 476-8800

PERFORMANCE

	3yr Annual	5yr Annual	10yr Annual	Bull	Bear
Return (%)	18.7	14.3	14.4	75.3	-9.3
Differ from Category (+/-)	2.3 abv av	1.8 abv av	2.0 abv av	5.2 abv av	2.3 abv av

Total Risk	Standard Deviation	Category Risk	Risk Index	Beta
high	15.9%	high	1.8	1.0

	1993	1992	1991	1990	1989	1988	1987	1986	1985	1984
Return (%)	16.4	17.5	22.3	-5.1	22.7	15.4	4.3	17.2	29.9	8.0
Differ from category (+/-) . . .	3.8	7.5	-5.4	0.5	1.1	-1.4	3.9	2.0	4.5	1.8

PER SHARE DATA

	1993	1992	1991	1990	1989	1988	1987	1986	1985	1984
Dividends, Net Income ($) .	0.10	0.18	0.34	0.74	0.75	0.64	0.69	0.43	0.64	0.72
Distrib'ns, Cap Gain ($) . . .	2.20	1.79	0.77	0.34	1.68	0.00	2.79	2.25	1.27	0.27
Net Asset Value ($)	20.62	19.69	18.44	16.02	18.06	16.72	15.06	17.37	17.16	14.85
Expense Ratio (%).	0.86	0.86	0.88	0.91	0.97	0.95	0.86	0.89	0.93	0.91
Net Income to Assets (%). .	0.83	1.23	2.84	4.53	3.96	3.28	2.93	3.23	4.80	5.44
Portfolio Turnover (%)	82	97	161	136	157	210	169	181	146	227
Total Assets (Millions $) . .	1,200	853	823	794	743	719	758	433	221	146

PORTFOLIO (as of 8/31/93)

Portfolio Manager: Michael Kassen - 1990

Investm't Category: Growth & Income

Cap Gain	Asset Allocation
✔ Cap & Income	Fund of Funds
Income	Index
	Sector
✔ Domestic	Small Cap
✔ Foreign	Socially Conscious
Country/Region	State Specific

Portfolio: stocks 94%   bonds 0%
convertibles 0%   other 0%   cash 6%

Largest Holdings: insurance 13%, health care 8%

Unrealized Net Capital Gains: 14% of portfolio value

SHAREHOLDER INFORMATION

Minimum Investment
Initial: $1,000   Subsequent: $100

Minimum IRA Investment
Initial: $250   Subsequent: $100

Maximum Fees
Load: none   12b-1: none
Other: none

Distributions
Income: Dec   Capital Gains: Dec

Exchange Options
Number Per Year: no limit   Fee: none
Telephone: yes (money market fund available)

Services
IRA, other pension, auto exchange, auto invest, auto withdraw

Neuberger & Berman
Select Sectors (NBSSX)

605 Third Ave., 2nd Fl.
New York, NY 10158
(800) 877-9700, (212) 476-8800

Growth

PERFORMANCE

	3yr Annual	5yr Annual	10yr Annual	Bull	Bear
Return (%)	20.6	16.4	13.5	81.4	-8.9
Differ from Category (+/-)	1.4 abv av	1.8 abv av	0.8 abv av	-3.3 av	3.5 abv av

Total Risk	Standard Deviation	Category Risk	Risk Index	Beta
abv av	12.3%	av	1.1	1.0

	1993	1992	1991	1990	1989	1988	1987	1986	1985	1984
Return (%).............	16.3	21.0	24.6	-5.9	29.7	16.4	0.6	10.0	22.3	4.8
Differ from category (+/-)...	3.1	10.0	-10.8	0.2	3.9	-1.3	-0.6	-4.5	-7.0	4.8

PER SHARE DATA

	1993	1992	1991	1990	1989	1988	1987	1986	1985	1984
Dividends, Net Income ($).	0.25	0.28	0.36	0.34	0.46	0.50	0.58	0.87	0.92	0.86
Distrib'ns, Cap Gain ($) ...	1.70	2.13	0.87	0.37	2.57	0.54	3.35	1.66	0.93	0.66
Net Asset Value ($)	23.06	21.50	19.97	17.06	18.93	16.96	15.49	18.47	19.14	17.26
Expense Ratio (%)	0.92	0.91	0.93	0.92	0.99	1.01	0.86	0.88	0.89	0.87
Net Income to Assets (%) .	1.18	1.46	2.01	2.34	2.39	2.64	2.21	4.08	4.60	4.70
Portfolio Turnover (%)......	52	77	60	66	60	66	88	28	18	22
Total Assets (Millions $)....	594	439	399	369	441	375	481	376	334	337

PORTFOLIO (as of 8/31/93)

Portfolio Manager: Lawrence Marx III - 1988, Kent Simons - 1988

Investm't Category: Growth

✔ Cap Gain
  Cap & Income
  Income

  Asset Allocation
  Fund of Funds
  Index
✔ Sector

✔ Domestic
✔ Foreign
  Country/Region

  Small Cap
  Socially Conscious
  State Specific

Portfolio: stocks 96%   bonds 0%
convertibles 0%   other 0%   cash 4%

Largest Holdings: financial services 35%, media & entertainment 17%

Unrealized Net Capital Gains: 26% of portfolio value

SHAREHOLDER INFORMATION

Minimum Investment
Initial: $1,000   Subsequent: $100

Minimum IRA Investment
Initial: $250   Subsequent: $100

Maximum Fees
Load: none   12b-1: none
Other: none

Distributions
Income: Sep, Dec   Capital Gains: Sep, Dec

Exchange Options
Number Per Year: no limit   Fee: none
Telephone: yes (money market fund available)

Services
IRA, other pension, auto exchange, auto invest, auto withdraw

Neuberger & Berman Ultra Short Bond (NBMMX)

605 Third Ave., 2nd Fl.
New York, NY 10158
(800) 877-9700, (212) 476-8800

General Bond

PERFORMANCE

	3yr Annual	5yr Annual	10yr Annual	Bull	Bear
Return (%)	4.7	6.3	na	17.6	5.8
Differ from Category (+/-)	-5.5 low	-3.5 low	na	-21.8 low	2.9 high

Total Risk	Standard Deviation	Category Risk	Risk Index	Avg Mat
low	69%	low	0.2	1.4 yrs

	1993	1992	1991	1990	1989	1988	1987	1986	1985	1984
Return (%)	3.2	3.6	7.4	8.3	9.3	6.8	5.5	—	—	—
Differ from category (+/-) . .	-6.0	-3.1	-7.2	1.4	-2.0	-0.8	3.0	—	—	—

PER SHARE DATA

	1993	1992	1991	1990	1989	1988	1987	1986	1985	1984
Dividends, Net Income ($) .	0.38	0.51	0.66	0.77	0.91	0.70	0.63	—	—	—
Distrib'ns, Cap Gain ($) . . .	0.00	0.00	0.00	0.00	0.00	0.00	0.00	—	—	—
Net Asset Value ($)	9.61	9.69	9.86	9.82	9.80	9.83	9.88	—	—	—
Expense Ratio (%).	0.65	0.65	0.65	0.65	0.65	0.50	0.50	—	—	—
Net Income to Assets (%) . .	4.37	5.70	6.97	8.14	9.06	6.72	6.03	—	—	—
Portfolio Turnover (%)	80	66	89	120	85	121	39	—	—	—
Total Assets (Millions $) . . .	105	103	98	86	103	125	67	—	—	—

PORTFOLIO (as of 4/30/93)

Portfolio Manager: Theresa Havell - 1986

Investm't Category: General Bond

Cap Gain	Asset Allocation
Cap & Income	Fund of Funds
✔ Income	Index
	Sector
✔ Domestic	Small Cap
Foreign	Socially Conscious
Country/Region	State Specific

Portfolio: stocks 0%   bonds 92%
convertibles 0%   other 0%   cash 8%

Largest Holdings: U.S government 63%, asset backed securities 13%

Unrealized Net Capital Gains: 0% of portfolio value

SHAREHOLDER INFORMATION

Minimum Investment
Initial: $2,000   Subsequent: $100

Minimum IRA Investment
Initial: $250   Subsequent: $100

Maximum Fees
Load: none   12b-1: none
Other: none

Distributions
Income: monthly   Capital Gains: Dec

Exchange Options
Number Per Year: no limit   Fee: none
Telephone: yes (money market fund available)

Services
IRA, other pension, auto exchange, auto invest, auto withdraw

New Century Capital Portfolio (NCCPX)

20 William St.
Wellesley, MA 02181
(617) 239-0445

Growth

PERFORMANCE

	3yr Annual	5yr Annual	10yr Annual	Bull	Bear
Return (%)	16.1	na	na	66.1	-10.4
Differ from Category (+/-)	-3.1 blw av	na	na	-18.6 blw av	2.0 av

Total Risk	Standard Deviation	Category Risk	Risk Index	Beta
abv av	11.9%	av	1.1	0.9

	1993	1992	1991	1990	1989	1988	1987	1986	1985	1984
Return (%)	13.8	0.5	37.0	-5.1	—	—	—	—	—	—
Differ from category (+/-) . . .	0.6	-10.5	1.6	1.0	—	—	—	—	—	—

PER SHARE DATA

	1993	1992	1991	1990	1989	1988	1987	1986	1985	1984
Dividends, Net Income ($) .	0.00	0.16	0.11	0.17	—	—	—	—	—	—
Distrib'ns, Cap Gain ($) . . .	0.00	1.56	0.26	0.00	—	—	—	—	—	—
Net Asset Value ($)	12.93	11.36	13.02	9.78	—	—	—	—	—	—
Expense Ratio (%)	1.54	1.58	1.76	1.90	—	—	—	—	—	—
Net Income to Assets (%) .	-0.53	-0.14	0.84	1.56	—	—	—	—	—	—
Portfolio Turnover (%).	133	224	156	286	—	—	—	—	—	—
Total Assets (Millions $).	38	36	36	33	—	—	—	—	—	—

PORTFOLIO (as of 10/31/93)

Portfolio Manager: Douglas Biggar - 1989

Investm't Category: Growth

✔ Cap Gain	Asset Allocation
Cap & Income	✔ Fund of Funds
Income	Index
	Sector
✔ Domestic	Small Cap
✔ Foreign	Socially Conscious
Country/Region	State Specific

Portfolio: stocks 0% bonds 0%
convertibles 0% other 99% cash 1%

Largest Holdings: Mutual Beacon 8%, Fidelity Equity Income 8%

Unrealized Net Capital Gains: 13% of portfolio value

SHAREHOLDER INFORMATION

Minimum Investment
Initial: $5,000   Subsequent: $100

Minimum IRA Investment
Initial: $500   Subsequent: $100

Maximum Fees
Load: none   12b-1: 0.25%
Other: none

Distributions
Income: Dec   Capital Gains: Dec

Exchange Options
Number Per Year: no limit   Fee: none
Telephone: yes (money market fund not available)

Services
IRA, other pension, auto invest, auto withdraw

New York Muni (NYMFX)

Tax-Exempt Bond

90 Washington St.
New York, NY 10006
(800) 225-6864, (212) 635-3005

PERFORMANCE

	3yr Annual	5yr Annual	10yr Annual	Bull	Bear
Return (%)	13.3	9.5	9.6	45.1	-0.5
Differ from Category (+/-)	3.0 high	0.3 av	0.0 av	5.0 abv av	-2.8 low

Total Risk	Standard Deviation	Category Risk	Risk Index	Avg Mat
av	6.3%	high	1.6	21.9 yrs

	1993	1992	1991	1990	1989	1988	1987	1986	1985	1984
Return (%)	12.5	11.7	15.8	-0.8	9.6	11.5	-7.2	20.0	20.3	8.2
Differ from category (+/-)	0.8	3.4	4.5	-7.2	0.6	1.0	-6.0	3.6	3.0	-0.1

PER SHARE DATA

	1993	1992	1991	1990	1989	1988	1987	1986	1985	1984
Dividends, Net Income ($)	0.06	0.05	0.05	0.06	0.07	0.07	0.07	0.09	0.09	0.08
Distrib'ns, Cap Gain ($)	0.11	0.00	0.00	0.00	0.00	0.00	0.03	0.05	0.00	0.00
Net Asset Value ($)	1.18	1.21	1.14	1.04	1.12	1.09	1.05	1.25	1.19	1.07
Expense Ratio (%)	1.92	1.69	1.78	1.65	1.69	1.74	2.04	1.48	1.60	1.62
Net Income to Assets (%)	4.92	5.16	5.47	6.43	6.47	6.94	6.97	6.91	7.88	7.82
Portfolio Turnover (%)	223	461	365	483	386	463	549	333	424	156
Total Assets (Millions $)	276	197	184	183	238	230	220	261	174	129

PORTFOLIO (as of 6/30/93)

Portfolio Manager: Lance Brofman - 1981

Investm't Category: Tax-Exempt Bond

Cap Gain	Asset Allocation
Cap & Income	Fund of Funds
✔ Income	Index
	Sector
✔ Domestic	Small Cap
Foreign	Socially Conscious
Country/Region	✔ State Specific

Portfolio:	stocks 0%	bonds 100%
convertibles 0%	other 0%	cash 0%

Largest Holdings: general obligation 28%

Unrealized Net Capital Gains: 0% of portfolio value

SHAREHOLDER INFORMATION

Minimum Investment
Initial: $1,000   Subsequent: $100

Minimum IRA Investment
Initial: na   Subsequent: na

Maximum Fees
Load: none   12b-1: 0.50%
Other: none

Distributions
Income: monthly   Capital Gains: Dec, Jan

Exchange Options
Number Per Year: no limit   Fee: none
Telephone: yes (money market fund available)

Services
auto exchange, auto invest, auto withdraw

Nicholas (NICSX)

Growth

700 N. Water St., #1010
Milwaukee, WI 53202
(800) 227-5987, (414) 272-6133

PERFORMANCE

	3yr Annual	5yr Annual	10yr Annual	Bull	Bear
Return (%)	19.1	15.0	14.1	86.5	-13.2
Differ from Category (+/-)	-0.1 av	0.4 av	1.5 abv av	1.8 av	-0.8 av

Total Risk	Standard Deviation	Category Risk	Risk Index	Beta
abv av	11.2%	blw av	1.0	0.9

	1993	1992	1991	1990	1989	1988	1987	1986	1985	1984
Return (%).	5.8	12.6	41.9	-4.3	24.5	17.9	-1.1	11.7	29.6	9.9
Differ from category (+/-). . .	-7.4	1.6	6.5	1.8	-1.3	0.2	-2.3	-2.8	0.3	9.9

PER SHARE DATA

	1993	1992	1991	1990	1989	1988	1987	1986	1985	1984
Dividends, Net Income ($).	0.81	0.71	0.67	0.81	0.92	1.02	1.84	0.88	0.57	0.82
Distrib'ns, Cap Gain ($) . . .	1.04	2.01	0.82	0.37	1.05	0.45	4.03	0.18	0.61	1.39
Net Asset Value ($)	53.64	52.47	49.17	35.76	38.61	32.63	28.94	34.87	32.18	25.84
Expense Ratio (%)	0.76	0.78	0.81	0.82	0.86	0.86	0.86	0.86	0.82	0.87
Net Income to Assets (%) .	1.53	1.60	2.17	2.56	2.84	3.04	3.13	4.11	3.24	2.69
Portfolio Turnover (%).	10	15	22	21	24	32	27	13	13	22
Total Assets (Millions $). .	3,067	2,234	1,643	1,390	1,172	1,118	1,299	955	309	153

PORTFOLIO (as of 9/30/93)

Portfolio Manager: Albert Nicholas - 1969

Investm't Category: Growth

✔ Cap Gain	Asset Allocation
Cap & Income	Fund of Funds
Income	Index
	Sector
✔ Domestic	Small Cap
Foreign	Socially Conscious
Country/Region	State Specific

Portfolio: stocks 93% bonds 0%
convertibles 0% other 0% cash 7%

Largest Holdings: insurance 17%, health care 15%

Unrealized Net Capital Gains: 30% of portfolio value

SHAREHOLDER INFORMATION

Minimum Investment
Initial: $500   Subsequent: $100

Minimum IRA Investment
Initial: $500   Subsequent: $100

Maximum Fees
Load: none   12b-1: none
Other: none

Distributions
Income: May, Dec   Capital Gains: May, Dec

Exchange Options
Number Per Year: no limit   Fee: $5 (telephone)
Telephone: 2/yr (money market fund available)

Services
IRA, other pension, auto exchange, auto invest, auto withdraw

Nicholas II (NCTWX)

Growth

700 N. Water St., #1010
Milwaukee, WI 53202
(800) 227-5987, (414) 272-6133

PERFORMANCE

	3yr Annual	5yr Annual	10yr Annual	Bull	Bear
Return (%)	17.5	12.3	14.6	76.6	-13.7
Differ from Category (+/-)	-1.7 blw av	-2.3 blw av	2.0 high	-8.1 blw av	-1.3 av

Total Risk	Standard Deviation	Category Risk	Risk Index	Beta
av	10.6%	blw av	1.0	0.7

	1993	1992	1991	1990	1989	1988	1987	1986	1985	1984
Return (%)	6.4	9.3	39.5	-6.2	17.6	17.2	7.7	10.3	33.8	16.9
Differ from category (+/-) ..	-6.8	-1.7	4.1	-0.1	-8.2	-0.5	6.5	-4.2	4.5	16.9

PER SHARE DATA

	1993	1992	1991	1990	1989	1988	1987	1986	1985	1984
Dividends, Net Income ($) .	0.27	0.23	0.24	0.34	0.31	0.33	0.34	0.41	0.19	0.09
Distrib'ns, Cap Gain ($) ...	1.40	0.80	0.40	0.14	0.67	0.07	1.30	0.51	0.03	0.18
Net Asset Value ($)	26.32	26.32	25.02	18.42	20.16	17.98	15.69	16.22	15.54	11.79
Expense Ratio (%)........	0.67	0.66	0.70	0.71	0.74	0.77	0.74	0.79	1.11	1.85
Net Income to Assets (%)..	0.79	1.01	1.24	1.78	1.43	1.97	1.37	2.70	3.29	1.98
Portfolio Turnover (%).....	27	11	12	19	8	18	26	14	10	29
Total Assets (Millions $) ...	704	646	491	337	422	380	432	299	140	11

PORTFOLIO (as of 9/30/93)

Portfolio Manager: David Nicholas - 1993

Investm't Category: Growth
✔ Cap Gain	Asset Allocation
Cap & Income	Fund of Funds
Income	Index
	Sector
✔ Domestic	✔ Small Cap
Foreign	Socially Conscious
Country/Region	State Specific

Portfolio: stocks 94%   bonds 0%
convertibles 0%   other 0%   cash 6%

Largest Holdings: health care 19%, banks & finance 15%

Unrealized Net Capital Gains: 29% of portfolio value

SHAREHOLDER INFORMATION

Minimum Investment
Initial: $1,000   Subsequent: $100

Minimum IRA Investment
Initial: $1,000   Subsequent: $100

Maximum Fees
Load: none   12b-1: none
Other: none

Distributions
Income: Dec   Capital Gains: Dec

Exchange Options
Number Per Year: no limit   Fee: $5 (telephone)
Telephone: 2/yr (money market fund available)

Services
IRA, other pension, auto exchange, auto invest, auto withdraw

Nicholas Income (NCINX)

Corporate High-Yield Bond

700 N. Water St., #1010
Milwaukee, WI 53202
(800) 227-5987, (414) 272-6133

PERFORMANCE

	3yr Annual	5yr Annual	10yr Annual	Bull	Bear
Return (%)	15.3	11.9	11.8	48.9	13.7
Differ from Category (+/-)	-5.2 low	1.1 high	0.1 av	-26.0 low	17.0 high

Total Risk	Standard Deviation	Category Risk	Risk Index	Avg Mat
low	3.2%	low	0.8	7.3 yrs

	1993	1992	1991	1990	1989	1988	1987	1986	1985	1984
Return (%)	12.9	10.3	23.0	10.4	3.9	11.5	2.6	11.4	21.2	12.7
Differ from category (+/-). . .	-6.3	-5.5	-4.3	14.6	2.6	-0.8	1.6	-3.8	-2.3	1.9

PER SHARE DATA

	1993	1992	1991	1990	1989	1988	1987	1986	1985	1984
Dividends, Net Income ($) .	0.28	0.29	0.34	0.75	0.38	0.37	0.46	0.37	0.41	0.44
Distrib'ns, Cap Gain ($) . . .	0.00	0.00	0.00	0.00	0.00	0.00	0.00	0.00	0.00	0.00
Net Asset Value ($)	3.52	3.38	3.34	3.01	3.44	3.68	3.64	4.01	3.96	3.65
Expense Ratio (%)	0.63	0.68	0.76	0.77	0.81	0.83	0.86	0.96	1.00	1.00
Net Income to Assets (%) .	8.38	9.23	10.70	11.74	10.46	10.03	9.79	10.22	12.57	12.82
Portfolio Turnover (%).	38	56	28	40	40	12	48	20	12	14
Total Assets (Millions $). . . .	159	119	80	61	75	78	70	65	25	17

PORTFOLIO (as of 6/30/93)

Portfolio Manager: Albert Nicholas - 1977

Investm't Category: Corp. High-Yield Bond

Cap Gain	Asset Allocation
✔ Cap & Income	Fund of Funds
Income	Index
	Sector
✔ Domestic	Small Cap
Foreign	Socially Conscious
Country/Region	State Specific

Portfolio: stocks 6% bonds 80%
convertibles 4% other 0% cash 10%

Largest Holdings: diversified products & services 20%, electric utilities 9%

Unrealized Net Capital Gains: 3% of portfolio value

SHAREHOLDER INFORMATION

Minimum Investment
Initial: $500   Subsequent: $100

Minimum IRA Investment
Initial: $500   Subsequent: $100

Maximum Fees
Load: none   12b-1: none
Other: none

Distributions
Income: quarterly   Capital Gains: Dec

Exchange Options
Number Per Year: no limit   Fee: none
Telephone: none

Services
IRA, other pension, auto exchange, auto invest, auto withdraw

Nicholas Limited Edition

(NCLEX)

700 N. Water St., #1010
Milwaukee, WI 53202
(800) 227-5987, (414) 272-6133

Growth

this fund is closed to new investors

PERFORMANCE

	3yr Annual	5yr Annual	10yr Annual	Bull	Bear
Return (%)	22.1	16.0	na	105.8	-12.9
Differ from Category (+/-)	2.9 abv av	1.4 abv av	na	21.1 abv av	-0.5 av

Total Risk	Standard Deviation	Category Risk	Risk Index	Beta
abv av	11.0%	blw av	1.0	0.7

	1993	1992	1991	1990	1989	1988	1987	1986	1985	1984
Return (%)	9.0	16.7	43.2	-1.7	17.3	27.2	—	—	—	—
Differ from category (+/-) ..	-4.2	5.7	7.8	4.4	-8.5	9.5	—	—	—	—

PER SHARE DATA

	1993	1992	1991	1990	1989	1988	1987	1986	1985	1984
Dividends, Net Income ($) .	0.08	0.08	0.12	0.12	0.14	0.09	—	—	—	—
Distrib'ns, Cap Gain ($) ...	1.67	0.82	0.24	0.12	0.61	0.25	—	—	—	—
Net Asset Value ($)	18.68	18.77	16.86	12.03	12.49	11.29	—	—	—	—
Expense Ratio (%)........	0.90	0.92	0.93	1.07	1.12	1.32	—	—	—	—
Net Income to Assets (%) ..	0.42	0.45	1.05	1.10	1.37	1.03	—	—	—	—
Portfolio Turnover (%).....	14	24	13	15	31	31	—	—	—	—
Total Assets (Millions $) ...	179	190	175	71	57	33	—	—	—	—

PORTFOLIO (as of 6/30/93)

Portfolio Manager: David Nicholas - 1993

Investm't Category: Growth

✔ Cap Gain	Asset Allocation
Cap & Income	Fund of Funds
Income	Index
	Sector
✔ Domestic	✔ Small Cap
Foreign	Socially Conscious
Country/Region	State Specific

Portfolio: stocks 95%   bonds 0%
convertibles 0%   other 0%   cash 5%

Largest Holdings: health care 14%, banks & finance 13%

Unrealized Net Capital Gains: 29% of portfolio value

SHAREHOLDER INFORMATION

Minimum Investment
Initial: $2,000   Subsequent: $100

Minimum IRA Investment
Initial: $2,000   Subsequent: $100

Maximum Fees
Load: none   12b-1: none
Other: none

Distributions
Income: Dec   Capital Gains: Dec

Exchange Options
Number Per Year: no limit   Fee: none
Telephone: none

Services
IRA, other pension, auto exchange, auto invest, auto withdraw

Nomura Pacific Basin
(NPBFX)
International Stock

180 Maiden Lane
New York, NY 10038
(800) 833-0018, (212) 509-7893

PERFORMANCE

	3yr Annual	5yr Annual	10yr Annual	Bull	Bear
Return (%)	11.1	7.3	na	52.2	-23.7
Differ from Category (+/-)	-3.4 blw av	-1.4 blw av	na	-2.9 av	-8.6 low

Total Risk	Standard Deviation	Category Risk	Risk Index	Beta
high	17.7%	high	1.5	0.3

	1993	1992	1991	1990	1989	1988	1987	1986	1985	1984
Return (%).............	40.4	-12.6	11.8	-15.3	22.7	16.3	32.7	74.3	—	—
Differ from category (+/-)...	1.9	-9.1	-1.1	-4.2	0.5	2.5	20.7	24.0	—	—

PER SHARE DATA

	1993	1992	1991	1990	1989	1988	1987	1986	1985	1984
Dividends, Net Income ($).	0.28	0.01	0.52	0.45	0.10	0.05	0.08	0.30	—	—
Distrib'ns, Cap Gain ($) ...	0.00	0.00	0.34	2.29	3.98	1.21	10.46	0.06	—	—
Net Asset Value ($)	17.47	12.64	14.51	13.75	19.40	19.39	17.75	21.13	—	—
Expense Ratio (%)	1.51	1.46	1.42	1.32	1.25	1.22	1.45	1.50	—	—
Net Income to Assets (%) .	0.01	0.00	0.28	0.04	0.07	0.28	0.14	0.88	—	—
Portfolio Turnover (%)......	55	41	76	46	37	61	46	3	—	—
Total Assets (Millions $).....	56	44	54	54	73	95	82	32	—	—

PORTFOLIO (as of 9/30/93)

Portfolio Manager: Takeo Nakamura - 1985

Investm't Category: International Stock

✔ Cap Gain	Asset Allocation
Cap & Income	Fund of Funds
Income	Index
	Sector
Domestic	Small Cap
✔ Foreign	Socially Conscious
✔ Country/Region	State Specific

Portfolio: stocks 100% bonds 0%
convertibles 0% other 0% cash 0%

Largest Holdings: Japan 62%, Australia 9%

Unrealized Net Capital Gains: 16% of port-folio value

SHAREHOLDER INFORMATION

Minimum Investment
Initial: $1,000   Subsequent: $0

Minimum IRA Investment
Initial: $1,000   Subsequent: $0

Maximum Fees
Load: none   12b-1: none
Other: none

Distributions
Income: May, Dec   Capital Gains: Dec

Exchange Options
Number Per Year: none Fee: na
Telephone: na

Services
IRA

Northeast Investors Growth (NTHFX)

50 Congress St.
Boston, MA 02109
(800) 225-6704, (617) 523-3588

Growth

PERFORMANCE

	3yr Annual	5yr Annual	10yr Annual	Bull	Bear
Return (%)	11.6	13.3	13.5	52.9	-7.7
Differ from Category (+/-)	-7.6 low	-1.3 blw av	1.1 abv av	-31.8 low	4.7 abv av

Total Risk	Standard Deviation	Category Risk	Risk Index	Beta
abv av	12.9%	abv av	1.2	1.1

	1993	1992	1991	1990	1989	1988	1987	1986	1985	1984
Return (%)	2.3	-0.6	36.9	1.3	32.9	12.8	-3.3	24.0	35.8	3.8
Differ from category (+/-) .	-10.9	-11.7	1.5	7.4	7.1	-4.9	-4.5	9.5	6.5	3.8

PER SHARE DATA

	1993	1992	1991	1990	1989	1988	1987	1986	1985	1984
Dividends, Net Income ($) .	0.19	0.20	0.36	0.25	0.28	0.26	0.12	0.12	0.05	0.11
Distrib'ns, Cap Gain ($) ...	4.46	1.57	0.55	0.33	0.29	0.46	0.61	0.52	0.09	0.30
Net Asset Value ($)	25.11	29.11	31.12	23.44	23.70	18.27	16.84	18.20	15.24	11.35
Expense Ratio (%)........	1.47	1.42	1.50	1.74	1.77	1.74	1.60	1.87	2.00	2.02
Net Income to Assets (%) ..	0.68	0.71	1.02	1.19	1.11	1.25	0.60	0.53	0.92	1.25
Portfolio Turnover (%)	na	29	16	37	23	16	36	12	36	34
Total Assets (Millions $)	38	43	41	27	27	19	21	20	6	4

PORTFOLIO (as of 6/30/93)

Portfolio Manager: William Oates, Jr. - 1980

Investm't Category: Growth

✔ Cap Gain	Asset Allocation
Cap & Income	Fund of Funds
Income	Index
	Sector
✔ Domestic	Small Cap
Foreign	Socially Conscious
Country/Region	State Specific

Portfolio: stocks 99% bonds 0%
convertibles 0% other 0% cash 1%

Largest Holdings: food & beverage 15%, telecommunications 14%

Unrealized Net Capital Gains: 19% of portfolio value

SHAREHOLDER INFORMATION

Minimum Investment
Initial: $1,000   Subsequent: $0

Minimum IRA Investment
Initial: $500   Subsequent: $0

Maximum Fees
Load: none   12b-1: none
Other: none

Distributions
Income: Dec   Capital Gains: Dec

Exchange Options
Number Per Year: no limit   Fee: none
Telephone: yes (money market fund not available)

Services
IRA, other pension, auto exchange, auto invest, auto withdraw

Northeast Investors Trust (NTHEX)

50 Congress St.
Boston, MA 02109
(800) 225-6704, (617) 523-3588

Corporate High-Yield Bond

PERFORMANCE

	3yr Annual	5yr Annual	10yr Annual	Bull	Bear
Return (%)	22.4	10.7	12.5	76.7	-5.7
Differ from Category (+/-)	1.9 abv av	-0.1 av	0.8 abv av	1.8 abv av	-2.4 av

Total Risk	Standard Deviation	Category Risk	Risk Index	Avg Mat
blw av	4.5%	av	1.2	8.2 yrs

	1993	1992	1991	1990	1989	1988	1987	1986	1985	1984
Return (%)	23.5	17.4	26.3	-9.1	0.0	14.0	0.1	20.3	25.5	13.8
Differ from category (+/-). . .	4.3	1.6	-1.0	-4.9	-1.3	1.7	-0.8	5.1	2.0	3.0

PER SHARE DATA

	1993	1992	1991	1990	1989	1988	1987	1986	1985	1984
Dividends, Net Income ($).	1.00	1.11	1.30	1.40	1.49	1.54	1.92	1.46	1.46	1.46
Distrib'ns, Cap Gain ($) . . .	0.00	0.00	0.00	0.00	0.00	0.00	0.00	0.00	0.00	0.00
Net Asset Value ($)	10.29	9.21	8.83	8.14	10.43	11.89	11.83	13.70	12.68	11.39
Expense Ratio (%)	1.21	0.79	0.88	0.78	0.72	0.75	0.76	1.24	1.34	1.34
Net Income to Assets (%)	10.53	12.36	15.38	14.35	12.68	13.16	11.59	11.53	12.70	12.92
Portfolio Turnover (%).	75	59	34	21	32	17	52	42	22	14
Total Assets (Millions $). . . .	562	453	311	277	386	405	348	313	217	168

PORTFOLIO (as of 9/30/93)

Portfolio Manager: Ernest Monrad - 1960

Investm't Category: Corp. High-Yield Bond

Cap Gain	Asset Allocation
✔ Cap & Income	Fund of Funds
Income	Index
	Sector
✔ Domestic	Small Cap
Foreign	Socially Conscious
Country/Region	State Specific

Portfolio: stocks 15% bonds 102%
convertibles 0% other 0% cash 0%

Largest Holdings: retail 11%, packaging & container 10%

Unrealized Net Capital Gains: 7% of portfolio value

SHAREHOLDER INFORMATION

Minimum Investment
Initial: $1,000   Subsequent: $0

Minimum IRA Investment
Initial: $500   Subsequent: $0

Maximum Fees
Load: none   12b-1: none
Other: none

Distributions
Income: quarterly   Capital Gains: Dec

Exchange Options
Number Per Year: no limit   Fee: none
Telephone: yes (money market fund not available)

Services
IRA, other pension, auto exchange, auto invest, auto withdraw

Oakmark (OAKMX)

Growth

Two N. LaSalle St.
Chicago, IL 60602
(800) 476-9625

PERFORMANCE

	3yr Annual	5yr Annual	10yr Annual	Bull	Bear
Return (%)	na	na	na	na	na
Differ from Category (+/-)	na	na	na	na	na

Total Risk	Standard Deviation	Category Risk	Risk Index	Beta
na	na	na	na	na

	1993	1992	1991	1990	1989	1988	1987	1986	1985	1984
Return (%)	30.5	48.8	—	—	—	—	—	—	—	—
Differ from category (+/-) . .	17.3	37.8	—	—	—	—	—	—	—	—

PER SHARE DATA

	1993	1992	1991	1990	1989	1988	1987	1986	1985	1984
Dividends, Net Income ($) .	0.23	0.03	—	—	—	—	—	—	—	—
Distrib'ns, Cap Gain ($) . . .	0.76	0.21	—	—	—	—	—	—	—	—
Net Asset Value ($)	23.93	19.13	—	—	—	—	—	—	—	—
Expense Ratio (%).	1.34	1.70	—	—	—	—	—	—	—	—
Net Income to Assets (%) . .	1.25	-0.24	—	—	—	—	—	—	—	—
Portfolio Turnover (%)	18	34	—	—	—	—	—	—	—	—
Total Assets (Millions $) . .	1,226	115	—	—	—	—	—	—	—	—

PORTFOLIO (as of 7/31/93)

Portfolio Manager: Robert Sanborn - 1991

Investm't Category: Growth

✔ Cap Gain	Asset Allocation
Cap & Income	Fund of Funds
Income	Index
	Sector
✔ Domestic	Small Cap
✔ Foreign	Socially Conscious
Country/Region	State Specific

Portfolio: stocks 87%   bonds 0%
convertibles 0%   other 0%   cash 13%

Largest Holdings: health care 15%, foreign securities 14%

Unrealized Net Capital Gains: 5% of portfolio value

SHAREHOLDER INFORMATION

Minimum Investment
Initial: $1,000   Subsequent: $100

Minimum IRA Investment
Initial: $1,000   Subsequent: $100

Maximum Fees
Load: none   12b-1: none
Other: none

Distributions
Income: Dec   Capital Gains: Dec

Exchange Options
Number Per Year: no limit   Fee: $5
Telephone: yes (money market fund available)

Services
IRA, auto invest, auto withdraw

Oakmark International
(OAKIX)

Two N. LaSalle St.
Chicago, IL 60602
(800) 476-9625

International Stock

PERFORMANCE

	3yr Annual	5yr Annual	10yr Annual	Bull	Bear
Return (%)	na	na	na	na	na
Differ from Category (+/-)	na	na	na	na	na

Total Risk	Standard Deviation	Category Risk	Risk Index	Beta
na	na	na	na	na

	1993	1992	1991	1990	1989	1988	1987	1986	1985	1984
Return (%)	53.5	—	—	—	—	—	—	—	—	—
Differ from category (+/-). .	15.0	—	—	—	—	—	—	—	—	—

PER SHARE DATA

	1993	1992	1991	1990	1989	1988	1987	1986	1985	1984
Dividends, Net Income ($)	0.07	—	—	—	—	—	—	—	—	—
Distrib'ns, Cap Gain ($) . . .	0.15	—	—	—	—	—	—	—	—	—
Net Asset Value ($)	14.79	—	—	—	—	—	—	—	—	—
Expense Ratio (%)	1.33	—	—	—	—	—	—	—	—	—
Net Income to Assets (%) .	2.21	—	—	—	—	—	—	—	—	—
Portfolio Turnover (%).	20	—	—	—	—	—	—	—	—	—
Total Assets (Millions $). .	1,193	—	—	—	—	—	—	—	—	—

PORTFOLIO (as of 4/30/93)

Portfolio Manager: David Herro - 1992

Investm't Category: International Stock

✔ Cap Gain	Asset Allocation
Cap & Income	Fund of Funds
Income	Index
	Sector
Domestic	Small Cap
✔ Foreign	Socially Conscious
Country/Region	State Specific

Portfolio: stocks 86% bonds 0%
convertibles 0% other 0% cash 14%

Largest Holdings: banks 10%, telecommunications 10%

Unrealized Net Capital Gains: 6% of portfolio value

SHAREHOLDER INFORMATION

Minimum Investment
Initial: $1,000   Subsequent: $100

Minimum IRA Investment
Initial: $1,000   Subsequent: $100

Maximum Fees
Load: none   12b-1: none
Other: none

Distributions
Income: Dec   Capital Gains: Dec

Exchange Options
Number Per Year: no limit   Fee: $5
Telephone: yes (money market fund available)

Services
IRA, auto invest, auto withdraw

Oberweis Emerging Growth (OBEGX)

One Constitution Drive
Aurora, IL 60506
(800) 323-6166, (708) 897-7100

Aggressive Growth

PERFORMANCE

	3yr Annual	5yr Annual	10yr Annual	Bull	Bear
Return (%)	34.1	24.7	na	181.6	-14.0
Differ from Category (+/-)	8.7 high	6.5 high	na	56.6 high	1.0 av

Total Risk	Standard Deviation	Category Risk	Risk Index	Beta
high	24.1%	high	1.6	1.2

	1993	1992	1991	1990	1989	1988	1987	1986	1985	1984
Return (%)	13.3	13.7	87.0	0.4	24.9	5.6	—	—	—	—
Differ from category (+/-) ..	-5.7	3.3	34.6	6.7	-2.1	-9.6	—	—	—	—

PER SHARE DATA

	1993	1992	1991	1990	1989	1988	1987	1986	1985	1984
Dividends, Net Income ($) .	0.00	0.00	0.00	0.00	0.00	0.00	—	—	—	—
Distrib'ns, Cap Gain ($) ...	0.74	0.00	4.27	0.00	0.00	0.00	—	—	—	—
Net Asset Value ($)	22.93	20.90	18.38	12.11	12.06	9.65	—	—	—	—
Expense Ratio (%)........	1.81	1.99	2.13	2.15	2.00	2.46	—	—	—	—
Net Income to Assets (%).	-0.98	-1.14	-1.27	-1.24	-1.19	-1.80	—	—	—	—
Portfolio Turnover (%)	na	63	114	63	112	67	—	—	—	—
Total Assets (Millions $) ...	104	54	20	12	13	16	—	—	—	—

PORTFOLIO (as of 6/30/93)

Portfolio Manager: James D. Oberweis - 1987

Investm't Category: Aggressive Growth

✔ Cap Gain	Asset Allocation
Cap & Income	Fund of Funds
Income	Index
	Sector
✔ Domestic	✔ Small Cap
Foreign	Socially Conscious
Country/Region	State Specific

Portfolio:	stocks 93%	bonds 7%
convertibles 0%	other 0%	cash 0%

Largest Holdings: telecommunications 11%, oil and gas 9%

Unrealized Net Capital Gains: 11% of portfolio value

SHAREHOLDER INFORMATION

Minimum Investment
Initial: $1,000   Subsequent: $100

Minimum IRA Investment
Initial: $1,000   Subsequent: $100

Maximum Fees
Load: none   12b-1: 0.50%
Other: none

Distributions
Income: Dec   Capital Gains: Dec

Exchange Options
Number Per Year: none   Fee: na
Telephone: na

Services
IRA, other pension, auto invest, auto withdraw

Olympic Equity Income
(OLEQX)
Growth & Income

800 W. 6th St., 5th Fl.
Los Angeles, CA 90017
(800) 346-7301, (213) 362-8900

PERFORMANCE

	3yr Annual	5yr Annual	10yr Annual	Bull	Bear
Return (%)	21.1	12.4	na	92.4	-24.3
Differ from Category (+/-)	4.7 high	-0.1 av	na	22.3 high	-12.7 low

Total Risk	Standard Deviation	Category Risk	Risk Index	Beta
abv av	11.4%	abv av	1.3	0.9

	1993	1992	1991	1990	1989	1988	1987	1986	1985	1984
Return (%)	15.7	13.9	34.6	-18.0	23.6	21.1	—	—	—	—
Differ from category (+/-)	3.1	3.9	6.9	-12.4	2.0	4.3	—	—	—	—

PER SHARE DATA

	1993	1992	1991	1990	1989	1988	1987	1986	1985	1984
Dividends, Net Income ($)	0.44	0.44	0.40	0.56	0.58	0.55	—	—	—	—
Distrib'ns, Cap Gain ($)	0.52	0.23	0.00	0.30	0.25	0.02	—	—	—	—
Net Asset Value ($)	15.97	14.66	13.48	10.34	13.65	11.75	—	—	—	—
Expense Ratio (%)	1.00	1.00	1.00	1.00	1.00	1.00	—	—	—	—
Net Income to Assets (%)	2.99	2.95	4.23	4.42	4.68	5.11	—	—	—	—
Portfolio Turnover (%)	25	32	39	39	9	20	—	—	—	—
Total Assets (Millions $)	83	72	63	65	47	29	—	—	—	—

PORTFOLIO (as of 6/30/93)

Portfolio Manager: George Wiley - 1987

Investm't Category: Growth & Income
Cap Gain	Asset Allocation
✔ Cap & Income	Fund of Funds
Income	Index
	Sector
✔ Domestic	Small Cap
✔ Foreign	Socially Conscious
Country/Region	State Specific

Portfolio: stocks 76%   bonds 9%
convertibles 0%   other 4%   cash 11%

Largest Holdings: auto & trucks 10%, financial services 8%

Unrealized Net Capital Gains: 13% of portfolio value

SHAREHOLDER INFORMATION

Minimum Investment
Initial: $10,000   Subsequent: $0

Minimum IRA Investment
Initial: $1,000   Subsequent: $0

Maximum Fees
Load: none   12b-1: none
Other: none

Distributions
Income: quarterly   Capital Gains: Dec

Exchange Options
Number Per Year: no limit   Fee: none
Telephone: yes (money market fund not available)

Services
IRA

Olympic Trust Balanced Income (OLBAX)

800 W. 6th St., 5th Fl.
Los Angeles, CA 90017
(800) 346-7301, (213) 362-8900

Balanced

PERFORMANCE

	3yr Annual	5yr Annual	10yr Annual	Bull	Bear
Return (%)	14.0	11.7	na	59.5	-7.3
Differ from Category (+/-)	-1.0 blw av	-0.4 blw av	na	-2.1 av	-1.5 blw av

Total Risk	Standard Deviation	Category Risk	Risk Index	Beta
blw av	5.9%	blw av	0.9	0.5

	1993	1992	1991	1990	1989	1988	1987	1986	1985	1984
Return (%)	12.5	9.4	20.5	-0.4	17.8	14.6	3.9	13.0	—	—
Differ from category (+/-) . .	-0.8	1.3	-3.4	0.1	0.2	2.6	1.6	-4.5	—	—

PER SHARE DATA

	1993	1992	1991	1990	1989	1988	1987	1986	1985	1984
Dividends, Net Income ($) .	0.89	0.72	0.79	0.85	0.93	0.73	0.79	0.54	—	—
Distrib'ns, Cap Gain ($) . . .	0.66	0.50	0.36	0.40	0.86	0.00	0.75	0.44	—	—
Net Asset Value ($)	16.44	16.02	15.79	14.10	15.44	14.67	13.46	14.44	—	—
Expense Ratio (%).	1.00	1.00	1.00	1.00	1.00	1.00	1.00	1.00	—	—
Net Income to Assets (%). .	4.77	4.90	5.58	5.59	5.77	5.51	4.87	5.67	—	—
Portfolio Turnover (%)	155	36	75	78	97	112	81	27	—	—
Total Assets (Millions $)	33	16	11	9	7	6	3	1	—	—

PORTFOLIO (as of 6/30/93)

Portfolio Manager: Roger DeBard - 1985

Investm't Category: Balanced
Cap Gain	✔ Asset Allocation
✔ Cap & Income	Fund of Funds
Income	Index
	Sector
✔ Domestic	Small Cap
✔ Foreign	Socially Conscious
Country/Region	State Specific

Portfolio: stocks 46%   bonds 48%
convertibles 0%   other 0%   cash 6%

Largest Holdings: bonds—mortgage-backed 23%, bonds—corporate 19%

Unrealized Net Capital Gains: 4% of portfolio value

SHAREHOLDER INFORMATION

Minimum Investment
Initial: $10,000   Subsequent: $0

Minimum IRA Investment
Initial: $1,000   Subsequent: $0

Maximum Fees
Load: none   12b-1: none
Other: none

Distributions
Income: quarterly   Capital Gains: Dec

Exchange Options
Number Per Year: no limit   Fee: none
Telephone: yes (money market fund not available)

Services
IRA

Oregon Municipal Bond
(ORBFX)

Tax-Exempt Bond

121 S.W. Morrison St.
Suite 1425
Portland, OR 97204
(800) 541-9732, (503) 295-0919

PERFORMANCE

	3yr Annual	5yr Annual	10yr Annual	Bull	Bear
Return (%)	8.6	7.9	na	32.2	3.2
Differ from Category (+/-)	-1.7 low	-1.3 low	na	-7.9 low	0.8 abv av

Total Risk	Standard Deviation	Category Risk	Risk Index	Avg Mat
low	3.1%	low	0.7	9.0 yrs

	1993	1992	1991	1990	1989	1988	1987	1986	1985	1984
Return (%)	8.9	7.3	9.8	6.3	7.5	7.6	0.6	—	—	—
Differ from category (+/-)	-2.7	-1.0	-1.5	0.0	-1.5	-2.5	1.9	—	—	—

PER SHARE DATA

	1993	1992	1991	1990	1989	1988	1987	1986	1985	1984
Dividends, Net Income ($)	0.56	0.61	0.63	0.64	0.67	0.65	0.68	—	—	—
Distrib'ns, Cap Gain ($)	0.00	0.10	0.09	0.06	0.02	0.09	0.01	—	—	—
Net Asset Value ($)	12.82	12.31	12.16	11.77	11.75	11.60	11.48	—	—	—
Expense Ratio (%)	1.04	1.11	1.21	1.38	1.04	1.21	1.31	—	—	—
Net Income to Assets (%)	4.71	5.04	5.36	5.41	5.82	5.53	6.43	—	—	—
Portfolio Turnover (%)	25	25	53	58	45	31	18	—	—	—
Total Assets (Millions $)	30	20	18	18	19	20	14	—	—	—

PORTFOLIO (as of 4/30/93)

Portfolio Manager: Jay Willoughby - na

Investm't Category: Tax-Exempt Bond

Cap Gain	Asset Allocation
Cap & Income	Fund of Funds
✔ Income	Index
	Sector
✔ Domestic	Small Cap
Foreign	Socially Conscious
Country/Region	✔ State Specific

Portfolio: stocks 0% bonds 100%
convertibles 0% other 0% cash 0%

Largest Holdings: general obligation 28%

Unrealized Net Capital Gains: 6% of portfolio value

SHAREHOLDER INFORMATION

Minimum Investment
Initial: $1,000 Subsequent: $500

Minimum IRA Investment
Initial: na Subsequent: na

Maximum Fees
Load: none 12b-1: 1.00%
Other: none

Distributions
Income: quarterly Capital Gains: Dec

Exchange Options
Number Per Year: no limit Fee: none
Telephone: yes (money market fund available)

Services
auto invest, auto withdraw

Pacifica Asset Preservation (PCASX)

237 Park Ave., Suite 910
New York, NY 10017
(800) 662-8417, (212) 808-3937

General Bond

PERFORMANCE

	3yr Annual	5yr Annual	10yr Annual	Bull	Bear
Return (%)	6.0	na	na	22.4	na
Differ from Category (+/-)	-4.2 low	na	na	-17.0 low	na

Total Risk	Standard Deviation	Category Risk	Risk Index	Avg Mat
low	1.1%	low	0.3	1.0 yrs

	1993	1992	1991	1990	1989	1988	1987	1986	1985	1984
Return (%)	4.5	4.6	9.0	—	—	—	—	—	—	—
Differ from category (+/-)	-4.7	-2.1	-5.6	—	—	—	—	—	—	—

PER SHARE DATA

	1993	1992	1991	1990	1989	1988	1987	1986	1985	1984
Dividends, Net Income ($)	0.44	0.54	0.67	—	—	—	—	—	—	—
Distrib'ns, Cap Gain ($)	0.00	0.00	0.00	—	—	—	—	—	—	—
Net Asset Value ($)	10.19	10.18	10.26	—	—	—	—	—	—	—
Expense Ratio (%)	0.80	0.75	0.62	—	—	—	—	—	—	—
Net Income to Assets (%)	4.64	5.52	6.90	—	—	—	—	—	—	—
Portfolio Turnover (%)	49	21	30	—	—	—	—	—	—	—
Total Assets (Millions $)	144	160	73	—	—	—	—	—	—	—

PORTFOLIO (as of 9/30/93)

Portfolio Manager: Mark Romano - 1990

Investm't Category: General Bond

Cap Gain	Asset Allocation
Cap & Income	Fund of Funds
✔ Income	Index
	Sector
✔ Domestic	Small Cap
✔ Foreign	Socially Conscious
Country/Region	State Specific

Portfolio: stocks 0% bonds 100%
convertibles 0% other 0% cash 0%

Largest Holdings: corporate bonds 39%,
commercial paper 35%

Unrealized Net Capital Gains: 0% of portfolio value

SHAREHOLDER INFORMATION

Minimum Investment
Initial: $500 Subsequent: $50

Minimum IRA Investment
Initial: $250 Subsequent: $50

Maximum Fees
Load: none 12b-1: 0.50%
Other: none

Distributions
Income: monthly Capital Gains: Dec

Exchange Options
Number Per Year: no limit Fee: none
Telephone: yes (money market fund available)

Services
IRA, auto invest, auto withdraw

Pacifica Short Term CA Tax-Free (PCATX)

237 Park Ave., Suite 910
New York, NY 10017
(800) 662-8417, (212) 808-3937

Tax-Exempt Bond

fund in existence since 1/20/93

PERFORMANCE

	3yr Annual	5yr Annual	10yr Annual	Bull	Bear
Return (%)	na	na	na	na	na
Differ from Category (+/-)	na	na	na	na	na

Total Risk	Standard Deviation	Category Risk	Risk Index	Avg Mat
na	na	na	na	3.0 yrs

	1993	1992	1991	1990	1989	1988	1987	1986	1985	1984
Return (%)	—	—	—	—	—	—	—	—	—	—
Differ from category (+/-)	—	—	—	—	—	—	—	—	—	—

PER SHARE DATA

	1993	1992	1991	1990	1989	1988	1987	1986	1985	1984
Dividends, Net Income ($)	0.34	—	—	—	—	—	—	—	—	—
Distrib'ns, Cap Gain ($)	0.00	—	—	—	—	—	—	—	—	—
Net Asset Value ($)	10.18	—	—	—	—	—	—	—	—	—
Expense Ratio (%)	0.28	—	—	—	—	—	—	—	—	—
Net Income to Assets (%)	3.53	—	—	—	—	—	—	—	—	—
Portfolio Turnover (%)	23	—	—	—	—	—	—	—	—	—
Total Assets (Millions $)	37	—	—	—	—	—	—	—	—	—

PORTFOLIO (as of 9/30/93)

Portfolio Manager: Keli Chaux - 1992

Investm't Category: Tax-Exempt Bond

Cap Gain	Asset Allocation
Cap & Income	Fund of Funds
✔ Income	Index
	Sector
✔ Domestic	Small Cap
Foreign	Socially Conscious
Country/Region	✔ State Specific

Portfolio: stocks 0%   bonds 100%
convertibles 0%   other 0%   cash 0%

Largest Holdings: na

Unrealized Net Capital Gains: 1% of portfolio value

SHAREHOLDER INFORMATION

Minimum Investment
Initial: $500   Subsequent: $50

Minimum IRA Investment
Initial: na   Subsequent: na

Maximum Fees
Load: none   12b-1: 0.50%
Other: none

Distributions
Income: monthly   Capital Gains: Dec

Exchange Options
Number Per Year: no limit   Fee: none
Telephone: yes (money market fund available)

Services
auto invest, auto withdraw

Paine Webber Atlas Global Growth "D"

103 Bellevue Parkway
Bloomington, DE 19809
(800) 647-1568

(PAGDX) *International Stock*

PERFORMANCE

	3yr Annual	5yr Annual	10yr Annual	Bull	Bear
Return (%)	na	na	na	na	na
Differ from Category (+/-)	na	na	na	na	na

Total Risk	Standard Deviation	Category Risk	Risk Index	Beta
na	na	na	na	na

	1993	1992	1991	1990	1989	1988	1987	1986	1985	1984
Return (%)	41.0	—	—	—	—	—	—	—	—	—
Differ from category (+/-) ...	2.5	—	—	—	—	—	—	—	—	—

PER SHARE DATA

	1993	1992	1991	1990	1989	1988	1987	1986	1985	1984
Dividends, Net Income ($) .	0.01	—	—	—	—	—	—	—	—	—
Distrib'ns, Cap Gain ($) ...	0.67	—	—	—	—	—	—	—	—	—
Net Asset Value ($)	17.18	—	—	—	—	—	—	—	—	—
Expense Ratio (%)........	1.90	—	—	—	—	—	—	—	—	—
Net Income to Assets (%) ..	0.04	—	—	—	—	—	—	—	—	—
Portfolio Turnover (%)....	258	—	—	—	—	—	—	—	—	—
Total Assets (Millions $)	50	—	—	—	—	—	—	—	—	—

PORTFOLIO (as of 8/31/93)

Portfolio Manager: Frank Jennings - 1983

Investm't Category: International Stock

✔ Cap Gain	Asset Allocation
Cap & Income	Fund of Funds
Income	Index
	Sector
✔ Domestic	Small Cap
✔ Foreign	Socially Conscious
Country/Region	State Specific

Portfolio: stocks 96%   bonds 0%
convertibles 0%   other 4%   cash 0%

Largest Holdings: United States 18%, Indonesia 10%

Unrealized Net Capital Gains: 12% of portfolio value

SHAREHOLDER INFORMATION

Minimum Investment
Initial: $1,000   Subsequent: $100

Minimum IRA Investment
Initial: $250   Subsequent: $100

Maximum Fees
Load: none   12b-1: 1.00%
Other: none

Distributions
Income: Aug   Capital Gains: Aug

Exchange Options
Number Per Year: no limit   Fee: $5
Telephone: none

Services
IRA, other pension, auto invest, auto withdraw

Paine Webber CA Tax-Free Inc. "D" (PCIDX)

103 Bellevue Parkway
Bloomington, DE 19809
(800) 647-1568

Tax-Exempt Bond

PERFORMANCE

	3yr Annual	5yr Annual	10yr Annual	Bull	Bear
Return (%)	na	na	na	na	na
Differ from Category (+/-)	na	na	na	na	na

Total Risk	Standard Deviation	Category Risk	Risk Index	Avg Mat
na	na	na	na	25.0 yrs

	1993	1992	1991	1990	1989	1988	1987	1986	1985	1984
Return (%)	10.9	—	—	—	—	—	—	—	—	—
Differ from category (+/-)	-0.6	—	—	—	—	—	—	—	—	—

PER SHARE DATA

	1993	1992	1991	1990	1989	1988	1987	1986	1985	1984
Dividends, Net Income ($)	0.51	—	—	—	—	—	—	—	—	—
Distrib'ns, Cap Gain ($)	0.28	—	—	—	—	—	—	—	—	—
Net Asset Value ($)	11.69	—	—	—	—	—	—	—	—	—
Expense Ratio (%)	1.48	—	—	—	—	—	—	—	—	—
Net Income to Assets (%)	5.06	—	—	—	—	—	—	—	—	—
Portfolio Turnover (%)	3	—	—	—	—	—	—	—	—	—
Total Assets (Millions $)	346	—	—	—	—	—	—	—	—	—

PORTFOLIO (as of 2/28/93)

Portfolio Manager: Gregory W. Serbe - 1992, Cynthia Bowa - 1992

Investm't Category: Tax-Exempt Bond
Cap Gain	Asset Allocation
Cap & Income	Fund of Funds
✔ Income	Index
	Sector
✔ Domestic	Small Cap
Foreign	Socially Conscious
Country/Region	✔ State Specific

Portfolio: stocks 0%   bonds 0%
convertibles 0%   other 0%   cash 0%

Largest Holdings: general obligation 12%

Unrealized Net Capital Gains: 9% of portfolio value

SHAREHOLDER INFORMATION

Minimum Investment
Initial: $1,000   Subsequent: $100

Minimum IRA Investment
Initial: na   Subsequent: na

Maximum Fees
Load: none   12b-1: 0.75%
Other: none

Distributions
Income: monthly   Capital Gains: Dec

Exchange Options
Number Per Year: no limit   Fee: $5
Telephone: none

Services
auto invest, auto withdraw

Paine Webber Capital Appreciation "D" (PWCDX)

103 Bellevue Parkway
Bloomington, DE 19809
(800) 647-1568

Aggressive Growth

PERFORMANCE

	3yr Annual	5yr Annual	10yr Annual	Bull	Bear
Return (%)	na	na	na	na	na
Differ from Category (+/-)	na	na	na	na	na

Total Risk	Standard Deviation	Category Risk	Risk Index	Beta
na	na	na	na	na

	1993	1992	1991	1990	1989	1988	1987	1986	1985	1984
Return (%)	15.2	—	—	—	—	—	—	—	—	—
Differ from category (+/-) . .	-3.8	—	—	—	—	—	—	—	—	—

PER SHARE DATA

	1993	1992	1991	1990	1989	1988	1987	1986	1985	1984
Dividends, Net Income ($) .	0.00	—	—	—	—	—	—	—	—	—
Distrib'ns, Cap Gain ($) . . .	0.00	—	—	—	—	—	—	—	—	—
Net Asset Value ($)	12.05	—	—	—	—	—	—	—	—	—
Expense Ratio (%).	na	—	—	—	—	—	—	—	—	—
Net Income to Assets (%)	na	—	—	—	—	—	—	—	—	—
Portfolio Turnover (%)	na	—	—	—	—	—	—	—	—	—
Total Assets (Millions $)	22	—	—	—	—	—	—	—	—	—

PORTFOLIO

Portfolio Manager: Todger Anders - na

Investm't Category: Aggressive Growth

✔ Cap Gain	Asset Allocation
Cap & Income	Fund of Funds
Income	Index
	Sector
✔ Domestic	Small Cap
Foreign	Socially Conscious
Country/Region	State Specific

Portfolio: stocks na   bonds na
convertibles na   other na   cash na

Largest Holdings: na

Unrealized Net Capital Gains: na

SHAREHOLDER INFORMATION

Minimum Investment
Initial: $1,000   Subsequent: $100

Minimum IRA Investment
Initial: $250   Subsequent: $100

Maximum Fees
Load: none   12b-1: 1.00%
Other: none

Distributions
Income: na   Capital Gains: na

Exchange Options
Number Per Year: no limit   Fee: $5
Telephone: none

Services
IRA, other pension, auto invest, auto withdraw

Paine Webber Dividend Growth "D" (PWDDX)

103 Bellevue Parkway
Bloomington, DE 19809
(800) 647-1568

Growth & Income

PERFORMANCE

	3yr Annual	5yr Annual	10yr Annual	Bull	Bear
Return (%)	na	na	na	na	na
Differ from Category (+/-)	na	na	na	na	na

Total Risk	Standard Deviation	Category Risk	Risk Index	Beta
na	na	na	na	na

	1993	1992	1991	1990	1989	1988	1987	1986	1985	1984
Return (%)	-3.2	—	—	—	—	—	—	—	—	—
Differ from category (+/-)	-15.8	—	—	—	—	—	—	—	—	—

PER SHARE DATA

	1993	1992	1991	1990	1989	1988	1987	1986	1985	1984
Dividends, Net Income ($)	0.13	—	—	—	—	—	—	—	—	—
Distrib'ns, Cap Gain ($)	0.03	—	—	—	—	—	—	—	—	—
Net Asset Value ($)	20.87	—	—	—	—	—	—	—	—	—
Expense Ratio (%)	1.87	—	—	—	—	—	—	—	—	—
Net Income to Assets (%)	0.61	—	—	—	—	—	—	—	—	—
Portfolio Turnover (%)	36	—	—	—	—	—	—	—	—	—
Total Assets (Millions $)	55	—	—	—	—	—	—	—	—	—

PORTFOLIO (as of 8/31/93)

Portfolio Manager: Whitney Merill - 1992

Investm't Category: Growth & Income

Cap Gain	Asset Allocation
✔ Cap & Income	Fund of Funds
Income	Index
	Sector
✔ Domestic	Small Cap
Foreign	Socially Conscious
Country/Region	State Specific

Portfolio: stocks 97% bonds 0%
convertibles 0% other 0% cash 3%

Largest Holdings: insurance 16%, banking 12%

Unrealized Net Capital Gains: 9% of portfolio value

SHAREHOLDER INFORMATION

Minimum Investment
Initial: $1,000   Subsequent: $100

Minimum IRA Investment
Initial: $250   Subsequent: $100

Maximum Fees
Load: none   12b-1: 1.00%
Other: none

Distributions
Income: quarterly   Capital Gains: Aug

Exchange Options
Number Per Year: no limit   Fee: $5
Telephone: none

Services
IRA, other pension, auto invest, auto withdraw

Paine Webber Global Income "D" (PWIDX)

103 Bellevue Parkway
Bloomington, DE 19809
(800) 647-1568

International Bond

PERFORMANCE

	3yr Annual	5yr Annual	10yr Annual	Bull	Bear
Return (%)	na	na	na	na	na
Differ from Category (+/-)	na	na	na	na	na

Total Risk	Standard Deviation	Category Risk	Risk Index	Avg Mat
na	na	na	na	8.9 yrs

	1993	1992	1991	1990	1989	1988	1987	1986	1985	1984
Return (%)	13.6	—	—	—	—	—	—	—	—	—
Differ from category (+/-)	0.8	—	—	—	—	—	—	—	—	—

PER SHARE DATA

	1993	1992	1991	1990	1989	1988	1987	1986	1985	1984
Dividends, Net Income ($)	0.74	—	—	—	—	—	—	—	—	—
Distrib'ns, Cap Gain ($)	0.09	—	—	—	—	—	—	—	—	—
Net Asset Value ($)	10.97	—	—	—	—	—	—	—	—	—
Expense Ratio (%)	na	—	—	—	—	—	—	—	—	—
Net Income to Assets (%)	na	—	—	—	—	—	—	—	—	—
Portfolio Turnover (%)	na	—	—	—	—	—	—	—	—	—
Total Assets (Millions $)	136	—	—	—	—	—	—	—	—	—

PORTFOLIO

Portfolio Manager: Stuart Waugh - 1992

Investm't Category: International Bond

Cap Gain	Asset Allocation
Cap & Income	Fund of Funds
✔ Income	Index
	Sector
✔ Domestic	Small Cap
✔ Foreign	Socially Conscious
Country/Region	State Specific

Portfolio: stocks na   bonds na
convertibles na   other na   cash na

Largest Holdings: na

Unrealized Net Capital Gains: na

SHAREHOLDER INFORMATION

Minimum Investment
Initial: $1,000   Subsequent: $100

Minimum IRA Investment
Initial: $250   Subsequent: $100

Maximum Fees
Load: none   12b-1: 0.75%
Other: none

Distributions
Income: quarterly   Capital Gains: Oct

Exchange Options
Number Per Year: no limit   Fee: $5
Telephone: none

Services
IRA, other pension, auto invest, auto withdraw

Paine Webber Growth "D" (PGRDX)

103 Bellevue Parkway
Bloomington, DE 19809
(800) 647-1568

Growth

PERFORMANCE

	3yr Annual	5yr Annual	10yr Annual	Bull	Bear
Return (%)	na	na	na	na	na
Differ from Category (+/-)	na	na	na	na	na

Total Risk	Standard Deviation	Category Risk	Risk Index	Beta
na	na	na	na	na

	1993	1992	1991	1990	1989	1988	1987	1986	1985	1984
Return (%).............	18.1	—	—	—	—	—	—	—	—	—
Differ from category (+/-)...	4.9	—	—	—	—	—	—	—	—	—

PER SHARE DATA

	1993	1992	1991	1990	1989	1988	1987	1986	1985	1984
Dividends, Net Income ($).	0.00	—	—	—	—	—	—	—	—	—
Distrib'ns, Cap Gain ($) ...	1.07	—	—	—	—	—	—	—	—	—
Net Asset Value ($)	20.85	—	—	—	—	—	—	—	—	—
Expense Ratio (%)	2.06	—	—	—	—	—	—	—	—	—
Net Income to Assets (%) .	-0.69	—	—	—	—	—	—	—	—	—
Portfolio Turnover (%)......	35	—	—	—	—	—	—	—	—	—
Total Assets (Millions $).....	23	—	—	—	—	—	—	—	—	—

PORTFOLIO (as of 8/31/93)

Portfolio Manager: Ellen Harris - 1992

Investm't Category: Growth

✔ Cap Gain	Asset Allocation
Cap & Income	Fund of Funds
Income	Index
	Sector
✔ Domestic	Small Cap
Foreign	Socially Conscious
Country/Region	State Specific

Portfolio: stocks 84% bonds 0%
convertibles 0% other 0% cash 16%

Largest Holdings: specialty—retail 10%, leisure & entertainment 9%

Unrealized Net Capital Gains: 25% of portfolio value

SHAREHOLDER INFORMATION

Minimum Investment
Initial: $1,000 Subsequent: $100

Minimum IRA Investment
Initial: $250 Subsequent: $100

Maximum Fees
Load: none 12b-1: 1.00%
Other: none

Distributions
Income: Aug Capital Gains: Aug

Exchange Options
Number Per Year: no limit Fee: $5
Telephone: none

Services
IRA, other pension, auto invest, auto withdraw

Paine Webber High Income "D" (PWHDX)

Corporate High-Yield Bond

103 Bellevue Parkway
Bloomington, DE 19809
(800) 647-1568

PERFORMANCE

	3yr Annual	5yr Annual	10yr Annual	Bull	Bear
Return (%)	na	na	na	na	na
Differ from Category (+/-)	na	na	na	na	na

Total Risk	Standard Deviation	Category Risk	Risk Index	Avg Mat
na	na	na	na	7.0 yrs

	1993	1992	1991	1990	1989	1988	1987	1986	1985	1984
Return (%)	22.6	—	—	—	—	—	—	—	—	—
Differ from category (+/-)	3.4	—	—	—	—	—	—	—	—	—

PER SHARE DATA

	1993	1992	1991	1990	1989	1988	1987	1986	1985	1984
Dividends, Net Income ($)	0.80	—	—	—	—	—	—	—	—	—
Distrib'ns, Cap Gain ($)	0.06	—	—	—	—	—	—	—	—	—
Net Asset Value ($)	8.79	—	—	—	—	—	—	—	—	—
Expense Ratio (%)	1.41	—	—	—	—	—	—	—	—	—
Net Income to Assets (%)	10.17	—	—	—	—	—	—	—	—	—
Portfolio Turnover (%)	na	—	—	—	—	—	—	—	—	—
Total Assets ($)	na	—	—	—	—	—	—	—	—	—

PORTFOLIO (as of 5/31/93)

Portfolio Manager: Evan Steen - 1992

Investm't Category: Corp. High-Yield Bond

Cap Gain	Asset Allocation
Cap & Income	Fund of Funds
✔ Income	Index
	Sector
✔ Domestic	Small Cap
Foreign	Socially Conscious
Country/Region	State Specific

Portfolio: stocks 3% bonds 87%
convertibles 2% other 4% cash 4%

Largest Holdings: gaming/hotel 18%, diversified/industrial 9%

Unrealized Net Capital Gains: 6% of portfolio value

SHAREHOLDER INFORMATION

Minimum Investment
Initial: $1,000 Subsequent: $100

Minimum IRA Investment
Initial: $250 Subsequent: $100

Maximum Fees
Load: none 12b-1: 0.75%
Other: none

Distributions
Income: monthly Capital Gains: Nov

Exchange Options
Number Per Year: no limit Fee: $5
Telephone: none

Services
IRA, other pension, auto invest, auto withdraw

Paine Webber Investment Growth Inc "D" (PIVDX) *Corporate Bond*

103 Bellevue Parkway
Bloomington, DE 19809
(800) 647-1568

PERFORMANCE

	3yr Annual	5yr Annual	10yr Annual	Bull	Bear
Return (%)	na	na	na	na	na
Differ from Category (+/-)	na	na	na	na	na

Total Risk	Standard Deviation	Category Risk	Risk Index	Avg Mat
na	na	na	na	15.3 yrs

	1993	1992	1991	1990	1989	1988	1987	1986	1985	1984
Return (%)	12.7	—	—	—	—	—	—	—	—	—
Differ from category (+/-). . .	1.3	—	—	—	—	—	—	—	—	—

PER SHARE DATA

	1993	1992	1991	1990	1989	1988	1987	1986	1985	1984
Dividends, Net Income ($).	0.70	—	—	—	—	—	—	—	—	—
Distrib'ns, Cap Gain ($) . . .	0.03	—	—	—	—	—	—	—	—	—
Net Asset Value ($)	11.08	—	—	—	—	—	—	—	—	—
Expense Ratio (%)	1.44	—	—	—	—	—	—	—	—	—
Net Income to Assets (%) .	6.69	—	—	—	—	—	—	—	—	—
Portfolio Turnover (%).	na	—	—	—	—	—	—	—	—	—
Total Assets ($)	na	—	—	—	—	—	—	—	—	—

PORTFOLIO (as of 5/31/93)

Portfolio Manager: Mary King - na

Investm't Category: Corporate Bond

Cap Gain	Asset Allocation
Cap & Income	Fund of Funds
✔ Income	Index
	Sector
✔ Domestic	Small Cap
Foreign	Socially Conscious
Country/Region	State Specific

Portfolio: stocks 0%   bonds 95%
convertibles 0%   other 0%   cash 5%

Largest Holdings: utilities 12%, finance 10%

Unrealized Net Capital Gains: 7% of portfolio value

SHAREHOLDER INFORMATION

Minimum Investment
Initial: $1,000   Subsequent: $100

Minimum IRA Investment
Initial: $250   Subsequent: $100

Maximum Fees
Load: none   12b-1: 0.75%
Other: none

Distributions
Income: monthly   Capital Gains: Nov

Exchange Options
Number Per Year: no limit   Fee: $5
Telephone: none

Services
IRA, other pension, auto invest, auto withdraw

Paine Webber Muni High Income "D" (PMIDX)

103 Bellevue Parkway
Bloomington, DE 19809
(800) 647-1568

Tax-Exempt Bond

PERFORMANCE

	3yr Annual	5yr Annual	10yr Annual	Bull	Bear
Return (%)	na	na	na	na	na
Differ from Category (+/-)	na	na	na	na	na

Total Risk	Standard Deviation	Category Risk	Risk Index	Avg Mat
na	na	na	na	25.0 yrs

	1993	1992	1991	1990	1989	1988	1987	1986	1985	1984
Return (%)	11.1	—	—	—	—	—	—	—	—	—
Differ from category (+/-)	-0.5	—	—	—	—	—	—	—	—	—

PER SHARE DATA

	1993	1992	1991	1990	1989	1988	1987	1986	1985	1984
Dividends, Net Income ($)	0.69	—	—	—	—	—	—	—	—	—
Distrib'ns, Cap Gain ($)	0.03	—	—	—	—	—	—	—	—	—
Net Asset Value ($)	10.97	—	—	—	—	—	—	—	—	—
Expense Ratio (%)	1.40	—	—	—	—	—	—	—	—	—
Net Income to Assets (%)	5.26	—	—	—	—	—	—	—	—	—
Portfolio Turnover (%)	10	—	—	—	—	—	—	—	—	—
Total Assets (Millions $)	35	—	—	—	—	—	—	—	—	—

PORTFOLIO (as of 2/28/93)

Portfolio Manager: Gregory Serbe - 1992

Investm't Category: Tax-Exempt Bond
- Cap Gain
- Cap & Income
- ✔ Income
- ✔ Domestic
- Foreign
- Country/Region
- Asset Allocation
- Fund of Funds
- Index
- Sector
- Small Cap
- Socially Conscious
- State Specific

Portfolio: stocks 0%   bonds 100%
convertibles 0%   other 0%   cash 0%

Largest Holdings: general obligation 2%

Unrealized Net Capital Gains: 8% of portfolio value

SHAREHOLDER INFORMATION

Minimum Investment
Initial: $1,000   Subsequent: $100

Minimum IRA Investment
Initial: na   Subsequent: na

Maximum Fees
Load: none   12b-1: 0.75%
Other: none

Distributions
Income: monthly   Capital Gains: Dec

Exchange Options
Number Per Year: no limit   Fee: $5
Telephone: none

Services
auto invest, auto withdraw

Paine Webber N.Y. Tax Free Income "D" (PNYDX)

103 Bellevue Parkway
Bloomington, DE 19809
(800) 647-1568

Tax-Exempt Bond

PERFORMANCE

	3yr Annual	5yr Annual	10yr Annual	Bull	Bear
Return (%)	na	na	na	na	na
Differ from Category (+/-)	na	na	na	na	na

Total Risk	Standard Deviation	Category Risk	Risk Index	Avg Mat
na	na	na	na	24.0 yrs

	1993	1992	1991	1990	1989	1988	1987	1986	1985	1984
Return (%)	11.0	—	—	—	—	—	—	—	—	—
Differ from category (+/-). . .	-0.6	—	—	—	—	—	—	—	—	—

PER SHARE DATA

	1993	1992	1991	1990	1989	1988	1987	1986	1985	1984
Dividends, Net Income ($) .	0.50	—	—	—	—	—	—	—	—	—
Distrib'ns, Cap Gain ($) . . .	0.00	—	—	—	—	—	—	—	—	—
Net Asset Value ($)	11.20	—	—	—	—	—	—	—	—	—
Expense Ratio (%)	0.90	—	—	—	—	—	—	—	—	—
Net Income to Assets (%) .	5.04	—	—	—	—	—	—	—	—	—
Portfolio Turnover (%).	5	—	—	—	—	—	—	—	—	—
Total Assets (Millions $). . . .	100	—	—	—	—	—	—	—	—	—

PORTFOLIO (as of 2/28/93)

Portfolio Manager: Gregory Serbe - 1992

Investm't Category: Tax-Exempt Bond
Cap Gain	Asset Allocation
Cap & Income	Fund of Funds
✔ Income	Index
	Sector
✔ Domestic	Small Cap
Foreign	Socially Conscious
Country/Region	✔ State Specific

Portfolio: stocks 0%   bonds 100%
convertibles 0%   other 0%   cash 0%

Largest Holdings: general obligation 8%

Unrealized Net Capital Gains: 8% of portfolio value

SHAREHOLDER INFORMATION

Minimum Investment
Initial: $1,000   Subsequent: $100

Minimum IRA Investment
Initial: na   Subsequent: na

Maximum Fees
Load: none   12b-1: 0.75%
Other: none

Distributions
Income: monthly   Capital Gains: na

Exchange Options
Number Per Year: no limit   Fee: $5
Telephone: none

Services
auto invest, auto withdraw

Paine Webber Nat'l Tax-Free Income "D"

103 Bellevue Parkway
Bloomington, DE 19809
(800) 647-1568

(PWNDX) *Tax-Exempt Bond*

PERFORMANCE

	3yr Annual	5yr Annual	10yr Annual	Bull	Bear
Return (%)	na	na	na	na	na
Differ from Category (+/-)	na	na	na	na	na

Total Risk	Standard Deviation	Category Risk	Risk Index	Avg Mat
na	na	na	na	26.0 yrs

	1993	1992	1991	1990	1989	1988	1987	1986	1985	1984
Return (%)	11.5	—	—	—	—	—	—	—	—	—
Differ from category (+/-) . .	-0.1	—	—	—	—	—	—	—	—	—

PER SHARE DATA

	1993	1992	1991	1990	1989	1988	1987	1986	1985	1984
Dividends, Net Income ($) .	0.56	—	—	—	—	—	—	—	—	—
Distrib'ns, Cap Gain ($) . . .	0.12	—	—	—	—	—	—	—	—	—
Net Asset Value ($)	12.25	—	—	—	—	—	—	—	—	—
Expense Ratio (%).	1.37	—	—	—	—	—	—	—	—	—
Net Income to Assets (%) . .	5.30	—	—	—	—	—	—	—	—	—
Portfolio Turnover (%)	5	—	—	—	—	—	—	—	—	—
Total Assets (Millions $) . . .	201	—	—	—	—	—	—	—	—	—

PORTFOLIO (as of 2/28/93)

Portfolio Manager: Gregory Serbe - 1992

Investm't Category: Tax-Exempt Bond

Cap Gain	Asset Allocation
Cap & Income	Fund of Funds
✔ Income	Index
	Sector
✔ Domestic	Small Cap
Foreign	Socially Conscious
Country/Region	State Specific

Portfolio: stocks 0%   bonds 100%
convertibles 0%   other 0%   cash 0%

Largest Holdings: general obligation 5%

Unrealized Net Capital Gains: 8% of portfolio value

SHAREHOLDER INFORMATION

Minimum Investment
Initial: $1,000   Subsequent: $100

Minimum IRA Investment
Initial: na   Subsequent: na

Maximum Fees
Load: none   12b-1: 0.75%
Other: none

Distributions
Income: monthly   Capital Gains: na

Exchange Options
Number Per Year: no limit   Fee: $5
Telephone: none

Services
auto invest, auto withdraw

Paine Webber Short Term U.S. Gov't Inc "D"

103 Bellevue Parkway
Bloomington, DE 19809
(800) 647-1568

(PSGDX) *General Bond*

fund in existence since 5/3/93

PERFORMANCE

	3yr Annual	5yr Annual	10yr Annual	Bull	Bear
Return (%)	na	na	na	na	na
Differ from Category (+/-)	na	na	na	na	na

Total Risk	Standard Deviation	Category Risk	Risk Index	Avg Mat
na	na	na	na	2.5 yrs

	1993	1992	1991	1990	1989	1988	1987	1986	1985	1984
Return (%)	—	—	—	—	—	—	—	—	—	—
Differ from category (+/-). . . .	—	—	—	—	—	—	—	—	—	—

PER SHARE DATA

	1993	1992	1991	1990	1989	1988	1987	1986	1985	1984
Dividends, Net Income ($) .	0.06	—	—	—	—	—	—	—	—	—
Distrib'ns, Cap Gain ($) . . .	0.00	—	—	—	—	—	—	—	—	—
Net Asset Value ($)	2.48	—	—	—	—	—	—	—	—	—
Expense Ratio (%)	na	—	—	—	—	—	—	—	—	—
Net Income to Assets (%) . . .	na	—	—	—	—	—	—	—	—	—
Portfolio Turnover (%).	na	—	—	—	—	—	—	—	—	—
Total Assets (Millions $). .	1,191	—	—	—	—	—	—	—	—	—

PORTFOLIO

Portfolio Manager: Ellen Griggs - 1993, Ed Rosenzweig - 1993

Investm't Category: General Bond

Cap Gain	Asset Allocation
Cap & Income	Fund of Funds
✔ Income	Index
	Sector
✔ Domestic	Small Cap
Foreign	Socially Conscious
Country/Region	State Specific

Portfolio: stocks na   bonds na
convertibles na   other na   cash na

Largest Holdings: na

Unrealized Net Capital Gains: na

SHAREHOLDER INFORMATION

Minimum Investment
Initial: $1,000   Subsequent: $100

Minimum IRA Investment
Initial: $250   Subsequent: $100

Maximum Fees
Load: none   12b-1: 0.75%
Other: none

Distributions
Income: monthly   Capital Gains: Nov

Exchange Options
Number Per Year: no limit   Fee: $5
Telephone: none

Services
IRA, other pension, auto invest, auto withdraw

Paine Webber Small Cap Value "D" (PSCDX)

103 Bellevue Parkway
Bloomington, DE 19809
(800) 647-1568

Growth

fund in existence since 5/3/93

PERFORMANCE

	3yr Annual	5yr Annual	10yr Annual	Bull	Bear
Return (%)	na	na	na	na	na
Differ from Category (+/-)	na	na	na	na	na

Total Risk	Standard Deviation	Category Risk	Risk Index	Beta
na	na	na	na	na

	1993	1992	1991	1990	1989	1988	1987	1986	1985	1984
Return (%)	—	—	—	—	—	—	—	—	—	—
Differ from category (+/-) ...	—	—	—	—	—	—	—	—	—	—

PER SHARE DATA

	1993	1992	1991	1990	1989	1988	1987	1986	1985	1984
Dividends, Net Income ($) .	0.06	—	—	—	—	—	—	—	—	—
Distrib'ns, Cap Gain ($) ...	0.08	—	—	—	—	—	—	—	—	—
Net Asset Value ($)	10.61	—	—	—	—	—	—	—	—	—
Expense Ratio (%)..........	na	—	—	—	—	—	—	—	—	—
Net Income to Assets (%)	na	—	—	—	—	—	—	—	—	—
Portfolio Turnover (%)	na	—	—	—	—	—	—	—	—	—
Total Assets (Millions $)	20	—	—	—	—	—	—	—	—	—

PORTFOLIO

Portfolio Manager: Chuck Royce - 1993

Investm't Category: Growth

✔ Cap Gain	Asset Allocation
Cap & Income	Fund of Funds
Income	Index
	Sector
✔ Domestic	✔ Small Cap
Foreign	Socially Conscious
Country/Region	State Specific

Portfolio: stocks na bonds na
convertibles na other na cash na

Largest Holdings: na

Unrealized Net Capital Gains: na

SHAREHOLDER INFORMATION

Minimum Investment
Initial: $1,000   Subsequent: $100

Minimum IRA Investment
Initial: $250   Subsequent: $100

Maximum Fees
Load: none   12b-1: 1.00%
Other: none

Distributions
Income: Dec   Capital Gains: Dec

Exchange Options
Number Per Year: no limit   Fee: $5
Telephone: none

Services
IRA, other pension, auto invest, auto withdraw

Paine Webber U.S. Gov't Income "D" (PWGDX)

103 Bellevue Parkway
Bloomington, DE 19809
(800) 647-1568

Mortgage-Backed Bond

PERFORMANCE

	3yr Annual	5yr Annual	10yr Annual	Bull	Bear
Return (%)	na	na	na	na	na
Differ from Category (+/-)	na	na	na	na	na

Total Risk	Standard Deviation	Category Risk	Risk Index	Avg Mat
na	na	na	na	8.9 yrs

	1993	1992	1991	1990	1989	1988	1987	1986	1985	1984
Return (%)	5.8	—	—	—	—	—	—	—	—	—
Differ from category (+/-)	-1.0	—	—	—	—	—	—	—	—	—

PER SHARE DATA

	1993	1992	1991	1990	1989	1988	1987	1986	1985	1984
Dividends, Net Income ($)	0.58	—	—	—	—	—	—	—	—	—
Distrib'ns, Cap Gain ($)	0.02	—	—	—	—	—	—	—	—	—
Net Asset Value ($)	10.02	—	—	—	—	—	—	—	—	—
Expense Ratio (%)	1.39	—	—	—	—	—	—	—	—	—
Net Income to Assets (%)	6.34	—	—	—	—	—	—	—	—	—
Portfolio Turnover (%)	na	—	—	—	—	—	—	—	—	—
Total Assets (Millions $)	979	—	—	—	—	—	—	—	—	—

PORTFOLIO (as of 5/31/93)

Portfolio Manager: Ellen Griggs - 1992,
Ed Rosenzweig - 1992

Investm't Category: Mortgage-Backed Bond

Cap Gain	Asset Allocation
Cap & Income	Fund of Funds
✔ Income	Index
	Sector
✔ Domestic	Small Cap
Foreign	Socially Conscious
Country/Region	State Specific

Portfolio: stocks 0% bonds 84%
convertibles 0% other 0% cash 16%

Largest Holdings: mortgage-backed 70%,
U.S. government & agencies 12%

Unrealized Net Capital Gains: 3% of portfolio value

SHAREHOLDER INFORMATION

Minimum Investment
Initial: $1,000   Subsequent: $100

Minimum IRA Investment
Initial: $250   Subsequent: $100

Maximum Fees
Load: none   12b-1: 0.75%
Other: none

Distributions
Income: monthly   Capital Gains: Nov

Exchange Options
Number Per Year: no limit   Fee: $5
Telephone: none

Services
IRA, other pension, auto invest, auto withdraw

Pax World (PAXWX)

Balanced

224 State St.
Portsmouth, NH 03801
(800) 767-1729, (603) 431-8022

PERFORMANCE

	3yr Annual	5yr Annual	10yr Annual	Bull	Bear
Return (%)	6.3	10.6	10.7	32.7	0.0
Differ from Category (+/-)	-8.7 low	-1.5 blw av	-1.3 low	-28.9 low	5.8 high

Total Risk	Standard Deviation	Category Risk	Risk Index	Beta
blw av	5.8%	blw av	0.9	0.3

	1993	1992	1991	1990	1989	1988	1987	1986	1985	1984
Return (%)	-1.0	0.6	20.6	10.4	24.8	11.6	2.4	8.4	25.8	7.4
Differ from category (+/-) .	-14.4	-7.5	-3.3	10.9	7.2	-0.4	0.1	-9.1	2.1	0.0

PER SHARE DATA

	1993	1992	1991	1990	1989	1988	1987	1986	1985	1984
Dividends, Net Income ($) .	0.50	0.67	0.76	0.61	0.62	0.61	0.75	0.50	0.51	0.50
Distrib'ns, Cap Gain ($) . . .	0.07	0.12	1.04	0.83	0.25	0.37	1.24	0.70	0.37	0.76
Net Asset Value ($)	13.55	14.27	14.99	13.98	13.98	11.93	11.57	13.19	13.35	11.47
Expense Ratio (%).	1.00	1.00	1.20	1.20	1.10	1.10	1.10	1.20	1.40	1.50
Net Income to Assets (%). .	3.40	3.70	5.10	5.40	5.80	5.00	4.10	3.20	4.30	6.50
Portfolio Turnover (%)	15	17	26	39	37	58	124	57	48	34
Total Assets (Millions $) . . .	464	469	270	120	93	74	66	54	33	17

PORTFOLIO (as of 6/30/93)

Portfolio Manager: Anthony Brown - 1971

Investm't Category: Balanced

Cap Gain	Asset Allocation
✔ Cap & Income	Fund of Funds
Income	Index
	Sector
✔ Domestic	Small Cap
Foreign	✔ Socially Conscious
Country/Region	State Specific

Portfolio: stocks 62% bonds 38%
convertibles 0% other 0% cash 0%

Largest Holdings: stocks—food 20%, stocks—natural gas 13%

Unrealized Net Capital Gains: 1% of portfolio value

SHAREHOLDER INFORMATION

Minimum Investment
Initial: $250   Subsequent: $50

Minimum IRA Investment
Initial: $250   Subsequent: $50

Maximum Fees
Load: none   12b-1: 0.25%
Other: none

Distributions
Income: Jul, Dec   Capital Gains: Dec

Exchange Options
Number Per Year: none   Fee: na
Telephone: na

Services
IRA, other pension, auto invest, auto withdraw

PBHG Growth (PBHGX)

Aggressive Growth

1255 Drummers Lane
Suite 300
Wayne, PA 19087
(800) 809-8008

PERFORMANCE

	3yr Annual	5yr Annual	10yr Annual	Bull	Bear
Return (%)	41.2	26.9	na	214.6	-19.1
Differ from Category (+/-)	15.8 high	8.7 high	na	89.6 high	-4.1 blw av

Total Risk	Standard Deviation	Category Risk	Risk Index	Beta
high	23.3%	high	1.5	1.3

	1993	1992	1991	1990	1989	1988	1987	1986	1985	1984
Return (%)	44.6	28.5	51.6	-9.7	29.4	6.8	11.9	—	—	—
Differ from category (+/-) . .	25.6	18.1	-0.8	-3.4	2.4	-8.4	15.0	—	—	—

PER SHARE DATA

	1993	1992	1991	1990	1989	1988	1987	1986	1985	1984
Dividends, Net Income ($) .	0.00	0.00	0.00	0.00	0.03	0.00	0.00	—	—	—
Distrib'ns, Cap Gain ($) . . .	0.00	2.45	2.43	0.79	2.81	0.02	4.24	—	—	—
Net Asset Value ($)	15.20	10.51	10.53	8.74	10.71	10.51	9.86	—	—	—
Expense Ratio (%)	2.39	1.52	1.50	1.32	1.19	1.21	1.31	—	—	—
Net Income to Assets (%) .	-1.69	-0.55	-0.09	-0.35	0.20	0.02	0.36	—	—	—
Portfolio Turnover (%).	209	114	228	219	175	208	213	—	—	—
Total Assets (Millions $). . . .	121	7	10	18	23	28	30	—	—	—

PORTFOLIO (as of 3/31/93)

Portfolio Manager: Gary Pilgrim - 1985, Harold Baxter - 1985

Investm't Category: Aggressive Growth
- ✔ Cap Gain
- Cap & Income
- Income
- Asset Allocation
- Fund of Funds
- Index
- Sector
- ✔ Domestic
- ✔ Foreign
- Country/Region
- ✔ Small Cap
- Socially Conscious
- State Specific

Portfolio: stocks 86% bonds 0% convertibles 0% other 0% cash 14%

Largest Holdings: computer software 18%, electronics 13%

Unrealized Net Capital Gains: 12% of portfolio value

SHAREHOLDER INFORMATION

Minimum Investment
Initial: $1,000   Subsequent: $0

Minimum IRA Investment
Initial: $0   Subsequent: $0

Maximum Fees
Load: none   12b-1: none
Other: none

Distributions
Income: Oct   Capital Gains: Oct

Exchange Options
Number Per Year: none   Fee: na
Telephone: na

Services
IRA, other pension, auto invest, auto withdraw

Pennsylvania Mutual
(PENNX)

Growth

1414 Avenue of the Americas
New York, NY 10019
(800) 221-4268, (212) 355-7311

this fund is closed to new investors

PERFORMANCE

	3yr Annual	5yr Annual	10yr Annual	Bull	Bear
Return (%)	19.4	11.9	na	76.5	-14.5
Differ from Category (+/-)	0.2 av	-2.7 blw av	na	-8.2 blw av	-2.1 blw av

Total Risk	Standard Deviation	Category Risk	Risk Index	Beta
av	10.4%	low	1.0	0.6

	1993	1992	1991	1990	1989	1988	1987	1986	1985	1984
Return (%)	11.2	16.1	31.8	-11.5	16.6	24.4	1.3	—	—	—
Differ from category (+/-) . .	-2.0	5.1	-3.6	-5.4	-9.2	6.7	0.1	—	—	—

PER SHARE DATA

	1993	1992	1991	1990	1989	1988	1987	1986	1985	1984
Dividends, Net Income ($) .	0.10	0.10	0.11	0.15	0.21	0.11	0.33	—	—	—
Distrib'ns, Cap Gain ($) . . .	0.47	0.37	0.20	0.11	0.40	0.28	1.30	—	—	—
Net Asset Value ($)	8.31	8.00	7.29	5.78	6.85	6.41	5.47	—	—	—
Expense Ratio (%)	0.97	0.91	0.95	0.96	0.97	1.01	0.99	—	—	—
Net Income to Assets (%) . .	1.28	1.48	1.73	2.62	2.93	2.35	2.02	—	—	—
Portfolio Turnover (%)	12	22	29	15	23	24	23	—	—	—
Total Assets (Millions $) . .	1,032	1,102	789	549	550	445	276	—	—	—

PORTFOLIO (as of 6/30/93)

Portfolio Manager: Thomas Ebright - 1978, Charles Royce - 1973

Investm't Category: Growth

✔ Cap Gain	Asset Allocation
Cap & Income	Fund of Funds
Income	Index
	Sector
✔ Domestic	✔ Small Cap
Foreign	Socially Conscious
Country/Region	State Specific

Portfolio:	stocks 74%	bonds 3%
convertibles 0%	other 0%	cash 23%

Largest Holdings: business & industrial products 20%, business & industrial services 16%

Unrealized Net Capital Gains: 21% of portfolio value

SHAREHOLDER INFORMATION

Minimum Investment
Initial: $2,000   Subsequent: $50

Minimum IRA Investment
Initial: $500   Subsequent: $50

Maximum Fees
Load: 1.00% redemption   12b-1: none
Other: redemption fee applies for 1 year

Distributions
Income: Dec   Capital Gains: Dec

Exchange Options
Number Per Year: no limit   Fee: none
Telephone: yes (money market fund not available)

Services
IRA, other pension, auto invest, auto withdraw

Permanent Portfolio

(PRPFX)

Balanced

P.O. Box 5847
Austin, TX 78763
(800) 531-5142, (512) 453-7558

PERFORMANCE

	3yr Annual	5yr Annual	10yr Annual	Bull	Bear
Return (%)	8.5	5.5	5.2	28.9	-4.5
Differ from Category (+/-)	-6.5 low	-6.6 low	-6.8 low	-32.7 low	1.3 abv av

Total Risk	Standard Deviation	Category Risk	Risk Index	Beta
blw av	4.8%	low	0.7	0.2

	1993	1992	1991	1990	1989	1988	1987	1986	1985	1984
Return (%)	15.5	2.5	8.0	-3.8	6.3	1.2	13.1	14.1	11.7	-12.9
Differ from category (+/-). . .	2.1	-5.6	-15.9	-3.3	-11.3	-10.8	10.8	-3.4	-12.0	-20.3

PER SHARE DATA

	1993	1992	1991	1990	1989	1988	1987	1986	1985	1984
Dividends, Net Income ($).	0.23	0.28	0.91	0.47	0.00	0.00	0.00	0.00	0.00	0.00
Distrib'ns, Cap Gain ($) . . .	0.00	0.00	0.00	0.00	0.00	0.01	0.11	0.00	0.00	0.00
Net Asset Value ($)	17.27	15.16	15.07	14.81	15.91	14.96	14.79	13.18	11.55	10.34
Expense Ratio (%)	1.25	1.27	1.36	1.17	1.17	1.15	1.17	0.90	0.90	0.92
Net Income to Assets (%) .	3.20	3.29	4.22	3.80	3.00	2.53	2.51	3.00	3.53	2.81
Portfolio Turnover (%).	70	8	32	61	24	22	31	17	10	0
Total Assets (Millions $).	81	72	81	94	98	90	73	72	71	68

PORTFOLIO (as of 7/31/93)

Portfolio Manager: Terry Coxon - 1982

Investm't Category: Balanced

Cap Gain	✔ Asset Allocation
✔ Cap & Income	Fund of Funds
Income	Index
	Sector
✔ Domestic	Small Cap
✔ Foreign	Socially Conscious
Country/Region	State Specific

Portfolio: stocks 30%   bonds 38%
convertibles 0%   other 32%   cash 0%

Largest Holdings: U.S. government 33%, gold 21%

Unrealized Net Capital Gains: 10% of portfolio value

SHAREHOLDER INFORMATION

Minimum Investment
Initial: $1,000   Subsequent: $100

Minimum IRA Investment
Initial: $1,000   Subsequent: $100

Maximum Fees
Load: none   12b-1: 0.25%
Other: $35 start-up fee; $1.50/mo maintenance fee

Distributions
Income: Dec   Capital Gains: Dec

Exchange Options
Number Per Year: no limit   Fee: $5
Telephone: yes (money market fund available)

Services
IRA, other pension, auto withdraw

Permanent Portfolio— Versatile Bond (PRVBX)

Corporate Bond

P.O. Box 5847
Austin, TX 78763
(800) 531-5142, (512) 453-7558

PERFORMANCE

	3yr Annual	5yr Annual	10yr Annual	Bull	Bear
Return (%)	na	na	na	na	na
Differ from Category (+/-)	na	na	na	na	na

Total Risk	Standard Deviation	Category Risk	Risk Index	Avg Mat
na	na	na	na	0.9 yrs

	1993	1992	1991	1990	1989	1988	1987	1986	1985	1984
Return (%)	3.7	5.5	—	—	—	—	—	—	—	—
Differ from category (+/-)	-7.7	-3.1	—	—	—	—	—	—	—	—

PER SHARE DATA

	1993	1992	1991	1990	1989	1988	1987	1986	1985	1984
Dividends, Net Income ($)	0.69	0.00	—	—	—	—	—	—	—	—
Distrib'ns, Cap Gain ($)	0.00	0.00	—	—	—	—	—	—	—	—
Net Asset Value ($)	54.37	53.07	—	—	—	—	—	—	—	—
Expense Ratio (%)	0.89	1.07	—	—	—	—	—	—	—	—
Net Income to Assets (%)	3.86	4.00	—	—	—	—	—	—	—	—
Portfolio Turnover (%)	224	600	—	—	—	—	—	—	—	—
Total Assets (Millions $)	36	1	—	—	—	—	—	—	—	—

PORTFOLIO (as of 7/31/93)

Portfolio Manager: Terry Coxon - 1991

Investm't Category: Corporate Bond

Cap Gain	Asset Allocation
Cap & Income	Fund of Funds
✔ Income	Index
	Sector
✔ Domestic	Small Cap
Foreign	Socially Conscious
Country/Region	State Specific

Portfolio: stocks 0% bonds 100%
convertibles 0% other 0% cash 0%

Largest Holdings: financial services 23%, utilities 12%

Unrealized Net Capital Gains: 10% of portfolio value

SHAREHOLDER INFORMATION

Minimum Investment
Initial: $1,000   Subsequent: $100

Minimum IRA Investment
Initial: $1,000   Subsequent: $100

Maximum Fees
Load: none   12b-1: 0.25%
Other: $35 start-up fee; $1.50/mo maintenance fee

Distributions
Income: Dec   Capital Gains: Dec

Exchange Options
Number Per Year: no limit   Fee: $5
Telephone: yes (money market fund available)

Services
IRA, other pension, auto withdraw

Permanent Treasury Bill
(PRTBX)
Government Bond

P.O. Box 5847
Austin, TX 78763
(800) 531-5142, (512) 453-7558

PERFORMANCE

	3yr Annual	5yr Annual	10yr Annual	Bull	Bear
Return (%)	3.4	5.1	na	12.6	5.4
Differ from Category (+/-)	-7.4 low	-5.3 low	na	-33.6 low	4.9 high

Total Risk	Standard Deviation	Category Risk	Risk Index	Avg Mat
low	40%	low	0.1	4.8 yrs

	1993	1992	1991	1990	1989	1988	1987	1986	1985	1984
Return (%)	2.2	2.8	5.2	7.3	8.1	6.3	—	—	—	—
Differ from category (+/-). . .	-8.2	-3.4	-9.8	0.8	-5.8	-1.3	—	—	—	—

PER SHARE DATA

	1993	1992	1991	1990	1989	1988	1987	1986	1985	1984
Dividends, Net Income ($)	1.08	2.41	1.30	0.43	0.00	0.02	—	—	—	—
Distrib'ns, Cap Gain ($) . . .	0.00	0.00	0.00	0.00	0.00	0.00	—	—	—	—
Net Asset Value ($)	64.67	64.30	64.86	62.85	58.96	54.53	—	—	—	—
Expense Ratio (%)	0.73	0.73	0.83	0.54	0.54	0.50	—	—	—	—
Net Income to Assets (%) .	2.97	4.87	6.74	7.87	6.70	5.32	—	—	—	—
Portfolio Turnover (%).	0	0	0	0	0	0	—	—	—	—
Total Assets (Millions $). . . .	139	320	208	61	31	7	—	—	—	—

PORTFOLIO (as of 7/31/93)

Portfolio Manager: Terry Coxon - 1987

Investm't Category: Government Bond

Cap Gain	Asset Allocation
Cap & Income	Fund of Funds
✔ Income	Index
	Sector
✔ Domestic	Small Cap
Foreign	Socially Conscious
Country/Region	State Specific

Portfolio: stocks 0%   bonds 100%
convertibles 0%   other 0%   cash 0%

Largest Holdings: U.S. government 100%

Unrealized Net Capital Gains: 0% of portfolio value

SHAREHOLDER INFORMATION

Minimum Investment
Initial: $1,000   Subsequent: $100

Minimum IRA Investment
Initial: $1,000   Subsequent: $100

Maximum Fees
Load: none   12b-1: 0.25%
Other: $35 start-up fee; $1.50/mo maintenance fee

Distributions
Income: Dec   Capital Gains: Dec

Exchange Options
Number Per Year: no limit   Fee: $5
Telephone: yes (money market fund available)

Services
IRA, other pension, auto withdraw

Perritt Capital Growth

(PRCGX)

Aggressive Growth

680 N. Lake Shore Dr.
2038 Tower Offices
Chicago, IL 60611
(800) 338-1579, (312) 649-6940

PERFORMANCE

	3yr Annual	5yr Annual	10yr Annual	Bull	Bear
Return (%)	15.8	5.7	na	61.8	-20.0
Differ from Category (+/-)	-9.6 low	-12.5 low	na	-63.2 low	-5.0 blw av

Total Risk	Standard Deviation	Category Risk	Risk Index	Beta
abv av	13.0%	low	0.8	0.8

	1993	1992	1991	1990	1989	1988	1987	1986	1985	1984
Return (%)	5.2	6.4	38.6	-16.7	2.0	—	—	—	—	—
Differ from category (+/-) .	-13.8	-4.0	-13.8	-10.4	-25.0	—	—	—	—	—

PER SHARE DATA

	1993	1992	1991	1990	1989	1988	1987	1986	1985	1984
Dividends, Net Income ($) .	0.00	0.00	0.00	0.06	0.17	—	—	—	—	—
Distrib'ns, Cap Gain ($) . . .	0.53	0.35	0.11	0.00	0.00	—	—	—	—	—
Net Asset Value ($)	12.48	12.37	11.96	8.71	10.54	—	—	—	—	—
Expense Ratio (%).	1.96	2.30	2.50	2.50	2.50	—	—	—	—	—
Net Income to Assets (%).	-1.10	-1.10	-0.02	0.90	1.80	—	—	—	—	—
Portfolio Turnover (%)	34	24	37	24	23	—	—	—	—	—
Total Assets (Millions $)	7	7	6	4	6	—	—	—	—	—

PORTFOLIO (as of 4/30/93)

Portfolio Manager: Gerald Perritt - 1988

Investm't Category: Aggressive Growth

✔ Cap Gain	Asset Allocation
Cap & Income	Fund of Funds
Income	Index
	Sector
✔ Domestic	✔ Small Cap
✔ Foreign	Socially Conscious
Country/Region	State Specific

Portfolio: stocks 97%   bonds 0%
convertibles 0%   other 0%   cash 3%

Largest Holdings: food 12%, environmental 11%

Unrealized Net Capital Gains: 7% of portfolio value

SHAREHOLDER INFORMATION

Minimum Investment
Initial: $1,000   Subsequent: $250

Minimum IRA Investment
Initial: $250   Subsequent: $250

Maximum Fees
Load: none   12b-1: none
Other: none

Distributions
Income: Dec   Capital Gains: Dec

Exchange Options
Number Per Year: none   Fee: na
Telephone: na

Services
IRA, other pension, auto invest, auto withdraw

Philadelphia (PHILX)

Growth & Income

1200 N. Federal Hwy.
Suite 424
Boca Raton, FL 33432
(800) 749-9933, (407) 395-2155

PERFORMANCE

	3yr Annual	5yr Annual	10yr Annual	Bull	Bear
Return (%)	14.1	11.8	10.2	58.2	-16.7
Differ from Category (+/-)	-2.3 blw av	-0.6 blw av	-2.2 blw av	-11.9 blw av	-5.1 low

Total Risk	Standard Deviation	Category Risk	Risk Index	Beta
av	8.7%	blw av	1.0	0.5

	1993	1992	1991	1990	1989	1988	1987	1986	1985	1984
Return (%)	17.5	19.7	5.7	-11.3	32.6	15.2	3.8	7.6	21.9	-3.2
Differ from category (+/-)	4.9	9.7	-22.0	-5.7	11.0	-1.6	3.4	-7.6	-3.5	-9.4

PER SHARE DATA

	1993	1992	1991	1990	1989	1988	1987	1986	1985	1984
Dividends, Net Income ($)	0.13	0.08	0.09	0.18	0.14	0.09	0.14	0.21	0.20	0.24
Distrib'ns, Cap Gain ($)	0.62	0.07	0.00	0.00	0.88	0.15	1.77	2.35	0.81	0.64
Net Asset Value ($)	7.01	6.61	5.66	5.44	6.34	5.57	5.05	6.70	8.54	7.87
Expense Ratio (%)	1.81	1.79	1.61	1.19	0.95	0.90	0.87	0.83	0.90	0.91
Net Income to Assets (%)	1.55	1.37	1.73	2.95	2.02	1.50	1.81	2.37	2.42	2.92
Portfolio Turnover (%)	24	39	49	43	9	16	152	147	60	42
Total Assets (Millions $)	94	86	82	88	110	91	89	109	108	101

PORTFOLIO (as of 5/31/93)

Portfolio Manager: Donald H. Baxter - 1987

Investm't Category: Growth & Income

Cap Gain	Asset Allocation
✔ Cap & Income	Fund of Funds
Income	Index
	Sector
✔ Domestic	Small Cap
✔ Foreign	Socially Conscious
Country/Region	State Specific

Portfolio: stocks 59% bonds 29%
convertibles 0% other 2% cash 10%

Largest Holdings: communications 12%, utilities 9%

Unrealized Net Capital Gains: 16% of portfolio value

SHAREHOLDER INFORMATION

Minimum Investment
Initial: $1,000   Subsequent: $0

Minimum IRA Investment
Initial: $1,000   Subsequent: $0

Maximum Fees
Load: none   12b-1: 0.50%
Other: none

Distributions
Income: quarterly   Capital Gains: Dec

Exchange Options
Number Per Year: none   Fee: na
Telephone: na

Services
IRA, other pension, auto invest, auto withdraw

Portico Balanced (POBKX)

Balanced

615 E. Michigan Street
P.O. Box 701
Milwaukee, WI 53201
(800) 228-1024, (414) 287-3808

PERFORMANCE

	3yr Annual	5yr Annual	10yr Annual	Bull	Bear
Return (%)	na	na	na	na	na
Differ from Category (+/-)	na	na	na	na	na

Total Risk	Standard Deviation	Category Risk	Risk Index	Beta
na	na	na	na	na

	1993	1992	1991	1990	1989	1988	1987	1986	1985	1984
Return (%)	8.2	—	—	—	—	—	—	—	—	—
Differ from category (+/-) . .	-5.2	—	—	—	—	—	—	—	—	—

PER SHARE DATA

	1993	1992	1991	1990	1989	1988	1987	1986	1985	1984
Dividends, Net Income ($) .	0.45	—	—	—	—	—	—	—	—	—
Distrib'ns, Cap Gain ($) . . .	0.00	—	—	—	—	—	—	—	—	—
Net Asset Value ($)	23.01	—	—	—	—	—	—	—	—	—
Expense Ratio (%)	0.75	—	—	—	—	—	—	—	—	—
Net Income to Assets (%) . .	2.37	—	—	—	—	—	—	—	—	—
Portfolio Turnover (%)	71	—	—	—	—	—	—	—	—	—
Total Assets (Millions $)	87	—	—	—	—	—	—	—	—	—

PORTFOLIO (as of 4/30/93)

Portfolio Manager: David Halford - 1992, Teresa Westman - 1992

Investm't Category: Balanced

Cap Gain	Asset Allocation
✔ Cap & Income	Fund of Funds
Income	Index
	Sector
✔ Domestic	Small Cap
✔ Foreign	Socially Conscious
Country/Region	State Specific

Portfolio: stocks 50% bonds 32%
convertibles 1% other 0% cash 17%

Largest Holdings: bonds—U.S. government 21%, bonds—corporate 7%

Unrealized Net Capital Gains: 4% of portfolio value

SHAREHOLDER INFORMATION

Minimum Investment
Initial: $1,000   Subsequent: $100

Minimum IRA Investment
Initial: $100   Subsequent: $100

Maximum Fees
Load: none   12b-1: 0.25%
Other: none

Distributions
Income: quarterly   Capital Gains: Dec

Exchange Options
Number Per Year: 4   Fee: none
Telephone: yes (money market fund available)

Services
IRA, other pension, auto exchange, auto invest, auto withdraw

Portico Bond IMMDEX
(POBIX)
General Bond

615 E. Michigan Street
P.O. Box 701
Milwaukee, WI 53201
(800) 228-1024, (414) 287-3808

PERFORMANCE

	3yr Annual	5yr Annual	10yr Annual	Bull	Bear
Return (%)	11.6	na	na	46.3	2.8
Differ from Category (+/-)	1.4 abv av	na	na	6.9 abv av	-0.1 av

Total Risk	Standard Deviation	Category Risk	Risk Index	Avg Mat
low	3.7%	abv av	1.3	10.5 yrs

	1993	1992	1991	1990	1989	1988	1987	1986	1985	1984
Return (%)	10.9	7.5	16.5	8.2	—	—	—	—	—	—
Differ from category (+/-). . .	1.7	0.8	1.9	1.3	—	—	—	—	—	—

PER SHARE DATA

	1993	1992	1991	1990	1989	1988	1987	1986	1985	1984
Dividends, Net Income ($).	1.65	1.76	1.88	1.90	—	—	—	—	—	—
Distrib'ns, Cap Gain ($) . . .	0.50	0.20	0.13	0.00	—	—	—	—	—	—
Net Asset Value ($)	27.82	27.04	27.03	25.05	—	—	—	—	—	—
Expense Ratio (%)	0.50	0.50	0.50	0.50	—	—	—	—	—	—
Net Income to Assets (%) .	6.50	6.92	7.85	8.10	—	—	—	—	—	—
Portfolio Turnover (%).	81	38	132	111	—	—	—	—	—	—
Total Assets (Millions $). . . .	258	181	90	44	—	—	—	—	—	—

PORTFOLIO (as of 4/30/93)

Portfolio Manager: Mary Ellen Stanek - 1989,
Teresa Westman - 1992

Investm't Category: General Bond

Cap Gain	Asset Allocation
Cap & Income	Fund of Funds
✔ Income	✔ Index
	Sector
✔ Domestic	Small Cap
✔ Foreign	Socially Conscious
Country/Region	State Specific

Portfolio: stocks 0%   bonds 96%
convertibles 0%   other 4%   cash 0%

Largest Holdings: Lehman Brothers Government/Corporate Bond Index

Unrealized Net Capital Gains: 4% of portfolio value

SHAREHOLDER INFORMATION

Minimum Investment
Initial: $1,000   Subsequent: $100

Minimum IRA Investment
Initial: $100   Subsequent: $100

Maximum Fees
Load: 0.25% charge   12b-1: 0.25%
Other: none

Distributions
Income: quarterly   Capital Gains: Dec

Exchange Options
Number Per Year: 4   Fee: none
Telephone: yes (money market fund available)

Services
IRA, other pension, auto exchange, auto invest, auto withdraw

Portico Equity Index

(POEIX)

Growth & Income

615 E. Michigan Street
P.O. Box 701
Milwaukee, WI 53201
(800) 228-1024, (414) 287-3808

PERFORMANCE

	3yr Annual	5yr Annual	10yr Annual	Bull	Bear
Return (%)	14.8	na	na	64.9	-10.8
Differ from Category (+/-)	-1.6 blw av	na	na	-5.2 blw av	0.8 av

Total Risk	Standard Deviation	Category Risk	Risk Index	Beta
av	10.5%	abv av	1.2	0.9

	1993	1992	1991	1990	1989	1988	1987	1986	1985	1984
Return (%)	9.1	6.9	29.9	-3.2	—	—	—	—	—	—
Differ from category (+/-) . .	-3.5	-3.1	2.2	2.4	—	—	—	—	—	—

PER SHARE DATA

	1993	1992	1991	1990	1989	1988	1987	1986	1985	1984
Dividends, Net Income ($) .	0.75	0.72	0.73	0.75	—	—	—	—	—	—
Distrib'ns, Cap Gain ($) . . .	0.00	0.00	0.01	0.06	—	—	—	—	—	—
Net Asset Value ($)	32.91	30.87	29.57	23.37	—	—	—	—	—	—
Expense Ratio (%).	0.50	0.50	0.50	0.49	—	—	—	—	—	—
Net Income to Assets (%). .	2.27	2.48	2.82	3.01	—	—	—	—	—	—
Portfolio Turnover (%)	13	6	1	9	—	—	—	—	—	—
Total Assets (Millions $)	77	81	51	36	—	—	—	—	—	—

PORTFOLIO (as of 4/30/93)

Portfolio Manager: D. Tranchita - 1992, M. E. Stanek - 1989

Investm't Category: Growth & Income

Cap Gain	Asset Allocation
✔ Cap & Income	Fund of Funds
Income	✔ Index
	Sector
✔ Domestic	Small Cap
Foreign	Socially Conscious
Country/Region	State Specific

Portfolio: stocks 100%   bonds 0%
convertibles 0%   other 0%   cash 0%

Largest Holdings: telecommunications 9%, drugs 7%

Unrealized Net Capital Gains: 15% of portfolio value

SHAREHOLDER INFORMATION

Minimum Investment
Initial: $1,000   Subsequent: $100

Minimum IRA Investment
Initial: $100   Subsequent: $100

Maximum Fees
Load: 0.25% charge   12b-1: 0.25%
Other: none

Distributions
Income: quarterly   Capital Gains: Dec

Exchange Options
Number Per Year: 4   Fee: none
Telephone: yes (money market fund available)

Services
IRA, other pension, auto exchange, auto invest, auto withdraw

Portico Growth & Income (POIGX)

Growth & Income

615 E. Michigan Street
P.O. Box 701
Milwaukee, WI 53201
(800) 228-1024, (414) 287-3808

	3yr Annual	5yr Annual	10yr Annual	Bull	Bear
Return (%)	11.1	na	na	47.0	-6.7
Differ from Category (+/-)	-5.3 low	na	na	-23.1 low	4.9 high

Total Risk	Standard Deviation	Category Risk	Risk Index	Beta
av	8.1%	blw av	0.9	0.7

	1993	1992	1991	1990	1989	1988	1987	1986	1985	1984
Return (%)	6.6	5.4	22.2	-0.2	—	—	—	—	—	—
Differ from category (+/-) . . .	-6.0	-4.6	-5.5	5.4	—	—	—	—	—	—

PER SHARE DATA

	1993	1992	1991	1990	1989	1988	1987	1986	1985	1984
Dividends, Net Income ($) .	0.50	0.68	0.77	0.86	—	—	—	—	—	—
Distrib'ns, Cap Gain ($) . . .	0.59	0.18	0.00	0.00	—	—	—	—	—	—
Net Asset Value ($)	23.18	22.79	22.46	19.06	—	—	—	—	—	—
Expense Ratio (%)	0.85	0.75	0.75	0.74	—	—	—	—	—	—
Net Income to Assets (%) .	2.84	3.16	3.93	4.39	—	—	—	—	—	—
Portfolio Turnover (%).	86	31	28	50	—	—	—	—	—	—
Total Assets (Millions $). . . .	164	136	103	66	—	—	—	—	—	—

PORTFOLIO (as of 4/30/93)

Portfolio Manager: Marian Zentmyer - 1993

Investm't Category: Growth & Income

Cap Gain	Asset Allocation
✔ Cap & Income	Fund of Funds
Income	Index
	Sector
✔ Domestic	Small Cap
✔ Foreign	Socially Conscious
Country/Region	State Specific

Portfolio: stocks 92%   bonds 0%
convertibles 7%   other 1%   cash 0%

Largest Holdings: drugs 12%, oil & gas 9%

Unrealized Net Capital Gains: 10% of portfolio value

SHAREHOLDER INFORMATION

Minimum Investment
Initial: $1,000   Subsequent: $100

Minimum IRA Investment
Initial: $100   Subsequent: $100

Maximum Fees
Load: none   12b-1: 0.25%
Other: none

Distributions
Income: quarterly   Capital Gains: Dec

Exchange Options
Number Per Year: 4   Fee: none
Telephone: yes (money market fund available)

Services
IRA, other pension, auto exchange, auto invest, auto withdraw

Portico Interm Bond Market (POIMX)

General Bond

615 E. Michigan Street
P.O. Box 701
Milwaukee, WI 53201
(800) 228-1024, (414) 287-3808

fund in existence since 1/6/93

PERFORMANCE

	3yr Annual	5yr Annual	10yr Annual	Bull	Bear
Return (%)	na	na	na	na	na
Differ from Category (+/-)	na	na	na	na	na

Total Risk	Standard Deviation	Category Risk	Risk Index	Avg Mat
na	na	na	na	4.5 yrs

	1993	1992	1991	1990	1989	1988	1987	1986	1985	1984
Return (%)	—	—	—	—	—	—	—	—	—	—
Differ from category (+/-)	—	—	—	—	—	—	—	—	—	—

PER SHARE DATA

	1993	1992	1991	1990	1989	1988	1987	1986	1985	1984
Dividends, Net Income ($)	0.43	—	—	—	—	—	—	—	—	—
Distrib'ns, Cap Gain ($)	0.09	—	—	—	—	—	—	—	—	—
Net Asset Value ($)	10.29	—	—	—	—	—	—	—	—	—
Expense Ratio (%)	0.49	—	—	—	—	—	—	—	—	—
Net Income to Assets (%)	4.82	—	—	—	—	—	—	—	—	—
Portfolio Turnover (%)	82	—	—	—	—	—	—	—	—	—
Total Assets (Millions $)	66	—	—	—	—	—	—	—	—	—

PORTFOLIO (as of 4/30/93)

Portfolio Manager: Mary Ellen Stanek - 1993, Teresa Westman - 1993

Investm't Category: General Bond
Cap Gain	Asset Allocation
Cap & Income	Fund of Funds
✔ Income	✔ Index
	Sector
✔ Domestic	Small Cap
Foreign	Socially Conscious
Country/Region	State Specific

Portfolio: stocks 0%   bonds 85%
convertibles 0%   other 0%   cash 15%

Largest Holdings: Lehman Brothers Intermediate Government/Corporate Bond Index

Unrealized Net Capital Gains: 1% of portfolio value

SHAREHOLDER INFORMATION

Minimum Investment
Initial: $1,000   Subsequent: $100

Minimum IRA Investment
Initial: $100   Subsequent: $100

Maximum Fees
Load: 0.25% charge   12b-1: none
Other: none

Distributions
Income: monthly   Capital Gains: Dec

Exchange Options
Number Per Year: 4   Fee: none
Telephone: yes (money market fund available)

Services
IRA, other pension, auto exchange, auto invest, auto withdraw

Portico MidCore Growth
(POMGX)
Growth

615 E. Michigan Street
P.O. Box 701
Milwaukee, WI 53201
(800) 228-1024, (414) 287-3808

Portico Short Term Bond Market (POSEX)

General Bond

615 E. Michigan Street
P.O. Box 701
Milwaukee, WI 53201
(800) 228-1024, (414) 287-3808

PERFORMANCE

	3yr Annual	5yr Annual	10yr Annual	Bull	Bear
Return (%)	8.8	na	na	32.3	4.9
Differ from Category (+/-)	-1.4 low	na	na	-7.1 blw av	2.0 abv av

Total Risk	Standard Deviation	Category Risk	Risk Index	Avg Mat
low	2.2%	blw av	0.7	2.6 yrs

	1993	1992	1991	1990	1989	1988	1987	1986	1985	1984
Return (%)	6.3	6.8	13.5	7.6	—	—	—	—	—	—
Differ from category (+/-) . .	-2.9	0.1	-1.1	0.6	—	—	—	—	—	—

PER SHARE DATA

	1993	1992	1991	1990	1989	1988	1987	1986	1985	1984
Dividends, Net Income ($) .	0.56	0.62	0.70	0.78	—	—	—	—	—	—
Distrib'ns, Cap Gain ($) . . .	0.12	0.14	0.02	0.00	—	—	—	—	—	—
Net Asset Value ($)	10.40	10.43	10.50	9.94	—	—	—	—	—	—
Expense Ratio (%)	0.53	0.60	0.60	0.60	—	—	—	—	—	—
Net Income to Assets (%) . .	5.75	6.00	7.13	7.93	—	—	—	—	—	—
Portfolio Turnover (%)	87	82	67	57	—	—	—	—	—	—
Total Assets (Millions $) . . .	138	129	63	23	—	—	—	—	—	—

PORTFOLIO (as of 4/30/93)

Portfolio Manager: Mary Ellen Stanek - 1989, Daniel Tranchita - 1993

Investm't Category: General Bond

Cap Gain	Asset Allocation
Cap & Income	Fund of Funds
✔ Income	✔ Index
	Sector
✔ Domestic	Small Cap
✔ Foreign	Socially Conscious
Country/Region	State Specific

Portfolio:	stocks 0%	bonds 96%
convertibles 0%	other 0%	cash 4%

Largest Holdings: Merrill Lynch U.S. Treasury Short-Term Bond Index

Unrealized Net Capital Gains: 1% of portfolio value

SHAREHOLDER INFORMATION

Minimum Investment
Initial: $1,000   Subsequent: $100

Minimum IRA Investment
Initial: $100   Subsequent: $100

Maximum Fees
Load: 0.25% charge   12b-1: 0.25%
Other: none

Distributions
Income: monthly   Capital Gains: Dec

Exchange Options
Number Per Year: 4   Fee: none
Telephone: yes (money market fund available)

Services
IRA, other pension, auto exchange, auto invest, auto withdraw

Portico Special Growth
(POSGX)
Growth

615 E. Michigan Street
P.O. Box 701
Milwaukee, WI 53201
(800) 228-1024, (414) 287-3808

PERFORMANCE

	3yr Annual	5yr Annual	10yr Annual	Bull	Bear
Return (%)	22.3	na	na	107.1	-10.7
Differ from Category (+/-)	3.1 abv av	na	na	22.4 high	1.7 av

Total Risk	Standard Deviation	Category Risk	Risk Index	Beta
high	14.8%	high	1.4	1.1

	1993	1992	1991	1990	1989	1988	1987	1986	1985	1984
Return (%)	8.0	7.2	57.9	1.0	—	—	—	—	—	—
Differ from category (+/-)	-5.2	-3.8	22.5	7.1	—	—	—	—	—	—

PER SHARE DATA

	1993	1992	1991	1990	1989	1988	1987	1986	1985	1984
Dividends, Net Income ($)	0.07	0.17	0.21	0.30	—	—	—	—	—	—
Distrib'ns, Cap Gain ($)	0.00	0.62	1.72	0.00	—	—	—	—	—	—
Net Asset Value ($)	33.37	30.96	29.67	20.16	—	—	—	—	—	—
Expense Ratio (%)	0.85	0.76	0.75	0.74	—	—	—	—	—	—
Net Income to Assets (%)	0.27	0.65	1.10	1.41	—	—	—	—	—	—
Portfolio Turnover (%)	58	32	48	42	—	—	—	—	—	—
Total Assets (Millions $)	355	205	96	39	—	—	—	—	—	—

PORTFOLIO (as of 4/30/93)

Portfolio Manager: J. Scott Harkness - 1989, Joseph J. Docter - 1989

Investm't Category: Growth

✔ Cap Gain	Asset Allocation
Cap & Income	Fund of Funds
Income	Index
	Sector
✔ Domestic	Small Cap
✔ Foreign	Socially Conscious
Country/Region	State Specific

Portfolio: stocks 83% bonds 0%
convertibles 0% other 0% cash 17%

Largest Holdings: retail 14%, health care services & supplies 9%

Unrealized Net Capital Gains: 10% of portfolio value

SHAREHOLDER INFORMATION

Minimum Investment
Initial: $1,000   Subsequent: $100

Minimum IRA Investment
Initial: $100   Subsequent: $100

Maximum Fees
Load: none   12b-1: 0.25%
Other: none

Distributions
Income: quarterly   Capital Gains: Dec

Exchange Options
Number Per Year: 4   Fee: none
Telephone: yes (money market fund available)

Services
IRA, other pension, auto exchange, auto invest, auto withdraw

PRA Real Estate Securities (PRREX)

Growth

900 North Michigan Avenue
Suite 1000
Chicago, IL 60611
(312) 915-3600

PERFORMANCE

	3yr Annual	5yr Annual	10yr Annual	Bull	Bear
Return (%)	20.4	na	na	74.6	-22.1
Differ from Category (+/-)	1.2 abv av	na	na	-10.1 blw av	-9.7 low

Total Risk	Standard Deviation	Category Risk	Risk Index	Beta
high	14.6%	high	1.4	0.5

	1993	1992	1991	1990	1989	1988	1987	1986	1985	1984
Return (%)	19.9	17.8	23.5	-22.1	—	—	—	—	—	—
Differ from category (+/-) ...	6.7	6.8	-11.9	-16.0	—	—	—	—	—	—

PER SHARE DATA

	1993	1992	1991	1990	1989	1988	1987	1986	1985	1984
Dividends, Net Income ($) .	0.40	0.44	0.52	0.72	—	—	—	—	—	—
Distrib'ns, Cap Gain ($) ...	0.66	0.00	0.00	0.10	—	—	—	—	—	—
Net Asset Value ($)	9.36	8.71	7.80	6.75	—	—	—	—	—	—
Expense Ratio (%)........	1.24	1.37	1.25	1.54	—	—	—	—	—	—
Net Income to Assets (%)..	4.37	5.75	7.36	7.25	—	—	—	—	—	—
Portfolio Turnover (%)	61	28	16	24	—	—	—	—	—	—
Total Assets (Millions $) ...	107	66	54	18	—	—	—	—	—	—

PORTFOLIO (as of 9/30/93)

Portfolio Manager: Michael Oliver - 1989, Dean Sotter - 1993

Investm't Category: Growth

Cap Gain	Asset Allocation
✔ Cap & Income	Fund of Funds
Income	Index
	✔ Sector
✔ Domestic	Small Cap
Foreign	Socially Conscious
Country/Region	State Specific

Portfolio:	stocks 90%	bonds 0%
convertibles 4%	other 1%	cash 5%

Largest Holdings: real estate investment trusts 90%, convertible bonds 4%

Unrealized Net Capital Gains: 17% of portfolio value

SHAREHOLDER INFORMATION

Minimum Investment
Initial: $2,000   Subsequent: $0

Minimum IRA Investment
Initial: $2,000   Subsequent: $0

Maximum Fees
Load: none   12b-1: none
Other: none

Distributions
Income: quarterly   Capital Gains: Dec

Exchange Options
Number Per Year: none   Fee: na
Telephone: na

Services
IRA

Preferred Asset Allocation (PFAAX)

Balanced

100 N. Adams Street
Peoria, IL 61629
(800) 662-4769, (309) 675-1000

PERFORMANCE

	3yr Annual	5yr Annual	10yr Annual	Bull	Bear
Return (%)	na	na	na	na	na
Differ from Category (+/-)	na	na	na	na	na

Total Risk	Standard Deviation	Category Risk	Risk Index	Beta
na	na	na	na	na

	1993	1992	1991	1990	1989	1988	1987	1986	1985	1984
Return (%)	10.5	—	—	—	—	—	—	—	—	—
Differ from category (+/-)	-2.9	—	—	—	—	—	—	—	—	—

PER SHARE DATA

	1993	1992	1991	1990	1989	1988	1987	1986	1985	1984
Dividends, Net Income ($)	0.31	—	—	—	—	—	—	—	—	—
Distrib'ns, Cap Gain ($)	0.21	—	—	—	—	—	—	—	—	—
Net Asset Value ($)	11.02	—	—	—	—	—	—	—	—	—
Expense Ratio (%)	1.27	—	—	—	—	—	—	—	—	—
Net Income to Assets (%)	3.25	—	—	—	—	—	—	—	—	—
Portfolio Turnover (%)	34	—	—	—	—	—	—	—	—	—
Total Assets (Millions $)	56	—	—	—	—	—	—	—	—	—

PORTFOLIO (as of 6/30/93)

Portfolio Manager: R. Jackson - 1992, T. Hazuka - 1992, E. Peters - 1992

Investm't Category: Balanced

Cap Gain	✔ Asset Allocation
✔ Cap & Income	Fund of Funds
Income	Index
	Sector
✔ Domestic	Small Cap
✔ Foreign	Socially Conscious
Country/Region	State Specific

Portfolio: stocks 59% bonds 34%
convertibles 0% other 0% cash 7%

Largest Holdings: bonds—U.S. government 34%, stocks—fuel 6%

Unrealized Net Capital Gains: 6% of portfolio value

SHAREHOLDER INFORMATION

Minimum Investment
Initial: $1,000   Subsequent: $50

Minimum IRA Investment
Initial: $250   Subsequent: $50

Maximum Fees
Load: none   12b-1: none
Other: none

Distributions
Income: Jun, Dec   Capital Gains: Dec

Exchange Options
Number Per Year: no limit   Fee: none
Telephone: yes (money market fund available)

Services
IRA, other pension, auto invest, auto withdraw

Preferred Fixed Income

(PFXIX)

General Bond

100 N. Adams Street
Peoria, IL 61629
(800) 662-4769, (309) 675-1000

PERFORMANCE

	3yr Annual	5yr Annual	10yr Annual	Bull	Bear
Return (%)	na	na	na	na	na
Differ from Category (+/-)	na	na	na	na	na

Total Risk	Standard Deviation	Category Risk	Risk Index	Avg Mat
na	na	na	na	7.7 yrs

	1993	1992	1991	1990	1989	1988	1987	1986	1985	1984
Return (%)	10.3	—	—	—	—	—	—	—	—	—
Differ from category (+/-) ...	1.1	—	—	—	—	—	—	—	—	—

PER SHARE DATA

	1993	1992	1991	1990	1989	1988	1987	1986	1985	1984
Dividends, Net Income ($) .	0.48	—	—	—	—	—	—	—	—	—
Distrib'ns, Cap Gain ($)	0.30	—	—	—	—	—	—	—	—	—
Net Asset Value ($)	10.34	—	—	—	—	—	—	—	—	—
Expense Ratio (%)........	1.05	—	—	—	—	—	—	—	—	—
Net Income to Assets (%)..	4.91	—	—	—	—	—	—	—	—	—
Portfolio Turnover (%)....	316	—	—	—	—	—	—	—	—	—
Total Assets (Millions $)	43	—	—	—	—	—	—	—	—	—

PORTFOLIO (as of 6/30/93)

Portfolio Manager: Edward P. Scovell - 1992, Laurence R. Smith - 1992

Investm't Category: General Bond

Cap Gain	Asset Allocation
Cap & Income	Fund of Funds
✔ Income	Index
	Sector
✔ Domestic	Small Cap
✔ Foreign	Socially Conscious
Country/Region	State Specific

Portfolio: stocks 0%   bonds 79%
convertibles 0%   other 0%   cash 21%

Largest Holdings: U.S. government 32%, corporate 27%

Unrealized Net Capital Gains: 3% of portfolio value

SHAREHOLDER INFORMATION

Minimum Investment
Initial: $1,000   Subsequent: $50

Minimum IRA Investment
Initial: $250   Subsequent: $50

Maximum Fees
Load: none   12b-1: none
Other: none

Distributions
Income: monthly   Capital Gains: Dec

Exchange Options
Number Per Year: no limit   Fee: none
Telephone: yes (money market fund available)

Services
IRA, other pension, auto invest, auto withdraw

Preferred Growth (PFGRX)

Growth

100 N. Adams Street
Peoria, IL 61629
(800) 662-4769, (309) 675-1000

PERFORMANCE

	3yr Annual	5yr Annual	10yr Annual	Bull	Bear
Return (%)	na	na	na	na	na
Differ from Category (+/-)	na	na	na	na	na

Total Risk	Standard Deviation	Category Risk	Risk Index	Beta
na	na	na	na	na

	1993	1992	1991	1990	1989	1988	1987	1986	1985	1984
Return (%).............	16.0	—	—	—	—	—	—	—	—	—
Differ from category (+/-)...	2.8	—	—	—	—	—	—	—	—	—

PER SHARE DATA

	1993	1992	1991	1990	1989	1988	1987	1986	1985	1984
Dividends, Net Income ($).	0.00	—	—	—	—	—	—	—	—	—
Distrib'ns, Cap Gain ($) ...	0.00	—	—	—	—	—	—	—	—	—
Net Asset Value ($)	13.82	—	—	—	—	—	—	—	—	—
Expense Ratio (%)	1.00	—	—	—	—	—	—	—	—	—
Net Income to Assets (%) .	0.07	—	—	—	—	—	—	—	—	—
Portfolio Turnover (%).....	58	—	—	—	—	—	—	—	—	—
Total Assets (Millions $)....	152	—	—	—	—	—	—	—	—	—

PORTFOLIO (as of 6/30/93)

Portfolio Manager: Lulu C. Wang - 1992

Investm't Category: Growth

✔ Cap Gain	Asset Allocation
Cap & Income	Fund of Funds
Income	Index
	Sector
✔ Domestic	Small Cap
✔ Foreign	Socially Conscious
Country/Region	State Specific

Portfolio: stocks 99% bonds 0%
convertibles 0% other 0% cash 1%

Largest Holdings: office equipment & computers 21%, discount/fashion retailing 13%

Unrealized Net Capital Gains: 17% of portfolio value

SHAREHOLDER INFORMATION

Minimum Investment
Initial: $1,000   Subsequent: $50

Minimum IRA Investment
Initial: $250   Subsequent: $50

Maximum Fees
Load: none   12b-1: none
Other: none

Distributions
Income: Dec   Capital Gains: Dec

Exchange Options
Number Per Year: no limit   Fee: none
Telephone: yes (money market fund available)

Services
IRA, other pension, auto invest, auto withdraw

Preferred International
(PFIFX)
International Stock

100 N. Adams Street
Peoria, IL 61629
(800) 662-4769, (309) 675-1000

PERFORMANCE

	3yr Annual	5yr Annual	10yr Annual	Bull	Bear
Return (%)	na	na	na	na	na
Differ from Category (+/-)	na	na	na	na	na

Total Risk	Standard Deviation	Category Risk	Risk Index	Beta
na	na	na	na	na

	1993	1992	1991	1990	1989	1988	1987	1986	1985	1984
Return (%)	41.5	—	—	—	—	—	—	—	—	—
Differ from category (+/-) . . .	3.0	—	—	—	—	—	—	—	—	—

PER SHARE DATA

	1993	1992	1991	1990	1989	1988	1987	1986	1985	1984
Dividends, Net Income ($) .	0.07	—	—	—	—	—	—	—	—	—
Distrib'ns, Cap Gain ($) . . .	0.05	—	—	—	—	—	—	—	—	—
Net Asset Value ($)	11.75	—	—	—	—	—	—	—	—	—
Expense Ratio (%)	1.60	—	—	—	—	—	—	—	—	—
Net Income to Assets (%) . .	1.83	—	—	—	—	—	—	—	—	—
Portfolio Turnover (%)	16	—	—	—	—	—	—	—	—	—
Total Assets (Millions $)	73	—	—	—	—	—	—	—	—	—

PORTFOLIO (as of 6/30/93)

Portfolio Manager: Peter F. Spano - 1992

Investm't Category: International Stock
- ✔ Cap Gain
- Cap & Income
- Income
- Domestic
- ✔ Foreign
- Country/Region
- Asset Allocation
- Fund of Funds
- Index
- Sector
- Small Cap
- Socially Conscious
- State Specific

Portfolio: stocks 96% bonds 0%
convertibles 0% other 0% cash 4%

Largest Holdings: United Kingdom 14%,
France 11%

Unrealized Net Capital Gains: -2% of portfolio value

SHAREHOLDER INFORMATION

Minimum Investment
Initial: $1,000 Subsequent: $50

Minimum IRA Investment
Initial: $250 Subsequent: $50

Maximum Fees
Load: none 12b-1: none
Other: none

Distributions
Income: Dec Capital Gains: Dec

Exchange Options
Number Per Year: no limit Fee: none
Telephone: yes (money market fund available)

Services
IRA, other pension, auto invest, auto withdraw

Preferred Short-Term Gov't Securities (PFSGX)

General Bond

100 N. Adams Street
Peoria, IL 61629
(800) 662-4769, (309) 675-1000

PERFORMANCE

	3yr Annual	5yr Annual	10yr Annual	Bull	Bear
Return (%)	na	na	na	na	na
Differ from Category (+/-)	na	na	na	na	na

Total Risk	Standard Deviation	Category Risk	Risk Index	Avg Mat
na	na	na	na	2.2 yrs

	1993	1992	1991	1990	1989	1988	1987	1986	1985	1984
Return (%)	5.5	—	—	—	—	—	—	—	—	—
Differ from category (+/-)	-3.7	—	—	—	—	—	—	—	—	—

PER SHARE DATA

	1993	1992	1991	1990	1989	1988	1987	1986	1985	1984
Dividends, Net Income ($)	0.38	—	—	—	—	—	—	—	—	—
Distrib'ns, Cap Gain ($)	0.02	—	—	—	—	—	—	—	—	—
Net Asset Value ($)	10.06	—	—	—	—	—	—	—	—	—
Expense Ratio (%)	0.78	—	—	—	—	—	—	—	—	—
Net Income to Assets (%)	3.87	—	—	—	—	—	—	—	—	—
Portfolio Turnover (%)	268	—	—	—	—	—	—	—	—	—
Total Assets (Millions $)	30	—	—	—	—	—	—	—	—	—

PORTFOLIO (as of 6/30/93)

Portfolio Manager: J.S. Orr - 1992, P.M. Pond - 1992, T.M. Sheridan - 1992

Investm't Category: General Bond
Cap Gain	Asset Allocation
Cap & Income	Fund of Funds
✔ Income	Index
	Sector
✔ Domestic	Small Cap
Foreign	Socially Conscious
Country/Region	State Specific

Portfolio: stocks 0%   bonds 69%
convertibles 0%   other 0%   cash 31%

Largest Holdings: U.S. government & agencies 55%, mortgage-backed 13%

Unrealized Net Capital Gains: 0% of portfolio value

SHAREHOLDER INFORMATION

Minimum Investment
Initial: $1,000   Subsequent: $50

Minimum IRA Investment
Initial: $250   Subsequent: $50

Maximum Fees
Load: none   12b-1: none
Other: none

Distributions
Income: monthly   Capital Gains: Dec

Exchange Options
Number Per Year: no limit   Fee: none
Telephone: yes (money market fund available)

Services
IRA, other pension, auto invest, auto withdraw

Preferred Value (PFVLX)

Growth & Income

100 N. Adams Street
Peoria, IL 61629
(800) 662-4769, (309) 675-1000

PERFORMANCE

	3yr Annual	5yr Annual	10yr Annual	Bull	Bear
Return (%)	na	na	na	na	na
Differ from Category (+/-)	na	na	na	na	na

Total Risk	Standard Deviation	Category Risk	Risk Index	Beta
na	na	na	na	na

	1993	1992	1991	1990	1989	1988	1987	1986	1985	1984
Return (%)	8.7	—	—	—	—	—	—	—	—	—
Differ from category (+/-) ..	-3.9	—	—	—	—	—	—	—	—	—

PER SHARE DATA

	1993	1992	1991	1990	1989	1988	1987	1986	1985	1984
Dividends, Net Income ($) .	0.16	—	—	—	—	—	—	—	—	—
Distrib'ns, Cap Gain ($) ...	0.10	—	—	—	—	—	—	—	—	—
Net Asset Value ($)	11.56	—	—	—	—	—	—	—	—	—
Expense Ratio (%)........	0.96	—	—	—	—	—	—	—	—	—
Net Income to Assets (%)..	1.79	—	—	—	—	—	—	—	—	—
Portfolio Turnover (%)	17	—	—	—	—	—	—	—	—	—
Total Assets (Millions $) ...	126	—	—	—	—	—	—	—	—	—

PORTFOLIO (as of 6/30/93)

Portfolio Manager: John G. Lindenthal - 1992

Investm't Category: Growth & Income

Cap Gain	Asset Allocation
✔ Cap & Income	Fund of Funds
Income	Index
	Sector
✔ Domestic	Small Cap
✔ Foreign	Socially Conscious
Country/Region	State Specific

Portfolio: stocks 90% bonds 0%
convertibles 0% other 0% cash 10%

Largest Holdings: non-bank financial 22%, health care 12%

Unrealized Net Capital Gains: 11% of portfolio value

SHAREHOLDER INFORMATION

Minimum Investment
Initial: $1,000   Subsequent: $50

Minimum IRA Investment
Initial: $250   Subsequent: $50

Maximum Fees
Load: none   12b-1: none
Other: none

Distributions
Income: Dec   Capital Gains: Dec

Exchange Options
Number Per Year: no limit   Fee: none
Telephone: yes (money market fund available)

Services
IRA, other pension, auto invest, auto withdraw

Primary Trend (PTFDX)

Growth & Income

First Financial Centre
700 N. Water St.
Milwaukee, WI 53202
(800) 443-6544, (414) 271-2726

PERFORMANCE

	3yr Annual	5yr Annual	10yr Annual	Bull	Bear
Return (%)	10.1	7.3	na	42.6	-8.0
Differ from Category (+/-)	-6.3 low	-5.2 low	na	-27.5 low	3.6 abv av

Total Risk	Standard Deviation	Category Risk	Risk Index	Beta
av	8.0%	low	0.9	0.6

	1993	1992	1991	1990	1989	1988	1987	1986	1985	1984
Return (%).	11.4	0.2	19.5	-1.7	8.9	18.3	3.6	—	—	—
Differ from category (+/-). . .	-1.2	-9.8	-8.2	3.9	-12.7	1.5	3.2	—	—	—

PER SHARE DATA

	1993	1992	1991	1990	1989	1988	1987	1986	1985	1984
Dividends, Net Income ($).	0.07	0.28	0.41	0.56	0.31	0.56	0.34	—	—	—
Distrib'ns, Cap Gain ($) . . .	0.12	0.86	0.28	0.68	0.30	0.10	0.07	—	—	—
Net Asset Value ($)	11.25	10.29	11.38	10.13	11.60	11.19	10.02	—	—	—
Expense Ratio (%)	1.20	1.10	1.20	1.10	1.10	1.20	1.30	—	—	—
Net Income to Assets (%) .	1.90	2.50	4.70	3.80	2.00	6.40	3.90	—	—	—
Portfolio Turnover (%).	40	66	77	32	30	17	20	—	—	—
Total Assets (Millions $). . . .	24	32	33	39	56	45	31	—	—	—

PORTFOLIO (as of 5/31/93)

Portfolio Manager: David Aushwitz - 1989

Investm't Category: Growth & Income
Cap Gain	Asset Allocation
✔ Cap & Income	Fund of Funds
Income	Index
	Sector
✔ Domestic	Small Cap
Foreign	Socially Conscious
Country/Region	State Specific

Portfolio: stocks 61%   bonds 4%
convertibles 0%   other 0%   cash 35%

Largest Holdings: oil & gas 12%, gold 4%

Unrealized Net Capital Gains: 5% of portfolio value

SHAREHOLDER INFORMATION

Minimum Investment
Initial: $2,500   Subsequent: $100

Minimum IRA Investment
Initial: $2,000   Subsequent: $100

Maximum Fees
Load: none   12b-1: none
Other: none

Distributions
Income: Aug, Dec   Capital Gains: Aug, Dec

Exchange Options
Number Per Year: 5   Fee: $5 (telephone)
Telephone: yes (money market fund available)

Services
IRA, other pension, auto exchange, auto invest, auto withdraw

Prudent Speculator

(PSLFX)

Aggressive Growth

P.O. Box 75231
Los Angeles, CA 90075
(800) 444-4778, (213) 778-7732

PERFORMANCE

	3yr Annual	5yr Annual	10yr Annual	Bull	Bear
Return (%)	19.4	0.6	na	88.7	-43.5
Differ from Category (+/-)	-6.0 blw av	-17.5 low	na	-36.3 blw av	-28.5 low

Total Risk	Standard Deviation	Category Risk	Risk Index	Beta
high	24.2%	high	1.6	1.1

	1993	1992	1991	1990	1989	1988	1987	1986	1985	1984
Return (%)	3.1	0.8	63.7	-37.5	-2.5	12.7	—	—	—	—
Differ from category (+/-) .	-15.9	-9.5	11.3	-31.2	-29.5	-2.5	—	—	—	—

PER SHARE DATA

	1993	1992	1991	1990	1989	1988	1987	1986	1985	1984
Dividends, Net Income ($) .	0.00	0.00	0.00	0.00	0.00	0.04	—	—	—	—
Distrib'ns, Cap Gain ($) . . .	0.34	0.31	0.00	0.00	0.00	0.00	—	—	—	—
Net Asset Value ($)	6.94	7.08	7.32	4.47	7.16	7.35	—	—	—	—
Expense Ratio (%).	4.17	3.83	4.09	7.42	4.26	2.81	—	—	—	—
Net Income to Assets (%) .	-3.89	-3.48	-3.20	-5.90	-1.37	-0.08	—	—	—	—
Portfolio Turnover (%)	36	81	107	108	88	20	—	—	—	—
Total Assets ($)	na	9	16	4	8	10	—	—	—	—

PORTFOLIO (as of 4/30/93)

Portfolio Manager: Edwin R. Bernstein - 1989

Investm't Category: Aggressive Growth
- ✔ Cap Gain
- Cap & Income
- Income
- Asset Allocation
- Fund of Funds
- Index
- Sector
- ✔ Domestic
- Foreign
- Country/Region
- ✔ Small Cap
- Socially Conscious
- State Specific

Portfolio: stocks 95% bonds 0%
convertibles 0% other 0% cash 5%

Largest Holdings: medical products 14%,
manufacturing 11%

Unrealized Net Capital Gains: 11% of portfolio value

SHAREHOLDER INFORMATION

Minimum Investment
Initial: $500   Subsequent: $100

Minimum IRA Investment
Initial: $500   Subsequent: $100

Maximum Fees
Load: none   12b-1: 0.25%
Other: none

Distributions
Income: Dec   Capital Gains: Dec

Exchange Options
Number Per Year: 6   Fee: none
Telephone: yes (money market fund available)

Services
IRA, other pension, auto invest, auto withdraw

Prudential Gov't Securities Interm Term

One Seaport Plaza
New York, NY 10292
(800) 225-1852, (908) 417-7555

(PBGVX)   *Government Bond*

PERFORMANCE

	3yr Annual	5yr Annual	10yr Annual	Bull	Bear
Return (%)	8.7	9.0	na	34.1	3.5
Differ from Category (+/-)	-2.1 blw av	-1.4 blw av	na	-12.1 blw av	3.0 av

Total Risk	Standard Deviation	Category Risk	Risk Index	Avg Mat
low	3.0%	blw av	0.7	3.8 yrs

	1993	1992	1991	1990	1989	1988	1987	1986	1985	1984
Return (%)	7.1	6.1	13.1	8.1	11.2	6.1	2.6	—	—	—
Differ from category (+/-). . .	-3.3	-0.1	-1.9	1.6	-2.7	-1.5	4.4	—	—	—

PER SHARE DATA

	1993	1992	1991	1990	1989	1988	1987	1986	1985	1984
Dividends, Net Income ($).	0.69	0.74	0.83	0.85	0.90	0.92	0.87	—	—	—
Distrib'ns, Cap Gain ($) . . .	0.00	0.00	0.00	0.04	0.00	0.10	0.07	—	—	—
Net Asset Value ($)	10.03	10.02	10.17	9.78	9.92	9.75	10.16	—	—	—
Expense Ratio (%)	0.80	0.79	0.79	0.88	0.86	0.83	0.72	—	—	—
Net Income to Assets (%) .	6.83	7.47	8.36	8.60	9.16	9.39	8.30	—	—	—
Portfolio Turnover (%).	na	60	151	68	186	28	59	—	—	—
Total Assets (Millions $). . . .	343	304	298	328	396	474	634	—	—	—

PORTFOLIO (as of 5/31/93)

Portfolio Manager: Kay Wilcox - 1991

Investm't Category: Government Bond

Cap Gain	Asset Allocation
Cap & Income	Fund of Funds
✔ Income	Index
	Sector
✔ Domestic	Small Cap
Foreign	Socially Conscious
Country/Region	State Specific

Portfolio: stocks 0%   bonds 95%
convertibles 0%   other 0%   cash 5%

Largest Holdings: U. S. government 89%, mortgage-backed 6%

Unrealized Net Capital Gains: 2% of portfolio value

SHAREHOLDER INFORMATION

Minimum Investment
Initial: $1,000   Subsequent: $100

Minimum IRA Investment
Initial: $0   Subsequent: $0

Maximum Fees
Load: none   12b-1: 0.25%
Other: none

Distributions
Income: monthly   Capital Gains: Dec

Exchange Options
Number Per Year: no limit   Fee: none
Telephone: yes (money market fund available)

Services
IRA, other pension, auto exchange, auto invest, auto withdraw

Rainbow (RBOWX)

Growth

255 Park Avenue
Suite 209
New York, NY 10169
(212) 983-2980

PERFORMANCE

	3yr Annual	5yr Annual	10yr Annual	Bull	Bear
Return (%)	8.5	4.7	6.6	33.0	-13.0
Differ from Category (+/-)	-10.7 low	-9.9 low	-6.0 low	-51.7 low	-0.6 av

Total Risk	Standard Deviation	Category Risk	Risk Index	Beta
abv av	12.9%	abv av	1.2	0.9

	1993	1992	1991	1990	1989	1988	1987	1986	1985	1984
Return (%)	-4.6	-2.6	37.9	-9.6	9.2	18.0	-4.0	15.8	20.6	-4.9
Differ from category (+/-) .	-17.8	-13.6	2.5	-3.5	-16.6	0.3	-5.2	1.3	-8.7	-4.9

PER SHARE DATA

	1993	1992	1991	1990	1989	1988	1987	1986	1985	1984
Dividends, Net Income ($)	0.00	0.00	0.05	0.00	0.44	0.00	0.13	0.00	0.00	0.00
Distrib'ns, Cap Gain ($) . . .	0.35	0.00	0.47	0.00	0.17	0.00	0.69	0.00	0.00	0.00
Net Asset Value ($)	5.21	5.84	6.00	4.76	5.27	5.36	4.54	5.41	4.67	3.87
Expense Ratio (%).	2.86	2.66	2.84	3.41	3.22	3.53	3.27	—	—	—
Net Income to Assets (%) .	-0.01	-0.05	0.19	0.10	1.11	-0.20	-0.85	—	—	—
Portfolio Turnover (%)	81	81	103	212	193	133	113	—	—	—
Total Assets (Millions $)	1	2	3	2	2	2	2	—	—	—

PORTFOLIO (as of 4/30/93)

Portfolio Manager: Robert Furman - 1974

Investm't Category: Growth

- ✔ Cap Gain
- Cap & Income
- Income
- ✔ Domestic
- ✔ Foreign
- Country/Region

- Asset Allocation
- Fund of Funds
- Index
- Sector
- Small Cap
- Socially Conscious
- State Specific

Portfolio: stocks 100% bonds 0%
convertibles 0% other 0% cash 0%

Largest Holdings: bank & financial services
13%, textile manufacturers 13%

Unrealized Net Capital Gains: 4% of portfolio value

SHAREHOLDER INFORMATION

Minimum Investment
Initial: $300   Subsequent: $50

Minimum IRA Investment
Initial: $300   Subsequent: $50

Maximum Fees
Load: none   12b-1: none
Other: none

Distributions
Income: Dec   Capital Gains: Dec

Exchange Options
Number Per Year: none   Fee: na
Telephone: na

Services
IRA

Regis ICM Small Company Port (ICSCX)

Growth

P.O. Box 2798
Boston, MA 02208
(800) 638-7983

PERFORMANCE

	3yr Annual	5yr Annual	10yr Annual	Bull	Bear
Return (%)	33.8	na	na	164.8	-16.1
Differ from Category (+/-)	14.6 high	na	na	80.2 high	-3.7 blw av

Total Risk	Standard Deviation	Category Risk	Risk Index	Beta
abv av	12.6%	abv av	1.2	0.8

	1993	1992	1991	1990	1989	1988	1987	1986	1985	1984
Return (%)	21.9	32.2	48.6	-7.3	—	—	—	—	—	—
Differ from category (+/-) . . .	8.7	21.2	13.2	-1.2	—	—	—	—	—	—

PER SHARE DATA

	1993	1992	1991	1990	1989	1988	1987	1986	1985	1984
Dividends, Net Income ($).	0.07	0.09	0.14	0.14	—	—	—	—	—	—
Distrib'ns, Cap Gain ($) . . .	2.33	1.16	0.36	0.00	—	—	—	—	—	—
Net Asset Value ($)	16.57	15.60	12.75	8.92	—	—	—	—	—	—
Expense Ratio (%)	0.97	0.95	1.02	1.14	—	—	—	—	—	—
Net Income to Assets (%) .	0.49	0.77	1.32	1.52	—	—	—	—	—	—
Portfolio Turnover (%).	47	34	49	40	—	—	—	—	—	—
Total Assets (Millions $).	92	58	44	19	—	—	—	—	—	—

PORTFOLIO (as of 4/30/93)

Portfolio Manager: Robert D. McDorman Jr. - 1989

Investm't Category: Growth

✔ Cap Gain	Asset Allocation
Cap & Income	Fund of Funds
Income	Index
	Sector
✔ Domestic	✔ Small Cap
Foreign	Socially Conscious
Country/Region	State Specific

Portfolio: stocks 94% bonds 0%
convertibles 0% other 0% cash 6%

Largest Holdings: technology 17%, basic industries 10%

Unrealized Net Capital Gains: 26% of portfolio value

SHAREHOLDER INFORMATION

Minimum Investment
Initial: $100,000 Subsequent: $1,000

Minimum IRA Investment
Initial: na Subsequent: na

Maximum Fees
Load: none 12b-1: none
Other: none

Distributions
Income: quarterly Capital Gains: Dec

Exchange Options
Number Per Year: no limit Fee: none
Telephone: yes (money market fund not available)

Services

Reich & Tang Equity

(RCHTX)

Growth

100 Park Ave.
New York, NY 10017
(212) 476-5050

PERFORMANCE

	3yr Annual	5yr Annual	10yr Annual	Bull	Bear
Return (%)	17.6	12.5	na	82.3	-15.7
Differ from Category (+/-)	-1.6 blw av	-2.1 blw av	na	-2.4 av	-3.3 blw av

Total Risk	Standard Deviation	Category Risk	Risk Index	Beta
av	9.9%	low	0.9	0.8

	1993	1992	1991	1990	1989	1988	1987	1986	1985	1984
Return (%)	13.8	16.3	23.0	-5.8	17.8	22.8	5.1	14.6	—	—
Differ from category (+/-) . . .	0.6	5.3	-12.4	0.3	-8.0	5.1	3.9	0.1	—	—

PER SHARE DATA

	1993	1992	1991	1990	1989	1988	1987	1986	1985	1984
Dividends, Net Income ($) .	0.20	0.22	0.36	0.36	0.44	0.44	0.40	0.28	—	—
Distrib'ns, Cap Gain ($) . . .	1.43	1.03	0.02	0.00	1.93	1.53	1.78	0.62	—	—
Net Asset Value ($)	17.61	16.92	15.64	13.05	14.24	14.11	13.11	14.50	—	—
Expense Ratio (%).	1.15	1.15	1.14	1.12	1.10	1.11	1.11	1.21	—	—
Net Income to Assets (%). .	1.15	1.35	2.33	2.56	2.68	2.87	2.07	2.51	—	—
Portfolio Turnover (%).	25	27	43	27	48	27	43	35	—	—
Total Assets (Millions $) . . .	109	93	83	97	112	102	102	110	—	—

PORTFOLIO (as of 12/31/93)

Portfolio Manager: Hoerle - 1985,
Wilson - 1985, Delafield - 1992, Sellecchia - 1992

Investm't Category: Growth
✔ Cap Gain   Asset Allocation
  Cap & Income   Fund of Funds
  Income   Index
                    Sector
✔ Domestic   Small Cap
✔ Foreign   Socially Conscious
  Country/Region   State Specific

Portfolio: stocks 96%   bonds 0%
convertibles 0%   other 0%   cash 4%

Largest Holdings: industrial products 19%, insurance 10%

Unrealized Net Capital Gains: 25% of portfolio value

SHAREHOLDER INFORMATION

Minimum Investment
Initial: $5,000   Subsequent: $0

Minimum IRA Investment
Initial: $250   Subsequent: $0

Maximum Fees
Load: none   12b-1: 0.05%
Other: none

Distributions
Income: quarterly   Capital Gains: Dec

Exchange Options
Number Per Year: no limit   Fee: none
Telephone: yes (money market fund available)

Services
IRA, other pension, auto withdraw

Reynolds Blue Chip Growth (RBCGX)

Growth & Income

Wood Island, 3rd Fl.
80 E. Sir Francis Drake Blvd.
Larkspur, CA 94939
(800) 338-1579, (415) 461-7860

PERFORMANCE

	3yr Annual	5yr Annual	10yr Annual	Bull	Bear
Return (%)	8.8	9.2	na	37.5	-6.2
Differ from Category (+/-)	-7.6 low	-3.3 low	na	-32.6 low	5.4 high

Total Risk	Standard Deviation	Category Risk	Risk Index	Beta
abv av	13.0%	high	1.5	1.0

	1993	1992	1991	1990	1989	1988	1987	1986	1985	1984
Return (%)	-5.2	0.0	35.9	0.0	20.6	—	—	—	—	—
Differ from category (+/-)	-17.8	-10.0	8.2	5.6	-1.0	—	—	—	—	—

PER SHARE DATA

	1993	1992	1991	1990	1989	1988	1987	1986	1985	1984
Dividends, Net Income ($)	0.13	0.08	0.08	0.14	0.15	—	—	—	—	—
Distrib'ns, Cap Gain ($)	0.00	0.00	0.00	0.00	0.04	—	—	—	—	—
Net Asset Value ($)	14.82	15.78	15.86	11.74	11.88	—	—	—	—	—
Expense Ratio (%)	0.66	1.50	1.70	2.10	2.00	—	—	—	—	—
Net Income to Assets (%)	2.67	0.60	1.20	0.80	2.70	—	—	—	—	—
Portfolio Turnover (%)	na	0	1	66	33	—	—	—	—	—
Total Assets (Millions $)	38	41	28	10	5	—	—	—	—	—

PORTFOLIO (as of 3/31/93)

Portfolio Manager: Frederick Reynolds - 1988

Investm't Category: Growth & Income
Cap Gain	Asset Allocation
✔ Cap & Income	Fund of Funds
Income	Index
	Sector
✔ Domestic	Small Cap
Foreign	Socially Conscious
Country/Region	State Specific

Portfolio: stocks 96%   bonds 0%
convertibles 0%   other 1%   cash 4%

Largest Holdings: drugs 16%, food 13%

Unrealized Net Capital Gains: 16% of portfolio value

SHAREHOLDER INFORMATION

Minimum Investment
Initial: $1,000   Subsequent: $100

Minimum IRA Investment
Initial: $1,000   Subsequent: $100

Maximum Fees
Load: none   12b-1: none
Other: none

Distributions
Income: Dec   Capital Gains: Dec

Exchange Options
Number Per Year: no limit   Fee: none
Telephone: yes (money market fund available)

Services
IRA, other pension, auto exchange, auto invest, auto withdraw

Rightime (RTFDX)

Growth

Forst Pavilion
Suite 3000
Wyncote, PA 19095
(800) 242-1421, (215) 887-8111

PERFORMANCE

	3yr Annual	5yr Annual	10yr Annual	Bull	Bear
Return (%)	13.1	10.2	na	44.3	0.8
Differ from Category (+/-)	-6.1 low	-4.4 low	na	-40.4 low	13.3 high

Total Risk	Standard Deviation	Category Risk	Risk Index	Beta
abv av	11.4%	av	1.1	0.9

	1993	1992	1991	1990	1989	1988	1987	1986	1985	1984
Return (%)	6.7	3.6	30.8	0.6	11.8	-1.3	19.1	10.6	—	—
Differ from category (+/-)	-6.5	-7.4	-4.6	6.7	-14.0	-19.0	17.9	-3.9	—	—

PER SHARE DATA

	1993	1992	1991	1990	1989	1988	1987	1986	1985	1984
Dividends, Net Income ($)	0.00	0.05	0.17	0.61	0.34	0.14	0.67	0.23	—	—
Distrib'ns, Cap Gain ($)	1.27	2.38	4.68	1.46	0.00	0.77	3.97	1.94	—	—
Net Asset Value ($)	35.32	34.29	35.43	30.93	32.79	29.64	30.97	29.80	—	—
Expense Ratio (%)	2.54	2.56	2.67	2.67	2.58	2.58	2.55	2.77	—	—
Net Income to Assets (%)	-0.41	0.12	0.45	1.52	0.14	0.53	1.20	-1.63	—	—
Portfolio Turnover (%)	na	73	136	383	168	187	166	231	—	—
Total Assets (Millions $)	165	171	163	134	167	235	211	145	—	—

PORTFOLIO (as of 4/30/93)

Portfolio Manager: David Rights - 1986

Investm't Category: Growth

✔ Cap Gain	Asset Allocation
Cap & Income	✔ Fund of Funds
Income	Index
	Sector
✔ Domestic	Small Cap
Foreign	Socially Conscious
Country/Region	State Specific

Portfolio: stocks 0%   bonds 0%
convertibles 0%   other 81%   cash 19%

Largest Holdings: 20th Century Growth Fund 5%, 20th Century Select Fund 5%

Unrealized Net Capital Gains: 4% of portfolio value

SHAREHOLDER INFORMATION

Minimum Investment
Initial: $2,000   Subsequent: $100

Minimum IRA Investment
Initial: $2,000   Subsequent: $0

Maximum Fees
Load: none   12b-1: 0.75%
Other: none

Distributions
Income: Dec   Capital Gains: Dec

Exchange Options
Number Per Year: no limit   Fee: none
Telephone: yes (money market fund available)

Services
IRA, other pension, auto withdraw

Robertson Stephens
Emerging Growth (RSEGX)

Aggressive Growth

555 California Street
Suite 2600
San Francisco, CA 94104
(800) 766-3863

PERFORMANCE

	3yr Annual	5yr Annual	10yr Annual	Bull	Bear
Return (%)	18.3	21.2	na	95.7	-7.1
Differ from Category (+/-)	-7.1 low	3.0 abv av	na	-29.3 blw av	7.9 high

Total Risk	Standard Deviation	Category Risk	Risk Index	Beta
high	23.4%	high	1.5	1.4

	1993	1992	1991	1990	1989	1988	1987	1986	1985	1984
Return (%).	7.2	-2.5	58.7	9.5	44.4	14.0	—	—	—	—
Differ from category (+/-). .	-11.8	-12.9	6.3	15.8	17.4	-1.2	—	—	—	—

PER SHARE DATA

	1993	1992	1991	1990	1989	1988	1987	1986	1985	1984
Dividends, Net Income ($).	0.00	0.00	0.00	0.00	0.00	0.00	—	—	—	—
Distrib'ns, Cap Gain ($) . . .	0.00	0.27	0.89	0.86	1.60	0.00	—	—	—	—
Net Asset Value ($)	17.98	16.77	17.50	11.67	11.46	9.09	—	—	—	—
Expense Ratio (%)	1.60	1.49	1.59	1.88	2.15	2.85	—	—	—	—
Net Income to Assets (%) .	-0.53	-0.92	-0.68	-0.02	-0.75	-2.44	—	—	—	—
Portfolio Turnover (%).	114	124	147	272	236	139	—	—	—	—
Total Assets (Millions $). . . .	166	277	142	23	13	8	—	—	—	—

PORTFOLIO (as of 9/30/93)

Portfolio Manager: Bob Czepiel - 1987

Investm't Category: Aggressive Growth
- ✔ Cap Gain
- Cap & Income
- Income
- ✔ Domestic
- Foreign
- Country/Region
- Asset Allocation
- Fund of Funds
- Index
- Sector
- ✔ Small Cap
- Socially Conscious
- State Specific

Portfolio:	stocks 96%	bonds 0%
convertibles 0%	other 0%	cash 4%

Largest Holdings: computer software 18%, semiconductors 13%

Unrealized Net Capital Gains: 17% of portfolio value

SHAREHOLDER INFORMATION

Minimum Investment
Initial: $5,000   Subsequent: $100

Minimum IRA Investment
Initial: $1,000   Subsequent: $1

Maximum Fees
Load: none   12b-1: 0.25%
Other: none

Distributions
Income: Dec   Capital Gains: Dec

Exchange Options
Number Per Year: no limit   Fee: none
Telephone: yes (money market fund not available)

Services
IRA, other pension, auto invest, auto withdraw

Robertson Stephens Value Plus (RSVPX)

Aggressive Growth

555 California Street
Suite 2600
San Francisco, CA 94104
(800) 766-3863

PERFORMANCE

	3yr Annual	5yr Annual	10yr Annual	Bull	Bear
Return (%)	na	na	na	na	na
Differ from Category (+/-)	na	na	na	na	na

Total Risk	Standard Deviation	Category Risk	Risk Index	Beta
na	na	na	na	na

	1993	1992	1991	1990	1989	1988	1987	1986	1985	1984
Return (%)	21.6	—	—	—	—	—	—	—	—	—
Differ from category (+/-)	2.6	—	—	—	—	—	—	—	—	—

PER SHARE DATA

	1993	1992	1991	1990	1989	1988	1987	1986	1985	1984
Dividends, Net Income ($)	0.00	—	—	—	—	—	—	—	—	—
Distrib'ns, Cap Gain ($)	0.33	—	—	—	—	—	—	—	—	—
Net Asset Value ($)	13.06	—	—	—	—	—	—	—	—	—
Expense Ratio (%)	1.85	—	—	—	—	—	—	—	—	—
Net Income to Assets (%)	-0.38	—	—	—	—	—	—	—	—	—
Portfolio Turnover (%)	172	—	—	—	—	—	—	—	—	—
Total Assets (Millions $)	23	—	—	—	—	—	—	—	—	—

PORTFOLIO (as of 9/30/93)

Portfolio Manager: Ron Elijah - 1992

Investm't Category: Aggressive Growth

✔ Cap Gain	Asset Allocation
Cap & Income	Fund of Funds
Income	Index
	Sector
✔ Domestic	✔ Small Cap
Foreign	Socially Conscious
Country/Region	State Specific

Portfolio: stocks 93% bonds 0%
convertibles 1% other 0% cash 6%

Largest Holdings: speciality retail 14%, energy 10%

Unrealized Net Capital Gains: 11% of portfolio value

SHAREHOLDER INFORMATION

Minimum Investment
Initial: $5,000   Subsequent: $100

Minimum IRA Investment
Initial: $1,000   Subsequent: $1

Maximum Fees
Load: none   12b-1: none
Other: none

Distributions
Income: Dec   Capital Gains: Dec

Exchange Options
Number Per Year: no limit   Fee: none
Telephone: yes (money market fund not available)

Services
IRA, other pension, auto invest, auto withdraw

Royce Equity Income Series (RYEQX)

1414 Avenue of the Americas
New York, NY 10019
(800) 221-4268

Growth & Income

PERFORMANCE

	3yr Annual	5yr Annual	10yr Annual	Bull	Bear
Return (%)	20.7	na	na	78.0	-16.3
Differ from Category (+/-)	4.3 high	na	na	7.9 abv av	-4.7 low

Total Risk	Standard Deviation	Category Risk	Risk Index	Beta
av	7.5%	low	0.8	0.5

	1993	1992	1991	1990	1989	1988	1987	1986	1985	1984
Return (%)	13.0	19.3	30.3	-15.3	—	—	—	—	—	—
Differ from category (+/-)	0.4	9.3	2.6	-9.7	—	—	—	—	—	—

PER SHARE DATA

	1993	1992	1991	1990	1989	1988	1987	1986	1985	1984
Dividends, Net Income ($)	0.20	0.21	0.21	0.21	—	—	—	—	—	—
Distrib'ns, Cap Gain ($)	0.40	0.15	0.09	0.00	—	—	—	—	—	—
Net Asset Value ($)	5.58	5.49	4.93	4.03	—	—	—	—	—	—
Expense Ratio (%)	1.00	0.99	0.99	1.00	—	—	—	—	—	—
Net Income to Assets (%)	4.20	4.31	4.58	4.74	—	—	—	—	—	—
Portfolio Turnover (%)	91	59	72	28	—	—	—	—	—	—
Total Assets (Millions $)	81	54	41	19	—	—	—	—	—	—

PORTFOLIO (as of 6/30/93)

Portfolio Manager: Thomas Ebright - 1989, Charles Royce - 1989

Investm't Category: Growth & Income

Cap Gain	Asset Allocation
✔ Cap & Income	Fund of Funds
Income	Index
	Sector
✔ Domestic	Small Cap
Foreign	Socially Conscious
Country/Region	State Specific

Portfolio: stocks 62% bonds 14%
convertibles 0% other 3% cash 21%

Largest Holdings: business & industrial products 20%, consumer products 12%

Unrealized Net Capital Gains: 5% of portfolio value

SHAREHOLDER INFORMATION

Minimum Investment
Initial: $2,000   Subsequent: $50

Minimum IRA Investment
Initial: $1,000   Subsequent: $50

Maximum Fees
Load: 1.00% redemption   12b-1: none
Other: redemption fee applies for 1 year

Distributions
Income: quarterly   Capital Gains: Dec

Exchange Options
Number Per Year: no limit   Fee: none
Telephone: yes (money market fund not available)

Services
IRA, other pension, auto invest, auto withdraw

Rushmore American GAS Index (GASFX)

4922 Fairmont Ave.
Bethesda, MD 20814
(800) 621-7874, (301) 657-1517

Growth & Income

PERFORMANCE

	3yr Annual	5yr Annual	10yr Annual	Bull	Bear
Return (%)	10.2	na	na	34.3	-10.6
Differ from Category (+/-)	-6.2 low	na	na	-35.8 low	1.0 av

Total Risk	Standard Deviation	Category Risk	Risk Index	Beta
abv av	11.3%	abv av	1.3	0.4

	1993	1992	1991	1990	1989	1988	1987	1986	1985	1984
Return (%)	16.5	11.3	3.2	-10.4	—	—	—	—	—	—
Differ from category (+/-) ...	3.9	1.3	-24.5	-4.8	—	—	—	—	—	—

PER SHARE DATA

	1993	1992	1991	1990	1989	1988	1987	1986	1985	1984
Dividends, Net Income ($) .	0.39	0.41	0.46	0.54	—	—	—	—	—	—
Distrib'ns, Cap Gain ($) ...	0.06	0.13	0.00	0.10	—	—	—	—	—	—
Net Asset Value ($)	11.96	10.65	10.09	10.24	—	—	—	—	—	—
Expense Ratio (%)........	0.85	0.85	0.79	0.75	—	—	—	—	—	—
Net Income to Assets (%)..	3.82	4.73	5.00	4.99	—	—	—	—	—	—
Portfolio Turnover (%)	21	30	30	25	—	—	—	—	—	—
Total Assets (Millions $)	11	129	131	86	—	—	—	—	—	—

PORTFOLIO (as of 9/30/93)

Portfolio Manager: Dan Gillespie - 1993

Investm't Category: Growth & Income
- Cap Gain
- ✔ Cap & Income
- Income
- ✔ Domestic
- Foreign
- Country/Region
- Asset Allocation
- Fund of Funds
- ✔ Index
- ✔ Sector
- Small Cap
- Socially Conscious
- State Specific

Portfolio: stocks 98% bonds 0%
convertibles 0% other 0% cash 2%

Largest Holdings: American Gas Association Index

Unrealized Net Capital Gains: 13% of portfolio value

SHAREHOLDER INFORMATION

Minimum Investment
Initial: $2,500   Subsequent: $0

Minimum IRA Investment
Initial: $500   Subsequent: $0

Maximum Fees
Load: none   12b-1: none
Other: none

Distributions
Income: quarterly   Capital Gains: Dec

Exchange Options
Number Per Year: 5   Fee: none
Telephone: yes (money market fund available)

Services
IRA, other pension, auto exchange, auto invest, auto withdraw

Rushmore Maryland Tax-Free (RSXLX)

Tax-Exempt Bond

4922 Fairmont Ave.
Bethesda, MD 20814
(800) 621-7874, (301) 657-1517

PERFORMANCE

	3yr Annual	5yr Annual	10yr Annual	Bull	Bear
Return (%)	10.0	7.9	8.4	39.2	-1.5
Differ from Category (+/-)	-0.3 blw av	-1.3 low	-1.2 low	-0.8 blw av	-3.8 low

Total Risk	Standard Deviation	Category Risk	Risk Index	Avg Mat
blw av	5.0%	high	1.2	15.1 yrs

	1993	1992	1991	1990	1989	1988	1987	1986	1985	1984
Return (%).............	11.9	8.0	10.2	2.8	6.6	9.6	1.0	11.7	16.1	7.0
Differ from category (+/-)...	0.3	-0.3	-1.1	-3.5	-2.4	-0.5	2.2	-4.7	-1.2	-1.3

PER SHARE DATA

	1993	1992	1991	1990	1989	1988	1987	1986	1985	1984
Dividends, Net Income ($).	0.56	0.60	0.59	0.61	0.68	0.70	0.73	0.79	0.83	0.82
Distrib'ns, Cap Gain ($) ...	0.00	0.00	0.00	0.00	0.00	0.00	0.00	0.00	0.00	0.00
Net Asset Value ($)	11.27	10.60	10.39	9.99	10.33	10.34	10.09	10.71	10.33	9.67
Expense Ratio (%)	0.50	0.50	0.62	0.93	0.92	0.93	0.93	0.95	0.87	0.84
Net Income to Assets (%) .	5.27	5.67	5.85	6.19	6.56	6.81	7.04	7.60	8.52	8.60
Portfolio Turnover (%)......	21	21	61	244	173	102	84	40	87	28
Total Assets (Millions $).....	58	44	24	10	1	9	9	10	6	4

PORTFOLIO (as of 6/30/93)

Portfolio Manager: Dan Gillespie - 1991

Investm't Category: Tax-Exempt Bond

Cap Gain	Asset Allocation
Cap & Income	Fund of Funds
✔ Income	Index
	Sector
✔ Domestic	Small Cap
Foreign	Socially Conscious
Country/Region	✔ State Specific

Portfolio: stocks 0% bonds 100%
convertibles 0% other 0% cash 0%

Largest Holdings: general obligation 98%

Unrealized Net Capital Gains: 6% of portfolio value

SHAREHOLDER INFORMATION

Minimum Investment
Initial: $2,500   Subsequent: $0

Minimum IRA Investment
Initial: na   Subsequent: na

Maximum Fees
Load: none   12b-1: none
Other: none

Distributions
Income: monthly   Capital Gains: Dec

Exchange Options
Number Per Year: no limit   Fee: none
Telephone: yes (money market fund available)

Services
auto exchange, auto invest, auto withdraw

Rushmore OTC Index Plus (RSOIX)

4922 Fairmont Ave.
Bethesda, MD 20814
(800) 621-7874, (301) 657-1517

Growth

PERFORMANCE

	3yr Annual	5yr Annual	10yr Annual	Bull	Bear
Return (%)	21.0	11.0	na	96.3	-25.4
Differ from Category (+/-)	1.8 abv av	-3.6 low	na	11.6 abv av	-13.0 low

Total Risk	Standard Deviation	Category Risk	Risk Index	Beta
high	17.6%	high	1.7	1.3

	1993	1992	1991	1990	1989	1988	1987	1986	1985	1984
Return (%)	12.7	4.6	50.5	-17.6	15.4	9.1	6.3	8.2	—	—
Differ from category (+/-)	-0.5	-6.4	15.1	-11.5	-10.4	-8.6	5.1	-6.3	—	—

PER SHARE DATA

	1993	1992	1991	1990	1989	1988	1987	1986	1985	1984
Dividends, Net Income ($)	0.26	0.00	0.00	0.01	0.11	0.11	0.10	0.18	—	—
Distrib'ns, Cap Gain ($)	0.22	0.00	0.42	0.00	1.63	0.00	0.00	0.00	—	—
Net Asset Value ($)	16.89	15.41	14.73	10.07	12.24	12.12	11.12	10.65	—	—
Expense Ratio (%)	1.00	0.87	0.91	1.00	1.00	0.95	0.76	1.00	—	—
Net Income to Assets (%)	0.99	-0.24	-0.03	0.91	1.79	0.93	1.18	0.64	—	—
Portfolio Turnover (%)	273	880	443	1,399	582	252	42	5	—	—
Total Assets (Millions $)	6	14	18	5	21	4	6	1	—	—

PORTFOLIO (as of 8/31/93)

Portfolio Manager: committee

Investm't Category: Growth

✔ Cap Gain	Asset Allocation
Cap & Income	Fund of Funds
Income	✔ Index
	Sector
✔ Domestic	Small Cap
Foreign	Socially Conscious
Country/Region	State Specific

Portfolio: stocks 86% bonds 0%
convertibles 0% other 0% cash 14%

Largest Holdings: Nasdaq - 100 Index

Unrealized Net Capital Gains: 2% of portfolio value

SHAREHOLDER INFORMATION

Minimum Investment
Initial: $2,500   Subsequent: $0

Minimum IRA Investment
Initial: $500   Subsequent: $0

Maximum Fees
Load: 0.50% redemption   12b-1: none
Other: redemption fee applies for 3 mos

Distributions
Income: Jun, Dec   Capital Gains: Dec

Exchange Options
Number Per Year: no limit   Fee: none
Telephone: yes (money market fund available)

Services
IRA, other pension, auto exchange, auto invest, auto withdraw

Rushmore Stock Market Index Plus (RSSIX)

4922 Fairmont Ave.
Bethesda, MD 20814
(800) 621-7874, (301) 657-1517

Growth & Income

PERFORMANCE

	3yr Annual	5yr Annual	10yr Annual	Bull	Bear
Return (%)	12.3	11.0	na	52.6	-10.0
Differ from Category (+/-)	-4.1 low	-1.5 blw av	na	-17.5 low	1.6 av

Total Risk	Standard Deviation	Category Risk	Risk Index	Beta
abv av	12.4%	high	1.4	1.0

	1993	1992	1991	1990	1989	1988	1987	1986	1985	1984
Return (%).............	10.0	1.7	26.6	-3.0	23.2	8.9	8.8	17.6	—	—
Differ from category (+/-)...	-2.6	-8.3	-1.1	2.6	1.6	-7.9	8.4	2.4	—	—

PER SHARE DATA

	1993	1992	1991	1990	1989	1988	1987	1986	1985	1984
Dividends, Net Income ($).	0.36	0.36	0.57	0.15	0.43	0.43	0.40	0.28	—	—
Distrib'ns, Cap Gain ($) ...	0.00	0.00	0.00	0.00	0.00	0.00	0.48	0.00	—	—
Net Asset Value ($)	18.37	17.04	17.11	14.00	14.60	12.23	11.64	11.48	—	—
Expense Ratio (%)	1.00	0.99	0.91	0.93	1.00	0.90	0.75	1.00	—	—
Net Income to Assets (%) .	1.83	2.00	2.66	2.31	3.72	3.41	3.08	3.13	—	—
Portfolio Turnover (%)......	45	423	583	576	370	621	188	6	—	—
Total Assets (Millions $)......	9	13	28	10	23	10	29	1	—	—

PORTFOLIO (as of 8/31/93)

Portfolio Manager: committee

Investm't Category: Growth & Income

Cap Gain	Asset Allocation
✔ Cap & Income	Fund of Funds
Income	✔ Index
	Sector
✔ Domestic	Small Cap
Foreign	Socially Conscious
Country/Region	State Specific

Portfolio: stocks 75% bonds 0%
convertibles 0% other 0% cash 25%

Largest Holdings: 100 largest stocks on the NYSE

Unrealized Net Capital Gains: 0% of portfolio value

SHAREHOLDER INFORMATION

Minimum Investment
Initial: $2,500   Subsequent: $0

Minimum IRA Investment
Initial: $500   Subsequent: $0

Maximum Fees
Load: 0.50% redemption   12b-1: none
Other: redemption fee applies for 3 mos

Distributions
Income: Jun, Dec   Capital Gains: Dec

Exchange Options
Number Per Year: no limit   Fee: none
Telephone: yes (money market fund available)

Services
IRA, other pension, auto exchange, auto invest, auto withdraw

Rushmore US Gov't Interm-Term (RSUIX)

Government Bond

4922 Fairmont Ave.
Bethesda, MD 20814
(800) 621-7874, (301) 657-1517

PERFORMANCE

	3yr Annual	5yr Annual	10yr Annual	Bull	Bear
Return (%)	11.6	11.2	na	48.0	0.1
Differ from Category (+/-)	0.8 abv av	0.8 abv av	na	1.8 abv av	-0.4 blw av

Total Risk	Standard Deviation	Category Risk	Risk Index	Avg Mat
blw av	5.7%	abv av	1.3	9.0 yrs

	1993	1992	1991	1990	1989	1988	1987	1986	1985	1984
Return (%)	11.8	7.0	16.3	6.4	14.8	6.8	0.6	10.4	—	—
Differ from category (+/-) . . .	1.4	0.8	1.3	-0.1	0.8	-0.8	2.5	-8.7	—	—

PER SHARE DATA

	1993	1992	1991	1990	1989	1988	1987	1986	1985	1984
Dividends, Net Income ($) .	0.52	0.68	0.69	0.72	0.77	0.83	0.66	0.64	—	—
Distrib'ns, Cap Gain ($) . . .	0.16	1.25	0.00	0.00	0.22	0.00	0.00	0.00	—	—
Net Asset Value ($)	9.84	9.42	10.65	9.82	9.95	9.58	9.77	10.37	—	—
Expense Ratio (%).	0.80	0.80	0.80	0.80	0.80	0.81	0.78	1.00	—	—
Net Income to Assets (%) . .	5.91	6.63	7.21	7.47	7.93	8.14	6.18	6.50	—	—
Portfolio Turnover (%)	113	200	196	424	461	1,754	87	na	—	—
Total Assets (Millions $)	21	16	23	4	7	1	1	1	—	—

PORTFOLIO (as of 8/31/93)

Portfolio Manager: committee

Investm't Category: Government Bond

Cap Gain	Asset Allocation
Cap & Income	Fund of Funds
✔ Income	Index
	Sector
✔ Domestic	Small Cap
Foreign	Socially Conscious
Country/Region	State Specific

Portfolio: stocks 0% bonds 82%
convertibles 0% other 0% cash 18%

Largest Holdings: U.S. government 82%

Unrealized Net Capital Gains: 6% of portfolio value

SHAREHOLDER INFORMATION

Minimum Investment
Initial: $2,500 Subsequent: $0

Minimum IRA Investment
Initial: $500 Subsequent: $0

Maximum Fees
Load: none 12b-1: none
Other: none

Distributions
Income: monthly Capital Gains: Dec

Exchange Options
Number Per Year: no limit Fee: none
Telephone: yes (money market fund available)

Services
IRA, other pension, auto exchange, auto invest, auto withdraw

Rushmore US Gov't Long-Term (RSGVX)

4922 Fairmont Ave.
Bethesda, MD 20814
(800) 621-7874, (301) 657-1517

Government Bond

PERFORMANCE

	3yr Annual	5yr Annual	10yr Annual	Bull	Bear
Return (%)	12.5	12.1	na	56.4	-4.7
Differ from Category (+/-)	1.7 abv av	1.7 abv av	na	10.2 abv av	-5.2 low

Total Risk	Standard Deviation	Category Risk	Risk Index	Avg Mat
av	7.4%	high	1.7	27.1 yrs

	1993	1992	1991	1990	1989	1988	1987	1986	1985	1984
Return (%)	15.3	6.1	16.5	4.4	18.9	7.9	0.4	8.9	—	—
Differ from category (+/-)	4.9	-0.1	1.5	-2.1	5.0	0.3	2.2	-10.2	—	—

PER SHARE DATA

	1993	1992	1991	1990	1989	1988	1987	1986	1985	1984
Dividends, Net Income ($)	0.60	0.68	0.71	0.72	0.73	0.75	0.75	0.86	—	—
Distrib'ns, Cap Gain ($)	0.77	0.47	0.00	0.00	0.00	0.00	0.00	0.00	—	—
Net Asset Value ($)	10.31	10.16	10.71	9.87	10.20	9.24	9.28	10.01	—	—
Expense Ratio (%)	0.80	0.80	0.80	0.80	0.80	0.83	0.78	1.00	—	—
Net Income to Assets (%)	6.08	6.80	7.43	7.28	7.73	8.05	7.90	8.83	—	—
Portfolio Turnover (%)	173	298	236	401	412	829	226	43	—	—
Total Assets (Millions $)	18	23	14	13	26	7	11	7	—	—

PORTFOLIO (as of 8/31/93)

Portfolio Manager: committee

Investm't Category: Government Bond

Cap Gain	Asset Allocation
Cap & Income	Fund of Funds
✔ Income	Index
	Sector
✔ Domestic	Small Cap
Foreign	Socially Conscious
Country/Region	State Specific

Portfolio: stocks 0%   bonds 62%
convertibles 0%   other 0%   cash 38%

Largest Holdings: U.S government 62%

Unrealized Net Capital Gains: 8% of portfolio value

SHAREHOLDER INFORMATION

Minimum Investment
Initial: $2,500   Subsequent: $0

Minimum IRA Investment
Initial: $500   Subsequent: $0

Maximum Fees
Load: none   12b-1: none
Other: none

Distributions
Income: monthly   Capital Gains: Dec

Exchange Options
Number Per Year: no limit   Fee: none
Telephone: yes (money market fund available)

Services
IRA, other pension, auto exchange, auto invest, auto withdraw

Rushmore Virginia Tax-Free (RSXIX)

4922 Fairmont Ave.
Bethesda, MD 20814
(800) 621-7874, (301) 657-1517

Tax-Exempt Bond

PERFORMANCE

	3yr Annual	5yr Annual	10yr Annual	Bull	Bear
Return (%)	10.2	8.5	8.3	39.4	0.1
Differ from Category (+/-)	-0.1 blw av	-0.6 low	-1.3 low	-0.6 blw av	-2.2 low

Total Risk	Standard Deviation	Category Risk	Risk Index	Avg Mat
blw av	4.8%	abv av	1.2	16.0 yrs

	1993	1992	1991	1990	1989	1988	1987	1986	1985	1984
Return (%)	11.7	8.0	10.8	4.4	7.9	7.4	-1.0	12.0	13.1	8.5
Differ from category (+/-) . . .	0.1	-0.3	-0.5	-1.9	-1.1	-2.7	0.2	-4.4	-4.2	0.2

PER SHARE DATA

	1993	1992	1991	1990	1989	1988	1987	1986	1985	1984
Dividends, Net Income ($) .	0.58	0.61	0.60	0.57	0.59	0.60	0.63	0.72	0.75	0.74
Distrib'ns, Cap Gain ($) . . .	0.00	0.00	0.00	0.00	0.00	0.00	0.00	0.00	0.00	0.00
Net Asset Value ($)	11.51	10.84	10.63	10.17	10.31	10.12	9.98	10.74	10.26	9.78
Expense Ratio (%)	0.50	0.50	0.61	0.93	0.93	0.93	0.92	0.94	0.89	0.84
Net Income to Assets (%) . .	5.30	5.71	5.91	5.70	5.82	5.92	6.18	6.87	7.55	7.73
Portfolio Turnover (%)	na	50	74	202	150	78	125	42	67	10
Total Assets (Millions $)	34	26	17	7	7	8	8	9	6	3

PORTFOLIO (as of 6/30/93)

Portfolio Manager: Dan Gillespie - 1991

Investm't Category: Tax-Exempt Bond
Cap Gain	Asset Allocation
Cap & Income	Fund of Funds
✔ Income	Index
	Sector
✔ Domestic	Small Cap
Foreign	Socially Conscious
Country/Region	✔ State Specific

Portfolio: stocks 0% bonds 100%
convertibles 0% other 0% cash 0%

Largest Holdings: general obligation 97%

Unrealized Net Capital Gains: 6% of portfolio value

SHAREHOLDER INFORMATION

Minimum Investment
Initial: $2,500   Subsequent: $0

Minimum IRA Investment
Initial: na   Subsequent: na

Maximum Fees
Load: none   12b-1: none
Other: none

Distributions
Income: monthly   Capital Gains: Dec

Exchange Options
Number Per Year: no limit   Fee: none
Telephone: yes (money market fund available)

Services
auto exchange, auto invest, auto withdraw

Safeco CA Tax-Free Income (SFCAX)

P.O. Box 34890
Seattle, WA 98124
(800) 426-6730, (206) 545-5530

Tax-Exempt Bond

PERFORMANCE

	3yr Annual	5yr Annual	10yr Annual	Bull	Bear
Return (%)	11.2	10.1	10.7	44.9	1.5
Differ from Category (+/-)	0.8 abv av	0.8 abv av	1.1 abv av	4.8 abv av	-0.8 blw av

Total Risk	Standard Deviation	Category Risk	Risk Index	Avg Mat
blw av	5.2%	high	1.3	24.0 yrs

	1993	1992	1991	1990	1989	1988	1987	1986	1985	1984
Return (%)	13.2	7.9	12.5	6.9	9.8	12.8	-2.0	19.6	21.0	7.5
Differ from category (+/-)	1.6	-0.4	1.2	0.6	0.8	2.7	-0.8	3.2	3.7	-0.8

PER SHARE DATA

	1993	1992	1991	1990	1989	1988	1987	1986	1985	1984
Dividends, Net Income ($)	0.66	0.68	0.70	0.71	0.72	0.75	0.76	0.81	0.84	0.84
Distrib'ns, Cap Gain ($)	0.34	0.13	0.07	0.06	0.18	0.00	0.43	0.11	0.00	0.00
Net Asset Value ($)	12.43	11.90	11.81	11.23	11.26	11.11	10.55	12.02	10.87	9.73
Expense Ratio (%)	0.66	0.67	0.67	0.68	0.71	0.72	0.70	0.76	0.77	0.89
Net Income to Assets (%)	5.71	6.13	6.32	6.42	6.86	6.99	6.71	7.66	8.79	8.09
Portfolio Turnover (%)	23	39	23	71	77	67	45	40	23	44
Total Assets (Millions $)	84	71	57	48	37	29	35	21	11	8

PORTFOLIO (as of 9/30/93)

Portfolio Manager: Stephen Bauer - 1983

Investm't Category: Tax-Exempt Bond
Cap Gain	Asset Allocation
Cap & Income	Fund of Funds
✔ Income	Index
	Sector
✔ Domestic	Small Cap
Foreign	Socially Conscious
Country/Region	✔ State Specific

Portfolio: stocks 0% bonds 99%
convertibles 0% other 0% cash 1%

Largest Holdings: general obligation 9%

Unrealized Net Capital Gains: 11% of portfolio value

SHAREHOLDER INFORMATION

Minimum Investment
Initial: $1,000   Subsequent: $100

Minimum IRA Investment
Initial: na   Subsequent: na

Maximum Fees
Load: none   12b-1: none
Other: none

Distributions
Income: monthly   Capital Gains: Apr, Oct

Exchange Options
Number Per Year: no limit   Fee: none
Telephone: yes (money market fund available)

Services
auto invest, auto withdraw

Safeco Equity (SAFQX)

Growth & Income

P.O. Box 34890
Seattle, WA 98124
(800) 426-6730, (206) 545-5530

PERFORMANCE

	3yr Annual	5yr Annual	10yr Annual	Bull	Bear
Return (%)	22.3	17.8	15.3	96.1	-14.7
Differ from Category (+/-)	5.9 high	5.3 high	2.9 high	26.0 high	-3.1 blw av

Total Risk	Standard Deviation	Category Risk	Risk Index	Beta
high	14.1%	high	1.6	1.0

	1993	1992	1991	1990	1989	1988	1987	1986	1985	1984
Return (%)	30.9	9.2	27.9	-8.5	35.7	25.2	-4.8	12.7	33.2	2.6
Differ from category (+/-) . .	18.3	-0.8	0.2	-2.9	14.1	8.4	-5.2	-2.5	7.8	-3.6

PER SHARE DATA

	1993	1992	1991	1990	1989	1988	1987	1986	1985	1984
Dividends, Net Income ($) .	0.17	0.13	0.17	0.19	0.39	0.20	0.24	0.29	0.39	0.45
Distrib'ns, Cap Gain ($) . . .	0.81	0.48	0.67	0.38	0.63	0.12	1.78	2.03	1.21	0.71
Net Asset Value ($)	13.18	10.87	10.59	8.97	10.48	8.55	7.09	9.54	10.50	9.22
Expense Ratio (%).	0.93	0.96	0.98	0.97	0.96	1.00	0.97	0.88	0.68	0.64
Net Income to Assets (%) . .	1.50	1.34	1.70	2.19	4.13	2.16	1.92	2.55	3.97	4.66
Portfolio Turnover (%)	37	40	45	51	64	88	85	86	56	20
Total Assets (Millions $) . . .	199	74	72	52	54	46	65	46	34	31

PORTFOLIO (as of 9/30/93)

Portfolio Manager: Doug Johnson - 1984

Investm't Category: Growth & Income

Cap Gain	Asset Allocation
✔ Cap & Income	Fund of Funds
Income	Index
	Sector
✔ Domestic	Small Cap
Foreign	Socially Conscious
Country/Region	State Specific

Portfolio: stocks 91% bonds 0%
convertibles 0% other 2% cash 7%

Largest Holdings: drugs & hospital supplies 17%, leisure time 12%

Unrealized Net Capital Gains: 20% of portfolio value

SHAREHOLDER INFORMATION

Minimum Investment
Initial: $1,000   Subsequent: $100

Minimum IRA Investment
Initial: $250   Subsequent: $100

Maximum Fees
Load: none   12b-1: none
Other: none

Distributions
Income: quarterly   Capital Gains: Sep, Dec

Exchange Options
Number Per Year: no limit   Fee: none
Telephone: yes (money market fund available)

Services
IRA, other pension, auto exchange, auto invest, auto withdraw

Safeco Growth (SAFGX)

Aggressive Growth

P.O. Box 34890
Seattle, WA 98124
(800) 426-6730, (206) 545-5530

PERFORMANCE

	3yr Annual	5yr Annual	10yr Annual	Bull	Bear
Return (%)	24.4	14.3	11.2	107.8	-21.1
Differ from Category (+/-)	-1.0 av	-3.9 blw av	-0.6 blw av	-17.2 av	-6.1 blw av

Total Risk	Standard Deviation	Category Risk	Risk Index	Beta
high	20.9%	high	1.4	1.3

	1993	1992	1991	1990	1989	1988	1987	1986	1985	1984
Return (%).	22.1	-3.0	62.6	-14.9	19.1	22.1	7.0	1.8	20.6	-7.1
Differ from category (+/-). . .	3.1	-13.4	10.2	-8.6	-7.9	6.9	10.4	-7.6	-10.4	2.3

PER SHARE DATA

	1993	1992	1991	1990	1989	1988	1987	1986	1985	1984
Dividends, Net Income ($).	0.00	0.00	0.04	0.08	0.42	0.43	0.32	0.31	0.50	0.51
Distrib'ns, Cap Gain ($) . . .	0.70	0.61	1.14	1.88	0.90	0.81	1.25	1.58	2.97	1.15
Net Asset Value ($)	20.06	17.00	18.31	12.01	16.61	15.04	13.36	14.00	15.56	16.07
Expense Ratio (%)	0.91	0.91	0.90	1.01	0.93	0.98	0.92	0.85	0.63	0.61
Net Income to Assets (%) .	-0.10	-0.10	0.36	0.88	3.27	2.37	1.46	1.90	2.94	2.89
Portfolio Turnover (%).	57	85	50	90	11	19	24	46	29	23
Total Assets (Millions $). . . .	163	128	155	59	82	74	83	68	66	63

PORTFOLIO (as of 9/30/93)

Portfolio Manager: Thomas M. Maguire - 1989

Investm't Category: Aggressive Growth

✔ Cap Gain	Asset Allocation
Cap & Income	Fund of Funds
Income	Index
	Sector
✔ Domestic	Small Cap
Foreign	Socially Conscious
Country/Region	State Specific

Portfolio: stocks 93%   bonds 0%
convertibles 0%   other 0%   cash 7%

Largest Holdings: financial services 13%, food & tobacco 12%

Unrealized Net Capital Gains: 29% of portfolio value

SHAREHOLDER INFORMATION

Minimum Investment
Initial: $1,000   Subsequent: $100

Minimum IRA Investment
Initial: $250   Subsequent: $100

Maximum Fees
Load: none   12b-1: none
Other: none

Distributions
Income: quarterly   Capital Gains: Sep, Dec

Exchange Options
Number Per Year: no limit   Fee: none
Telephone: yes (money market fund available)

Services
IRA, other pension, auto exchange, auto invest, auto withdraw

Safeco High Yield Bond
(SAFHX)

Corporate High-Yield Bond

P.O. Box 34890
Seattle, WA 98124
(800) 426-6730, (206) 545-5530

PERFORMANCE

	3yr Annual	5yr Annual	10yr Annual	Bull	Bear
Return (%)	18.2	10.2	na	63.6	-2.4
Differ from Category (+/-)	-2.3 blw av	-0.6 blw av	na	-11.3 blw av	0.8 high

Total Risk	Standard Deviation	Category Risk	Risk Index	Avg Mat
low	3.7%	blw av	1.0	8.9 yrs

	1993	1992	1991	1990	1989	1988	1987	1986	1985	1984
Return (%)	16.9	13.8	24.2	-3.5	1.9	—	—	—	—	—
Differ from category (+/-) ..	-2.3	-2.0	-3.1	0.6	0.6	—	—	—	—	—

PER SHARE DATA

	1993	1992	1991	1990	1989	1988	1987	1986	1985	1984
Dividends, Net Income ($) .	0.86	0.88	0.85	1.03	1.11	—	—	—	—	—
Distrib'ns, Cap Gain ($) ...	0.00	0.00	0.00	0.00	0.00	—	—	—	—	—
Net Asset Value ($)	9.30	8.73	8.48	7.58	8.91	—	—	—	—	—
Expense Ratio (%)........	1.09	1.05	1.11	1.15	1.11	—	—	—	—	—
Net Income to Assets (%)..	9.94	9.66	11.51	11.90	11.52	—	—	—	—	—
Portfolio Turnover (%).....	50	40	32	18	12	—	—	—	—	—
Total Assets (Millions $)	34	19	11	7	9	—	—	—	—	—

PORTFOLIO (as of 9/30/93)

Portfolio Manager: Ron Spaulding - 1988

Investm't Category: Corp. High-Yield Bond

Cap Gain	Asset Allocation
Cap & Income	Fund of Funds
✔ Income	Index
	Sector
✔ Domestic	Small Cap
Foreign	Socially Conscious
Country/Region	State Specific

Portfolio: stocks 0% bonds 100%
convertibles 0% other 0% cash 0%

Largest Holdings: retail 15%, hospital management 7%

Unrealized Net Capital Gains: 4% of portfolio value

SHAREHOLDER INFORMATION

Minimum Investment
Initial: $1,000   Subsequent: $100

Minimum IRA Investment
Initial: $250   Subsequent: $100

Maximum Fees
Load: none   12b-1: none
Other: none

Distributions
Income: monthly   Capital Gains: Sep, Dec

Exchange Options
Number Per Year: no limit   Fee: none
Telephone: yes (money market fund available)

Services
IRA, other pension, auto exchange, auto invest, auto withdraw

Safeco Income (SAFIX)

Balanced

P.O. Box 34890
Seattle, WA 98124
(800) 426-6730, (206) 545-5530

PERFORMANCE

	3yr Annual	5yr Annual	10yr Annual	Bull	Bear
Return (%)	15.6	10.4	12.3	63.1	-15.4
Differ from Category (+/-)	0.6 abv av	-1.7 low	0.3 av	1.5 av	-9.6 low

Total Risk	Standard Deviation	Category Risk	Risk Index	Beta
av	7.4%	abv av	1.2	0.6

	1993	1992	1991	1990	1989	1988	1987	1986	1985	1984
Return (%)	12.5	11.4	23.2	-10.7	19.1	18.9	-5.9	20.0	31.7	9.9
Differ from category (+/-)	-0.8	3.3	-0.6	-10.2	1.5	6.9	-8.2	2.5	8.0	2.5

PER SHARE DATA

	1993	1992	1991	1990	1989	1988	1987	1986	1985	1984
Dividends, Net Income ($)	0.78	0.78	0.80	0.85	0.81	0.78	1.00	0.77	0.74	0.87
Distrib'ns, Cap Gain ($)	0.00	0.04	0.05	0.09	0.08	0.00	0.83	0.72	0.55	1.16
Net Asset Value ($)	17.77	16.50	15.58	13.37	16.03	14.23	12.64	15.28	14.03	11.76
Expense Ratio (%)	0.90	0.90	0.93	0.92	0.92	0.97	0.93	0.95	0.73	0.62
Net Income to Assets (%)	4.55	5.06	5.58	5.59	5.28	5.58	4.53	5.08	6.41	7.02
Portfolio Turnover (%)	20	20	22	19	16	34	33	28	29	33
Total Assets (Millions $)	202	182	181	170	233	232	313	102	31	19

PORTFOLIO (as of 9/30/93)

Portfolio Manager: Arley Hudson - 1978

Investm't Category: Balanced

Cap Gain	Asset Allocation
✔ Cap & Income	Fund of Funds
Income	Index
	Sector
✔ Domestic	Small Cap
Foreign	Socially Conscious
Country/Region	State Specific

Portfolio: stocks 55%   bonds 22%
convertibles 0%   other 22%   cash 1%

Largest Holdings: stocks—telephone utilities 12%, real estate investment trusts 6%

Unrealized Net Capital Gains: 12% of portfolio value

SHAREHOLDER INFORMATION

Minimum Investment
Initial: $1,000   Subsequent: $100

Minimum IRA Investment
Initial: $250   Subsequent: $100

Maximum Fees
Load: none   12b-1: none
Other: none

Distributions
Income: quarterly   Capital Gains: Sep, Dec

Exchange Options
Number Per Year: no limit   Fee: none
Telephone: yes (money market fund available)

Services
IRA, other pension, auto exchange, auto invest, auto withdraw

Safeco Muni Bond
(SFCOX)

Tax-Exempt Bond

P.O. Box 34890
Seattle, WA 98124
(800) 426-6730, (206) 545-5530

PERFORMANCE

	3yr Annual	5yr Annual	10yr Annual	Bull	Bear
Return (%)	11.6	10.3	11.5	46.5	1.4
Differ from Category (+/-)	1.3 high	1.1 high	1.9 high	6.4 high	-0.8 blw av

Total Risk	Standard Deviation	Category Risk	Risk Index	Avg Mat
blw av	5.2%	high	1.3	22.8 yrs

	1993	1992	1991	1990	1989	1988	1987	1986	1985	1984
Return (%)	12.5	8.7	13.7	6.6	10.0	13.8	0.1	19.7	21.6	10.1
Differ from category (+/-) . . .	0.8	0.4	2.4	0.3	1.0	3.7	1.3	3.3	4.3	1.8

PER SHARE DATA

	1993	1992	1991	1990	1989	1988	1987	1986	1985	1984
Dividends, Net Income ($) .	0.77	0.82	0.85	0.86	0.89	0.94	0.96	1.01	1.05	1.07
Distrib'ns, Cap Gain ($) . . .	0.30	0.18	0.06	0.04	0.44	0.28	0.40	0.20	0.02	0.00
Net Asset Value ($)	14.43	13.82	13.68	12.88	12.97	13.05	12.60	13.97	12.76	11.46
Expense Ratio (%).	0.53	0.54	0.56	0.57	0.60	0.61	0.59	0.63	0.63	0.63
Net Income to Assets (%) . .	5.91	6.37	6.68	6.76	7.23	7.42	7.20	8.29	9.43	9.17
Portfolio Turnover (%)	31	25	39	66	136	72	23	21	46	92
Total Assets (Millions $) . . .	599	428	332	286	232	184	215	161	84	50

PORTFOLIO (as of 9/30/93)

Portfolio Manager: Stephen Bauer - 1981

Investm't Category: Tax-Exempt Bond

Cap Gain	Asset Allocation
Cap & Income	Fund of Funds
✔ Income	Index
	Sector
✔ Domestic	Small Cap
Foreign	Socially Conscious
Country/Region	State Specific

Portfolio: stocks 0% bonds 98%
convertibles 0% other 0% cash 2%

Largest Holdings: general obligation 17%

Unrealized Net Capital Gains: 11% of portfolio value

SHAREHOLDER INFORMATION

Minimum Investment
Initial: $1,000   Subsequent: $100

Minimum IRA Investment
Initial: na   Subsequent: na

Maximum Fees
Load: none   12b-1: none
Other: none

Distributions
Income: monthly   Capital Gains: Apr, Oct

Exchange Options
Number Per Year: no limit   Fee: none
Telephone: yes (money market fund available)

Services
auto invest, auto withdraw

Safeco Northwest
(SFNWX)

Growth

P.O. Box 34890
Seattle, WA 98124
(800) 426-6730, (206) 545-5530

PERFORMANCE

	3yr Annual	5yr Annual	10yr Annual	Bull	Bear
Return (%)	na	na	na	na	na
Differ from Category (+/-)	na	na	na	na	na

Total Risk	Standard Deviation	Category Risk	Risk Index	Beta
na	na	na	na	na

	1993	1992	1991	1990	1989	1988	1987	1986	1985	1984
Return (%)	1.0	14.0	—	—	—	—	—	—	—	—
Differ from category (+/-). .	-12.2	3.0	—	—	—	—	—	—	—	—

PER SHARE DATA

	1993	1992	1991	1990	1989	1988	1987	1986	1985	1984
Dividends, Net Income ($).	0.03	0.06	—	—	—	—	—	—	—	—
Distrib'ns, Cap Gain ($) . . .	0.23	0.31	—	—	—	—	—	—	—	—
Net Asset Value ($)	12.45	12.59	—	—	—	—	—	—	—	—
Expense Ratio (%)	1.11	1.11	—	—	—	—	—	—	—	—
Net Income to Assets (%) .	0.18	0.55	—	—	—	—	—	—	—	—
Portfolio Turnover (%).	14	33	—	—	—	—	—	—	—	—
Total Assets (Millions $).	40	40	—	—	—	—	—	—	—	—

PORTFOLIO (as of 9/30/93)

Portfolio Manager: Charles Driggs - 1992

Investm't Category: Growth

✔ Cap Gain	Asset Allocation
Cap & Income	Fund of Funds
Income	Index
	Sector
✔ Domestic	Small Cap
Foreign	Socially Conscious
Country/Region	State Specific

Portfolio: stocks 87% bonds 0%
convertibles 0% other 0% cash 13%

Largest Holdings: banks 13%, savings &
loans/savings banks 13%

Unrealized Net Capital Gains: 12% of portfolio value

SHAREHOLDER INFORMATION

Minimum Investment
Initial: $1,000   Subsequent: $100

Minimum IRA Investment
Initial: $250   Subsequent: $100

Maximum Fees
Load: none   12b-1: none
Other: none

Distributions
Income: quarterly   Capital Gains: Dec

Exchange Options
Number Per Year: no limit   Fee: none
Telephone: yes (money market fund available)

Services
IRA, other pension, auto exchange, auto invest,
auto withdraw

Safeco US Gov't Securities (SFUSX)

Mortgage-Backed Bond

P.O. Box 34890
Seattle, WA 98124
(800) 426-6730, (206) 545-5530

PERFORMANCE

	3yr Annual	5yr Annual	10yr Annual	Bull	Bear
Return (%)	9.4	9.9	na	36.9	4.0
Differ from Category (+/-)	0.2 av	0.0 av	na	0.2 av	-0.6 blw av

Total Risk	Standard Deviation	Category Risk	Risk Index	Avg Mat
low	2.8%	av	1.1	21.5 yrs

	1993	1992	1991	1990	1989	1988	1987	1986	1985	1984
Return (%)	7.0	6.6	14.8	8.6	12.9	7.8	0.8	—	—	—
Differ from category (+/-) ...	0.2	0.5	0.4	-0.8	0.6	0.8	-1.2	—	—	—

PER SHARE DATA

	1993	1992	1991	1990	1989	1988	1987	1986	1985	1984
Dividends, Net Income ($) .	0.64	0.72	0.76	0.76	0.78	0.87	0.82	—	—	—
Distrib'ns, Cap Gain ($) ...	0.00	0.00	0.00	0.00	0.00	0.00	0.00	—	—	—
Net Asset Value ($)	9.88	9.84	9.93	9.37	9.37	9.03	9.21	—	—	—
Expense Ratio (%)........	0.93	0.93	0.97	0.99	1.02	1.06	1.05	—	—	—
Net Income to Assets (%)..	6.71	7.49	8.23	8.28	8.83	9.51	8.59	—	—	—
Portfolio Turnover (%)	70	25	44	90	77	110	101	—	—	—
Total Assets (Millions $)	60	56	42	29	27	28	20	—	—	—

PORTFOLIO (as of 9/30/93)

Portfolio Manager: Paul Stevenson - 1988

Investm't Category: Mortgage-Backed Bond
Cap Gain	Asset Allocation
Cap & Income	Fund of Funds
✔ Income	Index
	Sector
✔ Domestic	Small Cap
Foreign	Socially Conscious
Country/Region	State Specific

Portfolio: stocks 0% bonds 96%
convertibles 0% other 0% cash 4%

Largest Holdings: mortgage-backed 70%, U.S. government 26%

Unrealized Net Capital Gains: 3% of portfolio value

SHAREHOLDER INFORMATION

Minimum Investment
Initial: $1,000   Subsequent: $100

Minimum IRA Investment
Initial: $250   Subsequent: $100

Maximum Fees
Load: none   12b-1: none
Other: none

Distributions
Income: monthly   Capital Gains: Sep, Dec

Exchange Options
Number Per Year: no limit   Fee: none
Telephone: yes (money market fund available)

Services
IRA, other pension, auto exchange, auto invest, auto withdraw

Salomon Brothers Capital (SACPX)

Aggressive Growth

7 World Trade Center
38th Floor
New York, NY 10048
(800) 725-6666, (212) 783-1301

PERFORMANCE

	3yr Annual	5yr Annual	10yr Annual	Bull	Bear
Return (%)	17.8	15.7	10.5	71.4	-13.1
Differ from Category (+/-)	-7.6 low	-2.5 blw av	-1.4 blw av	-53.6 low	1.9 av

Total Risk	Standard Deviation	Category Risk	Risk Index	Beta
high	15.2%	blw av	1.0	1.2

	1993	1992	1991	1990	1989	1988	1987	1986	1985	1984
Return (%)	16.9	4.8	33.4	-9.0	39.7	-4.5	1.3	13.7	23.6	-3.9
Differ from category (+/-) . . .	-2.1	-5.6	-19.0	-2.7	12.7	-19.7	4.7	4.3	-7.4	5.5

PER SHARE DATA

	1993	1992	1991	1990	1989	1988	1987	1986	1985	1984
Dividends, Net Income ($) .	0.03	0.10	0.32	0.28	0.00	0.00	0.12	0.25	0.18	0.62
Distrib'ns, Cap Gain ($) . . .	2.07	0.21	0.36	0.09	5.13	0.23	1.55	4.03	0.38	2.57
Net Asset Value ($)	20.80	19.67	19.06	14.86	16.75	15.58	16.58	17.87	19.75	16.52
Expense Ratio (%)	1.54	1.34	1.48	1.44	1.48	1.27	1.17	1.13	1.13	1.13
Net Income to Assets (%) .	0.20	0.58	1.87	1.59	0.33	0.03	0.19	0.65	1.22	2.88
Portfolio Turnover (%)	46	41	94	156	362	270	395	279	162	137
Total Assets (Millions $)	114	103	89	75	72	64	91	105	116	105

PORTFOLIO (as of 9/30/93)

Portfolio Manager: Robert S. Salomon, Jr. - 1990

Investm't Category: Aggressive Growth

✔ Cap Gain	Asset Allocation
Cap & Income	Fund of Funds
Income	Index
	Sector
✔ Domestic	Small Cap
✔ Foreign	Socially Conscious
Country/Region	State Specific

Portfolio: stocks 95% bonds 5%
convertibles 0% other 0% cash 0%

Largest Holdings: banks & trust 11%, chemicals 11%

Unrealized Net Capital Gains: 19% of portfolio value

SHAREHOLDER INFORMATION

Minimum Investment
Initial: $1,000   Subsequent: $100

Minimum IRA Investment
Initial: $250   Subsequent: $100

Maximum Fees
Load: none   12b-1: none
Other: none

Distributions
Income: Dec   Capital Gains: Feb, Dec

Exchange Options
Number Per Year: no limit   Fee: none
Telephone: yes (money market fund available)

Services
IRA, other pension, auto withdraw

Salomon Brothers Investors (SAIFX)

Growth & Income

7 World Trade Center
38th Floor
New York, NY 10048
(800) 725-6666, (212) 783-1301

PERFORMANCE

	3yr Annual	5yr Annual	10yr Annual	Bull	Bear
Return (%)	16.9	12.7	11.5	71.5	-12.8
Differ from Category (+/-)	0.5 abv av	0.2 av	-0.9 blw av	1.4 av	-1.2 blw av

Total Risk	Standard Deviation	Category Risk	Risk Index	Beta
abv av	10.9%	abv av	1.3	0.9

	1993	1992	1991	1990	1989	1988	1987	1986	1985	1984
Return (%)	15.1	7.4	29.3	-6.4	21.8	16.8	0.7	13.0	24.4	-0.6
Differ from category (+/-)	2.5	-2.6	1.6	-0.8	0.2	0.0	0.3	-2.2	-1.0	-6.9

PER SHARE DATA

	1993	1992	1991	1990	1989	1988	1987	1986	1985	1984
Dividends, Net Income ($)	0.32	0.40	0.45	0.55	0.62	0.52	0.50	0.54	0.55	0.61
Distrib'ns, Cap Gain ($)	2.52	1.79	1.10	0.49	1.59	1.10	2.26	4.55	1.50	3.18
Net Asset Value ($)	15.60	16.10	17.10	14.54	16.65	15.55	14.77	17.37	19.86	17.61
Expense Ratio (%)	0.71	0.68	0.70	0.68	0.63	0.67	0.58	0.57	0.62	0.60
Net Income to Assets (%)	1.95	2.47	2.67	3.13	3.76	3.32	2.37	2.56	3.32	3.35
Portfolio Turnover (%)	47	48	44	22	36	54	80	62	46	40
Total Assets (Millions $)	392	370	378	330	393	362	352	398	403	351

PORTFOLIO (as of 9/30/93)

Portfolio Manager: James Fleischmann - 1992, Allan R. White III - 1992

Investm't Category: Growth & Income

Cap Gain	Asset Allocation
✔ Cap & Income	Fund of Funds
Income	Index
	Sector
✔ Domestic	Small Cap
✔ Foreign	Socially Conscious
Country/Region	State Specific

Portfolio: stocks 92% bonds 3%
convertibles 0%   other 2%   cash 3%

Largest Holdings: financial services 16%, basic industries 15%

Unrealized Net Capital Gains: 20% of portfolio value

SHAREHOLDER INFORMATION

Minimum Investment
Initial: $500   Subsequent: $50

Minimum IRA Investment
Initial: $250   Subsequent: $50

Maximum Fees
Load: none   12b-1: none
Other: none

Distributions
Income: quarterly   Capital Gains: Dec

Exchange Options
Number Per Year: no limit   Fee: none
Telephone: yes (money market fund available)

Services
IRA, other pension, auto withdraw

Salomon Brothers Opportunity (SAOPX)

Growth

7 World Trade Center
38th Floor
New York, NY 10048
(800) 725-6666, (212) 783-1301

PERFORMANCE

	3yr Annual	5yr Annual	10yr Annual	Bull	Bear
Return (%)	18.8	11.2	13.1	82.5	-22.8
Differ from Category (+/-)	-0.4 av	-3.4 low	0.5 av	-2.2 av	-10.4 low

Total Risk	Standard Deviation	Category Risk	Risk Index	Beta
av	9.5%	low	0.9	0.7

	1993	1992	1991	1990	1989	1988	1987	1986	1985	1984
Return (%).	12.8	13.8	30.5	-15.9	20.9	23.2	4.3	6.4	32.8	10.9
Differ from category (+/-). . .	-0.4	2.8	-4.9	-9.8	-4.9	5.5	3.1	-8.1	3.5	10.9

PER SHARE DATA

	1993	1992	1991	1990	1989	1988	1987	1986	1985	1984
Dividends, Net Income ($).	0.63	0.34	0.50	0.62	0.81	0.54	0.75	0.58	0.47	0.40
Distrib'ns, Cap Gain ($) . . .	1.70	0.80	0.17	0.01	0.88	1.58	2.94	2.78	1.39	1.37
Net Asset Value ($)	30.01	28.70	26.24	20.65	25.35	22.40	19.91	22.60	24.29	19.75
Expense Ratio (%)	1.23	1.25	1.30	1.26	1.19	1.20	1.16	1.16	1.23	1.23
Net Income to Assets (%) .	1.86	1.28	2.31	2.38	3.20	2.29	1.92	2.44	2.71	2.44
Portfolio Turnover (%).	10	11	11	13	15	29	25	28	24	32
Total Assets (Millions $). . . .	115	102	103	90	119	93	114	110	71	48

PORTFOLIO (as of 8/31/93)

Portfolio Manager: Irving Brilliant - 1979

Investm't Category: Growth
- ✔ Cap Gain
- Cap & Income
- Income
- ✔ Domestic
- ✔ Foreign
- Country/Region

- Asset Allocation
- Fund of Funds
- Index
- Sector
- Small Cap
- Socially Conscious
- State Specific

Portfolio: stocks 96% bonds 40%
convertibles 0% other 0% cash 0%

Largest Holdings: insurance—property & casualty 22%, banks—commercial 13%

Unrealized Net Capital Gains: 45% of portfolio value

SHAREHOLDER INFORMATION

Minimum Investment
Initial: $1,000   Subsequent: $100

Minimum IRA Investment
Initial: $250   Subsequent: $100

Maximum Fees
Load: none   12b-1: none
Other: none

Distributions
Income: Dec   Capital Gains: Dec

Exchange Options
Number Per Year: no limit   Fee: none
Telephone: yes (money market fund available)

Services
IRA, other pension, auto withdraw

SBSF (SBFFX)

Growth

45 Rockefeller Plaza
New York, NY 10111
(800) 422-7273, (212) 903-1200

PERFORMANCE

	3yr Annual	5yr Annual	10yr Annual	Bull	Bear
Return (%)	15.2	14.7	13.3	58.8	-6.3
Differ from Category (+/-)	-4.0 blw av	0.1 av	0.6 av	-25.9 blw av	6.1 high

Total Risk	Standard Deviation	Category Risk	Risk Index	Beta
av	8.2%	low	0.8	0.6

	1993	1992	1991	1990	1989	1988	1987	1986	1985	1984
Return (%)	20.4	6.6	19.0	-2.6	33.9	17.1	-3.1	7.9	28.3	11.8
Differ from category (+/-) . . .	7.2	-4.4	-16.4	3.5	8.1	-0.6	-4.3	-6.6	-1.0	11.8

PER SHARE DATA

	1993	1992	1991	1990	1989	1988	1987	1986	1985	1984
Dividends, Net Income ($) .	0.30	0.40	0.56	0.58	0.50	0.41	0.46	0.48	0.40	0.18
Distrib'ns, Cap Gain ($) . . .	2.11	1.00	1.60	0.40	0.57	0.06	0.40	1.60	0.00	0.00
Net Asset Value ($)	15.71	15.07	15.46	14.83	16.26	12.97	11.49	12.72	13.75	11.08
Expense Ratio (%)	1.10	1.16	1.15	1.15	1.20	1.16	1.10	1.17	1.40	1.37
Net Income to Assets (%) . .	2.49	2.68	3.11	3.66	3.12	3.12	1.67	1.80	1.96	4.11
Portfolio Turnover (%)	na	45	50	42	44	47	66	65	80	87
Total Assets (Millions $) . . .	123	105	103	93	98	81	83	90	60	23

PORTFOLIO (as of 5/31/93)

Portfolio Manager: Louis R. Benzak - 1983

Investm't Category: Growth

✔ Cap Gain	Asset Allocation
Cap & Income	Fund of Funds
Income	Index
	Sector
✔ Domestic	Small Cap
Foreign	Socially Conscious
Country/Region	State Specific

Portfolio: stocks 63%   bonds 7%
convertibles 10%   other 0%   cash 20%

Largest Holdings: oil & gas 14%, insurance 11%

Unrealized Net Capital Gains: 14% of portfolio value

SHAREHOLDER INFORMATION

Minimum Investment
Initial: $5,000   Subsequent: $100

Minimum IRA Investment
Initial: $500   Subsequent: $100

Maximum Fees
Load: none   12b-1: 0.25%
Other: none

Distributions
Income: Jun, Dec   Capital Gains: Dec

Exchange Options
Number Per Year: no limit   Fee: none
Telephone: yes (money market fund available)

Services
IRA, other pension, auto exchange, auto invest, auto withdraw

SBSF Convertible Securities (SBFCX)

Growth & Income

45 Rockefeller Plaza
New York, NY 10111
(800) 422-7273, (212) 903-1200

	3yr Annual	5yr Annual	10yr Annual	Bull	Bear
Return (%)	19.5	14.0	na	75.1	-7.4
Differ from Category (+/-)	3.1 abv av	1.5 abv av	na	5.0 abv av	4.2 high

Total Risk	Standard Deviation	Category Risk	Risk Index	Beta
blw av	5.3%	low	0.6	0.3

	1993	1992	1991	1990	1989	1988	1987	1986	1985	1984
Return (%).............	20.0	11.2	27.7	-5.0	18.8	—	—	—	—	—
Differ from category (+/-)...	7.4	1.2	0.0	0.6	-2.8	—	—	—	—	—

PER SHARE DATA

	1993	1992	1991	1990	1989	1988	1987	1986	1985	1984
Dividends, Net Income ($).	0.63	0.68	0.68	0.89	0.81	—	—	—	—	—
Distrib'ns, Cap Gain ($) ...	0.23	0.23	0.15	0.02	0.18	—	—	—	—	—
Net Asset Value ($)	12.21	10.93	10.67	9.06	10.52	—	—	—	—	—
Expense Ratio (%)	1.22	1.32	1.37	1.52	1.15	—	—	—	—	—
Net Income to Assets (%) .	5.04	5.46	7.13	9.12	8.72	—	—	—	—	—
Portfolio Turnover (%)......	na	42	53	32	76	—	—	—	—	—
Total Assets (Millions $).....	63	42	28	15	12	—	—	—	—	—

PORTFOLIO (as of 5/31/93)

Portfolio Manager: Louis R. Benzak - 1988

Investm't Category: Growth & Income
Cap Gain	Asset Allocation
✔ Cap & Income	Fund of Funds
Income	Index
	Sector
✔ Domestic	Small Cap
Foreign	Socially Conscious
Country/Region	State Specific

Portfolio: stocks 17%   bonds 9%
convertibles 67%   other 0%   cash 7%

Largest Holdings: utilities 11%, oil & gas 11%

Unrealized Net Capital Gains: 7% of portfolio value

SHAREHOLDER INFORMATION

Minimum Investment
Initial: $5,000   Subsequent: $100

Minimum IRA Investment
Initial: $500   Subsequent: $100

Maximum Fees
Load: none   12b-1: 0.25%
Other: none

Distributions
Income: quarterly   Capital Gains: Dec

Exchange Options
Number Per Year: no limit   Fee: none
Telephone: yes (money market fund available)

Services
IRA, other pension, auto exchange, auto invest, auto withdraw

Schafer Value (SCHVX)

Growth & Income

645 5th Avenue
7th Floor
New York, NY 10022
(800) 343-0481, (212) 644-1800

PERFORMANCE

	3yr Annual	5yr Annual	10yr Annual	Bull	Bear
Return (%)	27.5	19.3	na	120.0	-15.2
Differ from Category (+/-)	11.1 high	6.8 high	na	49.9 high	-3.6 blw av

Total Risk	Standard Deviation	Category Risk	Risk Index	Beta
abv av	12.7%	high	1.5	1.0

	1993	1992	1991	1990	1989	1988	1987	1986	1985	1984
Return (%)	23.9	18.6	40.9	-10.1	30.0	17.9	-0.3	10.0	—	—
Differ from category (+/-) . .	11.3	8.6	13.2	-4.5	8.4	1.1	-0.6	-5.2	—	—

PER SHARE DATA

	1993	1992	1991	1990	1989	1988	1987	1986	1985	1984
Dividends, Net Income ($) .	0.18	0.38	0.51	0.57	1.26	0.21	0.00	0.31	—	—
Distrib'ns, Cap Gain ($) . . .	1.08	3.27	5.48	1.73	0.60	1.18	0.00	0.00	—	—
Net Asset Value ($)	36.78	30.70	28.98	24.91	30.28	24.86	22.42	22.51	—	—
Expense Ratio (%).	1.74	2.08	2.00	2.00	2.09	1.82	1.96	2.05	—	—
Net Income to Assets (%). .	0.79	1.20	1.26	1.45	1.81	2.32	1.20	1.80	—	—
Portfolio Turnover (%)	33	53	55	36	42	43	47	19	—	—
Total Assets (Millions $)	25	12	10	11	14	12	20	7	—	—

PORTFOLIO (as of 9/30/93)

Portfolio Manager: David K. Schafer - 1985

Investm't Category: Growth & Income
Cap Gain	Asset Allocation
✔ Cap & Income	Fund of Funds
Income	Index
	Sector
✔ Domestic	Small Cap
✔ Foreign	Socially Conscious
Country/Region	State Specific

Portfolio: stocks 99% bonds 0%
convertibles 0% other 0% cash 1%

Largest Holdings: banks 15%, retail 11%

Unrealized Net Capital Gains: 23% of portfolio value

SHAREHOLDER INFORMATION

Minimum Investment
Initial: $2,000   Subsequent: $1,000

Minimum IRA Investment
Initial: $2,000   Subsequent: $1,000

Maximum Fees
Load: none   12b-1: none
Other: none

Distributions
Income: Dec   Capital Gains: Dec

Exchange Options
Number Per Year: none Fee: na
Telephone: na

Services
IRA

Schroder US Equity
(SUSEX)
Growth

787 Seventh Ave.
New York, NY 10019
(800) 344-8332, (212) 841-3841

	3yr Annual	5yr Annual	10yr Annual	Bull	Bear
Return (%)	21.5	16.4	12.6	91.6	-10.1
Differ from Category (+/-)	2.3 abv av	1.8 abv av	0.0 av	6.9 abv av	2.3 abv av

Total Risk	Standard Deviation	Category Risk	Risk Index	Beta
abv av	12.6%	abv av	1.2	1.1

	1993	1992	1991	1990	1989	1988	1987	1986	1985	1984
Return (%)	12.6	15.2	38.2	-4.0	24.4	12.0	0.4	12.2	23.4	-1.6
Differ from category (+/-)	-0.6	4.2	2.8	2.1	-1.4	-5.7	-0.8	-2.3	-5.9	-1.6

PER SHARE DATA

	1993	1992	1991	1990	1989	1988	1987	1986	1985	1984
Dividends, Net Income ($)	0.05	0.03	0.12	0.12	0.25	0.14	0.36	0.23	0.22	0.30
Distrib'ns, Cap Gain ($)	2.51	1.10	0.57	0.00	0.42	0.45	5.47	0.73	0.00	0.36
Net Asset Value ($)	8.77	10.14	9.80	7.61	8.06	7.05	6.82	12.45	12.04	9.96
Expense Ratio (%)	na	1.40	1.39	1.34	1.49	1.60	1.30	1.16	1.16	1.12
Net Income to Assets (%)	na	0.42	1.30	1.59	1.99	1.89	1.60	2.25	2.66	2.56
Portfolio Turnover (%)	na	31	30	28	40	18	43	40	58	43
Total Assets (Millions $)	20	20	20	18	24	26	30	46	51	54

PORTFOLIO (as of 4/30/93)

Portfolio Manager: Fariba Talebi - 1991

Investm't Category: Growth

✔ Cap Gain	Asset Allocation
Cap & Income	Fund of Funds
Income	Index
	Sector
✔ Domestic	Small Cap
Foreign	Socially Conscious
Country/Region	State Specific

Portfolio: stocks 100% bonds 0%
convertibles 0% other 0% cash 0%

Largest Holdings: retail 14%, banks & financial services 9%

Unrealized Net Capital Gains: 29% of portfolio value

SHAREHOLDER INFORMATION

Minimum Investment
Initial: $500   Subsequent: $100

Minimum IRA Investment
Initial: na   Subsequent: na

Maximum Fees
Load: none   12b-1: none
Other: none

Distributions
Income: Jun, Dec   Capital Gains: Dec

Exchange Options
Number Per Year: none   Fee: na
Telephone: na

Services

Schwab 1000 (SNXFX)

Growth & Income

101 Montgomery St.
San Francisco, CA 94104
(800) 526-8600

PERFORMANCE

	3yr Annual	5yr Annual	10yr Annual	Bull	Bear
Return (%)	na	na	na	na	na
Differ from Category (+/-)	na	na	na	na	na

Total Risk	Standard Deviation	Category Risk	Risk Index	Beta
na	na	na	na	na

	1993	1992	1991	1990	1989	1988	1987	1986	1985	1984
Return (%)	9.5	8.5	—	—	—	—	—	—	—	—
Differ from category (+/-) . .	-3.1	-1.5	—	—	—	—	—	—	—	—

PER SHARE DATA

	1993	1992	1991	1990	1989	1988	1987	1986	1985	1984
Dividends, Net Income ($) .	0.25	0.24	—	—	—	—	—	—	—	—
Distrib'ns, Cap Gain ($) . . .	0.00	0.00	—	—	—	—	—	—	—	—
Net Asset Value ($)	12.85	11.96	—	—	—	—	—	—	—	—
Expense Ratio (%).	0.45	0.35	—	—	—	—	—	—	—	—
Net Income to Assets (%) . .	2.21	2.45	—	—	—	—	—	—	—	—
Portfolio Turnover (%)	na	1	—	—	—	—	—	—	—	—
Total Assets (Millions $) . . .	532	371	—	—	—	—	—	—	—	—

PORTFOLIO (as of 8/31/93)

Portfolio Manager: not specified

Investm't Category: Growth & Income
- Cap Gain
- ✔ Cap & Income
- Income
- ✔ Domestic
- Foreign
- Country/Region
- Asset Allocation
- Fund of Funds
- ✔ Index
- Sector
- Small Cap
- Socially Conscious
- State Specific

Portfolio: stocks 100% bonds 0%
convertibles 0% other 0% cash 0%

Largest Holdings: Schwab 1000 Index

Unrealized Net Capital Gains: 13% of portfolio value

SHAREHOLDER INFORMATION

Minimum Investment
Initial: $1,000   Subsequent: $100

Minimum IRA Investment
Initial: $500   Subsequent: $100

Maximum Fees
Load: 0.50% redemption   12b-1: none
Other: redemption fee applies for 6 mos

Distributions
Income: Jun, Dec   Capital Gains: Dec

Exchange Options
Number Per Year: no limit   Fee: none
Telephone: yes (money market fund available)

Services
IRA, other pension, auto invest

Schwab CA Long-Term Tax-Free (SWCAX)

101 Montgomery St.
San Francisco, CA 94104
(800) 526-8600

Tax-Exempt Bond

PERFORMANCE

	3yr Annual	5yr Annual	10yr Annual	Bull	Bear
Return (%)	na	na	na	na	na
Differ from Category (+/-)	na	na	na	na	na

Total Risk	Standard Deviation	Category Risk	Risk Index	Avg Mat
na	na	na	na	20.1 yrs

	1993	1992	1991	1990	1989	1988	1987	1986	1985	1984
Return (%)	12.8	—	—	—	—	—	—	—	—	—
Differ from category (+/-) . . .	1.2	—	—	—	—	—	—	—	—	—

PER SHARE DATA

	1993	1992	1991	1990	1989	1988	1987	1986	1985	1984
Dividends, Net Income ($) .	0.56	—	—	—	—	—	—	—	—	—
Distrib'ns, Cap Gain ($) . . .	0.12	—	—	—	—	—	—	—	—	—
Net Asset Value ($)	11.23	—	—	—	—	—	—	—	—	—
Expense Ratio (%)	0.60	—	—	—	—	—	—	—	—	—
Net Income to Assets (%) .	5.18	—	—	—	—	—	—	—	—	—
Portfolio Turnover (%)	na	—	—	—	—	—	—	—	—	—
Total Assets (Millions $)	132	—	—	—	—	—	—	—	—	—

PORTFOLIO (as of 8/31/93)

Portfolio Manager: Keighley - 1992, Ward - 1992

Investm't Category: Tax-Exempt Bond

Cap Gain	Asset Allocation
Cap & Income	Fund of Funds
✔ Income	Index
	Sector
✔ Domestic	Small Cap
Foreign	Socially Conscious
Country/Region	✔ State Specific

Portfolio: stocks 0% bonds 100%
convertibles 0% other 0% cash 0%

Largest Holdings: general obligation 0%

Unrealized Net Capital Gains: 5% of portfolio value

SHAREHOLDER INFORMATION

Minimum Investment
Initial: $1,000   Subsequent: $100

Minimum IRA Investment
Initial: na   Subsequent: na

Maximum Fees
Load: none   12b-1: none
Other: none

Distributions
Income: monthly   Capital Gains: Dec

Exchange Options
Number Per Year: no limit   Fee: none
Telephone: yes (money market fund available)

Services
auto invest

Schwab CA Short/Interm Tax-Free (SWCSX)

101 Montgomery St.
San Francisco, CA 94104
(800) 526-8600

Tax-Exempt Bond

fund in existence since 4/21/93

PERFORMANCE

	3yr Annual	5yr Annual	10yr Annual	Bull	Bear
Return (%)	na	na	na	na	na
Differ from Category (+/-)	na	na	na	na	na

Total Risk	Standard Deviation	Category Risk	Risk Index	Avg Mat
na	na	na	na	4.6 yrs

	1993	1992	1991	1990	1989	1988	1987	1986	1985	1984
Return (%)	—	—	—	—	—	—	—	—	—	—
Differ from category (+/-) ...	—	—	—	—	—	—	—	—	—	—

PER SHARE DATA

	1993	1992	1991	1990	1989	1988	1987	1986	1985	1984
Dividends, Net Income ($) .	0.24	—	—	—	—	—	—	—	—	—
Distrib'ns, Cap Gain ($) ...	0.00	—	—	—	—	—	—	—	—	—
Net Asset Value ($)	10.19	—	—	—	—	—	—	—	—	—
Expense Ratio (%)........	0.45	—	—	—	—	—	—	—	—	—
Net Income to Assets (%)..	3.49	—	—	—	—	—	—	—	—	—
Portfolio Turnover (%)	na	—	—	—	—	—	—	—	—	—
Total Assets (Millions $)	51	—	—	—	—	—	—	—	—	—

PORTFOLIO (as of 8/31/93)

Portfolio Manager: Keighley - 1992, Ward - 1992

Investm't Category: Tax-Exempt Bond

Cap Gain	Asset Allocation
Cap & Income	Fund of Funds
✔ Income	Index
	Sector
✔ Domestic	Small Cap
Foreign	Socially Conscious
Country/Region	✔ State Specific

Portfolio: stocks 0% bonds 100%
convertibles 0% other 0% cash 0%

Largest Holdings: general obligation 0%

Unrealized Net Capital Gains: 1% of portfolio value

SHAREHOLDER INFORMATION

Minimum Investment
Initial: $1,000   Subsequent: $100

Minimum IRA Investment
Initial: na   Subsequent: na

Maximum Fees
Load: none   12b-1: none
Other: none

Distributions
Income: monthly   Capital Gains: Dec

Exchange Options
Number Per Year: no limit   Fee: none
Telephone: yes (money market fund available)

Services
auto invest

Schwab Long-Term Tax-Free (SWNTX)

101 Montgomery St.
San Francisco, CA 94104
(800) 526-8600

Tax-Exempt Bond

PERFORMANCE

	3yr Annual	5yr Annual	10yr Annual	Bull	Bear
Return (%)	na	na	na	na	na
Differ from Category (+/-)	na	na	na	na	na

Total Risk	Standard Deviation	Category Risk	Risk Index	Avg Mat
na	na	na	na	19.3 yrs

	1993	1992	1991	1990	1989	1988	1987	1986	1985	1984
Return (%)	13.5	—	—	—	—	—	—	—	—	—
Differ from category (+/-)	1.9	—	—	—	—	—	—	—	—	—

PER SHARE DATA

	1993	1992	1991	1990	1989	1988	1987	1986	1985	1984
Dividends, Net Income ($)	0.53	—	—	—	—	—	—	—	—	—
Distrib'ns, Cap Gain ($)	0.07	—	—	—	—	—	—	—	—	—
Net Asset Value ($)	10.62	—	—	—	—	—	—	—	—	—
Expense Ratio (%)	0.45	—	—	—	—	—	—	—	—	—
Net Income to Assets (%)	5.30	—	—	—	—	—	—	—	—	—
Portfolio Turnover (%)	na	—	—	—	—	—	—	—	—	—
Total Assets (Millions $)	49	—	—	—	—	—	—	—	—	—

PORTFOLIO (as of 8/31/93)

Portfolio Manager: Keighley - 1992, Ward - 1992

Investm't Category: Tax-Exempt Bond

Cap Gain	Asset Allocation
Cap & Income	Fund of Funds
✔ Income	Index
	Sector
✔ Domestic	Small Cap
Foreign	Socially Conscious
Country/Region	State Specific

Portfolio: stocks 0%   bonds 100%
convertibles 0%   other 0%   cash 0%

Largest Holdings: general obligation 0%

Unrealized Net Capital Gains: 4% of portfolio value

SHAREHOLDER INFORMATION

Minimum Investment
Initial: $1,000   Subsequent: $100

Minimum IRA Investment
Initial: na   Subsequent: na

Maximum Fees
Load: none   12b-1: none
Other: none

Distributions
Income: monthly   Capital Gains: Dec

Exchange Options
Number Per Year: no limit   Fee: none
Telephone: yes (money market fund available)

Services
auto invest

Schwab Short/Interm Gov't Bond (SWBDX)

Government Bond

101 Montgomery St.
San Francisco, CA 94104
(800) 526-8600

fund in existence since 4/21/93

PERFORMANCE

	3yr Annual	5yr Annual	10yr Annual	Bull	Bear
Return (%)	na	na	na	na	na
Differ from Category (+/-)	na	na	na	na	na

Total Risk	Standard Deviation	Category Risk	Risk Index	Avg Mat
na	na	na	na	3.9 yrs

	1993	1992	1991	1990	1989	1988	1987	1986	1985	1984
Return (%)	7.7	6.0	—	—	—	—	—	—	—	—
Differ from category (+/-) . .	-2.7	-0.2	—	—	—	—	—	—	—	—

PER SHARE DATA

	1993	1992	1991	1990	1989	1988	1987	1986	1985	1984
Dividends, Net Income ($) .	0.54	0.59	—	—	—	—	—	—	—	—
Distrib'ns, Cap Gain ($) . . .	0.11	0.02	—	—	—	—	—	—	—	—
Net Asset Value ($)	10.38	10.26	—	—	—	—	—	—	—	—
Expense Ratio (%).	0.60	0.43	—	—	—	—	—	—	—	—
Net Income to Assets (%) . .	5.28	5.78	—	—	—	—	—	—	—	—
Portfolio Turnover (%)	na	185	—	—	—	—	—	—	—	—
Total Assets (Millions $) . . .	270	226	—	—	—	—	—	—	—	—

PORTFOLIO (as of 8/31/93)

Portfolio Manager: Regan - 1991, Ward - 1991

Investm't Category: Government Bond
Cap Gain	Asset Allocation
Cap & Income	Fund of Funds
✔ Income	Index
	Sector
✔ Domestic	Small Cap
Foreign	Socially Conscious
Country/Region	State Specific

Portfolio: stocks 0% bonds 97%
convertibles 0% other 0% cash 3%

Largest Holdings: mortgage-backed 53%, U.S. government & agencies 44%

Unrealized Net Capital Gains: 3% of portfolio value

SHAREHOLDER INFORMATION

Minimum Investment
Initial: $1,000   Subsequent: $100

Minimum IRA Investment
Initial: $500   Subsequent: $100

Maximum Fees
Load: none   12b-1: none
Other: none

Distributions
Income: monthly   Capital Gains: Dec

Exchange Options
Number Per Year: no limit   Fee: none
Telephone: yes (money market fund available)

Services
IRA, other pension, auto invest

Schwab Short/ Intermediate Tax-Free

101 Montgomery St.
San Francisco, CA 94104
(800) 526-8600

(SWITX) *Tax-Exempt Bond*

fund in existence since 4/21/93

PERFORMANCE

	3yr Annual	5yr Annual	10yr Annual	Bull	Bear
Return (%)	na	na	na	na	na
Differ from Category (+/-)	na	na	na	na	na

Total Risk	Standard Deviation	Category Risk	Risk Index	Avg Mat
na	na	na	na	4.8 yrs

	1993	1992	1991	1990	1989	1988	1987	1986	1985	1984
Return (%).	—	—	—	—	—	—	—	—	—	—
Differ from category (+/-). . . .	—	—	—	—	—	—	—	—	—	—

PER SHARE DATA

	1993	1992	1991	1990	1989	1988	1987	1986	1985	1984
Dividends, Net Income ($) .	0.24	—	—	—	—	—	—	—	—	—
Distrib'ns, Cap Gain ($) . . .	0.00	—	—	—	—	—	—	—	—	—
Net Asset Value ($)	10.20	—	—	—	—	—	—	—	—	—
Expense Ratio (%)	0.45	—	—	—	—	—	—	—	—	—
Net Income to Assets (%) .	3.63	—	—	—	—	—	—	—	—	—
Portfolio Turnover (%).	na	—	—	—	—	—	—	—	—	—
Total Assets (Millions $).	67	—	—	—	—	—	—	—	—	—

PORTFOLIO (as of 8/31/93)

Portfolio Manager: committee

Investm't Category: Tax-Exempt Bond

Cap Gain	Asset Allocation
Cap & Income	Fund of Funds
✔ Income	Index
	Sector
✔ Domestic	Small Cap
Foreign	Socially Conscious
Country/Region	State Specific

Portfolio: stocks 0% bonds 100%
convertibles 0% other 0% cash 0%

Largest Holdings: general obligation 0%

Unrealized Net Capital Gains: 1% of portfolio value

SHAREHOLDER INFORMATION

Minimum Investment
Initial: $1,000   Subsequent: $100

Minimum IRA Investment
Initial: na   Subsequent: na

Maximum Fees
Load: none   12b-1: none
Other: none

Distributions
Income: monthly   Capital Gains: Dec

Exchange Options
Number Per Year: no limit   Fee: none
Telephone: yes (money market fund available)

Services
auto invest

Scudder Balanced

(SCBAX)

Balanced

160 Federal St.
Boston, MA 02110
(800) 225-2470, (617) 439-4640

PERFORMANCE

	3yr Annual	5yr Annual	10yr Annual	Bull	Bear
Return (%)	na	na	na	na	na
Differ from Category (+/-)	na	na	na	na	na

Total Risk	Standard Deviation	Category Risk	Risk Index	Beta
na	na	na	na	na

	1993	1992	1991	1990	1989	1988	1987	1986	1985	1984
Return (%)	4.1	—	—	—	—	—	—	—	—	—
Differ from category (+/-) . .	-9.3	—	—	—	—	—	—	—	—	—

PER SHARE DATA

	1993	1992	1991	1990	1989	1988	1987	1986	1985	1984
Dividends, Net Income ($) .	0.25	—	—	—	—	—	—	—	—	—
Distrib'ns, Cap Gain ($) . . .	0.00	—	—	—	—	—	—	—	—	—
Net Asset Value ($)	12.23	—	—	—	—	—	—	—	—	—
Expense Ratio (%)	1.00	—	—	—	—	—	—	—	—	—
Net Income to Assets (%) . .	2.51	—	—	—	—	—	—	—	—	—
Portfolio Turnover (%)	87	—	—	—	—	—	—	—	—	—
Total Assets (Millions $)	65	—	—	—	—	—	—	—	—	—

PORTFOLIO (as of 6/30/93)

Portfolio Manager: H.F. Ward - 1993, B.F. Beaty - 1993, W. Hutchinson - 1993

Investm't Category: Balanced

Cap Gain	Asset Allocation
✔ Cap & Income	Fund of Funds
Income	Index
	Sector
✔ Domestic	Small Cap
✔ Foreign	Socially Conscious
Country/Region	State Specific

Portfolio: stocks 55% bonds 27%
convertibles 0% other 0% cash 18%

Largest Holdings: stocks—finance 11%, bonds—mortgage-backed 8%

Unrealized Net Capital Gains: 0% of portfolio value

SHAREHOLDER INFORMATION

Minimum Investment
Initial: $1,000   Subsequent: $100

Minimum IRA Investment
Initial: $500   Subsequent: $50

Maximum Fees
Load: none   12b-1: none
Other: none

Distributions
Income: quarterly   Capital Gains: Dec

Exchange Options
Number Per Year: no limit   Fee: none
Telephone: yes (money market fund available)

Services
IRA, other pension, auto exchange, auto invest, auto withdraw

Scudder CA Tax Free
(SCTFX)

Tax-Exempt Bond

160 Federal St.
Boston, MA 02110
(800) 225-2470, (617) 439-4640

	3yr Annual	5yr Annual	10yr Annual	Bull	Bear
Return (%)	11.9	10.4	10.3	47.6	1.1
Differ from Category (+/-)	1.6 high	1.2 high	0.6 av	7.5 high	-1.2 low

Total Risk	Standard Deviation	Category Risk	Risk Index	Avg Mat
blw av	5.3%	high	1.3	11.3 yrs

	1993	1992	1991	1990	1989	1988	1987	1986	1985	1984
Return (%)............	13.8	9.3	12.6	6.3	10.3	11.8	-1.6	16.8	18.4	7.0
Differ from category (+/-)...	2.2	1.0	1.3	0.0	1.3	1.7	-0.4	0.4	1.1	-1.3

PER SHARE DATA

	1993	1992	1991	1990	1989	1988	1987	1986	1985	1984
Dividends, Net Income ($).	0.55	0.58	0.62	0.63	0.66	0.68	0.69	0.72	0.75	0.81
Distrib'ns, Cap Gain ($) ...	0.68	0.48	0.27	0.09	0.18	0.00	0.26	0.29	0.00	0.00
Net Asset Value ($)	10.85	10.66	10.77	10.41	10.50	10.31	9.86	11.01	10.35	9.42
Expense Ratio (%)	0.79	0.81	0.84	0.83	0.89	0.88	0.84	0.88	0.99	1.00
Net Income to Assets (%) .	5.42	5.79	6.13	6.23	6.71	6.95	6.55	7.11	8.76	8.26
Portfolio Turnover (%)....	208	143	171	70	159	52	68	92	168	91
Total Assets (Millions $)....	349	242	209	193	171	153	195	132	73	38

PORTFOLIO (as of 3/31/93)

Portfolio Manager: Carleton - 1983, Ragus - 1989

Investm't Category: Tax-Exempt Bond

Cap Gain	Asset Allocation
Cap & Income	Fund of Funds
✔ Income	Index
	Sector
✔ Domestic	Small Cap
Foreign	Socially Conscious
Country/Region	✔ State Specific

Portfolio: stocks 0% bonds 90%
convertibles 0% other 0% cash 10%

Largest Holdings: general obligation 7%

Unrealized Net Capital Gains: 3% of portfolio value

SHAREHOLDER INFORMATION

Minimum Investment
Initial: $1,000 Subsequent: $100

Minimum IRA Investment
Initial: na Subsequent: na

Maximum Fees
Load: none 12b-1: none
Other: none

Distributions
Income: monthly Capital Gains: Jun, Nov

Exchange Options
Number Per Year: no limit Fee: none
Telephone: yes (money market fund available)

Services
auto exchange, auto invest, auto withdraw

Scudder Capital Growth
(SCDUX)

160 Federal St.
Boston, MA 02110
(800) 225-2470, (617) 439-4640

Growth

PERFORMANCE

	3yr Annual	5yr Annual	10yr Annual	Bull	Bear
Return (%)	22.4	15.3	15.4	105.7	-25.8
Differ from Category (+/-)	3.2 abv av	0.6 abv av	2.8 high	21.0 abv av	-13.4 low

Total Risk	Standard Deviation	Category Risk	Risk Index	Beta
high	15.4%	high	1.5	1.2

	1993	1992	1991	1990	1989	1988	1987	1986	1985	1984
Return (%)	20.0	7.0	42.9	-16.9	33.8	29.7	-0.6	16.5	36.6	0.4
Differ from category (+/-) . . .	6.8	-4.0	7.5	-10.8	8.0	12.0	-1.9	2.0	7.3	0.4

PER SHARE DATA

	1993	1992	1991	1990	1989	1988	1987	1986	1985	1984
Dividends, Net Income ($) .	0.00	0.10	0.21	0.37	0.15	0.07	0.19	0.23	0.23	0.28
Distrib'ns, Cap Gain ($) . . .	2.62	1.25	0.98	1.35	1.45	0.79	2.13	2.46	1.88	0.50
Net Asset Value ($)	21.26	19.91	19.86	14.81	19.91	16.13	13.14	15.59	15.64	13.14
Expense Ratio (%).	0.96	0.98	1.04	0.93	0.88	0.95	0.88	0.84	0.86	0.89
Net Income to Assets (%). .	0.22	0.57	1.24	1.56	1.22	0.63	0.86	1.50	1.74	2.17
Portfolio Turnover (%)	92	92	93	88	56	49	58	55	57	35
Total Assets (Millions $) . .	1,415	1,054	1,059	712	1,013	491	583	414	362	236

PORTFOLIO (as of 9/30/93)

Portfolio Manager: J. D. Cox - 1984,
S. Aronoff - 1989, W. F. Gadsden - 1989

Investm't Category: Growth

✔ Cap Gain	Asset Allocation
Cap & Income	Fund of Funds
Income	Index
	Sector
✔ Domestic	Small Cap
✔ Foreign	Socially Conscious
Country/Region	State Specific

Portfolio: stocks 95%   bonds 0%
convertibles 5%   other 0%   cash 0%

Largest Holdings: consumer discretionary
20%, communications 14%

Unrealized Net Capital Gains: 18% of portfolio value

SHAREHOLDER INFORMATION

Minimum Investment
Initial: $1,000   Subsequent: $100

Minimum IRA Investment
Initial: $500   Subsequent: $50

Maximum Fees
Load: none   12b-1: none
Other: none

Distributions
Income: Dec   Capital Gains: Dec

Exchange Options
Number Per Year: no limit   Fee: none
Telephone: yes (money market fund available)

Services
IRA, other pension, auto exchange, auto invest,
auto withdraw

Scudder Development
(SCDVX)

160 Federal St.
Boston, MA 02110
(800) 225-2470, (617) 439-4640

Aggressive Growth

PERFORMANCE

	3yr Annual	5yr Annual	10yr Annual	Bull	Bear
Return (%)	22.4	18.0	11.2	112.8	-12.4
Differ from Category (+/-)	-3.0 blw av	-0.2 av	-0.6 blw av	-12.2 av	2.6 abv av

Total Risk	Standard Deviation	Category Risk	Risk Index	Beta
high	20.0%	abv av	1.3	1.5

	1993	1992	1991	1990	1989	1988	1987	1986	1985	1984
Return (%)	8.8	-1.8	71.9	1.4	23.2	11.0	-1.5	7.6	19.8	-10.2
Differ from category (+/-)	-10.2	-12.2	19.5	7.7	-3.8	-4.2	1.9	-1.8	-11.2	-0.8

PER SHARE DATA

	1993	1992	1991	1990	1989	1988	1987	1986	1985	1984
Dividends, Net Income ($)	0.00	0.00	0.00	0.00	0.00	0.00	0.00	0.00	0.17	0.28
Distrib'ns, Cap Gain ($)	3.07	1.70	0.95	1.23	2.28	0.42	1.89	1.33	0.91	0.35
Net Asset Value ($)	33.51	33.62	36.25	21.73	22.69	20.32	18.69	20.71	20.43	18.02
Expense Ratio (%)	1.30	1.30	1.29	1.34	1.32	1.30	1.27	1.25	1.29	1.31
Net Income to Assets (%)	-0.83	-0.70	-0.40	-0.35	-0.47	-0.44	-0.33	-0.03	0.90	1.62
Portfolio Turnover (%)	49	54	71	40	32	39	24	29	25	20
Total Assets (Millions $)	749	700	476	361	275	356	387	359	254	206

PORTFOLIO (as of 6/30/93)

Portfolio Manager: Roy C. McKay - 1988

Investm't Category: Aggressive Growth
✔ Cap Gain   Asset Allocation
  Cap & Income   Fund of Funds
  Income   Index
                  Sector
✔ Domestic   ✔ Small Cap
✔ Foreign   Socially Conscious
  Country/Region State Specific

Portfolio: stocks 96% bonds 0%
convertibles 0% other 1% cash 3%

Largest Holdings: technology 23%, consumer discretionary 18%

Unrealized Net Capital Gains: 29% of portfolio value

SHAREHOLDER INFORMATION

Minimum Investment
Initial: $1,000   Subsequent: $100

Minimum IRA Investment
Initial: $500   Subsequent: $50

Maximum Fees
Load: none   12b-1: none
Other: none

Distributions
Income: Aug, Dec   Capital Gains: Aug, Dec

Exchange Options
Number Per Year: no limit   Fee: none
Telephone: yes (money market fund available)

Services
IRA, other pension, auto exchange, auto invest, auto withdraw

Scudder Global (SCOBX)

International Stock

160 Federal St.
Boston, MA 02110
(800) 225-2470, (617) 439-4640

PERFORMANCE

	3yr Annual	5yr Annual	10yr Annual	Bull	Bear
Return (%)	17.0	15.5	na	67.0	-10.1
Differ from Category (+/-)	2.7 abv av	6.8 high	na	11.9 abv av	5.0 high

Total Risk	Standard Deviation	Category Risk	Risk Index	Beta
av	9.5%	low	0.8	0.6

	1993	1992	1991	1990	1989	1988	1987	1986	1985	1984
Return (%)	31.1	4.4	17.0	-6.4	37.3	19.1	3.0	—	—	—
Differ from category (+/-) . .	-7.4	7.9	4.1	4.7	15.1	5.3	-9.0	—	—	—

PER SHARE DATA

	1993	1992	1991	1990	1989	1988	1987	1986	1985	1984
Dividends, Net Income ($) .	0.23	0.15	0.31	0.62	0.10	0.14	0.06	—	—	—
Distrib'ns, Cap Gain ($) . . .	0.25	0.34	0.66	0.57	0.63	0.07	0.24	—	—	—
Net Asset Value ($)	24.80	19.31	18.96	17.06	19.48	14.74	12.56	—	—	—
Expense Ratio (%).	1.48	1.59	1.70	1.81	1.98	1.71	1.84	—	—	—
Net Income to Assets (%) . .	0.90	1.09	2.21	1.77	1.22	1.23	0.63	—	—	—
Portfolio Turnover (%)	64	45	85	38	31	54	32	—	—	—
Total Assets (Millions $) . . .	965	371	268	257	91	81	102	—	—	—

PORTFOLIO (as of 6/30/93)

Portfolio Manager: William Holzer - 1986;
J. Gregory Garrett - 1986

Investm't Category: International Stock

✔ Cap Gain	Asset Allocation
Cap & Income	Fund of Funds
Income	Index
	Sector
✔ Domestic	Small Cap
✔ Foreign	Socially Conscious
Country/Region	State Specific

Portfolio: stocks 76% bonds 10%
convertibles 1% other 1% cash 12%

Largest Holdings: United States 23%, Switzer-land 9%

Unrealized Net Capital Gains: 12% of port-folio value

SHAREHOLDER INFORMATION

Minimum Investment
Initial: $1,000 Subsequent: $100

Minimum IRA Investment
Initial: $500 Subsequent: $50

Maximum Fees
Load: none 12b-1: none
Other: none

Distributions
Income: Nov, Dec Capital Gains: Nov, Dec

Exchange Options
Number Per Year: no limit Fee: none
Telephone: yes (money market fund available)

Services
IRA, other pension, auto exchange, auto invest, auto withdraw

Scudder Global Small Company (SGSCX)

160 Federal St.
Boston, MA 02110
(800) 225-2470, (617) 439-4640

International Stock

PERFORMANCE

	3yr Annual	5yr Annual	10yr Annual	Bull	Bear
Return (%)	na	na	na	na	na
Differ from Category (+/-)	na	na	na	na	na

Total Risk	Standard Deviation	Category Risk	Risk Index	Beta
na	na	na	na	na

	1993	1992	1991	1990	1989	1988	1987	1986	1985	1984
Return (%)	38.1	0.0	—	—	—	—	—	—	—	—
Differ from category (+/-)	-0.4	3.5	—	—	—	—	—	—	—	—

PER SHARE DATA

	1993	1992	1991	1990	1989	1988	1987	1986	1985	1984
Dividends, Net Income ($)	0.17	0.07	—	—	—	—	—	—	—	—
Distrib'ns, Cap Gain ($)	0.15	0.11	—	—	—	—	—	—	—	—
Net Asset Value ($)	16.53	12.20	—	—	—	—	—	—	—	—
Expense Ratio (%)	1.50	1.50	—	—	—	—	—	—	—	—
Net Income to Assets (%)	0.53	0.78	—	—	—	—	—	—	—	—
Portfolio Turnover (%)	54	23	—	—	—	—	—	—	—	—
Total Assets (Millions $)	216	55	—	—	—	—	—	—	—	—

PORTFOLIO (as of 10/31/93)

Portfolio Manager: A. Economos - 1991, C. L. Franklin - 1991, G. J. Moran - 1991

Investm't Category: International Stock

✔ Cap Gain	Asset Allocation
Cap & Income	Fund of Funds
Income	Index
	Sector
✔ Domestic	✔ Small Cap
✔ Foreign	Socially Conscious
Country/Region	State Specific

Portfolio: stocks 88% bonds 0%
convertibles 1% other 7% cash 5%

Largest Holdings: United States 24%, Japan 16%

Unrealized Net Capital Gains: 12% of portfolio value

SHAREHOLDER INFORMATION

Minimum Investment
Initial: $1,000   Subsequent: $100

Minimum IRA Investment
Initial: $1,000   Subsequent: $100

Maximum Fees
Load: none   12b-1: none
Other: none

Distributions
Income: Dec   Capital Gains: Dec

Exchange Options
Number Per Year: no limit   Fee: none
Telephone: yes (money market fund available)

Services
IRA, other pension, auto exchange, auto invest, auto withdraw

Scudder GNMA (SGMSX)

Mortgage-Backed Bond

160 Federal St.
Boston, MA 02110
(800) 225-2470, (617) 439-4640

	3yr Annual	5yr Annual	10yr Annual	Bull	Bear
Return (%)	9.2	10.1	na	37.1	4.7
Differ from Category (+/-)	0.0 av	0.2 abv av	na	0.4 abv av	0.1 blw av

Total Risk	Standard Deviation	Category Risk	Risk Index	Avg Mat
low	3.1%	abv av	1.2	7.2 yrs

	1993	1992	1991	1990	1989	1988	1987	1986	1985	1984
Return (%)	6.0	6.9	15.0	10.1	12.8	6.8	1.4	11.3	—	—
Differ from category (+/-)	-0.8	0.8	0.6	0.6	0.5	-0.2	-0.6	0.1	—	—

PER SHARE DATA

	1993	1992	1991	1990	1989	1988	1987	1986	1985	1984
Dividends, Net Income ($)	1.20	1.29	1.21	1.23	1.26	1.30	1.27	1.41	—	—
Distrib'ns, Cap Gain ($)	0.00	0.00	0.00	0.00	0.00	0.00	0.00	0.07	—	—
Net Asset Value ($)	15.06	15.36	15.62	14.72	14.56	14.09	14.43	15.50	—	—
Expense Ratio (%)	0.93	0.99	1.04	1.05	1.04	1.04	1.05	1.02	—	—
Net Income to Assets (%)	8.36	8.24	8.49	8.74	8.95	8.93	8.63	10.11	—	—
Portfolio Turnover (%)	87	147	52	71	128	92	59	123	—	—
Total Assets (Millions $)	618	350	264	251	242	252	294	153	—	—

PORTFOLIO (as of 9/30/93)

Portfolio Manager: Robert E. Pruyne - 1985, David H. Glen - 1985

Investm't Category: Mortgage-Backed Bond
Cap Gain	Asset Allocation
Cap & Income	Fund of Funds
✔ Income	Index
	Sector
✔ Domestic	Small Cap
Foreign	Socially Conscious
Country/Region	State Specific

Portfolio: stocks 0% bonds 94%
convertibles 0% other 0% cash 6%

Largest Holdings: mortgage-backed 91%, U.S. government 3%

Unrealized Net Capital Gains: 0% of portfolio value

SHAREHOLDER INFORMATION

Minimum Investment
Initial: $1,000   Subsequent: $100

Minimum IRA Investment
Initial: $500   Subsequent: $50

Maximum Fees
Load: none   12b-1: none
Other: none

Distributions
Income: monthly   Capital Gains: May

Exchange Options
Number Per Year: no limit   Fee: none
Telephone: yes (money market fund available)

Services
IRA, other pension, auto exchange, auto invest, auto withdraw

Scudder Gold (SCGDX)

Gold

160 Federal St.
Boston, MA 02110
(800) 225-2470, (617) 439-4640

PERFORMANCE

	3yr Annual	5yr Annual	10yr Annual	Bull	Bear
Return (%)	10.4	4.4	na	23.2	-8.8
Differ from Category (+/-)	-3.3 low	-7.9 low	na	-10.4 low	-54.7 abv av

Total Risk	Standard Deviation	Category Risk	Risk Index	Beta
high	20.1%	low	0.8	-0.2

	1993	1992	1991	1990	1989	1988	1987	1986	1985	1984
Return (%)	59.3	-9.0	-6.9	-16.6	10.6	—	—	—	—	—
Differ from category (+/-). .	-27.6	6.7	-2.1	-48.1	-14.1	—	—	—	—	—

PER SHARE DATA

	1993	1992	1991	1990	1989	1988	1987	1986	1985	1984
Dividends, Net Income ($) .	0.23	0.00	0.00	0.00	0.05	—	—	—	—	—
Distrib'ns, Cap Gain ($) . . .	0.00	0.00	0.00	0.00	0.03	—	—	—	—	—
Net Asset Value ($)	13.35	8.55	9.40	10.10	12.12	—	—	—	—	—
Expense Ratio (%)	2.17	2.54	2.54	2.60	3.00	—	—	—	—	—
Net Income to Assets (%) .	-0.81	-1.34	-0.59	0.34	-1.06	—	—	—	—	—
Portfolio Turnover (%).	59	58	71	81	35	—	—	—	—	—
Total Assets (Millions $). . . .	108	31	33	17	9	—	—	—	—	—

PORTFOLIO (as of 6/30/93)

Portfolio Manager: Douglas D. Donald -
1988; William J. Wallace - 1988

Investm't Category: Gold

✔ Cap Gain	Asset Allocation
Cap & Income	Fund of Funds
Income	Index
	✔ Sector
✔ Domestic	Small Cap
✔ Foreign	Socially Conscious
Country/Region	State Specific

Portfolio: stocks 69% bonds 0%
convertibles 0% other 22% cash 9%

Largest Holdings: Canadian gold mining companies 38%, gold bullion 22%

Unrealized Net Capital Gains: 15% of portfolio value

SHAREHOLDER INFORMATION

Minimum Investment
Initial: $1,000   Subsequent: $100

Minimum IRA Investment
Initial: $500   Subsequent: $50

Maximum Fees
Load: none   12b-1: none
Other: none

Distributions
Income: Nov, Dec   Capital Gains: Nov, Dec

Exchange Options
Number Per Year: no limit   Fee: none
Telephone: yes (money market fund available)

Services
IRA, other pension, auto exchange, auto invest,
auto withdraw

Scudder Growth & Income (SCDGX)

160 Federal St.
Boston, MA 02110
(800) 225-2470, (617) 439-4640

Growth & Income

PERFORMANCE

	3yr Annual	5yr Annual	10yr Annual	Bull	Bear
Return (%)	17.5	14.9	13.5	75.9	-9.9
Differ from Category (+/-)	1.1 abv av	2.4 high	1.1 abv av	5.8 abv av	1.7 abv av

Total Risk	Standard Deviation	Category Risk	Risk Index	Beta
av	9.1%	av	1.0	0.8

	1993	1992	1991	1990	1989	1988	1987	1986	1985	1984
Return (%)	15.5	9.5	28.1	-2.3	26.4	11.8	3.4	18.3	34.4	-3.7
Differ from category (+/-) ...	2.9	-0.5	0.4	3.3	4.8	-5.0	3.0	3.1	9.0	-9.9

PER SHARE DATA

	1993	1992	1991	1990	1989	1988	1987	1986	1985	1984
Dividends, Net Income ($) .	0.44	0.52	0.55	0.67	0.68	0.58	0.67	0.68	0.57	0.40
Distrib'ns, Cap Gain ($) ...	1.01	0.50	0.00	0.34	1.77	0.00	2.63	2.27	0.00	1.78
Net Asset Value ($)	17.24	16.20	15.76	12.77	14.14	13.17	12.31	15.02	15.35	11.90
Expense Ratio (%)........	0.88	0.93	0.97	0.95	0.87	0.92	0.89	0.83	0.84	0.88
Net Income to Assets (%)..	2.82	3.60	4.03	5.03	4.47	4.63	4.24	4.19	4.35	3.56
Portfolio Turnover (%).....	42	28	45	65	77	48	60	45	73	78
Total Assets (Millions $) ..	1,652	1,166	722	491	491	402	392	385	302	224

PORTFOLIO (as of 6/30/93)

Portfolio Manager: B. W. Thorndike - 1987, R. Hoffman - 1990, K. T. Millard - 1992

Investm't Category: Growth & Income

Cap Gain	Asset Allocation
✔ Cap & Income	Fund of Funds
Income	Index
	Sector
✔ Domestic	Small Cap
✔ Foreign	Socially Conscious
Country/Region	State Specific

Portfolio: stocks 82% bonds 0%
convertibles 13% other 0% cash 5%

Largest Holdings: financial 22%, manufacturing 15%

Unrealized Net Capital Gains: 22% of portfolio value

SHAREHOLDER INFORMATION

Minimum Investment
Initial: $1,000   Subsequent: $100

Minimum IRA Investment
Initial: $500   Subsequent: $50

Maximum Fees
Load: none   12b-1: none
Other: none

Distributions
Income: quarterly   Capital Gains: Dec

Exchange Options
Number Per Year: no limit   Fee: none
Telephone: yes (money market fund available)

Services
IRA, other pension, auto exchange, auto invest, auto withdraw

Scudder High Yield Tax-Free (SHYTX)

160 Federal St.
Boston, MA 02110
(800) 225-2470, (617) 439-4640

Tax-Exempt Bond

PERFORMANCE

	3yr Annual	5yr Annual	10yr Annual	Bull	Bear
Return (%)	12.7	10.8	na	48.7	2.1
Differ from Category (+/-)	2.4 high	1.6 high	na	8.6 high	-0.2 blw av

Total Risk	Standard Deviation	Category Risk	Risk Index	Avg Mat
blw av	4.8%	abv av	1.2	12.5 yrs

	1993	1992	1991	1990	1989	1988	1987	1986	1985	1984
Return (%)	13.8	10.9	13.4	6.0	10.3	13.4	—	—	—	—
Differ from category (+/-)	2.2	2.6	2.1	-0.3	1.3	3.3	—	—	—	—

PER SHARE DATA

	1993	1992	1991	1990	1989	1988	1987	1986	1985	1984
Dividends, Net Income ($)	0.67	0.72	0.76	0.76	0.75	0.82	—	—	—	—
Distrib'ns, Cap Gain ($)	0.28	0.26	0.20	0.04	0.05	0.00	—	—	—	—
Net Asset Value ($)	12.55	11.90	11.67	11.19	11.35	11.06	—	—	—	—
Expense Ratio (%)	0.98	0.98	1.00	1.00	1.00	0.67	—	—	—	—
Net Income to Assets (%)	5.53	6.10	6.65	6.88	6.72	7.65	—	—	—	—
Portfolio Turnover (%)	78	57	46	33	76	37	—	—	—	—
Total Assets (Millions $)	316	204	160	129	114	74	—	—	—	—

PORTFOLIO (as of 6/30/93)

Portfolio Manager: Condon - 1987, Manning - 1987

Investm't Category: Tax-Exempt Bond

Cap Gain	Asset Allocation
Cap & Income	Fund of Funds
✔ Income	Index
	Sector
✔ Domestic	Small Cap
Foreign	Socially Conscious
Country/Region	State Specific

Portfolio: stocks 0% bonds 100%
convertibles 0% other 0% cash 0%

Largest Holdings: general obligation 11%

Unrealized Net Capital Gains: 7% of portfolio value

SHAREHOLDER INFORMATION

Minimum Investment
Initial: $1,000   Subsequent: $100

Minimum IRA Investment
Initial: na   Subsequent: na

Maximum Fees
Load: none   12b-1: none
Other: none

Distributions
Income: monthly   Capital Gains: Dec

Exchange Options
Number Per Year: no limit   Fee: none
Telephone: yes (money market fund available)

Services
auto exchange, auto invest, auto withdraw

Scudder Income (SCSBX)

General Bond

160 Federal St.
Boston, MA 02110
(800) 225-2470, (617) 439-4640

PERFORMANCE

	3yr Annual	5yr Annual	10yr Annual	Bull	Bear
Return (%)	12.1	11.4	11.4	48.4	2.9
Differ from Category (+/-)	1.9 high	1.6 high	0.5 abv av	9.0 high	0.0 av

Total Risk	Standard Deviation	Category Risk	Risk Index	Avg Mat
blw av	4.1%	high	1.4	12.0 yrs

	1993	1992	1991	1990	1989	1988	1987	1986	1985	1984
Return (%)	12.7	6.7	17.3	8.3	12.6	8.9	0.6	14.7	21.7	12.1
Differ from category (+/-) . . .	3.5	0.0	2.7	1.4	1.3	1.3	-1.8	0.8	1.6	-0.2

PER SHARE DATA

	1993	1992	1991	1990	1989	1988	1987	1986	1985	1984
Dividends, Net Income ($) .	0.87	0.93	0.93	1.09	1.06	1.07	1.09	1.22	1.29	1.25
Distrib'ns, Cap Gain ($) . . .	0.57	0.39	0.11	0.00	0.00	0.00	0.00	0.00	0.00	0.00
Net Asset Value ($)	13.72	13.48	13.91	12.82	12.89	12.41	12.40	13.41	12.82	11.70
Expense Ratio (%).	0.93	0.93	0.97	0.95	0.93	0.93	0.93	0.88	0.91	1.02
Net Income to Assets (%) . .	6.67	7.05	7.13	8.21	8.23	8.53	8.37	9.12	10.57	11.04
Portfolio Turnover (%)	151	121	110	48	63	20	34	24	29	40
Total Assets (Millions $) . . .	512	456	403	302	272	245	242	249	172	123

PORTFOLIO (as of 6/30/93)

Portfolio Manager: William Hutchinson - 1986, Samuel Thorne, Jr. - 1990

Investm't Category: General Bond

Cap Gain	Asset Allocation
Cap & Income	Fund of Funds
✔ Income	Index
	Sector
✔ Domestic	Small Cap
Foreign	Socially Conscious
Country/Region	State Specific

Portfolio: stocks 0% bonds 100%
convertibles 0% other 0% cash 0%

Largest Holdings: corporate 38%, mortgage-backed 29%

Unrealized Net Capital Gains: 6% of portfolio value

SHAREHOLDER INFORMATION

Minimum Investment
Initial: $1,000   Subsequent: $100

Minimum IRA Investment
Initial: $500   Subsequent: $50

Maximum Fees
Load: none   12b-1: none
Other: none

Distributions
Income: quarterly   Capital Gains: Dec

Exchange Options
Number Per Year: no limit   Fee: none
Telephone: yes (money market fund available)

Services
IRA, other pension, auto exchange, auto invest, auto withdraw

Scudder International
(SCINX)

International Stock

160 Federal St.
Boston, MA 02110
(800) 225-2470, (617) 439-4640

PERFORMANCE

	3yr Annual	5yr Annual	10yr Annual	Bull	Bear
Return (%)	14.1	11.3	16.4	54.3	-12.3
Differ from Category (+/-)	-0.2 av	2.6 abv av	3.0 abv av	-0.8 av	2.8 abv av

Total Risk	Standard Deviation	Category Risk	Risk Index	Beta
abv av	12.2%	blw av	1.0	0.4

	1993	1992	1991	1990	1989	1988	1987	1986	1985	1984
Return (%)............	36.5	-2.6	11.7	-8.9	26.8	18.7	0.8	50.5	48.8	-0.6
Differ from category (+/-)...	-2.0	0.8	-1.2	2.2	4.6	4.9	-11.1	0.2	8.2	8.9

PER SHARE DATA

	1993	1992	1991	1990	1989	1988	1987	1986	1985	1984
Dividends, Net Income ($).	0.39	0.82	0.00	0.74	0.43	0.18	0.99	0.49	0.40	0.10
Distrib'ns, Cap Gain ($) ...	0.38	0.86	0.40	1.98	3.15	2.99	9.21	5.93	0.12	0.58
Net Asset Value ($)	44.10	32.93	35.53	32.15	38.20	33.10	30.60	39.79	31.03	21.32
Expense Ratio (%)	1.26	1.30	1.24	1.18	1.22	1.21	1.09	0.99	1.04	1.05
Net Income to Assets (%) .	1.13	1.25	2.22	1.33	1.20	1.16	1.19	2.60	2.34	1.02
Portfolio Turnover (%)......	29	50	70	49	48	55	67	36	19	17
Total Assets (Millions $)..	1,369	933	929	783	550	559	791	596	222	188

PORTFOLIO (as of 9/30/93)

Portfolio Manager: N. Bratt - 1976,
C. L. Franklin - 1989, I. Cheng - 1990

Investm't Category: International Stock
- ✔ Cap Gain
- Cap & Income
- Income
- Domestic
- ✔ Foreign
- Country/Region
- Asset Allocation
- Fund of Funds
- Index
- Sector
- Small Cap
- Socially Conscious
- State Specific

Portfolio: stocks 84% bonds 4%
convertibles 3% other 1% cash 8%

Largest Holdings: Japan 25%, United Kingdom 9%

Unrealized Net Capital Gains: 17% of portfolio value

SHAREHOLDER INFORMATION

Minimum Investment
Initial: $1,000   Subsequent: $100

Minimum IRA Investment
Initial: $500   Subsequent: $50

Maximum Fees
Load: none   12b-1: none
Other: none

Distributions
Income: Nov, Dec   Capital Gains: May, Dec

Exchange Options
Number Per Year: no limit   Fee: none
Telephone: yes (money market fund available)

Services
IRA, other pension, auto exchange, auto invest, auto withdraw

Scudder International Bond (SCIBX)

160 Federal St.
Boston, MA 02110
(800) 225-2470, (617) 439-4640

International Bond

PERFORMANCE

	3yr Annual	5yr Annual	10yr Annual	Bull	Bear
Return (%)	15.0	14.6	na	63.8	12.5
Differ from Category (+/-)	3.0 high	3.2 high	na	5.7 abv av	5.9 high

Total Risk	Standard Deviation	Category Risk	Risk Index	Avg Mat
av	7.8%	high	1.9	9.2 yrs

	1993	1992	1991	1990	1989	1988	1987	1986	1985	1984
Return (%)	15.8	7.5	22.2	21.0	7.2	—	—	—	—	—
Differ from category (+/-) . . .	3.1	2.7	7.3	9.5	5.0	—	—	—	—	—

PER SHARE DATA

	1993	1992	1991	1990	1989	1988	1987	1986	1985	1984
Dividends, Net Income ($) .	0.92	1.06	1.16	1.15	1.04	—	—	—	—	—
Distrib'ns, Cap Gain ($) . . .	0.38	0.61	0.82	0.28	0.00	—	—	—	—	—
Net Asset Value ($)	13.50	12.83	13.53	12.90	11.97	—	—	—	—	—
Expense Ratio (%).	1.25	1.25	1.25	1.25	1.00	—	—	—	—	—
Net Income to Assets (%) . .	7.69	8.31	9.48	9.57	8.58	—	—	—	—	—
Portfolio Turnover (%)	249	148	260	216	104	—	—	—	—	—
Total Assets (Millions $) . .	1,377	542	144	73	13	—	—	—	—	—

PORTFOLIO (as of 12/31/93)

Portfolio Manager: Adam M. Greshin - 1988, Margaret D. Hadzima - 1988

Investm't Category: International Bond
Cap Gain	Asset Allocation
Cap & Income	Fund of Funds
✔ Income	Index
	Sector
✔ Domestic	Small Cap
✔ Foreign	Socially Conscious
Country/Region	State Specific

Portfolio: stocks 0% bonds 89%
convertibles 0% other 4% cash 7%

Largest Holdings: United Kingdom 11%, Japan 10%

Unrealized Net Capital Gains: 0% of portfolio value

SHAREHOLDER INFORMATION

Minimum Investment
Initial: $1,000   Subsequent: $100

Minimum IRA Investment
Initial: $500   Subsequent: $50

Maximum Fees
Load: none   12b-1: none
Other: none

Distributions
Income: monthly   Capital Gains: Dec

Exchange Options
Number Per Year: no limit   Fee: none
Telephone: yes (money market fund available)

Services
IRA, other pension, auto exchange, auto invest, auto withdraw

Scudder Latin America
(SLAFX)
International Stock

160 Federal St.
Boston, MA 02110
(800) 225-2470, (617) 439-4640

PERFORMANCE

	3yr Annual	5yr Annual	10yr Annual	Bull	Bear
Return (%)	na	na	na	na	na
Differ from Category (+/-)	na	na	na	na	na

Total Risk	Standard Deviation	Category Risk	Risk Index	Beta
na	na	na	na	na

	1993	1992	1991	1990	1989	1988	1987	1986	1985	1984
Return (%)	74.3	—	—	—	—	—	—	—	—	—
Differ from category (+/-). .	35.8	—	—	—	—	—	—	—	—	—

PER SHARE DATA

	1993	1992	1991	1990	1989	1988	1987	1986	1985	1984
Dividends, Net Income ($).	0.05	—	—	—	—	—	—	—	—	—
Distrib'ns, Cap Gain ($) . . .	0.05	—	—	—	—	—	—	—	—	—
Net Asset Value ($)	21.68	—	—	—	—	—	—	—	—	—
Expense Ratio (%)	2.00	—	—	—	—	—	—	—	—	—
Net Income to Assets (%) .	0.44	—	—	—	—	—	—	—	—	—
Portfolio Turnover (%).	4	—	—	—	—	—	—	—	—	—
Total Assets (Millions $). . . .	372	—	—	—	—	—	—	—	—	—

PORTFOLIO (as of 10/31/93)

Portfolio Manager: Games - 1992, Truscott - 1992, Rathnam - 1992, Cornell - 1993

Investm't Category: International Stock

✔ Cap Gain	Asset Allocation
Cap & Income	Fund of Funds
Income	Index
	Sector
Domestic	Small Cap
✔ Foreign	Socially Conscious
✔ Country/Region	State Specific

Portfolio: stocks 89% bonds 0%
convertibles 0% other 0% cash 11%

Largest Holdings: Mexico 37%, Argentina 26%

Unrealized Net Capital Gains: 17% of portfolio value

SHAREHOLDER INFORMATION

Minimum Investment
Initial: $1,000 Subsequent: $100

Minimum IRA Investment
Initial: $500 Subsequent: $50

Maximum Fees
Load: 2.00% redemption 12b-1: none
Other: redemption fee applies for 1 year

Distributions
Income: Dec Capital Gains: Dec

Exchange Options
Number Per Year: no limit Fee: none
Telephone: yes (money market fund available)

Services
IRA, other pension, auto exchange, auto invest, auto withdraw

Scudder Managed Muni Bond (SCMBX)

160 Federal St.
Boston, MA 02110
(800) 225-2470, (617) 439-4640

Tax-Exempt Bond

PERFORMANCE

	3yr Annual	5yr Annual	10yr Annual	Bull	Bear
Return (%)	11.4	10.4	10.8	45.8	1.4
Differ from Category (+/-)	1.1 abv av	1.2 high	1.2 abv av	5.7 high	-0.8 blw av

Total Risk	Standard Deviation	Category Risk	Risk Index	Avg Mat
blw av	4.9%	high	1.2	12.1 yrs

	1993	1992	1991	1990	1989	1988	1987	1986	1985	1984
Return (%)	13.3	9.0	12.1	6.7	11.1	12.2	0.3	16.7	17.5	10.2
Differ from category (+/-) . . .	1.7	0.6	0.8	0.4	2.1	2.1	1.5	0.3	0.2	1.9

PER SHARE DATA

	1993	1992	1991	1990	1989	1988	1987	1986	1985	1984
Dividends, Net Income ($) .	0.47	0.50	0.52	0.55	0.58	0.60	0.60	0.60	0.59	0.71
Distrib'ns, Cap Gain ($) . . .	0.28	0.33	0.11	0.08	0.38	0.01	0.10	0.23	0.00	0.00
Net Asset Value ($)	9.09	8.72	8.80	8.45	8.54	8.60	8.24	8.93	8.40	7.69
Expense Ratio (%)	0.64	0.63	0.64	0.61	0.62	0.61	0.63	0.58	0.58	0.61
Net Income to Assets (%) . .	5.39	5.76	6.16	6.61	6.78	7.13	7.20	6.88	7.27	9.52
Portfolio Turnover (%)	63	60	32	72	90	76	73	78	98	120
Total Assets (Millions $) . . .	909	829	796	719	691	636	592	663	574	545

PORTFOLIO (as of 6/30/93)

Portfolio Manager: Carleton - 1986, Condon - 1987

Investm't Category: Tax-Exempt Bond

Cap Gain	Asset Allocation
Cap & Income	Fund of Funds
✔ Income	Index
	Sector
✔ Domestic	Small Cap
Foreign	Socially Conscious
Country/Region	State Specific

Portfolio: stocks 0%   bonds 100%
convertibles 0%   other 0%   cash 0%

Largest Holdings: general obligation 16%

Unrealized Net Capital Gains: 7% of portfolio value

SHAREHOLDER INFORMATION

Minimum Investment
Initial: $1,000   Subsequent: $100

Minimum IRA Investment
Initial: na   Subsequent: na

Maximum Fees
Load: none   12b-1: none
Other: none

Distributions
Income: monthly   Capital Gains: Dec

Exchange Options
Number Per Year: no limit   Fee: none
Telephone: yes (money market fund available)

Services
auto exchange, auto invest, auto withdraw

Scudder Mass Tax-Free
(SCMAX)
Tax-Exempt Bond

160 Federal St.
Boston, MA 02110
(800) 225-2470, (617) 439-4640

PERFORMANCE

	3yr Annual	5yr Annual	10yr Annual	Bull	Bear
Return (%)	12.4	10.6	na	48.9	1.5
Differ from Category (+/-)	2.1 high	1.4 high	na	8.8 high	-0.8 blw av

Total Risk	Standard Deviation	Category Risk	Risk Index	Avg Mat
blw av	4.6%	abv av	1.1	11.8 yrs

	1993	1992	1991	1990	1989	1988	1987	1986	1985	1984
Return (%)	14.3	10.8	12.2	6.3	9.8	12.3	—	—	—	—
Differ from category (+/-). . .	2.7	2.5	0.8	0.0	0.8	2.2	—	—	—	—

PER SHARE DATA

	1993	1992	1991	1990	1989	1988	1987	1986	1985	1984
Dividends, Net Income ($).	0.83	0.83	0.80	0.82	0.84	0.89	—	—	—	—
Distrib'ns, Cap Gain ($) . . .	0.12	0.16	0.08	0.00	0.10	0.20	—	—	—	—
Net Asset Value ($)	14.21	13.31	12.96	12.39	12.46	12.24	—	—	—	—
Expense Ratio (%)	0.00	0.48	0.60	0.60	0.51	0.50	—	—	—	—
Net Income to Assets (%) .	6.36	6.38	6.72	6.60	7.23	7.55	—	—	—	—
Portfolio Turnover (%).	29	23	27	46	111	96	—	—	—	—
Total Assets (Millions $). . . .	371	120	67	46	31	16	—	—	—	—

PORTFOLIO (as of 9/30/93)

Portfolio Manager: Condon - 1989, Meany - 1991

Investm't Category: Tax-Exempt Bond
Cap Gain	Asset Allocation
Cap & Income	Fund of Funds
✔ Income	Index
	Sector
✔ Domestic	Small Cap
Foreign	Socially Conscious
Country/Region	✔ State Specific

Portfolio: stocks 0% bonds 100%
convertibles 0% other 0% cash 0%

Largest Holdings: general obligation 21%

Unrealized Net Capital Gains: 8% of portfolio value

SHAREHOLDER INFORMATION

Minimum Investment
Initial: $1,000   Subsequent: $100

Minimum IRA Investment
Initial: na   Subsequent: na

Maximum Fees
Load: none   12b-1: none
Other: none

Distributions
Income: monthly   Capital Gains: Jun, Nov

Exchange Options
Number Per Year: no limit   Fee: none
Telephone: yes (money market fund available)

Services
auto exchange, auto invest, auto withdraw

Scudder Medium Term Tax Free (SCMTX)

160 Federal St.
Boston, MA 02110
(800) 225-2470, (617) 439-4640

Tax-Exempt Bond

PERFORMANCE

	3yr Annual	5yr Annual	10yr Annual	Bull	Bear
Return (%)	10.6	na	na	38.4	4.0
Differ from Category (+/-)	0.3 av	na	na	-1.7 blw av	1.7 high

Total Risk	Standard Deviation	Category Risk	Risk Index	Avg Mat
low	3.4%	low	0.8	7.2 yrs

	1993	1992	1991	1990	1989	1988	1987	1986	1985	1984
Return (%)	10.9	8.9	12.1	6.3	—	—	—	—	—	—
Differ from category (+/-) ..	-0.6	0.6	0.8	0.0	—	—	—	—	—	—

PER SHARE DATA

	1993	1992	1991	1990	1989	1988	1987	1986	1985	1984
Dividends, Net Income ($) .	0.60	0.64	0.67	0.54	—	—	—	—	—	—
Distrib'ns, Cap Gain ($) ...	0.05	0.03	0.00	0.00	—	—	—	—	—	—
Net Asset Value ($)	11.36	10.86	10.62	10.11	—	—	—	—	—	—
Expense Ratio (%)........	0.00	0.00	0.00	0.97	—	—	—	—	—	—
Net Income to Assets (%) ..	5.58	6.07	6.44	5.37	—	—	—	—	—	—
Portfolio Turnover (%)	28	22	14	117	—	—	—	—	—	—
Total Assets (Millions $) ..	1,025	661	268	27	—	—	—	—	—	—

PORTFOLIO (as of 6/30/93)

Portfolio Manager: Carleton - 1986, Patton - 1987

Investm't Category: Tax-Exempt Bond

Cap Gain	Asset Allocation
Cap & Income	Fund of Funds
✔ Income	Index
	Sector
✔ Domestic	Small Cap
Foreign	Socially Conscious
Country/Region	State Specific

Portfolio: stocks 0% bonds 100%
convertibles 0% other 0% cash 0%

Largest Holdings: general obligation 30%

Unrealized Net Capital Gains: 4% of portfolio value

SHAREHOLDER INFORMATION

Minimum Investment
Initial: $1,000   Subsequent: $100

Minimum IRA Investment
Initial: na   Subsequent: na

Maximum Fees
Load: none   12b-1: none
Other: none

Distributions
Income: monthly   Capital Gains: Dec

Exchange Options
Number Per Year: no limit   Fee: none
Telephone: yes (money market fund available)

Services
auto exchange, auto invest, auto withdraw

Scudder NY Tax Free
(SCYTX)

Tax-Exempt Bond

160 Federal St.
Boston, MA 02110
(800) 225-2470, (617) 439-4640

PERFORMANCE

	3yr Annual	5yr Annual	10yr Annual	Bull	Bear
Return (%)	12.5	10.3	10.0	48.8	-0.1
Differ from Category (+/-)	2.2 high	1.1 high	0.4 av	8.7 high	-2.4 low

Total Risk	Standard Deviation	Category Risk	Risk Index	Avg Mat
blw av	5.0%	high	1.2	10.4 yrs

	1993	1992	1991	1990	1989	1988	1987	1986	1985	1984
Return (%)	12.9	10.2	14.4	4.2	9.9	10.8	-0.6	14.1	16.0	9.2
Differ from category (+/-) . . .	1.3	1.9	3.1	-2.1	0.8	0.6	0.5	-2.3	-1.3	0.8

PER SHARE DATA

	1993	1992	1991	1990	1989	1988	1987	1986	1985	1984
Dividends, Net Income ($) .	0.56	0.61	0.66	0.67	0.69	0.72	0.73	0.74	0.78	0.83
Distrib'ns, Cap Gain ($) . . .	0.73	0.60	0.25	0.00	0.09	0.00	0.18	0.14	0.00	0.00
Net Asset Value ($)	11.17	11.08	11.21	10.65	10.88	10.64	10.28	11.30	10.73	9.96
Expense Ratio (%)	0.82	0.87	0.91	0.89	0.89	0.95	0.88	0.88	1.01	1.00
Net Income to Assets (%) .	5.36	5.96	6.29	6.39	6.89	7.05	6.70	7.01	8.42	8.31
Portfolio Turnover (%). . . .	201	168	225	114	132	44	72	40	166	150
Total Assets (Millions $). . . .	225	159	142	132	123	116	154	101	61	27

PORTFOLIO (as of 9/30/93)

Portfolio Manager: Carleton - 1986, Ragus - 1990

Investm't Category: Tax-Exempt Bond

Cap Gain	Asset Allocation
Cap & Income	Fund of Funds
✔ Income	Index
	Sector
✔ Domestic	Small Cap
Foreign	Socially Conscious
Country/Region	✔ State Specific

Portfolio: stocks 0% bonds 100%
convertibles 0% other 0% cash 0%

Largest Holdings: general obligation 23%

Unrealized Net Capital Gains: 5% of portfolio value

SHAREHOLDER INFORMATION

Minimum Investment
Initial: $1,000   Subsequent: $100

Minimum IRA Investment
Initial: na   Subsequent: na

Maximum Fees
Load: none   12b-1: none
Other: none

Distributions
Income: monthly   Capital Gains: Jun, Nov

Exchange Options
Number Per Year: no limit   Fee: none
Telephone: yes (money market fund available)

Services
auto exchange, auto invest, auto withdraw

Scudder Ohio Tax-Free
(SCOHX)

160 Federal St.
Boston, MA 02110
(800) 225-2470, (617) 439-4640

Tax-Exempt Bond

PERFORMANCE

	3yr Annual	5yr Annual	10yr Annual	Bull	Bear
Return (%)	10.9	9.8	na	43.9	1.3
Differ from Category (+/-)	0.6 av	0.6 av	na	3.8 abv av	-1.0 blw av

Total Risk	Standard Deviation	Category Risk	Risk Index	Avg Mat
blw av	4.5%	abv av	1.1	10.2 yrs

	1993	1992	1991	1990	1989	1988	1987	1986	1985	1984
Return (%)	12.3	8.8	11.8	6.6	9.5	12.8	—	—	—	—
Differ from category (+/-)	0.6	0.5	0.5	0.3	0.5	2.7	—	—	—	—

PER SHARE DATA

	1993	1992	1991	1990	1989	1988	1987	1986	1985	1984
Dividends, Net Income ($)	0.71	0.73	0.75	0.79	0.82	0.82	—	—	—	—
Distrib'ns, Cap Gain ($)	0.09	0.19	0.02	0.05	0.06	0.02	—	—	—	—
Net Asset Value ($)	13.59	12.85	12.69	12.09	12.17	11.96	—	—	—	—
Expense Ratio (%)	0.50	0.50	0.50	0.50	0.50	0.50	—	—	—	—
Net Income to Assets (%)	5.61	6.05	6.50	6.74	7.13	7.17	—	—	—	—
Portfolio Turnover (%)	34	13	23	16	36	106	—	—	—	—
Total Assets (Millions $)	83	51	37	25	12	6	—	—	—	—

PORTFOLIO (as of 9/30/93)

Portfolio Manager: Condon - 1988, Manning - 1987

Investm't Category: Tax-Exempt Bond

Cap Gain	Asset Allocation
Cap & Income	Fund of Funds
✔ Income	Index
	Sector
✔ Domestic	Small Cap
Foreign	Socially Conscious
Country/Region	✔ State Specific

Portfolio: stocks 0%   bonds 100%
convertibles 0%   other 0%   cash 0%

Largest Holdings: general obligation 26%

Unrealized Net Capital Gains: 9% of portfolio value

SHAREHOLDER INFORMATION

Minimum Investment
Initial: $1,000   Subsequent: $100

Minimum IRA Investment
Initial: na   Subsequent: na

Maximum Fees
Load: none   12b-1: none
Other: none

Distributions
Income: monthly   Capital Gains: May, Nov

Exchange Options
Number Per Year: no limit   Fee: none
Telephone: yes (money market fund available)

Services
auto exchange, auto invest, auto withdraw

Scudder Pacific Opportunities (SCOPX)

International Stock

160 Federal St.
Boston, MA 02110
(800) 225-2470, (617) 439-4640

PERFORMANCE

	3yr Annual	5yr Annual	10yr Annual	Bull	Bear
Return (%)	na	na	na	na	na
Differ from Category (+/-)	na	na	na	na	na

Total Risk	Standard Deviation	Category Risk	Risk Index	Beta
na	na	na	na	na

	1993	1992	1991	1990	1989	1988	1987	1986	1985	1984
Return (%)	60.0	—	—	—	—	—	—	—	—	—
Differ from category (+/-)	21.5	—	—	—	—	—	—	—	—	—

PER SHARE DATA

	1993	1992	1991	1990	1989	1988	1987	1986	1985	1984
Dividends, Net Income ($)	0.07	—	—	—	—	—	—	—	—	—
Distrib'ns, Cap Gain ($)	0.00	—	—	—	—	—	—	—	—	—
Net Asset Value ($)	19.07	—	—	—	—	—	—	—	—	—
Expense Ratio (%)	1.75	—	—	—	—	—	—	—	—	—
Net Income to Assets (%)	1.41	—	—	—	—	—	—	—	—	—
Portfolio Turnover (%)	9	—	—	—	—	—	—	—	—	—
Total Assets (Millions $)	433	—	—	—	—	—	—	—	—	—

PORTFOLIO (as of 10/31/93)

Portfolio Manager: A. Economos - 1992, N. Bratt - 1992, J. Cornell - 1993

Investm't Category: International Stock

✔ Cap Gain	Asset Allocation
Cap & Income	Fund of Funds
Income	Index
	Sector
✔ Domestic	Small Cap
✔ Foreign	Socially Conscious
Country/Region	State Specific

Portfolio: stocks 73% bonds 0%
convertibles 4% other 0% cash 23%

Largest Holdings: Hong Kong 24%, Malaysia 14%

Unrealized Net Capital Gains: 12% of portfolio value

SHAREHOLDER INFORMATION

Minimum Investment
Initial: $1,000   Subsequent: $100

Minimum IRA Investment
Initial: $500   Subsequent: $50

Maximum Fees
Load: none   12b-1: none
Other: none

Distributions
Income: Dec   Capital Gains: Dec

Exchange Options
Number Per Year: no limit   Fee: none
Telephone: yes (money market fund available)

Services
IRA, other pension, auto exchange, auto invest, auto withdraw

Scudder Penn Tax Free
(SCPAX)

Tax-Exempt Bond

160 Federal St.
Boston, MA 02110
(800) 225-2470, (617) 439-4640

PERFORMANCE

	3yr Annual	5yr Annual	10yr Annual	Bull	Bear
Return (%)	11.5	10.0	na	45.5	0.8
Differ from Category (+/-)	1.2 abv av	0.8 abv av	na	5.4 abv av	-1.4 low

Total Risk	Standard Deviation	Category Risk	Risk Index	Avg Mat
blw av	4.2%	av	1.0	9.8 yrs

	1993	1992	1991	1990	1989	1988	1987	1986	1985	1984
Return (%)	13.1	9.0	12.4	5.8	10.1	13.4	—	—	—	—
Differ from category (+/-)	1.5	0.6	1.1	-0.5	1.1	3.3	—	—	—	—

PER SHARE DATA

	1993	1992	1991	1990	1989	1988	1987	1986	1985	1984
Dividends, Net Income ($)	0.74	0.76	0.78	0.82	0.84	0.84	—	—	—	—
Distrib'ns, Cap Gain ($)	0.08	0.21	0.07	0.00	0.00	0.06	—	—	—	—
Net Asset Value ($)	13.99	13.14	12.98	12.35	12.48	12.14	—	—	—	—
Expense Ratio (%)	0.50	0.50	0.50	0.50	0.50	0.50	—	—	—	—
Net Income to Assets (%)	5.47	6.05	6.67	6.78	7.09	7.16	—	—	—	—
Portfolio Turnover (%)	20	11	8	2	14	98	—	—	—	—
Total Assets (Millions $)	75	39	26	18	11	5	—	—	—	—

PORTFOLIO (as of 9/30/93)

Portfolio Manager: Condon - 1987, Manning - 1987

Investm't Category: Tax-Exempt Bond

Cap Gain	Asset Allocation
Cap & Income	Fund of Funds
✔ Income	Index
	Sector
✔ Domestic	Small Cap
Foreign	Socially Conscious
Country/Region	✔ State Specific

Portfolio: stocks 0%   bonds 100%
convertibles 0%   other 0%   cash 0%

Largest Holdings: general obligation 19%

Unrealized Net Capital Gains: 9% of portfolio value

SHAREHOLDER INFORMATION

Minimum Investment
Initial: $1,000   Subsequent: $100

Minimum IRA Investment
Initial: na   Subsequent: na

Maximum Fees
Load: none   12b-1: none
Other: none

Distributions
Income: monthly   Capital Gains: Jun, Nov

Exchange Options
Number Per Year: no limit   Fee: none
Telephone: yes (money market fund available)

Services
auto exchange, auto invest, auto withdraw

Scudder Quality Growth (SCQGX)

Growth

160 Federal St.
Boston, MA 02110
(800) 225-2470, (617) 439-4640

PERFORMANCE

	3yr Annual	5yr Annual	10yr Annual	Bull	Bear
Return (%)	na	na	na	na	na
Differ from Category (+/-)	na	na	na	na	na

Total Risk	Standard Deviation	Category Risk	Risk Index	Beta
na	na	na	na	na

	1993	1992	1991	1990	1989	1988	1987	1986	1985	1984
Return (%)	0.0	6.6	—	—	—	—	—	—	—	—
Differ from category (+/-)	-13.2	-4.4	—	—	—	—	—	—	—	—

PER SHARE DATA

	1993	1992	1991	1990	1989	1988	1987	1986	1985	1984
Dividends, Net Income ($)	0.07	0.02	—	—	—	—	—	—	—	—
Distrib'ns, Cap Gain ($)	0.23	0.00	—	—	—	—	—	—	—	—
Net Asset Value ($)	15.92	16.23	—	—	—	—	—	—	—	—
Expense Ratio (%)	1.20	1.25	—	—	—	—	—	—	—	—
Net Income to Assets (%)	0.39	0.24	—	—	—	—	—	—	—	—
Portfolio Turnover (%)	111	27	—	—	—	—	—	—	—	—
Total Assets (Millions $)	124	101	—	—	—	—	—	—	—	—

PORTFOLIO (as of 10/31/93)

Portfolio Manager: B. Beaty - 1991, H. F. Ward - 1991, M. K. Shields - 1992

Investm't Category: Growth

✔ Cap Gain	Asset Allocation
Cap & Income	Fund of Funds
Income	Index
	Sector
✔ Domestic	Small Cap
✔ Foreign	Socially Conscious
Country/Region	State Specific

Portfolio: stocks 97% bonds 0%
convertibles 0% other 1% cash 2%

Largest Holdings: financial 16%, communications 15%

Unrealized Net Capital Gains: 11% of portfolio value

SHAREHOLDER INFORMATION

Minimum Investment
Initial: $1,000   Subsequent: $100

Minimum IRA Investment
Initial: $500   Subsequent: $100

Maximum Fees
Load: none   12b-1: none
Other: none

Distributions
Income: Dec   Capital Gains: Dec

Exchange Options
Number Per Year: no limit   Fee: none
Telephone: yes (money market fund available)

Services
IRA, other pension, auto exchange, auto invest, auto withdraw

Scudder Short-Term Bond (SCSTX)

General Bond

160 Federal St.
Boston, MA 02110
(800) 225-2470, (617) 439-4640

PERFORMANCE

	3yr Annual	5yr Annual	10yr Annual	Bull	Bear
Return (%)	9.2	10.1	na	34.4	6.6
Differ from Category (+/-)	-1.0 blw av	0.3 av	na	-5.0 blw av	3.7 high

Total Risk	Standard Deviation	Category Risk	Risk Index	Avg Mat
low	1.8%	low	0.6	3.0 yrs

	1993	1992	1991	1990	1989	1988	1987	1986	1985	1984
Return (%)	8.2	5.5	14.2	9.8	13.2	6.3	1.2	14.6	20.9	—
Differ from category (+/-) . .	-1.0	-1.2	-0.4	2.9	1.9	-1.3	-1.3	0.6	0.8	—

PER SHARE DATA

	1993	1992	1991	1990	1989	1988	1987	1986	1985	1984
Dividends, Net Income ($) .	0.77	0.96	1.08	1.08	0.82	0.71	0.72	0.81	0.95	—
Distrib'ns, Cap Gain ($) . . .	0.10	0.00	0.00	0.00	0.08	0.01	0.10	0.21	0.00	—
Net Asset Value ($)	12.01	11.93	12.24	11.72	11.71	11.19	11.23	11.92	11.35	—
Expense Ratio (%).	0.68	0.75	0.44	0.16	0.36	1.50	1.45	1.45	1.27	—
Net Income to Assets (%). .	7.75	8.01	8.96	9.36	7.97	6.48	6.34	6.89	8.82	—
Portfolio Turnover (%)	111	84	41	53	40	24	29	15	58	—
Total Assets (Millions $) . .	3,196	2,862	2,248	340	72	10	10	8	5	—

PORTFOLIO (as of 6/30/93)

Portfolio Manager: C. Gootkind - 1989, T. Poor - 1989, S. Martland - 1992

Investm't Category: General Bond

Cap Gain	Asset Allocation
Cap & Income	Fund of Funds
✔ Income	Index
	Sector
✔ Domestic	Small Cap
✔ Foreign	Socially Conscious
Country/Region	State Specific

Portfolio: stocks 0% bonds 84%
convertibles 0% other 12% cash 4%

Largest Holdings: mortgage-backed 32%, asset-backed 18%

Unrealized Net Capital Gains: 2% of portfolio value

SHAREHOLDER INFORMATION

Minimum Investment
Initial: $1,000   Subsequent: $100

Minimum IRA Investment
Initial: $500   Subsequent: $50

Maximum Fees
Load: none   12b-1: none
Other: none

Distributions
Income: monthly   Capital Gains: Dec

Exchange Options
Number Per Year: no limit   Fee: none
Telephone: yes (money market fund available)

Services
IRA, other pension, auto exchange, auto invest, auto withdraw

Scudder Short-Term Global Income (SSTGX)

International Bond

160 Federal St.
Boston, MA 02110
(800) 225-2470, (617) 439-4640

	3yr Annual	5yr Annual	10yr Annual	Bull	Bear
Return (%)	na	na	na	na	na
Differ from Category (+/-)	na	na	na	na	na

Total Risk	Standard Deviation	Category Risk	Risk Index	Avg Mat
na	na	na	na	1.7 yrs

	1993	1992	1991	1990	1989	1988	1987	1986	1985	1984
Return (%).	6.6	5.5	—	—	—	—	—	—	—	—
Differ from category (+/-). . .	-6.1	0.6	—	—	—	—	—	—	—	—

PER SHARE DATA

	1993	1992	1991	1990	1989	1988	1987	1986	1985	1984
Dividends, Net Income ($).	0.93	1.05	—	—	—	—	—	—	—	—
Distrib'ns, Cap Gain ($) . . .	0.00	0.01	—	—	—	—	—	—	—	—
Net Asset Value ($)	11.53	11.70	—	—	—	—	—	—	—	—
Expense Ratio (%)	1.00	1.00	—	—	—	—	—	—	—	—
Net Income to Assets (%) .	8.10	8.94	—	—	—	—	—	—	—	—
Portfolio Turnover (%).	259	274	—	—	—	—	—	—	—	—
Total Assets (Millions $). . . .	958	1,369	—	—	—	—	—	—	—	—

PORTFOLIO (as of 10/31/93)

Portfolio Manager: A. M. Greshin - 1991, M. Craddock - 1992, G. P. Johnson - 1992

Investm't Category: International Bond

Cap Gain	Asset Allocation
Cap & Income	Fund of Funds
✔ Income	Index
	Sector
✔ Domestic	Small Cap
✔ Foreign	Socially Conscious
Country/Region	State Specific

Portfolio: stocks 0%, bonds 92%
convertibles 0%, other 8%, cash 0%

Largest Holdings: United States 18%, New Zealand 13%

Unrealized Net Capital Gains: 0% of portfolio value

SHAREHOLDER INFORMATION

Minimum Investment
Initial: $1,000   Subsequent: $100

Minimum IRA Investment
Initial: $500   Subsequent: $50

Maximum Fees
Load: none   12b-1: none
Other: none

Distributions
Income: monthly   Capital Gains: Nov, Dec

Exchange Options
Number Per Year: no limit   Fee: none
Telephone: yes (money market fund available)

Services
IRA, other pension, auto exchange, auto invest, auto withdraw

Scudder Value (SCVAX)

Growth

160 Federal St.
Boston, MA 02110
(800) 225-2470, (617) 439-4640

PERFORMANCE

	3yr Annual	5yr Annual	10yr Annual	Bull	Bear
Return (%)	na	na	na	na	na
Differ from Category (+/-)	na	na	na	na	na

Total Risk	Standard Deviation	Category Risk	Risk Index	Beta
na	na	na	na	na

	1993	1992	1991	1990	1989	1988	1987	1986	1985	1984
Return (%)	11.6	—	—	—	—	—	—	—	—	—
Differ from category (+/-) . .	-1.6	—	—	—	—	—	—	—	—	—

PER SHARE DATA

	1993	1992	1991	1990	1989	1988	1987	1986	1985	1984
Dividends, Net Income ($) .	0.10	—	—	—	—	—	—	—	—	—
Distrib'ns, Cap Gain ($) . . .	0.43	—	—	—	—	—	—	—	—	—
Net Asset Value ($)	12.85	—	—	—	—	—	—	—	—	—
Expense Ratio (%)	1.25	—	—	—	—	—	—	—	—	—
Net Income to Assets (%) . .	1.56	—	—	—	—	—	—	—	—	—
Portfolio Turnover (%)	60	—	—	—	—	—	—	—	—	—
Total Assets (Millions $)	32	—	—	—	—	—	—	—	—	—

PORTFOLIO (as of 9/30/93)

Portfolio Manager: Donald E. Hall - 1992, William J. Wallace - 1992

Investm't Category: Growth

✔ Cap Gain	Asset Allocation
Cap & Income	Fund of Funds
Income	Index
	Sector
✔ Domestic	Small Cap
✔ Foreign	Socially Conscious
Country/Region	State Specific

Portfolio: stocks 81% bonds 0%
convertibles 6% other 0% cash 13%

Largest Holdings: financial 18%, health 10%

Unrealized Net Capital Gains: 1% of portfolio value

SHAREHOLDER INFORMATION

Minimum Investment
Initial: $1,000   Subsequent: $100

Minimum IRA Investment
Initial: $500   Subsequent: $50

Maximum Fees
Load: none   12b-1: none
Other: none

Distributions
Income: Dec   Capital Gains: Dec

Exchange Options
Number Per Year: no limit   Fee: none
Telephone: yes (money market fund available)

Services
IRA, other pension, auto exchange, auto invest, auto withdraw

Scudder Zero Coupon 2000 (SGZTX)

160 Federal St.
Boston, MA 02110
(800) 225-2470, (617) 439-4640

Government Bond

PERFORMANCE

	3yr Annual	5yr Annual	10yr Annual	Bull	Bear
Return (%)	14.6	13.6	na	66.6	-5.4
Differ from Category (+/-)	3.8 high	3.2 high	na	20.4 high	-5.9 low

Total Risk	Standard Deviation	Category Risk	Risk Index	Avg Mat
av	7.2%	high	1.7	8.4 yrs

	1993	1992	1991	1990	1989	1988	1987	1986	1985	1984
Return (%)	16.0	8.1	20.0	4.5	20.3	11.7	-8.0	—	—	—
Differ from category (+/-). . .	5.6	1.9	5.0	-2.0	6.4	4.1	-6.2	—	—	—

PER SHARE DATA

	1993	1992	1991	1990	1989	1988	1987	1986	1985	1984
Dividends, Net Income ($).	0.82	0.93	0.93	0.82	0.51	0.62	1.22	—	—	—
Distrib'ns, Cap Gain ($) . . .	0.88	1.38	0.00	0.07	0.02	0.00	0.10	—	—	—
Net Asset Value ($)	12.85	12.55	13.76	12.27	12.61	10.92	10.34	—	—	—
Expense Ratio (%)	1.00	1.00	1.00	1.00	1.00	1.00	1.00	—	—	—
Net Income to Assets (%) .	5.58	6.38	7.12	7.62	7.10	8.10	8.13	—	—	—
Portfolio Turnover (%).	94	119	91	99	87	149	37	—	—	—
Total Assets (Millions $).	30	29	33	33	32	5	2	—	—	—

PORTFOLIO (as of 6/30/93)

Portfolio Manager: Samuel Thorne, Jr. - 1986, Ruth Heisler - 1988, Renee Ross - 1990

Investm't Category: Government Bond

Cap Gain	Asset Allocation
Cap & Income	Fund of Funds
✔ Income	Index
	Sector
✔ Domestic	Small Cap
Foreign	Socially Conscious
Country/Region	State Specific

Portfolio: stocks 0%   bonds 100%
convertibles 0%   other 0%   cash 0%

Largest Holdings: U.S. government 100%

Unrealized Net Capital Gains: 8% of portfolio value

SHAREHOLDER INFORMATION

Minimum Investment
Initial: $1,000   Subsequent: $100

Minimum IRA Investment
Initial: $500   Subsequent: $50

Maximum Fees
Load: none   12b-1: none
Other: none

Distributions
Income: Dec   Capital Gains: Dec

Exchange Options
Number Per Year: no limit   Fee: none
Telephone: yes (money market fund available)

Services
IRA, other pension, auto exchange, auto invest, auto withdraw

Selected American Shares (SLASX)

Growth & Income

124 East Marcy Street
Sante Fe, NM 87501
(800) 243-1575

PERFORMANCE

	3yr Annual	5yr Annual	10yr Annual	Bull	Bear
Return (%)	17.7	13.5	15.2	79.2	-12.4
Differ from Category (+/-)	1.3 abv av	1.0 abv av	2.8 high	9.1 abv av	-0.8 av

Total Risk	Standard Deviation	Category Risk	Risk Index	Beta
abv av	13.9%	high	1.6	1.2

	1993	1992	1991	1990	1989	1988	1987	1986	1985	1984
Return (%)	5.4	5.7	46.3	-3.9	20.0	22.0	0.2	16.9	33.2	14.8
Differ from category (+/-) . .	-7.2	-4.3	18.6	1.7	-1.6	5.2	-0.2	1.7	7.8	8.6

PER SHARE DATA

	1993	1992	1991	1990	1989	1988	1987	1986	1985	1984
Dividends, Net Income ($) .	0.25	0.18	0.23	0.34	0.44	0.25	0.57	0.47	0.40	0.52
Distrib'ns, Cap Gain ($) . . .	3.22	2.19	0.00	0.11	2.10	0.00	0.75	2.29	0.17	0.00
Net Asset Value ($)	14.60	17.13	18.43	12.79	13.81	13.67	11.43	12.65	13.35	10.54
Expense Ratio (%).	1.09	1.17	1.19	1.35	1.08	1.11	1.11	0.85	0.87	0.99
Net Income to Assets (%). .	1.52	0.95	1.41	2.04	3.06	2.07	2.38	3.07	4.42	4.58
Portfolio Turnover (%)	na	50	21	48	46	35	45	40	33	49
Total Assets (Millions $) . . .	450	581	712	401	360	285	263	160	122	84

PORTFOLIO (as of 6/30/93)

Portfolio Manager: Shelby M.C. Davis - 1993

Investm't Category: Growth & Income

Cap Gain	Asset Allocation
✔ Cap & Income	Fund of Funds
Income	Index
	Sector
✔ Domestic	Small Cap
Foreign	Socially Conscious
Country/Region	State Specific

Portfolio: stocks 89%   bonds 0%
convertibles 5%   other 0%   cash 6%

Largest Holdings: financial 16%, insurance 15%

Unrealized Net Capital Gains: 17% of portfolio value

SHAREHOLDER INFORMATION

Minimum Investment
Initial: $1,000   Subsequent: $100

Minimum IRA Investment
Initial: $500   Subsequent: $100

Maximum Fees
Load: none   12b-1: 0.25%
Other: none

Distributions
Income: quarterly   Capital Gains: Dec

Exchange Options
Number Per Year: 4   Fee: none
Telephone: yes (money market fund available)

Services
IRA, other pension, auto invest, auto withdraw

Selected Special Shares
(SLSSX)

Growth

124 East Marcy Street
Sante Fe, NM 87501
(800) 243-1575

PERFORMANCE

	3yr Annual	5yr Annual	10yr Annual	Bull	Bear
Return (%)	14.6	12.5	10.6	64.2	-14.5
Differ from Category (+/-)	-4.6 blw av	-2.1 blw av	-2.0 blw av	-20.5 blw av	-2.1 blw av

Total Risk	Standard Deviation	Category Risk	Risk Index	Beta
abv av	12.6%	abv av	1.2	0.8

	1993	1992	1991	1990	1989	1988	1987	1986	1985	1984
Return (%)	10.8	8.4	25.5	-6.8	28.9	19.5	0.6	7.3	23.3	-4.6
Differ from category (+/-). . .	-2.4	-2.6	-9.9	-0.6	3.1	1.8	-0.6	-7.2	-6.0	-4.6

PER SHARE DATA

	1993	1992	1991	1990	1989	1988	1987	1986	1985	1984
Dividends, Net Income ($).	0.00	0.12	0.25	0.38	0.37	0.20	1.39	0.63	0.49	0.56
Distrib'ns, Cap Gain ($) . . .	2.60	1.08	1.95	0.05	1.65	1.75	0.64	3.45	0.64	4.28
Net Asset Value ($)	20.41	20.81	20.33	18.08	19.90	17.04	15.91	17.83	20.55	17.70
Expense Ratio (%)	1.41	1.41	1.39	1.41	1.22	1.24	1.10	1.08	1.23	1.38
Net Income to Assets (%) .	-0.29	0.56	1.11	1.81	2.11	1.09	0.85	2.47	3.23	2.67
Portfolio Turnover (%).	na	41	74	87	45	71	89	133	73	68
Total Assets (Millions $).	52	58	60	51	50	35	36	32	35	32

PORTFOLIO (as of 6/30/93)

Portfolio Manager: Shelby M.C. Davis - 1993

Investm't Category: Growth

✔ Cap Gain	Asset Allocation
Cap & Income	Fund of Funds
Income	Index
	Sector
✔ Domestic	Small Cap
Foreign	Socially Conscious
Country/Region	State Specific

Portfolio: stocks 77%   bonds 0%
convertibles 0%   other 0%   cash 23%

Largest Holdings: health care 11%, insurance 10%

Unrealized Net Capital Gains: 17% of portfolio value

SHAREHOLDER INFORMATION

Minimum Investment
Initial: $1,000   Subsequent: $100

Minimum IRA Investment
Initial: $500   Subsequent: $100

Maximum Fees
Load: none   12b-1: 0.25%
Other: none

Distributions
Income: Dec   Capital Gains: Dec

Exchange Options
Number Per Year: 4   Fee: none
Telephone: yes (money market fund available)

Services
IRA, other pension, auto invest, auto withdraw

Selected US Gov't Income (SSGTX)

Mortgage-Backed Bond

124 East Marcy Street
Sante Fe, NM 87501
(800) 243-1575

PERFORMANCE

	3yr Annual	5yr Annual	10yr Annual	Bull	Bear
Return (%)	8.9	8.9	na	35.8	3.4
Differ from Category (+/-)	-0.3 blw av	-1.0 low	na	-0.8 blw av	-1.2 low

Total Risk	Standard Deviation	Category Risk	Risk Index	Avg Mat
low	3.8%	high	1.5	22.0 yrs

	1993	1992	1991	1990	1989	1988	1987	1986	1985	1984
Return (%)	8.4	5.1	13.5	8.5	9.1	2.9	—	—	—	—
Differ from category (+/-)	1.6	-1.0	-0.8	-1.0	-3.2	-4.1	—	—	—	—

PER SHARE DATA

	1993	1992	1991	1990	1989	1988	1987	1986	1985	1984
Dividends, Net Income ($)	0.56	0.60	0.70	0.72	0.72	0.72	—	—	—	—
Distrib'ns, Cap Gain ($)	0.31	0.25	0.00	0.00	0.23	0.23	—	—	—	—
Net Asset Value ($)	9.20	9.31	9.70	9.22	9.20	9.34	—	—	—	—
Expense Ratio (%)	1.44	1.44	1.41	1.44	1.50	1.50	—	—	—	—
Net Income to Assets (%)	6.02	6.26	6.51	6.95	6.70	6.30	—	—	—	—
Portfolio Turnover (%)	na	53	36	29	76	76	—	—	—	—
Total Assets (Millions $)	10	14	22	21	28	15	—	—	—	—

PORTFOLIO (as of 6/30/93)

Portfolio Manager: B. Clark Stamper - 1993

Investm't Category: Mortgage-Backed Bond

Cap Gain	Asset Allocation
Cap & Income	Fund of Funds
✔ Income	Index
	Sector
✔ Domestic	Small Cap
Foreign	Socially Conscious
Country/Region	State Specific

Portfolio: stocks 0% bonds 100%
convertibles 5% other 0% cash 0%

Largest Holdings: mortgage-backed 83%, U.S. government 17%

Unrealized Net Capital Gains: 5% of portfolio value

SHAREHOLDER INFORMATION

Minimum Investment
Initial: $1,000   Subsequent: $100

Minimum IRA Investment
Initial: $500   Subsequent: $100

Maximum Fees
Load: none   12b-1: 0.25%
Other: none

Distributions
Income: monthly   Capital Gains: Dec

Exchange Options
Number Per Year: 4   Fee: none
Telephone: yes (money market fund available)

Services
IRA, other pension, auto invest, auto withdraw

Sentry (SNTRX)

Growth

1800 N. Point Dr.
Stevens Point, WI 54481
(800) 533-7827, (715) 346-7048

PERFORMANCE

	3yr Annual	5yr Annual	10yr Annual	Bull	Bear
Return (%)	13.6	13.8	12.6	61.9	-4.6
Differ from Category (+/-)	-5.6 low	-0.8 blw av	0.0 av	-22.8 blw av	7.8 high

Total Risk	Standard Deviation	Category Risk	Risk Index	Beta
av	9.2%	low	0.8	0.7

	1993	1992	1991	1990	1989	1988	1987	1986	1985	1984
Return (%)	5.9	7.4	28.8	5.2	24.0	16.9	-5.4	14.6	32.6	1.8
Differ from category (+/-)	-7.3	-3.6	-6.6	11.3	-1.8	-0.8	-6.6	0.1	3.3	1.8

PER SHARE DATA

	1993	1992	1991	1990	1989	1988	1987	1986	1985	1984
Dividends, Net Income ($)	0.20	0.25	0.37	0.34	0.37	0.21	0.30	0.31	0.34	0.25
Distrib'ns, Cap Gain ($)	0.98	0.36	1.14	0.64	0.73	0.30	1.47	1.21	0.60	0.18
Net Asset Value ($)	14.85	15.15	14.68	12.60	12.93	11.33	10.14	12.70	12.36	10.07
Expense Ratio (%)	na	0.88	0.84	0.68	0.65	0.66	0.67	0.72	0.71	0.75
Net Income to Assets (%)	na	1.95	2.56	2.84	2.90	1.85	1.80	2.55	2.83	2.72
Portfolio Turnover (%)	na	13	3	30	15	19	35	24	25	57
Total Assets (Millions $)	76	69	61	44	46	42	38	42	33	30

PORTFOLIO (as of 4/30/93)

Portfolio Manager: Keith Ringberg - 1977

Investm't Category: Growth

✔ Cap Gain	Asset Allocation
Cap & Income	Fund of Funds
Income	Index
	Sector
✔ Domestic	Small Cap
Foreign	Socially Conscious
Country/Region	State Specific

Portfolio: stocks 66% bonds 0%
convertibles 0% other 0% cash 34%

Largest Holdings: stocks—food & restaurant 13%, stocks—retail 12%

Unrealized Net Capital Gains: -2% of portfolio value

SHAREHOLDER INFORMATION

Minimum Investment
Initial: $200   Subsequent: $50

Minimum IRA Investment
Initial: $200   Subsequent: $50

Maximum Fees
Load: none   12b-1: none
Other: none

Distributions
Income: Jun, Dec   Capital Gains: Dec

Exchange Options
Number Per Year: none   Fee: na
Telephone: na

Services
IRA, auto invest, auto withdraw

Sequoia (SEQUX)

Growth & Income

1370 Avenue of the Americas
New York, NY 10019
(212) 245-4500

this fund is closed to new investors

PERFORMANCE

	3yr Annual	5yr Annual	10yr Annual	Bull	Bear
Return (%)	19.2	15.7	15.6	79.9	-9.3
Differ from Category (+/-)	2.8 abv av	3.2 high	3.2 high	9.8 abv av	2.3 abv av

Total Risk	Standard Deviation	Category Risk	Risk Index	Beta
abv av	11.4%	abv av	1.3	0.9

	1993	1992	1991	1990	1989	1988	1987	1986	1985	1984
Return (%)	10.7	9.3	40.0	-3.8	27.7	11.0	7.4	13.3	27.9	18.4
Differ from category (+/-) . .	-1.9	-0.6	12.3	1.8	6.1	-5.8	7.0	-1.9	2.5	12.2

PER SHARE DATA

	1993	1992	1991	1990	1989	1988	1987	1986	1985	1984
Dividends, Net Income ($) .	0.65	0.93	1.36	1.38	1.28	1.38	2.21	1.61	1.51	1.43
Distrib'ns, Cap Gain ($) . . .	7.19	0.62	3.58	1.78	1.43	2.23	1.59	8.54	3.77	2.58
Net Asset Value ($)	54.84	56.66	53.31	41.94	46.86	38.81	38.43	39.29	44.01	39.26
Expense Ratio (%).	1.00	1.00	1.00	1.00	1.00	1.00	1.00	1.00	1.00	1.00
Net Income to Assets (%). .	1.30	1.80	2.80	3.10	2.80	3.60	3.30	3.90	3.80	4.30
Portfolio Turnover (%)	na	28	36	29	44	39	43	40	44	39
Total Assets (Millions $) . .	1,512	1,389	1,251	870	924	714	721	696	599	443

PORTFOLIO (as of 6/30/93)

Portfolio Manager: William Ruane - 1970

Investm't Category: Growth & Income

Cap Gain	Asset Allocation
✔ Cap & Income	Fund of Funds
Income	Index
	Sector
✔ Domestic	Small Cap
✔ Foreign	Socially Conscious
Country/Region	State Specific

Portfolio: stocks 71%   bonds 0%
convertibles 0%   other 0%   cash 29%

Largest Holdings: services 23%, insurance 21%

Unrealized Net Capital Gains: 35% of portfolio value

SHAREHOLDER INFORMATION

Minimum Investment
Initial: na   Subsequent: na

Minimum IRA Investment
Initial: na   Subsequent: na

Maximum Fees
Load: none   12b-1: none
Other: none

Distributions
Income: Feb, Jun, Dec   Capital Gains: Feb, Dec

Exchange Options
Number Per Year: none   Fee: na
Telephone: na

Services
IRA, auto withdraw

Seven Seas Series— Matrix Equity (SSMTX)

Growth & Income

Two International Place
34th Floor
Boston, MA 02110
(800) 647-7327, (617) 654-6089

PERFORMANCE

	3yr Annual	5yr Annual	10yr Annual	Bull	Bear
Return (%)	na	na	na	na	na
Differ from Category (+/-)	na	na	na	na	na

Total Risk	Standard Deviation	Category Risk	Risk Index	Beta
na	na	na	na	na

	1993	1992	1991	1990	1989	1988	1987	1986	1985	1984
Return (%)	16.2	—	—	—	—	—	—	—	—	—
Differ from category (+/-)	3.6	—	—	—	—	—	—	—	—	—

PER SHARE DATA

	1993	1992	1991	1990	1989	1988	1987	1986	1985	1984
Dividends, Net Income ($)	0.18	—	—	—	—	—	—	—	—	—
Distrib'ns, Cap Gain ($)	0.18	—	—	—	—	—	—	—	—	—
Net Asset Value ($)	11.93	—	—	—	—	—	—	—	—	—
Expense Ratio (%)	0.60	—	—	—	—	—	—	—	—	—
Net Income to Assets (%)	2.13	—	—	—	—	—	—	—	—	—
Portfolio Turnover (%)	58	—	—	—	—	—	—	—	—	—
Total Assets (Millions $)	89	—	—	—	—	—	—	—	—	—

PORTFOLIO (as of 8/31/93)

Portfolio Manager: Doug Holmes - 1992

Investm't Category: Growth & Income

Cap Gain	Asset Allocation
✔ Cap & Income	Fund of Funds
Income	Index
	Sector
✔ Domestic	Small Cap
Foreign	Socially Conscious
Country/Region	State Specific

Portfolio: stocks 97% bonds 0%
convertibles 0% other 0% cash 3%

Largest Holdings: consumer basics 19%, utilities 14%

Unrealized Net Capital Gains: 0% of portfolio value

SHAREHOLDER INFORMATION

Minimum Investment
Initial: $1,000   Subsequent: $250

Minimum IRA Investment
Initial: na   Subsequent: na

Maximum Fees
Load: none   12b-1: 0.25%
Other: none

Distributions
Income: quarterly   Capital Gains: Dec

Exchange Options
Number Per Year: no limit   Fee: none
Telephone: yes (money market fund available)

Services

Seven Seas Series— S&P 500 (SVSPX)

Growth & Income

Two International Place
34th Floor
Boston, MA 02110
(800) 647-7327, (617) 654-6089

PERFORMANCE

	3yr Annual	5yr Annual	10yr Annual	Bull	Bear
Return (%)	na	na	na	na	na
Differ from Category (+/-)	na	na	na	na	na

Total Risk	Standard Deviation	Category Risk	Risk Index	Beta
na	na	na	na	na

	1993	1992	1991	1990	1989	1988	1987	1986	1985	1984
Return (%)	9.5	—	—	—	—	—	—	—	—	—
Differ from category (+/-) . .	-3.1	—	—	—	—	—	—	—	—	—

PER SHARE DATA

	1993	1992	1991	1990	1989	1988	1987	1986	1985	1984
Dividends, Net Income ($) .	0.19	—	—	—	—	—	—	—	—	—
Distrib'ns, Cap Gain ($) . . .	0.12	—	—	—	—	—	—	—	—	—
Net Asset Value ($)	10.63	—	—	—	—	—	—	—	—	—
Expense Ratio (%)	0.15	—	—	—	—	—	—	—	—	—
Net Income to Assets (%) . .	3.02	—	—	—	—	—	—	—	—	—
Portfolio Turnover (%)	48	—	—	—	—	—	—	—	—	—
Total Assets (Millions $) . . .	322	—	—	—	—	—	—	—	—	—

PORTFOLIO (as of 8/31/93)

Portfolio Manager: Ann Eisenberg - 1992

Investm't Category: Growth & Income

Cap Gain	Asset Allocation
✔ Cap & Income	Fund of Funds
Income	✔ Index
	Sector
✔ Domestic	Small Cap
Foreign	Socially Conscious
Country/Region	State Specific

Portfolio: stocks 99% bonds 0%
convertibles 0% other 0% cash 1%

Largest Holdings: S&P 500 Stock Price Index

Unrealized Net Capital Gains: 2% of portfolio value

SHAREHOLDER INFORMATION

Minimum Investment
Initial: $1,000 Subsequent: $250

Minimum IRA Investment
Initial: na Subsequent: na

Maximum Fees
Load: none 12b-1: 0.25%
Other: none

Distributions
Income: quarterly Capital Gains: Oct

Exchange Options
Number Per Year: none Fee: none
Telephone: yes (money market fund available)

Services

Seven Seas Series— S&P MidCap (SSMCX)

Growth & Income

Two International Place
34th Floor
Boston, MA 02110
(800) 647-7327, (617) 654-6089

PERFORMANCE

	3yr Annual	5yr Annual	10yr Annual	Bull	Bear
Return (%)	na	na	na	na	na
Differ from Category (+/-)	na	na	na	na	na

Total Risk	Standard Deviation	Category Risk	Risk Index	Beta
na	na	na	na	na

	1993	1992	1991	1990	1989	1988	1987	1986	1985	1984
Return (%)	12.9	—	—	—	—	—	—	—	—	—
Differ from category (+/-). . .	0.3	—	—	—	—	—	—	—	—	—

PER SHARE DATA

	1993	1992	1991	1990	1989	1988	1987	1986	1985	1984
Dividends, Net Income ($).	0.22	—	—	—	—	—	—	—	—	—
Distrib'ns, Cap Gain ($) . . .	0.60	—	—	—	—	—	—	—	—	—
Net Asset Value ($)	11.92	—	—	—	—	—	—	—	—	—
Expense Ratio (%)	0.25	—	—	—	—	—	—	—	—	—
Net Income to Assets (%) .	1.85	—	—	—	—	—	—	—	—	—
Portfolio Turnover (%).	81	—	—	—	—	—	—	—	—	—
Total Assets (Millions $).	37	—	—	—	—	—	—	—	—	—

PORTFOLIO (as of 8/31/93)

Portfolio Manager: Lynn Blake - 1992

Investm't Category: Growth & Income

Cap Gain	Asset Allocation
✔ Cap & Income	Fund of Funds
Income	✔ Index
	Sector
✔ Domestic	Small Cap
Foreign	Socially Conscious
Country/Region	State Specific

Portfolio: stocks 100% bonds 0%
convertibles 0% other 0% cash 0%

Largest Holdings: S&P 400 MidCap Index

Unrealized Net Capital Gains: 3% of portfolio value

SHAREHOLDER INFORMATION

Minimum Investment
Initial: $1,000   Subsequent: $250

Minimum IRA Investment
Initial: na   Subsequent: na

Maximum Fees
Load: none   12b-1: 0.25%
Other: none

Distributions
Income: quarterly   Capital Gains: Oct

Exchange Options
Number Per Year: none   Fee: none
Telephone: yes (money market fund available)

Services

Seven Seas Short Term Gov't Securities (SVSGX)

Government Bond

Two International Place
34th Floor
Boston, MA 02110
(800) 647-7327, (617) 654-6089

PERFORMANCE

	3yr Annual	5yr Annual	10yr Annual	Bull	Bear
Return (%)	na	na	na	na	na
Differ from Category (+/-)	na	na	na	na	na

Total Risk	Standard Deviation	Category Risk	Risk Index	Avg Mat
na	na	na	na	1.6 yrs

	1993	1992	1991	1990	1989	1988	1987	1986	1985	1984
Return (%)	4.7	—	—	—	—	—	—	—	—	—
Differ from category (+/-) ..	-5.7	—	—	—	—	—	—	—	—	—

PER SHARE DATA

	1993	1992	1991	1990	1989	1988	1987	1986	1985	1984
Dividends, Net Income ($) .	0.41	—	—	—	—	—	—	—	—	—
Distrib'ns, Cap Gain ($) ...	0.26	—	—	—	—	—	—	—	—	—
Net Asset Value ($)	9.90	—	—	—	—	—	—	—	—	—
Expense Ratio (%)........	0.64	—	—	—	—	—	—	—	—	—
Net Income to Assets (%) ..	4.62	—	—	—	—	—	—	—	—	—
Portfolio Turnover (%)	69	—	—	—	—	—	—	—	—	—
Total Assets (Millions $)	23	—	—	—	—	—	—	—	—	—

PORTFOLIO (as of 8/31/93)

Portfolio Manager: Steve Boxer - 1992

Investm't Category: Government Bond

Cap Gain	Asset Allocation
Cap & Income	Fund of Funds
✔ Income	Index
	Sector
✔ Domestic	Small Cap
Foreign	Socially Conscious
Country/Region	State Specific

Portfolio: stocks 0%   bonds 91%
convertibles 0%   other 0%   cash 9%

Largest Holdings: U.S. government & agencies 78%, mortgage-backed 12%

Unrealized Net Capital Gains: 1% of portfolio value

SHAREHOLDER INFORMATION

Minimum Investment
Initial: $1,000   Subsequent: $250

Minimum IRA Investment
Initial: na   Subsequent: na

Maximum Fees
Load: none   12b-1: 0.25%
Other: none

Distributions
Income: monthly   Capital Gains: Oct

Exchange Options
Number Per Year: no limit   Fee: none
Telephone: yes (money market fund available)

Services

Seven Seas Yield Plus
(SSYPX)
General Bond

Two International Place
34th Floor
Boston, MA 02110
(800) 647-7327, (617) 654-6089

PERFORMANCE

	3yr Annual	5yr Annual	10yr Annual	Bull	Bear
Return (%)	na	na	na	na	na
Differ from Category (+/-)	na	na	na	na	na

Total Risk	Standard Deviation	Category Risk	Risk Index	Avg Mat
na	na	na	na	0.1 yrs

	1993	1992	1991	1990	1989	1988	1987	1986	1985	1984
Return (%).	3.4	—	—	—	—	—	—	—	—	—
Differ from category (+/-). . .	-5.8	—	—	—	—	—	—	—	—	—

PER SHARE DATA

	1993	1992	1991	1990	1989	1988	1987	1986	1985	1984
Dividends, Net Income ($).	0.34	—	—	—	—	—	—	—	—	—
Distrib'ns, Cap Gain ($) . . .	0.00	—	—	—	—	—	—	—	—	—
Net Asset Value ($)	10.00	—	—	—	—	—	—	—	—	—
Expense Ratio (%)	0.38	—	—	—	—	—	—	—	—	—
Net Income to Assets (%) .	3.54	—	—	—	—	—	—	—	—	—
Portfolio Turnover (%). . . .	137	—	—	—	—	—	—	—	—	—
Total Assets (Millions $). .	1,288	—	—	—	—	—	—	—	—	—

PORTFOLIO (as of 8/31/93)

Portfolio Manager: Glen Migliozzi - 1992

Investm't Category: General Bond

Cap Gain	Asset Allocation
Cap & Income	Fund of Funds
✔ Income	Index
	Sector
✔ Domestic	Small Cap
✔ Foreign	Socially Conscious
Country/Region	State Specific

Portfolio:	stocks 0%	bonds 89%
convertibles 0%	other 0%	cash 11%

Largest Holdings: corporate 53%

Unrealized Net Capital Gains: 0% of portfolio value

SHAREHOLDER INFORMATION

Minimum Investment
Initial: $1,000   Subsequent: $250

Minimum IRA Investment
Initial: na   Subsequent: na

Maximum Fees
Load: none   12b-1: 0.25%
Other: none

Distributions
Income: montlhly   Capital Gains: Oct

Exchange Options
Number Per Year: no limit   Fee: none
Telephone: yes (money market fund available)

Services

SIT Growth (NBNGX)

Aggressive Growth

4600 Norwest Center
Minneapolis, MN 55402
(800) 332-5580, (612) 334-5888

PERFORMANCE

	3yr Annual	5yr Annual	10yr Annual	Bull	Bear
Return (%)	20.6	18.3	15.2	96.6	-12.3
Differ from Category (+/-)	-4.8 blw av	0.1 av	3.3 abv av	-28.4 blw av	2.7 abv av

Total Risk	Standard Deviation	Category Risk	Risk Index	Beta
high	16.4%	av	1.1	1.2

	1993	1992	1991	1990	1989	1988	1987	1986	1985	1984
Return (%)	8.5	-2.1	65.4	-2.0	35.0	9.7	5.6	10.2	43.6	-3.2
Differ from category (+/-)	-10.5	-12.5	13.0	4.3	8.0	-5.5	9.0	0.8	12.6	6.2

PER SHARE DATA

	1993	1992	1991	1990	1989	1988	1987	1986	1985	1984
Dividends, Net Income ($)	0.01	0.04	0.05	0.07	0.08	0.09	0.00	0.14	0.05	0.04
Distrib'ns, Cap Gain ($)	0.29	0.02	0.03	0.38	0.36	0.25	0.74	0.81	0.18	0.09
Net Asset Value ($)	12.66	11.95	12.28	7.47	8.10	6.33	6.08	6.34	6.59	4.79
Expense Ratio (%)	0.80	0.83	1.03	1.10	1.19	1.21	1.20	1.32	1.50	1.50
Net Income to Assets (%)	0.35	0.52	0.96	0.75	1.85	0.57	0.09	0.19	2.65	1.18
Portfolio Turnover (%)	45	25	37	55	88	78	81	98	129	79
Total Assets (Millions $)	329	242	123	74	54	48	56	40	19	13

PORTFOLIO (as of 9/30/93)

Portfolio Manager: Eugene C. Sit - 1981, Erik S. Anderson - 1985

Investm't Category: Aggressive Growth
- ✔ Cap Gain
- Cap & Income
- Income
- Asset Allocation
- Fund of Funds
- Index
- Sector
- ✔ Domestic
- Foreign
- Country/Region
- ✔ Small Cap
- Socially Conscious
- State Specific

Portfolio: stocks 97% bonds 0%
convertibles 1% other 0% cash 2%

Largest Holdings: financial services 25%, technology 20%

Unrealized Net Capital Gains: 17% of portfolio value

SHAREHOLDER INFORMATION

Minimum Investment
Initial: $2,000 Subsequent: $100

Minimum IRA Investment
Initial: $0 Subsequent: $0

Maximum Fees
Load: none 12b-1: none
Other: none

Distributions
Income: Dec Capital Gains: Dec

Exchange Options
Number Per Year: 4 Fee: none
Telephone: yes (money market fund available)

Services
IRA, other pension, auto exchange, auto invest, auto withdraw

SIT Growth & Income
(SNIGX)
Growth & Income

4600 Norwest Center
Minneapolis, MN 55402
(800) 332-5580, (612) 334-5888

PERFORMANCE

	3yr Annual	5yr Annual	10yr Annual	Bull	Bear
Return (%)	12.8	13.1	na	52.7	-8.2
Differ from Category (+/-)	-3.6 low	0.6 av	na	-17.4 low	3.4 abv av

Total Risk	Standard Deviation	Category Risk	Risk Index	Beta
av	10.4%	av	1.2	0.9

	1993	1992	1991	1990	1989	1988	1987	1986	1985	1984
Return (%)	3.0	4.9	32.7	-2.3	32.0	5.3	5.3	—	—	—
Differ from category (+/-)	-9.6	-5.1	5.0	3.3	10.4	-11.5	4.9	—	—	—

PER SHARE DATA

	1993	1992	1991	1990	1989	1988	1987	1986	1985	1984
Dividends, Net Income ($)	0.26	0.38	0.51	0.63	0.50	0.44	0.85	—	—	—
Distrib'ns, Cap Gain ($)	1.38	0.54	0.54	0.68	0.91	0.00	0.89	—	—	—
Net Asset Value ($)	24.92	25.79	25.49	20.06	21.90	17.69	17.22	—	—	—
Expense Ratio (%)	1.42	1.50	1.50	1.50	1.50	1.50	1.50	—	—	—
Net Income to Assets (%)	1.31	1.92	2.74	2.86	2.95	2.96	2.70	—	—	—
Portfolio Turnover (%)	47	73	70	55	82	67	61	—	—	—
Total Assets (Millions $)	37	32	21	18	14	12	10	—	—	—

PORTFOLIO (as of 9/30/93)

Portfolio Manager: Peter Mitchelson - 1981, Eugene C. Sit - 1981

Investm't Category: Growth & Income
Cap Gain	Asset Allocation
✔ Cap & Income	Fund of Funds
Income	Index
	Sector
✔ Domestic	Small Cap
Foreign	Socially Conscious
Country/Region	State Specific

Portfolio: stocks 86% bonds 13%
convertibles 0% other 0% cash 1%

Largest Holdings: technology 22%, financial services 15%

Unrealized Net Capital Gains: 18% of portfolio value

SHAREHOLDER INFORMATION

Minimum Investment
Initial: $2,000   Subsequent: $100

Minimum IRA Investment
Initial: $0   Subsequent: $0

Maximum Fees
Load: none   12b-1: none
Other: none

Distributions
Income: quarterly   Capital Gains: Dec

Exchange Options
Number Per Year: 4   Fee: none
Telephone: yes (money market fund available)

Services
IRA, other pension, auto exchange, auto invest, auto withdraw

SIT International Growth (SNGRX)

International Stock

4600 Norwest Center
Minneapolis, MN 55402
(800) 332-5580, (612) 334-5888

PERFORMANCE

	3yr Annual	5yr Annual	10yr Annual	Bull	Bear
Return (%)	na	na	na	na	na
Differ from Category (+/-)	na	na	na	na	na

Total Risk	Standard Deviation	Category Risk	Risk Index	Beta
na	na	na	na	na

	1993	1992	1991	1990	1989	1988	1987	1986	1985	1984
Return (%)	48.3	2.6	—	—	—	—	—	—	—	—
Differ from category (+/-)	9.8	6.1	—	—	—	—	—	—	—	—

PER SHARE DATA

	1993	1992	1991	1990	1989	1988	1987	1986	1985	1984
Dividends, Net Income ($)	0.09	0.02	—	—	—	—	—	—	—	—
Distrib'ns, Cap Gain ($)	0.05	0.00	—	—	—	—	—	—	—	—
Net Asset Value ($)	15.66	10.66	—	—	—	—	—	—	—	—
Expense Ratio (%)	1.85	1.85	—	—	—	—	—	—	—	—
Net Income to Assets (%)	-0.29	0.67	—	—	—	—	—	—	—	—
Portfolio Turnover (%)	52	19	—	—	—	—	—	—	—	—
Total Assets (Millions $)	63	25	—	—	—	—	—	—	—	—

PORTFOLIO (as of 9/30/93)

Portfolio Manager: Andrew Kim - 1991, Eugene Sit - 1991

Investm't Category: International Stock

✔ Cap Gain	Asset Allocation
Cap & Income	Fund of Funds
Income	Index
	Sector
Domestic	Small Cap
✔ Foreign	Socially Conscious
Country/Region	State Specific

Portfolio: stocks 94%   bonds 0%
convertibles 0%   other 0%   cash 6%

Largest Holdings: Japan 28%, United Kingdom 11%

Unrealized Net Capital Gains: 13% of portfolio value

SHAREHOLDER INFORMATION

Minimum Investment
Initial: $2,000   Subsequent: $100

Minimum IRA Investment
Initial: $0   Subsequent: $0

Maximum Fees
Load: none   12b-1: none
Other: none

Distributions
Income: Dec   Capital Gains: Dec

Exchange Options
Number Per Year: 4   Fee: none
Telephone: yes (money market fund available)

Services
IRA, other pension, auto exchange, auto invest, auto withdraw

SIT Tax Free Income
(SNTIX)

Tax-Exempt Bond

4600 Norwest Center
Minneapolis, MN 55402
(800) 332-5580, (612) 334-5888

PERFORMANCE

	3yr Annual	5yr Annual	10yr Annual	Bull	Bear
Return (%)	9.0	8.5	na	32.2	5.3
Differ from Category (+/-)	-1.3 low	-0.6 low	na	-7.9 low	3.0 high

Total Risk	Standard Deviation	Category Risk	Risk Index	Avg Mat
low	2.5%	low	0.6	15.7 yrs

	1993	1992	1991	1990	1989	1988	1987	1986	1985	1984
Return (%)	10.4	7.6	9.1	7.2	8.3	—	—	—	—	—
Differ from category (+/-). . .	-1.2	-0.6	-2.2	0.8	-0.6	—	—	—	—	—

PER SHARE DATA

	1993	1992	1991	1990	1989	1988	1987	1986	1985	1984
Dividends, Net Income ($) .	0.58	0.64	0.69	0.78	0.77	—	—	—	—	—
Distrib'ns, Cap Gain ($) . . .	0.08	0.03	0.00	0.00	0.00	—	—	—	—	—
Net Asset Value ($)	10.08	9.76	9.72	9.57	9.68	—	—	—	—	—
Expense Ratio (%)	0.80	0.80	0.80	0.80	0.80	—	—	—	—	—
Net Income to Assets (%) .	6.17	7.02	7.62	8.16	8.08	—	—	—	—	—
Portfolio Turnover (%).	58	80	74	87	132	—	—	—	—	—
Total Assets (Millions $). . . .	340	193	87	31	13	—	—	—	—	—

PORTFOLIO (as of 9/30/93)

Portfolio Manager: Michael C. Brilley - 1988

Investm't Category: Tax-Exempt Bond

Cap Gain	Asset Allocation
Cap & Income	Fund of Funds
✔ Income	Index
	Sector
✔ Domestic	Small Cap
Foreign	Socially Conscious
Country/Region	State Specific

Portfolio: stocks 0% bonds 100%
convertibles 0% other 0% cash 0%

Largest Holdings: general obligation 0%

Unrealized Net Capital Gains: 2% of portfolio value

SHAREHOLDER INFORMATION

Minimum Investment
Initial: $2,000   Subsequent: $100

Minimum IRA Investment
Initial: na   Subsequent: na

Maximum Fees
Load: none   12b-1: none
Other: none

Distributions
Income: monthly   Capital Gains: Dec

Exchange Options
Number Per Year: 4   Fee: none
Telephone: yes (money market fund available)

Services
auto exchange, auto invest, auto withdraw

SIT US Gov't Securities
(SNGVX)
Mortgage-Backed Bond

4600 Norwest Center
Minneapolis, MN 55402
(800) 332-5580, (612) 334-5888

	3yr Annual	5yr Annual	10yr Annual	Bull	Bear
Return (%)	8.4	9.4	na	33.8	5.8
Differ from Category (+/-)	-0.8 low	-0.5 low	na	-2.9 low	1.2 high

Total Risk	Standard Deviation	Category Risk	Risk Index	Avg Mat
low	2.3%	low	0.9	18.1 yrs

	1993	1992	1991	1990	1989	1988	1987	1986	1985	1984
Return (%)	7.3	5.4	12.8	10.9	11.0	7.8	—	—	—	—
Differ from category (+/-) . . .	0.5	-0.6	-1.6	1.4	-1.3	0.8	—	—	—	—

	1993	1992	1991	1990	1989	1988	1987	1986	1985	1984
Dividends, Net Income ($) .	0.68	0.70	0.79	0.78	0.84	0.83	—	—	—	—
Distrib'ns, Cap Gain ($) . . .	0.04	0.15	0.17	0.00	0.00	0.00	—	—	—	—
Net Asset Value ($)	10.63	10.60	10.89	10.56	10.27	10.05	—	—	—	—
Expense Ratio (%).	0.89	0.80	0.90	1.25	1.25	1.25	—	—	—	—
Net Income to Assets (%) . .	6.60	7.28	7.60	8.02	8.33	8.27	—	—	—	—
Portfolio Turnover (%)	76	134	118	126	139	136	—	—	—	—
Total Assets (Millions $)	39	35	30	13	12	11	—	—	—	—

Portfolio Manager: Michael C. Brilley - 1987

Investm't Category: Mortgage-Backed Bond
Cap Gain	Asset Allocation
Cap & Income	Fund of Funds
✔ Income	Index
	Sector
✔ Domestic	Small Cap
Foreign	Socially Conscious
Country/Region	State Specific

Portfolio: stocks 0% bonds 99%
convertibles 0% other 0% cash 1%

Largest Holdings: mortgage-backed 93%, U.S. government 6%

Unrealized Net Capital Gains: 2% of portfolio value

Minimum Investment
Initial: $2,000   Subsequent: $100

Minimum IRA Investment
Initial: $0   Subsequent: $0

Maximum Fees
Load: none   12b-1: none
Other: none

Distributions
Income: monthly   Capital Gains: Dec

Exchange Options
Number Per Year: 4   Fee: none
Telephone: yes (money market fund available)

Services
IRA, other pension, auto exchange, auto invest, auto withdraw

Skyline Special Equities II (SPEQX)

350 North Clark Street
Chicago, IL 60610
(800) 458-5222, (312) 670-6035

Growth

fund in existence since 2/9/93

PERFORMANCE

	3yr Annual	5yr Annual	10yr Annual	Bull	Bear
Return (%)	na	na	na	na	na
Differ from Category (+/-)	na	na	na	na	na

Total Risk	Standard Deviation	Category Risk	Risk Index	Beta
na	na	na	na	na

	1993	1992	1991	1990	1989	1988	1987	1986	1985	1984
Return (%)	—	—	—	—	—	—	—	—	—	—
Differ from category (+/-). . . .	—	—	—	—	—	—	—	—	—	—

PER SHARE DATA

	1993	1992	1991	1990	1989	1988	1987	1986	1985	1984
Dividends, Net Income ($).	0.12	—	—	—	—	—	—	—	—	—
Distrib'ns, Cap Gain ($) . . .	0.09	—	—	—	—	—	—	—	—	—
Net Asset Value ($)	10.79	—	—	—	—	—	—	—	—	—
Expense Ratio (%)	1.57	—	—	—	—	—	—	—	—	—
Net Income to Assets (%) .	0.10	—	—	—	—	—	—	—	—	—
Portfolio Turnover (%).	111	—	—	—	—	—	—	—	—	—
Total Assets (Millions $).	56	—	—	—	—	—	—	—	—	—

PORTFOLIO (as of 6/30/93)

Portfolio Manager: Kenneth S. Kailin - 1993

Investm't Category: Growth

✔ Cap Gain	Asset Allocation
Cap & Income	Fund of Funds
Income	Index
	Sector
✔ Domestic	✔ Small Cap
Foreign	Socially Conscious
Country/Region	State Specific

Portfolio: stocks 88% bonds 0%
convertibles 0% other 0% cash 12%

Largest Holdings: insurance 10%, health care 10%

Unrealized Net Capital Gains: 4% of portfolio value

SHAREHOLDER INFORMATION

Minimum Investment
Initial: $1,000 Subsequent: $100

Minimum IRA Investment
Initial: $1,000 Subsequent: $100

Maximum Fees
Load: none 12b-1: none
Other: none

Distributions
Income: Dec Capital Gains: Dec

Exchange Options
Number Per Year: none Fee: none
Telephone: yes (money market fund available)

Services
IRA, other pension, auto exchange, auto invest, auto withdraw

Smith Barney Muni Bond Ltd Term "A" (SBLTX)

1345 Avenue of the Americas
New York, NY 10105
(212) 698-5349

Tax-Exempt Bond

PERFORMANCE

	3yr Annual	5yr Annual	10yr Annual	Bull	Bear
Return (%)	8.8	8.3	na	32.6	4.4
Differ from Category (+/-)	-1.5 low	-0.8 low	na	-7.5 low	2.1 high

Total Risk	Standard Deviation	Category Risk	Risk Index	Avg Mat
low	3.3%	low	0.8	7.7 yrs

	1993	1992	1991	1990	1989	1988	1987	1986	1985	1984
Return (%)	9.3	8.1	9.0	7.4	7.8	—	—	—	—	—
Differ from category (+/-) ..	-2.3	-0.2	-2.3	1.1	-1.2	—	—	—	—	—

PER SHARE DATA

	1993	1992	1991	1990	1989	1988	1987	1986	1985	1984
Dividends, Net Income ($) .	0.37	0.39	0.42	0.40	0.44	—	—	—	—	—
Distrib'ns, Cap Gain ($) ...	0.00	0.00	0.00	0.00	0.00	—	—	—	—	—
Net Asset Value ($)	6.84	6.61	6.49	6.36	6.31	—	—	—	—	—
Expense Ratio (%)........	0.52	0.49	0.33	0.30	0.30	—	—	—	—	—
Net Income to Assets (%)	na	6.42	6.77	6.98	6.58	—	—	—	—	—
Portfolio Turnover (%)......	na	26	15	65	14	—	—	—	—	—
Total Assets (Millions $) ...	289	157	65	20	5	—	—	—	—	—

PORTFOLIO

Portfolio Manager: Peter Coffey - 1988

Investm't Category: Tax-Exempt Bond

Cap Gain	Asset Allocation
Cap & Income	Fund of Funds
✔ Income	Index
	Sector
✔ Domestic	Small Cap
Foreign	Socially Conscious
Country/Region	State Specific

Portfolio: stocks na bonds na
convertibles na other na cash na

Largest Holdings: general obligation 5%

Unrealized Net Capital Gains: na

SHAREHOLDER INFORMATION

Minimum Investment
Initial: $10,000   Subsequent: $50

Minimum IRA Investment
Initial: na   Subsequent: na

Maximum Fees
Load: 2.00% front   12b-1: none
Other: 2% load on reinvested dividends

Distributions
Income: monthly   Capital Gains: Dec

Exchange Options
Number Per Year: no limit   Fee: none
Telephone: none

Services
auto invest, auto withdraw

Smith Barney Short-Term US Treasury (SBSTX)

1345 Avenue of the Americas
New York, NY 10105
(212) 698-5349

Government Bond

PERFORMANCE

	3yr Annual	5yr Annual	10yr Annual	Bull	Bear
Return (%)	na	na	na	na	na
Differ from Category (+/-)	na	na	na	na	na

Total Risk	Standard Deviation	Category Risk	Risk Index	Avg Mat
na	na	na	na	na

	1993	1992	1991	1990	1989	1988	1987	1986	1985	1984
Return (%)	6.0	5.9	—	—	—	—	—	—	—	—
Differ from category (+/-)	-4.4	-0.3	—	—	—	—	—	—	—	—

PER SHARE DATA

	1993	1992	1991	1990	1989	1988	1987	1986	1985	1984
Dividends, Net Income ($)	0.18	0.19	—	—	—	—	—	—	—	—
Distrib'ns, Cap Gain ($)	0.02	0.01	—	—	—	—	—	—	—	—
Net Asset Value ($)	4.16	4.12	—	—	—	—	—	—	—	—
Expense Ratio (%)	0.85	0.91	—	—	—	—	—	—	—	—
Net Income to Assets (%)	na	4.76	—	—	—	—	—	—	—	—
Portfolio Turnover (%)	na	45	—	—	—	—	—	—	—	—
Total Assets ($)	na	130	—	—	—	—	—	—	—	—

PORTFOLIO

Portfolio Manager: not specified

Investm't Category: Government Bond

Cap Gain	Asset Allocation
Cap & Income	Fund of Funds
✔ Income	Index
	Sector
✔ Domestic	Small Cap
Foreign	Socially Conscious
Country/Region	State Specific

Portfolio: stocks na   bonds na
convertibles na   other na   cash na

Largest Holdings: na

Unrealized Net Capital Gains: na

SHAREHOLDER INFORMATION

Minimum Investment
Initial: $10,000   Subsequent: $50

Minimum IRA Investment
Initial: $1,000   Subsequent: $50

Maximum Fees
Load: none   12b-1: 0.35%
Other: none

Distributions
Income: monthly   Capital Gains: Dec

Exchange Options
Number Per Year: no limit   Fee: $5
Telephone: none

Services
IRA, other pension, auto invest

Smith Barney—Income Return "A" (SBNRX)

1345 Avenue of the Americas
New York, NY 10105
(212) 698-5349

Government Bond

PERFORMANCE

	3yr Annual	5yr Annual	10yr Annual	Bull	Bear
Return (%)	6.8	8.0	na	24.9	6.5
Differ from Category (+/-)	-4.0 low	-2.4 low	na	-21.3 low	6.0 high

Total Risk	Standard Deviation	Category Risk	Risk Index	Avg Mat
low	2.2%	low	0.5	na

	1993	1992	1991	1990	1989	1988	1987	1986	1985	1984
Return (%)	3.9	5.8	10.9	9.1	10.5	6.4	5.3	8.6	—	—
Differ from category (+/-) . .	-6.5	-0.4	-4.1	2.6	-3.4	-1.2	7.1	-10.5	—	—

PER SHARE DATA

	1993	1992	1991	1990	1989	1988	1987	1986	1985	1984
Dividends, Net Income ($) .	0.46	0.51	0.71	0.74	0.75	0.72	0.60	0.87	—	—
Distrib'ns, Cap Gain ($) . . .	0.00	0.00	0.00	0.00	0.00	0.00	0.05	0.00	—	—
Net Asset Value ($)	9.59	9.68	9.65	9.38	9.31	9.12	9.26	9.43	—	—
Expense Ratio (%).	0.52	0.50	0.49	0.43	0.43	0.44	0.35	0.28	—	—
Net Income to Assets (%). . . .	na	5.33	6.98	7.92	8.13	7.78	7.37	7.58	—	—
Portfolio Turnover (%)	na	84	30	28	33	124	68	304	—	—
Total Assets ($)	na	49	34	24	28	54	56	54	—	—

PORTFOLIO

Portfolio Manager: Patrick Sheehan - 1992

Investm't Category: Government Bond

Cap Gain	Asset Allocation
Cap & Income	Fund of Funds
✔ Income	Index
	Sector
✔ Domestic	Small Cap
Foreign	Socially Conscious
Country/Region	State Specific

Portfolio: stocks na bonds na
convertibles na other na cash na

Largest Holdings: na

Unrealized Net Capital Gains: na

SHAREHOLDER INFORMATION

Minimum Investment
Initial: $10,000 Subsequent: $50

Minimum IRA Investment
Initial: $1,000 Subsequent: $50

Maximum Fees
Load: 1.50% front 12b-1: none
Other: 1.5% load on reinvested dividends

Distributions
Income: monthly Capital Gains: Dec

Exchange Options
Number Per Year: no limit Fee: $5
Telephone: none

Services
IRA, other pension, auto invest

Sound Shore (SSHFX)

Growth

P.O. Box 1810
8 Sound Shore Dr.
Greenwich, CT 06836
(800) 551-1980, (203) 629-1980

PERFORMANCE

PERFORMANCE

	3yr Annual	5yr Annual	10yr Annual	Bull	Bear
Return (%)	21.5	14.4	na	84.1	-12.9
Differ from Category (+/-)	2.3 abv av	-0.2 av	na	-0.6 av	-0.5 av

Total Risk	Standard Deviation		Category Risk	Risk Index		Beta
abv av	11.2%		blw av	1.0		0.9

	1993	1992	1991	1990	1989	1988	1987	1986	1985	1984
Return (%)	11.9	21.1	32.2	-10.6	22.3	21.1	-3.6	20.4	—	—
Differ from category (+/-). . .	-1.3	10.1	-3.2	-4.5	-3.5	3.4	-4.8	5.9	—	—

PER SHARE DATA

	1993	1992	1991	1990	1989	1988	1987	1986	1985	1984
Dividends, Net Income ($) .	0.14	0.17	0.28	0.51	0.34	0.17	0.18	0.21	—	—
Distrib'ns, Cap Gain ($) . . .	1.54	1.95	0.09	0.00	1.41	1.17	1.21	0.38	—	—
Net Asset Value ($)	16.50	16.24	15.17	11.77	13.73	12.67	11.58	13.31	—	—
Expense Ratio (%)	1.29	1.37	1.30	1.33	1.24	1.40	1.45	1.48	—	—
Net Income to Assets (%) .	1.01	1.10	2.10	3.55	2.37	1.57	1.14	2.55	—	—
Portfolio Turnover (%).	na	88	100	105	91	134	91	82	—	—
Total Assets (Millions $)	59	40	32	29	54	29	32	14	—	—

PORTFOLIO (as of 6/30/93)

Portfolio Manager: Harry Burn III - 1985,
Gibb Kane - 1985

Investm't Category: Growth
- ✔ Cap Gain   Asset Allocation
-    Cap & Income   Fund of Funds
-    Income   Index
-      Sector
- ✔ Domestic   Small Cap
-    Foreign   Socially Conscious
-    Country/Region   State Specific

Portfolio: stocks 79%   bonds 20%
convertibles 0%   other 0%   cash 1%

Largest Holdings: U.S. government 20%, apparel/clothing/fabric 7%

Unrealized Net Capital Gains: 8% of portfolio value

SHAREHOLDER INFORMATION

Minimum Investment
Initial: $10,000   Subsequent: $0

Minimum IRA Investment
Initial: $250   Subsequent: $0

Maximum Fees
Load: none   12b-1: none
Other: none

Distributions
Income: Jun, Dec   Capital Gains: Dec

Exchange Options
Number Per Year: no limit   Fee: none
Telephone: yes (money market fund available)

Services
IRA, other pension, auto withdraw

Southeastern Asset Mgmt Small Cap (SAMSX)

860 Ridgelake Blvd., Suite 301
Memphis, TN 38120
(800) 445-9469, (901) 761-2474

Growth

PERFORMANCE

	3yr Annual	5yr Annual	10yr Annual	Bull	Bear
Return (%)	17.3	8.4	na	50.6	-24.9
Differ from Category (+/-)	-1.9 blw av	-6.2 low	na	-34.1 low	-12.5 low

Total Risk	Standard Deviation	Category Risk	Risk Index	Beta
av	10.5%	blw av	1.0	0.6

	1993	1992	1991	1990	1989	1988	1987	1986	1985	1984
Return (%)	19.8	6.8	26.3	-30.0	32.8	—	—	—	—	—
Differ from category (+/-) ...	6.6	-4.2	-9.1	-23.9	7.0	—	—	—	—	—

PER SHARE DATA

	1993	1992	1991	1990	1989	1988	1987	1986	1985	1984
Dividends, Net Income ($) .	0.00	0.00	0.05	0.36	0.14	—	—	—	—	—
Distrib'ns, Cap Gain ($) ...	0.16	0.00	0.00	0.22	0.36	—	—	—	—	—
Net Asset Value ($)	13.49	11.40	10.67	8.49	12.87	—	—	—	—	—
Expense Ratio (%)........	1.46	1.45	1.43	1.43	1.50	—	—	—	—	—
Net Income to Assets (%) .	-0.13	-0.03	0.60	3.48	1.63	—	—	—	—	—
Portfolio Turnover (%)	na	26	65	15	20	—	—	—	—	—
Total Assets (Millions $)	85	62	60	48	44	—	—	—	—	—

PORTFOLIO (as of 6/30/93)

Portfolio Manager: O. Mason Hawkins - 1991

Investm't Category: Growth

✔ Cap Gain	Asset Allocation
Cap & Income	Fund of Funds
Income	Index
	Sector
✔ Domestic	✔ Small Cap
✔ Foreign	Socially Conscious
Country/Region	State Specific

Portfolio: stocks 95%   bonds 0%
convertibles 0%   other 0%   cash 5%

Largest Holdings: business services 13%, publishing 13%

Unrealized Net Capital Gains: 4% of portfolio value

SHAREHOLDER INFORMATION

Minimum Investment
Initial: $50,000   Subsequent: $0

Minimum IRA Investment
Initial: $10,000   Subsequent: $0

Maximum Fees
Load: none   12b-1: none
Other: none

Distributions
Income: Jun, Dec   Capital Gains: Dec

Exchange Options
Number Per Year: no limit   Fee: none
Telephone: none

Services
IRA, other pension, auto withdraw

Southeastern Asset Mgmt Value Trust (SAMVX)

860 Ridgelake Blvd., Suite 301
Memphis, TN 38120
(800) 445-9469, (901) 761-2474

Growth

PERFORMANCE

	3yr Annual	5yr Annual	10yr Annual	Bull	Bear
Return (%)	27.0	16.1	na	116.5	-20.8
Differ from Category (+/-)	7.8 high	1.5 abv av	na	31.8 high	-8.4 low

Total Risk	Standard Deviation	Category Risk	Risk Index	Beta
av	10.5%	blw av	1.0	0.8

	1993	1992	1991	1990	1989	1988	1987	1986	1985	1984
Return (%)	22.2	20.5	39.1	-16.3	23.2	35.2	—	—	—	—
Differ from category (+/-) . . .	9.0	9.5	3.7	-10.2	-2.6	17.5	—	—	—	—

PER SHARE DATA

	1993	1992	1991	1990	1989	1988	1987	1986	1985	1984
Dividends, Net Income ($) .	0.09	0.07	0.05	0.14	0.15	0.05	—	—	—	—
Distrib'ns, Cap Gain ($) . . .	0.95	1.29	0.78	0.23	1.53	0.00	—	—	—	—
Net Asset Value ($)	16.92	14.70	13.34	10.21	12.62	11.60	—	—	—	—
Expense Ratio (%)	1.25	1.29	1.30	1.32	1.35	1.50	—	—	—	—
Net Income to Assets (%) .	0.78	0.50	0.42	1.13	1.37	1.40	—	—	—	—
Portfolio Turnover (%).	na	29	45	52	58	93	—	—	—	—
Total Assets (Millions $)	402	244	178	130	140	51	—	—	—	—

PORTFOLIO (as of 6/30/93)

Portfolio Manager: O. Mason Hawkins - 1987

Investm't Category: Growth

✔ Cap Gain	Asset Allocation
Cap & Income	Fund of Funds
Income	Index
	Sector
✔ Domestic	Small Cap
✔ Foreign	Socially Conscious
Country/Region	State Specific

Portfolio: stocks 98% bonds 0%
convertibles 0% other 0% cash 2%

Largest Holdings: food 15%, business services 13%

Unrealized Net Capital Gains: 17% of portfolio value

SHAREHOLDER INFORMATION

Minimum Investment
Initial: $50,000 Subsequent: $0

Minimum IRA Investment
Initial: $10,000 Subsequent: $0

Maximum Fees
Load: none 12b-1: none
Other: none

Distributions
Income: Jun, Dec Capital Gains: Dec

Exchange Options
Number Per Year: no limit Fee: none
Telephone: none

Services
IRA, other pension, auto withdraw

SteinRoe Capital Opportunities (SRFCX)

Aggressive Growth

P.O. Box 1143
Chicago, IL 60690
(800) 338-2550, (312) 368-7800

PERFORMANCE

	3yr Annual	5yr Annual	10yr Annual	Bull	Bear
Return (%)	28.5	15.5	10.0	128.7	-34.0
Differ from Category (+/-)	3.1 abv av	-2.7 blw av	-1.9 blw av	3.7 av	-19.0 low

Total Risk	Standard Deviation	Category Risk	Risk Index	Beta
high	15.1%	blw av	1.0	1.1

	1993	1992	1991	1990	1989	1988	1987	1986	1985	1984
Return (%)	27.5	2.4	62.7	-29.0	36.8	-3.8	9.3	16.7	24.5	-17.3
Differ from category (+/-) . . .	8.5	-8.0	10.3	-22.7	9.8	-19.0	12.7	7.3	-6.5	-7.9

PER SHARE DATA

	1993	1992	1991	1990	1989	1988	1987	1986	1985	1984
Dividends, Net Income ($) .	0.01	0.07	0.20	0.15	0.11	0.09	0.08	0.20	0.28	0.11
Distrib'ns, Cap Gain ($) . . .	0.00	0.00	0.00	0.15	5.06	0.11	6.73	0.84	0.00	2.55
Net Asset Value ($)	32.39	25.41	24.89	15.42	22.20	20.20	21.23	26.75	23.81	19.37
Expense Ratio (%).	1.06	1.06	1.18	1.14	1.09	1.01	0.95	0.95	0.95	0.92
Net Income to Assets (%). .	0.09	0.42	1.19	0.43	0.42	0.34	0.18	0.19	0.93	1.21
Portfolio Turnover (%)	55	46	69	171	245	164	133	116	90	85
Total Assets (Millions $) . . .	160	119	130	86	273	194	172	191	176	176

PORTFOLIO (as of 9/30/93)

Portfolio Manager: Gloria Santella - 1989, Bruce Dunn - 1991

Investm't Category: Aggressive Growth
- ✔ Cap Gain
- Cap & Income
- Income
- ✔ Domestic
- ✔ Foreign
- Country/Region

- Asset Allocation
- Fund of Funds
- Index
- Sector
- Small Cap
- Socially Conscious
- State Specific

Portfolio: stocks 75%   bonds 0%
convertibles 4%   other 0%   cash 21%

Largest Holdings: leisure & entertainment 13%, technology 12%

Unrealized Net Capital Gains: 31% of portfolio value

SHAREHOLDER INFORMATION

Minimum Investment
Initial: $2,500   Subsequent: $100

Minimum IRA Investment
Initial: $500   Subsequent: $50

Maximum Fees
Load: none   12b-1: none
Other: none

Distributions
Income: Dec   Capital Gains: Dec

Exchange Options
Number Per Year: no limit   Fee: none
Telephone: yes 8/yr (money market fund available)

Services
IRA, other pension, auto exchange, auto invest, auto withdraw

SteinRoe Gov't Income (SRGPX)

General Bond

P.O. Box 1143
Chicago, IL 60690
(800) 338-2550, (312) 368-7800

PERFORMANCE

	3yr Annual	5yr Annual	10yr Annual	Bull	Bear
Return (%)	12.0	11.5	na	48.1	2.8
Differ from Category (+/-)	1.8 abv av	1.7 high	na	8.7 high	-0.1 av

Total Risk	Standard Deviation	Category Risk	Risk Index	Avg Mat
blw av	5.8%	high	2.0	19.4 yrs

	1993	1992	1991	1990	1989	1988	1987	1986	1985	1984
Return (%)	15.0	6.1	14.9	8.4	13.2	6.8	1.6	—	—	—
Differ from category (+/-). . .	5.8	-0.6	0.3	1.5	1.9	-0.8	-0.8	—	—	—

PER SHARE DATA

	1993	1992	1991	1990	1989	1988	1987	1986	1985	1984
Dividends, Net Income ($).	0.56	0.69	0.72	0.76	0.78	0.75	0.88	—	—	—
Distrib'ns, Cap Gain ($) . . .	0.98	0.25	0.00	0.00	0.00	0.00	0.05	—	—	—
Net Asset Value ($)	10.16	10.22	10.55	9.86	9.84	9.42	9.54	—	—	—
Expense Ratio (%)	0.95	0.99	1.00	1.00	1.00	1.00	1.00	—	—	—
Net Income to Assets (%) .	6.25	7.05	7.65	7.90	8.19	7.68	7.13	—	—	—
Portfolio Turnover (%).	170	139	136	181	239	237	205	—	—	—
Total Assets (Millions $).	56	59	50	47	32	27	23	—	—	—

PORTFOLIO (as of 6/30/93)

Portfolio Manager: Michael Kennedy - 1988

Investm't Category: General Bond

Cap Gain	Asset Allocation
Cap & Income	Fund of Funds
✔ Income	Index
	Sector
✔ Domestic	Small Cap
Foreign	Socially Conscious
Country/Region	State Specific

Portfolio: stocks 0%   bonds 82%
convertibles 0%   other 0%   cash 18%

Largest Holdings: mortgage-backed 64%, U.S. government 17%

Unrealized Net Capital Gains: 3% of portfolio value

SHAREHOLDER INFORMATION

Minimum Investment
Initial: $2,500   Subsequent: $100

Minimum IRA Investment
Initial: $500   Subsequent: $50

Maximum Fees
Load: none   12b-1: none
Other: none

Distributions
Income: monthly   Capital Gains: Dec

Exchange Options
Number Per Year: no limit   Fee: none
Telephone: yes 8/yr (money market fund available)

Services
IRA, other pension, auto exchange, auto invest, auto withdraw

SteinRoe High Yield Muni (SRMFX)

P.O. Box 1143
Chicago, IL 60690
(800) 338-2550, (312) 368-7800

Tax-Exempt Bond

PERFORMANCE

	3yr Annual	5yr Annual	10yr Annual	Bull	Bear
Return (%)	8.5	8.9	na	32.3	4.0
Differ from Category (+/-)	-1.8 low	-0.3 blw av	na	-7.8 low	1.7 high

Total Risk	Standard Deviation	Category Risk	Risk Index	Avg Mat
low	3.9%	blw av	1.0	19.4 yrs

	1993	1992	1991	1990	1989	1988	1987	1986	1985	1984
Return (%)	10.4	5.3	9.8	7.6	11.4	13.6	1.6	19.1	21.1	—
Differ from category (+/-) . .	-1.2	-3.0	-1.5	1.3	2.4	3.5	2.8	2.7	3.8	—

PER SHARE DATA

	1993	1992	1991	1990	1989	1988	1987	1986	1985	1984
Dividends, Net Income ($) .	0.66	0.74	0.81	0.84	0.86	0.87	1.07	0.91	0.94	—
Distrib'ns, Cap Gain ($) . . .	0.23	0.17	0.18	0.16	0.20	0.03	0.10	0.14	0.00	—
Net Asset Value ($)	11.76	11.49	11.80	11.68	11.82	11.61	11.06	12.06	11.09	—
Expense Ratio (%).	0.73	0.68	0.71	0.71	0.73	0.76	0.73	0.76	0.80	—
Net Income to Assets (%) . .	6.04	6.75	7.00	7.22	7.54	7.87	8.20	7.77	8.89	—
Portfolio Turnover (%)	75	88	195	261	208	53	110	34	46	—
Total Assets (Millions $) . . .	348	411	374	311	278	201	182	225	99	—

PORTFOLIO (as of 6/30/93)

Portfolio Manager: James Grabovac - 1991

Investm't Category: Tax-Exempt Bond

Cap Gain	Asset Allocation
Cap & Income	Fund of Funds
✔ Income	Index
	Sector
✔ Domestic	Small Cap
Foreign	Socially Conscious
Country/Region	State Specific

Portfolio: stocks 0% bonds 100%
convertibles 0% other 0% cash 0%

Largest Holdings: general obligation 4%

Unrealized Net Capital Gains: 2% of portfolio value

SHAREHOLDER INFORMATION

Minimum Investment
Initial: $2,500 Subsequent: $100

Minimum IRA Investment
Initial: na Subsequent: na

Maximum Fees
Load: none 12b-1: none
Other: none

Distributions
Income: monthly Capital Gains: Dec

Exchange Options
Number Per Year: no limit Fee: none
Telephone: yes 8/yr (money market fund available)

Services
auto exchange, auto invest, auto withdraw

SteinRoe
Income (SRHBX)

Corporate Bond

P.O. Box 1143
Chicago, IL 60690
(800) 338-2550, (312) 368-7800

PERFORMANCE

	3yr Annual	5yr Annual	10yr Annual	Bull	Bear
Return (%)	13.0	10.4	na	50.4	2.0
Differ from Category (+/-)	1.0 abv av	0.3 abv av	na	4.3 abv av	0.2 blw av

Total Risk	Standard Deviation	Category Risk	Risk Index	Avg Mat
low	4.0%	abv av	1.4	8.5 yrs

	1993	1992	1991	1990	1989	1988	1987	1986	1985	1984
Return (%)	13.1	9.1	17.1	6.1	7.1	11.5	3.8	—	—	—
Differ from category (+/-) . . .	1.7	0.5	0.5	0.8	-2.4	2.5	2.0	—	—	—

PER SHARE DATA

	1993	1992	1991	1990	1989	1988	1987	1986	1985	1984
Dividends, Net Income ($) .	0.69	0.76	0.76	0.84	0.95	0.94	0.95	—	—	—
Distrib'ns, Cap Gain ($) . . .	0.00	0.00	0.00	0.00	0.00	0.00	0.00	—	—	—
Net Asset Value ($)	10.14	9.60	9.53	8.85	9.17	9.47	9.37	—	—	—
Expense Ratio (%)	0.82	0.90	0.95	0.93	0.90	0.91	0.96	—	—	—
Net Income to Assets (%) .	7.62	8.20	8.98	10.02	9.97	10.08	9.90	—	—	—
Portfolio Turnover (%)	39	76	77	90	94	158	153	—	—	—
Total Assets (Millions $)	162	113	94	89	110	97	92	—	—	—

PORTFOLIO (as of 6/30/93)

Portfolio Manager: Ann Henderson - 1990

Investm't Category: Corporate Bond

Cap Gain	Asset Allocation
✔ Cap & Income	Fund of Funds
Income	Index
	Sector
✔ Domestic	Small Cap
✔ Foreign	Socially Conscious
Country/Region	State Specific

Portfolio: stocks 0%   bonds 96%
convertibles 0%   other 0%   cash 4%

Largest Holdings: financial 12%, utilites 12%

Unrealized Net Capital Gains: 6% of portfolio value

SHAREHOLDER INFORMATION

Minimum Investment
Initial: $2,500   Subsequent: $100

Minimum IRA Investment
Initial: $500   Subsequent: $50

Maximum Fees
Load: none   12b-1: none
Other: none

Distributions
Income: monthly   Capital Gains: Dec

Exchange Options
Number Per Year: no limit   Fee: none
Telephone: yes 8/yr (money market fund available)

Services
IRA, other pension, auto exchange, auto invest, auto withdraw

SteinRoe Interm Bond
(SRBFX)

General Bond

P.O. Box 1143
Chicago, IL 60690
(800) 338-2550, (312) 368-7800

PERFORMANCE

	3yr Annual	5yr Annual	10yr Annual	Bull	Bear
Return (%)	10.5	10.2	11.0	40.7	2.7
Differ from Category (+/-)	0.3 av	0.4 av	0.1 av	1.3 av	-0.2 blw av

Total Risk	Standard Deviation	Category Risk	Risk Index	Avg Mat
low	3.4%	av	1.2	4.7 yrs

	1993	1992	1991	1990	1989	1988	1987	1986	1985	1984
Return (%)	8.9	7.6	15.1	7.1	12.5	7.2	2.5	16.3	22.9	11.3
Differ from category (+/-) . .	-0.3	0.8	0.5	0.2	1.2	-0.4	0.0	2.4	2.8	-1.0

PER SHARE DATA

	1993	1992	1991	1990	1989	1988	1987	1986	1985	1984
Dividends, Net Income ($) .	0.57	0.68	0.68	0.72	0.73	0.70	0.87	0.82	0.87	0.93
Distrib'ns, Cap Gain ($) . . .	0.23	0.00	0.00	0.00	0.00	0.00	0.13	0.74	0.00	0.00
Net Asset Value ($)	8.98	9.00	9.02	8.48	8.63	8.35	8.46	9.26	9.36	8.41
Expense Ratio (%).	0.67	0.70	0.73	0.74	0.73	0.73	0.68	0.68	0.70	0.77
Net Income to Assets (%) . .	7.22	7.87	8.17	8.60	8.71	7.97	7.94	9.03	10.65	11.15
Portfolio Turnover (%)	214	202	239	296	197	273	230	334	286	152
Total Assets (Millions $) . . .	326	243	185	161	165	162	189	183	134	86

PORTFOLIO (as of 6/30/93)

Portfolio Manager: Michael Kennedy - 1988

Investm't Category: General Bond

Cap Gain	Asset Allocation
Cap & Income	Fund of Funds
✔ Income	Index
	Sector
✔ Domestic	Small Cap
✔ Foreign	Socially Conscious
Country/Region	State Specific

Portfolio: stocks 0%   bonds 90%
convertibles 0%   other 0%   cash 10%

Largest Holdings: corporate 58%, mortgage-backed 31%

Unrealized Net Capital Gains: 1% of portfolio value

SHAREHOLDER INFORMATION

Minimum Investment
Initial: $2,500   Subsequent: $100

Minimum IRA Investment
Initial: $500   Subsequent: $50

Maximum Fees
Load: none   12b-1: none
Other: none

Distributions
Income: monthly   Capital Gains: Dec

Exchange Options
Number Per Year: no limit   Fee: none
Telephone: yes 8/yr (money market fund available)

Services
IRA, other pension, auto exchange, auto invest, auto withdraw

SteinRoe Interm Muni

(SRIMX)

Tax-Exempt Bond

P.O. Box 1143
Chicago, IL 60690
(800) 338-2550, (312) 368-7800

PERFORMANCE

	3yr Annual	5yr Annual	10yr Annual	Bull	Bear
Return (%)	9.6	8.9	na	36.9	3.5
Differ from Category (+/-)	-0.6 blw av	-0.3 blw av	na	-3.2 blw av	1.2 abv av

Total Risk	Standard Deviation	Category Risk	Risk Index	Avg Mat
low	3.9%	blw av	1.0	8.0 yrs

	1993	1992	1991	1990	1989	1988	1987	1986	1985	1984
Return (%).............	10.8	7.6	10.5	7.5	8.1	6.1	1.8	12.1	—	—
Differ from category (+/-)....	-0.8	-0.6	-0.8	1.2	-0.8	-4.0	3.0	-4.3	—	—

PER SHARE DATA

	1993	1992	1991	1990	1989	1988	1987	1986	1985	1984
Dividends, Net Income ($).	0.51	0.55	0.58	0.63	0.62	0.59	0.57	0.57	—	—
Distrib'ns, Cap Gain ($) ...	0.18	0.12	0.16	0.03	0.03	0.00	0.01	0.00	—	—
Net Asset Value ($)	11.62	11.13	10.99	10.65	10.55	10.39	10.37	10.77	—	—
Expense Ratio (%)	0.72	0.79	0.80	0.80	0.80	0.80	0.80	0.80	—	—
Net Income to Assets (%) .	4.79	5.23	5.79	5.96	5.96	5.66	5.47	5.45	—	—
Portfolio Turnover (%)......	96	109	96	141	83	22	49	10	—	—
Total Assets (Millions $)....	258	165	119	99	91	97	96	104	—	—

PORTFOLIO (as of 6/30/93)

Portfolio Manager: Joanne Costopoulos - 1991

Investm't Category: Tax-Exempt Bond

Cap Gain	Asset Allocation
Cap & Income	Fund of Funds
✔ Income	Index
	Sector
✔ Domestic	Small Cap
Foreign	Socially Conscious
Country/Region	State Specific

Portfolio: stocks 0% bonds 100%
convertibles 0% other 0% cash 0%

Largest Holdings: general obligation 26%

Unrealized Net Capital Gains: 5% of portfolio value

SHAREHOLDER INFORMATION

Minimum Investment
Initial: $2,500   Subsequent: $100

Minimum IRA Investment
Initial: na   Subsequent: na

Maximum Fees
Load: none   12b-1: none
Other: none

Distributions
Income: monthly   Capital Gains: Dec

Exchange Options
Number Per Year: no limit   Fee: none
Telephone: yes 8/yr (money market fund available)

Services
auto exchange, auto invest, auto withdraw

SteinRoe Managed Muni
(SRMMX)

P.O. Box 1143
Chicago, IL 60690
(800) 338-2550, (312) 368-7800

Tax-Exempt Bond

PERFORMANCE

	3yr Annual	5yr Annual	10yr Annual	Bull	Bear
Return (%)	10.4	9.7	11.7	40.7	2.5
Differ from Category (+/-)	0.1 blw av	0.5 av	2.1 high	0.6 av	0.2 av

Total Risk	Standard Deviation	Category Risk	Risk Index	Avg Mat
blw av	4.5%	abv av	1.1	16.0 yrs

	1993	1992	1991	1990	1989	1988	1987	1986	1985	1984
Return (%)	11.0	8.5	11.8	7.0	10.6	10.8	0.8	23.3	23.4	11.3
Differ from category (+/-) ..	-0.6	0.2	0.5	0.6	1.6	0.6	2.1	6.9	6.1	3.0

PER SHARE DATA

	1993	1992	1991	1990	1989	1988	1987	1986	1985	1984
Dividends, Net Income ($) .	0.49	0.55	0.55	0.57	0.60	0.60	0.65	0.78	0.68	0.64
Distrib'ns, Cap Gain ($) ...	0.16	0.15	0.20	0.05	0.25	0.02	0.13	0.92	0.02	0.00
Net Asset Value ($)	9.36	9.04	9.01	8.76	8.80	8.76	8.50	9.22	8.93	7.89
Expense Ratio (%)........	0.64	0.64	0.66	0.66	0.65	0.65	0.65	0.65	0.65	0.64
Net Income to Assets (%)..	5.65	6.17	6.39	6.66	7.00	7.03	6.99	7.04	8.11	8.74
Portfolio Turnover (%)	63	94	203	95	102	28	113	92	113	190
Total Assets (Millions $) ...	781	726	656	584	515	468	458	523	357	242

PORTFOLIO (as of 6/30/93)

Portfolio Manager: Jane McCart - 1991

Investm't Category: Tax-Exempt Bond

Cap Gain	Asset Allocation
Cap & Income	Fund of Funds
✔ Income	Index
	Sector
✔ Domestic	Small Cap
Foreign	Socially Conscious
Country/Region	State Specific

Portfolio: stocks 0% bonds 100%
convertibles 0% other 0% cash 0%

Largest Holdings: general obligation 13%

Unrealized Net Capital Gains: 8% of portfolio value

SHAREHOLDER INFORMATION

Minimum Investment
Initial: $2,500   Subsequent: $100

Minimum IRA Investment
Initial: na   Subsequent: na

Maximum Fees
Load: none   12b-1: none
Other: none

Distributions
Income: monthly   Capital Gains: Dec

Exchange Options
Number Per Year: no limit   Fee: none
Telephone: yes 8/yr (money market fund available)

Services
auto exchange, auto invest, auto withdraw

SteinRoe Prime Equities

(SRPEX)

Growth

P.O. Box 1143
Chicago, IL 60690
(800) 338-2550, (312) 368-7800

PERFORMANCE

	3yr Annual	5yr Annual	10yr Annual	Bull	Bear
Return (%)	17.9	16.1	na	72.8	-6.6
Differ from Category (+/-)	-1.3 av	1.5 abv av	na	-11.9 blw av	5.8 abv av

Total Risk	Standard Deviation	Category Risk	Risk Index	Beta
av	9.9%	low	0.9	0.8

	1993	1992	1991	1990	1989	1988	1987	1986	1985	1984
Return (%).	12.8	9.9	32.3	-1.7	30.9	9.0	—	—	—	—
Differ from category (+/-). . .	-0.4	-1.1	-3.1	4.4	5.1	-8.7	—	—	—	—

PER SHARE DATA

	1993	1992	1991	1990	1989	1988	1987	1986	1985	1984
Dividends, Net Income ($).	0.15	0.17	0.23	0.28	0.23	0.18	—	—	—	—
Distrib'ns, Cap Gain ($) . . .	0.70	0.75	0.34	0.36	0.00	0.00	—	—	—	—
Net Asset Value ($)	14.58	13.71	13.32	10.54	11.39	8.89	—	—	—	—
Expense Ratio (%)	0.88	0.97	1.00	1.08	1.24	1.47	—	—	—	—
Net Income to Assets (%) .	1.23	1.46	2.27	2.40	2.28	2.03	—	—	—	—
Portfolio Turnover (%).	50	40	48	51	63	105	—	—	—	—
Total Assets (Millions $). . . .	107	71	55	43	33	23	—	—	—	—

PORTFOLIO (as of 9/30/93)

Portfolio Manager: Ralph Segall - 1987

Investm't Category: Growth

✔ Cap Gain	Asset Allocation
Cap & Income	Fund of Funds
Income	Index
	Sector
✔ Domestic	Small Cap
✔ Foreign	Socially Conscious
Country/Region	State Specific

Portfolio: stocks 86% bonds 4%
convertibles 1% other 1% cash 8%

Largest Holdings: banks 13%, health care 8%

Unrealized Net Capital Gains: 21% of portfolio value

SHAREHOLDER INFORMATION

Minimum Investment
Initial: $2,500   Subsequent: $100

Minimum IRA Investment
Initial: $500   Subsequent: $50

Maximum Fees
Load: none   12b-1: none
Other: none

Distributions
Income: quarterly   Capital Gains: Dec

Exchange Options
Number Per Year: no limit   Fee: none
Telephone: yes 8/yr (money market fund available)

Services
IRA, other pension, auto exchange, auto invest, auto withdraw

SteinRoe Special (SRSPX)

Aggressive Growth

P.O. Box 1143
Chicago, IL 60690
(800) 338-2550, (312) 368-7800

PERFORMANCE

	3yr Annual	5yr Annual	10yr Annual	Bull	Bear
Return (%)	22.5	19.0	15.9	90.7	-9.1
Differ from Category (+/-)	-2.9 blw av	0.8 av	4.0 abv av	-34.3 blw av	5.9 abv av

Total Risk	Standard Deviation	Category Risk	Risk Index	Beta
abv av	11.8%	low	0.8	1.0

	1993	1992	1991	1990	1989	1988	1987	1986	1985	1984
Return (%)	20.4	14.0	34.0	-5.8	37.8	20.2	4.2	14.7	29.4	-1.0
Differ from category (+/-) ...	1.4	3.6	-18.4	0.5	10.8	5.0	7.6	5.3	-1.6	8.4

PER SHARE DATA

	1993	1992	1991	1990	1989	1988	1987	1986	1985	1984
Dividends, Net Income ($) .	0.21	0.18	0.36	0.34	0.39	0.22	0.57	0.34	0.18	0.23
Distrib'ns, Cap Gain ($) ...	1.77	1.16	0.30	1.31	2.08	0.05	3.89	3.80	0.54	2.28
Net Asset Value ($)	24.00	21.63	20.16	15.58	18.31	15.14	12.83	16.95	18.41	14.88
Expense Ratio (%)........	0.97	0.99	1.04	1.01	0.96	0.99	0.96	0.92	0.92	0.95
Net Income to Assets (%)..	0.92	0.99	2.11	2.33	2.12	1.31	1.32	1.75	2.07	1.99
Portfolio Turnover (%)	42	40	50	70	85	42	103	116	96	89
Total Assets (Millions $) ..	1,100	626	587	361	322	225	188	253	278	152

PORTFOLIO (as of 9/30/93)

Portfolio Manager: Bruce Dunn - 1991, Richard Peterson - 1991

Investm't Category: Aggressive Growth
✔ Cap Gain	Asset Allocation
Cap & Income	Fund of Funds
Income	Index
	Sector
✔ Domestic	Small Cap
✔ Foreign	Socially Conscious
Country/Region	State Specific

Portfolio: stocks 82% bonds 6%
convertibles 1% other 0% cash 11%

Largest Holdings: financial services 11%, energy & related services 10%

Unrealized Net Capital Gains: 24% of portfolio value

SHAREHOLDER INFORMATION

Minimum Investment
Initial: $2,500   Subsequent: $100

Minimum IRA Investment
Initial: $500   Subsequent: $50

Maximum Fees
Load: none   12b-1: none
Other: none

Distributions
Income: Dec   Capital Gains: Dec

Exchange Options
Number Per Year: no limit   Fee: none
Telephone: yes 8/yr (money market fund available)

Services
IRA, other pension, auto exchange, auto invest, auto withdraw

SteinRoe Stock (SRFSX)

Growth

P.O. Box 1143
Chicago, IL 60690
(800) 338-2550, (312) 368-7800

PERFORMANCE

	3yr Annual	5yr Annual	10yr Annual	Bull	Bear
Return (%)	17.5	17.3	12.0	73.4	-5.4
Differ from Category (+/-)	-1.7 blw av	2.7 abv av	-0.6 blw av	-11.3 blw av	7.0 high

Total Risk	Standard Deviation	Category Risk	Risk Index	Beta
abv av	12.9%	abv av	1.2	1.0

	1993	1992	1991	1990	1989	1988	1987	1986	1985	1984
Return (%).............	2.8	8.2	45.9	0.8	35.4	0.6	5.5	16.9	26.5	-10.9
Differ from category (+/-)..	-10.4	-2.8	10.5	7.0	9.6	-17.1	4.3	2.4	-2.8	-10.9

PER SHARE DATA

	1993	1992	1991	1990	1989	1988	1987	1986	1985	1984
Dividends, Net Income ($).	0.15	0.15	0.28	0.42	0.36	0.27	0.29	0.25	0.30	0.37
Distrib'ns, Cap Gain ($) ...	1.73	0.94	1.16	0.91	0.00	0.05	2.71	3.21	0.00	4.69
Net Asset Value ($)	24.39	25.59	24.67	17.97	19.14	14.43	14.67	16.97	17.43	14.04
Expense Ratio (%)	0.93	0.92	0.79	0.73	0.77	0.76	0.65	0.67	0.67	0.67
Net Income to Assets (%) .	0.59	0.75	1.63	2.03	2.05	1.62	1.25	1.34	1.89	2.55
Portfolio Turnover (%)......	29	23	34	40	47	84	143	137	114	195
Total Assets (Millions $)....	368	373	292	206	206	196	233	226	224	216

PORTFOLIO (as of 9/30/93)

Portfolio Manager: committee

Investm't Category: Growth

✔ Cap Gain	Asset Allocation
Cap & Income	Fund of Funds
Income	Index
	Sector
✔ Domestic	Small Cap
✔ Foreign	Socially Conscious
Country/Region	State Specific

Portfolio:	stocks 95%	bonds 0%
convertibles 0%	other 0%	cash 5%

Largest Holdings: telecommunications 13%, health care 9%

Unrealized Net Capital Gains: 29% of portfolio value

SHAREHOLDER INFORMATION

Minimum Investment
Initial: $2,500   Subsequent: $100

Minimum IRA Investment
Initial: $500   Subsequent: $50

Maximum Fees
Load: none   12b-1: none
Other: none

Distributions
Income: Dec   Capital Gains: Dec

Exchange Options
Number Per Year: no limit   Fee: none
Telephone: yes 8/yr (money market fund available)

Services
IRA, other pension, auto exchange, auto invest, auto withdraw

SteinRoe Total Return
(SRFBX)

Balanced

P.O. Box 1143
Chicago, IL 60690
(800) 338-2550, (312) 368-7800

PERFORMANCE

	3yr Annual	5yr Annual	10yr Annual	Bull	Bear
Return (%)	16.2	13.1	12.0	67.1	-7.7
Differ from Category (+/-)	1.2 abv av	1.0 av	0.0 av	5.5 abv av	-1.9 blw av

Total Risk	Standard Deviation	Category Risk	Risk Index	Beta
av	7.4%	abv av	1.2	0.6

	1993	1992	1991	1990	1989	1988	1987	1986	1985	1984
Return (%)	12.3	7.8	29.5	-1.7	20.3	7.8	0.6	17.1	25.7	4.8
Differ from category (+/-) ..	-1.1	-0.3	5.6	-1.2	2.7	-4.2	-1.6	-0.4	2.0	-2.6

PER SHARE DATA

	1993	1992	1991	1990	1989	1988	1987	1986	1985	1984
Dividends, Net Income ($) .	1.22	1.30	1.32	1.06	1.40	1.31	1.62	1.35	1.42	1.41
Distrib'ns, Cap Gain ($) ...	0.70	1.67	0.62	0.73	0.73	0.49	1.45	2.69	0.18	1.55
Net Asset Value ($)	26.85	25.69	26.62	22.16	24.41	22.15	22.25	25.07	25.04	21.37
Expense Ratio (%)........	0.81	0.85	0.87	0.88	0.90	0.87	0.80	0.79	0.77	0.73
Net Income to Assets (%)..	4.69	4.94	5.50	5.36	5.83	5.68	5.12	5.21	6.30	6.94
Portfolio Turnover (%)	53	59	71	75	93	85	86	108	25	50
Total Assets (Millions $) ...	226	173	151	125	145	134	140	149	128	95

PORTFOLIO (as of 9/30/93)

Portfolio Manager: Robert Christensen - 1981

Investm't Category: Balanced

Cap Gain	Asset Allocation
✔ Cap & Income	Fund of Funds
Income	Index
	Sector
✔ Domestic	Small Cap
✔ Foreign	Socially Conscious
Country/Region	State Specific

Portfolio: stocks 35% bonds 12%
convertibles 25% other 17% cash 11%

Largest Holdings: stocks—real estate 69%, stocks—telephone 4%

Unrealized Net Capital Gains: 17% of portfolio value

SHAREHOLDER INFORMATION

Minimum Investment
Initial: $2,500   Subsequent: $100

Minimum IRA Investment
Initial: $500   Subsequent: $50

Maximum Fees
Load: none   12b-1: none
Other: none

Distributions
Income: quarterly   Capital Gains: Dec

Exchange Options
Number Per Year: no limit   Fee: none
Telephone: yes 8/yr (money market fund available)

Services
IRA, other pension, auto exchange, auto invest, auto withdraw

Stratton Growth (STRGX)

Growth & Income

Plymouth Mtg. Exec. Campus
610 W. Germantown Pike, # 361
Plymouth Meeting, PA 19462
(800) 634-5726, (215) 941-0255

PERFORMANCE

	3yr Annual	5yr Annual	10yr Annual	Bull	Bear
Return (%)	11.5	9.8	9.7	45.5	-11.0
Differ from Category (+/-)	-4.9 low	-2.7 low	-2.7 low	-24.6 low	0.6 av

Total Risk	Standard Deviation	Category Risk	Risk Index	Beta
av	9.0%	blw av	1.0	0.7

	1993	1992	1991	1990	1989	1988	1987	1986	1985	1984
Return (%).............	6.4	6.7	22.1	-6.7	23.7	22.5	-3.8	10.6	27.4	-4.7
Differ from category (+/-)...	-6.2	-3.3	-5.6	-1.1	2.1	5.7	-4.2	-4.6	2.0	-10.9

PER SHARE DATA

	1993	1992	1991	1990	1989	1988	1987	1986	1985	1984
Dividends, Net Income ($).	0.50	0.56	0.72	0.81	0.70	0.52	0.69	0.28	0.20	0.14
Distrib'ns, Cap Gain ($) ...	0.90	0.81	0.43	0.46	2.49	1.49	1.53	2.07	0.61	0.69
Net Asset Value ($)	20.05	20.19	20.27	17.63	20.24	19.06	17.23	20.02	20.09	16.45
Expense Ratio (%)	1.39	1.35	1.41	1.38	1.41	1.48	1.50	1.49	1.61	1.61
Net Income to Assets (%) .	2.76	3.20	3.94	4.09	2.79	2.80	1.74	1.40	1.22	0.87
Portfolio Turnover (%)......	35	60	57	55	50	34	23	28	35	36
Total Assets (Millions $).....	24	25	25	23	20	17	19	19	14	11

PORTFOLIO (as of 5/31/93)

Portfolio Manager: James W. Stratton - 1972, John A. Affleck - 1979

Investm't Category: Growth & Income

Cap Gain	Asset Allocation
✔ Cap & Income	Fund of Funds
Income	Index
	Sector
✔ Domestic	Small Cap
Foreign	Socially Conscious
Country/Region	State Specific

Portfolio: stocks 93% bonds 2%
convertibles 0% other 0% cash 5%

Largest Holdings: consumer products/services 20%, health care 13%

Unrealized Net Capital Gains: 19% of portfolio value

SHAREHOLDER INFORMATION

Minimum Investment
Initial: $2,000   Subsequent: $100

Minimum IRA Investment
Initial: $0   Subsequent: $0

Maximum Fees
Load: none   12b-1: none
Other: none

Distributions
Income: Jul, Dec   Capital Gains: Jul, Dec

Exchange Options
Number Per Year: no limit   Fee: none
Telephone: yes (money market fund not available)

Services
IRA, other pension, auto invest, auto withdraw

Stratton Monthly Dividend Shares (STMDX)

Growth & Income

Plymouth Mtg. Exec. Campus
610 W. Germantown Pike, # 361
Plymouth Meeting, PA 19462
(800) 634-5726, (215) 941-0255

PERFORMANCE

	3yr Annual	5yr Annual	10yr Annual	Bull	Bear
Return (%)	16.6	12.6	12.8	69.1	-9.6
Differ from Category (+/-)	0.2 av	0.1 av	0.4 av	-1.0 av	2.0 abv av

Total Risk	Standard Deviation	Category Risk	Risk Index	Beta
av	8.0%	low	0.9	0.5

	1993	1992	1991	1990	1989	1988	1987	1986	1985	1984
Return (%)	6.5	10.3	35.0	-3.8	18.7	9.7	-11.4	20.4	29.9	21.1
Differ from category (+/-) ..	-6.1	0.3	7.3	1.8	-2.9	-7.1	-11.8	5.2	4.5	14.9

PER SHARE DATA

	1993	1992	1991	1990	1989	1988	1987	1986	1985	1984
Dividends, Net Income ($) .	1.95	1.94	1.95	2.20	2.05	2.08	2.09	2.28	2.16	2.04
Distrib'ns, Cap Gain ($) ...	0.00	0.00	0.00	0.00	0.00	0.00	0.64	0.50	0.00	0.00
Net Asset Value ($)	29.17	29.16	28.31	22.66	25.88	23.63	23.44	29.21	26.62	22.42
Expense Ratio (%)........	1.10	1.23	1.27	1.25	1.21	1.21	1.24	1.49	1.72	1.74
Net Income to Assets (%)..	6.74	7.63	8.79	8.19	8.54	7.52	6.90	8.36	9.77	9.03
Portfolio Turnover (%).....	35	44	14	39	15	24	15	13	28	30
Total Assets (Millions $) ...	178	46	31	33	34	36	54	21	10	9

PORTFOLIO (as of 7/31/93)

Portfolio Manager: Gerard E. Hefferman - 1980, James W. Stratton - 1980

Investm't Category: Growth & Income

Cap Gain	Asset Allocation
✔ Cap & Income	Fund of Funds
Income	Index
	Sector
✔ Domestic	Small Cap
Foreign	Socially Conscious
Country/Region	State Specific

Portfolio: stocks 88%   bonds 2%
convertibles 1%   other 5%   cash 4%

Largest Holdings: utilities 75%, real estate
health care 12%

Unrealized Net Capital Gains: 9% of portfolio value

SHAREHOLDER INFORMATION

Minimum Investment
Initial: $2,000   Subsequent: $100

Minimum IRA Investment
Initial: $0   Subsequent: $0

Maximum Fees
Load: none   12b-1: none
Other: none

Distributions
Income: monthly   Capital Gains: Dec

Exchange Options
Number Per Year: no limit   Fee: none
Telephone: yes (money market fund not available)

Services
IRA, other pension, auto invest, auto withdraw

Strong Advantage (STADX)

Corporate Bond

P.O. Box 2936
Milwaukee, WI 53201
(800) 368-1030, (414) 359-1400

PERFORMANCE

	3yr Annual	5yr Annual	10yr Annual	Bull	Bear
Return (%)	8.9	8.5	na	30.8	5.4
Differ from Category (+/-)	-3.1 low	-1.6 low	na	-15.3 low	3.6 high

Total Risk	Standard Deviation	Category Risk	Risk Index	Avg Mat
low	1.0%	low	0.3	1.8 yrs

	1993	1992	1991	1990	1989	1988	1987	1986	1985	1984
Return (%)	7.8	8.4	10.6	6.6	9.3	—	—	—	—	—
Differ from category (+/-)	-3.6	-0.2	-6.0	1.3	-0.2	—	—	—	—	—

PER SHARE DATA

	1993	1992	1991	1990	1989	1988	1987	1986	1985	1984
Dividends, Net Income ($)	0.58	0.70	0.75	0.82	1.02	—	—	—	—	—
Distrib'ns, Cap Gain ($)	0.00	0.00	0.00	0.00	0.00	—	—	—	—	—
Net Asset Value ($)	10.19	10.01	9.90	9.67	9.87	—	—	—	—	—
Expense Ratio (%)	0.90	1.00	1.20	1.20	1.10	—	—	—	—	—
Net Income to Assets (%)	6.10	7.00	7.80	8.50	10.00	—	—	—	—	—
Portfolio Turnover (%)	323	316	503	274	211	—	—	—	—	—
Total Assets (Millions $)	425	272	143	119	143	—	—	—	—	—

PORTFOLIO (as of 6/30/93)

Portfolio Manager: Jeffrey A. Koch - 1991

Investm't Category: Corporate Bond

Cap Gain	Asset Allocation
Cap & Income	Fund of Funds
✔ Income	Index
	Sector
✔ Domestic	Small Cap
✔ Foreign	Socially Conscious
Country/Region	State Specific

Portfolio: stocks 0% bonds 98%
convertibles 0% other 0% cash 2%

Largest Holdings: corporate 86%, U.S. government 12%

Unrealized Net Capital Gains: 1% of portfolio value

SHAREHOLDER INFORMATION

Minimum Investment
Initial: $1,000   Subsequent: $50

Minimum IRA Investment
Initial: $250   Subsequent: $50

Maximum Fees
Load: none   12b-1: none
Other: none

Distributions
Income: monthly   Capital Gains: Dec

Exchange Options
Number Per Year: 5   Fee: none
Telephone: yes (money market fund available)

Services
IRA, other pension, auto exchange, auto invest, auto withdraw

Strong Common Stock
(STCSX)
Aggressive Growth

P.O. Box 2936
Milwaukee, WI 53201
(800) 368-1030, (414) 359-1400

this fund is closed to new investors

PERFORMANCE

	3yr Annual	5yr Annual	10yr Annual	Bull	Bear
Return (%)	33.3	na	na	163.2	-8.9
Differ from Category (+/-)	7.9 high	na	na	38.2 abv av	6.1 abv av

Total Risk	Standard Deviation	Category Risk	Risk Index	Beta
high	14.3%	blw av	0.9	0.9

	1993	1992	1991	1990	1989	1988	1987	1986	1985	1984
Return (%)	25.1	20.7	57.0	0.8	—	—	—	—	—	—
Differ from category (+/-) ...	6.1	10.3	4.6	7.2	—	—	—	—	—	—

PER SHARE DATA

	1993	1992	1991	1990	1989	1988	1987	1986	1985	1984
Dividends, Net Income ($) .	0.17	0.01	0.00	0.08	—	—	—	—	—	—
Distrib'ns, Cap Gain ($) ...	0.73	0.38	2.58	0.00	—	—	—	—	—	—
Net Asset Value ($)	17.94	15.07	12.84	10.02	—	—	—	—	—	—
Expense Ratio (%)........	1.40	1.40	2.00	2.00	—	—	—	—	—	—
Net Income to Assets (%)..	0.60	0.10	-0.50	0.90	—	—	—	—	—	—
Portfolio Turnover (%)	89	292	2,461	291	—	—	—	—	—	—
Total Assets (Millions $) ...	788	179	49	2	—	—	—	—	—	—

PORTFOLIO (as of 6/30/93)

Portfolio Manager: Richard Weiss - 1991, Carlene Murphy - 1991

Investm't Category: Aggressive Growth

✔ Cap Gain	Asset Allocation
Cap & Income	Fund of Funds
Income	Index
	Sector
✔ Domestic	Small Cap
✔ Foreign	Socially Conscious
Country/Region	State Specific

Portfolio: stocks 82% bonds 0%
convertibles 0% other 0% cash 18%

Largest Holdings: financial services 13%, energy related 10%

Unrealized Net Capital Gains: 7% of portfolio value

SHAREHOLDER INFORMATION

Minimum Investment
Initial: $1,000 Subsequent: $50

Minimum IRA Investment
Initial: $250 Subsequent: $50

Maximum Fees
Load: none 12b-1: none
Other: none

Distributions
Income: quarterly Capital Gains: Dec

Exchange Options
Number Per Year: 5 Fee: none
Telephone: yes (money market fund available)

Services
IRA, other pension, auto exchange, auto invest, auto withdraw

Strong Discovery (STDIX)

Growth

P.O. Box 2936
Milwaukee, WI 53201
(800) 368-1030, (414) 359-1400

PERFORMANCE

	3yr Annual	5yr Annual	10yr Annual	Bull	Bear
Return (%)	27.8	20.2	na	114.1	-5.1
Differ from Category (+/-)	8.6 high	5.6 high	na	29.4 high	7.3 high

Total Risk	Standard Deviation	Category Risk	Risk Index	Beta
high	17.9%	high	1.7	1.3

	1993	1992	1991	1990	1989	1988	1987	1986	1985	1984
Return (%).............	22.2	1.9	67.5	-2.7	23.9	24.4	—	—	—	—
Differ from category (+/-)...	9.0	-9.1	32.1	3.4	-1.9	6.7	—	—	—	—

PER SHARE DATA

	1993	1992	1991	1990	1989	1988	1987	1986	1985	1984
Dividends, Net Income ($).	0.49	1.49	0.82	0.30	0.27	0.97	—	—	—	—
Distrib'ns, Cap Gain ($) ...	0.92	0.15	2.60	0.00	0.71	0.02	—	—	—	—
Net Asset Value ($)	18.05	16.01	17.49	12.51	13.18	11.44	—	—	—	—
Expense Ratio (%)	1.50	1.50	1.60	1.90	1.90	2.00	—	—	—	—
Net Income to Assets (%) .	0.00	-0.40	0.00	2.10	2.40	11.90	—	—	—	—
Portfolio Turnover (%).....	776	1,259	1,060	494	550	442	—	—	—	—
Total Assets (Millions $)....	304	193	162	56	58	14	—	—	—	—

PORTFOLIO (as of 6/30/93)

Portfolio Manager: Richard Strong - 1987

Investm't Category: Growth

✔ Cap Gain	Asset Allocation
Cap & Income	Fund of Funds
Income	Index
	Sector
✔ Domestic	✔ Small Cap
✔ Foreign	Socially Conscious
Country/Region	State Specific

Portfolio: stocks 91% bonds 0%
convertibles 0% other 0% cash 9%

Largest Holdings: real estate investment trusts 8%, oil field services/equipment 8%

Unrealized Net Capital Gains: 1% of portfolio value

SHAREHOLDER INFORMATION

Minimum Investment
Initial: $1,000   Subsequent: $50

Minimum IRA Investment
Initial: $250   Subsequent: $50

Maximum Fees
Load: none   12b-1: none
Other: none

Distributions
Income: quarterly   Capital Gains: Dec

Exchange Options
Number Per Year: 5   Fee: none
Telephone: yes (money market fund available)

Services
IRA, other pension, auto exchange, auto invest, auto withdraw

Strong Gov't Securities
(STVSX)

P.O. Box 2936
Milwaukee, WI 53201
(800) 368-1030, (414) 359-1400

General Bond

PERFORMANCE

	3yr Annual	5yr Annual	10yr Annual	Bull	Bear
Return (%)	12.8	11.3	na	48.6	4.9
Differ from Category (+/-)	2.6 high	1.5 abv av	na	9.2 high	2.0 abv av

Total Risk	Standard Deviation	Category Risk	Risk Index	Avg Mat
low	3.8%	abv av	1.3	13.1 yrs

	1993	1992	1991	1990	1989	1988	1987	1986	1985	1984
Return (%)	12.6	9.2	16.6	8.7	9.8	10.5	3.4	—	—	—
Differ from category (+/-) . . .	3.4	2.5	2.0	1.8	-1.5	2.9	0.8	—	—	—

PER SHARE DATA

	1993	1992	1991	1990	1989	1988	1987	1986	1985	1984
Dividends, Net Income ($) .	0.65	0.80	0.76	0.72	0.79	0.67	0.65	—	—	—
Distrib'ns, Cap Gain ($) . . .	0.40	0.48	0.17	0.09	0.05	0.09	0.00	—	—	—
Net Asset Value ($)	10.61	10.39	10.77	10.10	10.08	9.98	9.75	—	—	—
Expense Ratio (%)	0.80	0.70	0.80	1.30	1.30	0.40	1.00	—	—	—
Net Income to Assets (%) . .	6.40	7.70	7.50	7.20	7.60	6.90	6.60	—	—	—
Portfolio Turnover (%)	738	629	293	254	422	1,728	715	—	—	—
Total Assets (Millions $) . . .	234	82	52	41	35	25	11	—	—	—

PORTFOLIO (as of 6/30/93)

Portfolio Manager: Bradley C. Tank - 1990

Investm't Category: General Bond

Cap Gain	Asset Allocation
Cap & Income	Fund of Funds
✔ Income	Index
	Sector
✔ Domestic	Small Cap
Foreign	Socially Conscious
Country/Region	State Specific

Portfolio: stocks 0% bonds 85%
convertibles 0% other 0% cash 15%

Largest Holdings: U.S. government & agencies 46%, mortgage-backed 22%

Unrealized Net Capital Gains: 1% of portfolio value

SHAREHOLDER INFORMATION

Minimum Investment
Initial: $1,000   Subsequent: $50

Minimum IRA Investment
Initial: $250   Subsequent: $50

Maximum Fees
Load: none   12b-1: none
Other: none

Distributions
Income: monthly   Capital Gains: Dec

Exchange Options
Number Per Year: 5   Fee: none
Telephone: yes (money market fund available)

Services
IRA, other pension, auto exchange, auto invest, auto withdraw

Strong Income (SRNCX)

General Bond

P.O. Box 2936
Milwaukee, WI 53201
(800) 368-1030, (414) 359-1400

PERFORMANCE

	3yr Annual	5yr Annual	10yr Annual	Bull	Bear
Return (%)	13.6	6.6	na	45.7	-5.6
Differ from Category (+/-)	3.4 high	-3.2 low	na	6.3 abv av	-8.5 low

Total Risk	Standard Deviation	Category Risk	Risk Index	Avg Mat
low	3.5%	av	1.2	12.5 yrs

	1993	1992	1991	1990	1989	1988	1987	1986	1985	1984
Return (%)	16.7	9.3	14.8	-6.2	0.3	12.4	4.3	29.9	—	—
Differ from category (+/-)	7.5	2.6	0.2	-13.1	-11.0	4.8	1.8	16.0	—	—

PER SHARE DATA

	1993	1992	1991	1990	1989	1988	1987	1986	1985	1984
Dividends, Net Income ($)	0.69	0.81	0.76	1.05	1.40	1.16	1.51	0.69	—	—
Distrib'ns, Cap Gain ($)	0.00	0.00	0.00	0.00	0.00	0.00	0.05	0.00	—	—
Net Asset Value ($)	10.24	9.40	9.37	8.87	10.57	11.88	11.64	12.65	—	—
Expense Ratio (%)	1.20	1.30	1.50	1.40	1.20	1.20	1.10	1.00	—	—
Net Income to Assets (%)	7.20	8.70	8.40	11.20	12.10	9.80	10.60	11.30	—	—
Portfolio Turnover (%)	740	557	392	294	207	400	245	204	—	—
Total Assets (Millions $)	123	103	92	92	195	203	138	118	—	—

PORTFOLIO (as of 6/30/93)

Portfolio Manager: Jeff Koch - 1991

Investm't Category: General Bond

Cap Gain	Asset Allocation
✔ Cap & Income	Fund of Funds
Income	Index
	Sector
✔ Domestic	Small Cap
✔ Foreign	Socially Conscious
Country/Region	State Specific

Portfolio: stocks 0% bonds 95%
convertibles 0% other 1% cash 4%

Largest Holdings: corporate 88%, U.S. government agencies 6%

Unrealized Net Capital Gains: 2% of portfolio value

SHAREHOLDER INFORMATION

Minimum Investment
Initial: $1,000   Subsequent: $50

Minimum IRA Investment
Initial: $250   Subsequent: $50

Maximum Fees
Load: none   12b-1: none
Other: none

Distributions
Income: monthly   Capital Gains: Dec

Exchange Options
Number Per Year: 5   Fee: none
Telephone: yes (money market fund available)

Services
IRA, other pension, auto exchange, auto invest, auto withdraw

Strong Insured Muni Bond (STIMX)

Tax-Exempt Bond

P.O. Box 2936
Milwaukee, WI 53201
(800) 368-1030, (414) 359-1400

PERFORMANCE

	3yr Annual	5yr Annual	10yr Annual	Bull	Bear
Return (%)	na	na	na	na	na
Differ from Category (+/-)	na	na	na	na	na

Total Risk	Standard Deviation	Category Risk	Risk Index	Avg Mat
na	na	na	na	16.7 yrs

	1993	1992	1991	1990	1989	1988	1987	1986	1985	1984
Return (%)	12.8	13.0	—	—	—	—	—	—	—	—
Differ from category (+/-)	1.2	4.7	—	—	—	—	—	—	—	—

PER SHARE DATA

	1993	1992	1991	1990	1989	1988	1987	1986	1985	1984
Dividends, Net Income ($)	0.56	0.62	—	—	—	—	—	—	—	—
Distrib'ns, Cap Gain ($)	0.15	0.14	—	—	—	—	—	—	—	—
Net Asset Value ($)	11.46	10.82	—	—	—	—	—	—	—	—
Expense Ratio (%)	0.40	0.20	—	—	—	—	—	—	—	—
Net Income to Assets (%)	5.20	5.80	—	—	—	—	—	—	—	—
Portfolio Turnover (%)	136	290	—	—	—	—	—	—	—	—
Total Assets (Millions $)	404	21	—	—	—	—	—	—	—	—

PORTFOLIO (as of 6/30/93)

Portfolio Manager: Mary-Kay Bourbulas - 1991, Tom Conlin - 1991

Investm't Category: Tax-Exempt Bond

Cap Gain	Asset Allocation
Cap & Income	Fund of Funds
✔ Income	Index
	Sector
✔ Domestic	Small Cap
Foreign	Socially Conscious
Country/Region	State Specific

Portfolio: stocks 0% bonds 86%
convertibles 0% other 0% cash 14%

Largest Holdings: general obligation 12%

Unrealized Net Capital Gains: 2% of portfolio value

SHAREHOLDER INFORMATION

Minimum Investment
Initial: $2,500   Subsequent: $50

Minimum IRA Investment
Initial: na   Subsequent: na

Maximum Fees
Load: none   12b-1: none
Other: none

Distributions
Income: monthly   Capital Gains: Dec

Exchange Options
Number Per Year: 5   Fee: none
Telephone: yes (money market fund available)

Services
auto exchange, auto invest, auto withdraw

Strong International Stock (STISX)

International Stock

P.O. Box 2936
Milwaukee, WI 53201
(800) 368-1030, (414) 359-1400

PERFORMANCE

	3yr Annual	5yr Annual	10yr Annual	Bull	Bear
Return (%)	na	na	na	na	na
Differ from Category (+/-)	na	na	na	na	na

Total Risk	Standard Deviation	Category Risk	Risk Index	Beta
na	na	na	na	na

	1993	1992	1991	1990	1989	1988	1987	1986	1985	1984
Return (%).	47.7	—	—	—	—	—	—	—	—	—
Differ from category (+/-). . .	9.2	—	—	—	—	—	—	—	—	—

PER SHARE DATA

	1993	1992	1991	1990	1989	1988	1987	1986	1985	1984
Dividends, Net Income ($).	0.02	—	—	—	—	—	—	—	—	—
Distrib'ns, Cap Gain ($) . . .	0.22	—	—	—	—	—	—	—	—	—
Net Asset Value ($)	14.18	—	—	—	—	—	—	—	—	—
Expense Ratio (%)	2.00	—	—	—	—	—	—	—	—	—
Net Income to Assets (%) .	0.10	—	—	—	—	—	—	—	—	—
Portfolio Turnover (%).	101	—	—	—	—	—	—	—	—	—
Total Assets (Millions $). . . .	151	—	—	—	—	—	—	—	—	—

PORTFOLIO (as of 6/30/93)

Portfolio Manager: Anthony Cragg-92

Investm't Category: International Stock

✔ Cap Gain	Asset Allocation
Cap & Income	Fund of Funds
Income	Index
	Sector
Domestic	Small Cap
✔ Foreign	Socially Conscious
Country/Region	State Specific

Portfolio: stocks 90% bonds 0%
convertibles 0% other 0% cash 10%

Largest Holdings: Japan 37%, United Kingdom 16%

Unrealized Net Capital Gains: 1% of portfolio value

SHAREHOLDER INFORMATION

Minimum Investment
Initial: $1,000 Subsequent: $50

Minimum IRA Investment
Initial: $250 Subsequent: $50

Maximum Fees
Load: none 12b-1: none
Other: none

Distributions
Income: quarterly Capital Gains: Dec

Exchange Options
Number Per Year: 5 Fee: none
Telephone: yes (money market fund available)

Services
IRA, other pension, auto exchange, auto invest, auto withdraw

Strong Investment (STIFX)

Balanced

P.O. Box 2936
Milwaukee, WI 53201
(800) 368-1030, (414) 359-1400

PERFORMANCE

	3yr Annual	5yr Annual	10yr Annual	Bull	Bear
Return (%)	12.2	10.0	10.4	45.4	-0.1
Differ from Category (+/-)	-2.8 low	-2.1 low	-1.6 low	-16.2 low	5.7 high

Total Risk	Standard Deviation	Category Risk	Risk Index	Beta
av	6.9%	av	1.1	0.5

	1993	1992	1991	1990	1989	1988	1987	1986	1985	1984
Return (%)	14.4	3.2	19.6	2.7	11.1	9.1	-0.3	17.6	19.3	9.7
Differ from category (+/-) ...	1.0	-4.9	-4.3	3.2	-6.5	-2.9	-2.6	0.1	-4.4	2.3

PER SHARE DATA

	1993	1992	1991	1990	1989	1988	1987	1986	1985	1984
Dividends, Net Income ($) .	0.82	0.86	0.96	1.38	0.96	1.60	1.77	0.94	0.75	0.31
Distrib'ns, Cap Gain ($) ...	1.23	0.93	0.19	0.00	0.13	0.00	2.95	0.41	0.03	1.10
Net Asset Value ($)	19.06	18.49	19.68	17.50	18.41	17.57	17.60	22.18	20.12	17.62
Expense Ratio (%)........	1.20	1.20	1.30	1.30	1.30	1.20	1.10	1.10	1.10	1.20
Net Income to Assets (%)..	5.20	4.40	5.10	6.10	6.60	7.50	4.20	4.70	5.40	8.40
Portfolio Turnover (%)	332	320	418	320	207	426	337	80	143	76
Total Assets (Millions $) ...	257	208	215	204	241	256	273	339	220	146

PORTFOLIO (as of 6/30/93)

Portfolio Manager: J. Mueller - 1993,
A. Stephens - 1993, B. Tank - 1993

Investm't Category: Balanced

Cap Gain	Asset Allocation
✔ Cap & Income	Fund of Funds
Income	Index
	Sector
✔ Domestic	Small Cap
✔ Foreign	Socially Conscious
Country/Region	State Specific

Portfolio:　stocks 36%　bonds 58%
convertibles 1%　other 2%　cash 3%

Largest Holdings: bonds—corporate 46%, bonds—U.S. government

Unrealized Net Capital Gains: 3% of portfolio value

SHAREHOLDER INFORMATION

Minimum Investment
Initial: $250　　　Subsequent: $50

Minimum IRA Investment
Initial: $250　　　Subsequent: $50

Maximum Fees
Load: none　　　12b-1: none
Other: none

Distributions
Income: quarterly　　Capital Gains: Dec

Exchange Options
Number Per Year: 5　Fee: none
Telephone: yes (money market fund available)

Services
IRA, other pension, auto exchange, auto invest, auto withdraw

Strong Muni Bond (SXFIX)

Tax-Exempt Bond

P.O. Box 2936
Milwaukee, WI 53201
(800) 368-1030, (414) 359-1400

PERFORMANCE

	3yr Annual	5yr Annual	10yr Annual	Bull	Bear
Return (%)	12.1	9.6	na	47.2	0.2
Differ from Category (+/-)	1.8 high	0.4 av	na	7.1 high	-2.1 low

Total Risk	Standard Deviation	Category Risk	Risk Index	Avg Mat
blw av	4.3%	av	1.1	18.1 yrs

	1993	1992	1991	1990	1989	1988	1987	1986	1985	1984
Return (%)	10.9	12.1	13.3	4.6	7.0	7.5	-1.7	—	—	—
Differ from category (+/-) . . .	-0.6	3.8	2.0	-1.7	-2.0	-2.6	-0.5	—	—	—

PER SHARE DATA

	1993	1992	1991	1990	1989	1988	1987	1986	1985	1984
Dividends, Net Income ($) .	0.58	0.65	0.64	0.66	0.52	0.49	0.67	—	—	—
Distrib'ns, Cap Gain ($) . . .	0.24	0.25	0.00	0.00	0.00	0.00	0.00	—	—	—
Net Asset Value ($)	10.25	10.00	9.76	9.22	9.47	9.35	9.16	—	—	—
Expense Ratio (%)	0.60	0.10	0.10	0.30	1.70	1.30	1.00	—	—	—
Net Income to Assets (%) .	5.70	6.40	6.90	7.20	5.60	5.30	7.00	—	—	—
Portfolio Turnover (%)	165	324	465	586	243	344	284	—	—	—
Total Assets (Millions $)	402	290	115	32	19	18	19	—	—	—

PORTFOLIO (as of 6/30/93)

Portfolio Manager: Conlin - 1991, Bourbulas - 1991

Investm't Category: Tax-Exempt Bond

Cap Gain	Asset Allocation
Cap & Income	Fund of Funds
✔ Income	Index
	Sector
✔ Domestic	Small Cap
Foreign	Socially Conscious
Country/Region	State Specific

Portfolio: stocks 0%   bonds 95%
convertibles 0%   other 0%   cash 5%

Largest Holdings: general obligation 5%

Unrealized Net Capital Gains: 2% of portfolio value

SHAREHOLDER INFORMATION

Minimum Investment
Initial: $2,500   Subsequent: $50

Minimum IRA Investment
Initial: na   Subsequent: na

Maximum Fees
Load: none   12b-1: none
Other: none

Distributions
Income: monthly   Capital Gains: Dec

Exchange Options
Number Per Year: 5   Fee: none
Telephone: yes (money market fund available)

Services
auto exchange, auto invest, auto withdraw

Strong Opportunity
(SOPFX)

Growth

P.O. Box 2936
Milwaukee, WI 53201
(800) 368-1030, (414) 359-1400

PERFORMANCE

	3yr Annual	5yr Annual	10yr Annual	Bull	Bear
Return (%)	23.2	14.5	na	92.0	-13.5
Differ from Category (+/-)	4.0 abv av	-0.1 av	na	7.3 abv av	-1.1 av

Total Risk	Standard Deviation	Category Risk	Risk Index	Beta
abv av	11.8%	av	1.1	0.9

	1993	1992	1991	1990	1989	1988	1987	1986	1985	1984
Return (%)	21.1	17.3	31.6	-11.3	18.5	16.4	11.8	59.9	—	—
Differ from category (+/-) ...	7.9	6.3	-3.8	-5.2	-7.3	-1.3	10.6	45.4	—	—

PER SHARE DATA

	1993	1992	1991	1990	1989	1988	1987	1986	1985	1984
Dividends, Net Income ($) .	0.05	0.05	0.18	0.74	0.68	1.37	0.23	0.00	—	—
Distrib'ns, Cap Gain ($) ...	1.56	0.15	0.00	0.03	0.15	0.18	1.80	0.00	—	—
Net Asset Value ($)	28.23	24.70	21.24	16.29	19.21	16.90	15.87	15.99	—	—
Expense Ratio (%)........	1.40	1.50	1.70	1.70	1.60	1.60	1.50	1.70	—	—
Net Income to Assets (%)..	0.50	0.30	1.10	3.30	4.30	7.40	1.70	0.70	—	—
Portfolio Turnover (%)....	105	139	271	275	306	352	371	170	—	—
Total Assets (Millions $) ...	469	193	160	132	205	157	154	43	—	—

PORTFOLIO (as of 6/30/93)

Portfolio Manager: Carlene H. Murphy - 1991, Richard T. Weiss - 1991

Investm't Category: Growth

✔ Cap Gain	Asset Allocation
Cap & Income	Fund of Funds
Income	Index
	Sector
✔ Domestic	Small Cap
✔ Foreign	Socially Conscious
Country/Region	State Specific

Portfolio: stocks 82% bonds 0%
convertibles 0% other 0% cash 18%

Largest Holdings: energy related 13%, financial services 12%

Unrealized Net Capital Gains: 14% of portfolio value

SHAREHOLDER INFORMATION

Minimum Investment
Initial: $1,000   Subsequent: $50

Minimum IRA Investment
Initial: $250   Subsequent: $50

Maximum Fees
Load: none   12b-1: none
Other: none

Distributions
Income: quarterly   Capital Gains: Dec

Exchange Options
Number Per Year: 5   Fee: none
Telephone: yes (money market fund available)

Services
IRA, other pension, auto exchange, auto invest, auto withdraw

Strong Short-Term Bond (SSTBX)

P.O. Box 2936
Milwaukee, WI 53201
(800) 368-1030, (414) 359-1400

Corporate Bond

PERFORMANCE

	3yr Annual	5yr Annual	10yr Annual	Bull	Bear
Return (%)	10.1	8.7	na	37.4	2.3
Differ from Category (+/-)	-1.9 blw av	-1.4 low	na	-8.7 blw av	0.5 av

Total Risk	Standard Deviation	Category Risk	Risk Index	Avg Mat
low	1.9%	blw av	0.6	2.8 yrs

	1993	1992	1991	1990	1989	1988	1987	1986	1985	1984
Return (%)	9.3	6.6	14.6	5.2	8.2	10.1	—	—	—	—
Differ from category (+/-). . .	-2.1	-2.0	-2.0	-0.1	-1.3	1.1	—	—	—	—

PER SHARE DATA

	1993	1992	1991	1990	1989	1988	1987	1986	1985	1984
Dividends, Net Income ($).	0.66	0.78	0.74	0.81	1.00	0.86	—	—	—	—
Distrib'ns, Cap Gain ($) . . .	0.00	0.00	0.00	0.00	0.02	0.06	—	—	—	—
Net Asset Value ($)	10.23	9.99	10.12	9.53	9.86	10.09	—	—	—	—
Expense Ratio (%)	0.08	0.60	1.00	1.30	1.10	1.00	—	—	—	—
Net Income to Assets (%) .	6.70	7.30	7.80	8.60	9.70	8.50	—	—	—	—
Portfolio Turnover (%).	381	353	398	314	177	461	—	—	—	—
Total Assets (Millions $). .	1,569	757	165	80	130	102	—	—	—	—

PORTFOLIO (as of 6/30/93)

Portfolio Manager: Bradley C. Tank - 1990

Investm't Category: Corporate Bond

Cap Gain	Asset Allocation
Cap & Income	Fund of Funds
✔ Income	Index
	Sector
✔ Domestic	Small Cap
✔ Foreign	Socially Conscious
Country/Region	State Specific

Portfolio: stocks 0% bonds 95%
convertibles 0% other 3% cash 2%

Largest Holdings: corporate 83%, mortgage-backed 11%

Unrealized Net Capital Gains: 1% of portfolio value

SHAREHOLDER INFORMATION

Minimum Investment
Initial: $1,000   Subsequent: $50

Minimum IRA Investment
Initial: $250   Subsequent: $50

Maximum Fees
Load: none   12b-1: none
Other: none

Distributions
Income: monthly   Capital Gains: Dec

Exchange Options
Number Per Year: 5   Fee: none
Telephone: yes (money market fund available)

Services
IRA, other pension, auto exchange, auto invest, auto withdraw

Strong Short-Term Muni Bond (STSMX)

Tax-Exempt Bond

P.O. Box 2936
Milwaukee, WI 53201
(800) 368-1030, (414) 359-1400

PERFORMANCE

	3yr Annual	5yr Annual	10yr Annual	Bull	Bear
Return (%)	na	na	na	na	na
Differ from Category (+/-)	na	na	na	na	na

Total Risk	Standard Deviation	Category Risk	Risk Index	Avg Mat
na	na	na	na	2.8 yrs

	1993	1992	1991	1990	1989	1988	1987	1986	1985	1984
Return (%)	6.7	7.1	—	—	—	—	—	—	—	—
Differ from category (+/-) ..	-4.9	-1.2	—	—	—	—	—	—	—	—

PER SHARE DATA

	1993	1992	1991	1990	1989	1988	1987	1986	1985	1984
Dividends, Net Income ($) .	0.44	0.47	—	—	—	—	—	—	—	—
Distrib'ns, Cap Gain ($) ...	0.07	0.01	—	—	—	—	—	—	—	—
Net Asset Value ($)	10.36	10.20	—	—	—	—	—	—	—	—
Expense Ratio (%)........	0.50	0.20	—	—	—	—	—	—	—	—
Net Income to Assets (%)..	4.40	4.90	—	—	—	—	—	—	—	—
Portfolio Turnover (%)	92	140	—	—	—	—	—	—	—	—
Total Assets (Millions $) ...	217	111	—	—	—	—	—	—	—	—

PORTFOLIO (as of 6/30/93)

Portfolio Manager: G. Nolan Smith - 1992

Investm't Category: Tax-Exempt Bond

Cap Gain	Asset Allocation
Cap & Income	Fund of Funds
✔ Income	Index
	Sector
✔ Domestic	Small Cap
Foreign	Socially Conscious
Country/Region	State Specific

Portfolio: stocks 0% bonds 91%
convertibles 0% other 0% cash 9%

Largest Holdings: general obligation 18%

Unrealized Net Capital Gains: 1% of portfolio value

SHAREHOLDER INFORMATION

Minimum Investment
Initial: $2,500   Subsequent: $50

Minimum IRA Investment
Initial: na   Subsequent: na

Maximum Fees
Load: none   12b-1: none
Other: none

Distributions
Income: monthly   Capital Gains: Dec

Exchange Options
Number Per Year: 5   Fee: none
Telephone: yes (money market fund available)

Services
auto exchange, auto invest, auto withdraw

Strong Total Return
(STRFX)

Balanced

P.O. Box 2936
Milwaukee, WI 53201
(800) 368-1030, (414) 359-1400

PERFORMANCE

	3yr Annual	5yr Annual	10yr Annual	Bull	Bear
Return (%)	18.0	9.4	12.3	66.1	-7.9
Differ from Category (+/-)	3.0 high	-2.7 low	0.3 av	4.5 abv av	-2.1 blw av

Total Risk	Standard Deviation	Category Risk	Risk Index	Beta
abv av	12.6%	high	2.0	1.0

	1993	1992	1991	1990	1989	1988	1987	1986	1985	1984
Return (%)	22.5	0.5	33.5	-7.1	2.5	15.5	6.0	19.9	25.3	10.4
Differ from category (+/-) . . .	9.1	-7.6	9.6	-6.6	-15.1	3.5	3.7	2.4	1.6	3.0

PER SHARE DATA

	1993	1992	1991	1990	1989	1988	1987	1986	1985	1984
Dividends, Net Income ($) .	0.33	0.17	0.22	1.14	1.31	1.96	1.65	0.69	0.57	0.37
Distrib'ns, Cap Gain ($) . . .	0.05	0.00	0.00	0.00	0.50	0.25	3.17	1.04	0.20	1.29
Net Asset Value ($)	24.30	20.17	20.24	15.34	17.72	18.96	18.37	21.61	19.56	16.35
Expense Ratio (%)	1.20	1.30	1.40	1.40	1.20	1.20	1.10	1.10	1.10	1.30
Net Income to Assets (%) .	2.10	0.90	1.30	5.40	7.70	10.10	5.20	4.30	5.00	8.10
Portfolio Turnover (%)	245	372	426	312	305	281	224	153	304	183
Total Assets (Millions $)	628	588	691	646	1,066	1,005	802	518	233	106

PORTFOLIO (as of 6/30/93)

Portfolio Manager: Ronald C. Ognar - 1993

Investm't Category: Balanced

Cap Gain	Asset Allocation
✔ Cap & Income	Fund of Funds
Income	Index
	Sector
✔ Domestic	Small Cap
✔ Foreign	Socially Conscious
Country/Region	State Specific

Portfolio: stocks 94% bonds 0%
convertibles 1% other 0% cash 5%

Largest Holdings: stocks—oil field serv/equip 8%, stocks—consumer related products 8%

Unrealized Net Capital Gains: 11% of portfolio value

SHAREHOLDER INFORMATION

Minimum Investment
Initial: $250   Subsequent: $50

Minimum IRA Investment
Initial: $250   Subsequent: $50

Maximum Fees
Load: none   12b-1: none
Other: none

Distributions
Income: quarterly   Capital Gains: Dec

Exchange Options
Number Per Year: 5   Fee: none
Telephone: yes (money market fund available)

Services
IRA, other pension, auto exchange, auto invest, auto withdraw

Tocqueville (TOCQX)

Growth

1675 Broadway
16th Floor
New York, NY 10019
(800) 697-3863, (212) 698-0800

PERFORMANCE

	3yr Annual	5yr Annual	10yr Annual	Bull	Bear
Return (%)	17.2	13.9	na	71.1	-4.5
Differ from Category (+/-)	-2.0 blw av	-0.6 av	na	-13.6 blw av	7.9 high

Total Risk	Standard Deviation	Category Risk	Risk Index	Beta
av	7.1%	low	0.6	0.4

	1993	1992	1991	1990	1989	1988	1987	1986	1985	1984
Return (%)	22.5	16.9	12.4	1.4	17.5	20.4	—	—	—	—
Differ from category (+/-)	9.3	5.9	-23.0	7.5	-8.3	2.7	—	—	—	—

PER SHARE DATA

	1993	1992	1991	1990	1989	1988	1987	1986	1985	1984
Dividends, Net Income ($)	0.14	0.15	0.36	0.51	0.37	0.05	—	—	—	—
Distrib'ns, Cap Gain ($)	0.79	0.66	0.63	0.11	0.40	0.21	—	—	—	—
Net Asset Value ($)	13.23	11.57	10.59	10.37	10.84	9.89	—	—	—	—
Expense Ratio (%)	1.73	1.74	1.96	1.61	1.70	2.09	—	—	—	—
Net Income to Assets (%)	0.99	1.44	3.38	4.71	2.86	0.85	—	—	—	—
Portfolio Turnover (%)	68	89	97	125	34	65	—	—	—	—
Total Assets (Millions $)	29	19	17	13	17	15	—	—	—	—

PORTFOLIO (as of 4/30/93)

Portfolio Manager: Francois Sicart - 1987, Robert Kleinschmidt - 1991

Investm't Category: Growth
- ✔ Cap Gain
- Cap & Income
- Income
- Asset Allocation
- Fund of Funds
- Index
- Sector
- ✔ Domestic
- Foreign
- Country/Region
- Small Cap
- Socially Conscious
- State Specific

Portfolio: stocks 80% bonds 9%
convertibles 0% other 0% cash 11%

Largest Holdings: depressed industries/regions 20%, revitalized companies 17%

Unrealized Net Capital Gains: 8% of portfolio value

SHAREHOLDER INFORMATION

Minimum Investment
Initial: $5,000   Subsequent: $1,000

Minimum IRA Investment
Initial: $2,000   Subsequent: $1,000

Maximum Fees
Load: none   12b-1: 0.50%
Other: none

Distributions
Income: none   Capital Gains: none

Exchange Options
Number Per Year: no limit   Fee: none
Telephone: yes (money market fund not available)

Services
IRA, other pension

T Rowe Price Adjustable Rate US Gov't (PRARX)

10090 Red Run Blvd.
Owings Mills, MD 21117
(800) 638-5660, (410) 547-2308

Mortgage-Backed Bond

PERFORMANCE

	3yr Annual	5yr Annual	10yr Annual	Bull	Bear
Return (%)	na	na	na	na	na
Differ from Category (+/-)	na	na	na	na	na

Total Risk	Standard Deviation	Category Risk	Risk Index	Avg Mat
na	na	na	na	0.7 yrs

	1993	1992	1991	1990	1989	1988	1987	1986	1985	1984
Return (%)	2.7	3.9	—	—	—	—	—	—	—	—
Differ from category (+/-)	-4.1	-2.2	—	—	—	—	—	—	—	—

PER SHARE DATA

	1993	1992	1991	1990	1989	1988	1987	1986	1985	1984
Dividends, Net Income ($)	0.23	0.32	—	—	—	—	—	—	—	—
Distrib'ns, Cap Gain ($)	0.00	0.00	—	—	—	—	—	—	—	—
Net Asset Value ($)	4.77	4.87	—	—	—	—	—	—	—	—
Expense Ratio (%)	0.25	0.00	—	—	—	—	—	—	—	—
Net Income to Assets (%)	5.96	7.45	—	—	—	—	—	—	—	—
Portfolio Turnover (%)	110	98	—	—	—	—	—	—	—	—
Total Assets (Millions $)	266	343	—	—	—	—	—	—	—	—

PORTFOLIO (as of 8/31/93)

Portfolio Manager: Peter Dyke - 1991

Investm't Category: Mortgage-Backed Bond

Cap Gain	Asset Allocation
Cap & Income	Fund of Funds
✔ Income	Index
	Sector
✔ Domestic	Small Cap
Foreign	Socially Conscious
Country/Region	State Specific

Portfolio: stocks 0%   bonds 100%
convertibles 0%   other 0%   cash 0%

Largest Holdings: mortgage-backed 97%, U.S. government 3%

Unrealized Net Capital Gains: 0% of portfolio value

SHAREHOLDER INFORMATION

Minimum Investment
Initial: $2,500   Subsequent: $100

Minimum IRA Investment
Initial: $1,000   Subsequent: $50

Maximum Fees
Load: none   12b-1: none
Other: none

Distributions
Income: monthly   Capital Gains: Jan, Mar

Exchange Options
Number Per Year: 6   Fee: none
Telephone: yes (money market fund available)

Services
IRA, other pension, auto exchange, auto invest, auto withdraw

T Rowe Price Balanced
(RPBAX)

Balanced

10090 Red Run Blvd.
Owings Mills, MD 21117
(800) 638-5660, (410) 547-2308

PERFORMANCE

	3yr Annual	5yr Annual	10yr Annual	Bull	Bear
Return (%)	14.1	14.0	13.4	61.1	-0.8
Differ from Category (+/-)	-0.8 blw av	1.9 high	1.4 abv av	-0.5 av	4.9 high

Total Risk	Standard Deviation	Category Risk	Risk Index	Beta
av	7.3%	av	1.2	0.6

	1993	1992	1991	1990	1989	1988	1987	1986	1985	1984
Return (%)	13.3	7.7	21.9	7.2	20.6	8.9	-3.3	23.2	32.9	6.4
Differ from category (+/-) ..	-0.1	-0.4	-2.0	7.7	3.0	-3.1	-5.6	5.7	9.2	-1.0

PER SHARE DATA

	1993	1992	1991	1990	1989	1988	1987	1986	1985	1984
Dividends, Net Income ($) .	0.38	0.50	0.61	0.66	0.68	0.48	0.78	0.76	0.76	0.68
Distrib'ns, Cap Gain ($) ...	0.10	0.66	0.56	0.00	0.00	0.00	2.83	3.20	0.00	0.14
Net Asset Value ($)	12.02	11.07	11.42	10.37	10.32	9.14	8.84	12.80	13.80	11.07
Expense Ratio (%)........	1.00	1.03	1.10	0.93	1.15	1.25	1.18	0.98	0.74	0.76
Net Income to Assets (%)..	3.61	4.07	5.61	6.82	6.27	5.19	3.81	5.76	6.93	6.60
Portfolio Turnover (%)	8	208	240	127	219	251	324	239	97	87
Total Assets (Millions $) ...	340	239	175	157	167	164	196	180	152	141

PORTFOLIO (as of 6/30/93)

Portfolio Manager: Richard Whitney - 1991

Investm't Category: Balanced

Cap Gain	Asset Allocation
✔ Cap & Income	Fund of Funds
Income	Index
	Sector
✔ Domestic	Small Cap
✔ Foreign	Socially Conscious
Country/Region	State Specific

Portfolio: stocks 60% bonds 37%
convertibles 0% other 0% cash 3%

Largest Holdings: bonds—U.S. government
& agencies 20%, bonds—corp & foreign 17%

Unrealized Net Capital Gains: 7% of portfolio value

SHAREHOLDER INFORMATION

Minimum Investment
Initial: $2,500   Subsequent: $100

Minimum IRA Investment
Initial: $1,000   Subsequent: $50

Maximum Fees
Load: none   12b-1: none
Other: none

Distributions
Income: quarterly   Capital Gains: Dec

Exchange Options
Number Per Year: 6   Fee: none
Telephone: yes (money market fund available)

Services
IRA, other pension, auto exchange, auto invest, auto withdraw

T Rowe Price CA
Tax-Free Bond (PRXCX)

Tax-Exempt Bond

10090 Red Run Blvd.
Owings Mills, MD 21117
(800) 638-5660, (410) 547-2308

PERFORMANCE

	3yr Annual	5yr Annual	10yr Annual	Bull	Bear
Return (%)	11.1	9.5	na	43.8	1.0
Differ from Category (+/-)	0.8 av	0.3 av	na	3.7 abv av	-1.3 low

Total Risk	Standard Deviation	Category Risk	Risk Index	Avg Mat
blw av	4.4%	av	1.1	10.7 yrs

	1993	1992	1991	1990	1989	1988	1987	1986	1985	1984
Return (%).............	12.4	8.9	12.1	5.8	8.4	9.5	-6.8	—	—	—
Differ from category (+/-)...	0.8	0.6	0.8	-0.5	-0.6	-0.6	-5.6	—	—	—

PER SHARE DATA

	1993	1992	1991	1990	1989	1988	1987	1986	1985	1984
Dividends, Net Income ($).	0.56	0.57	0.58	0.59	0.58	0.56	0.56	—	—	—
Distrib'ns, Cap Gain ($) ...	0.23	0.00	0.00	0.00	0.00	0.00	0.00	—	—	—
Net Asset Value ($)	10.68	10.22	9.94	9.42	9.48	9.30	9.03	—	—	—
Expense Ratio (%)	0.60	0.60	0.73	0.93	1.00	1.00	0.85	—	—	—
Net Income to Assets (%) .	5.69	6.07	6.29	6.25	6.23	6.19	6.10	—	—	—
Portfolio Turnover (%)......	57	80	193	88	77	152	88	—	—	—
Total Assets (Millions $)....	154	108	84	65	43	36	44	—	—	—

PORTFOLIO (as of 8/31/93)

Portfolio Manager: Mary J. Miller - 1990

Investm't Category: Tax-Exempt Bond

Cap Gain	Asset Allocation
Cap & Income	Fund of Funds
✔ Income	Index
	Sector
✔ Domestic	Small Cap
Foreign	Socially Conscious
Country/Region	✔ State Specific

Portfolio: stocks 0%   bonds 100%
convertibles 0%   other 0%   cash 0%

Largest Holdings: general obligation 7%

Unrealized Net Capital Gains: 7% of portfolio value

SHAREHOLDER INFORMATION

Minimum Investment
Initial: $2,500   Subsequent: $100

Minimum IRA Investment
Initial: na   Subsequent: na

Maximum Fees
Load: none   12b-1: none
Other: none

Distributions
Income: monthly   Capital Gains: Jan, Mar

Exchange Options
Number Per Year: 6   Fee: none
Telephone: yes (money market fund available)

Services
auto exchange, auto invest, auto withdraw

T Rowe Price Capital Appreciation (PRWCX)

10090 Red Run Blvd.
Owings Mills, MD 21117
(800) 638-5660, (410) 547-2308

Growth

PERFORMANCE

	3yr Annual	5yr Annual	10yr Annual	Bull	Bear
Return (%)	15.4	13.0	na	65.5	-8.3
Differ from Category (+/-)	-3.8 blw av	-1.6 blw av	na	-19.2 blw av	4.1 abv av

Total Risk	Standard Deviation	Category Risk	Risk Index	Beta
blw av	5.8%	low	0.5	0.4

	1993	1992	1991	1990	1989	1988	1987	1986	1985	1984
Return (%)	15.6	9.3	21.5	-1.2	21.4	21.1	5.8	—	—	—
Differ from category (+/-) . . .	2.4	-1.7	-13.9	4.9	-4.4	3.4	4.6	—	—	—

PER SHARE DATA

	1993	1992	1991	1990	1989	1988	1987	1986	1985	1984
Dividends, Net Income ($) .	0.18	0.50	0.43	0.38	0.44	0.28	0.47	—	—	—
Distrib'ns, Cap Gain ($) . . .	0.33	0.15	0.63	0.31	1.36	0.37	1.85	—	—	—
Net Asset Value ($)	12.66	11.39	11.02	9.98	10.82	10.42	9.15	—	—	—
Expense Ratio (%).	1.09	1.08	1.20	1.25	1.50	1.50	1.20	—	—	—
Net Income to Assets (%) . .	2.40	4.28	3.90	3.44	3.85	2.76	3.03	—	—	—
Portfolio Turnover (%)	37	30	51	50	99	166	291	—	—	—
Total Assets (Millions $) . . .	534	359	216	142	133	101	64	—	—	—

PORTFOLIO (as of 6/30/93)

Portfolio Manager: Richard Howard - 1989

Investm't Category: Growth

✔ Cap Gain	Asset Allocation
Cap & Income	Fund of Funds
Income	Index
	Sector
✔ Domestic	Small Cap
✔ Foreign	Socially Conscious
Country/Region	State Specific

Portfolio: stocks 50% bonds 6%
convertibles 17% other 3% cash 24%

Largest Holdings: media & communications 6%, integrated petroleum 5%

Unrealized Net Capital Gains: 8% of portfolio value

SHAREHOLDER INFORMATION

Minimum Investment
Initial: $2,500   Subsequent: $100

Minimum IRA Investment
Initial: $1,000   Subsequent: $50

Maximum Fees
Load: none   12b-1: none
Other: none

Distributions
Income: Dec   Capital Gains: Dec

Exchange Options
Number Per Year: 6   Fee: none
Telephone: yes (money market fund available)

Services
IRA, other pension, auto exchange, auto invest, auto withdraw

T Rowe Price Dividend Growth (PRDGX)

10090 Red Run Blvd.
Owings Mills, MD 21117
(800) 638-5660, (410) 547-2308

Growth & Income

PERFORMANCE

	3yr Annual	5yr Annual	10yr Annual	Bull	Bear
Return (%)	na	na	na	na	na
Differ from Category (+/-)	na	na	na	na	na

Total Risk	Standard Deviation	Category Risk	Risk Index	Beta
na	na	na	na	na

	1993	1992	1991	1990	1989	1988	1987	1986	1985	1984
Return (%).............	19.4	—	—	—	—	—	—	—	—	—
Differ from category (+/-)...	6.8	—	—	—	—	—	—	—	—	—

PER SHARE DATA

	1993	1992	1991	1990	1989	1988	1987	1986	1985	1984
Dividends, Net Income ($).	0.28	—	—	—	—	—	—	—	—	—
Distrib'ns, Cap Gain ($) ...	0.15	—	—	—	—	—	—	—	—	—
Net Asset Value ($)	11.48	—	—	—	—	—	—	—	—	—
Expense Ratio (%)	1.00	—	—	—	—	—	—	—	—	—
Net Income to Assets (%) .	2.77	—	—	—	—	—	—	—	—	—
Portfolio Turnover (%)......	44	—	—	—	—	—	—	—	—	—
Total Assets (Millions $).....	40	—	—	—	—	—	—	—	—	—

PORTFOLIO (as of 6/30/93)

Portfolio Manager: William Stromborg - 1992

Investm't Category: Growth & Income
- Cap Gain
- ✔ Cap & Income
- Income
- ✔ Domestic
- ✔ Foreign
- Country/Region
- Asset Allocation
- Fund of Funds
- Index
- Sector
- Small Cap
- Socially Conscious
- State Specific

Portfolio: stocks 70% bonds 6%
convertibles 4% other 0% cash 20%

Largest Holdings: financial 12%, consumer non-durables 11%

Unrealized Net Capital Gains: 1% of portfolio value

SHAREHOLDER INFORMATION

Minimum Investment
Initial: $2,500   Subsequent: $100

Minimum IRA Investment
Initial: $1,000   Subsequent: $50

Maximum Fees
Load: none   12b-1: none
Other: none

Distributions
Income: quarterly   Capital Gains: Dec

Exchange Options
Number Per Year: 6   Fee: none
Telephone: yes (money market fund available)

Services
IRA, other pension, auto exchange, auto invest, auto withdraw

T Rowe Price Equity Income (PRFDX)

Growth & Income

10090 Red Run Blvd.
Owings Mills, MD 21117
(800) 638-5660, (410) 547-2308

PERFORMANCE

	3yr Annual	5yr Annual	10yr Annual	Bull	Bear
Return (%)	17.9	11.7	na	78.4	-14.2
Differ from Category (+/-)	1.5 abv av	-0.8 blw av	na	8.3 abv av	-2.6 blw av

Total Risk	Standard Deviation	Category Risk	Risk Index	Beta
av	8.0%	low	0.9	0.6

	1993	1992	1991	1990	1989	1988	1987	1986	1985	1984
Return (%)	14.8	14.1	25.2	-6.7	13.6	27.5	3.5	26.6	—	—
Differ from category (+/-)	2.2	4.1	-2.5	-1.1	-8.0	10.7	3.1	11.4	—	—

PER SHARE DATA

	1993	1992	1991	1990	1989	1988	1987	1986	1985	1984
Dividends, Net Income ($)	0.54	0.62	0.61	0.64	0.75	0.62	0.81	0.64	—	—
Distrib'ns, Cap Gain ($)	0.72	0.38	0.10	0.18	0.38	0.37	1.35	0.25	—	—
Net Asset Value ($)	16.65	15.63	14.62	12.27	14.06	13.38	11.29	12.96	—	—
Expense Ratio (%)	0.95	0.97	1.05	1.13	1.11	1.30	1.10	1.00	—	—
Net Income to Assets (%)	3.34	3.95	4.44	5.09	5.31	4.83	4.58	5.16	—	—
Portfolio Turnover (%)	39	30	34	24	34	36	80	72	—	—
Total Assets (Millions $)	2,800	2,092	1,335	862	968	501	185	93	—	—

PORTFOLIO (as of 6/30/93)

Portfolio Manager: Brian C. Rogers - 1989

Investm't Category: Growth & Income
Cap Gain	Asset Allocation
✔ Cap & Income	Fund of Funds
Income	Index
	Sector
✔ Domestic	Small Cap
✔ Foreign	Socially Conscious
Country/Region	State Specific

Portfolio: stocks 72% bonds 5%
convertibles 9% other 0% cash 14%

Largest Holdings: pharmaceuticals 7%, integrated petroleum—international 6%

Unrealized Net Capital Gains: 8% of portfolio value

SHAREHOLDER INFORMATION

Minimum Investment
Initial: $2,500   Subsequent: $100

Minimum IRA Investment
Initial: $1,000   Subsequent: $50

Maximum Fees
Load: none   12b-1: none
Other: none

Distributions
Income: quarterly   Capital Gains: Dec

Exchange Options
Number Per Year: 6   Fee: none
Telephone: yes (money market fund available)

Services
IRA, other pension, auto exchange, auto invest, auto withdraw

T Rowe Price European Stock (PRESX)

International Stock

10090 Red Run Blvd.
Owings Mills, MD 21117
(800) 638-5660, (410) 547-2308

PERFORMANCE

	3yr Annual	5yr Annual	10yr Annual	Bull	Bear
Return (%)	8.8	na	na	35.3	na
Differ from Category (+/-)	-5.5 low	na	na	-19.8 low	na

Total Risk	Standard Deviation	Category Risk	Risk Index	Beta
abv av	13.3%	av	1.1	0.6

	1993	1992	1991	1990	1989	1988	1987	1986	1985	1984
Return (%)	27.2	-5.5	7.3	—	—	—	—	—	—	—
Differ from category (+/-)	-11.3	-2.0	-5.6	—	—	—	—	—	—	—

PER SHARE DATA

	1993	1992	1991	1990	1989	1988	1987	1986	1985	1984
Dividends, Net Income ($)	0.03	0.17	0.07	—	—	—	—	—	—	—
Distrib'ns, Cap Gain ($)	0.00	0.00	0.00	—	—	—	—	—	—	—
Net Asset Value ($)	11.86	9.36	10.09	—	—	—	—	—	—	—
Expense Ratio (%)	1.39	1.48	1.71	—	—	—	—	—	—	—
Net Income to Assets (%)	2.38	1.23	1.04	—	—	—	—	—	—	—
Portfolio Turnover (%)	33	52	58	—	—	—	—	—	—	—
Total Assets (Millions $)	291	174	104	—	—	—	—	—	—	—

PORTFOLIO (as of 6/30/93)

Portfolio Manager: M. David Testa - 1990, Martin G. Wade - 1990

Investm't Category: International Stock
✔ Cap Gain   Asset Allocation
  Cap & Income   Fund of Funds
  Income   Index
                            Sector
  Domestic   Small Cap
✔ Foreign   Socially Conscious
✔ Country/Region   State Specific

Portfolio: stocks 94%   bonds 0%
convertibles 0%   other 1%   cash 5%

Largest Holdings: United Kingdom 31%, Netherlands 14%

Unrealized Net Capital Gains: 9% of portfolio value

SHAREHOLDER INFORMATION

Minimum Investment
Initial: $2,500   Subsequent: $100

Minimum IRA Investment
Initial: $1,000   Subsequent: $50

Maximum Fees
Load: none   12b-1: none
Other: none

Distributions
Income: Dec   Capital Gains: Dec

Exchange Options
Number Per Year: 6   Fee: none
Telephone: yes (money market fund available)

Services
IRA, other pension, auto exchange, auto invest, auto withdraw

T Rowe Price Global Gov't Bond (RPGGX)

International Bond

10090 Red Run Blvd.
Owings Mills, MD 21117
(800) 638-5660, (410) 547-2308

PERFORMANCE

	3yr Annual	5yr Annual	10yr Annual	Bull	Bear
Return (%)	8.6	na	na	na	na
Differ from Category (+/-)	-3.4 low	na	na	na	na

Total Risk	Standard Deviation	Category Risk	Risk Index	Avg Mat
blw av	4.2%	blw av	1.0	7.5 yrs

	1993	1992	1991	1990	1989	1988	1987	1986	1985	1984
Return (%)	11.2	3.6	11.3	—	—	—	—	—	—	—
Differ from category (+/-)	-1.5	-1.2	-3.6	—	—	—	—	—	—	—

PER SHARE DATA

	1993	1992	1991	1990	1989	1988	1987	1986	1985	1984
Dividends, Net Income ($)	0.61	0.75	0.77	—	—	—	—	—	—	—
Distrib'ns, Cap Gain ($)	0.28	0.00	0.00	—	—	—	—	—	—	—
Net Asset Value ($)	10.08	9.89	10.30	—	—	—	—	—	—	—
Expense Ratio (%)	1.20	1.20	1.20	—	—	—	—	—	—	—
Net Income to Assets (%)	5.90	7.51	8.07	—	—	—	—	—	—	—
Portfolio Turnover (%)	134	237	94	—	—	—	—	—	—	—
Total Assets (Millions $)	48	54	40	—	—	—	—	—	—	—

PORTFOLIO (as of 6/30/93)

Portfolio Manager: David Boardman - 1990

Investm't Category: International Bond

Cap Gain	Asset Allocation
Cap & Income	Fund of Funds
✔ Income	Index
	Sector
✔ Domestic	Small Cap
✔ Foreign	Socially Conscious
Country/Region	State Specific

Portfolio:
stocks 0%   bonds 100%
convertibles 0%   other 0%   cash 0%

Largest Holdings: United States 37%, Japan 10%

Unrealized Net Capital Gains: 2% of portfolio value

SHAREHOLDER INFORMATION

Minimum Investment
Initial: $2,500   Subsequent: $100

Minimum IRA Investment
Initial: $1,000   Subsequent: $50

Maximum Fees
Load: none   12b-1: none
Other: none

Distributions
Income: monthly   Capital Gains: Dec

Exchange Options
Number Per Year: 6   Fee: none
Telephone: yes (money market fund available)

Services
IRA, other pension, auto exchange, auto invest, auto withdraw

T Rowe Price GNMA
(PRGMX)

Mortgage-Backed Bond

10090 Red Run Blvd.
Owings Mills, MD 21117
(800) 638-5660, (410) 547-2308

T Rowe Price Growth & Income (PRGIX)

10090 Red Run Blvd.
Owings Mills, MD 21117
(800) 638-5660, (410) 547-2308

Growth & Income

PERFORMANCE

	3yr Annual	5yr Annual	10yr Annual	Bull	Bear
Return (%)	19.6	12.6	11.1	85.1	-17.6
Differ from Category (+/-)	3.2 abv av	0.1 av	-1.3 blw av	15.0 high	-6.0 low

Total Risk	Standard Deviation	Category Risk	Risk Index	Beta
av	10.2%	av	1.2	0.8

	1993	1992	1991	1990	1989	1988	1987	1986	1985	1984
Return (%)	12.9	15.3	31.5	-11.0	19.2	25.0	-4.2	7.9	19.8	1.8
Differ from category (+/-) ...	0.3	5.3	3.8	-5.4	-2.4	8.2	-4.6	-7.3	-5.6	-4.4

PER SHARE DATA

	1993	1992	1991	1990	1989	1988	1987	1986	1985	1984
Dividends, Net Income ($) .	0.46	0.60	0.56	0.56	0.63	0.49	0.87	0.70	0.61	0.79
Distrib'ns, Cap Gain ($) ...	0.47	0.15	0.00	0.00	0.79	0.46	1.04	1.57	0.00	0.05
Net Asset Value ($)	16.57	15.53	14.16	11.22	13.25	12.32	10.63	12.98	14.18	12.41
Expense Ratio (%)........	0.83	0.85	0.93	0.97	0.96	1.04	1.03	0.96	0.93	0.93
Net Income to Assets (%)..	2.89	3.75	4.23	4.68	4.70	3.94	4.80	5.26	4.53	6.63
Portfolio Turnover (%).....	36	30	48	35	57	50	114	99	120	51
Total Assets (Millions $) ..	1,171	840	655	475	554	445	366	388	356	309

PORTFOLIO (as of 6/30/93)

Portfolio Manager: Stephen Boesel - 1987

Investm't Category: Growth & Income

Cap Gain	Asset Allocation
✔ Cap & Income	Fund of Funds
Income	Index
	Sector
✔ Domestic	Small Cap
✔ Foreign	Socially Conscious
Country/Region	State Specific

Portfolio: stocks 72% bonds 4%
convertibles 7% other 1% cash 16%

Largest Holdings: bank & trust 7%, consumer products 6%

Unrealized Net Capital Gains: 15% of portfolio value

SHAREHOLDER INFORMATION

Minimum Investment
Initial: $2,500   Subsequent: $100

Minimum IRA Investment
Initial: $1,000   Subsequent: $50

Maximum Fees
Load: none   12b-1: none
Other: none

Distributions
Income: quarterly   Capital Gains: Dec

Exchange Options
Number Per Year: 6   Fee: none
Telephone: yes (money market fund available)

Services
IRA, other pension, auto exchange, auto invest, auto withdraw

T Rowe Price Growth Stock (PRGFX)

10090 Red Run Blvd.
Owings Mills, MD 21117
(800) 638-5660, (410) 547-2308

Growth

PERFORMANCE

	3yr Annual	5yr Annual	10yr Annual	Bull	Bear
Return (%)	17.8	14.4	13.3	77.8	-11.8
Differ from Category (+/-)	-1.4 av	-0.2 av	0.6 av	-6.9 av	0.6 av

Total Risk	Standard Deviation	Category Risk	Risk Index	Beta
abv av	12.1%	av	1.1	1.0

	1993	1992	1991	1990	1989	1988	1987	1986	1985	1984
Return (%).............	15.5	5.9	33.7	-4.3	25.4	6.0	3.6	21.8	35.2	-1.4
Differ from category (+/-)...	2.3	-5.1	-1.7	1.8	-0.4	-11.7	2.4	7.3	5.9	-1.4

PER SHARE DATA

	1993	1992	1991	1990	1989	1988	1987	1986	1985	1984
Dividends, Net Income ($).	0.14	0.18	0.25	0.43	0.34	0.31	0.62	0.37	0.34	0.36
Distrib'ns, Cap Gain ($) ...	0.99	1.03	0.62	0.43	1.58	0.25	2.66	4.18	0.63	0.44
Net Asset Value ($)	20.42	18.66	18.75	14.71	16.27	14.55	14.27	16.96	17.95	14.20
Expense Ratio (%)	0.85	0.83	0.85	0.76	0.68	0.77	0.67	0.57	0.52	0.51
Net Income to Assets (%) .	1.06	0.94	1.40	2.31	2.13	2.08	1.71	1.79	2.32	2.53
Portfolio Turnover (%)......	34	27	32	30	39	41	51	59	68	59
Total Assets (Millions $)..	1,980	1,946	1,846	1,397	1,516	1,295	1,268	1,273	1,158	965

PORTFOLIO (as of 6/30/93)

Portfolio Manager: M. David Testa - 1984

Investm't Category: Growth

✔ Cap Gain	Asset Allocation
Cap & Income	Fund of Funds
Income	Index
	Sector
✔ Domestic	Small Cap
✔ Foreign	Socially Conscious
Country/Region	State Specific

Portfolio: stocks 92% bonds 0%
convertibles 0% other 0% cash 8%

Largest Holdings: financial services 8%, pharmaceuticals 8%

Unrealized Net Capital Gains: 29% of portfolio value

SHAREHOLDER INFORMATION

Minimum Investment
Initial: $2,500   Subsequent: $100

Minimum IRA Investment
Initial: $1,000   Subsequent: $50

Maximum Fees
Load: none   12b-1: none
Other: none

Distributions
Income: Dec   Capital Gains: Dec

Exchange Options
Number Per Year: 6   Fee: none
Telephone: yes (money market fund available)

Services
IRA, other pension, auto exchange, auto invest, auto withdraw

T Rowe Price High Yield

(PRHYX)

Corporate High-Yield Bond

10090 Red Run Blvd.
Owings Mills, MD 21117
(800) 638-5660, (410) 547-2308

PERFORMANCE

	3yr Annual	5yr Annual	10yr Annual	Bull	Bear
Return (%)	22.2	9.9	na	75.9	-7.4
Differ from Category (+/-)	1.7 abv av	-0.8 low	na	1.0 av	-4.1 low

Total Risk	Standard Deviation	Category Risk	Risk Index	Avg Mat
blw av	4.5%	av	1.2	9.0 yrs

	1993	1992	1991	1990	1989	1988	1987	1986	1985	1984
Return (%)	21.7	14.7	30.8	-10.9	-1.4	17.9	2.9	15.0	22.4	—
Differ from category (+/-) . . .	2.5	-1.1	3.5	-6.7	-2.7	5.6	1.9	-0.2	-1.1	—

PER SHARE DATA

	1993	1992	1991	1990	1989	1988	1987	1986	1985	1984
Dividends, Net Income ($) .	0.81	0.82	0.89	1.11	1.26	1.25	1.25	1.29	1.35	—
Distrib'ns, Cap Gain ($) . . .	0.00	0.00	0.00	0.00	0.00	0.00	0.14	0.12	0.00	—
Net Asset Value ($)	9.22	8.29	7.98	6.86	8.88	10.25	9.82	10.87	10.75	—
Expense Ratio (%).	0.89	0.97	1.03	1.02	0.95	0.99	0.99	1.00	1.00	—
Net Income to Assets (%). .	9.85	11.22	14.02	13.01	12.32	12.10	11.57	13.01	16.69	—
Portfolio Turnover (%)	104	59	83	66	80	138	166	163	6	—
Total Assets (Millions $) . .	1,619	1,108	556	660	1,251	840	940	456	22	—

PORTFOLIO (as of 8/31/93)

Portfolio Manager: Richard Swingle - 1984

Investm't Category: Corp. High-Yield Bond

Cap Gain	Asset Allocation
✔ Cap & Income	Fund of Funds
Income	Index
	Sector
✔ Domestic	Small Cap
✔ Foreign	Socially Conscious
Country/Region	State Specific

Portfolio: stocks 2%   bonds 88%
convertibles 4%   other 1%   cash 5%

Largest Holdings: hotels & gaming 11%, manufacturing 8%

Unrealized Net Capital Gains: 2% of portfolio value

SHAREHOLDER INFORMATION

Minimum Investment
Initial: $2,500   Subsequent: $100

Minimum IRA Investment
Initial: $1,000   Subsequent: $50

Maximum Fees
Load: 1.00% redemption   12b-1: none
Other: redemption fee applies for 1 year

Distributions
Income: monthly   Capital Gains: Jan, Mar

Exchange Options
Number Per Year: 6   Fee: none
Telephone: yes (money market fund available)

Services
IRA, other pension, auto exchange, auto invest, auto withdraw

T Rowe Price
International Bond (RPIBX)

10090 Red Run Blvd.
Owings Mills, MD 21117
(800) 638-5660, (410) 547-2308

International Bond

PERFORMANCE

	3yr Annual	5yr Annual	10yr Annual	Bull	Bear
Return (%)	13.0	10.1	na	54.8	8.3
Differ from Category (+/-)	1.0 abv av	-1.3 blw av	na	-3.3 blw av	1.7 abv av

Total Risk	Standard Deviation	Category Risk	Risk Index	Avg Mat
av	9.2%	high	2.3	7.6 yrs

	1993	1992	1991	1990	1989	1988	1987	1986	1985	1984
Return (%)	19.9	2.3	17.7	16.0	-3.2	-1.2	27.5	—	—	—
Differ from category (+/-)	7.2	-2.5	2.8	4.5	-5.4	-3.6	14.1	—	—	—

PER SHARE DATA

	1993	1992	1991	1990	1989	1988	1987	1986	1985	1984
Dividends, Net Income ($)	0.67	0.83	0.77	0.82	0.74	0.91	1.01	—	—	—
Distrib'ns, Cap Gain ($)	0.46	0.15	0.00	0.17	0.00	0.25	0.00	—	—	—
Net Asset Value ($)	10.34	9.61	10.35	9.53	9.15	10.25	11.60	—	—	—
Expense Ratio (%)	1.02	1.08	1.24	1.15	1.23	1.20	1.25	—	—	—
Net Income to Assets (%)	6.90	8.66	8.11	9.04	8.11	8.73	9.47	—	—	—
Portfolio Turnover (%)	348	358	296	211	293	368	284	—	—	—
Total Assets (Millions $)	749	514	414	431	304	407	400	—	—	—

PORTFOLIO (as of 6/30/93)

Portfolio Manager: David Boardman - 1988

Investm't Category: International Bond

Cap Gain	Asset Allocation
Cap & Income	Fund of Funds
✔ Income	Index
	Sector
Domestic	Small Cap
✔ Foreign	Socially Conscious
Country/Region	State Specific

Portfolio: stocks 0% bonds 99%
convertibles 0% other 0% cash 1%

Largest Holdings: Japan 16%, Italy 12%

Unrealized Net Capital Gains: 0% of portfolio value

SHAREHOLDER INFORMATION

Minimum Investment
Initial: $2,500   Subsequent: $100

Minimum IRA Investment
Initial: $1,000   Subsequent: $50

Maximum Fees
Load: none   12b-1: none
Other: none

Distributions
Income: monthly   Capital Gains: Dec

Exchange Options
Number Per Year: 6   Fee: none
Telephone: yes (money market fund available)

Services
IRA, other pension, auto exchange, auto invest, auto withdraw

T Rowe Price International Discovery

10090 Red Run Blvd.
Owings Mills, MD 21117
(800) 638-5660, (410) 547-2308

(PRIDX) *International Stock*

T Rowe Price
International Stock (PRITX)

10090 Red Run Blvd.
Owings Mills, MD 21117
(800) 638-5660, (410) 547-2308

International Stock

PERFORMANCE

	3yr Annual	5yr Annual	10yr Annual	Bull	Bear
Return (%)	16.1	12.0	17.3	67.2	-14.6
Differ from Category (+/-)	1.8 abv av	3.3 high	3.9 high	12.1 abv av	0.5 av

Total Risk	Standard Deviation	Category Risk	Risk Index	Beta
abv av	12.9%	av	1.1	0.5

	1993	1992	1991	1990	1989	1988	1987	1986	1985	1984
Return (%).............	40.1	-3.4	15.8	-8.8	23.7	17.9	7.9	61.2	45.1	-5.8
Differ from category (+/-)...	1.6	0.1	2.9	2.3	1.5	4.1	-4.1	10.9	4.5	3.7

PER SHARE DATA

	1993	1992	1991	1990	1989	1988	1987	1986	1985	1984
Dividends, Net Income ($).	0.09	0.15	0.15	0.15	0.15	0.15	0.23	0.10	0.15	0.07
Distrib'ns, Cap Gain ($) ...	0.20	0.15	0.49	0.36	0.67	0.93	4.97	1.37	0.22	0.07
Net Asset Value ($)	12.16	8.89	9.54	8.81	10.24	8.97	8.54	12.89	9.04	6.59
Expense Ratio (%)	1.01	1.05	1.10	1.09	1.10	1.16	1.14	1.10	1.11	1.11
Net Income to Assets (%) .	1.52	1.49	1.51	2.16	1.63	1.78	0.93	0.89	1.54	2.29
Portfolio Turnover (%)......	30	38	45	47	48	42	77	56	62	38
Total Assets (Millions $)..	4,266	1,950	1,476	1,031	971	630	643	554	275	196

PORTFOLIO (as of 10/31/93)

Portfolio Manager: M. David Testa - 1980, Martin G. Wade - 1980

Investm't Category: International Stock
- ✔ Cap Gain
- Cap & Income
- Income
- Domestic
- ✔ Foreign
- Country/Region
- Asset Allocation
- Fund of Funds
- Index
- Sector
- Small Cap
- Socially Conscious
- State Specific

Portfolio:

stocks 87%	bonds 0%
convertibles 0%	other 1%	cash 12%

Largest Holdings: Japan 20%, United Kingdom 13%

Unrealized Net Capital Gains: 16% of portfolio value

SHAREHOLDER INFORMATION

Minimum Investment
Initial: $2,500   Subsequent: $100

Minimum IRA Investment
Initial: $1,000   Subsequent: $50

Maximum Fees
Load: none   12b-1: none
Other: none

Distributions
Income: Dec   Capital Gains: Dec

Exchange Options
Number Per Year: 6   Fee: none
Telephone: yes (money market fund available)

Services
IRA, other pension, auto exchange, auto invest, auto withdraw

T Rowe Price Japan (PRJPX)

International Stock

10090 Red Run Blvd.
Owings Mills, MD 21117
(800) 638-5660, (410) 547-2308

PERFORMANCE

	3yr Annual	5yr Annual	10yr Annual	Bull	Bear
Return (%)	na	na	na	na	na
Differ from Category (+/-)	na	na	na	na	na

Total Risk	Standard Deviation	Category Risk	Risk Index	Beta
na	na	na	na	na

	1993	1992	1991	1990	1989	1988	1987	1986	1985	1984
Return (%)	20.6	-13.4	—	—	—	—	—	—	—	—
Differ from category (+/-) .	-17.9	-9.9	—	—	—	—	—	—	—	—

PER SHARE DATA

	1993	1992	1991	1990	1989	1988	1987	1986	1985	1984
Dividends, Net Income ($) .	0.00	0.00	—	—	—	—	—	—	—	—
Distrib'ns, Cap Gain ($) . . .	0.85	0.00	—	—	—	—	—	—	—	—
Net Asset Value ($)	9.61	8.66	—	—	—	—	—	—	—	—
Expense Ratio (%).	1.50	1.50	—	—	—	—	—	—	—	—
Net Income to Assets (%) .	-0.56	-0.22	—	—	—	—	—	—	—	—
Portfolio Turnover (%)	46	42	—	—	—	—	—	—	—	—
Total Assets (Millions $)	71	46	—	—	—	—	—	—	—	—

PORTFOLIO (as of 6/30/93)

Portfolio Manager: Robert Howe - 1991

Investm't Category: International Stock

✔ Cap Gain	Asset Allocation
Cap & Income	Fund of Funds
Income	Index
	Sector
Domestic	Small Cap
✔ Foreign	Socially Conscious
✔ Country/Region	State Specific

Portfolio: stocks 93% bonds 0%
convertibles 0% other 0% cash 7%

Largest Holdings: electrical & electronics 18%, building materials & construction 16%

Unrealized Net Capital Gains: 12% of portfolio value

SHAREHOLDER INFORMATION

Minimum Investment
Initial: $2,500   Subsequent: $100

Minimum IRA Investment
Initial: $1,000   Subsequent: $50

Maximum Fees
Load: none   12b-1: none
Other: none

Distributions
Income: Dec   Capital Gains: Dec

Exchange Options
Number Per Year: 6   Fee: none
Telephone: yes (money market fund available)

Services
IRA, other pension, auto exchange, auto invest, auto withdraw

T Rowe Price Maryland Tax-Free (MDXBX)

Tax-Exempt Bond

10090 Red Run Blvd.
Owings Mills, MD 21117
(800) 638-5660, (410) 547-2308

PERFORMANCE

	3yr Annual	5yr Annual	10yr Annual	Bull	Bear
Return (%)	10.8	9.6	na	41.9	1.8
Differ from Category (+/-)	0.5 av	0.4 av	na	1.8 av	-0.5 blw av

Total Risk	Standard Deviation	Category Risk	Risk Index	Avg Mat
blw av	4.1%	av	1.0	16.1 yrs

	1993	1992	1991	1990	1989	1988	1987	1986	1985	1984
Return (%)	12.7	8.5	11.2	6.2	9.5	8.8	—	—	—	—
Differ from category (+/-)	1.1	0.2	-0.1	-0.1	0.5	-1.3	—	—	—	—

PER SHARE DATA

	1993	1992	1991	1990	1989	1988	1987	1986	1985	1984
Dividends, Net Income ($)	0.56	0.57	0.58	0.60	0.59	0.56	—	—	—	—
Distrib'ns, Cap Gain ($)	0.10	0.05	0.05	0.00	0.02	0.00	—	—	—	—
Net Asset Value ($)	10.67	10.08	9.89	9.50	9.53	9.29	—	—	—	—
Expense Ratio (%)	0.61	0.64	0.68	0.85	0.92	0.85	—	—	—	—
Net Income to Assets (%)	5.72	6.04	6.38	6.29	6.23	6.15	—	—	—	—
Portfolio Turnover (%)	22	22	52	58	64	178	—	—	—	—
Total Assets (Millions $)	825	475	301	194	113	63	—	—	—	—

PORTFOLIO (as of 8/31/93)

Portfolio Manager: Mary J. Miller - 1990

Investm't Category: Tax-Exempt Bond

Cap Gain	Asset Allocation
Cap & Income	Fund of Funds
✔ Income	Index
	Sector
✔ Domestic	Small Cap
Foreign	Socially Conscious
Country/Region	✔ State Specific

Portfolio: stocks 0% bonds 100%
convertibles 0% other 0% cash 0%

Largest Holdings: general obligation 19%

Unrealized Net Capital Gains: 8% of portfolio value

SHAREHOLDER INFORMATION

Minimum Investment
Initial: $2,500 Subsequent: $100

Minimum IRA Investment
Initial: na Subsequent: na

Maximum Fees
Load: none 12b-1: none
Other: none

Distributions
Income: monthly Capital Gains: Jan, Mar

Exchange Options
Number Per Year: 6 Fee: none
Telephone: yes (money market fund available)

Services
auto exchange, auto invest, auto withdraw

T Rowe Price MD Short-Term Tax-Free

10090 Red Run Blvd.
Owings Mills, MD 21117
(800) 638-5660, (410) 547-2308

(PRMDX) *Tax-Exempt Bond*

fund in existence since 1/29/93

PERFORMANCE

	3yr Annual	5yr Annual	10yr Annual	Bull	Bear
Return (%)	na	na	na	na	na
Differ from Category (+/-)	na	na	na	na	na

Total Risk	Standard Deviation	Category Risk	Risk Index	Avg Mat
na	na	na	na	2.6 yrs

	1993	1992	1991	1990	1989	1988	1987	1986	1985	1984
Return (%)	—	—	—	—	—	—	—	—	—	—
Differ from category (+/-) ...	—	—	—	—	—	—	—	—	—	—

PER SHARE DATA

	1993	1992	1991	1990	1989	1988	1987	1986	1985	1984
Dividends, Net Income ($) .	0.14	—	—	—	—	—	—	—	—	—
Distrib'ns, Cap Gain ($) ...	0.00	—	—	—	—	—	—	—	—	—
Net Asset Value ($)	5.12	—	—	—	—	—	—	—	—	—
Expense Ratio (%)........	0.65	—	—	—	—	—	—	—	—	—
Net Income to Assets (%)..	2.96	—	—	—	—	—	—	—	—	—
Portfolio Turnover (%).....	96	—	—	—	—	—	—	—	—	—
Total Assets (Millions $)	67	—	—	—	—	—	—	—	—	—

PORTFOLIO (as of 8/31/93)

Portfolio Manager: Mary J. Miller - 1993

Investm't Category: Tax-Exempt Bond

Cap Gain	Asset Allocation
Cap & Income	Fund of Funds
✔ Income	Index
	Sector
✔ Domestic	Small Cap
Foreign	Socially Conscious
Country/Region	✔ State Specific

Portfolio: stocks 0%   bonds 100%
convertibles 0%   other 0%   cash 0%

Largest Holdings: general obligation 34%

Unrealized Net Capital Gains: 0% of portfolio value

SHAREHOLDER INFORMATION

Minimum Investment
Initial: $2,500   Subsequent: $100

Minimum IRA Investment
Initial: na   Subsequent: na

Maximum Fees
Load: none   12b-1: none
Other: none

Distributions
Income: monthly   Capital Gains: Jan, Mar

Exchange Options
Number Per Year: 6   Fee: none
Telephone: yes (money market fund available)

Services
auto exchange, auto invest, auto withdraw

T Rowe Price Mid-Cap Growth (RPMGX)

10090 Red Run Blvd.
Owings Mills, MD 21117
(800) 638-5660, (410) 547-2308

Growth

PERFORMANCE

	3yr Annual	5yr Annual	10yr Annual	Bull	Bear
Return (%)	na	na	na	na	na
Differ from Category (+/-)	na	na	na	na	na

Total Risk	Standard Deviation	Category Risk	Risk Index	Beta
na	na	na	na	na

	1993	1992	1991	1990	1989	1988	1987	1986	1985	1984
Return (%)	26.2	—	—	—	—	—	—	—	—	—
Differ from category (+/-). .	13.0	—	—	—	—	—	—	—	—	—

PER SHARE DATA

	1993	1992	1991	1990	1989	1988	1987	1986	1985	1984
Dividends, Net Income ($).	0.00	—	—	—	—	—	—	—	—	—
Distrib'ns, Cap Gain ($) . . .	0.30	—	—	—	—	—	—	—	—	—
Net Asset Value ($)	15.18	—	—	—	—	—	—	—	—	—
Expense Ratio (%)	1.25	—	—	—	—	—	—	—	—	—
Net Income to Assets (%) .	-0.04	—	—	—	—	—	—	—	—	—
Portfolio Turnover (%).	70	—	—	—	—	—	—	—	—	—
Total Assets (Millions $).	63	—	—	—	—	—	—	—	—	—

PORTFOLIO (as of 6/30/93)

Portfolio Manager: Brian Berghius - 1992

Investm't Category: Growth

✔ Cap Gain	Asset Allocation
Cap & Income	Fund of Funds
Income	Index
	Sector
✔ Domestic	Small Cap
✔ Foreign	Socially Conscious
Country/Region	State Specific

Portfolio: stocks 85% bonds 0%
convertibles 1% other 0% cash 14%

Largest Holdings: machinery 12%, financial services 8%

Unrealized Net Capital Gains: 12% of portfolio value

SHAREHOLDER INFORMATION

Minimum Investment
Initial: $2,500 Subsequent: $100

Minimum IRA Investment
Initial: $1,000 Subsequent: $50

Maximum Fees
Load: none 12b-1: none
Other: none

Distributions
Income: Dec Capital Gains: Dec

Exchange Options
Number Per Year: 6 Fee: none
Telephone: yes (money market fund available)

Services
IRA, other pension, auto exchange, auto invest, auto withdraw

T Rowe Price New America Growth (PRWAX)

10090 Red Run Blvd.
Owings Mills, MD 21117
(800) 638-5660, (410) 547-2308

Growth

PERFORMANCE

	3yr Annual	5yr Annual	10yr Annual	Bull	Bear
Return (%)	27.8	20.4	na	134.2	-21.7
Differ from Category (+/-)	8.6 high	5.8 high	na	49.5 high	-9.3 low

Total Risk	Standard Deviation	Category Risk	Risk Index	Beta
high	16.8%	high	1.6	1.2

	1993	1992	1991	1990	1989	1988	1987	1986	1985	1984
Return (%)	17.4	9.8	61.9	-12.2	38.4	18.4	-9.3	14.3	—	—
Differ from category (+/-) ...	4.2	-1.2	26.5	-6.1	12.6	0.6	-10.5	-0.2	—	—

PER SHARE DATA

	1993	1992	1991	1990	1989	1988	1987	1986	1985	1984
Dividends, Net Income ($) .	0.00	0.00	0.00	0.17	0.00	0.00	0.05	0.10	—	—
Distrib'ns, Cap Gain ($) ...	1.13	0.18	0.87	0.00	0.23	0.00	1.39	0.30	—	—
Net Asset Value ($)	28.04	24.86	22.79	14.66	16.90	12.38	10.45	13.14	—	—
Expense Ratio (%)........	1.25	1.25	1.25	1.25	1.50	1.50	1.23	1.00	—	—
Net Income to Assets (%) .	-0.32	-0.44	-0.12	0.81	-0.02	-0.36	-0.08	0.38	—	—
Portfolio Turnover (%).....	36	26	42	42	40	45	72	80	—	—
Total Assets (Millions $) ...	615	480	232	96	134	66	62	83	—	—

PORTFOLIO (as of 6/30/93)

Portfolio Manager: John Laporte - 1985

Investm't Category: Growth

✔ Cap Gain   Asset Allocation
   Cap & Income   Fund of Funds
   Income   Index
          ✔ Sector
✔ Domestic   Small Cap
   Foreign   Socially Conscious
   Country/Region   State Specific

Portfolio: stocks 95%   bonds 0%
convertibles 2%   other 0%   cash 3%

Largest Holdings: entertainment & leisure 15%, specialty retailers 15%

Unrealized Net Capital Gains: 23% of portfolio value

SHAREHOLDER INFORMATION

Minimum Investment
Initial: $2,500   Subsequent: $100

Minimum IRA Investment
Initial: $1,000   Subsequent: $50

Maximum Fees
Load: none   12b-1: none
Other: none

Distributions
Income: Dec   Capital Gains: Dec

Exchange Options
Number Per Year: 6   Fee: none
Telephone: yes (money market fund available)

Services
IRA, other pension, auto exchange, auto invest, auto withdraw

T Rowe Price New Asia
(PRASX)

International Stock

10090 Red Run Blvd.
Owings Mills, MD 21117
(800) 638-5660, (410) 547-2308

PERFORMANCE

	3yr Annual	5yr Annual	10yr Annual	Bull	Bear
Return (%)	33.3	na	na	141.0	na
Differ from Category (+/-)	19.0 high	na	na	85.9 high	na

Total Risk	Standard Deviation	Category Risk	Risk Index	Beta
high	17.0%	high	1.4	0.3

	1993	1992	1991	1990	1989	1988	1987	1986	1985	1984
Return (%)	78.7	11.2	19.3	—	—	—	—	—	—	—
Differ from category (+/-). .	40.2	14.7	6.4	—	—	—	—	—	—	—

PER SHARE DATA

	1993	1992	1991	1990	1989	1988	1987	1986	1985	1984
Dividends, Net Income ($).	0.07	0.20	0.20	—	—	—	—	—	—	—
Distrib'ns, Cap Gain ($) . . .	0.37	0.25	0.00	—	—	—	—	—	—	—
Net Asset Value ($)	22.19	12.68	11.82	—	—	—	—	—	—	—
Expense Ratio (%)	1.29	1.51	1.75	—	—	—	—	—	—	—
Net Income to Assets (%) .	1.02	1.64	1.75	—	—	—	—	—	—	—
Portfolio Turnover (%).	40	36	49	—	—	—	—	—	—	—
Total Assets (Millions $). .	2,183	314	103	—	—	—	—	—	—	—

PORTFOLIO (as of 10/31/93)

Portfolio Manager: M. David Testa - 1990,
Martin Wade - 1990

Investm't Category: International Stock

✔ Cap Gain	Asset Allocation
Cap & Income	Fund of Funds
Income	Index
	Sector
Domestic	Small Cap
✔ Foreign	Socially Conscious
✔ Country/Region	State Specific

Portfolio: stocks 90% bonds 1%
convertibles 0% other 1% cash 8%

Largest Holdings: Malaysia 28%, Hong Kong 27%

Unrealized Net Capital Gains: 22% of portfolio value

SHAREHOLDER INFORMATION

Minimum Investment
Initial: $2,500   Subsequent: $100

Minimum IRA Investment
Initial: $1,000   Subsequent: $50

Maximum Fees
Load: none   12b-1: none
Other: none

Distributions
Income: Dec   Capital Gains: Dec

Exchange Options
Number Per Year: 6   Fee: none
Telephone: yes (money market fund available)

Services
IRA, other pension, auto exchange, auto invest, auto withdraw

T Rowe Price New Era
(PRNEX)

Growth

10090 Red Run Blvd.
Owings Mills, MD 21117
(800) 638-5660, (410) 547-2308

PERFORMANCE

	3yr Annual	5yr Annual	10yr Annual	Bull	Bear
Return (%)	10.5	8.8	11.3	34.6	-8.5
Differ from Category (+/-)	-8.7 low	-5.8 low	-1.3 blw av	-50.1 low	3.9 abv av

Total Risk	Standard Deviation	Category Risk	Risk Index	Beta
av	9.2%	low	0.8	0.7

	1993	1992	1991	1990	1989	1988	1987	1986	1985	1984
Return (%)	15.3	2.0	14.7	-8.8	24.2	10.2	17.8	15.9	23.4	3.3
Differ from category (+/-)	2.1	-9.0	-20.7	-2.7	-1.6	-7.5	16.6	1.4	-5.9	3.3

PER SHARE DATA

	1993	1992	1991	1990	1989	1988	1987	1986	1985	1984
Dividends, Net Income ($)	0.37	0.44	0.55	0.62	0.56	0.52	0.98	0.50	0.68	0.61
Distrib'ns, Cap Gain ($)	1.03	0.93	0.73	0.70	1.05	0.61	1.77	3.25	1.41	1.29
Net Asset Value ($)	20.35	18.88	19.86	18.48	21.73	18.79	18.08	17.76	18.67	17.13
Expense Ratio (%)	0.82	0.81	0.85	0.83	0.83	0.89	0.82	0.73	0.68	0.68
Net Income to Assets (%)	2.00	2.22	2.56	2.81	2.52	2.41	3.11	1.98	2.76	3.96
Portfolio Turnover (%)	20	17	9	9	19	16	30	32	36	38
Total Assets (Millions $)	755	700	757	707	827	727	757	496	529	472

PORTFOLIO (as of 6/30/93)

Portfolio Manager: George Roche - 1979

Investm't Category: Growth

✔ Cap Gain   Asset Allocation
   Cap & Income   Fund of Funds
   Income   Index
               ✔ Sector
✔ Domestic   Small Cap
✔ Foreign   Socially Conscious
   Country/Region   State Specific

Portfolio: stocks 89%   bonds 0%
convertibles 0%   other 0%   cash 11%

Largest Holdings: integrated petroleum 17%, precious metals 12%

Unrealized Net Capital Gains: 24% of portfolio value

SHAREHOLDER INFORMATION

Minimum Investment
Initial: $2,500   Subsequent: $100

Minimum IRA Investment
Initial: $1,000   Subsequent: $50

Maximum Fees
Load: none   12b-1: none
Other: none

Distributions
Income: Dec   Capital Gains: Dec

Exchange Options
Number Per Year: 6   Fee: none
Telephone: yes (money market fund available)

Services
IRA, other pension, auto exchange, auto invest, auto withdraw

T Rowe Price New Horizons (PRNHX)

10090 Red Run Blvd.
Owings Mills, MD 21117
(800) 638-5660, (410) 547-2308

Aggressive Growth

PERFORMANCE

	3yr Annual	5yr Annual	10yr Annual	Bull	Bear
Return (%)	27.1	18.5	10.7	133.1	-20.3
Differ from Category (+/-)	1.7 av	0.3 av	-1.2 blw av	8.1 abv av	-5.3 blw av

Total Risk	Standard Deviation	Category Risk	Risk Index	Beta
high	17.3%	av	1.1	1.2

	1993	1992	1991	1990	1989	1988	1987	1986	1985	1984
Return (%)............	22.0	10.5	52.3	-9.6	26.1	14.0	-7.2	-0.1	24.3	-9.6
Differ from category (+/-)...	3.0	0.1	-0.1	-3.3	-0.8	-1.2	-3.8	-9.5	-6.7	-0.2

PER SHARE DATA

	1993	1992	1991	1990	1989	1988	1987	1986	1985	1984
Dividends, Net Income ($).	0.00	0.00	0.05	0.09	0.07	0.07	0.05	0.09	0.14	0.15
Distrib'ns, Cap Gain ($) ...	2.70	1.76	0.38	0.52	1.01	0.02	1.93	2.64	0.51	3.72
Net Asset Value ($)	16.16	15.53	15.68	10.61	12.43	10.74	9.51	12.38	15.13	12.78
Expense Ratio (%)	0.97	0.93	0.92	0.82	0.79	0.84	0.78	0.73	0.70	0.70
Net Income to Assets (%) .	-0.24	-0.32	0.35	0.72	0.58	0.67	0.23	0.10	0.63	1.15
Portfolio Turnover (%)......	38	50	33	38	45	43	50	34	30	31
Total Assets (Millions $)..	1,623	1,547	1,470	855	1,043	915	856	1,033	1,474	1,273

PORTFOLIO (as of 6/30/93)

Portfolio Manager: John Laporte - 1987

Investm't Category: Aggressive Growth

✔ Cap Gain	Asset Allocation
Cap & Income	Fund of Funds
Income	Index
	Sector
✔ Domestic	✔ Small Cap
✔ Foreign	Socially Conscious
Country/Region	State Specific

Portfolio: stocks 91% bonds 0%
convertibles 3% other 0% cash 6%

Largest Holdings: health care services 11%, computer software 10%

Unrealized Net Capital Gains: 31% of portfolio value

SHAREHOLDER INFORMATION

Minimum Investment
Initial: $2,500   Subsequent: $100

Minimum IRA Investment
Initial: $1,000   Subsequent: $50

Maximum Fees
Load: none   12b-1: none
Other: none

Distributions
Income: Dec   Capital Gains: Dec

Exchange Options
Number Per Year: 6   Fee: none
Telephone: yes (money market fund available)

Services
IRA, other pension, auto exchange, auto invest, auto withdraw

T Rowe Price New Income (PRCIX)

10090 Red Run Blvd.
Owings Mills, MD 21117
(800) 638-5660, (410) 547-2308

General Bond

PERFORMANCE

	3yr Annual	5yr Annual	10yr Annual	Bull	Bear
Return (%)	9.9	10.1	10.3	39.6	3.4
Differ from Category (+/-)	-0.3 blw av	0.3 av	-0.6 low	0.2 av	0.5 abv av

Total Risk	Standard Deviation	Category Risk	Risk Index	Avg Mat
low	3.5%	av	1.2	8.6 yrs

	1993	1992	1991	1990	1989	1988	1987	1986	1985	1984
Return (%)	9.5	4.9	15.5	8.7	12.2	7.5	2.0	13.8	17.6	11.8
Differ from category (+/-)	0.3	-1.8	0.8	1.8	0.8	-0.1	-0.5	-0.1	-2.5	-0.5

PER SHARE DATA

	1993	1992	1991	1990	1989	1988	1987	1986	1985	1984
Dividends, Net Income ($)	0.53	0.59	0.67	0.70	0.75	0.80	0.74	0.76	0.90	0.93
Distrib'ns, Cap Gain ($)	0.07	0.00	0.01	0.00	0.00	0.00	0.00	0.00	0.00	0.00
Net Asset Value ($)	9.24	9.00	9.16	8.58	8.59	8.37	8.55	9.13	8.73	8.26
Expense Ratio (%)	0.84	0.87	0.88	0.86	0.91	0.80	0.65	0.66	0.64	0.62
Net Income to Assets (%)	6.36	7.64	8.33	8.85	9.50	8.77	8.22	10.39	11.53	11.13
Portfolio Turnover (%)	86	50	21	51	92	158	125	184	155	84
Total Assets (Millions $)	1,566	1,307	1,131	993	860	835	939	936	707	695

PORTFOLIO (as of 8/31/93)

Portfolio Manager: Charles Smith - 1986

Investm't Category: General Bond

Cap Gain	Asset Allocation
Cap & Income	Fund of Funds
✔ Income	Index
	Sector
✔ Domestic	Small Cap
✔ Foreign	Socially Conscious
Country/Region	State Specific

Portfolio: stocks 0% bonds 92%
convertibles 0% other 0% cash 8%

Largest Holdings: corporate 50%, U.S. government 27%

Unrealized Net Capital Gains: 6% of portfolio value

SHAREHOLDER INFORMATION

Minimum Investment
Initial: $2,500   Subsequent: $100

Minimum IRA Investment
Initial: $1,000   Subsequent: $50

Maximum Fees
Load: none   12b-1: none
Other: none

Distributions
Income: monthly   Capital Gains: Jan, Mar

Exchange Options
Number Per Year: 6   Fee: none
Telephone: yes (money market fund available)

Services
auto exchange, auto invest, auto withdraw

T Rowe Price NJ Tax-Free (NJTFX)

Tax-Exempt Bond

10090 Red Run Blvd.
Owings Mills, MD 21117
(800) 638-5660, (410) 547-2308

PERFORMANCE

	3yr Annual	5yr Annual	10yr Annual	Bull	Bear
Return (%)	na	na	na	na	na
Differ from Category (+/-)	na	na	na	na	na

Total Risk	Standard Deviation	Category Risk	Risk Index	Avg Mat
na	na	na	na	18.3 yrs

	1993	1992	1991	1990	1989	1988	1987	1986	1985	1984
Return (%).............	13.9	9.5	—	—	—	—	—	—	—	—
Differ from category (+/-)...	2.3	1.2	—	—	—	—	—	—	—	—

PER SHARE DATA

	1993	1992	1991	1990	1989	1988	1987	1986	1985	1984
Dividends, Net Income ($).	0.55	0.57	—	—	—	—	—	—	—	—
Distrib'ns, Cap Gain ($) ...	0.14	0.07	—	—	—	—	—	—	—	—
Net Asset Value ($)	11.45	10.69	—	—	—	—	—	—	—	—
Expense Ratio (%)	0.65	0.65	—	—	—	—	—	—	—	—
Net Income to Assets (%) .	5.47	5.86	—	—	—	—	—	—	—	—
Portfolio Turnover (%).....	103	152	—	—	—	—	—	—	—	—
Total Assets (Millions $).....	60	14	—	—	—	—	—	—	—	—

PORTFOLIO (as of 8/31/93)

Portfolio Manager: William Reynolds - 1991

Investm't Category: Tax-Exempt Bond
Cap Gain	Asset Allocation
Cap & Income	Fund of Funds
✔ Income	Index
	Sector
✔ Domestic	Small Cap
Foreign	Socially Conscious
Country/Region	✔ State Specific

Portfolio: stocks 0%   bonds 100%
convertibles 0%   other 0%   cash 0%

Largest Holdings: general obligation 19%

Unrealized Net Capital Gains: 7% of portfolio value

SHAREHOLDER INFORMATION

Minimum Investment
Initial: $2,500   Subsequent: $100

Minimum IRA Investment
Initial: na   Subsequent: na

Maximum Fees
Load: none   12b-1: none
Other: none

Distributions
Income: monthly   Capital Gains: Jan, Mar

Exchange Options
Number Per Year: 6   Fee: none
Telephone: yes (money market fund available)

Services
auto exchange, auto invest, auto withdraw

T Rowe Price NY Tax-Free (PRNYX)

Tax-Exempt Bond

10090 Red Run Blvd.
Owings Mills, MD 21117
(800) 638-5660, (410) 547-2308

PERFORMANCE

	3yr Annual	5yr Annual	10yr Annual	Bull	Bear
Return (%)	12.0	9.8	na	45.4	1.7
Differ from Category (+/-)	1.7 high	0.6 av	na	5.3 abv av	-0.6 blw av

Total Risk	Standard Deviation	Category Risk	Risk Index	Avg Mat
blw av	4.1%	av	1.0	19.3 yrs

	1993	1992	1991	1990	1989	1988	1987	1986	1985	1984
Return (%)	13.3	10.3	12.4	5.2	8.0	10.4	-2.4	—	—	—
Differ from category (+/-) . . .	1.7	2.0	1.1	-1.1	-1.0	0.3	-1.2	—	—	—

PER SHARE DATA

	1993	1992	1991	1990	1989	1988	1987	1986	1985	1984
Dividends, Net Income ($) .	0.59	0.62	0.62	0.62	0.62	0.60	0.60	—	—	—
Distrib'ns, Cap Gain ($) . . .	0.15	0.00	0.00	0.00	0.00	0.00	0.00	—	—	—
Net Asset Value ($)	11.21	10.59	10.19	9.65	9.78	9.65	9.31	—	—	—
Expense Ratio (%)	0.60	0.60	0.73	0.96	1.00	1.00	0.85	—	—	—
Net Income to Assets (%) . .	5.91	6.33	6.43	6.40	6.40	6.44	6.16	—	—	—
Portfolio Turnover (%)	41	49	62	72	89	147	126	—	—	—
Total Assets (Millions $) . . .	134	74	55	47	36	28	24	—	—	—

PORTFOLIO (as of 8/31/93)

Portfolio Manager: William T. Reynolds - 1986

Investm't Category: Tax-Exempt Bond

Cap Gain	Asset Allocation
Cap & Income	Fund of Funds
✔ Income	Index
	Sector
✔ Domestic	Small Cap
Foreign	Socially Conscious
Country/Region	✔ State Specific

Portfolio: stocks 0% bonds 100%
convertibles 0% other 0% cash 0%

Largest Holdings: general obligation 12%

Unrealized Net Capital Gains: 8% of portfolio value

SHAREHOLDER INFORMATION

Minimum Investment
Initial: $2,500 Subsequent: $100

Minimum IRA Investment
Initial: na Subsequent: na

Maximum Fees
Load: none 12b-1: none
Other: none

Distributions
Income: monthly Capital Gains: Jan, Mar

Exchange Options
Number Per Year: 6 Fee: none
Telephone: yes (money market fund available)

Services
auto exchange, auto invest, auto withdraw

T Rowe Price OTC
(OTCFX)

Aggressive Growth

10090 Red Run Blvd.
Owings Mills, MD 21117
(800) 638-5660, (410) 547-2308

	3yr Annual	5yr Annual	10yr Annual	Bull	Bear
Return (%)	23.1	12.1	10.5	92.8	-22.9
Differ from Category (+/-)	-2.3 av	-6.1 low	-1.4 blw av	-32.2 blw av	-7.9 blw av

Total Risk	Standard Deviation	Category Risk	Risk Index	Beta
abv av	12.4%	low	0.8	0.8

	1993	1992	1991	1990	1989	1988	1987	1986	1985	1984
Return (%)	18.4	13.9	38.6	-20.4	19.1	27.1	-12.5	4.7	35.4	-2.5
Differ from category (+/-) . . .	-0.6	3.5	-13.8	-14.1	-7.9	11.9	-9.1	-4.7	4.4	6.9

PER SHARE DATA

	1993	1992	1991	1990	1989	1988	1987	1986	1985	1984
Dividends, Net Income ($) .	0.00	0.07	0.09	0.08	0.12	0.12	0.31	0.05	0.15	0.10
Distrib'ns, Cap Gain ($) . . .	1.58	4.64	0.68	0.10	0.47	2.50	1.51	2.54	1.13	1.38
Net Asset Value ($)	15.39	14.37	16.86	12.72	16.23	14.14	13.19	17.04	18.68	14.93
Expense Ratio (%)	1.29	1.32	1.34	1.47	1.45	1.55	1.00	0.85	1.25	1.28
Net Income to Assets (%) .	-0.11	0.03	0.48	0.73	0.63	0.64	0.80	0.95	0.75	1.07
Portfolio Turnover (%)	41	31	31	35	33	27	49	30	31	21
Total Assets (Millions $)	202	187	267	215	316	292	212	247	147	84

PORTFOLIO (as of 6/30/93)

Portfolio Manager: Greg McCrickard - 1992

Investm't Category: Aggressive Growth

✔ Cap Gain	Asset Allocation
Cap & Income	Fund of Funds
Income	Index
	Sector
✔ Domestic	✔ Small Cap
✔ Foreign	Socially Conscious
Country/Region	State Specific

Portfolio: stocks 92%   bonds 0%
convertibles 2%   other 0%   cash 6%

Largest Holdings: bank & trust 10%, insurance 8%

Unrealized Net Capital Gains: 26% of portfolio value

SHAREHOLDER INFORMATION

Minimum Investment
Initial: $2,500   Subsequent: $100

Minimum IRA Investment
Initial: $1,000   Subsequent: $50

Maximum Fees
Load: none   12b-1: none
Other: none

Distributions
Income: Dec   Capital Gains: Dec

Exchange Options
Number Per Year: 6   Fee: none
Telephone: yes (money market fund available)

Services
IRA, other pension, auto exchange, auto invest, auto withdraw

T Rowe Price Science & Tech (PRSCX)

10090 Red Run Blvd.
Owings Mills, MD 21117
(800) 638-5660, (410) 547-2308

Aggressive Growth

PERFORMANCE

	3yr Annual	5yr Annual	10yr Annual	Bull	Bear
Return (%)	33.2	26.8	na	175.1	-15.1
Differ from Category (+/-)	7.8 high	8.6 high	na	50.1 high	-0.1 av

Total Risk	Standard Deviation	Category Risk	Risk Index	Beta
high	23.1%	high	1.5	1.5

	1993	1992	1991	1990	1989	1988	1987	1986	1985	1984
Return (%)	24.2	18.7	60.1	-1.2	40.5	13.2	—	—	—	—
Differ from category (+/-) . . .	5.2	8.3	7.7	5.1	13.5	-2.0	—	—	—	—

PER SHARE DATA

	1993	1992	1991	1990	1989	1988	1987	1986	1985	1984
Dividends, Net Income ($) .	0.00	0.00	0.00	0.09	0.05	0.07	—	—	—	—
Distrib'ns, Cap Gain ($) . . .	2.51	1.12	0.47	0.23	1.39	0.43	—	—	—	—
Net Asset Value ($)	18.95	17.33	15.57	10.05	10.52	8.57	—	—	—	—
Expense Ratio (%)	1.25	1.25	1.25	1.25	1.20	1.20	—	—	—	—
Net Income to Assets (%) .	-0.49	-0.81	-0.07	0.91	0.50	0.68	—	—	—	—
Portfolio Turnover (%)	210	144	148	183	203	92	—	—	—	—
Total Assets (Millions $) . . .	494	281	166	62	24	12	—	—	—	—

PORTFOLIO (as of 6/30/93)

Portfolio Manager: Charles Morris - 1991

Investm't Category: Aggressive Growth

✔ Cap Gain	Asset Allocation
Cap & Income	Fund of Funds
Income	Index
	✔ Sector
✔ Domestic	Small Cap
✔ Foreign	Socially Conscious
Country/Region	State Specific

Portfolio:
stocks 84%   bonds 0%
convertibles 0%   other 0%   cash 16%

Largest Holdings: computer software 23%, semiconductor related 17%

Unrealized Net Capital Gains: 16% of portfolio value

SHAREHOLDER INFORMATION

Minimum Investment
Initial: $2,500   Subsequent: $100

Minimum IRA Investment
Initial: $1,000   Subsequent: $50

Maximum Fees
Load: none   12b-1: none
Other: none

Distributions
Income: Dec   Capital Gains: Dec

Exchange Options
Number Per Year: 6   Fee: none
Telephone: yes (money market fund available)

Services
IRA, other pension, auto exchange, auto invest, auto withdraw

T Rowe Price Short-Term Bond (PRWBX)

10090 Red Run Blvd.
Owings Mills, MD 21117
(800) 638-5660, (410) 547-2308

General Bond

PERFORMANCE

	3yr Annual	5yr Annual	10yr Annual	Bull	Bear
Return (%)	7.5	8.2	na	28.1	5.5
Differ from Category (+/-)	-2.7 low	-1.6 low	na	-11.3 low	2.6 high

Total Risk	Standard Deviation	Category Risk	Risk Index	Avg Mat
low	2.1%	blw av	0.7	2.3 yrs

	1993	1992	1991	1990	1989	1988	1987	1986	1985	1984
Return (%)	6.6	4.9	11.2	8.6	9.9	5.5	5.2	8.9	12.8	—
Differ from category (+/-). . .	-2.6	-1.8	-3.4	1.7	-1.4	-2.1	2.7	-5.0	-7.3	—

PER SHARE DATA

	1993	1992	1991	1990	1989	1988	1987	1986	1985	1984
Dividends, Net Income ($) .	0.31	0.33	0.35	0.39	0.41	0.41	0.38	0.41	0.47	—
Distrib'ns, Cap Gain ($) . . .	0.00	0.00	0.00	0.03	0.00	0.00	0.00	0.00	0.00	—
Net Asset Value ($)	5.05	5.04	5.13	4.95	4.97	4.92	5.06	5.19	5.16	—
Expense Ratio (%)	0.76	0.88	0.93	0.95	0.93	0.91	0.93	1.31	0.90	—
Net Income to Assets (%) .	6.59	7.07	7.90	8.43	8.27	7.85	7.58	9.12	10.73	—
Portfolio Turnover (%).	68	381	980	161	309	203	7	20	73	—
Total Assets (Millions $). . . .	680	398	219	210	232	284	218	96	41	—

PORTFOLIO (as of 8/31/93)

Portfolio Manager: Veena A. Kutler - 1991

Investm't Category: General Bond

Cap Gain	Asset Allocation
Cap & Income	Fund of Funds
✔ Income	Index
	Sector
✔ Domestic	Small Cap
✔ Foreign	Socially Conscious
Country/Region	State Specific

Portfolio: stocks 0% bonds 92%
convertibles 0% other 0% cash 8%

Largest Holdings: mortgage-backed 33%, corporate 27%

Unrealized Net Capital Gains: 2% of portfolio value

SHAREHOLDER INFORMATION

Minimum Investment
Initial: $2,500 Subsequent: $100

Minimum IRA Investment
Initial: $1,000 Subsequent: $50

Maximum Fees
Load: none 12b-1: none
Other: none

Distributions
Income: monthly Capital Gains: Jan, Mar

Exchange Options
Number Per Year: 6 Fee: none
Telephone: yes (money market fund available)

Services
IRA, other pension, auto exchange, auto invest, auto withdraw

T Rowe Price Short-Term Global Inc (RPSGX)

10090 Red Run Blvd.
Owings Mills, MD 21117
(800) 638-5660, (410) 547-2308

International Bond

PERFORMANCE

	3yr Annual	5yr Annual	10yr Annual	Bull	Bear
Return (%)	na	na	na	na	na
Differ from Category (+/-)	na	na	na	na	na

Total Risk	Standard Deviation	Category Risk	Risk Index	Avg Mat
na	na	na	na	2.6 yrs

	1993	1992	1991	1990	1989	1988	1987	1986	1985	1984
Return (%)	7.8	—	—	—	—	—	—	—	—	—
Differ from category (+/-) . .	-4.9	—	—	—	—	—	—	—	—	—

PER SHARE DATA

	1993	1992	1991	1990	1989	1988	1987	1986	1985	1984
Dividends, Net Income ($) .	0.32	—	—	—	—	—	—	—	—	—
Distrib'ns, Cap Gain ($) . . .	0.00	—	—	—	—	—	—	—	—	—
Net Asset Value ($)	4.82	—	—	—	—	—	—	—	—	—
Expense Ratio (%)	1.00	—	—	—	—	—	—	—	—	—
Net Income to Assets (%) . .	7.02	—	—	—	—	—	—	—	—	—
Portfolio Turnover (%)	98	—	—	—	—	—	—	—	—	—
Total Assets (Millions $)	96	—	—	—	—	—	—	—	—	—

PORTFOLIO (as of 6/30/93)

Portfolio Manager: David P. Baandman - 1992

Investm't Category: International Bond

Cap Gain	Asset Allocation
Cap & Income	Fund of Funds
✔ Income	Index
	Sector
✔ Domestic	Small Cap
✔ Foreign	Socially Conscious
Country/Region	State Specific

Portfolio: stocks 0% bonds 95%
convertibles 0% other 0% cash 5%

Largest Holdings: France 14%, Spain 10%

Unrealized Net Capital Gains: 0% of portfolio value

SHAREHOLDER INFORMATION

Minimum Investment
Initial: $2,500   Subsequent: $100

Minimum IRA Investment
Initial: $1,000   Subsequent: $50

Maximum Fees
Load: none   12b-1: none
Other: none

Distributions
Income: monthly   Capital Gains: Dec

Exchange Options
Number Per Year: 6   Fee: none
Telephone: yes (money market fund available)

Services
IRA, other pension, auto exchange, auto invest, auto withdraw

T Rowe Price Small Cap Value (PRSVX)

10090 Red Run Blvd.
Owings Mills, MD 21117
(800) 638-5660, (410) 547-2308

Growth

this fund is closed to new investors

PERFORMANCE

	3yr Annual	5yr Annual	10yr Annual	Bull	Bear
Return (%)	25.9	15.9	na	109.8	-15.5
Differ from Category (+/-)	6.7 high	1.3 abv av	na	25.1 high	-3.1 blw av

Total Risk	Standard Deviation	Category Risk	Risk Index	Beta
av	9.0%	low	0.8	0.5

	1993	1992	1991	1990	1989	1988	1987	1986	1985	1984
Return (%)	23.3	20.8	34.1	-11.3	18.0	—	—	—	—	—
Differ from category (+/-)	10.1	9.8	-1.3	-5.2	-7.8	—	—	—	—	—

PER SHARE DATA

	1993	1992	1991	1990	1989	1988	1987	1986	1985	1984
Dividends, Net Income ($)	0.10	0.10	0.11	0.23	0.14	—	—	—	—	—
Distrib'ns, Cap Gain ($)	0.34	0.15	0.34	0.11	0.89	—	—	—	—	—
Net Asset Value ($)	14.68	12.28	10.37	8.09	9.53	—	—	—	—	—
Expense Ratio (%)	1.20	1.25	1.25	1.25	1.25	—	—	—	—	—
Net Income to Assets (%)	0.90	0.98	1.31	2.57	1.42	—	—	—	—	—
Portfolio Turnover (%)	9	12	31	33	43	—	—	—	—	—
Total Assets (Millions $)	449	264	53	26	33	—	—	—	—	—

PORTFOLIO (as of 6/30/93)

Portfolio Manager: Preston Athey - 1991

Investm't Category: Growth
✔ Cap Gain	Asset Allocation
Cap & Income	Fund of Funds
Income	Index
	Sector
✔ Domestic	✔ Small Cap
✔ Foreign	Socially Conscious
Country/Region	State Specific

Portfolio: stocks 81%   bonds 1%
convertibles 3%   other 0%   cash 15%

Largest Holdings: business services 6%, specialty merchandisers 6%

Unrealized Net Capital Gains: 15% of portfolio value

SHAREHOLDER INFORMATION

Minimum Investment
Initial: $2,500   Subsequent: $100

Minimum IRA Investment
Initial: $1,000   Subsequent: $50

Maximum Fees
Load: none   12b-1: none
Other: none

Distributions
Income: Dec   Capital Gains: Dec

Exchange Options
Number Per Year: 6   Fee: none
Telephone: yes (money market fund available)

Services
IRA, other pension, auto exchange, auto invest, auto withdraw

T Rowe Price Spectrum Growth (PRSGX)

10090 Red Run Blvd.
Owings Mills, MD 21117
(800) 638-5660, (410) 547-2308

Growth & Income

PERFORMANCE

	3yr Annual	5yr Annual	10yr Annual	Bull	Bear
Return (%)	18.9	na	na	81.3	na
Differ from Category (+/-)	2.5 abv av	na	na	11.2 abv av	na

Total Risk	Standard Deviation	Category Risk	Risk Index	Beta
av	10.2%	av	1.2	0.8

	1993	1992	1991	1990	1989	1988	1987	1986	1985	1984
Return (%)	20.9	7.2	29.8	—	—	—	—	—	—	—
Differ from category (+/-)	8.3	-2.8	2.1	—	—	—	—	—	—	—

PER SHARE DATA

	1993	1992	1991	1990	1989	1988	1987	1986	1985	1984
Dividends, Net Income ($)	0.15	0.20	0.20	—	—	—	—	—	—	—
Distrib'ns, Cap Gain ($)	0.72	0.55	0.31	—	—	—	—	—	—	—
Net Asset Value ($)	11.87	10.54	10.53	—	—	—	—	—	—	—
Expense Ratio (%)	0.00	0.00	0.00	—	—	—	—	—	—	—
Net Income to Assets (%)	0.96	2.15	2.77	—	—	—	—	—	—	—
Portfolio Turnover (%)	10	8	15	—	—	—	—	—	—	—
Total Assets (Millions $)	581	355	149	—	—	—	—	—	—	—

PORTFOLIO (as of 6/30/93)

Portfolio Manager: Peter Van Dyke - 1990

Investm't Category: Growth & Income

Cap Gain	Asset Allocation
✔ Cap & Income	✔ Fund of Funds
Income	Index
	Sector
✔ Domestic	Small Cap
✔ Foreign	Socially Conscious
Country/Region	State Specific

Portfolio: stocks 0%   bonds 0%
convertibles 0%   other 100%   cash 0%

Largest Holdings: T. Rowe Price New Horizons 20%, T. Rowe Price Int'l Stock 20%

Unrealized Net Capital Gains: 8% of portfolio value

SHAREHOLDER INFORMATION

Minimum Investment
Initial: $2,500   Subsequent: $100

Minimum IRA Investment
Initial: $1,000   Subsequent: $50

Maximum Fees
Load: none   12b-1: none
Other: none

Distributions
Income: Dec   Capital Gains: Dec

Exchange Options
Number Per Year: 6   Fee: none
Telephone: yes (money market fund available)

Services
IRA, other pension, auto exchange, auto invest, auto withdraw

T Rowe Price Spectrum Income (RPSIX)

10090 Red Run Blvd.
Owings Mills, MD 21117
(800) 638-5660, (410) 547-2308

Balanced

PERFORMANCE

	3yr Annual	5yr Annual	10yr Annual	Bull	Bear
Return (%)	13.1	na	na	51.1	na
Differ from Category (+/-)	-1.9 blw av	na	na	-10.5 blw av	na

Total Risk	Standard Deviation	Category Risk	Risk Index	Beta
low	3.0%	low	0.4	0.2

	1993	1992	1991	1990	1989	1988	1987	1986	1985	1984
Return (%).............	12.4	7.8	19.6	—	—	—	—	—	—	—
Differ from category (+/-)...	-1.0	-0.3	-4.3	—	—	—	—	—	—	—

PER SHARE DATA

	1993	1992	1991	1990	1989	1988	1987	1986	1985	1984
Dividends, Net Income ($).	0.69	0.76	0.82	—	—	—	—	—	—	—
Distrib'ns, Cap Gain ($) ...	0.18	0.07	0.05	—	—	—	—	—	—	—
Net Asset Value ($)	11.11	10.70	10.73	—	—	—	—	—	—	—
Expense Ratio (%)	0.00	0.00	0.00	—	—	—	—	—	—	—
Net Income to Assets (%) .	6.41	7.10	8.03	—	—	—	—	—	—	—
Portfolio Turnover (%)......	17	14	19	—	—	—	—	—	—	—
Total Assets (Millions $)....	595	377	148	—	—	—	—	—	—	—

PORTFOLIO (as of 6/30/93)

Portfolio Manager: Peter Van Dyke - 1990

Investm't Category: Balanced

Cap Gain	Asset Allocation
✔ Cap & Income	✔ Fund of Funds
Income	Index
	Sector
✔ Domestic	Small Cap
✔ Foreign	Socially Conscious
Country/Region	State Specific

Portfolio: stocks 0% bonds 0%
convertibles 0% other 100% cash 0%

Largest Holdings: T. Rowe Price New Income 25%, T. Rowe Price High Yield 20%

Unrealized Net Capital Gains: 4% of portfolio value

SHAREHOLDER INFORMATION

Minimum Investment
Initial: $2,500   Subsequent: $100

Minimum IRA Investment
Initial: $1,000   Subsequent: $50

Maximum Fees
Load: none   12b-1: none
Other: none

Distributions
Income: monthly   Capital Gains: Dec

Exchange Options
Number Per Year: 6   Fee: none
Telephone: yes (money market fund available)

Services
IRA, other pension, auto exchange, auto invest, auto withdraw

T Rowe Price Tax-Free High Yield (PRFHX)

Tax-Exempt Bond

10090 Red Run Blvd.
Owings Mills, MD 21117
(800) 638-5660, (410) 547-2308

PERFORMANCE

	3yr Annual	5yr Annual	10yr Annual	Bull	Bear
Return (%)	11.4	10.3	na	42.7	3.7
Differ from Category (+/-)	1.1 abv av	1.1 high	na	2.6 av	1.4 high

Total Risk	Standard Deviation	Category Risk	Risk Index	Avg Mat
low	3.4%	low	0.8	21.1 yrs

	1993	1992	1991	1990	1989	1988	1987	1986	1985	1984
Return (%)	12.9	9.5	11.7	7.1	10.5	11.1	0.2	20.4	—	—
Differ from category (+/-) . . .	1.3	1.2	0.4	0.8	1.5	1.0	1.4	4.0	—	—

PER SHARE DATA

	1993	1992	1991	1990	1989	1988	1987	1986	1985	1984
Dividends, Net Income ($) .	0.74	0.79	0.81	0.82	0.84	0.82	0.84	0.87	—	—
Distrib'ns, Cap Gain ($) . . .	0.23	0.10	0.10	0.02	0.05	0.00	0.25	0.00	—	—
Net Asset Value ($)	12.46	11.93	11.74	11.37	11.45	11.21	10.86	11.92	—	—
Expense Ratio (%)	0.81	0.83	0.85	0.88	0.92	0.96	0.98	1.00	—	—
Net Income to Assets (%) . .	6.58	7.01	7.30	7.38	7.45	7.49	7.45	8.47	—	—
Portfolio Turnover (%)	34	51	51	72	62	128	111	156	—	—
Total Assets (Millions $) . . .	959	624	505	444	331	281	324	168	—	—

PORTFOLIO (as of 8/31/93)

Portfolio Manager: C. Stephan Wolfe - 1993

Investm't Category: Tax-Exempt Bond

Cap Gain	Asset Allocation
Cap & Income	Fund of Funds
✔ Income	Index
	Sector
✔ Domestic	Small Cap
Foreign	Socially Conscious
Country/Region	State Specific

Portfolio: stocks 0% bonds 100%
convertibles 0% other 0% cash 0%

Largest Holdings: general obligation 7%

Unrealized Net Capital Gains: 8% of portfolio value

SHAREHOLDER INFORMATION

Minimum Investment
Initial: $2,500   Subsequent: $100

Minimum IRA Investment
Initial: na   Subsequent: na

Maximum Fees
Load: none   12b-1: none
Other: none

Distributions
Income: monthly   Capital Gains: Mar, Dec

Exchange Options
Number Per Year: 6   Fee: none
Telephone: yes (money market fund available)

Services
auto exchange, auto invest, auto withdraw

T Rowe Price Tax-Free Income (PRTAX)

10090 Red Run Blvd.
Owings Mills, MD 21117
(800) 638-5660, (410) 547-2308

Tax-Exempt Bond

PERFORMANCE

	3yr Annual	5yr Annual	10yr Annual	Bull	Bear
Return (%)	11.4	9.8	9.5	44.4	1.3
Differ from Category (+/-)	1.1 abv av	0.6 av	-0.1 blw av	4.3 abv av	-1.0 blw av

Total Risk	Standard Deviation	Category Risk	Risk Index	Avg Mat
blw av	. 4.5%	abv av	1.1	18.4 yrs

	1993	1992	1991	1990	1989	1988	1987	1986	1985	1984
Return (%)	12.7	9.3	12.1	5.8	9.1	7.8	-4.1	19.8	16.9	7.1
Differ from category (+/-). . .	1.1	1.0	0.8	-0.5	0.1	-2.3	-2.9	3.4	-0.4	-1.2

PER SHARE DATA

	1993	1992	1991	1990	1989	1988	1987	1986	1985	1984
Dividends, Net Income ($).	0.53	0.56	0.56	0.57	0.59	0.58	0.59	0.70	0.69	0.65
Distrib'ns, Cap Gain ($) . . .	0.18	0.00	0.00	0.00	0.00	0.00	0.54	0.00	0.00	0.00
Net Asset Value ($)	9.90	9.44	9.17	8.71	8.79	8.62	8.55	10.07	9.03	8.37
Expense Ratio (%)	0.61	0.62	0.63	0.64	0.66	0.65	0.61	0.63	0.63	0.66
Net Income to Assets (%) .	5.98	6.34	6.59	6.80	6.81	6.72	6.94	8.07	7.84	8.25
Portfolio Turnover (%).	76	58	80	141	116	181	237	187	277	220
Total Assets (Millions $). .	1,510	1,246	1,129	1,123	1,023	1,094	1,558	1,325	936	961

PORTFOLIO (as of 8/31/93)

Portfolio Manager: William T. Reynolds - 1990

Investm't Category: Tax-Exempt Bond

Cap Gain	Asset Allocation
Cap & Income	Fund of Funds
✔ Income	Index
	Sector
✔ Domestic	Small Cap
Foreign	Socially Conscious
Country/Region	State Specific

Portfolio: stocks 0% bonds 100%
convertibles 0% other 0% cash 0%

Largest Holdings: general obligation 15%

Unrealized Net Capital Gains: 8% of portfolio value

SHAREHOLDER INFORMATION

Minimum Investment
Initial: $2,500   Subsequent: $100

Minimum IRA Investment
Initial: na   Subsequent: na

Maximum Fees
Load: none   12b-1: none
Other: none

Distributions
Income: monthly   Capital Gains: Mar, Dec

Exchange Options
Number Per Year: 6   Fee: none
Telephone: yes (money market fund available)

Services
auto exchange, auto invest, auto withdraw

T Rowe Price Tax-Free Insured Interm (PTIBX)

10090 Red Run Blvd.
Owings Mills, MD 21117
(800) 638-5660, (410) 547-2308

Tax-Exempt Bond

PERFORMANCE

	3yr Annual	5yr Annual	10yr Annual	Bull	Bear
Return (%)	na	na	na	na	na
Differ from Category (+/-)	na	na	na	na	na

Total Risk	Standard Deviation	Category Risk	Risk Index	Avg Mat
na	na	na	na •	7.8 yrs

	1993	1992	1991	1990	1989	1988	1987	1986	1985	1984
Return (%)	12.6	—	—	—	—	—	—	—	—	—
Differ from category (+/-) . . .	1.0	—	—	—	—	—	—	—	—	—

PER SHARE DATA

	1993	1992	1991	1990	1989	1988	1987	1986	1985	1984
Dividends, Net Income ($) .	0.48	—	—	—	—	—	—	—	—	—
Distrib'ns, Cap Gain ($) . . .	0.06	—	—	—	—	—	—	—	—	—
Net Asset Value ($)	10.80	—	—	—	—	—	—	—	—	—
Expense Ratio (%)	0.00	—	—	—	—	—	—	—	—	—
Net Income to Assets (%) . .	5.08	—	—	—	—	—	—	—	—	—
Portfolio Turnover (%)	65	—	—	—	—	—	—	—	—	—
Total Assets (Millions $)	97	—	—	—	—	—	—	—	—	—

PORTFOLIO (as of 8/31/93)

Portfolio Manager: William Reynolds - 1992

Investm't Category: Tax-Exempt Bond

Cap Gain	Asset Allocation
Cap & Income	Fund of Funds
✔ Income	Index
	Sector
✔ Domestic	Small Cap
Foreign	Socially Conscious
Country/Region	State Specific

Portfolio: stocks 0% bonds 100%
convertibles 0% other 0% cash 0%

Largest Holdings: general obligation 11%

Unrealized Net Capital Gains: 2% of portfolio value

SHAREHOLDER INFORMATION

Minimum Investment
Initial: $2,500   Subsequent: $100

Minimum IRA Investment
Initial: na   Subsequent: na

Maximum Fees
Load: none   12b-1: none
Other: none

Distributions
Income: monthly   Capital Gains: Mar, Dec

Exchange Options
Number Per Year: 6   Fee: none
Telephone: yes (money market fund available)

Services
auto exchange, auto invest, auto withdraw

T Rowe Price Tax-Free Short-Interm (PRFSX)

10090 Red Run Blvd.
Owings Mills, MD 21117
(800) 638-5660, (410) 547-2308

Tax-Exempt Bond

PERFORMANCE

	3yr Annual	5yr Annual	10yr Annual	Bull	Bear
Return (%)	6.7	6.6	6.5	24.0	3.9
Differ from Category.(+/-)	-3.6 low	-2.6 low	-3.1 low	-16.1 low	1.6 high

Total Risk	Standard Deviation	Category Risk	Risk Index	Avg Mat
low	1.6%	low	0.4	3.3 yrs

	1993	1992	1991	1990	1989	1988	1987	1986	1985	1984
Return (%)	6.3	6.0	7.8	6.0	6.8	4.9	2.2	9.7	8.8	6.8
Differ from category (+/-)	-5.3	-2.3	-3.5	-0.3	-2.2	-5.2	3.4	-6.7	-8.5	-1.5

PER SHARE DATA

	1993	1992	1991	1990	1989	1988	1987	1986	1985	1984
Dividends, Net Income ($)	0.22	0.24	0.28	0.28	0.29	0.27	0.27	0.30	0.32	0.31
Distrib'ns, Cap Gain ($)	0.00	0.00	0.00	0.00	0.00	0.00	0.01	0.00	0.00	0.00
Net Asset Value ($)	5.38	5.28	5.22	5.11	5.10	5.06	5.09	5.27	5.09	4.98
Expense Ratio (%)	0.63	0.67	0.74	0.75	0.74	0.74	0.73	0.90	0.90	0.89
Net Income to Assets (%)	4.61	5.34	5.67	5.93	5.46	5.29	5.60	6.26	6.51	7.11
Portfolio Turnover (%)	38	81	190	191	53	225	120	128	300	110
Total Assets (Millions $)	530	329	233	223	249	292	405	155	68	23

PORTFOLIO (as of 8/31/93)

Portfolio Manager: Mary J. Miller - 1989

Investm't Category: Tax-Exempt Bond
Cap Gain	Asset Allocation
Cap & Income	Fund of Funds
✔ Income	Index
	Sector
✔ Domestic	Small Cap
Foreign	Socially Conscious
Country/Region	State Specific

Portfolio: stocks 0%   bonds 100%
convertibles 0%   other 0%   cash 0%

Largest Holdings: general obligation 24%

Unrealized Net Capital Gains: 2% of portfolio value

SHAREHOLDER INFORMATION

Minimum Investment
Initial: $2,500   Subsequent: $100

Minimum IRA Investment
Initial: na   Subsequent: na

Maximum Fees
Load: none   12b-1: none
Other: none

Distributions
Income: monthly   Capital Gains: Mar, Dec

Exchange Options
Number Per Year: 6   Fee: none
Telephone: yes (money market fund available)

Services
auto exchange, auto invest, auto withdraw

T Rowe Price US Treasury Interm (PRTIX)

10090 Red Run Blvd.
Owings Mills, MD 21117
(800) 638-5660, (410) 547-2308

Government Bond

PERFORMANCE

	3yr Annual	5yr Annual	10yr Annual	Bull	Bear
Return (%)	9.6	na	na	37.0	4.7
Differ from Category (+/-)	-1.2 av	na	na	-9.2 blw av	4.2 abv av

Total Risk	Standard Deviation	Category Risk	Risk Index	Avg Mat
low	3.5%	blw av	0.8	3.5 yrs

	1993	1992	1991	1990	1989	1988	1987	1986	1985	1984
Return (%)	7.9	6.2	14.7	8.9	—	—	—	—	—	—
Differ from category (+/-) . .	-2.5	0.0	-0.3	2.4	—	—	—	—	—	—

PER SHARE DATA

	1993	1992	1991	1990	1989	1988	1987	1986	1985	1984
Dividends, Net Income ($) .	0.29	0.32	0.35	0.40	—	—	—	—	—	—
Distrib'ns, Cap Gain ($) . . .	0.00	0.12	0.02	0.00	—	—	—	—	—	—
Net Asset Value ($)	5.38	5.27	5.41	5.08	—	—	—	—	—	—
Expense Ratio (%).	0.80	0.80	0.80	0.80	—	—	—	—	—	—
Net Income to Assets (%) . .	5.98	6.80	7.71	8.13	—	—	—	—	—	—
Portfolio Turnover (%)	23	91	175	195	—	—	—	—	—	—
Total Assets (Millions $) . . .	171	124	68	11	—	—	—	—	—	—

PORTFOLIO (as of 8/31/93)

Portfolio Manager: Charles P. Smith - 1989

Investm't Category: Government Bond

Cap Gain	Asset Allocation
Cap & Income	Fund of Funds
✔ Income	Index
	Sector
✔ Domestic	Small Cap
Foreign	Socially Conscious
Country/Region	State Specific

Portfolio: stocks 0%   bonds 100%
convertibles 0%   other 0%   cash 0%

Largest Holdings: U.S. government 92%, mortgage-backed 8%

Unrealized Net Capital Gains: 5% of portfolio value

SHAREHOLDER INFORMATION

Minimum Investment
Initial: $2,500   Subsequent: $100

Minimum IRA Investment
Initial: $1,000   Subsequent: $50

Maximum Fees
Load: none   12b-1: none
Other: none

Distributions
Income: monthly   Capital Gains: Jan, Mar

Exchange Options
Number Per Year: 6   Fee: none
Telephone: yes (money market fund available)

Services
IRA, other pension, auto exchange, auto invest, auto withdraw

T Rowe Price US Treasury Long Term

(PRULX)   Government Bond

10090 Red Run Blvd.
Owings Mills, MD 21117
(800) 638-5660, (410) 547-2308

PERFORMANCE

	3yr Annual	5yr Annual	10yr Annual	Bull	Bear
Return (%)	11.5	na	na	48.9	-0.4
Differ from Category (+/-)	0.6 abv av	na	na	2.7 abv av	-0.8 blw av

Total Risk	Standard Deviation	Category Risk	Risk Index	Avg Mat
blw av	5.5%	abv av	1.3	16.0 yrs

	1993	1992	1991	1990	1989	1988	1987	1986	1985	1984
Return (%).	12.9	5.8	16.2	6.6	—	—	—	—	—	—
Differ from category (+/-). . .	2.5	-0.4	1.2	0.1	—	—	—	—	—	—

PER SHARE DATA

	1993	1992	1991	1990	1989	1988	1987	1986	1985	1984
Dividends, Net Income ($).	0.67	0.72	0.77	0.81	—	—	—	—	—	—
Distrib'ns, Cap Gain ($) . . .	0.28	0.28	0.00	0.00	—	—	—	—	—	—
Net Asset Value ($)	10.71	10.36	10.78	10.01	—	—	—	—	—	—
Expense Ratio (%)	0.80	0.80	0.80	0.80	—	—	—	—	—	—
Net Income to Assets (%) .	6.75	7.66	8.01	8.23	—	—	—	—	—	—
Portfolio Turnover (%).	165	162	159	316	—	—	—	—	—	—
Total Assets (Millions $).	57	53	43	11	—	—	—	—	—	—

PORTFOLIO (as of 8/31/93)

Portfolio Manager: Peter Van Dyke - 1989

Investm't Category: Government Bond
Cap Gain	Asset Allocation
Cap & Income	Fund of Funds
✔ Income	Index
	Sector
✔ Domestic	Small Cap
Foreign	Socially Conscious
Country/Region	State Specific

Portfolio: stocks 0%   bonds 100%
convertibles 0%   other 0%   cash 0%

Largest Holdings: U.S. government 87%, mortgage-backed 13%

Unrealized Net Capital Gains: 10% of portfolio value

SHAREHOLDER INFORMATION

Minimum Investment
Initial: $2,500   Subsequent: $100

Minimum IRA Investment
Initial: $1,000   Subsequent: $50

Maximum Fees
Load: none   12b-1: none
Other: none

Distributions
Income: monthly   Capital Gains: Jan, Mar

Exchange Options
Number Per Year: 6   Fee: none
Telephone: yes (money market fund available)

Services
IRA, other pension, auto exchange, auto invest, auto withdraw

T Rowe Price Virginia Tax-Free Bond (PRVAX)

10090 Red Run Blvd.
Owings Mills, MD 21117
(800) 638-5660, (410) 547-2308

Tax-Exempt Bond

PERFORMANCE

	3yr Annual	5yr Annual	10yr Annual	Bull	Bear
Return (%)	na	na	na	na	na
Differ from Category (+/-)	na	na	na	na	na

Total Risk	Standard Deviation	Category Risk	Risk Index	Avg Mat
na	na	na	na	18.5 yrs

	1993	1992	1991	1990	1989	1988	1987	1986	1985	1984
Return (%)	12.5	9.2	—	—	—	—	—	—	—	—
Differ from category (+/-) . . .	0.8	0.8	—	—	—	—	—	—	—	—

PER SHARE DATA

	1993	1992	1991	1990	1989	1988	1987	1986	1985	1984
Dividends, Net Income ($) .	0.56	0.58	—	—	—	—	—	—	—	—
Distrib'ns, Cap Gain ($) . . .	0.15	0.02	—	—	—	—	—	—	—	—
Net Asset Value ($)	11.24	10.65	—	—	—	—	—	—	—	—
Expense Ratio (%).	0.65	0.65	—	—	—	—	—	—	—	—
Net Income to Assets (%) . .	5.53	5.80	—	—	—	—	—	—	—	—
Portfolio Turnover (%)	68	76	—	—	—	—	—	—	—	—
Total Assets (Millions $) . . .	162	44	—	—	—	—	—	—	—	—

PORTFOLIO (as of 8/31/93)

Portfolio Manager: Mary J. Miller - 1991

Investm't Category: Tax-Exempt Bond

Cap Gain	Asset Allocation
Cap & Income	Fund of Funds
✔ Income	Index
	Sector
✔ Domestic	Small Cap
Foreign	Socially Conscious
Country/Region	✔ State Specific

Portfolio:
stocks 0% bonds 100%
convertibles 0% other 0% cash 0%

Largest Holdings: general obligation 13%

Unrealized Net Capital Gains: 5% of portfolio value

SHAREHOLDER INFORMATION

Minimum Investment
Initial: $2,500   Subsequent: $100

Minimum IRA Investment
Initial: na   Subsequent: na

Maximum Fees
Load: none   12b-1: none
Other: none

Distributions
Income: monthly   Capital Gains: Jan, Mar

Exchange Options
Number Per Year: 6   Fee: none
Telephone: yes (money market fund available)

Services
auto exchange, auto invest, auto withdraw

Tweedy Browne Global Value (TBGVX)

International Stock

52 Vanderbilt Avenue
New York, NY 10017
(800) 432-4789

fund in existence since 6/15/93

PERFORMANCE

	3yr Annual	5yr Annual	10yr Annual	Bull	Bear
Return (%)	na	na	na	na	na
Differ from Category (+/-)	na	na	na	na	na

Total Risk	Standard Deviation	Category Risk	Risk Index	Beta
na	na	na	na	na

	1993	1992	1991	1990	1989	1988	1987	1986	1985	1984
Return (%)	—	—	—	—	—	—	—	—	—	—
Differ from category (+/-)	—	—	—	—	—	—	—	—	—	—

PER SHARE DATA

	1993	1992	1991	1990	1989	1988	1987	1986	1985	1984
Dividends, Net Income ($) .	0.00	—	—	—	—	—	—	—	—	—
Distrib'ns, Cap Gain ($) . . .	0.00	—	—	—	—	—	—	—	—	—
Net Asset Value ($)	11.54	—	—	—	—	—	—	—	—	—
Expense Ratio (%)	1.75	—	—	—	—	—	—	—	—	—
Net Income to Assets (%) .	0.44	—	—	—	—	—	—	—	—	—
Portfolio Turnover (%).	0	—	—	—	—	—	—	—	—	—
Total Assets (Millions $). . . .	154	—	—	—	—	—	—	—	—	—

PORTFOLIO (as of 9/30/93)

Portfolio Manager: Browne - 1993, Spears - 1993, McClark, Jr. - 1993

Investm't Category: International Stock

- ✔ Cap Gain
- Cap & Income
- Income
- ✔ Domestic
- ✔ Foreign
- Country/Region
- Asset Allocation
- Fund of Funds
- Index
- Sector
- ✔ Small Cap
- Socially Conscious
- State Specific

Portfolio: stocks 85%   bonds 0%
convertibles 0%   other 0%   cash 15%

Largest Holdings: Switzerland 23%, Netherlands 16%

Unrealized Net Capital Gains: 3% of portfolio value

SHAREHOLDER INFORMATION

Minimum Investment
Initial: $2,500   Subsequent: $500

Minimum IRA Investment
Initial: $500   Subsequent: $500

Maximum Fees
Load: none   12b-1: none
Other: none

Distributions
Income: Dec   Capital Gains: Dec

Exchange Options
Number Per Year: no limit   Fee: none
Telephone: yes (money market fund not available)

Services
IRA, other pension

Twentieth Century Balanced (TWBIX)

Balanced

4500 Main St.
P.O. Box 419200
Kansas City, MO 64141
(800) 345-2021, (816) 531-5575

PERFORMANCE

	3yr Annual	5yr Annual	10yr Annual	Bull	Bear
Return (%)	13.9	13.6	na	58.0	-4.6
Differ from Category (+/-)	-1.1 blw av	1.5 abv av	na	-3.6 blw av	1.2 abv av

Total Risk	Standard Deviation	Category Risk	Risk Index	Beta
abv av	11.5%	high	1.8	0.9

	1993	1992	1991	1990	1989	1988	1987	1986	1985	1984
Return (%)	7.2	-6.0	46.8	1.8	25.6	—	—	—	—	—
Differ from category (+/-) . .	-6.2	-14.1	22.9	2.3	8.0	—	—	—	—	—

PER SHARE DATA

	1993	1992	1991	1990	1989	1988	1987	1986	1985	1984
Dividends, Net Income ($) .	0.37	0.34	0.35	0.41	0.42	—	—	—	—	—
Distrib'ns, Cap Gain ($) . . .	0.00	0.00	0.00	0.00	0.31	—	—	—	—	—
Net Asset Value ($)	16.00	15.28	16.64	11.62	11.83	—	—	—	—	—
Expense Ratio (%)	1.00	1.00	1.00	1.00	1.00	—	—	—	—	—
Net Income to Assets (%) . .	2.40	2.40	3.10	3.80	4.20	—	—	—	—	—
Portfolio Turnover (%)	95	100	116	104	171	—	—	—	—	—
Total Assets (Millions $) . . .	687	654	255	66	30	—	—	—	—	—

PORTFOLIO (as of 10/31/93)

Portfolio Manager: committee

Investm't Category: Balanced

Cap Gain	Asset Allocation
✔ Cap & Income	Fund of Funds
Income	Index
	Sector
✔ Domestic	Small Cap
✔ Foreign	Socially Conscious
Country/Region	State Specific

Portfolio: stocks 59%   bonds 39%
convertibles 0%   other 0%   cash 2%

Largest Holdings: stocks—communications services 14%, bonds—mortgaged-backed 10%

Unrealized Net Capital Gains: 16% of portfolio value

SHAREHOLDER INFORMATION

Minimum Investment
Initial: $0   Subsequent: $25

Minimum IRA Investment
Initial: $0   Subsequent: $25

Maximum Fees
Load: none   12b-1: none
Other: none

Distributions
Income: quarterly   Capital Gains: Dec

Exchange Options
Number Per Year: 4   Fee: none
Telephone: yes (money market fund available)

Services
IRA, other pension, auto exchange, auto invest, auto withdraw

Twentieth Century Giftrust (TWGTX)

Aggressive Growth

4500 Main St.
P.O. Box 419200
Kansas City, MO 64141
(800) 345-2021, (816) 531-5575

PERFORMANCE

	3yr Annual	5yr Annual	10yr Annual	Bull	Bear
Return (%)	42.0	29.0	22.0	210.3 ·	-23.3
Differ from Category (+/-)	16.6 high	10.8 high	10.1 high	85.4 high	-8.3 low

Total Risk	Standard Deviation	Category Risk	Risk Index	Beta
high	23.4%	high	1.5	1.6

	1993	1992	1991	1990	1989	1988	1987	1986	1985	1984
Return (%)	31.4	17.9	84.9	-16.9	50.2	11.0	8.6	28.0	55.4	-14.2
Differ from category (+/-)	12.4	7.5	32.5	-10.6	23.2	-4.2	12.0	18.6	24.4	-4.8

PER SHARE DATA

	1993	1992	1991	1990	1989	1988	1987	1986	1985	1984
Dividends, Net Income ($)	0.00	0.00	0.00	0.00	0.00	0.00	0.00	0.00	0.02	0.00
Distrib'ns, Cap Gain ($)	1.91	1.43	0.69	0.02	0.92	0.20	0.85	1.42	0.00	0.00
Net Asset Value ($)	17.53	14.86	13.85	7.88	9.52	6.97	6.47	6.75	6.40	4.14
Expense Ratio (%)	1.00	1.00	1.00	1.00	1.00	1.00	1.00	1.01	1.01	1.01
Net Income to Assets (%)	-0.70	-0.70	-0.60	-0.60	-0.50	-0.10	-0.50	-0.40	-0.30	0.90
Portfolio Turnover (%)	143	134	143	137	160	157	130	123	134	135
Total Assets (Millions $)	163	77	55	25	23	13	10	7	3	1

PORTFOLIO (as of 10/30/93)

Portfolio Manager: committee

Investm't Category: Aggressive Growth
✔ Cap Gain   Asset Allocation
  Cap & Income   Fund of Funds
  Income   Index
             Sector
✔ Domestic   ✔ Small Cap
✔ Foreign   Socially Conscious
  Country/Region   State Specific

Portfolio: stocks 95%   bonds 0%
convertibles 0%   other 0%   cash 5%

Largest Holdings: electrical & electronic components 12%, retail 11%

Unrealized Net Capital Gains: 32% of portfolio value

SHAREHOLDER INFORMATION

Minimum Investment
Initial: $250   Subsequent: $25

Minimum IRA Investment
Initial: na   Subsequent: na

Maximum Fees
Load: none   12b-1: none
Other: none

Distributions
Income: Dec   Capital Gains: Dec

Exchange Options
Number Per Year: none   Fee: none
Telephone: none

Services
auto invest

Twentieth Century Growth (TWCGX)

Aggressive Growth

4500 Main St.
P.O. Box 419200
Kansas City, MO 64141
(800) 345-2021, (816) 531-5575

PERFORMANCE

	3yr Annual	5yr Annual	10yr Annual	Bull	Bear
Return (%)	18.8	18.2	14.2	80.2	-10.5
Differ from Category (+/-)	-6.6 low	0.0 av	2.3 abv av	-44.8 low	4.5 abv av

Total Risk	Standard Deviation	Category Risk	Risk Index	Beta
high	17.7%	abv av	1.2	1.4

	1993	1992	1991	1990	1989	1988	1987	1986	1985	1984
Return (%)	3.7	-4.2	69.0	-3.8	43.1	2.7	13.1	18.8	33.9	-11.0
Differ from category (+/-)	-15.3	-14.6	16.6	2.5	16.1	-12.5	16.5	9.4	2.9	-1.6

PER SHARE DATA

	1993	1992	1991	1990	1989	1988	1987	1986	1985	1984
Dividends, Net Income ($)	0.05	0.00	0.01	0.11	0.07	0.31	0.13	0.18	0.15	0.05
Distrib'ns, Cap Gain ($)	2.76	0.36	0.00	0.89	0.59	0.00	3.46	5.07	0.00	1.84
Net Asset Value ($)	22.40	24.36	25.83	15.29	16.95	12.31	12.30	14.06	16.21	12.25
Expense Ratio (%)	1.00	1.00	1.00	1.00	1.00	1.00	1.00	1.01	1.01	1.01
Net Income to Assets (%)	0.20	-0.10	0.20	0.60	0.50	2.40	0.20	0.60	1.30	1.40
Portfolio Turnover (%)	94	53	69	118	98	143	114	105	116	132
Total Assets (Millions $)	4,538	4,473	3,193	1,697	1,597	1,228	1,188	964	759	678

PORTFOLIO (as of 10/31/93)

Portfolio Manager: committee

Investm't Category: Aggressive Growth

✔ Cap Gain	Asset Allocation
Cap & Income	Fund of Funds
Income	Index
	Sector
✔ Domestic	Small Cap
✔ Foreign	Socially Conscious
Country/Region	State Specific

Portfolio: stocks 97%   bonds 0%
convertibles 0%   other 0%   cash 3%

Largest Holdings: electrical & electronic components 12%, communications

Unrealized Net Capital Gains: 23% of portfolio value

SHAREHOLDER INFORMATION

Minimum Investment
Initial: $0   Subsequent: $25

Minimum IRA Investment
Initial: $0   Subsequent: $25

Maximum Fees
Load: none   12b-1: none
Other: none

Distributions
Income: Dec   Capital Gains: Dec

Exchange Options
Number Per Year: 4   Fee: none
Telephone: yes (money market fund available)

Services
IRA, other pension, auto exchange, auto invest, auto withdraw

Twentieth Century Heritage (TWHIX)

Growth

4500 Main St.
P.O. Box 419200
Kansas City, MO 64141
(800) 345-2021, (816) 531-5575

PERFORMANCE

	3yr Annual	5yr Annual	10yr Annual	Bull	Bear
Return (%)	21.7	17.2	na	88.2	-12.9
Differ from Category (+/-)	2.5 abv av	2.6 abv av	na	3.5 av	-0.5 av

Total Risk	Standard Deviation	Category Risk	Risk Index	Beta
high	14.2%	high	1.3	1.1

	1993	1992	1991	1990	1989	1988	1987	1986	1985	1984
Return (%).............	20.4	10.1	35.9	-9.1	34.9	16.4	—	—	—	—
Differ from category (+/-)...	7.2	-0.8	0.5	-3.0	9.1	-1.3	—	—	—	—

PER SHARE DATA

	1993	1992	1991	1990	1989	1988	1987	1986	1985	1984
Dividends, Net Income ($).	0.06	0.09	0.11	0.11	0.06	0.06	—	—	—	—
Distrib'ns, Cap Gain ($) ...	0.50	0.67	0.00	0.00	0.69	0.00	—	—	—	—
Net Asset Value ($)	10.61	9.31	9.17	6.83	7.64	6.22	—	—	—	—
Expense Ratio (%)	1.00	1.00	1.00	1.00	1.00	1.00	—	—	—	—
Net Income to Assets (%) .	0.70	1.10	1.50	1.60	1.30	1.40	—	—	—	—
Portfolio Turnover (%).....	116	119	146	127	159	130	—	—	—	—
Total Assets (Millions $)....	725	369	269	199	117	55	—	—	—	—

PORTFOLIO (as of 10/31/93)

Portfolio Manager: committee

Investm't Category: Growth

✔ Cap Gain   Asset Allocation
   Cap & Income   Fund of Funds
   Income   Index
    Sector
✔ Domestic   Small Cap
✔ Foreign   Socially Conscious
   Country/Region   State Specific

Portfolio: stocks 96%   bonds 0%
convertibles 0%   other 0%   cash 4%

Largest Holdings: transportation 10%, energy (production & marketing) 9%

Unrealized Net Capital Gains: 19% of portfolio value

SHAREHOLDER INFORMATION

Minimum Investment
Initial: $0   Subsequent: $25

Minimum IRA Investment
Initial: $0   Subsequent: $25

Maximum Fees
Load: none   12b-1: none
Other: none

Distributions
Income: Dec   Capital Gains: Dec

Exchange Options
Number Per Year: 4   Fee: none
Telephone: yes (money market fund available)

Services
IRA, other pension, auto exchange, auto invest, auto withdraw

Twentieth Century International Equity

(TWIEX) *International Stock*

4500 Main St.
P.O. Box 419200
Kansas City, MO 64141
(800) 345-2021, (816) 531-5575

PERFORMANCE

	3yr Annual	5yr Annual	10yr Annual	Bull	Bear
Return (%)	na	na	na	na	na
Differ from Category (+/-)	na	na	na	na	na

Total Risk	Standard Deviation	Category Risk	Risk Index	Beta
na	na	na	na	na

	1993	1992	1991	1990	1989	1988	1987	1986	1985	1984
Return (%)	42.6	4.8	—	—	—	—	—	—	—	—
Differ from category (+/-)	4.1	8.3	—	—	—	—	—	—	—	—

PER SHARE DATA

	1993	1992	1991	1990	1989	1988	1987	1986	1985	1984
Dividends, Net Income ($)	0.00	0.19	—	—	—	—	—	—	—	—
Distrib'ns, Cap Gain ($)	0.40	0.00	—	—	—	—	—	—	—	—
Net Asset Value ($)	7.70	5.69	—	—	—	—	—	—	—	—
Expense Ratio (%)	1.90	1.91	—	—	—	—	—	—	—	—
Net Income to Assets (%)	0.25	0.95	—	—	—	—	—	—	—	—
Portfolio Turnover (%)	230	180	—	—	—	—	—	—	—	—
Total Assets (Millions $)	1,023	215	—	—	—	—	—	—	—	—

PORTFOLIO (as of 5/31/93)

Portfolio Manager: Mark Kopinski - 1991, Ted Tyson - 1991

Investm't Category: International Stock

✔ Cap Gain	Asset Allocation
Cap & Income	Fund of Funds
Income	Index
	Sector
Domestic	Small Cap
✔ Foreign	Socially Conscious
Country/Region	State Specific

Portfolio: stocks 90% bonds 5%
convertibles 1% other 1% cash 3%

Largest Holdings: Japan 16%, United Kingdom 11%

Unrealized Net Capital Gains: 9% of portfolio value

SHAREHOLDER INFORMATION

Minimum Investment
Initial: $0   Subsequent: $25

Minimum IRA Investment
Initial: $0   Subsequent: $25

Maximum Fees
Load: none   12b-1: none
Other: none

Distributions
Income: Dec   Capital Gains: Dec

Exchange Options
Number Per Year: 4   Fee: none
Telephone: yes (money market fund available)

Services
IRA, other pension, auto exchange, auto invest, auto withdraw

Twentieth Century Long-Term Bond (TWLBX)

General Bond

4500 Main St.
P.O. Box 419200
Kansas City, MO 64141
(800) 345-2021, (816) 531-5575

PERFORMANCE

	3yr Annual	5yr Annual	10yr Annual	Bull	Bear
Return (%)	10.9	10.5	na	45.4	-0.4
Differ from Category (+/-)	0.6 av	0.6 abv av	na	6.0 abv av	-3.3 low

Total Risk	Standard Deviation	Category Risk	Risk Index	Avg Mat
blw av	4.2%	high	1.5	8.6 yrs

	1993	1992	1991	1990	1989	1988	1987	1986	1985	1984
Return (%).	9.9	5.6	17.4	6.0	13.9	8.3	—	—	—	—
Differ from category (+/-). . .	0.6	-1.1	2.8	-0.8	2.6	0.6	—	—	—	—

PER SHARE DATA

	1993	1992	1991	1990	1989	1988	1987	1986	1985	1984
Dividends, Net Income ($).	0.60	0.63	0.72	0.79	0.82	0.83	—	—	—	—
Distrib'ns, Cap Gain ($) . . .	0.18	0.15	0.00	0.00	0.00	0.00	—	—	—	—
Net Asset Value ($)	9.88	9.72	9.98	9.17	9.45	9.06	—	—	—	—
Expense Ratio (%)	1.00	0.98	0.96	1.00	1.00	1.00	—	—	—	—
Net Income to Assets (%) .	6.54	6.30	8.06	8.81	8.83	9.15	—	—	—	—
Portfolio Turnover (%).	113	186	219	98	216	280	—	—	—	—
Total Assets (Millions $). . . .	157	154	114	77	62	26	—	—	—	—

PORTFOLIO (as of 10/31/93)

Portfolio Manager: Charles M. Duboc - 1987, Bud Hoops - 1989

Investm't Category: General Bond

Cap Gain	Asset Allocation
Cap & Income	Fund of Funds
✔ Income	Index
	Sector
✔ Domestic	Small Cap
✔ Foreign	Socially Conscious
Country/Region	State Specific

Portfolio: stocks 0% bonds 98%
convertibles 0% other 0% cash 2%

Largest Holdings: corporate 52%, mortgage-backed 17%

Unrealized Net Capital Gains: 5% of portfolio value

SHAREHOLDER INFORMATION

Minimum Investment
Initial: $0   Subsequent: $25

Minimum IRA Investment
Initial: $0   Subsequent: $25

Maximum Fees
Load: none   12b-1: none
Other: none

Distributions
Income: monthly   Capital Gains: Dec

Exchange Options
Number Per Year: 4   Fee: none
Telephone: yes (money market fund available)

Services
IRA, other pension, auto exchange, auto invest, auto withdraw

Twentieth Century Select (TWCIX)

4500 Main St.
P.O. Box 419200
Kansas City, MO 64141
(800) 345-2021, (816) 531-5575

Growth

PERFORMANCE

	3yr Annual	5yr Annual	10yr Annual	Bull	Bear
Return (%)	12.9	14.8	12.7	54.2	-6.9
Differ from Category (+/-)	-6.3 low	0.2 av	0.1 av	-30.5 low	5.5 abv av

Total Risk	Standard Deviation	Category Risk	Risk Index	Beta
abv av	12.8%	abv av	1.2	1.1

	1993	1992	1991	1990	1989	1988	1987	1986	1985	1984
Return (%)	14.6	-4.4	31.5	-0.4	39.5	5.6	5.6	20.5	33.9	-7.6
Differ from category (+/-) ...	1.4	-15.4	-3.9	5.7	13.7	-12.1	4.4	6.0	4.6	-7.6

PER SHARE DATA

	1993	1992	1991	1990	1989	1988	1987	1986	1985	1984
Dividends, Net Income ($) .	0.43	0.49	0.65	0.65	1.11	0.70	0.86	0.51	0.46	0.13
Distrib'ns, Cap Gain ($) ...	4.46	1.32	1.82	1.55	0.00	0.00	6.36	3.46	0.00	0.68
Net Asset Value ($)	39.46	38.72	42.40	34.14	36.51	26.98	26.22	31.61	29.56	22.53
Expense Ratio (%)........	1.00	1.00	1.00	1.00	1.00	1.00	1.00	1.01	1.01	1.01
Net Income to Assets (%)..	1.10	1.40	1.70	1.80	3.40	2.20	1.10	1.60	2.50	2.40
Portfolio Turnover (%)	82	95	84	83	93	140	123	85	119	112
Total Assets (Millions $) ..	4,908	4,535	4,163	2,953	2,721	2,367	2,417	1,978	1,143	840

PORTFOLIO (as of 10/31/93)

Portfolio Manager: committee

Investm't Category: Growth
✔ Cap Gain	Asset Allocation
Cap & Income	Fund of Funds
Income	Index
	Sector
✔ Domestic	Small Cap
✔ Foreign	Socially Conscious
Country/Region	State Specific

Portfolio: stocks 95% bonds 0%
convertibles 0% other 0% cash 5%

Largest Holdings: communications services 16%, energy (production & marketing) 12%

Unrealized Net Capital Gains: 22% of portfolio value

SHAREHOLDER INFORMATION

Minimum Investment
Initial: $0   Subsequent: $25

Minimum IRA Investment
Initial: $0   Subsequent: $25

Maximum Fees
Load: none   12b-1: none
Other: none

Distributions
Income: Dec   Capital Gains: Dec

Exchange Options
Number Per Year: 4   Fee: none
Telephone: yes (money market fund available)

Services
IRA, other pension, auto exchange, auto invest, auto withdraw

Twentieth Century Tax-Exempt Interm (TWTIX)

Tax-Exempt Bond

4500 Main St.
P.O. Box 419200
Kansas City, MO 64141
(800) 345-2021, (816) 531-5575

PERFORMANCE

	3yr Annual	5yr Annual	10yr Annual	Bull	Bear
Return (%)	8.7	7.8	na	32.4	3.0
Differ from Category (+/-)	-1.6 low	-1.4 low	na	-7.7 low	0.6 abv av

Total Risk	Standard Deviation	Category Risk	Risk Index	Avg Mat
low	2.8%	low	0.7	3.9 yrs

	1993	1992	1991	1990	1989	1988	1987	1986	1985	1984
Return (%)	8.9	7.1	10.0	6.2	6.6	5.9	—	—	—	—
Differ from category (+/-)	-2.7	-1.2	-1.3	-0.1	-2.4	-4.2	—	—	—	—

PER SHARE DATA

	1993	1992	1991	1990	1989	1988	1987	1986	1985	1984
Dividends, Net Income ($)	0.47	0.46	0.52	0.56	0.56	0.54	—	—	—	—
Distrib'ns, Cap Gain ($)	0.13	0.07	0.00	0.00	0.00	0.00	—	—	—	—
Net Asset Value ($)	10.66	10.35	10.19	9.76	9.73	9.66	—	—	—	—
Expense Ratio (%)	0.72	0.98	0.96	1.00	1.00	1.00	—	—	—	—
Net Income to Assets (%)	4.51	4.68	5.40	5.80	5.79	5.57	—	—	—	—
Portfolio Turnover (%)	38	36	62	102	74	86	—	—	—	—
Total Assets (Millions $)	96	77	45	26	21	14	—	—	—	—

PORTFOLIO (as of 10/31/93)

Portfolio Manager: committee

Investm't Category: Tax-Exempt Bond

Cap Gain	Asset Allocation
Cap & Income	Fund of Funds
✔ Income	Index
	Sector
✔ Domestic	Small Cap
Foreign	Socially Conscious
Country/Region	State Specific

Portfolio:	stocks 0%	bonds 95%
convertibles 0%	other 0%	cash 5%

Largest Holdings: general obligation 11%

Unrealized Net Capital Gains: 5% of portfolio value

SHAREHOLDER INFORMATION

Minimum Investment
Initial: $10,000   Subsequent: $25

Minimum IRA Investment
Initial: na   Subsequent: na

Maximum Fees
Load: none   12b-1: none
Other: none

Distributions
Income: monthly   Capital Gains: Dec

Exchange Options
Number Per Year: no limit   Fee: none
Telephone: yes (money market fund available)

Services
auto exchange, auto invest, auto withdraw

Twentieth Century Tax-Exempt Long (TWTLX)

Tax-Exempt Bond

4500 Main St.
P.O. Box 419200
Kansas City, MO 64141
(800) 345-2021, (816) 531-5575

PERFORMANCE

	3yr Annual	5yr Annual	10yr Annual	Bull	Bear
Return (%)	10.5	9.4	na	42.2	0.8
Differ from Category (+/-)	0.2 blw av	0.2 av	na	2.1 av	-1.5 low

Total Risk	Standard Deviation	Category Risk	Risk Index	Avg Mat
blw av	4.3%	av	1.1	15.0 yrs

	1993	1992	1991	1990	1989	1988	1987	1986	1985	1984
Return (%)	12.0	7.7	12.0	6.1	9.5	10.3	—	—	—	—
Differ from category (+/-) . . .	0.4	-0.6	0.6	-0.2	0.5	0.2	—	—	—	—

PER SHARE DATA

	1993	1992	1991	1990	1989	1988	1987	1986	1985	1984
Dividends, Net Income ($) .	0.52	0.53	0.56	0.60	0.62	0.60	—	—	—	—
Distrib'ns, Cap Gain ($) . . .	0.34	0.16	0.08	0.00	0.09	0.00	—	—	—	—
Net Asset Value ($)	10.80	10.43	10.35	9.86	9.88	9.70	—	—	—	—
Expense Ratio (%).	0.73	0.98	0.96	1.00	1.00	1.00	—	—	—	—
Net Income to Assets (%) . .	4.90	5.07	5.73	6.22	6.36	6.43	—	—	—	—
Portfolio Turnover (%)	81	88	110	144	120	215	—	—	—	—
Total Assets (Millions $)	67	62	39	28	20	12	—	—	—	—

PORTFOLIO (as of 10/31/93)

Portfolio Manager: committee

Investm't Category: Tax-Exempt Bond

Cap Gain	Asset Allocation
Cap & Income	Fund of Funds
✔ Income	Index
	Sector
✔ Domestic	Small Cap
Foreign	Socially Conscious
Country/Region	State Specific

Portfolio: stocks 0%   bonds 94%
convertibles 0%   other 0%   cash 6%

Largest Holdings: general obligation 13%

Unrealized Net Capital Gains: 6% of portfolio value

SHAREHOLDER INFORMATION

Minimum Investment
Initial: $10,000   Subsequent: $25

Minimum IRA Investment
Initial: na   Subsequent: na

Maximum Fees
Load: none   12b-1: none
Other: none

Distributions
Income: monthly   Capital Gains: Dec

Exchange Options
Number Per Year: no limit   Fee: none
Telephone: yes (money market fund available)

Services
auto exchange, auto invest, auto withdraw

Twentieth Century Tax-Exempt Short (TWTSX)

Tax-Exempt Bond

4500 Main St.
P.O. Box 419200
Kansas City, MO 64141
(800) 345-2021, (816) 531-5575

fund in existence since 3/1/93

PERFORMANCE

	3yr Annual	5yr Annual	10yr Annual	Bull	Bear
Return (%)	na	na	na	na	na
Differ from Category (+/-)	na	na	na	na	na

Total Risk	Standard Deviation	Category Risk	Risk Index	Avg Mat
na	na	na	na	1.3 yrs

	1993	1992	1991	1990	1989	1988	1987	1986	1985	1984
Return (%).	—	—	—	—	—	—	—	—	—	—
Differ from category (+/-). . . .	—	—	—	—	—	—	—	—	—	—

PER SHARE DATA

	1993	1992	1991	1990	1989	1988	1987	1986	1985	1984
Dividends, Net Income ($).	0.27	—	—	—	—	—	—	—	—	—
Distrib'ns, Cap Gain ($) . . .	0.00	—	—	—	—	—	—	—	—	—
Net Asset Value ($)	10.06	—	—	—	—	—	—	—	—	—
Expense Ratio (%)	0.00	—	—	—	—	—	—	—	—	—
Net Income to Assets (%) .	3.09	—	—	—	—	—	—	—	—	—
Portfolio Turnover (%).	3	—	—	—	—	—	—	—	—	—
Total Assets (Millions $). . . .	54	—	—	—	—	—	—	—	—	—

PORTFOLIO (as of 10/31/93)

Portfolio Manager: Robert Gahagn - 1986, Laurie Kirby - 1987, Bud Hoops - 1989

Investm't Category: Tax-Exempt Bond
  Cap Gain   Asset Allocation
  Cap & Income   Fund of Funds
✔ Income   Index
               Sector
✔ Domestic   Small Cap
  Foreign   Socially Conscious
  Country/Region   State Specific

Portfolio: stocks 0%   bonds 95%
convertibles 0%   other 0%   cash 5%

Largest Holdings: general obligation 21%

Unrealized Net Capital Gains: 0% of portfolio value

SHAREHOLDER INFORMATION

Minimum Investment
Initial: $10,000   Subsequent: $25

Minimum IRA Investment
Initial: na   Subsequent: na

Maximum Fees
Load: none   12b-1: none
Other: none

Distributions
Income: monthly   Capital Gains: Dec

Exchange Options
Number Per Year: 4   Fee: none
Telephone: yes (money market fund available)

Services
auto exchange, auto invest, auto withdraw

Twentieth Century Ultra
(TWCUX)
Aggressive Growth

4500 Main St.
P.O. Box 419200
Kansas City, MO 64141
(800) 345-2021, (816) 531-5575

PERFORMANCE

	3yr Annual	5yr Annual	10yr Annual	Bull	Bear
Return (%)	32.0	28.0	16.6	170.2	-6.9
Differ from Category (+/-)	6.6 abv av	9.8 high	4.7 high	45.2 abv av	8.1 high

Total Risk	Standard Deviation	Category Risk	Risk Index	Beta
high	23.4%	high	1.5	1.6

	1993	1992	1991	1990	1989	1988	1987	1986	1985	1984
Return (%)	21.8	1.2	86.4	9.3	36.9	13.3	6.6	10.2	26.1	-19.3
Differ from category (+/-) ...	2.8	-9.2	34.0	15.6	9.9	-1.9	10.0	0.8	-4.9	-9.9

PER SHARE DATA

	1993	1992	1991	1990	1989	1988	1987	1986	1985	1984
Dividends, Net Income ($) .	0.00	0.00	0.00	0.00	0.19	0.00	0.00	0.00	0.00	0.00
Distrib'ns, Cap Gain ($) ...	0.00	0.00	0.00	0.02	0.94	0.00	3.25	0.00	0.00	0.25
Net Asset Value ($)	21.39	17.56	17.34	9.30	8.53	7.06	6.23	8.92	8.10	6.42
Expense Ratio (%)........	1.00	1.00	1.00	1.00	1.00	1.00	1.00	1.01	1.01	1.01
Net Income to Assets (%) .	-0.60	-0.40	-0.50	-0.30	2.21	-0.30	-0.50	na	0.10	-0.30
Portfolio Turnover (%)	53	59	42	141	132	140	137	99	100	93
Total Assets (Millions $) ..	8,353	4,275	2,148	330	347	259	236	314	385	445

PORTFOLIO (as of 10/31/93)

Portfolio Manager: committee

Investm't Category: Aggressive Growth
✔ Cap Gain   Asset Allocation
  Cap & Income   Fund of Funds
  Income   Index
                    Sector
✔ Domestic   ✔ Small Cap
✔ Foreign   Socially Conscious
  Country/Region   State Specific

Portfolio: stocks 89%   bonds 0%
convertibles 0%   other 0%   cash 11%

Largest Holdings: computer software & services 12%, communications equipment 12%

Unrealized Net Capital Gains: 34% of portfolio value

SHAREHOLDER INFORMATION

Minimum Investment
Initial: $0   Subsequent: $25

Minimum IRA Investment
Initial: $0   Subsequent: $25

Maximum Fees
Load: none   12b-1: none
Other: none

Distributions
Income: Dec   Capital Gains: Dec

Exchange Options
Number Per Year: 4   Fee: none
Telephone: yes (money market fund available)

Services
IRA, other pension, auto exchange, auto invest, auto withdraw

Twentieth Century US Gov'ts (TWUSX)

Government Bond

4500 Main St.
P.O. Box 419200
Kansas City, MO 64141
(800) 345-2021, (816) 531-5575

PERFORMANCE

	3yr Annual	5yr Annual	10yr Annual	Bull	Bear
Return (%)	6.6	7.5	8.1	25.4	4.0
Differ from Category (+/-)	-4.2 low	-2.9 low	-1.6 low	-20.8 low	3.5 abv av

Total Risk	Standard Deviation	Category Risk	Risk Index	Avg Mat
low	2.0%	low	0.4	2.1 yrs

	1993	1992	1991	1990	1989	1988	1987	1986	1985	1984
Return (%).	4.1	4.4	11.6	7.5	9.9	5.6	3.8	9.8	12.9	12.3
Differ from category (+/-). . .	-6.3	-1.8	-3.4	1.0	-4.0	-2.0	5.6	-9.3	-6.2	-0.6

PER SHARE DATA

	1993	1992	1991	1990	1989	1988	1987	1986	1985	1984
Dividends, Net Income ($)	0.33	0.42	0.59	0.78	0.82	0.81	0.79	0.84	0.98	1.02
Distrib'ns, Cap Gain ($) . . .	0.00	0.00	0.00	0.00	0.00	0.00	0.12	0.05	0.00	0.00
Net Asset Value ($)	9.65	9.59	9.60	9.17	9.29	9.23	9.53	10.09	10.04	9.81
Expense Ratio (%)	1.00	0.99	0.99	1.00	1.00	1.00	1.00	1.01	1.01	1.01
Net Income to Assets (%) .	3.73	4.62	6.88	8.64	9.10	8.60	8.10	8.54	10.10	10.72
Portfolio Turnover (%).	413	391	779	620	567	578	468	464	573	352
Total Assets (Millions $). . . .	489	569	535	456	444	440	336	254	98	58

PORTFOLIO (as of 10/31/93)

Portfolio Manager: committee

Investm't Category: Government Bond

Cap Gain	Asset Allocation
Cap & Income	Fund of Funds
✔ Income	Index
	Sector
✔ Domestic	Small Cap
Foreign	Socially Conscious
Country/Region	State Specific

Portfolio: stocks 0% bonds 99%
convertibles 0% other 0% cash 1%

Largest Holdings: U. S. government & agencies 75%, mortgage-backed 24%

Unrealized Net Capital Gains: 0% of portfolio value

SHAREHOLDER INFORMATION

Minimum Investment
Initial: $0   Subsequent: $25

Minimum IRA Investment
Initial: $0   Subsequent: $25

Maximum Fees
Load: none   12b-1: none
Other: none

Distributions
Income: monthly   Capital Gains: Dec

Exchange Options
Number Per Year: 4   Fee: none
Telephone: yes (money market fund available)

Services
IRA, other pension, auto exchange, auto invest, auto withdraw

Twentieth Century Vista
(TWCVX)
Aggressive Growth

4500 Main St.
P.O. Box 419200
Kansas City, MO 64141
(800) 345-2021, (816) 531-5575

PERFORMANCE

	3yr Annual	5yr Annual	10yr Annual	Bull	Bear
Return (%)	21.4	18.1	12.4	94.3	-22.2
Differ from Category (+/-)	-4.0 blw av	-0.1 av	0.5 av	-30.7 blw av	-7.2 blw av

Total Risk	Standard Deviation	Category Risk	Risk Index	Beta
high	20.7%	abv av	1.4	1.5

	1993	1992	1991	1990	1989	1988	1987	1986	1985	1984
Return (%)	5.4	-2.1	73.6	-15.7	52.1	2.4	6.0	26.3	22.5	-16.2
Differ from category (+/-) .	-13.6	-12.5	21.2	-9.4	25.1	-12.8	9.4	16.9	-8.5	-6.8

PER SHARE DATA

	1993	1992	1991	1990	1989	1988	1987	1986	1985	1984
Dividends, Net Income ($) .	0.00	0.00	0.00	0.00	0.00	0.01	0.00	0.00	0.00	0.00
Distrib'ns, Cap Gain ($) ...	1.67	0.64	0.00	0.00	0.69	0.00	0.46	0.65	0.00	0.00
Net Asset Value ($)	10.27	11.35	12.28	7.07	8.39	5.97	5.84	5.95	5.22	4.27
Expense Ratio (%)........	1.00	1.00	1.00	1.00	1.00	1.00	1.00	1.01	1.01	1.01
Net Income to Assets (%) .	-0.60	-0.40	-0.30	-0.10	-0.40	0.20	-0.70	-0.30	-0.20	0.40
Portfolio Turnover (%)	133	87	92	103	125	145	123	121	174	97
Total Assets (Millions $) ...	786	830	622	340	264	206	187	159	146	105

PORTFOLIO (as of 10/31/93)

Portfolio Manager: committee

Investm't Category: Aggressive Growth

✔ Cap Gain
Cap & Income
Income

Asset Allocation
Fund of Funds
Index
Sector
✔ Small Cap
Socially Conscious
State Specific

✔ Domestic
✔ Foreign
Country/Region

Portfolio: stocks 98% bonds 0%
convertibles 0% other 0% cash 2%

Largest Holdings: computer software & services 17%, communications equipment 11%

Unrealized Net Capital Gains: 23% of portfolio value

SHAREHOLDER INFORMATION

Minimum Investment
Initial: $0 Subsequent: $25

Minimum IRA Investment
Initial: $0 Subsequent: $25

Maximum Fees
Load: none 12b-1: none
Other: none

Distributions
Income: Dec Capital Gains: Dec

Exchange Options
Number Per Year: 4 Fee: none
Telephone: yes (money market fund available)

Services
IRA, other pension, auto exchange, auto invest, auto withdraw

UMB Bond (UMBBX)

General Bond

Three Crown Center
2440 Pershing Rd., #G-15
Kansas City, MO 64108
(800) 422-2766, (816) 471-5200

PERFORMANCE

	3yr Annual	5yr Annual	10yr Annual	Bull	Bear
Return (%)	9.3	9.4	9.9	34.4	5.0
Differ from Category (+/-)	-0.8 blw av	-0.4 blw av	-1.0 low	-5.0 blw av	2.1 abv av

Total Risk	Standard Deviation	Category Risk	Risk Index	Avg Mat
low	2.6%	blw av	0.9	na

	1993	1992	1991	1990	1989	1988	1987	1986	1985	1984
Return (%)	8.3	6.5	13.2	8.0	11.3	5.8	2.9	12.4	18.3	13.4
Differ from category (+/-). . .	-0.8	-0.2	-1.4	1.1	0.0	-1.8	0.4	-1.5	-1.8	1.1

PER SHARE DATA

	1993	1992	1991	1990	1989	1988	1987	1986	1985	1984
Dividends, Net Income ($).	0.63	0.71	0.71	0.78	0.82	0.80	1.25	0.82	0.96	0.44
Distrib'ns, Cap Gain ($) . . .	0.03	0.00	0.00	0.00	0.00	0.02	0.01	0.02	0.23	0.00
Net Asset Value ($)	11.44	11.20	11.19	10.54	10.50	10.19	10.42	11.37	10.94	10.37
Expense Ratio (%)	0.87	0.87	0.87	0.88	0.88	0.87	0.87	0.88	0.88	0.87
Net Income to Assets (%) .	5.95	6.77	7.44	7.61	7.69	7.47	7.36	8.11	9.21	9.85
Portfolio Turnover (%).	19	24	21	13	8	7	12	23	51	0
Total Assets (Millions $). . . .	89	63	43	34	28	30	31	19	10	6

PORTFOLIO (as of 6/30/93)

Portfolio Manager: George Root - 1982

Investm't Category: General Bond

Cap Gain	Asset Allocation
Cap & Income	Fund of Funds
✔ Income	Index
	Sector
✔ Domestic	Small Cap
Foreign	Socially Conscious
Country/Region	State Specific

Portfolio: stocks 0% bonds 93%
convertibles 0% other 0% cash 7%

Largest Holdings: corporate 37%, mortgage-backed 25%

Unrealized Net Capital Gains: 5% of portfolio value

SHAREHOLDER INFORMATION

Minimum Investment
Initial: $1,000   Subsequent: $100

Minimum IRA Investment
Initial: $100   Subsequent: $0

Maximum Fees
Load: none   12b-1: none
Other: none

Distributions
Income: monthly   Capital Gains: Jun, Dec

Exchange Options
Number Per Year: no limit   Fee: none
Telephone: yes (money market fund available)

Services
IRA, other pension, auto exchange, auto invest, auto withdraw

UMB Heartland Fund

(UMBHX)

Growth

Three Crown Center
2440 Pershing Rd., #G-15
Kansas City, MO 64108
(800) 422-2766, (816) 471-5200

PERFORMANCE

	3yr Annual	5yr Annual	10yr Annual	Bull	Bear
Return (%)	na	na	na	na	na
Differ from Category (+/-)	na	na	na	na	na

Total Risk	Standard Deviation	Category Risk	Risk Index	Beta
na	na	na	na	na

	1993	1992	1991	1990	1989	1988	1987	1986	1985	1984
Return (%)	5.9	10.9	—	—	—	—	—	—	—	—
Differ from category (+/-)	-7.3	-0.1	—	—	—	—	—	—	—	—

PER SHARE DATA

	1993	1992	1991	1990	1989	1988	1987	1986	1985	1984
Dividends, Net Income ($)	0.13	0.11	—	—	—	—	—	—	—	—
Distrib'ns, Cap Gain ($)	0.00	0.00	—	—	—	—	—	—	—	—
Net Asset Value ($)	9.49	9.09	—	—	—	—	—	—	—	—
Expense Ratio (%)	na	1.06	—	—	—	—	—	—	—	—
Net Income to Assets (%)	na	1.91	—	—	—	—	—	—	—	—
Portfolio Turnover (%)	na	7	—	—	—	—	—	—	—	—
Total Assets (Millions $)	25	8	—	—	—	—	—	—	—	—

PORTFOLIO (as of 6/30/93)

Portfolio Manager: David Anderson - 1991

Investm't Category: Growth

✔ Cap Gain	Asset Allocation
Cap & Income	Fund of Funds
Income	Index
	Sector
✔ Domestic	✔ Small Cap
Foreign	Socially Conscious
Country/Region	State Specific

Portfolio: stocks 49% bonds 0%
convertibles 0% other 0% cash 57%

Largest Holdings: consumer cyclical 14%,
consumer staples 14%

Unrealized Net Capital Gains: 0% of portfolio value

SHAREHOLDER INFORMATION

Minimum Investment
Initial: $1,000   Subsequent: $100

Minimum IRA Investment
Initial: $100   Subsequent: $0

Maximum Fees
Load: none   12b-1: none
Other: none

Distributions
Income: Jun, Dec   Capital Gains: Dec

Exchange Options
Number Per Year: no limit   Fee: none
Telephone: yes (money market fund available)

Services
IRA, other pension, auto exchange, auto invest,
auto withdraw

UMB Stock (UMBSX)

Growth & Income

Three Crown Center
2440 Pershing Rd., #G-15
Kansas City, MO 64108
(800) 422-2766, (816) 471-5200

PERFORMANCE

	3yr Annual	5yr Annual	10yr Annual	Bull	Bear
Return (%)	13.9	11.4	11.7	57.5	-8.4
Differ from Category (+/-)	-2.5 blw av	-1.1 blw av	-0.6 blw av	-12.6 blw av	3.2 abv av

Total Risk	Standard Deviation	Category Risk	Risk Index	Beta
av	8.0%	low	0.9	0.7

	1993	1992	1991	1990	1989	1988	1987	1986	1985	1984
Return (%).............	10.6	7.1	24.7	-2.3	19.0	13.8	5.5	12.3	23.1	5.9
Differ from category (+/-)...	-2.0	-2.9	-3.0	3.3	-2.6	-3.0	5.1	-2.9	-2.3	-0.3

PER SHARE DATA

	1993	1992	1991	1990	1989	1988	1987	1986	1985	1984
Dividends, Net Income ($).	0.33	0.38	0.47	0.58	0.58	0.47	0.65	0.50	0.49	0.25
Distrib'ns, Cap Gain ($) ...	0.82	0.31	0.00	0.21	0.52	0.40	1.09	1.01	0.45	0.46
Net Asset Value ($)	16.24	15.77	15.40	12.76	13.87	12.62	11.87	12.78	12.74	11.20
Expense Ratio (%)	0.87	0.86	0.85	0.88	0.87	0.86	0.87	0.87	0.88	0.87
Net Income to Assets (%) .	2.30	2.91	4.03	4.23	4.08	3.41	3.08	3.75	4.36	4.38
Portfolio Turnover (%)......	21	12	8	9	17	33	50	38	65	80
Total Assets (Millions $)....	111	76	53	48	41	43	42	32	18	11

PORTFOLIO (as of 6/30/93)

Portfolio Manager: David Anderson - 1982

Investm't Category: Growth & Income
Cap Gain	Asset Allocation
✔ Cap & Income	Fund of Funds
Income	Index
	Sector
✔ Domestic	Small Cap
Foreign	Socially Conscious
Country/Region	State Specific

Portfolio: stocks 76%   bonds 0%
convertibles 1%   other 0%   cash 23%

Largest Holdings: consumer staples 18%, basic materials 11%

Unrealized Net Capital Gains: 11% of portfolio value

SHAREHOLDER INFORMATION

Minimum Investment
Initial: $1,000   Subsequent: $100

Minimum IRA Investment
Initial: $100   Subsequent: $0

Maximum Fees
Load: none   12b-1: none
Other: none

Distributions
Income: Jun, Dec   Capital Gains: Jun

Exchange Options
Number Per Year: no limit   Fee: none
Telephone: yes (money market fund available)

Services
IRA, other pension, auto exchange, auto invest, auto withdraw

US All American Equity

(GBTFX)

Growth & Income

P.O. Box 659
San Antonio, TX 78293
(800) 873-8637, (210) 308-1222

PERFORMANCE

	3yr Annual	5yr Annual	10yr Annual	Bull	Bear
Return (%)	13.7	8.8	7.7	54.0	-15.2
Differ from Category (+/-)	-2.7 blw av	-3.7 low	-4.7 low	-16.1 blw av	-3.6 blw av

Total Risk	Standard Deviation	Category Risk	Risk Index	Beta
av	10.3%	av	1.2	0.9

	1993	1992	1991	1990	1989	1988	1987	1986	1985	1984
Return (%)	10.0	5.6	26.6	-11.2	16.7	-3.1	0.5	11.2	23.9	2.6
Differ from category (+/-) . .	-2.6	-4.4	-1.1	-5.6	-4.9	-19.9	0.1	-4.0	-1.5	-3.6

PER SHARE DATA

	1993	1992	1991	1990	1989	1988	1987	1986	1985	1984
Dividends, Net Income ($) .	0.46	0.21	0.11	0.31	0.56	0.37	0.57	0.37	0.31	0.34
Distrib'ns, Cap Gain ($) . . .	0.31	0.00	0.00	0.00	0.00	0.00	0.00	0.00	0.00	0.00
Net Asset Value ($)	21.13	19.93	19.08	15.16	17.42	15.41	16.28	16.68	15.32	12.65
Expense Ratio (%)	1.03	2.03	2.80	2.10	1.97	1.43	1.35	1.40	1.50	1.45
Net Income to Assets (%) . .	1.86	0.78	0.83	2.63	2.62	1.68	1.68	1.98	2.38	2.54
Portfolio Turnover (%)	11	35	209	258	113	180	58	91	99	92
Total Assets (Millions $)	12	12	10	10	12	17	36	33	36	13

PORTFOLIO (as of 6/30/93)

Portfolio Manager: Frank Holmes - 1993

Investm't Category: Growth & Income
Cap Gain	Asset Allocation
✔ Cap & Income	Fund of Funds
Income	✔ Index
	Sector
✔ Domestic	Small Cap
Foreign	Socially Conscious
Country/Region	State Specific

Portfolio: stocks 100%   bonds 0%
convertibles 0%   other 0%   cash 0%

Largest Holdings: S&P 500 Composite Stock
Price Index

Unrealized Net Capital Gains: 16% of portfolio value

SHAREHOLDER INFORMATION

Minimum Investment
Initial: $1,000   Subsequent: $50

Minimum IRA Investment
Initial: $0   Subsequent: $0

Maximum Fees
Load: 0.10% redemption   12b-1: none
Other: redemption fee applies for 14 days; $10
close-out fee; $12/yr maintenance fee

Distributions
Income: quarterly   Capital Gains: Dec

Exchange Options
Number Per Year: no limit   Fee: $5
Telephone: yes (money market fund available)

Services
IRA, other pension, auto invest, auto withdraw

US European Income
(LOCFX)

International Stock

P.O. Box 659
San Antonio, TX 78293
(800) 873-8637, (210) 308-1222

PERFORMANCE

	3yr Annual	5yr Annual	10yr Annual	Bull	Bear
Return (%)	1.6	-5.3	na	-1.5	-21.3
Differ from Category (+/-)	-12.7 low	-14.0 low	na	-56.6 low	-6.2 low

Total Risk	Standard Deviation	Category Risk	Risk Index	Beta
abv av	11.9%	blw av	1.0	0.6

	1993	1992	1991	1990	1989	1988	1987	1986	1985	1984
Return (%)	11.6	-11.2	5.8	-26.2	-1.6	3.3	-13.1	-6.5	—	—
Differ from category (+/-) . .	-26.9	-7.7	-7.1	-15.1	-23.8	-10.5	-25.1	-56.8	—	—

PER SHARE DATA

	1993	1992	1991	1990	1989	1988	1987	1986	1985	1984
Dividends, Net Income ($) .	0.12	0.00	0.00	0.00	0.00	0.00	0.00	0.01	—	—
Distrib'ns, Cap Gain ($) . . .	0.00	0.00	0.00	0.00	0.00	0.00	0.00	0.00	—	—
Net Asset Value ($)	4.53	4.18	4.71	4.45	6.03	6.13	5.93	6.83	—	—
Expense Ratio (%)	2.35	3.78	6.14	3.64	2.63	2.43	2.27	1.84	—	—
Net Income to Assets (%) .	1.65	-0.20	-3.01	-1.18	-1.38	-0.76	-0.82	0.31	—	—
Portfolio Turnover (%)	88	145	200	104	34	39	52	70	—	—
Total Assets (Millions $)	2	2	1	2	1	3	4	3	—	—

PORTFOLIO (as of 6/30/93)

Portfolio Manager: Ralph Aldis - 1991

Investm't Category: International Stock

Cap Gain	✔ Asset Allocation
✔ Cap & Income	Fund of Funds
Income	Index
	Sector
Domestic	Small Cap
✔ Foreign	Socially Conscious
✔ Country/Region	State Specific

Portfolio: stocks 40% bonds 56%
convertibles 0% other 0% cash 4%

Largest Holdings: United Kingdom 47%, Germany 13%

Unrealized Net Capital Gains: 0% of portfolio value

SHAREHOLDER INFORMATION

Minimum Investment
Initial: $1,000   Subsequent: $50

Minimum IRA Investment
Initial: $0   Subsequent: $0

Maximum Fees
Load: 0.10% redemption   12b-1: none
Other: redemption fee applies for 14 days; $10
close-out fee; $12/yr maintenance fee

Distributions
Income: quarterly   Capital Gains: Dec

Exchange Options
Number Per Year: no limit   Fee: $5
Telephone: yes (money market fund available)

Services
IRA, other pension, auto invest, auto withdraw

US Global Resources
(PSPFX)

International Stock

P.O. Box 659
San Antonio, TX 78293
(800) 873-8637, (210) 308-1222

PERFORMANCE

	3yr Annual	5yr Annual	10yr Annual	Bull	Bear
Return (%)	6.5	4.4	1.0	14.0	-10.8
Differ from Category (+/-)	-7.8 low	-4.3 low	-12.4 low	-41.1 low	4.3 abv av

Total Risk	Standard Deviation	Category Risk	Risk Index	Beta
av	9.8%	low	0.8	0.4

	1993	1992	1991	1990	1989	1988	1987	1986	1985	1984
Return (%)	18.5	-2.7	5.0	-15.9	22.0	-12.1	25.3	29.0	3.7	-39.0
Differ from category (+/-) .	-20.0	0.8	-7.9	-4.8	-0.2	-25.9	13.3	-21.3	-36.9	-29.5

PER SHARE DATA

	1993	1992	1991	1990	1989	1988	1987	1986	1985	1984
Dividends, Net Income ($) .	0.00	0.03	0.07	0.03	0.50	0.00	0.00	0.00	0.00	0.00
Distrib'ns, Cap Gain ($) . . .	0.15	0.00	0.15	0.41	0.40	0.40	0.69	0.00	0.00	0.00
Net Asset Value ($)	6.50	5.62	5.82	5.76	7.40	6.80	8.20	7.10	5.50	5.30
Expense Ratio (%).	2.46	2.33	2.43	2.10	2.04	0.49	2.90	1.89	1.50	1.51
Net Income to Assets (%) . .	0.17	0.61	0.58	1.37	1.78	1.78	-1.64	0.45	0.01	0.73
Portfolio Turnover (%)	119	55	82	70	21	27	8	83	20	46
Total Assets (Millions $)	24	25	28	32	37	45	76	61	76	48

PORTFOLIO (as of 6/30/93)

Portfolio Manager: Ralph Aldis - 1992

Investm't Category: International Stock

✔ Cap Gain	Asset Allocation
Cap & Income	Fund of Funds
Income	Index
	✔ Sector
✔ Domestic	Small Cap
✔ Foreign	Socially Conscious
Country/Region	State Specific

Portfolio: stocks 90% bonds 5%
convertibles 0% other 0% cash 5%

Largest Holdings: petroleum refining & drilling 24%, natural gas transmission & distrib. 22%

Unrealized Net Capital Gains: 6% of portfolio value

SHAREHOLDER INFORMATION

Minimum Investment
Initial: $1,000 Subsequent: $50

Minimum IRA Investment
Initial: $0 Subsequent: $0

Maximum Fees
Load: 0.10% redemption 12b-1: none
Other: redemption fee applies for 14 days; $10 close-out fee

Distributions
Income: Dec Capital Gains: Dec

Exchange Options
Number Per Year: no limit Fee: $5
Telephone: yes (money market fund available)

Services
IRA, other pension, auto invest, auto withdraw

US Gold Shares (USERX)

Gold

P.O. Box 659
San Antonio, TX 78293
(800) 873-8637, (210) 308-1222

	3yr Annual	5yr Annual	10yr Annual	Bull	Bear
Return (%)	-2.4	0.1	-4.9	-16.1	-27.1
Differ from Category (+/-)	-16.1 low	-12.2 low	-7.8 low	-49.7 low	-73.0 low

Total Risk	Standard Deviation	Category Risk	Risk Index	Beta
high	35.7%	high	1.4	-0.7

	1993	1992	1991	1990	1989	1988	1987	1986	1985	1984
Return (%)............	123.9	-50.8	-15.6	-34.2	64.7	-35.6	31.5	37.5	-26.8	-29.7
Differ from category (+/-)..	37.0	-35.1	-10.8	-65.7	40.0	-16.7	-0.4	-0.1	-19.4	-3.5

PER SHARE DATA

	1993	1992	1991	1990	1989	1988	1987	1986	1985	1984
Dividends, Net Income ($).	0.05	0.05	0.07	0.15	0.17	0.21	0.54	0.28	0.27	0.31
Distrib'ns, Cap Gain ($) ...	0.00	0.00	0.00	0.00	0.00	0.00	0.00	0.00	0.00	0.05
Net Asset Value ($)	2.88	1.31	2.75	3.35	5.31	3.34	5.53	4.63	3.60	5.23
Expense Ratio (%)	1.88	1.54	1.54	1.46	1.54	1.31	1.32	1.27	1.15	1.06
Net Income to Assets (%) .	2.58	2.52	2.71	3.80	5.46	5.10	6.45	6.90	4.47	5.69
Portfolio Turnover (%)......	19	25	49	13	7	18	24	14	9	11
Total Assets (Millions $)....	305	188	343	295	239	238	408	215	390	443

PORTFOLIO (as of 6/30/93)

Portfolio Manager: Victor Flores - 1992

Investm't Category: Gold

✔ Cap Gain
  Cap & Income
  Income

  Asset Allocation
  Fund of Funds
  Index
✔ Sector

✔ Domestic
✔ Foreign
  Country/Region

  Small Cap
  Socially Conscious
  State Specific

Portfolio: stocks 85%   bonds 0%
convertibles 0%   other 0%   cash 15%

Largest Holdings: North American mining cos. 27%, gold/uranium mining cos. 22%

Unrealized Net Capital Gains: -10% of portfolio value

SHAREHOLDER INFORMATION

Minimum Investment
Initial: $1,000   Subsequent: $50

Minimum IRA Investment
Initial: $0   Subsequent: $0

Maximum Fees
Load: 0.10% redemption   12b-1: none
Other: redemption fee applies for 14 days; $10 close-out fee

Distributions
Income: Jun, Dec   Capital Gains: Dec

Exchange Options
Number Per Year: no limit   Fee: $5
Telephone: yes (money market fund available)

Services
IRA, other pension, auto invest, auto withdraw

US Growth (GRTHX)

Growth

P.O. Box 659
San Antonio, TX 78293
(800) 873-8637, (210) 308-1222

	3yr Annual	5yr Annual	10yr Annual	Bull	Bear
Return (%)	8.3	5.8	2.7	29.8	-15.0
Differ from Category (+/-)	-10.9 low	-8.8 low	-9.9 low	-54.9 low	-2.6 blw av

Total Risk	Standard Deviation	Category Risk	Risk Index	Beta
high	16.5%	high	1.6	1.0

	1993	1992	1991	1990	1989	1988	1987	1986	1985	1984
Return (%)	12.9	-11.3	26.9	-13.2	20.4	10.4	-11.2	11.5	21.0	-25.6
Differ from category (+/-)	-0.3	-22.3	-8.5	-7.1	-5.4	-7.3	-12.4	-3.0	-8.3	-25.6

PER SHARE DATA

	1993	1992	1991	1990	1989	1988	1987	1986	1985	1984
Dividends, Net Income ($)	0.00	0.00	0.11	0.50	0.05	0.17	0.09	0.07	0.05	0.07
Distrib'ns, Cap Gain ($)	0.87	0.00	0.69	0.00	0.28	0.33	1.55	0.00	0.00	0.00
Net Asset Value ($)	5.76	5.87	6.62	5.86	7.32	6.36	6.21	8.82	7.97	6.64
Expense Ratio (%)	2.79	2.42	2.75	2.40	2.26	2.03	1.71	1.52	1.67	1.45
Net Income to Assets (%)	-1.23	-1.02	-0.73	0.32	2.55	0.47	0.62	0.52	0.97	1.74
Portfolio Turnover (%)	99	138	109	41	58	94	64	59	163	161
Total Assets (Millions $)	4	5	5	5	5	6	9	12	12	6

PORTFOLIO (as of 6/30/93)

Portfolio Manager: Frank Holmes - 1993

Investm't Category: Growth

✔ Cap Gain	Asset Allocation
Cap & Income	Fund of Funds
Income	Index
	Sector
✔ Domestic	Small Cap
✔ Foreign	Socially Conscious
Country/Region	State Specific

Portfolio: stocks 91%   bonds 0%
convertibles 0%   other 0%   cash 9%

Largest Holdings: communications & media 19%, computer hardware & software 10%

Unrealized Net Capital Gains: 15% of portfolio value

SHAREHOLDER INFORMATION

Minimum Investment
Initial: $1,000   Subsequent: $50

Minimum IRA Investment
Initial: $0   Subsequent: $0

Maximum Fees
Load: 0.10% redemption   12b-1: none
Other: redemption fee applies for 14 days; $10 close-out fee

Distributions
Income: Jun, Dec   Capital Gains: Dec

Exchange Options
Number Per Year: no limit   Fee: $5
Telephone: yes (money market fund available)

Services
IRA, other pension, auto invest, auto withdraw

US Income (USINX)

Growth & Income

P.O. Box 659
San Antonio, TX 78293
(800) 873-8637, (210) 308-1222

PERFORMANCE

	3yr Annual	5yr Annual	10yr Annual	Bull	Bear
Return (%)	13.2	12.8	9.9	52.1	-12.6
Differ from Category (+/-)	-3.2 blw av	0.3 av	-2.5 low	-18.0 low	-1.0 av

Total Risk	Standard Deviation	Category Risk	Risk Index	Beta
av	8.0%	low	0.9	0.4

	1993	1992	1991	1990	1989	1988	1987	1986	1985	1984
Return (%)	17.7	8.0	14.3	-8.6	37.8	16.8	-4.2	5.4	15.3	3.9
Differ from category (+/-). . .	5.1	-2.0	-13.4	-3.0	16.2	0.0	-4.6	-9.8	-10.1	-2.3

PER SHARE DATA

	1993	1992	1991	1990	1989	1988	1987	1986	1985	1984
Dividends, Net Income ($).	0.31	0.28	0.34	0.40	0.44	0.47	0.68	0.58	0.34	0.50
Distrib'ns, Cap Gain ($) . . .	0.40	0.81	0.00	0.28	0.00	0.00	0.34	0.62	0.00	0.00
Net Asset Value ($)	14.08	12.57	12.66	11.41	13.25	9.98	8.97	10.43	11.05	9.90
Expense Ratio (%)	1.83	1.95	2.22	1.94	2.00	1.73	1.60	1.63	1.66	1.80
Net Income to Assets (%) .	2.34	2.47	2.99	3.55	4.61	6.19	6.14	3.27	5.58	6.34
Portfolio Turnover (%).	44	76	110	19	18	127	174	178	271	279
Total Assets (Millions $).	14	8	7	8	5	4	4	3	2	1

PORTFOLIO (as of 6/30/93)

Portfolio Manager: Frank Holmes - 1993

Investm't Category: Growth & Income

Cap Gain	Asset Allocation
✔ Cap & Income	Fund of Funds
Income	Index
	Sector
✔ Domestic	Small Cap
Foreign	Socially Conscious
Country/Region	State Specific

Portfolio: stocks 89% bonds 0%
convertibles 0% other 0% cash 11%

Largest Holdings: electric & water utilities 36%, natural gas transmission & distrib. 27%

Unrealized Net Capital Gains: 18% of portfolio value

SHAREHOLDER INFORMATION

Minimum Investment
Initial: $1,000   Subsequent: $50

Minimum IRA Investment
Initial: $0   Subsequent: $0

Maximum Fees
Load: 0.10% redemption   12b-1: none
Other: redemption fee applies for 14 days; $10 close-out fee

Distributions
Income: quarterly   Capital Gains: Dec

Exchange Options
Number Per Year: no limit   Fee: $5
Telephone: yes (money market fund available)

Services
IRA, other pension, auto invest, auto withdraw

US Real Estate (UNREX)

Growth & Income

P.O. Box 659
San Antonio, TX 78293
(800) 873-8637, (210) 308-1222

PERFORMANCE

	3yr Annual	5yr Annual	10yr Annual	Bull	Bear
Return (%)	17.6	7.0	na	75.0	-25.3
Differ from Category (+/-)	1.2 abv av	-5.5 low	na	4.9 abv av	-13.7 low

Total Risk	Standard Deviation	Category Risk	Risk Index	Beta
high	18.1%	high	2.1	1.1

	1993	1992	1991	1990	1989	1988	1987	1986	1985	1984
Return (%)	0.1	4.6	55.3	-19.8	7.3	20.8	—	—	—	—
Differ from category (+/-) .	-12.5	-5.4	27.6	-14.2	-14.3	4.0	—	—	—	—

PER SHARE DATA

	1993	1992	1991	1990	1989	1988	1987	1986	1985	1984
Dividends, Net Income ($) .	0.23	0.28	0.18	0.34	0.37	0.46	—	—	—	—
Distrib'ns, Cap Gain ($) . . .	0.00	0.00	0.00	0.00	0.27	0.00	—	—	—	—
Net Asset Value ($)	10.69	10.91	10.71	7.01	9.15	9.11	—	—	—	—
Expense Ratio (%).	1.40	1.63	2.63	2.51	2.14	0.00	—	—	—	—
Net Income to Assets (%) . .	1.55	3.17	2.66	3.50	4.70	6.76	—	—	—	—
Portfolio Turnover (%)	186	103	133	63	88	51	—	—	—	—
Total Assets (Millions $)	18	22	7	6	6	3	—	—	—	—

PORTFOLIO (as of 6/30/93)

Portfolio Manager: Allen Parker - 1987

Investm't Category: Growth & Income

Cap Gain	Asset Allocation
✔ Cap & Income	Fund of Funds
Income	Index
	✔ Sector
✔ Domestic	Small Cap
Foreign	Socially Conscious
Country/Region	State Specific

Portfolio: stocks 95% bonds 0%
convertibles 0% other 0% cash 5%

Largest Holdings: real estate investment trusts 71%, home builder 18%

Unrealized Net Capital Gains: 11% of portfolio value

SHAREHOLDER INFORMATION

Minimum Investment
Initial: $1,000   Subsequent: $50

Minimum IRA Investment
Initial: $0   Subsequent: $0

Maximum Fees
Load: 0.10% redemption   12b-1: none
Other: redemption fee applies for 14 days; $10 close-out fee

Distributions
Income: Jun, Dec   Capital Gains: Dec

Exchange Options
Number Per Year: no limit   Fee: $5
Telephone: yes (money market fund available)

Services
IRA, other pension, auto invest, auto withdraw

US Tax Free (USUTX)

Tax-Exempt Bond

P.O. Box 659
San Antonio, TX 78293
(800) 873-8637, (210) 308-1222

PERFORMANCE

	3yr Annual	5yr Annual	10yr Annual	Bull	Bear
Return (%)	9.6	8.6	na	38.6	0.6
Differ from Category (+/-)	-0.6 blw av	-0.6 blw av	na	-1.5 blw av	-1.6 low

Total Risk	Standard Deviation	Category Risk	Risk Index	Avg Mat
blw av	4.4%	av	1.1	8.1 yrs

	1993	1992	1991	1990	1989	1988	1987	1986	1985	1984
Return (%)	11.7	7.1	9.9	6.0	8.2	11.9	-0.2	17.0	11.1	—
Differ from category (+/-)	0.1	-1.2	-1.4	-0.3	-0.8	1.8	1.0	0.6	-6.2	—

PER SHARE DATA

	1993	1992	1991	1990	1989	1988	1987	1986	1985	1984
Dividends, Net Income ($)	0.68	0.67	0.54	0.62	0.61	0.81	0.81	0.85	0.46	—
Distrib'ns, Cap Gain ($)	0.12	0.02	0.20	0.00	0.00	0.00	0.00	0.11	0.00	—
Net Asset Value ($)	12.24	11.71	11.60	11.26	11.24	10.97	10.56	11.42	10.63	—
Expense Ratio (%)	0.32	1.27	1.93	1.61	1.23	0.00	0.05	0.38	1.44	—
Net Income to Assets (%)	5.48	5.38	5.09	5.64	6.38	7.60	6.99	8.57	5.94	—
Portfolio Turnover (%)	93	70	54	82	110	121	37	50	67	—
Total Assets (Millions $)	22	8	7	8	10	8	8	2	1	—

PORTFOLIO (as of 6/30/93)

Portfolio Manager: Allen Parker - 1992

Investm't Category: Tax-Exempt Bond

Cap Gain	Asset Allocation
Cap & Income	Fund of Funds
✔ Income	Index
	Sector
✔ Domestic	Small Cap
Foreign	Socially Conscious
Country/Region	State Specific

Portfolio: stocks 0% bonds 100%
convertibles 0% other 0% cash 0%

Largest Holdings: general obligation 20%

Unrealized Net Capital Gains: 3% of portfolio value

SHAREHOLDER INFORMATION

Minimum Investment
Initial: $1,000   Subsequent: $50

Minimum IRA Investment
Initial: na   Subsequent: na

Maximum Fees
Load: none   12b-1: none
Other: $10 close-out fee

Distributions
Income: monthly   Capital Gains: Dec

Exchange Options
Number Per Year: no limit   Fee: none
Telephone: yes (money market fund available)

Services
auto exchange, auto invest, auto withdraw

US World Gold (UNWPX)

Gold

P.O. Box 659
San Antonio, TX 78293
(800) 873-8637, (210) 308-1222

PERFORMANCE

	3yr Annual	5yr Annual	10yr Annual	Bull	Bear
Return (%)	20.4	71.1	na	57.5	700.0
Differ from Category (+/-)	6.7 high	58.8 high	na	23.9 high	654.0 high

Total Risk	Standard Deviation	Category Risk	Risk Index	Beta
high	28.2%	high	1.1	-0.4

	1993	1992	1991	1990	1989	1988	1987	1986	1985	1984
Return (%)	89.7	-4.7	-3.3	621.4	16.5	-18.7	31.0	38.5	—	—
Differ from category (+/-) . . .	2.8	11.0	1.5	589.9	-8.2	0.2	-0.8	0.8	—	—

PER SHARE DATA

	1993	1992	1991	1990	1989	1988	1987	1986	1985	1984
Dividends, Net Income ($) .	0.00	0.00	0.00	0.00	0.00	0.00	0.01	0.00	—	—
Distrib'ns, Cap Gain ($) . . .	0.00	0.00	0.00	0.00	0.00	0.00	0.20	0.01	—	—
Net Asset Value ($)	17.65	9.30	9.76	10.10	1.40	1.21	1.49	1.31	—	—
Expense Ratio (%)	2.00	2.20	2.22	1.95	2.00	1.47	1.47	1.51	—	—
Net Income to Assets (%) .	-1.15	-1.18	-0.95	-0.24	0.13	0.04	-0.05	0.01	—	—
Portfolio Turnover (%)	26	47	44	26	20	39	44	31	—	—
Total Assets (Millions $) . . .	163	58	65	73	85	104	127	27	—	—

PORTFOLIO (as of 6/30/93)

Portfolio Manager: Victor Flores - 1990

Investm't Category: Gold

✔ Cap Gain   Asset Allocation
  Cap & Income   Fund of Funds
  Income   Index
                ✔ Sector
✔ Domestic   Small Cap
✔ Foreign   Socially Conscious
  Country/Region State Specific

Portfolio: stocks 86%   bonds 4%
convertibles 0%   other 0%   cash 10%

Largest Holdings: gold producing cos. 74%, mining—finance 6%

Unrealized Net Capital Gains: 38% of portfolio value

SHAREHOLDER INFORMATION

Minimum Investment
Initial: $1,000   Subsequent: $50

Minimum IRA Investment
Initial: $0   Subsequent: $0

Maximum Fees
Load: 0.10% redemption   12b-1: none
Other: redemption fee applies for 14 days

Distributions
Income: Dec   Capital Gains: Dec

Exchange Options
Number Per Year: no limit   Fee: $5
Telephone: yes (money market fund available)

Services
IRA, other pension, auto invest, auto withdraw

USAA Aggressive Growth (USAUX)

Aggressive Growth

USAA Building
San Antonio, TX 78288
(800) 382-8722, (210) 498-6505

PERFORMANCE

	3yr Annual	5yr Annual	10yr Annual	Bull	Bear
Return (%)	19.3	11.7	7.7	97.3	-24.2
Differ from Category (+/-)	-6.1 blw av	-6.5 low	-4.2 low	-27.7 blw av	-9.2 low

Total Risk	Standard Deviation	Category Risk	Risk Index	Beta
high	19.6%	abv av	1.3	1.4

	1993	1992	1991	1990	1989	1988	1987	1986	1985	1984
Return (%)	8.1	-8.5	71.6	-11.9	16.5	14.2	-0.8	5.6	23.0	-18.1
Differ from category (+/-). .	-10.9	-18.9	19.2	-5.6	-10.5	-1.0	2.5	-3.8	-8.0	-8.7

PER SHARE DATA

	1993	1992	1991	1990	1989	1988	1987	1986	1985	1984
Dividends, Net Income ($).	0.01	0.00	0.00	0.10	0.18	0.14	0.11	0.07	0.10	0.07
Distrib'ns, Cap Gain ($) . . .	1.25	2.14	0.00	0.00	2.62	0.46	1.86	0.34	0.00	0.00
Net Asset Value ($)	20.22	19.93	24.42	14.23	16.28	16.34	14.85	17.10	16.57	13.56
Expense Ratio (%)	0.86	0.82	0.87	0.93	0.91	1.00	0.97	1.05	1.11	1.06
Net Income to Assets (%) .	0.10	-0.05	0.17	0.68	0.78	0.82	0.54	0.37	0.66	0.75
Portfolio Turnover (%).	113	74	50	78	98	68	35	57	74	51
Total Assets (Millions $). . . .	286	235	208	115	158	139	150	118	108	98

PORTFOLIO (as of 9/30/93)

Portfolio Manager: Mark Johnson - 1992

Investm't Category: Aggressive Growth

✔ Cap Gain	Asset Allocation
Cap & Income	Fund of Funds
Income	Index
	Sector
✔ Domestic	✔ Small Cap
Foreign	Socially Conscious
Country/Region	State Specific

Portfolio: stocks 96% bonds 0%
convertibles 0% other 0% cash 4%

Largest Holdings: retail—specialty 9%, textiles—apparel manufacturers 6%

Unrealized Net Capital Gains: 14% of portfolio value

SHAREHOLDER INFORMATION

Minimum Investment
Initial: $1,000   Subsequent: $50

Minimum IRA Investment
Initial: $1,000   Subsequent: $50

Maximum Fees
Load: none   12b-1: none
Other: none

Distributions
Income: Nov   Capital Gains: Nov

Exchange Options
Number Per Year: 6   Fee: none
Telephone: yes (money market fund available)

Services
IRA, other pension, auto exchange, auto invest, auto withdraw

USAA Balanced (USBLX)

Balanced

USAA Building
San Antonio, TX 78288
(800) 382-8722, (210) 498-6505

PERFORMANCE

	3yr Annual	5yr Annual	10yr Annual	Bull	Bear
Return (%)	11.0	na	na	43.1	-3.0
Differ from Category (+/-)	-4.0 low	na	na	-18.5 low	2.8 high

Total Risk	Standard Deviation	Category Risk	Risk Index	Beta
blw av	5.1%	low	0.8	0.4

	1993	1992	1991	1990	1989	1988	1987	1986	1985	1984
Return (%)	13.7	4.9	14.6	1.3	—	—	—	—	—	—
Differ from category (+/-)	0.3	-3.2	-9.3	1.8	—	—	—	—	—	—

PER SHARE DATA

	1993	1992	1991	1990	1989	1988	1987	1986	1985	1984
Dividends, Net Income ($)	0.44	0.46	0.50	0.54	—	—	—	—	—	—
Distrib'ns, Cap Gain ($)	0.37	0.00	0.00	0.00	—	—	—	—	—	—
Net Asset Value ($)	12.71	11.92	11.82	10.78	—	—	—	—	—	—
Expense Ratio (%)	0.86	0.92	1.00	1.00	—	—	—	—	—	—
Net Income to Assets (%)	3.81	4.31	4.91	5.05	—	—	—	—	—	—
Portfolio Turnover (%)	98	107	81	106	—	—	—	—	—	—
Total Assets (Millions $)	127	83	54	38	—	—	—	—	—	—

PORTFOLIO (as of 9/30/93)

Portfolio Manager: John W. Saunders Jr. - 1989

Investm't Category: Balanced

Cap Gain	Asset Allocation
✔ Cap & Income	Fund of Funds
Income	Index
	Sector
✔ Domestic	Small Cap
Foreign	Socially Conscious
Country/Region	State Specific

Portfolio: stocks 40% bonds 60%
convertibles 0% other 0% cash 0%

Largest Holdings: long-term tax-exempt 34%, short-term tax-exempt 28%

Unrealized Net Capital Gains: 8% of portfolio value

SHAREHOLDER INFORMATION

Minimum Investment
Initial: $1,000   Subsequent: $50

Minimum IRA Investment
Initial: na   Subsequent: na

Maximum Fees
Load: none   12b-1: none
Other: none

Distributions
Income: quarterly   Capital Gains: Nov

Exchange Options
Number Per Year: 6   Fee: none
Telephone: yes (money market fund available)

Services
auto exchange, auto invest, auto withdraw

USAA Cornerstone
(USCRX)

Balanced

USAA Building
San Antonio, TX 78288
(800) 382-8722, (210) 498-6505

PERFORMANCE

	3yr Annual	5yr Annual	10yr Annual	Bull	Bear
Return (%)	15.2	11.0	na	51.6	-8.4
Differ from Category (+/-)	0.2 av	-1.1 blw av	na	-10.0 blw av	-2.6 blw av

Total Risk	Standard Deviation	Category Risk	Risk Index	Beta
av	7.4%	abv av	1.2	0.4

	1993	1992	1991	1990	1989	1988	1987	1986	1985	1984
Return (%)	23.7	6.3	16.2	-9.2	21.8	8.3	8.9	40.7	14.7	—
Differ from category (+/-). .	10.3	-1.8	-7.7	-8.7	4.2	-3.7	6.6	23.2	-9.0	—

PER SHARE DATA

	1993	1992	1991	1990	1989	1988	1987	1986	1985	1984
Dividends, Net Income ($).	0.58	0.62	0.58	0.64	0.70	0.66	0.36	0.30	0.31	—
Distrib'ns, Cap Gain ($) . . .	0.28	0.00	0.00	0.00	0.00	0.00	0.01	0.20	0.05	—
Net Asset Value ($)	23.46	19.69	19.12	16.98	19.44	16.54	15.87	14.92	10.97	—
Expense Ratio (%)	1.18	1.18	1.18	1.21	1.21	1.21	1.07	1.50	1.50	—
Net Income to Assets (%) .	2.92	3.25	3.58	3.50	3.57	3.54	3.41	3.68	5.03	—
Portfolio Turnover (%).	45	33	28	41	33	28	15	70	15	—
Total Assets (Millions $). . . .	770	567	580	535	522	544	823	28	13	—

PORTFOLIO (as of 9/30/93)

Portfolio Manager: Harry W. Miller - 1990

Investm't Category: Balanced

Cap Gain	✔ Asset Allocation
✔ Cap & Income	Fund of Funds
Income	Index
	Sector
✔ Domestic	Small Cap
✔ Foreign	Socially Conscious
Country/Region	State Specific

Portfolio: stocks 77% bonds 23%
convertibles 0% other 0% cash 0%

Largest Holdings: real estate investment trusts 20%, bonds—U.S. government & agencies 12%

Unrealized Net Capital Gains: 14% of portfolio value

SHAREHOLDER INFORMATION

Minimum Investment
Initial: $1,000   Subsequent: $50

Minimum IRA Investment
Initial: $1,000   Subsequent: $50

Maximum Fees
Load: none   12b-1: none
Other: none

Distributions
Income: Nov   Capital Gains: Nov

Exchange Options
Number Per Year: 6   Fee: none
Telephone: yes (money market fund available)

Services
IRA, other pension, auto exchange, auto invest, auto withdraw

USAA GNMA Trust
(USGNX)

USAA Building
San Antonio, TX 78288
(800) 382-8722, (210) 498-6505

Mortgage-Backed Bond

PERFORMANCE

	3yr Annual	5yr Annual	10yr Annual	Bull	Bear
Return (%)	na	na	na	na	na
Differ from Category (+/-)	na	na	na	na	na

Total Risk	Standard Deviation	Category Risk	Risk Index	Avg Mat
na	na	na	na	na

	1993	1992	1991	1990	1989	1988	1987	1986	1985	1984
Return (%)	7.1	6.0	—	—	—	—	—	—	—	—
Differ from category (+/-)	0.3	-0.1	—	—	—	—	—	—	—	—

PER SHARE DATA

	1993	1992	1991	1990	1989	1988	1987	1986	1985	1984
Dividends, Net Income ($)	0.78	0.80	—	—	—	—	—	—	—	—
Distrib'ns, Cap Gain ($)	0.00	0.00	—	—	—	—	—	—	—	—
Net Asset Value ($)	10.28	10.34	—	—	—	—	—	—	—	—
Expense Ratio (%)	0.32	0.38	—	—	—	—	—	—	—	—
Net Income to Assets (%)	7.53	7.92	—	—	—	—	—	—	—	—
Portfolio Turnover (%)	81	36	—	—	—	—	—	—	—	—
Total Assets (Millions $)	278	219	—	—	—	—	—	—	—	—

PORTFOLIO (as of 9/30/93)

Portfolio Manager: Carl W. Shirley - 1991

Investm't Category: Mortgage-Backed Bond
Cap Gain	Asset Allocation
Cap & Income	Fund of Funds
✔ Income	Index
	Sector
✔ Domestic	Small Cap
Foreign	Socially Conscious
Country/Region	State Specific

Portfolio: stocks 0%   bonds 100%
convertibles 0%   other 0%   cash 0%

Largest Holdings: mortgage-backed 100%

Unrealized Net Capital Gains: 1% of portfolio value

SHAREHOLDER INFORMATION

Minimum Investment
Initial: $3,000   Subsequent: $50

Minimum IRA Investment
Initial: $1,000   Subsequent: $50

Maximum Fees
Load: none   12b-1: none
Other: none

Distributions
Income: monthly   Capital Gains: Dec

Exchange Options
Number Per Year: 6   Fee: none
Telephone: yes (money market fund available)

Services
IRA, other pension, auto exchange, auto invest,
auto withdraw

USAA Gold (USAGX)

Gold

USAA Building
San Antonio, TX 78288
(800) 382-8722, (210) 498-6505

PERFORMANCE

	3yr Annual	5yr Annual	10yr Annual	Bull	Bear
Return (%)	11.6	3.8	na	20.8	-15.3
Differ from Category (+/-)	-2.1 low	-8.5 low	na	-12.8 low	-61.2 low

Total Risk	Standard Deviation	Category Risk	Risk Index	Beta
high	24.4%	low	0.9	-0.3

	1993	1992	1991	1990	1989	1988	1987	1986	1985	1984
Return (%)	58.3	-7.9	-4.4	-26.5	18.1	-17.1	15.8	55.6	-20.6	—
Differ from category (+/-). .	-28.6	7.8	0.4	-58.0	-6.6	1.8	-16.1	18.0	-13.2	—

PER SHARE DATA

	1993	1992	1991	1990	1989	1988	1987	1986	1985	1984
Dividends, Net Income ($) .	0.00	0.03	0.07	0.05	0.15	0.12	0.05	0.10	0.11	—
Distrib'ns, Cap Gain ($) . . .	0.00	0.00	0.00	0.00	0.00	0.00	0.50	0.00	0.00	—
Net Asset Value ($)	9.49	6.00	6.56	6.95	9.55	8.21	10.06	9.23	6.00	—
Expense Ratio (%)	1.41	1.43	1.45	1.43	1.34	1.42	1.14	1.50	1.50	—
Net Income to Assets (%) .	0.25	1.02	1.55	0.93	1.92	0.50	0.73	1.49	3.71	—
Portfolio Turnover (%).	81	19	13	42	17	27	54	62	0	—
Total Assets (Millions $). . . .	184	114	121	157	165	174	310	29	15	—

PORTFOLIO (as of 9/30/93)

Portfolio Manager: Stuart H. Wester - 1992

Investm't Category: Gold

- ✔ Cap Gain
- Cap & Income
- Income
- Asset Allocation
- Fund of Funds
- Index
- ✔ Sector
- ✔ Domestic
- ✔ Foreign
- Country/Region
- Small Cap
- Socially Conscious
- State Specific

Portfolio: stocks 86% bonds 0%
convertibles 0% other 0% cash 14%

Largest Holdings: North American mining cos. 66%, mortgage-backed securities 10%

Unrealized Net Capital Gains: 2% of portfolio value

SHAREHOLDER INFORMATION

Minimum Investment
Initial: $1,000 Subsequent: $50

Minimum IRA Investment
Initial: $1,000 Subsequent: $50

Maximum Fees
Load: none 12b-1: none
Other: none

Distributions
Income: Nov Capital Gains: Nov

Exchange Options
Number Per Year: 6 Fee: none
Telephone: yes (money market fund available)

Services
IRA, other pension, auto exchange, auto invest, auto withdraw

USAA Growth (USAAX)

Growth & Income

USAA Building
San Antonio, TX 78288
(800) 382-8722, (210) 498-6505

PERFORMANCE

	3yr Annual	5yr Annual	10yr Annual	Bull	Bear
Return (%)	14.7	13.9	10.1	64.5	-8.3
Differ from Category (+/-)	-1.7 blw av	1.4 abv av	-2.3 low	-5.6 blw av	3.3 abv av

Total Risk	Standard Deviation	Category Risk	Risk Index	Beta
av	10.6%	abv av	1.2	0.9

	1993	1992	1991	1990	1989	1988	1987	1986	1985	1984
Return (%)	7.4	9.9	27.8	0.0	27.3	6.5	5.3	9.9	20.1	-7.4
Differ from category (+/-) . .	-5.2	-0.1	0.1	5.6	5.7	-10.3	4.9	-5.3	-5.3	-13.6

PER SHARE DATA

	1993	1992	1991	1990	1989	1988	1987	1986	1985	1984
Dividends, Net Income ($) .	0.15	0.31	0.40	0.46	0.46	0.34	0.37	0.18	0.28	0.22
Distrib'ns, Cap Gain ($) . . .	1.99	0.27	0.00	0.00	0.00	0.00	3.88	1.59	0.30	0.00
Net Asset Value ($)	17.69	18.51	17.40	13.96	14.45	11.72	11.32	14.76	15.03	13.03
Expense Ratio (%)	1.07	1.07	1.11	1.18	1.19	1.22	1.09	1.09	1.06	1.00
Net Income to Assets (%) . .	1.07	2.27	3.18	2.95	3.02	2.40	2.14	1.37	1.86	2.25
Portfolio Turnover (%)	96	39	37	56	95	109	124	109	128	69
Total Assets (Millions $) . . .	516	432	319	223	230	208	272	145	128	128

PORTFOLIO (as of 9/30/93)

Portfolio Manager: William Fries - 1989

Investm't Category: Growth & Income
Cap Gain	Asset Allocation
✔ Cap & Income	Fund of Funds
Income	Index
	Sector
✔ Domestic	Small Cap
Foreign	Socially Conscious
Country/Region	State Specific

Portfolio: stocks 99% bonds 1%
convertibles 0% other 0% cash 0%

Largest Holdings: retail—specialty 7%, electronics (semiconductors) 6%

Unrealized Net Capital Gains: 12% of portfolio value

SHAREHOLDER INFORMATION

Minimum Investment
Initial: $1,000   Subsequent: $50

Minimum IRA Investment
Initial: $1,000   Subsequent: $50

Maximum Fees
Load: none   12b-1: none
Other: none

Distributions
Income: Nov   Capital Gains: Nov

Exchange Options
Number Per Year: 6   Fee: none
Telephone: yes (money market fund available)

Services
IRA, other pension, auto exchange, auto invest, auto withdraw

USAA Growth & Income
(USGRX)

Growth & Income

USAA Building
San Antonio, TX 78288
(800) 382-8722, (210) 498-6505

fund in existence since 6/1/93

	3yr Annual	5yr Annual	10yr Annual	Bull	Bear
Return (%)	na	na	na	na	na
Differ from Category (+/-)	na	na	na	na	na

Total Risk	Standard Deviation	Category Risk	Risk Index	Beta
na	na	na	na	na

	1993	1992	1991	1990	1989	1988	1987	1986	1985	1984
Return (%)	—	—	—	—	—	—	—	—	—	—
Differ from category (+/-)	—	—	—	—	—	—	—	—	—	—

PER SHARE DATA

	1993	1992	1991	1990	1989	1988	1987	1986	1985	1984
Dividends, Net Income ($)	0.07	—	—	—	—	—	—	—	—	—
Distrib'ns, Cap Gain ($)	0.01	—	—	—	—	—	—	—	—	—
Net Asset Value ($)	10.38	—	—	—	—	—	—	—	—	—
Expense Ratio (%)	1.63	—	—	—	—	—	—	—	—	—
Net Income to Assets (%)	1.87	—	—	—	—	—	—	—	—	—
Portfolio Turnover (%)	na	—	—	—	—	—	—	—	—	—
Total Assets (Millions $)	94	—	—	—	—	—	—	—	—	—

PORTFOLIO (as of 9/30/93)

Portfolio Manager: David Parsons - 1994

Investm't Category: Growth & Income
Cap Gain   Asset Allocation
✔ Cap & Income   Fund of Funds
Income   Index
     Sector
✔ Domestic   Small Cap
Foreign   Socially Conscious
Country/Region   State Specific

Portfolio: stocks 91%   bonds 0%
convertibles 0%   other 0%   cash 9%

Largest Holdings: telephones 9%, aerospace/defense 6%

Unrealized Net Capital Gains: 2% of portfolio value

SHAREHOLDER INFORMATION

Minimum Investment
Initial: $1,000   Subsequent: $50

Minimum IRA Investment
Initial: $1000   Subsequent: $50

Maximum Fees
Load: none   12b-1: none
Other: none

Distributions
Income: quarterly   Capital Gains: Sep

Exchange Options
Number Per Year: 6   Fee: none
Telephone: yes (money market fund available)

Services
IRA, other pension, auto exchange, auto invest, auto withdraw

USAA Income (USAIX)

Balanced

USAA Building
San Antonio, TX 78288
(800) 382-8722, (210) 498-6505

PERFORMANCE

	3yr Annual	5yr Annual	10yr Annual	Bull	Bear
Return (%)	12.4	12.2	11.9	51.4	1.0
Differ from Category (+/-)	-2.6 blw av	0.1 av	-0.1 blw av	-10.2 blw av	6.8 high

Total Risk	Standard Deviation	Category Risk	Risk Index	Beta
blw av	4.2%	low	0.6	0.2

	1993	1992	1991	1990	1989	1988	1987	1986	1985	1984
Return (%)	9.9	8.3	19.3	7.6	16.1	9.9	3.5	12.6	18.9	13.9
Differ from category (+/-) ..	-3.5	0.2	-4.6	8.1	-1.5	-2.1	1.2	-4.9	-4.8	6.5

PER SHARE DATA

	1993	1992	1991	1990	1989	1988	1987	1986	1985	1984
Dividends, Net Income ($) .	0.87	0.93	0.95	0.94	1.03	1.07	1.14	1.28	1.20	1.07
Distrib'ns, Cap Gain ($) ...	0.25	0.00	0.00	0.07	0.02	0.00	0.25	0.05	0.01	0.00
Net Asset Value ($)	12.71	12.61	12.55	11.41	11.61	10.96	10.97	11.98	11.89	11.12
Expense Ratio (%)........	0.41	0.42	0.47	0.53	0.57	0.61	0.61	0.65	0.68	0.75
Net Income to Assets (%)..	7.00	7.78	8.61	9.19	9.36	9.57	9.13	9.69	10.96	10.97
Portfolio Turnover (%).....	44	22	15	12	14	11	36	37	78	116
Total Assets (Millions $) ..	1,546	1,359	827	435	332	285	250	213	138	92

PORTFOLIO (as of 9/30/93)

Portfolio Manager: John W. Saunders Jr. - 1985

Investm't Category: Balanced

Cap Gain	Asset Allocation
✔ Cap & Income	Fund of Funds
Income	Index
	Sector
✔ Domestic	Small Cap
Foreign	Socially Conscious
Country/Region	State Specific

Portfolio: stocks 17% bonds 82%
convertibles 0% other 0% cash 1%

Largest Holdings: bonds—mortgage-backed 71%, bonds—U.S. government 8%

Unrealized Net Capital Gains: 6% of portfolio value

SHAREHOLDER INFORMATION

Minimum Investment
Initial: $1,000   Subsequent: $50

Minimum IRA Investment
Initial: $1,000   Subsequent: $50

Maximum Fees
Load: none   12b-1: none
Other: none

Distributions
Income: monthly   Capital Gains: Nov

Exchange Options
Number Per Year: 6   Fee: none
Telephone: yes (money market fund available)

Services
IRA, other pension, auto exchange, auto invest, auto withdraw

USAA Income Stock
(USISX)

Growth & Income

USAA Building
San Antonio, TX 78288
(800) 382-8722, (210) 498-6505

	3yr Annual	5yr Annual	10yr Annual	Bull	Bear
Return (%)	15.2	13.9	na	69.3	-10.8
Differ from Category (+/-)	-1.2 blw av	1.4 abv av	na	-0.8 av	0.8 av

Total Risk	Standard Deviation	Category Risk	Risk Index	Beta
av	8.5%	blw av	1.0	0.7

	1993	1992	1991	1990	1989	1988	1987	1986	1985	1984
Return (%)	11.5	7.7	27.3	-1.3	27.1	19.3	—	—	—	—
Differ from category (+/-). . .	-1.1	-2.3	-0.4	4.3	5.5	2.5	—	—	—	—

PER SHARE DATA

	1993	1992	1991	1990	1989	1988	1987	1986	1985	1984
Dividends, Net Income ($).	0.70	0.69	0.68	0.64	0.56	0.47	—	—	—	—
Distrib'ns, Cap Gain ($) . . .	0.18	0.09	0.00	0.00	0.57	0.00	—	—	—	—
Net Asset Value ($)	14.13	13.48	13.27	11.01	11.85	10.28	—	—	—	—
Expense Ratio (%)	0.70	0.74	0.83	1.00	1.00	1.00	—	—	—	—
Net Income to Assets (%) .	5.43	5.99	6.30	5.75	5.10	4.72	—	—	—	—
Portfolio Turnover (%).	26	16	27	49	72	28	—	—	—	—
Total Assets (Millions $). .	1,140	481	179	81	55	31	—	—	—	—

PORTFOLIO (as of 9/30/93)

Portfolio Manager: Harry Miller - 1989

Investm't Category: Growth & Income

Cap Gain	Asset Allocation
✔ Cap & Income	Fund of Funds
Income	Index
	Sector
✔ Domestic	Small Cap
Foreign	Socially Conscious
Country/Region	State Specific

Portfolio: stocks 80% bonds 0%
convertibles 0% other 19% cash 1%

Largest Holdings: electric power 17%, real estate investment trusts 9%

Unrealized Net Capital Gains: 9% of portfolio value

SHAREHOLDER INFORMATION

Minimum Investment
Initial: $1,000   Subsequent: $50

Minimum IRA Investment
Initial: $1,000   Subsequent: $50

Maximum Fees
Load: none   12b-1: none
Other: none

Distributions
Income: quarterly   Capital Gains: Nov

Exchange Options
Number Per Year: 6   Fee: none
Telephone: yes (money market fund available)

Services
IRA, other pension, auto exchange, auto invest, auto withdraw

USAA International
(USIFX)

International Stock

USAA Building
San Antonio, TX 78288
(800) 382-8722, (210) 498-6505

PERFORMANCE

	3yr Annual	5yr Annual	10yr Annual	Bull	Bear
Return (%)	16.5	11.0	na	71.6	-16.3
Differ from Category (+/-)	2.2 abv av	2.3 abv av	na	16.5 high	-1.2 av

Total Risk	Standard Deviation	Category Risk	Risk Index	Beta
abv av	12.2%	blw av	1.0	0.4

	1993	1992	1991	1990	1989	1988	1987	1986	1985	1984
Return (%)	39.8	-0.1	13.4	-9.2	17.3	—	—	—	—	—
Differ from category (+/-) . . .	1.3	3.4	0.5	1.9	-4.9	—	—	—	—	—

PER SHARE DATA

	1993	1992	1991	1990	1989	1988	1987	1986	1985	1984
Dividends, Net Income ($) .	0.00	0.12	0.09	0.05	0.01	—	—	—	—	—
Distrib'ns, Cap Gain ($) . . .	0.34	0.00	0.00	0.05	0.44	—	—	—	—	—
Net Asset Value ($)	16.10	11.79	11.94	10.61	11.82	—	—	—	—	—
Expense Ratio (%)	1.50	1.69	1.82	2.09	2.30	—	—	—	—	—
Net Income to Assets (%) . .	0.72	1.05	1.26	0.81	0.48	—	—	—	—	—
Portfolio Turnover (%)	52	34	64	70	95	—	—	—	—	—
Total Assets (Millions $) . . .	141	43	29	21	13	—	—	—	—	—

PORTFOLIO (as of 9/30/93)

Portfolio Manager: David G. Peebles - 1988

Investm't Category: International Stock

✔ Cap Gain	Asset Allocation
Cap & Income	Fund of Funds
Income	Index
	Sector
Domestic	Small Cap
✔ Foreign	Socially Conscious
Country/Region	State Specific

Portfolio: stocks 93% bonds 0%
convertibles 0% other 0% cash 7%

Largest Holdings: Japan 22%, United Kingdom 9%

Unrealized Net Capital Gains: 12% of portfolio value

SHAREHOLDER INFORMATION

Minimum Investment
Initial: $1,000   Subsequent: $50

Minimum IRA Investment
Initial: $1,000   Subsequent: $50

Maximum Fees
Load: none   12b-1: none
Other: none

Distributions
Income: Nov   Capital Gains: Nov

Exchange Options
Number Per Year: 6   Fee: none
Telephone: yes (money market fund available)

Services
IRA, other pension, auto exchange, auto invest, auto withdraw

USAA Tax Exempt CA Bond (USCBX)

Tax-Exempt Bond

USAA Building
San Antonio, TX 78288
(800) 382-8722, (210) 498-6505

PERFORMANCE

	3yr Annual	5yr Annual	10yr Annual	Bull	Bear
Return (%)	10.6	na	na	42.4	2.9
Differ from Category (+/-)	0.3 av	na	na	2.3 av	0.6 abv av

Total Risk	Standard Deviation	Category Risk	Risk Index	Avg Mat
blw av	4.7%	abv av	1.2	23.4 yrs

	1993	1992	1991	1990	1989	1988	1987	1986	1985	1984
Return (%)	12.7	8.3	10.9	8.1	—	—	—	—	—	—
Differ from category (+/-). . .	1.1	0.0	-0.4	1.8	—	—	—	—	—	—

PER SHARE DATA

	1993	1992	1991	1990	1989	1988	1987	1986	1985	1984
Dividends, Net Income ($) .	0.59	0.63	0.66	0.66	—	—	—	—	—	—
Distrib'ns, Cap Gain ($) . . .	0.20	0.11	0.00	0.00	—	—	—	—	—	—
Net Asset Value ($)	10.94	10.44	10.36	9.97	—	—	—	—	—	—
Expense Ratio (%)	0.46	0.48	0.50	0.50	—	—	—	—	—	—
Net Income to Assets (%) .	5.94	6.44	6.73	6.81	—	—	—	—	—	—
Portfolio Turnover (%).	86	51	73	136	—	—	—	—	—	—
Total Assets (Millions $). . . .	427	306	192	108	—	—	—	—	—	—

PORTFOLIO (as of 9/30/93)

Portfolio Manager: Kenneth Willmann - 1989

Investm't Category: Tax-Exempt Bond

Cap Gain	Asset Allocation
Cap & Income	Fund of Funds
✔ Income	Index
	Sector
✔ Domestic	Small Cap
Foreign	Socially Conscious
Country/Region	✔ State Specific

Portfolio: stocks 0%   bonds 100%
convertibles 0%   other 0%   cash 0%

Largest Holdings: general obligation 7%

Unrealized Net Capital Gains: 8% of portfolio value

SHAREHOLDER INFORMATION

Minimum Investment
Initial: $3,000   Subsequent: $50

Minimum IRA Investment
Initial: na   Subsequent: na

Maximum Fees
Load: none   12b-1: none
Other: none

Distributions
Income: monthly   Capital Gains: Nov

Exchange Options
Number Per Year: 6   Fee: none
Telephone: yes (money market fund available)

Services
auto exchange, auto invest, auto withdraw

USAA Tax Exempt Interm-Term (USATX)

USAA Building
San Antonio, TX 78288
(800) 382-8722, (210) 498-6505

Tax-Exempt Bond

PERFORMANCE

	3yr Annual	5yr Annual	10yr Annual	Bull	Bear
Return (%)	10.3	9.3	9.4	38.3	3.6
Differ from Category (+/-)	0.0 blw av	0.1 blw av	-0.2 blw av	-1.8 blw av	1.3 abv av

Total Risk	Standard Deviation	Category Risk	Risk Index	Avg Mat
low	3.4%	low	0.8	9.2 yrs

	1993	1992	1991	1990	1989	1988	1987	1986	1985	1984
Return (%)	11.4	8.4	11.1	6.7	9.2	8.6	0.8	13.1	16.3	8.7
Differ from category (+/-) . .	-0.2	0.1	-0.2	0.4	0.2	-1.5	2.1	-3.3	-1.0	0.4

PER SHARE DATA

	1993	1992	1991	1990	1989	1988	1987	1986	1985	1984
Dividends, Net Income ($) .	0.70	0.75	0.80	0.82	0.83	0.83	0.83	0.91	0.98	0.98
Distrib'ns, Cap Gain ($) . . .	0.13	0.00	0.00	0.00	0.00	0.00	0.01	0.00	0.00	0.00
Net Asset Value ($)	13.26	12.68	12.41	11.93	11.98	11.76	11.61	12.35	11.75	11.00
Expense Ratio (%).	0.42	0.44	0.43	0.46	0.49	0.56	0.60	0.57	0.64	0.73
Net Income to Assets (%). .	5.85	6.45	6.91	6.95	7.10	7.16	7.07	8.36	9.09	8.84
Portfolio Turnover (%)	74	67	66	62	113	139	91	79	127	49
Total Assets (Millions $) . .	1,662	894	576	471	401	346	403	201	107	70

PORTFOLIO (as of 9/30/93)

Portfolio Manager: Clifford A. Gladson - 1993

Investm't Category: Tax-Exempt Bond

Cap Gain	Asset Allocation
Cap & Income	Fund of Funds
✔ Income	Index
	Sector
✔ Domestic	Small Cap
Foreign	Socially Conscious
Country/Region	State Specific

Portfolio: stocks 0% bonds 100%
convertibles 0% other 0% cash 0%

Largest Holdings: general obligation 29%

Unrealized Net Capital Gains: 7% of portfolio value

SHAREHOLDER INFORMATION

Minimum Investment
Initial: $3,000   Subsequent: $50

Minimum IRA Investment
Initial: na   Subsequent: na

Maximum Fees
Load: none   12b-1: none
Other: none

Distributions
Income: monthly   Capital Gains: May

Exchange Options
Number Per Year: 6   Fee: none
Telephone: yes (money market fund available)

Services
auto exchange, auto invest, auto withdraw

USAA Tax Exempt Long-Term (USTEX)

Tax-Exempt Bond

USAA Building
San Antonio, TX 78288
(800) 382-8722, (210) 498-6505

PERFORMANCE

	3yr Annual	5yr Annual	10yr Annual	Bull	Bear
Return (%)	11.1	10.1	10.6	43.0	2.2
Differ from Category (+/-)	0.8 av	0.8 abv av	1.0 abv av	2.9 abv av	-0.1 av

Total Risk	Standard Deviation	Category Risk	Risk Index	Avg Mat
blw av	4.1%	av	1.0	22.3 yrs

	1993	1992	1991	1990	1989	1988	1987	1986	1985	1984
Return (%).............	12.4	8.6	12.3	6.5	10.6	12.4	-1.8	17.2	19.6	10.3
Differ from category (+/-)...	0.8	0.3	1.0	0.2	1.6	2.3	-0.6	0.8	2.3	2.0

PER SHARE DATA

	1993	1992	1991	1990	1989	1988	1987	1986	1985	1984
Dividends, Net Income ($).	0.83	0.89	0.92	0.94	0.94	0.95	0.98	1.06	1.13	1.10
Distrib'ns, Cap Gain ($) ...	0.55	0.07	0.00	0.00	0.00	0.00	0.21	0.08	0.00	0.00
Net Asset Value ($)	14.18	13.90	13.73	13.09	13.21	12.84	12.31	13.79	12.81	11.73
Expense Ratio (%)	0.39	0.40	0.40	0.43	0.45	0.51	0.49	0.50	0.56	0.68
Net Income to Assets (%) .	6.35	6.83	7.22	7.23	7.58	7.75	7.64	8.94	9.78	9.34
Portfolio Turnover (%)......	88	76	91	92	124	169	83	122	150	64
Total Assets (Millions $)..	2,049	1,638	1,356	1,173	975	823	1,039	648	272	148

PORTFOLIO (as of 9/30/93)

Portfolio Manager: Kenneth Willmann - 1982

Investm't Category: Tax-Exempt Bond

Cap Gain	Asset Allocation
Cap & Income	Fund of Funds
✔ Income	Index
	Sector
✔ Domestic	Small Cap
Foreign	Socially Conscious
Country/Region	State Specific

Portfolio: stocks 0% bonds 100%
convertibles 0% other 0% cash 0%

Largest Holdings: general obligation 15%

Unrealized Net Capital Gains: 8% of portfolio value

SHAREHOLDER INFORMATION

Minimum Investment
Initial: $3,000   Subsequent: $50

Minimum IRA Investment
Initial: na   Subsequent: na

Maximum Fees
Load: none   12b-1: none
Other: none

Distributions
Income: monthly   Capital Gains: May, Nov

Exchange Options
Number Per Year: 6   Fee: none
Telephone: yes (money market fund available)

Services
auto exchange, auto invest, auto withdraw

USAA Tax Exempt NY Bond (USNYX)

USAA Building
San Antonio, TX 78288
(800) 382-8722, (210) 498-6505

Tax-Exempt Bond

PERFORMANCE

	3yr Annual	5yr Annual	10yr Annual	Bull	Bear
Return (%)	12.0	na	na	48.2	na
Differ from Category (+/-)	1.7 high	na	na	8.1 high	na

Total Risk	Standard Deviation	Category Risk	Risk Index	Avg Mat
blw av	4.3%	av	1.1	23.9 yrs

	1993	1992	1991	1990	1989	1988	1987	1986	1985	1984
Return (%)	13.4	8.9	13.7	—	—	—	—	—	—	—
Differ from category (+/-)	1.8	0.6	2.4	—	—	—	—	—	—	—

PER SHARE DATA

	1993	1992	1991	1990	1989	1988	1987	1986	1985	1984
Dividends, Net Income ($)	0.62	0.65	0.69	—	—	—	—	—	—	—
Distrib'ns, Cap Gain ($)	0.28	0.11	0.00	—	—	—	—	—	—	—
Net Asset Value ($)	11.83	11.27	11.09	—	—	—	—	—	—	—
Expense Ratio (%)	0.50	0.50	0.50	—	—	—	—	—	—	—
Net Income to Assets (%)	5.79	6.32	6.73	—	—	—	—	—	—	—
Portfolio Turnover (%)	107	111	128	—	—	—	—	—	—	—
Total Assets (Millions $)	62	28	12	—	—	—	—	—	—	—

PORTFOLIO (as of 9/30/93)

Portfolio Manager: Kenneth E. Willmann - 1990

Investm't Category: Tax-Exempt Bond

Cap Gain	Asset Allocation
Cap & Income	Fund of Funds
✔ Income	Index
	Sector
✔ Domestic	Small Cap
Foreign	Socially Conscious
Country/Region	✔ State Specific

Portfolio: stocks 0% bonds 100%
convertibles 0% other 0% cash 0%

Largest Holdings: general obligation 17%

Unrealized Net Capital Gains: 7% of portfolio value

SHAREHOLDER INFORMATION

Minimum Investment
Initial: $3,000 Subsequent: $50

Minimum IRA Investment
Initial: na Subsequent: na

Maximum Fees
Load: none 12b-1: none
Other: none

Distributions
Income: monthly Capital Gains: Nov

Exchange Options
Number Per Year: 6 Fee: none
Telephone: yes (money market fund available)

Services
auto exchange, auto invest, auto withdraw

USAA Tax Exempt Short-Term (USSTX)

Tax-Exempt Bond

USAA Building
San Antonio, TX 78288
(800) 382-8722, (210) 498-6505

PERFORMANCE

	3yr Annual	5yr Annual	10yr Annual	Bull	Bear
Return (%)	6.3	6.4	6.6	22.7	3.8
Differ from Category (+/-)	-4.0 low	-2.8 low	-3.0 low	-17.4 low	1.5 high

Total Risk	Standard Deviation	Category Risk	Risk Index	Avg Mat
low	1.2%	low	0.3	2.7 yrs

	1993	1992	1991	1990	1989	1988	1987	1986	1985	1984
Return (%).	5.5	5.9	7.6	5.8	7.4	6.0	2.8	8.6	9.4	7.5
Differ from category (+/-). . .	-6.1	-2.4	-3.7	-0.5	-1.6	-4.1	4.0	-7.8	-7.9	-0.8

PER SHARE DATA

	1993	1992	1991	1990	1989	1988	1987	1986	1985	1984
Dividends, Net Income ($).	0.46	0.52	0.61	0.67	0.67	0.62	0.60	0.64	0.71	0.72
Distrib'ns, Cap Gain ($) . . .	0.00	0.00	0.00	0.00	0.00	0.00	0.03	0.00	0.00	0.00
Net Asset Value ($)	10.70	10.59	10.50	10.34	10.42	10.35	10.36	10.71	10.47	10.24
Expense Ratio (%)	0.43	0.48	0.50	0.52	0.51	0.56	0.57	0.65	0.70	0.85
Net Income to Assets (%) .	4.75	5.59	6.48	6.47	6.14	5.81	5.78	6.85	7.19	6.67
Portfolio Turnover (%). . . .	138	107	96	87	146	148	142	100	158	56
Total Assets (Millions $). . . .	983	680	424	279	254	245	287	139	85	62

PORTFOLIO (as of 9/30/93)

Portfolio Manager: David G. Miller - 1992

Investm't Category: Tax-Exempt Bond

Cap Gain	Asset Allocation
Cap & Income	Fund of Funds
✔ Income	Index
	Sector
✔ Domestic	Small Cap
Foreign	Socially Conscious
Country/Region	State Specific

Portfolio:	stocks 0%	bonds 100%
convertibles 0%	other 0%	cash 0%

Largest Holdings: general obligation 19%

Unrealized Net Capital Gains: 2% of portfolio value

SHAREHOLDER INFORMATION

Minimum Investment
Initial: $3,000   Subsequent: $50

Minimum IRA Investment
Initial: na   Subsequent: na

Maximum Fees
Load: none   12b-1: none
Other: none

Distributions
Income: monthly   Capital Gains: May

Exchange Options
Number Per Year: no limit   Fee: none
Telephone: yes (money market fund available)

Services
auto exchange, auto invest, auto withdraw

USAA Tax-Exempt Virginia Bond (USVAX)

Tax-Exempt Bond

USAA Building
San Antonio, TX 78288
(800) 382-8722, (210) 498-6505

PERFORMANCE

	3yr Annual	5yr Annual	10yr Annual	Bull	Bear
Return (%)	11.0	na	na	na	na
Differ from Category (+/-)	0.6 av	na	na	na	na

Total Risk	Standard Deviation	Category Risk	Risk Index	Avg Mat
blw av	4.1%	av	1.0	24.1 yrs

	1993	1992	1991	1990	1989	1988	1987	1986	1985	1984
Return (%)	12.6	8.4	11.9	—	—	—	—	—	—	—
Differ from category (+/-) . . .	1.0	0.1	0.6	—	—	—	—	—	—	—

PER SHARE DATA

	1993	1992	1991	1990	1989	1988	1987	1986	1985	1984
Dividends, Net Income ($) .	0.62	0.64	0.68	—	—	—	—	—	—	—
Distrib'ns, Cap Gain ($) . . .	0.14	0.05	0.00	—	—	—	—	—	—	—
Net Asset Value ($)	11.47	10.90	10.73	—	—	—	—	—	—	—
Expense Ratio (%)	0.50	0.50	0.50	—	—	—	—	—	—	—
Net Income to Assets (%) . .	5.90	6.40	6.83	—	—	—	—	—	—	—
Portfolio Turnover (%)	91	87	143	—	—	—	—	—	—	—
Total Assets (Millions $) . . .	252	132	58	—	—	—	—	—	—	—

PORTFOLIO (as of 9/30/93)

Portfolio Manager: Kenneth E. Willmann - 1990

Investm't Category: Tax-Exempt Bond

Cap Gain	Asset Allocation
Cap & Income	Fund of Funds
✔ Income	Index
	Sector
✔ Domestic	Small Cap
Foreign	Socially Conscious
Country/Region	✔ State Specific

Portfolio: stocks 0% bonds 100%
convertibles 0% other 0% cash 0%

Largest Holdings: general obligation 4%

Unrealized Net Capital Gains: 6% of portfolio value

SHAREHOLDER INFORMATION

Minimum Investment
Initial: $3,000 Subsequent: $50

Minimum IRA Investment
Initial: na Subsequent: na

Maximum Fees
Load: none 12b-1: none
Other: none

Distributions
Income: monthly Capital Gains: Nov, May

Exchange Options
Number Per Year: 6 Fee: none
Telephone: yes (money market fund available)

Services
auto exchange, auto invest, auto withdraw

USAA World Growth
(USAWX)

International Stock

USAA Building
San Antonio, TX 78288
(800) 382-8722, (210) 498-6505

PERFORMANCE

	3yr Annual	5yr Annual	10yr Annual	Bull	Bear
Return (%)	na	na	na	na	na
Differ from Category (+/-)	na	na	na	na	na

Total Risk	Standard Deviation	Category Risk	Risk Index	Beta
na	na	na	na	na

	1993	1992	1991	1990	1989	1988	1987	1986	1985	1984
Return (%)	24.0	—	—	—	—	—	—	—	—	—
Differ from category (+/-)	-14.5	—	—	—	—	—	—	—	—	—

PER SHARE DATA

	1993	1992	1991	1990	1989	1988	1987	1986	1985	1984
Dividends, Net Income ($)	0.00	—	—	—	—	—	—	—	—	—
Distrib'ns, Cap Gain ($)	0.05	—	—	—	—	—	—	—	—	—
Net Asset Value ($)	12.70	—	—	—	—	—	—	—	—	—
Expense Ratio (%)	1.70	—	—	—	—	—	—	—	—	—
Net Income to Assets (%)	0.75	—	—	—	—	—	—	—	—	—
Portfolio Turnover (%)	45	—	—	—	—	—	—	—	—	—
Total Assets (Millions $)	100	—	—	—	—	—	—	—	—	—

PORTFOLIO (as of 9/30/93)

Portfolio Manager: David G. Peebles - 1992

Investm't Category: International Stock

✔ Cap Gain   Asset Allocation
   Cap & Income   Fund of Funds
   Income   Index
     Sector
✔ Domestic   Small Cap
✔ Foreign   Socially Conscious
   Country/Region   State Specific

Portfolio: stocks 90%   bonds 0%
convertibles 0%   other 0%   cash 10%

Largest Holdings: United States 29%, Japan 14%

Unrealized Net Capital Gains: 9% of portfolio value

SHAREHOLDER INFORMATION

Minimum Investment
Initial: $1,000   Subsequent: $50

Minimum IRA Investment
Initial: $250   Subsequent: $50

Maximum Fees
Load: none   12b-1: none
Other: none

Distributions
Income: Nov   Capital Gains: Nov

Exchange Options
Number Per Year: 6   Fee: none
Telephone: yes (money market fund available)

Services
IRA, other pension, auto exchange, auto invest, auto withdraw

Valley Forge (VAFGX)

Growth & Income

1375 Anthony Wayne Dr.
Wayne, PA 19087
(800) 548-1942, (215) 688-6839

PERFORMANCE

	3yr Annual	5yr Annual	10yr Annual	Bull	Bear
Return (%)	11.3	8.0	7.4	35.3	-3.4
Differ from Category (+/-)	-5.1 low	-4.5 low	-5.0 low	-34.8 low	8.2 high

Total Risk	Standard Deviation	Category Risk	Risk Index	Beta
low	4.0%	low	0.4	na

	1993	1992	1991	1990	1989	1988	1987	1986	1985	1984
Return (%)	17.1	9.3	7.8	-5.3	12.9	6.9	4.8	5.4	10.4	6.7
Differ from category (+/-) ...	4.5	-0.6	-19.9	0.3	-8.7	-9.9	4.4	-9.8	-15.0	0.5

PER SHARE DATA

	1993	1992	1991	1990	1989	1988	1987	1986	1985	1984
Dividends, Net Income ($) .	0.15	0.25	0.37	0.54	0.64	0.57	1.25	0.46	0.56	0.58
Distrib'ns, Cap Gain ($) ...	0.87	0.00	0.33	0.01	0.56	0.15	0.27	0.58	0.05	0.91
Net Asset Value ($)	9.51	9.00	8.48	8.52	9.60	9.57	9.63	10.67	11.16	10.71
Expense Ratio (%)........	1.40	1.40	1.40	1.40	1.40	1.40	1.30	1.40	1.40	1.70
Net Income to Assets (%)..	1.40	2.90	4.20	5.50	6.00	5.50	6.90	5.90	5.60	7.10
Portfolio Turnover (%).....	22	22	46	17	50	97	56	40	87	70
Total Assets (Millions $)	10	7	7	7	8	9	9	9	10	7

PORTFOLIO (as of 12/31/93)

Portfolio Manager: Bernard Klawans - 1971

Investm't Category: Growth & Income

Cap Gain	Asset Allocation
✔ Cap & Income	Fund of Funds
Income	Index
	Sector
✔ Domestic	Small Cap
Foreign	Socially Conscious
Country/Region	State Specific

Portfolio: stocks 24%   bonds 0%
convertibles 0%   other 0%   cash 73%

Largest Holdings: natural resources 4%, household furnishings 3%

Unrealized Net Capital Gains: 3% of portfolio value

SHAREHOLDER INFORMATION

Minimum Investment
Initial: $1,000   Subsequent: $100

Minimum IRA Investment
Initial: $250   Subsequent: $100

Maximum Fees
Load: none   12b-1: none
Other: none

Distributions
Income: Dec   Capital Gains: Dec

Exchange Options
Number Per Year: none   Fee: na
Telephone: na

Services
IRA, other pension

Value Line (VLIFX)

Growth

200 East 42nd Street
New York, NY 10017
(800) 223-0818, (212) 907-1500

PERFORMANCE

	3yr Annual	5yr Annual	10yr Annual	Bull	Bear
Return (%)	18.5	16.7	12.8	81.6	-9.0
Differ from Category (+/-)	-0.6 av	2.1 abv av	0.2 av	-3.1 av	3.4 abv av

Total Risk	Standard Deviation	Category Risk	Risk Index	Beta
high	14.1%	abv av	1.3	1.1

	1993	1992	1991	1990	1989	1988	1987	1986	1985	1984
Return (%)	6.8	4.6	48.8	-0.6	31.4	9.6	5.2	16.5	34.5	-14.7
Differ from category (+/-) . . .	-6.4	-6.4	13.4	5.4	5.6	-8.1	4.0	2.0	5.2	-14.7

PER SHARE DATA

	1993	1992	1991	1990	1989	1988	1987	1986	1985	1984
Dividends, Net Income ($) .	0.07	0.16	0.23	0.27	0.34	0.31	0.26	0.23	0.20	0.20
Distrib'ns, Cap Gain ($) . . .	1.39	2.73	0.92	0.23	1.80	0.24	2.64	1.75	0.00	0.00
Net Asset Value ($)	17.90	18.16	20.17	14.42	15.06	13.15	12.51	14.68	14.27	10.77
Expense Ratio (%)	0.80	0.84	0.71	0.71	0.70	0.71	0.68	0.73	0.81	0.82
Net Income to Assets (%) .	0.46	0.90	1.35	1.83	2.00	2.67	1.53	1.44	1.62	1.67
Portfolio Turnover (%).	na	129	109	84	125	108	118	145	129	110
Total Assets (Millions $). . . .	332	328	321	202	195	181	205	212	206	166

PORTFOLIO (as of 6/30/93)

Portfolio Manager: committee

Investm't Category: Growth

✔ Cap Gain	Asset Allocation
Cap & Income	Fund of Funds
Income	Index
	Sector
✔ Domestic	Small Cap
Foreign	Socially Conscious
Country/Region	State Specific

Portfolio: stocks 85%   bonds 0%
convertibles 0%   other 0%   cash 15%

Largest Holdings: financial services 6%, hotel/gaming 5%

Unrealized Net Capital Gains: 23% of portfolio value

SHAREHOLDER INFORMATION

Minimum Investment
Initial: $1,000   Subsequent: $100

Minimum IRA Investment
Initial: $1,000   Subsequent: $100

Maximum Fees
Load: none   12b-1: none
Other: none

Distributions
Income: quarterly   Capital Gains: Dec

Exchange Options
Number Per Year: 8   Fee: none
Telephone: yes (money market fund available)

Services
IRA, other pension, auto invest, auto withdraw

Value Line Adjustable Rate US Gov't (VLUGX)

200 East 42nd Street
New York, NY 10017
(800) 223-0818, (212) 907-1500

Mortgage-Backed Bond

PERFORMANCE

	3yr Annual	5yr Annual	10yr Annual	Bull	Bear
Return (%)	na	na	na	na	na
Differ from Category (+/-)	na	na	na	na	na

Total Risk	Standard Deviation	Category Risk	Risk Index	Avg Mat
na	na	na	na	28.0 yrs

	1993	1992	1991	1990	1989	1988	1987	1986	1985	1984
Return (%)	6.0	—	—	—	—	—	—	—	—	—
Differ from category (+/-)	-0.8	—	—	—	—	—	—	—	—	—

PER SHARE DATA

	1993	1992	1991	1990	1989	1988	1987	1986	1985	1984
Dividends, Net Income ($)	0.52	—	—	—	—	—	—	—	—	—
Distrib'ns, Cap Gain ($)	0.00	—	—	—	—	—	—	—	—	—
Net Asset Value ($)	9.97	—	—	—	—	—	—	—	—	—
Expense Ratio (%)	0.75	—	—	—	—	—	—	—	—	—
Net Income to Assets (%)	5.54	—	—	—	—	—	—	—	—	—
Portfolio Turnover (%)	na	—	—	—	—	—	—	—	—	—
Total Assets (Millions $)	42	—	—	—	—	—	—	—	—	—

PORTFOLIO (as of 4/30/93)

Portfolio Manager: committee

Investm't Category: Mortgage-Backed Bond

Cap Gain	Asset Allocation
Cap & Income	Fund of Funds
✔ Income	Index
	Sector
✔ Domestic	Small Cap
Foreign	Socially Conscious
Country/Region	State Specific

Portfolio: stocks 0% bonds 100%
convertibles 0% other 0% cash 0%

Largest Holdings: mortgage-backed 100%

Unrealized Net Capital Gains: 0% of portfolio value

SHAREHOLDER INFORMATION

Minimum Investment
Initial: $1,000   Subsequent: $250

Minimum IRA Investment
Initial: $1,000   Subsequent: $250

Maximum Fees
Load: none   12b-1: none
Other: none

Distributions
Income: monthly   Capital Gains: Dec

Exchange Options
Number Per Year: 8   Fee: none
Telephone: yes (money market fund available)

Services
IRA, other pension, auto invest, auto withdraw

Value Line Aggressive Income (VAGIX)

200 East 42nd Street
New York, NY 10017
(800) 223-0818, (212) 907-1500

Corporate High-Yield Bond

PERFORMANCE

	3yr Annual	5yr Annual	10yr Annual	Bull	Bear
Return (%)	19.1	10.7	na	74.3	-6.6
Differ from Category (+/-)	-1.4 av	-0.1 av	na	-0.6 av	-3.3 blw av

Total Risk	Standard Deviation	Category Risk	Risk Index	Avg Mat
blw av	4.5%	av	1.2	8.8 yrs

	1993	1992	1991	1990	1989	1988	1987	1986	1985	1984
Return (%)	19.0	12.1	26.6	-3.6	2.3	6.3	-2.0	—	—	—
Differ from category (+/-)	-0.2	-3.7	-0.6	0.6	1.0	-6.0	-3.0	—	—	—

PER SHARE DATA

	1993	1992	1991	1990	1989	1988	1987	1986	1985	1984
Dividends, Net Income ($)	0.66	0.67	0.75	0.77	0.87	0.93	1.17	—	—	—
Distrib'ns, Cap Gain ($)	0.00	0.00	0.00	0.00	0.00	0.00	0.00	—	—	—
Net Asset Value ($)	7.87	7.21	7.06	6.22	7.26	7.95	8.39	—	—	—
Expense Ratio (%)	1.15	1.18	1.43	1.30	1.14	1.22	1.33	—	—	—
Net Income to Assets (%)	9.40	10.74	11.74	11.46	11.61	12.29	12.02	—	—	—
Portfolio Turnover (%)	148	59	36	129	95	134	110	—	—	—
Total Assets (Millions $)	43	31	23	29	46	54	58	—	—	—

PORTFOLIO (as of 7/31/93)

Portfolio Manager: committee

Investm't Category: Corp. High-Yield Bond
Cap Gain	Asset Allocation
Cap & Income	Fund of Funds
✔ Income	Index
	Sector
✔ Domestic	Small Cap
Foreign	Socially Conscious
Country/Region	State Specific

Portfolio: stocks 0% bonds 92%
convertibles 0% other 0% cash 8%

Largest Holdings: homebuilding 15%, textile 7%

Unrealized Net Capital Gains: 3% of portfolio value

SHAREHOLDER INFORMATION

Minimum Investment
Initial: $1,000   Subsequent: $250

Minimum IRA Investment
Initial: $1,000   Subsequent: $250

Maximum Fees
Load: none   12b-1: none
Other: none

Distributions
Income: monthly   Capital Gains: Dec

Exchange Options
Number Per Year: 8   Fee: none
Telephone: yes (money market fund available)

Services
IRA, other pension, auto invest, auto withdraw

Value Line Convertible
(VALCX)

Growth & Income

200 East 42nd Street
New York, NY 10017
(800) 223-0818, (212) 907-1500

PERFORMANCE

	3yr Annual	5yr Annual	10yr Annual	Bull	Bear
Return (%)	18.9	12.3	na	73.1	-6.4
Differ from Category (+/-)	2.5 abv av	-0.2 av	na	3.0 av	5.2 high

Total Risk	Standard Deviation	Category Risk	Risk Index	Beta
av	7.9%	low	0.9	0.6

	1993	1992	1991	1990	1989	1988	1987	1986	1985	1984
Return (%)	14.8	13.8	28.7	-3.7	10.7	15.9	-6.1	16.2	—	—
Differ from category (+/-)	2.2	3.8	1.0	1.9	-10.9	-0.8	-6.5	1.0	—	—

PER SHARE DATA

	1993	1992	1991	1990	1989	1988	1987	1986	1985	1984
Dividends, Net Income ($)	0.66	0.64	0.60	0.66	0.72	0.47	0.81	0.50	—	—
Distrib'ns, Cap Gain ($)	1.66	0.00	0.00	0.00	0.00	0.00	0.48	0.70	—	—
Net Asset Value ($)	12.85	13.25	12.25	10.04	11.12	10.70	9.66	11.53	—	—
Expense Ratio (%)	1.10	1.14	1.19	1.05	1.03	1.06	1.04	1.31	—	—
Net Income to Assets (%)	4.80	5.45	5.50	5.81	6.32	4.78	5.12	5.37	—	—
Portfolio Turnover (%)	146	140	216	105	112	257	234	164	—	—
Total Assets (Millions $)	50	37	37	45	62	65	89	49	—	—

PORTFOLIO (as of 4/30/93)

Portfolio Manager: committee

Investm't Category: Growth & Income
Cap Gain	Asset Allocation
✔ Cap & Income	Fund of Funds
Income	Index
	Sector
✔ Domestic	Small Cap
Foreign	Socially Conscious
Country/Region	State Specific

Portfolio: stocks 0%   bonds 9%
convertibles 91%   other 0%   cash 0%

Largest Holdings: computer & peripherals 86%, electronics 8%

Unrealized Net Capital Gains: 5% of portfolio value

SHAREHOLDER INFORMATION

Minimum Investment
Initial: $1,000   Subsequent: $250

Minimum IRA Investment
Initial: $1,000   Subsequent: $250

Maximum Fees
Load: none   12b-1: none
Other: none

Distributions
Income: quarterly   Capital Gains: Dec

Exchange Options
Number Per Year: 8   Fee: none
Telephone: yes (money market fund available)

Services
IRA, other pension, auto invest, auto withdraw

Value Line Income
(VALIX)
Balanced

200 East 42nd Street
New York, NY 10017
(800) 223-0818, (212) 907-1500

PERFORMANCE

	3yr Annual	5yr Annual	10yr Annual	Bull	Bear
Return (%)	12.2	12.0	11.1	52.8	-5.5
Differ from Category (+/-)	-2.8 low	-0.1 av	-0.8 blw av	-8.8 blw av	0.3 av

Total Risk	Standard Deviation	Category Risk	Risk Index	Beta
av	8.7%	high	1.4	0.7

	1993	1992	1991	1990	1989	1988	1987	1986	1985	1984
Return (%)	8.2	1.7	28.5	1.9	22.5	12.1	-2.3	16.7	23.8	2.6
Differ from category (+/-). . .	-5.2	-6.4	4.6	2.4	4.9	0.1	-4.6	-0.8	0.1	-4.8

PER SHARE DATA

	1993	1992	1991	1990	1989	1988	1987	1986	1985	1984
Dividends, Net Income ($) .	0.21	0.27	0.31	0.38	0.46	0.39	0.53	0.47	0.47	0.47
Distrib'ns, Cap Gain ($) . . .	0.89	0.41	0.00	0.00	0.00	0.00	0.58	0.91	0.00	0.25
Net Asset Value ($)	6.77	7.29	7.86	6.39	6.66	5.84	5.57	6.81	7.09	6.16
Expense Ratio (%)	0.93	0.89	0.74	0.77	0.75	0.80	0.76	0.77	0.83	0.88
Net Income to Assets (%) .	2.80	3.69	4.37	5.59	7.38	6.76	5.95	6.43	7.62	7.17
Portfolio Turnover (%).	na	85	67	57	108	83	96	167	148	114
Total Assets (Millions $). . . .	163	163	172	141	148	133	140	162	134	117

PORTFOLIO (as of 6/30/93)

Portfolio Manager: committee

Investm't Category: Balanced

Cap Gain	✔ Asset Allocation
✔ Cap & Income	Fund of Funds
Income	Index
	Sector
✔ Domestic	Small Cap
✔ Foreign	Socially Conscious
Country/Region	State Specific

Portfolio: stocks 71% bonds 19%
convertibles 0% other 0% cash 10%

Largest Holdings: bonds—mortgage-backed 12%, stocks—petroleum integrated 7%

Unrealized Net Capital Gains: 7% of portfolio value

SHAREHOLDER INFORMATION

Minimum Investment
Initial: $1,000   Subsequent: $100

Minimum IRA Investment
Initial: $1,000   Subsequent: $100

Maximum Fees
Load: none   12b-1: none
Other: none

Distributions
Income: quarterly   Capital Gains: Dec

Exchange Options
Number Per Year: 8   Fee: none
Telephone: yes (money market fund available)

Services
IRA, other pension, auto invest, auto withdraw

Value Line Leveraged Growth (VALLX)

200 East 42nd Street
New York, NY 10017
(800) 223-0818, (212) 907-1500

Aggressive Growth

PERFORMANCE

	3yr Annual	5yr Annual	10yr Annual	Bull	Bear
Return (%)	18.3	16.6	12.9	82.3	-10.6
Differ from Category (+/-)	-7.1 low	-1.6 blw av	1.0 abv av	-42.7 low	4.4 abv av

Total Risk	Standard Deviation	Category Risk	Risk Index	Beta
high	15.7%	av	1.0	1.2

	1993	1992	1991	1990	1989	1988	1987	1986	1985	1984
Return (%)	16.1	-2.4	46.2	-1.6	32.3	6.4	2.8	23.0	27.1	-8.8
Differ from category (+/-) . .	-2.9	-12.8	-6.2	4.7	5.3	-8.8	6.2	13.6	-3.9	0.6

PER SHARE DATA

	1993	1992	1991	1990	1989	1988	1987	1986	1985	1984
Dividends, Net Income ($) .	0.05	0.15	0.22	0.36	0.38	0.43	0.45	0.34	0.12	0.31
Distrib'ns, Cap Gain ($) . . .	0.98	2.68	4.61	1.18	1.45	0.00	4.92	2.60	0.00	0.99
Net Asset Value ($)	24.67	22.15	25.64	21.16	23.10	18.87	18.15	22.79	20.90	16.56
Expense Ratio (%).	0.95	0.93	0.90	0.96	0.96	0.97	0.95	0.96	0.80	0.86
Net Income to Assets (%) . .	0.25	0.62	0.84	1.51	1.47	1.99	1.05	0.98	1.57	0.90
Portfolio Turnover (%)	na	208	250	94	122	143	148	115	121	89
Total Assets (Millions $) . . .	304	291	348	236	255	235	283	290	228	181

PORTFOLIO (as of 6/30/93)

Portfolio Manager: committee

Investm't Category: Aggressive Growth

✔ Cap Gain	Asset Allocation
Cap & Income	Fund of Funds
Income	Index
	Sector
✔ Domestic	Small Cap
Foreign	Socially Conscious
Country/Region	State Specific

Portfolio: stocks 93% bonds 0%
convertibles 0% other 0% cash 7%

Largest Holdings: financial services 8%, bank 8%

Unrealized Net Capital Gains: 19% of portfolio value

SHAREHOLDER INFORMATION

Minimum Investment
Initial: $1,000   Subsequent: $100

Minimum IRA Investment
Initial: $1,000   Subsequent: $100

Maximum Fees
Load: none   12b-1: none
Other: none

Distributions
Income: Dec   Capital Gains: Dec

Exchange Options
Number Per Year: 8   Fee: none
Telephone: yes (money market fund available)

Services
IRA, other pension, auto invest, auto withdraw

Value Line NY Tax-Exempt Trust (VLNYX)

Tax-Exempt Bond

200 East 42nd Street
New York, NY 10017
(800) 223-0818, (212) 907-1500

PERFORMANCE

	3yr Annual	5yr Annual	10yr Annual	Bull	Bear
Return (%)	12.5	9.9	na	46.1	1.7
Differ from Category (+/-)	2.2 high	0.6 abv av	na	6.0 high	-0.6 blw av

Total Risk	Standard Deviation	Category Risk	Risk Index	Avg Mat
blw av	5.8%	high	1.4	24.0 yrs

	1993	1992	1991	1990	1989	1988	1987	1986	1985	1984
Return (%)	13.9	9.5	14.3	4.1	7.9	10.8	—	—	—	—
Differ from category (+/-) . . .	2.3	1.2	3.0	-2.2	-1.1	0.6	—	—	—	—

PER SHARE DATA

	1993	1992	1991	1990	1989	1988	1987	1986	1985	1984
Dividends, Net Income ($) .	0.57	0.59	0.65	0.70	0.71	0.74	—	—	—	—
Distrib'ns, Cap Gain ($) . . .	0.41	0.14	0.00	0.00	0.03	0.05	—	—	—	—
Net Asset Value ($)	10.73	10.32	10.12	9.47	9.79	9.78	—	—	—	—
Expense Ratio (%)	0.85	0.92	0.91	1.01	0.76	0.00	—	—	—	—
Net Income to Assets (%) .	5.82	6.50	7.46	7.16	7.51	8.15	—	—	—	—
Portfolio Turnover (%)	137	124	61	39	73	17	—	—	—	—
Total Assets (Millions $)	44	35	32	29	26	20	—	—	—	—

PORTFOLIO (as of 8/31/93)

Portfolio Manager: committee

Investm't Category: Tax-Exempt Bond

Cap Gain	Asset Allocation
Cap & Income	Fund of Funds
✔ Income	Index
	Sector
✔ Domestic	Small Cap
Foreign	Socially Conscious
Country/Region	✔ State Specific

Portfolio: stocks 0% bonds 96%
convertibles 0% other 0% cash 4%

Largest Holdings: general obligation 16%

Unrealized Net Capital Gains: 9% of portfolio value

SHAREHOLDER INFORMATION

Minimum Investment
Initial: $1,000   Subsequent: $250

Minimum IRA Investment
Initial: na   Subsequent: na

Maximum Fees
Load: none   12b-1: none
Other: none

Distributions
Income: monthly   Capital Gains: Dec

Exchange Options
Number Per Year: 8   Fee: none
Telephone: yes (money market fund available)

Services
auto invest, auto withdraw

Value Line Special Situations (VALSX)

Aggressive Growth

200 East 42nd Street
New York, NY 10017
(800) 223-0818, (212) 907-1500

PERFORMANCE

	3yr Annual	5yr Annual	10yr Annual	Bull	Bear
Return (%)	14.6	11.8	4.5	59.8	-9.9
Differ from Category (+/-)	-10.8 low	-6.4 low	-7.4 low	-65.2 low	5.1 abv av

Total Risk	Standard Deviation	Category Risk	Risk Index	Beta
high	17.4%	av	1.1	1.1

	1993	1992	1991	1990	1989	1988	1987	1986	1985	1984
Return (%)	12.9	-3.4	38.1	-4.4	21.6	3.3	-9.0	5.1	21.0	-25.5
Differ from category (+/-) . .	-6.1	-13.8	-14.3	1.9	-5.4	-11.9	-5.6	-4.3	-10.0	-16.1

PER SHARE DATA

	1993	1992	1991	1990	1989	1988	1987	1986	1985	1984
Dividends, Net Income ($) .	0.00	0.00	0.22	0.16	0.22	0.08	0.11	0.03	0.04	0.01
Distrib'ns, Cap Gain ($) . . .	0.74	0.14	0.85	0.00	0.00	0.00	2.55	0.00	0.00	0.07
Net Asset Value ($)	16.95	15.69	16.41	12.72	13.49	11.27	10.99	15.07	14.37	11.91
Expense Ratio (%)	1.26	1.09	1.04	1.11	1.08	1.16	1.01	1.02	1.07	1.06
Net Income to Assets (%) .	-0.93	-0.33	0.24	0.92	1.84	0.68	0.26	0.29	0.22	0.60
Portfolio Turnover (%)	na	43	37	33	66	59	41	72	87	75
Total Assets (Millions $)	90	101	129	104	117	112	124	193	242	240

PORTFOLIO (as of 9/30/93)

Portfolio Manager: committee

Investm't Category: Aggressive Growth

✔ Cap Gain	Asset Allocation
Cap & Income	Fund of Funds
Income	Index
	Sector
✔ Domestic	Small Cap
Foreign	Socially Conscious
Country/Region	State Specific

Portfolio: stocks 93% bonds 0%
convertibles 0% other 0% cash 7%

Largest Holdings: computer software & services 13%, drug 12%

Unrealized Net Capital Gains: 21% of portfolio value

SHAREHOLDER INFORMATION

Minimum Investment
Initial: $1,000   Subsequent: $100

Minimum IRA Investment
Initial: $1,000   Subsequent: $100

Maximum Fees
Load: none   12b-1: none
Other: none

Distributions
Income: Dec   Capital Gains: Dec

Exchange Options
Number Per Year: 8   Fee: none
Telephone: yes (money market fund available)

Services
IRA, other pension, auto invest, auto withdraw

Value Line Tax Exempt High Yield (VLHYX)

200 East 42nd Street
New York, NY 10017
(800) 223-0818, (212) 907-1500

Tax-Exempt Bond

PERFORMANCE

	3yr Annual	5yr Annual	10yr Annual	Bull	Bear
Return (%)	10.5	9.2	na	40.3	2.4
Differ from Category (+/-)	0.2 blw av	0.0 blw av	na	0.2 blw av	0.1 av

Total Risk	Standard Deviation	Category Risk	Risk Index	Avg Mat
blw av	4.7%	abv av	1.2	20.7 yrs

	1993	1992	1991	1990	1989	1988	1987	1986	1985	1984
Return (%).............	11.5	7.8	12.2	6.5	8.3	10.9	0.5	13.4	19.2	—
Differ from category (+/-)...	-0.1	-0.5	0.8	0.2	-0.6	0.8	1.7	-3.0	1.9	—

PER SHARE DATA

	1993	1992	1991	1990	1989	1988	1987	1986	1985	1984
Dividends, Net Income ($).	0.60	0.63	0.69	0.77	0.79	0.79	0.81	0.91	0.93	—
Distrib'ns, Cap Gain ($) ...	0.20	0.00	0.00	0.00	0.00	0.00	0.05	0.34	0.00	—
Net Asset Value ($)	11.27	10.86	10.68	10.17	10.30	10.26	9.99	10.81	10.70	—
Expense Ratio (%)	0.60	0.58	0.60	0.62	0.63	0.64	0.68	0.66	0.17	—
Net Income to Assets (%) .	5.89	6.50	7.47	7.70	7.77	7.98	8.20	9.36	10.49	—
Portfolio Turnover (%).....	101	122	122	63	73	76	79	253	186	—
Total Assets (Millions $)....	290	300	278	272	266	259	312	133	36	—

PORTFOLIO (as of 8/31/93)

Portfolio Manager: committee

Investm't Category: Tax-Exempt Bond

Cap Gain	Asset Allocation
Cap & Income	Fund of Funds
✔ Income	Index
	Sector
✔ Domestic	Small Cap
Foreign	Socially Conscious
Country/Region	State Specific

Portfolio: stocks 0% bonds 94%
convertibles 0% other 0% cash 6%

Largest Holdings: general obligation 28%

Unrealized Net Capital Gains: 6% of portfolio value

SHAREHOLDER INFORMATION

Minimum Investment
Initial: $1,000   Subsequent: $250

Minimum IRA Investment
Initial: na   Subsequent: na

Maximum Fees
Load: none   12b-1: none
Other: none

Distributions
Income: monthly   Capital Gains: Dec

Exchange Options
Number Per Year: 8   Fee: none
Telephone: yes (money market fund available)

Services
auto invest, auto withdraw

Value Line US Gov't Securities (VALBX)

200 East 42nd Street
New York, NY 10017
(800) 223-0818, (212) 907-1500

Mortgage-Backed Bond

PERFORMANCE

	3yr Annual	5yr Annual	10yr Annual	Bull	Bear
Return (%)	10.7	10.8	11.0	42.4	5.2
Differ from Category (+/-)	1.5 high	0.8 high	0.3 av	5.7 high	0.6 high

Total Risk	Standard Deviation	Category Risk	Risk Index	Avg Mat
low	3.6%	high	1.4	23.7 yrs

	1993	1992	1991	1990	1989	1988	1987	1986	1985	1984
Return (%)	9.7	6.3	16.4	10.2	11.9	7.9	3.3	10.6	21.2	14.0
Differ from category (+/-)	2.9	0.2	2.0	0.6	-0.4	0.8	1.2	-0.6	1.9	0.6

PER SHARE DATA

	1993	1992	1991	1990	1989	1988	1987	1986	1985	1984
Dividends, Net Income ($)	0.94	0.88	0.94	1.00	1.10	1.01	1.50	1.32	1.31	1.28
Distrib'ns, Cap Gain ($)	0.33	0.10	0.00	0.00	0.00	0.00	0.00	0.37	0.00	0.00
Net Asset Value ($)	12.62	12.68	12.89	11.96	11.80	11.57	11.67	12.77	13.15	12.06
Expense Ratio (%)	0.61	0.64	0.64	0.67	0.66	0.67	0.72	0.76	0.85	0.92
Net Income to Assets (%)	7.29	7.47	8.54	9.25	10.05	10.09	9.49	10.10	11.01	11.63
Portfolio Turnover (%)	169	130	79	59	34	54	48	72	64	30
Total Assets (Millions $)	452	424	337	258	252	247	218	112	68	51

PORTFOLIO (as of 8/31/93)

Portfolio Manager: committee

Investm't Category: Mortgage-Backed Bond
- Cap Gain
- Cap & Income
- ✔ Income
- ✔ Domestic
- Foreign
- Country/Region
- Asset Allocation
- Fund of Funds
- Index
- Sector
- Small Cap
- Socially Conscious
- State Specific

Portfolio: stocks 0% bonds 100%
convertibles 0% other 0% cash 0%

Largest Holdings: mortgage-backed 94%, U.S. government 6%

Unrealized Net Capital Gains: 3% of portfolio value

SHAREHOLDER INFORMATION

Minimum Investment
Initial: $1,000   Subsequent: $250

Minimum IRA Investment
Initial: $1,000   Subsequent: $250

Maximum Fees
Load: none   12b-1: none
Other: none

Distributions
Income: quarterly   Capital Gains: Dec

Exchange Options
Number Per Year: 8   Fee: none
Telephone: yes (money market fund available)

Services
IRA, other pension, auto invest, auto withdraw

Vanguard Admiral Interm US Treas (VAITX)

Government Bond

Vanguard Financial Center
P.O. Box 2600
Valley Forge, PA 19482
(800) 662-7447, (215) 648-6000

PERFORMANCE

	3yr Annual	5yr Annual	10yr Annual	Bull	Bear
Return (%)	na	na	na	na	na
Differ from Category (+/-)	na	na	na	na	na

Total Risk	Standard Deviation	Category Risk	Risk Index	Avg Mat
na	na	na	na	6.6 yrs

	1993	1992	1991	1990	1989	1988	1987	1986	1985	1984
Return (%)	11.3	—	—	—	—	—	—	—	—	—
Differ from category (+/-). . .	0.8	—	—	—	—	—	—	—	—	—

PER SHARE DATA

	1993	1992	1991	1990	1989	1988	1987	1986	1985	1984
Dividends, Net Income ($) .	0.58	—	—	—	—	—	—	—	—	—
Distrib'ns, Cap Gain ($) . . .	0.12	—	—	—	—	—	—	—	—	—
Net Asset Value ($)	10.48	—	—	—	—	—	—	—	—	—
Expense Ratio (%)	0.15	—	—	—	—	—	—	—	—	—
Net Income to Assets (%) .	5.63	—	—	—	—	—	—	—	—	—
Portfolio Turnover (%).	159	—	—	—	—	—	—	—	—	—
Total Assets (Millions $). . . .	989	—	—	—	—	—	—	—	—	—

PORTFOLIO (as of 7/31/93)

Portfolio Manager: Ian MacKinnon - 1992

Investm't Category: Government Bond

Cap Gain	Asset Allocation
Cap & Income	Fund of Funds
✔ Income	Index
	Sector
✔ Domestic	Small Cap
Foreign	Socially Conscious
Country/Region	State Specific

Portfolio: stocks 0% bonds 99%
convertibles 0% other 0% cash 1%

Largest Holdings: U.S. government 99%

Unrealized Net Capital Gains: 1% of portfolio value

SHAREHOLDER INFORMATION

Minimum Investment
Initial: $50,000   Subsequent: $100

Minimum IRA Investment
Initial: $50,000   Subsequent: $100

Maximum Fees
Load: none   12b-1: none
Other: none

Distributions
Income: monthly   Capital Gains: Dec

Exchange Options
Number Per Year: 2   Fee: none
Telephone: yes (money market fund available)

Services
IRA, other pension, auto invest, auto withdraw

Vanguard Admiral Long US Treas (VALGX)

Government Bond

Vanguard Financial Center
P.O. Box 2600
Valley Forge, PA 19482
(800) 662-7447, (215) 648-6000

PERFORMANCE

	3yr Annual	5yr Annual	10yr Annual	Bull	Bear
Return (%)	na	na	na	na	na
Differ from Category (+/-)	na	na	na	na	na

Total Risk	Standard Deviation	Category Risk	Risk Index	Avg Mat
na	na	na	na	20.3 yrs

	1993	1992	1991	1990	1989	1988	1987	1986	1985	1984
Return (%)	16.6	—	—	—	—	—	—	—	—	—
Differ from category (+/-) . . .	6.2	—	—	—	—	—	—	—	—	—

PER SHARE DATA

	1993	1992	1991	1990	1989	1988	1987	1986	1985	1984
Dividends, Net Income ($) .	0.73	—	—	—	—	—	—	—	—	—
Distrib'ns, Cap Gain ($) . . .	0.26	—	—	—	—	—	—	—	—	—
Net Asset Value ($)	10.71	—	—	—	—	—	—	—	—	—
Expense Ratio (%)	0.15	—	—	—	—	—	—	—	—	—
Net Income to Assets (%) . .	6.74	—	—	—	—	—	—	—	—	—
Portfolio Turnover (%)	39	—	—	—	—	—	—	—	—	—
Total Assets (Millions $) . . .	831	—	—	—	—	—	—	—	—	—

PORTFOLIO (as of 7/31/93)

Portfolio Manager: Ian MacKinnon - 1992

Investm't Category: Government Bond

Cap Gain	Asset Allocation
Cap & Income	Fund of Funds
✔ Income	Index
	Sector
✔ Domestic	Small Cap
Foreign	Socially Conscious
Country/Region	State Specific

Portfolio: stocks 0% bonds 98%
convertibles 0% other 0% cash 2%

Largest Holdings: U.S. government 98%

Unrealized Net Capital Gains: 5% of portfolio value

SHAREHOLDER INFORMATION

Minimum Investment
Initial: $50,000   Subsequent: $100

Minimum IRA Investment
Initial: $50,000   Subsequent: $100

Maximum Fees
Load: none   12b-1: none
Other: none

Distributions
Income: monthly   Capital Gains: Dec

Exchange Options
Number Per Year: 2   Fee: none
Telephone: yes (money market fund available)

Services
IRA, other pension, auto invest, auto withdraw

Vanguard Admiral Short US Treas (VASTX)

Government Bond

Vanguard Financial Center
P.O. Box 2600
Valley Forge, PA 19482
(800) 662-7447, (215) 648-6000

PERFORMANCE

	3yr Annual	5yr Annual	10yr Annual	Bull	Bear
Return (%)	na	na	na	na	na
Differ from Category (+/-)	na	na	na	na	na

Total Risk	Standard Deviation	Category Risk	Risk Index	Avg Mat
na	na	na	na	2.5 yrs

	1993	1992	1991	1990	1989	1988	1987	1986	1985	1984
Return (%)	6.4	—	—	—	—	—	—	—	—	—
Differ from category (+/-)	-4.0	—	—	—	—	—	—	—	—	—

PER SHARE DATA

	1993	1992	1991	1990	1989	1988	1987	1986	1985	1984
Dividends, Net Income ($)	0.45	—	—	—	—	—	—	—	—	—
Distrib'ns, Cap Gain ($)	0.00	—	—	—	—	—	—	—	—	—
Net Asset Value ($)	10.23	—	—	—	—	—	—	—	—	—
Expense Ratio (%)	0.15	—	—	—	—	—	—	—	—	—
Net Income to Assets (%)	4.44	—	—	—	—	—	—	—	—	—
Portfolio Turnover (%)	62	—	—	—	—	—	—	—	—	—
Total Assets (Millions $)	704	—	—	—	—	—	—	—	—	—

PORTFOLIO (as of 7/31/93)

Portfolio Manager: Ian MacKinnon - 1992

Investm't Category: Government Bond

Cap Gain	Asset Allocation
Cap & Income	Fund of Funds
✔ Income	Index
	Sector
✔ Domestic	Small Cap
Foreign	Socially Conscious
Country/Region	State Specific

Portfolio: stocks 0% bonds 99%
convertibles 0% other 0% cash 1%

Largest Holdings: U.S. government 99%

Unrealized Net Capital Gains: 0% of portfolio value

SHAREHOLDER INFORMATION

Minimum Investment
Initial: $50,000   Subsequent: $100

Minimum IRA Investment
Initial: $50,000   Subsequent: $100

Maximum Fees
Load: none   12b-1: none
Other: none

Distributions
Income: monthly   Capital Gains: Dec

Exchange Options
Number Per Year: 2   Fee: none
Telephone: yes (money market fund available)

Services
IRA, other pension, auto invest, auto withdraw

Vanguard Asset Allocation (VAAPX)

Balanced

Vanguard Financial Center
P.O. Box 2600
Valley Forge, PA 19482
(800) 662-7447, (215) 648-6000

PERFORMANCE

	3yr Annual	5yr Annual	10yr Annual	Bull	Bear
Return (%)	15.2	13.8	na	66.8	-7.3
Differ from Category (+/-)	0.2 av	1.7 abv av	na	5.2 abv av	-1.5 blw av

Total Risk	Standard Deviation	Category Risk	Risk Index	Beta
av	7.5%	abv av	1.2	0.6

	1993	1992	1991	1990	1989	1988	1987	1986	1985	1984
Return (%)	13.4	7.5	25.5	0.8	23.6	—	—	—	—	—
Differ from category (+/-)	0.0	-0.6	1.6	1.3	6.0	—	—	—	—	—

PER SHARE DATA

	1993	1992	1991	1990	1989	1988	1987	1986	1985	1984
Dividends, Net Income ($)	0.47	0.58	0.58	0.62	0.50	—	—	—	—	—
Distrib'ns, Cap Gain ($)	0.52	0.17	0.18	0.12	0.15	—	—	—	—	—
Net Asset Value ($)	14.45	13.64	13.41	11.35	12.01	—	—	—	—	—
Expense Ratio (%)	0.49	0.52	0.44	0.50	0.49	—	—	—	—	—
Net Income to Assets (%)	4.07	4.95	5.28	5.53	5.53	—	—	—	—	—
Portfolio Turnover (%)	31	18	44	12	52	—	—	—	—	—
Total Assets (Millions $)	1,089	502	265	160	107	—	—	—	—	—

PORTFOLIO (as of 9/30/93)

Portfolio Manager: Thomas Hazuka - 1988

Investm't Category: Balanced

Cap Gain	✔ Asset Allocation
✔ Cap & Income	Fund of Funds
Income	Index
	Sector
✔ Domestic	Small Cap
Foreign	Socially Conscious
Country/Region	State Specific

Portfolio: stocks 70% bonds 28%
convertibles 0% other 0% cash 2%

Largest Holdings: S&P 500 stocks 70%, bonds—U.S. government 28%

Unrealized Net Capital Gains: 8% of portfolio value

SHAREHOLDER INFORMATION

Minimum Investment
Initial: $3,000   Subsequent: $100

Minimum IRA Investment
Initial: $500   Subsequent: $100

Maximum Fees
Load: none   12b-1: none
Other: none

Distributions
Income: Apr, Dec   Capital Gains: Dec

Exchange Options
Number Per Year: 2   Fee: none
Telephone: yes (money market fund available)

Services
IRA, other pension, auto exchange, auto invest, auto withdraw

Vanguard Balanced Index (VBINX)

Balanced

Vanguard Financial Center
P.O. Box 2600
Valley Forge, PA 19482
(800) 662-7447, (215) 648-6000

PERFORMANCE

	3yr Annual	5yr Annual	10yr Annual	Bull	Bear
Return (%)	na	na	na	na	na
Differ from Category (+/-)	na	na	na	na	na

Total Risk	Standard Deviation	Category Risk	Risk Index	Beta
na	na	na	na	na

	1993	1992	1991	1990	1989	1988	1987	1986	1985	1984
Return (%)	9.9	—	—	—	—	—	—	—	—	—
Differ from category (+/-)	-3.5	—	—	—	—	—	—	—	—	—

PER SHARE DATA

	1993	1992	1991	1990	1989	1988	1987	1986	1985	1984
Dividends, Net Income ($)	0.38	—	—	—	—	—	—	—	—	—
Distrib'ns, Cap Gain ($)	0.02	—	—	—	—	—	—	—	—	—
Net Asset Value ($)	10.91	—	—	—	—	—	—	—	—	—
Expense Ratio (%)	0.20	—	—	—	—	—	—	—	—	—
Net Income to Assets (%)	3.75	—	—	—	—	—	—	—	—	—
Portfolio Turnover (%)	41	—	—	—	—	—	—	—	—	—
Total Assets (Millions $)	385	—	—	—	—	—	—	—	—	—

PORTFOLIO (as of 6/30/93)

Portfolio Manager: George U. Sauter - 1992

Investm't Category: Balanced
- Cap Gain
- ✔ Cap & Income
- Income

- Asset Allocation
- Fund of Funds
- ✔ Index
- Sector
- Small Cap
- Socially Conscious
- State Specific

- ✔ Domestic
- Foreign
- Country/Region

Portfolio: stocks 60% bonds 39%
convertibles 0% other 0% cash 1%

Largest Holdings: Wilshire 5000 Index 60%, Lehman Brothers Aggregate Bond Index 40%

Unrealized Net Capital Gains: 3% of portfolio value

SHAREHOLDER INFORMATION

Minimum Investment
Initial: $3,000   Subsequent: $100

Minimum IRA Investment
Initial: $500   Subsequent: $100

Maximum Fees
Load: none   12b-1: none
Other: $10 account maintenance fee

Distributions
Income: quarterly   Capital Gains: Dec

Exchange Options
Number Per Year: 2   Fee: none
Telephone: none

Services
IRA, other pension, auto exchange, auto invest, auto withdraw

Vanguard Bond Index
(VBMFX)
General Bond

Vanguard Financial Center
P.O. Box 2600
Valley Forge, PA 19482
(800) 662-7447, (215) 648-6000

PERFORMANCE

	3yr Annual	5yr Annual	10yr Annual	Bull	Bear
Return (%)	10.6	10.8	na	42.5	3.2
Differ from Category (+/-)	0.4 av	1.0 abv av	na	3.1 av	0.3 av

Total Risk	Standard Deviation	Category Risk	Risk Index	Avg Mat
low	3.2%	blw av	1.1	9.0 yrs

	1993	1992	1991	1990	1989	1988	1987	1986	1985	1984
Return (%)	9.6	7.1	15.2	8.6	13.6	7.3	1.5	—	—	—
Differ from category (+/-) . . .	0.4	0.4	0.6	1.7	2.3	-0.3	-1.0	—	—	—

PER SHARE DATA

	1993	1992	1991	1990	1989	1988	1987	1986	1985	1984
Dividends, Net Income ($) .	0.63	0.69	0.76	0.79	0.79	0.80	0.87	—	—	—
Distrib'ns, Cap Gain ($) . . .	0.11	0.09	0.02	0.00	0.00	0.00	0.00	—	—	—
Net Asset Value ($)	10.06	9.88	9.99	9.41	9.44	9.05	9.20	—	—	—
Expense Ratio (%)	0.18	0.20	0.16	0.21	0.24	0.30	0.14	—	—	—
Net Income to Assets (%) . .	6.58	7.06	7.95	8.60	8.49	8.84	9.01	—	—	—
Portfolio Turnover (%)	73	49	31	29	33	21	77	—	—	—
Total Assets (Millions $) . .	1,559	1,067	849	277	139	58	43	—	—	—

PORTFOLIO (as of 6/30/93)

Portfolio Manager: Ian MacKinnon - 1986

Investm't Category: General Bond

Cap Gain	Asset Allocation
Cap & Income	Fund of Funds
✔ Income	✔ Index
	Sector
✔ Domestic	Small Cap
Foreign	Socially Conscious
Country/Region	State Specific

Portfolio: stocks 0% bonds 99%
convertibles 0% other 0% cash 1%

Largest Holdings: Lehman Brothers Aggregate Bond Index

Unrealized Net Capital Gains: 4% of portfolio value

SHAREHOLDER INFORMATION

Minimum Investment
Initial: $3,000   Subsequent: $100

Minimum IRA Investment
Initial: $500   Subsequent: $100

Maximum Fees
Load: none   12b-1: none
Other: $10 account maintenance fee

Distributions
Income: monthly   Capital Gains: Dec

Exchange Options
Number Per Year: 2   Fee: none
Telephone: yes (money market fund available)

Services
IRA, other pension, auto exchange, auto invest, auto withdraw

Vanguard CA Tax-Free Insured Long (VCITX)

Tax-Exempt Bond

Vanguard Financial Center
P.O. Box 2600
Valley Forge, PA 19482
(800) 662-7447, (215) 648-6000

PERFORMANCE

	3yr Annual	5yr Annual	10yr Annual	Bull	Bear
Return (%)	11.0	10.1	na	45.7	0.5
Differ from Category (+/-)	0.6 av	0.8 abv av	na	5.6 high	-1.8 low

Total Risk	Standard Deviation	Category Risk	Risk Index	Avg Mat
blw av	5.5%	high	1.4	11.3 yrs

	1993	1992	1991	1990	1989	1988	1987	1986	1985	1984
Return (%)............	12.8	9.3	11.0	6.9	10.4	12.1	-3.8	—	—	—
Differ from category (+/-)...	1.2	1.0	-0.3	0.6	1.4	2.0	-2.6	—	—	—

PER SHARE DATA

	1993	1992	1991	1990	1989	1988	1987	1986	1985	1984
Dividends, Net Income ($).	0.60	0.63	0.64	0.65	0.67	0.68	0.66	—	—	—
Distrib'ns, Cap Gain ($) ...	0.15	0.19	0.00	0.00	0.00	0.00	0.00	—	—	—
Net Asset Value ($)	11.37	10.77	10.64	10.20	10.18	9.85	9.43	—	—	—
Expense Ratio (%)	0.20	0.24	0.25	0.26	0.24	0.30	0.31	—	—	—
Net Income to Assets (%) .	5.48	5.92	6.24	6.57	6.67	6.83	6.86	—	—	—
Portfolio Turnover (%)......	29	54	19	6	3	4	37	—	—	—
Total Assets (Millions $)..	1,071	828	630	386	260	126	89	—	—	—

PORTFOLIO (as of 5/31/93)

Portfolio Manager: Ian MacKinnon - 1986

Investm't Category: Tax-Exempt Bond

Cap Gain	Asset Allocation
Cap & Income	Fund of Funds
✔ Income	Index
	Sector
✔ Domestic	Small Cap
Foreign	Socially Conscious
Country/Region	✔ State Specific

Portfolio: stocks 0% bonds 100%
convertibles 0% other 0% cash 0%

Largest Holdings: na

Unrealized Net Capital Gains: 7% of portfolio value

SHAREHOLDER INFORMATION

Minimum Investment
Initial: $3,000   Subsequent: $100

Minimum IRA Investment
Initial: na   Subsequent: na

Maximum Fees
Load: none   12b-1: none
Other: none

Distributions
Income: monthly   Capital Gains: Dec

Exchange Options
Number Per Year: 2   Fee: none
Telephone: yes (money market fund available)

Services
auto exchange, auto invest, auto withdraw

Vanguard Convertible Securities (VCVSX)

Growth & Income

Vanguard Financial Center
P.O. Box 2600
Valley Forge, PA 19482
(800) 662-7447, (215) 648-6000

PERFORMANCE

	3yr Annual	5yr Annual	10yr Annual	Bull	Bear
Return (%)	21.9	14.0	na	91.8	-13.1
Differ from Category (+/-)	5.5 high	1.5 abv av	na	21.7 high	-1.5 blw av

Total Risk	Standard Deviation	Category Risk	Risk Index	Beta
av	9.0%	blw av	1.0	0.6

	1993	1992	1991	1990	1989	1988	1987	1986	1985	1984
Return (%)	13.5	18.9	34.3	-8.1	15.8	15.7	-10.6	—	—	—
Differ from category (+/-)	0.8	8.9	6.6	-2.5	-5.8	-1.1	-11.0	—	—	—

PER SHARE DATA

	1993	1992	1991	1990	1989	1988	1987	1986	1985	1984
Dividends, Net Income ($)	0.52	0.52	0.54	0.56	0.56	0.56	0.56	—	—	—
Distrib'ns, Cap Gain ($)	0.91	0.00	0.00	0.00	0.00	0.00	0.11	—	—	—
Net Asset Value ($)	11.91	11.80	10.40	8.19	9.52	8.72	8.04	—	—	—
Expense Ratio (%)	0.74	0.85	0.81	0.88	0.84	0.88	0.85	—	—	—
Net Income to Assets (%)	4.49	4.80	5.72	6.35	5.60	6.52	6.13	—	—	—
Portfolio Turnover (%)	78	55	57	55	55	24	13	—	—	—
Total Assets (Millions $)	202	120	55	44	59	69	73	—	—	—

PORTFOLIO (as of 5/31/93)

Portfolio Manager: Rohit Desai - 1986

Investm't Category: Growth & Income

Cap Gain	Asset Allocation
✔ Cap & Income	Fund of Funds
Income	Index
	Sector
✔ Domestic	Small Cap
Foreign	Socially Conscious
Country/Region	State Specific

Portfolio: stocks 5% bonds 0%
convertibles 92% other 0% cash 3%

Largest Holdings: health care 11%, specialty training 9%

Unrealized Net Capital Gains: 6% of portfolio value

SHAREHOLDER INFORMATION

Minimum Investment
Initial: $3,000   Subsequent: $100

Minimum IRA Investment
Initial: $500   Subsequent: $100

Maximum Fees
Load: none   12b-1: none
Other: none

Distributions
Income: quarterly   Capital Gains: Dec

Exchange Options
Number Per Year: 2   Fee: none
Telephone: yes (money market fund available)

Services
IRA, other pension, auto exchange, auto invest, auto withdraw

Vanguard Equity Income (VEIPX)

Growth & Income

Vanguard Financial Center
P.O. Box 2600
Valley Forge, PA 19482
(800) 662-7447, (215) 648-6000

PERFORMANCE

	3yr Annual	5yr Annual	10yr Annual	Bull	Bear
Return (%)	16.2	11.8	na	66.3	-16.8
Differ from Category (+/-)	-0.2 av	-0.6 blw av	na	-3.8 blw av	-5.2 low

Total Risk	Standard Deviation	Category Risk	Risk Index	Beta
av	9.1%	av	1.0	0.8

	1993	1992	1991	1990	1989	1988	1987	1986	1985	1984
Return (%)	14.6	9.1	25.3	-11.9	26.4	—	—	—	—	—
Differ from category (+/-) . . .	2.0	-0.8	-2.4	-6.3	4.8	—	—	—	—	—

PER SHARE DATA

	1993	1992	1991	1990	1989	1988	1987	1986	1985	1984
Dividends, Net Income ($) .	0.61	0.58	0.64	0.73	0.69	—	—	—	—	—
Distrib'ns, Cap Gain ($) . . .	0.51	0.00	0.10	0.07	0.02	—	—	—	—	—
Net Asset Value ($)	13.66	12.92	12.40	10.54	12.86	—	—	—	—	—
Expense Ratio (%)	0.40	0.44	0.46	0.48	0.44	—	—	—	—	—
Net Income to Assets (%) .	4.39	4.74	5.52	5.67	6.01	—	—	—	—	—
Portfolio Turnover (%).	15	13	9	5	8	—	—	—	—	—
Total Assets (Millions $). .	1,058	778	518	353	267	—	—	—	—	—

PORTFOLIO (as of 9/30/93)

Portfolio Manager: Roger Newell - 1988

Investm't Category: Growth & Income
Cap Gain	Asset Allocation
✔ Cap & Income	Fund of Funds
Income	Index
	Sector
✔ Domestic	Small Cap
Foreign	Socially Conscious
Country/Region	State Specific

Portfolio: stocks 96% bonds 0%
convertibles 0% other 0% cash 4%

Largest Holdings: electric utility 16%, tele-communications 13%

Unrealized Net Capital Gains: 12% of portfolio value

SHAREHOLDER INFORMATION

Minimum Investment
Initial: $3,000   Subsequent: $100

Minimum IRA Investment
Initial: $500   Subsequent: $100

Maximum Fees
Load: none   12b-1: none
Other: none

Distributions
Income: quarterly   Capital Gains: Dec

Exchange Options
Number Per Year: 2   Fee: none
Telephone: yes (money market fund available)

Services
IRA, other pension, auto exchange, auto invest, auto withdraw

Vanguard Explorer
(VEXPX)

Aggressive Growth

Vanguard Financial Center
P.O. Box 2600
Valley Forge, PA 19482
(800) 662-7447, (215) 648-6000

PERFORMANCE

	3yr Annual	5yr Annual	10yr Annual	Bull	Bear
Return (%)	26.7	14.7	7.6	124.8	-19.2
Differ from Category (+/-)	1.3 av	-3.5 blw av	-4.3 low	-0.2 av	-4.2 blw av

Total Risk	Standard Deviation	Category Risk	Risk Index	Beta
high	14.8%	blw av	1.0	1.0

	1993	1992	1991	1990	1989	1988	1987	1986	1985	1984
Return (%)	15.5	12.9	55.9	-10.7	9.3	25.8	-6.9	-8.4	22.3	-19.5
Differ from category (+/-) . .	-3.5	2.5	3.5	-4.4	-17.7	10.6	-3.5	-17.8	-8.7	-10.1

PER SHARE DATA

	1993	1992	1991	1990	1989	1988	1987	1986	1985	1984
Dividends, Net Income ($) .	0.14	0.12	0.25	0.34	0.37	0.31	0.10	0.01	0.33	0.37
Distrib'ns, Cap Gain ($) . . .	5.17	0.77	0.00	0.00	1.01	1.59	1.96	3.27	1.29	0.20
Net Asset Value ($)	45.11	43.84	39.62	25.58	29.06	27.85	23.66	27.66	33.73	28.97
Expense Ratio (%)	0.70	0.68	0.56	0.67	0.58	0.65	0.62	0.76	0.80	1.00
Net Income to Assets (%) . .	0.44	0.38	0.85	1.11	1.24	0.99	0.28	0.05	1.02	1.27
Portfolio Turnover (%)	47	43	49	46	16	28	9	15	19	8
Total Assets (Millions $) . . .	787	519	381	208	271	266	210	271	334	260

PORTFOLIO (as of 4/30/93)

Portfolio Manager: Frank Wisneski - 1979, John Granahan - 1990

Investm't Category: Aggressive Growth
- ✔ Cap Gain
- Cap & Income
- Income
- ✔ Domestic
- ✔ Foreign
- Country/Region

- Asset Allocation
- Fund of Funds
- Index
- Sector
- ✔ Small Cap
- Socially Conscious
- State Specific

Portfolio: stocks 84% bonds 0%
convertibles 1% other 0% cash 15%

Largest Holdings: business, industrial & government services 17%, consumer services 16%

Unrealized Net Capital Gains: 10% of portfolio value

SHAREHOLDER INFORMATION

Minimum Investment
Initial: $3,000   Subsequent: $100

Minimum IRA Investment
Initial: $500   Subsequent: $100

Maximum Fees
Load: none   12b-1: none
Other: none

Distributions
Income: Dec   Capital Gains: Dec

Exchange Options
Number Per Year: 2   Fee: none
Telephone: none

Services
IRA, other pension, auto exchange, auto invest, auto withdraw

Vanguard Florida Insured Tax Free (VFLTX)

Tax-Exempt Bond

Vanguard Financial Center
P.O. Box 2600
Valley Forge, PA 19482
(800) 662-7447, (215) 648-6000

PERFORMANCE

	3yr Annual	5yr Annual	10yr Annual	Bull	Bear
Return (%)	na	na	na	na	na
Differ from Category (+/-)	na	na	na	na	na

Total Risk	Standard Deviation	Category Risk	Risk Index	Avg Mat
na	na	na	na	10.7 yrs

	1993	1992	1991	1990	1989	1988	1987	1986	1985	1984
Return (%)	13.5	—	—	—	—	—	—	—	—	—
Differ from category (+/-)	1.9	—	—	—	—	—	—	—	—	—

PER SHARE DATA

	1993	1992	1991	1990	1989	1988	1987	1986	1985	1984
Dividends, Net Income ($)	0.53	—	—	—	—	—	—	—	—	—
Distrib'ns, Cap Gain ($)	0.06	—	—	—	—	—	—	—	—	—
Net Asset Value ($)	10.99	—	—	—	—	—	—	—	—	—
Expense Ratio (%)	0.25	—	—	—	—	—	—	—	—	—
Net Income to Assets (%)	5.08	—	—	—	—	—	—	—	—	—
Portfolio Turnover (%)	75	—	—	—	—	—	—	—	—	—
Total Assets (Millions $)	267	—	—	—	—	—	—	—	—	—

PORTFOLIO (as of 5/31/93)

Portfolio Manager: Ian MacKinnon - 1992

Investm't Category: Tax-Exempt Bond

Cap Gain	Asset Allocation
Cap & Income	Fund of Funds
✔ Income	Index
	Sector
✔ Domestic	Small Cap
Foreign	Socially Conscious
Country/Region	✔ State Specific

Portfolio: stocks 0%   bonds 100%
convertibles 0%   other 0%   cash 0%

Largest Holdings: na

Unrealized Net Capital Gains: 3% of portfolio value

SHAREHOLDER INFORMATION

Minimum Investment
Initial: $3,000   Subsequent: $100

Minimum IRA Investment
Initial: na   Subsequent: na

Maximum Fees
Load: none   12b-1: none
Other: none

Distributions
Income: monthly   Capital Gains: Dec

Exchange Options
Number Per Year: 2   Fee: none
Telephone: yes (money market fund available)

Services
auto exchange, auto invest, auto withdraw

Vanguard GNMA (VFIIX)

Mortgage-Backed Bond

Vanguard Financial Center
P.O. Box 2600
Valley Forge, PA 19482
(800) 662-7447, (215) 648-6000

PERFORMANCE

	3yr Annual	5yr Annual	10yr Annual	Bull	Bear
Return (%)	9.7	10.8	11.0	39.1	4.7
Differ from Category (+/-)	0.5 abv av	0.8 high	0.3 av	2.4 abv av	0.1 blw av

Total Risk	Standard Deviation	Category Risk	Risk Index	Avg Mat
low	3.1%	abv av	1.2	6.0 yrs

	1993	1992	1991	1990	1989	1988	1987	1986	1985	1984
Return (%)	5.8	6.8	16.7	10.3	14.7	8.8	2.1	11.5	20.6	14.0
Differ from category (+/-) . .	-1.0	0.6	2.3	0.8	2.4	1.8	0.0	0.3	1.3	0.6

PER SHARE DATA

	1993	1992	1991	1990	1989	1988	1987	1986	1985	1984
Dividends, Net Income ($) .	0.65	0.78	0.83	0.85	0.87	0.88	0.89	0.97	1.08	1.07
Distrib'ns, Cap Gain ($) . . .	0.00	0.00	0.00	0.00	0.00	0.00	0.00	0.00	0.00	0.00
Net Asset Value ($)	10.37	10.42	10.52	9.79	9.70	9.27	9.35	10.05	9.94	9.23
Expense Ratio (%).	0.29	0.29	0.34	0.31	0.35	0.35	0.38	0.50	0.58	0.57
Net Income to Assets (%) . .	7.38	8.22	8.95	9.25	9.35	9.35	9.41	10.16	11.90	11.31
Portfolio Turnover (%)	7	1	1	9	8	22	28	32	23	21
Total Assets (Millions $) . .	7,081	5,208	2,712	2,129	1,908	1,909	2,380	1,262	298	172

PORTFOLIO (as of 7/31/93)

Portfolio Manager: Paul G. Sullivan - 1980

Investm't Category: Mortgage-Backed Bond

Cap Gain	Asset Allocation
Cap & Income	Fund of Funds
✔ Income	Index
	Sector
✔ Domestic	Small Cap
Foreign	Socially Conscious
Country/Region	State Specific

Portfolio: stocks 0%   bonds 94%
convertibles 0%   other 0%   cash 6%

Largest Holdings: mortgage-backed 94%

Unrealized Net Capital Gains: 4% of portfolio value

SHAREHOLDER INFORMATION

Minimum Investment
Initial: $3,000   Subsequent: $100

Minimum IRA Investment
Initial: $500   Subsequent: $100

Maximum Fees
Load: none   12b-1: none
Other: none

Distributions
Income: monthly   Capital Gains: Dec

Exchange Options
Number Per Year: 2   Fee: none
Telephone: yes (money market fund available)

Services
IRA, other pension, auto exchange, auto invest, auto withdraw

Vanguard High Yield Corporate (VWEHX)

Corporate High-Yield Bond

Vanguard Financial Center
P.O. Box 2600
Valley Forge, PA 19482
(800) 662-7447, (215) 648-6000

PERFORMANCE

	3yr Annual	5yr Annual	10yr Annual	Bull	Bear
Return (%)	20.3	10.8	11.5	77.0	-7.3
Differ from Category (+/-)	-0.2 av	0.0 abv av	-0.2 blw av	2.1 abv av	-4.0 low

Total Risk	Standard Deviation	Category Risk	Risk Index	Avg Mat
blw av	4.1%	blw av	1.1	9.5 yrs

	1993	1992	1991	1990	1989	1988	1987	1986	1985	1984
Return (%)	18.2	14.2	29.0	-5.8	1.8	13.5	2.6	16.8	21.9	7.8
Differ from category (+/-). . .	-1.0	-1.6	1.7	-1.6	0.5	1.2	1.6	1.6	-1.6	-3.0

PER SHARE DATA

	1993	1992	1991	1990	1989	1988	1987	1986	1985	1984
Dividends, Net Income ($).	0.69	0.73	0.77	0.91	1.00	1.01	1.01	1.09	1.18	1.20
Distrib'ns, Cap Gain ($) . . .	0.00	0.00	0.00	0.00	0.00	0.00	0.11	0.00	0.00	0.00
Net Asset Value ($)	8.02	7.41	7.16	6.22	7.55	8.39	8.32	9.20	8.86	8.33
Expense Ratio (%)	0.34	0.34	0.40	0.38	0.41	0.41	0.45	0.60	0.65	0.68
Net Income to Assets (%) .	9.82	11.13	13.35	12.56	12.07	11.47	11.43	12.51	13.61	12.75
Portfolio Turnover (%).	83	44	61	41	48	82	67	61	71	82
Total Assets (Millions $). .	2,518	1,594	698	829	1,235	994	1,370	634	252	116

PORTFOLIO (as of 7/31/93)

Portfolio Manager: Earl E. McEvoy - 1984

Investm't Category: Corp. High-Yield Bond
Cap Gain	Asset Allocation
✔ Cap & Income	Fund of Funds
Income	Index
	Sector
✔ Domestic	Small Cap
Foreign	Socially Conscious
Country/Region	State Specific

Portfolio: stocks 0% bonds 97%
convertibles 0% other 0% cash 3%

Largest Holdings: basic industries 15%, media & communications 13%

Unrealized Net Capital Gains: 3% of portfolio value

SHAREHOLDER INFORMATION

Minimum Investment
Initial: $3,000 Subsequent: $100

Minimum IRA Investment
Initial: $500 Subsequent: $100

Maximum Fees
Load: 1.00% redemption 12b-1: none
Other: redemption fee applies for 1 year

Distributions
Income: monthly Capital Gains: Dec

Exchange Options
Number Per Year: 2 Fee: none
Telephone: yes (money market fund available)

Services
IRA, other pension, auto exchange, auto invest, auto withdraw

Vanguard High-Yield Muni Bond (VWAHX)

Tax-Exempt Bond

Vanguard Financial Center
P.O. Box 2600
Valley Forge, PA 19482
(800) 662-7447, (215) 648-6000

PERFORMANCE

	3yr Annual	5yr Annual	10yr Annual	Bull	Bear
Return (%)	12.3	10.7	11.5	49.1	0.6
Differ from Category (+/-)	2.0 high	1.5 high	1.9 high	9.0 high	-1.6 low

Total Risk	Standard Deviation	Category Risk	Risk Index	Avg Mat
blw av	5.2%	high	1.3	12.6 yrs

	1993	1992	1991	1990	1989	1988	1987	1986	1985	1984
Return (%)	12.6	9.8	14.6	5.9	11.0	13.8	-1.6	19.6	21.6	9.7
Differ from category (+/-)	1.0	1.5	3.3	-0.4	2.0	3.7	-0.4	3.2	4.3	1.4

PER SHARE DATA

	1993	1992	1991	1990	1989	1988	1987	1986	1985	1984
Dividends, Net Income ($)	0.65	0.70	0.72	0.73	0.75	0.74	0.76	0.83	0.85	0.87
Distrib'ns, Cap Gain ($)	0.21	0.25	0.10	0.14	0.11	0.00	0.20	0.38	0.00	0.00
Net Asset Value ($)	11.01	10.57	10.53	9.96	10.26	10.05	9.52	10.67	10.00	8.99
Expense Ratio (%)	0.20	0.23	0.25	0.25	0.27	0.29	0.26	0.33	0.39	0.41
Net Income to Assets (%)	6.15	6.83	7.34	7.30	7.43	7.74	7.55	8.32	9.37	9.69
Portfolio Turnover (%)	34	64	58	82	80	40	83	38	41	90
Total Assets (Millions $)	1,873	1,506	1,215	963	866	690	791	794	451	238

PORTFOLIO (as of 8/31/93)

Portfolio Manager: Ian MacKinnon - 1981

Investm't Category: Tax-Exempt Bond

Cap Gain	Asset Allocation
Cap & Income	Fund of Funds
✔ Income	Index
	Sector
✔ Domestic	Small Cap
Foreign	Socially Conscious
Country/Region	State Specific

Portfolio: stocks 0% bonds 100%
convertibles 0% other 0% cash 0%

Largest Holdings: na

Unrealized Net Capital Gains: 9% of portfolio value

SHAREHOLDER INFORMATION

Minimum Investment
Initial: $3,000   Subsequent: $100

Minimum IRA Investment
Initial: na   Subsequent: na

Maximum Fees
Load: none   12b-1: none
Other: none

Distributions
Income: monthly   Capital Gains: Nov

Exchange Options
Number Per Year: 2   Fee: none
Telephone: yes (money market fund available)

Services
auto exchange, auto invest, auto withdraw

Vanguard Index Trust—500 (VFINX)

Growth & Income

Vanguard Financial Center
P.O. Box 2600
Valley Forge, PA 19482
(800) 662-7447, (215) 648-6000

PERFORMANCE

	3yr Annual	5yr Annual	10yr Annual	Bull	Bear
Return (%)	15.4	14.3	14.6	67.3	-11.2
Differ from Category (+/-)	-1.0 av	1.8 abv av	2.2 abv av	-2.8 av	0.4 av

Total Risk	Standard Deviation	Category Risk	Risk Index	Beta
av	10.5%	abv av	1.2	1.0

	1993	1992	1991	1990	1989	1988	1987	1986	1985	1984
Return (%)	9.8	7.4	30.1	-3.3	31.3	16.2	4.7	18.0	31.2	6.2
Differ from category (+/-) . . .	-2.8	-2.6	2.4	2.3	9.7	-0.6	4.3	2.8	5.8	0.0

PER SHARE DATA

	1993	1992	1991	1990	1989	1988	1987	1986	1985	1984
Dividends, Net Income ($) .	1.13	1.12	1.15	1.17	1.20	1.10	0.68	0.88	0.91	0.87
Distrib'ns, Cap Gain ($) . . .	0.02	0.10	0.11	0.10	0.75	0.31	0.17	2.02	1.61	0.47
Net Asset Value ($)	43.83	40.97	39.31	31.24	33.64	27.18	24.65	24.27	22.99	19.52
Expense Ratio (%)	0.19	0.19	0.20	0.22	0.21	0.22	0.26	0.28	0.28	0.27
Net Income to Assets (%) .	2.74	2.81	3.07	3.60	3.62	4.08	3.15	3.40	4.09	4.53
Portfolio Turnover (%).	9	4	5	23	8	10	15	29	36	14
Total Assets (Millions $) . .	8,366	6,547	4,346	2,173	1,804	1,055	827	485	394	289

PORTFOLIO (as of 6/30/93)

Portfolio Manager: George U. Sauter - 1987

Investm't Category: Growth & Income
- Cap Gain
- ✔ Cap & Income
- Income

- Asset Allocation
- Fund of Funds
- ✔ Index
- Sector

- ✔ Domestic
- Foreign
- Country/Region

- Small Cap
- Socially Conscious
- State Specific

Portfolio: stocks 100% bonds 0%
convertibles 0% other 0% cash 0%

Largest Holdings: S&P 500 composite price index

Unrealized Net Capital Gains: 13% of portfolio value

SHAREHOLDER INFORMATION

Minimum Investment
Initial: $3,000   Subsequent: $100

Minimum IRA Investment
Initial: $500   Subsequent: $100

Maximum Fees
Load: none   12b-1: none
Other: $10 account maintenance fee

Distributions
Income: quarterly   Capital Gains: Dec

Exchange Options
Number Per Year: 2   Fee: none
Telephone: none

Services
IRA, other pension, auto exchange, auto invest, auto withdraw

Vanguard Index Trust— Extended Market (VEXMX)

Growth

Vanguard Financial Center
P.O. Box 2600
Valley Forge, PA 19482
(800) 662-7447, (215) 648-6000

PERFORMANCE

	3yr Annual	5yr Annual	10yr Annual	Bull	Bear
Return (%)	22.2	14.2	na	96.5	-20.0
Differ from Category (+/-)	3.0 abv av	-0.4 av	na	11.8 abv av	-7.6 low

Total Risk	Standard Deviation	Category Risk	Risk Index	Beta
abv av	11.7%	av	1.1	0.9

	1993	1992	1991	1990	1989	1988	1987	1986	1985	1984
Return (%)	14.4	12.4	41.8	-14.0	23.9	19.7	—	—	—	—
Differ from category (+/-) . . .	1.2	1.4	6.4	-7.9	-1.9	2.0	—	—	—	—

PER SHARE DATA

	1993	1992	1991	1990	1989	1988	1987	1986	1985	1984
Dividends, Net Income ($) .	0.23	0.25	0.25	0.33	0.23	0.20	—	—	—	—
Distrib'ns, Cap Gain ($) . . .	0.20	0.18	0.20	0.15	0.23	0.15	—	—	—	—
Net Asset Value ($)	19.43	17.35	15.82	11.48	13.91	11.60	—	—	—	—
Expense Ratio (%).	0.19	0.20	0.19	0.23	0.23	0.24	—	—	—	—
Net Income to Assets (%). .	1.61	1.73	2.14	2.68	2.92	2.90	—	—	—	—
Portfolio Turnover (%)	15	9	11	9	14	26	—	—	—	—
Total Assets (Millions $) . . .	931	585	372	179	147	35	—	—	—	—

PORTFOLIO (as of 6/30/93)

Portfolio Manager: George U. Sauter - 1987

Investm't Category: Growth

✔ Cap Gain	Asset Allocation
Cap & Income	Fund of Funds
Income	✔ Index
	Sector
✔ Domestic	✔ Small Cap
Foreign	Socially Conscious
Country/Region	State Specific

Portfolio: stocks 100% bonds 0%
convertibles 0% other 0% cash 0%

Largest Holdings: Wilshire 4500 index

Unrealized Net Capital Gains: 18% of portfolio value

SHAREHOLDER INFORMATION

Minimum Investment
Initial: $3,000   Subsequent: $100

Minimum IRA Investment
Initial: $500   Subsequent: $100

Maximum Fees
Load: 1.00% charge   12b-1: none
Other: $10 account maintenance fee

Distributions
Income: Dec   Capital Gains: Dec

Exchange Options
Number Per Year: 2   Fee: none
Telephone: none

Services
IRA, other pension, auto exchange, auto invest, auto withdraw

Vanguard Index Trust— Growth Port (VIGRX)

Growth

Vanguard Financial Center
P.O. Box 2600
Valley Forge, PA 19482
(800) 662-7447, (215) 648-6000

PERFORMANCE

	3yr Annual	5yr Annual	10yr Annual	Bull	Bear
Return (%)	na	na	na	na	na
Differ from Category (+/-)	na	na	na	na	na

Total Risk	Standard Deviation	Category Risk	Risk Index	Beta
na	na	na	na	na

	1993	1992	1991	1990	1989	1988	1987	1986	1985	1984
Return (%).............	1.5	—	—	—	—	—	—	—	—	—
Differ from category (+/-)..	-11.7	—	—	—	—	—	—	—	—	—

PER SHARE DATA

	1993	1992	1991	1990	1989	1988	1987	1986	1985	1984
Dividends, Net Income ($).	0.20	—	—	—	—	—	—	—	—	—
Distrib'ns, Cap Gain ($) ...	0.00	—	—	—	—	—	—	—	—	—
Net Asset Value ($)	10.20	—	—	—	—	—	—	—	—	—
Expense Ratio (%)	0.21	—	—	—	—	—	—	—	—	—
Net Income to Assets (%) .	2.19	—	—	—	—	—	—	—	—	—
Portfolio Turnover (%)......	41	—	—	—	—	—	—	—	—	—
Total Assets (Millions $).....	50	—	—	—	—	—	—	—	—	—

PORTFOLIO (as of 6/30/93)

Portfolio Manager: George U. Sauter - 1992

Investm't Category: Growth

✔ Cap Gain   Asset Allocation
   Cap & Income   Fund of Funds
   Income   ✔ Index
           Sector
✔ Domestic   Small Cap
   Foreign   Socially Conscious
   Country/Region   State Specific

Portfolio: stocks 100%   bonds 0%
convertibles 0%   other 0%   cash 0%

Largest Holdings: Standard & Poor's/BARRA Growth Index

Unrealized Net Capital Gains: -1% of portfolio value

SHAREHOLDER INFORMATION

Minimum Investment
Initial: $3,000   Subsequent: $100

Minimum IRA Investment
Initial: $500   Subsequent: $100

Maximum Fees
Load: none   12b-1: none
Other: $10 account maintenance fee

Distributions
Income: quarterly   Capital Gains: Dec

Exchange Options
Number Per Year: 2   Fee: none
Telephone: none

Services
IRA, other pension, auto exchange, auto invest, auto withdraw

Vanguard Index Trust— Total Stock Mkt (VTSMX)

Growth & Income

Vanguard Financial Center
P.O. Box 2600
Valley Forge, PA 19482
(800) 662-7447, (215) 648-6000

PERFORMANCE

	3yr Annual	5yr Annual	10yr Annual	Bull	Bear
Return (%)	na	na	na	na	na
Differ from Category (+/-)	na	na	na	na	na

Total Risk	Standard Deviation	Category Risk	Risk Index	Beta
na	na	na	na	na

	1993	1992	1991	1990	1989	1988	1987	1986	1985	1984
Return (%)	10.6	—	—	—	—	—	—	—	—	—
Differ from category (+/-) ..	-2.0	—	—	—	—	—	—	—	—	—

PER SHARE DATA

	1993	1992	1991	1990	1989	1988	1987	1986	1985	1984
Dividends, Net Income ($) .	0.25	—	—	—	—	—	—	—	—	—
Distrib'ns, Cap Gain ($) ...	0.02	—	—	—	—	—	—	—	—	—
Net Asset Value ($)	11.69	—	—	—	—	—	—	—	—	—
Expense Ratio (%)........	0.20	—	—	—	—	—	—	—	—	—
Net Income to Assets (%)..	2.41	—	—	—	—	—	—	—	—	—
Portfolio Turnover (%)	1	—	—	—	—	—	—	—	—	—
Total Assets (Millions $) ...	533	—	—	—	—	—	—	—	—	—

PORTFOLIO (as of 6/30/93)

Portfolio Manager: George U. Sauter - 1992

Investm't Category: Growth & Income
Cap Gain	Asset Allocation
✔ Cap & Income	Fund of Funds
Income	✔ Index
	Sector
✔ Domestic	Small Cap
Foreign	Socially Conscious
Country/Region	State Specific

Portfolio: stocks 99%   bonds 0%
convertibles 0%   other 0%   cash 1%

Largest Holdings: Wilshire 5000 Index

Unrealized Net Capital Gains: 6% of portfolio value

SHAREHOLDER INFORMATION

Minimum Investment
Initial: $3,000   Subsequent: $100

Minimum IRA Investment
Initial: $500   Subsequent: $100

Maximum Fees
Load: 0.25% charge   12b-1: none
Other: $10 account maintenance fee

Distributions
Income: quarterly   Capital Gains: Dec

Exchange Options
Number Per Year: 2   Fee: none
Telephone: none

Services
IRA, other pension, auto exchange, auto invest, auto withdraw

Vanguard Index Trust— Value Port (VIVAX)

Growth & Income

Vanguard Financial Center
P.O. Box 2600
Valley Forge, PA 19482
(800) 662-7447, (215) 648-6000

PERFORMANCE

	3yr Annual	5yr Annual	10yr Annual	Bull	Bear
Return (%)	na	na	na	na	na
Differ from Category (+/-)	na	na	na	na	na

Total Risk	Standard Deviation	Category Risk	Risk Index	Beta
na	na	na	na	na

	1993	1992	1991	1990	1989	1988	1987	1986	1985	1984
Return (%).	18.3	—	—	—	—	—	—	—	—	—
Differ from category (+/-). . .	5.7	—	—	—	—	—	—	—	—	—

PER SHARE DATA

	1993	1992	1991	1990	1989	1988	1987	1986	1985	1984
Dividends, Net Income ($).	0.37	—	—	—	—	—	—	—	—	—
Distrib'ns, Cap Gain ($) . . .	0.05	—	—	—	—	—	—	—	—	—
Net Asset Value ($)	11.74	—	—	—	—	—	—	—	—	—
Expense Ratio (%)	0.20	—	—	—	—	—	—	—	—	—
Net Income to Assets (%) .	3.48	—	—	—	—	—	—	—	—	—
Portfolio Turnover (%).	34	—	—	—	—	—	—	—	—	—
Total Assets (Millions $). . . .	192	—	—	—	—	—	—	—	—	—

PORTFOLIO (as of 6/30/93)

Portfolio Manager: George U. Sauter - 1992

Investm't Category: Growth & Income

Cap Gain	Asset Allocation
✔ Cap & Income	Fund of Funds
Income	✔ Index
	Sector
✔ Domestic	Small Cap
Foreign	Socially Conscious
Country/Region	State Specific

Portfolio: stocks 100% bonds 0%
convertibles 0% other 0% cash 0%

Largest Holdings: Standard & Poor's/BARRA Value Index

Unrealized Net Capital Gains: 4% of portfolio value

SHAREHOLDER INFORMATION

Minimum Investment
Initial: $3,000   Subsequent: $100

Minimum IRA Investment
Initial: $500   Subsequent: $100

Maximum Fees
Load: none   12b-1: none
Other: $10 annual account maintenance fee

Distributions
Income: quarterly   Capital Gains: Dec

Exchange Options
Number Per Year: 2   Fee: none
Telephone: no

Services
IRA, other pension, auto exchange, auto invest, auto withdraw

Vanguard Insured Long-Term Muni (VILPX)

Tax-Exempt Bond

Vanguard Financial Center
P.O. Box 2600
Valley Forge, PA 19482
(800) 662-7447, (215) 648-6000

PERFORMANCE

	3yr Annual	5yr Annual	10yr Annual	Bull	Bear
Return (%)	11.5	10.4	na	47.0	1.0
Differ from Category (+/-)	1.2 abv av	1.2 high	na	6.9 high	-1.3 low

Total Risk	Standard Deviation	Category Risk	Risk Index	Avg Mat
blw av	5.4%	high	1.3	11.8 yrs

	1993	1992	1991	1990	1989	1988	1987	1986	1985	1984
Return (%)	13.0	9.1	12.4	7.0	10.5	12.7	0.0	18.6	19.3	—
Differ from category (+/-)	1.4	0.8	1.1	0.6	1.5	2.6	1.2	2.2	2.0	—

PER SHARE DATA

	1993	1992	1991	1990	1989	1988	1987	1986	1985	1984
Dividends, Net Income ($)	0.70	0.74	0.77	0.79	0.83	0.81	0.83	0.88	0.90	—
Distrib'ns, Cap Gain ($)	0.17	0.20	0.07	0.12	0.15	0.00	0.10	0.17	0.00	—
Net Asset Value ($)	12.81	12.14	12.03	11.50	11.64	11.45	10.92	11.86	10.94	—
Expense Ratio (%)	0.20	0.23	0.25	0.25	0.29	0.29	0.26	0.33	0.36	—
Net Income to Assets (%)	5.77	6.34	6.77	6.99	7.50	7.50	7.35	7.99	8.70	—
Portfolio Turnover (%)	30	42	33	47	36	28	50	20	16	—
Total Assets (Millions $)	2,127	1,948	1,551	1,122	934	735	793	709	335	—

PORTFOLIO

Portfolio Manager: Ian MacKinnon - 1984

Investm't Category: Tax-Exempt Bond

Cap Gain	Asset Allocation
Cap & Income	Fund of Funds
✔ Income	Index
	Sector
✔ Domestic	Small Cap
Foreign	Socially Conscious
Country/Region	State Specific

Portfolio: stocks 0%   bonds 100%
convertibles 0%   other 0%   cash 0%

Largest Holdings: na

Unrealized Net Capital Gains: 11% of portfolio value

SHAREHOLDER INFORMATION

Minimum Investment
Initial: $3,000   Subsequent: $100

Minimum IRA Investment
Initial: na   Subsequent: na

Maximum Fees
Load: none   12b-1: none
Other: none

Distributions
Income: monthly   Capital Gains: Nov

Exchange Options
Number Per Year: 2   Fee: none
Telephone: yes (money market fund available)

Services
auto exchange, auto invest, auto withdraw

Vanguard Int'l Equity Index—Europe (VEURX)

International Stock

Vanguard Financial Center
P.O. Box 2600
Valley Forge, PA 19482
(800) 662-7447, (215) 648-6000

PERFORMANCE

	3yr Annual	5yr Annual	10yr Annual	Bull	Bear
Return (%)	11.9	na	na	52.0	na
Differ from Category (+/-)	-2.4 blw av	na	na	-3.1 blw av	na

Total Risk	Standard Deviation	Category Risk	Risk Index	Beta
high	14.3%	abv av	1.2	0.7

	1993	1992	1991	1990	1989	1988	1987	1986	1985	1984
Return (%)	29.2	-3.3	12.4	—	—	—	—	—	—	—
Differ from category (+/-). . .	-9.3	0.2	-0.5	—	—	—	—	—	—	—

PER SHARE DATA

	1993	1992	1991	1990	1989	1988	1987	1986	1985	1984
Dividends, Net Income ($) .	0.17	0.25	0.25	—	—	—	—	—	—	—
Distrib'ns, Cap Gain ($) . . .	0.00	0.00	0.00	—	—	—	—	—	—	—
Net Asset Value ($)	11.89	9.33	9.92	—	—	—	—	—	—	—
Expense Ratio (%)	0.30	0.32	0.33	—	—	—	—	—	—	—
Net Income to Assets (%) .	3.27	3.05	3.06	—	—	—	—	—	—	—
Portfolio Turnover (%).	4	1	15	—	—	—	—	—	—	—
Total Assets (Millions $). . . .	616	256	161	—	—	—	—	—	—	—

PORTFOLIO (as of 6/30/93)

Portfolio Manager: George U. Sauter - 1990

Investm't Category: International Stock

Cap Gain	Asset Allocation
✔ Cap & Income	Fund of Funds
Income	✔ Index
	Sector
Domestic	Small Cap
✔ Foreign	Socially Conscious
✔ Country/Region	State Specific

Portfolio: stocks 99% bonds 0%
convertibles 0% other 0% cash 1%

Largest Holdings: Morgan Stanley Capital International Europe Index

Unrealized Net Capital Gains: 0% of portfolio value

SHAREHOLDER INFORMATION

Minimum Investment
Initial: $3,000   Subsequent: $100

Minimum IRA Investment
Initial: $500   Subsequent: $100

Maximum Fees
Load: 1.00% charge   12b-1: none
Other: $10 account maintenance fee

Distributions
Income: Dec   Capital Gains: Dec

Exchange Options
Number Per Year: 2   Fee: none
Telephone: none

Services
IRA, other pension, auto exchange, auto invest, auto withdraw

Vanguard Int'l Equity Index—Pacific (VPACX)

International Stock

Vanguard Financial Center
P.O. Box 2600
Valley Forge, PA 19482
(800) 662-7447, (215) 648-6000

PERFORMANCE

	3yr Annual	5yr Annual	10yr Annual	Bull	Bear
Return (%)	7.0	na	na	38.2	na
Differ from Category (+/-)	-7.3 low	na	na	-16.9 blw av	na

Total Risk	Standard Deviation	Category Risk	Risk Index	Beta
high	23.2%	high	2.0	0.4

	1993	1992	1991	1990	1989	1988	1987	1986	1985	1984
Return (%)	35.4	-18.1	10.7	—	—	—	—	—	—	—
Differ from category (+/-) . .	-3.1	-14.6	-2.2	—	—	—	—	—	—	—

PER SHARE DATA

	1993	1992	1991	1990	1989	1988	1987	1986	1985	1984
Dividends, Net Income ($) .	0.05	0.05	0.05	—	—	—	—	—	—	—
Distrib'ns, Cap Gain ($) . . .	0.05	0.10	0.00	—	—	—	—	—	—	—
Net Asset Value ($)	10.13	7.56	9.42	—	—	—	—	—	—	—
Expense Ratio (%)	0.31	0.32	0.32	—	—	—	—	—	—	—
Net Income to Assets (%) . .	0.87	0.92	0.70	—	—	—	—	—	—	—
Portfolio Turnover (%)	4	3	21	—	—	—	—	—	—	—
Total Assets (Millions $) . . .	500	207	84	—	—	—	—	—	—	—

PORTFOLIO (as of 6/30/93)

Portfolio Manager: George U. Sauter - 1990

Investm't Category: International Stock

✔ Cap Gain	Asset Allocation
Cap & Income	Fund of Funds
Income	✔ Index
	Sector
Domestic	Small Cap
✔ Foreign	Socially Conscious
✔ Country/Region	State Specific

Portfolio: stocks 97% bonds 0%
convertibles 0% other 0% cash 3%

Largest Holdings: Morgan Stanley Capital International Pacific Index

Unrealized Net Capital Gains: 15% of portfolio value

SHAREHOLDER INFORMATION

Minimum Investment
Initial: $3,000   Subsequent: $100

Minimum IRA Investment
Initial: $500   Subsequent: $100

Maximum Fees
Load: 1.00% charge   12b-1: none
Other: $10 account maintenance fee

Distributions
Income: Dec   Capital Gains: Dec

Exchange Options
Number Per Year: 2   Fee: none
Telephone: none

Services
IRA, other pension, auto exchange, auto invest, auto withdraw

Vanguard Int'l Growth
(VWIGX)
International Stock

Vanguard Financial Center
P.O. Box 2600
Valley Forge, PA 19482
(800) 662-7447, (215) 648-6000

PERFORMANCE

	3yr Annual	5yr Annual	10yr Annual	Bull	Bear
Return (%)	12.6	9.4	16.9	52.0	-17.3
Differ from Category (+/-)	-1.7 blw av	0.6 av	3.5 high	-3.1 blw av	-2.2 blw av

Total Risk	Standard Deviation	Category Risk	Risk Index	Beta
abv av	13.9%	abv av	1.2	0.5

	1993	1992	1991	1990	1989	1988	1987	1986	1985	1984
Return (%)	44.7	-5.7	4.7	-12.0	24.7	11.6	12.4	56.7	56.9	-0.8
Differ from category (+/-). . .	6.2	-2.2	-8.2	-0.8	2.5	-2.2	0.4	6.4	16.3	8.6

PER SHARE DATA

	1993	1992	1991	1990	1989	1988	1987	1986	1985	1984
Dividends, Net Income ($)	0.10	0.20	0.18	0.20	0.15	0.15	0.12	0.07	0.09	0.10
Distrib'ns, Cap Gain ($) . . .	0.00	0.00	0.11	0.68	0.28	1.07	2.43	0.80	0.64	0.37
Net Asset Value ($)	13.51	9.41	10.21	10.05	12.42	10.30	10.34	11.26	7.79	5.56
Expense Ratio (%)	0.59	0.58	0.67	0.68	0.64	0.67	0.66	0.52	0.56	0.63
Net Income to Assets (%) .	1.27	2.04	1.80	3.01	1.27	1.39	1.00	2.65	3.11	3.89
Portfolio Turnover (%).	51	58	49	45	50	71	77	24	29	8
Total Assets (Millions $). .	1,801	919	846	796	551	454	607	718	581	317

PORTFOLIO (as of 8/31/93)

Portfolio Manager: Richard R. Foulkes - 1981

Investm't Category: International Stock
- ✔ Cap Gain
- Cap & Income
- Income

- Domestic
- ✔ Foreign
- Country/Region

- Asset Allocation
- Fund of Funds
- Index
- Sector
- Small Cap
- Socially Conscious
- State Specific

Portfolio: stocks 94% bonds 0%
convertibles 0% other 0% cash 6%

Largest Holdings: Japan 25%, United Kingdom 13%

Unrealized Net Capital Gains: 13% of portfolio value

SHAREHOLDER INFORMATION

Minimum Investment
Initial: $3,000   Subsequent: $100

Minimum IRA Investment
Initial: $500   Subsequent: $100

Maximum Fees
Load: none   12b-1: none
Other: none

Distributions
Income: Dec   Capital Gains: Dec

Exchange Options
Number Per Year: 2   Fee: none
Telephone: yes (money market fund available)

Services
IRA, other pension, auto exchange, auto invest, auto withdraw

Vanguard Interm-Term Muni Bond (VWITX)

Tax-Exempt Bond

Vanguard Financial Center
P.O. Box 2600
Valley Forge, PA 19482
(800) 662-7447, (215) 648-6000

PERFORMANCE

	3yr Annual	5yr Annual	10yr Annual	Bull	Bear
Return (%)	10.8	9.9	10.3	42.0	2.7
Differ from Category (+/-)	0.5 av	0.6 abv av	0.6 av	1.9 av	0.4 av

Total Risk	Standard Deviation	Category Risk	Risk Index	Avg Mat
low	4.0%	blw av	1.0	6.9 yrs

	1993	1992	1991	1990	1989	1988	1987	1986	1985	1984
Return (%)	11.5	8.8	12.1	7.1	9.9	10.0	1.6	16.2	17.3	9.5
Differ from category (+/-) ..	-0.1	0.5	0.8	0.8	0.8	-0.1	2.8	-0.2	0.0	1.2

PER SHARE DATA

	1993	1992	1991	1990	1989	1988	1987	1986	1985	1984
Dividends, Net Income ($) .	0.69	0.72	0.78	0.81	0.84	0.80	0.82	0.87	0.90	0.91
Distrib'ns, Cap Gain ($) ...	0.07	0.12	0.07	0.09	0.06	0.00	0.09	0.01	0.00	0.00
Net Asset Value ($)	13.52	12.84	12.61	12.05	12.12	11.88	11.56	12.29	11.39	10.54
Expense Ratio (%)........	0.20	0.23	0.25	0.25	0.27	0.29	0.26	0.33	0.39	0.41
Net Income to Assets (%) ..	5.41	5.91	6.49	6.83	7.03	6.88	6.94	7.66	8.53	8.58
Portfolio Turnover (%)	15	32	27	54	56	89	57	13	26	55
Total Assets (Millions $) ..	5,114	3,102	2,006	1,259	1,005	795	920	811	411	209

PORTFOLIO (as of 8/31/93)

Portfolio Manager: Ian MacKinnon - 1981

Investm't Category: Tax-Exempt Bond

Cap Gain	Asset Allocation
Cap & Income	Fund of Funds
✔ Income	Index
	Sector
✔ Domestic	Small Cap
Foreign	Socially Conscious
Country/Region	State Specific

Portfolio: stocks 0% bonds 100%
convertibles 0% other 0% cash 0%

Largest Holdings: na

Unrealized Net Capital Gains: 7% of portfolio value

SHAREHOLDER INFORMATION

Minimum Investment
Initial: $3,000   Subsequent: $100

Minimum IRA Investment
Initial: na   Subsequent: na

Maximum Fees
Load: none   12b-1: none
Other: none

Distributions
Income: monthly   Capital Gains: Nov

Exchange Options
Number Per Year: 2   Fee: none
Telephone: yes (money market fund available)

Services
auto exchange, auto invest, auto withdraw

Vanguard Interm-Term US Treasury (VFITX)

Government Bond

Vanguard Financial Center
P.O. Box 2600
Valley Forge, PA 19482
(800) 662-7447, (215) 648-6000

PERFORMANCE

	3yr Annual	5yr Annual	10yr Annual	Bull	Bear
Return (%)	na	na	na	na	na
Differ from Category (+/-)	na	na	na	na	na

Total Risk	Standard Deviation	Category Risk	Risk Index	Avg Mat
na	na	na	na	6.7 yrs

	1993	1992	1991	1990	1989	1988	1987	1986	1985	1984
Return (%)	11.4	7.7	—	—	—	—	—	—	—	—
Differ from category (+/-)	1.0	1.5	—	—	—	—	—	—	—	—

PER SHARE DATA

	1993	1992	1991	1990	1989	1988	1987	1986	1985	1984
Dividends, Net Income ($)	0.62	0.67	—	—	—	—	—	—	—	—
Distrib'ns, Cap Gain ($)	0.41	0.01	—	—	—	—	—	—	—	—
Net Asset Value ($)	10.71	10.56	—	—	—	—	—	—	—	—
Expense Ratio (%)	0.26	0.26	—	—	—	—	—	—	—	—
Net Income to Assets (%)	6.44	6.47	—	—	—	—	—	—	—	—
Portfolio Turnover (%)	123	32	—	—	—	—	—	—	—	—
Total Assets (Millions $)	989	190	—	—	—	—	—	—	—	—

PORTFOLIO (as of 7/31/93)

Portfolio Manager: Robert Auwaerter - 1991, Ian Mackinnon - 1991

Investm't Category: Government Bond

Cap Gain	Asset Allocation
Cap & Income	Fund of Funds
✔ Income	Index
	Sector
✔ Domestic	Small Cap
Foreign	Socially Conscious
Country/Region	State Specific

Portfolio: stocks 0% bonds 99%
convertibles 0% other 0% cash 1%

Largest Holdings: U.S. government & agencies 99%

Unrealized Net Capital Gains: 3% of portfolio value

SHAREHOLDER INFORMATION

Minimum Investment
Initial: $3,000   Subsequent: $100

Minimum IRA Investment
Initial: $500   Subsequent: $100

Maximum Fees
Load: none   12b-1: none
Other: none

Distributions
Income: monthly   Capital Gains: Nov

Exchange Options
Number Per Year: 2   Fee: none
Telephone: yes (money market fund available)

Services
IRA, other pension, auto exchange, auto invest, auto withdraw

Vanguard Limited-Term Muni Bond (VMLTX)

Tax-Exempt Bond

Vanguard Financial Center
P.O. Box 2600
Valley Forge, PA 19482
(800) 662-7447, (215) 648-6000

PERFORMANCE

	3yr Annual	5yr Annual	10yr Annual	Bull	Bear
Return (%)	7.3	7.4	na	27.1	4.2
Differ from Category (+/-)	-3.0 low	-1.8 low	na	-13.0 low	1.9 high

Total Risk	Standard Deviation	Category Risk	Risk Index	Avg Mat
low	1.9%	low	0.4	2.8 yrs

	1993	1992	1991	1990	1989	1988	1987	1986	1985	1984
Return (%)	6.3	6.3	9.4	7.0	8.0	6.3	—	—	—	—
Differ from category (+/-) . .	-5.3	-2.0	-1.9	0.6	-1.0	-3.8	—	—	—	—

PER SHARE DATA

	1993	1992	1991	1990	1989	1988	1987	1986	1985	1984
Dividends, Net Income ($) .	0.46	0.51	0.59	0.63	0.64	0.60	—	—	—	—
Distrib'ns, Cap Gain ($) . . .	0.02	0.04	0.06	0.00	0.00	0.00	—	—	—	—
Net Asset Value ($)	10.82	10.65	10.56	10.27	10.22	10.09	—	—	—	—
Expense Ratio (%).	0.20	0.23	0.25	0.25	0.27	0.29	—	—	—	—
Net Income to Assets (%) . .	4.50	5.08	5.91	6.31	6.33	5.91	—	—	—	—
Portfolio Turnover (%)	20	37	57	55	89	122	—	—	—	—
Total Assets (Millions $) . .	1,782	873	420	245	166	162	—	—	—	—

PORTFOLIO (as of 8/31/93)

Portfolio Manager: Ian MacKinnon - 1987

Investm't Category: Tax-Exempt Bond

Cap Gain	Asset Allocation
Cap & Income	Fund of Funds
✔ Income	Index
	Sector
✔ Domestic	Small Cap
Foreign	Socially Conscious
Country/Region	State Specific

Portfolio: stocks 0% bonds 100%
convertibles 0% other 0% cash 0%

Largest Holdings: na

Unrealized Net Capital Gains: 0% of portfolio value

SHAREHOLDER INFORMATION

Minimum Investment
Initial: $3,000   Subsequent: $100

Minimum IRA Investment
Initial: na   Subsequent: na

Maximum Fees
Load: none   12b-1: none
Other: none

Distributions
Income: monthly   Capital Gains: Nov

Exchange Options
Number Per Year: 2   Fee: none
Telephone: yes (money market fund available)

Services
auto exchange, auto invest, auto withdraw

Vanguard Long Term Corp Bond (VWESX)

Corporate Bond

Vanguard Financial Center
P.O. Box 2600
Valley Forge, PA 19482
(800) 662-7447, (215) 648-6000

PERFORMANCE

	3yr Annual	5yr Annual	10yr Annual	Bull	Bear
Return (%)	14.9	13.1	12.5	61.6	-0.1
Differ from Category (+/-)	2.9 high	3.0 high	1.5 high	15.5 high	-1.9 low

Total Risk	Standard Deviation	Category Risk	Risk Index	Avg Mat
blw av	5.3%	high	1.9	16.9 yrs

	1993	1992	1991	1990	1989	1988	1987	1986	1985	1984
Return (%)	14.3	9.7	20.9	6.2	15.1	9.6	0.1	14.3	21.9	14.1
Differ from category (+/-)	2.9	1.1	4.3	0.8	5.6	0.6	-1.7	-0.4	2.2	3.0

PER SHARE DATA

	1993	1992	1991	1990	1989	1988	1987	1986	1985	1984
Dividends, Net Income ($)	0.62	0.68	0.70	0.72	0.73	0.74	0.77	0.88	1.00	1.00
Distrib'ns, Cap Gain ($)	0.25	0.15	0.00	0.00	0.00	0.00	0.12	0.00	0.00	0.00
Net Asset Value ($)	9.22	8.86	8.87	7.99	8.24	7.83	7.84	8.73	8.46	7.86
Expense Ratio (%)	0.31	0.31	0.37	0.34	0.38	0.37	0.41	0.55	0.62	0.67
Net Income to Assets (%)	7.68	8.46	9.16	9.07	9.40	9.40	9.41	10.78	12.50	11.80
Portfolio Turnover (%)	50	72	62	70	60	63	47	56	55	62
Total Assets (Millions $)	3,193	1,992	1,254	954	734	665	753	318	106	68

PORTFOLIO (as of 7/31/93)

Portfolio Manager: Bob Auwaeter - 1993

Investm't Category: Corporate Bond

Cap Gain	Asset Allocation
Cap & Income	Fund of Funds
✔ Income	Index
	Sector
✔ Domestic	Small Cap
Foreign	Socially Conscious
Country/Region	State Specific

Portfolio: stocks 0% bonds 93%
convertibles 0% other 0% cash 7%

Largest Holdings: industrial 40%, banks & finance 24%

Unrealized Net Capital Gains: 6% of portfolio value

SHAREHOLDER INFORMATION

Minimum Investment
Initial: $3,000   Subsequent: $100

Minimum IRA Investment
Initial: $500   Subsequent: $100

Maximum Fees
Load: none   12b-1: none
Other: none

Distributions
Income: monthly   Capital Gains: Dec

Exchange Options
Number Per Year: 2   Fee: none
Telephone: yes (money market fund available)

Services
IRA, other pension, auto exchange, auto invest, auto withdraw

Vanguard Long-Term Muni Bond (VWLTX)

Tax-Exempt Bond

Vanguard Financial Center
P.O. Box 2600
Valley Forge, PA 19482
(800) 662-7447, (215) 648-6000

PERFORMANCE

	3yr Annual	5yr Annual	10yr Annual	Bull	Bear
Return (%)	12.0	10.8	11.2	49.3	0.6
Differ from Category (+/-)	1.7 high	1.6 high	1.6 high	9.2 high	-1.7 low

Total Risk	Standard Deviation	Category Risk	Risk Index	Avg Mat
blw av	5.5%	high	1.4	13.0 yrs

	1993	1992	1991	1990	1989	1988	1987	1986	1985	1984
Return (%)	13.4	9.2	13.4	6.8	11.5	12.2	-1.0	19.4	20.8	8.5
Differ from category (+/-)	1.8	0.8	2.1	0.5	2.5	2.1	0.2	3.0	3.5	0.2

PER SHARE DATA

	1993	1992	1991	1990	1989	1988	1987	1986	1985	1984
Dividends, Net Income ($)	0.62	0.68	0.73	0.72	0.76	0.74	0.78	0.83	0.85	0.86
Distrib'ns, Cap Gain ($)	0.20	0.28	0.19	0.17	0.16	0.00	0.31	0.18	0.00	0.00
Net Asset Value ($)	11.29	10.71	10.72	10.31	10.53	10.31	9.88	11.12	10.23	9.24
Expense Ratio (%)	0.20	0.23	0.25	0.25	0.27	0.29	0.26	0.33	0.39	0.41
Net Income to Assets (%)	5.81	6.52	7.09	7.04	7.33	7.48	7.40	8.09	9.13	9.35
Portfolio Turnover (%)	36	63	62	110	99	34	67	32	72	99
Total Assets (Millions $)	1,086	962	798	684	626	531	617	627	410	289

PORTFOLIO (as of 8/31/93)

Portfolio Manager: Ian MacKinnon - 1981

Investm't Category: Tax-Exempt Bond

Cap Gain	Asset Allocation
Cap & Income	Fund of Funds
✔ Income	Index
	Sector
✔ Domestic	Small Cap
Foreign	Socially Conscious
Country/Region	State Specific

Portfolio: stocks 0%   bonds 100%
convertibles 0%   other 0%   cash 0%

Largest Holdings: na

Unrealized Net Capital Gains: 10% of portfolio value

SHAREHOLDER INFORMATION

Minimum Investment
Initial: $3,000   Subsequent: $100

Minimum IRA Investment
Initial: na   Subsequent: na

Maximum Fees
Load: none   12b-1: none
Other: none

Distributions
Income: monthly   Capital Gains: Nov

Exchange Options
Number Per Year: 2   Fee: none
Telephone: yes (money market fund available)

Services
auto exchange, auto invest, auto withdraw

Vanguard Long-Term US Treasury (VUSTX)

Government Bond

Vanguard Financial Center
P.O. Box 2600
Valley Forge, PA 19482
(800) 662-7447, (215) 648-6000

PERFORMANCE

	3yr Annual	5yr Annual	10yr Annual	Bull	Bear
Return (%)	13.7	12.9	na	60.6	-2.9
Differ from Category (+/-)	2.9 abv av	2.5 high	na	14.4 high	-3.4 low

Total Risk	Standard Deviation	Category Risk	Risk Index	Avg Mat
av	6.6%	abv av	1.5	23.5 yrs

	1993	1992	1991	1990	1989	1988	1987	1986	1985	1984
Return (%)	16.7	7.4	17.4	5.7	17.9	9.1	-2.9	—	—	—
Differ from category (+/-)	6.3	1.2	2.4	-0.8	4.0	1.5	-1.1	—	—	—

PER SHARE DATA

	1993	1992	1991	1990	1989	1988	1987	1986	1985	1984
Dividends, Net Income ($)	0.68	0.73	0.76	0.77	0.78	0.77	0.77	—	—	—
Distrib'ns, Cap Gain ($)	0.17	0.69	0.00	0.00	0.00	0.00	0.03	—	—	—
Net Asset Value ($)	10.57	9.82	10.54	9.70	9.96	9.16	9.13	—	—	—
Expense Ratio (%)	0.27	0.26	0.30	0.28	0.36	0.32	0.00	—	—	—
Net Income to Assets (%)	7.26	7.72	8.29	8.08	8.46	8.10	6.93	—	—	—
Portfolio Turnover (%)	170	89	147	83	387	182	182	—	—	—
Total Assets (Millions $)	831	833	722	456	172	83	35	—	—	—

PORTFOLIO (as of 4/31/93)

Portfolio Manager: Ian MacKinnon - 1986

Investm't Category: Government Bond

Cap Gain	Asset Allocation
Cap & Income	Fund of Funds
✔ Income	Index
	Sector
✔ Domestic	Small Cap
Foreign	Socially Conscious
Country/Region	State Specific

Portfolio: stocks 0% bonds 93%
convertibles 0% other 0% cash 7%

Largest Holdings: U.S. government & agencies 93%

Unrealized Net Capital Gains: 4% of portfolio value

SHAREHOLDER INFORMATION

Minimum Investment
Initial: $3,000   Subsequent: $100

Minimum IRA Investment
Initial: $500   Subsequent: $100

Maximum Fees
Load: none   12b-1: none
Other: none

Distributions
Income: monthly   Capital Gains: Dec

Exchange Options
Number Per Year: 2   Fee: none
Telephone: yes (money market fund available)

Services
IRA, other pension, auto exchange, auto invest, auto withdraw

Vanguard Morgan Growth (VMRGX)

Growth

Vanguard Financial Center
P.O. Box 2600
Valley Forge, PA 19482
(800) 662-7447, (215) 648-6000

PERFORMANCE

	3yr Annual	5yr Annual	10yr Annual	Bull	Bear
Return (%)	14.9	12.9	12.0	69.1	-11.4
Differ from Category (+/-)	-4.3 blw av	-1.7 blw av	-0.6 blw av	-15.6 blw av	1.0 av

Total Risk	Standard Deviation	Category Risk	Risk Index	Beta
abv av	11.6%	av	1.1	1.0

	1993	1992	1991	1990	1989	1988	1987	1986	1985	1984
Return (%)	7.3	9.5	29.3	-1.5	22.5	22.3	5.0	7.8	30.2	-6.0
Differ from category (+/-) . .	-5.9	-1.5	-6.1	4.6	-3.3	4.6	3.8	-6.7	0.8	-6.0

PER SHARE DATA

	1993	1992	1991	1990	1989	1988	1987	1986	1985	1984
Dividends, Net Income ($) .	0.18	0.18	0.28	0.34	0.28	0.23	0.20	0.43	0.25	0.31
Distrib'ns, Cap Gain ($) . . .	1.35	0.51	0.86	0.80	0.58	0.98	2.45	2.88	0.60	1.39
Net Asset Value ($)	12.01	12.65	12.20	10.40	11.72	10.27	9.39	11.50	13.82	11.45
Expense Ratio (%)	0.48	0.48	0.46	0.55	0.51	0.55	0.46	0.54	0.60	0.68
Net Income to Assets (%) . .	1.41	1.51	2.36	2.77	2.38	2.20	1.52	1.49	1.96	2.51
Portfolio Turnover (%)	57	64	52	73	27	32	43	31	42	38
Total Assets (Millions $) . .	1,137	1,116	957	697	733	622	538	594	665	467

PORTFOLIO (as of 6/30/93)

Portfolio Manager: F. Wisneski - 1979, N. August - 1990, J. Nagnoriak - 1990

Investm't Category: Growth

✔ Cap Gain	Asset Allocation
Cap & Income	Fund of Funds
Income	Index
	Sector
✔ Domestic	Small Cap
Foreign	Socially Conscious
Country/Region	State Specific

Portfolio: stocks 92% bonds 0%
convertibles 0% other 0% cash 8%

Largest Holdings: retail 11%, computers & services 10%

Unrealized Net Capital Gains: 15% of portfolio value

SHAREHOLDER INFORMATION

Minimum Investment
Initial: $3,000   Subsequent: $100

Minimum IRA Investment
Initial: $500   Subsequent: $100

Maximum Fees
Load: none   12b-1: none
Other: none

Distributions
Income: Dec   Capital Gains: Dec

Exchange Options
Number Per Year: 2   Fee: none
Telephone: yes (money market fund available)

Services
IRA, other pension, auto exchange, auto invest, auto withdraw

Vanguard NJ Tax Free Insured Long (VNJTX)

Tax-Exempt Bond

Vanguard Financial Center
P.O. Box 2600
Valley Forge, PA 19482
(800) 662-7447, (215) 648-6000

PERFORMANCE

	3yr Annual	5yr Annual	10yr Annual	Bull	Bear
Return (%)	11.2	10.3	na	46.6	1.2
Differ from Category (+/-)	0.8 abv av	1.1 high	na	6.5 high	-1.1 blw av

Total Risk	Standard Deviation	Category Risk	Risk Index	Avg Mat
blw av	5.0%	high	1.2	9.5 yrs

	1993	1992	1991	1990	1989	1988	1987	1986	1985	1984
Return (%)	13.3	9.3	11.2	7.6	10.4	—	—	—	—	—
Differ from category (+/-). . .	1.7	1.0	-0.1	1.3	1.4	—	—	—	—	—

PER SHARE DATA

	1993	1992	1991	1990	1989	1988	1987	1986	1985	1984
Dividends, Net Income ($).	0.63	0.65	0.67	0.68	0.70	—	—	—	—	—
Distrib'ns, Cap Gain ($) . . .	0.06	0.13	0.00	0.00	0.01	—	—	—	—	—
Net Asset Value ($)	11.91	11.15	10.95	10.49	10.42	—	—	—	—	—
Expense Ratio (%)	0.21	0.25	0.24	0.25	0.24	—	—	—	—	—
Net Income to Assets (%) .	5.62	5.99	6.33	6.73	6.88	—	—	—	—	—
Portfolio Turnover (%).	16	34	18	7	17	—	—	—	—	—
Total Assets (Millions $). . . .	767	572	433	245	129	—	—	—	—	—

PORTFOLIO (as of 5/31/93)

Portfolio Manager: Ian MacKinnon - 1988

Investm't Category: Tax-Exempt Bond

Cap Gain	Asset Allocation
Cap & Income	Fund of Funds
✔ Income	Index
	Sector
✔ Domestic	Small Cap
Foreign	Socially Conscious
Country/Region	✔ State Specific

Portfolio: stocks 0% bonds 100%
convertibles 0% other 0% cash 0%

Largest Holdings: na

Unrealized Net Capital Gains: 8% of portfolio value

SHAREHOLDER INFORMATION

Minimum Investment
Initial: $3,000   Subsequent: $100

Minimum IRA Investment
Initial: na   Subsequent: na

Maximum Fees
Load: none   12b-1: none
Other: none

Distributions
Income: monthly   Capital Gains: Dec

Exchange Options
Number Per Year: 2   Fee: none
Telephone: yes (money market fund available)

Services
auto exchange, auto invest, auto withdraw

Vanguard NY Insured Tax Free (VNYTX)

Tax-Exempt Bond

Vanguard Financial Center
P.O. Box 2600
Valley Forge, PA 19482
(800) 662-7447, (215) 648-6000

PERFORMANCE

	3yr Annual	5yr Annual	10yr Annual	Bull	Bear
Return (%)	11.8	10.4	na	48.2	0.3
Differ from Category (+/-)	1.5 high	1.2 high	na	8.1 high	-2.0 low

Total Risk	Standard Deviation	Category Risk	Risk Index	Avg Mat
blw av	4.9%	high	1.2	9.9 yrs

	1993	1992	1991	1990	1989	1988	1987	1986	1985	1984
Return (%)	13.0	9.7	12.8	6.2	10.3	11.9	-3.4	—	—	—
Differ from category (+/-) . . .	1.4	1.4	1.5	-0.1	1.3	1.8	-2.2	—	—	—

PER SHARE DATA

	1993	1992	1991	1990	1989	1988	1987	1986	1985	1984
Dividends, Net Income ($) .	0.59	0.62	0.63	0.63	0.63	0.64	0.62	—	—	—
Distrib'ns, Cap Gain ($) . . .	0.01	0.14	0.00	0.00	0.00	0.00	0.00	—	—	—
Net Asset Value ($)	11.15	10.42	10.23	9.67	9.72	9.41	9.01	—	—	—
Expense Ratio (%).	0.20	0.23	0.27	0.31	0.34	0.40	0.35	—	—	—
Net Income to Assets (%) . .	5.61	6.11	6.48	6.60	6.64	6.75	6.80	—	—	—
Portfolio Turnover (%)	14	28	19	17	10	4	31	—	—	—
Total Assets (Millions $) . . .	824	574	408	241	168	103	76	—	—	—

PORTFOLIO (as of 5/31/93)

Portfolio Manager: Ian MacKinnon - 1986

Investm't Category: Tax-Exempt Bond

Cap Gain	Asset Allocation
Cap & Income	Fund of Funds
✔ Income	Index
	Sector
✔ Domestic	Small Cap
Foreign	Socially Conscious
Country/Region	✔ State Specific

Portfolio: stocks 0% bonds 100%
convertibles 0% other 0% cash 0%

Largest Holdings: na

Unrealized Net Capital Gains: 7% of portfolio value

SHAREHOLDER INFORMATION

Minimum Investment
Initial: $3,000 Subsequent: $100

Minimum IRA Investment
Initial: na Subsequent: na

Maximum Fees
Load: none 12b-1: none
Other: none

Distributions
Income: monthly Capital Gains: Dec

Exchange Options
Number Per Year: 2 Fee: none
Telephone: yes (money market fund available)

Services
auto exchange, auto invest, auto withdraw

Vanguard Ohio Tax Free Insur Long (VOHIX)

Tax-Exempt Bond

Vanguard Financial Center
P.O. Box 2600
Valley Forge, PA 19482
(800) 662-7447, (215) 648-6000

PERFORMANCE

	3yr Annual	5yr Annual	10yr Annual	Bull	Bear
Return (%)	11.4	na	na	45.4	na
Differ from Category (+/-)	1.1 abv av	na	na	5.3 abv av	na

Total Risk	Standard Deviation	Category Risk	Risk Index	Avg Mat
blw av	4.7%	abv av	1.2	8.9 yrs

	1993	1992	1991	1990	1989	1988	1987	1986	1985	1984
Return (%)	12.7	9.4	11.9	—	—	—	—	—	—	—
Differ from category (+/-). . .	1.1	1.1	0.6	—	—	—	—	—	—	—

PER SHARE DATA

	1993	1992	1991	1990	1989	1988	1987	1986	1985	1984
Dividends, Net Income ($).	0.60	0.62	0.64	—	—	—	—	—	—	—
Distrib'ns, Cap Gain ($) . . .	0.03	0.14	0.00	—	—	—	—	—	—	—
Net Asset Value ($)	11.77	11.03	10.81	—	—	—	—	—	—	—
Expense Ratio (%)	0.22	0.31	0.27	—	—	—	—	—	—	—
Net Income to Assets (%) .	5.43	5.77	6.20	—	—	—	—	—	—	—
Portfolio Turnover (%).	20	27	20	—	—	—	—	—	—	—
Total Assets (Millions $). . . .	173	101	61	—	—	—	—	—	—	—

PORTFOLIO (as of 5/31/93)

Portfolio Manager: Ian MacKinnon - 1990

Investm't Category: Tax-Exempt Bond
Cap Gain	Asset Allocation
Cap & Income	Fund of Funds
✔ Income	Index
	Sector
✔ Domestic	Small Cap
Foreign	Socially Conscious
Country/Region	✔ State Specific

Portfolio: stocks 0% bonds 100%
convertibles 0% other 0% cash 0%

Largest Holdings: na

Unrealized Net Capital Gains: 5% of portfolio value

SHAREHOLDER INFORMATION

Minimum Investment
Initial: $3,000   Subsequent: $100

Minimum IRA Investment
Initial: na   Subsequent: na

Maximum Fees
Load: none   12b-1: none
Other: none

Distributions
Income: monthly   Capital Gains: Dec

Exchange Options
Number Per Year: 2   Fee: none
Telephone: yes (money market fund available)

Services
auto exchange, auto invest, auto withdraw

Vanguard Penn Tax-Free Insur Long (VPAIX)

Tax-Exempt Bond

Vanguard Financial Center
P.O. Box 2600
Valley Forge, PA 19482
(800) 662-7447, (215) 648-6000

PERFORMANCE

	3yr Annual	5yr Annual	10yr Annual	Bull	Bear
Return (%)	11.6	10.5	na	47.4	1.0
Differ from Category (+/-)	1.3 high	1.3 high	na	7.3 high	-1.3 low

Total Risk	Standard Deviation	Category Risk	Risk Index	Avg Mat
blw av	4.5%	abv av	1.1	8.4 yrs

	1993	1992	1991	1990	1989	1988	1987	1986	1985	1984
Return (%)	12.7	10.1	12.2	6.9	10.5	12.2	-1.2	—	—	—
Differ from category (+/-) ...	1.1	1.8	0.8	0.6	1.5	2.1	0.0	—	—	—

PER SHARE DATA

	1993	1992	1991	1990	1989	1988	1987	1986	1985	1984
Dividends, Net Income ($)	0.62	0.66	0.66	0.67	0.68	0.69	0.68	—	—	—
Distrib'ns, Cap Gain ($) ...	0.07	0.22	0.03	0.00	0.00	0.00	0.00	—	—	—
Net Asset Value ($)	11.44	10.80	10.64	10.14	10.15	9.83	9.41	—	—	—
Expense Ratio (%)........	0.21	0.24	0.25	0.25	0.26	0.33	0.31	—	—	—
Net Income to Assets (%) ..	5.73	6.17	6.46	6.77	6.87	6.95	7.06	—	—	—
Portfolio Turnover (%)	12	17	2	9	8	3	15	—	—	—
Total Assets (Millions $) ..	1,532	1,130	828	556	416	270	194	—	—	—

PORTFOLIO (as of 5/31/93)

Portfolio Manager: Ian MacKinnon - 1986

Investm't Category: Tax-Exempt Bond

Cap Gain	Asset Allocation
Cap & Income	Fund of Funds
✔ Income	Index
	Sector
✔ Domestic	Small Cap
Foreign	Socially Conscious
Country/Region	✔ State Specific

Portfolio: stocks 0% bonds 100%
convertibles 0% other 0% cash 0%

Largest Holdings: na

Unrealized Net Capital Gains: 6% of portfolio value

SHAREHOLDER INFORMATION

Minimum Investment
Initial: $3,000   Subsequent: $100

Minimum IRA Investment
Initial: na   Subsequent: na

Maximum Fees
Load: none   12b-1: none
Other: none

Distributions
Income: monthly   Capital Gains: Dec

Exchange Options
Number Per Year: 2   Fee: none
Telephone: yes (money market fund available)

Services
auto exchange, auto invest, auto withdraw

Vanguard Preferred Stock (VQIIX)

Growth & Income

Vanguard Financial Center
P.O. Box 2600
Valley Forge, PA 19482
(800) 662-7447, (215) 648-6000

PERFORMANCE

	3yr Annual	5yr Annual	10yr Annual	Bull	Bear
Return (%)	14.0	13.3	12.8	57.7	0.0
Differ from Category (+/-)	-2.4 blw av	0.8 av	0.4 av	-12.4 blw av	11.6 high

Total Risk	Standard Deviation	Category Risk	Risk Index	Beta
blw av	4.2%	low	0.5	0.2

	1993	1992	1991	1990	1989	1988	1987	1986	1985	1984
Return (%)............	13.0	8.4	20.9	6.3	18.7	8.0	-7.7	26.1	28.4	10.3
Differ from category (+/-)...	0.4	-1.6	-6.8	11.9	-2.9	-8.8	-8.1	10.9	3.0	4.1

PER SHARE DATA

	1993	1992	1991	1990	1989	1988	1987	1986	1985	1984
Dividends, Net Income ($).	0.71	0.73	0.72	0.77	0.74	0.77	0.64	0.80	0.89	0.93
Distrib'ns, Cap Gain ($) ...	0.14	0.00	0.00	0.00	0.00	0.00	0.12	0.05	0.00	0.00
Net Asset Value ($)	9.54	9.23	9.22	8.29	8.56	7.89	8.05	9.52	8.26	7.19
Expense Ratio (%)	0.59	0.58	0.63	0.65	0.67	0.66	0.64	0.58	0.59	0.66
Net Income to Assets (%) .	6.76	7.43	7.96	8.69	9.11	9.40	8.60	9.07	11.01	13.16
Portfolio Turnover (%)......	40	33	18	15	42	52	67	48	34	56
Total Assets (Millions $)....	882	187	89	53	63	77	84	153	85	62

PORTFOLIO (as of 4/30/93)

Portfolio Manager: Earl E. McEvoy - 1982

Investm't Category: Growth & Income
- Cap Gain
- ✔ Cap & Income
- Income

- Asset Allocation
- Fund of Funds
- Index
- Sector
- Small Cap
- Socially Conscious
- State Specific

- ✔ Domestic
- Foreign
- Country/Region

Portfolio: stocks 0% bonds 0%
convertibles 0% other 96% cash 4%

Largest Holdings: preferred stock—utilities 56%, preferred stock—banks 16%

Unrealized Net Capital Gains: 4% of portfolio value

SHAREHOLDER INFORMATION

Minimum Investment
Initial: $3,000   Subsequent: $100

Minimum IRA Investment
Initial: $500   Subsequent: $100

Maximum Fees
Load: none   12b-1: none
Other: none

Distributions
Income: quarterly   Capital Gains: Dec

Exchange Options
Number Per Year: 2   Fee: none
Telephone: yes (money market fund available)

Services
IRA, other pension, auto exchange, auto invest, auto withdraw

Vanguard Primecap
(VPMCX)
Growth

Vanguard Financial Center
P.O. Box 2600
Valley Forge, PA 19482
(800) 662-7447, (215) 648-6000

PERFORMANCE

	3yr Annual	5yr Annual	10yr Annual	Bull	Bear
Return (%)	19.6	15.1	na	95.6	-14.8
Differ from Category (+/-)	0.4 av	0.5 abv av	na	10.9 abv av	-2.4 blw av

Total Risk	Standard Deviation	Category Risk	Risk Index	Beta
abv av	13.9%	abv av	1.3	1.0

	1993	1992	1991	1990	1989	1988	1987	1986	1985	1984
Return (%)	18.0	8.9	33.1	-2.7	21.5	14.6	-2.3	23.5	35.7	—
Differ from category (+/-) . . .	4.8	-2.1	-2.3	3.4	-4.3	-3.1	-3.5	9.0	6.4	—

PER SHARE DATA

	1993	1992	1991	1990	1989	1988	1987	1986	1985	1984
Dividends, Net Income ($) .	0.07	0.11	0.15	0.12	0.15	0.13	0.10	0.14	0.00	—
Distrib'ns, Cap Gain ($) . . .	0.58	0.40	0.68	0.11	0.61	0.20	0.23	0.18	0.00	—
Net Asset Value ($)	18.42	16.19	15.36	12.21	12.81	11.18	10.05	10.64	8.89	—
Expense Ratio (%)	0.67	0.68	0.68	0.75	0.74	0.83	0.83	0.82	0.98	—
Net Income to Assets (%) . .	0.55	0.84	1.09	1.06	1.35	0.83	0.91	1.00	1.44	—
Portfolio Turnover (%)	18	7	24	11	15	26	21	15	14	—
Total Assets (Millions $) . . .	815	646	486	305	279	186	165	33	13	—

PORTFOLIO (as of 6/30/93)

Portfolio Manager: Howard Schow - 1984

Investm't Category: Growth

✔ Cap Gain	Asset Allocation
Cap & Income	Fund of Funds
Income	Index
	Sector
✔ Domestic	Small Cap
Foreign	Socially Conscious
Country/Region	State Specific

Portfolio: stocks 92% bonds 0%
convertibles 0% other 0% cash 8%

Largest Holdings: electronic components & instruments 16%, telecommunications 16%

Unrealized Net Capital Gains: 25% of portfolio value

SHAREHOLDER INFORMATION

Minimum Investment
Initial: $10,000   Subsequent: $1,000

Minimum IRA Investment
Initial: $500   Subsequent: $100

Maximum Fees
Load: none   12b-1: none
Other: none

Distributions
Income: Dec   Capital Gains: Dec

Exchange Options
Number Per Year: 2   Fee: none
Telephone: yes (money market fund available)

Services
IRA, other pension, auto exchange, auto invest, auto withdraw

Vanguard Quantitative Portfolio (VQNPX)

Growth & Income

Vanguard Financial Center
P.O. Box 2600
Valley Forge, PA 19482
(800) 662-7447, (215) 648-6000

PERFORMANCE

	3yr Annual	5yr Annual	10yr Annual	Bull	Bear
Return (%)	16.6	15.3	na	74.4	-11.2
Differ from Category (+/-)	0.2 av	2.8 high	na	4.3 abv av	0.4 av

Total Risk	Standard Deviation	Category Risk	Risk Index	Beta
av	10.8%	abv av	1.2	1.0

	1993	1992	1991	1990	1989	1988	1987	1986	1985	1984
Return (%)	13.8	7.0	30.2	-2.4	31.9	16.7	4.0	—	—	—
Differ from category (+/-)	1.2	-3.0	2.5	3.2	10.3	-0.1	3.6	—	—	—

PER SHARE DATA

	1993	1992	1991	1990	1989	1988	1987	1986	1985	1984
Dividends, Net Income ($)	0.38	0.43	0.46	0.46	0.46	0.34	0.25	—	—	—
Distrib'ns, Cap Gain ($)	1.69	0.70	0.43	0.03	0.00	0.00	0.05	—	—	—
Net Asset Value ($)	16.45	16.30	16.32	13.29	14.14	11.08	9.80	—	—	—
Expense Ratio (%)	0.45	0.40	0.43	0.48	0.53	0.64	0.64	—	—	—
Net Income to Assets (%)	2.34	2.67	2.95	3.34	3.35	3.38	2.79	—	—	—
Portfolio Turnover (%)	79	51	61	81	78	50	73	—	—	—
Total Assets (Millions $)	539	415	335	211	175	144	149	—	—	—

PORTFOLIO (as of 6/30/93)

Portfolio Manager: John Nagorniak - 1986

Investm't Category: Growth & Income

Cap Gain	Asset Allocation
✔ Cap & Income	Fund of Funds
Income	Index
	Sector
✔ Domestic	Small Cap
Foreign	Socially Conscious
Country/Region	State Specific

Portfolio: stocks 98% bonds 0%
convertibles 0% other 0% cash 2%

Largest Holdings: na

Unrealized Net Capital Gains: 12% of portfolio value

SHAREHOLDER INFORMATION

Minimum Investment
Initial: $3,000   Subsequent: $100

Minimum IRA Investment
Initial: $500   Subsequent: $100

Maximum Fees
Load: none   12b-1: none
Other: none

Distributions
Income: Jul, Dec   Capital Gains: Dec

Exchange Options
Number Per Year: 2   Fee: none
Telephone: none

Services
IRA, other pension, auto exchange, auto invest, auto withdraw

Vanguard Short-Term Corporate (VFSTX)

Corporate Bond

Vanguard Financial Center
P.O. Box 2600
Valley Forge, PA 19482
(800) 662-7447, (215) 648-6000

PERFORMANCE

	3yr Annual	5yr Annual	10yr Annual	Bull	Bear
Return (%)	9.0	9.5	9.9	33.8	5.9
Differ from Category (+/-)	-3.0 low	-0.6 blw av	-1.1 low	-12.3 low	4.1 high

Total Risk	Standard Deviation	Category Risk	Risk Index	Avg Mat
low	2.2%	blw av	0.8	2.5 yrs

	1993	1992	1991	1990	1989	1988	1987	1986	1985	1984
Return (%)	7.0	7.1	13.0	9.2	11.4	6.9	4.4	11.3	14.8	14.2
Differ from category (+/-) . .	-4.4	-1.5	-3.6	3.9	1.9	-2.1	2.6	-3.4	-4.9	3.1

PER SHARE DATA

	1993	1992	1991	1990	1989	1988	1987	1986	1985	1984
Dividends, Net Income ($) .	0.61	0.70	0.81	0.87	0.89	0.82	0.75	0.88	1.00	1.06
Distrib'ns, Cap Gain ($) . . .	0.09	0.16	0.00	0.00	0.00	0.00	0.18	0.00	0.00	0.00
Net Asset Value ($)	10.90	10.86	10.97	10.47	10.43	10.20	10.33	10.82	10.55	10.12
Expense Ratio (%).	0.27	0.26	0.31	0.28	0.34	0.33	0.38	0.49	0.62	0.56
Net Income to Assets (%). .	6.33	7.44	8.48	8.70	8.17	7.36	7.79	9.50	11.26	10.23
Portfolio Turnover (%)	71	99	107	121	165	258	278	460	270	121
Total Assets (Millions $) . .	3,473	1,912	829	597	493	429	401	198	119	135

PORTFOLIO (as of 7/31/93)

Portfolio Manager: Ian MacKinnon - 1982

Investm't Category: Corporate Bond

Cap Gain	Asset Allocation
Cap & Income	Fund of Funds
✔ Income	Index
	Sector
✔ Domestic	Small Cap
Foreign	Socially Conscious
Country/Region	State Specific

Portfolio: stocks 0%   bonds 98%
convertibles 0%   other 0%   cash 2%

Largest Holdings: utilities 19%, finance—diversified 15%

Unrealized Net Capital Gains: 2% of portfolio value

SHAREHOLDER INFORMATION

Minimum Investment
Initial: $3,000   Subsequent: $100

Minimum IRA Investment
Initial: $500   Subsequent: $100

Maximum Fees
Load: none   12b-1: none
Other: none

Distributions
Income: monthly   Capital Gains: Dec

Exchange Options
Number Per Year: 2   Fee: none
Telephone: yes (money market fund available)

Services
IRA, other pension, auto exchange, auto invest, auto withdraw

Vanguard Short-Term Federal (VSGBX)

Government Bond

Vanguard Financial Center
P.O. Box 2600
Valley Forge, PA 19482
(800) 662-7447, (215) 648-6000

PERFORMANCE

	3yr Annual	5yr Annual	10yr Annual	Bull	Bear
Return (%)	8.4	9.1	na	31.9	5.5
Differ from Category (+/-)	-2.4 low	-1.3 blw av	na	-14.3 low	5.0 high

Total Risk	Standard Deviation	Category Risk	Risk Index	Avg Mat
low	2.3%	low	0.5	2.5 yrs

	1993	1992	1991	1990	1989	1988	1987	1986	1985	1984
Return (%)	6.9	6.1	12.1	9.3	11.3	5.7	—	—	—	—
Differ from category (+/-) . . .	-3.5	-0.1	-2.9	2.8	-2.6	-1.9	—	—	—	—

PER SHARE DATA

	1993	1992	1991	1990	1989	1988	1987	1986	1985	1984
Dividends, Net Income ($) .	0.52	0.61	0.73	0.80	0.84	0.79	—	—	—	—
Distrib'ns, Cap Gain ($) . . .	0.10	0.16	0.06	0.00	0.00	0.00	—	—	—	—
Net Asset Value ($)	10.34	10.27	10.43	10.06	9.98	9.76	—	—	—	—
Expense Ratio (%)	0.27	0.26	0.30	0.28	0.32	0.00	—	—	—	—
Net Income to Assets (%) .	5.88	6.98	8.06	8.59	8.50	0.00	—	—	—	—
Portfolio Turnover (%)	70	111	141	133	228	0	—	—	—	—
Total Assets (Millions $) . .	1,919	1,275	508	228	159	6	—	—	—	—

PORTFOLIO (as of 7/31/93)

Portfolio Manager: Ian MacKinnon - 1987

Investm't Category: Government Bond

Cap Gain	Asset Allocation
Cap & Income	Fund of Funds
✔ Income	Index
	Sector
✔ Domestic	Small Cap
Foreign	Socially Conscious
Country/Region	State Specific

Portfolio: stocks 0%   bonds 98%
convertibles 0%   other 0%   cash 2%

Largest Holdings: U.S. government & agencies 67%, mortgage-backed 31%

Unrealized Net Capital Gains: 1% of portfolio value

SHAREHOLDER INFORMATION

Minimum Investment
Initial: $3,000   Subsequent: $100

Minimum IRA Investment
Initial: $500   Subsequent: $100

Maximum Fees
Load: none   12b-1: none
Other: none

Distributions
Income: monthly   Capital Gains: Dec

Exchange Options
Number Per Year: 2   Fee: none
Telephone: yes (money market fund available)

Services
IRA, other pension, auto exchange, auto invest, auto withdraw

Vanguard Short-Term Muni Bond (VWSTX)

Tax-Exempt Bond

Vanguard Financial Center
P.O. Box 2600
Valley Forge, PA 19482
(800) 662-7447, (215) 648-6000

PERFORMANCE

	3yr Annual	5yr Annual	10yr Annual	Bull	Bear
Return (%)	5.2	5.8	6.0	18.9	4.3
Differ from Category (+/-)	-5.1 low	-3.4 low	-3.6 low	-21.2 low	2.0 high

Total Risk	Standard Deviation	Category Risk	Risk Index	Avg Mat
low	89%	low	0.2	1.2 yrs

	1993	1992	1991	1990	1989	1988	1987	1986	1985	1984
Return (%)	3.8	4.7	7.1	6.5	7.0	5.6	4.1	7.3	6.9	6.8
Differ from category (+/-) . .	-7.8	-3.6	-4.2	0.2	-2.0	-4.5	5.3	-9.1	-10.4	-1.5

PER SHARE DATA

	1993	1992	1991	1990	1989	1988	1987	1986	1985	1984
Dividends, Net Income ($) .	0.57	0.66	0.82	0.91	0.89	0.81	0.76	0.86	0.94	0.97
Distrib'ns, Cap Gain ($) . . .	0.01	0.04	0.06	0.00	0.00	0.00	0.10	0.00	0.00	0.00
Net Asset Value ($)	15.63	15.64	15.63	15.43	15.36	15.21	15.19	15.44	15.22	15.14
Expense Ratio (%)	0.20	0.23	0.25	0.25	0.27	0.29	0.26	0.33	0.39	0.41
Net Income to Assets (%) . .	3.88	4.58	5.55	5.90	5.77	5.13	5.12	5.81	6.47	6.08
Portfolio Turnover (%)	46	60	104	78	54	113	12	57	55	102
Total Assets (Millions $) . .	1,443	1,061	840	751	700	841	1,105	906	536	353

PORTFOLIO (as of 8/31/93)

Portfolio Manager: Ian MacKinnon - 1981

Investm't Category: Tax-Exempt Bond

Cap Gain	Asset Allocation
Cap & Income	Fund of Funds
✔ Income	Index
	Sector
✔ Domestic	Small Cap
Foreign	Socially Conscious
Country/Region	State Specific

Portfolio: stocks 0% bonds 100%
convertibles 0% other 0% cash 0%

Largest Holdings: na

Unrealized Net Capital Gains: 1% of portfolio value

SHAREHOLDER INFORMATION

Minimum Investment
Initial: $3,000   Subsequent: $100

Minimum IRA Investment
Initial: na   Subsequent: na

Maximum Fees
Load: none   12b-1: none
Other: none

Distributions
Income: monthly   Capital Gains: Nov

Exchange Options
Number Per Year: 2   Fee: none
Telephone: yes (money market fund available)

Services
auto exchange, auto invest, auto withdraw

Vanguard Short-Term US Treasury (VFISX)

Government Bond

Vanguard Financial Center
P.O. Box 2600
Valley Forge, PA 19482
(800) 662-7447, (215) 648-6000

PERFORMANCE

	3yr Annual	5yr Annual	10yr Annual	Bull	Bear
Return (%)	na	na	na	na	na
Differ from Category (+/-)	na	na	na	na	na

Total Risk	Standard Deviation	Category Risk	Risk Index	Avg Mat
na	na	na	na	2.5 yrs

	1993	1992	1991	1990	1989	1988	1987	1986	1985	1984
Return (%)	6.3	6.7	—	—	—	—	—	—	—	—
Differ from category (+/-). . .	-4.1	0.5	—	—	—	—	—	—	—	—

PER SHARE DATA

	1993	1992	1991	1990	1989	1988	1987	1986	1985	1984
Dividends, Net Income ($).	0.48	0.52	—	—	—	—	—	—	—	—
Distrib'ns, Cap Gain ($) . . .	0.07	0.04	—	—	—	—	—	—	—	—
Net Asset Value ($)	10.39	10.31	—	—	—	—	—	—	—	—
Expense Ratio (%)	0.26	0.26	—	—	—	—	—	—	—	—
Net Income to Assets (%) .	5.12	5.22	—	—	—	—	—	—	—	—
Portfolio Turnover (%).	71	40	—	—	—	—	—	—	—	—
Total Assets (Millions $). . . .	704	102	—	—	—	—	—	—	—	—

PORTFOLIO (as of 7/31/93)

Portfolio Manager: Ian MacKinnon - 1991

Investm't Category: Government Bond

Cap Gain	Asset Allocation
Cap & Income	Fund of Funds
✔ Income	Index
	Sector
✔ Domestic	Small Cap
Foreign	Socially Conscious
Country/Region	State Specific

Portfolio: stocks 0% bonds 100%
convertibles 0% other 0% cash 0%

Largest Holdings: U.S. government & agencies 100%

Unrealized Net Capital Gains: 1% of portfolio value

SHAREHOLDER INFORMATION

Minimum Investment
Initial: $3,000   Subsequent: $100

Minimum IRA Investment
Initial: $500   Subsequent: $100

Maximum Fees
Load: none   12b-1: none
Other: none

Distributions
Income: monthly   Capital Gains: Nov

Exchange Options
Number Per Year: 2   Fee: none
Telephone: yes (money market fund available)

Services
IRA, other pension, auto exchange, auto invest, auto withdraw

Vanguard Small Cap Stock (NAESX)

Aggressive Growth

Vanguard Financial Center
P.O. Box 2600
Valley Forge, PA 19482
(800) 662-7447, (215) 648-6000

PERFORMANCE

	3yr Annual	5yr Annual	10yr Annual	Bull	Bear
Return (%)	26.7	13.0	7.0	116.0	-22.7
Differ from Category (+/-)	1.3 av	-5.2 low	-4.9 low	-9.0 av	-7.7 blw av

Total Risk	Standard Deviation	Category Risk	Risk Index	Beta
high	14.0%	blw av	0.9	0.9

	1993	1992	1991	1990	1989	1988	1987	1986	1985	1984
Return (%)	18.7	18.2	45.2	-18.1	10.4	24.6	-6.9	0.1	23.0	-25.1
Differ from category (+/-) . .	-0.3	7.8	-7.2	-11.8	-16.6	9.4	-3.5	-9.3	-8.0	-15.7

PER SHARE DATA

	1993	1992	1991	1990	1989	1988	1987	1986	1985	1984
Dividends, Net Income ($) .	0.18	0.18	0.18	0.18	0.12	0.05	0.00	0.00	0.15	0.00
Distrib'ns, Cap Gain ($) . . .	0.81	0.15	0.28	0.14	2.16	0.00	1.21	1.89	0.76	0.00
Net Asset Value ($)	15.67	14.07	12.19	8.74	11.07	11.97	9.65	11.70	13.56	11.95
Expense Ratio (%)	0.18	0.18	0.21	0.31	1.00	0.95	0.92	0.92	1.00	1.05
Net Income to Assets (%) . .	1.47	1.65	2.11	1.91	0.65	0.24	-0.25	-0.06	-0.28	1.11
Portfolio Turnover (%)	26	26	33	40	160	68	92	92	103	100
Total Assets (Millions $) . . .	465	202	111	40	20	27	35	10	1	12

PORTFOLIO (as of 9/30/93)

Portfolio Manager: George U. Sauter - 1989

Investm't Category: Aggressive Growth

✔ Cap Gain	Asset Allocation
Cap & Income	Fund of Funds
Income	✔ Index
	Sector
✔ Domestic	✔ Small Cap
Foreign	Socially Conscious
Country/Region	State Specific

Portfolio: stocks 97% bonds 0%
convertibles 0% other 0% cash 3%

Largest Holdings: Russell 2000 Small Stock Index

Unrealized Net Capital Gains: 13% of portfolio value

SHAREHOLDER INFORMATION

Minimum Investment
Initial: $3,000   Subsequent: $100

Minimum IRA Investment
Initial: $500   Subsequent: $100

Maximum Fees
Load: 1.00% charge   12b-1: none
Other: $10/yr maintenance fee

Distributions
Income: Dec   Capital Gains: Dec

Exchange Options
Number Per Year: 2   Fee: none
Telephone: none

Services
IRA, other pension, auto exchange, auto invest, auto withdraw

Vanguard Spec Port— Energy (VGENX)

Growth

Vanguard Financial Center
P.O. Box 2600
Valley Forge, PA 19482
(800) 662-7447, (215) 648-6000

PERFORMANCE

	3yr Annual	5yr Annual	10yr Annual	Bull	Bear
Return (%)	10.4	13.7	na	24.8	6.3
Differ from Category (+/-)	-8.8 low	-0.8 blw av	na	-59.9 low	18.7 high

Total Risk	Standard Deviation	Category Risk	Risk Index	Beta
high	15.8%	high	1.5	0.7

	1993	1992	1991	1990	1989	1988	1987	1986	1985	1984
Return (%)	26.5	6.1	0.2	-1.3	43.4	21.3	6.1	12.6	14.4	—
Differ from category (+/-)	13.3	-4.9	-35.2	4.8	17.6	3.6	4.9	-1.9	-14.9	—

PER SHARE DATA

	1993	1992	1991	1990	1989	1988	1987	1986	1985	1984
Dividends, Net Income ($)	0.28	0.36	0.41	0.46	0.36	0.37	0.75	0.43	0.14	—
Distrib'ns, Cap Gain ($)	1.38	0.18	0.41	0.87	0.56	0.00	1.41	0.05	0.07	—
Net Asset Value ($)	15.06	13.28	13.03	13.84	15.40	11.39	9.69	11.18	10.46	—
Expense Ratio (%)	0.21	0.30	0.35	0.38	0.40	0.38	0.65	0.92	0.55	—
Net Income to Assets (%)	2.47	2.78	3.24	3.05	3.07	3.70	3.43	4.40	3.75	—
Portfolio Turnover (%)	37	42	40	44	46	84	34	156	34	—
Total Assets (Millions $)	250	124	114	80	44	36	29	2	1	—

PORTFOLIO (as of 7/31/93)

Portfolio Manager: Ernst Von Metzsch - 1984

Investm't Category: Growth

- ✔ Cap Gain
- Cap & Income
- Income
- Asset Allocation
- Fund of Funds
- Index
- ✔ Sector
- ✔ Domestic
- ✔ Foreign
- Country/Region
- Small Cap
- Socially Conscious
- State Specific

Portfolio: stocks 95% bonds 0%
convertibles 0% other 0% cash 5%

Largest Holdings: petroleum 52%, foreign energy 23%

Unrealized Net Capital Gains: 11% of portfolio value

SHAREHOLDER INFORMATION

Minimum Investment
Initial: $3,000 Subsequent: $100

Minimum IRA Investment
Initial: $500 Subsequent: $100

Maximum Fees
Load: 1.00% charge 12b-1: none
Other: none

Distributions
Income: Dec Capital Gains: Dec

Exchange Options
Number Per Year: 3 Fee: none
Telephone: yes (money market fund available)

Services
IRA, other pension, auto exchange, auto invest, auto withdraw

Vanguard Spec Port— Gold & PM (VGPMX)

Gold

Vanguard Financial Center
P.O. Box 2600
Valley Forge, PA 19482
(800) 662-7447, (215) 648-6000

PERFORMANCE

	3yr Annual	5yr Annual	10yr Annual	Bull	Bear
Return (%)	17.6	11.1	na	51.2	-13.8
Differ from Category (+/-)	3.9 high	-1.2 high	na	17.6 high	-59.7 blw av

Total Risk	Standard Deviation	Category Risk	Risk Index	Beta
high	25.3%	blw av	1.0	-0.3

	1993	1992	1991	1990	1989	1988	1987	1986	1985	1984
Return (%)	93.3	-19.4	4.3	-19.9	30.3	-14.2	38.7	49.8	-5.0	—
Differ from category (+/-) ...	6.4	-3.7	9.1	-51.4	5.6	4.7	6.8	12.2	2.4	—

PER SHARE DATA

	1993	1992	1991	1990	1989	1988	1987	1986	1985	1984
Dividends, Net Income ($) .	0.20	0.18	0.25	0.31	0.34	0.25	0.47	0.20	0.05	—
Distrib'ns, Cap Gain ($) ...	0.00	0.00	0.00	0.00	0.00	0.00	1.14	0.00	0.00	—
Net Asset Value ($)	13.78	7.24	9.21	9.07	11.73	9.27	11.11	9.22	6.33	—
Expense Ratio (%)........	0.36	0.35	0.42	0.45	0.48	0.47	0.59	0.73	0.87	—
Net Income to Assets (%) ..	2.50	2.54	2.78	3.01	2.67	2.71	3.36	3.86	3.25	—
Portfolio Turnover (%)	2	3	10	17	18	44	32	40	11	—
Total Assets (Millions $) ...	586	178	144	223	126	128	70	30	6	—

PORTFOLIO (as of 7/31/93)

Portfolio Manager: David Hutchins - 1987

Investm't Category: Gold

✔ Cap Gain	Asset Allocation
Cap & Income	Fund of Funds
Income	Index
	✔ Sector
✔ Domestic	Small Cap
✔ Foreign	Socially Conscious
Country/Region	State Specific

Portfolio: stocks 87% bonds 0%
convertibles 0% other 7% cash 6%

Largest Holdings: N. American gold mining cos. 32%, S. African gold mining cos. 32%

Unrealized Net Capital Gains: 24% of portfolio value

SHAREHOLDER INFORMATION

Minimum Investment
Initial: $3,000   Subsequent: $100

Minimum IRA Investment
Initial: $500   Subsequent: $100

Maximum Fees
Load: 1.00% charge   12b-1: none
Other: none

Distributions
Income: Dec   Capital Gains: Dec

Exchange Options
Number Per Year: 3   Fee: none
Telephone: yes (money market fund available)

Services
IRA, other pension, auto exchange, auto invest, auto withdraw

Vanguard Spec Port— Health Care (VGHCX)

Growth

Vanguard Financial Center
P.O. Box 2600
Valley Forge, PA 19482
(800) 662-7447, (215) 648-6000

PERFORMANCE

	3yr Annual	5yr Annual	10yr Annual	Bull	Bear
Return (%)	17.2	20.0	na	89.4	-0.6
Differ from Category (+/-)	-2.0 blw av	5.4 high	na	4.7 av	11.7 high

Total Risk	Standard Deviation	Category Risk	Risk Index	Beta
high	14.7%	high	1.4	1.1

	1993	1992	1991	1990	1989	1988	1987	1986	1985	1984
Return (%)	11.8	-1.5	46.3	16.7	32.9	28.3	-0.5	21.4	45.7	—
Differ from category (+/-)	-1.4	-12.5	10.9	22.8	7.1	10.6	-1.7	6.9	16.4	—

PER SHARE DATA

	1993	1992	1991	1990	1989	1988	1987	1986	1985	1984
Dividends, Net Income ($)	0.75	0.69	0.52	0.55	0.49	0.34	0.56	0.12	0.07	—
Distrib'ns, Cap Gain ($)	1.97	1.20	0.52	0.83	0.72	1.29	1.39	0.80	0.10	—
Net Asset Value ($)	35.07	34.01	36.50	25.69	23.21	18.43	15.70	17.64	15.31	—
Expense Ratio (%)	0.22	0.30	0.36	0.39	0.62	0.51	0.61	0.83	0.59	—
Net Income to Assets (%)	2.06	1.98	2.54	2.34	1.85	1.65	1.47	1.52	2.41	—
Portfolio Turnover (%)	15	7	17	28	19	41	27	59	23	—
Total Assets (Millions $)	602	553	190	76	58	54	49	22	2	—

PORTFOLIO (as of 7/31/93)

Portfolio Manager: Edward Owens - 1984

Investm't Category: Growth

Cap Gain	Asset Allocation
✔ Cap & Income	Fund of Funds
Income	Index
	✔ Sector
✔ Domestic	Small Cap
✔ Foreign	Socially Conscious
Country/Region	State Specific

Portfolio:	stocks 97%	bonds 0%
convertibles 0%	other 0%	cash 3%

Largest Holdings: pharmaceuticals 64%, medical technology & services 33%

Unrealized Net Capital Gains: 6% of portfolio value

SHAREHOLDER INFORMATION

Minimum Investment
Initial: $3,000   Subsequent: $100

Minimum IRA Investment
Initial: $500   Subsequent: $100

Maximum Fees
Load: 1.00% charge   12b-1: none
Other: none

Distributions
Income: Dec   Capital Gains: Dec

Exchange Options
Number Per Year: 3   Fee: none
Telephone: yes (money market fund available)

Services
IRA, other pension, auto exchange, auto invest, auto withdraw

Vanguard Spec Port— Service Economy (VGSEX)

Growth

Vanguard Financial Center
P.O. Box 2600
Valley Forge, PA 19482
(800) 662-7447, (215) 648-6000

PERFORMANCE

	3yr Annual	5yr Annual	10yr Annual	Bull	Bear
Return (%)	18.5	13.0	na	80.2	-21.8
Differ from Category (+/-)	-0.6 av	-1.6 blw av	na	-4.5 av	-9.4 low

Total Risk	Standard Deviation	Category Risk	Risk Index	Beta
abv av	12.5%	av	1.2	1.0

	1993	1992	1991	1990	1989	1988	1987	1986	1985	1984
Return (%)	12.0	10.6	34.3	-15.4	31.3	19.1	-13.0	12.7	43.7	—
Differ from category (+/-) . .	-1.2	-0.4	-1.1	-9.3	5.5	1.4	-14.2	-1.8	14.4	—

PER SHARE DATA

	1993	1992	1991	1990	1989	1988	1987	1986	1985	1984
Dividends, Net Income ($) .	0.21	0.17	0.28	0.38	0.40	0.25	0.87	0.15	0.09	—
Distrib'ns, Cap Gain ($) . . .	0.93	0.00	0.03	0.27	0.83	0.00	2.05	0.69	0.11	—
Net Asset Value ($)	23.21	21.76	19.82	15.01	18.49	15.03	12.83	17.59	16.35	—
Expense Ratio (%)	0.56	0.48	0.59	0.43	0.86	0.44	0.48	0.57	0.58	—
Net Income to Assets (%) . .	0.93	1.47	1.99	2.10	1.57	2.08	1.61	2.24	2.92	—
Portfolio Turnover (%)	36	43	34	53	33	49	96	54	125	—
Total Assets (Millions $)	34	22	17	21	22	24	49	33	3	—

PORTFOLIO (as of 7/31/93)

Portfolio Manager: Matthew E. Megargel - 1984

Investm't Category: Growth

✔ Cap Gain	Asset Allocation
Cap & Income	Fund of Funds
Income	Index
	✔ Sector
✔ Domestic	Small Cap
✔ Foreign	Socially Conscious
Country/Region	State Specific

Portfolio:	stocks 94%	bonds 0%
convertibles 1%	other 0%	cash 5%

Largest Holdings: business services 30%, financial services 23%

Unrealized Net Capital Gains: 23% of portfolio value

SHAREHOLDER INFORMATION

Minimum Investment
Initial: $3,000   Subsequent: $100

Minimum IRA Investment
Initial: $500   Subsequent: $100

Maximum Fees
Load: 1.00% charge   12b-1: none
Other: none

Distributions
Income: Dec   Capital Gains: Dec

Exchange Options
Number Per Year: 3   Fee: none
Telephone: yes (money market fund available)

Services
IRA, other pension, auto exchange, auto invest, auto withdraw

Vanguard Spec Port— Tech (VGTCX)

Aggressive Growth

Vanguard Financial Center
P.O. Box 2600
Valley Forge, PA 19482
(800) 662-7447, (215) 648-6000

PERFORMANCE

	3yr Annual	5yr Annual	10yr Annual	Bull	Bear
Return (%)	23.0	14.7	na	109.8	-17.0
Differ from Category (+/-)	-2.4 blw av	-3.5 blw av	na	-15.2 av	-2.0 av

Total Risk	Standard Deviation	Category Risk	Risk Index	Beta
high	17.1%	av	1.1	1.2

	1993	1992	1991	1990	1989	1988	1987	1986	1985	1984
Return (%)	11.3	13.4	47.3	-6.5	14.5	9.4	-11.9	5.6	13.4	—
Differ from category (+/-). . .	-7.7	3.0	-5.1	-0.2	-12.5	-5.8	-8.5	-3.8	-17.6	—

PER SHARE DATA

	1993	1992	1991	1990	1989	1988	1987	1986	1985	1984
Dividends, Net Income ($).	0.12	0.11	0.20	0.21	0.15	0.15	0.18	0.07	0.05	—
Distrib'ns, Cap Gain ($) . . .	1.75	0.00	0.00	0.00	0.00	0.00	0.52	0.30	0.00	—
Net Asset Value ($)	18.33	18.22	16.16	11.11	12.12	10.71	9.93	11.93	11.64	—
Expense Ratio (%)	0.25	0.36	0.48	0.48	0.51	0.39	0.65	0.72	0.53	—
Net Income to Assets (%) .	0.90	1.25	1.64	1.20	1.23	1.02	0.82	1.35	1.85	—
Portfolio Turnover (%).	65	57	55	35	41	129	108	85	65	—
Total Assets (Millions $). . . .	72	33	20	11	17	18	26	12	5	—

PORTFOLIO (as of 7/31/93)

Portfolio Manager: Perry Traquina - 1984

Investm't Category: Aggressive Growth

✔ Cap Gain	Asset Allocation
Cap & Income	Fund of Funds
Income	Index
	✔ Sector
✔ Domestic	Small Cap
✔ Foreign	Socially Conscious
Country/Region	State Specific

Portfolio: stocks 87% bonds 0%
convertibles 0% other 0% cash 13%

Largest Holdings: computer service & software 41%, computer equipment 25%

Unrealized Net Capital Gains: 4% of portfolio value

SHAREHOLDER INFORMATION

Minimum Investment
Initial: $3,000   Subsequent: $100

Minimum IRA Investment
Initial: $500   Subsequent: $100

Maximum Fees
Load: 1.00% charge   12b-1: none
Other: none

Distributions
Income: Dec   Capital Gains: Dec

Exchange Options
Number Per Year: 3   Fee: none
Telephone: yes (money market fund available)

Services
IRA, other pension, auto exchange, auto invest, auto withdraw

Vanguard Spec Port— Utilities Income (VGSUX)

Growth & Income

Vanguard Financial Center
P.O. Box 2600
Valley Forge, PA 19482
(800) 662-7447, (215) 648-6000

PERFORMANCE

	3yr Annual	5yr Annual	10yr Annual	Bull	Bear
Return (%)	na	na	na	na	na
Differ from Category (+/-)	na	na	na	na	na

Total Risk	Standard Deviation	Category Risk	Risk Index	Beta
na	na	na	na	na

	1993	1992	1991	1990	1989	1988	1987	1986	1985	1984
Return (%)	15.0	—	—	—	—	—	—	—	—	—
Differ from category (+/-) ...	2.4	—	—	—	—	—	—	—	—	—

PER SHARE DATA

	1993	1992	1991	1990	1989	1988	1987	1986	1985	1984
Dividends, Net Income ($) .	0.56	—	—	—	—	—	—	—	—	—
Distrib'ns, Cap Gain ($) ...	0.40	—	—	—	—	—	—	—	—	—
Net Asset Value ($)	11.63	—	—	—	—	—	—	—	—	—
Expense Ratio (%)........	0.45	—	—	—	—	—	—	—	—	—
Net Income to Assets (%)..	4.70	—	—	—	—	—	—	—	—	—
Portfolio Turnover (%).....	20	—	—	—	—	—	—	—	—	—
Total Assets (Millions $) ...	781	—	—	—	—	—	—	—	—	—

PORTFOLIO (as of 7/31/93)

Portfolio Manager: John R. Ryan - 1992

Investm't Category: Growth & Income
Cap Gain	Asset Allocation
✔ Cap & Income	Fund of Funds
Income	Index
	✔ Sector
✔ Domestic	Small Cap
✔ Foreign	Socially Conscious
Country/Region	State Specific

Portfolio: stocks 77% bonds 22%
convertibles 0% other 0% cash 1%

Largest Holdings: electric 37%, telephone 30%

Unrealized Net Capital Gains: 7% of portfolio value

SHAREHOLDER INFORMATION

Minimum Investment
Initial: $3,000 Subsequent: $100

Minimum IRA Investment
Initial: $500 Subsequent: $100

Maximum Fees
Load: none 12b-1: none
Other: none

Distributions
Income: quarterly Capital Gains: Dec

Exchange Options
Number Per Year: 3 Fee: none
Telephone: yes (money market fund available)

Services
IRA, other pension, auto exchange, auto invest, auto withdraw

Vanguard Star (VGSTX)

Balanced

Vanguard Financial Center
P.O. Box 2600
Valley Forge, PA 19482
(800) 662-7447, (215) 648-6000

PERFORMANCE

	3yr Annual	5yr Annual	10yr Annual	Bull	Bear
Return (%)	15.0	11.7	na	63.6	-10.4
Differ from Category (+/-)	0.0 av	-0.4 blw av	na	2.0 av	-4.6 low

Total Risk	Standard Deviation	Category Risk	Risk Index	Beta
av	6.7%	av	1.1	0.6

	1993	1992	1991	1990	1989	1988	1987	1986	1985	1984
Return (%)	10.8	10.5	24.0	-3.6	18.7	18.9	1.6	13.7	—	—
Differ from category (+/-)	-2.6	2.4	0.1	-3.1	1.1	6.9	-0.6	-3.8	—	—

PER SHARE DATA

	1993	1992	1991	1990	1989	1988	1987	1986	1985	1984
Dividends, Net Income ($)	0.46	0.50	0.62	0.73	0.76	0.68	0.85	0.86	—	—
Distrib'ns, Cap Gain ($)	0.40	0.18	0.37	0.15	0.37	0.02	0.75	0.70	—	—
Net Asset Value ($)	13.41	12.89	12.29	10.73	12.05	11.12	9.98	11.34	—	—
Expense Ratio (%)	0.00	0.00	0.00	0.00	0.00	0.00	0.00	0.00	—	—
Net Income to Assets (%)	3.38	4.36	5.48	6.65	6.42	5.87	6.08	6.08	—	—
Portfolio Turnover (%)	4	3	11	12	7	21	0	17	—	—
Total Assets (Millions $)	3,664	2,490	1,575	1,039	949	682	568	567	—	—

PORTFOLIO (as of 6/30/93)

Portfolio Manager: committee

Investm't Category: Balanced
- Cap Gain
- ✔ Cap & Income
- Income

- Asset Allocation
- ✔ Fund of Funds
- Index
- Sector

- ✔ Domestic
- Foreign
- Country/Region

- Small Cap
- Socially Conscious
- State Specific

Portfolio: stocks 0%   bonds 0%
convertibles 0%   other 100%   cash 0%

Largest Holdings: Vanguard Windsor II 41%,
Vanguard Fixed Inc. Sec. Inv't Grade Corp. 12%

Unrealized Net Capital Gains: 8% of portfolio value

SHAREHOLDER INFORMATION

Minimum Investment
Initial: $500   Subsequent: $100

Minimum IRA Investment
Initial: $500   Subsequent: $100

Maximum Fees
Load: none   12b-1: none
Other: none

Distributions
Income: Jul, Dec   Capital Gains: Dec

Exchange Options
Number Per Year: 2   Fee: none
Telephone: yes (money market fund available)

Services
IRA, other pension, auto exchange, auto invest, auto withdraw

Vanguard Trustees' Equity—Int'l (VTRIX)

International Stock

Vanguard Financial Center
P.O. Box 2600
Valley Forge, PA 19482
(800) 662-7447, (215) 648-6000

PERFORMANCE

	3yr Annual	5yr Annual	10yr Annual	Bull	Bear
Return (%)	9.3	7.6	16.1	35.8	-15.4
Differ from Category (+/-)	-5.0 blw av	-1.1 blw av	2.7 av	-19.3 blw av	-0.3 av

Total Risk	Standard Deviation	Category Risk	Risk Index	Beta
abv av	12.8%	av	1.1	0.4

	1993	1992	1991	1990	1989	1988	1987	1986	1985	1984
Return (%)	30.5	-8.7	9.8	-12.2	25.9	18.6	23.6	50.5	40.3	-0.6
Differ from category (+/-) ..	-8.0	-5.2	-3.1	-1.1	3.7	4.8	11.6	0.2	-0.3	8.8

PER SHARE DATA

	1993	1992	1991	1990	1989	1988	1987	1986	1985	1984
Dividends, Net Income ($) .	0.81	0.67	0.76	0.94	0.79	0.99	0.75	1.03	0.93	1.13
Distrib'ns, Cap Gain ($) ...	0.00	0.28	0.61	1.01	2.08	4.58	18.32	6.55	2.54	0.07
Net Asset Value ($)	31.04	24.43	27.78	26.60	32.44	28.27	28.66	38.65	30.91	24.59
Expense Ratio (%)........	0.45	0.42	0.38	0.44	0.46	0.51	0.50	0.52	0.56	0.63
Net Income to Assets (%)..	2.16	2.48	2.87	3.62	2.61	2.55	2.44	2.65	3.11	3.89
Portfolio Turnover (%)	49	51	46	18	25	14	48	24	29	8
Total Assets (Millions $) ..	1,008	679	878	796	646	467	657	718	581	317

PORTFOLIO (as of 6/30/93)

Portfolio Manager: Jarrod Wilcox - 1991

Investm't Category: International Stock

Cap Gain	Asset Allocation
✔ Cap & Income	Fund of Funds
Income	Index
	Sector
Domestic	Small Cap
✔ Foreign	Socially Conscious
Country/Region	State Specific

Portfolio: stocks 96%   bonds 0%
convertibles 0%   other 0%   cash 4%

Largest Holdings: Japan 38%, United Kingdom 11%

Unrealized Net Capital Gains: 13% of portfolio value

SHAREHOLDER INFORMATION

Minimum Investment
Initial: $10,000   Subsequent: $1,000

Minimum IRA Investment
Initial: $500   Subsequent: $100

Maximum Fees
Load: none   12b-1: none
Other: none

Distributions
Income: quarterly   Capital Gains: Dec

Exchange Options
Number Per Year: 2   Fee: none
Telephone: yes (money market fund available)

Services
IRA, other pension, auto exchange, auto invest, auto withdraw

Vanguard Trustees' Equity—US (VTRSX)

Growth & Income

Vanguard Financial Center
P.O. Box 2600
Valley Forge, PA 19482
(800) 662-7447, (215) 648-6000

PERFORMANCE

	3yr Annual	5yr Annual	10yr Annual	Bull	Bear
Return (%)	16.4	11.1	11.2	71.9	-15.7
Differ from Category (+/-)	0.0 av	-1.4 blw av	-1.2 blw av	1.8 av	-4.1 blw av

Total Risk	Standard Deviation	Category Risk	Risk Index	Beta
av	10.7%	abv av	1.2	0.8

	1993	1992	1991	1990	1989	1988	1987	1986	1985	1984
Return (%).............	17.2	6.4	26.5	-8.3	17.1	24.6	1.5	15.2	20.5	-2.8
Differ from category (+/-)...	4.6	-3.6	-1.2	-2.7	-4.5	7.8	1.1	0.0	-4.9	-9.0

PER SHARE DATA

	1993	1992	1991	1990	1989	1988	1987	1986	1985	1984
Dividends, Net Income ($).	0.43	0.67	0.70	1.08	0.87	0.97	0.72	1.16	1.45	1.57
Distrib'ns, Cap Gain ($) ...	2.16	0.86	0.00	0.00	3.81	1.00	5.88	6.15	4.10	2.51
Net Asset Value ($)	30.65	28.43	28.20	22.90	26.15	26.35	22.77	28.69	31.15	30.56
Expense Ratio (%)	0.98	0.65	0.44	0.52	0.51	0.58	0.52	0.52	0.48	0.53
Net Income to Assets (%) .	1.63	2.33	2.67	4.18	2.90	3.86	2.77	3.46	4.42	4.74
Portfolio Turnover (%).....	158	209	84	81	72	90	44	19	23	33
Total Assets (Millions $)....	119	68	115	100	121	115	122	162	201	271

PORTFOLIO (as of 6/30/93)

Portfolio Manager: John Geewax - 1992

Investm't Category: Growth & Income

Cap Gain	Asset Allocation
✔ Cap & Income	Fund of Funds
Income	Index
	Sector
✔ Domestic	Small Cap
Foreign	Socially Conscious
Country/Region	State Specific

Portfolio: stocks 97% bonds 0%
convertibles 0% other 0% cash 3%

Largest Holdings: na

Unrealized Net Capital Gains: 15% of portfolio value

SHAREHOLDER INFORMATION

Minimum Investment
Initial: $10,000   Subsequent: $1,000

Minimum IRA Investment
Initial: $500   Subsequent: $100

Maximum Fees
Load: none   12b-1: none
Other: none

Distributions
Income: quarterly   Capital Gains: Dec

Exchange Options
Number Per Year: 2   Fee: none
Telephone: yes (money market fund available)

Services
IRA, other pension, auto exchange, auto invest, auto withdraw

Vanguard US Growth
(VWUSX)
Growth

Vanguard Financial Center
P.O. Box 2600
Valley Forge, PA 19482
(800) 662-7447, (215) 648-6000

PERFORMANCE

	3yr Annual	5yr Annual	10yr Annual	Bull	Bear
Return (%)	14.1	16.4	13.4	62.4	-4.3
Differ from Category (+/-)	-5.1 blw av	1.8 abv av	0.8 av	-22.3 blw av	8.1 high

Total Risk	Standard Deviation	Category Risk	Risk Index	Beta
abv av	13.8%	abv av	1.3	1.2

	1993	1992	1991	1990	1989	1988	1987	1986	1985	1984
Return (%)	-1.4	2.7	46.7	4.6	37.6	8.7	1.7	7.8	36.5	1.1
Differ from category (+/-) .	-14.6	-8.3	11.3	10.7	11.8	-9.0	0.5	-6.7	7.2	1.1

PER SHARE DATA

	1993	1992	1991	1990	1989	1988	1987	1986	1985	1984
Dividends, Net Income ($) .	0.20	0.18	0.18	0.18	0.12	0.05	0.31	0.28	0.25	0.31
Distrib'ns, Cap Gain ($) . . .	0.00	0.07	0.00	0.00	0.00	0.00	3.26	1.94	0.81	0.33
Net Asset Value ($)	14.93	15.36	15.20	10.49	10.21	7.51	6.96	10.32	11.69	9.49
Expense Ratio (%).	0.49	0.49	0.56	0.74	0.95	0.88	0.65	0.80	1.04	0.88
Net Income to Assets (%) . .	1.50	1.52	1.82	1.77	1.44	1.23	2.41	2.27	2.10	2.53
Portfolio Turnover (%)	37	24	30	49	48	38	142	77	61	70
Total Assets (Millions $) . .	1,821	1,441	747	339	184	130	184	187	211	180

PORTFOLIO (as of 8/31/93)

Portfolio Manager: J. Parker Hall, III - 1987

Investm't Category: Growth

✔ Cap Gain	Asset Allocation
Cap & Income	Fund of Funds
Income	Index
	Sector
✔ Domestic	Small Cap
Foreign	Socially Conscious
Country/Region	State Specific

Portfolio: stocks 86%   bonds 0%
convertibles 0%   other 0%   cash 14%

Largest Holdings: consumer 22%, finance & insurance 19%

Unrealized Net Capital Gains: 10% of portfolio value

SHAREHOLDER INFORMATION

Minimum Investment
Initial: $3,000   Subsequent: $100

Minimum IRA Investment
Initial: $500   Subsequent: $100

Maximum Fees
Load: none   12b-1: none
Other: none

Distributions
Income: Dec   Capital Gains: Dec

Exchange Options
Number Per Year: 2   Fee: none
Telephone: yes (money market fund available)

Services
IRA, other pension, auto exchange, auto invest, auto withdraw

Vanguard Wellesley Income (VWINX)

Balanced

Vanguard Financial Center
P.O. Box 2600
Valley Forge, PA 19482
(800) 662-7447, (215) 648-6000

PERFORMANCE

	3yr Annual	5yr Annual	10yr Annual	Bull	Bear
Return (%)	14.8	13.6	14.0	62.1	-3.1
Differ from Category (+/-)	-0.2 av	1.5 abv av	2.0 high	0.5 av	2.7 abv av

Total Risk	Standard Deviation	Category Risk	Risk Index	Beta
blw av	5.6%	blw av	0.9	0.3

	1993	1992	1991	1990	1989	1988	1987	1986	1985	1984
Return (%)	14.6	8.7	21.4	3.7	20.8	13.5	-1.8	18.3	27.3	16.6
Differ from category (+/-) . . .	1.2	0.6	-2.5	4.2	3.2	1.5	-4.1	0.8	3.6	9.2

PER SHARE DATA

	1993	1992	1991	1990	1989	1988	1987	1986	1985	1984
Dividends, Net Income ($) .	1.14	1.21	1.27	1.30	1.31	1.23	1.04	1.33	1.38	1.37
Distrib'ns, Cap Gain ($) . . .	0.40	0.20	0.00	0.07	0.23	0.00	0.37	0.46	0.10	0.00
Net Asset Value ($)	19.24	18.16	18.07	16.02	16.82	15.26	14.57	16.27	15.31	13.28
Expense Ratio (%)	0.36	0.35	0.40	0.45	0.45	0.51	0.49	0.58	0.60	0.71
Net Income to Assets (%) .	6.00	6.50	7.08	7.77	7.68	8.14	7.83	7.74	9.36	10.68
Portfolio Turnover (%)	na	21	28	23	23	20	40	32	20	36
Total Assets (Millions $) . .	6,092	3,178	1,935	1,022	788	567	495	510	224	114

PORTFOLIO (as of 6/30/93)

Portfolio Manager: Earl McEvoy - 1982, John Ryan - 1987

Investm't Category: Balanced

Cap Gain	Asset Allocation
✔ Cap & Income	Fund of Funds
Income	Index
	Sector
✔ Domestic	Small Cap
Foreign	Socially Conscious
Country/Region	State Specific

Portfolio: stocks 34% bonds 62%
convertibles 2% other 0% cash 2%

Largest Holdings: bonds—utility 18%, stocks—utility 15%

Unrealized Net Capital Gains: 9% of portfolio value

SHAREHOLDER INFORMATION

Minimum Investment
Initial: $3,000 Subsequent: $100

Minimum IRA Investment
Initial: $500 Subsequent: $100

Maximum Fees
Load: none 12b-1: none
Other: none

Distributions
Income: quarterly Capital Gains: Dec

Exchange Options
Number Per Year: 2 Fee: none
Telephone: yes (money market fund available)

Services
IRA, other pension, auto exchange, auto invest, auto withdraw

Vanguard Wellington
(VWELX)
Balanced

Vanguard Financial Center
P.O. Box 2600
Valley Forge, PA 19482
(800) 662-7447, (215) 648-6000

PERFORMANCE

	3yr Annual	5yr Annual	10yr Annual	Bull	Bear
Return (%)	14.8	12.3	13.6	63.4	-9.9
Differ from Category (+/-)	-0.2 av	0.2 av	1.6 abv av	1.8 av	-4.1 low

Total Risk	Standard Deviation	Category Risk	Risk Index	Beta
av	7.5%	abv av	1.2	0.6

	1993	1992	1991	1990	1989	1988	1987	1986	1985	1984
Return (%)	13.5	7.9	23.8	-2.9	21.6	16.1	2.2	18.4	28.5	10.6
Differ from category (+/-) . . .	0.1	-0.2	-0.1	-2.4	4.0	4.1	-0.1	0.8	4.8	3.2

PER SHARE DATA

	1993	1992	1991	1990	1989	1988	1987	1986	1985	1984
Dividends, Net Income ($) .	0.92	0.93	0.95	1.01	1.02	0.95	0.98	0.93	0.92	0.92
Distrib'ns, Cap Gain ($) . . .	0.37	0.15	0.23	0.00	0.60	0.57	0.14	0.34	0.30	0.47
Net Asset Value ($)	20.40	19.16	18.81	16.24	17.78	16.01	15.15	15.85	14.50	12.32
Expense Ratio (%).	0.35	0.33	0.35	0.43	0.42	0.47	0.43	0.53	0.64	0.59
Net Income to Assets (%). .	4.65	4.98	5.39	5.99	5.77	5.88	5.56	5.88	6.84	7.52
Portfolio Turnover (%)	36	24	35	33	30	28	27	25	27	27
Total Assets (Millions $) . .	8,221	5,358	3,473	2,317	2,035	1,528	1,274	1,102	778	604

PORTFOLIO (as of 5/31/93)

Portfolio Manager: Vincent Bajakian - 1972, Paul Sullivan - 1975

Investm't Category: Balanced
Cap Gain	Asset Allocation
✔ Cap & Income	Fund of Funds
Income	Index
	Sector
✔ Domestic	Small Cap
✔ Foreign	Socially Conscious
Country/Region	State Specific

Portfolio: stocks 58% bonds 38%
convertibles 2% other 0% cash 2%

Largest Holdings: stocks—basic industry 17%, bonds—industrial 10%

Unrealized Net Capital Gains: 15% of portfolio value

SHAREHOLDER INFORMATION

Minimum Investment
Initial: $3,000   Subsequent: $100

Minimum IRA Investment
Initial: $500   Subsequent: $100

Maximum Fees
Load: none   12b-1: none
Other: none

Distributions
Income: quarterly   Capital Gains: Dec

Exchange Options
Number Per Year: 2   Fee: none
Telephone: yes (money market fund available)

Services
IRA, other pension, auto exchange, auto invest, auto withdraw

Vanguard Windsor
(VWNDX)

Growth & Income

Vanguard Financial Center
P.O. Box 2600
Valley Forge, PA 19482
(800) 662-7447, (215) 648-6000

this fund is closed to new investors

PERFORMANCE

	3yr Annual	5yr Annual	10yr Annual	Bull	Bear
Return (%)	21.3	11.6	15.3	92.6	-21.6
Differ from Category (+/-)	4.9 high	-0.8 blw av	2.9 high	22.5 high	-10.0 low

Total Risk	Standard Deviation	Category Risk	Risk Index	Beta
abv av	11.0%	abv av	1.3	0.8

	1993	1992	1991	1990	1989	1988	1987	1986	1985	1984
Return (%)	19.3	16.4	28.5	-15.5	15.0	28.6	1.2	20.2	28.0	19.4
Differ from category (+/-) . . .	6.7	6.4	0.8	-9.9	-6.6	11.8	0.8	5.0	2.6	13.2

PER SHARE DATA

	1993	1992	1991	1990	1989	1988	1987	1986	1985	1984
Dividends, Net Income ($) .	0.37	0.49	0.56	0.74	0.75	0.62	0.87	0.85	0.79	0.75
Distrib'ns, Cap Gain ($) . . .	0.88	0.37	0.83	0.31	0.85	0.55	2.21	2.59	0.74	0.47
Net Asset Value ($)	13.91	12.74	11.72	10.30	13.41	13.07	11.11	13.95	14.50	12.64
Expense Ratio (%)	0.40	0.26	0.30	0.37	0.41	0.46	0.43	0.52	0.53	0.63
Net Income to Assets (%) .	2.68	3.89	4.84	5.82	5.07	5.08	4.86	5.28	6.19	6.72
Portfolio Turnover (%).	25	32	36	21	34	24	46	51	23	23
Total Assets (Millions $).	10,417	8,249	7,860	5,838	8,313	5,921	4,849	4,862	3,814	2,337

PORTFOLIO (as of 10/31/93)

Portfolio Manager: John C. Neff - 1964

Investm't Category: Growth & Income
Cap Gain	Asset Allocation
✔ Cap & Income	Fund of Funds
Income	Index
	Sector
✔ Domestic	Small Cap
Foreign	Socially Conscious
Country/Region	State Specific

Portfolio: stocks 78% bonds 8%
convertibles 1% other 0% cash 13%

Largest Holdings: banks 15%, oil & gas 13%

Unrealized Net Capital Gains: 12% of portfolio value

SHAREHOLDER INFORMATION

Minimum Investment
Initial: $10,000   Subsequent: $100

Minimum IRA Investment
Initial: $500   Subsequent: $100

Maximum Fees
Load: none   12b-1: none
Other: none

Distributions
Income: May, Dec   Capital Gains: Dec

Exchange Options
Number Per Year: 2   Fee: none
Telephone: yes (money market fund available)

Services
IRA, other pension, auto exchange, auto invest, auto withdraw

Vanguard Windsor II
(VWNFX)

Growth & Income

Vanguard Financial Center
P.O. Box 2600
Valley Forge, PA 19482
(800) 662-7447, (215) 648-6000

PERFORMANCE

	3yr Annual	5yr Annual	10yr Annual	Bull	Bear
Return (%)	17.8	13.5	na	78.9	-17.6
Differ from Category (+/-)	1.4 abv av	1.0 abv av	na	8.8 abv av	-6.0 low

Total Risk	Standard Deviation	Category Risk	Risk Index	Beta
av	9.7%	av	1.1	0.8

	1993	1992	1991	1990	1989	1988	1987	1986	1985	1984
Return (%)	13.6	11.9	28.7	-10.0	27.8	24.7	-2.0	21.3	—	—
Differ from category (+/-) . . .	1.0	1.9	1.0	-4.4	6.2	7.9	-2.4	6.1	—	—

PER SHARE DATA

	1993	1992	1991	1990	1989	1988	1987	1986	1985	1984
Dividends, Net Income ($) .	0.50	0.51	0.61	0.73	0.74	0.56	0.61	0.43	—	—
Distrib'ns, Cap Gain ($) . . .	0.50	0.21	0.43	0.28	0.61	0.00	0.80	0.51	—	—
Net Asset Value ($)	17.04	15.91	14.89	12.45	14.96	12.81	10.75	12.39	—	—
Expense Ratio (%).	0.39	0.41	0.48	0.52	0.53	0.58	0.49	0.65	—	—
Net Income to Assets (%). .	3.11	3.72	4.51	4.93	5.29	4.94	4.11	4.33	—	—
Portfolio Turnover (%)	26	23	41	20	22	25	46	50	—	—
Total Assets (Millions $) . .	7,467	4,879	3,297	2,087	2,161	1,486	1,323	813	—	—

PORTFOLIO (as of 10/31/93)

Portfolio Manager: Barrow - 1985, Ulrich - 1991, Tukman - 1991, Sauter - 1991

Investm't Category: Growth & Income

Cap Gain	Asset Allocation
✔ Cap & Income	Fund of Funds
Income	Index
	Sector
✔ Domestic	Small Cap
Foreign	Socially Conscious
Country/Region	State Specific

Portfolio: stocks 91% bonds 0%
convertibles 0% other 0% cash 9%

Largest Holdings: oil 13%, banks 11%

Unrealized Net Capital Gains: 15% of portfolio value

SHAREHOLDER INFORMATION

Minimum Investment
Initial: $3,000   Subsequent: $100

Minimum IRA Investment
Initial: $500   Subsequent: $100

Maximum Fees
Load: none   12b-1: none
Other: none

Distributions
Income: May, Dec   Capital Gains: Dec

Exchange Options
Number Per Year: 2   Fee: none
Telephone: yes (money market fund available)

Services
IRA, other pension, auto exchange, auto invest, auto withdraw

Vista Bond (TRBDX)

General Bond

P.O. Box 419392
Kansas City, MO 64141
(800) 348-4782

PERFORMANCE

	3yr Annual	5yr Annual	10yr Annual	Bull	Bear
Return (%)	10.7	na	na	na	na
Differ from Category (+/-)	0.5 av	na	na	na	na

Total Risk	Standard Deviation	Category Risk	Risk Index	Avg Mat
low	3.7%	abv av	1.3	8.4 yrs

	1993	1992	1991	1990	1989	1988	1987	1986	1985	1984
Return (%).............	10.3	7.1	15.0	—	—	—	—	—	—	—
Differ from category (+/-)...	1.1	0.4	0.4	—	—	—	—	—	—	—

PER SHARE DATA

	1993	1992	1991	1990	1989	1988	1987	1986	1985	1984
Dividends, Net Income ($).	0.68	0.79	0.72	—	—	—	—	—	—	—
Distrib'ns, Cap Gain ($) ...	0.08	0.07	0.01	—	—	—	—	—	—	—
Net Asset Value ($)	11.03	10.70	10.84	—	—	—	—	—	—	—
Expense Ratio (%)	0.31	0.30	0.29	—	—	—	—	—	—	—
Net Income to Assets (%) .	6.46	7.20	7.30	—	—	—	—	—	—	—
Portfolio Turnover (%).......	4	31	35	—	—	—	—	—	—	—
Total Assets (Millions $).....	57	41	37	—	—	—	—	—	—	—

PORTFOLIO (as of 4/30/93)

Portfolio Manager: Mark Buonaugurio - 1992

Investm't Category: General Bond

Cap Gain	Asset Allocation
Cap & Income	Fund of Funds
✔ Income	Index
	Sector
✔ Domestic	Small Cap
Foreign	Socially Conscious
Country/Region	State Specific

Portfolio: stocks 0%　　bonds 92%
convertibles 0%　　other 0%　　cash 8%

Largest Holdings: U.S. government 67%, corporate 19%

Unrealized Net Capital Gains: 6% of portfolio value

SHAREHOLDER INFORMATION

Minimum Investment
Initial: $2,500　　Subsequent: $100

Minimum IRA Investment
Initial: $250　　Subsequent: $25

Maximum Fees
Load: none　　12b-1: 0.25%
Other: none

Distributions
Income: monthly　　Capital Gains: Jul, Dec

Exchange Options
Number Per Year: no limit　　Fee: none
Telephone: yes (money market fund available)

Services
IRA, other pension, auto invest, auto withdraw

Vista Equity (TREQX)

Growth

P.O. Box 419392
Kansas City, MO 64141
(800) 348-4782

PERFORMANCE

	3yr Annual	5yr Annual	10yr Annual	Bull	Bear
Return (%)	14.5	na	na	na	na
Differ from Category (+/-)	-4.7 blw av	na	na	na	na

Total Risk	Standard Deviation	Category Risk	Risk Index	Beta
abv av	10.9%	blw av	1.0	1.0

	1993	1992	1991	1990	1989	1988	1987	1986	1985	1984
Return (%)	8.6	5.3	31.2	—	—	—	—	—	—	—
Differ from category (+/-) ..	-4.6	-5.7	-4.2	—	—	—	—	—	—	—

PER SHARE DATA

	1993	1992	1991	1990	1989	1988	1987	1986	1985	1984
Dividends, Net Income ($) .	0.30	0.35	0.23	—	—	—	—	—	—	—
Distrib'ns, Cap Gain ($) ...	0.76	0.44	0.10	—	—	—	—	—	—	—
Net Asset Value ($)	13.00	12.96	13.12	—	—	—	—	—	—	—
Expense Ratio (%)........	0.30	0.30	0.28	—	—	—	—	—	—	—
Net Income to Assets (%)..	2.19	2.29	2.81	—	—	—	—	—	—	—
Portfolio Turnover (%).....	14	14	19	—	—	—	—	—	—	—
Total Assets (Millions $) ...	117	92	95	—	—	—	—	—	—	—

PORTFOLIO (as of 4/30/93)

Portfolio Manager: David Khalil - 1991

Investm't Category: Growth

✔ Cap Gain	Asset Allocation
Cap & Income	Fund of Funds
Income	Index
	Sector
✔ Domestic	Small Cap
Foreign	Socially Conscious
Country/Region	State Specific

Portfolio: stocks 96% bonds 0%
convertibles 0% other 0% cash 4%

Largest Holdings: oil & gas 11%, food & beverage 7%

Unrealized Net Capital Gains: 12% of portfolio value

SHAREHOLDER INFORMATION

Minimum Investment
Initial: $2,500   Subsequent: $100

Minimum IRA Investment
Initial: $250   Subsequent: $25

Maximum Fees
Load: none   12b-1: 0.25%
Other: none

Distributions
Income: Jun, Dec   Capital Gains: Jun, Dec

Exchange Options
Number Per Year: no limit   Fee: none
Telephone: yes (money market fund available)

Services
IRA, other pension, auto invest, auto withdraw

Vista Short-Term Bond
(TRSBX)

General Bond

P.O. Box 419392
Kansas City, MO 64141
(800) 348-4782

PERFORMANCE

	3yr Annual	5yr Annual	10yr Annual	Bull	Bear
Return (%)	6.1	na	na	na	na
Differ from Category (+/-)	-4.1 low	na	na	na	na

Total Risk	Standard Deviation	Category Risk	Risk Index	Avg Mat
low	1.1%	low	0.3	1.0 yrs

	1993	1992	1991	1990	1989	1988	1987	1986	1985	1984
Return (%).	4.5	4.9	9.1	—	—	—	—	—	—	—
Differ from category (+/-). . .	-4.7	-1.8	-5.5	—	—	—	—	—	—	—

PER SHARE DATA

	1993	1992	1991	1990	1989	1988	1987	1986	1985	1984
Dividends, Net Income ($).	0.52	0.64	0.62	—	—	—	—	—	—	—
Distrib'ns, Cap Gain ($) . . .	0.00	0.00	0.00	—	—	—	—	—	—	—
Net Asset Value ($)	10.11	10.18	10.33	—	—	—	—	—	—	—
Expense Ratio (%)	0.31	0.30	0.29	—	—	—	—	—	—	—
Net Income to Assets (%) .	5.30	6.12	6.56	—	—	—	—	—	—	—
Portfolio Turnover (%).	7	29	1	—	—	—	—	—	—	—
Total Assets (Millions $).	67	71	71	—	—	—	—	—	—	—

PORTFOLIO (as of 4/30/93)

Portfolio Manager: Linda Struble - 1991

Investm't Category: General Bond

Cap Gain	Asset Allocation
Cap & Income	Fund of Funds
✔ Income	Index
	Sector
✔ Domestic	Small Cap
Foreign	Socially Conscious
Country/Region	State Specific

Portfolio: stocks 0% bonds 94%
convertibles 0% other 0% cash 6%

Largest Holdings: corporate 41%, U.S. government 34%

Unrealized Net Capital Gains: na

SHAREHOLDER INFORMATION

Minimum Investment
Initial: $2,500   Subsequent: $100

Minimum IRA Investment
Initial: $250   Subsequent: $25

Maximum Fees
Load: none   12b-1: 0.25%
Other: none

Distributions
Income: monthly   Capital Gains: Jul, Dec

Exchange Options
Number Per Year: no limit   Fee: none
Telephone: yes (money market fund available)

Services
IRA, other pension, auto withdraw

Volumetric (VOLMX)

Growth

87 Violet Dr.
Pearl River, NY 10965
(800) 541-3863, (914) 623-7637

PERFORMANCE

	3yr Annual	5yr Annual	10yr Annual	Bull	Bear
Return (%)	15.0	10.9	na	60.5	-9.8
Differ from Category (+/-)	-4.2 blw av	-3.7 low	na	-24.2 blw av	2.6 abv av

Total Risk	Standard Deviation	Category Risk	Risk Index	Beta
abv av	12.8%	abv av	1.2	1.0

	1993	1992	1991	1990	1989	1988	1987	1986	1985	1984
Return (%)	2.0	10.7	34.9	-5.0	15.9	19.9	—	—	—	—
Differ from category (+/-) .	-11.2	-0.3	-0.5	1.1	-9.9	2.2	—	—	—	—

PER SHARE DATA

	1993	1992	1991	1990	1989	1988	1987	1986	1985	1984
Dividends, Net Income ($) .	0.07	0.11	0.17	0.10	0.25	0.11	—	—	—	—
Distrib'ns, Cap Gain ($) ...	0.62	1.11	0.00	1.24	0.68	0.00	—	—	—	—
Net Asset Value ($)	16.09	16.48	16.11	12.11	14.10	13.10	—	—	—	—
Expense Ratio (%)........	1.99	2.01	2.03	2.02	2.07	2.09	—	—	—	—
Net Income to Assets (%) .	-0.06	0.66	0.90	1.49	0.82	1.98	—	—	—	—
Portfolio Turnover (%)	164	125	149	194	188	203	—	—	—	—
Total Assets (Millions $)	11	10	7	5	5	3	—	—	—	—

PORTFOLIO (as of 6/30/93)

Portfolio Manager: Gabriel Gibs - 1978

Investm't Category: Growth

✔ Cap Gain	Asset Allocation
Cap & Income	Fund of Funds
Income	Index
	Sector
✔ Domestic	Small Cap
Foreign	Socially Conscious
Country/Region	State Specific

Portfolio: stocks 84% bonds 0%
convertibles 0% other 0% cash 16%

Largest Holdings: electrical/electronics 9%, machinery 8%

Unrealized Net Capital Gains: 12% of portfolio value

SHAREHOLDER INFORMATION

Minimum Investment
Initial: $500 Subsequent: $200

Minimum IRA Investment
Initial: $500 Subsequent: $200

Maximum Fees
Load: none 12b-1: none
Other: none

Distributions
Income: Jan Capital Gains: Jan

Exchange Options
Number Per Year: none Fee: na
Telephone: na

Services
IRA, other pension

Vontobel EuroPacific
(VNEPX)

International Stock

450 Park Avenue
New York, NY 10022
(800) 445-8872, (212) 415-7000

PERFORMANCE

	3yr Annual	5yr Annual	10yr Annual	Bull	Bear
Return (%)	17.9	na	na	77.7	na
Differ from Category (+/-)	3.6 abv av	na	na	22.6 high	na

Total Risk	Standard Deviation	Category Risk	Risk Index	Beta
abv av	11.5%	low	1.0	0.5

	1993	1992	1991	1990	1989	1988	1987	1986	1985	1984
Return (%)	41.4	-2.3	18.7	—	—	—	—	—	—	—
Differ from category (+/-) . . .	2.9	1.2	5.8	—	—	—	—	—	—	—

PER SHARE DATA

	1993	1992	1991	1990	1989	1988	1987	1986	1985	1984
Dividends, Net Income ($) .	0.07	0.14	0.00	—	—	—	—	—	—	—
Distrib'ns, Cap Gain ($) . . .	0.00	0.00	0.00	—	—	—	—	—	—	—
Net Asset Value ($)	17.22	12.23	12.67	—	—	—	—	—	—	—
Expense Ratio (%)	1.84	1.98	2.71	—	—	—	—	—	—	—
Net Income to Assets (%) .	0.49	0.79	0.02	—	—	—	—	—	—	—
Portfolio Turnover (%).	na	27	3	—	—	—	—	—	—	—
Total Assets (Millions $)	138	47	25	—	—	—	—	—	—	—

PORTFOLIO (as of 6/30/93)

Portfolio Manager: Felix Rovelli - 1990

Investm't Category: International Stock

✔ Cap Gain	Asset Allocation
Cap & Income	Fund of Funds
Income	Index
	Sector
Domestic	Small Cap
✔ Foreign	Socially Conscious
✔ Country/Region	State Specific

Portfolio: stocks 90% bonds 0%
convertibles 0% other 1% cash 9%

Largest Holdings: Japan 16%, Great Britian 8%

Unrealized Net Capital Gains: 7% of portfolio value

SHAREHOLDER INFORMATION

Minimum Investment
Initial: $1,000   Subsequent: $100

Minimum IRA Investment
Initial: $1,000   Subsequent: $100

Maximum Fees
Load: none   12b-1: none
Other: none

Distributions
Income: Dec   Capital Gains: Dec

Exchange Options
Number Per Year: no limit   Fee: none
Telephone: yes (money market fund not available)

Services
IRA, auto invest, auto withdraw

Vontobel US Value
(VUSVX)

Growth

450 Park Avenue
New York, NY 10022
(800) 445-8872, (212) 415-7000

PERFORMANCE

	3yr Annual	5yr Annual	10yr Annual	Bull	Bear
Return (%)	22.4	na	na	100.0	na
Differ from Category (+/-)	3.2 abv av	na	na	15.3 abv av	na

Total Risk	Standard Deviation	Category Risk	Risk Index	Beta
abv av	13.4%	abv av	1.3	1.0

	1993	1992	1991	1990	1989	1988	1987	1986	1985	1984
Return (%)	15.4	15.9	37.2	—	—	—	—	—	—	—
Differ from category (+/-) . . .	2.2	4.9	1.8	—	—	—	—	—	—	—

PER SHARE DATA

	1993	1992	1991	1990	1989	1988	1987	1986	1985	1984
Dividends, Net Income ($) .	0.08	0.17	0.05	—	—	—	—	—	—	—
Distrib'ns, Cap Gain ($) . . .	1.11	0.99	0.74	—	—	—	—	—	—	—
Net Asset Value ($)	12.64	12.00	11.36	—	—	—	—	—	—	—
Expense Ratio (%).	1.96	1.96	2.54	—	—	—	—	—	—	—
Net Income to Assets (%) . .	1.94	0.76	0.92	—	—	—	—	—	—	—
Portfolio Turnover (%)	na	100	166	—	—	—	—	—	—	—
Total Assets (Millions $)	33	31	22	—	—	—	—	—	—	—

PORTFOLIO (as of 6/30/93)

Portfolio Manager: Ed Walzack - 1990

Investm't Category: Growth

✔ Cap Gain	Asset Allocation
Cap & Income	Fund of Funds
Income	Index
	Sector
✔ Domestic	Small Cap
Foreign	Socially Conscious
Country/Region	State Specific

Portfolio: stocks 94% bonds 0%
convertibles 0% other 0% cash 6%

Largest Holdings: banking 22%, aerospace 6%

Unrealized Net Capital Gains: 3% of portfolio value

SHAREHOLDER INFORMATION

Minimum Investment
Initial: $1,000 Subsequent: $100

Minimum IRA Investment
Initial: $1,000 Subsequent: $100

Maximum Fees
Load: none 12b-1: none
Other: none

Distributions
Income: Dec Capital Gains: Dec

Exchange Options
Number Per Year: no limit Fee: none
Telephone: yes (money market fund available)

Services
IRA, auto invest, auto withdraw

Warburg Pincus Cap Appreciation (CUCAX)

Growth

466 Lexington Ave., 10 Fl.
New York, NY 10017
(800) 257-5614, (212) 878-0600

PERFORMANCE

	3yr Annual	5yr Annual	10yr Annual	Bull	Bear
Return (%)	16.3	13.5	na	65.9	-10.2
Differ from Category (+/-)	-2.9 blw av	-1.1 blw av	na	-18.8 blw av	2.2 abv av

Total Risk	Standard Deviation	Category Risk	Risk Index	Beta
abv av	12.2%	av	1.1	1.0

	1993	1992	1991	1990	1989	1988	1987	1986	1985	1984
Return (%)............	15.8	7.6	26.2	-5.4	26.7	21.3	—	—	—	—
Differ from category (+/-)...	2.6	-3.4	-9.2	0.6	0.8	3.6	—	—	—	—

PER SHARE DATA

	1993	1992	1991	1990	1989	1988	1987	1986	1985	1984
Dividends, Net Income ($) .	0.07	0.05	0.11	0.21	0.35	0.19	—	—	—	—
Distrib'ns, Cap Gain ($) ...	1.18	0.75	0.05	0.00	0.23	0.13	—	—	—	—
Net Asset Value ($)	14.06	13.24	13.06	10.48	11.31	9.39	—	—	—	—
Expense Ratio (%)	1.01	1.06	1.08	1.04	1.10	1.07	—	—	—	—
Net Income to Assets (%) .	0.27	0.41	1.27	2.07	1.90	2.00	—	—	—	—
Portfolio Turnover (%)......	48	56	40	37	37	33	—	—	—	—
Total Assets (Millions $)....	155	118	115	77	57	29	—	—	—	—

PORTFOLIO (as of 4/30/93)

Portfolio Manager: Andrew Massie, Jr. - 1989

Investm't Category: Growth

✔ Cap Gain	Asset Allocation
Cap & Income	Fund of Funds
Income	Index
	Sector
✔ Domestic	Small Cap
✔ Foreign	Socially Conscious
Country/Region	State Specific

Portfolio: stocks 95% bonds 0%
convertibles 0% other 0% cash 5%

Largest Holdings: consumer 28%, finance 25%

Unrealized Net Capital Gains: 19% of portfolio value

SHAREHOLDER INFORMATION

Minimum Investment
Initial: $2,500   Subsequent: $500

Minimum IRA Investment
Initial: $500   Subsequent: $500

Maximum Fees
Load: none   12b-1: none
Other: none

Distributions
Income: Jun, Dec   Capital Gains: Dec

Exchange Options
Number Per Year: 36   Fee: none
Telephone: yes (money market fund available)

Services
IRA, other pension, auto exchange, auto invest, auto withdraw

Warburg Pincus
Emerging Grth (CUEGX)

466 Lexington Ave., 10 Fl.
New York, NY 10017
(800) 257-5614, (212) 878-0600

Aggressive Growth

PERFORMANCE

	3yr Annual	5yr Annual	10yr Annual	Bull	Bear
Return (%)	27.4	17.8	na	121.5	-15.9
Differ from Category (+/-)	2.0 abv av	-0.4 av	na	-3.5 av	-0.8 av

Total Risk	Standard Deviation	Category Risk	Risk Index	Beta
high	17.2%	av	1.1	1.1

	1993	1992	1991	1990	1989	1988	1987	1986	1985	1984
Return (%)	18.1	12.1	56.1	-9.9	21.8	—	—	—	—	—
Differ from category (+/-) . .	-0.8	1.7	3.7	-3.6	-5.2	—	—	—	—	—

PER SHARE DATA

	1993	1992	1991	1990	1989	1988	1987	1986	1985	1984
Dividends, Net Income ($) .	0.00	0.00	0.17	0.13	0.38	—	—	—	—	—
Distrib'ns, Cap Gain ($) . . .	1.35	0.37	0.19	0.00	0.15	—	—	—	—	—
Net Asset Value ($)	22.31	20.07	18.23	11.92	13.37	—	—	—	—	—
Expense Ratio (%).	1.20	1.24	1.25	1.25	1.25	—	—	—	—	—
Net Income to Assets (%) .	-0.55	-0.25	0.32	1.05	1.38	—	—	—	—	—
Portfolio Turnover (%).	61	63	98	107	100	—	—	—	—	—
Total Assets (Millions $) . . .	191	100	42	23	27	—	—	—	—	—

PORTFOLIO (as of 4/30/93)

Portfolio Manager: Elizabeth Dater - 1988

Investm't Category: Aggressive Growth
- ✔ Cap Gain
- Cap & Income
- Income
- ✔ Domestic
- ✔ Foreign
- Country/Region

- Asset Allocation
- Fund of Funds
- Index
- Sector
- ✔ Small Cap
- Socially Conscious
- State Specific

Portfolio: stocks 93%   bonds 0%
convertibles 1%   other 0%   cash 6%

Largest Holdings: consumer 40%, finance 16%

Unrealized Net Capital Gains: 18% of portfolio value

SHAREHOLDER INFORMATION

Minimum Investment
Initial: $2,500   Subsequent: $500

Minimum IRA Investment
Initial: $500   Subsequent: $500

Maximum Fees
Load: none   12b-1: none
Other: none

Distributions
Income: Jun, Dec   Capital Gains: Dec

Exchange Options
Number Per Year: 36   Fee: none
Telephone: yes (money market fund available)

Services
IRA, other pension, auto exchange, auto invest,
auto withdraw

Warburg Pincus Fixed Income (CUFIX)

466 Lexington Ave., 10 Fl.
New York, NY 10017
(800) 257-5614, (212) 878-0600

General Bond

PERFORMANCE

	3yr Annual	5yr Annual	10yr Annual	Bull	Bear
Return (%)	11.4	9.2	na	40.5	1.4
Differ from Category (+/-)	1.2 abv av	-0.6 blw av	na	1.1 av	-1.5 low

Total Risk	Standard Deviation	Category Risk	Risk Index	Avg Mat
low	3.2%	blw av	1.1	7.4 yrs

	1993	1992	1991	1990	1989	1988	1987	1986	1985	1984
Return (%)	11.1	6.6	16.8	2.8	9.2	8.6	—	—	—	—
Differ from category (+/-)	1.9	-0.1	2.2	-4.1	-2.1	1.0	—	—	—	—

PER SHARE DATA

	1993	1992	1991	1990	1989	1988	1987	1986	1985	1984
Dividends, Net Income ($)	0.56	0.67	0.70	0.86	0.93	0.87	—	—	—	—
Distrib'ns, Cap Gain ($)	0.09	0.00	0.00	0.00	0.00	0.01	—	—	—	—
Net Asset Value ($)	10.24	9.82	9.86	9.09	9.69	9.75	—	—	—	—
Expense Ratio (%)	0.75	0.75	0.75	0.75	0.75	0.74	—	—	—	—
Net Income to Assets (%)	6.47	6.82	7.85	9.35	9.34	8.80	—	—	—	—
Portfolio Turnover (%)	228	122	151	132	78	56	—	—	—	—
Total Assets (Millions $)	82	65	62	61	87	76	—	—	—	—

PORTFOLIO (as of 4/30/93)

Portfolio Manager: Dale C. Christensen - 1992

Investm't Category: General Bond

Cap Gain	Asset Allocation
Cap & Income	Fund of Funds
✔ Income	Index
	Sector
✔ Domestic	Small Cap
✔ Foreign	Socially Conscious
Country/Region	State Specific

Portfolio: stocks 0% bonds 88%
convertibles 0% other 10% cash 2%

Largest Holdings: U.S government 46%, corporate bonds 23%

Unrealized Net Capital Gains: 0% of portfolio value

SHAREHOLDER INFORMATION

Minimum Investment
Initial: $2,500   Subsequent: $500

Minimum IRA Investment
Initial: $500   Subsequent: $500

Maximum Fees
Load: none   12b-1: none
Other: none

Distributions
Income: monthly   Capital Gains: Dec

Exchange Options
Number Per Year: 36   Fee: none
Telephone: yes (money market fund available)

Services
IRA, other pension, auto exchange, auto invest, auto withdraw

Warburg Pincus Global Fixed Income (CGFIX)

466 Lexington Ave., 10 Fl.
New York, NY 10017
(800) 257-5614, (212) 878-0600

International Bond

PERFORMANCE

	3yr Annual	5yr Annual	10yr Annual	Bull	Bear
Return (%)	11.9	na	na	na	na
Differ from Category (+/-)	-0.1 blw av	na	na	na	na

Total Risk	Standard Deviation	Category Risk	Risk Index	Avg Mat
av	7.4%	abv av	1.8	8.3 yrs

	1993	1992	1991	1990	1989	1988	1987	1986	1985	1984
Return (%)	19.6	2.1	14.7	—	—	—	—	—	—	—
Differ from category (+/-) . . .	6.9	-2.7	-0.2	—	—	—	—	—	—	—

PER SHARE DATA

	1993	1992	1991	1990	1989	1988	1987	1986	1985	1984
Dividends, Net Income ($) .	0.74	0.97	0.59	—	—	—	—	—	—	—
Distrib'ns, Cap Gain ($) . . .	0.13	0.03	0.00	—	—	—	—	—	—	—
Net Asset Value ($)	11.13	10.06	10.84	—	—	—	—	—	—	—
Expense Ratio (%).	0.12	0.45	1.09	—	—	—	—	—	—	—
Net Income to Assets (%) . .	9.15	8.66	7.45	—	—	—	—	—	—	—
Portfolio Turnover (%)	100	93	186	—	—	—	—	—	—	—
Total Assets (Millions $)	71	17	12	—	—	—	—	—	—	—

PORTFOLIO (as of 4/30/93)

Portfolio Manager: Dale C. Christensen - 1990

Investm't Category: International Bond

Cap Gain	Asset Allocation
✔ Cap & Income	Fund of Funds
Income	Index
	Sector
✔ Domestic	Small Cap
✔ Foreign	Socially Conscious
Country/Region	State Specific

Portfolio: stocks 5% bonds 89%
convertibles 0% other 1% cash 5%

Largest Holdings: France 23%, Australian 8%

Unrealized Net Capital Gains: 1% of portfolio value

SHAREHOLDER INFORMATION

Minimum Investment
Initial: $2,500   Subsequent: $500

Minimum IRA Investment
Initial: $500   Subsequent: $500

Maximum Fees
Load: none   12b-1: none
Other: none

Distributions
Income: quarterly   Capital Gains: Dec

Exchange Options
Number Per Year: 36   Fee: none
Telephone: yes (money market fund available)

Services
IRA, other pension, auto exchange, auto invest, auto withdraw

Warburg Pincus Int'l Equity (CUIEX)

466 Lexington Ave., 10 Fl.
New York, NY 10017
(800) 257-5614, (212) 878-0600

International Stock

PERFORMANCE

	3yr Annual	5yr Annual	10yr Annual	Bull	Bear
Return (%)	20.3	na	na	84.4	-9.7
Differ from Category (+/-)	6.0 high	na	na	29.3 high	5.4 high

Total Risk	Standard Deviation	Category Risk	Risk Index	Beta
abv av	13.3%	av	1.1	0.5

	1993	1992	1991	1990	1989	1988	1987	1986	1985	1984
Return (%).	51.2	-4.3	20.6	-4.5	—	—	—	—	—	—
Differ from category (+/-). .	12.7	-0.8	7.7	6.6	—	—	—	—	—	—

PER SHARE DATA

	1993	1992	1991	1990	1989	1988	1987	1986	1985	1984
Dividends, Net Income ($).	0.03	0.05	0.32	0.39	—	—	—	—	—	—
Distrib'ns, Cap Gain ($) . . .	0.03	0.12	0.00	0.01	—	—	—	—	—	—
Net Asset Value ($)	18.98	12.60	13.36	11.35	—	—	—	—	—	—
Expense Ratio (%)	1.46	1.49	1.50	1.46	—	—	—	—	—	—
Net Income to Assets (%) .	1.14	0.88	1.19	3.73	—	—	—	—	—	—
Portfolio Turnover (%).	45	53	55	66	—	—	—	—	—	—
Total Assets (Millions $). . . .	536	102	73	39	—	—	—	—	—	—

PORTFOLIO (as of 4/30/93)

Portfolio Manager: Richard King - 1989

Investm't Category: International Stock

✔ Cap Gain	Asset Allocation
Cap & Income	Fund of Funds
Income	Index
	Sector
Domestic	Small Cap
✔ Foreign	Socially Conscious
Country/Region	State Specific

Portfolio: stocks 93% bonds 0%
convertibles 0% other 0% cash 7%

Largest Holdings: Japan 20%, United Kingdom 14%

Unrealized Net Capital Gains: 11% of portfolio value

SHAREHOLDER INFORMATION

Minimum Investment
Initial: $2,500 Subsequent: $500

Minimum IRA Investment
Initial: $500 Subsequent: $500

Maximum Fees
Load: none 12b-1: none
Other: none

Distributions
Income: Jun, Dec Capital Gains: Dec

Exchange Options
Number Per Year: 36 Fee: none
Telephone: yes (money market fund available)

Services
IRA, other pension, auto exchange, auto invest, auto withdraw

Warburg Pincus Interm Mat Gov't (CUIGX)

466 Lexington Ave., 10 Fl.
New York, NY 10017
(800) 257-5614, (212) 878-0600

Government Bond

PERFORMANCE

	3yr Annual	5yr Annual	10yr Annual	Bull	Bear
Return (%)	9.7	9.9	na	38.1	4.2
Differ from Category (+/-)	-1.1 av	-0.5 av	na	-8.1 av	3.7 abv av

Total Risk	Standard Deviation	Category Risk	Risk Index	Avg Mat
low	3.6%	blw av	0.8	4.6 yrs

	1993	1992	1991	1990	1989	1988	1987	1986	1985	1984
Return (%)	7.8	6.6	14.9	8.9	11.5	—	—	—	—	—
Differ from category (+/-)	-2.6	0.4	-0.1	2.4	-2.4	—	—	—	—	—

PER SHARE DATA

	1993	1992	1991	1990	1989	1988	1987	1986	1985	1984
Dividends, Net Income ($)	0.57	0.65	0.76	0.78	0.82	—	—	—	—	—
Distrib'ns, Cap Gain ($)	0.63	0.53	0.00	0.00	0.00	—	—	—	—	—
Net Asset Value ($)	10.29	10.67	11.15	10.42	10.33	—	—	—	—	—
Expense Ratio (%)	0.60	0.60	0.57	0.50	0.50	—	—	—	—	—
Net Income to Assets (%)	5.49	6.10	7.29	7.78	8.07	—	—	—	—	—
Portfolio Turnover (%)	47	166	39	113	23	—	—	—	—	—
Total Assets (Millions $)	64	113	89	64	27	—	—	—	—	—

PORTFOLIO (as of 4/30/93)

Portfolio Manager: Dale C. Christensen - 1991

Investm't Category: Government Bond

Cap Gain	Asset Allocation
Cap & Income	Fund of Funds
✔ Income	Index
	Sector
✔ Domestic	Small Cap
Foreign	Socially Conscious
Country/Region	State Specific

Portfolio: stocks 0% bonds 99%
convertibles 0% other 0% cash 1%

Largest Holdings: U.S. government 86%

Unrealized Net Capital Gains: 4% of portfolio value

SHAREHOLDER INFORMATION

Minimum Investment
Initial: $2,500   Subsequent: $500

Minimum IRA Investment
Initial: $500   Subsequent: $500

Maximum Fees
Load: none   12b-1: none
Other: none

Distributions
Income: monthly   Capital Gains: Dec

Exchange Options
Number Per Year: 36   Fee: none
Telephone: yes (money market fund available)

Services
IRA, other pension, auto exchange, auto invest, auto withdraw

Warburg Pincus NY Muni Bond (CNMBX)

466 Lexington Ave., 10 Fl.
New York, NY 10017
(800) 257-5614, (212) 878-0600

Tax-Exempt Bond

PERFORMANCE

	3yr Annual	5yr Annual	10yr Annual	Bull	Bear
Return (%)	8.9	7.9	na	32.9	3.0
Differ from Category (+/-)	-1.4 low	-1.3 low	na	-7.2 low	0.6 abv av

Total Risk	Standard Deviation	Category Risk	Risk Index	Avg Mat
low	3.2%	low	0.8	7.6 yrs

	1993	1992	1991	1990	1989	1988	1987	1986	1985	1984
Return (%)	9.9	7.5	9.5	5.9	6.8	6.3	—	—	—	—
Differ from category (+/-)	-1.7	-0.8	-1.8	-0.4	-2.2	-3.8	—	—	—	—

PER SHARE DATA

	1993	1992	1991	1990	1989	1988	1987	1986	1985	1984
Dividends, Net Income ($)	0.46	0.49	0.56	0.59	0.59	0.55	—	—	—	—
Distrib'ns, Cap Gain ($)	0.13	0.04	0.00	0.00	0.00	0.00	—	—	—	—
Net Asset Value ($)	10.55	10.16	9.97	9.64	9.68	9.63	—	—	—	—
Expense Ratio (%)	0.56	0.55	0.55	0.55	0.56	0.54	—	—	—	—
Net Income to Assets (%)	4.58	4.99	5.84	6.21	6.14	5.70	—	—	—	—
Portfolio Turnover (%)	103	48	67	70	74	145	—	—	—	—
Total Assets (Millions $)	74	54	29	22	20	28	—	—	—	—

PORTFOLIO (as of 4/30/93)

Portfolio Manager: Dale C. Christensen - 1992

Investm't Category: Tax-Exempt Bond

Cap Gain	Asset Allocation
Cap & Income	Fund of Funds
✔ Income	Index
	Sector
✔ Domestic	Small Cap
Foreign	Socially Conscious
Country/Region	✔ State Specific

Portfolio: stocks 0% bonds 90%
convertibles 0% other 0% cash 10%

Largest Holdings: general obligation 25%

Unrealized Net Capital Gains: 3% of portfolio value

SHAREHOLDER INFORMATION

Minimum Investment
Initial: $2,500   Subsequent: $500

Minimum IRA Investment
Initial: na   Subsequent: na

Maximum Fees
Load: none   12b-1: none
Other: none

Distributions
Income: monthly   Capital Gains: Dec

Exchange Options
Number Per Year: no limit   Fee: none
Telephone: yes (money market fund available)

Services
auto exchange, auto invest, auto withdraw

Wasatch Aggressive Equity (WAAEX)

68 South Main Street
Salt Lake City, UT 84101
(800) 551-1700, (801) 533-0778

Aggressive Growth

PERFORMANCE

	3yr Annual	5yr Annual	10yr Annual	Bull	Bear
Return (%)	24.5	22.4	na	132.7	-10.5
Differ from Category (+/-)	-0.8 av	4.2 abv av	na	7.7 abv av	4.5 abv av

Total Risk	Standard Deviation	Category Risk	Risk Index	Beta
high	16.6%	av	1.1	1.0

	1993	1992	1991	1990	1989	1988	1987	1986	1985	1984
Return (%)	22.5	4.7	50.3	7.8	32.0	-1.4	-4.8	—	—	—
Differ from category (+/-) . . .	3.5	-5.7	-2.1	14.1	5.0	-16.6	-1.4	—	—	—

PER SHARE DATA

	1993	1992	1991	1990	1989	1988	1987	1986	1985	1984
Dividends, Net Income ($) .	0.12	0.00	0.71	0.00	0.00	0.04	0.01	—	—	—
Distrib'ns, Cap Gain ($) . . .	1.10	0.66	0.17	0.00	0.00	0.00	1.04	—	—	—
Net Asset Value ($)	19.50	16.95	16.82	11.78	10.92	8.27	8.44	—	—	—
Expense Ratio (%)	1.50	1.51	1.51	1.56	1.50	1.50	1.26	—	—	—
Net Income to Assets (%) .	-0.77	-0.41	-0.36	0.08	-0.12	0.30	0.16	—	—	—
Portfolio Turnover (%)	70	32	41	74	82	71	58	—	—	—
Total Assets (Millions $)	26	12	7	2	1	1	1	—	—	—

PORTFOLIO (as of 9/30/93)

Portfolio Manager: Samuel S. Stewart - 1986

Investm't Category: Aggressive Growth

✔ Cap Gain	Asset Allocation
Cap & Income	Fund of Funds
Income	Index
	Sector
✔ Domestic	Small Cap
✔ Foreign	Socially Conscious
Country/Region	State Specific

Portfolio: stocks 97% bonds 0%
convertibles 0% other 0% cash 3%

Largest Holdings: retail 14%, health care services 11%

Unrealized Net Capital Gains: 17% of portfolio value

SHAREHOLDER INFORMATION

Minimum Investment
Initial: $2,000   Subsequent: $100

Minimum IRA Investment
Initial: $1,000   Subsequent: $100

Maximum Fees
Load: none   12b-1: none
Other: none

Distributions
Income: Dec   Capital Gains: Dec

Exchange Options
Number Per Year: 4   Fee: $5
Telephone: yes (money market fund available)

Services
IRA, auto invest, auto withdraw

Wayne Hummer Growth (WHGRX)

Growth

300 S. Wacker Drive
Chicago, IL 60606
(800) 621-4477, (312) 431-1700

PERFORMANCE

	3yr Annual	5yr Annual	10yr Annual	Bull	Bear
Return (%)	13.7	13.9	12.6	65.0	-6.2
Differ from Category (+/-)	-5.5 low	-0.6 av	0.0 av	-19.7 blw av	6.2 high

Total Risk	Standard Deviation	Category Risk	Risk Index	Beta
av	8.2%	low	0.8	0.7

	1993	1992	1991	1990	1989	1988	1987	1986	1985	1984
Return (%)	3.5	10.3	28.8	5.0	24.0	7.0	9.2	13.7	24.3	4.0
Differ from category (+/-)	-9.7	-0.6	-6.6	11.1	-1.8	-10.7	8.0	-0.8	-5.0	4.0

PER SHARE DATA

	1993	1992	1991	1990	1989	1988	1987	1986	1985	1984
Dividends, Net Income ($)	0.28	0.28	0.38	0.43	0.23	0.21	0.31	0.23	0.34	0.23
Distrib'ns, Cap Gain ($)	0.06	0.14	0.16	0.75	0.36	0.18	1.11	0.34	0.00	0.00
Net Asset Value ($)	22.06	21.64	20.02	16.00	16.41	13.74	13.22	13.33	12.25	10.17
Expense Ratio (%)	1.12	1.23	1.36	1.50	1.50	1.50	1.50	1.50	1.50	1.50
Net Income to Assets (%)	1.41	2.01	2.87	1.91	1.83	1.73	1.64	2.44	4.12	5.09
Portfolio Turnover (%)	1	3	13	3	12	10	28	27	26	0
Total Assets (Millions $)	99	56	32	25	21	21	19	10	4	1

PORTFOLIO (as of 9/30/93)

Portfolio Manager: Alan Bird - 1983

Investm't Category: Growth

✔ Cap Gain	Asset Allocation
Cap & Income	Fund of Funds
Income	Index
	Sector
✔ Domestic	Small Cap
Foreign	Socially Conscious
Country/Region	State Specific

Portfolio: stocks 83% bonds 0%
convertibles 0% other 0% cash 17%

Largest Holdings: chemical 13%, food, beverage & household 11%

Unrealized Net Capital Gains: 20% of portfolio value

SHAREHOLDER INFORMATION

Minimum Investment
Initial: $1,000   Subsequent: $500

Minimum IRA Investment
Initial: $500   Subsequent: $200

Maximum Fees
Load: none   12b-1: none
Other: none

Distributions
Income: quarterly   Capital Gains: Apr, Dec

Exchange Options
Number Per Year: no limit   Fee: none
Telephone: yes (money market fund available)

Services
IRA, other pension, auto invest, auto withdraw

Wayne Hummer Income (WHICX)

300 S. Wacker Drive
Chicago, IL 60606
(800) 621-4477, (312) 431-1700

General Bond

PERFORMANCE

	3yr Annual	5yr Annual	10yr Annual	Bull	Bear
Return (%)	na	na	na	na	na
Differ from Category (+/-)	na	na	na	na	na

Total Risk	Standard Deviation	Category Risk	Risk Index	Avg Mat
na	na	na	na	5.5 yrs

	1993	1992	1991	1990	1989	1988	1987	1986	1985	1984
Return (%)	10.7	—	—	—	—	—	—	—	—	—
Differ from category (+/-) . . .	1.5	—	—	—	—	—	—	—	—	—

PER SHARE DATA

	1993	1992	1991	1990	1989	1988	1987	1986	1985	1984
Dividends, Net Income ($) .	0.93	—	—	—	—	—	—	—	—	—
Distrib'ns, Cap Gain ($) . . .	0.04	—	—	—	—	—	—	—	—	—
Net Asset Value ($)	15.62	—	—	—	—	—	—	—	—	—
Expense Ratio (%).	1.39	—	—	—	—	—	—	—	—	—
Net Income to Assets (%) . .	5.58	—	—	—	—	—	—	—	—	—
Portfolio Turnover (%)	141	—	—	—	—	—	—	—	—	—
Total Assets (Millions $)	36	—	—	—	—	—	—	—	—	—

PORTFOLIO (as of 3/31/93)

Portfolio Manager: David Poitras - 1992

Investm't Category: General Bond

Cap Gain	Asset Allocation
Cap & Income	Fund of Funds
✔ Income	Index
	Sector
✔ Domestic	Small Cap
Foreign	Socially Conscious
Country/Region	State Specific

Portfolio: stocks 0% bonds 100%
convertibles 0% other 0% cash 0%

Largest Holdings: corporate 61%, mortgage-backed 26%

Unrealized Net Capital Gains: 1% of portfolio value

SHAREHOLDER INFORMATION

Minimum Investment
Initial: $2,500   Subsequent: $1,000

Minimum IRA Investment
Initial: $2,000   Subsequent: $500

Maximum Fees
Load: none   12b-1: none
Other: none

Distributions
Income: monthly   Capital Gains: Apr, Dec

Exchange Options
Number Per Year: no limit   Fee: none
Telephone: yes (money market fund available)

Services
IRA, other pension, auto invest, auto withdraw

Weitz Value Port
(WVALX)
Growth

9290 West Dodge Road
Suite 405
Omaha, NE 68114
(800) 232-4161, (402) 391-1980

PERFORMANCE

	3yr Annual	5yr Annual	10yr Annual	Bull	Bear
Return (%)	20.3	15.0	na	81.2	-8.9
Differ from Category (+/-)	1.1 abv av	0.4 av	na	-3.5 av	3.5 abv av

Total Risk	Standard Deviation	Category Risk	Risk Index	Beta
av	8.5%	low	0.8	0.6

	1993	1992	1991	1990	1989	1988	1987	1986	1985	1984
Return (%).	20.0	13.6	27.6	-5.2	22.0	16.4	-0.5	—	—	—
Differ from category (+/-). . .	6.8	2.6	-7.8	0.8	-3.8	-1.3	-1.7	—	—	—

PER SHARE DATA

	1993	1992	1991	1990	1989	1988	1987	1986	1985	1984
Dividends, Net Income ($).	0.02	0.27	0.32	0.37	0.42	0.31	0.48	—	—	—
Distrib'ns, Cap Gain ($) . . .	0.59	0.54	0.39	0.06	0.62	0.00	0.11	—	—	—
Net Asset Value ($)	16.80	14.54	13.57	11.21	12.30	10.97	9.70	—	—	—
Expense Ratio (%)	1.35	1.40	1.49	1.46	1.50	1.50	1.50	—	—	—
Net Income to Assets (%) .	1.66	2.75	2.71	3.71	3.30	3.47	3.72	—	—	—
Portfolio Turnover (%).	22	35	28	49	25	67	54	—	—	—
Total Assets (Millions $). . . .	105	35	27	24	16	9	7	—	—	—

PORTFOLIO (as of 9/30/93)

Portfolio Manager: Wally Weitz - 1986

Investm't Category: Growth

✔ Cap Gain	Asset Allocation
Cap & Income	Fund of Funds
Income	Index
	Sector
✔ Domestic	Small Cap
Foreign	Socially Conscious
Country/Region	State Specific

Portfolio: stocks 64%   bonds 4%
convertibles 0%   other 0%   cash 32%

Largest Holdings: cable television 15%, financial services 12%

Unrealized Net Capital Gains: 16% of portfolio value

SHAREHOLDER INFORMATION

Minimum Investment
Initial: $25,000   Subsequent: $5,000

Minimum IRA Investment
Initial: $10,000   Subsequent: $2,000

Maximum Fees
Load: none   12b-1: none
Other: none

Distributions
Income: April, Dec   Capital Gains: April, Dec

Exchange Options
Number Per Year: no limit   Fee: none
Telephone: none

Services
IRA, other pension, auto invest, auto withdraw

Westcore Trust Short-Term Gov't Bond (WTSTX)

General Bond

600 Seventeenth St.
Suite 1605 South
Denver, CO 80202
(800) 392-2673, (303) 623-2577

PERFORMANCE

	3yr Annual	5yr Annual	10yr Annual	Bull	Bear
Return (%)	6.9	8.2	na	26.3	6.9
Differ from Category (+/-)	-3.3 low	-1.6 low	na	-13.1 low	4.0 high

Total Risk	Standard Deviation	Category Risk	Risk Index	Avg Mat
low	1.6%	low	0.5	1.6 yrs

	1993	1992	1991	1990	1989	1988	1987	1986	1985	1984
Return (%)	4.3	5.4	11.2	10.3	10.0	—	—	—	—	—
Differ from category (+/-)	-4.9	-1.3	-3.4	3.4	-1.3	—	—	—	—	—

PER SHARE DATA

	1993	1992	1991	1990	1989	1988	1987	1986	1985	1984
Dividends, Net Income ($)	0.63	0.82	1.13	1.16	1.16	—	—	—	—	—
Distrib'ns, Cap Gain ($)	0.15	0.12	0.00	0.03	0.00	—	—	—	—	—
Net Asset Value ($)	15.64	15.75	15.87	15.35	15.05	—	—	—	—	—
Expense Ratio (%)	0.62	0.62	0.57	0.50	0.50	—	—	—	—	—
Net Income to Assets (%)	4.62	6.84	7.85	8.51	8.46	—	—	—	—	—
Portfolio Turnover (%)	163	100	96	38	50	—	—	—	—	—
Total Assets (Millions $)	33	30	18	8	7	—	—	—	—	—

PORTFOLIO (as of 5/31/93)

Portfolio Manager: Warren Hastings, III - 1990

Investm't Category: General Bond

Cap Gain	Asset Allocation
Cap & Income	Fund of Funds
✔ Income	Index
	Sector
✔ Domestic	Small Cap
Foreign	Socially Conscious
Country/Region	State Specific

Portfolio: stocks 0%   bonds 87%
convertibles 0%   other 0%   cash 13%

Largest Holdings: U.S. government 61%, mortgage-backed 19%

Unrealized Net Capital Gains: 0% of portfolio value

SHAREHOLDER INFORMATION

Minimum Investment
Initial: $1,000   Subsequent: $50

Minimum IRA Investment
Initial: $250   Subsequent: $50

Maximum Fees
Load: 2.00% front   12b-1: none
Other: none

Distributions
Income: monthly   Capital Gains: Dec

Exchange Options
Number Per Year: no limit   Fee: none
Telephone: yes (money market fund available)

Services
IRA, other pension, auto invest, auto withdraw

William Blair Growth Shares (WBGSX)

Growth

135 S. LaSalle St.
Chicago, IL 60603
(800) 742-7272, (312) 853-2424

PERFORMANCE

	3yr Annual	5yr Annual	10yr Annual	Bull	Bear
Return (%)	21.5	18.0	13.8	91.1	-7.9
Differ from Category (+/-)	2.3 abv av	3.4 high	1.2 abv av	6.4 av	4.5 abv av

Total Risk	Standard Deviation	Category Risk	Risk Index	Beta
abv av	13.7%	abv av	1.3	1.1

	1993	1992	1991	1990	1989	1988	1987	1986	1985	1984
Return (%)	15.5	7.6	44.3	-2.0	30.4	7.1	7.9	9.8	23.1	1.8
Differ from category (+/-) . . .	2.3	-3.4	8.9	4.1	4.6	-10.6	6.7	-4.7	-6.2	1.8

PER SHARE DATA

	1993	1992	1991	1990	1989	1988	1987	1986	1985	1984
Dividends, Net Income ($) .	0.03	0.05	0.07	0.12	0.12	0.15	0.13	0.14	0.73	1.65
Distrib'ns, Cap Gain ($) . . .	1.04	0.76	0.44	0.58	2.14	0.80	1.37	3.59	0.00	0.00
Net Asset Value ($)	9.73	9.39	9.49	6.97	7.84	7.81	8.21	9.10	11.82	10.29
Expense Ratio (%)	0.78	0.83	0.90	0.87	0.91	0.92	0.87	0.90	0.95	0.92
Net Income to Assets (%) .	0.73	1.34	0.83	1.70	1.36	1.46	1.46	1.69	1.96	2.06
Portfolio Turnover (%)	80	27	33	34	45	18	22	26	43	13
Total Assets (Millions $)	147	111	91	63	67	60	66	68	72	58

PORTFOLIO (as of 6/30/93)

Portfolio Manager: Rocky Barber - 1993, Mark Fuller - 1993

Investm't Category: Growth

✔ Cap Gain	Asset Allocation
Cap & Income	Fund of Funds
Income	Index
	Sector
✔ Domestic	Small Cap
Foreign	Socially Conscious
Country/Region	State Specific

Portfolio: stocks 84%   bonds 0%
convertibles 0%   other 0%   cash 16%

Largest Holdings: industrial products 15%, consumer retail 11%

Unrealized Net Capital Gains: 19% of portfolio value

SHAREHOLDER INFORMATION

Minimum Investment
Initial: $1,000   Subsequent: $250

Minimum IRA Investment
Initial: $500   Subsequent: $250

Maximum Fees
Load: none   12b-1: none
Other: none

Distributions
Income: Jul, Dec   Capital Gains: Dec

Exchange Options
Number Per Year: 4   Fee: none
Telephone: yes (money market fund available)

Services
IRA, other pension, auto invest, auto withdraw

William Blair Income Shares (WBRRX)

135 S. LaSalle St.
Chicago, IL 60603
(800) 742-7272, (312) 853-2424

General Bond

PERFORMANCE

	3yr Annual	5yr Annual	10yr Annual	Bull	Bear
Return (%)	9.9	na	na	38.4	na
Differ from Category (+/-)	-0.3 blw av	na	na	-1.0 av	na

Total Risk	Standard Deviation	Category Risk	Risk Index	Avg Mat
low	3.3%	av	1.1	na

	1993	1992	1991	1990	1989	1988	1987	1986	1985	1984
Return (%)	7.7	7.1	15.2	—	—	—	—	—	—	—
Differ from category (+/-) . .	-1.5	0.4	0.6	—	—	—	—	—	—	—

PER SHARE DATA

	1993	1992	1991	1990	1989	1988	1987	1986	1985	1984
Dividends, Net Income ($) .	0.65	0.82	0.90	—	—	—	—	—	—	—
Distrib'ns, Cap Gain ($) . . .	0.17	0.08	0.00	—	—	—	—	—	—	—
Net Asset Value ($)	10.58	10.60	10.77	—	—	—	—	—	—	—
Expense Ratio (%)	0.79	0.88	0.92	—	—	—	—	—	—	—
Net Income to Assets (%) . .	7.23	7.69	8.33	—	—	—	—	—	—	—
Portfolio Turnover (%)	60	47	64	—	—	—	—	—	—	—
Total Assets (Millions $) . . .	205	137	83	—	—	—	—	—	—	—

PORTFOLIO (as of 6/30/93)

Portfolio Manager: Bentley Myer - 1991

Investm't Category: General Bond

Cap Gain	Asset Allocation
Cap & Income	Fund of Funds
✔ Income	Index
	Sector
✔ Domestic	Small Cap
Foreign	Socially Conscious
Country/Region	State Specific

Portfolio: stocks 0%   bonds 89%
convertibles 0%   other 0%   cash 11%

Largest Holdings: mortgage-backed 54%, U.S. government & agency 33%

Unrealized Net Capital Gains: 2% of portfolio value

SHAREHOLDER INFORMATION

Minimum Investment
Initial: $2,500   Subsequent: $250

Minimum IRA Investment
Initial: $500   Subsequent: $250

Maximum Fees
Load: none   12b-1: none
Other: none

Distributions
Income: monthly   Capital Gains: Dec

Exchange Options
Number Per Year: 4   Fee: none
Telephone: yes (money market fund available)

Services
IRA, other pension, auto invest, auto withdraw

Woodward Equity Index
(WOEIX)
Growth & Income

P.O. Box 7058
Troy, MI 48007
(800) 688-3350, (313) 259-0729

PERFORMANCE

	3yr Annual	5yr Annual	10yr Annual	Bull	Bear
Return (%)	na	na	na	na	na
Differ from Category (+/-)	na	na	na	na	na

Total Risk	Standard Deviation	Category Risk	Risk Index	Beta
na	na	na	na	na

	1993	1992	1991	1990	1989	1988	1987	1986	1985	1984
Return (%)	9.0	—	—	—	—	—	—	—	—	—
Differ from category (+/-)	-3.6	—	—	—	—	—	—	—	—	—

PER SHARE DATA

	1993	1992	1991	1990	1989	1988	1987	1986	1985	1984
Dividends, Net Income ($)	0.26	—	—	—	—	—	—	—	—	—
Distrib'ns, Cap Gain ($)	0.12	—	—	—	—	—	—	—	—	—
Net Asset Value ($)	11.15	—	—	—	—	—	—	—	—	—
Expense Ratio (%)	0.21	—	—	—	—	—	—	—	—	—
Net Income to Assets (%)	2.65	—	—	—	—	—	—	—	—	—
Portfolio Turnover (%)	na	—	—	—	—	—	—	—	—	—
Total Assets (Millions $)	331	—	—	—	—	—	—	—	—	—

PORTFOLIO (as of 6/30/93)

Portfolio Manager: Fortunate - 1992, Simmons - 1992, Neumann - 1992, Beard - 1992

Investm't Category: Growth & Income
Cap Gain	Asset Allocation
✔ Cap & Income	Fund of Funds
Income	✔ Index
	Sector
✔ Domestic	Small Cap
Foreign	Socially Conscious
Country/Region	State Specific

Portfolio: stocks 100% bonds 0%
convertibles 0% other 0% cash 0%

Largest Holdings: S&P 500 Composite Stock Price Index

Unrealized Net Capital Gains: 7% of portfolio value

SHAREHOLDER INFORMATION

Minimum Investment
Initial: $1,000   Subsequent: $100

Minimum IRA Investment
Initial: $1,000   Subsequent: $100

Maximum Fees
Load: none   12b-1: 0.35%
Other: none

Distributions
Income: quarterly   Capital Gains: Dec

Exchange Options
Number Per Year: 12   Fee: none
Telephone: yes (money market fund available)

Services
IRA, other pension, auto invest, auto withdraw

WPG Gov't Securities
(WPGVX)

Government Bond

One New York Plaza, 30th Fl.
New York, NY 10004
(800) 223-3332, (212) 908-9582

PERFORMANCE

	3yr Annual	5yr Annual	10yr Annual	Bull	Bear
Return (%)	10.1	10.6	na	39.8	4.2
Differ from Category (+/-)	-0.6 av	0.2 abv av	na	-6.4 av	3.7 abv av

Total Risk	Standard Deviation	Category Risk	Risk Index	Avg Mat
low	3.0%	blw av	0.7	6.1 yrs

	1993	1992	1991	1990	1989	1988	1987	1986	1985	1984
Return (%)	8.8	7.8	13.9	8.9	14.0	7.9	2.4	—	—	—
Differ from category (+/-) ..	-1.6	1.6	-1.1	2.4	0.1	0.3	4.2	—	—	—

PER SHARE DATA

	1993	1992	1991	1990	1989	1988	1987	1986	1985	1984
Dividends, Net Income ($) .	0.78	0.77	0.79	0.82	0.87	0.78	0.72	—	—	—
Distrib'ns, Cap Gain ($) ...	0.15	0.40	0.00	0.00	0.00	0.00	0.07	—	—	—
Net Asset Value ($)	10.37	10.40	10.79	10.22	10.18	9.74	9.77	—	—	—
Expense Ratio (%)........	0.79	0.78	0.81	0.75	0.76	0.82	0.87	—	—	—
Net Income to Assets (%)..	7.62	7.36	7.64	8.13	8.64	7.97	7.41	—	—	—
Portfolio Turnover (%)....	118	137	190	184	159	130	108	—	—	—
Total Assets (Millions $) ...	337	263	194	131	91	79	76	—	—	—

PORTFOLIO (as of 6/30/93)

Portfolio Manager: David Hoyle - 1986

Investm't Category: Government Bond
Cap Gain	Asset Allocation
Cap & Income	Fund of Funds
✔ Income	Index
	Sector
✔ Domestic	Small Cap
Foreign	Socially Conscious
Country/Region	State Specific

Portfolio:	stocks 0%	bonds 98%
convertibles 0%	other 0%	cash 2%

Largest Holdings: U.S. government & agencies 72%, mortgage-backed 25%

Unrealized Net Capital Gains: 2% of portfolio value

SHAREHOLDER INFORMATION

Minimum Investment
Initial: $2,500   Subsequent: $100

Minimum IRA Investment
Initial: $250   Subsequent: $0

Maximum Fees
Load: none   12b-1: none
Other: none

Distributions
Income: monthly   Capital Gains: Dec

Exchange Options
Number Per Year: 6   Fee: none
Telephone: yes (money market fund available)

Services
IRA, other pension, auto invest, auto withdraw

WPG Growth & Income
(WPGFX)

Growth & Income

One New York Plaza, 30th Fl.
New York, NY 10004
(800) 223-3332, (212) 908-9582

PERFORMANCE

	3yr Annual	5yr Annual	10yr Annual	Bull	Bear
Return (%)	20.5	14.9	13.0	88.8	-16.5
Differ from Category (+/-)	4.1 abv av	2.4 high	0.6 av	18.7 high	-4.9 low

Total Risk	Standard Deviation	Category Risk	Risk Index	Beta
abv av	12.3%	high	1.4	1.0

	1993	1992	1991	1990	1989	1988	1987	1986	1985	1984
Return (%).............	9.5	13.7	40.7	-10.1	27.6	10.1	7.5	11.4	30.3	-1.6
Differ from category (+/-)...	-3.1	3.7	13.0	-4.5	6.0	-6.7	7.1	-3.8	4.9	-7.8

PER SHARE DATA

	1993	1992	1991	1990	1989	1988	1987	1986	1985	1984
Dividends, Net Income ($).	0.89	0.43	0.31	0.33	0.24	0.17	0.15	0.15	0.64	0.56
Distrib'ns, Cap Gain ($) ...	1.93	3.02	1.67	0.94	3.16	2.48	3.36	6.55	0.00	0.54
Net Asset Value ($)	23.34	23.89	24.07	18.53	22.05	19.95	18.73	20.64	24.42	19.32
Expense Ratio (%)	1.26	1.34	1.48	1.56	1.41	1.53	1.19	1.23	1.21	1.17
Net Income to Assets (%) .	2.15	1.79	1.28	1.21	1.04	0.82	0.65	1.88	2.28	3.79
Portfolio Turnover (%).	90	76	89	91	67	42	84	71	108	104
Total Assets (Millions $).....	63	49	42	30	33	34	35	36	42	32

PORTFOLIO (as of 6/30/93)

Portfolio Manager: Roy Knutsen - 1992

Investm't Category: Growth & Income
Cap Gain	Asset Allocation
✔ Cap & Income	Fund of Funds
Income	Index
	Sector
✔ Domestic	Small Cap
✔ Foreign	Socially Conscious
Country/Region	State Specific

Portfolio: stocks 68% bonds 15%
convertibles 11% other 0% cash 0%

Largest Holdings: insurance 8%, other capital goods 7%

Unrealized Net Capital Gains: 14% of portfolio value

SHAREHOLDER INFORMATION

Minimum Investment
Initial: $2,500   Subsequent: $100

Minimum IRA Investment
Initial: $250   Subsequent: $0

Maximum Fees
Load: none   12b-1: none
Other: none

Distributions
Income: quarterly   Capital Gains: Dec

Exchange Options
Number Per Year: 6   Fee: none
Telephone: yes (money market fund available)

Services
IRA, other pension, auto invest, auto withdraw

WPG Quantitative Equity (WPGQX)

One New York Plaza, 30th Fl.
New York, NY 10004
(800) 223-3332, (212) 908-9582

Growth & Income

PERFORMANCE

	3yr Annual	5yr Annual	10yr Annual	Bull	Bear
Return (%)	na	na	na	na	na
Differ from Category (+/-)	na	na	na	na	na

Total Risk	Standard Deviation	Category Risk	Risk Index	Beta
na	na	na	na	na

	1993	1992	1991	1990	1989	1988	1987	1986	1985	1984
Return (%)	13.9	—	—	—	—	—	—	—	—	—
Differ from category (+/-) . . .	1.3	—	—	—	—	—	—	—	—	—

PER SHARE DATA

	1993	1992	1991	1990	1989	1988	1987	1986	1985	1984
Dividends, Net Income ($) .	0.07	—	—	—	—	—	—	—	—	—
Distrib'ns, Cap Gain ($) . . .	0.03	—	—	—	—	—	—	—	—	—
Net Asset Value ($)	5.58	—	—	—	—	—	—	—	—	—
Expense Ratio (%).	1.47	—	—	—	—	—	—	—	—	—
Net Income to Assets (%) . .	2.07	—	—	—	—	—	—	—	—	—
Portfolio Turnover (%)	38	—	—	—	—	—	—	—	—	—
Total Assets (Millions $)	46	—	—	—	—	—	—	—	—	—

PORTFOLIO (as of 6/30/93)

Portfolio Manager: Joseph Pappo - 1993

Investm't Category: Growth & Income

Cap Gain	Asset Allocation
✔ Cap & Income	Fund of Funds
Income	Index
	Sector
✔ Domestic	Small Cap
Foreign	Socially Conscious
Country/Region	State Specific

Portfolio: stocks 92%   bonds 0%
convertibles 0%   other 0%   cash 8%

Largest Holdings: na

Unrealized Net Capital Gains: 4% of portfolio value

SHAREHOLDER INFORMATION

Minimum Investment
Initial: $5,000   Subsequent: $500

Minimum IRA Investment
Initial: $250   Subsequent: $0

Maximum Fees
Load: none   12b-1: none
Other: none

Distributions
Income: none   Capital Gains: Dec

Exchange Options
Number Per Year: 6   Fee: none
Telephone: yes (money market fund available)

Services
IRA, other pension, auto invest, auto withdraw

WPG Tudor (TUDRX)

Aggressive Growth

One New York Plaza, 30th Fl.
New York, NY 10004
(800) 223-3332, (212) 908-9582

PERFORMANCE

	3yr Annual	5yr Annual	10yr Annual	Bull	Bear
Return (%)	20.2	15.5	12.6	75.6	-6.1
Differ from Category (+/-)	-5.2 blw av	-2.7 blw av	0.6 av	-49.4 low	8.9 high

Total Risk	Standard Deviation	Category Risk	Risk Index	Beta
high	18.7%	abv av	1.2	1.3

	1993	1992	1991	1990	1989	1988	1987	1986	1985	1984
Return (%)	13.3	5.1	45.8	-5.1	25.0	15.1	1.1	12.3	31.2	-7.2
Differ from category (+/-) . . .	-5.7	-5.3	-6.6	1.2	-2.0	-0.1	4.5	2.9	0.2	2.2

PER SHARE DATA

	1993	1992	1991	1990	1989	1988	1987	1986	1985	1984
Dividends, Net Income ($) .	0.00	0.00	0.28	0.23	0.16	0.86	0.00	0.07	0.37	0.10
Distrib'ns, Cap Gain ($) . . .	4.73	2.06	0.00	6.78	0.74	0.00	0.86	5.48	0.00	1.56
Net Asset Value ($)	23.40	24.85	25.68	17.85	25.97	21.65	19.64	20.08	22.75	17.67
Expense Ratio (%)	1.24	1.21	1.17	1.11	1.10	1.14	1.03	1.01	0.95	1.01
Net Income to Assets (%) .	-0.72	-0.17	-0.11	0.84	0.76	0.22	-0.19	-0.16	0.63	2.42
Portfolio Turnover (%)	124	89	90	73	94	89	113	127	123	83
Total Assets (Millions $) . . .	227	273	264	162	157	157	143	163	155	93

PORTFOLIO (as of 6/30/93)

Portfolio Manager: Melville Straus - 1973

Investm't Category: Aggressive Growth

✔ Cap Gain	Asset Allocation
Cap & Income	Fund of Funds
Income	Index
	Sector
✔ Domestic	Small Cap
✔ Foreign	Socially Conscious
Country/Region	State Specific

Portfolio: stocks 98% bonds 0%
convertibles 0% other 0% cash 2%

Largest Holdings: computer software & services 14%, other consumer 8%

Unrealized Net Capital Gains: 16% of portfolio value

SHAREHOLDER INFORMATION

Minimum Investment
Initial: $2,500   Subsequent: $100

Minimum IRA Investment
Initial: $250   Subsequent: $0

Maximum Fees
Load: none   12b-1: none
Other: none

Distributions
Income: quarterly   Capital Gains: Dec

Exchange Options
Number Per Year: 6   Fee: none
Telephone: yes (money market fund available)

Services
IRA, other pension, auto invest, auto withdraw

Wright Int'l Blue Chip Equity (WIBCX)

1000 Lafayette Blvd.
Bridgeport, CT 06604
(800) 888-9471, (203) 333-6666

International Stock

PERFORMANCE

	3yr Annual	5yr Annual	10yr Annual	Bull	Bear
Return (%)	13.0	na	na	54.8	-13.2
Differ from Category (+/-)	-1.3 av	na	na	-0.3 av	1.9 av

Total Risk	Standard Deviation	Category Risk	Risk Index	Beta
abv av	12.3%	blw av	1.0	0.5

	1993	1992	1991	1990	1989	1988	1987	1986	1985	1984
Return (%)	28.2	-3.9	17.2	-6.9	—	—	—	—	—	—
Differ from category (+/-) .	-10.3	-0.4	4.3	4.2	—	—	—	—	—	—

PER SHARE DATA

	1993	1992	1991	1990	1989	1988	1987	1986	1985	1984
Dividends, Net Income ($) .	0.07	0.09	0.10	0.17	—	—	—	—	—	—
Distrib'ns, Cap Gain ($) ...	0.00	0.00	0.00	0.00	—	—	—	—	—	—
Net Asset Value ($)	13.41	10.52	11.04	9.52	—	—	—	—	—	—
Expense Ratio (%)........	1.70	1.51	1.67	1.65	—	—	—	—	—	—
Net Income to Assets (%)..	1.76	0.81	1.12	1.66	—	—	—	—	—	—
Portfolio Turnover (%)	na	15	23	13	—	—	—	—	—	—
Total Assets (Millions $) ...	175	74	52	19	—	—	—	—	—	—

PORTFOLIO (as of 6/30/93)

Portfolio Manager: committee

Investm't Category: International Stock

Cap Gain	Asset Allocation
✔ Cap & Income	Fund of Funds
Income	Index
	Sector
Domestic	Small Cap
✔ Foreign	Socially Conscious
Country/Region	State Specific

Portfolio: stocks 97% bonds 0%
convertibles 0% other 0% cash 3%

Largest Holdings: Japan 14%, France 11%

Unrealized Net Capital Gains: 9% of portfolio value

SHAREHOLDER INFORMATION

Minimum Investment
Initial: $1,000   Subsequent: $50

Minimum IRA Investment
Initial: $1,000   Subsequent: $50

Maximum Fees
Load: none   12b-1: 0.20%
Other: none

Distributions
Income: June, Dec   Capital Gains: Dec

Exchange Options
Number Per Year: no limit   Fee: none
Telephone: yes (money market fund available)

Services
IRA, other pension, auto exchange, auto invest, auto withdraw

Yacktman (YACKX)

Growth

303 West Madison Street
Chicago, IL 60606
(800) 525-8258

PERFORMANCE

	3yr Annual	5yr Annual	10yr Annual	Bull	Bear
Return (%)	na	na	na	na	na
Differ from Category (+/-)	na	na	na	na	na

Total Risk	Standard Deviation	Category Risk	Risk Index	Beta
na	na	na	na	na

	1993	1992	1991	1990	1989	1988	1987	1986	1985	1984
Return (%)	-6.5	—	—	—	—	—	—	—	—	—
Differ from category (+/-). .	-19.7	—	—	—	—	—	—	—	—	—

PER SHARE DATA

	1993	1992	1991	1990	1989	1988	1987	1986	1985	1984
Dividends, Net Income ($).	0.14	—	—	—	—	—	—	—	—	—
Distrib'ns, Cap Gain ($) . . .	0.00	—	—	—	—	—	—	—	—	—
Net Asset Value ($)	9.56	—	—	—	—	—	—	—	—	—
Expense Ratio (%)	1.19	—	—	—	—	—	—	—	—	—
Net Income to Assets (%) .	0.69	—	—	—	—	—	—	—	—	—
Portfolio Turnover (%).	na	—	—	—	—	—	—	—	—	—
Total Assets (Millions $). . . .	145	—	—	—	—	—	—	—	—	—

PORTFOLIO (as of 6/30/93)

Portfolio Manager: Donald Yacktman - 1992

Investm't Category: Growth

✔ Cap Gain	Asset Allocation
Cap & Income	Fund of Funds
Income	Index
	Sector
✔ Domestic	Small Cap
Foreign	Socially Conscious
Country/Region	State Specific

Portfolio: stocks 93%   bonds 0%
convertibles 0%   other 0%   cash 7%

Largest Holdings: drugs & medical 20%, food & beverage 18%

Unrealized Net Capital Gains: 8% of portfolio value

SHAREHOLDER INFORMATION

Minimum Investment
Initial: $2,500   Subsequent: $100

Minimum IRA Investment
Initial: $500   Subsequent: $100

Maximum Fees
Load: none   12b-1: 0.65%
Other: none

Distributions
Income: quarterly   Capital Gains: Dec

Exchange Options
Number Per Year: no limit   Fee: $5 (tel.)
Telephone: yes (money market fund available)

Services
IRA, other pension, auto invest, auto withdraw

Appendix A

Special Types of Funds

ASSET ALLOCATION FUNDS
  Aetna
  Bascom Hill Balanced
  Blanchard Global Growth
  Boston Co Asset Allocation
  Brinson Global
  Crabbe Huson Asset Allocation
  Dreyfus Balanced
  Evergreen Foundation
  Fidelity Asset Manager
  Fidelity Asset Manager—Growth
  Fidelity Asset Manager—Income
  Fidelity Global Balanced
  Fremont Global
  Galaxy Asset Allocation
  IAI Balanced
  INVESCO Value Trust—Total Return
  Janus Balanced
  Maxus Equity
  Maxus Income
  Merriman Asset Allocation
  Olympic Trust Balanced Income
  Permanent Portfolio
  Preferred Asset Allocation
  US European Income
  USAA Cornerstone
  Value Line Income
  Vanguard Asset Allocation

FUNDS INVESTING IN FUNDS
  American Pension Investors—Growth

Flex Muirfield
Maxus Prism
Merriman Asset Allocation
Merriman Capital Appreciation
New Century Capital Portfolio
Rightime
T Rowe Price Spectrum Growth
T Rowe Price Spectrum Income
Vanguard Star

GLOBAL FUNDS

Acorn International
Alliance World Income Trust
Bartlett Value International
Blanchard Global Growth
Blanchard Short-Term Global Income
Brinson Global
Bull & Bear Global Income
Bull & Bear US & Overseas
Columbia International Stock
Fidelity Global Balanced
Fidelity Global Bond
Fidelity International Growth & Income
Fidelity Latin America
Fidelity Short Term World Income
Fidelity Southeast Asia
Fidelity Worldwide
Flex Short Term Global Income
Founders World Wide Growth
Janus Worldwide
Legg Mason Global Government Trust
Lexington Global
Lexington Worldwide Emerging Markets
Managers International Equity
Paine Webber Atlas Global Growth "D"
Paine Webber Global Income "D"
Scudder Global
Scudder Global Small Company
Scudder International Bond
Scudder Pacific Opportunities
Scudder Short-Term Global Income

T Rowe Price Global Government Bond
T Rowe Price Short-Term Global Income
Tweedy Browne Global Value
US Global Resources
USAA World Growth
Warburg Pincus Global Fixed Income

INDEX MUTUAL FUNDS

Benham Gold Equities Index
Bull & Bear Financial News Composite
Corefund Equity Index
Dreyfus Edison Electric Index
Dreyfus Peoples Index
Dreyfus Peoples S&P MidCap Index
Fidelity Market Index
Portico Bond IMMDEX
Portico Equity Index
Portico Intermediate Bond Market
Portico Short Term Bond Market
Rushmore American GAS Index
Rushmore OTC Index Plus
Rushmore Stock Market Index Plus
Schwab 1000
Seven Seas Series—S&P 500
Seven Seas Series—S&P MidCap
US All American Equity
Vanguard Balanced Index
Vanguard Bond Index
Vanguard Index Trust—500
Vanguard Index Trust—Extended Market
Vanguard Index Trust—Growth Portfolio
Vanguard Index Trust—Total Stock Market
Vanguard Index Trust—Value Portfolio
Vanguard International Equity Index—Europe
Vanguard International Equity Index—Pacific
Vanguard Small Cap Stock
Woodward Equity Index

SECTOR FUNDS

America's Utility

Benham Gold Equities Index
Blanchard Precious Metals
BT Investments—Utility
Bull & Bear Gold Investors Ltd
Cappiello-Rushmore Utility Income
Century Shares Trust
Cohen & Steers Realty Shares
Dreyfus Edison Electric Index
Fidelity Real Estate Investment
Fidelity Select Air Transportation
Fidelity Select American Gold
Fidelity Select Automotive
Fidelity Select Biotechnology
Fidelity Select Broadcast & Media
Fidelity Select Broker & Investment Management
Fidelity Select Chemical
Fidelity Select Computers
Fidelity Select Construction & Housing
Fidelity Select Consumer Product
Fidelity Select Defense & Aerospace
Fidelity Select Developing Communications
Fidelity Select Electric Utilities
Fidelity Select Electronics
Fidelity Select Energy
Fidelity Select Energy Services
Fidelity Select Environmental Services
Fidelity Select Financial Services
Fidelity Select Food & Agriculture
Fidelity Select Health Care
Fidelity Select Home Finance
Fidelity Select Industrial Equipment
Fidelity Select Industrial Materials
Fidelity Select Insurance
Fidelity Select Leisure
Fidelity Select Medical Delivery
Fidelity Select Natural Gas Portfolio
Fidelity Select Paper & Forest Products
Fidelity Select Precious Metals
Fidelity Select Regional Banks
Fidelity Select Retailing
Fidelity Select Software & Computers
Fidelity Select Technology

Fidelity Select Telecommunications
Fidelity Select Transportation
Fidelity Select Utilities
Fidelity Utilities Income
INVESCO Strategic Portfolio—Energy
INVESCO Strategic Portfolio—Environmental
INVESCO Strategic Portfolio—Financial
INVESCO Strategic Portfolio—Gold
INVESCO Strategic Portfolio—Health Sciences
INVESCO Strategic Portfolio—Leisure
INVESCO Strategic Portfolio—Technology
INVESCO Strategic Portfolio—Utilities
Lexington GoldFund
Neuberger & Berman Select Sectors
PRA Real Estate Securities
Rushmore American GAS Index
Scudder Gold
T Rowe Price New America Growth
T Rowe Price New Era
T Rowe Price Science & Technology
US Global Resources
US Gold Shares
US Real Estate
US World Gold
USAA Gold
Vanguard Specialized Portfolio—Energy
Vanguard Specialized Portfolio—Gold & Precious Metals
Vanguard Specialized Portfolio—Health Care
Vanguard Specialized Portfolio—Service Economy
Vanguard Specialized Portfolio—Technology
Vanguard Specialized Portfolio—Utilities Income

SMALL CAPITALIZATION STOCK FUNDS

Acorn
Acorn International
Babson Enterprise
Babson Shadow Stock
Cappiello-Rushmore Emerging Growth
Columbia Special
Dreyfus New Leaders
Eclipse Equity

Evergreen
Evergreen Limited Market
FAM Value
Fidelity Emerging Growth
Fidelity Low-Priced Stock
Fidelity New Millenium
Fifty-Nine Wall St. Small Company
Founders Discovery
Founders Frontier
Galaxy Small Company Equity
GIT Equity—Special Growth
Gradison McDonald Opportunity Value
HighMark Special Growth Equity
IAI Emerging Growth
INVESCO Emerging Growth
Janus Venture
Kaufmann
Legg Mason Special Investment
Loomis Sayles Small Cap
Managers Special Equity
Meridian
Monetta
Montgomery Small Cap
Mutual Discovery
Neuberger & Berman Genesis
Nicholas II
Nicholas Limited Edition
Oberweis Emerging Growth
Paine Webber Small Cap Value "D"
PBHG Growth
Pennsylvania Mutual
Perritt Capital Growth
Prudent Speculator
Regis ICM Small Company Portfolio
Robertson Stephens Emerging Growth
Robertson Stephens Value Plus
Scudder Development
Scudder Global Small Company
SIT Growth
Skyline Special Equities II
Southeastern Asset Management Small Cap
Strong Discovery

T Rowe Price International Discovery
T Rowe Price New Horizons
T Rowe Price OTC
T Rowe Price Small Cap Value
Tweedy Browne Global Value
Twentieth Century Giftrust
Twentieth Century Ultra
Twentieth Century Vista
UMB Heartland Fund
USAA Aggressive Growth
Vanguard Explorer
Vanguard Index Trust—Extended Market
Vanguard Small Cap Stock
Warburg Pincus Emerging Growth

SOCIALLY CONSCIOUS FUNDS

Dreyfus Third Century
Pax World

STATE-SPECIFIC TAX-EXEMPT BOND FUNDS

California
Alliance Municipal Income—CA "C"
Benham CA Tax-Free High-Yield
Benham CA Tax-Free Insured
Benham CA Tax-Free Intermediate
Benham CA Tax-Free Long-Term
Benham CA Tax-Free Short-Term
Bernstein CA Muni Portfolio
Cal Muni
Cal Tax-Free Income
Dreyfus CA Intermediate Muni Bond
Dreyfus CA Tax Exempt Bond
Evergreen Short Intermediate Muni CA
Fidelity CA Tax-Free High Yield
Fidelity CA Tax-Free Insured
Fidelity Spartan CA Muni High Yield
Fremont CA Intermediate Tax-Free
General CA Muni Bond
Pacifica Short Term CA Tax-Free
Paine Webber CA Tax-Free Income "D"

Safeco CA Tax-Free Income
Schwab CA Long-Term Tax-Free
Schwab CA Short/Intermediate Tax-Free
Scudder CA Tax Free
T Rowe Price CA Tax-Free Bond
USAA Tax Exempt CA Bond
Vanguard CA Tax-Free Insured Long

Connecticut
Dreyfus Conn Intermediate Muni Bond
Fidelity Spartan Conn Tax-Free High-Yield

Florida
Dreyfus Florida Intermediate Muni
Fidelity Spartan Florida Muni Income
Vanguard Florida Insured Tax Free

Hawaii
First Hawaii Muni Bond

Kentucky
Dupree KY Tax-Free Income
Dupree KY Tax-Free Short to Medium

Maryland
Rushmore Maryland Tax-Free
T Rowe Price Maryland Tax-Free
T Rowe Price MD Short-Term Tax-Free

Massachusetts
Dreyfus Mass Intermediate Muni Bond
Dreyfus Mass Tax-Exempt Bond
Fidelity Mass Tax-Free High Yield
Scudder Mass Tax-Free

Michigan
Fidelity Michigan Tax-Free High Yield

Minnesota
Fidelity Minnesota Tax-Free

New Jersey
Dreyfus NJ Intermediate Muni Bond
Dreyfus NJ Muni Bond
Fidelity Spartan NJ Muni High Yield
T Rowe Price NJ Tax-Free
Vanguard NJ Tax Free Insured Long

New York
Bernstein NY Muni Portfolio
BNY Hamilton Intermediate NY Tax Exempt
Dreyfus NY Insured Tax-Exempt
Dreyfus NY Tax-Exempt
Dreyfus NY Tax-Exempt Intermediate
Fidelity NY Tax-Free High Yield
Fidelity NY Tax-Free Insured
Fidelity Spartan NY Muni High Yield
Galaxy NY Muni Bond
General NY Muni Bond
New York Muni
Paine Webber N.Y. Tax Free Inc"D"
Scudder NY Tax Free
T Rowe Price NY Tax-Free
USAA Tax Exempt NY Bond
Value Line NY Tax-Exempt Trust
Vanguard NY Insured Tax Free
Warburg Pincus NY Muni Bond

Ohio
Fidelity Ohio Tax-Free High Yield
Scudder Ohio Tax-Free
Vanguard Ohio Tax Free Insured Long

Oregon
Oregon Municipal Bond

Pennsylvania
Fidelity Spartan Penn Muni High Yield
Scudder Penn Tax Free
Vanguard Penn Tax-Free Insured Long

Virginia
GIT Tax-Free Virginia Portfolio
Rushmore Virginia Tax-Free
T Rowe Price Virginia Tax-Free Bond
USAA Tax-Exempt Virginia Bond

Wisconsin
Heartland Wisconsin Tax Free

Appendix B

Changes to the Funds

FUND NAME CHANGES

Former	Current
Dreyfus Short Interm Tax-Exempt Bond	Dreyfus Short-Interm Municipal
Financial Bond Shares—High Yield	INVESCO Income—High Yield
Financial Bond Shares—Select Income	INVESCO Income—Sel Income
Financial Bond Shares—U.S. Government	INVESCO Income—U.S. Gov't Sec
Financial Dynamics	INVESCO Dynamics
Financial Emerging Growth	INVESCO Emerging Growth
Financial Industrial	INVESCO Growth
Financial Industrial Income	INVESCO Industrial Income
Financial Series Trust—Equity	INVESCO Value Trust—Value Equity
Financial Series Trust—Flex	INVESCO Value Trust—Total Return
Financial Series Trust—Interm Gov't Bond	INVESCO Value Trust—Interm Gov't
Financial Series Trust—International Growth	INVESCO Int'l—Int'l Growth
Financial Strategic Portfolio—Energy	INVESCO Strat Port—Energy
Financial Strategic Portfolio—Environm'l Serv	INVESCO Strat Port—Environm'l
Financial Strategic Portfolio—European	INVESCO Int'l—European
Financial Strategic Portfolio—Fin'l Services	INVESCO Strat Port—Financial
Financial Strategic Portfolio—Gold	INVESCO Strat Port—Gold
Financial Strategic Portfolio—Health Sciences	INVESCO Strat Port—Health Sci
Financial Strategic Portfolio—Leisure	INVESCO Strat Port—Leisure
Financial Strategic Portfolio—Pacific Basin	INVESCO Int'l—Pacific Basin
Financial Strategic Portfolio—Technology	INVESCO Strat Port—Tech
Financial Strategic Portfolio—Utilities	INVESCO Strat Port—Utilities
Financial Tax-Free Income Shares	INVESCO Tax-Free Long-Term Bond
Founders Equity Income	Founders Balanced
Fremont Multi Asset	Fremont Global
IAI Stock	IAI Growth & Income
Merrill Lynch Municipal Income—Class A	Merrill Lynch Muni Interm "A"
Portico Income & Growth	Portico Growth & Income
Prudent Speculator Leveraged	Prudent Speculator
SBSF Growth	SBSF
Schwab U.S. Government Bond Short Interm	Schwab Short/Interm Gov't Bond
SIT New Beginning Growth	SIT Growth

Former	Current
SIT New Beginning Income & Growth	SIT Growth & Income
SIT New Beginning International Growth	SIT Int'l Growth
SIT New Beginning Tax Free Income	SIT Tax Free Income
SIT New Beginning U.S. Government Securities	SIT US Gov't Securities
SWRW Growth Plus	Matrix Growth
Vanguard Bond Market	Vanguard Bond Index
Vanguard Investment Grade Corporate	Vanguard Long Term Corp Bond
Vanguard World—International Growth	Vanguard Int'l Growth
Vanguard World—U.S. Growth	Vanguard US Growth

INVESTMENT CATEGORY CHANGES

Fund Name	Old	New
Babson Enterprise	Aggressive Growth	Growth
Babson Shadow Stock	Aggressive Growth	Growth
Boston Co Special Growth	Growth	Aggressive Growth
Century Shares Trust	Growth & Income	Growth
Fairmont	Growth	Aggressive Growth
Fidelity Real Estate Investment	Balanced	Growth & Income
Gradison McDonald Opport'y Val	Aggressive Growth	Growth
Merriman Flexible Bond	Government Bond	Bond—General
Safeco Growth	Growth	Aggressive Growth
Selected US Gov't Income	Government Bond	Bond—Mortgage-Backed
T Rowe Price Small Cap Value	Aggressive Growth	Growth
Vanguard Spec Port—Energy	Growth & Income	Growth
Vanguard Spec Port—Tech	Growth	Aggressive Growth

FUNDS DROPPED FROM THE *GUIDE*

Fund Name	Reason
Baker U.S. Capital Accumulation	Information was not supplied
Corefund Int'l Growth "B"	Imposed a 4.5% front-end sales charge
Dreyfus Convertible Securities	Merged into Dreyfus Growth & Income
Forty-Four Wall Street	Merged into Forty-Four Wall Street Equity
Gabelli Small Cap Growth	Imposed a 4.5% front-end load
Kleinwort Benson Int'l Equity	Imposed a 4.5% load on class B shares
Lexington Technical Strategy	Liquidated
MetLife—State Street Gov't Income	Converted to a multiple class loaded structure
Rushmore Nova	Liquidated
Sherman, Dean	Converted to a closed-end fund
SIT Money Market	Converted to a money market fund

Index

A

AARP Capital Growth, 42, 64

AARP GNMA & US Treasury, 50, 65

AARP Growth & Income, 44, 66

AARP High Quality Bond, 51, 67

AARP Insured Tax Free General Bond, 53, 68

Acorn, 36 - 38, 41, 58, 69, 893

Acorn Int'l, 55, 58, 70, 890, 893

Aetna, 47, 71, 889

Aetna Bond, 51, 72

Aetna Growth & Income, 46, 73

Aetna Int'l Growth, 56, 74

Alliance Bond—U.S. Gov't "C", 75

Alliance Mortgage Strategy "C", 76

Alliance Municipal Income—CA "C", 77, 895

Alliance Municipal Income—National "C", 78

Alliance World Income Trust, 57, 79, 890

Amana Income, 45, 80

America's Utility, 45, 81, 891

American Heritage, 38 - 39, 82

American Pension Investors—Growth, 41, 83, 889

Analytic Optioned Equity, 45, 84

Armstrong Associates, 42, 85

ASM, 45, 86

B

Babson Bond Trust—Port L, 51, 87

Babson Bond Trust—Port S, 51, 88

Babson Enterprise, 36, 38, 41, 58, 89, 893, 900

Babson Enterprise II, 41, 90

Babson Growth, 45, 91

Babson Shadow Stock, 42, 58, 92, 893, 900

Babson Tax-Free Income—Port L, 54, 93

Babson Tax-Free Income—Port S, 54, 94

Babson Value, 44, 95

Babson-Stewart Ivory Int'l, 56, 96

Baker U.S. Capital Accumulation, 900

Baron Asset, 39, 97

Bartlett Basic Value, 45, 98

Bartlett Fixed Income, 51, 99

Bartlett Value Int'l, 56, 100, 890

Bascom Hill Balanced, 47, 101, 889

BayFunds Bond Port, 102

BayFunds Equity Port, 103

BayFunds Short-Term Yield, 104

Beacon Hill Mutual, 35, 43, 105

Benham Adjustable Rate Gov't, 50, 106

Benham CA Tax-Free High-Yield, 53, 107, 895

Benham CA Tax-Free Insured, 52, 108, 895

Benham CA Tax-Free Interm, 54, 109, 895

Benham CA Tax-Free Long-Term, 52, 110, 895

Benham CA Tax-Free Short-Term, 55, 111, 895

Benham Equity Growth, 42, 112

Benham European Gov't Bond, 57, 113

Benham GNMA Income, 50, 114

Benham Gold Equities Index, 35, 57, 115, 891 - 892

Benham Income & Growth, 45, 116

Benham Long-Term Treasury & Agency, 48, 117

Benham Nat'l Tax-Free Interm Term, 54, 118

Benham Nat'l Tax-Free Long-Term, 52, 119

Benham Short-Term Treasury & Agency, 49, 120

Benham Target Mat Trust—1995, 49, 121

Benham Target Mat Trust—2000, 48, 122

Benham Target Mat Trust—2005, 48, 123

Benham Target Mat Trust—2010, 48, 124

Benham Target Mat Trust—2015, 48, 125
Benham Target Mat Trust—2020, 48, 126
Benham Treasury Note, 49, 127
Benham Utilities Income, 128
Berger One Hundred, 36 - 39, 129
Berger One Hundred & One, 38, 44, 130
Bernstein CA Muni Port, 54, 131, 895
Bernstein Diversified Muni Port, 54, 132
Bernstein Gov't Short Duration, 49, 133
Bernstein Int'l Value, 56, 134
Bernstein Interm Duration, 51, 135
Bernstein NY Muni Port, 54, 136, 897
Bernstein Short Duration Plus, 51, 137
Berwyn, 38, 41, 138
Berwyn Income, 46, 139
Blanchard American Equity, 35, 43, 140
Blanchard Flexible Income, 51, 141
Blanchard Global Growth, 56, 142, 889 - 890
Blanchard Precious Metals, 35, 57, 143, 892
Blanchard Short-Term Global Inc, 57, 144, 890
BNY Hamilton Equity Income, 45, 145
BNY Hamilton Interm Gov't, 48, 146
BNY Hamilton Interm NY Tax Exempt, 54, 147, 897
Boston Co Asset Allocation, 47, 148, 889
Boston Co Capital Appreciation, 41, 149
Boston Co Int'l, 56, 150
Boston Co Interm Term Gov't, 48, 151
Boston Co Managed Income, 51, 152
Boston Co Special Growth, 39, 153, 900
Boston Tax Free Muni Bond, 54, 154
Brandywine, 37 - 38, 41, 155
Brinson Global, 56, 156, 889 - 890
Bruce, 41, 157
Brundage Story & Rose Short/Interm, 51, 158
BT Investments—Utility, 45, 159, 892
Bull & Bear Financial News Composite, 45, 160, 891
Bull & Bear Global Income, 57, 161, 890
Bull & Bear Gold Investors Ltd, 35, 57, 162, 892
Bull & Bear Muni Income, 54, 163

Bull & Bear Special Equities, 38, 40, 164
Bull & Bear US & Overseas, 56, 165, 890
Bull & Bear US Gov't Securities, 50, 166

C

CA Investment Trust US Gov't, 48, 167
Cal Muni, 52, 168, 895
Cal Tax-Free Income, 52, 169, 895
Calvert Tax-Free Reserves Ltd Term, 55, 170
Cappiello-Rushmore Emerging Growth, 39, 58, 171, 893
Cappiello-Rushmore Utility Income, 46, 172, 892
Capstone Gov't Income, 49, 173
Century Shares Trust, 35 - 36, 43, 174, 892, 900
CGM Capital Development, 37 - 39, 175
CGM Fixed Income, 47, 176
CGM Mutual, 46, 177
Charter Capital Blue Chip Growth, 46, 178
Clipper, 42, 179
Cohen & Steers Realty Shares, 44, 180, 892
Columbia Balanced, 46, 181
Columbia Common Stock, 44, 182
Columbia Fixed Income Securities, 51, 183
Columbia Growth, 36, 42, 184
Columbia Int'l Stock, 56, 185, 890
Columbia Muni Bond, 54, 186
Columbia Special, 38 - 39, 58, 187, 893
Columbia US Gov't Securities, 49, 188
Connecticut Mutual Inv Acts Income, 51, 189
Copley, 45, 190
Corefund Equity Index, 45, 191, 891
Corefund Int'l Growth "B", 900
Crabbe Huson Asset Allocation, 46, 192, 889

D

Dodge & Cox Balanced, 36, 46, 193

Dodge & Cox Income, 51, 194
Dodge & Cox Stock, 36, 44, 195
Dreman Contrarian, 45, 196
Dreman High Return, 42, 197
Dreyfus, 46, 198
Dreyfus 100% US Treasury Interm Term, 48, 199
Dreyfus 100% US Treasury Long Term, 48, 200
Dreyfus 100% US Treasury Short Term, 49, 201
Dreyfus A Bonds Plus, 51, 202
Dreyfus Appreciation, 35, 43, 203
Dreyfus Balanced, 47, 204, 889
Dreyfus CA Interm Muni Bond, 52, 205, 895
Dreyfus CA Tax Exempt Bond, 54, 206, 895
Dreyfus Capital Growth, 36, 42, 207
Dreyfus Conn Interm Muni Bond, 53, 208, 896
Dreyfus Convertible Securities, 900
Dreyfus Edison Electric Index, 45, 209, 891 - 892
Dreyfus Florida Interm Muni, 53, 210, 896
Dreyfus GNMA, 50, 211
Dreyfus Growth & Income, 44, 212
Dreyfus Growth Opportunity, 43, 213
Dreyfus Insured Muni Bond, 53, 214
Dreyfus Interm Muni Bond, 54, 215
Dreyfus Investors GNMA, 50, 216
Dreyfus Mass Interm Muni Bond, 53, 217, 896
Dreyfus Mass Tax-Exempt Bond, 53, 218, 896
Dreyfus Muni Bond, 53, 219
Dreyfus New Leaders, 40, 58, 220, 893
Dreyfus NJ Interm Muni Bond, 53, 221, 896
Dreyfus NJ Muni Bond, 53, 222, 896
Dreyfus NY Insured Tax-Exempt, 54, 223, 897
Dreyfus NY Tax-Exempt, 53, 224, 897
Dreyfus NY Tax-Exempt Interm, 54, 225, 897
Dreyfus Peoples Index, 45, 226, 891

Dreyfus Peoples S&P MidCap Index, 44, 227, 891
Dreyfus Short Interm Gov't, 49, 228
Dreyfus Short Interm Tax-Exempt Bond, 899
Dreyfus Short Term Income, 51, 229
Dreyfus Short-Interm Municipal, 54, 230, 899
Dreyfus Third Century, 46, 231, 895
Dupree KY Tax-Free Income, 53, 232, 896
Dupree KY Tax-Free Short to Medium, 55, 233, 896

E

Eaton Vance Short-Term Treasury, 49, 234
Eclipse Equity, 41, 58, 235, 893
Evergreen, 40, 59, 236, 894
Evergreen American Retirement, 46, 237
Evergreen Foundation, 46, 238, 889
Evergreen Insured National Tax-Free, 52, 239
Evergreen Limited Market, 36, 40, 58, 240, 894
Evergreen Short Interm Muni CA, 54, 241, 895
Evergreen Short-Interm Muni, 54, 242
Evergreen Total Return, 45, 243
Evergreen Value Timing, 42, 244

F

Fairmont, 40, 245, 900
FAM Value, 35, 43, 59, 246, 894
Fidelity Aggressive Tax-Free, 52, 248
Fidelity Asset Manager, 46, 249, 889
Fidelity Asset Manager—Growth, 46, 250, 889
Fidelity Asset Manager—Income, 46, 251, 889
Fidelity Balanced, 46, 252
Fidelity Blue Chip Growth, 37, 41, 253
Fidelity Canada, 56, 254
Fidelity Capital & Income, 36, 38, 48, 255
Fidelity Capital Appreciation Port, 41, 256

Fidelity CA Tax-Free High Yield, 52, 257, 895

Fidelity CA Tax-Free Insured, 52, 258, 895

Fidelity Contrafund, 36 - 38, 41, 259

Fidelity Convertible Securities, 37, 44, 260

Fidelity Discipline Equity, 42, 261

Fidelity Diversified Int'l, 56, 262

Fidelity Emerging Growth, 38 - 39, 58, 263, 894

Fidelity Emerging Markets, 35, 55, 264

Fidelity Equity-Income, 44, 265

Fidelity Equity-Income II, 38, 44, 266

Fidelity Europe, 56, 267

Fidelity Fund, 44, 247

Fidelity Ginnie Mae, 50, 268

Fidelity Global Balanced, 269, 889 - 890

Fidelity Global Bond, 57, 270, 890

Fidelity Gov't Securities, 48, 271

Fidelity Growth & Income, 44, 272

Fidelity Growth Company, 36 - 37, 40, 273

Fidelity High Yield Tax Free Port, 53, 274

Fidelity Insured Tax-Free, 52, 275

Fidelity Int'l Growth & Income, 56, 276, 890

Fidelity Interm Bond, 51, 277

Fidelity Investment Grade, 51, 278

Fidelity Japan, 56, 279

Fidelity Latin America, 280, 890

Fidelity Limited Term Muni, 53, 281

Fidelity Low-Priced Stock, 38, 41, 58, 282, 894

Fidelity Magellan, 36 - 37, 41, 283

Fidelity Market Index, 45, 284, 891

Fidelity Mass Tax-Free High Yield, 53, 285, 896

Fidelity Michigan Tax-Free High Yield, 52, 286, 896

Fidelity Minnesota Tax-Free, 53, 287, 896

Fidelity Mortgage Securities, 50, 288

Fidelity Muni Bond, 53, 289

Fidelity New Millenium, 39, 58, 290, 894

Fidelity NY Tax-Free High Yield, 53, 291, 897

Fidelity NY Tax-Free Insured, 53, 292, 897

Fidelity Ohio Tax-Free High Yield, 53, 293, 897

Fidelity OTC Port, 40, 294

Fidelity Overseas, 55, 295

Fidelity Pacific-Basin, 35, 55, 296

Fidelity Puritan, 36, 46, 297

Fidelity Real Estate Investment, 45, 298, 892, 900

Fidelity Retirement Growth, 36, 41, 299

Fidelity Sel Air Transportation, 39, 300, 892

Fidelity Sel American Gold, 35, 57, 301, 892

Fidelity Sel Automotive, 37 - 39, 302, 892

Fidelity Sel Biotechnology, 35, 37, 40, 303, 892

Fidelity Sel Broadcast & Media, 38 - 39, 304, 892

Fidelity Sel Broker & Invest Mgmt, 37 - 39, 305, 892

Fidelity Sel Chemical, 42, 306, 892

Fidelity Sel Computers, 37, 39, 307, 892

Fidelity Sel Constr'n & Hous'g, 38 - 39, 308, 892

Fidelity Sel Consumer Product, 39, 309, 892

Fidelity Sel Defense & Aerospace, 39, 310, 892

Fidelity Sel Dev'ping Communic'ns, 38 - 39, 311, 892

Fidelity Sel Electric Utilities, 45, 312, 892

Fidelity Sel Electronics, 37 - 39, 313, 892

Fidelity Sel Energy, 41, 314, 892

Fidelity Sel Energy Services, 39, 315, 892

Fidelity Sel Environ'l Serv, 35, 40, 316, 892

Fidelity Sel Financial Services, 36 - 38, 41, 317, 892

Fidelity Sel Food & Agriculture, 40, 318, 892

Fidelity Sel Health Care, 36 - 37, 40, 319, 892

Fidelity Sel Home Finance, 37 - 39, 320, 892

Fidelity Sel Industrial Equipment, 39, 321, 892

Fidelity Sel Industrial Materials, 39, 322, 892

Fidelity Sel Insurance, 43, 323, 892

Fidelity Sel Leisure, 38 - 39, 324, 892

Fidelity Sel Medical Delivery, 37, 40, 325, 892

Fidelity Sel Natural Gas Port, 326, 892

Fidelity Sel Paper & Forest Prod, 39, 327, 892

Fidelity Sel Precious Metals, 35, 57, 328, 892

Fidelity Sel Regional Banks, 37 - 38, 42, 329, 892

Fidelity Sel Retailing, 37 - 38, 40, 330, 892

Fidelity Sel Software & Comp, 37 - 39, 331, 892

Fidelity Sel Technology, 37 - 39, 332, 892

Fidelity Sel Telecomm, 37, 41, 333, 893

Fidelity Sel Transportation, 37 - 39, 334, 893

Fidelity Sel Utilities, 36, 45, 335, 893

Fidelity Short-Interm Gov't, 49, 336

Fidelity Short-Term Bond, 47, 337

Fidelity Short Term World Income, 57, 338, 890

Fidelity Southeast Asia, 339, 890

Fidelity Spartan CA Muni High Yield, 52, 340, 895

Fidelity Spartan Conn Tax-Free High-Yield, 53, 341, 896

Fidelity Spartan Florida Muni Income, 52, 342, 896

Fidelity Spartan Ginnie Mae, 50, 343

Fidelity Spartan Gov't Income, 50, 344

Fidelity Spartan High Income, 48, 345

Fidelity Spartan Investment Grade, 47, 346

Fidelity Spartan Long-Term Gov't, 48, 347

Fidelity Spartan Ltd Maturity Gov't, 50, 348

Fidelity Spartan Muni Income, 52, 349

Fidelity Spartan NJ Muni High Yield, 53, 350, 896

Fidelity Spartan NY Muni High Yield, 52, 351, 897

Fidelity Spartan Penn Muni High Yield, 53, 352, 897

Fidelity Spartan Short Intermediate Gov't, 49, 353

Fidelity Spartan Short-Interm Muni, 54, 354

Fidelity Spartan Short-Term Bond, 47, 355

Fidelity Stock Selector, 42, 356

Fidelity Trend, 36, 41, 357

Fidelity Utilities Income, 44, 358, 893

Fidelity Value, 41, 359

Fidelity Worldwide, 56, 360, 890

Fiduciary Capital Growth, 42, 361

Fifty-Nine Wall St. European, 56, 362

Fifty-Nine Wall St. Pacific Basin, 35, 38, 55, 363

Fifty-Nine Wall St. Small Company, 40, 58, 364, 894

Financial Bond Shares—High Yield, 899

Financial Bond Shares—Select Income, 899

Financial Bond Shares—U.S. Government, 899

Financial Dynamics, 899

Financial Emerging Growth, 899

Financial Industrial, 899

Financial Industrial Income, 899

Financial Series Trust—Equity, 899

Financial Series Trust—Flex, 899

Financial Series Trust—Interm Gov't Bond, 899

Financial Series Trust—International Growth, 899

Financial Strategic Portfolio—Energy, 899

Financial Strategic Portfolio—Environm'l Serv, 899

Financial Strategic Portfolio—European, 899

Financial Strategic Portfolio—Fin'l Services, 899

Financial Strategic Portfolio—Gold, 899

Financial Strategic Portfolio—Health Sciences, 899

Financial Strategic Portfolio—Leisure, 899

Financial Strategic Portfolio—Pacific Basin, 899

Financial Strategic Portfolio—Technology, 899

Financial Strategic Portfolio—Utilities, 899
Financial Tax-Free Income Shares, 899
First Eagle Fund of America, 41, 365
First Hawaii Muni Bond, 54, 366, 896
Flex Bond, 48, 367
Flex Growth, 43, 368
Flex Muirfield, 43, 369, 890
Flex Short Term Global Income, 35, 57, 370, 890
Fontaine Capital Appreciation, 42, 371
Forty-Four Wall Street, 900
Forty-Four Wall Street Equity, 39, 372
Founders Balanced, 46, 373, 899
Founders Blue Chip, 44, 374
Founders Discovery, 38, 40, 58, 375, 894
Founders Equity Income, 899
Founders Frontier, 37, 40, 58, 376, 894
Founders Gov't Securities, 48, 377
Founders Growth, 36 - 37, 41, 378
Founders Special, 36 - 37, 40, 379
Founders World Wide Growth, 56, 380, 890
Franklin Short-Interm US Gov't, 49, 381
Fremont CA Interm Tax-Free, 54, 382, 895
Fremont Global, 46, 383, 889, 899
Fremont Growth, 43, 384
Fremont Multi Asset, 899
Fundamental US Gov't Strat Income, 48, 385

G

Gabelli Asset, 41, 386
Gabelli Equity Income, 44, 387
Gabelli Growth, 42, 388
Gabelli Small Cap Growth, 900
Galaxy Asset Allocation, 47, 389, 889
Galaxy Equity Growth, 43, 390
Galaxy Equity Income, 45, 391
Galaxy Equity Value, 44, 392
Galaxy High Quality Bond, 51, 393
Galaxy Interm Bond, 51, 394
Galaxy NY Muni Bond, 53, 395, 897
Galaxy Short Term Bond, 51, 396

Galaxy Small Company Equity, 39, 58, 397, 894
Galaxy Tax-Exempt Bond, 54, 398
Gateway Government Bond Plus, 49, 399
Gateway Index Plus, 45, 400
General CA Muni Bond, 52, 401, 895
General Muni Bond, 52, 402
General NY Muni Bond, 52, 403, 897
GE U.S. Equity, 404
Gintel, 43, 405
Gintel ERISA, 46, 406
GIT Equity—Special Growth, 40, 58, 407, 894
GIT Income—Gov't Port, 48, 408
GIT Income—Maximum, 48, 409
GIT Tax-Free High Yield, 54, 410
GIT Tax-Free Virginia Port, 53, 411, 897
Gradison McDonald Established Value, 36, 41, 412
Gradison McDonald Opportunity Value, 42, 58, 413, 894, 900
Greenspring, 44, 414

H

Harbor Bond, 51, 415
Harbor Capital Appreciation, 42, 416
Harbor Growth, 41, 417
Harbor Int'l, 55, 418
Harbor Short Duration, 52, 419
Harbor Value, 45, 420
Heartland Wisconsin Tax Free, 54, 421, 897
HighMark Bond, 51, 422
HighMark Income Equity, 45, 423
HighMark Special Growth Equity, 42, 58, 424, 894
Homestead Short-Term Bond, 47, 425
Homestead Value, 44, 426

I

IAI Balanced, 47, 427, 889
IAI Bond, 48, 428
IAI Emerging Growth, 40, 58, 429, 894

IAI Gov't, 48, 430
IAI Growth & Income, 42, 431, 899
IAI Int'l, 55, 432
IAI MidCap Growth, 41, 433
IAI Regional, 36, 42, 434
IAI Reserve, 52, 435
IAI Stock, 899
IAI Value, 41, 436
International Equity, 55, 437
INVESCO Growth, 899
INVESCO Dynamics, 37 - 39, 438, 899
INVESCO Emerging Growth, 39, 58, 439,
    894, 899
INVESCO Growth, 41, 440
INVESCO Income—High Yield, 48, 441,
    899
INVESCO Income—Sel Income, 47, 442,
    899
NVESCO Income—US Gov't Sec, 48, 443,
    899
INVESCO Industrial Income, 36, 46, 444,
    899
INVESCO Int'l—European, 56, 445, 899
INVESCO Int'l—Int'l Growth, 56, 446, 899
INVESCO Int'l—Pacific Basin, 55, 447,
    899
INVESCO Strat Port—Energy, 40, 448,
    893, 899
INVESCO Strat Port—Environm'l, 35, 40,
    449, 893, 899
INVESCO Strat Port—Financial, 37 - 38,
    41, 450, 893, 899
INVESCO Strat Port—Gold, 35, 57, 451,
    893, 899
INVESCO Strat Port—Health Sci, 35, 37,
    40, 452, 893, 899
INVESCO Strat Port—Leisure, 37 - 39,
    453, 893, 899
INVESCO Strat Port—Tech, 37 - 38, 40,
    454, 893, 899
INVESCO Strat Port—Utilities, 44, 455,
    893, 899
INVESCO Tax-Free Long-Term Bond, 54,
    456, 899
INVESCO Value Trust—Interm Gov't,
    48, 457, 899

INVESCO Value Trust—Total Return, 47,
    458, 889, 899
INVESCO Value Trust—Value Equity,
    45, 459, 899

J

Janus, 36 - 37, 42, 460
Janus Balanced, 47, 461, 889
Janus Enterprise, 40, 462
Janus Federal Tax-Exempt, 463
Janus Flexible Income, 47, 464
Janus Growth & Income, 45, 465
Janus Interm Gov't Securities, 49, 466
Janus Mercury, 467
Janus Short-Term Bond, 47, 468
Janus Twenty, 37, 43, 469
Janus Venture, 40, 58, 470, 894
Janus Worldwide, 56, 471, 890
Japan, 36, 56, 472

K

Kaufmann, 37 - 38, 40, 58, 473, 894
Kleinwort Benson Int'l Equity, 900

L

Laurel Intermediate Income, 51, 474
Laurel Stock Port, 45, 475
Leeb Personal Finance, 43, 476
Legg Mason Global Gov't Trust, 477, 890
Legg Mason Investment Grade, 51, 478
Legg Mason Special Investment, 37, 39,
    58, 479, 894
Legg Mason Total Return, 44, 480
Legg Mason US Gov't Interm Port, 51, 481
Legg Mason Value, 42, 482
Lepercq-Istel, 46, 483
Lexington Global, 56, 484, 890
Lexington GNMA Income, 50, 485
Lexington GoldFund, 35, 57, 486, 893
Lexington Growth & Income, 45, 487
Lexington Tax-Exempt Bond Trust, 54,
    488

Lexington Technical Strategy, 900
Lexington Worldwide Emerg Mkts, 35, 38, 55, 489, 890
Lindner, 44, 490
Lindner Dividend, 46, 491
LMH, 45, 492
Loomis Sayles Bond, 47, 493
Loomis Sayles Growth, 40, 494
Loomis Sayles Int'l Equity, 55, 495
Loomis Sayles Small Cap, 39, 58, 496, 894
L. Roy Papp Stock, 46, 497

M

Managers Bond, 51, 498
Managers Capital Appreciation, 40, 499
Managers Income Equity, 45, 500
Managers Interm Mortgage, 50, 501
Managers International Equity, 55, 502, 890
Managers Short & Interm Bond, 51, 503
Managers Short Gov't, 50, 504
Managers Special Equity, 40, 58, 505, 894
Mathers, 43, 506
Matrix Growth, 42, 507, 900
Maxus Equity, 41, 508, 889
Maxus Income, 51, 509, 889
Maxus Prism, 510, 890
Meridian, 37, 42, 58, 511, 894
Merrill Lynch Corp Interm "A", 47, 512
Merrill Lynch Muni Interm "A", 54, 513, 899
Merrill Lynch Muni Ltd Mat "A", 55, 514
Merrill Lynch Municipal Income—Class A, 899
Merriman Asset Allocation, 46, 515, 889 - 890
Merriman Blue Chip, 46, 516
Merriman Capital Appreciation, 43, 517, 890
Merriman Flexible Bond, 51, 518, 900
MetLife—State Street Gov't Income, 900
MIM Bond Income, 47, 519
MIM Stock Appreciation, 37, 40, 520
MIM Stock Growth, 43, 521
MIM Stock Income, 35, 46, 522

Monetta, 35, 43, 59, 523, 894
Montgomery Emerging Markets, 35, 55, 524
Montgomery Short Duration Gov't, 50, 525
Montgomery Small Cap, 38 - 39, 58, 526, 894
Morgan Grenfell Fixed Income, 51, 527
Morgan Grenfell Muni Bond, 53, 528
M.S.B. Fund, 41, 529
Mutual Beacon, 44, 530
Mutual Discovery, 531, 894
Mutual Qualified, 36, 44, 532
Mutual Shares, 36, 44, 533

N

National Industries, 43, 534
Neuberger & Berman Genesis, 40, 58, 535, 894
Neuberger & Berman Guardian, 36, 44, 536
Neuberger & Berman Ltd Mat Bond, 51, 537
Neuberger & Berman Manhattan, 36, 42, 538
Neuberger & Berman Muni Securities, 54, 539
Neuberger & Berman Partners, 36, 44, 540
Neuberger & Berman Sel Sectors, 41, 541, 893
Neuberger & Berman Ultra Short Bond, 52, 542
New Century Capital Port, 42, 543, 890
New York Muni, 53, 544, 897
Nicholas, 36, 43, 545
Nicholas II, 36, 43, 59, 546, 894
Nicholas Income, 48, 547
Nicholas Limited Edition, 42, 58, 548, 894
Nomura Pacific Basin, 55, 549
Northeast Investors Growth, 43, 550
Northeast Investors Trust, 48, 551

O

Oakmark, 41, 552
Oakmark Int'l, 55, 553
Oberweis Emerging Growth, 37 - 38, 40, 58, 554, 894
Olympic Equity Income, 44, 555
Olympic Trust Balanced Income, 47, 556, 889
Oregon Municipal Bond, 54, 557, 897

P

Pacifica Asset Preservation, 52, 558
Pacifica Short Term CA Tax-Free, 559, 895
Paine Webber Atlas Global Growth "D", 55, 560, 890
Paine Webber CA Tax-Free Inc. "D", 54, 561, 895
Paine Webber Capital Appreciation "D", 40, 562
Paine Webber Dividend Growth "D", 35, 46, 563
Paine Webber Global Income "D", 57, 564, 890
Paine Webber Growth "D", 41, 565
Paine Webber High Income "D", 48, 566
Paine Webber Investment Gr Inc "D", 47, 567
Paine Webber Muni High Inc "D", 54, 568
Paine Webber N.Y. Tax Free Inc"D", 54, 569, 897
Paine Webber Nat'l Tax-Free Income "D", 54, 570
Paine Webber Short Term U.S. Gov't Inc "D", 571
Paine Webber Small Cap Value "D", 572, 894
Paine Webber U.S. Gov't Income "D", 50, 573
Pax World, 35, 47, 574, 895
PBHG Growth, 37 - 39, 58, 575, 894
Pennsylvania Mutual, 42, 58, 576, 894
Permanent Port, 46, 577, 889
Permanent Port—Versatile Bond, 47, 578
Permanent Treasury Bill, 49, 579

Perritt Capital Growth, 40, 59, 580, 894
Philadelphia, 44, 581
Portico Balanced, 47, 582
Portico Bond IMMDEX, 51, 583, 891
Portico Equity Index, 45, 584, 891
Portico Growth & Income, 46, 585, 899
Portico Income & Growth, 899
Portico Interm Bond Market, 586, 891
Portico MidCore Growth, 42, 587
Portico Short Term Bond Market, 51, 588, 891
Portico Special Growth, 43, 589
PRA Real Estate Securities, 41, 590, 893
Preferred Asset Allocation, 47, 591, 889
Preferred Fixed Income, 51, 592
Preferred Growth, 42, 593
Preferred Int'l, 55, 594
Preferred Short-Term Gov't Securities, 51, 595
Preferred Value, 45, 596
Primary Trend, 45, 597
Prudent Speculator, 40, 59, 598, 894, 899
Prudent Speculator Leveraged, 899
Prudential Gov't Securities Interm Term, 49, 599

R

Rainbow, 35, 43, 600
Regis ICM Small Company Port, 38, 41, 58, 601, 894
Reich & Tang Equity, 42, 602
Reynolds Blue Chip Growth, 35, 46, 603
Rightime, 43, 604, 890
Robertson Stephens Emerg Grth, 37, 40, 59, 605, 894
Robertson Stephens Value Plus, 39, 58, 606, 894
Royce Equity Income Series, 45, 607
Rushmore American GAS Index, 44, 608, 891, 893
Rushmore Maryland Tax-Free, 54, 609, 896
Rushmore Nova, 900
Rushmore OTC Index Plus, 42, 610, 891

Rushmore Stock Market Index Plus, 45, 611, 891
Rushmore US Gov't Interm-Term, 48, 612
Rushmore US Gov't Long-Term, 48, 613
Rushmore Virginia Tax-Free, 54, 614, 897

S

Safeco CA Tax-Free Income, 53, 615, 896
Safeco Equity, 36, 44, 616
Safeco Growth, 39, 617, 900
Safeco High Yield Bond, 48, 618
Safeco Income, 47, 619
Safeco Muni Bond, 53, 620
Safeco Northwest, 35, 43, 621
Safeco US Gov't Securities, 50, 622
Salomon Brothers Capital, 40, 623
Salomon Brothers Investors, 44, 624
Salomon Brothers Opportunity, 42, 625
SBSF, 41, 626, 899
SBSF Convertible Securities, 44, 627
SBSF Growth, 899
Schafer Value, 37 - 38, 44, 628
Schroder US Equity, 42, 629
Schwab 1000, 45, 630, 891
Schwab CA Long-Term Tax-Free, 53, 631, 896
Schwab CA Short/Interm Tax-Free, 632, 896
Schwab Long-Term Tax-Free, 52, 633
Schwab Short/Interm Gov't Bond, 49, 634, 899
Schwab Short/Intermediate Tax-Free, 635
Schwab U.S. Government Bond Short Interm, 899
Scudder Balanced, 47, 636
Scudder CA Tax Free, 52, 637, 896
Scudder Capital Growth, 36, 41, 638
Scudder Development, 40, 58, 639, 894
Scudder Global, 56, 640, 890
Scudder Global Small Company, 55, 58, 641, 890, 894
Scudder GNMA, 50, 642
Scudder Gold, 35, 57, 643, 893
Scudder Growth & Income, 44, 644

Scudder High Yield Tax-Free, 52, 645
Scudder Income, 51, 646
Scudder Int'l, 36, 56, 647
Scudder Int'l Bond, 57, 648, 890
Scudder Latin America, 35, 55, 649
Scudder Managed Muni Bond, 52, 650
Scudder Mass Tax-Free, 52, 651, 896
Scudder Medium Term Tax Free, 54, 652
Scudder NY Tax Free, 53, 653, 897
Scudder Ohio Tax-Free, 53, 654, 897
Scudder Pacific Opportunities, 35, 55, 655, 890
Scudder Penn Tax Free, 53, 656, 897
Scudder Quality Growth, 43, 657
Scudder Short-Term Bond, 51, 658
Scudder Short-Term Global Income, 57, 659, 890
Scudder Value, 42, 660
Scudder Zero Coupon 2000, 48, 661
Selected American Shares, 36, 46, 662
Selected Special Shares, 42, 663
Selected US Gov't Income, 50, 664, 900
Sentry, 43, 665
Sequoia, 36, 45, 666
Seven Seas Series—Matrix Equity, 44, 667
Seven Seas Series—S&P 500, 45, 668, 891
Seven Seas Series—S&P MidCap, 45, 669, 891
Seven Seas Short Term Gov't Securities, 49, 670
Seven Seas Yield Plus, 52, 671
1784 Growth and Income, 62
1784 U.S. Gov't Medium Term Income, 63
Sherman, Dean, 900
SIT Growth, 36, 40, 58, 672, 894, 899
SIT Growth & Income, 46, 673, 900
SIT Int'l Growth, 55, 674, 900
SIT Money Market, 900
SIT New Beginning Growth, 899
SIT New Beginning Income & Growth, 900
SIT New Beginning International Growth, 900
SIT New Beginning Tax Free Income, 900
SIT New Beginning U.S. Government Securities, 900

SIT Tax Free Income, 54, 675, 900
SIT US Gov't Securities, 50, 676, 900
Skyline Special Equities II, 677, 894
Smith Barney Muni Bond Ltd Term "A", 54, 678
Smith Barney Short-Term US Treasury, 49, 679
Smith Barney—Income Return "A", 49, 680
Sound Shore, 42, 681
Southeastern Asset Mgmt Small Cap, 41, 58, 682, 894
Southeastern Asset Mgmt Value Trust, 41, 683
SteinRoe Capital Opportunities, 38 - 39, 684
SteinRoe Gov't Income, 51, 685
SteinRoe High Yield Muni, 54, 686
SteinRoe Income, 47, 687
SteinRoe Interm Bond, 51, 688
SteinRoe Interm Muni, 54, 689
SteinRoe Managed Muni, 54, 690
SteinRoe Prime Equities, 42, 691
SteinRoe Special, 36, 39, 692
SteinRoe Stock, 43, 693
SteinRoe Total Return, 47, 694
Stratton Growth, 46, 695
Stratton Monthly Dividend Shares, 46, 696
Strong Advantage, 47, 697
Strong Common Stock, 38 - 39, 698
Strong Discovery, 37 - 38, 41, 58, 699, 894
Strong Gov't Securities, 51, 700
Strong Income, 51, 701
Strong Insured Muni Bond, 53, 702
Strong Int'l Stock, 55, 703
Strong Investment, 46, 704
Strong Muni Bond, 54, 705
Strong Opportunity, 41, 706
Strong Short-Term Bond, 47, 707
Strong Short-Term Muni Bond, 54, 708
Strong Total Return, 46, 709
SWRW Growth Plus, 900

T

Tocqueville, 41, 710
T Rowe Price Adjustable Rate US Gov't, 50, 711
T Rowe Price Balanced, 47, 712
T Rowe Price CA Tax-Free Bond, 53, 713, 896
T Rowe Price Capital Appreciation, 42, 714
T Rowe Price Dividend Growth, 44, 715
T Rowe Price Equity Income, 44, 716
T Rowe Price European Stock, 56, 717
T Rowe Price Global Gov't Bond, 57, 718, 891
T Rowe Price GNMA, 50, 719
T Rowe Price Growth & Income, 45, 720
T Rowe Price Growth Stock, 42, 721
T Rowe Price High Yield, 48, 722
T Rowe Price Int'l Bond, 57, 723
T Rowe Price Int'l Discovery, 55, 58, 724, 895
T Rowe Price Int'l Stock, 36, 55, 725
T Rowe Price Japan, 56, 726
T Rowe Price Maryland Tax-Free, 53, 727, 896
T Rowe Price MD Short-Term Tax-Free, 728, 896
T Rowe Price Mid-Cap Growth, 41, 729
T Rowe Price New America Growth, 37 - 38, 41, 730, 893
T Rowe Price New Asia, 35, 38, 55, 731
T Rowe Price New Era, 42, 732, 893
T Rowe Price New Horizons, 39, 58, 733, 895
T Rowe Price New Income, 51, 734
T Rowe Price NJ Tax-Free, 52, 735, 896
T Rowe Price NY Tax-Free, 52, 736, 897
T Rowe Price OTC, 39, 58, 737, 895
T Rowe Price Science & Tech, 37 - 39, 738, 893
T Rowe Price Short-Term Bond, 51, 739
T Rowe Price Short-Term Global Inc, 57, 740, 891
T Rowe Price Small Cap Value, 41, 58, 741, 895, 900

T Rowe Price Spectrum Growth, 44, 742, 890

T Rowe Price Spectrum Income, 47, 743, 890

T Rowe Price Tax-Free High Yield, 53, 744

T Rowe Price Tax-Free Income, 53, 745

T Rowe Price Tax-Free Insured Interm, 53, 746

T Rowe Price Tax-Free Short-Interm, 55, 747

T Rowe Price US Treasury Interm, 49, 748

T Rowe Price US Treasury Long Term, 48, 749

T Rowe Price Virginia Tax-Free Bond, 53, 750, 897

Tweedy Browne Global Value, 751, 891, 895

Twentieth Century Balanced, 47, 752

Twentieth Century Giftrust, 36 - 39, 58, 753, 895

Twentieth Century Growth, 36, 40, 754

Twentieth Century Heritage, 41, 755

Twentieth Century Int'l Equity, 55, 756

Twentieth Century Long-Term Bond, 51, 757

Twentieth Century Sel, 42, 758

Twentieth Century Tax-Exempt Interm, 54, 759

Twentieth Century Tax-Exempt Long, 54, 760

Twentieth Century Tax-Exempt Short, 761

Twentieth Century Ultra, 36 - 39, 58, 762, 895

Twentieth Century US Gov'ts, 49, 763

Twentieth Century Vista, 40, 59, 764, 895

U

UMB Bond, 51, 765

UMB Heartland Fund, 43, 59, 766, 895

UMB Stock, 45, 767

US All American Equity, 45, 768, 891

US European Income, 56, 769, 889

US Global Resources, 56, 770, 891, 893

US Gold Shares, 35, 57, 771, 893

US Growth, 42, 772

US Income, 44, 773

US Real Estate, 35, 46, 774, 893

US Tax Free, 54, 775

US World Gold, 35, 37, 57, 776, 893

USAA Aggressive Growth, 40, 59, 777, 895

USAA Balanced, 46, 778

USAA Cornerstone, 46, 779, 889

USAA GNMA Trust, 50, 780

USAA Gold, 35, 57, 781, 893

USAA Growth, 45, 782

USAA Growth & Income, 783

USAA Income, 47, 784

USAA Income Stock, 45, 785

USAA Int'l, 55, 786

USAA Tax Exempt CA Bond, 53, 787, 896

USAA Tax Exempt Interm-Term, 54, 788

USAA Tax Exempt Long-Term, 53, 789

USAA Tax Exempt NY Bond, 52, 790, 897

USAA Tax Exempt Short-Term, 55, 791

USAA Tax-Exempt Virginia Bond, 53, 792, 897

USAA World Growth, 56, 793, 891

V

Valley Forge, 44, 794

Value Line, 43, 795

Value Line Adjustable Rate US Gov't, 50, 796

Value Line Aggressive Income, 48, 797

Value Line Convertible, 44, 798

Value Line Income, 47, 799, 889

Value Line Leveraged Growth, 40, 800

Value Line NY Tax-Exempt Trust, 52, 801, 897

Value Line Special Situations, 40, 802

Value Line Tax Exempt High Yield, 54, 803

Value Line US Gov't Securities, 50, 804

Vanguard Admiral Interm US Treas, 48, 805

Vanguard Admiral Long US Treas, 48, 806

Vanguard Admiral Short US Treas, 49, 807
Vanguard Asset Allocation, 47, 808, 889
Vanguard Balanced Index, 47, 809, 891
Vanguard Bond Index, 51, 810, 891, 900
Vanguard Bond Market, 900
Vanguard CA Tax-Free Insured Long, 53, 811, 896
Vanguard Convertible Securities, 45, 812
Vanguard Equity Income, 44, 813
Vanguard Explorer, 40, 58, 814, 895
Vanguard Florida Insured Tax Free, 52, 815, 896
Vanguard GNMA, 50, 816
Vanguard High Yield Corporate, 48, 817
Vanguard High-Yield Muni Bond, 53, 818
Vanguard Index Trust—500, 36, 45, 819, 891
Vanguard Index Trust—Ext Market, 42, 58, 820, 891, 895
Vanguard Index Trust—Growth Port, 43, 821, 891
Vanguard Index Trust—Tot Stock Mkt, 45, 822, 891
Vanguard Index Trust—Value Port, 44, 823, 891
Vanguard Insured Long-Term Muni, 53, 824
Vanguard Int'l Equity Index—Europe, 56, 825, 891
Vanguard Int'l Equity Index—Pacific, 56, 826, 891
Vanguard Int'l Growth, 36, 55, 827, 900
Vanguard Interm-Term Muni Bond, 54, 828
Vanguard Interm-Term US Treasury, 48, 829
Vanguard Investment Grade Corporate, 900
Vanguard Limited-Term Muni Bond, 55, 830
Vanguard Long Term Corp Bond, 47, 831, 900
Vanguard Long-Term Muni Bond, 52, 832
Vanguard Long-Term US Treasury, 48, 833

Vanguard Morgan Growth, 43, 834
Vanguard NJ Tax Free Insured Long, 53, 835, 896
Vanguard NY Insured Tax Free, 53, 836, 897
Vanguard Ohio Tax Free Insur Long, 53, 837, 897
Vanguard Penn Tax-Free Insur Long, 53, 838, 897
Vanguard Preferred Stock, 45, 839
Vanguard Primecap, 41, 840
Vanguard Quantitative Port, 44, 841
Vanguard Short-Term Corporate, 47, 842
Vanguard Short-Term Federal, 49, 843
Vanguard Short-Term Muni Bond, 55, 844
Vanguard Short-Term US Treasury, 49, 845
Vanguard Small Cap Stock, 39, 58, 846, 891, 895
Vanguard Spec Port—Energy, 41, 847, 893, 900
Vanguard Spec Port—Gold & PM, 35, 57, 848, 893
Vanguard Spec Port—Health Care, 37, 42, 849, 893
Vanguard Spec Port—Service Econ, 42, 850, 893
Vanguard Spec Port—Tech, 40, 851, 893, 900
Vanguard Spec Port—Utilities Income, 44, 852, 893
Vanguard Star, 47, 853, 890
Vanguard Trustees' Equity—Int'l, 36, 56, 854
Vanguard Trustees' Equity—US, 44, 855
Vanguard US Growth, 35, 43, 856, 900
Vanguard Wellesley Income, 36, 46, 857
Vanguard Wellington, 46, 858
Vanguard Windsor, 36, 44, 859
Vanguard Windsor II, 44, 860
Vanguard World—International Growth, 900
Vanguard World—U.S. Growth, 900
Vista Bond, 51, 861
Vista Equity, 43, 862
Vista Short-Term Bond, 52, 863

Volumetric, 43, 864
Vontobel EuroPacific, 55, 865
Vontobel US Value, 42, 866

W

Warburg Pincus Cap Appreciation, 42, 867
Warburg Pincus Emerging Grth, 39, 58, 868, 895
Warburg Pincus Fixed Income, 51, 869
Warburg Pincus Global Fixed Income, 57, 870, 891
Warburg Pincus Int'l Equity, 55, 871
Warburg Pincus Interm Mat Gov't, 49, 872
Warburg Pincus NY Muni Bond, 54, 873, 897

Wasatch Aggressive Equity, 37, 39, 874
Wayne Hummer Growth, 43, 875
Wayne Hummer Income, 51, 876
Weitz Value Port, 41, 877
Westcore Trust Short-Term Gov't Bond, 52, 878
William Blair Growth Shares, 36, 42, 879
William Blair Income Shares, 51, 880
Woodward Equity Index, 45, 881, 891
WPG Gov't Securities, 48, 882
WPG Growth & Income, 45, 883
WPG Quantitative Equity, 44, 884
WPG Tudor, 40, 885
Wright Int'l Blue Chip Equity, 56, 886

Y

Yacktman, 35, 43, 887

INVESTING BASICS
Videocourse

In this three-and-a-half hour videotape, you will learn the techniques and strategies you should know to be a successful investor. The accompanying workbook reproduces the graphics and tables used in the video; the videotape format allows you to stop at any point during the course to go over in the workbook the section you just covered. In addition, the workbook includes a bibliography of information sources at the end of each section. The videocourse includes:

- **Part I: Basic Financial Concepts**—Risk, return, the risk/return trade-off, the time value of money, how to calculate future values.

- **Part II: Bonds and Other Fixed-Income Investments**—Characteristics of bonds; how to read bond quotes in the newspaper; other fixed-income investment alternatives; and how to purchase bonds.

- **Part III: Investing in Common Stocks**—Risk and return; stock valuation methods; how to read stock quotations; stock indexes and indicators; stock mutual funds.

- **Part IV: Building a Portfolio of Investments**—Diversification, asset allocation, modifying portfolio risk, calculating portfolio return.

The complete videocourse with accompanying workbook is available to AAII members for $98 and to non-members for $129.

For more information, contact the American Association of Individual Investors, 625 N. Michigan Avenue, Suite 1900, Chicago, IL 60611; (312) 280-0170.

AAII
AMERICAN
ASSOCIATION OF
INDIVIDUAL
INVESTORS®

Quarterly Low-Load Mutual Fund Update®

Keep up-to-date on all the funds you've read about in this book with the *Quarterly Low-Load Mutual Fund Update*.

This quarterly newsletter covers over 800 no-load and low-load mutual funds. Information reported for each fund includes:

- Performance by quarter over the last year
- Annual total return for the last year, three years and five years
- The difference between a fund's performance and that of an average of funds of the same category for all reported periods
- Risk index
- Yield
- Expense ratio
- Maximum load or 12b-1 charge, if any
- Telephone number

Lists of top-performing funds and the performance of major indexes make your fund's performance easy to monitor and evaluate. *The Quarterly Update* will also keep you abreast of fund developments such as a change in a portfolio manager.

The Quarterly Update is also available for IBM-compatible and Macintosh computers with a computerized menu-driven program that provides fund returns and investment category comparisons of these returns by quarter over the last year, last three years and last five years. Returns are also provided for each of the last eight years and over the most recent bull and bear market periods. Risk statistics provided include standard deviation, investment category risk index, beta for stock funds and average maturity for bond funds. The IBM version requires an IBM PC or compatible with 540K free RAM and 2MB hard drive storage space. The Mac version requires a Mac Plus or higher with 2MB hard disk storage.

Annual subscription to *The Quarterly Update,* $24 (non-members, $30); newsletter plus computer program, $39 (non-members, $50). For more information, contact the American Association of Individual Investors, 625 N. Michigan Avenue, Suite 1900, Chicago, IL 60611; (312) 280-0170.

AAII

AMERICAN
ASSOCIATION OF
INDIVIDUAL
INVESTORS®

Fourth Quarter
1993

	Last Qtr.	Cat. +/-	Last 2 Qtrs.	Cat. +/-	Last 3 Qtrs.	Cat. +/-	Last Year	Cat. +/-	Last 3 Years	Cat. +/-	Last 5 Years	Cat. +/-	Risk Index	Yield (%)	Exp. Ratio (%)	Max. Load (%)	Max. 12b-1 (%)	Phone
Balanced Funds																		
T Rowe Price Spectrum Income	ff 1.7	0.0	4.4	(1.1)	7.4	(0.3)	12.4	(0.9)	13.1	(2.1)	na	na	0.48	8.2	0.00	—	—	(800) 638-5660
Twentieth Century Balanced	(0.5)	(2.5)	3.4	(2.1)	6.2	(1.5)	7.2	(6.1)	13.9	(1.9)	13.6	1.4	1.35	2.3	1.00	—	—	(800) 345-2021
USAA Balanced	2.3	0.6	4.7	(0.5)	9.0	1.3	13.7	0.4	11.0	(4.2)	na	na	0.82	3.5	0.92	—	—	(800) 382-8722
USAA Cornerstone	aa 3.9	2.2	8.6	3.1	12.4	4.7	23.7	10.4	15.2	0.0	11.1	(1.1)	1.19	2.5	1.18	—	—	(800) 382-8722
USAA Income	(0.2)	(1.9)	1.9	(3.6)	4.9	(2.8)	9.9	(3.4)	12.4	(2.8)	12.2	0.0	0.68	6.9	0.42	—	—	(800) 382-8722
Value Line Income	aa 0.0	(1.7)	1.0	(4.5)	4.4	(3.3)	8.2	(5.1)	12.2	(3.0)	12.0	(0.2)	1.40	3.1	0.89	—	—	(800) 223-0818
Vanguard Asset Allocation	1.2	(0.5)	5.2	(0.3)	7.4	(0.3)	13.4	0.1	15.2	0.0	13.9	1.7	1.21	3.3	0.52	—	—	(800) 662-7447
Vanguard Balanced Index	idx 0.9	(0.9)	4.4	(1.1)	5.8	(1.9)	9.9	(3.4)	na	na	na	na	na	3.5	na	—	—	(800) 662-7447
Vanguard Star	ff 0.6	(1.1)	4.6	(0.9)	5.9	(1.8)	10.8	(2.5)	15.0	(0.2)	11.7	(0.5)	1.08	3.5	0.00	—	—	(800) 662-7447
Vanguard Wellesley Income	(0.8)	(2.5)	4.1	(1.4)	7.3	(0.4)	14.6	1.3	14.8	(0.4)	13.7	1.5	0.90	5.9	0.35	—	—	(800) 662-7447
Vanguard Wellington	2.0	0.3	4.9	(0.6)	7.9	0.2	13.5	0.2	14.8	(0.4)	12.3	0.1	1.21	4.5	0.33	—	—	(800) 662-7447
BALANCED FUND AVERAGE	1.7	0.0	5.5	0.0	7.7	0.0	13.3	0.0	15.2	0.0	12.2	0.0	1.00	3.3	1.04	—	—	SD 6.2%
Corporate Bond Funds																		
CGM Fixed Income	2.7	1.8	6.5	2.7	10.8	4.3	18.9	7.5	na	na	na	na	na	6.0	na	—	—	(800) 345-4048
Fidelity Short-Term Bond	1.6	0.7	3.6	(0.2)	5.5	(1.0)	9.1	(2.3)	10.1	(1.9)	9.3	(0.8)	0.67	na	0.77	—	—	(800) 544-8888
Fidelity Spartan Investment Grade Bond	(0.5)	(1.5)	4.5	0.7	8.8	2.3	15.7	4.3	na	na	na	na	na	na	0.65	—	—	(800) 544-8888
Fidelity Spartan Short-Term Bond	1.5	0.6	3.5	(0.3)	5.5	(1.0)	9.0	(2.4)	na	na	na	na	na	7.7	na	—	—	(800) 544-8888
Homestead Short-Term Bond	0.5	(0.4)	2.1	(1.7)	3.4	(3.1)	6.6	(4.8)	na	na	na	na	na	4.6	0.75	—	—	(800) 258-3030
INVESCO Income—Sel Income	1.4	0.5	3.1	(0.7)	6.1	(0.4)	11.3	(0.1)	13.3	1.3	10.5	0.4	0.96	7.5	na	—	0.250	(800) 525-8085
Janus Flexible Income	1.7	0.8	5.8	2.0	9.8	3.3	15.6	4.2	na	na	na	na	1.19	7.7	1.00	—	—	(800) 525-3713
Janus Short-Term Bond	0.6	(0.3)	2.4	(1.4)	3.7	(2.8)	6.1	(3.3)	na	na	na	na	na	4.8	1.00	—	—	(800) 525-3713
Loomis Sayles Bond	3.2	2.3	7.7	3.9	13.5	7.0	22.2	10.9	na	na	na	na	na	7.0	1.00	—	—	(800) 633-3330
Merrill Lynch Corp Interm "A"	(0.3)	(1.2)	3.4	(0.4)	6.0	(0.5)	10.7	0.4	na	na	11.0	0.9	na	6.2	0.62	2.00f	—	(609) 282-2800
Paine Webber Investment Gr Inc "D"	0.1	(0.8)	4.0	0.2	7.0	0.5	na	1.3	na	na	na	na	na	6.3	na	—	0.750	(800) 647-1568
Permanent Port—Versatile Bond	0.5	(0.4)	1.4	(2.4)	2.0	(4.5)	7.7	na	na	na	na	na	na	1.2	0.89	—	0.250	(800) 531-5142
SteinRoe Income	0.5	(0.4)	3.6	na	na	na	na	13.0	na	10.4	0.3	1.46	6.8	0.82	—	—	(800) 338-2550
Strong Advantage	1.8	0.9	3.4	(0.4)	na	na	na	3.6	8.9	(1.1)	8.5	(1.6)	0.37	5.7	1.00	—	—	(800) 368-1030
Strong Short-Term Bond	1.8	na	3.4	(0.4)	na	na	na	(2.1)	10.1	(1.9)	8.7	(1.4)	0.70	6.5	0.60	—	—	(800) 368-1030
Vanguard Long Term Corp Bond	(0.6)	(1.5)	na	(0.1)	na	1.1	na	2.9	14.9	2.9	13.1	3.0	1.96	6.8	0.31	—	—	(800) 662-7447
Vanguard Short-Term Corporate	0.6	na	2.2	na	3.8	na	7.0	(4.4)	9.0	(3.0)	9.5	(0.6)	0.81	5.6	0.27	—	—	(800) 662-7447
CORPORATE BOND FUND AVERAGE	0.9	0.0	na	0.0	na	0.0	11.4	0.0	12.0	0.0	10.1	0.0	1.00	6.1	0.72	—	—	SD 2.7%
Corporate High-Yield Bond Funds																		
Fidelity Capital & Income	na	0.3	6.9	0.5	14.2	3.3	24.8	6.4	27.5	7.0	14.0	3.5	1.47	8.4	0.91	1.50r	—	(800) 544-8888
Fidelity Spartan High Income	na	1.0	7.9	1.5	13.6	2.7	21.8	3.4	25.7	5.2	na	na	1.36	9.2	0.70	1.00r	—	(800) 544-8888
GIT Income—Maximum	1.9	0.6	6.0	(0.4)	9.1	(1.8)	15.0	(3.4)	17.4	(3.1)	9.0	(1.5)	1.14	8.0	1.54	—	—	(800) 336-3063
INVESCO Income—High Yield	3.7	(0.5)	5.2	(1.2)	9.2	(1.7)	15.6	(2.8)	17.8	(2.7)	10.1	(0.4)	0.92	8.0	1.00	—	0.250	(800) 525-8085
Nicholas Income	2.4	(1.8)	4.7	(1.7)	7.5	(3.4)	12.9	(5.5)	15.3	(5.2)	9.5	(1.0)	0.89	8.2	0.68	—	—	(800) 227-5987
Northeast Investors Trust	6.0	1.8	8.5	2.1	13.9	3.0	23.5	5.1	22.4	1.9	10.7	0.2	1.25	9.7	0.79	—	—	(800) 225-6704
Paine Webber High Income "D"	3.3	(0.9)	6.3	(0.1)	8.1	(2.8)	13.6	(4.8)	na	na	na	na	na	6.7	na	—	0.750	(800) 647-1568
Safeco High Yield Bond	3.0	(1.2)	5.3	(1.1)	9.7	(1.2)	16.9	(1.5)	18.2	(2.3)	10.2	(0.3)	1.03	9.2	1.00	—	—	(800) 426-6730
T Rowe Price High Yield	4.7	0.5	6.5	0.1	12.6	1.7	21.7	3.3	22.2	1.7	9.9	(0.6)	1.25	8.8	0.97	1.00r	—	(800) 638-5660
Value Line Aggressive Income	5.4	1.2	7.6	1.2	11.6	0.7	19.0	0.6	19.1	(1.4)	10.7	0.2	1.25	8.4	1.15	—	—	(800) 223-0818
Vanguard High Yield Corporate	3.5	(0.7)	6.0	(0.4)	10.7	(0.2)	18.2	(0.2)	20.3	(0.2)	10.8	0.3	1.14	8.6	0.34	1.00r	—	(800) 662-7447
CORPORATE HIGH-YIELD FUND AVERAGE	4.2	0.0	6.4	0.0	10.9	0.0	18.4	0.0	20.5	0.0	10.5	0.0	1.00	8.4	0.91	—	—	SD 3.6%
Government Bond Funds																		
1784 U.S. Gov't Medium Term Income	0.0	0.5	2.0	(0.7)	na	na	na	na	na	na	na	na	na	na	na	—	0.250	(800) 252-1784
Alliance Bond—U.S. Gov't "C"	(0.2)	0.3	2.2	(0.5)	na	na	na	na	na	na	na	na	na	na	na	—	1.000	(800) 221-5672
BNY Hamilton Interm Gov't	(0.6)	(0.1)	1.6	(0.9)	4.2	(1.5)	8.0	(2.4)	na	na	na	na	na	5.0	0.75	—	0.250	(800) 426-9363
Benham Long Term Treasury and Agency	(1.8)	(1.3)	5.0	2.3	10.4	4.7	17.6	7.2	na	na	na	na	na	6.4	0.00	—	—	(800) 321-8321
Benham Short-Term Treasury & Agency	0.4	0.9	1.7	(1.0)	2.7	(3.0)	5.4	(5.0)	na	na	na	na	na	3.9	0.00	—	—	(800) 321-8321
Benham Target Mat Trust—1995	0.4	0.9	1.8	(0.8)	3.2	(2.5)	6.9	(3.5)	10.0	(0.8)	10.9	0.5	0.86	0.0	0.62	—	—	(800) 321-8321
Benham Target Mat Trust—2000	(1.1)	(0.6)	2.8	0.1	7.5	1.8	15.4	5.0	14.7	3.9	13.9	3.5	1.87	0.0	0.86	—	—	(800) 321-8321
Benham Target Mat Trust—2005	(2.4)	(1.9)	4.0	1.3	12.0	6.3	21.5	11.1	17.3	6.5	15.7	5.3	2.21	0.0	0.63	—	—	(800) 321-8321
Benham Target Mat Trust—2010	(2.1)	(1.6)	6.3	3.6	16.3	10.6	26.2	15.8	18.8	8.0	16.5	6.1	2.56	0.0	0.70	—	—	(800) 321-8321

INVESTMENT HOME STUDY

Investment Home Study is a comprehensive course on investing designed for individuals who already understand the basics. It explores in depth the concepts, strategies and analytical methods useful for successful investing and portfolio management. The 10 lessons include:

- **Lesson I:** Concepts of Investment Risk and Return—*Measures of risk and return; the impact of diversification.*

- **Lesson II:** Investment Alternatives—*Risk considerations and analysis; market factors.*

- **Lesson III:** Stocks—*Risk and return; valuation; investment strategies.*

- **Lesson IV:** Options—*Valuation models; strategies.*

- **Lesson V:** Debt Investment—*Analyzing different types of bonds; investment approaches.*

- **Lesson VI:** Mutual Funds—*How they work; tax implications; risk and return; guidelines for selecting funds.*

- **Lesson VII:** International Investments—*Risks, diversification benefits, ways to invest internationally.*

- **Lesson VIII:** Futures Markets—*Trading mechanics; speculation; hedging.*

- **Lesson IX:** Real Estate—*Risk and return; the market; tax considerations.*

- **Lesson X:** Other Investments—*Collectibles; analysis and investment guidelines.*

The entire curriculum is shipped in a three-ring binder for easy reference and storage. AAII members receive free updates and revisions as they are developed, which are available to non-members for a nominal charge. The complete course is available to AAII members (for themselves or as a gift) for $55.00 and to non-members for $75.00. For more information, contact the American Association of Individual Investors, 625 N. Michigan Avenue, Suite 1900, Chicago, IL 60611; (312) 280-0170.